ROTH RUGBY UNION YEARBOOK

1998-99

**Editors: Mick Cleary
and John Griffiths**

ROTHMANS

HEADLINE

First published in 1998
by HEADLINE BOOK PUBLISHING

Cover photographs.
Front, L to R: Jeff Wilson of New Zealand in their match at Wembley against Wales
on 29 November 1997; Lawrence Dallaglio (England) wins a line-out against
New Zealand at Old Trafford on 22 November 1997; Will Greenwood (England)
tackled by Henry Honiball (South Africa) at Twickenham on 29 November 1997.
Back, L to R: Gary Teichmann (South Africa) and Laurent Cabannes (France) at
Parc des Princes on 22 November 1997; Phil de Glanville (England) and
Jonah Lomu (New Zealand) at Old Trafford on 22 November 1997.

All photographs by Colorsport unless otherwise credited.

10 9 8 7 6 5 4 3 2 1

ISBN 0 7472 7653 6

Copy-editing by Andrew Kinsman, First Rank Publishing, Brighton

Typeset by Letterpart Limited, Reigate, Surrey

Printed and bound in Great Britain by
Mackays of Chatham plc, Chatham, Kent

HEADLINE BOOK PUBLISHING
A division of Hodder Headline PLC
338 Euston Road
London NW1 3BH

CONTENTS

ABBREVIATIONS USED IN THIS YEARBOOK

International Teams

A – Australia; Arg – Argentina; AW – Anglo-Welsh; B – British Forces and Home Unions teams; Bb – Barbarians; Be – Belgium; BI – British Isles teams; Bu – Bulgaria; C – Canada; Cr – Croatia; Cv – New Zealand Cavaliers; Cz – Czechoslovakia; E – England; F – France; Fj – Fiji; I – Ireland; It – Italy; Iv – Ivory Coast; J – Japan; K – New Zealand Services; M – Maoris; Mo – Morocco; NAm – North America; Nm – Namibia; NZ – New Zealand; NZA – New Zealand Army; P – President's XV; Po – Poland; Pt – Portugal; R – Romania; Ru – Russia; S – Scotland; SA – South Africa; SAm – South America; SK – South Korea; Sp – Spain; Tg – Tonga; US – United States; W – Wales; Wld – World Invitation XV; WS – Western Samoa; Y – Yugoslavia; Z – Zimbabwe.

Other Abbreviations used in the International Listings

(R) – Replacement or substitute; (t) – temporary replacement; [ ] – Rugby World Cup appearances.

NB: When a series has taken place, figures are used to denote the particular matches in which players have featured. Thus NZ 1,3, would indicate that a player has appeared in the First and Third Tests of the relevant series against New Zealand.

Irish Clubs

CIYMS – Church of Ireland Young Men's Society; KCH – King's College Hospital; NIFC – North of Ireland Football Club.

French Clubs

ASF – Association Sportive Française; BEC – Bordeaux Etudiants Club; CASG – Club Athlétique des Sports Generaux; PUC – Paris Université Club; RCF – Racing Club de France; SB – Stade Bordelais; SBUC – Stade Bordelais Université; SCUF – Sporting Club Universitaire de France; SF – Stade Français; SOE – Stade Olympien des Etudiants; TOEC – Toulouse Olympique Employés Club.

South African Provinces

BB – Blue Bulls; Bol – Boland; Bor – Border; EP – Eastern Province; GL – Gauteng Lions; GW – Griqualand West; N – Natal; NT – Northern Transvaal; OFS – Orange Free State; R – Rhodesia; SET – South-East Transvaal; SWA – South-West Africa; SWD – South-West Districts; Tvl – Transvaal; WP – Western Province; WT – Western Transvaal; Z–R – Zimbabwe–Rhodesia.

Australian States

ACT – Australian Capital Territory; NSW – New South Wales; Q – Queensland; V – Victoria; WA – Western Australia.

EDITORIAL PREFACE

When the *Rothmans* series of Rugby Union Yearbooks was launched in 1972, the International Board comprised seven nations. By the end of 1997 membership had increased more than tenfold to 79. The Yearbook, we hope, has also expanded in its coverage of world events during the intervening seasons and this, the 27th edition, is mainly one of further consolidation.

Certainly our decision last season to devote a special section to the game in Italy was timely. Early this year the organisers of the International Championship which, since the 1880s has variously taken the form of a Three, Four and Five Nations tournament, took the decision to admit the *azzurri* to an enlarged competition which after next year's World Cup will presumably become known as the Six Nations.

We have therefore decided to extend our Italian section to include their principal national records, and for his considerable research and help in this area we should like to acknowledge Walter Pigatto of Padua. He, like all of our faithful statisticians in the Home Unions, France and overseas, has taken great pains down the years to ensure that full details of Test matches are regularly checked and conveyed to us. Our thanks, once again, go out to them as well as to our regular correspondents who file copy from far and wide.

The past season was dominated by the overseas nations on the international front and it will come as no surprise to learn that New Zealand's John Hart (personality) and France's Christian Califano (player) feature among the *Rothmans* awards. Saracens, we felt, deserved the title 'club of the year'. For the first 126 years of the RFU's existence, Watford had been a rugby wilderness. Saracens' playing style, success and inspired marketing at Vicarage Road last year turned the town into rugby's unlikeliest Mecca.

Finally we should like to express our gratitude to David Llewellyn and Chris Rhys, without whom many pages in this Yearbook would be blank, and also to Andrew Kinsman of First Rank Publishing and Chris Leggett of Letterpart Ltd for their technical excellence behind the scenes.

Mick Cleary
John Griffiths

NOTE: Statistical sections of the Yearbook are complete up to **30 April 1998**.

5

ROTHMANS AWARDS 1997-98

Player of the Year – Christian Califano (Stade Toulousain and France)

We've seen it all before. A Frenchman takes the ball in a crowded midfield. Suddenly, with a shimmy and a burst of speed, he is away, weaving through the traffic as if he is a Sunday cyclist freewheeling down a country lane. The defenders fall away in his wake, unable to compete for pace or angle of running. It's the classic French break, the hallmark of a Blanco, a Sella or a Maso. It suggests beauty, grace, nerve and genius. The one thing it doesn't suggest is prop forward.

Christian Califano is a freak, a marvellous contravention of the old lore which states that props should neither be seen nor heard, should be foursquare, hefty and slow, and should never dare to put their stubby mitts round that precious commodity known as the ball. Califano breaks every stereotype in the book. Or at least those regarding open play.

He is fast, dynamic and perceptive, as England found to their cost during the Five Nations. The 26-year-old loosehead scattered the English defence on several occasions as he charged upfield. On the day the English threequarters were ponderous by comparison. Califano has run the 100 metres in 12 seconds and has recorded a mark of just over three seconds in training for a 20-metre sprint.

And yet Califano is no lightweight. He more than carries his weight in the scrummage. Again England were on the receiving end when Califano and his mates took their front row to pieces in the championship match at the Stade de France. Califano has done the same things many times over for his club, Stade Toulousain. He has become the prototype modern prop, a man fully in tune with the demands of the game. He poses a formidable threat in the primary phase, never seeing it as a means to an end. But once that segment is over and done with, Califano unleashes himself into open field, never there merely to make up the numbers but to be an integral part of the show.

Califano was born into a working-class housing estate in Toulon. It was a tough upbringing with difficult circumstances at home. 'Without rugby, I would have ended up very badly,' says Califano. 'I realised that I could become something very good.'

Califano left Toulon six years ago to join Stade Toulousain and to work his way into the French team. It wasn't all smooth sailing. 'Things had gone to my head at Toulouse,' admits Califano. 'I was living it up and my weight was up to 123 kilos. But the coaches sat me down late in 1993 and told me that if I put my mind to it, I could become an international player.'

Eight months later, and 18 kilos lighter, he did. Califano won the first of his 39 caps against New Zealand in the summer of 1994, a series that France were to win 2-0. He has been an ever-present in the French side over the last year. Califano is a popular, modest and honest man, ingrained with the game's most cherished traditions. He also happens to be the finest prop in the world.

The shape of a prop, the talent of a threequarter – Christian Califano, Stade Toulousain and France, Rothmans Player of the Year.

Team of the Year – Saracens

Everyone used to love Saracens. Particularly the dozen or so clubs who invariably finished above them in the league every year. Saracens, homely and friendly, used to find it impossible to switch off the hospitality when kick-off time came around. All that has changed. Or at least the losing habit has. Saracens only had one team ahead of them in the league last season, Newcastle pipping them by a point in the Allied Dunbar Premiership. It was a

7

Saracens celebrate victory in the Tetley's Bitter Cup, accompanied by some enthusiastic fez-wearing supporters.

thrilling, close-run race. Saracens had more to spare in the cup. They beat the former league champions, Wasps, 48-18, in a glorious final at Twickenham to take the Tetley's Bitter Cup for the first time in their history.

Saracens had taken the hard route to Twickenham. They won easily enough at Blackheath, 59-13, but then scraped home 14-13 at home to Leicester in the next round. A difficult trip away to Richmond was their reward, which they survived 36-30. On paper a semi-final at Northampton was going to be the toughest call of all, coming just a few days after a draining midweek league defeat at Newcastle. Yet, in winning 25-10, Saracens showed all the traits which were to carry them through the season. They were hard, durable, committed but also inventive and opportunist. The victory was a reward for their spirit as much as their undoubted class.

They weren't a bad act off the field either. There were a few eyebrows raised when Saracens announced that they would be sharing a playing home with Watford FC at Vicarage Road. The move, though, was a resounding success. Gates shot up by almost 200% on average. The crucial league game with Newcastle drew a record league crowd of just under 20,000. One of Saracens' best signings of the entire season was marketing director, Peter Deakin.

Deakin had transformed Bradford Bulls of the Super League and set about doing a similar number on Saracens. In came the dancing girls, the loud music and a motorised kicking tee. There were many sceptics, but not on the terraces. The fans joined in the spirit. A small group took to wearing fez hats. By the end of the season the red-topped gang had become cult figures.

It wasn't all about gimmicks. Saracens did a huge amount of work in the local community. They rewarded over 150 clubs and groups on their cashback ticket scheme. They also sent players on a daily basis to help with coaching clinics in schools. Their corporate revenue for last year was just over £1 million. Two years before it had been £180,000. Season-ticket sales then were about 100. Now they are over 1000.

Saracens created an environment of excellence. And it was never just about star names. Even though it had been the likes of Francois Pienaar, Michael Lynagh and Philippe Sella who stole the early headlines, there were many unsung contributions to applaud. Three players – centre Steve Ravenscroft, hooker George Chuter, flanker Ben Sturnham – were to come through to England A honours while lock Danny Grewcock was one of England's finds of the season. There was so much to admire, too, in the play of Argentinian prop, Roberto Grau, and Australian wing, Ryan Constable.

Saracens came so close to a double of league and cup. They proved a class act in every respect.

Personality of the Year – John Hart, New Zealand coach

He coped pretty well with the unfamiliar circumstances. There was John Hart, coach to the All Blacks, having to digest an awful calamity. His team had failed to win a match. Just one match that is, across an entire calendar year. True, they had won all eleven games prior to the unexpected 26-26 draw with England, but when excellence is your constant point of reference on the barometer, then any drop of pressure at all signals storm clouds on the horizon.

But Hart, who has lost only one match in his 22 games in charge of the All Blacks (22-32 to South Africa in Johannesburg in August 1996) took it all in his confident stride. Sure, it had been a great match. Yes, England had surpassed expectations. But, come on, hadn't it been a tremendous advert for the sport?

Yes, it had. But inside Hart must have been fuming. It had been a terrific game, but his team had spurned several gilt-edged opportunities to wrap up the match, the tour and the entire year itself. Hart has never acquired the losing habit. And he wasn't about to start. He will have upbraided his players for being on the plane home before the match kicked off, for being distracted at the thought of it being Zinzan Brooke's last game in an All Black shirt, for not playing with focus, intelligence, composure and self-belief for the entire 80 minutes. These are the hallmarks of any Hart team.

Hart will not rest easily. His attention to detail is all-consuming. He knows that if the All Blacks could falter against England in an end-of-tour game then, in theory, it could happen again in a World Cup final. It did in 1995 when the All Blacks, as overwhelming favourites, were beaten by South Africa. The coach then was Laurie Mains. In came John Hart to make sure that there were no slip-ups next time around.

Hart had been involved with the All Black set-up before. He was assistant coach to Alex Wyllie during the 1991 World Cup, but that partnership never flourished. The pair were chalk and cheese. Wyllie, 'Grizz' by nickname and grizzly by nature; Hart, urbane, accessible, slick and media-friendly. He was too much of a show pony for some in the New Zealand hierarchy. He was also, they said, too interested in power, too fond of the limelight. It was a mean-spirited, short-sighted appraisal. For Hart was a proven winner.

He coached Auckland for five seasons in the mid-eighties, turning them from a middling, inconsistent outfit to being the greatest non-Test team in the world. Auckland won three provincial championships under Hart, acquired the Ranfurly Shield and won 80 of their 91 games. In 1987, when he stepped aside, Auckland provided 14 players to New Zealand's World Cup winning side. In 1982 they had provided just two All Blacks. Hart created the template of invincibility which Auckland have carried with them ever since.

So too his All Blacks. The class of 1997 were hailed as one of the greatest sides ever to visit these shores. Not only were they unbeaten across the land, they played with verve and style. They took visible pride in performance and in self-expression. We had Christian Cullen, Jeff Wilson, Josh Kronfeld, Andrew Mehrtens and big Jonah himself, nursed back to health by the medics and to his true confident self by Hart.

Hart is the corporate man with the human touch.

New Zealand coach John Hart (right) shares a joke with new captain Taine Randell at the press open day, Auckland, New Zealand, 9 June 1998.

SO MUCH TO WRITE HOME ABOUT IF ONLY YOU COULD FIND THE TIME

REVIEW OF THE 1997-98 SEASON
Mick Cleary

Lawrence Dallaglio, who had replaced Phil de Glanville as England captain, was voted Player of the Year by the Rugby Writers. He came to the podium at the awards ceremony in early January to collect his trophy and, in time-honoured fashion, to say a few words. 'When I came into the job Phil passed me three envelopes,' said Dallaglio. 'He told me to open them only if the going got tough and I needed advice. So, after we'd struggled to a draw with Australia in the first match I thought I'd sneak a look. I opened the first envelope and it said: "Blame the previous regime, everyone else has." The following week we lost to the All Blacks at Old Trafford and I needed some moral support. So I opened the next envelope. It said: "Blame the structured season, everyone else does." Fair enough. Then the third game came along and we were hammered by the Springboks. So again I reached into my pocket to see what Phil suggested. I opened the envelope. It said: "Start writing three more envelopes." '

The season was a succession of envelopes. Just when we thought there was no more bad news to come, bad news duly came knocking on the door right through to England's disastrous tour of the southern hemisphere. The tour was ill-conceived and poorly executed. The only positive to emerge from the five-week torment was the realisation that it must never be allowed to happen again.

Before a ball had been kicked in anger there had been an unseemly end to the career of England coach Jack Rowell. There were reports during the summer that a succession of people had been lined up to replace Rowell, all of which was news to Rowell himself. Auckland's Graham Henry was approached first and then British Lions coach Ian McGeechan, fresh from victory in South Africa, was sounded out. McGeechan did the decent thing, albeit tempted by the approach, and formally pulled out of the reckoning. Rowell had had enough. He resigned on August 20th.

The undignified courting of other people while Rowell was still in office set the tone for what was a troubled, often sordid season off the field. The political game was a desperate, irritating affair. It was a duplicitous, bitter, vindictive, gratuitous, tangled, long-running saga. If it had been policed with anything like the same rigour and vigilance as the game itself then there would have been umpteen red cards for unbecoming behaviour.

Rugby Union made a habit of grabbing the headlines for all the wrong reasons across the season. There was Rowell's resignation, the Pontypridd-Brive brawl on pitch and in town, Will Carling's will-he, won't-he retirement and the power-battle at Harlequins, the Simon Fenn missing earlobe outrage which saw Bath's Kevin Yates banned for six months after being found guilty of taking a chunk out of the London Scottish player's ear, a charge Yates denied all the way through the courts, Northampton owner Keith Barwell threatening to pull his players from England duty, and running throughout the entire season, rugby's equivalent of *The Mousetrap*, the fight for power between the RFU and the clubs.

The whole sorry dispute was a mix of John Le Carré and Sid James, part intrigue, part farce. It was at times impossible to locate the truth. The mystery around the riddle wrapped up in an enigma was the state of the union. And yet we had thought we were all sorted out when the season began earlier than ever in mid-August. There had been a drawn-out fight the year before between two central figures at the RFU, acting chief executive Tony Hallett and chairman of the Management Board, Cliff Brittle. The AGM of summer '97 saw the floor endorse Brittle. A month later Hallett was statesmanlike enough to resign, giving a magnanimous gesture of support for Brittle as he stepped down. 'I would like to have continued,' said Hallett. 'But it was important we didn't embark on an ego trip. Cliff was elected on an overwhelming majority. Cliff and I have disagreed on fundamental issues. For the benefit of the game I have decided to leave rather than appear to prolong the discord that has sadly been all too evident in recent months.'

That, we thought, might be the end of all that. Think again. Brittle was at loggerheads with several factions, including his own union, for the entire season. The chairman of the Management Board may have enjoyed support from the country (although that premise was open to challenge) but he never managed to woo the doubters within his own committee. By the end of the season the schism was complete. Brittle was removed from the front-line of negotiations with the leading clubs. These talks had stumbled along through months and months (if not years) of unproductive debate. Within six weeks of the removal of Brittle from the equation a solution, or at least a way forward, was found.

The Mayfair Agreement announced on Friday, May 8th was acclaimed as a peace treaty, an end to the tussle between club and union. Its value was symbolic as much as actual. For the first time there seemed to be a desire by the two sides to work together, as partners rather than as rivals. The principle of release periods for international players was enshrined; there would be a tripartite contract between union, club and player; there would be no attempt to organise provincial rugby at senior level and the limit for top players would be 37 matches a season.

The Premiership was increased from 12 to 14 clubs for the top two divisions. This meant that there was no automatic relegation from the Premiership for the season just ended. Instead there was a home and away play-off between the bottom two clubs, London Irish and Bristol and the third and fourth sides in the Second Division, Rotherham and London Scottish. The upshot was that Bristol dropped out of the top flight for the first time in their 110 year history. London Scottish replaced them. London Irish retained their status, while Bedford and West Hartlepool were promoted automatically from Division Two. Worcester were champions of Jewson One with Leeds, London Welsh and Rugby also promoted.

The major concession made by the clubs was to agree to play through international weekends for the forthcoming season. They agreed that they would not seek to postpone matches even though some players would be away on international duty. Clubs like Newcastle and Saracens could effectively lose well over half a side to England, Wales, Scotland and Ireland on a Five Nations weekend. Several clubs were unhappy with the proposal, but they have a simple choice. Either they put up with it or we go back to the chaotic mess of the old order. In a compromise deal both ends have to give somewhere along the line. The deal is not perfect, far from it, but it is a way forward. If the clubs should buck the accord, then they will be playing right into the hands of those who remain deeply suspicious of them.

Fran Cotton, manager of the successful British Lions tour to South Africa, was co-opted on to the RFU Management Board to be vice-chairman of playing. His primary role was to look after the affairs of the England team. In that regard he did a good job. Clive Woodward was brought in to replace Rowell and became England's first full-time professional coach. Rowell had never been able to devote himself full-time to the task. Woodward, as we shall see, got on with the job.

But Cotton was also closely aligned with Cliff Brittle. The pair published documents during the year on the future development of the game in England. Brittle's thesis – Vision 2000 – was followed by Cotton's – Club England. The central thrust of both papers was that the top end of the game needed to be streamlined, that the cause of the English team was paramount to the success of the sport.

Brittle made some radical suggestions. He proposed that a line should be drawn between the amateur and professional game, though he didn't declare where this line should be drawn or quite what the consequences should be. Many aspiring junior clubs took umbrage, fearing that they would not be allowed to pay their players and so would effectively be prevented from moving up the leagues into the professional strata. Brittle never did specify exactly what he meant by it all. It is likely that he wanted to cut off the subsidy to clubs below a certain level, an eminently sensible proposal if these funds were only to be used for paying players. Certainly those clubs who wished to pay players from their own means should be allowed to do so.

Brittle's other really contentious aim was to dismantle the 62-man RFU Council. He suggested that this tier of government was unwieldy and outdated. He was right. Unfortunately it was like asking turkeys to vote for Christmas. The RFU Council were none too keen on doing themselves out of a job. In another climate even they might have seen the sense of what was being proposed. Unfortunately the prevailing climate was one of suspicion and hostility. There was an enormous lack of trust in the game. Everyone's motives were questioned.

And so it was with Brittle and Cotton. Whatever they said, or whatever they did, the senior clubs always felt that they were both out to strip the clubs of power and significance. That may not have been the reality but it was the perception. The two of them had made no secret of the fact that they preferred a provincial set-up for the game. In an ideal world, said Cotton in his document, the senior England side would be underpinned by a Super-12 type competition featuring regional sides from the northern hemisphere. Cotton stressed that he was a supporter of club rugby in England. Only one small problem. The clubs didn't believe him. Cotton had long expressed his concern, too, at the number of overseas players playing in the Premiership. His proposed Super-16 tournament was for national players only.

So much for the backdrop. It was a prolonged and angry fight. In the end Cotton could stand no more. When, on the eve of the England-Ireland match in early April, Brittle was moved aside from the firing line of negotiations, Cotton resigned his position of vice-chairman of playing. But he was far from finished.

A few days later Cotton was painting a doom-laden scenario about the imminent collapse of the game. His rationale was that the senior clubs were about to take control not just of their own competitions but the entire international game. The clubs had recently made a submission to the European Commission in an attempt to clarify their legal position on commercial rights. They maintained that the RFU was acting outside the law of the land with regard to certain commercial activities to do with broadcasting and sponsorship. The clubs wanted these matters explained and clarified, hence the 42 page submission, which had been sent by mistake to Clive Woodward. The contents were then dissected by Cotton and Brittle's legal teams. As they saw it this clearly showed the covert intentions of the clubs to take over.

And so ensued another battle. Clive Woodward allied himself with the Cotton-Brittle faction. The Mayfair Agreement, which is supposedly binding for seven years, ought to have ended the matter. But the threat of an SGM lingered. And then into the fray came an Australian by the name of Dick McGruther, chairman of the Australian Union. After Clive Woodward had named 17 uncapped players in his original 37-man squad to tour Australia, New Zealand and South Africa in the summer, McGruther reacted with all the sensitivity and subtlety of TV's Les Patterson. 'The biggest English sell-out since Gallipoli,' spluttered McGruther in tasteless fashion.

There were a dozen star names missing from Woodward's list, including captain Lawrence Dallaglio and Lions captain Martin Johnson. Both needed operations: Dallaglio on his shoulder, Johnson on his groin. Also absent were Kyran Bracken, Mike Catt, Tim Rodber, Richard Hill, Tony Underwood and Will Greenwood, all of whom were injured or needed treatment, while Jeremy Guscott, Paul Grayson and Phil de Glanville were all excused duty for personal reasons. It was a hefty roll-call of absentees. McGruther and others claimed that it proved that the clubs were holding players back.

Actually talking to people to find out the truth was obviously too onerous a task for McGruther. The situation was complex. No club willingly held back players. One or two might have been more helpful in resting their men earlier, but until the Mayfair Agreement was signed no-one knew for certain whether there was to be promotion or relegation, or if Europe was to be on or off the agenda. At the time of going to press the English clubs were not part of the European competition.

It was a massive setback. The English clubs had withdrawn even prior to the Heineken final in January, objecting to what they saw as the unfair divide of money and power within European Rugby Cup Ltd (ERC). England felt that they, along with France, held the whip hand in both commercial and sporting terms and that this advantage should be reflected in voting rights. Their plea fell on deaf ears so they pulled out.

It was a great shame, all the more so given that an English club, Bath, won the competition for the first time, beating the holders, Brive, 19-18 in Bordeaux. There was a capacity 36,500 crowd at the Stade Lescure although they made the noise of 136,500. It was a marvellous backdrop. An estimated TV audience of over 35 million in some 70 countries tuned into the event. The match itself was not a classic, although the tension throughout was gripping, Bath clinching victory in the final moments through the boot of Jon Callard who scored all his side's points.

Brive might have been kicking themselves for failing to capitalise on their many chances. The 1997 champions knew though that they had been fortunate to scrape through in the semi-final against Toulouse, going through only on a 2-1 try count after the match was tied 22-22 after extra time.

The Heineken competition grew in appeal and status across the season. It is an utter farce that some middle ground cannot be reached so that the full tournament can take place. Without the English clubs the competition has little meaning. 'It is not a true European Cup without the English clubs,' said Brive coach, Laurent Seigne.

There were some cracking matches throughout the pool rounds. However, the headlines were dominated by a torrid encounter in Brive. A mass punch-up saw Pontypridd's Dale McIntosh and Brive's Lionel Mallier sent off. Sadly more bad blood was to be spilled. Later that night at Le Bar Toulzac in central Brive players from both teams again got caught up in a fight. Windows were smashed, riot police were called and three Brive players – Christophe Lamaison, David Venditti and Philippe Carbonneau – were taken to hospital. Pontypridd's Phil John, Dale McIntosh and Andre Barnard were questioned by police. 'I have never seen anything so violent in my life,' said Lamaison. 'It was like a Western. People were throwing doors, chairs, glasses, they were all hysterical. I even saw bottles smashed to be used as weapons.'

McIntosh and Mallier were later banned for 30 days each by the ERC for their on-field misdemeanour. The sour taste lingered for many weeks. The clubs met a fortnight later at Pontypridd. That the match went ahead at all was some achievement. The week before, when Brive travelled to Bath, Seigne had called Pontypridd 'semi-civilised animals'.

The game went ahead under tight security with Brive heading straight for a charter flight home barely 45 minutes after the final whistle. Incredibly the two sides had to meet for a third time when Pontypridd qualified as the best third-placed pool team, this time back in Brive.

The two clubs were fined £30,000 for their part in the brawl. Llanelli and Pau also suffered financial penalties when they were fined £20,000 for an outbreak of violence in their group game.

The game took a pummelling from unsavoury incidents. Next into the dock was Bath's Kevin Yates. The loosehead prop was suspended by his club after allegations that a London Scottish player, Simon Fenn, had had his ear bitten during the Tetley's Bitter Cup match between the clubs. London Scottish originally cited the entire Bath front row, Yates, Federico Mendez and Victor Ubogu, but the inquiry then focused on Yates. Yates denied the charge through the courts at a personal cost of over £90,000.

Finally though an RFU tribunal found him guilty and suspended him for six months.

Later in the season graphic newspaper photos of Newcastle's Paul Van Zandvliet appeared to show the prop with his teeth clamped round the head of Leicester's Neil Back. The case was unproven. In the same match Leicester centre Will Greenwood was sent off. The dismissal was deemed sufficient punishment. Earlier in the year Gloucester's Phil Vickery was cleared after being cited for punching Welsh flanker Colin Charvis. The English disciplinary committee needs to be very wary of treading too softly. Other countries already feel that double standards apply as far as England is concerned.

The game on the field though was in good order. The Allied Dunbar Premiership saw the best action in the ten-year life span of leagues. In an exciting, draining climax, Newcastle just had enough in the tank to deny Saracens. In the Tetley's Bitter Cup Saracens gave a thrilling demonstration of their all-round ability in comprehensively beating Wasps. The star turns of the domestic scene were variously Newcastle's Samoan flanker Pat Lam, Saracens lock Danny Grewcock and half-backs Kyran Bracken and Michael Lynagh.

Attendances at Premiership games showed an increase of just over 20%, with Saracens and Newcastle drawing a record crowd of almost 20,000 to Vicarage Road for their showdown. The clubs were all still strapped for cash with Saracens reporting a £2.2million deficit for the year ended April 1997. However, the success of their switch to Vicarage Road, with attendances up by nearly 200%, means that they are forecasting break even by next year. Richmond are to follow Saracens' lead this season, taking the bold gamble to head out to Reading for home Premiership matches. Lower down problems are more acute. Blackheath went into liquidation with Moseley also hitting the buffers.

Swansea were crowned Welsh champions, with Llanelli taking their tenth Welsh Cup title, beating Ebbw Vale in the final. Shannon won the league in Ireland for the fourth year in succession while Watsonians came through in Scotland to win the SRU Tennents Premiership. Glasgow Hawks, an amalgamation of Glasgow High and Glasgow Academicals, won the Tennents Cup.

The international card was packed. England played four Test matches in succession from mid-November onwards, meeting Australia, New Zealand (twice) and South Africa. New coach, Clive Woodward, new captain, Lawrence Dallaglio, and five new caps for the opening fixture against the Wallabies, only managed a draw. England played the first match against the All Blacks at Old Trafford. Even though they lost, the switch was a great success.

The All Blacks excited great interest. They almost finished the

England captain Lawrence Dallaglio leads from the front in the Five Nations match against Ireland. David Corkery is his closest pursuer.

year with a clean sweep, only for England to deny them at the last with a 26-26 draw at Twickenham. It was good to see Jonah Lomu back on the field after his serious kidney illness.

The Springboks had a great tour of the northern hemisphere, hammering France 52-10 in Paris, and then seeing off both Scotland and England. Australia were also successful in Scotland. In May there was a real danger of South Africa being sent back into sporting isolation. The South African government itself vigorously objected to the way the sport was being run in the country and called on SARFU chief, Louis Luyt, to resign. Luyt refused and a tour boycott was called. Finally, after huge pressure, Luyt did step aside.

France recovered to win the Five Nations Championship and historic back-to-back Grand Slams. England, beaten in Paris, won their fourth Triple Crown in succession. Ireland, whose coach Brian Ashton resigned, were whitewashed although their improvement under new coach Warren Gatland deserved better. Irish manager, Pat Whelan, was also to resign. Scotland too saw their coaches leave prior to the championship, Jim Telfer stepping in to replace Richie Dixon. By the end of the championship Wales and coach Kevin Bowring had parted company. Pontypridd's Dennis John was the caretaker coach for Wales's tour to South Africa. If the Celts had a rough time of it at senior level there was better news lower down the age scale. Scotland won a Grand Slam in the A team Five Nations while Ireland won a Triple Crown at under-19 and universities level.

Heads rolled on the domestic front too, notably at Leicester where Bob Dwyer was sacked and at London Irish where Willie Anderson was moved aside for Dick Best.

In far less acrimonious circumstances we also saw the last of All Blacks Zinzan Brooke, who had moved to Harlequins, as well as the great Fitzy. All Black captain Sean Fitzpatrick finally bowed to Mother Nature and admitted early in the New Zealand season that his knee was not up to scratch and so headed into retirement. Northampton lock Martin Bayfield gave in to the inevitable after battling for two years against injury. Michael Lynagh and Philippe Sella also called it a day after their successful English sojourns. Welsh captain Gwyn Jones suffered serious neck injuries in December when playing for Cardiff against Swansea. South Africa's World Cup winning coach, Kitch Christie, died after a long fight against cancer. There were welcomes to be extended, however, notably to Italy who were admitted to the International Championship from the year 2000.

It was the longest, most densely-packed season in the history of the game. The professionals are earning their money.

ENGLAND TO AUSTRALIA, NEW ZEALAND & SOUTH AFRICA 1998

THE TOURING PARTY

Manager RM Uttley   **Coach** CR Woodward   **Assistant Coaches** JEP Mitchell and WB Ashton   **Captain** MJS Dawson

Full-backs: MB Perry (Bath), TRG Stimpson (Leicester)

Threequarters: ND Beal (Northampton), TD Beim (Sale), S Brown (Richmond), DE Chapman (Richmond), AS Healey (Leicester), M Moore (Sale), JJN Baxendell (Sale), S Potter (Leicester), SCW Ravenscroft (Saracens), * PC Sampson (Wasps)

Half-backs: OJ Lewsey (Bristol, Wasps), JP Wilkinson (Newcastle), S Benton (Gloucester), P Richards (London Irish), MJS Dawson (Northampton)

Forwards: GC Rowntree (Leicester), D Bell (Sale), D Crompton (Richmond), T Windo (Gloucester), G Chuter (Saracens), R Cockerill (Leicester), PBT Greening (Gloucester), GS Archer (Newcastle), DJ Grewcock (Saracens), D Sims (Gloucester), RJ Fidler (Gloucester), BB Clarke (Richmond), L Moody (Leicester), SO Ojomoh (Gloucester), RJ Pool-Jones (Stade Français-CASG), PH Sanderson (Sale), B Sturnham (Saracens), AJ Diprose (Saracens)

* *Replacement on tour*

TOUR RECORD

All matches: Played 7   Lost 7   Points for 88   Against 328
International matches: Played 4   Lost 4   Points for 32   Against 198

SCORING DETAILS

All matches					International matches			
For:	11T	9C	5PG	88 Pts	4T	3C	2PG	32 Pts
Against:	46T	31C	12PG	328 Pts	28T	17C	8PG	198 Pts

MATCH DETAILS

1998	OPPONENTS	VENUE	RESULT
6 June	AUSTRALIA	Brisbane	L 0-76
13 June	New Zealand A	Hamilton	L 10-18
16 June	New Zealand Academy	Invercargill	L 32-50
20 June	NEW ZEALAND	Dunedin	L 22-64
23 June	New Zealand Maori	Rotorua	L 14-62
27 June	NEW ZEALAND	Auckland	L 10-40
4 July	SOUTH AFRICA	Cape Town	L 0-18

The cards were stacked high and they duly came toppling down. England's four Test tour of the southern hemisphere was a disaster in waiting. From the moment the arduous schedule was put in place it was odds-on that England would struggle. As it was, shorn of 17 front-line players, the heavily-depleted squad had no chance of winning any of the international matches. England gave 14 new caps on tour. There were 20 uncapped players on the 37-man tour roster.

This was the worst ever return from a senior country on tour. In the four Tests England conceded 28 tries and scored just four, a ratio of 7-1. They also recorded their three worst ever results in 127 years of international rugby. It was not a happy five weeks.

MATCH 1   6 June, Suncorp Stadium, Brisbane   Test Match
AUSTRALIA 76 (6G 3PG 5T)   ENGLAND 0

The slim hope that England might at least be marginally competitive on this trip was blown away on a warm Brisbane evening. At the first sign of real pressure the team caved in. England scrapped away for about half an hour only to then to concede four tries in 11 minutes just before half-time. They suffered a similar collapse at the end of the match, four more tries scored in the last 12 minutes. In all England conceded a record 11 tries. This was England's worst ever defeat in international rugby. The Australian score and winning margin are new records for a match between senior members of the International Board.

AUSTRALIA: M Burke (Eastwood & NSW); BN Tune (GPS & Queensland), DJ Herbert (GPS & Queensland), TJ Horan (Souths & Queensland), JW Roff (Canberra & ACT); SJ Larkham (Canberra & ACT), GM Gregan (Randwick & ACT); RLL Harry (Sydney University & NSW), PN Kearns (Randwick & NSW), AT Blades (Gordon & NSW), TM Bowman (Eastern Suburbs & NSW), JA Eales (Brothers & Queensland) (*capt*), MJ Cockbain (GPS & Queensland), TS Kefu (Souths & Queensland), DJ Wilson (Easts & Queensland) *Substitutions:* ODA Finegan (Randwick & ACT) for Cockbain (45 mins); V Ofahengaue (Manly & NSW) for Kefu (50 mins); DJ Crowley (Souths & Queensland) for Harry (61 mins); JS Little (Souths & Queensland) for Burke (66 mins)
Scorers *Tries:* Larkham (3), Tune (3), Horan (2), Burke, Gregan, Kefu *Conversions:* Burke (4), Larkham (2) *Penalty Goals:* Burke (3)
ENGLAND: Stimpson; Brown, Perry, Ravenscroft, Healey; Wilkinson, Benton; Vickery, Cockerill, Rowntree, Archer, Grewcock, Sturnham, Diprose (*capt*), Pool-Jones *Substitutions:* Clarke for Pool-Jones (temp 26-40 mins); Potter for Ravenscroft (temp 26-34 mins); Chapman for Stimpson (66 mins)
Referee A Watson (South Africa)

MATCH 2   13 June, Rugby Park, Hamilton

New Zealand A 18 (1G 2PG 1T)   **England XV 10** (1G 1PG)
New Zealand A: AR Cashmore (Auckland); GM Osborne (North Harbour), CS Ralph (Auckland), JD O'Halloran (Wellington), JT Lomu (Counties); L Stensness (Auckland), RJ Duggan (Waikato); KT Nepia (Canterbury), NJ Hewitt (Southland) (*capt*), KJ Meeuws (Otago), BP Larsen (Northland), NM Maxwell (Canterbury), AF Blowers (Auckland), XJ Rush (Auckland), SM Robertson (Canterbury) *Substitutions:* JP Preston (Wellington) for Duggan (40 mins); R Willis (Waikato) for Maxwell (40 mins); TJF Umaga (Wellington) for Lomu (52 mins); GL Slater (Taranaki) for Willis (67 mins)
Scorers *Tries:* Ralph, Stensness *Conversion:* Cashmore *Penalty Goals:* Cashmore (2)
England XV: Beim; Moore, Beal, Baxendell, Chapman; Lewsey, Dawson (*capt*); Windo, Greening, Green, Sims, Fidler, Clarke, Ojomoh, Sanderson *Substitution:* Crompton for Green (68 mins)
Scorers *Try:* Fidler *Conversion:* Lewsey *Penalty Goal:* Lewsey
Referee PD O'Brien (Southland)

MATCH 3   16 June, Homestead Rugby Stadium, Invercargill

New Zealand Academy 50 (6G 1PG 1T)   **England XV 32** (3G 2PG 1T)
NZ Academy: DPE Gibson (Canterbury); DC Howlett (Auckland), PF Alatini (Southland), RM Ranby (Manawatu), BT Reihana (Waikato); BR Feeney (Counties), B Kelleher (Otago); MJ Collins (Waikato), SAA Tiatia (Wellington), GE Feek (Taranaki), S Maling (Otago), CS Davis (Manawatu) (*capt*), RD Thorne

(Canterbury), I Maka (Otago), SF Maka (Auckland) *Substitutions:* DE Holwell (Northland) for Feeney (38 mins); KJ Meeuws (Otago) for Feek (45 mins); DJO Blakie (Otago) for F Maka (69 mins)
Scorers *Tries:* I Maka (2), Reihana (2), Kelleher (2), Alatini *Conversions:* Feeney (3), Holwell (2), Reihana *Penalty Goal:* Holwell
England XV: Stimpson; Moore, Potter, Baxendell, Chapman; King, Benton; Windo, Chuter, Crompton, Sims, Fidler, Sturnham, Diprose *(capt)*, Moody *Substitutions:* Cockerill for Chuter (31 mins); Bell for Windo (41 mins); Pool-Jones for Moody (45 mins); Lewsey for Moore (45 mins); Ravenscroft for Potter (55 mins); Richards for Benton (66 mins)
Scorers *Tries:* Benton (2), Chuter, Chapman *Conversions:* Stimpson (3) *Penalty Goals:* Stimpson (2)
Referee CJ Hawke (South Canterbury)

Matt Cockbain, supported by the Australian pack, breaks through the English defence in the record 76-0 victory at the Suncorp Stadium.

MATCH 4   20 June, Carisbrook, Dunedin   1st Test
NEW ZEALAND 64 (5G 3PG 4T)   ENGLAND 22 (2G 1PG 1T)

Another Test, another record defeat. The final scoreline does not tell the whole tale. England were fiery and resilient in the opening stages only to be completely thrown by the dismissal after half an hour of second row Danny Grewcock. The Saracens lock kicked All Black hooker Anton Oliver on the head after a scrum collapsed. Thereafter England were firmly on the back foot as New Zealand scored three tries in quick succession. A brief rally in the second half saw England score tries through

Matt Dawson and Tom Beim. Richard Cockerill also scored just before half-time. All Black lock Ian Jones was cited for stamping on Graham Rowntree but was cleared by a disciplinary hearing. Grewcock was banned for five weeks.

NEW ZEALAND: CM Cullen (Wellington); JW Wilson (Otago), MA Mayerhofler (Canterbury), WK Little (North Harbour), JT Lomu (Counties); AP Mehrtens (Canterbury), OFJ Tonu'u (Auckland); CW Dowd (Auckland), AD Oliver (Otago), OM Brown (Auckland), ID Jones (North Harbour), RM Brooke (Auckland), MN Jones (Auckland), TC Randell (Otago) (*capt*), JA Kronfeld (Otago) *Substitutions:* TJ Blackadder (Canterbury) for M Jones (20 mins); MD Robinson (North Harbour) for Tonu'u (62 mins)
Scorers *Tries:* Cullen (2), Randell (2), Wilson (2), Lomu, Kronfeld, Mayerhofler *Conversions:* Mehrtens (5) *Penalty Goals:* Mehrtens (3)
ENGLAND: Perry; Stimpson, Beal, Lewsey, Healey; Wilkinson, Dawson (*capt*); Rowntree, Cockerill, Vickery, Archer, Grewcock, Clarke, Ojomoh, Sanderson *Substitutions:* Beim for Wilkinson (43 mins); Green for Rowntree (temp 10-18 mins) and for Vickery (55 mins); Sturnham for Ojomoh (temp 35-55 mins); Greening for Cockerill (55 mins); Sims for Archer (76 mins)
Scorers *Tries:* Cockerill, Dawson, Beim *Conversions:* Stimpson (2) *Penalty Goal:* Stimpson
Referee WJ Erickson (Australia)

MATCH 5   23 June, Rotorua International Stadium

New Zealand Maori 62 (7G 1PG 2T)   **England XV 14** (2G)
New Zealand Maori: AR Cashmore (Auckland); RQ Randle (Waikato), NR Berryman (Northland), T Marsh (Counties), DPE Gibson (Canterbury); TE Brown (Otago), RJ Duggan (Waikato); KT Nepia (Canterbury), SP McFarland (North Harbour), KJ Meeuws (Otago), JN Coe (Counties), T Flavell (North Harbour), A Parker (Canterbury), EF Brain (Counties) (*capt*), DJ Seymour (Wellington) *Substitutions:* J Kerr (Canterbury) for Gibson (40 mins); DAG Waller (Manawatu) for Parker (62 mins); LL Lidgard (Counties) for Nepia (69 mins); DD Muir (Waikato) for Flavell (77 mins)
Scorers *Tries:* Berryman (2), Coe, Brown, Seymour, Duggan, Cashmore, Marsh, Randle *Conversions:* Cashmore (7) *Penalty Goal:* Cashmore
England XV: Stimpson; Brown, Baxendell, Ravenscroft, Moore; King. Richards; Windo, Greening, Crompton, Fidler, Sturnham, Pool-Jones, Diprose (*capt*), Moody *Substitutions:* Ojomoh for Pool-Jones (39 mins); Beim for King (46 mins); Benton for Richards (46 mins)
Scorers *Tries:* Brown, Diprose *Conversions:* Stimpson (2)
Referee PA Macfie (Southland)

MATCH 6   27 June, Eden Park, Auckland   2nd Test
NEW ZEALAND 40 (5G 1T)   ENGLAND 10 (1G 1PG)

For an hour England finally played some rugby on this beleaguered tour. They took the game to the All Blacks, showing craft and patience. The forwards, with Gloucester locks Dave Sims and Rob Fidler making their full debuts, were stroppy and positive. New Zealand led 14-7 at the break but were lucky that England's Ben Clarke had a try disallowed on the stroke of half-time. Four All Black tries in the last quarter put a significant gloss on the scoreboard for New Zealand. England captain, Matt Dawson, scored a wonderfully impudent try in the 26th minute, the scrum-half breaking from a ruck, jinking past Taine Randell and dummying inside Christian Cullen. Jeff Wilson was the lone star for New Zealand, the All Black winger scoring two tries to take his total to 28 in 37 Tests.

NEW ZEALAND: CM Cullen (Wellington); JW Wilson (Otago), CS Ralph (Auckland), MA Mayerhofler (Canterbury), JT Lomu (Counties); AP Mehrtens (Canterbury), OFJ Tonu'u (Auckland); CW Dowd (Auckland), AD Oliver (Otago), OM Brown (Auckland), ID Jones (North Harbour), RM Brooke (Auckland), TJ Blackadder (Canterbury), TC Randell (Otago) (*capt*), JA Kronfeld (Otago) *Substitutions:* CJ Spencer (Auckland) for Mayerhofler (40 mins); NJ Hewitt (Southland) for Oliver (temp 40-50 mins and 71-76 mins); I Maka (Otago) for Blackadder (50 mins); J Vidiri (Counties) for Lomu (62 mins); MP Carter (Auckland) for I Jones (65 mins); CH Hoeft for Dowd (temp 7-9 mins and 75 mins); Dowd for Hewitt (76 mins)
Scorers *Tries:* Wilson (2), Mayerhofler, Vidiri, Maka, Randell *Conversions:* Spencer (3), Mehrtens (2)
ENGLAND: Perry; Beim, Beal, Baxendell, Healey; Lewsey, Dawson (*capt*); Rowntree, Cockerill, Vickery, Fidler, Sims, Clarke, Diprose, Sanderson *Substitutions:* Sturnham for Sanderson (temp 19-21 mins); Stimpson for Beim (36 mins); Ravenscroft for Healey (70 mins); Greening for Cockerill (76 mins)
Scorer *Try:* Dawson *Conversion:* Dawson *Penalty Goal:* Dawson
Referee PL Marshall (Australia)

MATCH 7　　4 July, Newlands, Cape Town　　Test Match
SOUTH AFRICA 18 (1G 2PG 1T)　　ENGLAND 0

The Newlands pitch was a quagmire, a state of affairs which no-one in the English camp was complaining about. Springbok coach Nick Mallett felt that his team would have scored 50 points on a dry surface. Mallett was being a touch fanciful for the simple reason that his pack never gained the ascendancy necessary for posting such a score. South Africa were always in control, however, and might have bolstered their score if they'd chosen to move the ball wide more often. It would have been difficult and dangerous to do so but England looked vulnerable when they were stretched. South Africa's first try in the 21st minute from Joost van der Westhuizen came from a charge-down on Josh Lewsey. The second, just before half-time, was more sculpted, Percy Montgomery hitting the line to put Stefan Terblanche over for his seventh try in four Tests.

SOUTH AFRICA: PC Montgomery (Western Province); CS Terblanche (Boland), AH Snyman (Blue Bulls), PG Muller (Natal), PWG Rossouw (Western Province); HW Honiball (Natal), JH van der Westhuizen (Blue Bulls); RB Kempson (Natal), J Dalton (Gauteng Lions), AC Garvey (Natal), K Otto (Blue Bulls), MG Andrews (Natal), JC Erasmus (Free State), GH Teichmann (Natal) (*capt*), AG Venter (Free State) *Substitutions:* RB Skinstad (Western Province) for Otto (temp 10-19 mins); A-H Le Roux (Natal) for Kempson (75 mins)
Scorers *Tries:* van der Westhuizen, Terblanche *Conversion:* Montgomery *Penalty Goals:* Montgomery (2)
ENGLAND: Perry; Brown, Beal, Baxendell, Sampson; Lewsey, Dawson (*capt*); Rowntree, Cockerill, Vickery, Sims, Fidler, Clarke, Diprose, Sanderson *Substitution:* Stimpson for Sampson (55 mins)
Referee CJ Hawke (New Zealand)

FRANCE ALL THE WAY

THE INTERNATIONAL CHAMPIONSHIP 1998

Do we go with the heart or the head? The head tells you that more points were scored by one team, England (146) than in any other championship, that the highest aggregate for a match was passed, (England 60, Wales 26), that records tumbled out of the statisticians' notebooks faster than snow falling in a December blizzard – biggest margin of victory (51-0, France against Wales), record equalling number of tries in the championship, 55, matching the mark set in 1911, an unprecedented back-to-back Grand Slam for France. We know all of these things as fact. Therefore all must be rosy with the Five Nations Championship.

But the heart lay uneasy. Deep within, an anxiety nagged away as the championship unfolded, an anxiety which the deluge of points, tries and records could not wash away. The concern goes something like this: how much longer will people tune in to watch, or cross the seas and borders to be there live, when the outcome is so predictable? We all said beforehand that the big boys, France and England, would have the championship to themselves. They did. What is worse, the die was cast on the very first Saturday of the championship when France saw off England with unexpected ease at their new £270 million home, the Stade de France, in the northern suburbs of Paris. And that was it. Two halves of wham-bang-wallop rugby from the French and the title was decided.

Sure, Ireland were true to form in not being true to form when they travelled to Paris. Sure, they almost pulled off one of the biggest upsets in the history of the championship by running France so close, the home side only coming home 18-16 thanks to a late try by their captain, hooker Raphael Ibañez. But Ibañez did score and Ireland did not win. They have still not won in Paris for 26 years.

The imbalance between the Celts and the rest is growing alarmingly. On the second Saturday of the tournament England were racking up 60 points against Wales while France were cutting loose across the tartan landscape to score 51 points. The Celts have only won four matches in the entire decade against England. It's a sorry litany of failure.

Of course the championship has always relied for its appeal on events off the field as much as for what happens on it. The great social crusade to the capital cities of northern Europe is a fixed point in the calendar for many thousands of supporters. The game itself is an important part of the weekend, but it is not the only part. 20,000 Welsh fans travelled to Dublin. They certainly didn't all go in expectation of some decent rugby. They didn't get it either, though it's a good bet that they all returned home poorer in the back pocket but altogether richer for the experience. As long as that remains the case then it would be wrong to advocate dismantling the championship.

But nor is there reason to be complacent. Might it not be an idea to seed the fixtures, so that the supposedly strongest countries meet towards the end of the championship? The seedings would be based on performance over the previous five seasons. The system would not be perfect and there would be anomalies in the pattern of results. At least though there would be a better chance of some sense of climax being restored to the championship. Of course there have been times when it has evolved naturally, most famously at Murrayfield in 1990. It would be good to try and engineer that crescendo rather than just sit with fingers crossed and hope that it happens.

The Five Nations committee, not the most progressive bunch of men by reputation, acted with admirable foresight in admitting Italy to the championship. The Italians will take their place in 2000, a deserved return for their sustained good showing in recent years. They beat both Ireland and Scotland last season.

There was also a more unwelcome innovation in this champion-ship – Sunday rugby. There were two games played on the Sabbath, Scotland against England and Wales against France. The change, instigated by the BBC, was not at all popular. It disrupted the travel plans of many fans and broke the easy routine of the weekend. Let's hope that it is not repeated.

There were some outstanding performances in the 1998 champi-onship – Thomas Castaignède's tormenting of Wales, Olivier Magne's high-energy openside exhibition against Scotland, Neil Back's diligent and intelligent work throughout – but very little which really set the soul alight.

France, deserved champions, had a major blip in the middle when they trotted out as 33-1 on favourites against Ireland and thought that they could win without breaking sweat. By the final whistle of an extraordinary match their brows were drenched in the sweat of simple fear. France found themselves in the course of the championship, transformed from the limp lot who were rolled over by the Springboks just before Christmas. Ibañez was a marvellous leader, Philippe Carbonneau and Thomas Castaignède a potent combination at half-back.

Ireland were whitewashed for the first time in six years, yet it was not a dismal championship for them. Their overall points difference was only minus 30, an average margin of defeat of just over seven points. They unearthed another good lock, Malcolm O'Kelly, a back-up hooker in Ross Nesdale, and saw heartening performances

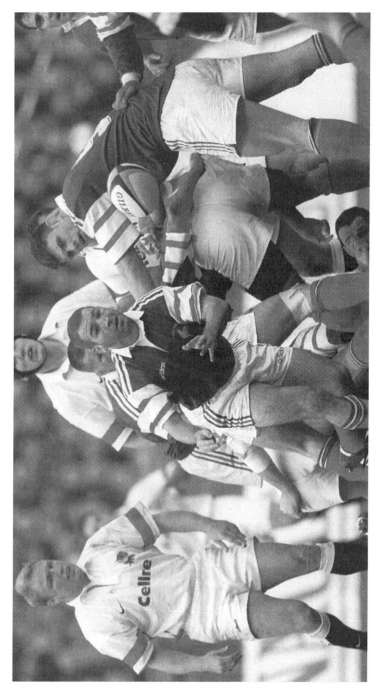

Philippe Carbonneau recycles the ball for France in the Grand Slam 'decider' against England at the new Stade de France.

from Victor Costello at No 8 and Conor McGuinness at scrum-half.

Wales, even though they managed two wins, did not have a good time of it. They had to come from some way back to beat Scotland at Wembley and were only marginally the better of two poor sides in Dublin. Their pack was underpowered and showed little heart. Allan Bateman, in contrast, was all heart and all class in the centre.

Scotland came into the tournament looking to save face. They had just lost to Italy, a defeat which prompted the departure of their coaches. On to the scene yet again strode big Jim Telfer and immediately Scotland began to play with more shape and purpose. They won by a point in Dublin and then actually played better than the scoreline suggests in conceding 51 points to France. Scotland should have won at Wembley but were then flattered by the final score in the Calcutta Cup.

England flopped in Paris and then spent the next two months stitching together their morale. They did so admirably, the team playing with great verve to put a record 60 points on Wales. In fits and starts England promised much for the future in taking the Triple Crown for the fourth time in succession.

FINAL TABLE

	P	W	D	L	F	A	Pts
France	4	4	0	0	144	49	8
England	4	3	0	1	146	87	6
Wales	4	2	0	2	75	145	4
Scotland	4	1	0	3	66	120	2
Ireland	4	0	0	4	70	100	0

The points tally was 501, only ten shy of the Five Nations record set the season before.

The points comprised 55 tries (equalling the all-time Five Nations record set in 1911), 41 conversions, 44 penalty goals and four dropped goals.

The leading individual scorers were: 66 – Paul Grayson (England); 39 – Christophe Lamaison (France); 29 – Neil Jenkins (Wales); 29 – Eric Elwood (Ireland); 26 – Craig Chalmers (Scotland). Grayson, who was also the top scorer the season before, finished one point short of the Five Nations record set by Jonathan Webb in 1992. Philippe Bernat-Salles (four for France), Allan Bateman (three for Wales) and Denis Hickie (three for Ireland) were the leading try-scorers.

7 February, Lansdowne Road, Dublin
IRELAND 16 (1G 2PG 1DG)   SCOTLAND 17 (4PG 1T)

Scotland stretched their unbeaten record against Ireland to 11 games with this narrow victory. Such a milestone must have been far from their thoughts just eight days before. Scotland had lost to Italy, coach Richie Dixon had been invited to resign while his assistant, David Johnston, was considering legal action for wrongful dismissal. There was also a whole battery of former internationals, two of them recent captains, David Sole and Finlay Calder, sniping from the sidelines about the poor direction and morale of Scottish rugby. Apart from all that, everything was just dandy.

But into the picture came Jim Telfer. The former Grand Slam winning coach and Lions assistant coach just six months earlier, had

had little intention of donning the tracksuit once again. But don it he did. Immediately there was a harder edge as well as shape to the Scottish team. Craig Chalmers came back in at fly-half with Gregor Townsend moving into the centre. On the day there were solid performances from No 8 Peter Walton and a cameo replacement's showing from prop Dave Hilton. He shored up the Scottish scrum in the final quarter.

Ireland, too, had their problems, troubles which were to come to a head in the wake of this loss when coach Brian Ashton resigned. On the field they looked devoid of confidence and purpose. They made enough openings to have won the game but simply lacked the self-belief and inner calm to finish the job. They led 16-11 going into the final quarter only to squander two gilt-edged try-scoring chances when Mark McCall ignored an overlap and then the forwards failed to take advantage of six scrums on the Scottish line.

Craig Chalmers steadied the ship for Scotland. In the second half he kicked two goals from two attempts after Rowen Shepherd had landed only two from six in the first half. David Humphreys landed three penalties from three attempts and also dropped a goal.

IRELAND: C M P O'Shea (London Irish); R M Wallace (Saracens), K M Maggs (Bristol), M C McCall (London Irish), D A Hickie (St Mary's College); D G Humphreys (London Irish), B T O'Meara (Cork Constitution); R Corrigan (Greystones), K G M Wood (Harlequins) *(capt)*, P S Wallace (Saracens), P S Johns (Saracens), M E O'Kelly (London Irish), D S Corkery (Bristol), E R P Miller (Leicester), K Dawson (London Irish) *Substitutions:* N J Popplewell (Newcastle) for P Wallace (temp 60-62 mins); V C P Costello (St Mary's College) for Dawson (66 mins)
Scorer *Try:* penalty try *Conversion:* Humphreys *Penalty Goals:* Humphreys (2) *Dropped Goal:* Humphreys
SCOTLAND: R J S Shepherd (Melrose); C A Joiner (Leicester), A V Tait (Newcastle), G P J Townsend (Northampton), K M Logan (Wasps); C M Chalmers (Melrose), G Armstrong (Newcastle) *(capt)*; G Graham (Newcastle), G C Bulloch (West of Scotland), M J Stewart (Northampton), G W Weir (Newcastle), D F Cronin (Wasps), R I Wainwright (Dundee HSFP), P Walton (Newcastle), S D Holmes (London Scottish) *Substitutions:* A G Stanger (Hawick) for Joiner (14 mins); D I W Hilton (Bath) for Graham (59 mins); S B Grimes (Watsonians) for Cronin (63 mins); D J Lee (London Scottish) for Shepherd (77 mins)
Scorers *Try:* Tait *Penalty Goals:* Shepherd (2), Chalmers (2)
Referee A Watson (South Africa)

7 February, Stade de France, Paris
FRANCE 24 (1G 2PG 2DG 1T)   **ENGLAND 17** (4PG 1T)
All week there had been fears about the frozen pitch at the new £270 million Stade de France. English supporters ought to have been more concerned that their team might freeze. England were a pale imitation of the side which had battled to an exhilarating 26-26 draw with New Zealand prior to Christmas. France, in pointed contrast, were a far remove from the feeble team who allowed the Springboks to score 52 points in the autumn.

The stadium and the French team were towering, futuristic and impressive. England were not. They made mistakes all over the field, were naive in their attempts to seek wide movement and singularly failed to establish any sort of forward platform. If France had managed to finish with the same style and precision they showed in all other phases then England would have been buried under an avalanche of points.

'The scoreline flattered us,' admitted England coach Clive Woodward.

This was France's fourth win in succession against England, a sharp reversal of the run which saw England win eight times on the trot through the nineties. The defeat meant that England had gone seven matches in succession without a win, their worst run in 26 years.

France made eight changes in the wake of the Springbok debacle. New captain, hooker Raphael Ibañez, brought much-needed focus and composure. England recalled Jeremy Guscott to the centre after a six month lay-off with injury, moved Mike Catt to full-back in place of Matt Perry and gave Paul Grayson a chance to show what he could do at fly-half.

England were given a fearful going over in the tight scrummage. The French front row, and particularly Toulouse loosehead, Christian Califano, were rampant.

Philippe Bernat-Salles skipped over for France's first try in the 10th minute after good build-up work from Philippe Benetton and Philippe Carbonneau. Nine minutes later debutant wing Christophe Dominici sliced past Mike Catt to score. Neil Back's try for England six minutes after the interval came from a line-out drive. Grayson's third penalty goal in the 56th minute closed the scores to 18-14. Christophe Lamaison hit his second goal 11 minutes later, Grayson replied in kind only for Jean-Luc Sadourny to bring down the curtain on a deserved French victory with a drop goal a minute from time.

FRANCE: J-L Sadourny (Colomiers); P Bernat-Salles (Pau), C Lamaison (Brive), S Glas (Bourgoin), C Dominici (Stade Français); T Castaignède (Castres), P Carbonneau (Brive); C Califano (Toulouse), R Ibañez (Dax) *(capt)*, F Tournaire (Narbonne), O Brouzet (Bègles-Bordeaux), F Pelous (Dax), P Benetton (Agen), T Lièvremont (Perpignan), O Magne (Brive) *Substitutions:* M Lièvremont (Stade Français) for Benetton (15 mins); T Cléda (Pau) for T Lièvremont (54 mins)
Scorers *Tries:* Bernat-Salles, Dominici *Conversion:* Lamaison
Penalty Goals: Lamaison (2) *Dropped Goals:* Castaignède, Sadourny
ENGLAND: M J Catt (Bath); D L Rees (Sale), W J H Greenwood (Leicester), J C Guscott (Bath), A S Healey (Leicester); P J Grayson (Northampton), K P P Bracken (Saracens); J Leonard (Harlequins), M P Regan (Bath), D J Garforth (Leicester), M O Johnson (Leicester), G S Archer (Newcastle), L B N Dallaglio (Wasps) *(capt)*, R A Hill (Saracens), N A Back (Leicester)
Substitution: D E West (Leicester) for Regan (70 mins)
Scorers *Try:* Back *Penalty Goals:* Grayson (4)
Referee D T M McHugh (Ireland)

21 February, Twickenham
ENGLAND 60 (7G 2PG 1T)   **WALES 26** (3G 1T)

It was difficult to know whether to weep with joy or regret. England rattled up a record score for the championship, beating the 49-14 mark set, ironically, by Wales against France in 1910. The match aggregate, 86 points, was also a record while England also equalled their highest ever mark in Test rugby. For the first time since the 1880s, England have now beaten Wales in five successive matches.

All these landmarks to revel in, and yet the heart lay uneasy. In the aftermath of this overwhelming victory there was a real sense that the championship itself was the loser. Indeed there was a muted air around Twickenham, a stunned awareness of how easy it had all been once England got into their stride.

For the first 28 minutes Wales were more than a match for their opponents. They actually led 12-6 and had scored two well-crafted tries. The first came when Matt Perry took his eye off a high hanging kick, allowing Allan Bateman to nip in and score. Bateman's second try was the result of a devastating counterattack from behind the Welsh posts initiated by Gareth Thomas.

And then it all went horribly wrong. The front five disappeared without trace and the back row were mere straws in the wind. 'We were blown apart,' said Welsh captain, Robert Howley.

England scored three tries in seven minutes towards the end of the first half. David Rees fastened onto an inside pass from Will Greenwood to score, Neil Back touched down from a line-out drive before Kyran Bracken went over near the posts in the 35th minute.

The second half confirmed the worst fears of Welsh supporters. They scored two more tries, from Arwel Thomas in the 54th minute and Scott Gibbs on the stroke of full-time, but they were never at the races. Rees scored his second after a beguiling run from Jerry Guscott. Austin Healey breezed disdainfully past Neil Jenkins in the 57th minute to score. Rees put Greenwood over after 69 minutes before Matt Dawson, one of six England replacements used, raced in unopposed from 50 metres for the final try. It all looked so easy. For once appearances were not deceptive.

England prop, Phil Vickery, who was making his debut, was later cited for foul play. He was eventually cleared.

ENGLAND: M B Perry (Bath); D L Rees (Sale), W J H Greenwood (Leicester), J C Guscott (Bath), A S Healey (Leicester); P J Grayson (Northampton), K P P Bracken (Saracens); J Leonard (Harlequins), R Cockerill (Leicester), P J Vickery (Gloucester), M O Johnson (Leicester), G S Archer (Newcastle), L B N Dallaglio (Wasps)(capt), R A Hill (Saracens), N A Back (Leicester) *Substitutions:* D J Grewcock (Saracens) for Johnson (56 mins); D J Garforth (Leicester) for Vickery (56 mins); A J Diprose (Saracens) for Hill (56 mins); M J Catt (Bath) for Grayson (70 mins); P R de Glanville (Bath) for Greenwood (70 mins); M J S Dawson (Northampton) for Bracken (70 mins)
Scorers *Tries:* Rees (2), Back, Bracken, Dallaglio, Healey, Greenwood, Dawson *Conversions:* Grayson (7) *Penalty Goals:* Grayson (2)
WALES: N R Jenkins (Pontypridd); G Thomas (Bridgend), A G Bateman (Richmond), I S Gibbs (Swansea), N K Walker (Cardiff); A C Thomas (Swansea), R Howley (Cardiff)(capt); A L P Lewis (Cardiff), B H Williams (Richmond), D Young (Swansea), G O Llewellyn (Harlequins), M J Voyle (Llanelli), C L Charvis (Swansea), L S Quinnell (Richmond), M E Williams (Pontypridd) *Substitutions:* W T Proctor (Llanelli) for Walker (3 mins); R C Appleyard

(Swansea) for Quinnell (48 mins); L B Davies (Cardiff) for Bateman (65 mins); J M Humphreys (Cardiff) for B Williams (65 mins); C Stephens (Bridgend) for Voyle (73 mins); L Mustoe (Cardiff) for Lewis (77 mins)
Scorers *Tries:* Bateman (2), G Thomas, Gibbs *Conversions:* Jenkins (3)
Referee C J Hawke (New Zealand)

21 February, Murrayfield
SCOTLAND 16 (1G 3PG) FRANCE 51 (5G 2PG 2T)

The French had travelled to Murrayfield in times past with heavy heart. They had only won once in the previous 20 years in Edinburgh. By the end of an invigorating afternoon the only strain on French cardiac systems had come from over-excitement.

France played some of the best rugby of the championship in posting their highest ever score in the Five Nations and equalling their biggest margin of victory (45-10 against Ireland two years earlier).

It was not that Scotland rolled over and died. There was plenty of heart and purpose in the play. But they had no equal to the pace, sharpness and intelligence of the French attack. Neither could they match France for individual quality, particularly at openside flanker where Olivier Magne gave one of the greatest displays ever seen from a No 7.

France scored seven tries to one, despite losing their way for 20 minutes in the second half when the mercurial Thomas Castaignede went walkabout. Magne, though, had no such lapses. He was an ever-present in support, relentless in the tackle, devastating in open play and even had time to slide through inch-perfect grubber kicks.

Scotland had set out to take the game to France, notably in their selection of young London Scottish full-back, Derrick Lee. However, they had few opportunities for Lee to show what he could do in the open field. He did feature in their one and only try in the 69th minute. A mistake by Castaignède was latched on to by Lee, Rob Wainwright and Alan Tait. Stanger, winning his 50th cap, needed no second bidding. But, three penalty goals by Craig Chalmers apart, that was the sum of Scotland's offering.

France were in their element. Marc Lievremont opened their account with a try in the 14th minute. The floodgates duly opened. Brouzet added another try seven minutes later before Philippe Bernat-Salles crossed in the 32nd minute. The second half saw tries from Christian Califano and Bernat-Salles again before Philippe Carbonneau and Thomas Castaignede gave the scoreboard a resounding flourish with two injury-time tries.

SCOTLAND: D J Lee (London Scottish); A G Stanger (Hawick), A V Tait (Newcastle), G P J Townsend (Northampton), K M Logan (Wasps); C M Chalmers (Melrose), G Armstrong (Newcastle) *(capt)*; D I W Hilton (Bath), G C Bulloch (West of Scotland), M J Stewart (Northampton), D F Cronin (Wasps), G W Weir (Newcastle), R I Wainwright (Dundee HSFP), P Walton (Newcastle), S D Holmes (London Scottish) *Substitutions:* S B Grimes (Watsonians) for Cronin (19 mins); G Graham (Newcastle) for Hilton (64 mins);

A J Roxburgh (Kelso) for Walton (64 mins); S L Longstaff (Dundee HSFP) for Chalmers (78 mins)
Scorers *Try:* Stanger *Conversion:* Chalmers *Penalty Goals:* Chalmers (3)
FRANCE: J-L Sadourny (Colomiers); P Bernat-Salles (Pau), C Lamaison (Brive), S Glas (Bourgoin), C Dominici (Stade Français); T Castaignède (Castres), P Carbonneau (Brive); C Califano (Toulouse), R Ibañez (Dax) *(capt)*, F Tournaire (Narbonne), O Brouzet (Bègles-Bordeaux), F Pelous (Dax), M Lièvremont (Stade Français), T Lièvremont (Perpignan), O Magne (Brive) *Substitutions:* D Aucagne (Pau) for Lamaison (40 mins); P Benetton (Agen) for T Lièvremont (77 mins); C Soulette (Béziers) for Tournaire (77 mins); T Cléda (Pau) for Pelous (81 mins)
Scorers *Tries:* Bernat-Salles (2), Brouzet, M Lièvremont, Califano, Carbonneau, Castaignède *Conversions:* Lamaison (2), Castaignède (3) *Penalty Goals:* Lamaison, Castaignède
Referee P D O'Brien (New Zealand)

7 March, Stade de France, Paris
FRANCE 18 (1G 2PG 1T) IRELAND 16 (1G 3PG)

Humble pie was on every menu across Paris after this astonishing reversal of form. France had been quoted at 33-1 on and the local papers had speculated as to whether their team would get close to New Zealand's Test record score of 145 points recorded against Japan. Ireland, who had seen their coach Brian Ashton resign 12 days earlier to be replaced by New Zealander Warren Gatland, were staring down a barrel.

The gun was loaded with blanks. France failed to fire while Ireland played as if their lives depended on it, which, in sporting terms, it did. France only got their noses in front with seven minutes remaining when their captain Raphael Ibañez was worked over from a rolling maul. In a country where style usually holds sway over substance, the French couldn't give a damn how prosaic the match-winning score had been. They had lived to fight another day and the Grand Slam was still a possibility.

Gatland could not have asked for more from his squad. He had made a big play of restoring morale by installing a fax line in the team hotel. Over 2,000 messages of support were received. The players responded. The Connacht half-backs, where Gatland had coached, were outstanding. Conor McGuinness was a thorn at scrum-half, prickly in defence and sharp in attack while Eric Elwood was precise and ordered. The pack saw big performances from locks Paddy Johns and Malcolm O'Kelly as well as new boy, Kiwi Andy Ward plucked from Third Division Ballynahinch.

Ireland led 13-6 at half-time. Elwood and Christophe Lamaison exchanged penalty goals before Denis Hickie stunned the home crowd by intercepting a Lamaison pass and running in from halfway. It was the first try scored by an Irishman in Paris since Freddie McLennan's in 1980. Elwood converted and then added another penalty.

France began to stir from their torpor on the hour, Philippe Bernat-Salles crossing for his fourth try of the championship. The finale was thrilling, both sides going close. The Gods were to side with France as Ibañez scored. 'We must regain respect,' said Gatland beforehand. Ireland certainly managed that.

FRANCE: J-L Sadourny (Colomiers); P Bernat-Salles (Pau), C Lamaison (Brive), S Glas (Bourgoin), X Garbajosa (Toulouse); T Castaignède (Castres), P Carbonneau (Brive); C Califano (Toulouse), R Ibañez (Dax) *(capt)*, F Tournaire (Narbonne), O Brouzet (Bègles-Bordeaux), F Pelous (Dax), M Lièvremont (Stade Français), T Lièvremont (Perpignan), O Magne (Brive) *Substitutions:* P Benetton (Agen) for M Lièvremont (53 mins); C Soulette (Béziers) for Tournaire (65 mins); T Cléda (Pau) for Pelous (71 mins)
Scorers *Tries:* Bernat-Salles, Ibañez *Conversion:* Lamaison
Penalty Goals: Lamaison (2)
IRELAND: C M P O'Shea (London Irish); R M Wallace (Saracens), R A J Henderson (Wasps), K M Maggs (Bristol), D A Hickie (St Mary's College); E P Elwood (Galwegians), C D McGuinness (St Mary's College); R Corrigan (Greystones), K G M Wood (Harlequins) *(capt)*, P S Wallace (Saracens), P S Johns (Saracens), M E O'Kelly (London Irish), D S Corkery (Bristol), V C P Costello (St Mary's College), A J Ward (Ballynahinch) *Substitutions:* N J Popplewell (Newcastle) for Corrigan (58 mins); R P Nesdale (Newcastle) for Wood (58 mins); P M Clohessy (Young Munster) for P Wallace (64 mins); M J Galwey (Shannon) for Johns (64 mins)
Scorers *Try:* Hickie *Conversion:* Elwood *Penalty Goals:* Elwood (3)
Referee J M Fleming (Scotland)

7 March, Wembley
WALES 19 (1G 4PG)   SCOTLAND 13 (1PG 2T)

The away day turned into a hooray day. The trip up the M4 to the temporary home of Wembley was a resounding success, on and off the pitch. The old stadium provided a wonderful backdrop.

It was not a classic match but it was fast and breathless. At the end the sense of sheer relief among Welsh supporters swept down from the terraces and engulfed the team celebrating an unexpected victory. After the hammering by England, victory by any means and any margin was to be cherished.

Wales had made five changes in personnel after the Twickenham horror show, four of them in the pack. Garin Jenkins came in at hooker, Andy Moore at lock, Rob Appleyard on the blindside and Kingsley Jones on the open. Welsh coach, Kevin Bowring, with only two wins from nine championship games in charge, knew that his future was under threat.

Bowring's brow must have had a few more furrows added to it during the first half. Five minutes before the interval Scotland led 13-3 and it might have been more. They had scored tries in the seventh and 35th minutes but had several other chances. Gregor Townsend linked beautifully with Shaun Longstaff, the New Zealand-born winger winning his first full cap, to score the first try from a long way out. Damian Cronin's try was rather more pedestrian, the Scottish lock judged to have touched the ball down amidst a pile of bodies.

Wales were transformed in the second half. Their forwards began to play with real bite, clattering into ruck and maul, forcing the pace of the game rather than sitting lamely back on the receiving end. David Young mustered support in the scrum, Mike Voyle became more influential at lock and Colin Charvis impressed at No 8.

Welsh captain and scrum-half, Robert Howley, was as shrewd as ever but the real damage was caused by centre Allan Bateman, a clear winner of man-of-the-match. His defence and angles of running were quite superb.

Four minutes after the restart Scottish full-back Rowen Shepherd made a dreadful hash of a high ball. Wales piled forward, recycling the ball to eventually put Wayne Proctor over in the corner. Arwel Thomas, who replaced the injured Neil Jenkins after just 18 minutes, converted and then added another penalty to go with his two early successes.

WALES: K A Morgan (Pontypridd); W T Proctor (Llanelli), A G Bateman (Richmond), I S Gibbs (Swansea), G Thomas (Bridgend); N R Jenkins (Pontypridd), R Howley (Cardiff) *(capt)*; A L P Lewis (Cardiff), G R Jenkins (Swansea), D Young (Swansea), M J Voyle (Llanelli), A P Moore (Swansea), R C Appleyard (Swansea), C L Charvis (Swansea), K P Jones (Ebbw Vale) *Substitutions:* A C Thomas (Swansea) for N Jenkins (18 mins); L S Quinnell (Richmond) for Appleyard (59 mins); J M Humphreys (Cardiff) for G Jenkins (69 mins)
Scorers *Try:* Proctor *Conversion:* A Thomas *Penalty Goals:* N Jenkins, A Thomas (3)
SCOTLAND: D J Lee (London Scottish); A G Stanger (Hawick), G P J Townsend (Northampton), A V Tait (Newcastle), S L Longstaff (Dundee HSFP); C M Chalmers (Melrose), G Armstrong (Newcastle) *(capt)*; D I W Hilton (Bath), G C Bulloch (West of Scotland), M J Stewart (Northampton), D F Cronin (Wasps), G W Weir (Newcastle), R I Wainwright (Dundee HSFP), E W Peters (Bath), A J Roxburgh (Kelso) *Substitutions:* R J S Shepherd (Melrose) for Lee (28 mins); S B Grimes (Watsonians) for Cronin (51 mins); G Graham (Newcastle) for Stewart (65 mins)
Scorers *Tries:* Townsend, Cronin *Penalty Goal:* Chalmers
Referee J Dumé (France)

21 March, Lansdowne Road, Dublin
IRELAND 21 (1G 3PG 1T)   WALES 30 (3G 3PG)

Wales continued to live the roller-coaster life. In absolute despair only a month ago after being humiliated by England, their supporters (and there were 20,000 of them in Dublin) were able to celebrate back-to-back victories. There was plenty else to toast in Ireland's capital city but fine rugby was not one of them.

It was a poor, scrappy, halting match. There was no shape or continuity about proceedings; not one individual able to rise above the pervasive mediocrity. There were so many unforced errors in general play that you wondered what on earth had put the players so on edge. Tackles were missed and passes spilled. Of course such mistakes can lend an air of excitement to a match.

Ireland, after the heroics of Paris, duly reverted to type. Anti-climax has been too frequent a visitor to these parts down the years for anyone to get unduly excited about one sterling performance. The Irish backs were woeful. They singularly failed to find each other with any sort of conviction, and this despite the fact that their forwards did actually manage to send some ball their way. Malcolm O'Kelly and Victor Costello chiselled away purposefully but they were on their own.

Neil Jenkins was the dominant figure for Wales. The fly-half scored 20 points to set a new record for a Welshman in a Five Nations match. Jenkins scored a try in the last minute after a storming break by replacement back-row forward, Stuart Davies. He also scored three conversions and three penalties. But it was his astute tactical kicking which kept Wales in the game during the first half. The Welsh line-out failed to function at all.

Ireland scored two tries in the opening 25 minutes, the first from flanker Andy Ward after sustained pressure, the second from Costello who blasted off a wheeled scrum. Wales hit straight back, Allan Bateman skipping over almost directly from the re-start.

The second half belonged to Wales. Kevin Morgan scored in the 44th minute after good work from Leigh Davies and Rob Appleyard. Jenkins was then to have the last word. His namesake, Garin Jenkins, equalled Bryn Meredith's Welsh record of 34 caps for a hooker.

IRELAND: C P Clarke (Terenure College); R M Wallace (Saracens), K M Maggs (Bristol), R A J Henderson (Wasps), D A Hickie (St Mary's College); E P Elwood (Galwegians), C D McGuinness (St Mary's College); R Corrigan (Greystones), K G M Wood (Harlequins)*(capt)*, P S Wallace (Saracens), P S Johns (Saracens), M E O'Kelly (London Irish), D S Corkery (Bristol), V C P Costello (St Mary's College), A J Ward (Ballynahinch) *Substitutions:* R P Nesdale (Newcastle) for Wood (60 mins); P M Clohessy (Young Munster) for P Wallace (60 mins); E R P Miller (Leicester) for Ward (69 mins)
Scorers *Tries:* Ward, Costello *Conversion:* Elwood *Penalty Goals:* Elwood (3)
WALES: K A Morgan (Pontypridd); W T Proctor (Llanelli), A G Bateman (Richmond), L B Davies (Cardiff), G Thomas (Bridgend); N R Jenkins (Pontypridd), R Howley (Cardiff)*(capt)*; A L P Lewis (Cardiff), G R Jenkins (Swansea), D Young (Swansea), M J Voyle (Llanelli), A P Moore (Swansea), R C Appleyard (Swansea), C L Charvis (Swansea), K P Jones (Ebbw Vale) *Substitutions:* J M Humphreys (Cardiff) for G Jenkins (64 mins); S Davies (Swansea) for Jones (64 mins); L Mustoe (Cardiff) for Young (75 mins)
Scorers *Tries:* Bateman, Morgan, N Jenkins *Conversions:* N Jenkins (3)
Penalty Goals: N Jenkins (3)
Referee E F Morrison (England)

22 March, Murrayfield
SCOTLAND 20 (2G 2PG)   ENGLAND 34 (4G 1PG 1DG)

Much to the disgust of many locals the match was staged on a Sunday. For much of this game it seemed that several of the players were also staging their own Sabbath protest. Certainly the general tempo of play was in keeping with the sedate pace of Sunday activity.

Scotland managed to rouse themselves at different stages of the game. Their resistance was compelling at times but it was never sustained. England, who had made four changes through injury, were never seriously threatened once they decided to revert to old habits and play through the forwards. Scotland simply did not have the fire power to compete once that happened. They owed their relative good standing on the scoreboard to two injury-time tries. Tony Stanger scored in the 81st minute to equal the Scottish record of 24 tries set by Ian Smith between 1924 and 1933. Scotland's second try was scored by the other winger, Shaun Longstaff. Both tries owed much to dynamic bursts from back-row forward, Adam Roxburgh.

England were rushed and anxious for much of the first half, again trying too hard to force the pace. After half-time they cut out the frills and concentrated on the direct game. It worked wonders. England aimed straight at the soft underbelly of this Scottish side, the tight scrummage. Shortly after the interval Scotland had to withstand eight minutes of pressure on the line. A series of scrums buckled and twisted, Welsh referee Clayton Thomas finally awarding England a penalty try. 'That score was harsh,' said Scottish captain, Gary Armstrong. 'Our spirits went down after that.'

And so they did. England scored three tries through Matt Dawson, Austin Healey and Paul Grayson within 13 minutes at the mid-point of the second half. Grayson finished with a full house of points – try, four conversions, dropped goal and penalty goal – the first England player to achieve the feat in a Five Nations match. This was England's highest Murrayfield score, passing the 30-18 win that sealed the 1980 Grand Slam. The match aggregate of 54 points equalled the series record set the previous year.

Scotland had finished their campaign by losing to England for the ninth time in succession.

SCOTLAND: D J Lee (London Scottish); A G Stanger (Hawick), G P J Townsend (Northampton), A V Tait (Newcastle), S L Longstaff (Dundee HSFP); C M Chalmers (Melrose), G Armstrong (Newcastle) *(capt)*; D I W Hilton (Bath), G C Bulloch (West of Scotland), A P Burnell (London Scottish), D F Cronin (Wasps), G W Weir (Newcastle), R I Wainwright (Dundee HSFP), E W Peters (Bath), A J Roxburgh (Kelso) *Substitutions:* S B Grimes (Watsonians) for Cronin (53 mins); C A Murray (Hawick) for Chalmers (72 mins)
Scorers *Tries:* Stanger, Longstaff *Conversions:* Lee (2) *Penalty Goals:* Chalmers (2)
ENGLAND: M B Perry (Bath); A S Healey (Leicester), W J H Greenwood (Leicester), J C Guscott (Bath), A A Adebayo (Bath); P J Grayson (Northampton), M J S Dawson (Northampton); J Leonard (Harlequins), R Cockerill (Leicester), D J Garforth (Leicester), M O Johnson (Leicester), G S Archer (Newcastle), L B N Dallaglio (Wasps) *(capt)*, D Ryan (Newcastle), N A Back (Leicester) *Substitutions:* A J Diprose (Saracens) for Ryan (68 mins); P R de Glanville (Bath) for Healey (71 mins); D J Grewcock (Saracens) for Johnson (74 mins); D E West (Leicester) for Cockerill (83 mins)
Scorers *Tries:* penalty try, Dawson, Healey, Grayson *Conversions:* Grayson (4) *Penalty Goal:* Grayson *Dropped Goal:* Grayson
Referee C Thomas (Wales)

4 April, Twickenham
ENGLAND 35 (3G 3PG 1T)   IRELAND 17 (2G 1PG)

A fourth Triple Crown in succession, and a new record aggregate mark for the championship (146 points), were the tangible returns from this victory. However the mood in the English camp immediately afterwards was one of sober reflection, of work still to be done.

Once more they played in fits and starts. When they clicked they produced some delightful rugby. However, they were unable to sustain the momentum. This was due to three factors – their own incompetence, the swirling wind and the hustling Irish. Ireland ended their championship season with the wooden spoon and their first whitewash in six years. As with this match they did not get due merit from the bald statement of finishing last. They were combative throughout, a trait which was in marked evidence here. The marks were largely on the back of English bodies, Ireland raking their opponents clear from many a piled-up ruck. Referee Derek Bevan was happy to let this pass; England were none too happy that he did so. There was an unseemly running battle between Ireland's David Corkery and England captain, Lawrence Dallaglio.

Matt Perry was put in after three minutes by neat build-up work by Will Greenwood and Jeremy Guscott. Fifteen minutes later it was a deft link and pass by Neil Back which sent Richard Cockerill to the try-line, the hooker celebrating the score in typically unrestrained fashion. But then England froze, perhaps as a result of the interception try they gave Denis Hickie in the 34th minute, Paul Grayson's pass finding the Irish wing rather than an English shirt.

Even a try in the 40th minute by Mike Catt, selected as a wing, did not calm the English jitters. Hickie scored his second try of the match in the 55th minute courtesy of a beautiful behind-the-back pass from Eric Elwood. Phil de Glanville scored England's fourth try in the 65th minute. Jonny Wilkinson came on to the field as a replacement two minutes from time to become, at 18 years and 314 days, the youngest English cap for 71 years.

A sickening clash of heads between Elwood and Mark McCall ended with McCall stretchered from the field. Happily he recovered in the dressing-room. The only other good news on the day came from Victor Costello's chase-back tackle on the fleeing Guscott. The England centre will never live it down.

ENGLAND: M B Perry (Bath); M J Catt (Bath), W J H Greenwood (Leicester), J C Guscott (Bath), A S Healey (Leicester); P J Grayson (Northampton), M J S Dawson (Northampton); J Leonard (Harlequins), R Cockerill (Leicester), D J Garforth (Leicester), M O Johnson (Leicester), G S Archer (Newcastle), L B N Dallaglio (Wasps)*(capt)*, A J Diprose (Saracens), N A Back (Leicester) *Substitutions:* D J Grewcock (Saracens) for Archer (52 mins); P R de Glanville (Bath) for Greenwood (52 mins); J P Wilkinson for Catt (78 mins) **Scorers** *Tries:* Perry, Catt, Cockerill, de Glanville *Conversions:* Grayson (3) *Penalty Goals:* Grayson (3)
IRELAND: C P Clarke (Terenure College); R M Wallace (Saracens), K M Maggs (Bristol), M C McCall (London Irish), D A Hickie (St Mary's College); E P Elwood (Galwegians), C D McGuinness (St Mary's College); R Corrigan (Greystones), K G M Wood (Harlequins)*(capt)*, P S Wallace (Saracens), P S Johns (Saracens), M E O'Kelly (London Irish), D S Corkery (Bristol), V C P Costello (St Mary's College), A J Ward (Ballynahinch) *Substitutions:* K P Keane (Garryowen) for McCall (45 mins); D G Humphreys (London Irish) for Clarke (69 mins) **Scorers** *Tries:* Hickie (2) *Conversions:* Elwood (2) *Penalty Goal:* Elwood
Referee W D Bevan (Wales)

5 April, Wembley
WALES 0   FRANCE 51 (5G 2PG 2T)

There have been many celebrated occasions when the French have frozen in the face of opportunity, betrayed by their own nerves and lack of self-belief. An unprecedented feat of back-to-back Grand Slams was the tantalising possibility on offer at Wembley. History was made in style.

France produced one of the most stunning performances of this or any other championship. They scored seven tries en route to the biggest ever win recorded in a Five Nations match, equalling their own record points total recorded earlier in the championship against Scotland. But the match was about more than mere numbers. It was the sheer effrontery of the French play, the cocky charm of their attack, the breezy insouciance of their breaks from the defence, which really caught the eye and captivated the soul. One man in particular, French fly-half, Thomas Castaignède, stole the show.

The bleached-blond Castres stand-off was voted man-of-the-match by every single one of the 81 journalists who voted. That's what you call unanimous. And on the day Castaignède was what you call a genius. He set out to make the life of Neil Jenkins, the Welsh No 10, a misery. He succeeded. Castaignède scorched past him with disdain on numerous occasions, often from inside his own half.

It was a marvellous virtuoso performance. The French superiority was not just reflected in their attack. They defended their line with desperate zeal throughout, even in the dying moments when the contest was long decided. There were outstanding contributions from the two giants of the front row, hooker and captain Raphael Ibañez and prop Christian Califano, openside flanker Olivier Magne, centre Stephane Glas and full-back Jean-Luc Sadourny.

Wales were a crushing disappointment, their defence pitiful. Sadourny had scored two tries within the opening 13 minutes. Thomas Lièvremont then picked up from a scrum to go over unmolested before Ibañez teed-up France's fourth try with a galloping run which eventually saw Glas cross. The second half brought no respite. Xavier Garbajosa scored the first of his two tries within three minutes of the restart. The 10,000 French supporters were exultant. And well they might be.

WALES: K A Morgan (Pontypridd); W T Proctor (Llanelli), L B Davies (Cardiff), N Boobyer (Llanelli), G Thomas (Bridgend); N R Jenkins (Pontypridd), R Howley (Cardiff)*(capt)*; A L P Lewis (Cardiff), G R Jenkins (Swansea), D Young (Swansea), M J Voyle (Llanelli), A P Moore (Swansea), R C Appleyard (Swansea), S Davies (Swansea), C L Charvis (Swansea) *Substitutions:* J M Humphreys (Cardiff) for G Jenkins (55 mins); L Mustoe (Cardiff) for Lewis (55 mins); D R James (Pontypridd) for Boobyer (56 mins); K P Jones (Ebbw Vale) for Appleyard (65 mins)

FRANCE: J-L Sadourny (Colomiers); P Bernat-Salles (Pau), C Lamaison (Brive), S Glas (Bourgoin), X Garbajosa (Toulouse); T Castaignède (Castres), P Carbonneau (Brive); C Califano (Toulouse), R Ibañez (Dax) *(capt)*, F Tournaire (Narbonne), O Brouzet (Bègles-Bordeaux), F Pelous (Dax), M Lièvremont (Stade Français), T Lièvremont (Perpignan), O Magne (Brive) *Substitutions:* P Benetton (Agen) for M Lièvremont (63 mins); C Soulette (Béziers) for Califano (67 mins); F Galthié (Colomiers) for Carbonneau (67 mins); D Aucagne (Pau) for Castaignède (67 mins); M Dal Maso (Agen) for Ibañez (71 mins); T Cléda (Pau) for Brouzet (77 mins); J-M Aué (Castres) for Lamaison (77 mins)

Scorers *Tries:* Sadourny (2), Garbajosa (2), T Lièvremont, Glas, Galthié *Conversions:* Lamaison (5) *Penalty Goals:* Lamaison (2)

Referee P Marshall (Australia)

NEW ZEALAND'S SECOND CLEAN SWEEP

THE TRI-NATIONS SERIES 1997

Hopes that the Lions' triumphs in South Africa would presage a British and Irish challenge to the southern hemisphere's long domination of international rugby evaporated during the 1997 Tri-Nations series that began less than a fortnight after the Lions had returned home. New Zealand repeated the clean sweep they had achieved in 1996, once again setting new benchmarks of fitness and skill for the rest of the world to aspire to.

The ease with which the All Blacks swept to 55 points in their home tie with the Springboks put the Lions' achievements firmly into perspective. The South African side which contested the Tri-Nations was drawn from essentially the same squad which under coach Carel du Plessis had gone down 2-1 to Martin Johnson's tourists, but by the end of the tournament the Springboks were clearly shown to be some way below the standard set by the All Blacks, a fact that precipitated the downfall of du Plessis. He was not the only one to go. Greg Smith, Australia's coach, was supplanted by Rod Macqueen in the wake of the Wallabies' 61-22 defeat in Pretoria in the last match of the series.

Big crowds poured in to see the matches, with the All Blacks the top draw card. Their match in Australia was the first international staged on the Melbourne Cricket Ground and more than 80,000 tickets were snapped up within days of going on sale. The final gate of 90,119 set a new record for a Test involving the All Blacks.

FINAL TABLE

	P	W	D	L	F	A	Bonus	Pts
New Zealand	4	4	0	0	159	109	2	18
South Africa	4	1	0	3	148	144	3	7
Australia	4	1	0	3	96	150	2	6

(The 403 points scored comprised 48 tries, 35 conversions, 29 penalty goals and two dropped goals. Carlos Spencer was the leading points scorer with 84 and Christian Cullen (four) scored most tries.)

19 July, Ellis Park, Johannesburg
SOUTH AFRICA 32 (2G 4PG 2DG)   **NEW ZEALAND 35** (3G 3PG 1T)

'That was an epic match,' said John Hart, New Zealand's coach, after this entertaining international. The two sides boldly engaged in the kind of free-flowing, high-scoring play that characterises the Super-12s, yet also managed to create a match of intense excitement with the outcome in the balance until the final whistle.

Jannie de Beer scored 22 points, a new high for a Springbok against

New Zealand, and helped his side accelerate into a 23-7 lead in the first 32 minutes. Sean Fitzpatrick rallied his men and the All Blacks quickly raised their game, tries by Jeff Wilson and Carlos Spencer making the score 23-19 to South Africa by the break. Midway through the second spell Spencer eventually put the visitors ahead for the first time, only for de Beer to tie the scores at 32-all with another penalty. Spencer edged New Zealand back into the lead with his third penalty 11 minutes from time. Although that was the final score, it was not the last thrill: two minutes from the end de Beer, after placing six goals from six attempts, fluffed a penalty kick that would have squared the match.

James Small, who came on for his 39th Test appearance at half-time, became South Africa's most capped player.

SOUTH AFRICA: RG Bennett (Border); AH Snyman (Blue Bulls), PC Montgomery (Western Province), D van Schalkwyk (Blue Bulls), PWG Rossouw (Western Province); JH de Beer (Free State), JH van der Westhuizen (Blue Bulls); JP du Randt (Free State), AE Drotské (Free State), MH Hurter (Blue Bulls), K Otto (Blue Bulls), MG Andrews (Natal), RJ Kruger (Blue Bulls), GH Teichmann (Natal)(*capt*), AG Venter (Free State)
Substitutions: JT Small (Western Province) for Bennett (40 mins); FJ van Heerden (Western Province) for Andrews (69 mins); DF Theron (Griqualand West) for du Randt (71 mins); HW Honiball (Natal) for Montgomery (77 mins)
Scorers *Tries:* Drotské, Bennett *Conversions:* de Beer (2) *Penalty Goals:* de Beer (4) *Dropped Goals:* de Beer (2)
NEW ZEALAND: CM Cullen (Manawatu); JW Wilson (Otago), FE Bunce (North Harbour), L Stensness (Auckland), TJF Umaga (Wellington); CJ Spencer (Auckland), JW Marshall (Canterbury); CW Dowd (Auckland), SBT Fitzpatrick (Auckland)(*capt*), OM Brown (Auckland), ID Jones (North Harbour), RM Brooke (Auckland), TC Randell (Otago), ZV Brooke (Auckland), JA Kronfeld (Otago)
Substitutions: A Ieremia (Wellington) for Umaga (29 mins); NJ Hewitt (Southland) for Fitzpatrick (49 mins)
Scorers *Tries:* Bunce (2), Wilson, Spencer *Conversions:* Spencer (3)
Penalty Goals: Spencer (3)
Referee PL Marshall (Australia)

26 July, Melbourne Cricket Ground
AUSTRALIA 18 (1G 2PG 1T)   **NEW ZEALAND 33** (3G 4PG)
New Zealand's second away victory of the tournament more or less guaranteed back-to-back Tri-Nations titles. Their ruthless efficiency under the MCG floodlights, and in front of a record attendance for a southern hemisphere international, was sublime. Backs and forwards combined effectively to tear holes in an Australian defence unable to cope with the waves of second- and third-phase attacks.

The All Blacks were out of sight at 23-6 by half-time and maintained the pressure in the second period. Carlos Spencer's last penalty brought up his Test century of points in only his fifth international, equalling the world record set by his compatriots Simon Culhane and Andrew Mehrtens, while Sean Fitzpatrick appeared in his 71st winning Test, passing the previous world record set by France's Philippe Sella.

AUSTRALIA: M Burke (NSW); BN Tune (Queensland), JS Little (Queensland), J Holbeck (ACT), JW Roff (ACT); TJ Horan (Queensland), GM Gregan (ACT); RLL Harry (NSW), MA Foley (Queensland), A Heath (NSW), GJ Morgan

(Queensland), JA Eales (Queensland)(*capt*), DT Manu (NSW), MC Brial (NSW), BJ Robinson (ACT) *Substitutions:* T Coker (ACT) for Brial (33 mins); SJ Larkham (ACT) for Horan (40 mins); DJ Wilson (Queensland) for Robinson (60 mins); SJ Payne (NSW) for Burke (77 mins)
Scorers *Tries:* Gregan, Little *Conversion:* Burke *Penalty Goals:* Burke (2)
NEW ZEALAND: CM Cullen (Manawatu); JW Wilson (Otago), FE Bunce (North Harbour), A Ieremia (Wellington), GM Osborne (North Harbour); CJ Spencer (Auckland), JW Marshall (Canterbury); CW Dowd (Auckland), SBT Fitzpatrick (Auckland)(*capt*), OM Brown (Auckland), ID Jones (North Harbour), RM Brooke (Auckland), TC Randell (Otago), ZV Brooke (Auckland), JA Kronfeld (Otago) *Substitution:* AR Cashmore (Auckland) for Wilson (40 mins)
Scorers *Tries:* Bunce, Wilson, Cullen *Conversions:* Spencer (3)
Penalty Goals: Spencer (4)
Referee EF Morrison (England)

2 August, Suncorp Stadium, Brisbane
AUSTRALIA 32 (3G 2PG 1T)   **SOUTH AFRICA** 20 (1G 1PG 2T)
David Knox, the 33-year-old ACT fly-half first capped in 1985, was dramatically recalled from his playing contract with Natal in South Africa to replace the injured Tim Horan in the Aussie Test side. The veteran made a spectacular return and, in his ninth international, maintained his record of never having played in a losing Test side.

His shrewd tactical control, particularly in the first half, and his accurate place-kicking provided the platform for Australia's win. The Wallabies led 26-10 at the pause, having conjured spectacular tries in the 8th, 17th, 27th and 40th minutes, and finished with their record score for a Test against South Africa.

AUSTRALIA: SJ Larkham (ACT); BN Tune (Queensland), JS Little (Queensland), J Holbeck (ACT), JW Roff (ACT); DJ Knox (ACT), GM Gregan (ACT); RLL Harry (NSW), MA Foley (Queensland), A Heath (NSW), ODA Finegan (ACT), JA Eales (Queensland)(*capt*), M Cockbain (Queensland), DT Manu (NSW), DJ Wilson (Queensland) *Substitutions:* T Coker (ACT) for Cockbain (57 mins); BJ Robinson (ACT) for Manu (60 mins); AT Blades (NSW) for Heath (73 mins); Heath returned for Harry (77 mins)
Scorers *Tries:* Tune (2), Larkham, Manu *Conversions:* Knox (3)
Penalty Goals: Knox (2)
SOUTH AFRICA: RG Bennett (Border); AH Snyman (Blue Bulls), PC Montgomery (Western Province), D van Schalkwyk (Blue Bulls), PWG Rossouw (Western Province); JH de Beer (Free State), JH van der Westhuizen (Blue Bulls); JP du Randt (Free State), AE Drotské (Free State), DF Theron (Griqualand West), K Otto (Blue Bulls), MG Andrews (Natal), RJ Kruger (Blue Bulls), GH Teichmann (Natal)(*capt*), AG Venter (Free State) *Substitutions:* JT Small (Western Province) for Snyman (50 mins); AC Garvey (Natal) for du Randt (temp 62-70 mins); HW Honiball (Natal) for van Schalkwyk (83 mins)
Scorers *Tries:* du Randt, de Beer, Andrews *Conversion:* de Beer
Penalty Goal: de Beer
Referee CJ Hawke (New Zealand)

9 August, Eden Park, Auckland
NEW ZEALAND 55 (4G 4PG 3T)   **SOUTH AFRICA** 35 (5G)
The lead swayed to and fro in an intoxicating first half in which both sides contributed fully to a match played at a blistering pace. New

Zealand held a slender 23-21 interval lead, but pulled clear in a second half of perpetual action, some of which however was of a violent nature. The ugliest incident came in the 47th minute when Springbok flanker André Venter stamped on Sean Fitzpatrick's face, prompting the South African's dismissal by Welsh referee Derek Bevan.

New Zealand's total was the highest ever scored by any Test XV against the Springboks and the winning margin was their biggest against South Africa. On the day when Sean Fitzpatrick led New Zealand for the 50th time in a Test, Carlos Spencer's 25-point contribution was a new individual record for an All Black against South Africa.

NEW ZEALAND: CM Cullen (Manawatu); JW Wilson (Otago), FE Bunce (North Harbour), A Ieremia (Wellington), TJF Umaga (Wellington); CJ Spencer (Auckland), JW Marshall (Canterbury); CW Dowd (Auckland), SBT Fitzpatrick (Auckland)(*capt*), OM Brown (Auckland), ID Jones (North Harbour), RM Brooke (Auckland), TC Randell (Otago), ZV Brooke (Auckland), JA Kronfeld (Otago) *Substitutions:* AP Mehrtens (Canterbury) for Spencer (68 mins); CC Riechelmann (Auckland) for Z Brooke then R Brooke (temp 57-67 mins); MR Allen (Manawatu) for Dowd (75 mins)
Scorers *Tries:* Cullen (2), Ieremia, Umaga, Spencer, Marshall, Randell *Conversions:* Spencer (4) *Penalty Goals:* Spencer (4)
SOUTH AFRICA: RG Bennett (Border); JT Small (Western Province), PC Montgomery (Western Province), HW Honiball (Natal), AH Snyman (Blue Bulls); JH de Beer (Free State), JH van der Westhuizen (Blue Bulls); JP du Randt (Free State), J Dalton (Gauteng Lions), MH Hurter (Blue Bulls), K Otto (Blue Bulls), MG Andrews (Natal), RJ Kruger (Blue Bulls), GH Teichmann (Natal)(*capt*), AG Venter (Free State) *Substitutions:* FJ van Heerden (Western Province) for Kruger (10 mins); AE Drotské (Free State) for Otto (58 mins); PWG Rossouw (Western Province) for de Beer (66 mins); DF Theron (Griqualand West) for Hurter (74 mins)
Scorers *Tries:* Kruger, Teichmann, Montgomery, van der Westhuizen, Rossouw *Conversions:* De Beer (3), Honiball (2)
Referee WD Bevan (Wales)

16 August, Carisbrook, Dunedin
NEW ZEALAND 36 (3G 5PG)   AUSTRALIA 24 (2G 2T)

Sean Fitzpatrick had his hands full showing off the substantial Tri-Nations and Bledisloe Cup silverware after New Zealand ended their season with an unblemished record of eight wins from eight Tests. This win also completed back-to-back Tri-Nations Grand Slams for Fitzpatrick's men.

The All Blacks were unstoppable, powering to an unassailable 36-0 lead by the break. Their three tries were augmented by Carlos Spencer's immaculate place-kicking. He landed eight out of eight in the first half to finish the tournament with 84 points from four games.

Australia's spirited second-half comeback provided the statisticians with the oddity that all 60 points were scored at the same end of the ground. Yet the Wallabies never really threatened to pinch a match that as a spectacle was spoiled by the incessant whistling of French referee Joel Dumé, who overall awarded 38 penalties. For New Zealand, the front row of Olo Brown, Sean Fitzpatrick and Craig Dowd were together for the 34th time in a Test, a new All Black record.

NEW ZEALAND: CM Cullen (Manawatu); JW Wilson (Otago), FE Bunce (North Harbour), A Ieremia (Wellington), GM Osborne (North Harbour); CJ Spencer (Auckland), JW Marshall (Canterbury); CW Dowd (Auckland), SBT Fitzpatrick (Auckland)(*capt*), OM Brown (Auckland), ID Jones (North Harbour), RM Brooke (Auckland), TC Randell (Otago), ZV Brooke (Auckland), JA Kronfeld (Otago) *Substitutions:* OFJ Tonu'u (Auckland) for Marshall (63 mins); MR Allen (Manawatu) for I Jones (76 mins)
Scorers *Tries:* Randell, Cullen, Marshall *Conversions:* Spencer (3) *Penalty Goals:* Spencer (5)
AUSTRALIA: SJ Larkham (ACT); BN Tune (Queensland), JS Little (Queensland), J Holbeck (ACT), JW Roff (ACT); DJ Knox (ACT), GM Gregan (ACT); RLL Harry (NSW), MA Foley (Queensland), AT Blades (NSW), ODA Finegan (ACT), JF Langford (ACT), SF Finau (NSW), T Coker (ACT), DJ Wilson (Queensland)(*capt*) *Substitutions:* BJ Robinson (ACT) for Langford (64 mins); MD Hardy (ACT) for Roff (69 mins)
Scorers *Tries:* Larkham (2), Roff, Tune *Conversions:* Knox (2)
Referee J Dumé (France)

23 August, Loftus Versfeld, Pretoria
SOUTH AFRICA 61 (6G 3PG 2T) **AUSTRALIA 22** (2G 1PG 1T)
André Joubert, who was called into the Springbok side as a late replacement for the injured Russell Bennett, was the catalyst of Australia's heaviest-ever Test defeat. The Wallabies were leading 15-13 when, on the stroke of half-time, Joubert gathered a kick ahead and launched a coruscating counterattack from his own half which led to a try by James Dalton. Thereafter South Africa never looked back. Copying Joubert's freedom of spirit, they ran all their possession at the Wallabies in an exhilarating second half to clock up 43 points.

History was made late in the game when James Holbeck became the first player to be sin-binned in a Test match. The rule had been introduced for the 1997 Super-12s and was extended as an experiment for the Tri-Nations series. It was only when Holbeck returned a minute from time that many of those present realised that the player had not in fact been sent off.

SOUTH AFRICA: AJ Joubert (Natal); JT Small (Western Province), PC Montgomery (Western Province), HW Honiball (Natal), AH Snyman (Blue Bulls); JH de Beer (Free State), JH van der Westhuizen (Blue Bulls); JP du Randt (Free State), J Dalton (Gauteng Lions), MH Hurter (Blue Bulls), JJ Strydom (Gauteng Lions), MG Andrews (Natal), W Brosnihan (Gauteng Lions), GH Teichmann (Natal)(*capt*), JC Erasmus (Free State) *Substitutions:* PWG Rossouw (Western Province) for Snyman (29 mins); S Bekker (Blue Bulls) for Teichmann (temp 50-52 mins); WW Els (Free State) for Strydom (68 mins); W Swanepoel (Free State) for Small (84 mins)
Scorers *Tries:* Montgomery (2), Erasmus, Dalton, Andrews, Rossouw, Brosnihan, de Beer *Conversions:* de Beer (6) *Penalty Goals:* de Beer (3)
AUSTRALIA: SJ Larkham (ACT); BN Tune (Queensland), JS Little (Queensland), J Holbeck (ACT), JW Roff (ACT); DJ Knox (ACT), GM Gregan (ACT); RLL Harry (NSW), MA Foley (Queensland), AT Blades (NSW), ODA Finegan (ACT), JF Langford (ACT), M Cockbain (Queensland), T Coker (ACT), DJ Wilson (Queensland)(*capt*) *Substitutions:* BJ Robinson (ACT) for Coker (57 mins); T Kefu (Queensland) for Cockbain (78 mins)
Scorers *Tries:* Knox, Roff, Little *Conversions:* Knox (2) *Penalty Goal:* Knox
Referee PD O'Brien (New Zealand)

FRANCE WIN BUT FAIL TO IMPRESS

LATIN CUP 1997

The second Latin Cup tournament took place in France in October 1997, the host nation retaining the trophy they had won at the inaugural competition held in Argentina two years earlier. Yet despite their victory, it has to be said that France showed little of the enterprise that was to ignite their subsequent Five Nations campaign. In fact, the truth was that France performed like a tired outfit at the end of an exhausting season rather than a squad coming together to stake its claim for back-to-back European championship titles. Their own supporters, moreover, booed them off the pitches at all three matches.

In 1995, Jean-Claude Skrela had made his national coaching debut at the Latin Cup, after Pierre Berbizier's demise in the wake of France's failure to lift the World Cup in South Africa. On that occasion Skrela had blooded several new caps with a view to providing them with international experience which, he hoped, would stand them in good stead for the 1999 World Cup. He was happy to leave behind the old guard of Thierry Lacroix and Laurent Cabannes, experimenting instead with the new talents of Thomas Castaignède, Philippe Carbonneau and Fabien Pelous.

How odd, therefore, that the same coach, two years into his reign, should decide to use the 1997 Latin Cup to rehabilitate Lacroix and Cabannes? The decision proved to be a retrograde step. France were unable to forge any kind of style in their play and, without a game plan, they lacked tactical purpose. Their approach was defensively effective but dreadfully dull, and it was the dullness that irritated the home supporters: never before could critics remember France winning three internationals at home and getting such a frosty reception from their supporters.

The first round of double-headers pitched the French against the up-and-coming Italians in Auch. Here, after a long lay-off and even before their own domestic competition had started, the *azzurri* were unable to repeat the golden performance of six months earlier when they had seen off the Five Nations champions 40-32 in Grenoble. Even so, the Italians showed that their drive for Six Nations status was gathering momentum. They were exceptionally well-organised defensively and showed a refreshing readiness to turn defence into attack when opportunities arose. Paulo Vaccari, their right-wing who has turned down several lucrative offers to play elsewhere in Europe, scored the try of the match early in the second half. He set off on an arcing run from inside his own half before linking up with Marcello Cuttitta on the other wing.

Receiving a return pass, Vaccari then sprinted nearly 40 metres to touch down. In the process, he earned the warmest ovation of the entire tournament.

The four nations assembled at Lourdes, the miracle city, in midweek. Here Romania, who had been thumped by Argentina in the first round, knew that they would need the powers of all the saints to hold France. The saints, predictably perhaps, deserted them, France winning 39-3, but once again it was a mediocre performance by the home team. Lourdes was the centre of the rise of French rugby in the 1950s. Though the local club has slipped of late, its rugby followers have lost none of their love and appreciation of the open game. They expressed their disapproval of the lacklustre French play by booing their men off the pitch at the end of the match.

In the other game staged at Lourdes, Italy and Argentina shared the spoils of a ding-dong battle in which Argentina scored two tries but could not overcome the deadly accurate boot of their expatriate Diego Dominguez, who kicked all six of Italy's penalty goals in an 18-all draw.

So on to Tarbes for the final round of the tournament. Italy duly despatched the hapless Romanians, while France, after a stuttering start, eventually scraped home against Argentina at the end of a rough match in which two players received yellow cards and one of the Argentinian back row was sent off.

FINAL TABLE

	P	W	D	L	F	A	Pts
France	3	3	0	0	101	49	9
Argentina	3	1	1	1	90	68	6
Italy	3	1	1	1	92	80	6
Romania	3	0	0	3	53	139	3

Previous winner: 1995 France

ARGENTINA **Captain** P Sporleder   **Managers** JL Rolandi, A Coscia
Coaches JL Imhoff, A Wyllie

Full-backs: E Jurado (Jockey Club, Rosario), D Giannantonio (Piacenza, Italy)
Threequarters: D Albanese (San Isidro Club), F Soler (Tala, Cordoba), E Simone (Liceo Naval), F Turnes (Banco Nacion), J Orengo (Atletico Rosario)
Half-backs: JC Fernandez-Miranda (Hindu), L Arbizu (Brive, France), N Fernandez-Miranda (Hindu), A Pichot (Richmond, England)
Forwards: F Mendez (Bath, England), C Promanzio (Duendes, Rosario), M Ledesma (Curupayti), D Alberdi (CU Buenos Aires), O Hasan-Jalil (Wellington, NZ), M Scelzo (Hindu), M Reggiardo (Castres, France), M Ruiz (Teque, Cuyo), G Llanes (Bath, England), P Sporleder (Curupayti), A Allub (Jockey Club, Rosario), P Bouza (Duendes, Rosario), S Phelan (San Isidro Club), R Martin (Richmond, England), R Travaglini (CA San Isidro), P Camerlinckx (Regetas Bella Vista)

FRANCE **Captain** P Saint-André **Managers** J Maso, J Dunyach
Coaches JC Skrela, P Villepreux

Full-backs: JL Sadourny (Colomiers), N Brusque (Pau)
Threequarters: P Saint-Andrè (Gloucester, England), T Castaignède (Castres),
S Glas (Bourgoin-Jallieu), C Lamaison (Brive), L Leflamand (Bourgoin-Jallieu),
P Bondouy (Toulouse)
Half-backs: T Lacroix (Harlequins, England), F Galthié (Colomiers), D Aucagne
(Pau), J Cazabou (Toulouse), P Mignoni (Béziers)
Forwards: M Dal Maso (Agen), R Ibanez (Dax), C Califano (Toulouse),
F Tournaire (Toulouse), C Soulette (Béziers), O Merle (Montferrand), O Brouzet
(Bègles-Bordeaux), P Benetton (Agen), A Benazzi (Agen), L Cabannes
(Harlequins, England), F Pelous (Toulouse), O Magne (Brive), N Bacqué (Pau)

ITALY **Captain** M Giovanelli **Manager** F Cimino **Coach** G Costes

Full-backs: J Pertile (Roma), C Pilat (Treviso), M Ravazzolo (Calvisano)
Threequarters: Marcello Cuttitta (Milan), P Vaccari (Calvisano), I Francescato
(Treviso), C Stoica (Narbonne, France), L Martin (Padova), M Dallan (Treviso)
Half-backs: D Dominguez (Stade Francais), F Mazzariol (Treviso), A Troncon
(Treviso), G Guidi (L'Aquila)
Forwards: Massimo Cuttitta (Harlequins, England), F Properzi-Curti (Milan),
A Castellani (L'Aquila), G De Carli (Roma), C Orlandi (Milan), A Moretti
(Padova), G Croci (Milan), W Cristofoletto (Treviso), C Caione (L'Aquila),
A Sgorlon (Treviso), M Giovanelli (Narbonne, France), R Piovan (Padova),
C Checchinato (Treviso)

ROMANIA **Captain** T Brinza **Manager** S Fuicu **Coach** M Paraschiv

Full-backs: V Maftei (Cluj University), P Mitu (Steaua Bucharest)
Threequarters: G Solomie (Timisoara), G Brezoianu (Timisoara), D Talaba (Farul
Constanta), L Colceriu (Steaua Bucharest), I Rotaru (Dinamo Bucharest),
R Gontineac (Pau, France)
Half-backs: M Iacob (Dinamo Bucharest), C Dragnea (Petrosani), I Tofan (Conaig
Giughu), S Guranescu (Dinamo Bucharest)
Forwards: G Vlad (Narbonne, France), D Nicolae (Romans, France), C Stan
(Dinamo Bucharest), D Bozian (Steaua Bucharest), A Salageanu (Dinamo
Bucharest), M Radoi (Dinamo Bucharest), L Dumitrescu (Grivita Rosie),
V Nedelcu (Dinamo Bucharest), T Brinza (Narbonne, France), V Doja (Dinamo
Bucharest), S Socol (Brive, France), M Dragomir (Steaua Bucharest),
C Draguceanu (Steaua Bucharest), A Girbu (Oyonnax, France), O Slusariuc
(Dinamo Bucharest), I Ruxanda (Farul Constanta), E Septar (Farul Constanta),
S Ciorascu (Auch, France), T Constantin (Tarbes, France)

MATCH 1 **18 October, Stade Moulias, Auch**

ARGENTINA 45 (3G 3PG 3T) **ROMANIA 18** (1G 2PG 1T)
ARGENTINA: Jurado; Albanese, Simone, Arbizu, Soler; JC Fernandez-Mranda,
N Fernandez-Miranda; Reggiardo, Ledesma, Hasan, Sporleder (*capt*), Llanes,
Travaglini, Camerlinckx, Ruiz *Substitutions:* Orengo for Simone (60 mins); Turnes
for Arbizu (62 mins); Scelzo for Reggiardo (66 mins); Bouza for Llanes (72 mins);
Phelan for Ruiz (temp 38-40 mins) and for Travaglini (temp 70-75 mins)
Scorers *Tries:* Simone (2), Scelzo (2), Soler, Albanese
Conversions: JC Fernandez-Miranda (3) *Penalty Goals:* JC Fernandez-Miranda (3)
ROMANIA: Mitu; Colceriu, Solomie, Gontineac, Rotaru; Tofan, Dragnea;
Nicolae, Radoi, Vlad, Brinza (*capt*), Nedelcu, Girbu, Draguceanu, Slusariuc

Substitutions: Iacob for Dragnea (66 mins); Dumitrescu for Girbu (66 mins); Bozian for Vlad (temp 47-53 mins); Guranescu for Tofan (temp 50-53 mins)
Scorers *Tries:* Solomie, Tofan *Conversion:* Tofan *Penalty Goals:* Tofan (2)
Referee C Giacomel (Italy)

MATCH 2   18 October, Stade Moulias, Auch

FRANCE 30 (1G 6PG 1T)   **ITALY 19** (1G 3PG 1DG)
FRANCE: Sadourny; Leflamand, Lamaison, Castaignède, Saint-André (*capt*); Lacroix, Galthié; Califano, Dal Maso, Tournaire, Merle, Brouzet, Benazzi, Pelous, Cabannes *Substitutions:* Cazalbou for Galthie (31 mins); Glas for Castaignède (39 mins); Magne for Merle (53 mins); Benetton for Cabannes (67 mins); Ibanez for Dal Maso (80 mins)
Scorers *Tries:* Califano, Saint-André *Conversion:* Lamaison
Penalty Goals: Lamaison (6)
ITALY: Ravazzolo; Vaccari, Stoica, Francescato, Marcello Cuttitta; Dominguez, Troncon; Massimo Cuttitta, Orlandi, Properzi Curti, Croci, Cristofoletto, Giovanelli (*capt*), Checchinato, Sgorlon *Substitutions:* Martin for Stoica (28 mins); Caione for Cristofoletto (59 mins)
Scorers *Try:* Vaccari *Conversion:* Dominguez *Penalty Goals:* Dominguez (3)
Dropped Goal: Dominguez
Referee S Borsani (Argentina)

MATCH 3   22 October, Stade Antoine-Beguere, Lourdes

ARGENTINA 18 (1G 2PG 1T)   **ITALY 18** (6PG)
ARGENTINA: Jurado; Albanese, Orengo, Arbizu, Soler; JC Fernandez-Miranda, Pichot; Hasan, Ledesma, Scelzo, Sporleder (*capt*), Llanes, Martin, Camerlinckx, Ruiz *Substitutions:* Phelan for Llanes (71 mins); Giannantonio for Soler (71 mins)
Scorers *Tries:* Scelzo, JC Fernandez-Miranda *Conversion:* JC Fernandez-Miranda
Penalty Goals: JC Fernandez-Miranda (2)
ITALY: Ravazzolo; Vaccari, Dallan, Francescato, Marcello Cuttitta; Dominguez, Troncon; Massimo Cuttitta, Orlandi, Properzi-Curti, Croci, Cristofoletto, Giovanelli (*capt*), Checchinato, Sgorlon *Substitutions:* Guidi for Troncon (46 mins); Castellani for Properzi Curti (temp 48-52 mins)
Scorer *Penalty Goals:* Dominguez (6)
Referee V Stancu (Romania)

MATCH 4   22 October, Stade Antoine-Beguere, Lourdes

FRANCE 39 (4G 2PG 1T)   **ROMANIA 3** (1PG)
FRANCE: Sadourny; Bondouy, Lamaison, Glas, Saint-André (*capt*); Lacroix, Cazalbou; Soulette, Ibanez, Tournaire, Merle, Pelous, Bacqué, Benetton, Magne *Substitutions:* Brusque for Sadourny (41 mins); Aucagne for Lacroix (51 mins); Benazzi for Pelous (51 mins); Mignoni for Cazalbou (65 mins); Califano for Tournaire (65 mins)
Scorers *Tries:* Saint-André, Tournaire, Merle, Penalty try, Benazzi
Conversions: Lamaison (4) *Penalty Goals:* Lamaison (2)
ROMANIA: Maftei; Colceriu, Solomie, Gontineac, Rotaru; Tofan, Dragnea; Nicolae, Radoi, Vlad, Ciorascu, Brinza (*capt*), Girbu, Slusariuc, Draguceanu *Substitutions:* Nedelcu for Slusariuc (11 mins); Talaba for Tofan (41 mins); Iacob for Rotaru (70 mins); Salageanu for Nicolae (78 mins)
Scorer *Penalty Goal:* Tofan
Referee S Borsani (Argentina)

MATCH 5   26 October, Stade Maurice Trelut, Tarbes

FRANCE 32 (3G 2PG 1T)   **ARGENTINA 27** (3G 1PG 1DG)
FRANCE: Sadourny; Leflamand, Lamaison, Glas, Saint-André *(capt)*; Lacroix, Cazalbou; Califano, Dal Maso, Tournaire, Pelous, Brouzet, Benetton, Benazzi, Cabannes *Substitutions:* Magne for Benetton (65 mins); Mignoni for Cazalbou (temp 45-50 mins)
Scorers *Tries:* Leflamand, Dal Maso, Benazzi, Sadourny *Conversions:* Lacroix (2), Lamaison *Penalty Goals:* Lacroix (2)
ARGENTINA: Jurado; Albanese, Simone, Turnes, Soler; Arbizu, Pichot; Reggiardo, Ledesma, Hasan, Sporleder *(capt)*, Llanes, Martin, Camerlinckx, Ruiz *Substitutions:* Scelzo for Hasan (55 mins); Allub for Llanes (57 mins); Travaglini for Camerlinckx (78 mins)
Scorers *Tries:* Sporleder, Turnes, Martin *Conversions:* Arbizu (3)
Penalty Goal: Arbizu *Dropped Goal:* Arbizu
Referee C Giacomel (Italy)

MATCH 6   26 October, Stade Maurice Trelut, Tarbes

ITALY 55 (5G 5PG 1T)   **ROMANIA 32** (3G 2PG 1T)
ITALY: Ravazzolo; Vaccari, Dallan, Francescato, Marcello Cuttitta; Dominguez, Guidi; De Carli, Orlandi, Castellani, Croci, Checchinato, Giovanelli *(capt)*, Piovan, Sgorlon *Substitutions:* Mazzariol for Francescato (64 mins); Moretti for Orlandi (73 mins)
Scorers *Tries:* Francescato (2), Dallan, De Carli, Sgorlon, Vaccari
Conversions: Dominguez (5) *Penalty Goals:* Dominguez (5)
ROMANIA: Mitu; Colceriu, Solomie, Gontineac, Talaba; Tofan, Dragnea; Nicolae, Radoi, Vlad, Constantin, Ciorascu, Girbu, Brinza *(capt)*, Draguceanu *Substitutions:* Iacob for Dragnea (70 mins); Nedelcu for Constantin (67 mins); Dumitrescu for Brinza (78 mins)
Scorers *Tries:* Radoi (2), Girbu, Solomie *Conversions:* Tofan (3)
Penalty Goals: Tofan (2)
Referee R Duhau (France)

OTHER MAJOR INTERNATIONAL MATCHES 1997-98

1 June, Dinamo Stadium, Bucharest
ROMANIA 20 (2G 2PG) FRANCE 51 (3G 6T)

ROMANIA: V Brici (Farul Constanta); L Colceriu (Steaua Bucharest), G Solomie (Timisoara U), R Gontineac (Pau, France), G Brezoianu (Timisoara U); N Nichitean (Cluj U), V Flutur (Cluj U); D Nicolae (Steaua Bucharest), M Radoï (Dinamo Bucharest), L Costea (Steaua Bucharest), C Branescu (Albertville, France), V Nedelcu (Dinamo Bucharest), F Corodeanu (Steaua Bucharest), T Brinza (Narbonne, France)(*capt*), A Girbu (Farul Constanta) *Substitutions:* A Manta (Dinamo Bucharest) for Girbu (40 mins); A Stanca (Steaua Bucharest) for Costea (67 mins); C Stan (Dinamo Bucharest) for Nicolae (67 mins); C Dragnea (Petrosani U) for Brezoianu (67 mins)
Scorers *Tries:* Gontineac, Radoï *Conversions:* Nichitean (2)
Penalty Goals: Nichitean (2)
FRANCE: J-L Sadourny (Colomiers); P Bernat-Salles (Pau), C Lamaison (Brive), D Dantiacq (Pau), D Venditti (Brive); A Penaud (Brive), F Torossian (Pau); D Casadeï (Brive), R Ibañez (Dax), F Tournaire (Narbonne), O Merle (Montferrand), O Brouzet (Bègles-Bordeaux), A Benazzi (Agen)(*capt*), F Pelous (Dax), M Lièvremont (Perpignan) *Substitutions:* S Viars (Brive) for Venditti (40 mins); O Magne (Dax) for Pelous (61 mins); D Aucagne (Pau) for Penaud (66 mins); P Carbonneau (Brive) for Torossian (66 mins); D Laperne (Dax) for Tournaire (66 mins); M Dal Maso (Agen) for Ibañez (66 mins)
Scorers *Tries:* Venditti (2), Bernat-Salles (2), Viars (2), Lièvremont, Penaud, Merle *Conversions:* Lamaison (2), Viars
Referee C Giacomel (Italy)

5 July, Lancaster Park, Christchurch (Bledisloe Cup)
NEW ZEALAND 30 (2G 2PG 2T) AUSTRALIA 13 (1G 2PG)

NEW ZEALAND: CM Cullen (Manawatu); JW Wilson (Otago), FE Bunce (North Harbour), L Stensness (Auckland), TJF Umaga (Wellington); CJ Spencer (Auckland), JW Marshall (Canterbury); CW Dowd (Auckland), SBT Fitzpatrick (Auckland)(*capt*), OM Brown (Auckland), ID Jones (North Harbour), RM Brooke (Auckland), TC Randell (Otago), ZV Brooke (Auckland), JA Kronfeld (Otago) *Substitutions:* CC Riechelmann (Auckland) for Z Brooke (68 mins); A Ieremia (Wellington) for Umaga (68 mins); MP Carter (Auckland) for Kronfeld (78 mins)
Scorers *Tries:* Kronfeld (2), Z Brooke (2) *Conversions:* Spencer (2)
Penalty Goals: Spencer (2)
AUSTRALIA: SJ Larkham (ACT); BN Tune (Queensland), DJ Herbert (Queensland), PW Howard (ACT), JW Roff (ACT); TJ Horan (Queensland), GM Gregan (ACT); RLL Harry (NSW), M Caputo (ACT), EJA McKenzie (ACT), M Cockbain (Queensland), JA Eales (Queensland)(*capt*), BJ Robinson (ACT), T Coker (ACT), DJ Wilson (Queensland) *Substitutions:* DT Manu (NSW) for Coker (temp 40-60 mins); J Holbeck (ACT) for Howard (53 mins); MD Hardy (ACT) for Roff (69 mins); MA Foley (Queensland) for Caputo (69 mins); AT Blades (NSW) for Harry (80 mins)
Scorers *Try:* Horan *Conversion:* Eales *Penalty Goals:* Eales (2)
Referee EF Morrison (England)

12 July, Sydney Football Stadium (Cook Cup)
AUSTRALIA 25 (1G 1PG 3T)   ENGLAND 6 (1PG 1DG)

AUSTRALIA: M Burke (NSW); BN Tune (Queensland), JS Little (Queensland), J Holbeck (ACT), JW Roff (ACT); TJ Horan (Queensland), GM Gregan (ACT); CD Blades (NSW), MA Foley (Queensland), EJA McKenzie (ACT), GJ Morgan (Queensland), JA Eales (Queensland)*(capt)*, DT Manu (NSW), T Coker (ACT), BJ Robinson (ACT) *Substitutions:* DJ Wilson (Queensland) for Coker (temp 37-56 mins and 75 mins); AT Blades (NSW) for McKenzie (65 mins)
Scorers *Tries:* Burke, Tune, Gregan, Horan *Conversion:* Burke *Penalty Goal:* Eales
ENGLAND: TRG Stimpson (Newcastle); J Bentley (Newcastle), NJJ Greenstock (Wasps), PR de Glanville (Bath)*(capt)*, ND Beal (Northampton); MJ Catt (Bath), MJS Dawson (Northampton); GC Rowntree (Leicester), MP Regan (Bristol), DJ Garforth (Leicester), NC Redman (Bath), SD Shaw (Wasps), LBN Dallaglio (Wasps), TAK Rodber (Northampton), RA Hill (Saracens) *Substitutions:* AS Healey (Leicester) for Dawson (40 mins); BB Clarke (Richmond) for Hill (60 mins)
Scorers *Penalty Goal:* Stimpson *Dropped Goal:* Catt
Referee PD O'Brien (New Zealand)

20 December, Stadio Dall'Ara, Bologna
ITALY 37 (2G 6PG 1T)   IRELAND 22 (1G 5PG)

ITALY: C Pilat (Treviso); P Vaccari (Calvisano), AC Stoica (Narbonne, France), M Dallan (Treviso), Marcello Cuttitta (Milan); D Dominguez (SF-CASG, France), A Troncon (Treviso); Massimo Cuttitta (Harlequins, England), C Orlandi (Milan), A Castellani (L'Aquila), C Checchinato (Treviso), G Croci (Milan), M Giovanelli (Narbonne, France)*(capt)*, JM Gardner (Treviso), A Sgorlon (Treviso) *Substitutions:* O Arancio (Toulon, France) for Giovanelli (temp 20-23 mins) and for Gardner (temp 25-28 mins); W Cristofoletto (Treviso) for Checchinato (83 mins)
Scorers *Tries:* Dominguez, Pilat, Stoica *Conversions:* Dominguez (2) *Penalty Goals:* Dominguez (6)
IRELAND: KW Nowlan (St Mary's Coll); DA Hickie (St Mary's Coll), KM Maggs (Bristol), MC McCall (London Irish), DW O'Mahony (Moseley); DG Humphreys (London Irish), NA Hogan (London Irish)); R Corrigan (Greystones), KGM Wood (Harlequins) *(capt)*, PM Clohessy (Young Munster), PS Johns (Saracens), ME O'Kelly (London Irish), DJ Erskine (Sale), ERP Miller (Leicester), D O'Grady (Sale) *Substitutions:* EP Elwood (Galwegians) for Humphreys (63 mins); ATH Clarke (Northampton) for Wood (73 mins); VCP Costello (St Mary's Coll) for Erskine (77 mins)
Scorers *Try:* O'Mahony *Conversion:* Elwood *Penalty Goals:* Humphreys (4), Elwood
Referee D Mené (France)

24 January, Stadio Monigo, Treviso
ITALY 25 (1G 6PG)   SCOTLAND 21 (1G 3PG 1T)

ITALY: C Pilat (Treviso); P Vaccari (Calvisano), AC Stoica (Narbonne, France), L Martin (Padova), Marcello Cuttitta (Milan); D Dominguez (SF-CASG, France), A Troncon (Treviso); G-P de Carli (Roma), C Orlandi (Milan), A Castellani (L'Aquila), W Cristofoletto (Treviso), G Croci (Milan), M Giovanelli (Narbonne, France)*(capt)*, JM Gardner (Treviso), A Sgorlon (Treviso) *Substitution:* O Arancio (Toulon, France) for Sgorlon (79 mins)
Scorers *Try:* Vaccari *Conversion:* Dominguez *Penalty Goals:* Dominguez (6)
SCOTLAND: RJS Shepherd (Melrose); AG Stanger (Hawick), AV Tait (Newcastle), CM Chalmers (Melrose), CA Joiner (Leicester); GPJ Townsend (Northampton), G Armstrong (Newcastle); DIW Hilton (Bath), GC Bulloch

(West of Scotland), MJ Stewart (Northampton), GW Weir (Newcastle),
S Murray (Bedford), R I Wainwright (Dundee HSFP)*(capt)*, AJ Roxburgh (Kelso),
S D Holmes (London Scottish)
Scorers *Tries:* Tait, Shepherd *Conversion:* Shepherd *Penalty Goals:* Shepherd (3)
Referee DR Davies (Wales)

7 February, Stradey Park, Llanelli
WALES 23 (2G 3PG)   ITALY 20 (2G 2PG)

WALES: N R Jenkins (Pontypridd); IC Evans (Bath), A G Bateman (Richmond),
I S Gibbs (Swansea), G Thomas (Bridgend); A C Thomas (Swansea), R Howley
(Cardiff) *(capt)*; A L P Lewis (Cardiff), B H Williams (Richmond), D Young
(Swansea), G O Llewellyn (Harlequins), M J Voyle (Llanelli), RC Appleyard
(Swansea), L S Quinnell (Richmond), M E Williams (Pontypridd)
Substitutions: J M Humphreys (Cardiff) for B Williams (70 mins); C L Charvis
(Swansea) for M Williams (70 mins)
Scorers *Tries:* penalty try, G Thomas *Conversions:* Jenkins (2)
Penalty Goals: Jenkins (3)
ITALY: C Pilat (Treviso); P Vaccari (Calvisano), AC Stoica (Narbonne, France),
L Martin (Padova), Marcello Cuttitta (Milan); D Dominguez (SF-CASG, France),
A Troncon (Treviso); Massimo Cuttita (Harlequins, England), C Orlandi (Milan),
A Castellani (L'Aquila), W Cristofoletto (Treviso), G Croci (Milan), M Giovanelli
(Narbonne, France)*(capt)*, JM Gardner (Treviso), A Sgorlon (Treviso)
Scorers *Tries:* Stoica, Sgorlon *Conversions:* Dominguez (2)
Penalty Goals: Dominguez (2)
Referee SJ Lander (England)

18 April, Krasnoiarsk
RUSSIA 18 (1G 2PG 1T)   ITALY 48 (4G 5PG 1T)

RUSSIA: Zakarliuk; Epimachov, Ratchkov, Patlasov, Kuzin; Nikolaev, Kranobaev;
Choclov, Nikolaychic, Bikbov, Kisielov, Ilvovski, Diatlov, Graciov, Negodin
Substitutions: Kasheev for Graciov (52 mins); Baciurin for Negodin (80 mins)
Scorers *Tries:* Nikolaev, Graciov *Conversion:* Nikolaev *Penalty Goals:* Nikolaev (2)
ITALY: J-A Pertile (Roma); F Roselli (Roma), AC Stoica (Narbonne, France),
L Martin (Padova), Marcello Cuttitta (Milan); D Dominguez (SF-CASG, France),
A Troncon (Treviso); Massimo Cuttitta (Harlequins, England), S Saviozzi
(Treviso), A Castellani (L'Aquila), W Cristofoletto (Treviso), C Checchinato
(Treviso), M Giovanelli (Narbonne, France)*(capt)*, A Sgorlon (Treviso), C Caione
(L'Aquila) *Substitutions:* G-P de Carli (Roma) for Castellani (15 mins); A Moretti
(Padova) for Saviozzi (82 mins)
Scorers *Tries:* Stoica, Roselli, Pertile, Martin, Marcello Cuttitta
Conversions: Dominguez (4) *Penalty Goals:* Dominguez (5)
Referee N Lasaga (France)
*(Italy awarded full caps for this World Cup qualifying match. For the World Cup matches
against Denmark and Georgia the Italians fielded their A XV.)*

WORLD CUP 1999

The World Cup is now firmly established as the major event in the game's calendar and by the time the 20 finalists (four more than before) assemble in Britain, Ireland and France in October 1999 for the closing stages of the fourth competition, 65 nations will have participated in the qualifying rounds. Wales, the host union, England, Scotland, Ireland and France will each stage pool matches before the five pool winners automatically progress to the quarter-finals. A new development for 1999 is that the five runners-up from the pools, together with the best third-placed team, will then play-off in three knock-out matches to determine the remaining quarter-finalists.

Cardiff will stage the opening match, Wales's matches, the third/fourth place play-off and the final at the new Millennium Stadium. Sited on the Cardiff Arms Park, the new stadium is expected to accommodate 73,500 spectators and will be the first in the rugby world to have a fully retractable roof. Construction is on schedule as the principality's capital city prepares to stage its most important sporting event since the 1958 Empire Games.

South Africa (as winners), New Zealand (runners-up) and France (play-off winners) automatically qualified from the 1995 event to join the hosts. For all other unions entering the tournament, there will be a series of qualifying events to negotiate before passage to the finals is booked. The tournament is already well underway, having started in September 1996 in Riga where Latvia beat Norway in the first of the 179 matches that will culminate in the World Cup final on 6 November 1999.

Results to date:

ROUND A

Europe Pool One *6 Oct 1996* Ukraine 60, Yugoslavia 0 (Kiev); *26 Oct* Austria 3, Yugoslavia 0 (Vienna: default result – Yugoslavia did not turn up); *2 Nov* Switzerland 0, Ukraine 30 (Nyon); *23 Nov* Israel 15, Austria 3 (Tel Aviv); *30 Nov* Israel 9, Switzerland 9 (Tel Aviv); *1 Mar 1997* Yugoslavia 8, Switzerland 0 (Belgrade); *26 Apr* Austria 6, Ukraine 36 (Vienna); *10 May* Yugoslavia 10, Israel 7 (Pancevo); *17 May* Ukraine 51, Israel 15 (Odessa); *24 May* Switzerland 31, Austria (Basle). **Qualifier: Ukraine**

Europe Pool Two *5 Oct 1996* Latvia 44, Norway 6 (Riga); *12 Oct* Bulgaria 6, Moldova 14 (Sofia); *12 Oct* Norway 7, Croatia 43 (Oslo); *19 Oct* Moldova 3, Latvia 8 (Chisinau); *26 Oct* Bulgaria 31, Croatia 46 (Sofia); *3 May 1997* Moldova 31, Norway 7 (Chisinau); *10 May* Latvia 89, Bulgaria 0 (Riga); *10 May* Croatia 60, Moldova 5 (Makarska); *17 May* Croatia 43, Latvia 24 (Split); *24 May* Norway 22, Bulgaria 7 (Oslo). **Qualifier: Croatia**

Europe Pool Three *5 Oct 1996* Lithuania 26, Luxembourg 3 (Vilnius); *19 Oct* Andorra 54, Lithuania 24 (Andorra La Vella); *19 Oct* Sweden 39, Hungary 17 (Vanersborg); *2 Nov* Luxembourg 3, Hungary 12 (Cessange); *2 Nov* Andorra 21, Sweden 20 (Andorra La Vella); *15 Mar 1997* Luxembourg 16, Andorra 30 (Cessange); *19 Apr* Sweden 48, Luxembourg 5 (Karlskrona); *3 May* Lithuania 17, Sweden 84 (Plunge); *31 May* Hungary 16, Lithuania 3 (Budapest); *14 Jun* Hungary 5, Andorra 34 (Budapest). **Qualifier: Andorra**

Americas Pool One *11 Nov 1996* Trinidad & Tobago 41, Brazil 0 (Port of Spain). **Qualifier: Trinidad & Tobago** *(Guyana withdrew from the pool)*

Americas Pool Two *22 Mar 1997* Bahamas 3, Bermuda 24 (Nassau); *5 Apr* Barbados 23, Bahamas 37 (Bridgetown); *19 Apr* Bermuda 52, Barbados 3 (Bermuda). **Qualifier: Bermuda**

Asia Pool *1 Feb 1997* Singapore 11, Thailand 16 (Singapore); *15 Feb* Thailand 15, Sri Lanka 30 (Bangkok); *30 Mar* Sri Lanka 18, Singapore 15 (Kuala Lumpur). **Qualifier: Sri Lanka**

Pacific Pool *22 Nov 1996* Cook Islands 22, Papua New Guinea 19 (Rarotonga); *8 Feb 1997* Papua New Guinea 92, Tahiti 6 (Port Moresby); *20 Feb* Tahiti 0, Cook Islands 40 (Papeeta). **Qualifier: Cook Islands**

Africa Pool *18 Apr 1997* Arabian Gulf 53, Botswana 13 (Bahrain); *25 Apr* Zambia 30, Arabian Gulf 44 (Luanshya); *17 May* Botswana 13, Zambia 20 (Jwaneng). **Qualifier: Arabian Gulf**

ROUND B

Europe Pool One *12 Oct 1997* Georgia 29, Croatia 15 (Tbilisi); *18 Oct* Denmark 8, Georgia 19 (Frederiksburg); *18 Oct* Croatia 23, Russia 16 (Makarska); *1 Nov* Italy 102, Denmark 3 (Brescia); *11 Apr 1998* Italy 31, Georgia 14 (L'Aquila); *18 Apr* Russia 18, Italy 48 (Krasnoiarsk); *3 May* Russia 45, Denmark 9 (Penza); *16 May* Denmark 6, Croatia 40 (Aalborg); *20 May* Georgia 12, Russia 6 (Tbilisi); *6 Jun* Croatia 29, Italy 39 (Makarska). **Qualifiers: Italy and Georgia**

Europe Pool Two *5 Oct 1997* Belgium 13, Romania 83 (Brussels); *18 Oct* Ukraine 48, Belgium 5 (Kiev); *26 Oct* Holland 49, Poland 7 (Amsterdam); *1 Nov* Holland 35, Ukraine 13 (Amsterdam); *28 Mar 1998* Poland 30, Belgium 10 (Gdynia); *18 Apr* Belgium 16, Holland 19 (Brussels); *25 Apr* Romania 42, Holland 3 (Bucharest); *2 May* Romania 74, Poland 13 (Bucharest); *16 May* Poland 8, Ukraine 19 (Gdansk); *30 May* Ukraine 17, Romania 39 (Kharkov). **Qualifiers: Romania and Holland**

Europe Pool Three *13 Sept 1997* Czech Republic 45, Andorra 20 (Prague); *4 Oct* Andorra 11, Germany 56 (Andorra La Vella); *19 Oct* Germany 31, Czech Republic 17 (Hanover); *8 Nov* Andorra 3, Spain 62 (Andorra La Vella); *29 Nov* Spain 39, Czech Republic 8 (Santander); *4 Apr 1998* Portugal 30, Germany 6 (Lisbon); *18 Apr* Czech Republic 10, Portugal 15 (Prague); *26 Apr* Germany 9, Spain 24 (Heidelberg); *3 May* Spain 33, Portugal 22 (Madrid); *30 May* Portugal 53, Andorra 11 (Lousa). **Qualifiers: Spain and Portugal**

Americas Pool *20 Sep 1997* Trinidad & Tobago 6, Chile 35 (Port of Spain); *5 Oct* Bermuda 52, Trinidad 6 (Bermuda); *18 Oct* Chile 65, Bermuda 8 (Santiago). **Qualifier: Chile**

Asia Pool *29 Nov 1997* Malaysia 15, Sri Lanka 37 (Kuala Lumpur); *20 Dec* Chinese Taipei 51, Malaysia 13 (Kuala Lumpur); *10 Jan 1998* Sri Lanka 27, Chinese Taipei 31 (Bangkok). **Qualifier: Chinese Taipei**

Pacific Pool *21 Jun 1997* Fiji 20, Tonga 10 (Suva); *27 Jun* Cook Islands 7, Fiji 53 (Rarotonga); *5 Jul* Tonga 68, Cook Islands 12 (Nuku'Alofa). **Qualifiers: Fiji & Tonga**

Africa Pool *6 Sep 1997* Kenya 37, Arabian Gulf 18 (Nairobi); *13 Jun* Arabian Gulf 12, Tunisia 11 (Bahrain); *20 Sep* Tunisia 52, Kenya 5 (Tunis). **Qualifier: Tunisia**

ROUND C

Africa Pool *4 Apr 1998* Zimbabwe 43, Tunisia 9 (Bulawayo); *18 Apr 1998* Tunisia 20, Namibia 17 (Tunis); *9 May* Namibia 32, Zimbabwe 26 (Windhoek). **Qualifiers: Namibia and Zimbabwe**

Americas Pool *21 Mar 1998* Chile 54, Paraguay 6 (Santiago); *28 Mar* Paraguay 3, Uruguay 43 (Asuncion); *4 Apr* Uruguay 20, Chile 14 (Montevideo). **Qualifier: Uruguay**

A INTERNATIONAL CHAMPIONSHIP 1998

Scotland performed the Grand Slam in the first complete Championship at A international level. In previous campaigns it had become common for there to be eight or nine A matches among the Unions, but the first ever meeting between England A and Wales A at Leicester opened the way for a long overdue meaningful second XV competition. The final table read:

	P	W	D	L	F	A	Pts
SCOTLAND	4	4	0	0	97	53	8
FRANCE	4	2	1	1	109	89	5
WALES	4	2	0	2	111	94	4
ENGLAND	4	1	0	3	93	147	2
IRELAND	4	0	1	3	96	123	1

6 February, Stade de la Vallée-du-Cher, Tours
FRANCE A 32 (3G 2PG 1T)   ENGLAND A 17 (4PG 1T)

France A were more than a match for a plucky yet limited England side. The home forwards were livelier in the loose than their opponents and scrum-half Christophe Laussucq, who scored two of France's four tries, flourished behind an eight which served up quality possession for its backs. George Chuter, the young Saracens hooker, enjoyed a successful senior representative debut and scored England's only try.

FRANCE A: R Dourthe (Dax); M Biboulet (Colomiers), S Roque (Colomiers), J-M Aué (Castres), J Bory (Montferrand); B Bellot (Perpignan), C Laussucq (Stade Français); P Collazo (Bègles-Bordeaux), Y Bru (Colomiers), J-M Gonzalez (Pau), F Belot (Toulouse), Y Manhès (Brive), M Raynaud (Narbonne)*(capt)*, P Raschi (Bourgoin), R Castel (Béziers) *Substitutions:* S Marconnet (Stade Français) for Collazo (58 mins); T Mentières (Pau) for Manhès (69 mins)
Scorers *Tries:* Laussucq (2), Collazo, Raynaud *Conversions:* Bellot (3) *Penalty Goals:* Bellot (2)
ENGLAND A: C Catling (Gloucester); B Johnson (Gloucester), N J J Greenstock (Wasps), M C Allen (Northampton), D Chapman (Richmond); M S Mapletoft (Gloucester), A C T Gomarsall (Wasps); D Molloy (Wasps), G Chuter (Saracens), V E Ubogu (Bath), S D Shaw (Wasps), R Fidler (Gloucester), R H J Jenkins (Harlequins), B B Clarke (Richmond)*(capt)*, M J Corry (Leicester)
Substitutions: S Ravenscroft (Saracens) for Catling (68 mins); C Gillies (Richmond) for Fidler (70 mins)
Scorers *Try:* Chuter *Penalty Goals:* Mapletoft (4)
Referee C Muir (Scotland)

6 February, Donnybrook, Dublin
IRELAND A 9 (3PG)   SCOTLAND A 11 (2PG 1T)

Scotland went ahead through a Shaun Longstaff try from a break by Bryan Redpath after only 30 seconds, and held the lead for the rest of the match. Paul Burke and Duncan Hodge exchanged penalty goals and Scotland went into the break 8-3 ahead. Hodge then stretched

Scotland's advantage early in the second half with another penalty, but two subsequent penalties by Burke in the difficult conditions kept Ireland's hopes alive. The Irish, in fact, ended the match strongly, but poor finishing deprived their pack of a winning score.

IRELAND A: K W Nowlan (St Mary's College); J Cunningham (Ballymena), K P Keane (Garryowen), M Lynch (Young Munster), D W O'Mahony (Moseley); P A Burke (Bristol)*(capt)*, S T Bell (Dungannon); J Fitzpatrick (London Irish), A T H Clarke (Northampton), G Walsh (Garryowen), B Cusack (Bath), A Quinlan (Shannon), M J Galwey (Shannon), D O'Grady (Sale), D Erskine (Sale) *Substitutions:* G Longwell (Ballymena) for Cusack (76 mins); D Wallace (Garryowen) for Quinlan (76 mins)
Scorers *Penalty Goals:* Burke (3)
SCOTLAND A: H R Gilmour (Heriot's FP); S L Longstaff (Dundee HSFP), A G Shiel (Melrose), J McLaren (Stirling County), J Kerr (Watsonians); D W Hodge (Watsonians), B W Redpath (Melrose)*(capt)*; P H Wright (West of Scotland), K D McKenzie (Stirling County), W Anderson (Kirkcaldy), S Murray (Bedford), A Lucking (Currie), E W Peters (Bath), S J Reid (Boroughmuir), A C Pountney (Northampton) *Substitutions:* S J Brotherstone (Melrose) for McKenzie (73 mins); G R McIlwham (Glasgow Hawks) for Anderson (73 mins)
Scorers *Try:* Longstaff *Penalty Goals:* Hodge (2)
Referee N Williams (Wales)

20 February, Goldenacre, Edinburgh
SCOTLAND A 24 (1G 4PG 1T)   FRANCE A 20 (1G 1PG 2T)

Scotland A staged a spirited second-half rally to maintain their unbeaten record in the championship. The French led 15-11 at the interval and were a trifle unlucky to lose, outscoring their hosts by three tries to two. Scotland A were again grateful for Duncan Hodge's place-kicking: the Watsonian landed four penalties and converted his own 15th-minute second-half try.

SCOTLAND A: H R Gilmour (Heriot's FP); C A Joiner (Leicester), C Murray (Hawick), I C Jardine (Stirling County), J Kerr (Watsonians); D W Hodge (Watsonians), B W Redpath (Melrose)*(capt)*; P H Wright (West of Scotland), S J Brotherstone (Melrose), W Anderson (Kirkcaldy), S Murray (Bedford), R Metcalfe (Newcastle), E W Peters (Bath), S J Reid (Boroughmuir), A C Pountney (Northampton) *Substitutions:* D Officer (Currie) for Jardine (43 mins); G R McIlwham (Glasgow Hawks) for Wright (57 mins); G W Scott (Dundee HSFP) for Anderson (temp 75-76 mins)
Scorers *Tries:* Gilmour, Hodge *Conversion:* Hodge *Penalty Goals:* Hodge (4)
FRANCE A: R Dourthe (Dax); M Biboulet (Colomiers), J Sieurac (Colomiers), J-M Aué (Castres), F Schizano (Narbonne); M Carrée (Colomiers), A Hueber (Toulon); P Collazo (Bègles-Bordeaux), M de Rougemont (Toulon), J-M Gonzalez (Pau), F Belot (Toulouse), Y Manhès (Brive), M Raynaud (Narbonne)*(capt)*, P Raschi (Bourgoin), B de Giusti (Colomiers) *Substitutions:* C Porcu (Agen) for Manhès (40 mins); R Castel (Béziers) for de Giusti (40 mins)
Scorers *Tries:* Sieurac, Raschi, Hueber *Conversion:* Dourthe *Penalty Goal:* Dourthe
Referee H A Smith (Ireland)

20 February, Welford Road, Leicester
ENGLAND A 22 (1G 5PG)   WALES A 41 (3G 5PG 1T)

Wales, with a late burst of scoring, won the inaugural game between these two nations at A level. Leading 15-3 at half-time, the Welsh were in sharp form, scoring four tries to one. Byron Hayward, the Ebbw Vale outside-half, enjoyed a productive evening, harvesting 26 points. England A lost their captain Ben Clarke for a period in the second half. The big Richmond No 8 was the victim of a punch which was unseen by the match officials.

ENGLAND A: C Catling (Gloucester); B Johnson (Gloucester), J Baxendell (Sale), M C Allen (Northampton), A A Adebayo (Bath); M S Mapletoft (Gloucester), A C T Gomarsall (Wasps); V E Ubogu (Bath), G Chuter (Saracens), W R Green (Wasps), S D Shaw (Wasps), C Gillies (Richmond), R H J Jenkins (Harlequins), B B Clarke (Richmond)*(capt)*, P Sanderson (Sale)
Substitutions: N J J Greenstock (Wasps) for Allen (73 mins); R Winters (Bedford) for Clarke (temp 56-62 mins)
Scorers *Try:* Ubogu *Conversion:* Mapletoft *Penalty Goals:* Mapletoft (5)
WALES A: K A Morgan (Pontypridd); G Wyatt (Pontypridd), M Taylor (Swansea), J Lewis (Pontypridd), D R James (Pontypridd); B Hayward (Ebbw Vale), A P Moore (Richmond); A Griffiths (Pontypridd), G R Jenkins (Swansea), C T Anthony (Swansea), W S Roy (Pontypridd), Andrew Moore (Swansea), M Lloyd (Pontypridd), C Wyatt (Llanelli), K P Jones (Ebbw Vale)*(capt)*
Substitutions: I Boobyer (Neath) for Lloyd (65 mins); V Cooper (Llanelli) for Roy (70 mins)
Scorers *Tries:* Hayward, Jenkins, A P Moore, James *Conversions:* Hayward (3)
Penalty Goals: Hayward (5)
Referee E Murray (Scotland)

6 March, Quimper
FRANCE A 30 (2G 2PG 2T)   IRELAND A 30 (1G 6PG 1T)

In a superb start, France A threatened to run away with the match. Outside-half Benoit Bellot controlled the tactical run of the game up to half-time and scored two of the tries which gave the home side an apparently commanding 20-9 interval lead. But a brilliant second-half display by the other outside-half, Ireland A captain Paul Burke, forced a miraculous change in fortunes. Ireland scored two tries and Burke landed four goals, the last four minutes from time, to tie the scores.

FRANCE A: N Brusque (Pau); M Biboulet (Colomiers), L Lafforgue (Bègles-Bordeaux), J Sieurac (Colomiers), S Roque (Colomiers); B Bellot (Perpignan), S Castaignède (Montferrand); M de Rougemont (Toulon), J-J Taofifenua (Grenoble), J-M Gonzalez (Pau), F Belot (Toulouse)*(capt)*, Y Manhès (Brive), B de Giusti (Colomiers), L Mallier (Brive), E Gouloumet (Biarritz) *Substitutions:* P Bondouy (Toulouse) for Biboulet (57 mins); P Collazo (Bègles-Bordeaux) for Taofifenua (71 mins); C Dongieu (Bègles-Bordeaux) for Manhès (79 mins)
Scorers *Tries:* Bellot (2), Biboulet, Gonzalez *Conversions:* Bellot (2)
Penalty Goals: Bellot (2)
IRELAND A: K W Nowlan (St Mary's College); J P J McWeeney (St Mary's College), K P Keane (Garryowen), M P Murphy (Galwegians), D W O'Mahony (Moseley); P A Burke (Bristol)*(capt)*, S C McIvor (Garryowen); J Fitzpatrick (London Irish), A T H Clarke (Northampton), G Walsh (Garryowen), G M Fulcher (London Irish), G Longwell (Ballymena), E O Halvey (Shannon), D Wallace (Garryowen), D Erskine (Sale)
Scorers *Tries:* McWeeney, Longwell *Conversion:* Burke *Penalty Goals:* Burke (6)
Referee R Davies (Wales)

6 March, Rodney Parade, Newport
WALES A 10 (1G 1PG)   SCOTLAND A 18 (1G 2PG 1T)

Scotland A successfully negotiated the third leg of their Grand Slam in difficult conditions. Driving rain fell throughout the match, turning the pitch into a paddy field. For all that, the Scots deserved their victory. Their forwards were more determined in the loose and had a greater appetite for work in the tight, particularly in the second half when they faced the elements nursing a slender 6-3 lead. Late tries by Steve Brotherstone and Kenny Logan sealed their win.

WALES A: W J L Thomas (Cardiff); G Wyatt (Pontypridd), N Boobyer (Llanelli), J Lewis (Pontypridd), D R James (Pontypridd); B Hayward (Ebbw Vale), A P Moore (Richmond) *(capt)*; A Griffiths (Pontypridd), B H Williams (Richmond), C T Anthony (Swansea), G O Llewellyn (Harlequins), C Stephens (Bridgend), M Lloyd (Pontypridd), C Wyatt (Llanelli), M E Williams (Pontypridd) *Substitutions:* I Boobyer (Neath) for Lloyd (54 mins); R C McBryde (Llanelli) for B Williams (62 mins); M Lloyd returned for Wyatt (65 mins)
Scorers *Try:* Lloyd *Conversion:* Hayward *Penalty Goal:* Hayward
SCOTLAND A: H R Gilmour (Heriot's FP); K M Logan (Wasps), D Officer (Currie), J McLaren (Stirling County), J Kerr (Watsonians); D W Hodge (Watsonians), G Burns (Watsonians); P H Wright (West of Scotland), S J Brotherstone (Melrose), W Anderson (Kirkcaldy), S Murray (Bedford), R Metcalfe (Newcastle), P Walton (Newcastle), S J Reid (Boroughmuir)*(capt)*, G Flockhart (Stirling County) *Substitutions:* G Metcalfe (Glasgow Hawks) for McLaren (64 mins); C Mather (Watsonians) for Walton (78 mins); G R McIlwham (Glasgow Hawks) for Wright (69 mins); G Perrett (West of Scotland) for R Metcalfe (temp 2-17 mins)
Scorers *Tries:* Brotherstone, Logan *Conversion:* Hodge *Penalty Goals:* Hodge (2)
Referee P Thomas (France)

20 March, Inverleith, Edinburgh
SCOTLAND A 44 (4G 2PG 2T)   ENGLAND A 14 (3PG 1T)

Scotland A carried off the Grand Slam, disposing of England with ease. They began positively, a try by skipper Stuart Reid opening the scoring in the first minute, and never looked back. It was 27-9 at the break and after half-time a John Kerr corner try and two memorable efforts by centre David Officer took the Scots past the 40-point mark. This was England A's fourth successive defeat of the season.

SCOTLAND A: R J S Shepherd (Melrose); G Metcalfe (Glasgow Hawks), D Officer (Currie), B R S Eriksson (London Scottish), J Kerr (Watsonians); D W Hodge (Watsonians), G Burns (Watsonians); G R McIlwham (Glasgow Hawks), S J Brotherstone (Melrose), W Anderson (Kirkcaldy), S Murray (Bedford), R Metcalfe (Newcastle), P Walton (Newcastle), S J Reid (Boroughmuir)*(capt)*, G Flockhart (Stirling County) *Substitutions:* M Proudfoot (Melrose) for Anderson (54 mins); C Mather (Watsonians) for Walton (54 mins)
Scorers *Tries:* Officer (2), Reid, penalty try, Hodge, Kerr *Conversions:* Hodge (4) *Penalty Goals:* Hodge (2)
ENGLAND A: C Catling (Gloucester); B Johnson (Gloucester), N J J Greenstock (Wasps), M C Allen (Northampton), D Chapman (Richmond); R Butland (Bath), P C Richards (London Irish); D Barnes (Newcastle), M P Regan (Bath), V E Ubogu (Bath), R Fidler (Gloucester), C Gillies (Richmond), R Winters (Bedford), B B Clarke (Richmond)*(capt)*, P Sanderson (Sale) *Substitutions:* M Shaw (Newcastle) for Allen (37 mins); R H J Jenkins (Harlequins) for Sanderson

(54 mins); S Brown (Richmond) for Johnson (65 mins); O J Lewsey (Bristol) for
Butland (69 mins); C Harrison (Orrell) for Richards (69 mins); J A Mallett (Bath)
for Ubogu (69 mins); G Chuter (Saracens) for Catling (74 mins)
Scorers *Try:* Chapman *Penalty Goals:* Butland (3)
Referee G Borreani (France)

20 March, Thomond Park, Limerick
IRELAND A 27 (3G 2PG)   WALES A 42 (4G 3PG 1T)

Arwel Thomas, discarded from Wales's senior team, was the personality of a thoroughly entertaining match, scoring a lovely try and
contributing 22 points. The game was staged in Limerick to mark the
centenary of the only previous international played there: Wales's 11-3
win in the 1898 Test. John McWeeney put Ireland ahead with a
35th-second try and by the half-hour Ireland A were 17-6 in front.
Wales recovered to 17-14 before the interval and took the game by the
scruff of the neck in the second half to coast to a satisfying victory.
IRELAND A: K W Nowlan (St Mary's College); J P J McWeeney (St Mary's
College), K P Keane (Garryowen), M P Murphy (Galwegians), D W O'Mahony
(Moseley); P A Burke (Bristol)*(capt)*, S C McIvor (Garryowen); J Fitzpatrick
(London Irish), A T H Clarke (Northampton), G Walsh (Garryowen), G M
Fulcher (London Irish), G Longwell (Ballymena), E O Halvey (Shannon), D
Wallace (Garryowen), K Dawson (London Irish) *Substitutions:* M Lynch (Young
Munster) for Burke (54 mins); B Jackman (Clontarf) for Clarke (62 mins); B
Cusack (Bath) for Longwell (71 mins); G S Leslie (Dungannon) for Walsh (71
mins); D Erskine (Sale) for Fulcher (79 mins)
Scorers *Tries:* McWeeney, Burke, McIvor *Conversions:* Burke (2), Keane *Penalty
Goals:* Burke (2)
WALES A: W J L Thomas (Cardiff); G Wyatt (Pontypridd), D R James
(Pontypridd), J Lewis (Pontypridd), R Rees (Swansea); A C Thomas (Swansea),
A P Moore (Richmond)*(capt)*; A Griffiths (Pontypridd), R C McBryde (Llanelli),
C T Anthony (Swansea), G O Llewellyn (Harlequins), C Stephens (Bridgend),
M Lloyd (Pontypridd), C Wyatt (Llanelli), M E Williams (Pontypridd)
Substitutions: D Weatherley (Swansea) for J Thomas (31 mins); C Warlow (Llanelli)
for G Wyatt (75 mins); N Eynon (Pontypridd) for Griffiths (82 mins); I Gough
(Newport) for Stephens (temp 62-71 mins); I Boobyer (Neath) for C Wyatt (78
mins)
Scorers *Tries:* Weatherley (2), A Moore, A Thomas, C Wyatt
Conversions: A Thomas (4) *Penalty Goals:* A Thomas (3)
Referee J Gastou (France)

3 April, Brewery Field, Bridgend
WALES A 18 (1G 2PG 1T)   FRANCE A 27 (3G 2PG)

Three yellow cards were shown in a fractious match. Wales A started
confidently and led through an Arwel Thomas penalty until French
flair opened the game up in the second quarter. It was only 13-6 to the
visitors at the break but Wales, despite a stiff breeze in their favour,
were unable to contain the French thereafter. France added a second
try barely a minute after the restart and were home and dry after Iain
Ramage awarded a penalty try for an obstruction on Pascal Fauthoux
seven minutes from time.

WALES A: W J L Thomas (Cardiff); S D Hill (Cardiff), J Lewis (Pontypridd), M Taylor (Swansea), R Rees (Swansea); A C Thomas (Swansea), A P Moore (Richmond) *(capt)*; A Griffiths (Pontypridd), R C McBryde (Llanelli), C T Anthony (Swansea), G O Llewellyn (Harlequins), C Stephens (Bridgend), M Lloyd (Pontypridd), C Wyatt (Llanelli), I Boobyer (Neath) *Substitutions:* D Thomas (Swansea) for Boobyer (50 mins); D Weatherley (Swansea) for Lewis (67 mins); D Llewellyn (Ebbw Vale) for Moore (70 mins); I Gough (Newport) for Stephens (70 mins)
Scorers *Tries:* D Thomas, Wyatt *Conversion:* A Thomas
Penalty Goals: A Thomas (2)
FRANCE A: P Fauthoux (Bègles-Bordeaux); C Heymans (Agen), J-C Cistacq (Agen), D Plana (Perpignan), P Bondouy (Toulouse); B Bellot (Perpignan), C Laussucq (SF); P Collazo (Bègles-Bordeaux), M de Rougemont (Toulon), J-M Gonzalez (Pau), F Belot (Toulouse) *(capt)*, J Daude (Bourgoin), M Raynaud (Narbonne), E Gouloumet (Biarritz), G Combes (Aurillac) *Substitutions:* L Mallier (Brive) for Combes (58 mins); S de Besombes (Perpignan) for Collazo (58 mins); G Sudre (Agen) for Laussucq (60 mins); D Barrier (Montferrand) for Gouloumet (70 mins)
Scorers *Tries:* Plana, Fauthoux, penalty try *Conversions:* Bellot (3)
Penalty Goals: Bellot (2)
Referee D I Ramage (Scotland)

3 April, Athletic Ground, Richmond
ENGLAND A 40 (2G 2PG 4T)   **IRELAND A 30** (3G 3PG)

Two tries in the opening eight minutes set up England A's first international win of the season in this free-flowing match. A boisterous crowd of nearly 5,000 were given a nine-try, 70-point feast. Josh Lewsey, the Bristol utility back who also possesses a Welsh qualification, was a steadying influence at fly-half, while Spencer Brown and Dominic Chapman on the wings and Rob Fidler at lock turned in creditable performances.
ENGLAND A: T R G Stimpson (Newcastle); S Brown (Richmond), S Ravenscroft (Saracens), P Mensah (Harlequins), D Chapman (Richmond); O J Lewsey (Bristol), P C Richards (London Irish); D Barnes (Newcastle), P B T Greening (Gloucester), J A Mallett (Bath), R Fidler (Gloucester), C Gillies (Richmond), R H J Jenkins (Harlequins) *(capt)*, B Sturnham (Saracens), R J Hutton (Richmond) *Substitutions:* M Cornwell (Gloucester) for Gillies (65 mins); W R Green (Wasps) for Mallett (67 mins); A Bennett (Saracens) for Jenkins (67 mins); A D King (Wasps) for Stimpson (74 mins); G Chuter (Saracens) for Greening (77 mins); M C Allen (Northampton) for Hutton (77 mins)
Scorers *Tries:* Brown, Sturnham, Lewsey, Fidler, Mensah, Gillies
Conversions: Stimpson (2) *Penalty Goals:* Stimpson (2)
IRELAND A: S McDowell (Ballymena); J P J McWeeney (St Mary's College), P Duignan (Galwegians), M P Murphy (Galwegians), N K P J Woods (London Irish); B G Everitt (Garryowen), S C McIvor (Garryowen); J M Fitzpatrick (London Irish), B J Jackman (Clontarf), G Walsh (Garryowen), B Cusack (Bath), G M Fulcher (London Irish), T Brennan (Bective Rangers), D O'Cuinneagain (Sale), K Dawson (London Irish) *Substitutions:* M McDermott (Shannon) for Jackman (26 mins); A G Foley (Shannon) for Dawson (65 mins); D J Crotty (Garryowen) for McWeeney (68 mins); S Leahy (Garryowen) for Fulcher (77 mins)
Scorers *Tries:* McWeeney, Murphy, Everitt *Conversions:* Woods (3)
Penalty Goals: Woods (3)
Referee G Morandin (Italy)
Results and teams in other A internationals will be found in tour details.

BATH GIVE LAST-MINUTE COLD SHOWER TO BRIVE

HEINEKEN EUROPEAN CUP 1997-98

The crowd loved it, the locals were in raptures, the players pushed themselves to the limit, the broadcasters went into overdrive, the media too – and yet we all trooped away from a wild weekend in Bordeaux not knowing if we were heading towards a bright dawn for this marvellous tournament or a dreary dusk.

The final itself had been fractured, halting and, in pure run of play, disappointing. But the occasion itself surpassed all expectations. The Stade Lescure in Bordeaux was teeming. There could be simply no disputing the fact that both the attendance and the atmosphere would have been hugely diminished if there had been regional and not club sides in this final.

That was one argument rumbling around the hotel lobbies of Bordeaux. Far louder, and far more ominous, were the heated words being exchanged over England's continued involvement in the competition. The English clubs pulled out of the 1998-99 tournament prior to the final of this year's competition. They had long been unhappy with the distribution of both money and power. They felt that they and France were the draw cards both on and off the field. The English clubs objected in particular to the way that they could be outmanoeuvred by the Celtic countries on every significant vote. 'This just can't carry on,' said one English club official. 'We need to have this out once and for all.'

The origin of the latest dispute concerned fixture scheduling for the following year. The English clubs, in debt up to their eyeballs, were keen to free up the calendar in order to play more domestic games. There was concern that the current format was designed primarily to suit the Irish and Scots regional sides in their build-up to the November tranche of internationals and then the Five Nations.

The whole thing was a mess. And more's the pity. For once again there was plenty of riveting action. There was controversy too. The Brive-Pontypridd pool match made headlines of the wrong sort. The action on the field was grim enough with Dale McIntosh of Pontypridd sent off along with Lionel Mallier of Brive after a mass punch-up. There was more brawling later that night with the Bar Toulzac in Brive taking a fearful pounding from fighting players. Three Brive players – Philippe Carbonneau, Christophe Lamaison and David Venditti – required hospital treatment. McIntosh and Pontypridd hooker, Phil John, were accused by Brive of triggering events in Bar Toulzac. The accusations were strenuously denied.

Fingers pointed every which way. Brive had won the match itself 32-31 courtesy of a controversial last-minute try awarded by Scottish referee Ed Murray.

The two clubs were fined £30,000 each and Pau and Llanelli were fined £20,000 each for poor conduct during a pool match at the Stade Municipal de Hameau on the same weekend. The return Pool C match between Pontypridd and Brive attracted interest far beyond rugby's normal constituency. And then, to cap it all, the pair came together again in the quarter-final play-off. Civility won the day, so too Brive who went through 25-20. The tension between the clubs will remain for many a day, however.

Pool C was the toughest of the groups. Bath came out on top and so enjoyed home advantage until the final. They lost in Brive (29-12) but Brive were to lose at the Recreation Ground (27-25), just a week after the trauma of the Toulzac and then also drop a point in the 29-29 draw at Pontypridd. The Welsh club qualified for the play-offs as the best of the pool finishers in third place.

Pau finished top of their group ahead of Llanelli by a massive points differential of 112 points. Wasps came through the easiest pool, just hanging on to their unblemished record with a 29-28 victory over Swansea on the last weekend, while in Pool D Harlequins let slip their grasp on home advantage by losing on the same weekend in Munster (23-16). As a result they had to travel to Toulouse for their quarter-final. Leicester, beaten finalists the previous year, had an uneven ride. They lost in Leinster (16-9), won in Toulouse (22-17) but then lost at home to the French champions (23-22).

The play-off round for the second-place finishers plus the best third-place side (Pontypridd) proved a mixed bag. Glasgow, who had enjoyed a good tournament with three wins from six matches in Pool B, were hammered 90-19 by Leicester. In the other games Cardiff saw off Llanelli 24-20 in the all-Welsh affair and Brive came through unscathed in all senses against Pontypridd.

The reigning champions had a tough looking assignment in the quarter-final. However, their power and self-belief shone through as they beat Wasps 25-18 at Loftus Road. The other games all went the way of the home side. Toulouse took Harlequins apart, 51-10, Bath got the better of Cardiff in a tough encounter, 32-21, while Pau had too much class for Leicester, winning 35-18.

The semi-finals threw up different stories. Bath won comfortably enough at home to Pau, 20-14, but an extraordinary match in Toulouse saw Brive reach their second final in succession by the narrowest of margins. The match was tied 22-22 after extra time but Brive went through on try count, 2-1. Toulouse had dominated the match but were pegged back right on full-time by a try from Sebastien Carrat. Christophe Lamaison only had to convert from in front of the posts for Brive to go through. He missed, although he later made amends by striking the penalty which levelled the scores in extra time.

The 70 matches produced 385 tries and attracted some 500,000 spectators through the turnstiles. An estimated TV audience of over 35 million in 70 countries watched the final live. The 1997-98 tournament certainly never wanted for drama.

FINAL
31 January 1998, Stade Lescure, Bordeaux
Brive 18 (5PG 1DG) Bath 19 (1G 4PG)

The key move for Bath occurred long before the first whistle sounded on this, the third Heineken Cup final. Seven days earlier Bath coach Andy Robinson had seen his side knocked out of the domestic Tetley's Bitter Cup by Richmond. Bath's goal-kicking had been woeful. Robinson decided there and then that the young adventurer, Matt Perry, was to make way for the trusty boot of Jon Callard. The hunch paid off handsomely.

It wasn't just that Callard scored all his side's points. It was the manner in which he did so. Bath had trailed from the second minute until the 80th. Then, with the clock ticking and hearts racing, Bath were awarded a penalty when wing Adedayo Adebayo was obstructed as he followed a kick. It was a marginal decision. The stadium seethed but Callard stayed cool, stroking the ball between the posts from about 30 metres, halfway out to touch.

Even then the drama was not over. Brive too had a shot at glory in injury time. Christophe Lamaison's kick fell short only for the Bath captain, Andy Nicol, to fumble the catch. The scrum five metres out offered up a chance for Lisandro Arbizu to drop a goal. Somehow he missed from about 15 metres, the ball slewing wide of the posts to be chased by a band of demented players all trying to ground the bobbing ball. Richard Webster got there first and the Heineken Cup was Bath's.

How Brive must have kicked themselves. In a tight game they always looked to have more fire power than their opponents, more punch in the back row and more pace on the wide outside. But they froze. They seemed petrified by the burden of their own expectations. Whereas they had flowed across the turf in the previous year's final, here they inched forward cautiously. They were good value, nonetheless, for their 15-6 lead at the interval, all their points coming from Lamaison.

Just after half-time they had a succession of scrums on the Bath line. Seven times they went for the pushover; seven times Bath resisted. It was the crucial turning point. Bath struck minutes later. A flickering run by Jeremy Guscott in the 58th minute, followed by a deft pass by Phil de Glanville, opened up the Brive defence. From the scrum Dan Lyle drove right and linked with Nicol who found Guscott. And there, on hand, to deliver, was Callard. It was his day.

Brive: A Penaud; J Carrat, C Lamaison, D Venditti, S Carrat; L Arbizu, P Carbonneau *(capt)*; D Casadei, L Travers, R Crespy, E Alegret, Y Manhes, L van der Linden, F Duboisset, O Magne *Substitutions:* D Laperne for Crespy (50 mins); R Sonnes for Duboisset (71 mins); S Viars for S Carrat (76 mins)
Scorers *Penalty Goals:* Lamaison (5) *Dropped Goal:* Penaud
Bath: J Callard; I Evans, P de Glanville, J Guscott, A Adebayo; M Catt, A Nicol *(capt)*; D Hilton, M Regan, V Ubogu, M Haag, N Redman, N Thomas, D Lyle, R Webster *Substitutions:* R Earnshaw for Thomas (71 mins); F Mendez for Regan (78 mins)
Scorers *Try:* Callard *Conversion:* Callard *Penalty Goals:* Callard (4)
Referee J Fleming (Scotland)

QUARTER-FINALS
8 November 1997, Recreation Ground, Bath
Bath 32 (1G 5PG 2T)   Cardiff 21 (1G 3PG 1T)

A bitter finish to a punishing match. French referee Didier Mene was threatened by Cardiff fans straight after blowing for full-time; it was felt that he should not have disallowed Craig Morgan's 16th-minute try (for pushing off the ball). Police later escorted M. Mene to his car. Then it was the turn of the respective coaches. Bath's Andy Robinson accused Cardiff of perpetrating 'the most cynical, professional fouls I've seen in a long time.' Alex Evans countered with: '. . . he [Robinson] is a bit wet behind the ears . . . I think those remarks are in pretty poor taste.' That all detracted from a fascinating tie which included a stunning try by Phil de Glanville, and provided Bath with revenge following their defeat against the same side at the same stage of the competition last season.

Bath: J Callard; I Evans, P de Glanville, M Perry, A Adebayo; M Catt, A Nicol *(capt)*; K Yates, A Long, V Ubogu, G Llanes, N Redman, N Thomas, D Lyle, E Peters *Substitution:* R Webster for Peters (62 mins)
Scorers *Tries:* de Glanville, Ubogu, Lyle *Conversion:* Callard
Penalty Goals: Callard (5)
Cardiff: J Thomas; N Walker, L Davies, M Hall, C Morgan; L Jarvis, R Howley; A Lewis, J Humphreys *(capt)*, D Young, J Tait, D Jones, G Kacala, S Williams, G Jones *Substitutions:* S John for Lewis (47 mins); L Mustoe for Young (65 mins)
Scorers *Tries:* Davies (2) *Conversion:* Jarvis *Penalty Goals:* Jarvis (3)
Referee D Mene (France)

8 November 1997, Stade Toulousain, Toulouse
Toulouse 51 (3G 5PG 3T)   Harlequins 10 (1G 1PG)

Not an English name on the scoresheet, just French ones. Emile Ntamack started it all, ghosting out of the smoke from the numerous flares in the third minute for the first of six scintillating tries by the Rouges et Noirs. It set the pattern for the game. Harlequins were knocked back in the tackle, left standing in defence and hopelessly outplayed from riveting start to stupendous finish. Will Carling said afterwards that he had not been on the end of anything similar since the All Blacks in the semi-final of the 1995 World Cup and he called it, '. . . one of the great performances by a club team.' Quins' reply, including a well-taken try, came via Thierry Lacroix, who himself had never been on the winning side against Toulouse, not even when he played for Dax.

Toulouse: S Ougier, E Ntamack, R Paillat, P Bondouy, P Lapoutge; Y Delaigue, J Cazalbou (*capt*); C Califano, P Soula, F Tournaire, H Miorin, P Pelous, D Lacroix, S Dispagne, C Labit *Substitutions:* M Marfaing for Ntamack (57 mins); F Belot for Labit (57 mins); J-L Jordana for Tournaire (62 mins); J Tilloles for Cazalbou (66 mins); J Begue for Soula (70 mins)
Scorers *Tries:* Ntamack, Lapoutge, Bondouy (2), Dispagne, D Lacroix *Conversions:* Delaigue (2), Ougier *Penalty Goals:* Ougier (5)
Harlequins: J Williams, D O'Leary, W Carling, J Ngauamo, T Tollett; T Lacroix, H Harries; A Ozdemir, K Wood (*capt*); J Leonard, G Llewellyn, L Gross, R Jenkins, B Davison, L Cabannes *Substitutions:* D Rouse for Ozdemir (53 mins); N Walshe for Harries (55 mins); J Keyter for O'Leary (77 mins)
Scorers *Try:* D Lacroix *Conversion:* D Lacroix *Penalty Goal:* D Lacroix
Referee D Bevan (Wales)

9 November 1997, Stade Municipal de Hameau
Pau 35 (3G 3PG 1T) Leicester 18 (1G 2PG 1T)

Maybe it was the £10,000 suspended fine, but there was not so much as a hint of the indiscipline which had characterised Pau's play in the round-robin stages of the tournament. Their pack powered through Leicester's inadequate shower and their backs proved deadly when given any room. Tigers' coach Bob Dwyer seethed about replacement referee David Davies's handling of the game, intimating a bias towards the home team, but it was Leicester who had the biggest let-off late in the tie when hooker Richard Cockerill cynically took out Pau flanker Nicolas Bacque, but was not even shown a yellow card. Full-back Nicolas Brusque set up the opening try and scored the fourth and final one to round off a fine performance. Leicester never offered enough in attack; eventually their defence caved in.

Pau: N Brusque; P Bernat-Salles, D Dantiacq, F Leloir, Y Martin; D Aucagne, F Torossian; P Triep-Capdeville, J Rey (*capt*), J-M Gonzalez, T Mentieres, T Cleda, S Keith, F Rolles, N Bacque *Substitutions:* S Vignolo for Keith (53 mins); S Bria for Triep-Capdeville (63 mins); A Lagouarde for Mentieres (69 mins)
Scorers *Tries:* Cleda, Leloir, Bernat-Salles, Brusque *Conversions:* Aucagne (3) *Penalty Goals:* Aucagne (3)
Leicester: M Horak; A Healey, W Greenwood, S Potter, L Lloyd; J Stransky, W Serevi; G Rowntree, R Cockerill, D Garforth, M Johnson (*capt*), D Richards, M Corry, E Miller, N Back *Substitutions:* J Wells for Richards (63 mins); P Freshwater for Garforth (temp 75-80 mins)
Scorers *Tries:* Back, Serevi *Conversion:* Stransky *Penalty Goals:* Stransky (2)
Referee D Davies (Wales)

9 November 1997, Loftus Road
Wasps 18 (6PG)   Brive 25 (2G 2PG 1T)

The defending champions overcame the loss of Sebastien Viars after half an hour, a penalty count that would have crippled many another side and seven minutes of unwarranted injury time; they also outplayed Wasps in every area. The English club resorted to reliance on the boot of Gareth Rees, their full-back, as they failed to score a single try. In contrast the Carrat brothers, Sebastien and Jerome, as well as the telling touchdown by flanker Loic van der Linden on the stroke of half-time, following a crucial fumble by scrum-half Martyn Wood, earned Brive a deserved victory. A claim by lock Andy Reed that he had been bitten on the arm by a Brive player late in the contest was ignored by Scottish referee Chuck Muir, although he did speak to Brive captain Philippe Carbonneau.

Wasps: G Rees; S Roiser, N Greenstock, R Henderson, K Logan; A King, M Wood; D Molloy, S Mitchell, W Green, D Cronin, A Reed, L Dallaglio *(capt)*, C Sheasby, P Volley *Substitutions:* S Shaw for Cronin (56 mins); D Macer for Mitchell (82 mins)
Scorers *Penalty Goals:* Rees (6)
Brive: S Viars; J Carrat, C Lamaison, D Venditti, S Carrat; P Carbonneau *(capt)*, S Bonnet; D Casadei, L Travers, R Crespy, E Alegret, Y Manhes, L van der Linden, P Duboisset, O Magne *Substitutions:* P Bomati for Viars (32 mins); R Sonnes for Duboisset (41 mins), L Mallier for van der Linden (50 mins); O Gouaillard for Casadei (70 mins); L Arbo for Bonnet (78 mins)
Scorers *Tries:* S Carrat, van der Linden, J Carrat   *Conversions:* Lamaison (2) *Penalty Goals:* Lamaison (2)
Referee C Muir (Scotland)

SEMI-FINALS
20 December 1997, Recreation Ground, Bath
Bath 20 (5PG 1T)   Pau 14 (3PG 1T)

What this lacked in entertainment, it more than made up for in commitment. Pau's pacey backline was restricted to one try; Bath's threequarters did not even manage that. They owed their try to prop Victor Ubogu, and their domination at the line-out and at just about every breakdown to the stalwart Nigel 'Ollie' Redman. The result was all the more remarkable given that, only a week before, Bath had been on the wrong end of a 50-23 scoreline in an Allied Dunbar Premiership match at Saracens. Against Pau they had to draw on reserves everyone thought they had forgotten about. They dogged it out. It was not pretty, but it was absorbing, watching them contain the formidable Pau pack and restrict the use of the lively backs. Philippe Bernat-Salles scored a superb try after David Dantiacq's long pass left Adedayo Adebayo stranded. But Callard's five penalties and the odd stroke of good fortune set Bath on their way to victory. Adebayo might have conceded a penalty try when, shortly after scoring his try, Bernat-Salles chased hard after a

Nicolas Brusque grubber, and the Bath wing gave the Frenchman an unsporting shove. It won him no friends in the Pyrenees, but he got away with it and Bath hung on.

Bath: J Callard; I Evans, P de Glanville, M Perry, A Adebayo; M Catt, A Nicol (*capt*); K Yates, M Regan, V Ubogu, G Llanes, N Redman, N Thomas, D Lyle, R Webster *Substitutions:* E Peters for Lyle (82 mins); R Butland for de Glanville (temp 43-51 mins)
Scorers *Try:* Ubogu *Penalty Goals:* Callard (5)
Pau: N Brusque; P Bernat-Salles, D Dantiacq, F Leloir, Y Martin; D Aucagne, F Torossian; P Triep-Capdeville, J Rey (*capt*), J-M Gonzalez, A Lagouarde, T Cleda, S Keith, F Rolles, N Bacque *Substitutions:* S Vignolo for Rolles (55 mins); T Mentieres for Cleda (62 mins); S Bria for Triep-Capdeville (72 mins)
Scorers *Try:* Bernat-Salles *Penalty Goals:* Aucagne (3)
Referee D Bevan (Wales)

21 December 1997, Stade Toulousain, Toulouse
Toulouse 22 (1G 5PG)   **Brive 22** (4PG 2T) *after extra time; score at 80 mins 16-16. Brive won on tries scored*

This had Hollywood epic written all over it; but not even the film-makers could have dreamed up the twists and turns of this tie. Holders Brive could see the cup slipping from their grasp, when, in the third minute of injury time, a last desperate surge took them to within 10 yards of the Toulouse line, play switched left and Sebastien Carrat crossed for the try that levelled the scores at 16-16. The conversion looked a formality, a fact acknowledged by the now hysterical Brive support. Christophe Lamaison, Mr Reliable with the boot, stepped up, swung his foot and then watched with incredulity as the ball sailed three inches wide of the right-hand post. It condemned his team-mates and the army of fans to an agonising 30 minutes more, in which time Lamaison kept Brive in the tie with two penalties which cancelled out a pair by Yann Delaigue. (When Lamaison lined up his second penalty just 60 seconds remained of the closely-fought tie.) Toulouse had crept into a five-point lead through a couple of Christophe Deylaud penalties and Pierre Bondouy's fine individual try, which countered an excellently worked effort by the outstanding Brive flanker Olivier Magne midway through the first half. Unfortunately Magne suffered an injured hip in scoring the try and was replaced immediately after the restart; otherwise, perhaps, Brive would have managed to assert themselves as they had threatened to do and so avoided those 30 extra minutes.

Toulouse: S Ougier; E Ntamack, P Bondouy, Y Delaigue, P Lapoutge; C Deylaud, J Cazalbou (*capt*); C Califano, P Soula, F Tournaire, H Miorin, P Pelous, D Lacroix, S Dispagne, C Labit *Substitutions:* F Belot for Pelous (57 mins); J-L Jordana for Tournaire (89 mins); N Martin for Deylaud (99 mins); X Garbajosa for Lapoutge (107 mins); N Spanghero for Lacroix (107 mins)
Scorers *Try:* Bondouy *Conversion:* Delaigue *Penalty Goals:* Deylaud (2), Delaigue (3)

Brive: A Penaud; J Carrat, C Lamaison, D Venditti, S Carrat; L Arbizu,
P Carbonneau (*capt*); D Casadei, L Travers, D Laperne, E Alegret, Y Manhes,
L van der Linden, F Duboisset, O Magne *Substitutions:* L Mallier for Magne
(21 mins); R Sonnes for Duboisset (41 mins); J C Vicard for Travers (77 mins);
P Bomati for S Carrat (95 mins); O Gouaillard for van der Linden (107 mins)
Scorers *Tries:* Magne, S Carrat   *Penalty Goals:* Lamaison (4)
Referee D McHugh (Ireland)

Previous finals
1996 Toulouse 21, Cardiff 18 (Cardiff)
1997 Brive 28, Leicester 9 (Cardiff)

*From left to right, Mike Catt, Adedayo Adebayo, Dave Hilton and Nigel Redman hold aloft
the European Cup after Bath's 19-18 defeat of Brive at the Stade Lescure, Bordeaux.*

69

ELIMINATION ROUND

Pool A	P	W	D	L	F	A	Pts
Toulouse	6	5	0	1	200	121	10
Leicester	6	4	0	2	163	117	8
Leinster	6	2	0	4	137	167	4
Milan	6	1	0	5	111	206	2

Results: Leinster 25, Toulouse 34; Leicester 26, Milan 10; Leinster 16, Leicester 9; Milan 14, Toulouse 19; Milan 33, Leinster 32; Toulouse 17, Leicester 22; Toulouse 69, Milan 19; Leicester 47, Leinster 22; Leicester 22, Toulouse 23; Leinster 23, Milan 6; Toulouse 38, Leinster 19; Milan 29, Leicester 37

Pool B	P	W	D	L	F	A	Pts
Wasps	6	6	0	0	243	104	12
Glasgow	6	3	0	3	132	167	6
Swansea	6	2	0	4	157	161	4
Ulster	6	1	0	5	95	195	2

Results: Swansea 25, Wasps 31; Ulster 12, Glasgow 18; Swansea 33, Ulster 16; Glasgow 22, Wasps 46; Glasgow 35, Swansea 21; Wasps 56, Ulster 3; Ulster 28, Swansea 20; Wasps 43, Glasgow 5; Ulster 31, Wasps 38; Swansea 30, Glasgow 22; Glasgow 30, Ulster 15; Wasps 29, Swansea 28

Pool C	P	W	D	L	F	A	Pts
Bath	6	5	0	1	141	119	10
Brive	6	4	1	1	210	146	9
Pontypridd	6	2	1	3	154	147	5
Scottish Borders	6	0	0	6	129	222	0

Results: Brive 56, Scottish Border 18; Pontypridd 15, Bath 21; Brive 32, Pontypridd 31; Scottish Border 17, Bath 31; Bath 27, Brive 25; Scottish Borders 16, Pontypridd 23; Bath 27, Scottish Borders 23; Pontypridd 29, Brive 29; Pontypridd 46, Scottish Borders 26; Brive 29, Bath 12; Bath 23, Pontypridd 10; Scottish Borders 29, Brive 39

Pool D	P	W	D	L	F	A	Pts
Harlequins	6	4	0	2	198	141	8
Cardiff	6	4	0	2	184	146	8
Munster	6	2	0	4	141	180	4
Bourgoin	6	2	0	4	93	149	4

Results: Bourgoin 26, Cardiff 25; Harlequins 48, Munster 40; Harlequins 45, Bourgoin 7; Cardiff 43, Munster 23; Munster 17, Bourgoin 15; Cardiff 21, Harlequins 28; Munster 32, Cardiff 37; Bourgoin 18, Harlequins 30; Bourgoin 21, Munster 6; Harlequins 31, Cardiff 32; Cardiff 26, Bourgoin 6; Munster 23, Harlequins 16

Pool E	P	W	D	L	F	A	Pts
Pau	6	4	0	2	203	89	8
Llanelli	6	4	0	2	144	142	8
Treviso	6	2	0	4	146	162	4
Caledonia	6	2	0	4	89	189	4

Results: Benetton Treviso 18, Pau 19; Caledonia 18, Llanelli 23; Pau 44, Llanelli 12; Caledonia 17, Benetton Treviso 9; Llanelli 39, Benetton Treviso 18; Pau 50, Caledonia 8; Benetton Treviso 52, Caledonia 6; Llanelli 14, Pau 10; Benetton Treviso 42, Llanelli 25; Caledonia 30, Pau 24; Llanelli 31, Caledonia 10; Pau 56, Benetton Treviso 7

Quarter-final play-offs
Brive 25, Pontypridd 20; Leicester 90, Glasgow 19; Cardiff 24, Llanelli 20

FRENCH AGAIN DOMINANT

HEINEKEN EUROPEAN CONFERENCE 1997-98

The European Conference was once again dominated by the French clubs, no surprise perhaps in that they provided 16 of the 32 teams for the pool matches. Only Newcastle came close to upsetting the French dominance, losing just 12-9 at Agen in the semi-final. Connacht were the surprise pick of the group winners, the Irish province heading a group which included Northampton, Bègles-Bordeaux and Nice. Gloucester, too, enjoyed success, winning five of their six pool games to head the likes of Toulon and Beziers. The dream ended for both clubs though in the quarter-finals with Gloucester going down 53-22 at Stade Français, while Connacht were beaten 40-27 in Agen.

FINAL
1 February 1998, Stade Toulousain, Toulouse
Colomiers 43 (4G 3T)   **Agen 5** (1T)

Colomiers, whose home is but a few miles from the Stade Toulousain, thrilled a crowd of 12,500 with their power running, scoring seven tries in all to live up to their billing of pre-match favourites. They never allowed Agen, who were handicapped by the absence of their injured captain Abdel Benazzi, to settle. Colomiers had come into the final on a run of form, dispatching the highly-fancied Stade Français in the semi-finals and then seeing off the likes of Beziers and Biarritz in their domestic championship.

French international full-back, Jean-Luc Sadourny, paid tribute to the backing his team received from their fans. 'This was not a small final,' said Sadourny. 'We take great pleasure in winning. We were ready for it and willing to play good rugby.' Scrum-half Fabien Galthie was also generous in his praise of the support. 'I am thrilled because this cup is the first one won by Colomiers,' said Galthie. 'I would like to associate this honour to the players at the club in previous seasons. The spirit at the club was developed by them.'

Colomiers: J-L Sadourny *(capt)*; M Biboulet, S Roque, J Sieurac, D dal Pos; M Carre, F Galthie; J-P Beyssen, Y Bru, P Pages, J-P Revaillier, J-M Lorenzi, B de Giusti, H Manent, S Peysson *Substitutions:* R Nones for Beyssen (40 mins); P Tabacco for Manent (40 mins); D Skrela for Pos (40 mins); C Barrau for Roque (55 mins); S Milhas for Sadourny (57 mins); G Moro for Lorenzi (70 mins); J-P Beyssen for Pages (75 mins)
Scorers *Tries:* de Giusti (2), Biboulet, Roque, Sieurac, Galthie, Bru
Conversions: Carre (4)

Agen: C Heymans; J-C Cistaq, O Campan, J Mateo, J-F Mateo; G Bouic, D Tastet; E Rodriguez, M dal Maso, P Piacentini, N Mekkaoui, C Porcu, P Benetton *(capt)*, J Troader, S Bohn *Substitutions:* V Thomas for J Mateo (40 mins); G Sudre for Tastet (40 mins); S Prosper for Bouic (40 mins); F Bourdeilh for Bohn (46 mins); L Lubrano for Benetton (55 mins); S Terle for Piacentini (62 mins)
Scorer *Try:* Porcu
Referee E Morrison (England)

EARLY ROUNDS

Quarter-finals
Stade Français 53, Gloucester 22
Agen 40, Connacht 27
Colomiers 23, Montferrand 13
Newcastle 44, Castres 0

Semi-finals
Agen 12, Newcastle 9
Colomiers 19, Stade Français 13

Final
Colomiers 43, Agen 5

Previous final
1997 Bougoin 18, Castres 9 (Béziers)

ELIMINATION ROUND

POOL A
Bristol 33, La Rochelle 14; Ebbw Vale 16, Agen 27; Ebbw Vale 28, Bristol 15; La Rochelle 20, Agen 33; Agen 45, Bristol 18; La Rochelle 25, Ebbw Vale 24; Bristol 18, Ebbw Vale 16; Agen 21, La Rochelle 15; Ebbw Vale 21, La Rochelle 19; Bristol 24, Agen 42; Agen 51, Ebbw Vale 12; La Rochelle 35, Bristol 7.
1 Agen 12 pts; 2 La Rochelle 4 pts; 3 Ebbw Vale 4 pts; 4 Bristol 4 pts

POOL B
Newport 42, Montpellier 17; Montferrand 25, Sale 16; Montferrand 58, Newport 32; Montpellier 30, Sale 12; Montpellier 16, Montferrand 18; Sale 61, Newport 27; Newport 26, Montferrand 31; Sale 43, Montpellier 3; Newport 17, Sale 11; Montferrand 56, Montpellier 10; Sale 20, Montferrand 15; Montpellier 14, Newport 28.
1 Montferrand 10 pts; 2 Sale 6 pts; 3 Newport 6 pts; 4 Montpellier 2 pts

POOL C
Dax 32, Farul Constanta 20; London Irish 25, Stade Français 41; Dax 34, London Irish 19; Stade Français 83, Farul Constanta 10; Stade Français 65, Dax 19; Farul Constanta 9, London Irish 26; Farul Constanta 28, Stade Français 85; London Irish 24, Dax 11; Dax 20, Stade Français 35; London Irish 46, Farul Constanta 10; Farul Constanta 17, Dax 23; Stade Français 28, London Irish 29.
1 Stade Français 10 pts; 2 London Irish 8 pts; 3 Dax 6 pts; 4 Farul Constanta 0 pts

POOL D
Nice 24, Bègles-Bordeaux 25; Connacht 43, Northampton 13; Northampton 23, Bègles-Bordeaux 13; Nice 20, Connacht 16; Northampton 66, Nice 7; Bègles-Bordeaux 9, Connacht 15; Connacht 28, Nice 25; Bègles-Bordeaux 23, Northampton 16; Connacht 22, Bègles-Bordeaux 15; Nice 10, Northampton 26; Bègles-Bordeaux 27, Nice 8; Northampton 15, Connacht 20.

1 Connacht 10 pts; 2 Northampton 6 pts; 3 Bègles-Bordeaux 6 pts; 4 Nice 2 pts

POOL E
Colomiers 34, Richmond 18; Grenoble 33, Bridgend 35; Richmond 43, Bridgend 14; Colomiers 60, Grenoble 10; Richmond 37, Grenoble 8; Bridgend 24, Colomiers 49; Bridgend 12, Richmond 44; Grenoble 24, Colomiers 29; Grenoble 16, Richmond 29; Colomiers 69, Bridgend 20; Bridgend 25, Grenoble 21; Richmond 25, Colomiers 49.

1 Colomiers 12 pts; 2 Richmond 8 pts; 3 Bridgend 4 pts; 4 Grenoble 0 pts

POOL F
Toulon 19, Beziers 14; Gloucester 43, Padova 10; Gloucester 18, Toulon 15; Beziers 40, Padova 23; Padova 13, Toulon 54; Beziers 27, Gloucester 29; Padova 26, Beziers 26; Toulon 16, Gloucester 13; Toulon 20, Padova 20; Gloucester 38, Beziers 17; Beziers 26, Toulon 12; Padova 16, Gloucester 29.

1 Gloucester 10 pts; 2 Toulon 7 pts; 3 Beziers 5 pts; 4 Padova 2 pts

POOL G
Newcastle 37, Biarritz 10; Perpignan 21, Edinburgh 9; Newcastle 60, Perpignan 3; Edinburgh 15, Biarritz 32; Biarritz 18, Perpignan 6; Edinburgh 16, Newcastle 40; Biarritz 25, Edinburgh 27; Perpignan 13, Newcastle 27; Newcastle 72, Edinburgh 24; Perpignan 40, Biarritz 6; Biarritz 32, Newcastle 28; Edinburgh 18, Perpignan 15.

1 Newcastle 10 pts; 2 Biarritz 6 pts; 3 Perpignan 4 pts; 4 Edinburgh 4 pts

POOL H
Neath 12, Castres 36; Narbonne 16, Saracens 18; Neath 10, Narbonne 50; Saracens 26, Castres 21; Castres 24, Narbonne 19; Saracens 69, Neath 30; Castres 32, Saracens 18; Narbonne 52, Neath 21; Neath 12, Saracens 26; Narbonne 14, Castres 25; Castres 68, Neath 8; Saracens 40, Narbonne 17.

1 Castres 10 pts; 2 Saracens 10 pts; 3 Narbonne 4 pts; 4 Neath 0 pts

CRUSADERS TOPPLE BLUES

THE SUPER-12 SERIES 1998

Neutral observers described the 1998 Super-12 as the best yet. For a start, the competition for semi-final places remained wide open until the last weeks of the round-robin phase. Then there was the phenomenal rise of the Crusaders, alias the Canterbury side who had wrested the domestic provincial title from Auckland in 1997. The Crusaders languished at the foot of the Super-12 table with one win from their first four matches before enjoying a magnificent six-match winning run to reach the last four.

The biggest surprise of the series was the decline of the three Australian State sides. The Brumbies, who were runners-up in 1997, finished third from the bottom of the round-robin, and though the Waratahs and Queensland Reds were in contention for a semi-final place, for the first time no Australian side reached the knock-out phase.

Refereeing interpretations continued to cause controversy. In the northern hemisphere, eyebrows have long been raised at the loose reading by Super-12 referees of the tackle law. Doubts were again expressed about rulings that invariably benefited the team in possession while there were also criticisms regarding inconsistency of interpretation. Ian McIntosh, coach of the Coastal Sharks, was particularly puzzled after his side were beaten 36-32 in the second of the semi-finals. 'I think we could almost say the referees decide who goes through to the finals these days,' he said in frustration at some of Peter Marshall's rulings regarding playing the ball on the ground.

FINAL
30 May, Auckland
Canterbury Crusaders 20 (2G 2PG)   **Auckland Blues 13** (1G 1PG 1DG)

For the first time two New Zealand sides came face to face in a Super-12 final and for the first time the Auckland Blues lost a Super-12 match at Eden Park. Andrew Mehrtens's role in the Crusaders' victory was pivotal. He had been out of form earlier in the campaign, but once he regained his confidence the influence he held on the side was a telling factor in their unbeaten run up to the Eden Park showdown. His tactical authority and fine kicking in the final, where he faced his rival for the New Zealand No 10 shirt, Carlos Spencer, effectively undermined the efforts of an Auckland side that should comfortably have won the title.

This was an absorbing match between the best two sides of the competition. Canterbury made first use of the breeze but had only a Mehrtens penalty, kicked in the 31st minute, on the scoreboard at half-time. The Blues, minus Sean Fitzpatrick and Zinzan Brooke (both retired) and without Jonah Lomu, came out after the interval to play with furious determination. James Christian finished off a jinking break made by Lee Stensness to score a try under the posts which Adrian Cashmore converted in the second minute, and Cashmore extended the lead to 10-3 with a lovely 40-metre dropped goal 12 minutes later. The Blues were in commanding form at this stage, but despite piling the pressure on the Crusaders' defence they were unable to create another score.

Mehrtens at length lifted the siege, kicking his side out of trouble midway through the half. Lock Norm Maxwell crossed for an opportunist's try in the 21st minute and Mehrtens's conversion tied the match. An exchange of penalties between Cashmore and Mehrtens brought the scores to 13-all as the game entered its final five minutes. Then, with extra time looming, Mehrtens chipped the ball into the Auckland 22 where two defenders appeared to have it covered. The ball, however, bobbed out of their reach for James Kerr to flop on it for the winning score.

Mehrtens, who added the conversion points, summed up his side's win moments later, saying, 'Most of the game I didn't really consider we were probably in it. Their defence was so awesome. We were a bit lucky with the tries we did get.'

Canterbury Crusaders: D Gibson; J Kerr, T Matson, M Mayerhofler, N Berryman; A Mehrtens, A Flynn; K Nepia, M Hammett, S Loe, R Thorne, N Maxwell, T Blackadder (*capt*), S Surridge, S Robertson *Substitutions:* T Marsh for Matson (46 mins); D Lilley for Berryman (52 mins); A Gardiner for Robertson (58 mins); G Feek for Nepia (61 mins); B Feeney for Mayerhofler (72 mins)
Scorers *Tries:* Maxwell, Kerr *Conversions:* Mehrtens (2) *Penalty Goals:* Mehrtens (2)
Auckland Blues: A Cashmore; J Vidiri, E Clarke, L Stensness, C Ralph; C Spencer, O Tonu'u; C Dowd, J Christian, O Brown, R Brooke, R Willis, M Jones (*capt*), X Rush, M Carter
Scorers *Try:* Christian *Conversion:* Cashmore *Penalty Goals:* Cashmore *Dropped Goal:* Cashmore
Referee P D O'Brien (New Zealand)

SEMI-FINALS
23 May, Auckland
Auckland Blues 37 (4G 3PG)   **Otago Highlanders 31** (2G 4PG 1T)

Auckland Blues: A Cashmore; J Vidiri, E Clarke, L Stensness, J Lomu; C Spencer, O Tonu'u; C Dowd, A Roose, O Brown, R Brooke, R Willis, M Jones (*capt*), X Rush, M Carter *Substitution:* A Blowers for M Jones (67 mins)
Scorers *Tries:* Cashmore (2), Vidiri, Stensness *Conversions:* Cashmore (4) *Penalty Goals:* Cashmore (3)
Otago Highlanders: B Laney; J Wilson, P Alatini, J Leslie, J Stanley; S Culhane, R Duggan; C Hoeft, A Oliver, K Meeuws, B Timmins, J Blaikie, K Middleton, T Randell (*capt*), J Kronfeld *Substitutions:* T Brown for Culhane (49 mins); I Maka for Middleton (49 mins); D Heaps for Oliver (temp 39-49 mins and 59-63 mins); P Fili for Stanley (77 mins)

Scorers *Tries:* Wilson, Randell, Maka *Conversions:* Culhane, Brown *Penalty Goals:* Culhane (3), Brown
Referee C Hawke (New Zealand)

24 May, Christchurch
Canterbury Crusaders 36 (2G 4PG 2T) **Coastal Sharks 32** (2G 1PG 3T)

Canterbury Crusaders: D Gibson; J Kerr, T Matson, M Mayerhofler, N Berryman; A Mehrtens, A Flynn; K Nepia, M Hammett, S Loe, R Thorne, N Maxwell, T Blackadder *(capt)*, S Surridge, A Gardiner *Substitutions:* D Lilley for Gibson (48 mins); S Robertson for Gardiner (48 mins); T Marsh for Matson (57 mins)
Scorers *Tries:* Berryman (2), Gibson, Lilley *Conversions:* Mehrtens (2) *Penalty Goals:* Mehrtens (4)
Coastal Sharks: A Joubert; S Payne, J Thomson, J Gillingham, S Terblanche; B Wessels, K Putt; O le Roux, C Rossouw, R Kempson, S Atherton, M Andrews, D Kriese, G Teichmann *(capt)*, W Brosnihan *Substitutions:* M Visser for Rossouw (temp 22-25 mins); R Bennett for Gillingham (50 mins); A Garvey for le Roux (58 mins); W Minaar for Kriese (72 mins); J Slade for Atherton (73 mins)
Scorers *Tries:* le Roux (2), Payne, Terblanche, Putt *Conversions:* Joubert (2) *Penalty Goal:* Joubert
Referee P Marshall (Australia)

ROUND-ROBIN SUMMARY

27 Feb	Highlanders 26, Reds 19	*(Dunedin)*
27 Feb	Hurricanes 45, Stormers 31	*(Cape Town)*
28 Feb	Chiefs 25, Crusaders 23	*(Albany)*
28 Feb	Golden Cats 39, Northern Bulls 32	*(Pretoria)*
28 Feb	Coastal Sharks 24, Blues 8	*(Durban)*
1 Mar	Waratahs 32, Brumbies 7	*(Sydney)*
6 Mar	Brumbies 34, Highlanders 26	*(Canberra)*
6 Mar	Crusaders 33, Waratahs 12	*(Christchurch)*
6 Mar	Hurricanes 37, Northern Bulls 19	*(Pretoria)*
7 Mar	Chiefs 28, Reds 25	*(Brisbane)*
7 Mar	Blues 38, Golden Cats 37	*(Johannesburg)*
7 Mar	Sharks 32, Stormers 17	*(Durban)*
13 Mar	Waratahs 25, Golden Cats 10	*(Sydney)*
13 Mar	Hurricanes 22, Chiefs 19	*(Hamilton)*
14 Mar	Blues 41, Highlanders 22	*(Auckland)*
14 Mar	Sharks 41, Brumbies 23	*(Canberra)*
14 Mar	Stormers 35, Northern Bulls 18	*(Cape Town)*
14 Mar	Reds 35, Crusaders 9	*(Brisbane)*
20 Mar	Highlanders 41, Coastal Sharks 35	*(Dunedin)*
21 Mar	Blues 25, Chiefs 23	*(Auckland)*
21 Mar	Brumbies 37, Golden Cats 3	*(Canberra)*
21 Mar	Northern Bulls 34, Waratahs 19	*(Witbank)*
22 Mar	Reds 41, Hurricanes 33	*(Wellington)*
27 Mar	Blues 31, Crusaders 24	*(Christchurch)*
28 Mar	Highlanders 57, Golden Cats 27	*(Invercargill)*
28 Mar	Stormers 35, Waratahs 33	*(Wellington, SA)*
28 Mar	Northern Bulls 24, Brumbies 7	*(Brakpan)*
29 Mar	Coastal Sharks 39, Hurricanes 23	*(Palmerston North)*
3 Apr	Stormers 34, Brumbies 3	*(Cape Town)*
3 Apr	Hurricanes 30, Golden Cats 15	*(New Plymouth)*
4 Apr	Highlanders 29, Chiefs 11	*(Dunedin)*
4 Apr	Reds 33, Blues 18	*(Brisbane)*

5 Apr	Crusaders 31, Northern Bulls 20	*(Christchurch)*
5 Apr	Waratahs 51, Coastal Sharks 18	*(Sydney)*
11 Apr	Chiefs 37, Northern Bulls 25	*(Hamilton)*
11 Apr	Crusaders 38, Brumbies 26	*(Timaru)*
11 Apr	Reds 19, Stormers 14	*(Brisbane)*
11 Apr	Coastal Sharks 30, Golden Cats 18	*(Durban)*
13 Apr	Blues 47, Waratahs 25	*(Auckland)*
17 Apr	Blues 34, Northern Bulls 24	*(Pukekohe)*
18 Apr	Crusaders 37, Stormers 25	*(Christchurch)*
18 Apr	Reds 17, Waratahs 17	*(Brisbane)*
18 Apr	Chiefs 36, Golden Cats 35	*(Bloemfontein)*
19 Apr	Highlanders 29, Hurricanes 8	*(Dunedin)*
24 Apr	Crusaders 40, Highlanders 24	*(Christchurch)*
24 Apr	Hurricanes 32, Brumbies 29	*(Canberra)*
25 Apr	Coastal Sharks 52, Chiefs 18	*(Port Elizabeth)*
25 Apr	Reds 28, Northern Bulls 15	*(Brisbane)*
26 Apr	Blues 74, Stormers 28	*(Auckland)*
1 May	Waratahs 23, Highlanders 22	*(Sydney)*
1 May	Crusaders 39, Hurricanes 17	*(Napier)*
2 May	Chiefs 26, Stormers 7	*(Rotorua)*
2 May	Blues 27, Brumbies 24	*(Canberra)*
2 May	Northern Bulls 12, Coastal Sharks 8	*(Pretoria)*
3 May	Reds 20, Golden Cats 16	*(Johannesburg)*
8 May	Chiefs 35, Brumbies 15	*(Hamilton)*
8 May	Waratahs 36, Hurricanes 32	*(Sydney)*
9 May	Highlanders 36, Stormers 15	*(Cape Town)*
9 May	Crusaders 34, Golden Cats 25	*(Bloemfontein)*
10 May	Coastal Sharks 30, Reds 20	*(Durban)*
15 May	Waratahs 33, Chiefs 21	*(Albany)*
15 May	Highlanders 31, Northern Bulls 26	*(Pretoria)*
16 May	Blues 45, Hurricanes 34	*(Wellington)*
16 May	Brumbies 23, Reds 16	*(Canberra)*
17 May	Crusaders 32, Coastal Sharks 20	*(Durban)*
17 May	Golden Cats 41, Stormers 7	*(Johannesburg)*

FINAL TABLE

	P	W	D	L	F	A	Bonus	Pts
Auckland Blues	11	9	0	2	388	296	7	43
Canterbury Crusaders	11	8	0	3	340	260	9	41
Coastal Sharks	11	7	0	4	329	263	8	36
Otago Highlanders	11	7	0	4	343	279	6	34
Queensland Reds	11	6	1	4	273	229	5	31
NSW Waratahs	11	6	1	4	306	276	4	30
Waikato Chiefs	11	6	0	5	279	291	5	29
Wellington Hurricanes	11	5	0	6	313	342	6	26
Western Stormers	11	3	0	8	246	364	6	18
ACT Brumbies	11	3	0	8	228	308	5	17
Northern Bulls	11	3	0	8	249	306	4	16
Golden Cats	11	2	0	9	266	346	7	15

The leading scorers in the round-robin were: 180 – Andrew Mehrtens (Canterbury Crusaders); 145 – Adrian Cashmore (Auckland Blues); 112 – Jon Preston (Wellington Hurricanes).
The top try-scorers were: 9 – Stefan Terblanche (Coastal Sharks); Jeff Wilson (Otago Highlanders); Jannie van der Walt (Golden Cats) and Joeli Vidiri (Auckland Blues).

OLD ORDER CHANGES

THE 1997-98 SEASON IN ENGLAND
David Llewellyn

This was a season when the old order was shunted aside in one way or another at most levels and in most facets of the game. It was also a year when the southern hemisphere reasserted itself as the breeding ground for excellence, setting standards that England aspired to but could not quite attain. At club level, amidst the politics and infighting that seemed to be the norm at Twickenham, there was a perceptible raising of standards on the playing front, coinciding with a rise in gates for Allied Dunbar Premiership matches. Here too the traditional cocks-of-the-walk, Bath and Leicester, found themselves being challenged, and beaten, by the moneyed upstarts. Newcastle and Saracens took the Allied Dunbar Premiership by storm; Sarries indeed were within a whisker of pulling off a cup and league double. In the end they had to settle for a comprehensive, record-equalling rout of woeful Wasps in the Tetley's Bitter Cup final at Twickenham.

The cup was marred early on by the infamous ear-biting incident, when London Scottish flanker Simon Fenn lost a chunk of his left lobe, for which Bath prop Kevin Yates was found guilty and banned for six months from the date of the offence. The incident itself, the original decision by Scottish to cite all three members of the Bath front row, and the handling of the subsequent disciplinary hearing, did not help the game's image. In this so-called professional age a protocol needs to be established which will embrace not only the laws of the game, but the law of the land where players may resort to the courts for restitution when they have suffered injury on the field. The whole sordid affair was sad for the sport and there was further cause for concern when there was a brief buzz of more biting when Leicester travelled to Newcastle as the season neared its climax. The RFU, having insisted on examining the various reports, concluded that there was insufficient evidence to indicate whether there had been an attempt by Paul Van Zandvliet to deprive Neil Back of part of his scalp.

There was sadness in Bristol as well, where a once mighty force sank into the lower division after the humiliation of a play-off defeat against London Scottish, although London Irish survived against Rotherham. Bristol had parted company with coach Alan Davies following the trouncing they received at the hands of Newcastle, but the soccer-style managerial merry-go-round picked up speed as Willie Anderson left London Irish and Bob Dwyer

The England squad which faced France in Paris. L-R, back row: D E West (replacement), P R de Glanville (replacement), A J Diprose (replacement), P J Vickery (replacement), W J H Greenwood, G S Archer, M O Johnson, R A Hill, D L Rees, J Leonard, D J Garforth, G C Rowntree (replacement), M B Perry (replacement), D J Grewcock (replacement); front row: N A Back, J C Guscott, P J Grayson, L B N Dallaglio (capt), M J Catt, A S Healey, M P Regan, K P P Bracken

departed Leicester. By the end of the season there were question marks over a number of other coaches as well.

Back on the playing front Allied Dunbar Two saw Bedford finish runaway champions, and just below the top level, Worcester were worthy champions. Cornwall, as has been their wont of late, reached the Tetley's Bitter County Championship final, where they lost 14-21 to Cheshire, newcomers to the Twickenham stage at this level. The Rugby Football Union was the winner in this fixture, Trelawney's Army was some 35,000-strong, outnumbering the Cheshire support by an incredible 70:1 and helping to swell the Twickenham coffers by around £500,000. The Middlesex Sevens raised damn near that amount for charity as The Barbarians, once again featuring some classy Fijians among their number, repeated their triumph of the previous year and breezed past everyone, although a talented young Leicester squad promise much for the future after putting up a fine fight in the final. The BaaBaas secretary Geoff Windsor-Lewis later hinted that they are unlikely to return next year. The Air France Sevens tournament beckons instead.

There was a crass moment politically when Cliff Brittle attempted to compromise Tetley's by threatening to withhold the brewery's cup money from the senior clubs if they pushed for an enlarged Premiership One and Two. That was nipped in the bud, but there was a great deal of posturing pettiness before an agreement was thrashed out, and even then Fran Cotton and Brittle found apparently democratic decisions hard to swallow. Compromise was clearly not within their compass, nor was gracious acceptance of defeat; all they seemed to offer, to their critics, by the end was what they had proffered from the start, a belief that they were right and that everyone else was wrong.

The new season began with the departure of England coach Jack Rowell; the end of a reign of some three years. The decision to turn Rowell's job into a full-time post persuaded the great man that it was time to step aside and he retired, to be succeeded by former England and Leicester centre Clive Woodward, who had just taken charge at Bath. There was certainly an element of the new broom having a good clean sweep, but Woodward's good sense stopped short of scrubbing bare.

New faces did appear, but generally with overwhelming support from pundits and fans alike. Lawrence Dallaglio was not just the management's choice as captain to take over from Phil de Glanville, he was the populist choice, having the acclaim of professionals, pundits and public alike. His on-field dynamism brought a new dimension to the leadership; off the field he was articulate, intelligent and frank-speaking. The public persona of England rugby rose a few welcome notches with Lorenzo Bruno Dallaglio at the helm.

New routines were established and Club England hardened from a concept into an entity on and off the pitch; players were made to feel that they belonged and, more importantly, were not being overlooked for further honours. This management was watching everyone, assessing the qualities of players all over the country, not just everywhere south of Watford and east of Bristol. However, there was not a great deal of time for Woodward and his coaching cohorts to prepare for one of the toughest looking pre-Christmas fixture lists ever dreamed up by the match-makers at HQ. Marriages arranged in hell was to understate the case.

Yet, at the time, everyone said it was a good idea. A month of concentrated, high-octane Tests. Four consecutive Saturdays against the best in the world to see where England, and English, rugby was going. They would open with Australia, and then travel up to Old Trafford, home of Manchester United, where they would tackle the mighty All Blacks of New Zealand, in an innovative move to spread the word and share the glamour of top international rugby with a public for so long – and so wrongly – starved of such fixtures. Having completed the first leg of a two-match series with New Zealand, it would be back to Twickenham where they would take on South Africa before finally, just a week later, squaring up once more to the All Blacks. It was a combustible month, foretelling, if anyone had realised at the time, a combustible year. It is a moot point as to whether England came through unscathed in their trial by southern hemisphere. They still had the Five Nations to contend with. The opening match, against France, was being billed as the Grand Slam 'decider' even before Christmas.

First up though it was the England 'Wannabes' against the Australian Wallabies. Woodward adopted a bold approach, selecting a side with five new caps: in the front row, hooker Andy Long and prop Will Green; and out in the backs, Will Greenwood at centre, David Rees on the right wing and Matt Perry at full-back. The two teams were competing for the Cook Cup, but all either side could serve up was some half-baked rugby. Australia won a moral victory, outscoring England by two tries to nil, but a draw was probably a reasonably accurate reflection of the game. Long, sadly, looked out of place and in fact spent the rest of the season leading the under-21s. By the time he returns to top-flight rugby he will be better prepared. The others though were not half bad in an error-strewn match.

Seven days later and a first time for everyone. Old Trafford was packed with enthusiastic people and the players later said that they wanted more games in the intimacy of the all-seater stadium. No new caps, just a battle royal with New Zealand. Martin Johnson went over the top with his aggression and was later cited for a punch on All Black captain Justin Marshall. Retribution was swift.

Woodward suspended the British Lions captain for a match, which meant that he missed out on the South Africa Test the following week. There was a fair bit of controversy in fact. Richard Cockerill, living up to his nickname Cocky, had steam coming out of All Black ears when he brazenly fronted up to his opposite number Norm Hewitt during the ritual Haka. It did not matter that England lost 8-25, because they gave such a good account of themselves. They tackled till they dropped, putting so much pressure on their opponents that the habitually perfect New Zealanders made uncharacteristic errors throughout a passionate match. Even so, as good as the performance might have been, England still lost, so their subsequent lap of honour – a mark of gratitude to the fans, maintained the players – was a trifle hard to swallow. But Dallaglio's men had engendered hope in the breast of every watching Englishman of greater things to come.

Unfortunately those greater things were not in evidence when the World Champions South Africa arrived at Twickenham fresh from a resounding 52-10 win against France in Paris the previous week. England fielded an inexperienced team, four of whom were making their Twickenham debuts, Nick Greenstock, John Bentley, Darren Garforth and lock Danny Grewcock. The outcome was not as bad as the French one, but South Africa still ended with their biggest winning margin at HQ. England went well for an hour, and led for much of that time, but with a shift in tactics at half-time England found the Springboks forwards practically unstoppable in the loose and it became a matter of time before the rampaging South Africans burst through the home side's defence. To their credit England tackled to the end and managed to limit the damage, but they still needed to prove that they could do more than that one thing in a match. It is all very well defending, but you also have to attack and breach your opponent's line as well in order to win a match. This they were finding difficult to do against the all-round skills of the faster-thinking southern hemisphere sides.

New Zealand Part II saw a recall for Paul Grayson at fly-half and Austin Healey moving out to the wing among a half a dozen changes made by Woodward. How England did not win is a mystery. They went 20-3 ahead at one stage only to allow the All Blacks to counter. It was one of the most thrilling games ever staged at Twickenham according to some pundits. It certainly had everything, panache, pizzazz, power play and passion again. England matched the All Blacks in every department. Woodward later tried to play it down by saying it was 'just an outstanding one-off performance', and he had a point. The All Blacks after all were coming to the end of 10 months of hard grind. But it was still glorious to wallow in a bath of optimism for the future. Playing like this, even though it ended, as the hectic schedule had begun, with a draw (the highest in international rugby), England should surely pulverise France in that Grand Slam decider.

In fact when New Zealand left for home it would appear that they took with them all the spirit that had made England such doughty opponents. When the Five Nations Championship got under way that Grand Slam decider was a no-contest. England lost badly to the Gauls. The seven-point margin was no reflection of the gulf between the two sides by the end. French flair told in this match as it did throughout the tournament. All that was left was the Triple Crown. This had to be won in style and the 60-26 thrashing that England handed out to a stunned Wales at least underlined that there was a widening gulf which the Celtic nations were struggling increasingly to bridge.

A Sunday in March at Murrayfield saw them duly complete the second leg of their mission, although the Scots were able to harass and harry for a long time. Grayson emerged with 19 points, including his first try for England and Garath Archer was beginning to look like a seriously skilful international lock. All that remained was Ireland, who did not endear themselves to Dallaglio and his cronies by accusing the English of 'arrogance' prior to the match. Come the day and England stood on their dignity, claiming that numbers of the Irish had stood on them. There was even a childish incident at the end when Dallaglio appeared to refuse to shake hands with David Corkery amidst dark mutterings and mumblings of skulduggery and thuggery in the 35-17 win.

NEWCASTLE REALISE THEIR AMBITIONS

ALLIED DUNBAR PREMIERSHIP 1997-98
David Llewellyn

So money does buy success. Newcastle's emphatic trouncing of a flabby Harlequins side brought to a climax a fascinating season and fulfilled all Sir John Hall's and Rob Andrew's ambitions a couple of years ahead of schedule. And, it has to be said, they were worthy winners of the inaugural Allied Dunbar Premiership title. Under the abrasive, but effective leadership of Dean Ryan, the Falcons, as Newcastle have styled themselves, outscored and out-defended everyone else, losing only three matches and winning the remaining 19, just pipping their rivals in the tight run-in, Saracens. As bravely as the Londoners fought they did not do quite enough. It was not the 10-10 draw at Leicester which cost them the title either, although it was a contributory factor, because had they beaten the Tigers they would have had to have done so by a seriously big score to have been able to challenge Newcastle's 258-point difference. It was rather an inability to maintain consistency of quality and purpose. Never mind. They still provided a worrying and worthy challenge to Newcastle and won the marketing battle hands down. No-one was remotely in their league in promoting the game as they did at Watford FC's Vicarage Road stadium.

Of course the season was littered with politics and there was the farcical situation of uncertainty over whether there was going to be relegation, or whether there would be an enlarged Premiership One in the new season, until the last week of the long campaign. Relegation was retained, but the bottom two in Division One had to play off against third and fourth in Division Two. That resulted in the end of an era as Bristol, anything but shipshape in this new age of professionalism, having earlier in the season parted company with their coach Alan Davies, finally departing the top flight as they lost the play-offs against London Scottish. But those great survivors London Irish saw off the threat of Rotherham in the other play-off, thanks as much as anything to the input from their consultant, part-time coach Dick Best.

The season began so early that it was almost still the old one. The Lions had no sooner stumbled home licking their wounds following their awesome achievements in South Africa, when their clubs were back in action in mid-August – we had not even had the Bank Holiday. It was obscene. For the new sponsors, however, it probably could not have begun soon enough. Allied Dunbar put their all into the programme and took the leagues onto the Internet. There was the odd change: 10-minute breaks at half-time, six substitutes and – before a ball had been kicked in anger – the introduction of a sin-bin. This last was announced a trifle prematurely. The idea had to be put up for approval by the International Board; but by the time they sanctioned it the nation was on the brink of celebrating the Gunpowder Plot.

Rugby had its own plotters; early on there was talk that the top clubs wanted to create a closed shop, something to which the Premiership Two clubs took great exception. In the end the idea was dropped and everyone got on with playing. Saracens set startling standards off the field, filling their Vicarage Road stadium at Watford with almost 20,000 people to create a record for a league match. And in general a survey run by the sponsors revealed that attendances were up by more than 21 per cent. Individually, relegated Bristol were down by 1.7 per cent, no surprise there, while Saracens, in contrast, with their razzmatazz, fez, and radio-controlled kicking tee transporter, were up by nearly 200 per cent.

On the field the *nouveaux riches* were spelling out that it was time for a change from the outset, with the eventual champions travelling to the Recreation Ground for their opening league match and coming away with both points, to leave Bath on the back foot for the rest of the campaign. Although the Falcons fluttered briefly and allowed Saracens to take over at the top, they got back on the right track in time to beat their closest rivals at home, while the old guard of Bath and Leicester were left in the frame, but only just.

Bath's Phil de Glanville tackles Newcastle's Va'aiga Tuigamala in the opening match of the season at the Recreation Ground. Newcastle's victory in this encounter set the scene for their first Premiership success.

The decision to expand Premierships One and Two to 14 teams meant that runaway Second Division champions Bedford and runners-up West Hartlepool went up and were joined by play-off winners London Scottish. That let in four from Jewson National League One, champions Worcester, runners-up Leeds, London Welsh and Rugby. Thankfully sanity returns and there will be no more August starts. It can only get better.

Previous champions

1988	Leicester	1993	Bath
1989	Bath	1994	Bath
1990	Wasps	1995	Leicester
1991	Bath	1996	Bath
1992	Bath	1997	Wasps

ENGLISH LEAGUES 1997-98

*indicates points deducted

ALLIED DUNBAR PREMIERSHIP

Allied Dunbar One

	P	W	D	L	F	A	Pts
Newcastle	22	19	0	3	645	387	38
Saracens	22	18	1	3	584	396	37
Bath	22	13	0	9	575	455	26
Leicester	22	12	2	8	569	449	26
Richmond	22	12	0	10	607	499	24
Sale	22	10	2	10	605	558	22
Gloucester	22	11	1	10	512	528	21*
Northampton	22	9	1	12	493	472	19
Wasps	22	8	1	13	490	609	17
NEC H'quins	22	8	0	14	516	645	16
London Irish	22	6	0	16	457	673	12
Bristol	22	2	0	20	351	733	4

Allied Dunbar Two

	P	W	D	L	F	A	Pts
Bedford	22	20	0	2	791	365	38*
West Hartlepool	22	15	1	6	617	431	31
London Scottish	22	14	1	7	517	404	29
Rotherham	22	14	0	8	566	386	28
Orrell	22	12	0	10	533	400	24
Moseley	22	11	1	10	478	421	23
Coventry	22	11	1	10	444	532	23
Waterloo	22	11	0	11	510	525	22
Blackheath	22	8	0	14	474	621	16
Wakefield	22	6	0	16	382	556	12
Exeter	22	6	0	16	334	553	12
Fylde	22	2	0	20	258	710	4

JEWSON NATIONAL LEAGUE

National 1

	P	W	D	L	F	A	Pts
Worcester	26	24	0	2	1001	331	48
Leeds	26	21	1	4	858	407	43
London Welsh	26	21	1	4	848	478	43
Rugby Lions	26	21	0	5	733	405	42
Rosslyn Park	26	13	1	12	486	537	27
Nottingham	26	13	0	13	527	602	26
Newbury	26	12	2	12	639	545	24*
Reading	26	11	1	14	620	697	23
Otley	26	10	1	15	447	682	21
Wharfedale	26	8	3	15	476	684	19
Liverpool St H	26	8	1	17	430	767	15*
Lydney	26	5	0	21	361	575	10
Morley	26	5	0	21	372	844	10
Harrogate	26	4	1	21	463	707	9

National 2 North

	P	W	D	L	F	A	Pts
B'ham/S'hull	26	23	0	3	805	334	56
Manchester	26	21	2	3	1029	472	44
Kendal	26	18	2	6	619	357	38
Preston Gshs	26	14	2	10	549	469	30
Sedgley Park	26	14	2	10	655	595	30
Stourbridge	26	14	0	12	685	605	28
Nuneaton	26	13	0	13	453	570	26
Sandal	26	13	1	12	485	547	25*
Aspatria	26	11	0	15	524	783	22
Sheffield	26	10	2	14	557	539	20*
Walsall	26	9	1	16	539	723	19
Hinckley	26	6	1	19	429	726	13
Lichfield	26	4	1	21	365	694	9
Winnington Park	26	5	0	21	470	750	8*

National 2 South

	P	W	D	L	F	A	Pts
Camberley	26	23	1	2	803	372	47
Henley	26	22	0	4	772	384	44
Barking	26	20	0	6	762	450	40
Esher	26	18	1	7	651	448	37
Cheltenham	26	14	1	11	627	514	29
Tabard	26	14	0	12	556	532	28
North Walsham	26	12	1	13	431	373	25
Bridgwater	26	12	0	14	535	664	24
Redruth	26	10	0	16	720	580	20
Weston-s-Mare	26	10	0	16	468	651	20
Clifton	26	8	1	17	414	611	17
Havant	26	8	1	17	388	643	17
Plymouth	26	6	0	20	472	756	12
Met Police	26	2	0	24	320	941	2*

LONDON DIVISION

London 1

	P	W	D	L	F	A	Pts
Norwich	16	15	0	1	525	151	30
Staines	16	14	1	1	598	177	29
Basingstoke	16	11	2	3	413	271	24
G'ford & G'ming	16	12	0	4	435	307	24
Harlow	16	11	1	4	537	234	23
Wimbledon	16	10	0	6	432	305	20
Sudbury	16	9	1	6	323	310	19
Thanet Wand	16	9	0	7	371	320	18
Ruislip	16	8	1	7	327	265	17
Sutton & Epsom	16	7	2	7	365	349	16
Cheshunt	16	6	0	10	305	379	12
Old Whifgiftian	16	5	0	11	266	402	10
Old Colfeians	16	5	0	11	336	504	10
Thurrock	16	4	0	12	179	473	8
Charlton Park	16	2	1	13	229	422	5
Southend	16	2	1	13	199	494	5
Askeans	16	1	0	15	110	587	2

London 2 North

	P	W	D	L	F	A	Pts
Woodford	16	15	1	0	505	173	31
Bishop's S'ford	16	13	0	3	430	230	26
Cambridge	16	11	1	4	412	188	23
Diss	16	11	1	4	349	229	23
Ipswich	16	10	0	6	503	247	20
Old Albanians	16	9	2	5	401	270	20
Welwyn	16	9	0	7	240	264	18
Finchley	16	8	0	8	315	320	16
Old Verulamians	16	8	0	8	305	373	16
Colchester	16	7	1	8	354	358	15
Braintree	16	7	0	9	283	342	14
Old Mer Taylors	16	7	0	9	307	457	14
Barnet	16	6	0	10	217	240	12
R'ford & Gid Pk	16	5	0	11	296	364	10
Brentwood	16	4	0	12	158	356	8
Chingford	16	3	0	13	180	525	6
Ealing	16	0	0	16	167	486	-10*

London 2 South

	P	W	D	L	F	A	Pts
Westcombe Park	15	15	0	0	703	138	30
Winchester	15	13	0	2	541	140	26
Haywards Heath	15	11	1	3	560	202	23
Gravesend	15	11	0	4	413	201	22
Sevenoaks	15	10	1	4	500	182	21
Old Blues	15	9	1	5	350	233	19
Lewes	15	9	1	5	309	244	19
O Wimb'donians	15	7	0	8	365	299	14
Beckenham	15	7	0	8	289	301	14
O Guildfordians	15	6	0	9	216	295	12
Warlingham	15	6	0	9	321	433	10*
Old Juddian	15	6	0	9	266	338	8*
Horsham	15	4	0	11	256	453	6*
Dorking	15	3	0	12	151	519	4*
Old Reigatian	15	1	0	14	173	647	-4*
S'ham-Croydon	15	0	0	15	127	915	-4*
Brockleians	0	0	0	0	0	0	-5

London 3 North-East

	P	W	D	L	F	A	Pts
L'stoft & Yarm'th	16	13	0	3	534	204	26
Bury St Edmunds	16	12	1	3	392	231	25
Campion	16	12	0	4	503	264	24
Chelmsford	16	9	1	6	364	250	19
Basildon	16	9	1	6	297	291	19
Newmarket	16	9	1	6	241	254	19
Wymondham	16	8	2	6	340	246	16*
Woodbridge	16	8	0	8	244	318	16
Canvey Island	16	7	0	9	342	318	14
Eton Manor	16	7	0	9	221	222	14
Old Edwardians	16	7	0	9	291	309	14
Maldon	16	7	0	9	263	324	14
West Norfolk	16	7	0	9	331	325	12*
Rochford	16	6	0	10	290	309	12
Shelford	16	6	0	10	292	320	12
Holt	16	5	0	11	223	342	10
Upminster	16	1	0	5	133	774	0*

London 3 North-West

	P	W	D	L	F	A	Pts
Harpenden	16	15	0	1	555	180	30
Hertford	16	13	0	3	578	178	26
Chiswick	16	12	0	4	410	222	24
Old Millhillians	16	11	1	4	477	190	23
Old Gaytonians	16	11	0	5	336	251	22
Grasshoppers	16	9	1	6	452	247	19
Uxbridge	16	9	1	6	360	295	19
Tring	16	8	2	6	286	298	18
Hampstead	16	9	1	6	420	326	17*
Letchworth	16	7	0	9	377	273	14
St Albans	16	6	0	10	333	410	12
Fullerians	16	5	1	10	315	364	11
Lensbury	16	5	1	10	236	358	11
Kingsburians	16	5	0	11	209	299	10
Mill Hill	16	4	0	12	186	632	8
Haringey	16	2	0	14	168	593	4
Hackney	16	1	0	15	168	750	2

London 3 South-East

	P	W	D	L	F	A	Pts
Canterbury	16	15	0	1	639	129	30
Worthing	16	15	0	1	577	175	30
Maidstone	16	13	0	3	573	183	26
Sidcup	16	11	0	5	317	268	22
Cranbrook	16	9	1	6	264	182	19
H'field & Waldr'n	16	9	1	6	338	267	19
East Grinstead	16	9	1	6	334	290	19
Tunbridge Wells	16	8	1	7	356	302	17
Brighton	16	7	2	7	345	261	16
Crawley	16	7	0	9	288	375	14
Medway	16	6	1	9	229	332	13
Chichester	16	6	1	9	220	452	13
Beccehamians	16	4	1	11	211	402	9
Park House	16	4	0	12	259	474	8
Uckfield	16	3	1	12	182	406	7
Sheppey	16	2	1	13	162	423	5
Bognor	16	2	1	13	165	538	5

London 3 South-West

	P	W	D	L	F	A	Pts
Alton	16	15	1	0	506	164	31
Jersey	16	12	2	2	475	215	26
Gosport	16	13	0	3	403	153	26
Old Alleynian	16	12	0	4	368	217	24
Portsmouth	16	10	0	6	520	251	20
Purley	16	10	0	6	354	247	20
Effingham	16	9	1	6	296	278	19
Uni Vandals	16	9	1	6	284	296	19
Old Emanuel	16	8	1	7	384	270	17
Old Reedonians	16	6	1	9	318	388	13
Southampton	16	5	1	10	247	339	11
Barnes	16	5	0	11	252	335	10
Farnborough	16	3	1	12	253	469	5*
Old Whitgiftians	16	2	1	13	233	480	3*
Esso	16	1	0	15	168	542	2
Old Walcountians	16	1	0	15	146	631	2
Guy's Hospital	16	9	2	5	348	280	-4*

Eastern Counties 1

	P	W	D	L	F	A	Pts
Hadleigh	18	17	0	1	723	166	34
Bancroft	18	15	0	3	501	181	30
Ilford Wanderers	18	11	1	6	272	252	23
Ely	18	11	0	7	455	292	22
Westcliffe	18	10	0	8	305	304	20
Felixstowe	18	7	0	11	260	492	12*
Cantabrigian	18	5	1	12	235	449	11
Saffron Walden	18	5	0	13	256	413	10
Wanstead	18	3	2	13	292	479	8
Harw' & D'court	18	4	0	14	200	471	8

Eastern Counties 2

	P	W	D	L	F	A	Pts
Met Pol Chigwell	14	12	0	2	473	188	24
Thetford	14	11	1	2	485	149	23
Old Cooperians	14	10	1	3	388	218	21
Sth W'ham Fers	14	9	0	5	372	227	16*
Mersea Island	14	5	0	9	277	288	10
Old Palmerians	14	5	0	9	192	287	10
Southwold	14	1	0	13	105	645	2
Thames	14	2	0	12	140	430	-2*
Loughton	0	0	0	0	0	0	-3*
Fakenham	0	0	0	0	0	0	-3*

Eastern Counties 3 North

	P	W	D	L	F	A	Pts
Beccles	16	13	1	2	415	161	25*
Crusaders	16	12	1	3	335	169	25
Ipswich YM	16	12	0	4	461	212	24
March	16	8	1	7	315	217	17
Thurston	16	8	1	7	313	345	17
Broadland	16	7	0	9	339	266	14
Stowmarket	16	5	0	11	165	310	10
Lakenham Hwtt	16	4	0	12	221	418	8
Brightlinsea	16	1	0	15	117	583	0*

Eastern Counties 3 South

	P	W	D	L	F	A	Pts
Billericay	14	14	0	0	686	57	28
East London	14	12	0	2	535	106	24
Ongar	14	10	0	4	278	186	20
B'ham-on-Crou'	14	5	0	9	156	378	10
Sawston	14	6	0	8	170	406	10*
Stanford	14	5	0	9	177	273	6*
Ravens	14	3	0	11	116	439	6
Haverhill	14	1	0	13	140	413	2

Eastern Counties 4 North

	P	W	D	L	F	A	Pts
Wisbech	10	10	0	0	486	46	20
Swaffham	10	7	0	3	318	181	14
RAF Lakenheath	10	5	0	5	183	245	10
Norwich Union	10	5	0	5	281	199	8*
Mistley	10	1	0	9	50	307	2
Clacton	10	2	0	8	100	440	2*
Watton	0	0	0	0	0	0	-4*

Eastern Counties 4 South

	P	W	D	L	F	A	Pts
Old Brentwoods	14	14	0	0	714	75	28
Witham	14	11	0	3	402	160	22
Millwall Albion	14	10	0	4	454	164	20
May & Baker	14	8	0	6	307	298	16
Old Bealonians	14	5	0	9	204	373	8*
Dagenham	14	3	0	11	138	460	4*
Rayleigh	14	2	0	12	166	438	2*
Fair'-Chigwell	14	3	0	11	165	582	2*

Hampshire 1

	P	W	D	L	F	A	Pts
Andover	16	15	0	1	560	85	30
Millbrook	16	14	0	2	524	242	28
US Portsmouth	16	11	1	4	357	266	21*
Tottonians	16	10	0	6	365	367	20
Isle of Wight	16	7	1	8	372	309	15
Guernsey	16	6	0	10	351	419	8*
Overton	16	3	0	13	212	446	6
Petersfield	16	5	0	11	265	448	4*
Eastleigh	16	0	0	16	168	592	0

Hampshire 2

	P	W	D	L	F	A	Pts
Ventnor	16	14	0	2	689	142	28
Trojans	16	14	0	2	506	114	28
Romsey	16	10	0	6	304	286	18*
New Milton	16	8	0	8	415	265	16
S'down & S'klin	16	7	0	9	261	294	12*
Fareham Heath	16	6	0	10	267	384	12
Fordingbridge	16	5	1	10	188	445	11
S'hampton Inst	16	5	0	11	259	468	10
Nomads	16	2	1	13	127	618	3*

Hampshire 3

	P	W	D	L	F	A	Pts
Hampshire Cons	14	14	0	0	656	81	28
Hamble	14	11	1	2	330	123	23
Alresford	14	7	2	5	268	170	14*
Waterlooville	14	8	0	6	285	285	14*
Fleet	14	5	0	9	251	229	10
A C Delco	14	6	1	7	252	299	9*
Kingsclere	14	2	0	12	139	442	2*
Ellingham	14	1	0	13	51	603	2

Herts/Middx 1

	P	W	D	L	F	A	Pts
Twickenham	13	13	0	0	586	129	24*
Lon Nigerians	14	12	0	2	467	153	24
Imperial Medics	14	11	0	3	520	157	22
HAC	13	9	0	4	312	268	18
Harrow	14	8	0	6	252	234	16
Stevenage Town	14	8	0	6	298	318	16
Hemel H'stead	14	6	0	8	277	247	12
Enfield Ignatians	14	7	0	7	256	236	12*
Upper Clapton	14	6	0	8	223	362	12
London NZ	14	6	0	8	338	252	10*
Old Haberdash's	14	5	0	9	242	301	10
Civil Service	14	5	0	9	172	372	10
Old Hamptonians	14	4	0	10	289	346	8
Wembley	14	3	0	11	135	548	2*
Hendon	14	1	0	13	174	618	0*
Centaurs	0	0	0	0	0	0	-4*

Herts/Middx 2

	P	W	D	L	F	A	Pts
UCS Old Boys	11	9	0	2	338	103	18
Feltham	11	9	0	2	385	188	18
Hitchin	11	9	0	2	273	105	18
Bank of England	11	7	0	4	304	216	14
Datchworth	11	7	0	4	194	144	14
London French	11	6	0	5	250	168	12
Old Actonians	11	6	0	5	204	133	12
Old Abbots'	11	5	0	6	188	211	10
Roxeth Man'r OB	11	4	0	7	205	259	8
Barclays Bank	11	3	0	8	161	250	6
Watford	11	1	0	10	121	501	2
Sudbury Court	11	0	0	11	101	446	-2*
London Exiles	0	0	0	0	0	0	-6*

Herts/Middx 3

	P	W	D	L	F	A	Pts
St Nicholas OB	9	8	0	1	344	51	16
H'smith & F'ham	9	8	0	1	186	108	16
Northold	9	6	0	3	282	103	12
Old Ashmoleans	9	6	0	3	225	140	12
Millfield OB	9	5	0	4	251	148	10
Old Isleworthians	9	4	0	5	147	201	8
Southgate	9	4	0	5	135	192	6*
Old Grammar's	9	2	0	7	87	156	4
Royston	9	2	0	7	96	272	2*
Pinner & Gram's	9	0	0	9	42	424	-2*

Herts/Middx 4 North

	P	W	D	L	F	A	Pts
Old Tottonians	7	6	0	1	212	66	12
Old Streetonians	7	7	0	0	201	98	10*
Cuffley	7	4	0	3	212	103	8
Hatfield	7	4	0	3	77	128	8
Belsize Park	7	3	0	4	119	92	4*
Kodak	7	2	0	5	62	241	4
QE II Hospital	7	1	0	6	107	173	2
Kilburn Cosmos	7	1	0	6	70	159	2

Herts/Middx 4 South

	P	W	D	L	F	A	Pts
Quintin	6	5	0	1	239	55	10
British Airways	6	5	0	1	109	44	10
Orleans FP	6	3	1	2	85	61	7
GWR	6	3	1	2	58	38	7
Osterley	6	2	0	4	100	131	4
Thamesians	6	2	0	4	91	176	4
Hayes	6	0	0	6	44	221	0
Meadhurst	0	0	0	0	0	0	-1*

Kent 1

	P	W	D	L	F	A	Pts
Folkestone	15	15	0	0	532	162	30
Dartfordians	15	14	0	1	562	169	28
Old Dunstonians	15	10	2	3	492	228	22
Ashford	15	8	2	5	289	229	18
Old Shooters'	15	9	0	6	279	230	18
Gill'ham Anchor	15	7	3	5	298	269	17
Bromley	15	7	2	6	217	267	16
Betteshanger	15	7	0	8	173	319	14
Nat West Bank	15	5	1	9	312	384	11
Dover	15	5	1	9	216	290	11
Lordswood	15	5	1	9	206	304	11
Met Police Hayes	15	5	1	9	182	306	9*
Sittingbourne	15	5	0	10	219	324	8*
Whitstable	15	4	0	11	212	354	8
Snowdown CW	15	5	0	10	167	379	8*
Deal	15	2	1	12	192	334	5

Kent 2

	P	W	D	L	F	A	Pts
Midland Bank	13	12	0	1	506	148	24
Tonbridge	13	12	0	1	449	93	24
New Ash Green	13	11	1	1	438	119	23
Old Williams'	13	10	0	3	286	257	20
Aylesford	13	9	0	4	346	145	18

	P	W	D	L	F	A	Pts
Old Elthamians	13	7	1	5	287	217	15
Bexley	13	7	0	6	194	232	12*
Vigo	13	5	1	7	179	226	11
Old Olavians	13	3	0	10	184	322	6
Footscray	13	3	0	10	130	324	6
Old Gravesend'	13	3	0	10	126	328	6
Orpington	13	4	0	9	137	370	6*
G'wich Academs	13	3	1	9	143	347	5*
Edenbridge	13	0	0	13	107	384	0

Kent 3

	P	W	D	L	F	A	Pts
Erith	10	10	0	0	302	47	20
Faversham	10	7	0	3	190	100	14
Greenwich	10	7	0	3	178	98	12*
Darenth Valley	10	4	0	6	130	189	6*
Canterbury Exls	10	2	0	8	75	201	4
Meopham	10	0	0	10	41	281	0

Surrey 1

	P	W	D	L	F	A	Pts
Cranleigh	12	10	0	2	411	154	20
Chobham	12	10	0	2	278	143	20
Old Cranleighans	12	9	1	2	225	155	19
Chipstead	12	9	1	2	242	175	19
Farnham	12	7	0	5	177	159	14
Woking	12	5	0	7	210	170	10
KCS Old Boys	12	5	0	7	238	249	10
Raynes Park	12	5	0	7	181	226	10
Wandsworthians	12	6	0	6	128	256	10*
Old Caterhams	12	4	0	8	197	232	8
Old Paulines	12	4	0	8	135	193	6*
Battersea Iron's	12	2	0	10	135	287	4
Kingston	12	1	0	11	125	283	0*

Surrey 2

	P	W	D	L	F	A	Pts
Cobham	12	11	0	1	427	103	22
Merton	12	10	0	2	427	161	20
Old Tiffinians	12	10	0	2	408	153	20
Old Rutlishians	12	8	0	4	242	185	16
Antlers	12	6	2	4	200	165	14
Old Wellington's	12	7	1	4	384	168	13
Shirley W'derers	12	5	2	5	161	241	12
Law Society	12	5	0	7	248	313	10
Old Hailey's	12	4	2	6	244	297	8*
London Media	12	3	1	8	257	331	7
Reigate & Redhill	12	4	0	8	195	257	6*
Old Suttonians	12	0	0	12	110	614	0
Old Freemans	12	1	0	11	59	374	-2*

Surrey 3

	P	W	D	L	F	A	Pts
London Cornish	11	10	0	1	365	133	20
London FB	11	8	1	2	268	158	17
Haslemere	11	8	0	3	345	118	16
Lightwater	11	9	0	2	317	149	16*
Mitcham	11	7	0	4	352	131	14
Worth Old Boys	11	8	0	3	336	197	14*
Kings Coll Hos	11	5	1	5	256	174	11
Egham	11	3	0	8	111	285	4*

	P	W	D	L	F	A	Pts
Bec Old Boys	11	2	0	9	126	349	4
Croydon	11	2	0	9	109	320	2*
Old Johnians	11	2	0	9	110	530	-2*
Old Bevonians	11	1	0	10	124	275	-4*

Surrey 4

	P	W	D	L	F	A	Pts
Surrey University	8	8	0	0	320	81	14*
St Georges Hos	8	6	0	2	278	96	12
Economicals	8	3	0	5	126	194	6
Racal-Decca	8	1	0	7	93	287	2
Surrey Police	8	2	0	6	132	291	0*
Oxted	0	0	0	0	0	0	-3*

Sussex 1

	P	W	D	L	F	A	Pts
Eastbourne	16	15	1	0	818	168	31
Hove	16	13	1	2	489	118	27
Crowborough	16	11	0	5	345	201	22
Seaford	16	10	1	5	351	208	21
Sun A Horsham	16	7	1	8	209	284	15
H'stings & B'hill	16	6	0	10	321	282	12
Ditchling	16	5	0	11	193	534	10
BA Wingspan	16	2	1	13	166	539	5
Pulborough	16	0	1	15	154	712	1

Sussex 2

	P	W	D	L	F	A	Pts
Burgess Hill	12	10	0	2	314	148	20
Old Brightonians	12	9	1	2	346	137	19
St Francis	12	8	0	4	228	142	16
Newick	12	5	0	7	133	250	10
Shoreham	12	4	0	8	179	206	8
Hellingly	12	4	1	7	207	208	5*
Rye	12	1	0	11	67	383	2
Sussex Police	0	0	0	0	0	0	0

Sussex 3

	P	W	D	L	F	A	Pts
Chichester Inst	10	10	0	0	518	69	20
Robertsbridge	10	7	0	3	198	159	14
Barns Green	10	4	1	5	145	239	9
Midhurst	10	4	1	5	152	248	9
Plumpton	10	3	1	6	179	216	7
Arun	10	0	1	9	45	306	1

MIDLANDS DIVISION

Midlands 1

	P	W	D	L	F	A	Pts
Whitchurch	16	16	0	0	537	210	32
Banbury	16	14	0	2	411	221	28
Broadstreet	16	13	1	2	420	211	27
Scunthorpe	16	10	0	6	415	279	20
Burton	16	9	1	6	311	222	19
Westleigh	16	9	0	7	333	283	18
Stoke on Trent	16	8	1	7	290	278	17
Syston	16	8	1	7	241	254	17
Barkers Butts	16	7	1	8	322	403	15

	P	W	D	L	F	A	Pts
Leighton Buzzard	16	7	0	9	325	397	14
Kenilworth	16	6	0	10	325	343	12
Hereford	16	6	1	9	260	295	11*
Mansfield	16	5	1	10	265	390	11
Belgrave	16	5	0	11	214	293	10
Camp Hill	16	3	2	11	287	422	8
Wolverhampton	16	4	0	12	227	430	8
Derby	16	1	1	14	185	437	3

Midlands 2

	P	W	D	L	F	A	Pts
Bedford Athletic	16	16	0	0	718	151	32
Dudley	16	14	1	1	528	145	29
Old Laurentians	16	12	1	3	480	246	25
Longton	16	12	0	4	445	206	24
Bromsgrove	16	11	1	4	282	255	23
Luctonians	16	9	0	7	377	318	18
Kettering	16	7	0	9	255	284	14
Newport	16	7	0	9	291	331	14
Stafford	16	7	0	9	268	403	14
Moderns	16	6	1	9	299	416	13
Stockwood Park	16	6	0	10	286	362	12
Huntingdon	16	6	0	10	215	340	12
Ampthill	16	6	1	9	289	326	11*
Sutton Coldfield	16	5	1	10	232	391	11
Leamington	16	4	0	12	201	437	6*
Towcestrians	16	3	0	13	149	507	6
Paviors	16	2	0	14	215	412	4

Midlands East 1

	P	W	D	L	F	A	Pts
Lincoln	16	14	0	2	358	170	28
Northampton OS	16	13	0	3	524	177	26
Wellingborough	16	12	0	4	500	213	24
Peterborough	16	11	0	5	392	257	22
Lutterworth	16	10	0	6	288	205	20
Old N'thampt's	16	10	0	6	276	234	20
Spalding	16	8	1	7	369	226	17
N'thampton MO	16	7	2	7	352	367	16
Stoneygate	16	7	1	8	278	286	15
Ilkeston	16	7	1	8	238	265	15
Coalville	16	7	0	9	204	268	14
Newark	16	7	0	9	288	359	14
Vipers	16	6	0	10	231	281	12
Stewarts & Ll'ds	16	5	1	10	189	369	11
Long Buckby	16	4	0	12	234	435	6*
Matlock	16	2	2	12	228	445	6
Ashbourne	16	2	0	14	160	552	2*

Midlands East 2

	P	W	D	L	F	A	Pts
Dunstablians	16	15	0	1	513	135	30
Oadby Wyggest's	16	14	0	2	290	162	28
Luton	16	13	0	3	587	156	26
Loughborough	16	13	0	3	412	248	26
South Leicester	16	12	0	4	548	275	24
Kibworth	16	10	1	5	367	333	21
Stamford	16	8	0	8	306	316	16
Grimsby	16	7	0	9	281	327	14
West Bridgford	16	7	0	9	320	374	14
Long Eaton	16	6	1	9	275	290	13

	P	W	D	L	F	A	Pts
Kesteven	16	6	0	10	319	400	12
Nottingham Cas	16	6	1	9	202	352	11*
Biggleswade	16	5	1	10	191	364	11
Buxton	16	4	1	11	217	319	9
Amber Valley	16	4	1	11	216	403	9
N'hampton B Bri	16	3	0	13	207	429	6
Bedford Queens	16	0	0	16	126	494	0

East Midlands/Leics 1

	P	W	D	L	F	A	Pts
Leicester Forest	16	15	0	1	758	107	30
Loughborough St	16	13	1	2	662	205	27
Oakham	16	14	0	2	879	159	26*
Market Bosworth	16	12	1	3	663	212	25
Melton Mowbray	16	12	0	4	365	239	24
R'den & Higham	16	10	1	5	309	247	21
Bedford Swifts	16	7	2	7	369	297	16
Daventry	16	8	0	8	247	353	16
St Ives	16	6	2	8	201	377	14
Bugbrooke	16	6	0	10	202	312	12
St Neots	16	6	0	10	170	518	12
Well'borough OG	16	6	1	9	187	457	11*
Brackley	16	6	1	9	218	559	11*
Old Ashbeians	16	5	0	11	223	480	10
Deepings	16	3	1	12	176	541	7
Colworth House	16	1	1	14	206	366	3
Ayles' St James	16	0	1	15	108	514	1

East Midlands

	P	W	D	L	F	A	Pts
N'hampton Cas	15	15	0	0	595	62	30
Oundle	16	11	1	4	307	220	23
Vauxhall Motors	16	10	0	6	362	230	20
Kempston	16	7	1	8	275	250	15
Biddenham	15	6	1	8	177	204	13
Thorney	15	6	1	8	252	284	13
Corby	15	5	0	10	170	289	10
N'hamp' Heath	15	5	0	10	185	366	10
Westwood	15	2	0	13	111	529	4

Leics 1

	P	W	D	L	F	A	Pts
Wigston	8	8	0	0	368	66	16
Old Newtonians	8	5	0	3	222	96	10
Aylestonians	8	3	0	5	127	186	6
New Parks	8	4	0	4	164	190	4*
Burbage	8	0	0	8	70	413	0

Leics 2

	P	W	D	L	F	A	Pts
Braunstone Town	6	5	0	1	194	34	10
Anstey	6	5	0	1	189	54	8*
Aylestone Athl'	6	2	0	4	51	169	4
Cosby	6	0	0	6	16	193	0

Notts, Lincs & Derby 1

	P	W	D	L	F	A	Pts
Glossop	15	14	1	0	510	139	29
Ashfield	15	14	0	1	342	118	28
Mellish	15	12	0	3	398	228	24

	P	W	D	L	F	A	Pts
Southwell	15	11	0	4	283	207	22
Keyworth	15	10	0	5	276	257	20
Melbourne	15	8	1	6	290	211	17
Worksop	15	6	2	7	228	266	14
Leesbrook	15	7	0	8	183	298	14
Bakewell Manner	15	6	0	9	271	237	12
Dronfield	15	6	0	9	190	285	12
Mkt R & Louth	15	5	1	9	257	255	11
Castle Donington	15	5	1	9	172	283	11
Boots Athletic	15	5	0	10	229	288	10
Stamford College	15	4	0	11	196	316	8
East Retford	15	4	0	11	147	288	8
Chesterfield	15	0	0	15	134	430	0

Notts, Lincs & Derby 2

	P	W	D	L	F	A	Pts
Belper	14	12	0	2	483	103	24
Sleaford	14	11	1	2	343	138	23
Nottinghamians	14	9	1	4	251	181	19
East Leake	14	8	2	4	325	177	18
Meden Vale	14	9	0	5	174	194	18
Boston	14	9	0	5	260	139	16*
Cotgrave	14	8	0	6	252	167	16
Hope Valley	14	7	1	6	185	138	15
Rolls Royce	14	6	0	8	356	266	10*
North Kesteven	14	5	0	9	159	309	10
Bourne	14	4	1	9	158	237	9
Barton & District	14	5	0	9	201	308	8*
Notts Cons	14	4	1	9	170	193	7*
Ollerton	14	3	0	11	90	487	6
Gainsborough	14	1	1	12	114	483	3

Notts, Lincs & Derby 3

	P	W	D	L	F	A	Pts
Cleethorpes	14	13	0	1	463	130	26
Skegness	14	13	0	1	340	132	26
Tupton	14	8	1	5	365	202	17
Uni of Derby	14	5	1	8	183	356	11
Bingham	14	5	0	9	209	282	10
Yarborough Bees	14	4	2	8	201	288	10
Horncastle	14	3	2	9	135	278	8
Whitwell	14	2	0	12	127	355	4

Midlands West 1

	P	W	D	L	F	A	Pts
Newbold	16	13	0	3	402	168	26
Keresley	16	12	2	2	335	153	26
Malvern	16	11	3	2	488	177	25
Woodrush	16	11	1	4	307	247	23
Selly Oak	16	10	0	6	424	358	20
Willenhall	16	8	3	5	323	309	19
Stratford	16	9	0	7	322	263	18
Old Leamingtons	16	9	0	7	243	217	18
Old Coventrians	16	8	1	7	321	263	17
Old Halesonians	16	8	0	8	290	252	16
Bedworth	16	8	0	8	272	348	16
Leek	16	7	1	8	310	299	15
Telford	16	4	0	12	224	410	8
Aston Old Ed	16	4	0	12	243	446	8
Ludlow	16	3	1	12	178	308	7
Kings Norton	16	2	1	13	186	350	5
Nuneaton O Eds	16	2	1	13	204	504	5

Midlands West 2

	P	W	D	L	F	A	Pts
Shrewsbury	16	15	0	1	641	80	30
Evesham	16	13	1	2	373	123	27
Old Yardleians	16	12	1	3	459	186	25
B'ham Exiles	16	12	0	4	417	185	24
Pershore	16	11	0	5	502	258	22
Dixonians	16	9	2	5	392	276	20
Stoke Old Boys	16	9	0	7	321	290	18
Manor Park	16	8	0	8	310	297	16
Berkswell & Bal	16	7	0	9	251	275	14
Southam	16	7	0	9	352	298	12*
Edwardians	16	5	2	9	213	249	12
Warley	16	5	1	10	231	391	11
Tamworth	16	4	2	10	267	294	10
GPT Coventry	16	6	0	10	235	354	10*
Erdington	16	6	1	9	239	282	9*
Old Griffinians	16	2	0	14	166	554	2*
Cov'try Saracens	16	0	0	16	68	1045	-2*

North Midlands 1

	P	W	D	L	F	A	Pts
Kidderminster	16	16	0	0	574	91	32
Old Saltleians	16	14	0	2	500	228	28
Ledbury	16	13	0	3	564	215	26
Bridgnorth	16	12	0	4	550	194	24
Droitwich	16	11	1	4	307	182	23
Five Way O E'd	16	10	0	6	412	242	20
Bromyard	16	8	0	8	362	220	16
Upton-on-Severn	16	7	1	8	361	294	15
Redditch	16	7	0	9	317	235	14
Tenbury	16	6	1	9	277	349	13
Bishops Castle	16	6	0	10	240	346	12
Oswestry	16	6	0	10	347	528	12
Veseyans	16	5	0	11	216	347	10
Ross-on-Wye	16	4	1	11	193	414	9
B'ham Civil Ser	16	4	0	12	149	380	8
Old Centrals	16	3	0	13	174	779	6
Kynoch	16	2	0	14	138	637	4

North Midlands 2

	P	W	D	L	F	A	Pts
Yardley & District	16	13	1	2	404	177	27
Birchfield	16	13	1	2	392	158	25*
C'bury Mortimer	16	11	1	4	344	172	23
Bourneville	16	9	1	6	542	229	17*
Stourport	16	8	0	8	208	241	16
Harborne	16	7	0	9	295	228	14
Witton	16	6	0	10	191	304	12
Bredon Star	16	1	2	13	119	432	4
Wulfrun	16	1	0	15	114	668	0*

Staffs/Warwicks 1

	P	W	D	L	F	A	Pts
N'castle (Staffs)	16	15	1	0	482	116	31
Spartans	16	12	0	4	374	185	24
Handsworth	16	11	2	3	375	206	22*
Dunlop	16	11	0	5	255	198	22
Claverdon	16	9	1	6	281	227	19
Trentham	16	9	1	6	242	190	19
S'ton-on-Stour	16	8	0	8	258	198	16

	P	W	D	L	F	A	Pts
Silhillians	16	7	1	8	357	306	15
Alcester	16	7	1	8	229	290	15
Trinity Guild	16	7	0	9	279	287	14
Earlsdon	16	7	0	9	226	333	12*
GEC St Leonards	16	6	0	10	199	367	12
Coventry Welsh	16	5	1	10	194	303	11
Burntwood	16	3	3	10	238	319	9
Pinley	16	5	1	10	171	313	9*
Old Wheatleyans	16	4	0	12	203	366	8
R'by St Andrews	16	4	0	12	180	339	6*

Staffordshire

	P	W	D	L	F	A	Pts
Wednesbury	14	13	0	1	427	153	26
Cannock	14	11	0	3	296	148	20*
Uttoxeter	14	9	0	5	295	183	18
Bloxwich	14	7	0	7	216	266	14
Linley	14	6	0	8	142	214	12
Rubery Owen	14	5	0	9	200	267	8*
Wheaton Aston	14	3	0	11	152	288	6
Rugeley	14	2	0	12	161	370	2*

Warwickshire

	P	W	D	L	F	A	Pts
Harbury	18	15	2	1	623	100	32
Atherstone	18	15	1	2	743	139	31
Standard	18	13	1	4	554	174	27
Ford	18	13	1	4	528	220	27
Old Warwickians	18	11	0	7	437	246	22
C'try Technical	18	8	1	9	267	439	17
Coventrians	18	4	0	14	210	536	6*
Rugby Welsh	18	4	0	14	147	480	4*
Shottery	18	2	0	16	111	716	4
Warwick	18	2	0	16	131	701	2*

NORTH DIVISION

North 1

	P	W	D	L	F	A	Pts
New Brighton	22	17	2	3	599	293	36
Doncaster	22	17	2	3	489	285	36
Middlesbrough	22	16	0	6	530	312	32
Widnes	21	14	1	6	378	396	29
Tynedale	22	13	2	7	510	332	28
Broughton Park	22	9	0	13	399	412	18
Stockton	22	8	2	12	355	456	18
Macclesfield	22	8	0	14	303	395	16
Wigton	21	7	0	14	338	436	14
Hull Ionians	21	5	3	13	397	524	13
Bridlington	22	5	2	15	304	532	12
W' Pk Bramhope	21	4	0	17	304	533	8

North 2

	P	W	D	L	F	A	Pts
Northern	22	20	1	1	714	256	41
Blaydon	22	19	1	2	568	251	37*
Vale of Lune	22	16	1	5	483	330	33
Driffield	22	16	1	5	507	356	33
B'ford & Bingley	22	10	0	12	498	439	20
Morpeth	22	9	0	13	410	529	18

Huddersfield	22	8	0	14	379	465	16
Blackburn	22	7	0	15	469	536	14
Alnwick	22	7	0	15	361	449	14
York	22	7	0	15	339	498	14
Lymm	22	7	0	15	243	523	14
Halifax	22	4	0	18	341	680	8

North-East 1

	P	W	D	L	F	A	Pts
Percy Park	18	11	1	6	417	273	23
Old Crossleyans	18	11	1	6	372	315	23
Pontefract	18	10	0	8	401	329	20
Horden	18	7	3	8	346	336	17
Old Brodleians	18	8	1	9	305	307	17
Beverley	18	8	1	9	316	365	17
Durham City	18	9	1	8	316	387	17*
Goole	18	7	1	10	261	274	15
Wheatley Hills	18	6	3	9	257	330	15
Gateshead Fell	18	7	0	11	323	398	12*

North-East 2

	P	W	D	L	F	A	Pts
D'ton M'den Pk	18	17	0	1	617	147	34
Keighley	18	14	0	4	385	257	28
Cleckheaton	18	11	0	7	403	301	22
Hull	18	11	0	7	374	313	22
Darlington	18	8	0	10	309	366	16
North Ribbles'	18	8	0	10	306	391	16
H'pool Rovers	18	7	0	11	279	334	14
Roundhegians	18	6	0	12	322	466	12
Ashington	18	6	0	12	242	470	12
Westoe	18	2	0	16	237	429	4

North-East 3

	P	W	D	L	F	A	Pts
Pocklington	18	13	1	4	437	244	27
Redcar	18	14	0	4	457	241	26*
Ripon	18	12	1	5	373	260	25
W Hart TDSOB	18	10	0	8	354	336	20
Selby	18	9	0	9	356	301	18
Yarnbury	18	9	0	9	287	294	18
Thornesians	18	7	0	11	273	360	14
Sunderland	18	6	2	10	255	375	12*
Bramley	18	5	0	13	248	405	10
Whitby	18	3	0	15	236	460	6

Yorkshire 1

	P	W	D	L	F	A	Pts
Bradford Salem	18	15	0	3	426	189	30
Northallerton	18	12	1	5	364	180	25
Castleford	18	11	1	6	433	227	23
Wath on Dearne	18	10	0	8	338	302	20
Old Otliensians	18	7	0	11	264	295	14
Ilkley	18	7	0	11	267	419	14
Malton & Norton	18	7	0	11	275	441	14
Leodiensians	18	6	1	11	330	354	13
Dinnington	18	7	1	10	311	429	13*
Moortown	18	6	0	12	200	372	12

Yorkshire 2

	P	W	D	L	F	A	Pts
H'field YMCA	16	16	0	0	714	64	32
West Leeds	16	10	3	3	357	253	23
Sheffield Oaks	16	8	1	7	251	227	17
Barnsley	16	7	1	8	205	326	15
Scarborough	16	7	0	9	267	290	14
Hullensians	16	7	0	9	211	301	14
Halifax Vandals	16	6	1	9	190	327	13
Sheffield Tigers	16	6	0	10	224	335	12
Old Modernians	16	2	0	14	135	431	4

Yorkshire 3

	P	W	D	L	F	A	Pts
Hemsworth	18	14	2	2	689	182	30
Stanley Rodillians	18	15	0	3	428	226	30
York RI	18	11	2	5	529	232	24
Leeds Corinths	18	10	2	6	374	172	22
Hessle	18	10	0	8	382	304	20
Stocksbridge	18	9	0	9	268	294	18
Wetherby	18	9	0	9	361	393	18
Skipton	18	5	1	12	338	407	11
Aireborough	18	2	1	15	221	470	5
Hornsea	18	1	0	17	91	1001	2

Yorkshire 4

	P	W	D	L	F	A	Pts
Heath	16	14	1	1	369	123	29
Baildon	16	13	1	2	435	171	27
Knottingley	16	11	4	1	387	123	26
Old Rishworth's	15	9	1	5	296	162	19
Mosborough	16	6	1	9	204	312	13
Garforth	15	5	0	10	145	243	10
Marist	16	4	0	12	174	316	8
Burley	16	4	0	12	159	325	8
Knaresborough	16	1	0	15	125	519	-2*

Yorkshire 5

	P	W	D	L	F	A	Pts
Ossett	16	13	2	1	421	163	26*
Rowntrees	16	11	2	3	424	180	24
Rawmarsh	16	10	1	5	291	154	21
Leeds Med & Ds	16	10	0	6	413	218	18*
BP Chemicals	16	9	0	7	268	213	18
Adwick Le Street	16	8	0	8	238	213	16
De La S' (Sheff)	16	4	1	11	260	215	9
Withernsea	16	4	0	12	168	503	8
Danum Phoenix	16	0	0	16	58	682	0

Durham & Northumbria 1

	P	W	D	L	F	A	Pts
Ryton	18	16	0	2	499	181	32
Acklam	18	16	0	2	384	167	32
Medicals	18	9	1	8	432	346	19
Winlaton Vulcans	18	9	1	8	316	332	19
North Shields	18	9	0	9	321	239	18
Whitley Bay Rock	18	7	3	8	270	315	17
Blyth	18	7	0	11	332	361	14
Consett	18	6	1	11	240	384	13
Bishop Auckland	18	4	1	13	255	415	9
North Durham	18	3	1	14	173	482	7

Durham & Northumbria 2

	P	W	D	L	F	A	Pts
Billingham	18	15	1	2	548	225	31
Novocastrians	18	16	0	2	522	175	30*
Seghill	18	14	0	4	421	178	26*
Ponteland	18	9	1	8	250	267	19
Hartlepool	18	9	1	8	269	344	19
Barnard Castle	18	9	0	9	284	361	18
South Tynes Coll	18	6	1	11	265	333	13
Chester-le-Street	18	5	0	13	252	383	10
Guisborough	18	4	0	14	238	454	8
Seaton Carew	18	1	0	17	178	507	2

Durham & Northumbria 3

	P	W	D	L	F	A	Pts
Gosforth	16	15	1	0	723	107	31
Houghton	16	13	1	2	554	133	27
Richmondshire	16	12	0	4	310	107	24
Wallsend	16	10	0	6	357	210	20
H'pool BBOB	16	6	0	10	252	427	12
Seaham	16	5	0	11	191	332	10
H'pool Athletic	16	4	0	12	246	542	8
Sedgefield	16	3	0	13	156	382	6
Wensleydale	16	3	0	13	152	701	6

Durham & Northumbria 4

	P	W	D	L	F	A	Pts
W H'pool Amat	12	12	0	0	365	55	24
Wearside	12	8	1	3	222	91	17
Durham Cons	12	7	1	4	220	135	15
Jarrovians	12	5	2	5	200	148	12
Prudhoe	12	5	0	7	123	123	10
Shildon Town	12	2	0	10	78	459	4
Newton Aycliffe	12	1	0	11	119	316	2

North-West 1

	P	W	D	L	F	A	Pts
Chester	18	17	0	1	521	172	34
Old Park (St H)	17	13	2	2	571	227	28
Old Aldwinians	18	11	0	7	349	247	22
Aspull	18	10	1	7	352	288	19*
Oldershaw	18	8	1	9	321	399	17
Penrith	18	8	0	10	421	358	16
Vagabonds (IoM)	17	8	0	9	316	355	16
Birkenhead Park	18	6	0	12	291	506	12
A'ton on Mersey	18	5	0	13	245	493	10
Wilmslow	18	1	0	17	181	523	2

North-West 2

	P	W	D	L	F	A	Pts
Caldy	18	14	0	4	595	248	28
Kirkby Lonsdale	18	13	0	5	464	252	26
Egremont	18	12	0	6	428	205	24
Leigh	18	11	1	6	443	310	23
Netherhall	18	9	2	7	313	301	20
Carlisle	18	7	2	9	343	292	16
Merseyside Police	18	6	3	9	298	336	15
Northwich	18	7	0	11	198	496	14
Fleetwood	18	5	2	11	274	462	12
Old Salians	18	1	0	17	102	556	2

North-West 3

	P	W	D	L	F	A	Pts
Stockport	18	15	1	2	591	131	31
Altri'ham Kersal	18	15	1	2	558	175	31
Workington	18	12	0	6	412	226	24
Wigan	18	11	0	7	480	226	22
St Benedicts	18	9	2	7	201	228	20
Rossendale	18	9	1	8	272	278	19
Calder Vale	18	8	0	10	274	471	16
Cockermouth	18	4	0	14	190	558	8
Sandbach	18	3	1	14	262	487	7
Windermere	18	1	0	17	161	621	2

South Lancs/Cheshire 1

	P	W	D	L	F	A	Pts
Warrington	16	14	0	2	449	156	28
Southport	16	12	1	3	516	230	25
Wirral	16	12	0	4	460	184	24
Crewe & Nant	16	10	0	6	243	204	20
St Edwards OB	15	8	1	6	423	273	17
Ruskin Park	16	6	0	10	206	368	12
Old Anselmians	16	3	2	11	232	383	8
Eagle	16	4	0	12	194	433	8
South Liverpool	0	0	0	0	0	0	0
N'ton-le-Willows	15	0	0	15	39	531	-2*

South Lancs/Cheshire 2

	P	W	D	L	F	A	Pts
Wallasey	18	14	2	2	346	205	30
Birchfield	18	14	1	3	487	216	29
St Mary's OB	18	12	1	5	356	213	25
Dukinfield	18	11	0	7	339	180	22
Congleton	18	9	0	9	254	202	18
Marple	18	9	0	9	181	249	16*
Bowdon	18	7	0	11	225	266	14
Sefton	18	6	0	12	223	262	12
Old Parkonians	18	4	0	14	155	432	8
Didsbury TOC H	18	2	0	16	207	548	2*

South Lancs/Cheshire 3

	P	W	D	L	F	A	Pts
Shell Stanlow	14	13	1	0	560	104	27
Prenton	14	10	2	2	362	207	22
Douglas (IoM)	14	9	0	5	445	303	18
Helsby	14	7	0	7	215	359	14
L'pool Collegiate	14	6	0	8	139	286	12
Port Sunlight	14	5	0	9	230	315	10
Hoylake	14	3	1	10	209	339	7
Halton	14	1	0	13	140	387	2

South Lancs/Cheshire 4

	P	W	D	L	F	A	Pts
Moore	12	10	0	2	443	137	20
Vulcan	12	10	0	2	333	124	18*
Whitehouse Park	12	6	1	5	144	146	13
Mossley Hill	12	6	0	6	195	228	12
Holmes Chapel	12	4	1	7	148	259	9
Lucas	12	4	0	8	160	263	8
Hightown	12	1	0	11	114	380	2

North Lancs/Cumbria

	P	W	D	L	F	A	Pts
Rochdale	18	17	0	1	478	128	34
Blackpool	18	13	0	5	476	259	26
Vickers	18	12	2	4	373	245	26
Furness	18	9	3	6	242	279	21
Tyldesley	18	10	0	8	356	278	20
Trafford MV	18	9	1	8	311	216	19
Keswick	18	4	2	12	237	401	10
Ormskirk	18	4	2	12	241	478	10
Upper Eden	18	4	0	14	219	431	8
Ashton-U-Lyne	18	3	0	15	209	427	6

North Lancs 1

	P	W	D	L	F	A	Pts
Oldham	18	15	1	2	464	133	31
Bury	18	11	2	5	358	296	22*
De La Salle (Sal)	18	10	2	6	363	304	22
Old Bedians	18	9	2	7	294	276	20
Eccles	18	9	0	9	296	274	18
Heaton Moor	18	7	2	9	320	379	16
Broughton	18	7	0	11	240	325	14
Bolton	18	5	2	11	274	344	12
T'ton Cleveleys	18	6	0	12	215	386	12
Littleborough	18	4	3	11	235	342	11

North Lancs 2

	P	W	D	L	F	A	Pts
Colne & Nelson	12	12	0	0	333	51	24
Chorley	12	8	0	4	372	124	16
Clitheroe	12	6	0	6	254	197	12
Lostock	12	4	1	7	138	300	9
North Man	12	5	0	7	133	220	8*
Montell Car'ton	12	3	1	8	160	258	5*
Burnage	12	3	0	9	72	312	2*

Cumbria

	P	W	D	L	F	A	Pts
Ambleside	14	13	0	1	344	96	26
Moresby	14	12	0	2	321	87	24
Whitehaven	14	7	0	7	252	233	12*
Carnforth	14	5	2	7	238	260	12
Creighton	14	5	1	8	179	203	11
Greengarth	14	4	1	9	181	289	9
Silloth	14	4	0	10	186	368	8
Millom	14	3	2	9	193	358	6*

SOUTH-WEST DIVISION

South-West 1

	P	W	D	L	F	A	Pts
Bracknell	22	18	2	2	786	271	38
Launceton	22	17	1	4	614	263	35
Glouc Old Boys	21	16	0	5	518	282	32
Penzance-Newlyn	22	14	1	7	599	361	29
Maidenhead	22	12	1	9	512	345	25
Barnstaple	22	11	1	10	466	384	23
Matson	21	10	1	10	301	418	21
Stroud	22	9	0	13	445	602	18
Torquay	22	8	0	14	315	448	16

	P	W	D	L	F	A	Pts
Berry Hill	22	7	0	15	308	471	12*
St Ives	22	5	1	16	293	652	11
High Wycombe	22	0	0	22	208	868	-2*

South-West 2 East

	P	W	D	L	F	A	Pts
Salisbury	22	17	1	4	537	251	35
Marlow	22	17	1	4	621	341	35
Swanage	22	16	0	6	495	277	32
Chinnor	22	12	1	9	361	374	25
A'sham & Chilt	21	11	2	8	357	361	24
Dorchester	22	11	0	11	483	396	22
Bournemouth	22	10	1	12	403	445	20
Abbey	22	9	1	12	414	391	19
Aylesbury	21	8	0	13	277	424	16
Stow-on-the-W	22	7	0	15	266	434	14
Sherborne	22	5	1	16	309	643	11
Oxford	22	4	1	17	371	557	7*

South-West 2 West

	P	W	D	L	F	A	Pts
Old Patesians	22	19	0	3	485	287	38
Keynsham	22	18	0	4	724	271	36
Cinderford	22	17	0	5	657	363	34
Spartans	22	14	1	7	458	330	29
Camborne	22	12	0	10	493	470	24
Brixham	22	10	2	10	544	480	22
Dings Crusaders	22	10	1	11	442	351	21
Clevedon	22	9	2	11	395	472	20
Taunton	22	8	0	14	436	415	16
Tiverton	22	6	0	16	275	702	12
Penryn	22	3	2	17	284	608	8
Okehampton	22	2	0	20	289	733	4

Western Counties North

	P	W	D	L	F	A	Pts
St Mary's Old B's	16	15	0	1	492	140	30
Cleve	16	12	1	3	300	212	25
Old Richians	16	12	0	4	426	245	24
Coney Hill	16	10	1	5	371	189	21
Cheltenham N	16	10	1	5	342	218	21
Old Redcliffians	16	10	0	6	348	212	20
Hornets	16	10	0	6	315	284	20
North Bristol	16	8	1	7	375	349	17
Drybrook	16	8	0	8	305	308	16
Cirencester	16	6	0	10	308	323	12
Oldfield Old Boys	16	6	0	10	277	384	12
Thornbury	16	5	1	10	274	372	11
Avonmouth	16	5	0	11	193	378	10
Gordon League	16	4	1	11	163	347	9
Whitehall	16	3	2	11	190	330	8
B'tol Harlequins	16	4	0	12	180	368	8
Old Culverhays	16	4	0	12	226	426	8

Western Counties West

	P	W	D	L	F	A	Pts
St Austell	18	13	1	4	506	281	27
Kingsbridge	18	11	1	6	314	252	23
Ivybridge	18	10	1	7	278	256	21
Hayle	18	10	0	8	330	289	20
South Molton	18	9	1	8	288	247	19

	P	W	D	L	F	A	Pts
Wellington	18	9	1	8	333	296	19
Paignton	18	8	2	8	326	303	18
Devonpt Services	18	8	0	10	329	319	16
Sidmouth	18	4	1	13	239	492	9
Bideford	18	4	0	14	209	417	8

Southern Counties North

	P	W	D	L	F	A	Pts
Slough	18	15	0	3	427	163	30
Olney	18	13	0	5	401	183	24*
Beaconsfield	18	11	0	7	418	350	22
Bicester	18	9	0	9	337	333	18
Buckingham	18	8	0	10	347	331	16
Bletchley	18	8	0	10	265	304	16
Oxf'd Harlequins	18	7	0	11	312	399	14
Chipping Norton	18	7	0	11	281	419	14
Witney	18	6	0	12	327	432	12
Milton Keynes	18	6	0	12	204	405	12

Southern Counties South

	P	W	D	L	F	A	Pts
Wimborne	18	16	0	2	579	199	32
Chippenham	18	13	2	3	581	246	28
Devizes	18	14	0	4	414	211	28
Wootton Bassett	18	13	1	4	459	192	27
Swindon	18	10	2	6	514	227	22
North Dorset	18	7	0	11	397	601	14
Windsor	18	6	1	11	340	444	11*
Blandford	18	5	0	13	263	521	10
Weymouth	18	3	0	15	153	617	6
Westbury	18	0	0	18	127	569	0

Cornwall & Devon

	P	W	D	L	F	A	Pts
Truro	18	15	0	3	436	196	30
Crediton	18	13	0	5	480	257	26
Exmouth	18	12	0	6	459	258	24
Withycombe	18	11	1	6	317	274	23
Falmouth	18	10	0	8	333	452	20
Teignmouth	18	7	2	9	256	308	16
Bude	18	6	1	11	232	361	13
Old Plymothian	18	6	0	12	269	383	12
Saltash	18	5	0	13	243	312	10
Honiton	18	3	0	15	187	411	6

Cornwall 1

	P	W	D	L	F	A	Pts
Newquay	18	16	0	2	442	125	32
Waderbridge	18	14	1	3	527	252	29
Bodmin	18	12	1	5	269	241	25
Perranporth	18	11	1	6	365	227	23
Illogan Park	18	8	4	6	299	284	20
St Just	18	6	1	11	235	342	13
Helston	18	6	0	12	220	368	12
Stithians	18	4	2	12	258	329	10
St Agnes	18	4	2	12	232	468	10
Liskeard-Looe	18	3	0	15	175	385	6

Cornwall 2

	P	W	D	L	F	A	Pts
Redruth Albany	12	11	0	1	275	74	22
Veor	12	9	0	3	284	137	18
Roseland	12	8	0	4	220	165	16
St Day	12	5	1	6	189	159	11
Callington	12	2	2	8	117	213	6
Lankelly Fowey	12	3	0	9	106	424	4*
Camborne SoM	12	2	1	9	135	154	-1*

Devon 1

	P	W	D	L	F	A	Pts
Newton Abbot	18	17	0	1	618	162	34
Old Technicians	17	12	0	5	403	160	24
Torrington	18	11	0	7	301	347	22
Ilfracombe	18	10	0	8	384	297	18*
Topsham	18	9	0	9	439	466	16*
Tavistock	18	7	1	10	320	299	15
Plymouth CS	18	7	1	10	248	322	15
Old Public Oaks	18	5	3	10	188	370	11*
Exeter Saracens	18	5	0	13	238	348	10
Dartmouth	17	3	1	13	218	586	7

Devon 2

	P	W	D	L	F	A	Pts
Cullompton	18	17	0	1	589	135	34
Wessex	18	16	0	2	626	83	32
Totnes	18	13	0	5	386	262	24*
Marjons	18	12	0	6	545	243	20*
Tamar Saracens	18	9	0	9	297	202	16*
Prince Rock	18	8	0	10	210	317	16
Salcombe	18	6	0	12	260	396	12
Ply'th Argaum	18	5	0	13	208	436	8*
North Taunton	18	4	0	14	159	511	8
Bovey Tracey	18	0	0	18	90	785	0

Devon 3

	P	W	D	L	F	A	Pts
D'port HSOB	12	12	0	0	346	120	24
Plymstock	12	9	0	3	296	143	18
Plym'n-Victoria	12	7	0	5	234	176	12*
Buckfastleigh	12	6	0	6	202	190	12
Woodland Fort	12	4	0	8	188	215	8
St Columba	12	3	0	9	111	207	4*
Plymouth YMCA	12	1	0	11	105	431	2

Gloucester & Somerset

	P	W	D	L	F	A	Pts
St Bernadette OB	16	14	1	1	403	159	29
Wiveliscombe	16	12	2	2	269	183	26
Barton Hill	16	12	0	4	401	179	24
Walcot Old Boys	16	12	0	4	386	228	24
Yatton	16	11	0	5	375	205	22
Longlevens	16	10	0	6	381	233	20
Combe Down	16	8	0	8	293	230	16
Tor	16	7	2	7	256	254	16
Bream	16	8	0	8	220	267	16
Gordano	16	7	1	8	198	253	15
Mids Norton	16	5	1	10	224	298	11
Bristol Saracens	16	5	0	11	221	259	10

Chard	16	5	0	11	248	388	10
F'ton Cotterell	16	4	1	11	198	375	9
Brockworth	16	5	0	11	204	392	8*
Old Sulians	16	4	0	12	167	430	8
Wells	16	2	2	12	172	283	6

Gloucester 1

	P	W	D	L	F	A	Pts
Old Centralians	12	10	0	2	384	146	20
Chosen Hill FP	12	10	0	2	325	139	20
Ashley Down OB	12	8	1	3	190	153	17
Old Bristolians	12	8	0	4	300	240	16
Chelt'ham Civil S	12	7	0	5	205	174	14
Southmead	12	7	0	5	181	172	14
Painswick	12	6	0	6	173	200	12
Tredworth	12	6	0	6	220	285	10*
Cainscross	12	4	1	7	176	202	9
Hucclecote	12	4	0	8	166	182	8
Old Cryptians	12	3	0	9	182	288	6
Chltnhm Saras	12	3	0	9	155	296	6
Bristol Tel's	12	1	0	11	189	369	2

Gloucester 2

	P	W	D	L	F	A	Pts
Chipping S'bury	12	12	0	0	360	65	24
Aretians	12	10	1	1	283	143	21
Bishopston	12	8	1	3	247	154	17
Tewkesbury	12	8	0	4	240	146	16
Westbury on S'n	12	7	0	5	262	195	14
Tetbury	12	6	0	6	206	165	12
Smiths (Ind)	12	6	0	6	220	229	12
Kingswood	12	5	0	7	170	275	10
Dursley	12	4	0	8	248	237	8
Widden Old Boys	12	4	0	8	121	235	8
Old Elizabethians	12	4	0	8	203	368	8
Cotham Park	12	3	0	9	170	243	6
Old Colstonians	12	0	0	12	85	360	0

Gloucester 3

	P	W	D	L	F	A	Pts
Glouc All Blues	8	8	0	0	236	14	14*
Minchinhampton	8	7	0	1	246	45	14
Dowty	8	4	0	4	104	167	8
Bristol Aerop's	8	4	1	3	88	114	7*
Newent	8	3	1	4	76	133	7
Gloucester CS	8	3	0	5	91	167	6
St Brendans OB	8	3	0	5	84	173	6
Wotton-u-Edge	8	3	0	5	58	170	6
Pilning	8	0	0	8	0	0	0

Somerset 1

	P	W	D	L	F	A	Pts
Chew Valley	18	17	0	1	747	177	34
Frome	18	16	1	1	600	150	33
Nailsea & B'well	18	9	0	9	266	339	18
Imperial	18	8	1	9	245	252	15*
Winscombe	18	7	1	10	298	460	15
Minehead Barbs	18	6	1	11	258	411	13
North Petherton	18	7	0	11	285	396	12*
Stothert & Pitt	18	7	0	11	260	455	12*
Blagdon	18	6	0	12	254	389	10*
Avonvale	18	5	0	13	237	421	8*

Somerset 2

	P	W	D	L	F	A	Pts
Avon	14	14	0	0	469	125	28
Old Ashtonians	14	7	2	5	303	166	16
British Gas	14	7	0	7	181	250	14
Cheddar Valley	14	6	1	7	172	189	11*
Broad Plain	14	6	0	8	187	258	10*
Burnham on Sea	14	5	0	9	134	322	10
Castle Cary	14	5	1	8	208	233	9*
Crewkerne	14	4	0	10	164	274	8

Somerset 3

	P	W	D	L	F	A	Pts
Bath O Edwards	8	8	0	0	290	74	16
Bath Saracens	8	5	0	3	201	92	10
Morganians	8	4	0	4	98	131	8
Martock	8	2	0	6	137	192	4
Wincanton	8	1	0	7	87	324	2

Berks, Dorset & Wilts 1

	P	W	D	L	F	A	Pts
Tadley	18	16	1	1	414	147	33
Redlingansians	18	15	0	3	407	177	30
Ivel Barbarians	18	14	0	4	464	104	28
Trowbridge	18	12	0	6	382	261	24
Corsham	18	6	2	10	252	292	14
Thatcham	18	6	2	10	265	339	14
Melksham	18	6	0	12	286	416	10*
Calne	18	4	1	13	118	505	9
Aldermaston	18	3	2	13	259	394	8
Marlborough	18	4	0	14	238	450	6*

Berks, Dorset & Wilts 2

	P	W	D	L	F	A	Pts
Swindon College	18	14	1	3	381	209	29
Portcastrians	18	13	0	5	354	189	26
Minety	18	11	1	6	357	198	23

Colerne	18	8	2	8	356	254	18
Christchurch	18	9	0	9	360	357	18
Bridport	18	9	0	9	284	327	18
Oakmeadians	18	9	0	9	255	315	18
Lytchett Minster	18	8	0	10	288	271	16
Berks Shire Hall	18	5	1	12	264	474	11
Supermarine	18	1	1	16	151	456	3

Berks, Dorset & Wilts 3

	P	W	D	L	F	A	Pts
Puddletown	12	9	0	3	363	144	18
Hungerford	12	9	0	3	285	107	18
Warminster	12	9	0	3	304	141	18
Pewsey Vale	12	6	0	6	153	176	12
Bradford on Avon	12	6	0	6	273	150	8*
Poole	12	3	0	9	161	279	6
Verwood	12	0	0	12	44	586	-2*

Bucks/Oxon 1

	P	W	D	L	F	A	Pts
Cholsey	12	10	0	2	288	135	20
Pennanians	12	10	0	2	202	91	20
Littlemore	12	6	0	6	185	128	12
Drifters	12	5	0	7	221	167	10
Phoenix	12	5	0	7	141	223	10
Wheatley	12	4	0	8	189	297	6*
Grove	12	2	0	10	140	325	2*

Bucks/Oxon 2

	P	W	D	L	F	A	Pts
Chesham	10	10	0	0	290	76	20
Abingdon	10	7	0	3	168	115	14
G'ford All Blacks	10	5	0	5	268	159	10
Harwell	10	4	0	6	187	179	8
Didcot	10	4	0	6	133	199	8
Winslow	10	0	0	10	25	343	-2*

SARRIES MARCH TO TRIUMPH

TETLEY'S BITTER CUP 1997-98
David Llewellyn

9 May 1998, Twickenham
Saracens 48 (5G 1DG 2T) **Wasps 18** (1G 2PG 1T)

They may have been regarded as antiques, too old for Test rugby, but three old masters can sit proudly in rugby's hall of fame after a stunning showpiece occasion culminated in a superlative performance by Saracens as they left Wasps devastated and devoid of any credibility. Francois Pienaar, Michael Lynagh and Philippe Sella masterminded a magnificent win in the first ever all-London final. For these last two it was their swansong and there could have been no more perfect exit for any star than to inspire Saracens to lift the first major trophy in their history by equalling the record for most points set by Bath in their 48-6 win against Gloucester in 1990.

Wasps could draw small consolation from the fact that the match aggregate of 66 points was also a record for the final, although interestingly, but perhaps not so surprisingly, only 25 of those points were scored by Englishmen.

But what the hell. It was a day when, overseas or home-grown, the 65,000 spectators crammed into Twickenham were treated to a display of rugby as passionate as any seen lately. Messrs Lynagh, Pienaar and Sella inspired their younger, less experienced teammates. After the highs of World Cup wins in 1991 and 1995 it was remarkable that Lynagh and Pienaar could want anything so badly as a cup final. But want it they did.

Pienaar led from the front. He put his body on the line time after time, put in a crunching, try-saving hit on Andy Reed late into the match and generally let the opponents know that he was not only around, but standing full square in their faces.

The influence that the likes of Sella – 111 caps for France – and Lynagh – 911 Test points for Australia – have had on the more junior members of the Saracens side cannot be underestimated. Steve Ravenscroft, while not exactly a clone of the great man, is having a serious stab at emulating Sella. His was one of seven tries scored by the Watford-based club. Naturally though the opening score came from Sella. With a scant seven minutes on the clock Saracens won a line-out through the good offices of the teak-hard Danny Grewcock. Pienaar spearheaded a drive before the ball was released; Gavin Johnson rounded Mark Denney then slipped the ball inside to Sella who powered through the flapping Wasps

Scrum-half Kyran Bracken (Saracens) in typically aggressive mood in the Tetley's Bitter Cup final against Wasps at Twickenham.

defence for the try which Lynagh converted – the first of five such kicks for the Australian maestro.

Shortly after that try, and following the first of Gareth Rees's two penalties for Wasps, Lynagh popped over a drop goal. Then came another electric score. Australian Sevens captain Ryan Constable was sent away by Sella; he skinned Laurence Scrase and crossed on the right. By the time they trooped in at half-time Sarries had opened up an embarrassingly comfortable 23-point lead.

Under the flawless direction of Lynagh they increased that lead within minutes of the restart. The Saracens fly-half set up a great position with a cunning diagonal kick deep into the Wasps' nest. At the resultant line-out Saracens won the ball against the throw; yet another explosive burst from Sella, a cute chip by Lynagh and Ravenscroft raced over.

There then followed a brief fightback by Wasps. It so nearly came to something. First Paul Volley peeled off a forward drive, then Shane Roiser, a dentist who adds bite to the backs, scored under the posts. The conversion looked a formality for Rees. But the Canadian international, making his second final appearance 12 years after his first as a teenager for Wasps, somehow contrived to miss the kick. Thereafter it was all Saracens again.

Later on Lynagh, who scored 13 points in all in the final, admitted the unthinkable. 'After all I'd been through in the previous 15 years I was still as nervous as hell before the kick-off. I always wanted to go out on a high, to retire in the knowledge that I'd been competitive right to the end. What happened out there vindicates my decision to retire now. In obvious ways there are links between this victory and the World Cup win with Australia in 1991. I'm back at Twickenham and my parents are there in the Rose Room drinking tea, just as they were seven years ago.'

Saracens: G Johnson; R Constable, P Sella, S Ravenscroft, B Daniel; M Lynagh, K Bracken; R Grau, G Chuter, P Wallace, P Johns, D Grewcock, B Sturnham, A Diprose (*capt*), F Pienaar *Substitutions:* R Wallace for Daniel (28 mins); G Botterman for Chuter (76 mins); A Olver for Grau (79 mins); M Singer for Sella (79 mins); M Olsen for Bracken (79 mins)
Scorers *Tries:* Sella, Constable, Johnson, Grewcock, Ravenscroft, Bracken, R Wallace *Conversions:* Lynagh (5) *Dropped Goal:* Lynagh
Wasps: G Rees; S Roiser, M Denney, R Henderson, L Scrase; A King, M Friday; D Molloy, S Mitchell, W Green, M Weedon, S Shaw, J Worsley, L Dallaglio (*capt*), P Volley *Substitutions:* P Sampson for Scrase (52 mins); M White for Worsley (57 mins); T Leota for Mitchell (65 mins); A Gomarsall for Friday (74 mins); A Black for Molloy (74 mins); A Reed for Weedon (74 mins)
Scorers *Tries:* Volley, Roiser *Conversion:* Rees *Penalty Goals:* Rees (2)

Earlier Rounds

It began in relative anonymity, with no name – but plenty of pack drill – and no backer. There was also the threat of a boycott by the top clubs over the share-out of the spoils. By the time Carlsberg-Tetley were on board the record first-round field of 84 had been reduced by half; among those clubs who made it to the second-round draw was Isle of Man club Vagabonds, which must have cheered a well-known resident of the tax haven, Cliff Brittle. Sadly, though, that was as far as they got on their debut in the competition. Cheltenham went into the hat on the back of a score of 138 – a record for the competition – and their opponents, Okehampton, did not manage any sort of reply. The brewer's deal had created, by the third round, the Tetley's Bitter Cup and the nine fruitful years with Pilkington were consigned to history.

By the fourth round that was also true of a number of former giants of the game. London Welsh and Bedford, both winners of the cup in the first of its incarnations, were dismissed by Gloucester and Northampton respectively, and the eventual finalists Wasps accounted for two-time winners Harlequins. A little local difficulty at Richmond, where they and ground share partners London

Scottish had both won home ties, resulted in the Exiles having to concede ground advantage to 10-times cup holders Bath, but Scottish came within an ace of knocking out the famous cup fighters on their own patch. It took an injury-time penalty by Jon Callard to rob the Exiles of what would have been a famous victory. The tie will be remembered for an infamous moment however. It was revealed that Scottish flanker Simon Fenn had been bitten on his left ear by a Bath player. After a great deal of wrangling and wriggling, which itself brought the game into disrepute, an independent hearing was set up and Bath prop Kevin Yates was found guilty and banned for six months. The player protested his innocence before, during and after, but despite a declaration that the matter would be taken to the High Court nothing more was said.

The fourth round had been disrupted by the weather, Bath and Scottish were playing a week late. Worcester and Bristol played some 10 days later. When they did, a once shipshape club foundered miserably upon the rocks of the Jewson National League One; full-back Tim Smith, the former Gloucester player, booting out the Premiership side with the last kick of the game.

Not to be outdone, the fifth round also threw up its share of drama, although in this case it was of the more conventional sort. Richmond beat Bath, although they needed extra time to do so; the sides were level at 14-14 when the final whistle went, but then they cut loose with a couple of tries. The eventual winners Saracens had a hard time of it before eventually dumping cup holders Leicester. Inevitably it was the old maestro Michael Lynagh who won it with a late penalty.

The quarter-finals did not have a single previous cup holder in the line-up, unless you count Newcastle, who as Gosforth did lift the trophy twice in the early years. Saracens found Richmond no real problem once they got into their stride, Northampton did for the much-vaunted Newcastle, last year's finalists Sale accounted for West Hartlepool and Wasps blew away London Irish. The semis were anti-climatic: Wasps slugged it out with Sale and not a try in sight; Saracens cruised, troublefree, past outclassed Northampton and the all-London final was set up.

RESULTS

First round

Aspatria 24, Stockton 13; Barking 26, Swanage & Wareham 18; Basingstoke 10, Weston-super-Mare 39; Birmingham/Solihull 22, Westleigh 10; Bridgewater 18, Met Police 30; Broadstreet 25, Walsall 17; Camberley 38, Barnstaple 16; Cheltenham 138, Okehampton 0; Coney Hill 5, Preston Grasshoppers 16; Haywards Heath 26, Plymouth 25; Henley 64, Cambridge 12; Hornets 28, Havant 72; Launceston 58, Bicester 6; Lewes 12, Wimbledon 11; Lichfield 10, Manchester 28; Longton 22, Widnes 38; Maidenhead 14, Amersham & Chiltern 36; Matson 8, Bishops Stortford 3; North Walsham 19, Esher 18; Northern 49, Derby 3; Norwich 14, Bracknell 25; Nuneaton 11, Sedgley Park 7; Old Coventrians 13, Huddersfield 35; Olney 18, St Ives 20; Sandal 30, Chester 22; Scunthorpe 6, Doncaster 23; Selly Oak 31, Syston 19; Sevenoaks 32, Cheshunt 13; Sheffield 38,

Old Northamptonians 14; Sherborne 19, Clifton 30; St Benedicts 9, Wigton 24; Staines 35, Redruth 25; Sunderland 8, Kendal 27; Sutton & Epsom 23, Banbury 25; Tabard 23, Harlow 0; Taunton 34, Canterbury 12; Tynedale 32, Hinckley 8; Vagabonds 18, Old Brodleians 15; Vale of Lune 27, Ampthill 25; Whitchurch 28, Stourbridge 35; Winchester 20, Ruislip 0; Winnington Park 64, Stoke 12

Second round

Aspatria 27 Widnes 18; Birmingham/Solihull 9 Otley 10; Bracknell 35 Met Police 14; Broadstreet 41 Huddersfield 3; Cheltenham 20 Sevenoaks 18; Havant 19 Matson 10; Hayward's Heath 20 Launceston 22; Henley 3 Camberley 16; Kendal 9 Harrogate 5; Lewes 10 North Walsham 42; London Welsh 65 Clifton 17; Lydney 67 Amersham/Chiltern 0; Morley 41 Selly Oak 5; Northern 5 Tynedale 22; Nottingham 20 Doncaster 24; Preston Grasshoppers 8 Manchester 33; Rugby 46 Vagabonds 0; Sandal 22 Nuneaton 16; Sheffield 42 Vale of Lune 20; St Ives 6 Barking 53; Staines 32 Banbury 12; Stourbridge 69 Taunton 5; Tabard 0 Rosslyn Park 31; Weston-super-Mare 17 Newbury 36; Wharfedale 35 Wigton 10; Winchester 12 Reading 26; Winnington Park 24 Liverpool St Helens 26; Worcester 28 Leeds 11

Third round

Barking 13 Exeter 17; Bedford 76 Staines 15; Blackheath 32 Sandal 3; Broadstreet 15 Bracknell 21; Camberley 32 Kendal 20; Coventry 83 Sheffield 19; Doncaster 24 Tynedale 11; Fylde 48 Aspatria 5; Havant 22 Rugby 32; London Welsh 36 Waterloo 34; Lydney 3 London Scottish 45; Moseley 79 Liverpool St Helens 10; North Walsham 11 Rosslyn Park 27; Orrell 16 Newbury 26; Otley 24 Manchester 25; Rotherham 67 Launceston 15; Stourbridge 7 Reading 58; Wakefield 53 Morley 14; West Hartlepool 41 Cheltenham 5; Wharfedale 8 Worcester 29

Fourth round

Bath 24, London Scottish 23; Blackheath 31, Saracens 59; Bracknell 3, Rotherham 26; Camberley 10, Newbury 11; Coventry 14, Leicester 50; Fylde 20, Rosslyn Park 5; London Welsh 18,

Gloucester 34; Manchester 13, London Irish 36; Moseley 11, Sale 18; Newcastle 34, Exeter 10; Northampton 31, Bedford 26; Richmond 58, Doncaster 8; Rugby 26, Reading 17; Wasps 31, Harlequins 26; West Hartlepool 23, Wakefield 13; Worcester 14, Bristol 12

Fifth round

Bath 17, Richmond 29; London Irish 27, Rotherham 14; Northampton 30, Gloucester 11; Sale 38, Newbury 11; Saracens 14, Leicester 13; Wasps 34, Fylde 8; West Hartlepool 42, Rugby 11; Worcester 0, Newcastle 10

Quarter-finals

London Irish 7, Wasps 41; Northampton 17, Newcastle 7; Richmond 30, Saracens 36; West Hartlepool 21, Sale 36

Semi-finals

Northampton 10, Saracens 25; Wasps 15, Sale 9

Final (at *Twickenham*)

Saracens 48, Wasps 18

Previous finals (*all at Twickenham*)

1972 Gloucester 17, Moseley 6
1973 Coventry 27, Bristol 15
1974 Coventry 26, London Scottish 6
1975 Bedford 28, Rosslyn Park 12
1976 Gosforth 23, Rosslyn Park 14
1977 Gosforth 27, Waterloo 11
1978 Gloucester 6, Leicester 3
1979 Leicester 15, Moseley 12
1980 Leicester 21, London Irish 9
1981 Leicester 22, Gosforth 15
1982 Gloucester 12, Moseley 12
     (*title shared*)
1983 Bristol 28, Leicester 22
1984 Bath 10, Bristol 9
1985 Bath 24, London Welsh 15
1986 Bath 25, Wasps 17
1987 Bath 19, Wasps 12
1988 Harlequins 28, Bristol 22
1989 Bath 10, Leicester 6
1990 Bath 48, Gloucester 6
1991 Harlequins 25, Northampton 13
     (*aet*)
1992 Bath 15, Harlequins 12 (*aet*)
1993 Leicester 23, Harlequins 16
1994 Bath 21, Leicester 9
1995 Bath 36, Wasps 16
1996 Bath 16, Leicester 15
1997 Leicester 9, Sale 3

TROPHY HEADS HOME

CHELTENHAM & GLOUCESTER CUP 1997-98

3 April 1998, Franklin's Gardens, Northampton
Gloucester 33 (2G 1PG 2DG 2T) **Bedford 25** (2G 1PG 1DG 1T)

The first (and perhaps only) Cheltenham & Gloucester Cup competition was set up at short notice in the autumn of 1997. The point of the new tournament was to provide meaningful club rugby in England on the eight weekends when the national side were in action. Clubs were free to field as strong a XV as was available and a prize of £20,000 was on offer for the winners.

Cambridge University joined 19 clubs from the Allied Dunbar Championship – Bath, Harlequins, Newcastle, Saracens and Wasps did not compete – in four groups of five for the league phase of the tournament. Gloucester went forward to beat Leicester 53-15 in one semi-final while Second Division Bedford disposed of Sale 31-20 in the other.

The final, played at Northampton before a crowd of 6000 on the eve of the England-Ireland clash, was a personal triumph for Gloucester fly-half Mark Mapletoft. He created two tries in the first half, scored another when Bedford staged a spirited comeback in the second, and altogether contributed 18 of his side's points. Bedford provided stiff opposition and a rousing try by Junior Paramore in the closing stages warned the Division One club that it could ill-afford to rest on its laurels.

With England's clubs committed to league rugby on international weekends in the seasons ahead, the future for a competition which offered clubs the opportunity of blooding new recruits could be in jeopardy.

Gloucester: A Lumsden; R Jewell, T Fanolua, R Tombs, P Saint-André;
M Mapletoft, L Beck; T Woodman, N McCarthy, A Deacon, R Ward, D Sims,
S Ojomoh, S Devereux, P Glanville (*capt*) *Substitution:* A Gibbs for Ward (71 mins)
Scorers *Tries:* Fanolua, Ward, penalty try, Mapletoft *Conversions:* Mapletoft (2)
Penalty Goal: Mapletoft *Dropped Goals :* Mapletoft (2)
Bedford: M Rayer; B Whetstone, J Paramore, M Pechey, R Underwood;
P Turner, S Crabb; N Hatley, J Richards, C Boyd, S Murray, S Platford,
R Winters, R Straeuli (*capt*), J Forster
Scorers *Tries:* Crabb, penalty try, Paramore *Conversions:* Rayer (2) *Penalty Goal:*
Rayer *Dropped Goal:* Whetstone
Referee B Campsall (Yorkshire)

ENGLAND TO ARGENTINA 1997

THE TOURING PARTY

Manager J Rowell   **Coach** L Cusworth   **Captain** PR de Glanville
Full-backs: J Mallinder (Sale), MS Mapletoft (Gloucester), *JEB Callard (Bath)
Threequarters: AA Adebayo (Bath), JM Sleightholme (Bath), PR de Glanville
(Bath), NJJ Greenstock (Wasps), MC Allen (Northampton), JJN Baxendell (Sale),
DL Rees (Sale), D O'Leary (Harlequins)
Half-backs: MJ Catt (Bath), AD King (Wasps), KPP Bracken (Saracens),
ACT Gomarsall (Wasps)
Forwards: J Mallett (Bath), KP Yates (Bath), DJ Garforth (Leicester),
RJK Hardwick (Coventry), R Cockerill (Leicester), PBT Greening (Gloucester),
NC Redman (Bath), M Haag (Bath), DN Baldwin (Sale), DJ Grewcock
(Coventry), BB Clarke (Richmond), MJ Corry (Bristol), AJ Diprose (Saracens),
RHJ Jenkins (Harlequins), SO Ojomoh (Bath), CMA Sheasby (Wasps),
*S Diamond (Sale), *WR Green (Wasps)
* *Replacements on tour*

TOUR RECORD

All matches   Played 6   Won 4   Lost 2   Points for 213   Against 122
International matches   Played 2   Won 1   Lost 1   Points for 59   Against 53

SCORING DETAILS

All matches					International matches					
For:	30T	18C	9PG		213 Pts	For:	8T	5C	3PG		59 Pts
Against:	14T	5C	12PG	2DG	122 Pts	Against:	7T	3C	3PG	1DG	53 Pts

MATCH DETAILS

1997	OPPONENTS	VENUE	RESULT
21 May	Cordoba	Cordoba	W 38-21
24 May	Buenos Aires XV	Buenos Aires	L 21-23
27 May	Argentina A	Buenos Aires	W 58-17
31 May	ARGENTINA	Buenos Aires	W 46-20
3 June	Cuyo	Mendoza	W 37-8
7 June	ARGENTINA	Buenos Aires	L 13-33

MATCH 1   21 May, Chateau Carreras Stadium, Cordoba

Cordoba 21 (1G 3PG 1T)   **England XV 38** (5G 1PG)
Cordoba: F Soler; J Luna, G Sagrera, J Legora, G Tomalino; H Herrera,
C Barrea; A Rodriguez, G Benardi (*capt*), D Munoz, J Simes, E Giaimo, M Viola,
L Bedoya, D Rotondo
Scorers *Tries:* Simes, Barrea *Conversion:* Luna *Penalty Goals:* Luna (3)
England XV: Mallinder; Sleightholme, Greenstock, de Glanville (*capt*), Adebayo;
Catt, Bracken; Hardwick, Greening, Garforth, Haag, Redman, Clarke, Sheasby,
Jenkins *Substitution:* Diprose for Sheasby (66 mins)
Scorers *Tries:* Bracken (2), de Glanville, Redman, Catt *Conversions:* Catt (5)
Penalty Goal: Catt
Referee E Blengio (Uruguay)

MATCH 2   24 May, Buenos Aires Cricket & Rugby Ground

Buenos Aires XV 23 (5PG 1DG 1T)   **England XV 21** (2PG 3T)
Buenos Aires XV: D Cuesta-Silva; O Bartolucci, J Orengo, E Simone, T Solari;
J-L Cilley, N Fernandez-Miranda; F Werner, J Angelillo (*capt*), M Urbano,
R Petti, P Sporleder, C Viel. P Camerlinckx, I Fernandez-Lobbe
Scorers *Try:* Solari *Penalty Goals:* Cilley (5) *Dropped Goal:* Cilley
England XV: Mallinder; Sleightholme, Greenstock, de Glanville (*capt*), Rees;
King, Gomarsall; Yates, Cockerill, Mallett, Baldwin, Redman, Clarke, Ojomoh,
Diprose *Substitutions:* Mapletoft for King (60 mins); Corry for Clarke (68 mins);
Baxendell for de Glanville (74 mins)
Scorers *Tries:* Clarke, de Glanville, Mallinder *Penalty Goals:* King (2)
Referee I Rogers (South Africa)

MATCH 3   27 May, Buenos Aires Cricket & Rugby Ground

Argentina A 17 (1G 2T)   **England XV 58** (6G 2PG 2T)
Argentina A: F Todeschini; G Aristide, J Legora, F del Castillo, F Schacht;
J-L Cilley (*capt*), C Barrea; F Diaz-Alberdi, M Ledesma, O Hasan-Jalil,
G Ugartemendia, J Simes, R Travaglini, C Viel, G Orsetti
Scorers *Tries:* Legora, penalty try, Viel *Conversion:* Cilley
England XV: Mapletoft; O'Leary, Baxendell, Allen, Rees; King, Gomarsall; Yates,
Cockerill, Garforth, Haag, Grewcock, Corry, Diprose (*capt*), Jenkins
Scorers *Tries:* Baxendell (2), Rees (2), Catt, Gomarsall, Haag, O'Leary
Conversions: Mapletoft (6) *Penalty Goals:* Mapletoft (2)
Referee J Kaplan (South Africa)

MATCH 4   31 May, Ferro Carril Oeste Stadium, Buenos Aires   1st Test

ARGENTINA 20 (1G 1DG 2T)   ENGLAND 46 (5G 2PG 1T)

ARGENTINA: E Jurado (Jockey Club, Rosario); T Solari (Hindu), E Simone
(Liceo Naval), L Arbizu (Belgrano Athletic)(*capt*), F Soler (Tala); G Quesada
(Hindu), N Fernandez-Miranda (Hindu); RD Grau (Gauteng Lions, South
Africa), FE Mendez (Bath, England), M Reggiardo (Castres, France), GA Llanes
(Bath, England), PL Sporleder (Curupayti), RA Martin (San Isidro Club),
P Bouza (Duendes), PJ Camerlinckx (Regatas Bella Vista)
Substitutions: C Promanzio (Duendes) for Mendez (38 mins); O Hasan-Jalil
(Natacion y Gimnasia) for Reggiardo (59 mins); I Fernandez-Lobbe (Liceo Naval)
for Sporleder (65 mins)
Scorers *Tries:* Quesada, Arbizu, Solari *Conversion:* Quesada *Dropped Goal:*
Quesada
ENGLAND: Mallinder; Sleightholme, de Glanville (*capt*), Greenstock, Adebayo;
Catt, Bracken; Yates, Greening, Garforth, Haag, Redman, Corry, Diprose, Clarke
Substitutions: Cockerill for Greening (25 mins); Sheasby for Corry (58 mins)
Scorers *Tries:* Adebayo (2), Greenstock, Diprose, Clarke, Catt
Conversions: Catt (5*) Penalty Goals:* Catt (2)
Referee I Rogers (South Africa)

MATCH 5   3 June, Mendoza Rugby Club

Cuyo 8 (1PG 1T)   **England XV 37** (2G 1PG 4T)
Cuyo: M Castro; M Brandi, L Speroni, F Serpa, S Cantu; A Gioeni, M Diaz;
F Bartolini, P-P Arnut, F Stoerman, G-L Correa, R Marchiori, F Rodriguez,

J-G Chiapetta, M Bertranou (*capt*) *Substitutions:* C Bajach for Correa (54 mins);
A Avila for Arnut (68 mins)
Scorers *Try:* Brandi *Penalty Goal:* Gioeni
England XV: Mapletoft; O'Leary, Baxendell, Allen, Adebayo; King, Gomarsall;
Hardwick, Diamond, Green, Baldwin, Grewcock, Ojomoh, Sheasby (*capt*), Jenkins
Substitutions: Mallender for Adebayo (21 mins); Greenstock for Mallinder
(78 mins); Corry for Sheasby (79 mins)
Scorers *Tries:* Mallinder (2), Baxendell, Gomarsall, Grewcock, Mapletoft
Conversions: Mapletoft (2) *Penalty Goal:* Mapletoft
Referee J Meeuwesen (Namibia)

MATCH 6 7 June, Ferro Carril Oeste Stadium, Buenos Aires   2nd Test

ARGENTINA 33 (2G 3PG 2T)   ENGLAND 13 (1PG 2T)

ARGENTINA: E Jurado (Jockey Club, Rosario); T Solari (Hindu), E Simone
(Liceo Naval), L Arbizu (Belgrano Athletic)(*capt*), F Soler (Tala); G Quesada
(Hindu), N Fernandez-Miranda (Hindu); RD Grau (Gauteng Lions, South
Africa), C Promanzio (Duendes), M Reggiardo (Castres, France), GA Llanes
(Bath, England), PL Sporleder (Curupayti), RA Martin (San Isidro),
PJ Camerlinckx (Regatas Bella Vista), I Fernandez-Lobbe (Liceo Naval)
Substitutions: O Hasan-Jalil (Natacion y Gimnasia) for Reggiardo (57 mins);
G Aristide (Rosario) for Solari (68 mins); C Viel (Newman) for Martin (76 mins)
Scorers *Tries:* Soler (2), Grau, Simone *Conversions:* Quesada (2)
Penalty Goals: Quesada (3)
ENGLAND: Mallinder; Sleightholme, de Glanville (*capt*), Greenstock, Adebayo;
Mapletoft, Bracken; Yates, Cockerill, Garforth, Haag, Grewcock, Corry, Diprose,
Clarke *Substitutions:* Sheasby for Corry (53 mins); King for Mallinder (57 mins);
Gomarsall for Adebayo (72 mins)
Scorers *Tries:* King, Grewcock *Penalty Goal:* Mapletoft
Referee J Kaplan (South Africa)

ENGLISH INTERNATIONAL PLAYERS
(up to 30 April 1998)

Note: Years given for Five Nations' matches are for second half of season; eg 1972 means season 1971-72. Years for all other matches refer to the actual year of the match. When a series has taken place, figures have been used to denote the particular matches in which players have featured. Thus 1984 *SA* 2 indicates that a player appeared in the second Test of the series.

Aarvold, C D (Cambridge U, W Hartlepool, Headingley, Blackheath) 1928 *A, W, I, F, S,* 1929 *W, I, F,* 1931 *W, S, F,* 1932 *SA, W, I, S,* 1933 *W*
Ackford, P J (Harlequins) 1988 *A,* 1989 *S, I, F, W, R, Fj,* 1990 *I, F, W, S, Arg* 3, 1991 *W, S, I, F, A, [NZ, It, F, S, A]*
Adams, A A (London Hospital) 1910 *F*
Adams, F R (Richmond) 1875 *I, S,* 1876 *S,* 1877 *I,* 1878 *S,* 1879 *S, I*
Adebayo, A A (Bath) 1996, *It,* 1997 *Arg* 1,2, *A* 2, *NZ* 1, 1998 *S*
Adey, G J (Leicester) 1976 *I, F*
Adkins, S J (Coventry) 1950 *I, F, S,* 1953 *W, I, F, S*
Agar, A E (Harlequins) 1952 *SA, W, S, I, F,* 1953 *W, I*
Alcock, A (Guy's Hospital) 1906 *SA*
Alderson, F H R (Hartlepool R) 1891 *W, I, S,* 1892 *W, S,* 1893 *W*
Alexander, H (Richmond) 1900 *I, S,* 1901 *W, I, S,* 1902 *W, I*
Alexander, W (Northern) 1927 *F*
Allison, D F (Coventry) 1956 *W, I, S, F,* 1957 *W,* 1958 *W, S*
Allport, A (Blackheath) 1892 *W,* 1893 *I,* 1894 *W, I, S*
Anderson, S (Rockcliff) 1899 *I*
Anderson, W F (Orrell) 1973 *NZ* 1
Anderton, C (Manchester FW) 1889 *M*
Andrew, C R (Cambridge U, Nottingham, Wasps, Toulouse, Newcastle) 1985 *R, F, S, I, W,* 1986 *W, S, I, F,* 1987 *I, F, W, [J (R), US],* 1988 *S, I* 1,2, *A* 1,2, *Fj, A,* 1989 *S, I, F, W, R, Fj,* 1990 *I, F, W, S, Arg* 3, 1991 *W, S, I, F, Fj, A, [NZ, It, US, F, S, A],* 1992 *S, I, F, W, C, SA,* 1993 *F, W, NZ,* 1994 *S, I, F, W, SA* 1,2, *R, C,* 1995 *I, F, W, S, [Arg, It, A, NZ, F],* 1997 *W(R)*
Archer, G S (Bristol, Army, Newcastle) 1996 *S, I,* 1997 *A* 2, *NZ* 1, *SA, NZ* 2, 1998 *F, W*
Archer, H (Bridgwater A) 1909 *W, F, I*
Armstrong, R (Northern) 1925 *W*
Arthur, T G (Wasps) 1966 *W, I*
Ashby, R C (Wasps) 1966 *I, F,* 1967 *A*
Ashcroft, A (Waterloo) 1956 *W, I, S, F,* 1957 *W, I, F, S,* 1958 *W, A, I, F, S,* 1959 *I, F, S*
Ashcroft, A H (Birkenhead Park) 1909 *A*
Ashford, W (Richmond) 1897 *W, I,* 1898 *S, W*
Ashworth, A (Oldham) 1892 *I*
Askew, J G (Cambridge U) 1930 *W, I, F*
Aslett, A R (Richmond) 1926 *W, I, F, S,* 1929 *S, F*
Assinder, E W (O Edwardians) 1909 *A, W*
Aston, R L (Blackheath) 1890 *S, I*
Auty, J R (Headingley) 1935 *S*

Back, N A (Leicester) 1994 *S, I,* 1995 *[Arg* (t), *It, WS],* 1997 *NZ* 1 (R), *SA, NZ* 2, 1998 *F, W, S, I*
Bailey, M D (Cambridge U, Wasps) 1984 *SA* 1,2, 1987 *[US],* 1989 *Fj,* 1990 *I, F, S* (R)
Bainbridge, S (Gosforth, Fylde) 1982 *F, W,* 1983 *F, W, S, I, NZ,* 1984 *S, I, F, W,* 1985 *NZ* 1,2, 1987 *F, W, S, [J, US]*
Baker, D G S (OMTs) 1955 *W, I, F, S*
Baker, E M (Moseley) 1895 *W, I, S,* 1896 *W, I, S,* 1897 *W*
Baker, H C (Clifton) 1887 *W*
Bance, J F (Bedford) 1954 *S*
Barley, B (Wakefield) 1984 *I, F, W, A,* 1988 *A* 1,2, *Fj*
Barnes, S (Bristol, Bath) 1984 *A,* 1985 *R* (R), *NZ* 1,2, 1986 *S* (R), *F,* 1987 *I* (R), 1988 *Fj,* 1993 *S, I*
Barr, R J (Leicester) 1932 *SA, W, I*
Barrett, E I M (Lennox) 1903 *S*
Barrington, T J M (Bristol) 1931 *W, I*
Barrington-Ward, L E (Edinburgh U) 1910 *W, I, F, S*
Barron, J H (Bingley) 1896 *S,* 1897 *W, I*
Bartlett, J T (Waterloo) 1951 *W*
Bartlett, R M (Harlequins) 1957 *W, I, F, S,* 1958 *I, F, S*
Barton, J (Coventry) 1967 *I, F, W,* 1972 *F*
Batchelor, T B (Oxford U) 1907 *F*

Bates, S M (Wasps) 1989 *R*
Bateson, A H (Otley) 1930 *W, I, F, S*
Bateson, H D (Liverpool) 1879 *I*
Batson, T (Blackheath) 1872 *S,* 1874 *S,* 1875 *I*
Batten, J M (Cambridge U) 1874 *S*
Baume, J L (Northern) 1950 *S*
Baxter, J (Birkenhead Park) 1900 *W, I, S*
Bayfield, M C (Northampton) 1991 *Fj, A,* 1992 *S, I, F, W, C, SA,* 1993 *F, W, S, I,* 1994 *S, I, SA* 1,2, *R, C,* 1995 *I, F, W, S, [Arg, It, A, NZ, F], SA, WS,* 1996 *F, W*
Bazley, R C (Waterloo) 1952 *I, F,* 1953 *W, I, F, S,* 1955 *W, I, F, S*
Beal, N D (Northampton) 1996 *Arg,* 1997 *A* 1
Beaumont, W B (Fylde) 1975 *I, A* 1(R),2, 1976 *A, W, S, I, F,* 1977 *S, I, F, W,* 1978 *F, W, S, I, NZ,* 1979 *S, I, F, W, NZ,* 1980 *I, F, W, S,* 1981 *W, S, I, F, Arg* 1,2, 1982 *A, S*
Bedford, H (Morley) 1889 *M,* 1890 *S, I*
Bedford, L L (Headingley) 1931 *W, I*
Beer, I D S (Harlequins) 1955 *F, S*
Beese, M C (Liverpool) 1972 *W, I, F*
Bell, F J (Northern) 1900 *W*
Bell, H (New Brighton) 1884 *I*
Bell, J L (Darlington) 1878 *I*
Bell, P J (Blackheath) 1968 *W, I, F, S*
Bell, R W (Northern) 1900 *W, I, S*
Bendon, G J (Wasps) 1959 *W, I, F, S*
Bennett, N O (St Mary's Hospital, Waterloo) 1947 *W, S, F,* 1948 *A, W, I, S*
Bennett, W N (Bedford, London Welsh) 1975 *S, A1,* 1976 *S* (R), 1979 *S, I, F, W*
Bennetts, B B (Penzance) 1909 *A, W*
Bentley, J (Sale, Newcastle) 1988 *I* 2, *A* 1, 1997 *A* 1, *SA*
Bentley, J E (Gipsies) 1871 *S,* 1872 *S*
Berridge, M J (Northampton) 1949 *W, I*
Berry, H (Gloucester) 1910 *W, I, F, S*
Berry, J (Tyldesley) 1891 *W, I, S*
Berry, J T W (Leicester) 1939 *W, I, S*
Beswick, E (Swinton) 1882 *I, S*
Biggs, J M (UCH) 1878 *S,* 1879 *I*
Birkett, J G G (Harlequins) 1906 *S, F, SA,* 1907 *F, W, S,* 1908 *F, W,I, S,* 1910 *W, I, S,* 1911 *W, F, I, S,* 1912 *W, I, S, F*
Birkett, L (Clapham R) 1875 *S,* 1877 *I, S*
Birkett, R H (Clapham R) 1871 *S,* 1875 *S,* 1876 *S,* 1877 *I*
Bishop, C C (Blackheath) 1927 *F*
Black, B H (Blackheath) 1930 *W, I, F, S,* 1931 *W, I, S, F,* 1932 *S,* 1933 *W*
Blacklock, J H (Aspatria) 1898 *I,* 1899 *I*
Blakeway, P J (Gloucester) 1980 *I, F, W, S,* 1981 *W, S, I, F,* 1982 *I, F, W,* 1984 *I, F, W, SA* 1, 1985 *R, F, S, I*
Blakiston, A F (Northampton) 1920 *S,* 1921 *W, I, S, F,* 1922 *W,* 1923 *S, F,* 1924 *W, I, F, S,* 1925 *NZ, W, I, S, F*
Blatherwick, T (Manchester) 1878 *I*
Body, J A (Gipsies) 1872 *S,* 1873 *S*
Bolton, C A (United Services) 1909 *F*
Bolton, R (Harlequins) 1933 *W,* 1936 *S,* 1937 *S,* 1938 *W, I*
Bolton, W N (Blackheath) 1882 *I, S,* 1883 *W, I, S,* 1884 *W, I, S,* 1885 *I,* 1887 *I, S*
Bonaventura, M S (Blackheath) 1931 *W*
Bond, A M (Sale) 1978 *NZ,* 1979 *S, I, NZ,* 1980 *I,* 1982 *I*
Bonham-Carter, E (Oxford U) 1891 *S*
Bonsor, F (Bradford) 1886 *W, I, S,* 1887 *W, S,* 1889 *M*
Boobbyer, B (Rosslyn Park) 1950 *W, I, F, S,* 1951 *W, F,* 1952 *S, I, F*
Booth, L A (Headingley) 1933 *W, I, S,* 1934 *S,* 1935 *W, I, S*
Botting, I J (Oxford U) 1950 *W, I*
Boughton, H J (Gloucester) 1935 *W, I, S*
Boyle, C W (Oxford U) 1873 *S*
Boyle, S B (Gloucester) 1983 *W, S, I*
Boylen, F (Hartlepool R) 1908 *F, W, I, S*

Bracken, K P P (Bristol, Saracens) 1993 *NZ*, 1994 *S, I, C*, 1995 *I, F, W, S, [It, WS* (t)], *SA*, 1996 *It* (R), 1997 *Arg* 1,2, *A* 2, *NZ* 1,2, 1998 *F, W*
Bradby, M S (United Services) 1922 *I, F*
Bradley, R (W Hartlepool) 1903 *W*
Bradshaw, H (Bramley) 1892 *S*, 1893 *W, I, S*, 1894 *W, I, S*
Brain, S E (Coventry) 1984 *SA* 2, *A* (R), 1985 *R, F, S, I, W, NZ* 1,2, 1986 *W, S, I, F*
Braithwaite, J (Leicester) 1905 *NZ*
Braithwaite-Exley, B (Headingley) 1949 *W*
Brettargh, A T (Liverpool OB) 1900 *W*, 1903 *I, S*, 1904 *W, I, S*, 1905 *I, S*
Brewer, J (Gipsies) 1876 *I*
Briggs, A (Bradford) 1892 *W, I, S*
Brinn, A (Gloucester) 1972 *W, I, S*
Broadley, T (Bingley) 1893 *W, S*, 1894 *W, I, S*, 1896 *S*
Bromet, W E (Richmond) 1891 *W, I*, 1892 *W, I, S*, 1893 *W, I, S*, 1895 *W, I, S*, 1896 *I*
Brook, P W P (Harlequins) 1930 *S*, 1931 *F*, 1936 *S*
Brooke, T J (Richmond) 1968 *F, S*
Brooks, F G (Bedford) 1906 *SA*
Brooks, M J (Oxford U) 1874 *S*
Brophy, T J (Liverpool) 1964 *I, F, S*, 1965 *W, I*, 1966 *W, I, F*
Brough, J W (Silloth) 1925 *NZ, W*
Brougham, H (Harlequins) 1912 *W, I, S, F*
Brown, A A (Exeter) 1938 *S*
Brown, L G (Oxford U, Blackheath) 1911 *W, F, I, S*, 1913 *SA, W, F, I, S*, 1914 *W, I, S, F*, 1921 *W, I, S, F*, 1922 *W*
Brown, T W (Bristol) 1928 *S*, 1929 *W, I, S, F*, 1932 *S*, 1933 *W, I, S*
Brunton, J (N Durham) 1914 *W, I, S*
Brutton, E B (Cambridge U) 1886 *S*
Bryden, C C (Clapham R) 1876 *I*, 1877 *S*
Bryden, H A (Clapham R) 1874 *S*
Buckingham, R A (Leicester) 1927 *F*
Bucknall, A L (Richmond) 1969 *SA*, 1970 *I, W, S, F*, 1971 *W, I, F, S* (2[1C])
Buckton, J R D (Saracens) 1988 *A* (R), 1990 *Arg* 1,2
Budd, A (Blackheath) 1878 *I*, 1879 *S, I*, 1881 *W, S*
Budworth, R T D (Blackheath) 1890 *W*, 1891 *W, S*
Bull, A G (Northampton) 1914 *W*
Bullough, E (Wigan) 1892 *W, I, S*
Bulpitt, M P (Blackheath) 1970 *S*
Bulteel, A J (Manchester) 1876 *I*
Bunting, W L (Moseley) 1897 *I, S*, 1898 *I, S, W*, 1899 *S*, 1900 *S*, 1901 *I, S*
Burland, D W (Bristol) 1931 *W, I, F*, 1932 *I, S*, 1933 *W, I, S*
Burns, B H (Blackheath) 1871 *S*
Burton, G W (Blackheath) 1879 *S, I*, 1880 *S*, 1881 *I, W, S*
Burton, H C (Richmond) 1926 *W*
Burton, M A (Gloucester) 1972 *W, I, F, S, SA*, 1974 *F, W*, 1975 *S, A* 1,2, 1976 *A, W, S, I, F*, 1978 *F, W*
Bush, J A (Clifton) 1872 *S*, 1873 *S*, 1875 *S*, 1876 *I, S*
Butcher, C J S (Harlequins) 1984 *SA* 1,2, *A*
Butcher, W V (Streatham) 1903 *S*, 1904 *W, I, S*, 1905 *W, I, S*
Butler, A G (Harlequins) 1937 *W, I*
Butler, P E (Gloucester) 1975 *A* 1, 1976 *F*
Butterfield, J (Northampton) 1953 *F, S*, 1954 *W, NZ, I, S, F*, 1955 *W, I, F, S*, 1956 *W, I, S, F*, 1957 *W, I, F, S*, 1958 *W, A, I, F, S*, 1959 *W, I, F, S*
Byrne, F A (Moseley) 1897 *W*
Byrne, J F (Moseley) 1894 *W, I, S*, 1895 *I, S*, 1896 *I*, 1897 *W, I, S*, 1898 *I, S, W*, 1899 *I*

Cain, J J (Waterloo) 1950 *W*
Callard, J E B (Bath) 1993 *NZ*, 1994 *S, I*, 1995 *[WS]*, 1993
Campbell, D A (Cambridge U) 1937 *W, I*
Candler, P L (St Bart's Hospital) 1935 *W*, 1936 *NZ, W, I, S*, 1937 *W, I, S*, 1938 *W, S*
Cannell, L B (Oxford U, St Mary's Hospital) 1948 *F*, 1949 *W, I, F, S*, 1950 *W, I, F, S*, 1952 *SA, W*, 1953 *W, I, F*, 1956 *I, S, F*, 1957 *W, I*
Caplan, D W N (Headingley) 1978 *S, I*
Cardus, R M (Roundhay) 1979 *F, W*
Carey, G M (Blackheath) 1895 *W, I, S*, 1896 *W, I*
Carleton, J (Orrell) 1979 *NZ*, 1980 *I, F, W, S*, 1981 *W, S, I, F, Arg* 1,2, 1982 *A, S, I, F, W*, 1983 *F, W, S, I, NZ*, 1984 *S, I, F, W, A*

Carling, W D C (Durham U, Harlequins) 1988 *F, W, S, I* 1,2, *A2, Fj, A*, 1989 *S, I, F, W, Fj*, 1990 *I, F, W, S, Arg* 1,2,3, 1991 *W, S, I, F, Fj, A, [NZ, It, US, F, S, A]*, 1992 *S, I, F, W, C, SA*, 1993 *F, W, S, I, NZ*, 1994 *S, I, F, W, SA* 1,2, *R, C*, 1995 *I, F, W, S, [Arg, WS, A, NZ, F], SA, WS*, 1996 *F, W, S, I, It, Arg*, 1997 *S, I, F, W*
Carpenter, A D (Gloucester) 1932 *SA*
Carr, R S L (Manchester) 1939 *W, I, S*
Cartwright, V H (Nottingham) 1903 *W, I, S*, 1904 *W, S*, 1905 *W, I, S, NZ*, 1906 *W, I, S, F, SA*
Catcheside, H C (Percy Park) 1924 *W, I, F, S*, 1926 *W, I*, 1927 *I, S*
Catt, M J (Bath) 1994 *W* (R), *C* (R), 1995 *I, F, W, S, [Arg, It, WS, A, NZ, F], SA, WS*, 1996 *F, W, S, I, It, Arg*, 1997 *W, Arg* 1, *A* 1,2, *NZ* 1, *SA*, 1998 *F, W* (R), *I*
Cattell, R H B (Blackheath) 1895 *W, I, S*, 1896 *W, I, S*, 1900 *W*
Cave, J W (Richmond) 1889 *M*
Cave, W T C (Blackheath) 1905 *W*
Challis, R (Bristol) 1957 *I, F, S*
Chambers, E L (Bedford) 1908 *F*, 1910 *W, I*
Chantrill, B S (Bristol) 1924 *W, I, F, S*
Chapman, C E (Cambridge U) 1884 *W*
Chapman, F E (Hartlepool) 1910 *W, I, F, S*, 1912 *W*, 1914 *W, I*
Cheesman, W I (OMTs) 1913 *SA, W, F, I*
Cheston, E C (Richmond) 1873 *S*, 1874 *S*, 1875 *I, S*, 1876 *S*
Chilcott, G J (Bath) 1984 *A*, 1986 *I, F*, 1987 *F* (R), *W, [J, US, W* (R)], 1988 *I* 2 (R), *Fj*, 1989 *I* (R), *F, W, R*
Christopherson, P (Blackheath) 1891 *W, S*
Clark, C W H (Liverpool) 1876 *I*
Clarke, A J (Coventry) 1935 *W, I, S*, 1936 *NZ, W, I*
Clarke, B B (Bath, Richmond) 1992 *SA*, 1993 *F, W, S, I, NZ*, 1994 *S, I, F, W, SA* 1,2, *R, C*, 1995 *I, F, W, S, [Arg, It, A, NZ, F], SA, WS*, 1996 *W, S, I, Arg* (R), 1997 *W, Arg* 1,2, *A* 1 (R)
Clarke, S J S (Cambridge U, Blackheath) 1963 *W, I, F, S, NZ* 1,2, *A*, 1964 *NZ, W, I*, 1965 *I, F, S*
Clayton, J H (Liverpool) 1871 *S*
Clements, J W (O Cranleighans) 1959 *I, F, S*
Cleveland, C R (Blackheath) 1887 *W, S*
Clibborn, W G (Richmond) 1886 *W, I, S*, 1887 *W, I, S*
Clough, F J (Cambridge U, Orrell) 1986 *I, F*, 1987 *[J* (R), *US]*
Coates, C H (Yorkshire W) 1880 *S*, 1881 *S*, 1882 *S*
Coates, V H M (Bath) 1913 *SA, W, F, I, S*
Cobby, W (Hull) 1900 *W*
Cockerham, A (Bradford Olicana) 1900 *W*
Cockerill, R (Leicester) 1997 *Arg* 1 (R), 2, *A* 2 (t + R), *NZ* 1, *SA, NZ* 2, 1998 *W, S, I*
Colclough, M J (Angoulême, Wasps, Swansea) 1978 *S, I*, 1979 *NZ*, 1980 *F, W, S*, 1981 *W, S, I, F*, 1982 *A, S, I, F, W*, 1983 *F, NZ*, 1984 *S, I, F, W*, 1986 *W, S, I, F*
Coley, E (Northampton) 1929 *F*, 1932 *W*
Collins, P J (Camborne) 1952 *S, I, F*
Collins, W E (O Cheltonians) 1874 *S*, 1875 *I, S*, 1876 *I, S*
Considine, S G U (Bath) 1925 *F*
Conway, G S (Cambridge U, Rugby, Manchester) 1920 *F, I, S*, 1921 *F*, 1922 *W, I, F, S*, 1923 *W, I, S, F*, 1924 *W, I, F, S*, 1925 *NZ*, 1927 *W*
Cook, J G (Bedford) 1937 *S*
Cook, P W (Richmond) 1965 *I, F*
Cooke, D A (Harlequins) 1976 *W, S, I, F*
Cooke, D H (Harlequins) 1981 *W, S, I, F*, 1984 *I*, 1985 *R, F, S, I, W, NZ* 1,2
Cooke, P (Richmond) 1939 *W, I*
Coop, T (Leigh) 1892 *S*
Cooper, J G (Moseley) 1909 *A, W*
Cooper, M J (Moseley) 1973 *F, S, NZ* 2 (R), 1975 *F, W*, 1976 *A, W*, 1977 *S, I, F, W*
Cooper, S F (Blackheath) 1900 *W*, 1902 *W, I*, 1905 *W, I, S*, 1907 *W*
Corbett, L J (Bristol) 1921 *F*, 1923 *W, I*, 1924 *W, I, F, S*, 1925 *NZ, W, I, S, F*, 1927 *W, I, S, F*
Corless, B J (Coventry, Moseley) 1976 *A, I* (R), 1977 *S, I, F, W*, 1978 *F, W, S, I*
Corry, M J (Bristol) 1997 *Arg* 1,2
Cotton, F E (Loughborough Colls, Coventry, Sale) 1971 *S* (2[1C]), *P*, 1973 *W, I, F, S, NZ* 2, *A*, 1974 *S, I*, 1975 *I, F, W*, 1976 *A, W, S, I, F*, 1977 *S, I, F, W*, 1978 *S, I*, 1979 *NZ*, 1980 *I, F, W, S*, 1981 *W*
Coulman, M J (Moseley) 1967 *A, I, F, S, W*, 1968 *W, I, F, S*
Coulson, T J (Coventry) 1927 *W*, 1928 *A, W*

Forrest, R (Wellington) 1899 *W*, 1900 *S*, 1902 *I, S*, 1903 *I, S*
Foulds, R T (Waterloo) 1929 *W, I*
Fowler, F D (Manchester) 1878 *S*, 1879 *S*
Fowler, H (Oxford U) 1878 *S*, 1881 *W, S*
Fowler, R H (Leeds) 1877 *I*
Fox, F H (Wellington) 1890 *W, S*
Francis, T E S (Cambridge U) 1926 *W, I, F, S*
Frankcom, G P (Cambridge U, Bedford) 1965 *W, I, F, S*
Fraser, E C (Blackheath) 1875 *I*
Fraser, G (Richmond) 1902 *W, I, S*, 1903 *W, I*
Freakes, H D (Oxford U) 1938 *W*, 1939 *W, I*
Freeman, H (Marlborough N) 1872 *S*, 1873 *S*, 1874 *S*
French, R J (St Helens) 1961 *W, I, F, S*
Fry, H A (Liverpool) 1934 *W, I, S*
Fry, T W (Queen's House) 1880 *I, S*, 1881 *W*
Fuller, H G (Cambridge U) 1882 *I, S*, 1883 *W, I, S*, 1884 *W*

Gadney, B C (Leicester, Headingley) 1932 *I, S*, 1933 *I, S*, 1934 *W, I, S*, 1935 *S*, 1936 *NZ, W, I, S*, 1937 *S*, 1938 *W*
Gamlin, H T (Blackheath) 1899 *W, S*, 1900 *W, I, S*, 1901 *S*, 1902 *W, I, S*, 1903 *W, I, S*, 1904 *W, I*
Gardner, E R (Devonport Services) 1921 *W, I, S*, 1922 *W, I, F*, 1923 *W, I, S, F*
Gardner, H P (Richmond) 1878 *I*
Garforth, D J (Leicester) 1997 *W* (R), *Arg* 1,2, *A* 1, *NZ* 1, *SA, NZ* 2, 1998 *F, W* (R), *S, I*
Garnett, H W T (Bradford) 1877 *S*
Gavins, M N (Leicester) 1961 *W*
Gay, D J (Bath) 1968 *W, I, F, S*
Gent, D R (Gloucester) 1905 *NZ*, 1906 *W, I*, 1910 *W, I*
Genth, J S M (Manchester) 1874 *S*, 1875 *S*
George, J T (Falmouth) 1947 *S, F*, 1949 *I*
Gerrard, R A (Bath) 1932 *SA, W, I, S*, 1933 *W, I, S*, 1934 *W, I, S*, 1936 *NZ, W, I, S*
Gibbs, G A (Bristol) 1947 *F*, 1948 *I*
Gibbs, J C (Harlequins) 1925 *NZ, W*, 1926 *F*, 1927 *W, I, S, F*
Gibbs, N (Harlequins) 1954 *S, F*
Giblin, L F (Blackheath) 1896 *W, I*, 1897 *S*
Gibson, A S (Manchester) 1871 *S*
Gibson, C O P (Northern) 1901 *W*
Gibson, G R (Northern) 1899 *W*, 1901 *S*
Gibson, T A (Northern) 1905 *W, S*
Gilbert, F G (Devonport Services) 1923 *W, I*
Gilbert, R (Devonport A) 1908 *W, I, S*
Giles, J L (Coventry) 1935 *W, I*, 1937 *W, I*, 1938 *I, S*
Gittings, W J (Coventry) 1967 *NZ*
Glover, P B (Bath) 1967 *A*, 1971 *F, P*
Godfray, R E (Richmond) 1905 *NZ*
Godwin, H O (Coventry) 1959 *F, S*, 1963 *S, NZ* 1,2, *A*, 1964 *NZ, I, F, S*, 1967 *NZ*
Gomarsall, A C T (Wasps) 1996 *It, Arg*, 1997 *S, I, F, Arg* 2 (R)
Gordon-Smith, G W (Blackheath) 1900 *W, I, S*
Gotley, A L H (Oxford U) 1910 *F, S*, 1911 *W, F, I, S*
Graham, D (Aspatria) 1901 *W*
Graham, H J (Wimbledon H) 1875 *I, S*, 1876 *I, S*
Graham, J D G (Wimbledon H) 1876 *I*
Gray, A (Otley) 1947 *W, I, S*
Grayson, P J (Northampton) 1995 *WS*, 1996 *F, W, S, I*, 1997 *S, I, F, A* 2 (t), *SA* (R), *NZ* 2, 1998 *F, W, S, I*
Green, J (Skipton) 1905 *I*, 1906 *S, F, SA*, 1907 *F, W, I, S*
Green, J F (West Kent) 1871 *S*
Green, W R (Wasps) 1997 *A* 2
Greening, P B T (Gloucester) 1996 *It* (R), 1997 *W* (R), *Arg* 1
Greenstock, N J J (Wasps) 1997 *Arg* 1,2, *A* 1, *SA*
Greenwell, J H (Rockcliff) 1893 *W, I*
Greenwood, J E (Cambridge U, Leicester) 1912 *F*, 1913 *SA, W, F, I, S*, 1914 *W, S, F*, 1920 *W, F, I, S*
Greenwood, J R H (Waterloo) 1966 *I, F, S*, 1967 *A*, 1969 *I*
Greenwood, W J H (Leicester) 1997 *A* 2, *NZ* 1, *SA, NZ* 2, 1998 *F, W, S, I*
Greg, W (Manchester) 1876 *I, S*
Gregory, G G (Bristol) 1931 *I, S, F*, 1932 *SA, W, I, S*, 1933 *W, I, S*, 1934 *W, I, S*
Gregory, J A (Blackheath) 1949 *W*
Grewcock, D J (Coventry, Saracens) 1997 *Arg* 2, *SA*, 1998 *W* (R), *S* (R), *I* (R)
Grylls, W M (Redruth) 1905 *I*
Guest, R H (Waterloo) 1939 *W, I, S*, 1947 *W, I, S, F*, 1948 *A, W, I, S*, 1949 *F, S*
Guillemard, A G (West Kent) 1871 *S*, 1872 *S*

Gummer, C H A (Plymouth A) 1929 *F*
Gunner, C R (Marlborough N) 1876 *I*
Gurdon, C (Richmond) 1880 *I, S*, 1881 *I, W, S*, 1882 *I, S*, 1883 *S*, 1884 *W, S*, 1885 *I*, 1886 *W, I, S*
Gurdon, E T (Richmond) 1878 *S*, 1879 *I*, 1880 *S*, 1881 *I, W, S*, 1882 *S*, 1883 *W, I, S*, 1884 *W, I, S*, 1885 *W, I*, 1886 *S*
Guscott, J C (Bath) 1989 *R, Fj*, 1990 *I, F, W, S, Arg* 3, 1991 *W, S, I, F, Fj, A*, [*NZ, It, F, S, A*], 1992 *S, I, F, W, C, SA*, 1993 *F, W, S, I*, 1994 *R, C*, 1995 *I, F, W, S*, [*Arg, It, A, NZ, F*], *SA, WS*, 1996 *F, W, S, I, Arg*, 1997 *I* (R), *W* (R), 1998 *F, W, S, I*

Haag, M (Bath) 1997 *Arg* 1,2
Haigh, L (Manchester) 1910 *W, I, S*, 1911 *W, F, I, S*
Hale, P M (Moseley) 1969 *SA*, 1970 *I, W*
Hall, C (Gloucester) 1901 *I, S*
Hall, J (N Durham) 1894 *W, I, S*
Hall, J P (Bath) 1984 *S* (R), *I, F, SA* 1,2, *A*, 1985 *R, F, S, I, W, NZ* 1,2, 1986 *W, S*, 1987 *I, F, W, S*, 1990 *Arg* 3, 1994 *S*
Hall, N M (Richmond) 1947 *W, I, S, F*, 1949 *W, I*, 1952 *SA, W, S, I, F*, 1953 *W, I, F, S*, 1955 *W, I*
Halliday, S J (Bath, Harlequins) 1986 *W, S*, 1987 *S*, 1988 *S, I* 1,2, *A* 1, *A*, 1989 *S, I, F, W, R, Fj* (R), 1990 *W, S*, 1991 [*US, S, A*], 1992 *S, I, F, W*
Hamersley, A St G (Marlborough N) 1871 *S*, 1872 *S*, 1873 *S*, 1874 *S*
Hamilton-Hill, E A (Harlequins) 1936 *NZ, W, I*
Hamilton-Wickes, R H (Cambridge U) 1924 *I*, 1925 *NZ, W, I, S, F*, 1926 *W, I, S*, 1927 *W*
Hammett, E D G (Newport) 1920 *W, F, S*, 1921 *W, I, S, F*, 1922 *W*
Hammond, C E L (Harlequins) 1905 *S, NZ*, 1906 *W, I, S, F*, 1908 *W, I*
Hancock, A W (Northampton) 1965 *F, S*, 1966 *F*
Hancock, G E (Birkenhead Park) 1939 *W, I, S*
Hancock, J H (Newport) 1955 *W, I*
Hancock, P F (Blackheath) 1886 *W, I*, 1890 *W*
Hancock, P S (Richmond) 1904 *W, I, S*
Handford, F G (Manchester) 1909 *W, F, I, S*
Hands, R H M (Blackheath) 1910 *F, S*
Hanley, J (Plymouth A) 1927 *W, S, F*, 1928 *W, I, F, S*
Hannaford, R C (Bristol) 1971 *W, I, F*
Hanvey, R J (Aspatria) 1926 *W, I, F, S*
Harding, E H (Devonport Services) 1931 *I*
Harding, R M (Bristol) 1985 *R, F, S*, 1987 *S*, [*A, J, W*], 1988 *I* 1 (R),2, *A* 1,2, *Fj*
Harding, V S J (Saracens) 1961 *F, S*, 1962 *W, I, F, S*
Hardwick, P F (Percy Park) 1902 *I, S*, 1903 *W, I, S*, 1904 *W, I, S*
Hardwick, R J K (Coventry) 1996 *It* (R)
Hardy, E M P (Blackheath) 1951 *I, F, S*
Hare, W H (Nottingham, Leicester) 1974 *W*, 1978 *F, NZ*, 1979 *NZ*, 1980 *I, F, W, S*, 1981 *W, S, Arg* 1,2, 1982 *F, W*, 1983 *F, W, S, I, NZ*, 1984 *S, I, F, W, SA* 1,2
Harper, C H (Exeter) 1899 *W*
Harriman, A T (Harlequins) 1988 *A*
Harris, S W (Blackheath) 1920 *I, S*
Harris, T W (Northampton) 1929 *S*, 1932 *I*
Harrison, A C (Hartlepool R) 1931 *I, S*
Harrison, A L (United Services, RN) 1914 *I, F*
Harrison, G (Hull) 1877 *I, S*, 1879 *S, I*, 1880 *S*, 1885 *W, I*
Harrison, H C (United Services, RN) 1909 *S*, 1914 *I, S, F*
Harrison, M E (Wakefield) 1985 *NZ* 1,2, 1986 *S, I, F*, 1987 *I, F, W, S*, [*A, J, US, W*], 1988 *F, W*
Hartley, B C (Blackheath) 1901 *S*, 1902 *S*
Haslett, L W (Birkenhead Park) 1926 *I, F*
Hastings, G W D (Gloucester) 1955 *W, I, F, S*, 1957 *W, I, F, S*, 1958 *W, A, I, F, S*
Havelock, H (Hartlepool R) 1908 *F, W, I*
Hawcridge, J J (Bradford) 1885 *W, I*
Hayward, L W (Cheltenham) 1910 *I*
Hazell, D St G (Leicester) 1955 *W, I, F, S*
Healey, A S (Leicester) 1997 *I* (R), *W, A* 1 (R), 2 (R), *NZ* 1 (R), *SA* (R), *NZ* 2, 1998 *F, W, S, I*
Hearn, R D (Bedford) 1966 *F, S*, 1967 *I, F, S, W*
Heath, A H (Oxford U) 1876 *S*
Heaton, J (Waterloo) 1935 *W, I, S*, 1939 *W, I, S*, 1947 *I, S, F*
Henderson, A P (Edinburgh Wands) 1947 *W, I, S, F*, 1948 *I, S, F*, 1949 *W, I*
Henderson, R S F (Blackheath) 1883 *W, S*, 1884 *W, S*, 1885 *W*
Heppell, W G (Devonport A) 1903 *I*
Herbert, A J (Wasps) 1958 *F, S*, 1959 *W, I, F, S*

England's Will Greenwood is tackled by Thomas Castaignède and Philippe Benetton (France) in the Five Nations match at Stade de France, 7 February 1998.

Hesford, R (Bristol) 1981 *S* (R), 1982 *A, S, F* (R), 1983 *F* (R), 1985 *R, F, S, I, W*
Heslop, N J (Orrell) 1990 *Arg* 1,2,3, 1991 *W, S, I, F, [US, F],* 1992 *W* (R)
Hetherington, J G G (Northampton) 1958 *A, I,* 1959 *W, I, F, S*
Hewitt, E N (Coventry) 1951 *W, I, F*
Hewitt, W W (Queen's House) 1881 *I, W, S,* 1882 *I*
Hickson, J L (Bradford) 1887 *W, I, S,* 1890 *W, S, I*
Higgins, R (Liverpool) 1954 *W, NZ, I, S,* 1955 *W, I, F, S,* 1957 *W, I, F, S,* 1959 *W*
Hignell, A J (Cambridge U, Bristol) 1975 *A 2,* 1976 *A, W, S, I,* 1977 *S, I, F, W,* 1978 *W,* 1979 *S, I, F, W*
Hill, B A (Blackheath) 1903 *I, S,* 1904 *W, I,* 1905 *W, NZ,* 1906 *SA,* 1907 *F, W*
Hill, R A (Saracens) 1997 *S, I, F, W, A* 1,2, *NZ* 1, *SA, NZ* 2, 1998 *F, W*
Hill, R J (Bath) 1984 *SA* 1,2, 1985 *I* (R), *NZ* 2 (R), 1986 *F* (R), 1987 *I, F, W, [US],* 1989 *Fj,* 1990 *I, F, W, S, Arg* 1,2,3, 1991 *W, S, I, F, Fj, A, [NZ, It, US, F, S, A]*
Hillard, R J (Oxford U) 1925 *NZ*
Hiller, R (Harlequins) 1968 *W, I, F, S,* 1969 *I, F, S, W, SA,* 1970 *I, W, S,* 1971 *I, F, S* (2[1C]), *P,* 1972 *W, I*
Hind, A E (Leicester) 1905 *NZ,* 1906 *W*
Hind, G R (Blackheath) 1910 *S,* 1911 *I*
Hobbs, R F A (Blackheath) 1899 *S,* 1903 *W*
Hobbs, R G S (Richmond) 1932 *SA, W, I, S*

Hodges, H A (Nottingham) 1906 *W, I*
Hodgkinson, S D (Nottingham) 1989 *R, Fj,* 1990 *I, F, W, S, Arg* 1,2,3, 1991 *W, S, I, F, [US]*
Hodgson, J McD (Northern) 1932 *SA, W, I, S,* 1934 *W, I,* 1936 *I*
Hodgson, S A M (Durham City) 1960 *W, I, F, S,* 1961 *SA, W,* 1962 *W, I, F, S,* 1964 *W*
Hofmeyr, M B (Oxford U) 1950 *W, F, S*
Hogarth, T B (Hartlepool R) 1906 *F*
Holford, G (Gloucester) 1920 *W, F*
Holland, D (Devonport A) 1912 *W, I, S*
Holliday, T E (Aspatria) 1923 *S, F,* 1925 *I, S, F,* 1926 *F, S*
Holmes, C B (Manchester) 1947 *S,* 1948 *I, F*
Holmes, E (Manningham) 1890 *S, I*
Holmes, W A (Nuneaton) 1950 *W, I, F, S,* 1951 *W, I, F, S,* 1952 *SA, S, I, F,* 1953 *W, I, F, S*
Holmes, W B (Cambridge U) 1949 *W, I, F, S*
Hook, W G (Gloucester) 1951 *S,* 1952 *SA, W*
Hooper, C A (Middlesex W) 1894 *W, I, S*
Hopley, D P (Wasps) 1995 *[WS* (R)*], SA, WS*
Hopley, F J V (Blackheath) 1907 *F, W,* 1908 *I*
Hordern, P C (Gloucester) 1931 *I, S, F,* 1934 *W*
Horley, C H (Swinton) 1885 *I*
Hornby, A N (Manchester) 1877 *I, S,* 1878 *S, I,* 1880 *I,* 1881 *I, S,* 1882 *I, S*

Horrocks-Taylor, J P (Cambridge U, Leicester, Middlesbrough) 1958 *W, A*, 1961 *S*, 1962 *S*, 1963 *NZ* 1,2, *A*, 1964 *NZ, W*
Horsfall, E L (Harlequins) 1949 *W*
Horton, A L (Blackheath) 1965 *W, I, F, S*, 1966 *F, S*, 1967 *NZ*
Horton, J P (Bath) 1978 *W, S, I, NZ*, 1980 *I, F, W, S*, 1981 *W*, 1983 *S, I*, 1984 *SA* 1,2
Horton, N E (Moseley, Toulouse) 1969 *I, F, S, W*, 1971 *I, F, S*, 1974 *S*, 1975 *W*, 1977 *S, I, F, W*, 1978 *F, W*, 1979 *S, I, F, W*, 1980 *I*
Hosen, R W (Bristol, Northampton) 1963 *NZ* 1,2, *A*, 1964 *F, S*, 1967 *A, I, F, S, W*
Hosking, G R d'A (Devonport Services) 1949 *W, I, F, S*, 1950 *W*
Houghton, S (Runcorn) 1892 *I*, 1896 *W*
Howard, P D (O Millhillians) 1930 *W, I, F, S*, 1931 *W, I, S, F*
Hubbard, G C (Blackheath) 1892 *W, I*
Hubbard, J C (Harlequins) 1930 *S*
Hudson, A (Gloucester) 1906 *W, I, F,* 1908 *F, W, I, S*, 1910 *F*
Hughes, G E (Barrow) 1896 *S*
Hull, P A (Bristol, RAF) 1994 *SA* 1,2, *R, C*
Hulme, F C (Birkenhead Park) 1903 *W, I*, 1905 *W, I*
Hunt, J T (Manchester) 1882 *I, S*, 1884 *W*
Hunt, R (Manchester) 1880 *I*, 1881 *W, S*, 1882 *I*
Hunt, W H (Manchester) 1876 *S*, 1877 *I, S*, 1878 *I*
Hunter, I (Northampton) 1992 *C*, 1993 *F, W*, 1994 *F, W*, 1995 [*WS, F*]
Huntsman, R P (Headingley) 1985 *NZ* 1,2
Hurst, A C B (Wasps) 1962 *S*
Huskisson, T F (OMTs) 1937 *W, I, S*, 1938 *W, I*, 1939 *W, I, S*
Hutchinson, F (Headingley) 1909 *F, I, S*
Hutchinson, J E (Durham City) 1906 *I*
Hutchinson, W C (RIE Coll) 1876 *S*, 1877 *I*
Hutchinson, W H H (Hull) 1875 *I*, 1876 *I*
Huth, H (Huddersfield) 1879 *S*
Hyde, J P (Northampton) 1950 *F, S*
Hynes, W B (United Services, RN) 1912 *F*

Ibbitson, E D (Headingley) 1909 *W, F, I, S*
Imrie, H M (Durham City) 1906 *NZ*, 1907 *I*
Inglis, R E (Blackheath) 1886 *W, I, S*
Irvin, S H (Devonport A) 1905 *W*
Isherwood, F W (Ravenscourt Park) 1872 *S*

Jackett, E J (Leicester, Falmouth) 1905 *NZ*, 1906 *W, I, S, F, SA*, 1907 *W, I, S*, 1909 *W, F, I, S*
Jackson, A H (Blackheath) 1878 *I*, 1880 *I*
Jackson, B S (Broughton Park) 1970 *S* (R), *F*
Jackson, P B (Coventry) 1956 *W, I, F*, 1957 *W, I, F, S*, 1958 *W, A, F, S*, 1959 *W, I, F, S*, 1961 *S*, 1963 *W, I, F, S*
Jackson, W J (Halifax) 1894 *S*
Jacob, F (Cambridge U) 1897 *W, I, S*, 1898 *I, S, W*, 1899 *W, I*
Jacob, H P (Blackheath) 1924 *W, I, F, S*, 1930 *F*
Jacob, P G (Blackheath) 1898 *I*
Jacobs, C R (Northampton) 1956 *W, I, S, F*, 1957 *W, I, F, S*, 1958 *W, A, I, F, S*, 1960 *W, I, F, S*, 1961 *SA, W, I, F, S*, 1963 *NZ* 1,2, *A*, 1964 *W, I, F, S*
Jago, R A (Devonport A) 1906 *W, I, SA*, 1907 *W, I*
Janion, J P A G (Bedford) 1971 *W, I, F, S* (2[1C]), *P*, 1972 *W, S, SA*, 1973 *A*, 1975 *A* 1,2
Jarman, J W (Bristol) 1900 *W*
Jeavons, N C (Moseley) 1981 *S, I, F, Arg* 1,2, 1982 *A, S, I, F, W*, 1983 *F, W, S, I*
Jeeps, R E G (Northampton) 1956 *W*, 1957 *W, I, F, S*, 1958 *W, A, I, F, S*, 1959 *I*, 1960 *W, I, F, S*, 1961 *SA, W, I, F, S*, 1962 *W, I, F, S*
Jeffery, G L (Blackheath) 1886 *W, I, S*, 1887 *W, I, S*
Jennins, C R (Waterloo) 1967 *A, I, F*
Jewitt, J (Hartlepool R) 1902 *W*
Johns, W A (Gloucester) 1909 *W, F, I, S*, 1910 *W, I, F*
Johnson, M O (Leicester) 1993 *F, NZ*, 1994 *S, I, F, W, R, C*, 1995 *I, F, W, S*, [*Arg, It, WS, A, NZ, F*], *SA, WS*, 1996 *F, W, S, I, It, Arg*, 1997 *S, I, F, W, A 2, NZ* 1,2, 1998 *F, W, S, I*
Johnston, W R (Bristol) 1910 *W, I*, 1912 *W, I, S, F*, 1913 *SA, W, F, I, S*, 1914 *W, I, S, F*
Jones, F P (New Brighton) 1893 *S*
Jones, H A (Barnstaple) 1950 *W, I, F*

Jorden, A M (Cambridge U, Blackheath, Bedford) 1970 *F*, 1973 *I, F, S*, 1974 *F*, 1975 *W, S*
Jowett, D (Heckmondwike) 1889 *M*, 1890 *S, I*, 1891 *W, I, S*
Judd, P E (Coventry) 1962 *W, I, F, S*, 1963 *S, NZ* 1,2, *A*, 1964 *NZ*, 1965 *I, F, S*, 1966 *W, I, F, S*, 1967 *A, I, F, S, W, NZ*

Kayll, H E (Sunderland) 1878 *S*
Keeling, J H (Guy's Hospital) 1948 *A, W*
Keen, B W (Newcastle U) 1968 *W, I, F, S*
Keeton, G H (Leicester) 1904 *W, I, S*
Kelly, G A (Bedford) 1947 *W, I, S*, 1948 *W*
Kelly, T S (London Devonians) 1906 *W, I, S, F, SA*, 1907 *F, W, I, S*, 1908 *F, I, S*
Kemble, A T (Liverpool) 1885 *W, I*, 1887 *I*
Kemp, D T (Blackheath) 1935 *W*
Kemp, T A (Richmond) 1937 *W, I*, 1939 *S*, 1948 *A, W*
Kendall, P D (Birkenhead Park) 1901 *S*, 1902 *W*, 1903 *S*
Kendall-Carpenter, J MacG K (Oxford U, Bath) 1949 *I, F, S*, 1950 *W, I, F, S*, 1951 *I, F, S*, 1952 *SA, W, S, I, F*, 1953 *W, I, F, S*, 1954 *W, NZ, I, F*
Kendrew, D A (Leicester) 1930 *W, I*, 1933 *I, S*, 1934 *S*, 1935 *W, I*, 1936 *NZ, W, I*
Kennedy, R D (Camborne S of M) 1949 *I, F, S*
Kent, C P (Rosslyn Park) 1977 *S, I, F, W*, 1978 *F* (R)
Kent, T (Salford) 1891 *W, I, S*, 1892 *W, I, S*
Kershaw, C A (United Services, RN) 1920 *W, F, I, S*, 1921 *W, I, S, F*, 1922 *W, I, F, S*, 1923 *W, I, S, F*
Kewley, E (Liverpool) 1874 *S*, 1875 *S*, 1876 *I, S*, 1877 *I, S*, 1878 *S*
Kewney, A L (Leicester) 1906 *W, I, S, F*, 1909 *A, W, F, I, S*, 1911 *W, F, I, S*, 1912 *I, S*, 1913 *SA*
Key, A (O Cranleighans) 1930 *I*, 1933 *W*
Keyworth, M (Swansea) 1976 *A, W, S, I*
Kilner, B (Wakefield T) 1880 *I*
Kindersley, R S (Exeter) 1883 *W*, 1884 *S*, 1885 *W*
King, A D (Wasps) 1997 *Arg* 2 (R)
King, I (Harrogate) 1954 *W, NZ, I*
King, J A (Headingley) 1911 *W, F, I, S*, 1912 *W, I, S*, 1913 *SA, W, F, I, S*
King, Q E M A (Army) 1921 *S*
Kingston, P (Gloucester) 1975 *A* 1,2, 1979 *I, F, W*
Kitching, A E (Blackheath) 1913 *I*
Kittermaster, H J (Harlequins) 1925 *NZ, W, I*, 1926 *W, I, F, S*
Knight, F (Plymouth) 1909 *A*
Knight, P M (Bristol) 1972 *F, S, SA*
Knowles, E (Millom) 1896 *S*, 1897 *S*
Knowles, T C (Birkenhead Park) 1931 *S*
Krige, J A (Guy's Hospital) 1920 *W*

Labuschagne, N A (Harlequins, Guy's Hospital) 1953 *W*, 1955 *W, I, F, S*
Lagden, R O (Richmond) 1911 *S*
Laird, H C C (Harlequins) 1927 *W, I, S*, 1928 *A, W, I, F, S*, 1929 *W, I*
Lambert, D (Harlequins) 1907 *F*, 1908 *F, W, S*, 1911 *W, F, I*
Lampkowski, M S (Headingley) 1976 *A, W, S, I*
Lapage, W N (United Services, RN) 1908 *F, W, I, S*
Larter, P J (Northampton, RAF) 1967 *A, NZ*, 1968 *W, I, F, S*, 1969 *I, F, S, W, SA*, 1970 *I, W, F, S*, 1971 *W, I, F, S* (2[1C]), *P*, 1972 *SA*, 1973 *NZ* 1, *W*
Law, A F (Richmond) 1877 *S*
Law, D E (Birkenhead Park) 1927 *I*
Lawrence, Hon H A (Richmond) 1873 *S*, 1874 *S*, 1875 *I, S*
Lawrie, P W (Leicester) 1910 *S*, 1911 *S*
Lawson, R G (Workington) 1925 *I*
Lawson, T M (Workington) 1928 *A, W*
Leadbetter, M M (Broughton Park) 1970 *F*
Leadbetter, V H (Edinburgh Wands) 1954 *S, F*
Leake, W R M (Harlequins) 1891 *W, I, S*
Leather, G (Liverpool) 1907 *I*
Lee, F H (Marlborough N) 1876 *S*, 1877 *I*
Lee, H (Blackheath) 1907 *F*
Le Fleming, J (Blackheath) 1887 *W*
Leonard, J (Saracens, Harlequins) 1990 *Arg* 1,2,3, 1991 *W, S, I, F, Fj, A*, [*NZ, It, US, F, S, A*], 1992 *S, I, F, W, C, SA*, 1993 *F, W, S, I, NZ*, 1994 *S, I, F, W, SA* 1,2, *R, C*, 1995 *I, F, W, S*, [*Arg, It, A, NZ, F*], *SA, WS*, 1996 *F, W, S, I, It, Arg*, 1997 *S, I, F, W, A 2, NZ* 1, *SA, NZ* 2, 1998 *F, W, S, I*

113

Leslie-Jones, F A (Richmond) 1895 *W, I*
Lewis, A O (Bath) 1952 *SA, W, S, I, F*, 1953 *W, I, F, S*, 1954 *F*
Leyland, R (Waterloo) 1935 *W, I, S*
Linnett, M S (Moseley) 1989 *Fj*
Livesay, R O'H (Blackheath) 1898 *W*, 1899 *W*
Lloyd, R H (Harlequins) 1967 *NZ*, 1968 *W, I, F, S*
Locke, H M (Birkenhead Park) 1923 *S, F*, 1924 *W, F, S*, 1925 *W, I, S, F*, 1927 *W, I, S*
Lockwood, R E (Heckmondwike) 1887 *W, I, S*, 1889 *M*, 1891 *W, I, S*, 1892 *W, I, S*, 1893 *W, I*, 1894 *W, I*
Login, S H M (RN Coll) 1876 *I*
Lohden, F C (Blackheath) 1893 *W*
Long, A E (Bath) 1997 *A* 2
Longland, R J (Northampton) 1932 *S*, 1933 *W, S*, 1934 *W, I, S*, 1935 *W, I, S*, 1936 *NZ, W, I, S*, 1937 *W, I, S*, 1938 *W, I, S*
Lowe, C N (Cambridge U, Blackheath) 1913 *SA, W, F, I, S*, 1914 *W, I, S, F*, 1920 *W, F, I, S*, 1921 *W, I, S, F*, 1922 *W, I, F, S*, 1923 *W, I, S, F*
Lowrie, F (Wakefield T) 1889 *M*, 1890 *W*
Lowry, W M (Birkenhead Park) 1920 *F*
Lozowski, R A P (Wasps) 1984 *A*
Luddington, W G E (Devonport Services) 1923 *W, I, S, F*, 1924 *W, I, F, S*, 1925 *W, I, S, F*, 1926 *W*
Luscombe, F (Gipsies) 1872 *S*, 1873 *S*, 1875 *I, S*, 1876 *I, S*
Luscombe, J H (Gipsies) 1871 *S*
Luxmoore, A F C C (Richmond) 1900 *S*, 1901 *W*
Luya, H F (Waterloo, Headingley) 1948 *W, I, S, F*, 1949 *W*
Lyon, A (Liverpool) 1871 *S*
Lyon, G H d'O (United Services, RN) 1908 *S*, 1909 *A*

McCanlis, M A (Gloucester) 1931 *W, I*
McFadyean, C W (Moseley) 1966 *I, F, S*, 1967 *A, I, F, S, W, NZ*, 1968 *W, I*
MacIlwaine, A H (United Services, Hull & E Riding) 1912 *W, I, S, F*, 1920 *I*
Mackie, O G (Wakefield T, Cambridge U) 1897 *S*, 1898 *I*
Mackinlay, J E H (St George's Hospital) 1872 *S*, 1873 *S*, 1875 *I*
MacLaren, W (Manchester) 1871 *S*
MacLennan, R R F (OMTs) 1925 *I, S, F*
McLeod, N F (RIE Coll) 1879 *S, I*
Madge, R J P (Exeter) 1948 *A, W, I, S*
Malir, F W S (Otley) 1930 *W, I, S*
Mallett, J A (Bath) 1995 [*WS* (R)]
Mallinder, J (Sale) 1997 *Arg* 1,2
Mangles, R H (Richmond) 1897 *W, I*
Manley, D C (Exeter) 1963 *W, I, F, S*
Mann, W E (United Services, Army) 1911 *W, F, I*
Mantell, N D (Rosslyn Park) 1975 *A* 1
Mapletoft, M S (Gloucester) 1997 *Arg* 2
Markendale, E T (Manchester R) 1880 *I*
Marques, R W D (Cambridge U, Harlequins) 1956 *W, I, S, F*, 1957 *W, I, F, S*, 1958 *W, A, I, F, S*, 1959 *W, I, F, S*, 1960 *W, I, F, S*, 1961 *SA, W*
Marquis, J C (Birkenhead Park) 1900 *I, S*
Marriott, C J B (Blackheath) 1884 *W, I, S*, 1886 *W, I, S*, 1887 *I*
Marriott, E E (Manchester) 1876 *I*
Marriott, V R (Harlequins) 1963 *NZ* 1,2, *A*, 1964 *NZ*
Marsden, G H (Morley) 1900 *W, I, S*
Marsh, H (RIE Coll) 1873 *S*
Marsh, J (Swinton) 1892 *I*
Marshall, H (Blackheath) 1893 *W*
Marshall, M W (Blackheath) 1873 *S*, 1874 *S*, 1875 *I, S*, 1876 *I, S*, 1877 *I, S*, 1878 *S, I*
Marshall, R M (Oxford U) 1938 *I, S*, 1939 *W, I, S*
Martin, C R (Bath) 1985 *F, S, I, W*
Martin, N O (Harlequins) 1972 *F* (R)
Martindale, S A (Kendal) 1929 *F*
Massey, E J (Leicester) 1925 *W, I, S*
Mathias, J L (Bristol) 1905 *W, I, S, NZ*
Matters, J C (RNE Coll) 1899 *S*
Matthews, J R C (Harlequins) 1949 *F, S*, 1950 *I, F, S*, 1952 *SA, W, S, I, F*
Maud, P (Blackheath) 1893 *W, I*
Maxwell, A W (New Brighton, Headingley) 1975 *A* 1, 1976 *A, W, S, I, F*, 1978 *F*
Maxwell-Hyslop, J E (Oxford U) 1922 *I, F, S*
Maynard, A F (Cambridge U) 1914 *W, I, S*
Meikle, G W C (Waterloo) 1934 *W, I, S*
Meikle, S S C (Waterloo) 1929 *S*
Mellish, F W (Blackheath) 1920 *W, F, I, S*, 1921 *W, I*

Melville, N D (Wasps) 1984 *A*, 1985 *I, W, NZ* 1,2, 1986 *W, S, I, F*, 1988 *F, W, S, I* 1
Merriam, L P B (Blackheath) 1920 *W, F*
Michell, A T (Oxford U) 1875 *I, S*, 1876 *I*
Middleton, B B (Birkenhead Park) 1882 *I*, 1883 *I*
Middleton, J A (Richmond) 1922 *S*
Miles, J H (Leicester) 1903 *W*
Millett, H (Richmond) 1920 *F*
Mills, F W (Marlborough N) 1872 *S*, 1873 *S*
Mills, S G F (Gloucester) 1981 *Arg* 1,2, 1983 *W*, 1984 *SA* 1, *A*
Mills, W A (Devonport A) 1906 *W, I, S, F, SA*, 1907 *F, W, I, S*, 1908 *F, W*
Milman, D L K (Bedford) 1937 *W*, 1938 *W, I, S*
Milton, C H (Camborne S of M) 1906 *I*
Milton, J G (Camborne S of M) 1904 *W, I, S*, 1905 *S*, 1907 *I*
Milton, W H (Marlborough N) 1874 *S*, 1875 *I*
Mitchell, F (Blackheath) 1895 *W, I, S*, 1896 *W, I, S*
Mitchell, W G (Richmond) 1890 *W, S, I*, 1891 *W, I, S*, 1893 *S*
Mobbs, E R (Northampton) 1909 *A, W, F, I, S*, 1910 *I, F*
Moberley, W O (Ravenscourt Park) 1872 *S*
Moore, B C (Nottingham, Harlequins) 1987 *S*, [*A, J, W*], 1988 *F, W, S, I* 1,2, *A* 1, 2, *Fj, A*, 1989 *S, I, F, W, R, Fj*, 1990 *I, F, W, S, Arg* 1,2, 1991 *W, S, I, F, Fj, A*, [*NZ, It, F, S, A*], 1992 *S, I, F, W, SA*, 1993 *F, W, S, I, NZ*, 1994 *S, I, F, W, SA* 1,2, *R, C*, 1995 *I, F, W, S*, [*Arg, It, WS* (R), *A, NZ, F*]
Moore, E J (Blackheath) 1883 *I, S*
Moore, N J N H (Bristol) 1904 *W, I, S*
Moore, P B C (Blackheath) 1951 *W*
Moore, W K T (Leicester) 1947 *W, I*, 1949 *F, S*, 1950 *I, F, S*
Mordell, R J (Rosslyn Park) 1978 *W*
Morfitt, S (W Hartlepool) 1894 *W, I, S*, 1896 *W, I, S*
Morgan, J R (Hawick) 1920 *W*
Morgan, W G D (Medicals, Newcastle) 1960 *W, I, F, S*, 1961 *SA, W, I, F, S*
Morley, A J (Bristol) 1972 *SA*, 1973 *NZ* 1, *W, I*, 1975 *S, A* 1,2
Morris, A D W (United Services, RN) 1909 *A, W, F*
Morris, C D (Liverpool St Helens, Orrell) 1988 *A*, 1989 *S, I, F, W*, 1992 *S, I, F, W, C, SA*, 1993 *F, W, S, I*, 1994 *F, W, SA* 1,2, *R*, 1995 *S* (t), [*Arg, WS, A, NZ, F*]
Morrison, P H (Cambridge U) 1890 *W, S, I*, 1891 *I*
Morse, S (Marlborough N) 1873 *S*, 1874 *S*, 1875 *S*
Mortimer, W (Marlborough N) 1899 *W*
Morton, H J S (Blackheath) 1909 *I, S*, 1910 *W, I*
Moss, F (Broughton) 1885 *W, I*, 1886 *W*
Mullins, A R (Harlequins) 1989 *Fj*
Mycock, J (Sale) 1947 *W, I, S, F*, 1948 *A*
Myers, E (Bradford) 1920 *I, S*, 1921 *W, I*, 1922 *W, I, F, S*, 1923 *W, I, S, F*, 1924 *W, I, F, S*, 1925 *S, F*
Myers, H (Keighley) 1898 *I*

Nanson, W M B (Carlisle) 1907 *F, W*
Nash, E H (Richmond) 1875 *I*
Neale, B A (Rosslyn Park) 1951 *I, F, S*
Neale, M E (Blackheath) 1912 *F*
Neame, S (O Cheltonians) 1879 *S, I*, 1880 *I, S*
Neary, A (Broughton Park) 1971 *W, I, F, S* (2[1C]), *P*, 1972 *W, I, F, S, SA*, 1973 *NZ* 1, *W, I, F, S, NZ* 2, *A*, 1974 *S, I, F, W*, 1975 *I, F, W, S, A* 1, 1976 *A, W, S, I, F*, 1977 *I*, 1978 *F* (R), 1979 *S, I, F, NZ*, 1980 *I, F, W, S*
Nelmes, B G (Cardiff) 1975 *A* 1,2, 1978 *W, S, I, NZ*
Newbold, C J (Blackheath) 1904 *W, I, S*, 1905 *W, I, S*
Newman, S C (Oxford U) 1947 *F*, 1948 *A, W*
Newton, A W (Blackheath) 1907 *S*
Newton, P A (Blackheath) 1882 *S*
Newton-Thompson, J O (Oxford U) 1947 *S, F*
Nichol, W (Brighouse R) 1892 *W, S*
Nicholas, P L (Exeter) 1902 *W*
Nicholson, B E (Harlequins) 1938 *W, I*
Nicholson, E S (Leicester) 1935 *W, I, S*, 1936 *NZ, W*
Nicholson, E T (Birkenhead Park) 1900 *W, I*
Nicholson, T (Rockcliff) 1893 *I*
Ninnes, B F (Coventry) 1971 *W*
Norman, D J (Leicester) 1932 *SA, W*
North, E H G (Blackheath) 1891 *W, I, S*
Northmore, S (Millom) 1897 *I*
Novak, M J (Harlequins) 1970 *W, S, F*
Novis, A L (Blackheath) 1929 *S, F*, 1930 *W, I, F*, 1933 *I, S*

Rimmer, G (Waterloo) 1949 *W, I*, 1950 *W*, 1951 *W, I, F*, 1952 *SA, W*, 1954 *W, NZ, I, S*
Rimmer, L I (Bath) 1961 *SA, W, I, F, S*
Ripley, A G (Rosslyn Park) 1972 *W, I, F, S, SA*, 1973 *NZ* 1*, W, I, F, S, NZ* 2*, A*, 1974 *S, I, F, W*, 1975 *I, F, S, A* 1,2, 1976 *A, W, S*
Risman, A B W (Loughborough Coll) 1959 *W, I, F, S*, 1961 *SA, W, I, F*
Ritson, J A S (Northern) 1910 *F, S*, 1912 *F*, 1913 *SA, W, F, I, S*
Rittson-Thomas, G C (Oxford U) 1951 *W, I, F*
Robbins, G L (Coventry) 1986 *W, S*
Robbins, P G D (Oxford U, Moseley, Coventry) 1956 *W, I, S, F*, 1957 *W, I, F, S*, 1958 *W, A, I, S*, 1960 *W, I, F, S*, 1961 *SA, W*, 1962 *S*
Roberts, A D (Northern) 1911 *W, F, I, S*, 1912 *I, S, F*, 1914 *I*
Roberts, E W (RNE Coll) 1901 *W, I*, 1905 *NZ*, 1906 *W, I*, 1907 *S*
Roberts, G D (Harlequins) 1907 *S*, 1908 *F, W*
Roberts, J (Sale) 1960 *W, I, F, S*, 1961 *SA, W, I, F, S*, 1962 *W, I, F, S*, 1963 *W, I, F, S*, 1964 *NZ*
Roberts, R S (Coventry) 1932 *I*
Roberts, S (Swinton) 1887 *W, I*
Roberts, V G (Penryn, Harlequins) 1947 *F*, 1949 *W, I, F, S*, 1950 *I, F, S*, 1951 *W, I, F, S*, 1956 *W, I, S, F*
Robertshaw, A R (Bradford) 1886 *W, I, S*, 1887 *W, S*
Robinson, A (Blackheath) 1889 *M*, 1890 *W, S, I*
Robinson, E T (Coventry) 1954 *S*, 1961 *I, F, S*
Robinson, G C (Percy Park) 1897 *I, S*, 1898 *I*, 1899 *W*, 1900 *I, S*, 1901 *I, S*
Robinson, J J (Headingley) 1893 *S*, 1902 *W, I, S*
Robinson, R A (Bath) 1988 *A* 2, *Fj, A*, 1989 *S, I, F, W*, 1995 *SA*
Robson, A (Northern) 1924 *W, I, F, S*, 1926 *W*
Robson, M (Oxford U) 1930 *W, I, F, S*
Rodber, T A K (Army, Northampton) 1992 *S, I*, 1993 *NZ*, 1994 *I, F, W, SA* 1,2, *R, C*, 1995 *I, F, W, S*, [*Arg, It, WS* (R), *A, NZ, F*], *SA, WS*, 1996 *W S* (R), *I* (t), *It, Arg*, 1997 *S, I, F, W, A* 1
Rogers, D P (Bedford) 1961 *I, F, S*, 1962 *W, I, F*, 1963 *W, I, F, S, NZ* 1,2, *A*, 1964 *NZ, W, I, F, S*, 1965 *W, I, F, S*, 1966 *W, I, F, S*, 1967 *A, S, W, NZ*, 1969 *I, F, S, W*
Rogers, J H (Moseley) 1890 *W, S, I*, 1891 *S*
Rogers, W L Y (Blackheath) 1905 *W, I*
Rollitt, D M (Bristol) 1967 *I, F, S, W*, 1969 *I, F, S, W*, 1975 *S, A* 1,2
Roncoroni, A D S (West Herts, Richmond) 1933 *W, I, S*
Rose, W M H (Cambridge U, Coventry, Harlequins) 1981 *I, F*, 1982 *A, S, I*, 1987 *I, F, W, S*, [*A*]
Rossborough, P A (Coventry) 1971 *W*, 1973 *NZ* 2, *A*, 1974 *S, I*, 1975 *I, F*
Rosser, D W A (Wasps) 1965 *W, I, F, S*, 1966 *W*
Rotherham, Alan (Richmond) 1883 *W, S*, 1884 *W, S*, 1885 *W, I*, 1886 *W, I, S*, 1887 *W, I, S*
Rotherham, Arthur (Richmond) 1898 *S, W*, 1899 *W, I, S*
Roughley, D (Liverpool) 1973 *A*, 1974 *S, I*
Rowell, R E (Leicester) 1964 *W*, 1965 *W*
Rowley, A J (Coventry) 1932 *SA*
Rowley, H C (Manchester) 1879 *S, I*, 1880 *I, S*, 1881 *I, W, S*, 1882 *I, S*
Rowntree, G C (Leicester) 1995 *S* (t), [*It, WS*], *WS*, 1996 *F, W, S, I, It, Arg*, 1997 *S, I, F, W, A* 1
Royds, P M R (Blackheath) 1898 *S, W*, 1899 *W*
Royle, A V (Broughton R) 1889 *M*
Rudd, E L (Liverpool) 1965 *W, I, S*, 1966 *W, I, S*
Russell, R F (Leicester) 1905 *NZ*
Rutherford, D (Percy Park, Gloucester) 1960 *W, I, F, S*, 1961 *SA*, 1965 *W, I, F, S*, 1966 *W, I, F, S*, 1967 *NZ*
Ryalls, H J (New Brighton) 1885 *W, I*
Ryan, D (Wasps, Newcastle) 1990 *Arg* 1,2, 1992 *C,* 1998 *S*
Ryan, P H (Richmond) 1955 *W, I*

Sadler, E H (Army) 1933 *I, S*
Sagar, J W (Cambridge U) 1901 *W, I*
Salmon, J L B (Harlequins) 1985 *NZ* 1,2, 1986 *W, S*, 1987 *I, F, W, S*, [*A, J, US, W*]
Sample, C H (Cambridge U) 1884 *I*, 1885 *I*, 1886 *S*
Sanders, D L (Harlequins) 1954 *W, NZ, I, S, F*, 1956 *W, I, S, F*
Sanders, F W (Plymouth A) 1923 *I, S, F*
Sandford, J R P (Marlborough N) 1906 *I*
Sangwin, R D (Hull and E Riding) 1964 *NZ, W*

Sargent, G A F (Gloucester) 1981 *I* (R)
Savage, K F (Northampton) 1966 *W, I, F, S*, 1967 *A, I, F, S, W, NZ*, 1968 *W, F, S*
Sawyer, C M (Broughton) 1880 *S*, 1881 *I*
Saxby, L E (Gloucester) 1932 *SA, W*
Schofield, J W (Manchester) 1880 *I*
Scholfield, J A (Preston Grasshoppers) 1911 *W*
Schwarz, R O (Richmond) 1899 *S*, 1901 *W, I*
Scorfield, E S (Percy Park) 1910 *F*
Scott, C T (Blackheath) 1900 *W, I*, 1901 *W, I*
Scott, E K (St Mary's Hospital, Redruth) 1947 *W*, 1948 *A, W, I, S*
Scott, F S (Bristol) 1907 *W*
Scott, H (Manchester) 1955 *F*
Scott, J P (Rosslyn Park, Cardiff) 1978 *F, W, S, I, NZ*, 1979 *S* (R), *I, F, W, NZ*, 1980 *I, F, W, S*, 1981 *W, S, I, F, Arg* 1,2, 1982 *I, F, W*, 1983 *F, W, S, I, NZ*, 1984 *S, I, F, W, SA* 1,2
Scott, J S M (Oxford U) 1958 *F*
Scott, M T (Cambridge U) 1887 *I*, 1890 *S, I*
Scott, W M (Cambridge U) 1889 *M*
Seddon, R L (Broughton R) 1887 *W, I, S*
Sellar, K A (United Services, RN) 1927 *W, I, S*, 1928 *A, W, I, F*
Sever, H S (Sale) 1936 *NZ, W, I, S*, 1937 *W, I, S*, 1938 *W, I, S*
Shackleton, I R (Cambridge U) 1969 *SA*, 1970 *I, W, S*
Sharp, R A W (Oxford U, Wasps, Redruth) 1960 *W, I, F, S*, 1961 *I, F*, 1962 *W, I, F*, 1963 *W, I, F, S*, 1967 *A*
Shaw, C H (Moseley) 1906 *S, SA*, 1907 *F, W, I, S*
Shaw, F (Cleckheaton) 1898 *I*
Shaw, J F (RNE Coll) 1898 *S, W*
Shaw, S D (Bristol, Wasps) 1996 *It, Arg*, 1997 *S, I, F, W, A* 1, *SA* (R)
Sheasby, C M A (Wasps) 1996 *It, Arg*, 1997 *W* (R), *Arg* 1 (R), 2 (R), *SA* (R), *NZ* 2 (t)
Sheppard, A (Bristol) 1981 *W* (R), 1985 *W*
Sherrard, C W (Blackheath) 1871 *S*, 1872 *S*
Sherriff, G A (Saracens) 1966 *S*, 1967 *A, NZ*
Shewring, H E (Bristol) 1905 *I, NZ*, 1906 *W, S, F, SA*, 1907 *F, W, I, S*
Shooter, J H (Morley) 1899 *I, S*, 1900 *I, S*
Shuttleworth, D W (Headingley) 1951 *S*, 1953 *S*
Sibree, H J H (Harlequins) 1908 *F*, 1909 *I, S*
Silk, N (Harlequins) 1965 *W, I, F, S*
Simms, K G (Cambridge U, Liverpool, Wasps) 1985 *R, F, S, I, W*, 1986 *I, F*, 1987 *I, F, W*, [*A, J, W*], 1988 *F, W*
Simpson, C P (Harlequins) 1965 *W*
Simpson, P D (Bath) 1983 *NZ*, 1984 *S*, 1987 *I*
Simpson, T (Rockcliff) 1902 *S*, 1903 *W, I, S*, 1904 *I, S*, 1905 *I, S*, 1906 *S, SA*, 1909 *F*
Skinner, M G (Harlequins) 1988 *F, W, S, I* 1,2, 1989 *Fj*, 1990 *I, F, W, S, Arg* 1,2, 1991 *Fj* (R), [*US, F, S, A*], 1992 *S, I, F, W*
Sladen, G M (United Services, RN) 1929 *W, I, S*
Sleightholme, J M (Bath) 1996 *F, W, S, I, It, Arg*, 1997 *S, I, F, W, Arg* 1,2
Slemen, M A C (Liverpool) 1976 *I, F*, 1977 *S, I, F, W*, 1978 *F, W, S, I, NZ*, 1979 *S, I, F, W, NZ*, 1980 *I, F, W, S*, 1981 *W, S, I, F*, 1982 *A, S, I, F, W*, 1983 *NZ*, 1984 *S*
Slocock, L A N (Liverpool) 1907 *F, W, I, S*, 1908 *F, W, I, S*
Slow, C F (Leicester) 1934 *S*
Small, H D (Oxford U) 1950 *W, I, F, S*
Smallwood, A M (Leicester) 1920 *F, I*, 1921 *W, I, S, F*, 1922 *I, S*, 1923 *W, I, S, F*, 1925 *I, S*
Smart, C E (Newport) 1979 *F, W, NZ*, 1981 *S, I, F, Arg* 1,2, 1982 *A, S, I, F, W*, 1983 *F, W, S, I*
Smart, S E J (Gloucester) 1913 *SA, W, F, I, S*, 1914 *W, I, S, F*, 1920 *W, I, S*
Smeddle, R W (Cambridge U) 1929 *W, I, S*, 1931 *F*
Smith, C C (Gloucester) 1901 *W*
Smith, D F (Richmond) 1910 *W, I*
Smith, J V (Cambridge U, Rosslyn Park) 1950 *W, I, F, S*
Smith, K (Roundhay) 1974 *F, W*, 1975 *W, S*
Smith, M J K (Oxford U) 1956 *W*
Smith, S J (Sale) 1973 *I, F, S, A*, 1974 *I, F*, 1975 *W* (R), 1976 *F*, 1977 *F* (R), 1979 *NZ*, 1980 *I, F, W, S*, 1981 *W, S, I, F, Arg* 1,2, 1982 *A, S, I, F, W*, 1983 *F, W, S*
Smith, S R (Richmond) 1959 *W, F, S*, 1964 *F, S*
Smith, S T (Wasps) 1985 *R, F, S, I, W, NZ* 1,2, 1986 *W, S*
Smith, T H (Northampton) 1951 *W*
Soane, F (Bath) 1893 *S*, 1894 *W, I, S*
Sobey, W H (O Millhillians) 1930 *W, F, S*, 1932 *SA, W*
Solomon, B (Redruth) 1910 *W*

Sparks, R H W (Plymouth A) 1928 *I, F, S*, 1929 *W, I, S*, 1931 *I, S, F*
Speed, H (Castleford) 1894 *W, I, S*, 1896 *S*
Spence, F W (Birkenhead Park) 1890 *I*
Spencer, J (Harlequins) 1966 *W*
Spencer, J S (Cambridge U, Headingley) 1969 *I, F, S, W, SA*, 1970 *I, W, S, F*, 1971 *W, I, S* (2[1C]), *P*
Spong, R S (O Millhillians) 1929 *F*, 1930 *W, I, F, S*, 1931 *F*, 1932 *SA, W*
Spooner, R H (Liverpool) 1903 *W*
Springman, H H (Liverpool) 1879 *S*, 1887 *S*
Spurling, A (Blackheath) 1882 *I*
Spurling, N (Blackheath) 1886 *I, S*, 1887 *W*
Squires, P J (Harrogate) 1973 *F, S, NZ* 2, *A*, 1974 *S, I, F, W*, 1975 *I, F, W, S, A* 1,2, 1976 *A, W*, 1977 *S, I, F, W*, 1978 *F, W, S, I, NZ*, 1979 *S, I, F, W*
Stafford R C (Bedford) 1912 *W, I, S, F*
Stafford, W F H (RE) 1874 *S*
Stanbury, E (Plymouth A) 1926 *W, I, S*, 1927 *W, I, S, F*, 1928 *A, W, I, F, S*, 1929 *W, I, S, F*
Standing, G (Blackheath) 1883 *W, I*
Stanger-Leathes, C F (Northern) 1905 *I*
Stark, K J (O Alleynians) 1927 *W, I, S, F*, 1928 *A, W, I, F, S*
Starks, A (Castleford) 1896 *W, I*
Starmer-Smith, N C (Harlequins) 1969 *SA*, 1970 *I, W, S, F*, 1971 *S* (C), *P*
Start, S P (United Services, RN) 1907 *S*
Steeds, J H (Saracens) 1949 *F, S*, 1950 *I, F, S*
Steele-Bodger, M R (Cambridge U) 1947 *W, I, S, F*, 1948 *A, W, I, S, F*
Steinthal, F E (Ilkley) 1913 *W, F*
Stevens, C B (Penzance-Newlyn, Harlequins) 1969 *SA*, 1970 *I, W, S*, 1971 *P*, 1972 *W, I, F, S, SA*, 1973 *NZ* 1, *W, I, F, S, NZ* 2, *A*, 1974 *S, I, F, W*, 1975 *I, F, W, S*
Still, E R (Oxford U, Ravenscourt P) 1873 *S*
Stimpson, T R G (Newcastle) 1996 *It*, 1997 *S, I, F, W, A* 1, *NZ* 2 (t + R)
Stirling, R V (Leicester, RAF, Wasps) 1951 *W, I, F, S*, 1952 *SA, W, S, I, F*, 1953 *W, I, F, S*, 1954 *W, NZ, I, S, F*
Stoddart, A E (Blackheath) 1885 *W, I*, 1886 *W, I, S*, 1889 *M*, 1890 *W, I*, 1893 *W, S*
Stoddart, W B (Liverpool) 1897 *W, I, S*
Stokes, F (Blackheath) 1871 *S*, 1872 *S*, 1873 *S*
Stokes, L (Blackheath) 1875 *I*, 1876 *S*, 1877 *I, S*, 1878 *S*, 1879 *S, I*, 1880 *I, S*, 1881 *I, W, S*
Stone, F le S (Blackheath) 1914 *F*
Stoop, A D (Harlequins) 1905 *S*, 1906 *S, F, SA*, 1907 *F, W*, 1910 *W, I, S*, 1911 *W, F, I, S*, 1912 *W, S*
Stoop, F M (Harlequins) 1910 *S*, 1911 *F, I*, 1913 *SA*
Stout, F M (Richmond) 1897 *W, I*, 1898 *I, S, W*, 1899 *I, S*, 1903 *S*, 1904 *W, I, S*, 1905 *W, I, S*
Stout, P W (Richmond) 1898 *S, W*, 1899 *W, I, S*
Stringer, C (Wasps) 1982 *A* (R), 1983 *NZ* (R), 1984 *SA* 1 (R), *A*, 1985 *R*
Strong, E L (Oxford U) 1884 *W, I, S*
Summerscales, G E (Durham City) 1905 *NZ*
Sutcliffe, J W (Heckmondwike) 1889 *M*
Swarbrick, D W (Oxford U) 1947 *W, I, F*, 1948 *A, W*, 1949 *I*
Swayne, D H (Oxford U) 1931 *W*
Swayne, J W R (Bridgwater) 1929 *W*
Swift, A H (Swansea) 1981 *Arg* 1,2, 1983 *F, W, S*, 1984 *SA* 2
Syddall, J P (Waterloo) 1982 *I*, 1984 *A*
Sykes, A R V (Blackheath) 1914 *F*
Sykes, F D (Northampton) 1955 *F, S*, 1963 *NZ* 2, *A*
Sykes, P W (Wasps) 1948 *F*, 1952 *S, I, F*, 1953 *W, I, F*
Syrett, R E (Wasps) 1958 *W, A, I, F*, 1960 *W, I, F, S*, 1962 *W, I, F*

Tallent, J A (Cambridge U, Blackheath) 1931 *S, F*, 1932 *SA, W*, 1935 *I*
Tanner, C C (Cambridge U, Gloucester) 1930 *S*, 1932 *SA, W, I, S*
Tarr, F N (Leicester) 1909 *A, W, F*, 1913 *S*
Tatham, W M (Oxford U) 1882 *S*, 1883 *W, I, S*, 1884 *W, I, S*
Taylor, A S (Blackheath) 1883 *W, I*, 1886 *W, I*
Taylor, E W (Rockcliff) 1892 *I*, 1893 *I*, 1894 *W, I, S*, 1895 *W, I, S*, 1896 *W, I*, 1897 *W, I, S*, 1899 *I*
Taylor, F (Leicester) 1920 *F, I*
Taylor, F M (Leicester) 1914 *W*
Taylor, H H (Blackheath) 1879 *S*, 1880 *S*, 1881 *I, W*, 1882 *S*

Taylor, J T (W Hartlepool) 1897 *I*, 1899 *I*, 1900 *I*, 1901 *W, I*, 1902 *W, I, S*, 1903 *W, I*, 1905 *S*
Taylor, P J (Northampton) 1955 *W, I*, 1962 *W, I, F, S*
Taylor, R B (Northampton) 1966 *W*, 1967 *I, F, S, W, NZ*, 1969 *F, S, W, SA*, 1970 *I, W, S, F*, 1971 *S* (2[1C])
Taylor, W J (Blackheath) 1928 *A, W, I, F, S*
Teague, M C (Gloucester, Moseley) 1985 *F* (R), *NZ* 1, 2, 1989 *S, I, F, W, R*, 1990 *F, W, S*, 1991 *W, S, I, F, Fj, A, [NZ, It, F, S, A]*, 1992 *SA*, 1993 *F, W, S, I*
Teden, D E (Richmond) 1939 *W, I, S*
Teggin, A (Broughton R) 1884 *I*, 1885 *W*, 1886 *I, S*, 1887 *I, S*
Tetley, T S (Bradford) 1876 *S*
Thomas, C (Barnstaple) 1895 *W, I, S*, 1899 *I*
Thompson, P H (Headingley, Waterloo) 1956 *W, I, S, F*, 1957 *W, I, F, S*, 1958 *W, A, I, F, S*, 1959 *W, I, F, S*
Thomson, G T (Halifax) 1878 *S*, 1882 *I, S*, 1883 *W, I, S*, 1884 *I, S*, 1885 *I*
Thomson, W B (Blackheath) 1892 *W*, 1895 *W, I, S*
Thorne, J D (Bristol) 1963 *W, I, F*
Tindall, V R (Liverpool U) 1951 *W, I, F, S*
Tobin, F (Liverpool) 1871 *S*
Todd, A F (Blackheath) 1900 *I, S*
Todd, R (Manchester) 1877 *S*
Toft, H B (Waterloo) 1936 *S*, 1937 *W, I, S*, 1938 *W, I, S*, 1939 *W, I, S*
Toothill, J T (Bradford) 1890 *S, I*, 1891 *W, I*, 1892 *W, I, S*, 1893 *W, I, S*, 1894 *W, I*
Tosswill, L R (Exeter) 1902 *W, I, S*
Touzel, C J C (Liverpool) 1877 *I, S*
Towell, A C (Bedford) 1948 *F*, 1951 *S*
Travers, B H (Harlequins) 1947 *W, I*, 1948 *A, W*, 1949 *F, S*
Treadwell, W T (Wasps) 1966 *I, F, S*
Trick, D M (Bath) 1983 *I*, 1984 *SA* 1
Tristram, H B (Oxford U) 1883 *S*, 1884 *W, S*, 1885 *W*, 1887 *S*
Troop, C L (Aldershot S) 1933 *I, S*
Tucker, J S (Bristol) 1922 *W*, 1925 *NZ, W, I, S, F*, 1926 *W, I, F, S*, 1927 *W, I, S, F*, 1928 *A, W, I, F, S*, 1929 *W, I, F*, 1930 *W, I, F, S*, 1931 *W*
Tucker, W E (Blackheath) 1894 *W, I*, 1895 *W, I, S*
Tucker, W E (Blackheath) 1926 *I*, 1930 *W, I*
Turner, D P (Richmond) 1871 *S*, 1872 *S*, 1873 *S*, 1874 *S*, 1875 *I, S*
Turner, E B (St George's Hospital) 1876 *I*, 1877 *I*, 1878 *I*
Turner, G R (St George's Hospital) 1876 *S*
Turner, H J C (Manchester) 1871 *S*
Turner, M F (Blackheath) 1948 *S, F*
Turquand-Young, D (Richmond) 1928 *A, W*, 1929 *I, S, F*
Twynam, H T (Richmond) 1879 *I*, 1880 *I*, 1881 *W*, 1882 *I*, 1883 *I*, 1884 *W, I, S*

Ubogu, V E (Bath) 1992 *C, SA*, 1993 *NZ*, 1994 *S, I, F, W, SA* 1,2, *R, C*, 1995 *I, F, W, S, [Arg, WS, A, NZ, F], SA*
Underwood, A M (Exeter) 1962 *W, I, F, S*, 1964 *I*
Underwood, R (Leicester, RAF) 1984 *I, F, W, A*, 1985 *R, F, S, I, W*, 1986 *W, I, F, W, S, [A, J, W]*, 1988 *F, W, S, I* 1,2, *A* 1,2, *Fj, A*, 1989 *S, I, F, W, R, Fj*, 1990 *I, F, W, S, Arg* 3, 1991 *W, S, I, F, Fj, A, [NZ, It, US, F, S, A]*, 1992 *S, I, F, W, SA*, 1993 *F, W, S, I, NZ*, 1994 *S, I, F, W, SA* 1,2, *R, C*, 1995 *I, F, W, S, [Arg, It, WS, A, NZ, F], SA, WS*, 1996 *F, W, S, I*
Underwood, T (Leicester, Newcastle) 1992 *C, SA*, 1993 *S, I, NZ*, 1994 *S, I, W, SA* 1,2, *R, C*, 1995 *I, F, W, S, [Arg, It, A, NZ]*, 1996 *Arg*, 1997 *S, I, F, W*
Unwin, E J (Rosslyn Park, Army) 1937 *S*, 1938 *W, I, S*
Unwin, G T (Blackheath) 1898 *S*
Uren, R (Waterloo) 1948 *I, S, F*, 1950 *I*
Uttley, R M (Gosforth) 1973 *I, F, S, NZ* 2, *A*, 1974 *I, F, W*, 1975 *F, W, S, A* 1,2, 1977 *S, I, F, W*, 1978 *NZ* 1979 *S*, 1980 *I, F, W, S*

Valentine J (Swinton) 1890 *W*, 1896 *W, I, S*
Vanderspar, C H R (Richmond) 1873 *S*
Van Ryneveld, C B (Oxford U) 1949 *W, I, F, S*
Varley, H (Liversedge) 1892 *S*
Vassall, H (Blackheath) 1881 *W, S*, 1882 *I, S*, 1883 *W*
Vassall, H H (Blackheath) 1908 *I*
Vaughan, D B (Headingley) 1948 *A, W, I, S*, 1949 *I, F, S*, 1950 *W*
Vaughan-Jones, A (Army) 1932 *I, S*, 1933 *W*
Verelst, C L (Liverpool) 1876 *I*, 1878 *I*
Vernon, G F (Blackheath) 1878 *S, I*, 1880 *I, S*, 1881 *I*
Vickery, G (Aberavon) 1905 *I*

ENGLISH INTERNATIONAL RECORDS
(*up to 30 April 1998*)

MATCH RECORDS

MOST CONSECUTIVE TEST WINS

10 1882 *W*, 1883 *I, S*, 1884 *W, I, S*,
   1885 *W, I*, 1886 *W, I*
10 1994 *R, C*, 1995 *I, F, W, S, Arg, It,
   WS, A*

MOST CONSECUTIVE TESTS WITHOUT DEFEAT

P	W	D	Period
12	10	2	1882–87
11	10	1	1922–24
10	6	4	1878–82
10	10	0	1994–95

MOST POINTS IN A MATCH
by the team

Pts	Opp	Venue	Year
60	J	Sydney	1987
60	C	Twickenham	1994
60	W	Twickenham	1998
58	R	Bucharest	1989
58	Fj	Twickenham	1989
54	R	Twickenham	1994
54	It	Twickenham	1996

by a player
30 by C R Andrew v Canada at
   Twickenham   1994
27 by C R Andrew v South Africa
   at Pretoria   1994
24 by J M Webb v Italy at
   Twickenham   1991
24 by C R Andrew v Romania at
   Twickenham   1994
24 by C R Andrew v Scotland at
   Twickenham   1995
24 by C R Andrew v Argentina at
   Durban   1995

MOST TRIES IN A MATCH
by the team

T	Opp	Venue	Year
13	W	Blackheath	1881
10	J	Sydney	1987
10	Fj	Twickenham	1989
9	F	Paris	1906
9	F	Richmond	1907
9	F	Paris	1914
9	R	Bucharest	1989

by a player
5 by D Lambert v France at
   Richmond   1907
5 by R Underwood v Fiji at
   Twickenham   1989
4 by G W Burton v Wales at
   Blackheath   1881
4 by A Hudson v France at Paris   1906
4 by R W Poulton v France at Paris 1914
4 by C Oti v Romania at Bucharest 1989

MOST CONVERSIONS IN A MATCH
by the team

C	Opp	Venue	Year
8	R	Bucharest	1989
7	W	Blackheath	1881
7	J	Sydney	1987
7	Arg	Twickenham	1990
7	W	Twickenham	1998

by a player
8 by S D Hodgkinson v Romania
   at Bucharest   1989
7 by J M Webb v Japan at Sydney   1987
7 by S D Hodgkinson v Argentina
   at Twickenham   1990
7 by P J Grayson v Wales at
   Twickenham   1998

MOST PENALTY GOALS IN A MATCH
by the team

P	Opp	Venue	Year
7	W	Cardiff	1991
7	S	Twickenham	1995
6	W	Twickenham	1986
6	C	Twickenham	1994
6	Arg	Durban	1995
6	S	Murrayfield	1996
6	I	Twickenham	1996

by a player
7 by S D Hodgkinson v Wales at
   Cardiff   1991
7 by C R Andrew v Scotland at
   Twickenham   1995
6 by C R Andrew v Wales at
   Twickenhan   1986
6 by C R Andrew v Canada at
   Twickenham   1994
6 by C R Andrew v Argentina at
   Durban   1995

6 by P J Grayson v Scotland at Murrayfield		1996
6 by P J Grayson v Ireland at Twickenham		1996

MOST DROPPED GOALS IN A MATCH
by the team

D	Opp	Venue	Year
2	I	Twickenham	1970
2	F	Paris	1978
2	F	Paris	1980
2	R	Twickenham	1985
2	Fj	Suva	1991
2	Arg	Durban	1995
2	F	Paris	1996

by a player

2 by R Hiller v Ireland at Twickenham	1970
2 by A G B Old v France at Paris	1978
2 by J P Horton v France at Paris	1980
2 by C R Andrew v Romania at Twickenham	1985
2 by C R Andrew v Fiji at Suva	1991
2 by C R Andrew v Argentina at Durban	1995
2 by P J Grayson v France at Paris	1996

CAREER RECORDS

MOST CAPPED PLAYERS

Caps	Player	Career
85	R Underwood	1984–96
72	W D C Carling	1988–97
71	C R Andrew	1985–97
64	B C Moore	1987–95
63	J Leonard	1990–98
58	P J Winterbottom	1982–93
55	W A Dooley	1985–93
52	J C Guscott	1989–98
48	D Richards	1986–96
43	A Neary	1971–80

MOST CONSECUTIVE TESTS

Tests	Player	Span
44	W D C Carling	1989–95
40	J Leonard	1990–95
36	J V Pullin	1968–75
33	W B Beaumont	1975–82
30	R Underwood	1992–96

MOST TESTS AS CAPTAIN

Tests	Captain	Span
59	W D C Carling	1988–96
21	W B Beaumont	1978–82
13	W W Wakefield	1924–26
13	N M Hall	1949–55
13	R E G Jeeps	1960–62
13	J V Pullin	1972–75

MOST TESTS IN INDIVIDUAL POSITIONS

Full-back J M Webb	33	1987–93
Wing R Underwood	85	1984–96
Centre W D C Carling	72	1988–97
Fly-half C R Andrew	70	1985–97
Scrum-half R J Hill	29	1984–91
Prop J Leonard	63	1990–98
Hooker B C Moore	63★	1987–95
Lock W A Dooley	55	1985–93
Flanker P J Winterbottom	58	1982–93
No 8 D Richards	47★	1986–96

★ *excludes an appearance as a temporary replacement*

MOST POINTS IN TESTS

Pts	Player	Tests	Career
396	C R Andrew	71	1985–97
296	J M Webb	33	1987–93
240	W H Hare	25	1974–84
210	R Underwood	85	1984–96
210	P J Grayson	15	1995–98

MOST TRIES IN TESTS

Tries	Player	Tests	Career
49	R Underwood	85	1984–96
18	C N Lowe	25	1913–23
18	J C Guscott	52	1989–98
13	T Underwood	25	1992–97
12	W D C Carling	72	1988–97

MOST CONVERSIONS IN TESTS

Cons	Player	Tests	Career
41	J M Webb	33	1987–93
35	S D Hodgkinson	14	1989–91
33	C R Andrew	71	1985–97
23	P J Grayson	15	1995–98
17	L Stokes	12	1875–81

MOST PENALTY GOALS IN TESTS

Pens	Player	Tests	Career
86	C R Andrew	71	1985–97
67	W H Hare	25	1974–84

66	J M Webb	33	1987–93
48	P J Grayson	15	1995–98
43	S D Hodgkinson	14	1989–91

MOST DROPPED GOALS IN TESTS

Drops	Player	Tests	Career
21	C R Andrew	71	1985–97
5	P J Grayson	15	1995–98
4	J P Horton	13	1978–84

INTERNATIONAL CHAMPIONSHIP RECORDS

Record	Detail		Set
Most points in season	146	in four matches	1998
Most tries in season	20	in four matches	1914
Highest score	60	60–26 v Wales	1998
Biggest win	40	46–6 v Ireland	1997
Highest score conceded	37	12–37 v France	1972
Biggest defeat	27	6–33 v Scotland	1986
Most appearances	50	R Underwood	1984–96
Most points in matches	185	C R Andrew	1985–97
Most points in season	67	J M Webb	1992
Most points in match	24	C R Andrew	v Scotland, 1995
Most tries in matches	18	C N Lowe	1913–23
	18	R Underwood	1984–96
Most tries in season	8	C N Lowe	1914
Most tries in match	4	R W Poulton	v France, 1914
Most cons in matches	21	P J Grayson	1996–98
Most cons in season	14	P J Grayson	1998
Most cons in match	7	P J Grayson	v Wales, 1998
Most pens in matches	50	W H Hare	1974–84
Most pens in season	18	S D Hodgkinson	1991
Most pens in match	7	S D Hodgkinson	v Wales, 1991
	7	C R Andrew	v Scotland, 1995
Most drops in matches	9	C R Andrew	1985–97
Most drops in season	3	P J Grayson	1996
Most drops in match	2	R Hiller	v Ireland, 1970
	2	A G B Old	v France, 1978
	2	J P Horton	v France, 1980
	2	P J Grayson	v France, 1996

MAJOR TOUR RECORDS

Record	Detail	Year	Place
Most individual points	58 by C R Andrew	1994	South Africa
Most points in match	36 by W N Bennett	1975 v W Australia	Perth
Most tries in match	4 by A J Morley	1975 v W Australia	Perth
	4 by P S Preece	1975 v NSW	Sydney

MISCELLANEOUS RECORDS

Record	Holder	Detail
Longest Test career	G S Pearce	14 seasons, 1978–79 to 1991–92
Youngest Test cap	H C C Laird	18 yrs 134 days in 1927
Oldest Test cap	F Gilbert	38 yrs in 1923

ENGLISH INTERNATIONAL CAREER RECORDS (*up to 30 April 1998*)

Player	Debut	Caps since last season	Caps	T	C	PG	DG	Pts
J Mallinder	1997 v Arg	1997 *Arg* 1,2	2	0	0	0	0	0
T R G Stimpson	1996 v It	1997 *A* 1, *NZ* 2 (t&R)	7	1	0	1	0	8
N D Beal	1996 v Arg	1997 *A* 1	2	0	0	0	0	0
M B Perry	1997 v A	1997 *A* 2, *NZ* 1, *SA*, *NZ* 2, 1998 *W, S, I*	7	1	0	0	0	5
D L Rees	1997 v A	1997 *A* 2, *NZ* 1, *SA*, *NZ* 2, 1998 *F, W*	6	3	0	0	0	15
A A Adebayo	1996 v It	1997 *Arg* 1,2, *A* 2, *NZ* 1, 1998 *S*	6	2	0	0	0	10
J Bentley	1988 v I	1997 *A* 1, *SA*	4	1	0	0	0	4
J M Sleightholme	1996 v F	1997 *Arg* 1,2	12	4	0	0	0	20
T Underwood	1992 v C		25	13	0	0	0	65
J P Wilkinson	1998 v I	1998 *I* (R)	1	0	0	0	0	0
N J J Greenstock	1997 v Arg	1997 *Arg* 1,2, *A* 1, *SA*	4	2	0	0	0	10
W J H Greenwood	1997 v A	1997 *A* 2, *NZ* 1, *SA*, *NZ* 2, 1998 *F, W, S, I*	8	1	0	0	0	5
P R de Glanville	1992 v SA	1997 *Arg* 1,2, *A* 1,2, *NZ* 1,2, 1998 *W* (R), *S* (R), *I* (R)	30	5	0	0	0	25
J C Guscott	1989 v R	1998 *F, W, S, I*	52	18	0	0	2	83
M J Catt	1994 v W	1997 *Arg* 1, *A* 1,2, *NZ* 1, *SA*, 1998 *F, W* (R), *I*	29	4	14	20	2	114
P J Grayson	1995 v WS	1997 *A* 2 (t), *SA* (R), *NZ* 2, 1998 *F, W, S, I*	15	1	23	48	5	210
A D King	1997 v Arg	1997 *Arg* 2 (R)	1	1	0	0	0	5
M S Mapletoft	1997 v Arg	1997 *Arg* 2	1	0	0	1	0	3
M J S Dawson	1995 v WS	1997 *A* 1, *SA*, *NZ* 2 (R), 1998 *W* (R), *S, I*	11	2	0	0	0	10
A C T Gomarsall	1996 v It	1997 *Arg* 2 (R)	6	4	0	0	0	20
A S Healey	1997 v I	1997 *A* 1 (R),2 (R), *NZ* 1 (R), *SA* (R), *NZ* 2, 1998 *F, W, S, I*	11	2	0	0	0	10
K P P Bracken	1993 v NZ	1997 *Arg* 1,2, *A* 2, *NZ* 1,2, 1998 *F, W*	19	2	0	0	0	10
M P Regan	1995 v SA	1997 *A* 1, *NZ* 2 (R), 1998 *F*	15	0	0	0	0	0
R Cockerill	1997 v Arg	1997 *Arg* 1 (R),2, *A* 2 (t&R), *NZ* 1, *SA*, *NZ* 2, 1998 *W, S, I*	9	1	0	0	0	5
D E West	1998 v F	1998 *F* (R), *S* (R)	2	0	0	0	0	0
A E Long	1997 v A	1997 *A* 2	1	0	0	0	0	0
P B T Greening	1996 v It	1997 *Arg* 1	3	0	0	0	0	0
K P Yates	1997 v Arg	1997 *Arg* 1,2	2	0	0	0	0	0

W R Green	1997 v A	1997 *A* 2	1	0	0	0	0	0
D J Garforth	1997 v W	1997 *Arg* 1,2, *A* 1, *NZ* 1, *SA*, *NZ* 2, 1998 *F*, *W* (R), *S*, *I*	11	0	0	0	0	0
J Leonard	1990 v Arg	1997 *A* 2, *NZ* 1, *SA*, *NZ* 2, 1998 *F*, *W*, *S*, *I*	63	1	0	0	0	5
P J Vickery	1998 v W	1998 *W*	1	0	0	0	0	0
G C Rowntree	1995 v S	1997 *A* 1	15	0	0	0	0	0
G S Archer	1996 v S	1997 *A* 2, *NZ* 1, *SA*, *NZ* 2, 1998 *F*, *W*, *S*, *I*	10	0	0	0	0	0
D J Grewcock	1997 v Arg	1997 *Arg* 2, *SA*, 1998 *W* (R), *S*(R), *I* (R)	5	1	0	0	0	5
M Haag	1997 v Arg	1997 *Arg* 1,2	2	0	0	0	0	0
N C Redman	1984 v A	1997 *Arg* 1, *A* 1	20	1	0	0	0	4
M O Johnson	1993 v F	1997 *A* 2, *NZ* 1,2, 1998 *F*, *W*, *S*, *I*	37	1	0	0	0	5
S D Shaw	1996 v It	1997 *A* 1, *SA* (R)	8	0	0	0	0	0
M J Corry	1997 v Arg	1997 *Arg* 1,2	2	0	0	0	0	0
R A Hill	1997 v S	1997 *A* 1,2, *NZ* 1, *SA*, *NZ* 2, 1998 *F*, *W*	11	3	0	0	0	15
L B N Dallaglio	1995 v SA	1997 *A* 1,2, *NZ* 1, *SA*, *NZ* 2, 1998 *F*, *W*, *S*, *I*	20	5	0	0	0	25
T A K Rodber	1992 v S	1997 *A* 1	32	3	0	0	0	15
N A Back	1994 v S	1997 *NZ* 1 (R), *SA*, *NZ* 2, 1998 *F*, *W*, *S*, *I*	12	3	0	0	0	15
B B Clarke	1992 v SA	1997 *Arg* 1,2, *A* 1 (R)	33	3	0	0	0	15
D Ryan	1990 v Arg	1998 *S*	4	1	0	0	0	4
A J Diprose	1997 v Arg	1997 *Arg* 1,2, *A* 2, *NZ* 1, 1998 *W* (R), *S* (R), *I*	7	1	0	0	0	5
C M A Sheasby	1996 v It	1997 *Arg* 1 (R), 2 (R), *SA* (R), *NZ* 2 (t)	7	1	0	0	0	5

ENGLISH CLUBS 1997-98

Bath

Year of formation 1865
Ground Recreation Ground, London Road, Bath BA2 6PW Tel: Bath (01225) 325200
Colours Blue, white and black hoops; royal blue shorts
Captain 1997-98 A D Nicol
Allied Dunbar Leagues 1997-98 Div 1 3rd **Tetley's Bitter Cup 1997-98** Lost 17-29 to Richmond (5th round)

How are the mighty fallen, on and off the field! The fly-on-the-wall documentary left them ridiculed and reviled and on the domestic competition front things went from bad to worse. First, there was no domestic silverware for the second season running, and while they did lift the Heineken European Cup by beating a talented Brive outfit to become the first English winners, it was hardly executed with their usual style and panache. Bath's appearance in the English knock-out competition turned the sponsors inaugural season into the 'Tetley's Biter Cup'. The fourth-round clash with London Scottish had had its own problems anyway, first because it should have been played at Richmond Athletic ground, but the Exiles could not agree a compromise with groundshare partners Richmond, and then it was postponed for a week because of the weather. Maybe someone was trying to tell the two clubs something, because when it finally got under way Kevin Yates, as it subsequently emerged, bit a chunk out of Scottish flanker Simon Fenn's left ear. A later hearing, after Scottish had cited the whole of the Bath front row when no-one had the guts to own up to the appalling deed, saw Yates banned for six months; he was also fined by the club. Bath just scraped through that tie but did not survive the fifth round where they lost to Richmond.

Their Allied Dunbar Premiership campaign was not a lot better. They opened with a home defeat, lost a further eight games – one a record defeat when they conceded 50 points at Saracens – and only a rally towards the end saw them secure third place on points difference.

They were without the services of their England centre Jeremy Guscott until the New Year; they also lost coach Clive Woodward at the start when he took the England job. Andy Robinson took over, with Jon Callard adopting a player-coach role. They sold Jon Sleightholme to Northampton, Steve Ojomoh to Gloucester, signed Ieuan Evans, appointed Andy Nicol as captain and saw not a thing of Simon Geoghegan as the Ireland wing battled with a wicked toe injury. There were a couple of big money deals with Adidas and Blackthorn Cider; and Federico Mendez and German Llanes were shipped back home to Argentina at the end of the season.

League Record 1997-98

Date	Venue	Opponents	Result	Scorers
23 Aug	H	Newcastle	13-20	*T:* Perry *C:* Catt *P:* Catt 2
30 Aug	A	Harlequins	27-20	*T:* Butland, pen try *C:* Butland *P:* Butland 5
18 Oct	H	Bristol	44-15	*T:* Adebayo, Callard, de Glanville, Earnshaw, Nicol, Peters, Sleightholme *C:* Callard 2, Catt *P:* Callard
25 Oct	A	Leicester	22-33	*T:* Webster *C:* Callard *P:* Callard 5
1 Nov	H	Richmond	47-31	*T:* Evans 2, de Glanville, Nicol, Redman, Tsimba, Thomas *C:* Callard 2, Balshaw *P:* Callard 2
14 Dec	A	Saracens	23-50	*T:* Butland, Regan *C:* Callard 2 *P:* Callard 3
27 Dec	A	Sale	13-11	*T:* Butland *C:* Catt *P:* Catt 2
30 Dec	H	Northampton	26-3	*T:* Earnshaw, Nicol *C:* Callard 2 *P:* Callard 4

11 Feb	H	Gloucester	47-3	T: Peters 3, Adebayo, de Glanville, Earnshaw
				C: Callard 4 P: Callard 3
14 Feb	H	Wasps	43-27	T: Guscott, Evans, de Glanville, Lyle, pen try
				C: Callard 3 P: Callard 4
28 Feb	H	Harlequins	39-13	T: Catt, Earnshaw, Evans, Nicol, Peters,
				Ubogu C: Callard 3 P: Callard
8 Mar	A	Bristol	22-16	T: Nicol, Perry, Ubogu C: Callard 2
				P: Callard
14 Mar	A	Leicester	16-5	T: Guscott C: Butland P: Butland 3
28 Mar	A	London Irish	49-35	T: Evans 2, Nicol 2, Guscott, Peters, pen try
				C: Callard 4 P: Callard, Butland
10 Apr	H	Saracens	13-29	T: Adebayo C: Callard P: Callard 2
13 Apr	A	Richmond	14-32	T: Balshaw P: Callard 3
18 Apr	A	Gloucester	17-27	T: Earnshaw, Peters C: Butland 2 P: Butland
25 Apr	H	Sale	19-29	T: Guscott , Butland P: Butland 3
28 Apr	H	London Irish	20-3	T: Butland, Evans, Nicol C: Callard
				P: Callard
2 May	A	Northampton	15-16	T: Adebayo, Nicol C: Callard P: Callard
11 May	A	Newcastle	15-20	P: Callard 5
17 May	A	Wasps	31-17	T: Peters, Adebayo, Evans, Guscott
				C: Callard 4 P: Callard

Bedford

Year of formation 1886
Ground Goldington Road, Bedford, MK40 3NF Tel: Bedford (01234) 347980
Colours Oxford and Cambridge blue hoops; navy blue shorts
Captain 1997-98 R Kirke/A Murdoch/R Straeuli
Allied Dunbar Leagues 1997-98 Div 2 *Winners – promoted* **Tetley's Bitter Cup 1997-98**
Lost 26-31 to Northampton (4th round)

So Frank Warren's shrewd investment paid off. With a pairing of Geoff Cooke, the former England manager and coach, and Paul Turner to run things, there was little doubt that they would progress. They not only finished as Division Two champions but also reached the final of the Cheltenham & Gloucester Cup, where they were beaten by Gloucester. The league was not quite a one-horse race, but the Allied Dunbar Premiership Two title chase was still won at a canter. Technically they won it twice. The first time they had enough points but were docked two for fielding three overseas players – centre Alistair Murdoch (Australia), Western Samoan Junior Paramore, and South Africa's Rudi Straeuli – for the last 10 minutes of their game against Fylde in January. They had so completely dominated affairs in the Second Division that they went undefeated for 18 straight games, and that first defeat was by a point at Rotherham in April.

Theirs was a remarkable season but sadly they lost a remarkable player. The 39-year-old Paul Turner, to whom they owe so much, retired from playing. He will be missed.

League Record 1997-98

Date	Venue	Opponents	Result	Scorers
30 Aug	H	Rotherham	18-11	P: Rayer 6
13 Sep	A	Exeter	32-17	T: Murdoch, Whetstone, Yapp, pen try
				C: Rayer 3 P: Rayer 2
20 Sep	H	L Scottish	45-33	T: Whetstone 2, Murdoch, O'Neill, Oliver,
				Turner C: Rayer 3 P: Rayer 3
27 Sep	A	Coventry	22-15	T: Whetstone C: Rayer P: Rayer 4
				D: Yapp
4 Oct	H	Waterloo	34-21	T: Underwood 2, Murdoch C: Pfluger 2
				P: Pfluger 5

11 Oct	A	Moseley	35-16	*T:* Forster 2, Boyd, Yapp *C:* Rayer 3 *P:* Rayer 3
18 Oct	H	W Hartlepool	22-9	*T:* pen try *C:* Rayer *P:* Rayer 5
25 Oct	A	L Scottish	22-15	*T:* Rayer *C:* Rayer *P:* Rayer 5
8 Nov	H	Coventry	77-3	*T:* Whetstone 3, Rayer 2, Deans, Forster, Murdoch, Pechey, Turner, Underwood *C:* Rayer 8 *P:* Rayer 2
13 Dec	A	Waterloo	28-14	*T:* Crabb, Hinkins, Kirke, Whetstone *C:* Rayer 4
20 Dec	H	Moseley	32-16	*T:* Murdoch 2, Rayer 2, Forster *C:* Rayer 2 *P:* Rayer
27 Dec	A	Fylde	67-7	*T:* Forster 3, Whetstone 2, Deans, Murdoch, Murray, pen try *C:* Rayer 8 *P:* Rayer 2
17 Jan	H	Fylde	50-14	*T:* Forster 4, Hatley, Murray, Platford, Underwood *C:* Rayer 5
31 Jan	H	Orrell	47-22	*T:* Turner 2, Webster 2, Stone, Underwood *C:* Rayer 4 *P:* Rayer 3
14 Feb	A	Wakefield	24-13	*T:* Paramore, Wells, Whetsone, Winters *C:* Rayer 2
7 Mar	A	Blackheath	37-13	*T:* Whetsone 2, Crabb, Forster, Underwood *C:* Rayer 3 *P:* Rayer 2
14 Mar	H	Wakefield	36-10	*T:* Crabb, Ewens, Whiston, Winters, pen try *C:* Rayer 4 *P:* Rayer
28 Mar	A	Orrell	29-16	*T:* Deans, Forster, Paramore, Whetstone, Winters *C:* Rayer 2
11 Apr	A	Rotherham	17-18	*T:* pen try, Whetstone *C:* Rayer 2 *P:* Rayer
18 Apr	H	Exeter	16-3	*T:* Rayer, Whetstone *P:* Rayer 2
25 Apr	H	Blackheath	72-31	*T:* Stone 3, Brading, Ewens, Forster, Hatley, Howard, Murray, Paramore, Underwood *C:* Rayer 7 *P:* Rayer
2 May	A	W Hartlepool	29-48	*T:* Brown, Ewens, Paramore, Straeuli, Winters *C:* Rayer 2

Blackheath

Year of formation 1858
Ground Rectory Field, Charlton Road, Blackheath, London SE3 8SR Tel: 0181 858 1578
Colours Red and black hoops with blue lines; black shorts
Captain 1997-98 J A Gallagher
Allied Dunbar Leagues 1997-98 Div 2 9th   **Tetley's Bitter Cup 1997-98** Lost 31-59 to
Saracens (4th round)

A sad reflection of the new age and the downside of professionalism, was the news
that the 'Club' have had to put their trading company into the hands of the receiver
after the long hoped for, and innovative, merger with Auckland fell through. The
New Zealanders withdrew their proposed £500,000 investment in April, after
Blackheath fell £300,000 short on their side of the deal. They now plan to run a
team (like so many others in the lower financial reaches) on a reduced budget. That
will not help their precarious status in the league. They did finish clear of the danger
zone by some four points, but by the same token there was a substantial gap between
them and the club above them, Waterloo. Their defence was the second worst in the
division, conceding more than 600 points, one of only two to do so, the other being
bottom side Fylde, who managed to top 700. They were unfortunate in coming up
against eventual winners Saracens in the Tetley's Bitter Cup, but they did give a
good account of themselves, going down 31-59.

League Record 1997-98

Date	Venue	Opponents	Result	Scorers
30 Aug	A	Orrell	17-26	T: Coyne, Wilkins C: Braithwaite 2 P: Braithwaite
7 Sep	A	L Scottish	6-34	P: Braithwaite D: Braithwaite
13 Sep	H	Wakefield	29-27	T: Clarke 2, Fitzgerald, Graham C: Braithwaite 3 P: Braithwaite
20 Sep	H	Fylde	50-16	T: Clarke 4, Wilkins 2, Ridgway, Schuster C: Braithwaite 3, Schuster 2
27 Sep	A	Waterloo	16-51	T: Ridgway C: Schuster P: Schuster 3
4 Oct	H	Coventry	28-27	T: Clarke C: Schuster P: Schuster 6 D: Penaluna
11 Oct	A	W Hartlepool	21-32	T: Clarke, Fitzgerald, Graham P: Penaluna 2
18 Oct	H	Moseley	11-19	T: Clarke P: Penaluna 2
25 Oct	A	Fylde	31-6	T: Clarke, pen try, McCorduck C: Calder 2 P: Calder 4
8 Nov	H	Waterloo	14-15	T: Ridgway, Russell C: Braithwaite 2
13 Dec	A	Coventry	22-24	T: Ridgway C: Braithwaite P: Braithwaite 5
20 Dec	H	W Hartlepool	25-22	T: Clarke, Pawson, Ridgway C: Braithwaite 2 P: Braithwaite 2
17 Jan	H	L Scottish	34-25	T: Christian, Clarke, Gallagher, Pawson, Ridgway C: Braithwaite 3 P: Braithwaite
31 Jan	A	Exeter	18-20	T: Clarke, Griffiths, Penaluna P: Braithwaite
14 Feb	H	Rotherham	18-31	T: Percival, Wilkins C: Braithwaite P: Braithwaite 2
28 Feb	A	Moseley	16-29	T: Percival C: Mason P: Mason 3
7 Mar	H	Bedford	13-37	T: Cooke C: Mason P: Mason 2
14 Mar	A	Rotherham	10-40	T: Pawson C: Mason P: Mason
28 Mar	H	Exeter	26-15	T: Fitzgerald, Boyle C: Mason 2 P: Mason 4
11 Apr	A	Orrell	14-32	T: Wilkins P: Mason 3
18 Apr	A	Wakefield	24-21	T: Griffiths, Mason, Pawson C: Mason 3 P: Mason
25 Apr	A	Bedford	31-72	T: Stanley 2, Braithwaite, Pawson C: Mason 4 P: Mason

Bristol

Year of formation 1888
Ground Memorial Ground, Filton Avenue, Horfield, Bristol, BS7 0AQ Tel: Bristol (0117) 951448
Colours Navy blue and white stripes
Captain 1997-98 R N Jones
Allied Dunbar Leagues 1997-98 Div 1 12th; lost Division One/Two play-off with London Scottish 40-46 on aggregate – *relegated*   **Tetley's Bitter Cup 1997-98** Lost 12-14 to Worcester (4th round)

Shipshape they are not. Not any more. Their play-off defeat against London Scottish was the saddest of ends for this once proud club whose style of rugby had been dubbed 'Bristol fashion'. As the realisation that for the first time in their history they are no longer in the top flight dawned on them, so the recriminations began. If the troubles are rooted in the relative successes of a decade ago though, there were ample problems this past season. They lost Mark Regan to Bath, Martin Corry to Leicester, parted company with Alan Davies and found themselves floundering again in a financial mire that has dogged them since the game went professional. Their lack of a backer of the calibre of Saracens' Nigel Wray or Wasps' Chris Wright became too much of a handicap. While they could always turn, and frequently did, to chairman Arthur Holmes, it was not satisfactory. A proposed deal to sell the Memorial Ground in a lease-back deal with Amtrak fell through. This chronic shortage of cash meant that it was impossible to attract big enough names to the club to help put bums on seats and points in the bag. Finally a consortium of around 120 businessman with ties either to the rugby club or Bristol Rovers, ploughed £2.3 million into purchasing the Memorial Ground to secure its future.

But it was an unequal struggle on the playing front. Captain Robert Jones had his work cut out to lift a side whose morale was at its nadir. Two victories in 22 league matches was the record of a very poor club. The first humiliation came when they were knocked out of the Tetley's Bitter Cup, a competition in which they had featured in prominently during the 1980s, winning it in 1983, by Jewson National League One side Worcester in the fourth round. Brian Ashton having turned down the vacant coaching job, caretakers Darryl Jones and his assistant Dave Egerton were handed the reins, but they did not have the time, nor indeed the playing staff, to prevent the inevitable. If anyone had harboured hopes that Bristol would escape the drop, as they had done in the play-offs against Bedford in the previous season, they were quickly disabused of the notion by London Scottish who triumphed 46-40 over the two legs.

League Record 1997-98

Date	Venue	Opponents	Result	Scorers
23 Aug	A	Gloucester	13-35	*T:* Corkery *C:* Burke *P:* Burke 2
30 Aug	H	Wasps	21-38	*T:* Lewsey, Tiueti, pen try *C:* Burke 3
18 Oct	A	Bath	15-44	*T:* Maggs, Pearce *C:* Burke *P:* Burke
26 Oct	H	Northampton	22-15	*T:* Tiueti *C:* Burke *P:* Burke 3 *D:* Burke 2
2 Nov	A	Saracens	9-31	*P:* Burke 3
9 Nov	A	Sale	0-76	
13 Dec	H	Richmond	12-13	*P:* Burke 4
27 Dec	H	Newcastle	8-50	*T:* Tiueti *P:* Burke
31 Dec	A	Harlequins	40-38	*T:* Burke, Lewsey, Browning, Tiueti *C:* Burke 4 *P:* Burke 4
18 Jan	H	Gloucester	13-14	*T:* pen try *C:* Burke *P:* Burke 2
1 Feb	A	Wasps	18-32	*T:* Lewsey, Tiueti *C:* Burke *P:* Burke 2
14 Feb	H	Saracens	20-37	*T:* Larkin, Lewsey *C:* Burke 2 *P:* Burke 2
20 Feb	A	London Irish	23-38	*T:* Larkin, Tiueti *C:* Burke 2 *P:* Burke 3
28 Feb	H	Leicester	24-27	*T:* Baber, Larkin, Pearce *C:* Burke 3 *P:* Burke
8 Mar	H	Bath	16-22	*T:* Burke *C:* Burke *P:* Burke 3
14 Mar	A	Northampton	12-35	*T:* Baber, Yapp *C:* Lewsey
10 Apr	A	Richmond	3-43	*P:* Hull
15 Apr	H	Sale	15-25	*T:* Tiueti, Martin *C:* Hull *P:* Hull
19 Apr	H	London Irish	5-17	*T:* Martin
26 Apr	A	Newcastle	18-43	*T:* Yapp 2, Moore *P:* Lewsey
3 May	H	Harlequins	19-26	*T:* Lewsey, Landreau *P:* Lewsey 2, Hull
10 May	A	Leicester	25-34	*T:* Corkery, Chesney, Rollitt *C:* Burke 2 *P:* Armstrong 2
Play-Offs				
17 May	A	L Scottish	25-29	*T:* Chesney, Hull, Maggs *C:* Burke 2 *P:* Burke 2
23 May	H	L Scottish	15-17	*P:* Burke 5

Coventry

Year of formation 1874
Ground Barker Butts Lane, Coundon Road, Coventry, CV6 1DU Tel: Coventry (01203) 601174
Colours Navy blue and white stripes; blue shorts
Captain 1997-98 R J K Hardwick

Allied Dunbar Leagues 1997-98 Div 2 7th **Tetley's Bitter Cup 1997-98** Lost 14-50 to Leicester (4th round)

There was little to smile about as 78 years at Coundon Road ended with an overwhelming vote to sell the ground to Bryant Homes for a sum reputed to be between £1.2 and £2 million, and find somewhere else to set up home. But if anyone was surprised at the financial problems, they should not have been, not once the contents of a confidential document were made public. In it it was alleged that Eves was being paid £120,000 per annum and that the average player received £50,000. The document, which was stolen from the club's office and then faxed to members and the media, detailed not just wages, but expenses as well. The total revealed that with win bonuses on top the total liability to staff could have exceeded £1 million, despite a trading loss in the previous financial year in excess of £400,000. In the end there were only 11 victories in the league, while their cup run ended in round four with a 50-14 thrashing at home to Leicester.

League Record 1997-98

Date	Venue	Opponents	Result	Scorers
30 Aug	H	Moseley	20-12	T: Horrobin P: Harris 5
7 Sep	H	Exeter	29-8	T: Dawson, McAdam, Smallwood C: Brown P: Brown 4
13 Sep	A	Fylde	23-15	T: Horrobin P: Harris 6
20 Sep	A	Wakefield	17-6	T: Eves, Curtis, Smallwood C: Brown
27 Sep	H	Bedford	15-22	T: Patten, Robinson C: Brown P: Brown
4 Oct	A	Blackheath	27-28	T: Curtis, Robinson C: Harris P: Harris 5
11 Oct	H	Rotherham	18-12	P: Harris 4 D: Gallagher, Harris
18 Oct	A	Orrell	13-38	T: Kilford 2 P: Brown
25 Oct	H	Wakefield	24-17	T: Blackmore, Dawson, Irwin P: Harris 3
8 Nov	A	Bedford	3-77	P: Harris
13 Dec	H	Blackheath	24-22	T: Hewlett, Robinson C: Harris P: Harris 4
20 Dec	A	Rotherham	8-46	T: Kilford P: Harris
17 Jan	A	Exeter	14-18	T: Kilford P: Brown 3
24 Jan	H	Orrell	21-30	P: Harris 6 D: Harris
31 Jan	H	W Hartlepool	21-16	T: Curtis, Gallagher C: Brown P: Brown D: Brown, Gallagher
14 Feb	A	L Scottish	18-18	T: Dulay 2 C: Brown P: Brown 2
7 Mar	H	Waterloo	41-33	T: Minshull 3, Gallagher, Horrobin, Smallwood C: Brown P: Brown, Harris D: Gallagher
14 Mar	H	L Scottish	37-10	T: Dawson 2, Smallwood 2, Jones C: Brown 3 P: Brown 2
28 Mar	A	W Hartlepool	31-42	T: Horrobin 3, Addleton, Gallagher C: Harris 2, Brown
18 Apr	H	Fylde	16-7	T: Eves C: Harris P: Harris 3
22 Apr	A	Moseley	3-31	P: Brown
25 Apr	A	Waterloo	21-24	T: Irwin, Lloyd C: Brown P: Brown 3

Exeter

Year of formation 1872
Ground County Ground, Church Road, St Thomas, Exeter, Devon EX2 9BQ
Tel: Exeter (01392) 78759
Colours Black; black shorts
Captain 1997-98 Robert Baxter
Allied Dunbar Leagues 1997-98 Div 2 11th **Tetley's Bitter Cup 1997-98** Lost 10-34 to Newcastle (4th round)

It would be tempting, after such a harrowing year, just to sit back as one of the fortunate beneficiaries of the collective will of the senior clubs, and enjoy the fact that because the Allied Dunbar Premiership has been increased for the coming season, there is really nothing to worry about. But that is unlikely to be the Exeter approach, not now they have a new rugby manager. If Ian Bremner's CV is anything to go by, the club and its supporters can expect a turnaround this year. Bremner has coached the Swedish national side and Ireland under-21 as well as being involved in London Irish, Cardiff and Aberavon among other notable institutions.

The acquisition of Craig Barrow from Bristol last year paid off and while Andy Maunder's departure was a sad end to a distinguished career, it is improbable that the club will repeat the mistakes of last season, when they were badly let down by the likes of Canadian Matthew McLoughlin, who made just six appearances, and the French-Iranian Farhad Tchahardehi, who blazed in one match, scoring all 23 points in the C&G Cup against Orrell, but was not seen again.

League Record 1997-98

Date	Venue	Opponents	Result	Scorers
30 Aug	A	Wakefield	19-15	*T:* Woodman *C:* Fabian *P:* Fabian 4
7 Sep	A	Coventry	8-29	*T:* Woodman *P:* Fabian
13 Sep	H	Bedford	17-32	*T:* John *P:* Fabian 2 *D:* Patidar 2
20 Sep	H	Waterloo	24-20	*T:* Fabian 2 *C:* Fabian *P:* Fabian 3 *D:* McLoughlin
27 Sep	A	Moseley	22-23	*T:* Wasley *C:* Fabian *P:* Fabian 5
4 Oct	H	W Hartlepool	19-20	*T:* Alvis *C:* Fabian *P:* Fabian 4
11 Oct	A	Fylde	10-18	*T:* pen try *C:* Fabian *P:* Fabian
18 Oct	H	L Scottish	16-22	*T:* Maunder, Southern *P:* Patidar *D:* Tchahardehi
25 Oct	A	Waterloo	13-44	*T:* Hodinson *C:* Fabian *P:* Fabian 2
8 Nov	H	Moseley	10-20	*T:* Thomas *C:* Fabian *P:* Fabian
13 Dec	A	W Hartlepool	14-34	*T:* Armstrong, Barrow *C:* Fabian 2
20 Dec	H	Fylde	24-15	*T:* Alvis, Curry *C:* Fabian *P:* Fabian 4
17 Jan	H	Coventry	18-14	*T:* Alvis, Richard Baxter *C:* Fabian *P:* Fabian 2
24 Jan	A	L Scottish	10-22	*T:* Woodman, Birkett
31 Jan	H	Blackheath	20-18	*T:* Alvis, Richard Baxter *C:* Fabian 2 *P:* Fabian 2
14 Feb	A	Orrell	3-38	*P:* Fabian
7 Mar	H	Rotherham	8-33	*T:* Barrow *P:* Fabian
14 Mar	H	Orrell	17-14	*T:* Woodman *P:* Fabian 4
28 Mar	A	Blackheath	15-26	*T:* Alvis, Carter *C:* Fabian *P:* Fabian
11 Apr	H	Wakefield	17-30	*T:* Carter, Gibbons, John *C:* Fabian
18 Apr	A	Bedford	3-16	*P:* Fabian
25 Apr	A	Rotherham	27-50	*T:* Alvis, Carter *C:* Fabian *P:* Fabian 5

Fylde

Year of formation 1919
Ground Woodlands Memorial Ground, Blackpool Road, Ansdell, Lytham St Annes, Lancashire FY8 1AB Tel: Lytham (01253) 734733
Colours Claret, white and gold hoops; white shorts
Captain 1997-98 G Russell
Allied Dunbar Leagues 1997-98 Div 2 12th   **Tetley's Bitter Cup 1997-98** Lost 8-34 to Wasps (5th round)

The good news is that Andy Macfarlane is staying on as rugby manager, despite the disastrous nature of last year. They finished bottom of the Allied Dunbar Premiership and unsurprisingly conceded more points than any of the other clubs. A record of 710 points against, while scoring a meagre 258, tells its own sorry tale. If Bedford were the runaway leaders of the Second Division, Fylde were not remotely challenged for last place. They had some bizarre luck; their two overseas players, Karl Kumbier and Brian McCarthy ended up playing for Germany and Canada respectively just when their club needed them.

They did finish top of something – unfortunately it was the Premiership's disciplinary table. A sending-off, two sin bins and 19 yellow cards needs no further explanation. The imposition of pay cuts to players in January was not well received and outside-half Steve Gough, their leading points-scorer the season before, was expected to leave over the summer. The final straw came in the Lancashire Cup final when they lost to Manchester of Jewson League Two North. A year to forget.

League Record 1997-98

Date	Venue	Opponents	Result	Scorers
30 Aug	A	L Scottish	9-35	*P:* Gough 3
13 Sep	H	Coventry	15-23	*T:* Duggan, Preston *C:* Gough *P:* Gough
20 Sep	A	Blackheath	16-50	*T:* Evans *C:* Gough *P:* Gough 3
27 Sep	H	Rotherham	18-25	*T:* Barclay, Gough *C:* Gough *P:* Gough 2
4 Oct	A	Orrell	9-35	*P:* Peacock 3
11 Oct	H	Exeter	18-10	*P:* Peacock 6
18 Oct	A	Wakefield	17-35	*T:* Preston *P:* Peacock 4
25 Oct	H	Blackheath	6-31	*P:* Gough 2
8 Nov	A	Rotherham	16-32	*T:* Gough *C:* Gough *P:* Gough 3
13 Dec	H	Orrell	9-21	*P:* Peacock 3
20 Dec	A	Exeter	15-24	*T:* Moffatt, Scott *C:* Gough *P:* Gough
27 Dec	H	Bedford	7-67	*T:* pen try *C:* Gough
17 Jan	A	Bedford	14-50	*T:* Preston *P:* Peacock 2 *D:* Peacock
31 Jan	H	Waterloo	10-25	*T:* Preston 2
14 Feb	A	W Hartlepool	12-66	*T:* McCarthy, Preston *C:* Gough
28 Feb	H	Wakefield	10-30	*T:* Scott *C:* Peacock *P:* Peacock
14 Mar	H	W Hartlepool	8-34	*T:* Moffat *P:* Peacock
28 Mar	A	Waterloo	12-22	*T:* Duggan, Evans *C:* Gough
4 Apr	H	Moseley	14-13	*T:* Evans *P:* Gough 3
11 Apr	H	L Scottish	7-22	*T:* Barclay *C:* Gough
18 Apr	A	Coventry	7-16	*T:* Ashurst *C:* Gough
25 Apr	A	Moseley	9-44	*P:* Gough 3

Gloucester

Year of formation 1873
Ground Kingsholm, Kingsholm Road, Gloucester, GL1 3AX Tel: Gloucester (01452) 381087
Colours Cherry and white stripes; black shorts
Captain 1997-98 P Glanville
Allied Dunbar Leagues 1997-98 Div 1 7th   **Tetley's Bitter Cup 1997-98** Lost 11-30 to Northampton (5th round)

A gleam of silverware at last. It may only have been the inaugural Cheltenham and Gloucester Cup, but what an appropriate trophy to win. And in fact there were more tangible signs that coach Richard Hill is getting it right on the field with the number of players selected for representative honours. Indeed England's tour party set off for the southern hemisphere with no fewer than seven Kingsholm regulars, Scott Benton, Phil Vickery, Phil Greening, Tony Windo, Rob Fidler, Dave Sims and Steve Ojomoh. That is a testament to what Hill is achieving for the club. The former Bath and England scrum-half has made some astute signings in his time in charge. His latest, Simon Mannix, made at the end of the season, could prove to be as good as the earlier ones, Ojomoh, Army wing Brian Johnson and centre Terry Fanolua, who so endeared himself to The Shed. This trio contributed to some cracking matches at home for the crowd to enjoy. The frustrating thing is that this is one side that suffers from collective homesickness. Winning away proved too difficult most of the time and it is a very real problem which Hill recognises and is determined to stamp out this time around.

Gloucester's finest hour probably came at Franklin's Gardens when they sneaked away with a rare victory over Northampton in the final Allied Dunbar Premiership match of the season which would have sealed a place in the top six, a highly respectable position considering that away handicap for the rest of the time, except that they were then docked two points for fielding an ineligible player.

In Europe they finished a creditable second in their pool, while the Tetley's Bitter Cup contained a nostalgic visit (and another rare away win) when they travelled to Old Deer Park for a fourth round tie against London Welsh. The Exiles had them worried for a while, stealing into the lead, but superior skills told and wing Robert Jewell ran in a couple of tries to underline his potential. As it happened the fifth round took them up to Franklin's Gardens for a first visit to the Saints, who marched all over Gloucester and ended their cup hopes in convincing style. But the C&G Cup final gave them no problems, even though that too was at Franklin's Gardens. Bedford may have dominated the Second Division, but they were unable to assert themselves over Gloucester. Hill promised more signings over the summer and, the way they ended the season, the players promise much in the year ahead.

League Record 1997-98

Date	Venue	Opponents	Result	Scorers
23 Aug	H	Bristol	35-13	T: P St-André 2, Fidler, Windo C: Mapletoft 3 P: Mapletoft 3
30 Aug	A	Leicester	16-33	T: Mapletoft C: Mapletoft P: Mapletoft 2 D: Mapletoft
19 Oct	H	London Irish	29-7	T: Fanolua, Tombs, pen try, Glanville C: Mapletoft 3 P: Mapletoft
26 Oct	A	Saracens	24-42	T: Tombs 2, Fanolua, Mapletoft C: Mapletoft 2
2 Nov	H	Harlequins	16-17	T: Fanolua C: Mapletoft P: Mapletoft 3
14 Dec	A	Newcastle	27-37	T: Catling, Jewell, pen try C: Mapletoft 3 P: Mapletoft 2
27 Dec	H	Richmond	26-20	T: Lumsden, Fanolua, Johnson C: Mapletoft P: Mapletoft 3
30 Dec	A	Sale	24-24	T: Vickery, pen try C: Mapletoft P: Mapletoft 4
11 Jan	A	Wasps	20-26	T: Fanolua, Fortey, Carter C: Mapletoft P: Mapletoft
18 Jan	A	Bristol	14-13	T: Fidler P: Mapletoft 3
1 Feb	H	Leicester	32-25	T: Mapletoft, Benton C: Mapletoft 2 P: Mapletoft 6
11 Feb	A	Bath	3-47	P: Mapletoft
14 Feb	H	Northampton	20-15	T: Fanolua, Lumsden C: Mapletoft 2 P: Mapletoft 2
11 Mar	H	Wasps	22-15	T: Fidler, Johnson, Tombs C: Mapletoft 2 P: Mapletoft
15 Mar	H	Saracens	38-15	T: Fidler, Johnson, Benton, Windo C: Mapletoft 3 P: Mapletoft 4
24 Mar	A	London Irish	19-23	T: Devereux C: Mapletoft P: Mapletoft 3 D: Mapletoft
29 Mar	A	Harlequins	16-36	T: pen try C: Mapletoft P: Mapletoft 3
11 Apr	H	Newcastle	27-29	T: Ojomoh, P St-André C: Mapletoft P: Mapletoft 5
18 Apr	H	Bath	27-17	T: Fidler, P St-André C: Mapletoft P: Mapletoft 5
25 Apr	A	Richmond	22-33	T: Mapletoft, Ojomoh, P St-André C: Mapletoft 2 P: Mapletoft

2 May	H	Sale	31-19	T: McCarthy, Fanolua, Johnson, P St-André
				C: Mapletoft 4 P: Mapletoft
17 May	A	Northampton	24-22	T: Johnson, Mapletoft C: Mapletoft
				P: Mapletoft 4

Harlequins

Year of formation 1866
Ground Stoop Memorial Ground, Craneford Way, Twickenham, Middlesex, TW2 7SQ Tel: 0181 892 0822
Colours Light blue, magenta, chocolate, French grey, black and light green; white shorts
Captain 1997-98 K G M Wood
Allied Dunbar Leagues 1997-98 Div 1 10th   **Tetley's Bitter Cup 1997-98** Lost 26-31 to Wasps (4th round)

It was a troubled season for the so-called top people's club. It may still be that, but it was not the top club, not by any stretch of the imagination. Even Jason Leonard tried to leave at the start of the season. And after it was all over they parted company with Andy Keast, their director of rugby. Financially it was unsound until Peter Beckwith was persuaded to sell out his holding to Australian businessman Duncan Saville for a reputed £3 million. Saville then ploughed a further £1 million into the coffers once he had done the deal. Not long after All Black legend Zinzan Brooke was signed up, a private settlement was agreed with Dick Best, their former director of rugby and Will Carling called it a day. The ex-England captain left in somewhat acrimonious circumstances, which was sad, in the New Year. He was reported to have been interested in joining London rivals Wasps, although that was vigorously denied by the North London club's management.

Strangely a Wasp rejoined Quins. Chris Sheasby returned after a couple of years away. By then Quins had long been eclipsed in the Heineken European Cup, although not before causing a stir by citing Cardiff lock Tony Rees for stamping on Gareth Llewellyn; Cardiff's counter that Thierry Lacroix had kicked their scrum-half was dismissed by the Londoners. Their abysmal quarter-final showing in the European Cup, when they were blitzed by a brilliant Toulouse side who ran in a half century of points, left them with red faces.

The Quins' Tetley's Bitter Cup campaign ended in the fourth round at Wasps, while their attempts to string together some consistent winning performances in the league came to nothing, or at least, third from bottom by the end of an arduous Allied Dunbar Premiership programme. Admittedly there was a gap between themselves and London Irish of four points, but having escaped the ignominy of the play-offs, they were not spared anything when they visited London Irish. The Exiles had every reason to want to beat Quins, since they had just been put in the care of one Dick Best, who had initially gone to Sunbury on a caretaker-consultant basis. Irish certainly took care of Quins. They thrashed them 62-14 – the heaviest defeat Harlequins have suffered in the 11 years of league rugby. By then Brooke had taken over the coaching role from Best's successor Andy Keast.

League Record 1997-98

Date	Venue	Opponents	Result	Scorers
23 Aug	A	Northampton	26-23	T: O'Leary, Carling C: Lacroix 2
				P: Lacroix 4
30 Aug	H	Bath	20-27	T: Ngauamo, Williams C: Lacroix 2
				P: Lacroix 2
18 Oct	A	Richmond	16-37	T: Stewart C: Liley P: Liley 3
25 Oct	H	Sale	52-41	T: O'Leary 2, Bromley, Davison, Jenkins, Leach, Tollett C: Liley 7 D: O'Leary
2 Nov	A	Gloucester	17-16	T: GO Llewellyn, Williams C: Lacroix 2
				P: Lacroix

13 Dec	H	Wasps	53-17	*T:* O'Leary 2, Keyter, Lacroix, Williams, pen try *C:* Lacroix 3, Challinor *P:* Lacroix 3 *D:* Lacroix 2
20 Dec	A	Leicester	3-27	*P:* Lacroix
27 Dec	H	London Irish	26-24	*T:* Davison, Nebbitt *C:* Lacroix 2 *P:* Lacroix 4
31 Dec	H	Bristol	38-40	*T:* Keyter 2, Challinor, Liley, Luger, Ngauamo *C:* Liley 3, Lacroix
11 Jan	A	Saracens	16-25	*T:* Luger *C:* Lacroix *P:* Lacroix 3
18 Jan	H	Northampton	5-30	*T:* Tollett
15 Feb	A	Newcastle	15-43	*T:* Luger, O'Leary *C:* Liley *P:* Liley
28 Feb	A	Bath	13-39	*T:* Luger *C:* Liley *P:* Liley 2
7 Mar	H	Richmond	41-12	*T:* O'Leary 2, Davison, Mensah, Lacroix *C:* Lacroix 5 *P:* Lacroix 2
14 Mar	A	Sale	13-23	*T:* Luger *C:* Lacroix *P:* Lacroix 2
29 Mar	H	Gloucester	36-16	*T:* Mensah, O'Leary, GO Llewellyn, Sheasby, Walshe *C:* Liley 4 *P:* Liley
12 Apr	A	Wasps	26-29	*T:* Liley 2, Ngauamo, Luger *C:* Liley 3
18 Apr	H	Leicester	14-23	*T:* Keyter, Leach *C:* Liley 2
25 Apr	A	London Irish	14-62	*T:* Keyter, pen try *C:* Lacroix, Walshe
29 Apr	H	Saracens	26-28	*T:* Lacroix, Williams *C:* Lacroix 2 *P:* Lacroix 4
3 May	A	Bristol	26-19	*T:* Luger, Wood *C:* Lacroix 2 *P:* Lacroix 4
17 May	H	Newcastle	20-44	*T:* Harries, Luger *C:* Lacroix 2 *P:* Lacroix 2

Leicester

Year of formation 1880
Ground Welford Road, Leicester, LE2 7LF Tel: Leicester (0116) 2541607
Colours Scarlet, green and white stripes; white shorts
Captain 1997-98 M O Johnson
Allied Dunbar Leagues 1997-98 Div 1 4th   **Tetley's Bitter Cup 1997-98** Lost 13-14 to Saracens (5th round)

This was not a good season for Leicester, who were pipped at the post by Bath for third place in the Allied Dunbar Premiership. Their Heineken European Cup assault came to grief at Pau in the quarter-finals of the tournament and, as holders, they lost out by a point to Saracens in the fifth round of the Tetley's Bitter Cup. Altogether a very unhappy season.

The sacking of Bob Dwyer following a lengthy board meeting presaged the entry of Leicester icon Dean Richards, aided by back-row stalwart and another former Tigers captain John Wells, as coach. It ended an 18-month reign by Dwyer who had guided them to a Pilkington Cup final victory, as well as taking them to the Heineken Cup runners-up spot in the previous season. But, significantly, the man who had guided Australia to World Cup victory in 1991, was unable to instil the consistency needed to dominate the Allied Dunbar Premiership. Dwyer's contract was due for renewal anyway and the Leicester board, after consultation with the players and a review of recent results, felt that fresh ideas were needed. The defeat at Gloucester had prompted Dwyer to predict his demise when he said at the time: 'If a player is not producing the goods he should look elsewhere, and if a coach is not producing the goods he should also look elsewhere.' At that point they had just lost to Gloucester.

Richards' first match in charge saw Tigers maul their way to a narrow victory at Bristol, but the consistency was still lacking and by the end of the season there were mutterings of unrest at Welford Road. They had begun the year by signing Martin Corry from Bristol and, even under the threat of legal action over the way the player had left his previous club, they stuck to their guns.

It is debatable whether Waisale Serevi, the Fijian Sevens specialist, was a good signing. He was asked to play out of position at scrum-half and anyway looked out of his depth in the 15-man game. His compatriot Vunibaka turned out to be a pig in a poke and Lewis Capes, the giant son of Olympic shot-putter Geoff, was also no great revelation. There had also been problems with the acquisition of Fritz van Heerden. Tigers were denied his expertise until after their European Cup was over.

League Record 1997-98

Date	Venue	Opponents	Result	Scorers
30 Aug	H	Gloucester	33-16	T: Back, Greenwood, Horak C: Stransky 3
				P: Stransky 4
18 Oct	A	Northampton	6-25	P: Stransky 2
25 Oct	H	Bath	33-22	T: Greenwood, Healey, Stransky
				C: Stransky 3 P: Stransky 4
13 Dec	H	Sale	55-15	T: Horak 2, Gustard, M Johnson, Moody, West,
				pen try C: Stransky 4 P: Stransky 4
16 Dec	A	Richmond	15-32	T: Greenwood, Potter C: Horak P: Horak
20 Dec	H	Harlequins	27-3	T: Back, Greenwood, pen try C: Serevi 2,
				Horak P: Serevi, Horak
26 Dec	A	Saracens	22-21	T: van Heerden C: Stransky P: Stransky 4
				D: Stransky
30 Dec	H	Newcastle	19-25	T: pen try C: Stransky P: Stransky 4
17 Jan	H	Wasps	45-21	T: Healey, Horak, Serevi, Stransky, pen try
				C: Stransky 4 P: Stransky 4
1 Feb	A	Gloucester	25-32	T: Horak 2, Joiner C: Serevi 2 P: Stransky 2
14 Feb	H	London Irish	34-19	T: Greenwood 2, Lloyd C: Stransky 2
				P: Stransky 5
28 Feb	A	Bristol	27-24	T: Back, Lloyd, Potter C: Stransky 3
				P: Stransky 2
7 Mar	H	Northampton	15-15	T: Cockerill, Joiner C: Stransky P: Stransky
14 Mar	A	Bath	5-16	T: Joiner
28 Mar	H	Richmond	42-19	T: Greenwood 3, Back, Potter, Rowntree
				C: Stransky 3 P: Stransky D: Stransky
11 Apr	A	Sale	21-35	T: Cockerill, Miller C: Stransky
				P: Stransky 3
18 Apr	A	Harlequins	23-14	T: Lloyd, Stransky C: Stransky 2
				P: Stransky 2 D: Stransky
25 Apr	H	Saracens	10-10	T: Hamilton C: Stransky P: Stransky
29 Apr	A	Wasps	13-17	T: Joiner 2 P: Stransky
4 May	A	Newcastle	10-27	T: Back C: Stransky P: Stransky
10 May	H	Bristol	34-25	T: Stransky 2, Healey, Joiner, Gustard
				C: Stransky 3 P: Stransky
17 May	A	London Irish	55-16	T: Back 2, Gustard 2, Horak 2, Hamilton,
				Barlow C: Stransky 6 P: Stransky

London Irish

Year of formation 1898
Ground The Avenue, Sunbury-on-Thames, Middlesex, TW16 5EQ Tel: Sunbury (01932) 783034
Colours Emerald green; white shorts
Captain 1997-98 C M P O'Shea
Allied Dunbar Leagues 1997-98 Div 1 11th; won Division One/Two play-off against Rotherham 42-27 on aggregate   **Tetley's Bitter Cup 1997-98** Lost 7-41 to Wasps (quarter-final)

They should be renamed the great survivors. Yet again they came sailing through the tense play-offs. Mind you, by the time they got to the second leg of the struggle to stay in the top flight they must have known Rotherham pretty well, since it was the fourth time the two sides had met during the season, after earlier encounters in the Tetley's Bitter Cup and the C&G Cup. At the start of the season Ireland lock Jeremy Davidson's decision to stay was cheering news, but his subsequent loss, through injury, was a big blow. Malcolm O'Kelly though revealed himself to be a more than capable deputy.

Second place in their European Conference Pool promised something for the rest of the season, but it was not to be. The sacking of Willie Anderson became inevitable as the defeats in the Allied Dunbar Premiership piled up. Under Anderson they won just one league match. When Dick Best was brought in on a caretaker basis as coaching consultant things changed rapidly. They opened up under new management with a resounding win at Sunbury over fellow strugglers Bristol and, although their resurgence was too late to avoid the play-offs, they had created a convincing gap between themselves and the bottom of Premiership One by the end of the season thanks to a further four victories.

One of those league wins late in the season probably meant more to Best than to any single Irishman at Sunbury. It was the complete and utter destruction of Harlequins, the club Best had parted company with the season before. Irish were as outstanding as Quins were hopeless. The 62-14 scoreline was but half the story. Woods helped himself to 32 of those, converting all eight tries, kicking two penalties and scoring two tries himself. It was the first time that the Exiles had ever run up a half century of points at this level. They got everything right on the day. By then though they had already been given a pounding by Wasps in the quarter-finals of the cup, but had done really well to reach that stage of the competition. Conor O'Shea proved an inspirational captain throughout Irish's troubles and the return of Davidson should mean that the Exiles will be a side to be feared in the coming year, particularly as Best is staying on to mastermind things. It will be interesting to see if the club adopts the black and cream kit – the colours of its sponsors – in favour of the traditional green this year.

League Record 1997-98

Date	Venue	Opponents	Result	Scorers
23 Aug	A	Richmond	12-32	*P:* Woods 4
30 Aug	H	Sale	20-26	*T:* Bird, O'Shea *C:* Woods 2 *P:* Woods
				D: Humphreys
19 Oct	A	Gloucester	7-29	*T:* Woods *C:* Woods
26 Oct	H	Wasps	22-17	*T:* N Burrows *C:* Woods *P:* Woods 3
				D: Humphreys, O'Shea
1 Nov	H	Newcastle	19-35	*T:* Hogan *C:* Corcoran *P:* Corcoran 4
13 Dec	H	Northampton	10-51	*T:* McCall *C:* Woods *P:* Woods
27 Dec	A	Harlequins	24-26	*T:* O'Shea 2, Bishop *C:* Woods 3 *P:* Woods
30 Dec	H	Saracens	10-25	*T:* O'Shea *C:* Woods *P:* Woods
11 Jan	A	Newcastle	13-46	*T:* Bishop *C:* Woods *P:* Woods
				D: Humphreys
17 Jan	H	Richmond	14-45	*T:* Woods *P:* Woods 3
1 Feb	A	Sale	16-41	*T:* Fitzpatrick *C:* Woods *P:* Woods 3
14 Feb	A	Leicester	19-34	*T:* Dawson *C:* Woods *P:* Woods 4
20 Feb	H	Bristol	38-23	*T:* Feaunati, Woods, O'Shea, Bishop
				C: Woods 3 *P:* Woods 4
15 Mar	A	Wasps	38-19	*T:* Feaunati, McLoughlin, O'Shea, Humphreys
				C: Woods 3 *P:* Woods 4
24 Mar	H	Gloucester	23-19	*T:* Woods 2, Richards *C:* Woods *P:* Woods 2
28 Mar	H	Bath	35-49	*T:* Feaunati 2, Richards, pen try *C:* Woods 3
				P: Woods 3
19 Apr	A	Bristol	17-5	*T:* Burns, Feaunati *C:* Woods 2 *P:* Woods
22 Apr	A	Northampton	18-33	*T:* Harvey, O'Shea *C:* Woods *P:* Woods 2
25 Apr	H	Harlequins	62-14	*T:* Bishop 3, Woods 2, Hogan, O'Kelly,
				O'Shea *C:* Woods 8 *P:* Woods 2

28 Apr	A	Bath	3-20	P: Woods
3 May	A	Saracens	21-29	T: Hogan, Woods C: Woods P: Woods 2
				D: Humphreys
17 May	H	Leicester	16-55	T: Amor, Jarvis P: Amor 2
Play-Offs				
20 May	A	Rotherham	16-13	T: Bishop C: Woods P: Woods 3
24 May	H	Rotherham	26-14	T: Bishop P: Woods 7

London Scottish

Year of formation 1878
Ground Richmond Athletic Ground, Kew Foot Road, Richmond, Surrey TW9 2SS Tel: 0181 332 2473
Colours Blue jersey with red lion crest; blue shorts
Captain 1997-98 B R S Eriksson
Allied Dunbar Leagues 1997-98 Div 2 3rd; won Division One/Two play-off against Bristol 46-40 on aggregate – *promoted* **Tetley's Bitter Cup 1997-98** Lost 23-24 to Bath (4th round)

The needless left hook thrown by Derrick Lee, which felled David Corkery like a log during the last minutes of the first leg of their vital play-off against Bristol, could have cost them dear. As things turned out, however, London Scottish triumphed and returned to the upper echelons of the game which they last graced in the first year of the then Courage Leagues back in 1987. Lee missed the return leg but his stand-in Iain McAusland did well enough with a drop goal and three penalties to ensure an overall 46-40 margin of victory. All in all, what with the notorious ear-biting incident at Bath when they ran the 10-times cup holders close in the fourth round, and the sudden departure of John Allan, then his equally unexpected return from South Africa in time for the play-offs, it was quite an interesting season for Scottish. The thorny issue of sharing the cramped Athletic Ground, a conflict which saw the Exiles relinquishing a home draw in the cup to travel to Bath for that fateful fourth-round tie, was resolved with Richmond moving to Reading and London Scottish to ground-share with Harlequins.

League Record 1997-98

Date	Venue	Opponents	Result	Scorers
30 Aug	H	Fylde	35-9	T: Eriksson 3, Lee, Sharman C: Cameron, Lee P: Cameron 2
7 Sep	H	Blackheath	34-6	T: Cameron, Eriksson, G Smith C: Cameron, Lee P: Lee 3, Cameron D: Lee
13 Sep	A	Waterloo	36-17	T: Sharman 2, Cook, Hunter C: Lee 2 P: Lee 3 D: Lee
20 Sep	A	Bedford	33-45	T: Sharman 3, pen try C: Lee 2 P: Lee 3
27 Sep	H	Orrell	20-19	T: Sharman P: McAusland 5
4 Oct	A	Rotherham	3-24	P: McAusland
11 Oct	H	Wakefield	30-13	T: Sharman 2, Cameron, Johnson, G Smith C: Lee P: Lee
18 Oct	A	Exeter	22-16	T: Lee, Thompson P: Lee 4
25 Oct	H	Bedford	15-22	T: Jackson, Watson C: McAusland P: Cameron
8 Nov	A	Orrell	27-13	T: Lee, Millard, Milligan, Watson C: Lee, McAusland D: McAusland
13 Dec	H	Rotherham	35-29	T: Cameron, Holmes, Milligan, Tarbuck C: Lee 3 P: Lee 2 D: Cameron
20 Dec	A	Wakefield	10-15	T: Johnstone C: McAusland P: Lee
17 Jan	A	Blackheath	25-34	T: Sharman, Tarbuck, pen try C: McAusland 2 P: McAusland 2
24 Jan	H	Exeter	22-10	T: Cameron, Jankovich, Milligan C: Cameron 2 P: Cameron

31 Jan	A	Moseley	29-18	T: Millard, Raynor C: Cameron, Lee P: Cameron 3, Lee 2
14 Feb	H	Coventry	18-18	T: Eriksson, Lee, Tarbuck P: Lee
8 Mar	H	W Hartlepool	31-17	T: Cameron, French, Todd C: Cameron 2 P: Cameron 4
14 Mar	A	Coventry	10-37	T: Sharman, Watson
28 Mar	H	Moseley	24-18	T: Eriksson, Todd, Watson, Sharman C: Lee 2
11 Apr	A	Fylde	22-7	T: Sharman 2 P: Lee 4
18 Apr	H	Waterloo	26-6	T: Millard 2, Lee C: Lee P: Lee 3
25 Apr	A	W Hartlepool	10-11	T: Watson C: Lee P: Lee
Play-Offs				
17 May	H	Bristol	29-25	T: Cameron, Davies, Holmes, Sharman C: Lee 3 P: Lee
23 May	A	Bristol	17-15	T: Sharman P: McAusland 3 D: McAusland

Moseley

Year of formation 1873
Ground The Reddings, Reddings Road, Moseley, Birmingham B13 8LW Tel: 0121 499 2149
Colours Red and black; black shorts
Captain 1997-98 R Denhardt
Allied Dunbar Leagues 1997-98 Div 2 6th   **Tetley's Bitter Cup 1997-98** Lost 11-18 to Sale (4th round)

Given the off-field shenanigans at The Reddings, Moseley's showing in the Allied Dunbar Premiership Two was something of a minor miracle. They began with the right personnel who were quite capable of taking them up a division; but, scandalously, the shedding of around a dozen of the playing staff in the New Year sealed their fate. The club went into administration in the winter with debts approaching £1 million. They had been unable to pay players their full wages from before Christmas. The involved sale of their famous ground to Bryant Homes, who seem to have found a cast-iron source of land in the ailing world of professional Rugby Union given that they have also agreed to purchase Coventry's ground, angered many long-standing members and former players. Warwickshire County Cricket Club though could well be the way forward as far as a groundshare goes. They took up a 25 per cent stake in the club and from season 2000-2001 the rugby club will play at Edgbaston in what is planned to be a multi-sports stadium.

League Record 1997-98

Date	Venue	Opponents	Result	Scorers
30 Aug	A	Coventry	12-20	T: Hackney, O'Mahony C: Liley
13 Sep	H	W Hartlepool	16-21	T: Liley C: Liley P: Liley 3
20 Sep	A	Orrell	19-30	T: Smith, O'Mahony, Martin C: Liley 2
27 Sep	H	Exeter	23-22	T: Binns, Mulraine, O'Mahony C: Liley P: Liley 2
4 Oct	A	Wakefield	27-15	T: O'Mahony 2, Geraghty, Moore C: Liley 2 P: Liley
11 Oct	H	Bedford	16-35	T: Harris C: Jones P: Jones 3
18 Oct	A	Blackheath	19-11	T: Martin C: Jones P: Jones 4
25 Oct	H	Orrell	18-9	T: Hall, Jones C: Liley P: Jones 2
8 Nov	A	Exeter	20-10	T: Hall, O'Mahony C: Jones 2 P: Liley 2
13 Dec	H	Wakefield	28-10	T: Drake-Lee, Jones, MacKinnon C: Jones 2 P: Jones 3
20 Dec	A	Bedford	16-32	T: McAtamney C: Jones P: Jones 2 D: Jones
27 Dec	H	Rotherham	23-25	T: Charron, Denhardt, Liley C: Jones P: Jones D: Jones

17 Jan	A	Rotherham	16-10	*T:* Harris *C:* Jones *P:* Jones 2 *D:* Jones
31 Jan	H	L Scottish	18-29	*T:* Colderley, O'Mahony *C:* Jones *P:* Jones 2
14 Feb	A	Waterloo	31-36	*T:* O'Mahony 3, Martin, Leu'u *C:* Jones 3
28 Feb	H	Blackheath	29-16	*T:* Denhardt, Massey, Mitchell, O'Mahony *C:* Jones 3 *P:* Jones
14 Mar	H	Waterloo	23-22	*T:* Harris, Martin *C:* Jones 2 *P:* Jones 3
28 Mar	A	L Scottish	18-24	*T:* O'Mahony 2 *C:* Jones *P:* Jones 2
4 Apr	A	Fylde	13-14	*T:* Binns *C:* Jones *P:* Jones *D:* Binns
18 Apr	A	W Hartlepool	18-18	*T:* Cockle, Mitchell *C:* Jones *P:* Jones 2
22 Apr	H	Coventry	31-3	*T:* Burns, Colderley, Massey, O'Mahony *C:* Jones *P:* Jones 3
25 Apr	H	Fylde	44-9	*T:* O'Mahony 3, Jones, Martin, Massey *C:* Jones 4 *P:* Jones 2

Newcastle

Year of formation 1877, reformed in 1995
Ground Kingston Park, Brunton Road, Kenton Bank Foot, Newcastle upon Tyne, NE13 8AF
Tel: 0191 214 0422
Colours Black and white stripes; black shorts
Captain 1997-98 D Ryan
Allied Dunbar Leagues 1997-98 Div 1 *Winners* **Tetley's Bitter Cup 1997-98** Lost 7-17 to
Northampton (quarter-final)

They had a dream, Sir John Hall and Rob Andrew, to win the Allied Dunbar
Premiership One championship within five years. In fact it took just two. They were
under a lot of pressure and fell away at one point. Having won their first 12 games,
they lost that 100 per cent record to gritty Richmond in March when the London
club had been reduced to 14 men following the sending-off of Scott Quinnell. A
second, far more telling defeat, came the following month at Saracens and allowed
their nearest rivals to get to within touching distance of the leadership. The lead
changed hands regularly from then on, due primarily to the vagaries of the fixture
lists and also to a third defeat. But with a game in hand and a fraction more
resilience and hardness than their North London challengers, the self-styled Falcons
were eventually crowned champions following a classy demolition of a member of
the old guard, Harlequins, in the final Premiership match of the season at The
Stoop. They ran in six tries that day and ended up as the First Division's leading
scorers (one of only three sides to top 600 points) and tightest defences.

If ever there were an omen it had to have been on the opening day of the season,
in high summer of 1997, when they travelled to Bath and came away with victory.
They later beat Leicester at Welford Road and the writing was on the pitch. The new
boys were taking over the block. Newcastle reached the European Conference
semi-finals, where they lost to Agen after playing well on the way.

But it was a season not without its problems. Tim Stimpson languished after
reportedly having a fall-out with Andrew, similarly Lions and England wing John
Bentley. The latter went on loan to Rotherham for a while and at the end of the
season returned to Rugby League. There was anger at Kingston Park when
inspirational captain Dean Ryan was banned for a month retrospectively. This
followed Cliff Brittle's intervention after Ryan was caught on camera racing fully 20
metres to land a punch on Nathan Thomas in retaliation for the Bath player's stamp
on Newcastle's full-back Stimpson in that opening game of the season. Typically,
once the sin bin was introduced at the beginning of November, Ryan was the first
Premiership player to be consigned to it for the statutory 10 minutes. They then
thankfully avoided a biting scandal following the bruising encounter with Leicester,
when it was deemed that there was insufficient evidence to pursue allegations against
Paul Van Zandvliet.

Newcastle finished on a high note. The victory over a World XV – the first by a

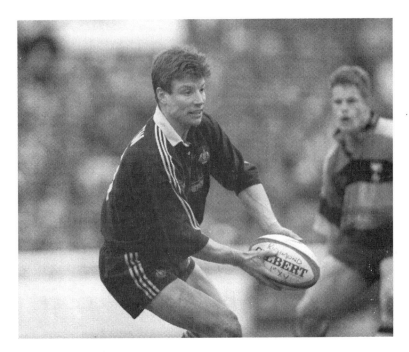

Rob Andrew, once more the fulcrum of a successful side, guiding Newcastle, as once he did Wasps and England, to success on and off the field.

club since the showpiece match was introduced – just served to confirm Newcastle's status as a top club – *the* top club.

League Record 1997-98

Date	Venue	Opponents	Result	Scorers
23 Aug	A	Bath	20-13	*T:* Legg, Tuigamala *C:* Stimpson 2 *P:* Stimpson 2
8 Oct	H	Northampton	37-12	*T:* Naylor 2, Armstrong, Lam, Popplewell *C:* Stimpson 3 *P:* Stimpson 2
18 Oct	A	Sale	33-26	*T:* Archer, Lam, S O'Neill, Ryan *C:* Andrew 2 *P:* Andrew 3
26 Oct	H	Richmond	18-12	*P:* Andrew 6
1 Nov	A	London Irish	35-19	*T:* Popplewell 2, Lam, Nesdale *C:* Andrew 3 *P:* Andrew 3
14 Dec	H	Gloucester	37-27	*T:* Armstrong 2, Legg, Metcalfe, Ryan, Underwood, Van Zandvliet *C:* Andrew
27 Dec	A	Bristol	50-8	*T:* Armstrong 3, Childs, Naylor, Tait, Tuigamala, Lam *C:* Andrew 2 *P:* Andrew 2
30 Dec	A	Leicester	25-19	*T:* Lam 2, Popplewell *C:* Andrew 2 *P:* Andrew *D:* Andrew
11 Jan	H	London Irish	46-13	*T:* Naylor 3, Archer 2, Armstrong, Nesdale, Tuigamala *C:* Andrew 2,Legg
31 Jan	A	Northampton	21-17	*T:* Naylor, Tuigamala *C:* Andrew *P:* Andrew 3

15 Feb	H	Harlequins	43-15	T: Underwood 2, Naylor, Ryan, Shaw, Tait C: Andrew 5 P: Andrew
10 Mar	H	Sale	23-18	T: Childs, Underwood, Andrew C: Andrew P: Andrew 2
14 Mar	A	Richmond	17-30	T: Underwood, pen try C: Andrew 2 P: Andrew
25 Mar	H	Saracens	30-25	T: Legg, Popplewell, Walton C: Andrew 3 P: Andrew 3
7 Apr	H	Wasps	20-13	T: Legg 2, Andrew C: Andrew P: Andrew
11 Apr	A	Gloucester	29-27	T: Andrew 2, Walton, pen try C: Andrew 3 P: Andrew
19 Apr	A	Saracens	10-12	T: Lam C: Andrew P: Andrew
22 Apr	A	Wasps	17-18	T: Armstrong 2 C: Andrew 2 P: Andrew
26 Apr	H	Bristol	43-18	T: Childs 2, Armstrong, Andrew, Legg, Shaw, pen try C: Andrew 4
4 May	H	Leicester	27-10	T: Armstrong, Lam, Walton C: Andrew 3 P: Andrew 2
11 May	H	Bath	20-15	T: Underwood, Arnold C: Andrew 2 P: Andrew 2
17 May	A	Harlequins	44-20	T: Armstrong 2, Arnold, Andrew, Popplewell, Lam C: Andrew 4 P: Andrew 2

Northampton

Year of formation 1880
Ground Franklins Gardens, Weedon Road, Northampton, NN5 5BG Tel: Northampton (01604) 751543
Colours Black, green and gold bands; black shorts
Captain 1997-98 T A K Rodber
Allied Dunbar Leagues 1997-98 Div 1 8th   **Tetley's Bitter Cup 1997-98** Lost 10-25 to Saracens (semi-final)

It was probably no big surprise when Gregor Townsend, the mercurial and highly talented threequarter, decided to move on. But his destination, Brive, probably was. The reason is fairly straightforward, though. Townsend regards himself as an outside-half, but unfortunately that spot belongs to England's Paul Grayson. So when Alain Penaud signed for Saracens, Brive decided that Townsend was the player they wanted as replacement for their fly-half. He will undoubtedly be missed by the Saints, but probably not as badly as their captain Tim Rodber was in the latter half of the season. Knee ligament damage kept him on the sidelines from where he watched his team limp into eighth place. They had been as high as fifth and as low as 10th at various times during the year.

The signing of Garry Pagel was a shrewd move and Jon Sleightholme's arrival galvanised things out wide. But injury problems were never far away. Apart from Rodber's troubles they also lost the services of Nick Beal for a substantial chunk of the season. Then there was the stand they made against England's tour demands. The club apparently decided not to release Rodber, Grayson and Matt Dawson for the southern hemisphere tour. They were clearly hoping for support from the other First Division clubs, but quickly found themselves out on a limb. They climbed down fairly smartly after feeling the chill of isolation and it was just as well, because when Clive Woodward finally announced the squad he also named scrum-half Dawson as the captain in place of Lawrence Dallaglio, a signal honour for the club.

If the European Conference, in which they finished runners-up in their pool, and the league were unfulfilling, the Tetley's Bitter Cup was quite the opposite. Saints appeared to be marching to glory. The fourth round, against Bedford was possibly the most troublesome of the ties, and the best came in the quarter-finals which had thrown Northampton in with Newcastle. A foregone conclusion according to certain pundits and Falcons fans. Come the day and Saints scrapped like the heroes they are. They repulsed everything Newcastle could throw at them, including a thunderous second-half tackle by Rodber on the one-man tank known as Va'aiga Tuigamala. It finished 17-7 but that was it for Saints. They were unable to draw on their reserves in the semi-final when they lost to Saracens.

League Record 1997-98

Date	Venue	Opponents	Result	Scorers
23 Aug	H	Harlequins	23-26	T: Dawson, Phillips, Tatupu C: Dawson P: Townsend 2
8 Oct	A	Newcastle	12-37	P: Hepher 3 D: Townsend
18 Oct	H	Leicester	25-6	T: Grayson, Rodber P: Dawson 4, Townsend
26 Oct	A	Bristol	15-22	P: Dawson 5
8 Nov	H	Saracens	13-19	T: Moir C: Dawson P: Dawson 2
13 Dec	A	London Irish	51-10	T: Allen, Dawson, Grayson, Pagel, Pountney, Townsend C: Grayson 6 P: Grayson 3
21 Dec	A	Richmond	24-21	P: Grayson 7 D: Grayson
27 Dec	H	Wasps	18-10	P: Grayson 6
30 Dec	A	Bath	3-26	P: Grayson
10 Jan	H	Sale	33-14	T: Allen 2, Townsend C: Grayson 3 P: Grayson 4
18 Jan	A	Harlequins	30-5	T: Allen 2, Townsend, Sleightholme C: Grayson 2 P: Grayson 2
31 Jan	H	Newcastle	17-21	T: Johnson P: Grayson 4
14 Feb	A	Gloucester	15-20	T: Seely, Thorneycroft C: Grayson P: Grayson
7 Mar	A	Leicester	15-15	P: Grayson 4 D: Grayson
14 Mar	H	Bristol	35-12	T: Thorneycroft 3, Allen, Chandler, Johnson C: Grayson P: Grayson
18 Apr	H	Richmond	39-47	T: Dawson, Phillips, Pountney, pen try, Thorneycroft C: Grayson 4 P: Grayson 2
22 Apr	H	London Irish	33-18	T: Pagel, Pountney, Bell C: Grayson 3 P: Grayson 4
26 Apr	A	Wasps	15-31	T: Allen, Seely C: Grayson P: Grayson
2 May	H	Bath	16-15	T: Bell C: Dawson P: Dawson 3
10 May	A	Sale	19-30	T: Dawson 2, Foale C: Dawson 2
14 May	A	Saracens	20-43	T: Beal, Tatupu, Grayson C: Grayson P: Grayson
17 May	H	Gloucester	22-24	T: Grayson C: Grayson P: Grayson 4 D: Grayson

Orrell

Year of formation 1927
Ground Edge Hall Road, Orrell, Wigan, Lancashire WN5 8TL Tel: Upholland (01695) 623193
Colours Black and amber; black shorts
Captain 1997-98 P Manley
Allied Dunbar Leagues 1997-98 Div 2 5th   **Tetley's Bitter Cup 1997-98** Lost 16-26 to Newbury (3rd round)

A fine beginning with three wins on the trot, including a veritable trouncing of Rotherham, raised hopes too high. But the lack of an established, consistent goal-kicker cost them dear when they travelled to London Scottish. They lost by a point, but had they had the services of a regular boot man they could just as easily have come away with the win. Orrell should still have been competing for promotion at the end, but key defeats thereafter saw their aspirations drift away from them. The final straw came at struggling Exeter where they lost 14-17. That effectively was that.
    The kicking duties were shunted around all season between three players

generally, Simon Verbickas, Neil Ryan and Neil McCarthy, until he returned to Pontypridd. They will need to sort that out for the new season. Injuries did not help their cause either. Their classy overseas player Doug Trivella, the Zimbabwe full-back, was sidelined midway through the season and that was a savage blow. Charlie Harrison, the Bath scrum-half, joined on loan and made an impact.

League Record 1997-98

Date	Venue	Opponents	Result	Scorers
30 Aug	H	Blackheath	26-17	*T:* Rudge 2, Wright, Verbickas *P:* Trivella, Verbickas
14 Sep	A	Rotherham	29-14	*T:* Cronin, Verbickas, Wright *C:* Verbickas *P:* Verbickas 4
20 Sep	H	Moseley	30-19	*T:* Ryan 2, Silcock, pen try *C:* Verbickas 2 *P:* Verbickas, McCarthy
27 Sep	A	L Scottish	19-20	*T:* Rees, Verbickas, Trivella *C:* Silcock 2
4 Oct	H	Fylde	35-9	*T:* Heslop 3, Silcock *C:* McCarthy 3 *P:* McCarthy 3
11 Oct	A	Waterloo	14-25	*T:* Ryan *P:* McCarthy 2 *D:* McCarthy
18 Oct	H	Coventry	38-13	*T:* Manley 2, Ryan 2, Trivella, Walsh *C:* Verbickas 2, Ryan 2
25 Oct	A	Moseley	9-18	*P:* Verbickas 2, Ryan
8 Nov	H	L Scottish	13-27	*T:* Heslop *C:* Verbickas *P:* Verbickas 2
13 Dec	A	Fylde	21-9	*T:* Heslop, Millichip *C:* Scott *P:* Scott 3
20 Dec	H	Waterloo	23-6	*T:* Richardson, Wright *C:* Scott 2 *P:* Scott 3
17 Jan	H	W Hartlepool	30-35	*T:* Oliver, Ryan, pen try *C:* Scott 3 *P:* Scott 3
24 Jan	A	Coventry	30-21	*T:* Verbickas 3, Oliver *C:* Scott 2 *P:* Scott 2
31 Jan	A	Bedford	22-47	*T:* Verbickas, Manley, pen try *C:* Verbickas 2 *P:* Scott
14 Feb	H	Exeter	38-3	*T:* Verbickas 2, Bartle, Cusani, Harrison, Manley *C:* Verbickas 3, Ryan
22 Feb	A	W Hartlepool	11-20	*T:* Bartle *P:* Verbickas 2
7 Mar	A	Wakefield	26-20	*T:* Oliver, Trivella *C:* Verbickas 2 *P:* Verbickas 4
14 Mar	A	Exeter	14-17	*T:* Oliver *P:* Scott 3
28 Mar	H	Bedford	16-29	*T:* Harrison, Lyon *P:* Verbickas 2
11 Apr	A	Blackheath	32-14	*T:* Harrison 2, Huxley, Lyon, Verbickas *C:* Verbickas 2 *P:* Verbickas
18 Apr	H	Rotherham	3-9	*P:* Scott
25 Apr	H	Wakefield	54-8	*T:* Verbickas 3, Lyon 2, Cronin, Manley, Wright *C:* Verbickas 7

Richmond

Year of formation 1861
Ground Richmond Athletic Ground, Kew Foot Road, Richmond, Surrey, TW9 2SS Tel: 0181 332 7112
Colours Old gold, red and black; black shorts
Captain 1997-98 B B Clarke
Allied Dunbar Leagues 1997-98 Div 1 5th **Tetley's Bitter Cup 1997-98** Lost 30-36 to Saracens (quarter-finals)

The proposed move down the M4 Motorway to play their home games at Reading FC's purpose-built 25,000 seater stadium may well rankle with the die-hard few but it certainly makes financial sense. They had effectively outgrown the Richmond Athletic Ground and the council's refusal to allow them any sensible development finally forced their hand. Millionaire backer Ashley Levett's repeated calls for additional financial support fell on deaf money-men's ears by all accounts, and his early season threat to quit because he felt he was pouring money down the drain were illustrations of the parlous state of the professional game. If the wealthy are feeling the pinch then the writing must be on the wall. But much will need to be achieved on the playing front to attract cash through the gates in the shape of fans and across the table in terms of additional backers.

For all that coach John Kingston worked wonders and made some outstanding signings. Australian full-back Matt Pini was a revelation, so too was Barry Williams in the front row. In the threequarters there were some world-class performances from Allan Bateman in the centre, while Adrian Davies and Andy Moore proved to be a fine half-back pairing; and in Dominic Chapman and Spencer Brown Richmond possess two of the most potent wings in the Allied Dunbar Premiership. Both grew in stature and their inclusion, together with that of captain Ben Clarke and prop Darren Crompton, in England's tour party for the summer's venture into the southern hemisphere, owed as much to Kingston's hard work as it did to the obvious talents of the players.

The greatest loss of the season was not so much a match, but rather Richmond's home record. It fell in December when Northampton, and specifically their fly-half Paul Grayson, came to town. Although Richmond outscored their opponents by three tries to nil, Grayson with seven penalties and a drop goal ensured that a run of 25 consecutive home wins was stopped in its tracks. In the end this free-scoring side's attractive all-round game saw them finish just outside the top four. In the Tetley's Bitter Cup perhaps their best moment came in the fifth round when they travelled to Bath and won; in the next round they succumbed to eventual winners Saracens.

League Record 1997-98

Date	Venue	Opponents	Result	Scorers
23 Aug	H	London Irish	32-12	*T:* Vander 2, Wright 2, S Quinnell *C:* A Davies 2 *P:* A Davies
8 Oct	A	Saracens	9-15	*P:* A Davies 2 *D:* Pini
18 Oct	H	Harlequins	37-16	*T:* Bateman, Chapman, Martin, C Quinnell *C:* Va'a 4 *P:* Va'a 3
26 Oct	A	Newcastle	12-18	*P:* Va'a 4
1 Nov	A	Bath	31-47	*T:* Bateman, Cottrell, J Davies, Fallon, S Quinnell *C:* Mason 3
13 Dec	A	Bristol	13-12	*T:* Wright 2 *P:* Pini
16 Dec	H	Leicester	32-15	*T:* Cottrell, Clarke, Gillies, Chapman, S Quinnell *C:* Pini 2 *P:* Pini
21 Dec	H	Northampton	21-24	*T:* Chapman, S Quinnell, Wright *P:* Pini 2
27 Dec	A	Gloucester	20-26	*T:* Bateman, Fallon, Williams *C:* Mason *P:* Mason
30 Dec	A	Wasps	18-22	*T:* Chapman 2 *C:* Pini *P:* Pini 2
17 Jan	A	London Irish	45-14	*T:* Chapman 2, Bateman, Moore, Va'a, S Quinnell *C:*A Davies 3 *P:*A Davies 3
31 Jan	H	Saracens	10-15	*T:* Fallon *C:* A Davies *P:* A Davies
15 Feb	H	Sale	20-28	*T:* Fallon *P:* A Davies 5
7 Mar	A	Harlequins	12-41	*T:* A Davies, Hutton *C:* A Davies
14 Mar	H	Newcastle	30-17	*T:* C Quinnell, Chapman, Moore, Wright *C:* A Davies 2 *P:* A Davies 2
28 Mar	A	Leicester	19-42	*T:* Bateman 2, Brown *C:* A Davies 2
10 Apr	H	Bristol	43-3	*T:* Chapman 3, C Quinnell 2, Brown, Bateman *C:* A Davies 4
13 Apr	H	Bath	32-14	*T:* S Quinnell, Clarke, Va'a, pen try *C:* A Davies 3 *P:* A Davies 2
18 Apr	A	Northampton	47-39	*T:* Chapman 2, Bateman, Clarke, Pini, Wright *C:* A Davies 4 *P:* A Davies 3

25 Apr	H	Gloucester	33-22	T: Chapman 2, S Quinnell, Wright, pen try
				C: A Davies 4
2 May	H	Wasps	51-29	T: Brown 2, A Davies 2, Pini 2, Clarke,
				S Quinnell C: A Davies 4 P: A Davies
17 May	A	Sale	40-28	T: Chapman 2, S Quinnell 2, Fallon
				C: A Davies 3 P: A Davies 3

Rotherham

Year of formation 1923
Ground Clifton Lane Grounds, Badsley Moor Lane, Rotherham, South Yorkshire S65 2AA
Tel: Rotherham (01709) 370763
Colours Maroon, sky blue and navy blue stripes; black shorts
Captain 1997-98 A J Buzza/G Austin
Allied Dunbar Leagues 1997-98 Div 2 4th; lost Division One/Two play-off against London Irish 27-42 on aggregate **Tetley's Bitter Cup 1997-98** Lost 14-27 to London Irish (5th round)

So near and yet, after four confrontations with London Irish (all of which they lost) during the season in various competitions, there was still a little distance left that Rotherham failed to cover. Their rise through the league ranks has been little short of unbelievable. If they had beaten the Exiles in the play-offs it would have been their seventh promotion in 11 seasons. However, despite a fine showing in Allied Dunbar Premiership Two, their efforts all came to naught.

They had lost the services of Ged Glynn as coach last May, but Geoff Wappett, who had worked alongside Glynn, stayed on and the team benefited from the continuity of control. Wappett was helped by Kevin Plant and Barry Forster. Sadly his commitments to Sedbergh School may preclude his staying on in a full-time role. Rotherham's recruitment policy paid off. Mike Umaga, the Western Samoa full-back and brother of All Black Tana, and Canadian No 8 Mike Schmid were unquestionably outstanding successes. These two joined a settled squad. Off the field the *nous* of finance manager Mike Yarlett and rugby manager Steve Cousins ensured no cash flow problems or player unrest. Expect a big challenge for honours this time around.

League Record 1997-98

Date	Venue	Opponents	Result	Scorers
30 Aug	A	Bedford	11-18	T: Austin P: Binns 2
14 Sep	H	Orrell	14-29	T: Sinclair P: Binns 3
20 Sep	H	W Hartlepool	33-21	T: Shepherd 2, Dudley , Easterby C: Binns 2
				P: Binns 2 D: Binns
27 Sep	A	Fylde	25-18	T: Shepherd, Moffatt, Spence C: Binns 2
				P: Binns 2
4 Oct	H	L Scottish	24-3	T: Binns, West C: Binns P: Binns 4
11 Oct	A	Coventry	12-18	P: Binns 4
18 Oct	H	Waterloo	16-26	T: Dudley C: Lax P: Binns 3
25 Oct	A	W Hartlepool	21-22	T: Wade, West C: Binns P: Binns 3
8 Nov	H	Fylde	32-16	T: Austin, Moffatt, Elliott C: Binns
				P: Binns 5
13 Dec	A	L Scottish	29-35	T: Austin, Binns, Harper, Lax C: Binns 3
				P: Binns
20 Dec	H	Coventry	46-8	T: Harper 2, Austin, Dudley, Easterby, Schmid
				C: Binns 5 P: Binns 2
27 Dec	A	Moseley	25-23	T: Binns, Wade, pen try C: Lax 2
				P: Binns, Lax
10 Jan	A	Waterloo	32-26	T: Easterby 2, Austin, Binns, Lax C: Binns 2
				P: Binns
17 Jan	H	Moseley	10-16	T: Dawson 2

145

31 Jan	H	Wakefield	41-9	*T:* Austin 3, Binns 2, Schmid 2 *C:* Binns 3
14 Feb	A	Blackheath	31-18	*T:* Schmid 2, Harper *C:* Binns 2 *P:* Binns 4
7 Mar	A	Exeter	33-8	*T:* Austin, Bunting, Dawson, Schmid, Umaga *C:* Binns 4
14 Mar	H	Blackheath	40-10	*T:* Austin 2, Dawson, Harper, Umaga, Wade *C:* Binns 5
28 Mar	A	Wakefield	14-15	*T:* Dawson 2 *C:* Binns 2
11 Apr	H	Bedford	18-17	*T:* Austin, Harper *C:* Binns *P:* Binns 2
18 Apr	A	Orrell	9-3	*P:* Binns 3
25 Apr	H	Exeter	50-27	*T:* Wade 4, Binns 2, Dudley, Umaga *C:* Binns 5

Play-Offs

20 May	H	London Irish	13-16	*T:* Lax *C:* Binns *P:* Binns 2
24 May	A	London Irish	14-26	*T:* Austin, Lax *C:* Binns 2

Sale

Year of formation 1861
Ground Heywood Road, Brooklands, Sale, Cheshire, M33 3WB Tel: 0161 973 6348
Colours Royal blue and white; blue shorts
Captain 1997-98 J Mallinder
Allied Dunbar Leagues 1997-98 Div 1 6th   **Tetley's Bitter Cup 1997-98** Lost 9-15 to
Wasps (semi-final)

There is little doubt that Sale have the playing personnel to mount a serious challenge for the top prizes. The fall-out with fly-half Simon Mannix, who was released and joined Gloucester after the end of the season, was somewhat cushioned by what was an overall good season, although his intuitive skills and fine footballing brain will certainly be missed. The actual cause of the difference between Mannix and the club was never made clear, but there were mutterings that he wanted to run the whole show and that was not something the club wanted him to do.

Sale have some gems in Dion O'Cuinneagain, the South African Irishman, Simon Raiwalui, the Fijian forward, and Shane Howarth, an English qualified New Zealander with sound kicking skills. But Sale also breed their own talent. Patrick Sanderson proved an abrasive, quick thinking back-row man and apparently his brother Craig is destined for great things. Graham Dawe provided useful cover for the excellent Steve Diamond at hooker, and indeed the former Bath player will be helping on the coaching front in the coming season. John Mitchell's commitment to England's cause of necessity meant enforced absences and his influence was possibly lacking for certain key matches. But Sale did themselves justice overall. They did not let themselves down in the European Conference, where they finished runners-up in their pool. Their eventual sixth place in the league, after Gloucester had been docked two points, was their worst finish since they returned to the top flight, but there was no disgrace in that.

Captain Jim Mallinder had another fine season and he, like Dawe, will be helping on the coaching front, looking after the backs. The Tetley's Bitter Cup once more provided Sale's faithful following with their best memories. After swatting aside Moseley in the weather-hit fourth round, last year's beaten finalists had a comfortable home win against lesser lights Newbury. The quarter-final pairing was a tough-looking clash at West Hartlepool, but they outscored the Second Division outfit by five tries to two just to underline their superiority. Sadly they came to grief in the semi-finals in a tense, but scrappy match at Wasps. The scoreline owed everything to footwork. In Sale's case Howarth's, who landed three penalties. They were not enough though and hopes of a second successive final appearance at Twickenham were dashed by the boot of Gareth Rees.

League Record 1997-98

Date	Venue	Opponents	Result	Scorers
24 Aug	H	Saracens	10-19	T: Erskine C: Howarth D: Howarth
30 Aug	A	London Irish	26-20	T: Yates, Ellis C: Howarth 2 P: Howarth 4
18 Oct	H	Newcastle	26-33	T: Moore, R Smith C: Howarth 2 P: Howarth 4
25 Oct	A	Harlequins	41-52	T: Yates, Ellis, Moore, Sanderson, Beim C: Howarth 5 P: Howarth 2
2 Nov	A	Wasps	38-22	T: Rees 2, Mannix, Sanderson C: Howarth 3 P: Howarth 3 D: Howarth
9 Nov	H	Bristol	76-0	T: Beim 4, Rees 3, Winstanley 2, Ellis, Mallinder, Sanderson C: Howarth 8
13 Dec	A	Leicester	15-55	T: Howarth, Raiwalui C: Howarth P: Howarth
27 Dec	H	Bath	11-13	T: Beim P: Howarth 2
30 Dec	H	Gloucester	24-24	T: Baxendell, Ellis C: Howarth P: Howarth 4
10 Jan	A	Northampton	14-33	T: Beim 2 C: Mannix 2
1 Feb	H	London Irish	41-16	T: Sanderson 2, Bell, Ellis, Yates C: Mannix 2 P: Mannix 4
15 Feb	A	Richmond	28-20	T: Baxendall, Mallinder, O'Cuinneagain C: Mannix 2 P: Mannix 2, Howarth
24 Feb	A	Saracens	20-42	T: Beim 2 C: Mannix 2 P: Mannix 2
10 Mar	A	Newcastle	18-23	T: Beim, Erskine C: Howarth P: Howarth 2
14 Mar	H	Harlequins	23-13	T: Bell, O'Cuinneagain, Winstanley C: Howarth P: Howarth 2
11 Apr	H	Leicester	35-21	T: Moore 2, Baxendell, Beim, Ellis C: Howarth 2 P: Howarth 2
15 Apr	A	Bristol	25-15	T: Raiwalui, Baxendell, Anglesea C: Howarth 2 P: Howarth 2
18 Apr	H	Wasps	28-28	T: Moore C: Howarth P: Howarth 7
25 Apr	A	Bath	29-19	T: Baxendell, Moore, Sanderson, R Smith C: Howarth 3 P: Howarth
2 May	A	Gloucester	19-31	T: Beim, Erskine, Howarth C: Howarth 2
10 May	H	Northampton	30-19	T: Mallinder, Howarth, Murphy C: Howarth 3 P: Howarth 3
17 May	H	Richmond	28-40	T: Beim, Howarth, O'Cuinneagain, Winstanley C: Howarth P: Howarth D: Yates

Saracens

Year of formation 1876
Ground Vicarage Road Stadium, Watford, Hertfordshire, WD1 8ER Tel: Watford (01923)
496200
Colours Black with red and white hoops on sleeve; black shorts
Captain 1997-98 A J Diprose
Allied Dunbar Leagues 1997-98 Div 1 2nd   **Tetley's Bitter Cup 1997-98** *Winners* - beat
Wasps 48-18 (final)

For a handful of weeks the improbable looked to be possible as Francois Pienaar's
charges stayed on course to pull off that most difficult of feats, a league and cup
double. In the end they had to be content with the Tetley's Bitter Cup, a trophy
which they lifted in style. Silly slip-ups along the way meant that they ran out of
games with which to challenge Newcastle for the Allied Dunbar Premiership
championship, but at least they forced it to the last game of the season. Their
appearance in the European Conference saw them finish runners-up in their pool
having gained invaluable experience.

Saracens also set another record. It fell to Peter Deakin, their marketing genius, to

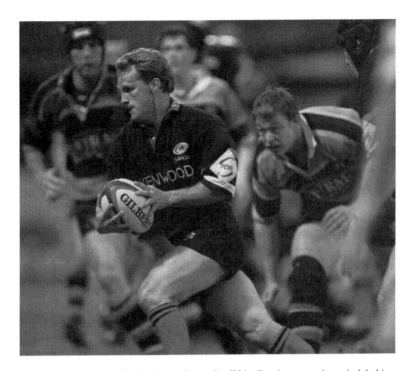

The glorious swansong. Michael Lynagh rounds off his glittering career in typical fashion, breaking here against Northampton in Saracens' final league game.

sell the game of Rugby Union to the people of Watford. It took most of the season to do this but eventually, by the time of the big showdown with Newcastle, Deakin was packing them in. Fully 20,000 – a record for an English club match outside Twickenham – crammed into Vicarage Road. Overall gates went up by nearly 200%, which fully vindicated Saracens' decision to quit Southgate and Enfield. So with the Allied Dunbar Premiership title going elsewhere, it was just as well that Saracens reached the Tetley's Bitter Cup final for the first time. They marked that debut, in what was billed as the Cockney Cup final, by equalling Bath's record score for the final, as they thrashed a hopelessly outclassed Wasps side. It was the perfect send-off for their two old masters, Michael Lynagh and Philippe Sella, who retired at the end of the season still on top of their game. Of course if Saracens had had their way the cup would have been won with another seasoned campaigner, Jason Leonard, back in the side. A written request to Harlequins for permission to approach the England prop resulted in a prohibitive price tag being hung around Leonard's ample neck and Saracens lost interest.

They had their share of injuries, the most notable being England scrum-half Kyran Bracken's shoulder problems, which ultimately forced him out of England's southern hemisphere jaunt. If Lynagh and Sella had been money well spent, the same could also be said for Ryan Constable, who scored some sensational tries, Brendon Daniel, Gavin Johnson and especially lock Danny Grewcock, who established himself as a second-row forward out of the top drawer, and dynamic back-row forward Ben Sturnham as well as centre Steve Ravenscroft.

League Record 1997-98

Date	Venue	Opponents	Result	Scorers
24 Aug	A	Sale	19-10	*T:* Diprose *C:* Lynagh *P:* Lynagh 4
8 Oct	H	Richmond	15-9	*P:* Lynagh 5
19 Oct	A	Wasps	19-15	*T:* Constable *C:* Lynagh *P:* Lynagh 4
26 Oct	H	Gloucester	42-24	*T:* Botterman, Chuter, Lynagh, Sella, P Wallace *C:* Lynagh 4 *P:* Lynagh 3
2 Nov	H	Bristol	31-9	*T:* Lynagh 2, Pienaar, Singer, D Thompson *C:* Lynagh 3
8 Nov	A	Northampton	19-13	*T:* Constable, Lynagh *P:* Lynagh 3
14 Dec	H	Bath	50-23	*T:* Johnson 2, R Wallace 2, Daniel, Ravenscroft *C:* Lynagh 4 *P:* Lynagh 4
26 Dec	A	Leicester	21-22	*T:* Constable, R Wallace *C:* Lynagh *P:* Lynagh 2 *D:* Lynagh
30 Dec	A	London Irish	25-10	*T:* Constable, Daniel, Lynagh *C:* Lynagh 2 *P:* Lynagh 2
11 Jan	H	Harlequins	25-16	*T:* pen try *C:* Lynagh *P:* Lynagh 6
31 Jan	A	Richmond	15-10	*T:* Diprose 2 *C:* Lynagh *P:* Lynagh
14 Feb	A	Bristol	37-20	*T:* R Wallace 3, Bracken, Sella *C:* Lynagh 3 *P:* Lynagh 2
24 Feb	H	Sale	42-20	*T:* Ravenscroft, Pienaar, pen try, Sturnham, Olver *C:* Lynagh 4 *P:* Lynagh 2 *D:* Johnson
8 Mar	H	Wasps	33-27	*T:* Olsen, Singer, pen try *C:* Lynagh 3 *P:* Lynagh 4
15 Mar	A	Gloucester	15-38	*T:* Pienaar 2 *C:* Lynagh *P:* Lynagh
25 Mar	A	Newcastle	25-30	*T:* Diprose *C:* Lynagh *P:* Lynagh 6
10 Apr	A	Bath	29-13	*T:* R Wallace, Pienaar *C:* Lynagh 2 *P:* Lynagh 5
19 Apr	H	Newcastle	12-10	*P:* Lynagh 3 *D:* Lynagh
25 Apr	A	Leicester	10-10	*T:* Lee *C:* Johnson *P:* Johnson
29 Apr	A	Harlequins	28-26	*T:* Ravenscroft, Copsey, Reidy *C:* Johnson 2 *P:* Johnson 3
3 May	H	London Irish	29-21	*T:* Daniel 2, Sturnham *C:* Johnson *P:* Johnson 4
14 May	H	Northampton	43-20	*T:* Olsen 2, R Wallace, Pienaar, Ravenscroft, Diprose *C:* Lynagh 5 *P:* Lynagh

Wakefield

Year of formation 1901
Ground Pinderfields Road, College Grove, Wakefield, WF1 3RR Tel: Wakefield (01924) 374801
Colours Black and gold quarters; black shorts
Captain 1997-98 P Stewart
Allied Dunbar Leagues 1997-98 Div 2 10th   **Tetley's Bitter Cup 1997-98** Lost 13-23 to West Hartlepool (4th round)

Huge debts and overspending of budgets caused real headaches and it looked as if the money problems had spilled over onto the pitch, with players understandably unhappy at having big pay cuts imposed on them. Indeed the players felt let down by the club and one or two subsequently decided to fight the club in the courts over the matter.

Whether or not the parlous state of financial affairs was to blame is debatable, but they certainly got off to a bad start, with defeat after defeat. It was not until shortly before Christmas, when they were second from bottom of Allied Dunbar Premiership Two, that things began to look up. Former Wasps forward Matt Greenwood, the player-coach, was instrumental in engineering the result which proved to be the turning point of their season, the 15-10 defeat of London Scottish. They finished with six victories out of 22 matches and just had the edge when it came to points difference over Exeter. Lock Simon Croft marked his retirement by nailing his boots to the dressing room door after their last match at Orrell

League Record 1997-98

Date	Venue	Opponents	Result	Scorers
30 Aug	H	Exeter	15-19	*P:* Scully 5
7 Sep	A	Waterloo	18-30	*T:* Rushforth, Thompson *C:* Cholewa *P:* Cholewa 2
13 Sep	A	Blackheath	27-29	*T:* Scully 2, Cholewa *C:* Jackson 3 *P:* Jackson 2
20 Sep	H	Coventry	6-17	*P:* Jackson 2
27 Sep	A	W Hartlepool	20-31	*T:* Hendry, Stewart *C:* Jackson 2 *P:* Jackson 2
4 Oct	H	Moseley	15-27	*T:* White, Garnett *C:* Cholewa *P:* Cholewa
11 Oct	A	L Scottish	13-30	*T:* Croft, Thompson *P:* Irving
18 Oct	H	Fylde	35-17	*T:* Garnett, Miller, Woodward, pen try *C:* Miller 3 *P:* Miller 3
25 Oct	A	Coventry	17-24	*T:* Summers *P:* Miller 4
8 Nov	H	W Hartlepool	12-28	*T:* pen try, Stewart *C:* Miller
13 Dec	A	Moseley	10-28	*T:* Scully *C:* Miller *P:* Miller
20 Dec	H	L Scottish	15-10	*P:* Miller 5
17 Jan	H	Waterloo	23-20	*T:* Maynard, Miller, Stewart *C:* Miller *P:* Miller 2
31 Jan	A	Rotherham	9-41	*P:* Miller 3
14 Feb	H	Bedford	13-24	*T:* White *C:* Scully *P:* Scully 2
28 Feb	A	Fylde	30-10	*T:* Croft, Elisara, White, Summers *C:* Miller 2 *P:* Miller 2
7 Mar	H	Orrell	20-26	*T:* Scully, Wilson, Yates *C:* Miller *P:* Miller
14 Mar	A	Bedford	10-36	*T:* Summers *C:* Miller *P:* Scully
28 Mar	H	Rotherham	15-14	*P:* Scully 2, Miller *D:* Miller 2
11 Apr	A	Exeter	30-17	*T:* Elisara, Greenwood, Scully, Thompson *C:* Miller 2 *P:* Miller 2
18 Apr	H	Blackheath	21-24	*P:* Miller 6 *D:* Miller
25 Apr	A	Orrell	8-54	*T:* Miller *P:* Miller

Wasps

Year of formation 1867
Ground Loftus Road Stadium, South Africa Road, Shepherds Bush, London W12 7PA Tel: 0181 743 0262
Colours Black with gold wasp on left breast; black shorts
Captain 1997-98 L B N Dallaglio
Allied Dunbar Leagues 1997-98 Div 1 9th   **Tetley's Bitter Cup 1997-98** Lost 18-48 to Saracens (final)

There were times during the season when Wasps could have put out a Casualty XV, so badly hit were they by injuries. Key men such as half-backs Andy Gomarsall and Alex King were sidelined for crucial periods, but injuries alone, especially in these days of first-team squads, as opposed to simple first teams, do not account for the way they tumbled from heroes to zeroes in one year. As reigning league champions they just did not approach even a half-hearted defence of their title, so hard won the year before. It was not until the New Year that they recorded their second Allied Dunbar Premiership One victory, but that was hardly a convincing one. By then they had already been hustled out of the Heineken European Cup at the quarter-final stage 25-18 by the eventual winners Brive, having gone through the pool matches unbeaten, although there was not a French side in that particular group.

For too long afterwards Wasps hovered dangerously close to the Premiership One dropping zone. In the end they did well to finish where they did, above Harlequins, whither Chris Sheasby had returned earlier in the season, but still not quite in touch with their peers, Bath, Leicester and the like. And they had to swallow a humiliating defeat at the hands of Quins, a 53-17 hammering at The Stoop on one of those rare days when the Fancy Dans of rugby got everything right.

So thank goodness for the cup. At least everyone was able to stay focused for that, well, up to the final anyway. In the fourth round they dealt with Quins; the fifth was a formality as they brushed aside Fylde; London Irish were not particularly troublesome in the quarter-finals either. At this point though the significance of their cup run perhaps got to them. It was all they had left in their season. Hence the tense and bitty struggle to overcome an equally edgy Sale in the semi-final.

No-one could have foreseen the misery that awaited them against Saracens at Twickenham in the first all-London final. A record-equalling defeat. Apart from one all too brief period in the second half when they fought back, they were hopelessly outplayed and outgunned, an epitaph for the whole of their season.

League Record 1997-98

Date	Venue	Opponents	Result	Scorers
31 Aug	A	Bristol	38-21	T: Greenstock, Rees, Logan, Weedon C: Rees 3 P: Rees 3, Ufton
19 Oct	H	Saracens	15-19	P: Rees 5
26 Oct	A	London Irish	17-22	T: Scrase, Wood C: Rees, Logan P: Rees
2 Nov	H	Sale	22-38	T: Wood C: Rees P: Rees 5
13 Dec	A	Harlequins	17-53	T: Ions, pen try C: Rees 2 P: Rees
27 Dec	A	Northampton	10-18	T: Friday C: Rees P: Rees
30 Dec	H	Richmond	22-18	T: Sampson C: Rees P: Rees 5
11 Jan	H	Gloucester	26-20	T: Friday, pen try C: Rees 2 P: Rees 4
17 Jan	A	Leicester	21-45	T: Logan 2 C: Rees P: Rees 3
1 Feb	H	Bristol	32-18	T: Scrivener, pen try C: Rees 2 P: Rees 5 D: Rees
14 Feb	A	Bath	27-43	T: Logan, Scrivener, Sheasby C: Rees 3 P: Rees 2
8 Mar	A	Saracens	27-33	T: Greenstock, Sampson, pen try C: Rees 3 P: Rees 2
11 Mar	A	Gloucester	15-22	T: Scrivener, Friday C: Rees P: Rees
15 Mar	H	London Irish	19-38	T: Green, Shaw P: Rees 3
7 Apr	A	Newcastle	13-20	T: King C: Rees P: Rees 2
12 Apr	H	Harlequins	29-26	T: Green, pen try C: Rees 2 P: Rees 5
18 Apr	A	Sale	28-28	T: Leota 2, Friday C: Rees 2 P: Rees 2 D: Rees
22 Apr	H	Newcastle	18-17	T: Scrase, Friday C: Rees P: Rees 2
26 Apr	H	Northampton	31-15	T: Dallaglio, Green, Sampson, Weedon C: Rees 4 P: Rees
29 Apr	H	Leicester	17-13	T: Mitchell P: Rees 3 D: Rees
2 May	A	Richmond	29-51	T: Black, Roiser, Gomarsall, Scrivener C: Rees 3 P: Rees
17 May	H	Bath	17-31	T: Ufton, Sampson, Ions C: Ufton

Waterloo

Year of formation 1882
Ground St Anthony's Road, Blundellsands, Liverpool, L23 8TW Tel: 0151 924 4552
Colours Green, red and white hoops; green shorts
Captain 1997-98 D Blyth
Allied Dunbar Leagues 1997-98 Div 2 8th   **Tetley's Bitter Cup 1997-98** Lost 34-36 to London Welsh (3rd round)

Waterloo got off to a real flier and by the end of October were in second place in Allied Dunbar Premiership Two, having won six of their first nine matches. Among those early scalps were West Hartlepool and Rotherham away and Orrell at home. And this from a team with no real stars, although Marcus Coast, a centre from New Zealand, looked particularly tasty, as did the half-back pairing of Lyndon Griffiths and Wayne Morris.

The slide began with defeat at home to Bedford in December, with a fairly comprehensive 13-28 scoreline. Alongside that came a narrow fall in the third round of the Tetley's Bitter Cup, 34-36 to London Welsh. They remained with an outside chance of a play-off place for a while but could not maintain the form or the consistency, and director of rugby Tony Russ had to be content with the fact that in the end they did manage to win half their 22 league matches, leaving plenty of room for improvement next time around.

League Record 1997-98

Date	Venue	Opponents	Result	Scorers
30 Aug	A	W Hartlepool	21-19	*T:* Blyth, Beckett, Coast *P:* Griffiths 2
7 Sep	H	Wakefield	30-18	*T:* Coast, Holt, Mullins *C:* Griffiths 3 *P:* Griffiths 3
13 Sep	H	L Scottish	17-36	*T:* Coast, Hart *C:* Griffiths 2 *P:* Griffiths
20 Sep	A	Exeter	20-24	*T:* Holt, Morris *C:* Griffiths 2 *P:* Griffiths 2
27 Sep	H	Blackheath	51-16	*T:* Beckett 2, Coast, Graham, Morris, Woof *C:* Griffiths 6 *P:* Griffiths 3
4 Oct	A	Bedford	21-34	*T:* Coast, Woof *C:* Griffiths *P:* Griffiths 3
11 Oct	H	Orrell	25-14	*T:* Morris 2, Graham, Woof *C:* Griffiths *P:* Griffiths
18 Oct	A	Rotherham	26-16	*T:* Graham, Morris *C:* Griffiths, Thompson *P:* Griffiths 4
25 Oct	H	Exeter	44-13	*T:* Coast, Graham, Thomas, Woof *C:* Griffiths 2, Thompson *P:* Griffiths 6
8 Nov	A	Blackheath	15-14	*P:* Griffiths 5
13 Dec	H	Bedford	14-28	*T:* Morris *P:* Griffiths 3
20 Dec	A	Orrell	6-23	*P:* Griffiths 2
10 Jan	H	Rotherham	26-32	*T:* Holt, Mullins, Hart, O'Shaughnessy *C:* Griffiths 3
17 Jan	A	Wakefield	20-23	*T:* Hart *P:* Griffiths 5
31 Jan	A	Fylde	25-10	*T:* Woof 2, O'Shaughnessy *C:* Griffiths 2 *P:* Griffiths 2
14 Feb	H	Moseley	36-31	*T:* Clapinson, O'Shaughnessy, Thomas, Woof *C:* Griffiths 2 *P:* Griffiths 4
7 Mar	A	Coventry	33-41	*T:* Blyth 2, Hackney, Temmen *C:* Griffiths 2 *P:* Griffiths 3
14 Mar	A	Moseley	22-23	*T:* Griffiths *C:* Griffiths *P:* Griffiths 5
28 Mar	H	Fylde	22-12	*T:* O'Shaughnessy, Thomas *P:* Griffiths 4
11 Apr	H	W Hartlepool	6-51	*P:* Griffiths 2
18 Apr	A	L Scottish	6-26	*P:* Griffiths 2
25 Apr	H	Coventry	24-21	*T:* Coast, Hackney *C:* Griffiths *P:* Griffiths 4

West Hartlepool

Year of formation 1881
Ground Brierton Lane, Hartlepool, Cleveland TS25 5DR Tel: Hartlepool (01429) 233149
Colours Red, white and green; white and green shorts
Captain 1997-98 D Mitchell/T Niu'ualiti'ia
Allied Dunbar Leagues 1997-98 Div 2 2nd – *promoted*   **Tetley's Bitter Cup 1997-98** Lost 21-36 to Sale (quarter-finals)

The best thing about West's season was one of the earliest signings they made – New Zealander Mike Brewer as coach. The former All Black soon knocked the squad into shape. He made a colossal impact and also recruited well. Three signings in particular, locks Philippe Farner (France) and Mark Giacheri (Italy) as well as scrum-half Tiu Nu'ualiti'ia from Western Samoa made a significant contribution to the side. Brewer did not play until January, but he too was soon making his presence felt.

Victories over London Scottish and Bedford right at the end of the league programme guaranteed promotion back into the First Division after an absence of 10 seasons. The win over Bedford had a particularly satisfying look to it, 48-29 was no mean feat against such a formidable side who had run away with the Second Division championship. They progressed well in the cup until they came up against last year's beaten finalists Sale in the quarter-finals. Even so they did not disgrace themselves, as a scoreline of 21-36 suggests, and on the way they accounted for some vigorous, if not glamorous, opponents, including Rugby and Wakefield.

League Record 1997-98

Date	Venue	Opponents	Result	Scorers
30 Aug	H	Waterloo	19-21	*T:* S John *C:* Vile *P:* Vile 4
13 Sep	A	Moseley	21-16	*T:* Morgan, Nu'ualiti'ia *C:* Vile *P:* Vile 2 *D:* Vile
20 Sep	A	Rotherham	21-33	*T:* Botham, Farrell *C:* Vile *P:* Vile, S John *D:* Vile
27 Sep	H	Wakefield	31-20	*T:* Connolly 2, Nu'ualiti'ia *C:* Vile 2 *P:* Vile 3, Belgian
4 Oct	A	Exeter	20-19	*T:* Farrell *P:* Vile 4, Farrell
11 Oct	H	Blackheath	32-21	*T:* Jones 2, Morgan 2, Farner *C:* Vile 2 *P:* Vile
18 Oct	A	Bedford	9-22	*P:* Vile 3
25 Oct	H	Rotherham	22-21	*T:* S John, Vile *P:* Vile 3, Belgian
8 Nov	A	Wakefield	28-12	*T:* Belgian, S John, Ponton *C:* Benson 2 *P:* Benson 3
13 Dec	H	Exeter	34-14	*T:* Vile 2, Benson, Farrell, S John *C:* Vile 3 *P:* Vile
20 Dec	A	Blackheath	22-25	*T:* Wood *C:* Vile *P:* Vile 5
17 Jan	A	Orrell	35-30	*T:* S John, Farrell *C:* Vile 2 *P:* Vile 6 *D:* Farrell
31 Jan	A	Coventry	16-21	*T:* S John *C:* Vile *P:* Vile 3
14 Feb	H	Fylde	66-12	*T:* Sparks 2, Farrell 2, Vile 2, S John, Ponton, Redpath, pen try *C:* Vile 8
22 Feb	H	Orrell	20-11	*T:* Benson, Wood, Vile *C:* Vile *P:* Vile
8 Mar	A	L Scottish	17-31	*T:* Benson, Connolly, Nu'ualiti'ia *C:* Belgian
14 Mar	A	Fylde	34-8	*T:* Belgian, Farrell, Giacheri, Ponton, Nu'ualiti'ia *C:* Vile 3 *P:* Vile
28 Mar	H	Coventry	42-31	*T:* Farner, Giacheri, Hyde, Morgan, Vile *C:* Vile 4 *P:* Vile 3
11 Apr	A	Waterloo	51-6	*T:* Farrell 2, Bishop, Morgan, Sparks, Wood, Vile, Nu'ualiti'ia *C:* Vile 3, Belgian *P:* Vile
18 Apr	H	Moseley	18-18	*P:* Belgian 6
25 Apr	H	L Scottish	11-10	*T:* Morgan *P:* Belgian, Benson
2 May	H	Bedford	48-29	*T:* Mitchell 2, Bishop, Cassidy, Connolly, Farrell *C:* Belgian 3 *P:* Belgian 4

BACK-UP BOYS COME TO THE FORE

THE 1997-98 SEASON IN SCOTLAND
Bill McMurtrie

A chronicle of Scottish rugby's 1997-98 international season would best be consigned to a file at the back of a drawer in an old cabinet in the cellar. Only one victory was achieved in seven internationals, an all-time record defeat was suffered at South Africa's hands at Murrayfield, and Scotland fell to even lower depths when they were humbled in a 25-21 loss to Italy in Treviso. The immediate consequence of those results was the resignation of the two coaches, Richie Dixon and David Johnston, before the Five Nations Championship had even begun.

However, as a strong counter-balance, Scotland's A team recovered so well from a 31-15 defeat by Northern Bulls, the South African Super-12 team, that they recorded the first clean sweep by any of the five nations at that level.

Scotland's senior team opened their programme with a 37-8 defeat by Australia at Murrayfield in November. The result was passed off as the norm for Scotland in pre-Christmas internationals, but worse was to follow two weeks later, with South Africa in rampant mood for a 68-10 win. The South Africans notched 10 tries as they ran up 54 points in a devastating second half. Scotland battled gamely throughout that international, but they were no match for the clinically skilful South Africans. The one Scottish try was scored by Derek Stark, ironically playing his only international of the season.

When Scotland visited Italy in January they seemed to have left even their national pride at home. By the end of the game it was the Italians who were showing all the determination, undaunted even when they were denied what would have been a late winning try because a touch judge had flagged. Italy came back for Paolo Vaccari to snatch a victory that was deserved even though Scotland scored two tries to one.

Within a week the Scottish coaches had departed. The Scottish Rugby Union turned to the Lions' successful pair, Ian McGeechan and Jim Telfer, along with a new back-up team. Telfer, the SRU's director of rugby, resumed as head coach, supported by McGeechan and two other former caps, Roy Laidlaw and David Leslie. Laidlaw was already Telfer's right-hand man in rugby administration at Murrayfield, and Leslie was promoted for the under-21 squad.

Telfer and his triumvirate were successful first time out, albeit a narrow win against Ireland at Lansdowne Road. Scotland were the

The Scotland squad which faced Ireland in Dublin. L-R, back row: G W Scott (replacement), A J Roxburgh (replacement), A G Stanger (replacement), M J Stewart, G C Bulloch, P Walton, D F Cronin, G W Weir, R I Wainwright, A V Tait, S B Grimes (replacement), D I W Hilton (replacement), A D Nicol (replacement), D J Lee (replacement); front row: C A Joiner, R J S Shepherd, G Graham, S D Holmes, G Armstrong (capt), K M Logan, G P J Townsend, C M Chalmers

more adaptable, and they came through to win 17-16 and preserve their record of not having lost to Ireland since 1988. Yet it ought not to have been that close. Rowen Shepherd scored with only two of his six first-half penalty shots. It was, however, Shepherd's inside pass that put Alan Tait through for the try which put Scotland 11-10 ahead at the interval, and Craig Chalmers took over the place-kicking for the two penalty goals that edged the game.

Scotland, however, succumbed again when France, appetites whetted for a second successive Grand Slam, ran in seven tries at Murrayfield in winning 51-16, a record for the series between the countries. A month later it was England's turn to inflict a Murrayfield defeat, the margin narrowed to 34-20 by late tries from Tony Stanger and Shaun Longstaff. Stanger's try was his 24th in international rugby, equalling the Scottish record held by Ian Smith for more than 70 years.

Between those Murrayfield internationals Scotland visited Wembley and lost a match which they really ought to have won against Wales, by 13-19. Gregor Townsend and Longstaff showed the way by opening up the Welsh for a try by the former, Derrick Lee threatened just about every time he touched the ball, and the Scots built up a 13-0 lead that should have been the foundation for victory. However, Lee departed injured after less than half an hour, and Wales worked their way back to a four-point deficit at half-time and on to what – after the first quarter – had seemed an unlikely triumph.

Scotland called on no fewer than 32 players for their seven internationals. Only Townsend was in the starting XV for all of those matches. Yet chopping and changing did not upset Scotland's A team on their way to a clean sweep. Here too 32 players were called on for the Five Nations matches, but the A team had more strands of continuity, with Duncan Hodge, John Kerr, Stuart Reid, Scott Murray and Willie Anderson starting in all four matches. Reid led the Scots against the Welsh and English after injury to the original captain, Bryan Redpath.

Each of the Scots' away A games was played in a downpour on a sodden pitch. Shaun Longstaff's first-minute try at Donnybrook set the Scots on the way to beating the Irish by 11-9, and again they were the more adaptable side in victory over the Welsh by 18-10 on a pitch that the Scots believed was unplayable at Rodney Parade, Newport.

Conditions were much more amenable for Scotland's A matches at home. Between the Dublin and Newport games the Scots recovered from a 3-15 deficit after quarter of an hour to beat the French 24-20 at Goldenacre, a deserved victory even though the visitors scored three tries to two, and in the final match, when the

English visited Inverleith, the Scots ran in five tries in their substantial 44-14 victory.

Scotland's age-group XVs met with mixed fortunes. The under-21 team lost three games but won away matches against Italy by 41-15 and Wales by 10-3, the latter game belatedly switched from Caerphilly to Llanwern because of heavy rain. It was Scotland's first win in six visits to Wales for under-21 matches. The Scottish under-19 team opened their season with a thoroughly satisfying victory over Canada by 39-6 at Myreside, but a 41-0 loss to England at Penrith preceded a poor performance in the FIRA world junior tournament in France. Defeats by Chile and Wales before wins over Spain and Russia left the Scots in 13th position, their worst placing in four ventures in the competition. Scotland's under-18 team beat Spain's under-19 side by 33-7 at Stirling but lost to their Irish and Welsh contemporaries – 14-25 at Ravenhill and 11-13 at Glasgow Southern. However, the Welsh snatched victory only with a last-minute try.

In the European club competitions the Scottish teams had a more productive season than they had had in 1996-97 – seven wins in 25 games contrasting with two out of 17. Glasgow progressed to the Heineken Cup knock-out stage as runners-up behind Wasps in their pool through victories over Ulster (home and away) and Swansea (at Scotstoun Stadium). However, a 90-19 trouncing by Leicester brought Glasgow back to earth in a quarter-final qualifying play-off at Welford Road. Caledonia won two of their six Heineken matches, both at the St Johnstone football ground, McDiarmid Park – 17-19 against Treviso, and 30-24 against Pau. Edinburgh, too, had a couple of wins, both against French clubs, in the European Conference – 27-25 away to Biarritz, and 18-15 against Perpignan at Goldenacre.

Edinburgh also won the Inter-District Championship, though it was only by a try-count tie-break that they took the title for the first time since 1989. Three teams finished level with two wins and one defeat each, with Edinburgh scoring eight tries, Glasgow six, and Caledonia (the defending champions) three. Edinburgh produced a stylish finish in the snow at Inverleith to snatch the title with five tries in a 31-10 win over Scottish Borders.

However, the Borders took the under-21 and under-19 trophies, each with a clean sweep. Glasgow were the under-18 champions, also winning all of their games, though they lived dangerously, finishing with a points difference of only plus five.

Both principal club trophies left the Borders. Watsonians edged Melrose by the margin of one bonus point for the SRU Tennents Velvet Premiership title, only the fourth time in the competition's 25 years that it has not been won by a Border club, and Glasgow Hawks beat Kelso by 36-14 in the cup final. Gala won the Border

League title for the first time since 1981, and Kelso took the Kings of the Sevens championship contested over all the tournaments on the Border circuit.

SRU TENNENTS VELVET PREMIERSHIP AND NATIONAL LEAGUE REVIEW 1997-98

Watsonians broke the Melrose grasp on the Scottish club trophy. It was only the second time in seven years that the Borderers had failed to win the title, and in the end the championship was settled by a margin of only one bonus point. Watsonians and Melrose each won nine of their 13 SRU Tennents Velvet Premiership games, but the Edinburgh club took eight bonus points whereas the Borderers had seven. Only Heriot's, Boroughmuir, and Stirling County had previously interrupted Border clubs' hold on the championship.

Defeat by Jed-Forest by 31-15 in Watsonians' first away match of the championship was an unexpected early upset for the Edinburgh club. Further losses followed against Boroughmuir and West of Scotland, but Watsonians stated their emphatic championship challenge with a home win against Melrose by 33-24 to complete the first stage of the league in February. At that point each of the three Premier divisions split into two sections, with the top five playing each other for the title, and at that cut-off Watsonians were just one point ahead of the champions, with Currie and Hawick two more adrift. West made up the championship play-off quintet.

Watsonians continued on a roll, with two substantial away wins – 45-20 against Hawick, and 56-5 against Currie. John Kerr ran in three tries in the Currie match, but that was nothing to the scoring domination that Duncan Hodge exerted on Watsonians' 34-8 victory against West at Myreside, a result that all but tied up the championship. The capped stand-off scored all of his club's points with three tries and seven goals in a victory that meant Watsonians had only to avoid losing by more than 67 points on their visit to Melrose the following week. The Edinburgh club lost that game by 17-37, but they could still celebrate.

Melrose set the championship's early pace in winning their first four league matches before they fell at home against Hawick by 8-19. It ended a run of 26 league matches without defeat, their previous loss also having been against Hawick.

West came through strongly in the second stage of the championship, beating Melrose (by 36-13 at Burnbrae), Hawick, and Currie and losing only on their visit to Watsonians. That surge lifted West into third place only a year after their return to the First Division, and their city rivals, Glasgow Hawks, the one-year-old amalgam of GHK and Glasgow Academicals, won the Second Division, securing the championship with a 100% sequence before their one and only league defeat – 5-14 on an April evening visit to Kilmarnock. Hawks went on to complete a double by beating Kelso in the Scottish Cup final.

Selkirk returned to the Second Division by winning the third whereas East Kilbride and Berwick continued to rise through the ranks as the promoted pair from the National League to the Premiership. It was the third successive year in which Berwick had been promoted. Annan did even better – as the National League's Second Division champions, they were promoted for the sixth season in a row. Hamilton Academicals took the National Seventh Division title by winning all of their 18 games and scoring 783 points, an average of well over 40 per match.

SRU TENNENTS PREMIERSHIP

* Bonus points (B) were awarded for the first time in 1997/98.

Division 1A	P	W	D	L	F	A	B	Pts
Watsonians	13	9	0	4	397	201	8	44
Melrose	13	9	0	4	331	230	7	43
W. of Scotland	13	8	0	5	301	233	7	39
Currie	13	7	0	6	260	335	4	32
Hawick	13	6	0	7	262	269	2	26

Division 1B	P	W	D	L	F	A	B	Pts
Boroughmuir	13	8	0	5	316	213	5	37
Stirling County	13	6	0	7	208	236	3	27
Jed-Forest	13	5	0	8	219	388	2	22
Heriot's FP**	13	5	0	8	255	302	1	21
Edinburgh Acads	13	2	0	11	209	353	5	13

Hawick have won the Scottish Championship 10 times, 1973-74 to 1977-78, 1981-82, 1983-84 to 1986-87; Melrose six times, 1989-90, 1991-92 to 1993-94, 1995-96 and 1996-97; Gala three times, 1979-80, 1980-81 and 1982-83; Kelso twice, 1987-88 1988-89; Heriot's FP 1978-79; Boroughmuir 1990-91; Stirling County 1994-95; Watsonians 1997-98

Division 2A	P	W	D	L	F	A	B	Pts
Glasgow Hks	13	12	0	1	521	180	10	58
Kelso**	13	8	1	4	330	282	6	40
Dundee HSFP	13	7	0	6	333	270	9	37
Gala	13	7	0	6	301	323	6	34
Kilmarnock	13	6	0	7	228	234	5	29

**Heriot's retained First Division status by beating Kelso (Second Division runners-up) in a play-off at Pennypit Park on May 16

Division 2B	P	W	D	L	F	A	B	Pts
Kirkcaldy	13	8	0	5	365	227	6	38
Biggar	13	5	0	7	225	211	7	31
Musselburgh	13	5	2	6	213	312	1	25
Peebles	13	3	1	9	173	374	5	19
Preston Lg FP	13	1	0	12	152	428	4	8

Division 3A	P	W	D	L	F	A	B	Pts
Selkirk	13	11	0	2	258	135	4	48
A'deen GSFP	13	10	0	3	274	154	6	46
Gordonians	13	7	1	5	247	200	4	34
Stewart's M FP	13	7	0	6	222	279	4	32
Grangemouth	13	6	0	7	300	266	6	30

Division 3B	P	W	D	L	F	A	B	Pts
Glenrothes	13	8	0	5	269	166	5	37
Glasgow S.	13	7	0	6	309	249	4	32
Ayr	13	5	1	7	189	190	5	27
Stewartry	13	1	1	11	183	424	4	10
Hillhead/Jhill	13	1	1	11	151	339	3	9

SRU TENNENTS NATIONAL LEAGUE

Division 1	P	W	D	L	F	A	B	Pts
East Kilbride	18	17	0	1	525	204	11	79
Berwick	18	17	0	1	475	162	11	79
Langholm	18	11	0	7	380	249	10	54
Duns	18	8	1	9	379	364	8	42
Hutchesons A.	18	8	1	9	327	409	7	41
Corstorphine	18	7	0	11	407	385	7	35
Trinity Acads	18	7	0	11	389	402	7	35
Haddington	18	6	1	11	219	360	3	29
Dunfermline	18	3	2	13	284	511	2	18
Edinburgh U	18	3	1	14	259	598	4	18

Division 2	P	W	D	L	F	A	B	Pts
Annan	18	15	2	1	526	193	8	72
Livingston	18	14	0	4	425	208	9	65
Dalziel	18	12	0	6	436	189	8	56
Murrayfield W	18	11	1	6	366	229	7	53
Royal High	18	8	1	9	307	373	5	39
St Boswells	18	8	0	10	279	402	3	35
Cambuslang	18	7	0	11	357	397	4	32
Portobello FP	18	6	0	12	285	374	7	31
Howe of Fife	18	6	0	12	292	350	6	30
Wigtownshire	18	1	0	17	172	730	2	6

Division 3	P	W	D	L	F	A	B	Pts
Linlithgow	18	16	1	1	517	172	10	76
Ross High	18	14	1	3	554	267	11	69
Madras Col FP	18	13	0	5	452	250	10	62
Cartha Q's Pk	18	12	1	5	348	269	7	57
Perthshire	18	9	1	8	314	368	4	42
Morgan FP	18	7	0	11	315	281	10	38
Dumfries	18	7	0	11	245	432	6	34
Allan Glen's	18	5	1	12	279	395	6	28
Lismore	18	3	1	14	230	425	4	18
Ardrossan As	18	1	0	17	108	503	3	7

Division 4	P	W	D	L	F	A	B	Pts
Garnock	18	15	0	3	396	180	8	68
Alloa	18	13	1	4	331	173	5	59
Cumbernauld	18	11	2	5	303	211	8	56
Clydebank	18	11	1	6	346	249	6	52
Highland	18	10	1	7	349	265	6	48
Aberdeenshire	18	7	3	8	363	242	9	43
Penicuik	18	8	0	10	212	325	3	35
Paisley	18	6	0	12	235	417	3	27
Hillfoots	18	3	0	15	219	435	7	19
Leith Acads	18	2	0	16	160	417	5	13

Division 5	P	W	D	L	F	A	B	Pts
Lochaber	18	14	0	4	543	189	14	70
W'side/Drum	18	15	1	2	449	207	6	68
Whitecraigs	18	11	1	6	430	257	11	57
Lasswade	18	11	1	6	349	184	10	56
North Berwick	18	10	0	8	429	311	9	49
Greenock W	18	9	1	8	378	265	7	45
Lenzie	18	8	0	10	394	383	6	38
Aberdeen U	18	5	0	13	362	642	7	27
Falkirk	18	3	1	14	260	628	3	17
Dunbar	18	1	1	16	298	826	5	11

Division 6	P	W	D	L	F	A	B	Pts
C'noust HSFP	18	16	0	2	583	170	13	77
Helensburgh	18	16	0	2	583	140	11	75
Forrester FP	18	15	0	3	508	179	10	70
Cumnock	18	11	0	7	372	309	6	50
RAF Kinloss	18	9	0	9	300	315	6	42
Earlston	18	6	0	12	209	436	7	31
Marr	18	4	0	14	247	317	12	28
Moray	18	5	0	13	212	671	4	24
Irvine	18	3	2	13	231	442	5	21
St Andrews U	18	3	2	13	212	478	5	21

Division 7	P	W	D	L	F	A	B	Pts
Hamilton A	18	18	0	0	783	140	11	83

RAF L'mouth	18	15	0	3	590	204	9	69
Orkney	18	11	0	7	487	300	11	55
Broughton FP	18	10	0	8	303	245	9	49
Newton St	18	10	0	8	349	361	7	40
Panmure	18	8	0	10	363	298	8	40
Dalkeith	18	7	0	11	271	326	9	37
Walkerburn	18	7	0	11	241	546	4	32
Rosyth & D	18	3	1	14	141	589	4	14
Inverleith	18	0	1	17	119	638	3	5

(Four points for a win; two for a draw)

District League Champions

Edinburgh: Heriot-Watt University
Glasgow: Strathendrick
Midlands: Strathmore
North: Ellon

Strathendrick and Ellon won promotion to the National League's Seventh Division through a round-robin competition contested by the four District League champions.

BANK OF SCOTLAND BORDER LEAGUE

	P	W	D	L	F	A	B	Pts
Gala	14	12	0	2	403	172	13	51
Hawick	14	13	0	1	350	152	6	46
Melrose	12	7	0	5	252	229	7	33
Jed-Forest	13	5	0	8	284	288	7	30
Kelso	12	4	0	8	180	223	1	21
Langholm	12	3	0	9	141	303	3	21
Selkirk	11	4	0	7	177	246	1	20
Peebles	12	2	0	10	155	329	0	16

(Three points for a win; one for a defeat)

INTER-DISTRICT CHAMPIONSHIP

	P	W	D	L	F	A	Tries	Pts
Edinburgh	3	2	0	1	76	55	8	4
Glasgow	3	2	0	1	67	49	6	4
Caledonia	3	2	0	1	49	54	3	4
Borders	3	0	0	3	34	68	3	0

Edinburgh won Championship on tie-break by virtue of scoring most tries.

SCOTTISH INTER-DISTRICT CHAMPIONSHIP 1997-98

17 October, Riverside Park, Jedburgh

Scottish Borders 15 (1G 1PG 1T) **Caledonia 20** (5PG 1T)
Scottish Borders: G J Aitchison (Kelso); S A Nichol (Melrose), A G Stanger (Hawick) *(capt)*, C A Murray (Hawick), M Dods (Gala); S W Welsh (Hawick), I T Fairley (Kelso); P H Wright (West of Scotland), J A Hay (Hawick), S W Ferguson (Peebles), R R Brown (Melrose), I A Fullarton (Kelso), S A Aitken (Melrose), C D Hogg (Melrose), A J Roxburgh (Kelso) *Substitutions:* N A McIlroy (Jed-Forest) for Wright (39 mins); A C Redpath (Melrose) for Aitken (71 mins); K Utterson (Kelso) for Stanger (79 mins)
Scorers *Tries:* Nichol, Stanger *Conversion:* Aitchison *Penalty Goal:* Welsh
Caledonia: R J S Shepherd (Melrose); S Longstaff (Dundee HSFP), P R Rouse (Dundee HSFP), D G Officer (Currie), J A Kerr (Watsonians); M McKenzie (Stirling County), D W Patterson (Heriot's FP);

W D Anderson (Kirkcaldy), G W Scott (Dundee HSFP), A Penman (Kirkcaldy), S J Campbell (Dundee HSFP), S D Grimes (Watsonians), D J McIvor (Glenrothes), G N Flockhart (Stirling County), R I Wainwright (Dundee HSFP) (*capt*) *Substitutions:* N A Renton (Kirkcaldy) for Shepherd (48 mins); M Waite (Watsonians) for Flockhart (48 mins); J J Manson (West of Scotland) for Anderson (56 mins); D J Herrington (Kirkcaldy) for Penman (56 mins); J P R White (Watsonians) for Waite (69 mins)
Scorers *Try:* Patterson *Penalty Goals:* McKenzie, Shepherd (4)
Referee R J Dickson (Madras College FP)

---

19 October, Scotstoun Stadium

Glasgow 36 (3G 5PG) **Edinburgh 20** (5PG 1T)
Glasgow: C M Sangster (Stirling County); D A Stark (Glasgow Hawks), C T Simmers (Glasgow Hawks), M McGrandles (Glasgow Hawks), J M Craig (West of Scotland); T Hayes (Glasgow Hawks), F H Stott (West of Scotland); G R McIlwham (Glasgow Hawks), G C Bulloch (West of Scotland) (*capt*), A J Kittle (Stirling County), M Norval (Stirling County), G C Perrett (West of Scotland), M I Wallace (Glasgow Hawks), D R McLeish (Watsonians), I W Sinclair (Watsonians) *Substitutions:* G Fraser (Kilmarnock) for Sangster (67 mins); F D Wallace (Glasgow Hawks) for McLeish (74 mins)
Scorers *Tries:* Craig (2), Hayes *Conversions:* Hayes (3) *Penalty Goals:* Hayes (5)
Edinburgh: C R Aitken (Boroughmuir); S D Reed (Boroughmuir), L Graham (Boroughmuir), S Hastings (Watsonians), A McLean (Boroughmuir); D W Hodge (Watsonians), G G Burns (Watsonians); R B McNulty (Boroughmuir), G McKelvey (Watsonians), B D Stewart (Edinburgh Academicals), D G Burns (Boroughmuir), M Blair (Currie), T A McVie (Heriot's FP), S J Reid (Boroughmuir) (*capt*), G F Dall (Heriot's FP) *Substitutions:* P T Jennings (Boroughmuir) for Blair (52 mins); N Penny (Watsonians) for Reed (55 mins)
Scorers *Try:* McLean *Penalty Goals:* Hodge (5)
Referee D I Ramage (Berwick)

---

24 October, Philiphaugh, Selkirk

Scottish Borders 9 (3PG) **Glasgow 17** (4PG 1T)
Scottish Borders: G J Aitchison (Kelso); S A Nichol (Melrose), A G Stanger (Hawick) (*capt*), C A Murray (Hawick), M Dods (Gala); C M Chalmers (Melrose), I T Fairley (Kelso); N A McIlroy (Jed-Forest), J A Hay (Hawick), S W Ferguson (Peebles), R R Brown (Melrose), I A Fullarton (Kelso), A C Redpath (Melrose), C D Hogg (Melrose), A J Roxburgh (Kelso) *Substitutions:* S W Welsh (Hawick) for Chalmers (60 mins); S A Aitken (Melrose) for Redpath (77 mins)
Scorer *Penalty Goals:* Chalmers (3)
Glasgow: C M Sangster (Stirling County); D A Stark (Glasgow Hawks), C T Simmers (Glasgow Hawks), M McGrandles (Glasgow Hawks), J M Craig (West of Scotland); T Hayes (Glasgow Hawks), F H Stott (West of Scotland); G R McIlwham (Glasgow Hawks), G C Bulloch (West of Scotland) (*capt*), A J Kittle (Stirling County), M Norval (Stirling County), G C Perrett (West of Scotland), M I Wallace (Glasgow Hawks), D R McLeish (West of Scotland), J D Shaw (West of Scotland) *Substitutions:* F D Wallace (Glasgow Hawks) for M I Wallace (13 mins); G Fraser (Kilmarnock) for Craig (52 mins); G H Metcalfe (Glasgow Hawks) for Simmers (72 mins)
Scorers *Try:* Stark *Penalty Goals:* Hayes (4)
Referee J C Bacigalupo (Murrayfield Wanderers)

---

26 October, Inverleith

Edinburgh 25 (5PG 2T) **Caledonia 9** (3PG)
Edinburgh: C R Aitken (Boroughmuir); G C Caldwell (Currie), S Hastings (Watsonians), D W Hodge (Watsonians), A McLean (Boroughmuir); G Ross (Heriot's FP), G G Burns (Watsonians); R B McNulty (Boroughmuir), G McKelvey (Watsonians), B D Stewart (Edinburgh Academicals), D G Burns (Boroughmuir), M Blair (Currie), T A McVie (Heriot's FP), S J Reid (Boroughmuir) (*capt*), G F Dall (Heriot's FP) *Substitutions:* F M Henderson (Watsonians) for McLean (48 mins); G Beveridge (Boroughmuir) for G G Burns (75 mins); S W Paul (Watsonians) for McNulty (75 mins)
Scorers *Tries:* D G Burns, Dall *Penalty Goals:* Hodge (5)
Caledonia: R J S Shepherd (Melrose); D G Officer (Currie), S Longstaff (Dundee HSFP), P R Rouse (Dundee HSFP), J A Kerr (Watsonians); M McKenzie (Stirling County), D W Patterson (Heriot's FP); W D Anderson (Kirkcaldy), G W Scott (Dundee HSFP), A Penman (Kirkcaldy), S J Campbell (Dundee HSFP), S D Grimes (Watsonians), D J McIvor (Glenrothes), G N Flockhart (Stirling County), R I Wainwright (Dundee HSFP) (*capt*) *Substitutions:* J P R White (Watsonians) for McIvor (43 mins); J J Manson (West of Scotland) for Wainwright (58 mins); B R Easson (Edinburgh Academicals) for McKenzie (61 mins)
Scorer *Penalty Goals:* Shepherd (3)
Referee C B Muir (Langholm)

---

4 January, Rubislaw, Aberdeen

Caledonia 20 (2G 2PG) **Glasgow 14** (2G)
Caledonia: R J S Shepherd (Melrose); S Longstaff (Dundee HSFP), P R Rouse (Dundee HSFP), J McLaren

(Stirling County), J A Kerr (Watsonians); M McKenzie (Stirling County), D W Patterson (Heriot's FP);
J J Manson (West of Scotland), G W Scott (Dundee HSFP), W D Anderson (Kirkcaldy), J P R White
(Watsonians), S D Grimes (Watsonians), D J McIvor (Glenrothes), G N Flockhart (Stirling County),
R I Wainwright (Dundee HSFP) (*capt*) *Substitutions:* D J Herrington (Kirkcaldy) for Anderson (56 mins);
M Waite (Watsonians) for Flockhart (56 mins); D G Officer (Currie) for Rouse (68 mins), J Petrie (Dundee
HSFP) for McIvor (71 mins); D Short (Stirling County) for Patterson (75 mins)
Scorers *Tries:* McIvor, Manson *Conversions:* Shepherd (2) *Penalty Goals:* Shepherd (2)
Glasgow: C M Sangster (Stirling County); D A Stark (Glasgow Hawks), A Bulloch (West of Scotland),
C T Simmers (Glasgow Hawks), G H Metcalfe (Glasgow Hawks); T Hayes (Glasgow Hawks), F H Stott
(West of Scotland); G R McIlwham (Glasgow Hawks), G C Bulloch (West of Scotland) (*capt*), M Beckham
(Glasgow Hawks), M Norval (Stirling County), G C Perrett (West of Scotland), M I Wallace (Glasgow
Hawks), F D Wallace (Glasgow Hawks), J D Shaw (West of Scotland) *Substitutions:* G T Mackay (Glasgow
Hawks) for Shaw (56 mins); D R McLeish (West of Scotland) for F D Wallace (56 mins); D Porte (Glasgow
Hawks) for McIlwham (temp 65-68 mins)
Scorers *Tries:* G C Bulloch, Simmers *Conversions:* Hayes (2)
Referee J M Fleming (Boroughmuir)

---

4 January, Inverleith

Edinburgh 31 (3G 2T) **Scottish Borders 10** (1G 1PG)
Edinburgh: H R Gilmour (Heriot's FP); I C Glasgow (Heriot's FP), S Hastings (Watsonians), M J M Mayer
(Watsonians), S D Reed (Boroughmuir); D W Hodge (Watsonians), G G Burns (Watsonians); R B McNulty
(Boroughmuir), K R Allan (Boroughmuir), B D Stewart (Edinburgh Academicals), D G Burns
(Boroughmuir), M Blair (Currie), T A McVie (Heriot's FP), S J Reid (Boroughmuir) (*capt*), C G Mather
(Watsonians) *Substitutions:* S W Paul (Watsonians) for Stewart (16 mins); G F Dall (Heriot's FP) for Mather
(62 mins); A McLean (Boroughmuir) for Glasgow (75 mins); D Rogerson (Currie) for G G Burns (77 mins)
Scorers *Tries:* Blair, Glasgow, Hodge, McLean, Mayer *Conversions:* Hodge (3)
Scottish Borders: C A Murray (Hawick); S A Nichol (Melrose), A G Stanger (Hawick), A G Shiel
(Melrose), M Moncrieff (Melrose); C M Chalmers (Melrose), B W Redpath (Melrose) (*capt*); P H Wright
(West of Scotland), J A Hay (Hawick), S W Ferguson (Peebles), R R Brown (Melrose), I A Fullarton (Kelso),
A C Redpath (Melrose), B L Renwick (Hawick), A J Roxburgh (Kelso) *Substitutions:* S Bennet (Kelso) for
A C Redpath (51 mins); M Dods (Gala) for Murray (62 mins)
Scorers *Try:* Nichol *Conversion:* Chalmers *Penalty Goal:* Chalmers
Referee J Pearson (England)

SRU TENNENTS VELVET CUP 1997-98

9 May 1998, Murrayfield
Glasgow Hawks 36 (2G 4PG 2T) Kelso 14 (2G)

Glasgow Hawks completed what could long remain a unique
double by beating Kelso to win the SRU Tennents Velvet Cup to
add to the Premiership Second Division trophy. Indeed, the cup
final, attracting a crowd of more than 23,000, was a rarity also in
that it was contested by two Second Division clubs, though well
before the end Hawks were flying high, convincingly justifying their
status as odds-on pre-match favourites.

Hawks, though less than a year old, were undoubtedly the club of
the Scottish season. A 1997 close-season amalgam of the Anniesland neighbours, Glasgow Academicals and GHK, the fledglings
had won the Second Division title with three of their 14 games still
to play, and on their way to the cup final they ousted no fewer than
three First Division clubs – Jed-Forest by 67-21, Watsonians (later
to become Scottish champions) by 21-6 and Boroughmuir 37-12.
Only the last of those was at home.

Kelso too had won past three clubs from the top flight. A 10-3
victory against West of Scotland at Poynder Park was followed,

again at home, by an 18-13 win over Melrose, the defending cup holders, and in the semi-final Kelso edged past Currie by only 18-17 at Malleny Park.

Kelso threatened an upset in the final when John Wearne's precise pass sent Iain Fairley in at the posts. Wearne's conversion took Kelso to a 7-3 lead, but the masterful Tommy Hayes responded by creating space for a try on the right by Derek Stark, who had played for the cup-winning team the previous year. Hayes converted, and the Cook Islands' World Cup stand-off edged Hawks to 16-7 with a couple of penalty goals. Another Hayes penalty in the second half was the prelude to Hawks' two killer punches in the last quarter, with Ally Common squeezing in on the left and Gordon Mackay also crossing.

Only then, with Hawks safe at 31-7, did Kelso score again, Graeme Cowe putting Wearne over. Yet Hawks still had the last word with Common's second try.

Hayes was voted official man-of-the-match. Yet none did more than Mackay, Hawks' No 8, to take the game to Kelso with his forceful running. The same in Kelso's cause could be said of Adam Roxburgh, the Borderers' captain and international breakaway forward. Both Mackay and Roxburgh thrived in the school of hard knocks.

Glasgow Hawks: G H Metcalfe; D A Stark, C T Simmers, D Wilson (*capt*), A N Common; T Hayes, S M Simmers; G R McIlwham, C P Docherty, M Beckham, C Afuakwah, S C Hutton, F D Wallace, G T Mackay, M I Wallace *Substitutions:* C E Little for S M Simmers (49 mins); A G Ness for Mackay (71 mins); M C Blackie for Beckham (77 mins); K Horton for Docherty (77 mins); C G MacGregor for Hayes (77 mins); M N McGrandles for C T Simmers (78 mins)
Scorers *Tries*: Common (2), Mackay, Stark *Conversions*: Hayes (2) *Penalty Goals*: Hayes (4)
Kelso: D J Baird; S A Ross, G Laing, I T Fairley, C A Jackson; S J Wearne, G Cowe; S T Murray, K D Thomson, D D Howlett, I A Fullarton, S Laing, S Bennet, S I Forsyth, A J Roxburgh (*capt*) *Substitutions:* S C M Rowley for S Laing (72 mins); R J Hogarth for Murray (75 mins)
Scorers *Tries*: Fairley, Wearne *Conversions*: Wearne (2)
Referee C B Muir (Langholm)

Earlier Rounds

Currie set a Scottish Cup record by notching 169 points in a third-round rout of Allan Glen's, from the National League's Division Three. Kelso, Watsonians, and Grangemouth also ran up three-figure scores in the same round. Strathendrick, who went on to win the Glasgow and District League title, upset the rankings with a 22-14 win over Falkirk, from the National League's Fifth Division. East Kilbride, however, were the most notable 'giant-killers' in the early rounds. The ultimate National League First

Division champions removed two Premiership clubs with home victories in the third and fourth rounds – 38-13 against Stewartry, and 28-24 against Dundee High School FP, who were then still challenging for promotion from the Second Division. Even when East Kilbride came up against Hawick, the 1996 cup winners, the new-town club gave a good account of themselves: the Borderers were relieved to depart from the Torrance House ground with a 28-15 win.

East Kilbride's performance was all the more creditable as they were the only club outside the Premiership's First and Second Divisions to survive to the fifth round. At the next stage, the quarter-finals, only Glasgow Hawks and Kelso prevented a First Division monopoly. Yet it was those two who went on to the final.

Boroughmuir seemed strong cup contenders when they left Mansfield Park with a 48-5 victory over Hawick, winners of the first cup final in 1996. That quarter-final was a personal triumph for Campbell Aitken, Boroughmuir's full-back, who scored 28 points with three tries, five conversions and a penalty goal.

A try by Darren Burns from a tapped penalty gave Boroughmuir hope of another away win when they led 5-3 on their visit to New Anniesland for the semi-final. Glasgow Hawks soon regained the lead when Chas Afuakwah chased through on to a cross kick by Tommy Hayes, and two minutes later the scorer's fellow lock, Scott Hutton, was driven over for a try after Hawks had stolen a Boroughmuir throw-in. It was, though, only in the last quarter with tries by Derek Stark and Glenn Metcalfe that Hawks added the substance to their winning margin of 37-12.

Melrose, cup winners in 1997, had an uncomfortable visit to Kilmarnock before edging through the fifth round by 16-9. The match could well have swung in the Second Division club's favour, and it was opposition from those ranks who broke Melrose's hold on the trophy, when the champions lost 13-18 to Kelso at Poynder Park. Iain Fairley, the Kelso scrum-half playing at centre, made two telling thrusts – first for a try by Kevin Thomson, then for one of his own.

Kelso toppled First Division opponents in the semi-final, too, though it was a close-run contest which Currie seemed to have won when David Officer capitalised on a series of five-metre scrums for a try which Ally Donaldson converted for 17-13 with only six minutes left. The Borderers, however, peeled round the front of a line-out for an Adam Roxburgh try that snatched the one-point win.

Selkirk have improved every year through the ranks of the knock-out competitions – runners-up in the SRU Tennents Bowl in 1996, winners of that trophy in 1997, and victorious in the 1998 Shield final, though it was only a last-act try by Cameron Cochrane that snatched a 17-11 victory over Berwick. Perthshire won the Bowl by beating Carnoustie 10-8 in an all-Tayside final.

RESULTS

Third round

Alloa 3, Aberdeen GSFP 31; Berwick 7, Heriot's FP 24; Biggar 28, Hillhead/Jordanhill 15; Boroughmuir 64, Livingston 0; Corstorphine 22, Linlithgow 24; Currie 169, Allan Glen's 3; Dalziel 14, Duns 13; Dundee HSFP 35, Stewart's Melville FP 8; Dunfermline 0, Kirkcaldy 5; East Kilbride 38, Stewartry 13; Falkirk 14, Strathendrick 22; Gala 60, Hawick Trades 17; Garnock 34, Hamilton Academicals 0; Glasgow Hawks 95 Cumbernauld 6; Glasgow Southern 54, RAF Lossiemouth 10; Gordonians 19, Preston Lodge FP 11; Grangemouth 101, Dumfries 0; Haddington 0, Hawick 54; Howe of Fife 8, Stirling County 60; Hutchesons'/Aloysians 7, Annan 9; Jed-Forest 67, Lochaber 14; Kinross 5, Kelso 112; Langholm 39, Forrester FP 3; Madras College FP 3, Kilmarnock Falcons 26; Melrose 48, Glenrothes 7; Murrayfield Wanderers 18, Aberdeenshire 9; Musselburgh 82, Cumnock 0; Peebles 19, Ayr 16; St Boswells 3, Edinburgh Academicals 69; Selkirk 5, West of Scotland 39; Trinity Academicals 39, Penicuik 8; Wigtownshire 9, Watsonians 107

Fourth round

Aberdeen GSFP 10 Glasgow Hawks 39; Biggar 0, Kilmarnock 13; East Kilbride 28, Dundee HSFP 24; Edinburgh Academicals 50, Dalziel 10; Kirkcaldy 44, Trinity Academicals 12; Hawick 27, Langholm 5; Heriot's FP 58, Annan 6; Jed-Forest 27, Garnock 5; Linlithgow 5, Boroughmuir 77; Melrose 41, Grangemouth 12; Murrayfield Wanderers 16, Kelso 32; Musselburgh 32, Currie 41; Peebles 12, Gala 30; Stirling County 27, Gordonians 14; Strathendrick 0, Watsonians 41; West of Scotland 38, Glasgow Southern 22

Fifth round

Currie 38, Gala 13; East Kilbride 15, Hawick 28; Edinburgh Academicals 22, Watsonians 55; Heriot's FP 38, Stirling County 46; Jed-Forest 21, Glasgow Hawks 67; Kelso 10, West of Scotland 3; Kilmarnock 9, Melrose 16; Kirkcaldy 16, Boroughmuir 24

Quarter-finals

Stirling County 14, Currie 27; Hawick 5, Boroughmuir 48; Kelso 18, Melrose 13; Watsonians 6, Glasgow Hawks 21

Semi-finals

Currie 17, Kelso 18; Glasgow Hawks 37, Boroughmuir 12

Final *(at Murrayfield)*

Glasgow Hawks 36, Kelso 14

Previous finals *(all at Murrayfield)*

1996 Hawick 17, Watsonians 15
1997 Melrose 31, Boroughmuir 23

SCOTLAND XV TO SOUTHERN AFRICA 1997

THE TOURING PARTY

Manager D W Morgan   **Coach** G C Hogg   **Assistant Coach** H Campbell
Captain A D Nicol

Full-backs: D J Lee (London Scottish), R J S Shepherd (Melrose)

Threequarters: *M Dods (Northampton), B R S Eriksson (London Scottish),
H R Gilmour (Heriot's FP), *S Hastings (Watsonians), C A Joiner (Leicester),
S L Longstaff (Dundee HSFP), M J M Mayer (Watsonians), C A Murray
(Hawick), S A Nichol (Melrose), A G Stanger (Hawick)

Half-backs: G G Burns (Watsonians), C M Chalmers (Melrose), D W Hodge
(Watsonians), A D Nicol (Bath)

Forwards: S J Brotherstone (Melrose), N J R Broughton (Melrose), G C Bulloch
(West of Scotland), S J Campbell (Melrose), G Graham (Newcastle), S B Grimes
(Watsonians), D I W Hilton (Bath), S D Holmes (London Scottish), C D Hogg
(Melrose), A Lucking (Currie), C G Mather (Watsonians), S Murray (Bedford),
E W Peters (Bath), I R Smith (Moseley), B D Stewart (Edinburgh Acads),
M J Stewart (Northampton), P Walton (Newcastle)

*Replacement during tour

TOUR RECORD

All matches   Played 6   Won 3   Lost 3   Points for 200   Against 146

SCORING DETAILS

All matches

For:	23T	17C	16PG	1DG	200 Pts
Against:	17T	11C	13PG		146 Pts

MATCH DETAILS

1997	OPPONENTS	VENUE	RESULT
17 June	Zimbabwe	Harare	W 55-10
21 June	Gauteng Lions	Johannesburg	L 20-42
25 June	Gauteng Falcons	Brakpan	L 35-38
27 June	Northern Transvaal	Pretoria	W 33-22
1 July	Mpumalanga	Nelspruit	L 21-24
4 July	Eastern Province	Port Elizabeth	W 36-10

SCOTTISH INTERNATIONAL PLAYERS
(*up to 30 April 1998*)

Note: Years given for Five Nations' matches are for second half of season; eg 1972 means season 1971-72. Years for all other matches refer to the actual year of the match. When a series has taken place, figures have been used to denote the particular matches in which players have featured. Thus 1981 *NZ* 1,2 indicates that a player appeared in the first and second Tests of the series. The abandoned game with Ireland at Belfast in 1885 is now included as a cap match.

Abercrombie, C H (United Services) 1910 *I, E,* 1911 *F, W,* 1913 *F, W*
Abercrombie, J G (Edinburgh U) 1949 *F, W, I,* 1950 *F, W, I, E*
Agnew, W C C (Stewart's Coll FP) 1930 *W, I*
Ainslie, R (Edinburgh Inst FP) 1879 *I, E,* 1880 *I, E,* 1881 *E,* 1882 *I, E*
Ainslie, T (Edinburgh Inst FP) 1881 *E,* 1882 *I, E,* 1883 *W, I, E,* 1884 *W, I, E,* 1885 *W, I* 1,2
Aitchison, G R (Edinburgh Wands) 1883 *I*
Aitchison, T G (Gala) 1929 *W, I, E*
Aitken, A I (Edinburgh Inst FP) 1889 *I*
Aitken, G G (Oxford U) 1924 *W, I, E,* 1925 *F, W, I, E,* 1929 *F*
Aitken, J (Gala) 1977 *E, I, F,* 1981 *F, W, E, I, NZ* 1,2, *R, A,* 1982 *E, I, F, W,* 1983 *F, W, E, NZ,* 1984 *W, E, I, F, R*
Aitken, R (London Scottish) 1947 *W*
Allan, B (Glasgow Acads) 1881 *I*
Allan, J (Edinburgh Acads) 1990 *NZ* 1, 1991, *W, I, R,* [*J, I, WS, E, NZ*]
Allan, J L (Melrose) 1952 *F, W, I,* 1953 *W*
Allan, J L F (Cambridge U) 1957 *I, E*
Allan, J W (Melrose) 1927 *F,* 1928 *F, I, E,* 1929 *F, W, I, E,* 1930 *F, E,* 1931 *F, W, I, E,* 1932 *SA, W, I,* 1934 *I, E*
Allan, R C (Hutchesons' GSFP) 1969 *I*
Allardice, W D (Aberdeen GSFP) 1947 *A,* 1948 *F, W, I,* 1949 *F, W, I, E*
Allen, H W (Glasgow Acads) 1873 *E*
Anderson, A H (Glasgow Acads) 1894 *I*
Anderson, D G (London Scottish) 1889 *I,* 1890 *W, I, E,* 1891 *W, E,* 1892 *W, E*
Anderson, E (Stewart's Coll FP) 1947 *I, E*
Anderson, J W (W of Scotland) 1872 *E*
Anderson, T (Merchiston) 1882 *I*
Angus, A W (Watsonians) 1909 *W,* 1910 *F, W, E,* 1911 *W, I,* 1912 *F, W, I, E, SA,* 1913 *F, W,* 1914 *E,* 1920 *F, W, I, E*
Anton, P A (St Andrew's U) 1873 *E*
Armstrong, G (Jedforest, Newcastle) 1988 *A,* 1989 *W, E, I, F, Fj, R,* 1990 *I, F, W, E, NZ* 1,2, *Arg,* 1991 *F, W, E, I, R,* [*J, I, WS, E, NZ*], 1993 *I, F, W, E,* 1994 *E, I,* 1996 *NZ,* 1,2, *A,* 1997 *W, SA* (R), 1998 *It, I, F, W, E*
Arneil, R J (Edinburgh Acads, Leicester and Northampton) 1968 *I, E, A,* 1969 *W, I, E, SA,* 1970 *F, W, I, E, A,* 1971 *F, W, I, E* (2[1C]), 1972 *F, W, E, NZ*
Arthur, A (Glasgow Acads) 1875 *E,* 1876 *E*
Arthur, J W (Glasgow Acads) 1871 *E,* 1872 *E*
Asher, A G G (Oxford U) 1882 *I,* 1884 *W, I, E,* 1885 *W,* 1886 *I, E*
Auld, W (W of Scotland) 1889 *W,* 1890 *W*
Auldjo, L J (Abertay) 1878 *E*

Bain, D McL (Oxford U) 1911 *E,* 1912 *F, W, E, SA,* 1913 *F, W, I, E,* 1914 *W, I*
Baird, G R T (Kelso) 1981 *A,* 1982 *E, I, F, W, A* 1,2, 1983 *I, F, W, E, NZ,* 1984 *W, E, I, F, A,* 1985 *I, W, E,* 1986 *F, W, E, I, R,* 1987 *E,* 1988 *I*
Balfour, A (Watsonians) 1896 *W, I, E,* 1897 *E*
Balfour, L M (Edinburgh Acads) 1872 *E*
Bannerman, E M (Edinburgh Acads) 1872 *E,* 1873 *E*
Bannerman, J M (Glasgow HSFP) 1921 *F, W, I, E,* 1922 *F, W, I, E,* 1923 *F, W, I, E,* 1924 *F, W, I, E,* 1925 *F, W, I, E,* 1926 *F, W, I, E,* 1927 *F, W, I, E, A,* 1928 *F, W, I, E,* 1929 *F, W, I, E*
Barnes, I A (Hawick) 1972 *W,* 1974 *F* (R), 1975 *E* (R), *NZ,* 1977 *I, F, W*
Barrie, R W (Hawick) 1936 *E*
Bearne, K R F (Cambridge U, London Scottish) 1960 *F, W*
Beattie, J A (Hawick) 1929 *F, W,* 1930 *W,* 1931 *F, W, I, E,* 1932 *SA, W, I, E,* 1933 *W, E, I,* 1934 *I, E,* 1935 *W, I, E,* 1936 *W, I, E*

Beattie, J R (Glasgow Acads) 1980 *I, F, W, E,* 1981 *F, W, E, I,* 1983 *F, W, E, NZ,* 1984 *F, W,* 1985 *I,* 1986 *F, W, E, I, R,* 1987 *I, F, W, E*
Bedell-Sivright, D R (Cambridge U, Edinburgh U) 1900 *W,* 1901 *W, I, E,* 1902 *W, I, E,* 1903 *W, I,* 1904 *W, I, E,* 1905 *NZ,* 1906 *W, I, E, SA,* 1907 *W, I, E,* 1908 *W, I*
Bedell-Sivright, J V (Cambridge U) 1902 *W*
Begbie, T A (Edinburgh Wands) 1881 *I, E*
Bell, D L (Watsonians) 1975 *I, F, W, E*
Bell, J A (Clydesdale) 1901 *W, I, E,* 1902 *W, I, E*
Bell, L H I (Edinburgh Acads) 1900 *E,* 1904 *W, I*
Berkeley, W V (Oxford U) 1926 *F,* 1929 *F, W, I*
Berry, C W (Fettesian-Lorettonians) 1884 *I, E,* 1885 *W, I* 1, 1887 *I, W, E,* 1888 *W, I*
Bertram, D M (Watsonians) 1922 *F, W, I, E,* 1923 *F, W, I, E,* 1924 *W, I, E*
Biggar, A G (London Scottish) 1969 *SA,* 1970 *F, I, E, A,* 1971 *F, W, I, E* (2[1C]), 1972 *F, W*
Biggar, M A (London Scottish) 1975 *I, F, W, E,* 1976 *W, E, I,* 1977 *I, F, W,* 1978 *I, F, W, E, NZ,* 1979 *W, E, I, F, NZ,* 1980 *I, F, W, E*
Birkett, G A (Harlequins, London Scottish) 1975 *NZ*
Bishop, J M (Glasgow Acads) 1893 *I*
Bisset, A A (RIE Coll) 1904 *W*
Black, A (Edinburgh U) 1947 *F, W,* 1948 *E,* 1950 *W, I, E*
Black, W P (Glasgow HSFP) 1948 *F, W, I, E,* 1951 *E*
Blackadder, W F (W of Scotland) 1938 *E*
Blaikie, C F (Heriot's FP) 1963 *I, E,* 1966 *E,* 1968 *A,* 1969 *F, W, I, E*
Blair, P C B (Cambridge U) 1912 *SA,* 1913 *F, W, I, E*
Bolton, W H (W of Scotland) 1876 *E*
Borthwick, J B (Stewart's Coll FP) 1938 *W, I*
Bos, F H ten (Oxford U, London Scottish) 1959 *E,* 1960 *F, W, SA,* 1961 *F, SA, W, I, E,* 1962 *F, W, I, E,* 1963 *F, W, I, E*
Boswell, J D (W of Scotland) 1889 *W, I,* 1890 *W, I, E,* 1891 *W, I, E,* 1892 *W, I, E,* 1893 *I, E,* 1894 *I, E*
Bowie, T C (Watsonians) 1913 *I, E,* 1914 *I, E*
Boyd, G M (Glasgow HSFP) 1926 *E*
Boyd, J L (United Services) 1912 *E, SA*
Boyle, A C W (London Scottish) 1963 *F, W, I*
Boyle, A H W (St Thomas's Hospital, London Scottish) 1966 *A,* 1967 *F, NZ,* 1968 *F, W, I*
Brash, J C (Cambridge U) 1961 *E*
Breakey, R W (Gosforth) 1978 *E*
Brewis, N T (Edinburgh Inst FP) 1876 *E,* 1878 *E,* 1879 *I, E,* 1880 *I, E*
Brewster, A K (Stewart's-Melville FP) 1977 *E,* 1980 *I, F,* 1986 *E, I, F*
Brown, A H (Heriot's FP) 1928 *E,* 1929 *F, W*
Brown, A R (Gala) 1971 *E* (2[1C]), 1972 *F, W, E*
Brown, C H C (Dunfermline) 1929 *E*
Brown, D I (Cambridge U) 1933 *W, E, I*
Brown, G L (W of Scotland) 1969 *SA,* 1970 *F, W* (R), *I, E, A,* 1971 *F, W, I, E* (2[1C]), 1972 *F, W, E, NZ,* 1973 *E* (R), *P,* 1974 *W, E, I, F,* 1975 *I, F, W, E, A,* 1976 *F, W, E, I*
Brown, J A (Glasgow Acads) 1908 *W, I*
Brown, J B (Glasgow Acads) 1879 *I, E,* 1880 *I, E,* 1881 *I, E,* 1882 *I, E,* 1883 *W, I, E,* 1884 *W, I, E,* 1885 *I* 1,2, 1886 *W, I, E*
Brown, P C (W of Scotland, Gala) 1964 *F, NZ, W, I, E,* 1965 *I, E, SA,* 1966 *A,* 1969 *I, E,* 1970 *W, E,* 1971 *F, W, I, E* (2[1C]), 1972 *F, W, E, NZ,* 1973 *F, W, I, E, P*
Brown, T G (Heriot's FP) 1929 *W*
Brown, W D (Glasgow Acads) 1871 *E,* 1872 *E,* 1873 *E,* 1874 *E,* 1875 *E*
Brown, W S (Edinburgh Inst FP) 1880 *I, E,* 1882 *I, E,* 1883 *W, E*
Browning, A (Glasgow HSFP) 1920 *I,* 1922 *F, W, I,* 1923 *W, I, E*

Bruce, C R (Glasgow Acads) 1947 *F, W, I, E,* 1949 *F, W, I, E*
Bruce, N S (Blackheath, Army and London Scottish) 1958 *F, A, I, E,* 1959 *F, W, I, E,* 1960 *F, W, I, E, SA,* 1961 *F, SA, W, I, E,* 1962 *F, W, I, E,* 1963 *F, W, I, E,* 1964 *F, NZ, W, I, E*
Bruce, R M (Gordonians) 1947 *A,* 1948 *F, W, I*
Bruce-Lockhart, J H (London Scottish) 1913 *W,* 1920 *E*
Bruce-Lockhart, L (London Scottish) 1948 *E,* 1950 *F, W,* 1953 *I, E*
Bruce-Lockhart, R B (Cambridge U and London Scottish) 1937 *I,* 1939 *I, E*
Bryce, C C (Glasgow Acads) 1873 *E,* 1874 *E*
Bryce, R D H (W of Scotland) 1973 *I* (R)
Bryce, W E (Selkirk) 1922 *W, I, E,* 1923 *F, W, I, E,* 1924 *F, W, I, E*
Brydon, W R C (Heriot's FP) 1939 *W*
Buchanan, A (Royal HSFP) 1871 *E*
Buchanan, F G (Kelvinside Acads and Oxford U) 1910 *F,* 1911 *F, W*
Buchanan, J C R (Stewart's Coll FP) 1921 *W, I, E,* 1922 *W, I, E,* 1923 *F, W, I, E,* 1924 *F, W, I, E,* 1925 *F, I*
Buchanan-Smith, G A E (London Scottish, Heriot's FP) 1989 *Fj* (R), 1990 *Arg*
Bucher, A M (Edinburgh Acads) 1897 *E*
Budge, G M (Edinburgh Wands) 1950 *F, W, I, E*
Bullmore, H H (Edinburgh U) 1902 *I*
Bulloch, G C (West of Scotland) 1997 *SA,* 1998 *It, I, F, W, E*
Burnell, A P (London Scottish) 1989 *E, I, F, Fj, R,* 1990 *I, F, W, E, Arg,* 1991 *F, W, E, I, R, [J, Z, I, WS, E, NZ],* 1992 *E, I, F, W, A,* 1993 *I, F, W, E, NZ,* 1994 *W, E, I, F, Arg 1,2, SA,* 1995 *[Iv, Tg* (R), *F* (R)], *WS,* 1998 *E*
Burnet, P J (London Scottish and Edinburgh Acads) 1960 *SA*
Burnet, W (Hawick) 1912 *E*
Burnet, W A (W of Scotland) 1934 *W,* 1935 *W, I, E, NZ,* 1936 *W, I, E*
Burnett, J N (Heriot's FP) 1980 *I, F, W, E*
Burrell, G (Gala) 1950 *F, W, I,* 1951 *SA*

Cairns, A G (Watsonians) 1903 *W, I, E,* 1904 *W, I, E,* 1905 *W, I, E,* 1906 *W, I, E*
Calder, F (Stewart's-Melville FP) 1986 *F, W, E, I, R,* 1987 *I, F, W, E, [F, Z, R, NZ],* 1988 *I, F, W, E,* 1989 *W, E, I, F, R,* 1990 *I, F, W, E, NZ 1,2,* 1991 *R, [J, I, WS, E, NZ]*
Calder, J H (Stewart's-Melville FP) 1981 *F, W, E, I, NZ 1,2, R, A,* 1982 *E, I, F, W, A 1,2,* 1983 *I, F, W, E, NZ,* 1984 *W, E, I, F, A,* 1985 *I, F, W*
Callander, G J (Kelso) 1984 *R,* 1988 *I, F, W, E, A*
Cameron, A (Glasgow HSFP) 1948 *W,* 1950 *I, E,* 1951 *F, W, I, E, SA,* 1953 *I, E,* 1955 *F, W, I, E,* 1956 *F, W, I*
Cameron, A D (Hillhead HSFP) 1951 *F,* 1954 *F, W*
Cameron, A W (Watsonians) 1887 *W,* 1893 *W,* 1894 *I*
Cameron, D (Glasgow HSFP) 1953 *I, E,* 1954 *F, NZ, I, E*
Cameron, N W (Glasgow U) 1952 *E,* 1953 *F, W*
Campbell, A J (Hawick) 1984 *I, F, R,* 1985 *I, F, W, E,* 1986 *F, W, E, I, R,* 1988 *F, W, A*
Campbell, G T (London Scottish) 1892 *W, I, E,* 1893 *I, E,* 1894 *W, I, E,* 1895 *W, I, E,* 1896 *W, I, E,* 1897 *I,* 1899 *I,* 1900 *E*
Campbell, H H (Cambridge U, London Scottish) 1947 *I, E,* 1948 *I, E*
Campbell, J A (Cambridge U) 1900 *I*
Campbell, J A (W of Scotland) 1878 *E,* 1879 *I, E,* 1881 *I, E*
Campbell, N M (London Scottish) 1956 *F, W*
Campbell, S J (Dundee HSFP) 1995 *C, I, F, W, E, R, [Iv, NZ* (R)], WS (t), 1996 *I, F, W, E,* 1997 *A, SA*
Campbell-Lamerton, J R E (London Scottish) 1986 *F,* 1987 *[Z, R*(R)]
Campbell-Lamerton, M J (Halifax, Army, London Scottish) 1961 *F, SA, W, I,* 1962 *F, W, I, E,* 1963 *F, W, I, E,* 1964 *I, E,* 1965 *F, W, I, E, SA,* 1966 *F, W, I, E*
Carmichael, A B (W of Scotland) 1967 *I, NZ,* 1968 *F, W, I, E, A,* 1969 *F, W, I, E, SA,* 1970 *F, W, I, E, A,* 1971 *F, W, I, E* (2[1C]), 1972 *F, W, E, NZ,* 1973 *F, W, I, E, P,* 1974 *W, E, I, F,* 1975 *I, F, W, E, NZ, A,* 1976 *W, E, I,* 1977 *E, I* (R), *F, W,* 1978 *I*
Carmichael, J H (Watsonians) 1921 *F, W, I*
Carrick, J S (Glasgow Acads) 1876 *E,* 1877 *E*
Cassels, D Y (W of Scotland) 1880 *E,* 1881 *I,* 1882 *I, E,* 1883 *W, I, E*
Cathcart, C W (Edinburgh U) 1872 *E,* 1873 *E,* 1876 *E*
Cawkwell, G L (Oxford U) 1947 *F*

Chalmers, C M (Melrose) 1989 *W, E, I, F, Fj,* 1990 *I, F, W, E, NZ 1,2, Arg,* 1991 *F, W, E, I, R, [J, Z(R), I, WS, E, NZ],* 1992 *E, I, F, W, A,* 1993 *I, F, W, E, NZ, SA,* 1995 *C, I, F, W, E, R, [Iv, Tg, F, NZ], WS,* 1996 *A, It,* 1997 *W, I, F, A* (R), *SA,* 1998 *It, I, F, W, E*
Chalmers, T (Glasgow Acads) 1871 *E,* 1872 *E,* 1873 *E,* 1874 *E,* 1875 *E,* 1876 *E*
Chambers, H F T (Edinburgh U) 1888 *W, I,* 1889 *W, I*
Charters, R G (Hawick) 1955 *W, I, E*
Chisholm, D H (Melrose) 1964 *I, E,* 1965 *E, SA,* 1966 *F, I, E, A,* 1967 *F, W, NZ,* 1968 *F, W, I*
Chisholm, R W T (Melrose) 1955 *I, E,* 1956 *F, W, I, E,* 1958 *F, W, A, I,* 1960 *SA*
Church, W C (Glasgow Acads) 1906 *W*
Clark, R L (Edinburgh Wands, Royal Navy) 1972 *F, W, E, NZ,* 1973 *W, I, E, P*
Clauss, P R A (Oxford U) 1891 *W, I, E,* 1892 *W, E,* 1895 *I*
Clay, A T (Edinburgh Acads) 1886 *W, I, E,* 1887 *I, W, E,* 1888 *W*
Clunies-Ross, A (St Andrew's U) 1871 *E*
Coltman, S (Hawick) 1948 *I,* 1949 *F, W, I, E*
Colville, A G (Merchistonians, Blackheath) 1871 *E,* 1872 *E*
Connell, G C (Trinity Acads and London Scottish) 1968 *E, A,* 1969 *F, E,* 1970 *F*
Cooper, M McG (Oxford U) 1936 *W, I*
Corcoran, I (Gala) 1992 *A* 1(R)
Cordial, I F (Edinburgh Wands) 1952 *F, W, I, E*
Cotter, J L (Hillhead HSFP) 1934 *I, E*
Cottington, G S (Kelso) 1934 *I, E,* 1935 *W, I,* 1936 *E*
Coughtrie, S (Edinburgh Acads) 1959 *F, W, I, E,* 1962 *W, I, E,* 1963 *F, W, I, E*
Couper, J H (W of Scotland) 1896 *W, I,* 1899 *I*
Coutts, F H (Melrose, Army) 1947 *W, I, E*
Coutts, I D F (Old Alleynians) 1951 *F,* 1952 *E*
Cowan, R C (Selkirk) 1961 *F,* 1962 *F, W, I, E*
Cowie, W L K (Edinburgh Wands) 1953 *E*
Cownie, W B (Watsonians) 1893 *W, I, E,* 1894 *W, I, E,* 1895 *W, I, E*
Crabbie, G E (Edinburgh Acads) 1904 *W*
Crabbie, J E (Edinburgh Acads, Oxford U) 1900 *W,* 1902 *I,* 1903 *W, I,* 1904 *E,* 1905 *W*
Craig, J B (Heriot's FP) 1939 *W*
Craig, J M (West of Scotland) 1997 *A*
Cramb, R I (Harlequins) 1987 *[R*(R)], 1988 *I, F, A*
Cranston, A G (Hawick) 1976 *W, E, I,* 1977 *E, W,* 1978 *F* (R), *W, E, NZ,* 1981 *NZ 1,2*
Crawford, J A (Army, London Scottish) 1934 *I*
Crawford, W H (United Services, RN) 1938 *W, I, E,* 1939 *W, E*
Crichton-Miller, D (Gloucester) 1931 *W, I, E*
Crole, G B (Oxford U) 1920 *F, W, I, E*
Cronin, D F (Bath, London Scottish, Bourges, Wasps) 1988 *I, F, W, E, A,* 1989 *W, E, I, F, Fj, R,* 1990 *I, F, W, E, NZ 1,2,* 1991 *W, E, I, R, [Z],* 1992 *A 2,* 1993 *I, F, W, E, NZ,* 1995 *C, I, F, [Tg, F, NZ], WS,* 1996 *NZ 1,2, A, It,* 1997 *F* (R), 1998 *I, F, W, E*
Cross, M (Merchistonians) 1875 *E,* 1876 *E,* 1877 *I, E,* 1878 *E,* 1879 *I, E,* 1880 *I, E*
Cross, W (Merchistonians) 1871 *E,* 1872 *E*
Cumming, R S (Aberdeen U) 1921 *F, W*
Cunningham, G (Oxford U) 1908 *W, I,* 1909 *W, E,* 1910 *F, I, E,* 1911 *E*
Cunningham, R F (Gala) 1978 *NZ,* 1979 *W, E*
Currie, L R (Dunfermline) 1947 *A,* 1948 *F, W, I,* 1949 *F, W, I, E*
Cuthbertson, W (Kilmarnock, Harlequins) 1980 *I,* 1981 *W, E, I, NZ 1,2, R, A,* 1982 *E, I, F, W, A 1,2,* 1983 *I, F, W, NZ,* 1984 *W, E, A*

Dalgleish, A (Gala) 1890 *W, E,* 1891 *W, I,* 1892 *W,* 1893 *W,* 1894 *W, I*
Dalgleish, K J (Edinburgh Wands, Cambridge U) 1951 *I, E,* 1953 *F, W*
Dallas, J D (Watsonians) 1903 *E*
Davidson, J A (London Scottish, Edinburgh Wands) 1959 *E,* 1960 *I, E*
Davidson, J N G (Edinburgh U) 1952 *F, W, I, E,* 1953 *F, W,* 1954 *F*
Davidson, J P (RIE Coll) 1873 *E,* 1874 *E*
Davidson, R S (Royal HSFP) 1893 *E*
Davies, D S (Hawick) 1922 *F, W, I, E,* 1923 *F, W, I, E,* 1924 *F, E,* 1925 *W, I, E,* 1926 *F, W, I, E,* 1927 *F, W, I*

Dawson, J C (Glasgow Acads) 1947 *A*, 1948 *F, W*, 1949 *F, W, I*, 1950 *F, W, I, E*, 1951 *F, W, I, E, SA*, 1952 *F, W, I, E*, 1953 *E*

Deans, C T (Hawick) 1978 *F, W, E, NZ*, 1979 *W, E, I, F, NZ*, 1980 *I, F, W, E, I, NZ* 1,2, *R, A*, 1982 *E, I, F, W, A* 1,2, 1983 *I, F, W, E, NZ*, 1984 *W, E, I, F, A*, 1985 *I, F, W, E*, 1986 *F, W, E, I, R*, 1987 *I, F, W, E*, [*F, Z, R, NZ*]

Deans, D T (Hawick) 1968 *E*

Deas, D W (Heriot's FP) 1947 *F, W*

Dick, L G (Loughborough Colls, Jordanhill, Swansea) 1972 *W* (R), *E*, 1974 *W, E, I, F*, 1975 *I, F, W, E, NZ, A*, 1976 *F*, 1977 *E*

Dick, R C S (Cambridge U, Guy's Hospital) 1934 *W, I, E*, 1935 *W, I, E, NZ*, 1936 *W, I, E*, 1937 *W*, 1938 *W, I, E*

Dickson, G (Gala) 1978 *NZ*, 1979 *W, E, I, F, NZ*, 1980 *W*, 1981 *F*, 1982 *W* (R)

Dickson, M R (Edinburgh U) 1905 *I*

Dickson, W M (Blackheath, Oxford U) 1912 *F, W, E, SA*, 1913 *F, W, I*

Dobson, J (Glasgow Acads) 1911 *E*, 1912 *F, W, I, E, SA*

Dobson, J D (Glasgow Acads) 1910 *I*

Dobson, W G (Heriot's FP) 1922 *W, I, E*

Docherty, J T (Glasgow HSFP) 1955 *F, W*, 1956 *E*, 1958 *F, W, A, I, E*

Dods, F P (Edinburgh Acads) 1901 *I*

Dods, J H (Edinburgh Acads) 1895 *W, I, E*, 1896 *W, I, E*, 1897 *I, E*

Dods, M (Gala, Northampton) 1994 *I* (t), *Arg* 1,2, 1995 *WS*, 1996 *I, F, W, E*

Dods, P W (Gala) 1983 *I, F, W, E, NZ*, 1984 *W, E, I, F, R, A*, 1985 *I, F, W, E*, 1989 *W, E, I, F*, 1991 *I* (R), *R*, [*Z, NZ* (R)]

Donald, D G (Oxford U) 1914 *W, I*

Donald, R L H (Glasgow HSFP) 1921 *W, I, E*

Donaldson, W P (Oxford U, W of Scotland) 1893 *I*, 1894 *I*, 1895 *E*, 1896 *I, E*, 1899 *I*

Don-Wauchope, A R (Fettesian-Lorettonians) 1881 *E*, 1882 *E*, 1883 *W*, 1884 *W, I, E*, 1885 *W, I* 1,2, 1886 *W, I, E*, 1888 *I*

Don-Wauchope, P H (Fettesian-Lorettonians) 1885 *I* 1,2, 1886 *W*, 1887 *I, W, E*

Dorward, A F (Cambridge U, Gala) 1950 *F*, 1951 *SA*, 1952 *W, I, E*, 1953 *F, W, E*, 1955 *F*, 1956 *I, E*, 1957 *F, W, I, E*

Dorward, T F (Gala) 1938 *W, I, E*, 1939 *I, E*

Douglas, G (Jedforest) 1921 *W*

Douglas, J (Stewart's Coll FP) 1961 *F, SA, W, I, E*, 1962 *F, W, I, E*, 1963 *F, W, I*

Douty, P S (London Scottish) 1927 *A*, 1928 *F, W*

Drew, D (Glasgow Acads) 1871 *E*, 1876 *E*

Druitt, W A H (London Scottish) 1936 *W, I, E*

Drummond, A H (Kelvinside Acads) 1938 *W, I*

Drummond, C W (Melrose) 1947 *F, W, I, E*, 1948 *F, I, E*, 1950 *F, W, I, E*

Drybrough, A S (Edinburgh Wands, Merchistonians) 1902 *I*, 1903 *I*

Dryden, R H (Watsonians) 1937 *E*

Drysdale, D (Heriot's FP) 1923 *F, W, I, E*, 1924 *F, W, I, E*, 1925 *F, W, I, E*, 1926 *F, W, I, E*, 1927 *F, W, I, E, A*, 1928 *F, W, I, E*, 1929 *F*

Duff, P L (Glasgow Acads) 1936 *W, I*, 1938 *W, I, E*, 1939 *W*

Duffy, H (Jedforest) 1955 *F*

Duke, A (Royal HSFP) 1888 *W, I*, 1889 *W, I*, 1890 *W, I*

Duncan, A W (Edinburgh U) 1901 *W, I, E*, 1902 *W, I, E*

Duncan, D D (Oxford U) 1920 *F, W, I, E*

Duncan, M D F (W of Scotland) 1986 *F, W, E, R*, 1987 *I, F, W, E*, [*F, Z, R, NZ*], 1988 *I, F, W, E, A*, 1989 *W*

Duncan, M M (Fettesian-Lorettonians) 1888 *W*

Dunlop, J W (W of Scotland) 1875 *E*

Dunlop, Q (W of Scotland) 1971 *E* (2[1C])

Dykes, A S (Glasgow Acads) 1932 *E*

Dykes, J C (Glasgow Acads) 1922 *F, E*, 1924 *I*, 1925 *F, W, I*, 1926 *F, W, I, E*, 1927 *F, W, I, E, A*, 1928 *F, I*, 1929 *F, W, I*

Dykes, J M (Clydesdale, Glasgow HSFP) 1898 *I, E*, 1899 *W, E*, 1900 *W, I*, 1901 *W, I, E*, 1902 *E*

Edwards, D B (Heriot's FP) 1960 *I, E, SA*

Edwards, N G B (Harlequins, Northampton) 1992 *E, I, F, W, A* 1, 1994 *W*

Elgie, M K (London Scottish) 1954 *NZ, I, E, W*, 1955 *F, W, I, E*

Elliot, C (Langholm) 1958 *E*, 1959 *F*, 1960 *F*, 1963 *E*, 1964 *F, NZ, W, I, E*, 1965 *F, W, I*

Elliot, T (Hawick) 1895 *W*, 1896 *E*, 1897 *I, E*, 1898 *I, E*

Elliot, T (Gala) 1905 *E*

Elliot, T (Gala) 1955 *W, I, E*, 1956 *F, W, I, E*, 1957 *F, W, I, E*, 1958 *W, A, I*

Elliot, T G (Langholm) 1968 *W, A*, 1969 *F, W*, 1970 *E*

Elliot, W I D (Edinburgh Acads) 1947 *F, W, E, A*, 1948 *F, W, I, E*, 1949 *F, W, I, E*, 1950 *F, W, I, E*, 1951 *F, W, I, E, SA*, 1952 *F, W, I, E*, 1954 *NZ, I, E, W*

Ellis, D G (Currie) 1997 *W, E, I, F*

Emslie, W D (Royal HSFP) 1930 *F*, 1932 *I*

Eriksson, B R S (London Scottish) 1996 *NZ* 1, *A*, 1997 *E*

Evans, H L (Edinburgh U) 1885 *I* 1,2

Ewart, E N (Glasgow Acads) 1879 *E*, 1880 *I, E*

Fahmy, Dr E C (Abertillery) 1920 *F, W, I, E*

Fasson, F H (London Scottish, Edinburgh Wands) 1900 *W*, 1901 *W, I*, 1902 *W, E*

Fell, A N (Edinburgh U) 1901 *W, I, E*, 1902 *W, E*, 1903 *W, E*

Ferguson, J H (Gala) 1928 *W*

Ferguson, W G (Royal HSFP) 1927 *A*, 1928 *F, W, I, E*

Fergusson, E A J (Oxford U) 1954 *F, NZ, I, E, W*

Finlay, A B (Edinburgh Acads) 1875 *E*

Finlay, J F (Edinburgh Acads) 1871 *E*, 1872 *E*, 1874 *E*, 1875 *E*

Finlay, N J (Edinburgh Acads) 1875 *E*, 1876 *E*, 1878 *E*, 1879 *I, E*, 1880 *I, E*, 1881 *I, E*

Finlay, R (Watsonians) 1948 *E*

Fisher, A T (Waterloo, Watsonians) 1947 *I, E*

Fisher, C D (Waterloo) 1975 *NZ, A*, 1976 *W, E, I*

Fisher, D (W of Scotland) 1893 *I*

Fisher, J P (Royal HSFP, London Scottish) 1963 *E*, 1964 *F, NZ, W, I, E*, 1965 *F, W, I, E, SA*, 1966 *F, W, I, E, A*, 1967 *F, W, I, E, NZ*, 1968 *F, W, I, E*

Fleming, C J N (Edinburgh Wands) 1896 *I, E*, 1897 *I*

Fleming, G R (Glasgow Acads) 1875 *E*, 1876 *E*

Fletcher, H N (Edinburgh U) 1904 *E*, 1905 *W*

Flett, A B (Edinburgh U) 1901 *W, I, E*, 1902 *W, I*

Forbes, J L (Watsonians) 1905 *W*, 1906 *I, E*

Ford, D St C (United Services, RN) 1930 *I, E*, 1931 *E*, 1932 *W, I*

Ford, J R (Gala) 1893 *I*

Forrest, J E (Glasgow Acads) 1932 *SA*, 1935 *E, NZ*

Forrest, J G S (Cambridge U) 1938 *W, I, E*

Forrest, W T (Hawick) 1903 *W, I, E*, 1904 *W, I, E*, 1905 *W, I*

Forsayth, H H (Oxford U) 1921 *F, W, I, E*, 1922 *W, I, E*

Forsyth, I W (Stewart's Coll FP) 1972 *NZ*, 1973 *F, W, I, E, P*

Forsyth, J (Edinburgh U) 1871 *E*

Foster, R A (Hawick) 1930 *W*, 1932 *SA, I, E*

Fox, J (Gala) 1952 *F, W, I, E*

Frame, J N M (Edinburgh U, Gala) 1967 *NZ*, 1968 *F, W, I, E*, 1969 *W, I, E, SA*, 1970 *F, W, I, E, A*, 1971 *F, W, I, E* (2[1C]), 1972 *F, W, E*, 1973 *P* (R)

France, C (Kelvinside Acads) 1903 *I*

Fraser, C F P (Glasgow U) 1888 *W*, 1889 *W*

Fraser, J W (Edinburgh Inst FP) 1881 *E*

Fraser, R (Cambridge U) 1911 *F, W, I, E*

French, J (Glasgow Acads) 1886 *W*, 1887 *I, W, E*

Frew, A (Edinburgh U) 1901 *W, I, E*

Frew, G M (Glasgow HSFP) 1906 *SA*, 1907 *W, I, E*, 1908 *W, I, E*, 1909 *W, I, E*, 1910 *F, W, I*, 1911 *I, E*

Friebe, J P (Glasgow HSFP) 1952 *E*

Fulton, A K (Edinburgh U, Dollar Acads) 1952 *F*, 1954 *F*

Fyfe, K C (Cambridge U, Sale, London Scottish) 1933 *W, E*, 1934 *E*, 1935 *W, I, E, NZ*, 1936 *W, E*, 1939 *I*

Gallie, G H (Edinburgh Acads) 1939 *W*

Gallie, R A (Glasgow Acads) 1920 *F, W, I, E*, 1921 *F, W, I, E*

Gammell, W B B (Edinburgh Wands) 1977 *I, F, W*, 1978 *W, E*

Geddes, I C (London Scottish) 1906 *SA*, 1907 *W, I, E*, 1908 *W, E*

Geddes, K I (London Scottish) 1947 *F, W, I, E*

Gedge, H T S (Oxford U, London Scottish, Edinburgh Wands) 1894 *W, I, E*, 1896 *E*, 1899 *W, E*

Gedge, P M S (Edinburgh Wands) 1933 *I*

Gemmill, R (Glasgow HSFP) 1950 *F, W, I, E*, 1951 *F, W, I*

Irvine, D R (Edinburgh Acads) 1878 *E*, 1879 *I, E*
Irvine, R W (Edinburgh Acads) 1871 *E*, 1872 *E*, 1873 *E*, 1874 *E*, 1875 *E*, 1876 *E*, 1877 *I, E*, 1878 *E*, 1879 *I, E*, 1880 *I, E*
Irvine T W (Edinburgh Acads) 1885 *I* 1,2, 1886 *W, I, E*, 1887 *I, W, E*, 1888 *W, I*, 1889 *I*

Jackson, K L T (Oxford U) 1933 *W, E, I*, 1934 *W*
Jackson, T G H (Army) 1947 *F, W, E, A*, 1948 *F, W, I, E*, 1949 *F, W, I, E*
Jackson, W D (Hawick) 1964 *I*, 1965 *E, SA*, 1968 *A*, 1969 *F, W, E*
Jamieson, J (W of Scotland) 1883 *W, I, E*, 1884 *W, I, E*, 1885 *W, I* 1,2
Jardine, I C (Stirling County) 1993 *NZ*, 1994 *W, E* (R), *Arg* 1,2, 1995 *C, I, F*, [*Tg, F* (t & R), *NZ* (R)], 1996 *I, F, W, E, NZ* 1,2
Jeffrey, J (Kelso) 1984 *A*, 1985 *I, E*, 1986 *F, W, E, I, R*, 1987 *I, F, W, E*, [*F, Z, R*], 1988 *I, W, A*, 1989 *W, E, I, F, Fj, R*, 1990 *I, F, W, E, NZ* 1,2, *Arg*, 1991 *F, W, E, I,* [*J, I, WS, E, NZ*]
Johnston, D I (Watsonians) 1979 *NZ*, 1980 *I, F, W, E*, 1981 *R, A*, 1982 *E, I, F, W, A* 1,2, 1983 *I, F, W, NZ*, 1984 *W, E, I, F, R*, 1986 *F, W, E, I, R*
Johnston, H H (Edinburgh Collegian FP) 1877 *I, E*
Johnston, J (Melrose) 1951 *SA*, 1952 *F, W, I, E*
Johnston, W C (Glasgow HSFP) 1922 *F*
Johnston, W G S (Cambridge U) 1935 *W, I*, 1937 *W, I, E*
Joiner, C A (Melrose, Leicester) 1994 *Arg* 1,2, 1995 *C, I, F, W, E, R,* [*Iv, Tg, F, NZ*], 1996 *I, F, W, E, NZ* 1, 1997 *SA*, 1998 *It, I*
Jones, P M (Gloucester) 1992 *W* (R)
Junor, J E (Glasgow Acads) 1876 *E*, 1877 *I, E*, 1878 *E*, 1879 *E*, 1881 *I*

Keddie, R R (Watsonians) 1967 *NZ*
Keith, G J (Wasps) 1968 *F, W*
Keller, D H (London Scottish) 1949 *F, W, I, E*, 1950 *F, W, I*
Kelly, R F (Watsonians) 1927 *A*, 1928 *F, W, E*
Kemp, J W Y (Glasgow HSFP) 1954 *W*, 1955 *F, W, I, E*, 1956 *F, W, I, E*, 1957 *F, W, I, E*, 1958 *F, W, A, I, E*, 1959 *F, W, I, E*, 1960 *F, W, I, E, SA*
Kennedy, A E (Watsonians) 1983 *NZ*, 1984 *W, E, A*
Kennedy, F (Stewart's Coll FP) 1920 *F, W, I, E*, 1921 *E*
Kennedy, N (W of Scotland) 1903 *W, I, E*
Ker, A B M (Kelso) 1988 *W, E*
Ker, H T (Glasgow Acads) 1887 *I, W, E*, 1888 *I*, 1889 *W*, 1890 *I, E*
Kerr, D S (Heriot's FP) 1923 *F, W*, 1924 *F*, 1926 *I, E*, 1927 *W, I, E*, 1928 *I, E*
Kerr, G C (Old Dunelmians, Edinburgh Wands) 1898 *I, E*, 1899 *I, W, E*, 1900 *W, I, E*
Kerr, J M (Heriot's FP) 1935 *NZ*, 1936 *I, E*, 1937 *W, I*
Kerr, W (London Scottish) 1953 *E*
Kidston, D W (Glasgow Acads) 1883 *W, E*
Kidston, W H (W of Scotland) 1874 *E*
Kilgour, I J (RMC Sandhurst) 1921 *F*
King, J H F (Selkirk) 1953 *F, W, E*, 1954 *E*
Kininmonth, P W (Oxford U, Richmond) 1949 *F, W, I, E*, 1950 *F, W, I, E*, 1951 *F, W, I, E, SA*, 1952 *F, W, I*, 1954 *F, NZ, I, E, W*
Kinnear, R M (Heriot's FP) 1926 *F, W, I*
Knox, J (Kelvinside Acads) 1903 *W, I, E*
Kyle, W E (Hawick) 1902 *W, I, E*, 1903 *W, I, E*, 1904 *W, I, E*, 1905 *W, I, E, NZ*, 1906 *W, I, E*, 1908 *E*, 1909 *W, I, E*, 1910 *W*

Laidlaw, A S (Hawick) 1897 *I*
Laidlaw, F A L (Melrose) 1965 *F, W, I, E, SA*, 1966 *F, W, I, E, A*, 1967 *W, I, E, NZ*, 1968 *F, W, I, A*, 1969 *F, W, I, E, SA*, 1970 *F, W, I, E, A*, 1971 *F, W, I*
Laidlaw, R J (Jedforest) 1980 *I, F, W, E*, 1981 *F, W, E, I, NZ* 1,2, *R, A*, 1982 *E, I, F, W, A* 1,2, 1983 *I, F, W, E, NZ*, 1984 *W, E, I, F, R, A*, 1985 *I, F*, 1986 *F, W, E, I, R*, 1987 *I, F, W, E,* [*F, R, NZ*], 1988 *I, F, W, E*
Laing, A D (Royal HSFP) 1914 *W, I, E*, 1920 *F, W, I*, 1921 *F*
Lambie, I K (Watsonians) 1978 *NZ* (R), 1979 *W, E, NZ*
Lambie, L B (Glasgow HSFP) 1934 *W, I, E*, 1935 *W, I, E, NZ*
Lamond, G A W (Kelvinside Acads) 1899 *W, E*, 1905 *E*
Lang, D (Paisley) 1876 *E*, 1877 *I*
Langrish, R W (London Scottish) 1930 *F*, 1931 *F, W, I*

Lauder, W (Neath) 1969 *I, E, SA*, 1970 *F, W, I, A*, 1973 *F*, 1974 *W, E, I, F*, 1975 *I, F, NZ, A*, 1976 *F*, 1977 *E*
Laughland, I H P (London Scottish) 1959 *F*, 1960 *F, W, I, E*, 1961 *SA, W, I, E*, 1962 *F, W, I, E*, 1963 *F, W, I*, 1964 *F, NZ, W, I, E*, 1965 *F, W, I, E, SA*, 1966 *F, W, I, E*, 1967 *E*
Lawrie, J R (Melrose) 1922 *F, W, I, E*, 1923 *F, W, I, E*, 1924 *W, I, E*
Lawrie, K G (Gala) 1980 *F* (R), *W, E*
Lawson, A J M (Edinburgh Wands, London Scottish) 1972 *F* (R), *E*, 1973 *F*, 1974 *W, E*, 1976 *E, I*, 1977 *E*, 1978 *NZ*, 1979 *W, E, I, F, NZ*, 1980 *W* (R)
Lawther, T H B (Old Millhillians) 1932 *SA, W*
Ledingham, G A (Aberdeen GSFP) 1913 *F*
Lee, D J (London Scottish) 1998 *I* (R), *F, W, E*
Lees, J B (Gala) 1947 *I, A*, 1948 *F, W, E*
Leggatt, H T O (Watsonians) 1891 *W, I, E*, 1892 *W, I*, 1893 *W, E*, 1894 *I, E*
Lely, W G (Cambridge U, London Scottish) 1909 *I*
Leslie, D G (Dundee HSFP, W of Scotland, Gala) 1975 *I, F, W, E, NZ, A*, 1976 *F, W, E, I*, 1978 *NZ*, 1980 *E*, 1981 *W, E, I, NZ* 1,2, *R, A*, 1982 *E*, 1983 *I, F, W, E*, 1984 *W, E, I, F, R*, 1985 *F, W, E*
Liddell, E H (Edinburgh U) 1922 *F, W, I*, 1923 *F, W, I, E*
Lind, H (Dunfermline) 1928 *I*, 1931 *F, W, I, E*, 1932 *SA, W, E*, 1933 *W, E, I*, 1934 *W, I, E*, 1935 *I*, 1936 *E*
Lindsay, A B (London Hospital) 1910 *I*, 1911 *I*
Lindsay, G C (London Scottish) 1884 *W*, 1885 *I* 1, 1887 *W, E*
Lindsay-Watson, R H (Hawick) 1909 *I*
Lineen, S R P (Boroughmuir) 1989 *W, E, I, F, Fj, R*, 1990 *I, F, W, E, NZ* 1,2, *Arg*, 1991 *F, W, E, I, R,* [*J, Z, I, E, NZ*], 1992 *E, I, F, W, A* 1,2
Little, A W (Hawick) 1905 *W*
Logan, K M (Stirling County, Wasps) 1992 *A* 2, 1993 *E* (R), *NZ* (t), 1994 *W, E, I, F, Arg* 1,2, 1995 *C, I, F, W, E, R,* [*Iv, Tg, F, NZ*], *WS*, 1996 *W* (R), *NZ* 1,2, *A, It*, 1997 *W, E, I, F, A*, 1998 *I, F*
Logan, W R (Edinburgh U, Edinburgh Wands) 1931 *E*, 1932 *SA, W, I*, 1933 *W, E, I*, 1934 *W, I, E*, 1935 *W, I, E, NZ*, 1936 *W, I, E*, 1937 *W, I, E*
Longstaff, S L (Dundee HSFP) 1998 *F* (R), *W, E*
Lorraine, H D B (Oxford U) 1933 *W, E, I*
Loudoun-Shand, E G (Oxford U) 1913 *E*
Lowe, J D (Heriot's FP) 1934 *W*
Lumsden, I J M (Bath, Watsonians) 1947 *F, W, A*, 1949 *F, W, I, E*
Lyall, G G (Gala) 1947 *I, A*, 1948 *F, W, I, E*
Lyall, W J C (Edinburgh Acads) 1871 *E*

Mabon, J T (Jedforest) 1898 *I, E*, 1899 *I*, 1900 *I*
Macarthur, J P (Waterloo) 1932 *E*
MacCallum, J C (Watsonians) 1905 *E, NZ*, 1906 *W, I, E, SA*, 1907 *W, I, E*, 1908 *W, I, E*, 1909 *W, I, E*, 1910 *F, W, I, E*, 1911 *F, I, E*, 1912 *F, W, I, E*
McClung, T (Edinburgh Acads) 1956 *I, E*, 1957 *W, I, E*, 1959 *F, W, I*, 1960 *W*
McClure, G B (W of Scotland) 1873 *E*
McClure, J H (W of Scotland) 1872 *E*
McCowan, D (W of Scotland) 1880 *I, E*, 1881 *I, E*, 1882 *I, E*, 1883 *I, E*, 1884 *I, E*
McCowat, R H (Glasgow Acads) 1905 *I*
McCrae, I G (Gordonians) 1967 *E*, 1968 *I*, 1969 *F* (R), *W*, 1972 *F, NZ*
McCrow, J W S (Edinburgh Acads) 1921 *I*
Macdonald, A E D (Heriot's FP) 1993 *NZ*
McDonald, C (Jedforest) 1947 *A*
Macdonald, D C (Edinburgh U) 1953 *F, W*, 1958 *I, E*
Macdonald, D S M (Oxford U, London Scottish, W of Scotland) 1977 *E, I, F, W*, 1978 *I, W, E*
Macdonald, J D (London Scottish, Army) 1966 *F, W, I, E*, 1967 *F, W, I, E*
Macdonald, J M (Edinburgh Wands) 1911 *W*
Macdonald, J S (Edinburgh U) 1903 *E*, 1904 *W, I, E*, 1905 *W*
Macdonald, K R (Stewart's Coll FP) 1956 *F, W, I*, 1957 *W, I, E*
Macdonald, R (Edinburgh U) 1950 *F, W, I, E*
McDonald, W A (Glasgow U) 1889 *W*, 1892 *I, E*
Macdonald, W G (London Scottish) 1969 *I* (R)
Macdougall, J B (Greenock Wands, Wakefield) 1913 *F*, 1914 *I*, 1921 *F, I, E*
McEwan, M C (Edinburgh Acads) 1886 *E*, 1887 *I, W, E*, 1888 *W, I*, 1889 *W, I*, 1890 *W, I, E*, 1891 *W, I, E*, 1892 *E*

MacEwan, N A (Gala, Highland) 1971 *F, W, I, E* (2[1C]), 1972 *F, W, E, NZ*, 1973 *F, W, I, E, P*, 1974 *W, E, I, F*, 1975 *W, E*
McEwan, W M C (Edinburgh Acads) 1894 *W, E*, 1895 *W, E*, 1896 *W, I, E*, 1897 *I, E*, 1898 *I, E*, 1899 *I, W, E*, 1900 *W, E*
MacEwen, R K G (Cambridge U, London Scottish) 1954 *F, NZ, I, W*, 1956 *F, W, I, E*, 1957 *F, W, I, E*, 1958 *W*
Macfarlan, D J (London Scottish) 1883 *W*, 1884 *W, I, E*, 1886 *W, I*, 1887 *I*, 1888 *I*
McFarlane, J L H (Edinburgh U) 1871 *E*, 1872 *E*, 1873 *E*
McGaughey, S K (Hawick) 1984 *R*
McGeechan, I R (Headingley) 1972 *NZ*, 1973 *F, W, I, E, P*, 1974 *W, E, I, F*, 1975 *I, F, W, E, NZ, A*, 1976 *F, W, E, I*, 1977 *E, I, F, W*, 1978 *I, F, W, NZ*, 1979 *W, E, I, F*
McGlashan, T P L (Royal HSFP) 1947 *F, I, E*, 1954 *F, NZ, I, E, W*
MacGregor, D G (Watsonians, Pontypridd) 1907 *W, I, E*
MacGregor, G (Cambridge U) 1890 *W, I, E*, 1891 *W, I, E*, 1893 *W, I, E*, 1894 *W, I, E*, 1896 *E*
MacGregor, I A A (Hillhead HSFP, Llanelli) 1955 *I, E*, 1956 *F, W, I, E*, 1957 *F, W, I*
MacGregor, J R (Edinburgh U) 1909 *I*
McGuinness, G M (W of Scotland) 1982 *A* 1,2, 1983 *I*, 1985 *I, F, W, E*
McHarg, A F (W of Scotland, London Scottish) 1968 *I, E, A*, 1969 *F, W, I, E*, 1971 *F, W, I, E* (2[1C]), 1972 *F, E, NZ*, 1973 *F, W, I, E, P*, 1974 *W, E, I, F*, 1975 *I, F, W, E, NZ, A*, 1976 *F, W, E, I*, 1977 *E, I, F, W*, 1978 *I, F, W, NZ*, 1979 *W, E*
McIndoe, F (Glasgow Acads) 1886 *W, I*
MacIntyre, I (Edinburgh Wands) 1890 *W, I, E*, 1891 *W, I, E*
McIvor, D J (Edinburgh Acads) 1992 *E, I, F, W*, 1993 *NZ*, 1994 *SA*
Mackay, E B (Glasgow Acads) 1920 *W*, 1922 *E*
McKeating, E (Heriot's FP) 1957 *F, W*, 1961 *SA, W, I, E*
McKelvey, G (Watsonians) 1997 *A*
McKendrick, J G (W of Scotland) 1889 *I*
Mackenzie, A D G (Selkirk) 1984 *A*
Mackenzie, C J G (United Services) 1921 *E*
Mackenzie, D D (Edinburgh U) 1947 *W, I, E*, 1948 *F, W, I*
Mackenzie, D K A (Edinburgh Wands) 1939 *I, E*
Mackenzie, J M (Edinburgh U) 1905 *NZ*, 1909 *W, I, E*, 1910 *W, I, E*, 1911 *W, I*
McKenzie, K D (Stirling County) 1994 *Arg* 1,2, 1995 *R, [Iv]*, 1996 *I, F, W, E, NZ* 1,2, *A, It*
Mackenzie, R C (Glasgow Acads) 1877 *I, E*, 1881 *I, E*
Mackie, G Y (Highland) 1975 *A*, 1976 *F, W*, 1978 *F*
MacKinnon, A (London Scottish) 1898 *I, E*, 1899 *I, W, E*, 1900 *E*
Mackintosh, C E W C (London Scottish) 1924 *F*
Mackintosh, H S (Glasgow U, W of Scotland) 1929 *F, W, I, E*, 1930 *F, W, I, E*, 1931 *F, W, I, E*, 1932 *SA, W, I, E*
MacLachlan, L P (Oxford U, London Scottish) 1954 *NZ, I, E, W*
Maclagan, W E (Edinburgh Acads) 1878 *E*, 1879 *I, E*, 1880 *I, E*, 1881 *I, E*, 1882 *I, E*, 1883 *W, I, E*, 1884 *W, I, E*, 1885 *W, I* 1,2, 1887 *I, W, E*, 1888 *W, I*, 1890 *W, I, E*
McLaren, A (Durham County) 1931 *F*
McLaren, E (London Scottish, Royal HSFP) 1923 *F, W, I, E*, 1924 *F*
McLauchlan, J (Jordanhill) 1969 *E, SA*, 1970 *F, W*, 1971 *F, W, I, E* (2[1C]), 1972 *F, W, E, NZ*, 1973 *F, W, I, E, P*, 1974 *W, E, I, F*, 1975 *I, F, W, E, NZ, A*, 1976 *F, W, E, I*, 1977 *W*, 1978 *I, F, W, E, NZ*, 1979 *W, E, I, F, NZ*
McLean, D I (Royal HSFP) 1947 *I, E*
Maclennan, W D (Watsonians) 1947 *F, I*
MacLeod, D A (Glasgow U) 1886 *I, E*
MacLeod, G (Edinburgh Acads) 1878 *E*, 1882 *I*
McLeod, H F (Hawick) 1954 *F, NZ, I, E, W*, 1955 *F, W, I, E*, 1956 *F, W, I, E*, 1957 *F, W, I, E*, 1958 *F, W, A, I, E*, 1959 *F, W, I, E*, 1960 *F, W, I, E, SA*, 1961 *F, SA, W, I, E*, 1962 *F, W, I, E*
MacLeod, K G (Cambridge U) 1905 *NZ*, 1906 *W, I, E, SA*, 1907 *W, I, E*, 1908 *I, E*
MacLeod, L M (Cambridge U) 1904 *W, I, E*, 1905 *W, I, NZ*
Macleod, W M (Fettesian-Lorettonians, Edinburgh Wands) 1886 *W, I*
McMillan, K H D (Sale) 1953 *F, W, I, E*

MacMillan, R G (London Scottish) 1887 *W, I, E*, 1890 *W, I, E*, 1891 *W, E*, 1892 *W, I, E*, 1893 *W, E*, 1894 *W, I, E*, 1895 *W, I, E*, 1897 *I, E*
MacMyn, D J (Cambridge U, London Scottish) 1925 *F, W, I, E*, 1926 *F, W, I, E*, 1927 *E, A*, 1928 *F*
McNeil, A S B (Watsonians) 1935 *I*
McPartlin, J J (Harlequins, Oxford U) 1960 *F, W*, 1962 *F, W, I, E*
Macphail, J A R (Edinburgh Acads) 1949 *E*, 1951 *SA*
Macpherson, D G (London Hospital) 1910 *I, E*
Macpherson, G P S (Oxford U, Edinburgh Acads) 1922 *F, W, I, E*, 1924 *W, E*, 1925 *F, W, E*, 1927 *F, W, I, E*, 1928 *F, W, E*, 1929 *I, E*, 1930 *F, W, I, E*, 1931 *W, E*, 1932 *SA, E*
Macpherson, N C (Newport) 1920 *W, I, E*, 1921 *F, E*, 1923 *I, E*
McQueen, S B (Waterloo) 1923 *F, W, I, E*
Macrae, D J (St Andrew's U) 1937 *W, I, E*, 1938 *W, I, E*, 1939 *W, I, E*
Madsen, D F (Gosforth) 1974 *W, E, I, F*, 1975 *I, F, W, E*, 1976 *F*, 1977 *E, I, F, W*, 1978 *I*
Mair, N G R (Edinburgh U) 1951 *F, W, I, E*
Maitland, G (Edinburgh Inst FP) 1885 *W, I* 2
Maitland, R (Edinburgh Inst FP) 1881 *E*, 1882 *I, E*, 1884 *W*, 1885 *W*
Maitland, R P (Royal Artillery) 1872 *E*
Malcolm, A G (Glasgow U) 1888 *I*
Manson, J J (Dundee HSFP) 1995 *E* (R)
Marsh, J (Edinburgh Inst FP) 1889 *W, I*
Marshall, A (Edinburgh Acads) 1875 *E*
Marshall, G R (Selkirk) 1988 *A* (R), 1989 *Fj*, 1990 *Arg*, 1991 *[Z]*
Marshall, J C (London Scottish) 1954 *F, NZ, I, E, W*
Marshall, K W (Edinburgh Acads) 1934 *W, I, E*, 1935 *W, I, E*, 1936 *W*, 1937 *E*
Marshall, T R (Edinburgh Acads) 1871 *E*, 1872 *E*, 1873 *E*, 1874 *E*
Marshall, W (Edinburgh Acads) 1872 *E*
Martin, H (Edinburgh Acads, Oxford U) 1908 *W, I, E*, 1909 *W, E*
Masters, W H (Edinburgh Inst FP) 1879 *I*, 1880 *I, E*
Maxwell, F T (Royal Engineers) 1872 *E*
Maxwell, G H H P (Edinburgh Acads, RAF, London Scottish) 1913 *I, E*, 1914 *W, I, E*, 1920 *W, E*, 1921 *F, W, I, E*, 1922 *F, E*
Maxwell, J M (Langholm) 1957 *I*
Mein, J (Edinburgh Acads) 1871 *E*, 1872 *E*, 1873 *E*, 1874 *E*, 1875 *E*
Melville, C L (Army) 1937 *W, I, E*
Menzies, H F (W of Scotland) 1893 *W, I*, 1894 *W, E*
Methuen, A (London Scottish) 1889 *W, I*
Michie, E J S (Aberdeen U, Aberdeen GSFP) 1954 *F, NZ, I, E*, 1955 *W, I, E*, 1956 *F, W, I, E*, 1957 *F, W, I, E*
Millar, J N (W of Scotland) 1892 *W, I, E*, 1893 *W*, 1895 *I, E*
Millar, R K (London Scottish) 1924 *I*
Millican, J G (Edinburgh U) 1973 *W, I, E*
Milne, C J B (Fettesian-Lorettonians, W of Scotland) 1886 *W, I, E*
Milne, D F (Heriot's FP) 1991 *[J(R)]*
Milne, I G (Heriot's FP, Harlequins) 1979 *I, F, NZ*, 1980 *I, F*, 1981 *NZ* 1,2, *R, A*, 1982 *E, I, F, W, A* 1,2, 1983 *I, F, W, E, NZ*, 1984 *W, E, I, F, A*, 1985 *F, W, E*, 1986 *F, W, E, I, R*, 1987 *I, F, W, E, [F, Z, NZ]*, 1988 *A*, 1989 *W*, 1990 *NZ* 1,2
Milne, K S (Heriot's FP) 1989 *W, E, I, F, Fj, R*, 1990 *I, F, W, E, NZ* 2, *Arg*, 1991 *F, W* (R), *E, [Z]*, 1992 *E, I, F, W, A* 1, 1993 *I, F, W, E, NZ*, 1994 *W, E, I, F, SA*, 1995 *C, I, F, W, E, [Tg, F, NZ]*
Milne, W M (Glasgow Acads) 1904 *I, E*, 1905 *W, I*
Milroy, E (Watsonians) 1910 *W*, 1911 *E*, 1912 *W, I, E, SA*, 1913 *F, W, I, E*, 1914 *I, E*
Mitchell, G W E (Edinburgh Wands) 1967 *NZ*, 1968 *F, W*
Mitchell, J G (W of Scotland) 1885 *W, I* 1,2
Moncreiff, F J (Edinburgh Acads) 1871 *E*, 1872 *E*, 1873 *E*
Monteith, H G (Cambridge U, London Scottish) 1905 *E*, 1906 *W, I, E, SA*, 1907 *W, I*, 1908 *E*
Monypenny, D B (London Scottish) 1899 *I, W, E*
Moodie, A R (St Andrew's U) 1909 *E*, 1910 *F*, 1911 *F*
Moore, A (Edinburgh Acads) 1990 *NZ* 2, *Arg*, 1991 *F, W, E*
Morgan, D W (Stewart's-Melville FP) 1973 *W, I, E, P*, 1974 *I, F*, 1975 *I, F, W, E, NZ, A*, 1976 *F, W*, 1977 *I, F, W*, 1978 *I, F, W, E*
Morrison, I R (London Scottish) 1993 *I, F, W, E*, 1994 *W, SA*, 1995 *C, I, F, W, E, R, [Tg, F, NZ]*

Ross, K I (Boroughmuir FP) 1961 *SA, W, I, E,* 1962 *F, W, I, E,* 1963 *F, W, E*
Ross, W A (Hillhead HSFP) 1937 *W, E*
Rottenburg, H (Cambridge U, London Scottish) 1899 *W, E,* 1900 *W, I, E*
Roughead, W N (Edinburgh Acads, London Scottish) 1927 *A,* 1928 *F, W, I, E,* 1930 *I, E,* 1931 *F, W, I, E,* 1932 *W*
Rowan, N A (Boroughmuir) 1980 *W, E,* 1981 *F, W, E, I,* 1984 *R,* 1985 *I,* 1987 *[R],* 1988 *I, F, W, E*
Rowand, R (Glasgow HSFP) 1930 *F, W,* 1932 *E,* 1933 *W, E, I,* 1934 *W*
Roxburgh, A J (Kelso) 1997 *A,* 1998 *It, F* (R), *W, E*
Roy, A (Waterloo) 1938 *W, I, E,* 1939 *W, I, E*
Russell, W L (Glasgow Acads) 1905 *NZ,* 1906 *W, I, E*
Rutherford, J Y (Selkirk) 1979 *W, E, I, F, NZ,* 1980 *I, F, E,* 1981 *F, W, E, I, NZ* 1,2, *A,* 1982 *E, I, F, W, A* 1,2, 1983 *E, NZ,* 1984 *W, E, I, F, R,* 1985 *I, F, W, E,* 1986 *F, W, E, I, R,* 1987 *I, F, W, E, [F]*

Sampson, R W F (London Scottish) 1939 *W,* 1947 *W*
Sanderson, G A (Royal HSFP) 1907 *W, I, E,* 1908 *I*
Sanderson, J L P (Edinburgh Acads) 1873 *E*
Schulze, D G (London Scottish) 1905 *E,* 1907 *I, E,* 1908 *W, I, E,* 1909 *W, I, E,* 1910 *W, I, E,* 1911 *W*
Scobie, R M (Royal Military Coll) 1914 *W, I, E*
Scotland, K J F (Heriot's FP, Cambridge U, Leicester) 1957 *F, W, I, E,* 1958 *E,* 1959 *F, W, I, E,* 1960 *F, W, I, E,* 1961 *F, SA, W, I, E,* 1962 *F, W, I, E,* 1963 *F, W, I, E,* 1965 *F*
Scott, D M (Langholm, Watsonians) 1950 *I, E,* 1951 *W, I, E, SA,* 1952 *F, W, I,* 1953 *F*
Scott, J M B (Edinburgh Acads) 1907 *E,* 1908 *W, I, E,* 1909 *W, I, E,* 1910 *F, W, I, E,* 1911 *F, W, I,* 1912 *W, I, E, SA,* 1913 *W, I, E*
Scott, J S (St Andrew's U) 1950 *E*
Scott, J W (Stewart's Coll FP) 1925 *F, W, I, E,* 1926 *F, W, I, E,* 1927 *F, W, I, E, A,* 1928 *F, W, E,* 1929 *E,* 1930 *F*
Scott, M (Dunfermline) 1992 *A* 2
Scott, R (Hawick) 1898 *I,* 1900 *I, E*
Scott, T (Langholm, Hawick) 1896 *W,* 1897 *I, E,* 1898 *I, E,* 1899 *I, W, E,* 1900 *W, I, E*
Scott, T M (Hawick) 1893 *E,* 1895 *W, I, E,* 1896 *W, E,* 1897 *I, E,* 1898 *I, E,* 1900 *W, I*
Scott, W P (W of Scotland) 1900 *I, E,* 1902 *I, E,* 1903 *W, I, E,* 1904 *W, I, E,* 1905 *W, I, E, NZ,* 1906 *W, I, E, SA,* 1907 *W, I, E*
Scoular, J G (Cambridge U) 1905 *NZ,* 1906 *W, I, E, SA*
Selby, J A R (Watsonians) 1920 *W, I*
Shackleton, J A P (London Scottish) 1959 *E,* 1963 *F, W,* 1964 *NZ, W,* 1965 *I, SA*
Sharp, A V (Bristol) 1994 *E, I, F, Arg* 1,2 *SA*
Sharp, G (Stewart's FP, Army) 1960 *F,* 1964 *F, NZ, W*
Shaw, G D (Sale) 1935 *NZ,* 1936 *W,* 1937 *W, I, E,* 1939 *I*
Shaw, I (Glasgow HSFP) 1937 *I*
Shaw, J N (Edinburgh Acads) 1921 *W, I*
Shaw, R W (Glasgow HSFP) 1934 *W, I, E,* 1935 *W, I, E, NZ,* 1936 *W, I, E,* 1937 *W, I, E,* 1938 *W, I, E,* 1939 *W, I, E,* 1946 *W, I, E,* 1937 *W, I, E,* 1938 *W, I, E,* 1939 *W, I, E*
Shedden, D (W of Scotland) 1972 *NZ,* 1973 *F, W, I, E, P,* 1976 *W, E, I,* 1977 *I, F, W,* 1978 *I, F, W*
Shepherd, R J S (Melrose) 1995 *WS,* 1996 *I, F, W, E, NZ* 1,2, *A, It,* 1997 *W, E, SA,* 1998 *It, I, W* (R)
Shiel, A G (Melrose) 1991 *[I* (R), *WS],* 1993 *I, F, W, E, NZ,* 1994 *Arg* 1,2, *SA,* 1995 *R, [Iv, F, NZ], WS*
Shillinglaw, R B (Gala, Army) 1960 *I, E, SA,* 1961 *F, SA*
Simmers, B M (Glasgow Acads) 1965 *F, W,* 1966 *A,* 1967 *F, W, I,* 1971 *F* (R)
Simmers, W M (Glasgow Acads) 1926 *W, I, E,* 1927 *F, W, I, E, A,* 1928 *F, W, I, E,* 1929 *F, W, I, E,* 1930 *F, W, I, E,* 1931 *F, W, I, E,* 1932 *SA, W, I, E*
Simpson, J W (Royal HSFP) 1893 *I, E,* 1894 *W, I, E,* 1895 *W, I, E,* 1896 *W, I,* 1897 *E,* 1899 *W, E*
Simpson, R S (Glasgow Acads) 1923 *I*
Simson, E D (Edinburgh U, London Scottish) 1902 *E,* 1903 *W, I, E,* 1904 *W, I, E,* 1905 *W, I, E, NZ,* 1906 *W, I, E,* 1907 *W, I, E*
Simson, J T (Watsonians) 1905 *NZ,* 1909 *W, I, E,* 1910 *F, W, I,* 1911 *I*
Simson, R F (London Scottish) 1911 *E*
Sloan, A T (Edinburgh Acads) 1914 *W,* 1920 *F, W, I, E,* 1921 *F, W, I, E*
Sloan, D A (Edinburgh Acads, London Scottish) 1950 *F, W, E,* 1951 *W, I, E,* 1953 *F*
Sloan, T (Glasgow Acads, Oxford U) 1905 *NZ,* 1906 *W, SA,* 1907 *W, E,* 1908 *W,* 1909 *I*
Smeaton, P W (Edinburgh Acads) 1881 *I,* 1883 *I, E*

Smith, A R (Oxford U) 1895 *W, I, E,* 1896 *W, I,* 1897 *I, E,* 1898 *I, E,* 1900 *I, E*
Smith, A R (Cambridge U, Gosforth, Ebbw Vale, Edinburgh Wands) 1955 *W, I, E,* 1956 *F, W, I, E,* 1957 *F, W, I, E,* 1958 *F, W, A, I,* 1959 *F, W, I, E,* 1960 *F, W, I, E, SA,* 1961 *F, SA, W, I, E,* 1962 *F, W, I, E*
Smith, D W C (London Scottish) 1949 *F, W, I, E,* 1950 *F, W, I,* 1953 *I*
Smith, E R (Edinburgh Acads) 1879 *I*
Smith, G K (Kelso) 1957 *I, E,* 1958 *F, W, A,* 1959 *F, W, I, E,* 1960 *F, W, I, E,* 1961 *F, SA, W, I, E*
Smith, H O (Watsonians) 1895 *W,* 1896 *W, I, E,* 1898 *I, E,* 1899 *W, I, E,* 1900 *E,* 1902 *E*
Smith, I R (Gloucester, Moseley) 1992 *E, I, W, A* 1,2, 1994 *E, I, F, Arg* 1,2, 1995 *[Iv],* WS, 1996 *I, F, W, E, NZ* 1,2, *A, It,* 1997 *E, I, F, A, SA*
Smith, I S (Oxford U, Edinburgh U) 1924 *W, I, E,* 1925 *F, W, I, E,* 1926 *F, W, I, E,* 1927 *F, I, E,* 1929 *F, W, I, E,* 1930 *F, W, I,* 1931 *F, W, I, E,* 1932 *SA, W, I, E,* 1933 *W, E, I*
Smith, I S G (London Scottish) 1969 *SA,* 1970 *F, W, I, E,* 1971 *F, W, I*
Smith, M A (London Scottish) 1970 *W, I, E, A*
Smith, R T (Kelso) 1929 *F, W, I, E,* 1930 *F, W, I*
Smith, S H (Glasgow Acads) 1877 *I,* 1878 *E*
Smith, T J (Gala) 1983 *E, NZ,* 1985 *I, F*
Smith T J (Watsonians) 1997 *E, I, F*
Sole, D M B (Bath, Edinburgh Acads) 1986 *F, W,* 1987 *I, F, W, E, [F, Z, R, NZ],* 1988 *I, F, W, E, A,* 1989 *W, E, I, F, Fj, R,* 1990 *I, F, W, E, NZ* 1,2, *Arg,* 1991 *F, W, E, I, R, [J, I, WS, E, NZ],* 1992 *E, I, F, W, A* 1,2
Somerville, D (Edinburgh Inst FP) 1879 *I,* 1882 *I,* 1883 *W, I, E,* 1884 *W*
Speirs, L M (Watsonians) 1906 *SA,* 1907 *W, I, E,* 1908 *W, I, E,* 1910 *F, W, E*
Spence, K M (Oxford U) 1953 *I*
Spencer, E (Clydesdale) 1898 *I*
Stagg, P K (Sale) 1965 *F, W, E, SA,* 1966 *F, W, I, E, A,* 1967 *F, W, I, E, NZ,* 1968 *F, W, I, E, A,* 1969 *F, W, I* (R), *SA,* 1970 *F, W, I, E, A*
Stanger, A G (Hawick) 1989 *Fj, R,* 1990 *I, F, W, E, NZ* 1,2, *Arg,* 1991 *F, W, E, I, R, [J, Z, I, WS, E, NZ],* 1992 *E, I, F, W, A* 1,2, 1993 *I, F, W, E, NZ,* 1994 *W, E, I, F, SA,* 1995 *R, [Iv],* 1996 *NZ* 2, *A, It,* 1997 *W, E, I, F, A, SA,* 1998 *It, I* (R), *F, W, E*
Stark, D A (Boroughmuir, Melrose, Glasgow Hawks) 1993 *I, F, W, E,* 1996 *NZ* 2(R), *It* (R), 1997 *W* (R), *E, SA*
Steele, W C C (Langholm, Bedford, RAF, London Scottish) 1969 *E,* 1971 *F, W, I, E* (2[1C]), 1972 *F, W, E, NZ,* 1973 *F, W, I, E,* 1975 *I, F, W, E, NZ* (R), 1976 *W, E, I,* 1977 *E*
Stephen, A E (W of Scotland) 1885 *W,* 1886 *I*
Steven, P D (Heriot's FP) 1984 *A,* 1985 *F, W, E*
Steven, R (Edinburgh Wands) 1962 *I*
Stevenson, A K (Glasgow Acads) 1922 *F,* 1923 *F, W, E*
Stevenson, A M (Glasgow U) 1911 *F*
Stevenson, G D (Hawick) 1956 *E,* 1957 *F,* 1958 *F, W, A, I, E,* 1959 *W, I, E,* 1960 *W, I, E, SA,* 1961 *F, SA, W, I, E,* 1963 *F, W, I,* 1964 *E,* 1965 *F*
Stevenson, H J (Edinburgh Acads) 1888 *W, I,* 1889 *W, I,* 1890 *W, I, E,* 1891 *W, I, E,* 1892 *W, I, E,* 1893 *I, E*
Stevenson, L E (Edinburgh U) 1888 *W*
Stevenson, R C (London Scottish) 1897 *I, E,* 1898 *E,* 1899 *I, W, E*
Stevenson, R C (St Andrew's U) 1910 *F, I, E,* 1911 *F, W, I*
Stevenson, W H (Glasgow Acads) 1925 *F*
Stewart, A K (Edinburgh U) 1874 *E,* 1876 *E*
Stewart, A M (Edinburgh Acads) 1914 *W*
Stewart, B D (Edinburgh Acads) 1996 *NZ* 2, *A*
Stewart, C A R (W of Scotland) 1880 *I, E*
Stewart, C E B (Kelso) 1960 *W,* 1961 *F*
Stewart, J (Glasgow HSFP) 1930 *F*
Stewart, J L (Edinburgh Acads) 1921 *I*
Stewart M J (Northampton) 1996 *It,* 1997 *W, E, I, F, A, SA,* 1998 *It, I, F, W*
Stewart, M S (Stewart's Coll FP) 1932 *SA, W, I,* 1933 *W, E, I,* 1934 *W, I, E*
Stewart, W A (London Hospital) 1913 *F, W, I,* 1914 *W*
Steyn, S S L (Oxford U) 1911 *E,* 1912 *I*
Strachan, G M (Jordanhill) 1971 *E* (C) (R), 1973 *W, I, E, P*
Stronach, R S (Glasgow Acads) 1901 *W, E,* 1905 *W, I, E*
Stuart, C D (W of Scotland) 1909 *I,* 1910 *F, W, I, E,* 1911 *I, E*

Stuart, L M (Glasgow HSFP) 1923 *F, W, I, E*, 1924 *F*, 1928 *E*, 1930 *I, E*
Suddon, N (Hawick) 1965 *W, I, E, SA*, 1966 *A*, 1968 *E, A*, 1969 *F, W, I*, 1970 *I, E, A*
Sutherland, W R (Hawick) 1910 *W, E*, 1911 *F, E*, 1912 *F, W, E, SA*, 1913 *F, W, I, E*, 1914 *W*
Swan, J S (Army, London Scottish, Leicester) 1953 *E*, 1954 *F, NZ, I, E, W*, 1955 *F, W, I, E*, 1956 *F, W, I, E*, 1957 *F, W*, 1958 *F*
Swan, M W (Oxford U, London Scottish) 1958 *F, W, A, I, E*, 1959 *F, W, I*
Sweet, J B (Glasgow HSFP) 1913 *E*, 1914 *I*
Symington, A W (Cambridge U) 1914 *W, E*

Tait, A V (Kelso, Newcastle) 1987 *[F(R), Z, R, NZ]*, 1988 *I, F, W, E*, 1997 *I, F, A*, 1998 *It, I, F, W, E*
Tait, J G (Edinburgh Acads) 1880 *I*, 1885 *I 2*
Tait, P W (Royal HSFP) 1935 *E*
Taylor, E G (Oxford U) 1927 *W, A*
Taylor, R C (Kelvinside-West) 1951 *W, I, E, SA*
Telfer, C M (Hawick) 1968 *A*, 1969 *F, W, I, E*, 1972 *F, W, E*, 1973 *W, I, E, P*, 1974 *W, E, I*, 1975 *A*, 1976 *F*
Telfer, J W (Melrose) 1964 *F, NZ, W, I, E*, 1965 *F, W, I*, 1966 *F, W, I, E*, 1967 *W, I, E*, 1968 *E, A*, 1969 *F, W, I, E, SA*, 1970 *F, W, I*
Tennent, J M (W of Scotland) 1909 *W, I, E*, 1910 *F, W, E*
Thom, D A (London Scottish) 1934 *W*, 1935 *W, I, E, NZ*
Thom, G (Kirkcaldy) 1920 *F, W, I, E*
Thom, J R (Watsonians) 1933 *W, E, I*
Thomson, A E (United Services) 1921 *F, W, E*
Thomson, A M (St Andrew's U) 1949 *I*
Thomson, B E (Oxford U) 1953 *F, W, I*
Thomson, I H M (Heriot's FP, Army) 1951 *W, I*, 1952 *F, W, I*, 1953 *I, E*
Thomson, J S (Glasgow Acads) 1871 *E*
Thomson, R H (London Scottish, PUC) 1960 *I, E, SA*, 1961 *F, SA, W, I, E*, 1963 *F, W, I, E*, 1964 *F, NZ, W*
Thomson, W H (W of Scotland) 1906 *SA*
Thomson, W J (W of Scotland) 1899 *W, E*, 1900 *W*
Timms, A B (Edinburgh U, Edinburgh Wands) 1896 *W*, 1900 *W, I*, 1901 *W, I, E*, 1902 *W, E*, 1903 *W, E*, 1904 *I, E*, 1905 *I, E*
Tod, H B (Gala) 1911 *F*
Tod, J (Watsonians) 1884 *W, I, E*, 1885 *W, I 1,2*, 1886 *W, I, E*
Todd, J K (Glasgow Acads) 1874 *E*, 1875 *E*
Tolmie, J M (Glasgow HSFP) 1922 *E*
Tomes, A J (Hawick) 1976 *E, I*, 1977 *E, I*, 1978 *I, F, W, E, NZ*, 1979 *W, E, I, F, NZ*, 1980 *F, W, E*, 1981 *F, W, E, I, NZ 1,2, A, R, A*, 1982 *E, I, F, W, A 1,2*, 1983 *I, F, W*, 1984 *W, E, I, F, R, A*, 1985 *W, E*, 1987 *I, F, E (R), [F, Z, R, NZ]*
Torrie, T J (Edinburgh Acads) 1877 *E*
Townsend, G P J (Gala, Northampton) 1993 *E (R)*, 1994 *W, E, I, F, Arg 1,2*, 1995 *C, I, F, W, E, WS*, 1996 *I, F, W, E, NZ 1,2, A, It*, 1997 *W, E, I, F, A, SA*, 1998 *It, I, F, W, E*
Tukalo, I (Selkirk) 1985 *I*, 1987 *I, F, W, E, [F, Z, R, NZ]*, 1988 *F, W, E, A*, 1989 *W, E, I, F, Fj*, 1990 *I, F, W, E, NZ 1*, 1991 *I, R, [J, Z, I, WS, E, NZ]*, 1992 *E, I, F, W, A 1,2*
Turk, A S (Langholm) 1971 *E (R)*
Turnbull, D J (Hawick) 1987 *[NZ]*, 1988 *F, E*, 1990 *E (R)*, 1991 *F, W, E, I, R, [Z]*, 1993 *I, F, W, E*, 1994 *W*
Turnbull, F O (Kelso) 1951 *F, SA*
Turnbull, G O (W of Scotland) 1896 *I, E*, 1897 *I, E*, 1904 *W*
Turnbull, P (Edinburgh Acads) 1901 *W, I, E*, 1902 *W, I, E*
Turner, F H (Oxford U, Liverpool) 1911 *F, W, I, E*, 1912 *F, W, I, E, SA*, 1913 *F, W, I, E*, 1914 *I, E*
Turner, J W C (Gala) 1966 *W, A*, 1967 *F, W, I, E, NZ*, 1968 *F, W, I, E, A*, 1969 *F*, 1970 *E, A*, 1971 *F, W, I, E* (2[1C])

Usher, C M (United Services, Edinburgh Wands) 1912 *E*, 1913 *F, W, I, E*, 1914 *E*, 1920 *F, W, I, E*, 1921 *W, E*, 1922 *F, W, I, E*

Valentine, A R (RNAS, Anthorn) 1953 *F, W, I*
Valentine, D D (Hawick) 1947 *I, E*
Veitch, J P (Royal HSFP) 1882 *E*, 1883 *I*, 1884 *W, I, E*, 1885 *I 1,2*, 1886 *E*
Villar, C (Edinburgh Wands) 1876 *E*, 1877 *I, E*

Waddell, G H (London Scottish, Cambridge U) 1957 *E*, 1958 *F, W, A, I, E*, 1959 *F, W, I, E*, 1960 *I, E, SA*, 1961 *F*, 1962 *F, W, I, E*

Waddell, H (Glasgow Acads) 1924 *F, W, I, E*, 1925 *I, E*, 1926 *F, W, I, E*, 1927 *F, W, I, E*, 1930 *W*
Wade, A L (London Scottish) 1908 *E*
Wainwright, R I (Edinburgh Acads, West Hartlepool, Watsonians, Army, Dundee HSFP) 1992 *I (R), F, A 1,2*, 1993 *NZ*, 1994 *W, E*, 1995 *C, I, F, W, E, R, [Iv, Tg, F, NZ]*, *WS*, 1996 *I, F, W, E, NZ 1,2*, 1997 *W, E, I, F, SA*, 1998 *It, I, F, W, E*
Walker, A (W of Scotland) 1881 *I*, 1882 *E*, 1883 *W, I, E*
Walker, A W (Cambridge U, Birkenhead Park) 1931 *F, W, I, E*, 1932 *I*
Walker, J G (W of Scotland) 1882 *E*, 1883 *W*
Walker, M (Oxford U) 1952 *F*
Wallace, A C (Oxford U) 1923 *F*, 1924 *F, W, E*, 1925 *F, W, I, E*, 1926 *F*
Wallace, W M (Cambridge U) 1913 *E*, 1914 *W, I, E*
Wallace, M I (Glasgow High Kelvinside) 1996 *A, It*, 1997 *W*
Walls, W A (Glasgow Acads) 1882 *E*, 1883 *W, I, E*, 1884 *W, I, E*, 1886 *W, I, E*
Walter, M W (London Scottish) 1906 *I, E, SA*, 1907 *W, I*, 1908 *W, I*, 1910 *I*
Walton, P (Northampton, Newcastle) 1994 *E, I, F, Arg 1,2*, 1995 *[Iv]*, 1997 *W, E, I, F, SA (R)*, 1998 *I, F*
Warren, J R (Glasgow Acads) 1914 *I*
Warren, R C (Glasgow Acads) 1922 *W, I*, 1930 *W, I, E*
Waters, F H (Cambridge U, London Scottish) 1930 *F, W, I, E*, 1932 *SA, W, I*
Waters, J A (Selkirk) 1933 *W, E, I*, 1934 *W, I, E*, 1935 *W, I, E, NZ*, 1936 *W, I, E*, 1937 *W, I, E*
Waters, J B (Cambridge U) 1904 *I, E*
Watherston, J G (Edinburgh Wands) 1934 *I, E*
Watherston, W R A (London Scottish) 1963 *F, W, I*
Watson, D H (Glasgow Acads) 1876 *E*, 1877 *I, E*
Watson, W S (Boroughmuir) 1974 *W, E, I, F*, 1975 *NZ*, 1977 *I, F, W*, 1979 *I, F*
Watt, A G J (Glasgow High Kelvinside) 1991 *[Z]*, 1993 *I, NZ*, 1994 *Arg 2* (t & R)
Watt, A G M (Edinburgh Acads) 1947 *F, W, I, A*, 1948 *F, W*
Weatherstone, T G (Stewart's Coll FP) 1952 *E*, 1953 *I, E*, 1954 *F, NZ, I, E, W*, 1955 *F*, 1958 *W, A, I, E*, 1959 *W, I, E*
Weir, G W (Melrose, Newcastle) 1990 *Arg*, 1991 *R, [J, Z, I, WS, E, NZ]*, 1992 *E, I, F, W, A 1,2*, 1993 *I, F, W, E, NZ*, 1994 *W (R), E, I, F, SA*, 1995 *F (R), W, E, R, [Iv, Tg, F, NZ], WS*, 1996 *I, F, W, E, NZ 1,2, A, It (R)*, 1997 *W, E, I, F*, 1998 *It, I, F, W, E*
Welsh, R (Watsonians) 1895 *W, I, E*, 1896 *W*
Welsh, R B (Hawick) 1967 *I, E*
Welsh, W B (Hawick) 1927 *A*, 1928 *F, W, I*, 1929 *I, E*, 1930 *F, W, I, E*, 1931 *F, W, I, E*, 1932 *SA, W, I, E*, 1933 *W, E, I*
Welsh, W H (Edinburgh U) 1900 *I, E*, 1901 *W, I, E*, 1902 *W, I, E*
Wemyss, A (Gala, Edinburgh Wands) 1914 *W, I*, 1920 *F, E*, 1922 *F, W, I*
West, L (Edinburgh U, West Hartlepool) 1903 *W, I, E*, 1905 *I, E, NZ*, 1906 *W, I, E*
Weston, V G (Kelvinside Acads) 1936 *I, E*
White, D B (Gala, London Scottish) 1982 *F, W, A 1,2*, 1987 *W, E, [F, R, NZ]*, 1988 *I, F, W, E, A*, 1989 *W, E, I, F, Fj, R*, 1990 *I, F, W, E, NZ 1,2*, 1991 *F, W, E, R, [J, Z, I, WS, E, NZ]*, 1992 *E, I, F, W*
White, D M (Kelvinside Acads) 1963 *F, W, I, E*
White, T B (Edinburgh Acads) 1888 *W, I*, 1889 *W*
Whittington, T P (Merchistonians) 1873 *E*
Whitworth, R J E (London Scottish) 1936 *I*
Whyte, D J (Edinburgh Wands) 1965 *W, I, E, SA*, 1966 *F, W, I, E, A*, 1967 *F, W, I, E*
Will, J G (Cambridge U) 1912 *F, W, I, E*, 1914 *W, I, E*
Wilson, A W (Dunfermline) 1931 *F, I, E*
Wilson, G A (Oxford U) 1949 *F, W, E*
Wilson, G R (Royal HSFP) 1886 *E*, 1890 *W, I, E*, 1891 *I*
Wilson, J H (Watsonians) 1953 *I*
Wilson, J S (St Andrew's U) 1931 *F, W, I, E*, 1932 *E*
Wilson, J S (United Services, London Scottish) 1908 *I*, 1909 *W*
Wilson, R (London Scottish) 1976 *E, I*, 1977 *E, I, F*, 1978 *I, F*, 1981 *R*, 1983 *I*
Wilson, R L (Gala) 1951 *F, W, I, E, SA*, 1953 *F, W, E*
Wilson, R W (W of Scotland) 1873 *E*, 1874 *E*
Wilson, S (Oxford U, London Scottish) 1964 *F, NZ, W, I, E*, 1965 *W, I, E, SA*, 1966 *F, W, I, A*, 1967 *F, W, I, E, NZ*, 1968 *F, W, I, E*

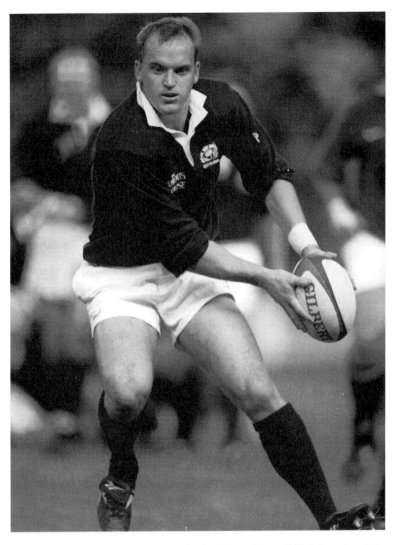

Gregor Townsend (Scotland), Scotland v South Africa at Murrayfield, 6 December 1997.

Wood, A (Royal HSFP) 1873 *E*, 1874 *E*, 1875 *E*
Wood, G (Gala) 1931 *W, I*, 1932 *W, I, E*
Woodburn, J C (Kelvinside Acads) 1892 *I*
Woodrow, A N (Glasgow Acads) 1887 *I, W, E*
Wotherspoon, W (W of Scotland) 1891 *I*, 1892 *I*, 1893 *W, E*, 1894 *W, I, E*
Wright, F A (Edinburgh Acads) 1932 *E*
Wright, H B (Watsonians) 1894 *W*
Wright, K M (London Scottish) 1929 *F, W, I, E*
Wright, P H (Boroughmuir) 1992 *A* 1,2, 1993 *F, W, E*, 1994 *W*, 1995 *C, I, F, W, E, R, [Iv, Tg, F, NZ]*, 1996 *W, E, NZ* 1
Wright, R W J (Edinburgh Wands) 1973 *F*

Wright, S T H (Stewart's Coll FP) 1949 *E*
Wright, T (Hawick) 1947 *A*
Wyllie, D S (Stewart's-Melville FP) 1984 *A*, 1985 *W* (R), *E*, 1987 *I, F, [F, Z, R, NZ]*, 1989 *R*, 1991 *R, [J (R), Z]*, 1993 *NZ* (R), 1994 *W* (R), *E, I, F*

Young, A H (Edinburgh Acads) 1874 *E*
Young, E T (Glasgow Acads) 1914 *E*
Young, R G (Watsonians) 1970 *W*
Young, T E B (Durham) 1911 *F*
Young, W B (Cambridge U, London Scottish) 1937 *W, I, E*, 1938 *W, I, E*, 1939 *W, I, E*, 1948 *E*

succumbed to Glasgow Hawks. Campbell Aitken, the former Scotland under-21 full-back, was Boroughmuir's leading scorer in the league with 103 points.

League Record 1997-98

Date	Venue	Opponents	Result	Scorers
15 Nov	A	Melrose	3-21	P: Reekie
29 Nov	H	Heriot's FP	13-5	T: Aitken, Finnie P: Aitken
		(match abandoned after 68 minutes)		
13 Dec	A	Hawick	18-6	T: Burns, Kiddie, Wyllie P: Aitken
20 Dec	A	West of Scotland	5-23	T: Scown
27 Dec	A	Watsonians	14-12	T: Reid P: Aitken 2 D: Wyllie
10 Jan	H	Edinburgh Acads	29-19	T: Aitken 2, Anderson, McLean, Walters C: Aitken 2
13 Jan	H	Heriot's FP	20-9	T: Aitken, McNulty C: Aitken 2 P: Aitken 2
17 Jan	A	Jed-Forest	14-21	T: Aitken P: Aitken 3
31 Jan	H	Currie	17-11	T: Graham P: Aitken 4
14 Feb	A	Stirling County	9-18	P: Aitken 3
14 Mar	H	Stirling County	39-7	T: Allan, Burns, Graham, Kiddie, McCallum 2, McLean C: Kiddie 2
28 Mar	A	Edinburgh Acads	63-23	T: Aitken, Burns, Cunningham, Graham 3, M Murray 3, Walters, Wyllie C: Aitken 3, Reekie
8 Apr	A	Heriot's FP	15-33	T: M Murray 2 C: Aitken P: Aitken
2 May	H	Jed-Forest	66-10	T: Graham 2, Kirkpatrick, McLean 2, D Murray, M Murray 2, Scown 2 C: Aitken 7, Wyllie

Currie

Year of formation 1970
Ground Malleny Park, Balerno, Edinburgh EH14 5HA Tel: (0131) 449 2432
Colours Amber and black
Captain 1997-98 M Blair
SRU Tennents Championship 1997-98 Div 1A 4th   **SRU Tennents Cup 1997-98** Lost 17-18 to Kelso (semi-final)

Currie were in the hunt for the championship until the last series of four league matches. At the mid-season cut-off they were third behind Watsonians and Melrose only on the bonus-points count. Currie's six wins included one at home against Melrose, the defending champions, and when they opened the second stage with a second victory over Hawick they were outright league leaders. However, they lost their last three matches, a home defeat by Watsonians being the second time in the league that they had conceded a half-century to the eventual champions. Currie reached the semi-final stage in the Scottish Cup, and they would have gone farther but for the late try with which Kelso snatched an 18-17 victory. Ally Donaldson, as usual, was Currie's top league scorer (88 points).

League Record 1997-98

Date	Venue	Opponents	Result	Scorers
15 Nov	A	Hawick	14-26	T: Blair, Donaldson C: Donaldson 2
13 Dec	A	Watsonians	0-58	
27 Dec	A	Jed-Forest	43-13	T: Blair, Caldwell, Campbell, Officer, Rogerson, Tonkin 2 C: Mallinson 3, Officer
10 Jan	H	Melrose	20-17	T: Mallinson, Officer C: Donaldson 2 P: Donaldson 2
14 Jan	H	Edinburgh Acads	36-10	T: Blair, Clark, Mainwaring, Mallinson, Ward C: Donaldson 4 P: Donaldson

17 Jan	H	Stirling County	19-11	T: Caldwell, Mallinson P: Donaldson 3
31 Jan	A	Boroughmuir	11-17	T: Officer P: Donaldson 2
10 Feb	H	West of Scotland	15-12	T: Caldwell, Campbell C: Donaldson P: Donaldson
14 Feb	H	Heriot's FP	24-13	T: Blair, Campbell, Tonkin C: Donaldson 3 P: Donaldson
14 Mar	H	Hawick	26-24	T: Officer 2, Wilson C: Donaldson P: Donaldson 3
28 Mar	A	West of Scotland	18-37	T: Campbell, Simpson C: Donaldson P: Donaldson 2
22 Apr	H	Watsonians	5-56	T: Caldwell
25 Apr	A	Melrose	29-41	T: Caldwell 2, Officer, Wilson C: Donaldson 3 P: Donaldson

Dundee High School FP

Year of formation 1880
Ground Mayfield, Arbroath Road, Dundee Tel: Dundee (01382) 453517 (ground) and 451045 (clubhouse)
Colours Dark blue with red band
Captain 1997-98 D R Hamilton
SRU Tennents Championship 1997-98 Div 2A 3rd   **SRU Tennents Cup 1997-98** Lost 24-28 to East Kilbride (4th round)

For the second successive season Dundee High School FP missed out on promotion by finishing third in the Second Division. Their first-stage campaign produced five wins, including successes against two other potential championship contenders, Gala and Kilmarnock, and when Dundee avenged those defeats after the division's mid-season split they were strongly in contention in second place. However, successive defeats by Kelso and Glasgow Hawks forced them back into third place. Another low point of the Dundee season was the Scottish Cup fourth-round defeat by a National League club, East Kilbride. More had been expected of Dundee when two Lions, Rob Wainwright and Tom Smith, were recruited to the Mayfield ranks to join their fellow Scottish international forward, Stewart Campbell. However, Smith did not play at all and the others' seasons were interrupted, all by injury.

League Record 1997-98

Date	Venue	Opponents	Result	Scorers
15 Nov	H	Kelso	17-21	T: Millard, Rouse C: CJ Milne 2 P: CJ Milne
29 Nov	A	Glasgow Hawks	6-36	P: CJ Milne 2
13 Dec	H	Gala	26-24	T: Longstaff, D Milne, J Petrie 2 P: CJ Milne 2
27 Dec	H	Peebles	59-8	T: Gray 3, Lamont, Longstaff, McWhirter, Pearson 2, Rouse C: Pearson 4 P: Pearson 2
10 Jan	A	Kirkcaldy	3-15	P: Patterson
17 Jan	A	Kilmarnock	12-11	T: Longstaff, W Robertson C: Hamilton
31 Jan	H	Preston Lodge FP	62-7	T: Gray 2, Hayter, Longstaff 2, CJ Milne, D Milne 2, Petrie, Scott C: CJ Milne 6
10 Feb	H	Musselburgh	27-16	T: McWhirter, D Milne, J Petrie, S Petrie C: CJ Milne 2 P: CJ Milne
14 Feb	A	Biggar	7-20	T: Rouse C: CJ Milne
14 Mar	H	Kilmarnock	34-25	T: Hayter, Longstaff 2, CJ Milne 2, W Robertson C: CJ Milne 2
28 Mar	A	Gala	37-35	T: Gray, Hayter, Mason, Pearson 2 C: CJ Milne 3 P: CJ Milne 2
25 Apr	A	Kelso	20-24	T: Pearson, Scott 2 C: CJ Milne P: CJ Milne

2 May	H	Glasgow Hawks	23-28	*T:* Featherstone, CJ Milne, Pearson
				C: CJ Milne *P:* CJ Milne 2

Edinburgh Academicals

Year of formation 1857
Ground Raeburn Place, Stockbridge, Edinburgh EH4 1HQ Tel: (0131) 332 1070 and 315 3298
Colours Blue and white hoops
Captain 1997-98 R Hoole
SRU Tennents Championship 1997-98 Div 1B 5th (relegated) **SRU Tennents Cup 1997-98** Lost 22-55 to Watsonians (5th round)

Edinburgh Academicals, champions of the Second Division in 1997, slipped back down, winning only two of their league games, both at home. Victory by 23-9 against Stirling was their only success in the first stage, though they grabbed a possible lifeline for survival when they beat Jed-Forest 33-6 at Raeburn Place in late April. It was cut short when in their final match at neighbouring Goldenacre they lost to Heriot's by 13-42. Well before the end of the league season Academicals had parted company with their coach, Roger Whittaker.

League Record 1997-98

Date	Venue	Opponents	Result	Scorers
15 Nov	A	Watsonians	10-35	*T:* Porter *C:* Easson *P:* Easson
29 Nov	H	Melrose	0-20	
13 Dec	H	Jed-Forest	15-20	*T:* Andreou, Barber *C:* Easson *P:* Easson
27 Dec	H	Stirling County	23-9	*T:* Hoole, Reid, Troup *C:* Stent *P:* Barber, Stent
10 Jan	A	Boroughmuir	19-29	*T:* Macdonald, McVie, van der Esch *C:* Barber 2
14 Jan	A	Currie	10-36	*T:* Harley, Harrison
17 Jan	H	Heriot's FP	14-33	*T:* Macdonald, pen try *C:* Hay-Smith, Stent
31 Jan	A	Hawick	16-20	*T:* Karaintiana *C:* Easson *P:* Easson 3
14 Feb	H	West of Scotland	20-22	*T:* Barber, Stent 2 *C:* Stent *P:* Stent
28 Mar	H	Boroughmuir	23-63	*T:* Burns, Porter 2 *C:* Easson *P:* Easson 2
22 Apr	A	Stirling County	13-18	*T:* McVie *C:* Easson *P:* Easson 2
25 Apr	H	Jed-Forest	33-6	*T:* Day, Howison, Light, Stent *C:* Easson 2 *P:* Easson 3
2 May	A	Heriot's FP	13-42	*T:* Hamilton *C:* Easson *P:* Easson 2

Gala

Year of formation 1875
Ground Netherdale, Nether Road, Galashiels TD1 3HE Tel: (01896) 755 145
Colours Maroon
Captain 1997-98 R Gray
SRU Tennents Championship 1997-98 Div 2A 4th **SRU Tennents Cup 1997-98** Lost 13-38 to Currie (5th round)

Gala were in second place behind Glasgow Hawks when the Second Division split in two, but they slipped in the latter stage to finish fourth. Their campaign in the first series produced six wins and three defeats, one by only 24-26 away against Dundee High School FP. However, they lost three of their four second-stage games, again by two points against Dundee (35-37), though in their final match Gala avenged their earlier defeat by Kilmarnock. Gary Parker, Gala's player-coach import from neighbours Melrose, was the club's leading points-scorer in the league with 88. Gala compensated for Premiership disappointments by winning the Border League for the first time since 1981.

League Record 1997-98

Date	Venue	Opponents	Result	Scorers
15 Nov	A	Peebles	20-14	T: M Changleng, Parker, CD Paterson C: CD Paterson P: CD Paterson
29 Nov	H	Kirkcaldy	26-13	T: CD Paterson, Townsend C: Parker 2 P: Parker 4
13 Dec	A	Dundee HSFP	24-26	T: M Changleng, Crooks C: CD Paterson P: CD Paterson 4
20 Dec	H	Preston Lodge FP	27-8	T: Ballantyne, M Changleng 2, Parker C: Parker 2 P: Parker
27 Dec	A	Biggar	8-3	T: Ballantyne P: Parker
10 Jan	H	Kelso	27-10	T: M Changleng, CD Paterson, Townsend, Weir C: Parker 2 P: Parker
17 Jan	A	Glasgow Hawks	11-46	T: M Changleng P: Parker 2
31 Jan	A	Kilmarnock	8-32	T: Scott P: Parker
14 Feb	H	Musselburgh	47-17	T: Amos, M Changleng 2, Harrison, Parker, CD Paterson, Townsend C: Parker 6
14 Mar	H	Glasgow Hawks	20-67	T: Amos, Harrison C: Parker 2 P: Parker 2
28 Mar	H	Dundee HSFP	35-37	T: Dods, Parker 2, Townsend C: Parker 3 P: Parker 2 D: CD Paterson
22 Apr	A	Kelso	22-32	T: Weir C: Aitchison P: Aitchison 5
25 Apr	H	Kilmarnock	26-18	T: Crooks, Johnstone C: Aitchison 2 P: Aitchison 3 D: Aitchison

Glasgow Hawks

Year of formation 1997 (association of Glasgow Academicals and GHK, the latter a 1982 amalgamation of Glasgow High RFC and Kelvinside Academicals)
Grounds New Anniesland, Helensburgh Drive, Glasgow Tel: (0141) 959 4569
Old Anniesland, 637 Crow Road, Glasgow Tel: (0141) 959 1154
Colours Red, white and back bands divided by narrow green stripes
Captain 1997-98 D Wilson
SRU Tennents Championship 1997-98 Div 2A *Winners – promoted*   **SRU Tennents Cup 1997-98** *Winners* – beat Kelso 36-14 (final)

Glasgow Hawks combined the resources of GHK and Glasgow Academicals so effectively with the Glasgow representative team's Cook Islands internationals, Tommy Hayes and Mike Beckham, that the fledgling club won the Premiership's Second Division title and the Scottish Cup. So dominant were Hawks in the league, running up four half-centuries in successive matches, that they had secured the division trophy with three games to spare. Their 100% record was broken only in the penultimate match, when they lost 5-14 on a visit to Kilmarnock. Hayes was the leading scorer in the Premiership with 185 points, and three Hawks, Derek Stark, Ally Common, and Glenn Metcalfe, led the list of Second Division try-scorers with respective hauls of 16, 10 and eight. Stark scored four tries in the 79-19 win at Musselburgh.

League Record 1997-98

Date	Venue	Opponents	Result	Scorers
15 Nov	A	Kirkcaldy	20-11	T: Common, pen try C: Hayes 2 P: Hayes 2
29 Nov	H	Dundee HSFP	36-6	T: Docherty, Hayes, Little, Ness 2 C: Hayes 4 P: Hayes
13 Dec	A	Preston Lodge FP	37-8	T: Hayes, Hutton, Metcalfe, Stark 2 C: Hayes 3 P: Hayes 2
20 Dec	H	Biggar	43-15	T: Common, Hawkes, Metcalfe, Stark 2, MI Wallace C: Hayes 3, MacGregor 2 P: MacGregor

27 Dec	A	Kelso	33-13	T: Hayes, Metcalfe, Stark, MI Wallace
				C: Hayes 2 P: Hayes 3
10 Jan	H	Kilmarnock	19-12	T: McGrandles, Matthewson, Stark
				C: Hayes 2
17 Jan	H	Gala	46-11	T: Common, Hayes, Little, Metcalfe 2, Stark
				C: Hayes 5 P: Hayes 2
31 Jan	A	Musselburgh	75-19	T: Common, Hawkes, Hayes 2, Little,
				McGrandles, Mackay, Stark 4 C: Hayes 7
				P: Hayes 2
14 Feb	H	Peebles	62-3	T: Common 3, Docherty, Hayes, Mackay,
				Stark 2, pen try C: Hayes 7 P: Hayes
14 Mar	A	Gala	67-20	T: Beckham, Common 3, Metcalfe 4, Simmers,
				Wilson C: Hayes 7 P: Hayes
28 Mar	H	Kelso	50-25	T: Common 2, Docherty, Hayes, Hutton,
				Metcalfe, Stark 2 C: Hayes 5
8 Apr	A	Kilmarnock	5-14	T: McGrandles
2 May	A	Dundee HSFP	28-23	T: Little, McIlwham, Stark, MI Wallace
				C: Hayes 4

Hawick

Year of formation 1873
Ground Mansfield Park, Mansfield Road, Hawick Tel: (01450) 737 429
Colours Green
Captain 1997-98 A G Stanger
SRU Tennents Championship 1997-98 Div 1A 5th
SRU Tennents Cup 1997-98 Lost 5-48 to Boroughmuir (quarter-final)

Hawick were in the running for the championship when the First Division split in two, but they could not follow through in the second stage of the competition. Six victories in nine games, including a notable win away to Melrose, the defending champions, meant that Hawick reached the cut-off with the same playing record as three other clubs. It was only on bonus points that Hawick were as low as fourth place. However, they lost all of their four matches in the second stage and slipped back to fifth place. Hawick, Scottish Cup winners in the initial season, 1995-96, slipped out of this year's competition with a 48-5 home defeat by Boroughmuir in the quarter-finals.

League Record 1997-98

Date	Venue	Opponents	Result	Scorers
15 Nov	H	Currie	26-14	T: Menzies 2, Scott C: Welsh P: Welsh 3
29 Nov	A	Stirling County	12-27	T: Davidson, Harris C: Welsh
13 Dec	H	Boroughmuir	6-18	P: Welsh 2
27 Dec	A	Melrose	19-8	T: Howe C: Welsh P: Colin Murray 2,
				Welsh 2
10 Jan	H	West of Scotland	23-15	T: Landels, Renwick, Wear C: Colin Murray
				P: Colin Murray, Sharp
17 Jan	A	Watsonians	9-20	P: Welsh 3
31 Jan	H	Edinburgh Acads	20-16	T: Stanger, Suddon C: Sharp, Welsh
				P: Sharp 2
10 Feb	A	Heriot's FP	34-3	T: Stanger 2, Suddon, Wear 2 C: Sharp 3
				P: Sharp
14 Feb	A	Jed-Forest	34-20	T: McDonnell, Scott, Sharp C: Sharp 2
				P: Sharp 5
14 Mar	A	Currie	24-26	T: Hay, Reid, Suddon C: Sharp 3 P: Sharp
28 Mar	H	Watsonians	20-45	T: Harris, Cameron Murray 2 C: Sharp
				P: Sharp
8 Apr	H	Melrose	18-28	T: Davidson, Suddon C: Sharp P: Sharp 2

| 2 May | A | West of Scotland | 17-29 | *T:* Cameron Murray, Stanger *C:* Sharp 2 *P:* Sharp |

Heriot's FP

Year of formation 1890
Ground Goldenacre, Bangholm Terrace, Edinburgh EH3 5QN Tel: (0131) 552 5925
Colours Blue with white horizontal stripes
Captain 1997-98 G F Dall
SRU Tennents Championship 1997-98 Div 1B 2nd **SRU Tennents Cup 1997-98** Lost 38-46 to Stirling County after extra time (5th round)

Heriot's retained the distinction of being only one of three clubs who have never been out of the First Division, though they had to go as far as defending that status in a play-off against Kelso, runners-up in the Second Division. At the 'cut' Heriot's were ninth of 10, after beating only Edinburgh Academicals and Jed-Forest. However, the Goldenacre club finished strongly with successive wins against Boroughmuir, Stirling, and Edinburgh Academicals to ensure that they avoided the certain relegation place. Heriot's exit from the Scottish Cup was in a close match which went to extra time before they lost to Stirling by 38-46. Gordon Ross, the Scotland under-21 stand-off, scored 111 points in total, including 21 in the 33-12 play-off victory over Kelso.

League Record 1997-98

Date	Venue	Opponents	Result	Scorers
15 Nov	H	Stirling County	5-37	*T:* Bell
29 Nov	A	Boroughmuir *(match abandoned after 68 minutes)*	5-13	*T:* Turnbull
13 Dec	A	Melrose	22-31	*T:* Fowler, Livingston, Payot *C:* Ross 2 *P:* Ross
27 Dec	A	West of Scotland	10-39	*T:* Keenan *C:* Ross *P:* Ross
10 Jan	H	Watsonians	20-31	*T:* Binnie, Gilmour, Lawrie *C:* Ross *P:* Ross
13 Jan	A	Boroughmuir	9-20	*P:* Ross 3
17 Jan	A	Edinburgh Acads	33-14	*T:* Bryce, G F Dall, Proctor *C:* Ross 3 *P:* Ross 3 *D:* Ross
31 Jan	H	Jed-Forest	21-6	*T:* Binnie, pen try *C:* Ross *P:* Ross 2 *D:* Ross
10 Feb	H	Hawick	3-34	*P:* Ross
14 Feb	A	Currie	13-24	*T:* Bell *C:* Ross *P:* Ross 2
14 Mar	A	Jed-Forest	19-29	*T:* G F Dall, Lawson, Turnbull *C:* Ross 2
8 Apr	H	Boroughmuir	33-15	*T:* Binnie, Boswell, Payot *C:* Ross 3 *P:* Ross 3 *D:* Ross
25 Apr	A	Stirling County	25-3	*T:* Binnie, A K Dall, Payot *C:* Ross 2 *P:* Ross 2
2 May	H	Edinburgh Acads	42-13	*T:* Binnie, G F Dall, Fowler, Gilmour, Payot *C:* Ross 4 *P:* Ross 3
Play-Off (at Pennypit Park)				
16 May		Kelso	33-12	*T:* Lawson, Payot, Smith *C:* Ross 3 *P:* Ross 4

Jed-Forest

Year of formation 1884
Ground Riverside Park, Jedburgh Tel: (01835) 862 855 and 862 232
Colours Royal blue
Captain 1997-98 Calum Brown

SRU Tennents Championship 1997-98 Div 1B 3rd   **SRU Tennents Cup 1997-98** Lost 21-67 to Glasgow Hawks (5th round)

Jed-Forest had a notable victory in their first home league match, winning emphatically by 31-15 against Watsonians, the eventual champions. Victory followed against Edinburgh Academicals, but Jed could not maintain that early impetus as they had to contest the lower half of the First Division in the second stage of the programme. Victories against Heriot's and Stirling left Jed in a position that neither Heriot's nor Edinburgh Academicals could overtake. Chris Richards, the former Scotland under-21 full-back, was leading scorer with 79 points.

League Record 1997-98

Date	Venue	Opponents	Result	Scorers
15 Nov	A	West of Scotland	6-51	*P:* Richards 2
29 Nov	H	Watsonians	31-15	*T:* C Brown, M Brown, Laidlaw, Richards *C:* Richards *P:* Richards 3
13 Dec	A	Edinburgh Acads	20-15	*T:* M Brown, Forster, McIlroy *C:* Richards *P:* Richards
20 Dec	H	Melrose	15-28	*T:* McIlroy, Renwick *C:* Richards *P:* Richards
27 Dec	H	Currie	13-43	*T:* Smith *C:* Richards *P:* Richards 2
10 Jan	A	Stirling County	12-32	*T:* C Brown, Renwick *C:* Richards
17 Jan	H	Boroughmuir	21-14	*T:* M Brown, Dungait *C:* Richards *P:* Richards 3
31 Jan	A	Heriot's FP	6-21	*P:* Richards 2
14 Feb	H	Hawick	20-34	*T:* Dungait, Richards *C:* Richards 2 *P:* Richards 2
14 Mar	H	Heriot's FP	29-19	*T:* M Brown 2, Liddle, Richards *C:* Richards 3 *P:* Richards
28 Mar	H	Stirling County	30-17	*T:* Amos, Dungait, Smith *C:* Amos 3 *P:* Amos 3
25 Apr	A	Edinburgh Acads	6-33	*P:* Amos 2
2 May	A	Boroughmuir	10-66	*T:* C Brown, Tunnah

Kelso

Year of formation 1876
Ground Poynder Park, Bowmont Street, Kelso Tel: (01573) 224 300 (club) and (01573) 223 773 (committee room)
Colours Black and white
Captain 1997-98 A J Roxburgh
SRU Tennents Championship 1997-98 Div 2A 2nd   **SRU Tennents Cup 1997-98** Lost 14-36 to Glasgow Hawks (final)

Kelso were runners-up to Glasgow Hawks in both the Premier Second Division and the national cup competition, but second place in the division did not earn them a step up as they lost to Heriot's by 12-33 in a promotion play-off. Successive defeats by Kilmarnock, Hawks, and Gala and a draw with Musselburgh left Kelso in fourth place at the mid-season split, and they secured that position only with a 46-34 win against Kirkcaldy. Kelso, however, finished strongly with three successive wins to climb into second place. League and cup disappointments for Adam Roxburgh, Kelso's captain, were balanced by his performances in his first international season.

League Record 1997-98

Date	Venue	Opponents	Result	Scorers
15 Nov	A	Dundee HSFP	21-17	*T:* Baird, Utterson *C:* Aitchison *P:* Aitchison 3

29 Nov	H	Preston Lodge FP	36-3	*T:* Aitchison, Baird 2, Dunkley, Thomson *C:* Aitchison 4 *P:* Aitchison
13 Dec	A	Biggar	32-13	*T:* Cowe, Fairlie, S Laing 2 *C:* Aitchison 3 *P:* Aitchison 2
20 Dec	H	Kilmarnock	13-23	*T:* R Laing *C:* Hogarth *P:* Hogarth 2
27 Dec	H	Glasgow Hawks	13-33	*T:* Fairlie *C:* Hogarth *P:* Hogarth 2
10 Jan	A	Gala	10-27	*T:* Cowe *C:* Baird *P:* Baird
17 Jan	H	Musselburgh	13-13	*T:* Carruthers, Ross *P:* Baird
31 Jan	A	Peebles	24-19	*T:* G Laing 2 *C:* Wearne *P:* Baird, Wearne 3
14 Feb	H	Kirkcaldy	46-34	*T:* Baird, Bennet, Cowe, Ross 2, Roxburgh, Thomson *C:* Wearne 4 *P:* Wearne
28 Mar	A	Glasgow Hawks	25-50	*T:* Baird, Fairley, Roxburgh, Wearne *C:* Wearne *P:* Wearne
22 Apr	H	Gala	32-22	*T:* Baird, Fairley 2, Ross *C:* Wearne 3 *P:* Wearne *D:* Roxburgh
25 Apr	H	Dundee HSFP	24-20	*T:* Ross, Roxburgh *C:* Wearne *P:* Wearne 4
2 May	A	Kilmarnock	41-10	*T:* Baird, Fairley 2, Ross, Rowley, Roxburgh, Wearne *C:* Wearne 3

Play-Off (at Pennypit Park)

16 May		Heriot's FP	12-33	*P:* Wearne 4

Kilmarnock

Year of formation 1868
Ground Bellsland, Queen's Drive, Kilmarnock Tel: Kilmarnock (01563) 522 314
Colours Red and white with Maltese Cross
Captain 1997-98 J Sharp
SRU Tennents Championship 1997-98 Div 2A 5th   **SRU Tennents Cup 1997-98** Lost 9-16 to Melrose (5th round)

Kilmarnock handicapped their campaign by losing two of their first three matches, both of which to clubs who were to finish up in the lower half of the Second Division at the cut-off point. Those early defeats prompted the resignation of their coach, John McHarg. His assistant, Campbell Bone, took over, with occasional help from Keith Robertson, Glasgow's New Zealand coach, and Kilmarnock's fortunes turned with notable victories over Kelso and Gala as well as a crucial win against Kirkcaldy. Those were enough for Kilmarnock to edge into the division's top half at the split, though by only the margin of a bonus point ahead of Kirkcaldy and Biggar. That form did not continue into the championship play-off phase, in which Kilmarnock won just one match, though that was by inflicting the only league defeat on Glasgow Hawks, who by then had already won the division championship. Robbie Stewart was the club's top-scorer again, with 118 points.

League Record 1997-98

Date	Venue	Opponents	Result	Scorers
15 Nov	H	Musselburgh	14-13	*T:* Pattie *P:* Stewart 3
29 Nov	A	Biggar	22-25	*T:* Fraser, Stewart, pen try *C:* Stewart 2 *P:* Stewart
13 Dec	H	Peebles	8-19	*T:* Stewart *P:* Stewart
20 Dec	A	Kelso	23-13	*T:* Pattie, Sinclair 2 *C:* Stewart *P:* Stewart 2
27 Dec	H	Kirkcaldy	18-10	*T:* Finnegan, Sinclair *C:* Stewart *P:* Stewart 2
10 Jan	A	Glasgow Hawks	12-19	*P:* Stewart 3 *D:* Graham
17 Jan	H	Dundee HSFP	11-12	*T:* Finnegan *P:* Stewart 2
31 Jan	H	Gala	32-8	*T:* Finnegan, Pattie, Stewart, pen try *C:* Stewart 3 *P:* Stewart 2
14 Feb	A	Preston Lodge FP	21-9	*P:* Stewart 7

14 Mar	A	Dundee HSFP	25-34	*T:* J W R Adams, Carswell, Graham, Sharp
				C: Stewart *P:* Stewart
8 Apr	H	Glasgow Hawks	14-5	*T:* Pattie, pen try *C:* Stewart 2
25 Apr	A	Gala	18-26	*T:* Pattie, pen try *C:* Stewart *P:* Stewart 2
2 May	H	Kelso	10-41	*T:* Sinclair, Stewart

Kirkcaldy

Year of formation 1873
Ground Beveridge Park, Kirkcaldy Tel: (01592) 263 470
Colours Royal blue
Captain 1997-98 W D Anderson
SRU Tennents Championship 1997-98 Div 2B *Winners*   **SRU Tennents Cup 1997-98** Lost
16-24 to Boroughmuir (5th round)

Kirkcaldy had to play the second stage of the Premier programme in the lower half
of the Second Division after having been edged out by Kilmarnock by the margin of
just one bonus point. The Fife club's notable result in the first stage was to beat the
high-flying Dundee High School FP without conceding a try, and they finished at
the top of the lower half of the division despite an upset defeat at Musselburgh.
Kirkcaldy completed their league season in fine style with two emphatic home wins,
scoring eight tries against Preston Lodge and 15 against Peebles.

League Record 1997-98

Date	Venue	Opponents	Result	Scorers
15 Nov	H	Glasgow Hawks	11-20	*T:* Meredith *P:* Gilmour 2
29 Nov	A	Gala	13-26	*T:* Trewartha *C:* J R Mitchell
				P: J R Mitchell 2
13 Dec	H	Musselburgh	31-5	*T:* Ferguson, Henderson, J R Mitchell,
				Parsons 2 *C:* Gilmour, J R Mitchell 2
20 Dec	A	Peebles	24-21	*T:* Gilmour, Hannah, Herrington
				C: Gilmour 3 *P:* Gilmour
27 Dec	A	Kilmarnock	10-18	*T:* Parsons *C:* Gilmour *P:* Gilmour
10 Jan	H	Dundee HSFP	15-3	*T:* Ferguson, Renton *C:* Ferguson
				P: Ferguson
31 Jan	H	Biggar	19-13	*T:* Macdonald, Parsons *P:* Ferguson,
				P J W Smith 2
10 Feb	A	Preston Lodge FP	47-8	*T:* Henderson 2, Imrie, Macdonald, Meredith,
				Trewartha *C:* Ferguson 4 *P:* Ferguson 2
				D: Ferguson
14 Feb	A	Kelso	34-46	*T:* Henderson 2, Macdonald 2, Renton
				C: Ferguson 2, P J W Smith *P:* Ferguson
14 Mar	A	Biggar	9-6	*P:* Gilmour, P J W Smith 3
28 Mar	A	Musselburgh	21-25	*T:* Parsons, Simpson, pen try *C:* Ferguson 3
25 Apr	H	Preston Lodge FP	42-29	*T:* Ferguson, Goodall, Henderson, Imrie, J
				R Mitchell, Renton, Syme, Simpson
				C: Gilmour
2 May	H	Peebles	91-7	*T:* Gilmour 2, Goodall, Hannah, Henderson,
				Imrie 3, J R Mitchell 2, Raeside 2, Renton,
				Syme, pen try *C:* Gilmour 2, J R Mitchell 3,
				Phil Smith 3

Melrose

Year of formation 1877
Ground The Greenyards, Melrose, Roxburghshire TD6 9SA Tel: (01896) 822 993 (office)
and (01896) 822 559 (clubrooms)
Colours Yellow and black
Captain 1997-98 C D Hogg

SRU Tennents Championship 1997-98 Div 1A 2nd **SRU Tennents Cup 1997-98** Lost 13-18 to Kelso (quarter-final)

Melrose lost all three of the 15-a-side trophies that they had won in 1996-97, though it was only by one bonus point that they conceded the Premier title to Watsonians. The margin was the same when the First Division split into two sections, with Melrose having lost to Hawick, Currie, and Watsonians, and the defending champions' second stage started with an away defeat by West of Scotland. The increased margin was too much for Melrose to recoup even though they beat Watsonians at home in the final league match. Melrose had to be content with the runners-up spot, and they slipped to third in the Border League, which they had won six times in the previous eight years. They exited from the Scottish Cup at the quarter-final stage in an away defeat by Kelso, the eventual beaten finalists. The one major trophy Melrose retained was in their own sevens.

League Record 1997-98

Date	Venue	Opponents	Result	Scorers
15 Nov	H	Boroughmuir	21-3	*T:* Dalgleish 2 *C:* Chalmers *P:* Chalmers 2, Shepherd
29 Nov	A	Edinburgh Acads	20-0	*T:* Lawrie, Nichol, Purves *C:* Shepherd *P:* Shepherd
13 Dec	H	Heriot's FP	31-22	*T:* Dalgleish, Hogg, Moncrieff 2 *C:* Shepherd *P:* Shepherd 3
20 Dec	A	Jed-Forest	28-15	*T:* Brotherstone, Broughton, Dalgleish, AC Redpath *C:* Shepherd *P:* Shepherd 2
27 Dec	H	Hawick	8-19	*T:* Dalgleish *P:* Ruthven
10 Jan	A	Currie	17-20	*T:* BW Redpath, Watt *C:* Shepherd 2 *P:* Shepherd
17 Jan	H	West of Scotland	49-7	*T:* Brotherstone, Broughton, Dalgleish, Moncrieff 2, Shiel *C:* Chalmers 2 *P:* Chalmers 4, Nichol
31 Jan	H	Stirling County	14-11	*T:* Chalmers *P:* Shepherd 3
14 Feb	A	Watsonians	24-33	*T:* MG Browne, Dalgleish, Purves, B W Redpath *C:* Shiel 2
14 Mar	A	West of Scotland	13-36	*T:* Shepherd *C:* Shepherd *P:* Shepherd 2
8 Apr	A	Hawick	28-18	*T:* RNC Brown, MG Browne, Dalgleish, Ruthven *C:* Shepherd *P:* Shepherd 2
25 Apr	H	Currie	41-29	*T:* MG Browne, Hogg 2, Ruthven *C:* Shepherd 3 *P:* Shepherd 5
2 May	H	Watsonians	37-17	*T:* Ruthven, Shepherd, pen try *C:* Shepherd 2 *P:* Shepherd 5 *D:* Shepherd

Musselburgh

Year of formation 1921
Ground Stoneyhill, Stoneyhill Farm Road, Musselburgh EH21 6RN Tel: (0131) 665 3435
Colours Navy blue and white hoops
Captain 1997-98 C Livingston
SRU Tennents Championship 1997-98 Div 2B 3rd **SRU Tennents Cup 1997-98** Lost 32-41 to Currie (4th round)

Musselburgh consolidated a Second Division place by finishing eighth, though they reached that status in 1997 only because of league revamping and the GHK-Glasgow Academicals amalgamation. Yet their first-stage record hinted at less than that as their only win in nine games was by just four points against their neighbours, Preston Lodge. However, Musselburgh came through strongly by winning all of their four matches in the second section. Cliff Livingston was again Musselburgh's principal gatherer of points – 103 of the club's 213 in the league, four tries out of 26.

League Record 1997-98

Date	Venue	Opponents	Result	Scorers
15 Nov	A	Kilmarnock	13-14	T: D Archibald, I Archibald P: Livingston
29 Nov	H	Peebles	8- 8	T: Cringan P: Livingston
13 Dec	A	Kirkcaldy	5-31	T: Thomas
27 Dec	A	Preston Lodge FP	18-14	T: D Archibald, Livingston C: Livingston P: Livingston 2
10 Jan	H	Biggar	17-37	T: D Archibald, Connorton, Walker C: Livingston
17 Jan	A	Kelso	13-13	T: G Jamieson C: Livingston P: Livingston D: Livingston
31 Jan	H	Glasgow Hawks	19-75	T: D Archibald, McCracken, Thomas C: Livingston 2
10 Feb	A	Dundee HSFP	16-27	T: Thomas C: Livingston P: Livingston 3
14 Feb	A	Gala	17-47	T: Jamieson, Livingston, Thomas C: Livingston
14 Mar	A	Peebles	22-10	T: D Archibald, Walker P: Livingston 4
28 Mar	H	Kirkcaldy	25-21	T: Bain, Cringan, Livingston C: Livingston 2 P: Livingston D: Livingston
8 Apr	H	Preston Lodge FP	21-3	T: Cringan, Livingston, Stewart C: Livingston 3
25 Apr	A	Biggar	19-12	T: Jameson C: Livingston P: Livingston 4

Peebles

Year of formation 1922
Ground The Gytes Leisure Centre, Walkershaugh, Peebles EH45 8NN Tel: (01721) 723 688
Clubrooms 19 Eastgate, Peebles EH45 8AD Tel: (01721) 720 494
Colours Red and white hoops
Captain 1997-98 D Gray
SRU Tennents Championship 1997-98 Div 2B 4th (relegated)   **SRU Tennents Cup 1997-98** Lost 12-30 to Gala (4th round)

Peebles were promoted in 1997 through league restructuring, and their Second Division sojourn lasted only the one season. Their most notable league scalp was to beat Kilmarnock away from home, but it was only towards the end of the season that they won again, with victories against Preston Lodge (away) and Biggar (at home) before finishing with a fearsomely heavy defeat by 91-7 at Kirkcaldy.

League Record 1997-98

Date	Venue	Opponents	Result	Scorers
15 Nov	H	Gala	14-20	T: Stumbles P: Nisbet 3
29 Nov	A	Musselburgh	8-8	T: Cleghorn P: Nisbet
13 Dec	A	Kilmarnock	19-8	T: Muller C: Muller P: Muller 4
20 Dec	H	Kirkcaldy	21-24	T: Farmer, Muller C: Muller P: Muller 3
27 Dec	A	Dundee HSFP	8-59	T: Nisbet P: Muller
10 Jan	H	Preston Lodge FP	16-17	T: Muller, Murray P: Muller 2
17 Jan	A	Biggar	8-9	T: Nisbet P: Muller
31 Jan	H	Kelso	19-24	T: Gray C: Rutherford P: Rutherford 4
14 Feb	A	Glasgow Hawks	3-62	P: Rutherford
14 Mar	H	Musselburgh	10-22	T: Hattingh C: Muller P: Rutherford
28 Mar	A	Preston Lodge FP	32-27	T: Cleghorn, Muller C: Muller, Rutherford P: Muller 2, Rutherford 4
8 Apr	H	Biggar	8-3	T: Nisbet P: Nisbet
2 May	A	Kirkcaldy	7-91	T: Currie C: Nisbet

Preston Lodge FP

Year of formation 1931
Ground Pennypit Park, Rope Walk, Prestonpans, East Lothian Tel: (01875) 810 309
Colours Black with maroon band edged in white
Captain 1997-98 N Clyde
SRU Tennents Championship 1997-98 Div 2B 5th (relegated)   **SRU Tennents Cup 1997-98** Lost 11-19 to Gordonians (3rd round)

Promotion from the Third Division in 1997 through league reorganisation was a step too far for Preston Lodge. One league victory was all they had to show of their efforts, and even that was by only one point against Peebles away from home. They lost the return match even though the try-count was 4-2 in Preston Lodge's favour. Their Scottish Cup interest was cut short by a third-round defeat by Third Division Gordonians.

League Record 1997-98

Date	Venue	Opponents	Result	Scorers
15 Nov	H	Biggar	14-25	*T:* McMillan *P:* Sim 3
29 Nov	A	Kelso	3-36	*P:* Kinross
13 Dec	H	Glasgow Hawks	8-37	*T:* Gilliland *P:* Kinross
20 Dec	A	Gala	8-27	*T:* Brotherston *P:* Kinross
27 Dec	H	Musselburgh	14-18	*T:* Redpath *P:* Sim 3
10 Jan	A	Peebles	17-16	*T:* McSorley, Sim *C:* Sim 2 *P:* Sim
31 Jan	A	Dundee HSFP	7-62	*T:* Sim *C:* Sim
10 Feb	H	Kirkcaldy	8-47	*T:* McMillan *D:* Kinross
14 Feb	H	Kilmarnock	9-21	*P:* Sim 3
28 Mar	H	Peebles	27-32	*T:* Allan, Anderson, Kinross, McSorley *C:* Kinross 2 *P:* Kinross
8 Apr	A	Musselburgh	3-21	*P:* Sim
25 Apr	A	Kirkcaldy	29-42	*T:* Allan, Anderson, Payne, Sim *C:* Sim 3 *P:* Sim
29 Apr	H	Biggar	5-44	*T:* Anderson

Stirling County

Year of formation 1904
Ground Bridgehaugh, Causewayhead Road, Stirling Tel: (01786) 474 827 (clubhouse) and (01786) 478 866 (office)
Colours Red, white and black
Captain 1997-98 I C Jardine
SRU Tennents Championship 1997-98 Div 1B 2nd   **SRU Tennents Cup 1997-98** Lost 14-27 to Currie (quarter-final)

A new coach from New Zealand, Tom Coventry, picked Stirling County up after their dismal 1996-97 season, when they won only two league games. They opened 1997-98 with successive victories against Heriot's, Hawick, and West of Scotland, and it was only by the narrowest margin that they failed to make a place in the top five for the championship play-off. An 18-9 win over Boroughmuir at home was not quite enough to earn them a place in the top quintet. A month later they lost to the same Edinburgh club by 7-39 in the return match, and thereafter they lost their way with only an 18-13 victory over Heriot's in the second stage of the programme. They went as far as the quarter-finals of the Scottish Cup before falling to Currie.

League Record 1997-98

Date	Venue	Opponents	Result	Scorers
15 Nov	A	Heriot's FP	37-5	*T:* Brough, Imrie, McLaren, Mailer, Norval *C:* M McKenzie 3 *P:* M McKenzie 2
29 Nov	H	Hawick	27-12	*T:* Flockhart 2, McLaren *C:* M McKenzie 3 *P:* M McKenzie *D:* M McKenzie
13 Dec	A	West of Scotland	11-6	*T:* Ireland *P:* M McKenzie 2
20 Dec	H	Watsonians	7-29	*T:* Brough *C:* M McKenzie
27 Dec	A	Edinburgh Acads	9-23	*P:* M McKenzie 3
10 Jan	H	Jed-Forest	32-12	*T:* Flockhart 2, McLaren 2, MacPhail *C:* Mailer 2 *P:* Mailer
17 Jan	A	Currie	11-19	*T:* Flockhart *P:* M McKenzie, Mailer
31 Jan	A	Melrose	11-14	*T:* Jardine *P:* M McKenzie 2
14 Feb	H	Boroughmuir	18-9	*T:* Ireland, Jardine, K D McKenzie *P:* M McKenzie
14 Mar	A	Boroughmuir	7-39	*T:* Flockhart *C:* M McKenzie
28 Mar	A	Jed-Forest	17-30	*T:* Ireland, pen try *C:* Mailer 2 *P:* Mailer
22 Apr	H	Edinburgh Acads	18-13	*T:* McLaren, pen try *C:* Mailer *P:* Mailer 2
25 Apr	H	Heriot's FP	3-25	*P:* Mailer

Watsonians

Year of formation 1875
Ground Myreside, Myreside Road, Edinburgh EH10 5DB Tel: (0131) 447 5200 (office) and (0131) 447 9261 (clubroom)
Colours Maroon and white
Captain 1997-98 G McKelvey
SRU Tennents Championship 1997-98 Div 1A *Winners*   **SRU Tennents Cup 1997-98** Lost 6-21 to Glasgow Hawks (quarter-final)

Watsonians at last broke through from the also-rans to take the Scottish title for the first time, though only by the margin of one bonus point ahead of Melrose, the defending champions. The margin was exactly the same at the end of the first half of the league season, when the premier divisions each split in two, and Watsonians held off the champions' challenge with a substantial victory against Hawick, Currie, and West of Scotland. Watsonians notched a half-century in each of their two league games against Currie, but the individual scoring feat of the championship was Duncan Hodge's monopoly against West – all the points in a 38-8 win which all but tied up the title. In all, Hodge, Watsonians' capped stand-off, scored 167 points in the championship whereas his club colleague, John Kerr, Caledonia's European Cup left wing, was the leading try-scorer in the First Division with nine, including three in each of the two matches against Currie.

League Record 1997-98

Date	Venue	Opponents	Result	Scorers
15 Nov	H	Edinburgh Acads	35-10	*T:* di Rollo, Hodge, Kerr, Penny *C:* Hodge 3 *P:* Hodge 3
29 Nov	A	Jed-Forest	15-31	*T:* Mather, Penny *C:* Hodge *P:* Hodge
13 Dec	H	Currie	58-0	*T:* Burns, Hastings, Henderson, Hodge, Kerr 3, Mayer *C:* Hodge 6 *P:* Hodge 2
20 Dec	A	Stirling County	29-7	*T:* Grimes, Hastings, Henderson *C:* Hodge *P:* Hodge 4
27 Dec	H	Boroughmuir	12-14	*T:* Dickson, Mather *C:* Hodge
10 Jan	A	Heriot's FP	31-20	*T:* Burns, Kerr, Mather, Waite, pen try *C:* Hodge 3
17 Jan	H	Hawick	20-9	*T:* Di Rollo, Waite, pen try *C:* Hodge *P:* Hodge

31 Jan	A	West of Scotland	12-16	*T:* Dickson, Mather *C:* Hodge
14 Feb	H	Melrose	33-24	*T:* Garry, Mather, Mayer 2 *C:* Hodge 2
				P: Hodge 3
28 Mar	A	Hawick	45-20	*T:* di Rollo 2, Hodge 2, Mather, Mayer, White
				C: Hodge 2 *P:* Hodge 2
8 Apr	A	Currie	56-5	*T:* Henderson, Kerr 3, Weston 2, Scott, White
				C: Hodge 5 *P:* Hodge 2
25 Apr	H	West of Scotland	34-8	*T:* Hodge 3 *C:* Hodge 2 *P:* Hodge 5
2 May	A	Melrose	17-37	*T:* Garry, Grimes *C:* Hodge 2 *P:* Hodge

West of Scotland

Year of formation 1865
Ground Burnbrae, Glasgow Road, Milngavie, Glasgow G62 6HX Tel: (0141) 956 3116
Colours Red and yellow hoops
Captain 1997-98 G C Bulloch
SRU Tennents Championship 1997-98 Div 1A 3rd   **SRU Tennents Cup 1997-98** Lost
3-10 to Kelso (5th round)

West of Scotland, promoted in 1996-97 with the last kick of their final league game,
finished a highly creditable third behind Watsonians and Melrose. Their progression
was a commendation of the efforts of the coaching duo, Brian Edwards and Muff
Scobbie. A half-century against Jed-Forest sent West on the way on their return to
First Division rugby, and a 16-12 win over Watsonians, the eventual champions, was
the highlight of the first section of the Premier programme. They were fifth at the
'cut' to qualify for the championship play-off section, though it was only victory
against Edinburgh Academicals by 22-20 that let West through to the top quintet.
They finished strongly, home victories against Melrose (the defending champions),
Currie, and Hawick more than compensating for an away defeat by Watsonians.
New Zealander Warren Chamberlin was heading for a league century with 61 in six
games when his Scottish sojourn was cut short by injury.

League Record 1997-98

Date	Venue	Opponents	Result	Scorers
15 Nov	H	Jed-Forest	51-6	*T:* Collins 2, R Craig, McLeish, Shaw, Sheridan, Thompson 2 *C:* Chamberlin 4
				P: Chamberlin
13 Dec	H	Stirling County	6-11	*P:* Thompson 2
20 Dec	A	Boroughmuir	23-5	*T:* G C Bulloch, Chamberlin 2
				C: Chamberlin *P:* Chamberlin 2
27 Dec	H	Heriot's FP	39-10	*T:* A Bulloch 2, Chamberlin, N Craig, Steele, Wright *C:* Chamberlin 2, Williamson
				P: Chamberlin
10 Jan	A	Hawick	15-23	*T:* G C Bulloch, Chamberlin *C:* Chamberlin
				P: Chamberlin
17 Jan	A	Melrose	7-49	*T:* Chamberlin *C:* Chamberlin
31 Jan	H	Watsonians	16-12	*T:* Houston, Steele *P:* Chamberlin, Williamson
10 Feb	A	Currie	12-15	*P:* Williamson 4
14 Feb	A	Edinburgh Acads	22-20	*T:* Houston, Shaw, Stott *C:* Williamson 2
				P: Williamson
14 Mar	H	Melrose	36-13	*T:* Collins, Houston, McKee, Stott
				C: Williamson 2 *P:* Williamson 4
28 Mar	H	Currie	37-18	*T:* A Bulloch 2, G C Bulloch, McKechnie, McLeish, Williamson *C:* Williamson 2
				P: Williamson
25 Apr	A	Watsonians	8-34	*T:* Curtis *P:* Curtis
2 May	H	Hawick	29-17	*T:* A Bulloch, G C Bulloch 2, Stott
				C: Curtis 3 *P:* Curtis

HOPE FOR FUTURE LIES IN IRISH YOUTH

THE SEASON IN IRELAND 1997-98
Sean Diffley *Irish Independent*

The Irish situation was summed up, succinctly, by Noel Murphy, who will be the Irish Rugby Football Union president for the 1998-99 season. 'Our problem,' he said at the IRFU annual meeting in June, 'was to translate the success of our youngsters into success for the national senior team.'

And Murphy called for an effort from all concerned with the Irish game to maximise their efforts towards that end. The reigning president is, of course, one of the most experienced player-administrators in the world game. He has been involved at every level of the game: a much-capped Irish flanker, captain, coach and manager; a Lions Test player and coach.

Murphy's call came after a quite remarkable successful season by Irish under-age sides, the highlight of which was the triumph of the Irish under-19 team in the IRB-FIRA World Youth (under-19) Championship in France in April. This young side began with a 47-13 win over the USA, drew 17-17 with South Africa two days later but won, on an appeal, after a penalty shoot-out and then beat Argentina 18-3. In the final in Toulouse they had a great 18-0 victory over France.

In the schools section, where the Irish have been doing so well in the nineties, they beat Scotland (49-0), Wales (13-6) but failed to England (26-22). The under-18 youth were victorious over Italy, Wales and Scotland. The under-21 team beat England, Scotland and Wales, failing only to France (36-28). Altogether then, plenty of evidence that the talent is there. And, as Murphy said, 'We must nurture it and ensure that Ireland remains among the major nations in the comity of rugby countries.'

At top international level the situation was bizarre, to say the least, and a 'whitewash' in the Five Nations was probably the natural outcome. The problems on the pitch, though, were compounded by a certain lack of empathy between players and coach Brian Ashton, not helped by plenty of speculation that all was not hunky-dory either between coach Ashton and team manager Pat Whelan. Following the defeat in the first Five Nations match by Scotland, Brian Ashton departed. He frankly admitted that he did not quite gel with Irish rugby, feeling that his task of watching players should be mostly confined to England where so many were employed. He never considered it a priority to watch the activities in the AIB All Ireland League. And although he never referred to

The Ireland team which faced Scotland in Dublin. L-R, back row: E R P Miller, K Dawson, M E O'Kelly, P S Johns, D S Corkery, R Corrigan; front row: C M P O'Shea, K M Maggs, D G Humphreys, M C McCall, K G M Wood (capt), team mascot, Mr N H Brophy (president IRFU), B T O'Meara, D A Hickie. Absent from photograph: R M Wallace & P S Wallace

any problems with management, it was noted that he did not go out of his way to deny that affairs were strained. As it happened Whelan also departed the scene later, citing business pressures as his reason, a resignation that occurred at around the same time as a highly publicised affray with a rugby journalist in a bar in Limerick.

The replacement for Brian Ashton was the New Zealander, Warren Gatland, who had already been resident in Galway for several years and been highly successful with the club, Galwegians, and then, spectacularly so with the Irish 'Cinderella' province, Connacht, in the European Conference.

Connacht were the revelation of the season, beating Northampton twice, at home and away, and Bègles-Bordeaux, to win their pool. They lost in the quarter-final to Agen who went on to the final. So Gatland's CV spoke for itself and he has been given the role of Irish coach with no shadows hovering over his shoulders. Donal Lenihan was appointed manager but obviously in a supportive capacity. Gatland is the boss but signs from the summer's South Africa tour suggest that the two will work well and harmoniously.

The pernicious anaemia afflicting the Irish game at top level is the fact that so many players have been enticed to take the large salaries on offer from English clubs. But there are signs that this movement may have been arrested and many players are returning to quite decent contracts at home. The four provinces now have professional managers and will be allowed to contract up to thirty players in each province with full-timers being paid up to £25,000 and part-timers £7,500 with match fees and win bonuses thrown in. A contracts sub-committee of the IRFU has been working to encourage the players to play at home.

Altogether it cost the IRFU £4.5 million last season in fees to players, a figure that emphasises the importance of gate receipts from the Five Nations matches, and it is a figure that will have to increase in the future. But the IRFU generated £13 million last season, which was a record.

The AIB All Ireland League had a new, very debatable, format in Division One, the top four teams engaging in a knock-out method of deciding the outcome. But justice prevailed and Shannon, who led the league after thirteen games, defeated fellow Limerick opponents, Garryowen, in the final at Lansdowne Road. And that was Shannon's fourth All Ireland League triumph in succession. In fact, three Limerick clubs headed the table, Shannon, Garryowen and Young Munster, once again highlighting the fact that Limerick City is Ireland's rugby capital.

AIB LEAGUE 1997-98

Division 1	P	W	D	L	F	A	Pts
Shannon	13	12	0	1	367	142	24
Garryowen	13	9	1	3	360	224	19
Young Munster	13	9	1	3	224	176	19
St Mary's Coll	13	9	0	4	409	274	18
Cork Const	13	8	0	5	289	217	16
Ballymena	13	7	0	6	344	287	14
Clontarf	13	7	0	6	276	266	14
Terenure Coll	13	5	1	7	241	262	11
Lansdowne	13	4	2	7	264	328	10
Blackrock Coll	13	4	1	8	249	326	9
Dungannon	13	4	0	9	239	309	8
Dolphin	13	3	2	8	227	345	8
Old Crescent	13	4	0	9	168	298	8
Old Belvedere	13	2	0	11	208	431	4

Division 2	P	W	D	L	F	A	Pts
Galwegians	13	13	0	0	336	164	26
Buccaneers	12	11	0	1	311	102	22*
Sunday's Well	13	7	2	4	254	227	16
City of Derry	13	8	0	5	277	255	16
Univ. C. Cork	13	6	1	6	204	282	13
Skerries	13	6	0	7	248	224	12
DL Salle Palm.	13	6	0	7	280	269	12
Old Wesley	13	5	1	7	256	248	11
Greystones	13	5	1	7	204	212	11
Bective Rang.	13	5	1	7	210	233	11
Malone	13	5	0	8	210	255	10
Wanderers	12	5	0	7	200	254	10*
Monkstown	13	3	0	10	207	336	6
Instonians	13	2	0	11	205	341	4

Division 3	P	W	D	L	F	A	Pts
Portadown	10	10	0	0	212	106	20
Ballynahinch	10	8	0	2	285	125	16
Univ.C. Dublin	10	8	0	2	222	126	16
Highfield	10	7	0	3	170	87	14
Bohemians	10	6	0	4	195	165	12
NIFC	10	5	0	5	190	160	10
Galway Cor'th.	10	4	0	6	178	214	8
Dublin Univ.	10	3	0	7	163	225	6
Collegians	10	2	1	7	130	229	5
Suttonians	10	1	1	8	153	250	3
Queens Univ.	10	0	0	10	128	339	0

Division 4	P	W	D	L	F	A	Pts
County Carlow	9	8	0	1	284	56	16
Richmond	9	7	1	1	171	113	15
Bangor	9	5	1	3	175	144	11
Ballina	9	5	0	4	169	128	10
Waterpark	9	5	0	4	131	155	10
Omagh Acad.	9	4	0	5	137	147	8
Ards	9	4	0	5	109	158	8
CIYMS	9	3	1	5	122	202	7
Sligo	9	2	1	6	111	147	5
Creggs	9	0	0	9	89	248	0

Midleton and Banbridge replace relegated Sligo and Creggs in Division Four.

* Match postponed and not played

In the play-off for the All Ireland Division One title Shannon beat Garryowen at Lansdowne Road to become All Ireland champions for the fourth consecutive time. For this season it was decided that the top four finishers in Division one should have a cup-style finish to the competition. Shannon and Garryowen eliminated the third and fourth placed league finishers, Young Munster and St Mary's College, and Shannon duly beat Garryowen in the final match.

Andrew Thompson, the Shannon threequarter, was once again the top points-scorer, piling up 155 points. The top try-scorer was the St Mary's College international wing, Denis Hickie, with 14 tries.

Guinness Inter-Provincial Tournament 1997

16 August, Sportsground, Galway

Munster 29 (1G 3PG 1DG 2T)   **Connacht 9** (3PG)
Munster: D Crotty (Garryowen); A Horgan (Cork Constitution), S McCahill (Sunday's Well), M Lynch (Young Munster), A Thompson (Shannon); R O'Gara (Cork Constitution), B O'Meara (Cork Constitution); I Murray (Cork Constitution), P Cunningham (Garryowen), P Clohessy (Young Munster), M Galwey (Shannon), S Leahy (Garryowen), E Halvey (Shannon), D Wallace (Garryowen), A Foley (Shannon)
Scorers *Tries:* Galwey, Halvey, O'Gara *Conversion:* O'Gara *Penalty Goals:* O' Gara (3) *Dropped Goal:* O'Gara
Connacht: W Ruane (Galwegians); N Barry (Clontarf), P Duignan (Galwegians), S Allnutt (Corinthians), N Carolan (Galwegians); E Elwood (Galwegians), C McGuinness (St Mary's College); J Maher (Bective Rangers), W Mulcahy

(Skerries), M Cahill (Bohemians), G Heaslip (Galwegians), M McConnell (Buccaneers), R Rogers (Blackrock College), J Charlie (Galwegians), B Gavin (Galwegians)
Scorers *Penalty Goals:* Elwood (3)
Referee A Lewis

16 August, Donnybrook, Dublin

Leinster 26 (1G 3PG 2T) **Ulster 25** (1G 6PG)
Leinster: C Clarke (Terenure College); D Hickie (St Mary's College), M Ridge (Old Belvedere), K McQuilkin (Lansdowne), D O'Mahony (Moseley); R Governey (Lansdowne), A Rolland (Wanderers); H Hurley (Old Wesley), S Byrne (Blackrock College), A McKeen (Lansdowne), D O'Brien (DLSP), A Freeman (Lansdowne), T Brennan (St Mary's College), S Rooney (Lansdowne), V Costello (St Mary's College)
Scorers *Tries:* Hickie, O'Mahony, Rolland *Conversion:* Governey *Penalty Goals:* Governey (3)
Ulster: R Morrow (Dungannon); J Cunningham (Ballymena), S Coulter (Ballymena), S McDowell (Ballymena), G McCluskey (Portadown); S Laing (Portadown), S Bell (Dungannon); R Mackey (Malone), S Ritchie (Ballymena), G Leslie (Dungannon), T McWhirter (Ballymena), G Longwell (Ballymena), S Duncan (Malone), A Ward (Ballynahinch), S McKinty (Bangor)
Scorers *Try:* Laing *Conversion:* Laing *Penalty Goals:* Laing (6)
Referee D McHugh

23 August, Musgrave Park, Cork

Munster 15 (4PG 1DG) **Leinster 12** (4PG)
Munster: D Crotty (Garryowen); A Horgan (Cork Constitution), S McCahill (Sunday's Well), M Lynch (Young Munster), A Thompson (Shannon); R O'Gara (Cork Constitution), B O'Meara (Cork Constitution); G Walsh (Garryowen), P Cunningham (Garryowen) P Clohessy (Young Munster), M Galwey (Shannon), S Leahy (Garryowen), E Halvey (Shannon), D Wallace (Garryowen), A Foley (Shannon)
Scorers *Penalty Goals:* O'Gara, Thompson (3) *Dropped Goal:* O'Gara
Leinster: C Clarke (Terenure College); D Hickie (St Mary's College) M Ridge (Old Belvedere), K McQuilkin (Lansdowne), D O'Mahony (Moseley); A McGowan (Blackrock College), D O'Mahony (Lansdowne); H Hurley (Moseley), S Byrne (Blackrock College), A McKeen (Lansdowne), S Jameson (St Mary's College), A Freeman (Lansdowne), C McEntee (Lansdowne), T Brennan (St Mary's College), V Costello (St Mary's College)
Scorers *Penalty Goals:* McGowan (4)
Referee B Stirling

23 August, Sportsground, Galway

Connacht 27 (3G 2PG) **Ulster 17** (2G 1PG)
Connacht: W Ruane (Ballina); N Barry (Clontarf), S Allnutt (Corinthians), P Duignan (Galwegians), N Carolan (Galwegians); E Elwood (Galwegians), C McGuinness (St Mary's College); J Maher (Bective Rangers), W Mulcahy (Skerries), M Finley (Galwegians), M McConnell (Buccaneers), G Heaslip (Cork Constitution), S McEntee (Wanderers), J Charlie (Galwegians), B Gavin (Galwegians)
Scorers *Tries:* McEntee, Charlie, Murphy *Conversions:* Elwood (3) *Penalty Goals:* Elwood (2)

Ulster: R Morrow (Dungannon); A Park (Ballymena), S McDowell (Ballymena), S Coulter (Ballymena), J Cunningham (Ballymena); S Laing (Portadown), S Bell (Dungannon); R Mackey (Malone), S Ritchie (Ballymena), G Leslie (Dungannon), T McWhirter (Ballymena), G Longwell (Ballymena), S McKinty (Ballymena), A Ward (Ballynahinch), R Wilson (Instonians)
Scorers *Tries:* McDowell (2)   *Conversions:* Laing (2)   *Penalty Goal:* Laing
Referee L Mayne

30 August, Ravenhill, Belfast

Ulster 22 (1G 4PG 1DG) **Munster 12** (4PG)
Ulster: S McDowell (Ballymena); J Cunningham (Ballymena), M Field (Malone), S Coulter (Ballymena), A Park (Ballymena); S Laing (Portadown), S Bell (Dungannon); R Mackey (Malone), S Ritchie (Ballymena), G Leslie (Dungannon), T McWhirter (Ballymena), G Longwell (Ballymena), S McKinty (Bangor), A Ward (Ballynahinch), K Gallick (City of Derry)
Scorers *Try:* Park   *Conversion:* Laing   *Penalty Goals:* Laing (4)   *Dropped Goal:* Laing
Munster: D Crotty (Garryowen); A Horgan (Cork Constitution), C Mahony (Dolphin), S McCahill (Sunday's Well), M Lynch (Young Munster); R O'Gara (Cork Constitution), S McIvor (Garryowen); A McSweeney (UCC), P Cunningham (Garryowen), P Clohessy (Young Munster), M Galwey (Shannon), S Leahy (Garryowen), E Halvey (Shannon), D Wallace (Garryowen), A Foley (Shannon)
Scorer *Penalty Goals:* O'Gara (4)
Referee M White

30 August, Donnybrook, Dublin

Leinster 23 (2G 3PG) **Connacht 6** (2PG)
Leinster: K Nowlan (St Mary's College); D Hickie (St Mary's College), M Ridge (Old Belvedere), K McQuilkin (Lansdowne), J McWeeney (St Mary's College); A McGowan (Blackrock College), D O'Mahony (Lansdowne); R Corrigan (Greystones), S Byrne (Blackrock College), A McKeen (Lansdowne), S Jameson (St Mary's College), A Freeman (Lansdowne), T Brennan (St Mary's College), A Goldfinch (Blackrock College), V Costello (St Mary's College)
Scorers *Tries:* Ridge, Nowlan   *Conversions:* McGowan (2)   *Penalty Goals:* McGowan (3)
Connacht: W Ruane (Ballina); N Barry (Clontarf), P Duignan (Galwegians), S Allnutt (Corinthians), N Carolan (Galwegians); E Elwood (Galwegians), C McGuinness (St Mary's College); J Maher (Bective Rangers), W Mulcahy (Skerries), M Finlay (Galwegians), G Heaslip (Galwegians), M McConnell (Buccaneers), R Rogers (Blackrock College), S McEntee (Wanderers), B Gavin (Galwegians)
Scorers *Penalty Goals:* Elwood (2)

FINAL TABLE

	P	W	D	L	F	A	Pts
Leinster	3	2	0	1	61	46	4
Munster	3	2	0	1	56	43	4
Ulster	3	1	0	2	64	65	2
Connacht	3	1	0	2	42	69	2

IRELAND A TO NEW ZEALAND & WESTERN SAMOA 1997

THE TOURING PARTY

Manager P C Whelan **Coach** W B Ashton **Assistant Coach** D Haslett
Captain G F Halpin

Full-backs: C P Clarke (Terenure Coll), C M P O'Shea (London Irish)

Threequarters: N K P J Woods (London Irish), D Coleman (Terenure Coll),
K M Maggs (Bristol), M Dillon (Lansdowne), R A J Henderson (Wasps),
M Lynch (Young Munster), J Bishop (London Irish), A McGrath (Shannon)

Half-backs: D G Humphreys (London Irish), R Governey (Lansdowne),
B T O'Meara (Cork Constitution), S C McIvor (Garryowen), A Matchett
(Portadown)

Forwards: D Molloy (Wasps), S J Byrne (Blackrock Coll), J Fitzpatrick (London
Irish), G F Halpin (London Irish), G L Walsh (Northampton), S Ritchie
(Ballymena), B McConnell (Bristol), G M Fulcher (London Irish), M E O'Kelly
(London Irish), B Cusack (Bath), R Sheriff (Shannon), K Dawson (London Irish),
E O Halvey (Shannon), A G Foley (Shannon), D Erskine (Sale), D Macartney
(Ballymena), D Wallace (Garryowen)

TOUR RECORD

All matches Played 7   Won 1   Lost 6   Points for 169   Against 337

SCORING DETAILS

All matches

For:	23T	12C	10PG	169 Pts
Against:	47T	36C	10PG	337 Pts

MATCH DETAILS

1997	OPPONENTS	VENUE	RESULT
22 May	Northland	Whangarei	L 16-69
26 May	NZ Academy	Albany	L 15-74
29 May	Bay of Plenty	Rotorua	L 39-52
1 June	Thames Valley	Paeroa	W 38-12
6 June	King Country	Taupo	L 26-32
10 June	NZ Maori	Palmerston North	L 10-41
14 June	Western Samoa	Apia	L 25-57

CANADA TO IRELAND 1997

THE TOURING PARTY

Manager R Witt   **Coach** PJ Parfrey   **Assistant Coaches** D Docherty D Clark **Captain** GL Rees

Full-backs: DS Stewart (UBC Old Boys & Harlequins, England), J Pagano (Yeoman and Ontario)

Threequarters: DC Lougheed (Balmy Beach & Ontario), R Toews (Meraloma & British Columbia), W Stanley (Vancouver Kats & Blackheath, England), C Smith (Meraloma & London Scottish, England), C Robertson (Montreal Wanderers & CCSD)

Half-backs: GL Rees (Oak Bay Castaways & Wasps, England), RP Ross (James Bay & Cardiff, Wales), R Card (Oak Bay Castaways & CCSD), JD Graf (UBC Old Boys & British Columbia)

Forwards: R Bice (Vancouver Rowing Club & Valence d'Agen, France), EA Evans (UBC Old Boys & IBM, Japan), RGA Snow (Dogs, Newfoundland & Newport, Wales), J Thiel (Bayside & CCSD), ME Cardinal (James Bay & British Columbia), AJ Charron (Ottowa Irish & Moseley, England), A Healy (James Bay & CCSD), M James (Burnaby Lake & Perpignan, France), G Rowlands (Saskatchewan & Newport, Wales), J Tait (Barrie & Cardiff, Wales), J Hutchinson (UBC Old Boys & IBM, Japan), K Morgan (Ajax Wanderers & Ontario), R Robson (James Bay & British Columbia), C McKenzie (Burnaby Lake & British Columbia), M Schmid (Abbotsford & Rotherham, England)

TOUR RECORD

All matches   Played 2   Lost 2   Points for 21   Against 59
International match   Played 1   Lost 1   Points for 11   Against 33

SCORING DETAILS

All matches					International matches				
For:	2T	1C	3PG	21 Pts	For:	1T		2PG	11 Pts
Against:	7T	3C	6PG	59 Pts	Against:	5T	1C	2PG	33 Pts

MATCH DETAILS

1997	OPPONENTS	VENUE	RESULT
26 Nov	Ireland A	Belfast	L 10-26
30 Nov	IRELAND	Dublin	L 11-33

MATCH 1   26 November, Ravenhill, Belfast

Ireland A 26 (2G 4PG)   **Canadians 10** (1G 1PG)
Ireland A: *Tries:* Clohessy, O'Mahony *Conversions:* Burke (2)
Penalty Goals: Burke (4)
Canadians *Try:* Ross *Conversion:* Ross *Penalty Goal:* Ross

Spunner, H F (Wanderers) 1881 *E, S*, 1884 *W*
Stack, C R R (Dublin U) 1889 *S*
Stack, G H (Dublin U) 1875 *W*
Staples, J E (London Irish, Harlequins) 1991 *W, E, S, Nm* 1,2, *[Z, J, S, A]*, 1992 *W, E, NZ* 1,2, *A*, 1995 *F, W, It, [NZ], Fj*, 1996 *US, S, F, A*, 1997 *W, E, S*
Steele, H W (Ballymena) 1976 *E*, 1977 *F*, 1978 *F, W, E*, 1979 *F, W, E, A* 1,2
Stephenson, G V (Queen's U, Belfast, London Hosp) 1920 *F*, 1921 *E, S, W, F*, 1922 *E, S, W, F*, 1923 *E, S, W, F*, 1924 *F, E, S, W, NZ*, 1925 *F, E, S, W*, 1926 *F, E, S, W*, 1927 *F, E, S, W, A*, 1928 *F, E, S, W*, 1929 *F, E, W*, 1930 *F, E, S, W*
Stephenson, H W V (United Services) 1922 *S, W, F*, 1924 *F, E, S, W, NZ*, 1925 *F, E, S, W*, 1927 *A*, 1928 *E*
Stevenson, J (Dungannon) 1888 *M*, 1889 *S*
Stevenson, J B (Instonians) 1958 *A, E, S, W, F*
Stevenson, R (Dungannon) 1887 *E, S, W*, 1888 *M*, 1889 *S, W*, 1890 *S, W, E*, 1891 *W*, 1892 *W*, 1893 *E, S, W*
Stevenson, T H (Belfast Acad) 1895 *E, W*, 1896 *E, S, W*, 1897 *E, S*
Stewart, A L (NIFC) 1913 *W, F*, 1914 *F*
Stewart, W J (Queen's U, Belfast, NIFC) 1922 *F*, 1924 *S*, 1928 *F, E, S, W*, 1929 *F, E, S, W*
Stoker, E W (Wanderers) 1888 *W, S*
Stoker, F O (Wanderers) 1886 *S*, 1888 *W, M*, 1889 *S*, 1891 *W*
Stokes, O S (Cork Bankers) 1882 *E*, 1884 *E*
Stokes, P (Garryowen) 1913 *E, S*, 1914 *F*, 1920 *E, S, W, F*, 1921 *E, S, F*, 1922 *W, F*
Stokes, R D (Queen's Coll, Cork) 1891 *S, W*
Strathdee, E (Queen's U, Belfast) 1947 *E, S, W, A*, 1948 *W, F*, 1949 *E, S, W*
Stuart, C P (Clontarf) 1912 *SA*
Stuart, I M B (Dublin U) 1924 *E, S*
Sugars, H S (Dublin U) 1905 *NZ*, 1906 *SA*, 1907 *S*
Sugden, M (Wanderers) 1925 *F, E, S, W*, 1926 *F, E, S, W*, 1927 *E, S, W, A*, 1928 *F, E, S, W*, 1929 *F, E, S, W*, 1930 *F, E, S, W*, 1931 *F, E, S, W*
Sullivan, D B (UC Dublin) 1922 *E, S, W, F*
Sweeney, J A (Blackrock Coll) 1907 *E, S, W*
Symes, G R (Monkstown) 1895 *E*
Synge, J S (Lansdowne) 1929 *S*

Taggart, T (Dublin U) 1887 *W*
Taylor, A S (Queen's Coll, Belfast) 1910 *E, S, W*, 1912 *F*
Taylor, J D R (Queen's Coll, Belfast) 1903 *E*
Taylor, J (Belfast Collegians) 1914 *E, S, W*
Taylor, J W (NIFC) 1879 *S*, 1880 *E, S*, 1881 *S*, 1882 *E, S*, 1883 *E, S*
Tector, W R (Wanderers) 1955 *F, E, S*
Tedford, A (Malone) 1902 *E, S, W*, 1903 *E, S, W*, 1904 *E, S, W*, 1905 *E, S, W, NZ*, 1906 *E, S, W, SA*, 1907 *E, S, W*, 1908 *E, S, W*
Teehan, C (UC Cork) 1939 *E, S, W*
Thompson, C (Belfast Collegians) 1907 *E, S*, 1908 *E, S, W*, 1909 *E, S, W, F*, 1910 *E, S, W, F*
Thompson, J A (Queen's Coll, Belfast) 1885 *S* 1,2
Thompson, J K S (Dublin U) 1921 *W*, 1922 *E, S, F*, 1923 *E, S, W, F*
Thompson, R G (Lansdowne) 1882 *W*
Thompson, R H (Instonians) 1951 *SA*, 1952 *F*, 1954 *NZ, F, E, S, W*, 1955 *F, E, S, W*, 1956 *W*
Thornhill, T (Wanderers) 1892 *E, S, W*, 1893 *E*
Thrift, H (Dublin U) 1904 *W*, 1905 *E, S, W, NZ*, 1906 *E, W, SA*, 1907 *E, S, W*, 1908 *E, S, W*, 1909 *E, S, W, F*
Tierney, D (UC Cork) 1938 *S, W*, 1939 *E*
Tillie, C R (Dublin U) 1887 *E, S*, 1888 *W, S*
Todd, A W P (Dublin U) 1913 *W, F*, 1914 *F*
Topping, J A (Ballymena) 1996 *WS, A*, 1997 *It* 1, *F, E*
Torrens, J D (Bohemians) 1938 *W*, 1939 *E, S, W*
Tucker, C C (Shannon) 1979 *F, W*, 1980 *F* (R)
Tuke, B B (Bective Rangers) 1890 *E*, 1891 *E, S*, 1892 *E*, 1894 *E, S, W*, 1895 *E, S*
Turley, N (Blackrock Coll) 1962 *E*
Tweed, D A (Ballymena) 1995 *F, W, It, [J]*
Tydings, J J (Young Munster) 1968 *A*
Tyrrell, W (Queen's U, Belfast) 1910 *F*, 1913 *E, S, W, F*, 1914 *F, E, S, W*

Uprichard, R J H (Harlequins, RAF) 1950 *S, W*

Waide, S L (Oxford U, NIFC) 1932 *E, S, W*, 1933 *E, W*

Waites, J (Bective Rangers) 1886 *S*, 1888 *M*, 1889 *W*, 1890 *S, W, E*, 1891 *E*
Waldron, O C (Oxford U, London Irish) 1966 *S, W*, 1968 *A*
Walker, S (Instonians) 1934 *E, S*, 1935 *E, S, W, NZ*, 1936 *E, S, W*, 1937 *E, S, W*, 1938 *E, S, W*
Walkington, D B (NIFC) 1887 *E, W*, 1888 *W*, 1890 *W, E*, 1891 *E, S, W*
Walkington, R B (NIFC) 1875 *E*, 1876 *E*, 1877 *E, S*, 1878 *E*, 1879 *S*, 1880 *E, S*, 1882 *E, S*
Wall, H (Dolphin) 1965 *S, W*
Wallace, Jas (Wanderers) 1904 *E, S*
Wallace, Jos (Wanderers) 1903 *S, W*, 1904 *E, S, W*, 1905 *E, S, W, NZ*, 1906 *W*
Wallace, P S (Blackrock Coll, Saracens) 1995 *[J], Fj*, 1996 *US, W, E, WS, A*, 1997 *It* 1, *F, W, E, S, NZ, C*, 1998 *S, F, W, E*
Wallace, R M (Garryowen, Saracens) 1991 *Nm* 1 (R), 1992 *W, E, S, F, A*, 1993 *S, F, W, E, R*, 1994 *F, W, E, S*, 1995 *W, It, [NZ, J, W], Fj*, 1996 *US, S, F, WS*, 1998 *S, F, W, E*
Wallace, T H (Cardiff) 1920 *E, S, W*
Wallis, A K (Wanderers) 1892 *E, S, W*, 1893 *E, W*
Wallis, C O'N (Old Cranleighans, Wanderers) 1935 *NZ*
Wallis, T G (Wanderers) 1921 *F*, 1922 *E, S, W, F*
Wallis, W A (Wanderers) 1880 *S*, 1881 *E, S*, 1882 *W*, 1883 *S*
Walmsley, G (Bective Rangers) 1894 *E*
Walpole, A (Dublin U) 1888 *S, M*
Walsh, E J (Lansdowne) 1887 *E, S, W*, 1892 *E, S, W*, 1893 *E*
Walsh, H D (Dublin U) 1875 *E*, 1876 *E*
Walsh, J C (UC Cork, Sunday's Well) 1960 *S, SA*, 1961 *E, S, F, SA*, 1963 *E, S, W, NZ*, 1964 *E, S, W, F*, 1965 *F, S, W, SA*, 1966 *F, S, W*, 1967 *E, S, W, F, A* 2
Ward, A J (Ballynahinch) 1998 *F, W, E*
Ward, A J P (Garryowen, St Mary's Coll, Greystones) 1978 *S, F, W, E, NZ*, 1979 *F, W, E, S*, 1981 *W, E, S, A*, 1983 *E* (R), 1984 *E, S*, 1986 *S*, 1987 *[C, Tg]*
Warren, J P (Kingstown) 1883 *E*
Warren, R G (Lansdowne) 1884 *W*, 1885 *E, S* 1,2, 1886 *E*, 1887 *E, S, W*, 1888 *W, S, M*, 1889 *S, W*, 1890 *S, W, E*
Watson, R (Wanderers) 1912 *SA*
Wells, H G (Bective Rangers) 1891 *S, W*, 1894 *E, S*
Westby, A J (Dublin U) 1876 *E*
Wheeler, G H (Queen's Coll, Belfast) 1884 *S*, 1885 *E*
Wheeler, J R (Queen's U, Belfast) 1922 *E, S, W, F*, 1924 *E*
Whelan, P C (Garryowen) 1975 *E, S*, 1976 *NZ*, 1977 *W, E, S, F*, 1978 *S, F, W, E, NZ*, 1979 *F, W, E, S*, 1981 *F, W, E*
White, M (Queen's Coll, Cork) 1906 *E, S, W, SA*, 1907 *E, W*
Whitestone, A M (Dublin U) 1877 *E*, 1879 *S, E*, 1880 *E*, 1883 *S*
Whittle, D (Bangor) 1988 *F*
Wilkinson, C R (Malone) 1993 *S*
Wilkinson, R W (Wanderers) 1947 *A*
Williamson, F W (Dolphin) 1930 *E, S, W*
Willis, W J (Lansdowne) 1879 *E*
Wilson, F (CIYMS) 1977 *W, E, S*
Wilson, H G (Glasgow U, Malone) 1905 *E, S, W, NZ*, 1906 *E, S, W, SA*, 1907 *E, S, W*, 1908 *E, S, W*, 1909 *E, S, W*, 1910 *W*
Wilson, W H (Bray) 1877 *E, S*
Withers, H H C (Army, Blackheath) 1931 *F, E, S, W, SA*
Wolfe, E J (Armagh) 1882 *E*
Wood, G H (Dublin U) 1913 *W*, 1914 *F*
Wood, B G M (Garryowen) 1954 *E, S*, 1956 *F, E, S, W*, 1957 *F, E, S, W*, 1958 *A, E, S, W, F*, 1959 *E, S, W, F*, 1960 *E, S, W, F, SA*, 1961 *E, S, W, F*
Wood, K G M (Garryowen, Harlequins) 1994 *A* 1,2, *US*, 1995 *E, S, [J]*, 1996 *A*, 1997 *It* 1, *F*, 1997 *NZ, It* 2, 1998 *S, F, W, E*
Woods, D C (Bessbrook) 1888 *M*, 1889 *S*
Woods, N K P J (Blackrock Coll) 1994 *A* 1,2, 1995 *E, F*, 1996 *F, W, E*
Wright, R A (Monkstown) 1912 *S*

Yeates, R A (Dublin U) 1889 *S, W*
Young, G (UC Cork) 1913 *E*
Young, R M (Collegians) 1965 *F, E, S, W, SA*, 1966 *F, E, S, W*, 1967 *W, F*, 1968 *W, A*, 1969 *F, E, S, W*, 1970 *SA, F, E, S, W*, 1971 *F, E, S, W*

IRISH INTERNATIONAL RECORDS

(up to 30 April 1998)

MATCH RECORDS

MOST CONSECUTIVE TEST WINS
6 1968 *S, W, A,* 1969 *F, E, S*

MOST CONSECUTIVE TESTS WITHOUT DEFEAT

P	W	D	Period
7	6	1	1968–69
5	4	1	1972–73

MOST POINTS IN A MATCH
by the team

Pts	Opp	Venue	Year
60	R	Dublin	1986
55	Z	Dublin	1991
50	J	Bloemfontein	1995
49	WS	Dublin	1988
46	C	Dunedin	1987

by a player
24 by P A Burke v Italy at Dublin — 1997
23 by R P Keyes v Zimbabwe at Dublin — 1991
21 by S O Campbell v Scotland at Dublin — 1982
21 by S O Campbell v England at Dublin — 1983
20 by M J Kiernan v Romania at Dublin — 1986
20 by E P Elwood v Romania at Dublin — 1993
20 by S J P Mason v Western Samoa at Dublin — 1996

MOST TRIES IN A MATCH
by the team

T	Opp	Venue	Year
10	R	Dublin	1986
8	WS	Dublin	1988
8	Z	Dublin	1991
7	J	Bloemfontein	1995

by a player
4 by B F Robinson v Zimbabwe at Dublin — 1991
3 by R Montgomery v Wales at Birkenhead — 1887
3 by J P Quinn v France at Cork — 1913
3 by E O'D Davy v Scotland at Murrayfield — 1930
3 by S J Byrne v Scotland at Murrayfield — 1953
3 by K D Crossan v Romania at Dublin — 1986
3 by B J Mullin v Tonga at Brisbane — 1987

MOST CONVERSIONS IN A MATCH
by the team

C	Opp	Venue	Year
7	R	Dublin	1986
6	J	Bloemfontein	1995
5	C	Dunedin	1987

by a player
7 by M J Kiernan v Romania at Dublin — 1986
6 by P A Burke v Japan at Bloemfontein — 1995
5 by M J Kiernan v Canada at Dunedin — 1987

MOST PENALTY GOALS IN A MATCH
by the team

P	Opp	Venue	Year
8	It	Dublin	1997
6	S	Dublin	1982
6	R	Dublin	1993
6	US	Atlanta	1996
6	WS	Dublin	1996

by a player
8 by P A Burke v Italy at Dublin — 1997
6 by S O Campbell v Scotland at Dublin — 1982
6 by EP Elwood v Romania at Dublin — 1993
6 by S J P Mason v Western Samoa at Dublin — 1996

MOST DROPPED GOALS IN A MATCH
by the team

D	Opp	Venue	Year
2	A	Dublin	1967
2	F	Dublin	1975
2	A	Sydney	1979
2	E	Dublin	1981
2	C	Dunedin	1987
2	E	Dublin	1993

by a player

2 by C M H Gibson v Australia at Dublin		1967
2 by W M McCombe v France at Dublin		1975
2 by S O Campbell v Australia at Sydney		1979
2 by E P Elwood v England at Dublin		1993

CAREER RECORDS

MOST CAPPED PLAYERS

Caps	Player	Career
69	C M H Gibson	1964–79
63	W J McBride	1962–75
61	J F Slattery	1970–84
58	P A Orr	1976–87
55	B J Mullin	1984–95
54	T J Kiernan	1960–73
52	D G Lenihan	1981–92
51	M I Keane	1974–84
48	N J Popplewell	1989–98
46	J W Kyle	1947–58

MOST CONSECUTIVE TESTS

Tests	Player	Span
52	W J McBride	1964–75
49	P A Orr	1976–86
43	D G Lenihan	1981–89
39	M I Keane	1974–81
37	G V Stephenson	1920–29

MOST TESTS AS CAPTAIN

Tests	Captain	Span
24	T J Kiernan	1963–73
19	C F Fitzgerald	1982–86
17	J F Slattery	1979–81
17	D G Lenihan	1986–90

MOST TESTS IN INDIVIDUAL POSITIONS

Full-back	T J Kiernan	54	1960–73
Wing	K D Crossan	41	1982–92
Centre	B J Mullin	55	1984–95
Fly-half	J W Kyle	46	1947–58
Scrum-half	M T Bradley	40	1984–95
Prop	P A Orr	58	1976–87
Hooker	K W Kennedy	45	1965–75
Lock	W J McBride	63	1962–75
Flanker	J F Slattery	61	1970–84
No 8	W P Duggan	39	1975–84

MOST POINTS IN TESTS

Pts	Player	Tests	Career
308	M J Kiernan	43	1982–91
217	S O Campbell	22	1976–84
214	E P Elwood	25	1993–98
158	T J Kiernan	54	1960–73
113	A J P Ward	19	1978–87

MOST TRIES IN TESTS

Tries	Player	Tests	Career
17	B J Mullin	55	1984–95
14	G V Stephenson	42	1920–30
12	K D Crossan	41	1982–92
11	A T A Duggan	25	1963–72
11	S P Geoghegan	37	1991–96

MOST CONVERSIONS IN TESTS

Cons	Player	Tests	Career
40	M J Kiernan	43	1982–91
26	T J Kiernan	54	1960–73
20	E P Elwood	25	1993–98
16	R A Lloyd	19	1910–20
15	S O Campbell	22	1976–84

MOST PENALTY GOALS IN TESTS

Pens	Player	Tests	Career
62	M J Kiernan	43	1982–91
56	E P Elwood	25	1993–98
54	S O Campbell	22	1976–84
31	T J Kiernan	54	1960–73
29	A J P Ward	19	1978–87

MOST DROPPED GOALS IN TESTS

Drops	Player	Tests	Career
7	R A Lloyd	19	1910–20
7	S O Campbell	22	1976–84
6	C M H Gibson	69	1964–79
6	B J McGann	25	1969–76
6	M J Kiernan	43	1982–91

INTERNATIONAL CHAMPIONSHIP RECORDS

Record	Detail		Set
Most points in seaon	71	in four matches	1983
Most tries in season	12	in four matches	1928 & 1953
Highest score	30	30–17 v Wales	1996
Biggest win	24	24–0 v France	1913
Highest score conceded	46	6–46 v England	1997
Biggest defeat	40	6–46 v England	1997
Most appearances	56	C M H Gibson	1964–79
Most points in matches	207	M J Kiernan	1982–91
Most points in season	52	S O Campbell	1983
Most points in match	21	S O Campbell	v Scotland, 1982
	21	S O Campbell	v England, 1983
Most tries in matches	14	G V Stephenson	1920–30
Most tries in season	5	J E Arigho	1928
Most tries in match	3	R Montgomery	v Wales, 1887
	3	J P Quinn	v France, 1913
	3	E O'D Davy	v Scotland, 1930
	3	S J Byrne	v Scotland, 1953
Most cons in matches	21	M J Kiernan	1982–91
Most cons in season	7	R A Lloyd	1913
Most cons in match	4	P F Murray	v Scotland, 1932
	4	R J Gregg	v Scotland, 1953
Most pens in matches	48	S O Campbell	1980–84
Most pens in season	14	S O Campbell	1983
	14	E P Elwood	1994
Most pens in match	6	S O Campbell	v Scotland, 1982
Most drops in matches	7	R A Lloyd	1910–20
Most drops in season	2	on several occasions	
Most drops in match	2	W M McCombe	v France, 1975
	2	E P Elwood	v England, 1993

MAJOR TOUR RECORDS

Record	Detail	Year	Place
Most individual points	60 by S O Campbell	1979	Australia
Most points in match	19 by A J P Ward	1979 v A C T	Canberra
	19 by S O Campbell	1979 v Australia	Brisbane
	19 by E P Elwood	1994 v W Australia	Perth
Most tries in match	3 by A T A Duggan	1967 v Victoria	Melbourne
	3 by J F Slattery	1981 v SA President's XV	East London (SA)
	3 by M J Kiernan	1981 v Gold Cup XV	Oudtshoorn (SA)
	3 by M J Field	1994 v W Australia	Perth

MISCELLANEOUS RECORDS

Record	Holder	Detail
Longest Test career	A J F O'Reilly	16 seasons, 1954–55 to 1969–70
	C M H Gibson	16 seasons, 1963–64 to 1979
Youngest Test cap	F S Hewitt	17 yrs 157 days in 1924
Oldest Test cap	C M H Gibson	36 yrs 195 days in 1979

IRISH INTERNATIONAL CAREER RECORDS (*up to 30 April 1998*)

Player	Debut	Caps since last season	Caps	T	C	PG	DG	Pts
C M P O'Shea	1993 v R	1998 *S, F*	18	0	1	3	1	14
S J P Mason	1996 v W		3	0	3	12	0	42
J E Staples	1991 v W		26	5	2	0	0	25
K W Nowlan	1997 v NZ	1997 *NZ, C, It* 2	3	2	0	0	0	10
C P Clarke	1993 v F	1998 *W, E*	5	0	0	0	1	3
J P J McWeeney	1997 v NZ	1997 *NZ*	1	0	0	0	0	0
K M Maggs	1997 v NZ	1997 *NZ* (R), *C, It* 2, 1998 *S, F, W, E*	7	1	0	0	0	5
R M Wallace	1991 v Nm	1998 *S, F, W, E*	29	5	0	0	0	23
J A Topping	1996 v WS		5	0	0	0	0	0
S P Geoghegan	1991 v F		37	11	0	0	0	51
D A Hickie	1997 v W	1997 *NZ, C, It* 2, 1998 *S, F, W, E*	10	5	0	0	0	25
N K P J Woods	1994 v A		7	1	0	0	0	5
M C McCall	1992 v NZ	1997 *NZ, C, It* 2, 1998 *S, E*	11	0	0	0	0	0
K P Keane	1998 v E	1998 *E* (R)	1	0	0	0	0	0
J C Bell	1994 v A		21	3	0	0	0	15
R A J Henderson	1996 v WS	1997 *NZ, C,* 1998 *F, W*	5	0	0	0	0	0
K P McQuilkin	1996 v US		5	0	0	0	0	0
M J Field	1994 v E		17	0	0	0	0	0
D W O'Mahony	1995 v It	1997 *It* 2	3	1	0	0	0	5
D G Humphreys	1996 v F	1997 *It* 2, 1998 *S, E* (R)	9	0	3	8	2	36
P A Burke	1995 v E		10	0	11	26	1	103
E P Elwood	1993 v W	1997 *NZ, C, It* 2 (R), 1998 *F, W, E*	25	0	20	56	2	214
N A Hogan	1995 v E	1997 *It* 2	13	1	0	0	0	5
B T O'Meara	1997 v E	1997 *NZ* (R), 1998 *S*	4	0	0	0	0	0
S C McIvor	1996 v A		3	0	0	0	0	0
C D McGuinness	1997 v NZ	1997 *NZ, C,* 1998 *F, W, E*	5	1	0	0	0	5
A T H Clarke	1995 v Fj	1997 *It* 2 (R)	6	0	0	0	0	0
R P Nesdale	1997 v W	1997 *NZ* (R), *C,* 1998 *F* (R), *W* (R)	7	0	0	0	0	0
K G M Wood	1994 v A	1997 *NZ, It* 2, 1998 *S, F, W, E*	15	2	0	0	0	10
N J Popplewell	1989 v NZ	1997 *NZ, C,* 1998 *S* (t), *F* (R)	48	3	0	0	0	13
R Corrigan	1997 v C	1997 *C* (R), *It* 2, 1998 *S, F, W, E*	6	0	0	0	0	0

P S Wallace	1995 v J	1997 *NZ, C,* 1998 *S, F, W, E*	18	2	0	0	0	10
P M Clohessy	1993 v F	1997 *It* 2, 1998 *F* (R), *W* (R)	19	2	0	0	0	10
G F Halpin	1990 v E		11	1	0	0	0	5
G M Fulcher	1994 v A		19	1	0	0	0	5
J W Davidson	1995 v Fj		12	0	0	0	0	0
M E O'Kelly	1997 v NZ	1997 *NZ, C, It* 2, 1998 *S, F, W, E*	7	0	0	0	0	0
P S Johns	1990 v Arg	1997 *NZ, C, It* 2, 1998 *S, F, W, E*	41	2	0	0	0	10
M J Galwey	1991 v F	1998 *F* (R)	23	1	0	0	0	5
E O Halvey	1995 v F	1997 *NZ, C* (R)	8	2	0	0	0	10
D J Erskine	1997 v NZ	1997 *NZ* (R), *C, It* 2	3	0	0	0	0	0
D O'Grady	1997 v It	1997 *It* 2	1	0	0	0	0	0
A J Ward	1998 v F	1998 *F, W, E*	3	1	0	0	0	5
K Dawson	1997 v NZ	1997 *NZ, C,* 1998 *S*	3	0	0	0	0	0
D S Corkery	1994 v A	1998 *S, F, W, E*	25	3	0	0	0	15
V C P Costello	1996 v US	1997 *C, It* 2 (R), 1998 *S* (R), *F, W, E*	11	2	0	0	0	10
A G Foley	1995 v E		9	1	0	0	0	5
E R P Miller	1997 v It	1997 *NZ, It* 2, 1998 *S, W* (R)	8	1	0	0	0	5

IRISH CLUBS 1997-98

Ballymena

Year of formation 1922
Ground Eaton Park, Raceview Road, Ballymena Tel: Ballymena 656746
Colours Black
Captain 1997-98 S Ritchie
Insurance Corporation League Div 1 6th **First Trust Bank Ulster Senior Cup** Lost
11-28 to Malone (quarter-final)

A season that promised so much was ultimately a disappointment for the Ulster side who were again coached by South African, Nelie Smith. Their six straight wins at the start of the season were built on a dominant pack and a quick back three, which included James Topping who was selected for the Irish tour to South Africa. However, they suffered a surprise defeat, when league leaders, to Old Crescent and from that point on their season began to unravel. They had been referred to as the best ever Ulster side in the All Ireland League after pushing Shannon very close, but despite this accolade they lost to all four Limerick sides, which underlines the current stark differences between the two areas. Ballymena supplied nine of the Ulster squad and three to the Ireland A side and were particularly well served by back-row forward Keith Gallick, who had joined from City of Derry, and Andy Dougan and scrum-half Andy Matchett, who had returned to the club from Portadown.

League Record 1997-98

Date	Venue	Opponents	Result	Scorers
22 Nov	H	Dolphin	45-16	*T:* Cunningham, Longwell, Matchett 3, Gallick, pen try *C:* McAleese 5
6 Dec	A	Old Belvedere	26-12	*T:* Machett, pen try *C:* McAleese 2 *P:* McAleese 2 *D:* McAleese 2
13 Dec	H	Blackrock College	44-6	*T:* Matchett, McDowell, Gallick, Dougan, Cunningham, Topping *C:* McAleese 3, Park *P:* McAleese 2
3 Jan	A	Terenure College	25-5	*T:* Topping 2, Matchett 2 *C:* McAleese *D:* McAleese
10 Jan	H	Dungannon	27-12	*T:* Irwin, Gallick, Parke, Topping *C:* McAleese 2 *P:* McAleese
17 Jan	A	Old Crescent	6-9	*P:* McAleese 2
24 Jan	H	Clontarf	46-18	*T:* Dougan 2, McDowell, Park, Irwin, Longwell, pen try *C:* McAleese 4 *P:* McAleese
31 Jan	A	Shannon	13-19	*T:* McDowell *C:* McAleese *P:* McAleese 2
14 Feb	H	Cork Constitution	6-19	*P:* McAleese 2
21 Feb	A	St Mary's College	33-64	*T:* Matchett 2, Dougan, Andrews, Boyd *C:* Park 4
14 Mar	H	Lansdowne	31-20	*T:* Cunningham, Gallick, McDowell, pen try *C:* McAleese 4 *P:* McAleese
28 Mar	H	Young Munster	13-21	*T:* Boyd *C:* McAleese *P:* McAleese 2
11 Apr	A	Garryowen	29-66	*T:* Irwin, McDowell, Topping, Matchett *C:* McAleese 3 *P:* McAleese

Blackrock College

Year of formation 1882
Ground Stradbrook Road, Blackrock, Dublin Tel: Dublin 2805967
Colours Royal blue and white hoops
Captain 1997-98 H Kos
Insurance Corporation League Div 1 10th **Heineken Leinster Senior Cup** Lost 20-26
to Bective Rangers (2nd round)

A young Blackrock side missed the strength and character of Dean Oswald, who had returned to New Zealand, but with the undoubted coaching abilities of George Hook and Tony Smeeth they set the realistic target this season of First Division survival. However, with some inconsistent displays throughout the campaign, they were only able to achieve this on the last Saturday when they had to rely on results elsewhere to hold the last automatic First Division place. Captain Hubie Kos was an outstanding performer throughout the year, and together with former Ireland squad member Shane Byrne created a solid platform up front from which their exciting back line were able to develop. The return of Paddy Dunne after two years dogged by injury was important, as were the kicking abilities of both Owen Cobbe and Alan McGowan, who kicked 65 and 75 points respectively in the league campaign.

League Record 1997-98

Date	Venue	Opponents	Result	Scorers
22 Nov	A	St Mary's College	23-41	*T:* Scally, McGowan *C:* McGowan 2 *P:* McGowan 3
6 Dec	H	Lansdowne	54-32	*T:* Dunne 3, Byrne, McGowan, Keating, Guinan 2 *C:* McGowan 7
13 Dec	A	Ballymena	6-44	*P:* McGowan 2
3 Jan	H	Garryowen	8-29	*T:* Guinan *P:* McGowan
10 Jan	A	Dolphin	13-13	*T:* Cuffe *C:* McGowan *P:* McGowan 2
17 Jan	H	Old Belvedere	44-19	*T:* Goldfinch, Moore, Hackett, Johnson, Keating *C:* Cobbe 3, McGowan 2 *P:* Cobbe 2, McGowan
24 Jan	A	Young Munster	16-26	*T:* Cobbe *C:* Cobbe *P:* Cobbe 3
31 Jan	A	Terenure College	20-13	*T:* Guinan *P:* Cobbe 4 *D:* Cobbe
14 Feb	H	Dungannon	23-9	*T:* Kos, McGowan *C:* McGowan 2 *P:* McGowan 2, Cobbe
21 Feb	A	Old Crescent	3-5	*P:* McGowan
28 Feb	H	Clontarf	13-29	*T:* Kos *C:* McGowan *P:* McGowan, Cobbe
28 Mar	A	Shannon	6-37	*P:* McGowan 2
11 Apr	H	Cork Constitution	20-29	*T:* Guinan 2, Kavanagh *C:* Cobbe *P:* Cobbe

Clontarf

Year of formation 1876
Ground Castle Avenue, Clontarf, Dublin Tel: Dublin 8332621
Colours Scarlet and royal blue hoops
Captain 1997-98 B Jackman
Insurance Corporation League Div 1 7th   **Heineken Leinster Senior Cup** Lost 20-32 to Skerries (quarter-final)

In their first season in Division One Clontarf were the league's surprise package. Their first fixture against Old Crescent was billed as an early relegation battle but by the end of the season they were attracting large crowds to North Dublin and were justifiably hailed as the top Dublin team, having beaten all four of their rivals in the capital. Especially pleasing was their victory over eventual play-off semi-finalists St Mary's, who had won 70-23 the week before meeting Brent Pope's Clontarf side. They will have learnt much for next season when they will again build around players such as New Zealander Craig Brownlie at No 8, who was the inspiration in a light, but extremely mobile pack, and ex-Greystones outside-half Richie Murphy, who contributed 154 points, the second highest in the league. Club captain and hooker, Bernard Jackman, was selected for the Ireland summer tour of South Africa.

League Record 1997-98

Date	Venue	Opponents	Result	Scorers
22 Nov	H	Old Crescent	11-8	*T:* Barry *P:* Murphy 2
6 Dec	A	Young Munster	19-25	*T:* Barry, Noble *P:* Murphy 3

13 Dec	A	Shannon	6-31	*P:* Murphy 2
3 Jan	H	Cork Constitution	3-11	*P:* Murphy
10 Jan	A	St Mary's College	23-12	*T:* O'Reilly 2 *C:* Murphy 2 *P:* Murphy 2 *D:* Murphy
17 Jan	H	Lansdowne	42-10	*T:* Brownley 2, Dignam, Woods, Noble, Guerin *C:* Murphy 6
24 Jan	A	Ballymena	18-46	*T:* Woods, pen try *C:* Murphy *P:* Murphy 2
31 Jan	H	Garryowen	14-16	*T:* Benson *P:* Murphy 3
14 Feb	A	Dolphin	46-21	*T:* Hoffman, Smith, Brownley, Murphy *C:* Murphy 4 *P:* Murphy 4 *D:* Murphy 2
21 Feb	H	Old Belvedere	17-10	*T:* Murphy *P:* Murphy 4
28 Feb	A	Blackrock College	29-13	*T:* Woods, Smith *C:* Murphy 2 *P:* Murphy 5
28 Mar	H	Terenure College	36-17	*T:* Meredith, Fitzsimmons, Power *C:* Murphy 3 *P:* Murphy 4 *D:* Murphy
11 Apr	A	Dungannon	12-47	*T:* Woods, Noble *C:* Noble

Cork Constitution

Year of formation 1892
Ground Temple Hill, Ballintemple, Cork Tel: Cork 292563
Colours White
Captain 1997-98 U O'Callaghan
Insurance Corporation League Div 1 5th   **Carling Munster Senior Cup** Lost 16-25 to Shannon (semi-final)

Constitution suffered several injuries in the early part of their league campaign, and managed only two wins from their first five games while using 29 players. However, this bad start came to an end with a one-point defeat to Shannon, in a game where they competed with the eventual champions for the full 80 minutes, which was more than could be said for many sides. This result seemed to galvanise the side and they lost only two further games. Defeat by Garryowen ultimately robbed them of a play-off place, but the displays of the back row, the line-out dominance exerted by Roger Newell and Ken Murphy and the work at half-back of international Brian O'Meara and under-21 cap Ronan O'Gara provided encouragement for next season.

League Record 1997-98

Date	Venue	Opponents	Result	Scorers
22 Nov	H	Terenure College	15-18	*T:* O'Meara, McLaughlin *C:* O'Gara *P:* O'Gara
6 Dec	A	Dungannon	9-18	*P:* O'Gara 3
14 Dec	A	Old Crescent	17-10	*T:* O'Gara, Kehilly, Kelly *C:* O'Gara
3 Jan	A	Clontarf	11-3	*T:* Horgan *P:* O'Gara 2
10 Jan	H	Shannon	11-12	*T:* Horgan *P:* O'Gara 2
17 Jan	H	Young Munster	16-9	*T:* J Murray *C:* O'Gara *P:* O'Gara 2 *D:* O'Gara
24 Jan	A	St Mary's College	23-38	*T:* O'Meara 2, J Murray *C:* O'Gara *P:* O'Gara 2
31 Jan	H	Lansdowne	26-19	*T:* J Murray, pen try *C:* O'Gara 2 *P:* O'Gara 4
14 Feb	A	Ballymena	19-6	*T:* McLoughlin *C:* O'Gara *P:* O'Gara 3 *D:* O'Gara
21 Feb	H	Garryowen	15-23	*P:* O'Gara 5
28 Feb	A	Dolphin	35-29	*T:* Callaghan, J Murray, O'Driscoll, pen try *C:* O'Brien 2, Kiernan *P:* Kiernan 3
28 Mar	H	Old Belvedere	63-12	*T:* Kelly 3, J Murray 2, N Murray 2, Lawlor 2, O'Brien, Doyle *C:* O'Gara 4
11 Apr	A	Blackrock College	29-20	*T:* O'Brien 2, O'Meara, Kelly *C:* O'Gara 3 *P:* O'Gara

Dolphin

Year of formation 1902
Ground Musgrave Park, Pearse Road, Cork Tel: Cork 962435
Colours Navy blue, yellow and white
Captain 1997-98 P Scott
Insurance Corporation League Div 1 12th – *Relegated* **Carling Munster Senior Cup**
Lost 13-21 to Young Munster (1st round)

Newly promoted Dolphin gave it their all throughout the season and were unlucky not to hold their position in the top flight. They finished only a point away from security and lost out to Dungannon for a play-off chance on points difference. Michael Kiernan prepared a fine side who showed their strength of character when coming from 11 points behind to defeat Garryowen and when narrowly losing their first Cork derby in the league to Constitution. Former international hooker Terry Kingston was inspirational in a pack where Steve Jackson and Dave Pomeroy in the back row were key defensive players, putting in an immense amount of work. Outside-half John O'Mahony was not only a valuable kicker of the ball but also an excellent running player, emphasised by his 35-metre run for a try against Old Belvedere.

League Record 1997-98

Date	Venue	Opponents	Result	Scorers
22 Nov	A	Ballymena	16-45	*T:* Cian Mahony *C:* Conor Mahony *P:* Conor Mahony 3
6 Dec	H	Garryowen	25-24	*T:* Dineen, O'Dowd, Jackson *C:* Conor Mahony 2 *P:* Conor Mahony 2
13 Dec	H	Young Munster	15-31	*T:* O'Donovan, Pomeroy *C:* Conor Mahony *P:* Conor Mahony
3 Jan	A	Old Belvedere	23-15	*T:* Conor Mahony, O'Mahony, McCoitier *C:* Conor Mahony *P:* Conor Mahony *D:* O'Mahony
10 Jan	H	Blackrock College	13-13	*T:* O'Dowd *C:* Conor Mahony *P:* Conor Mahony 2
17 Jan	A	Terenure College	10-23	*T:* Jackson *C:* Conor Mahony *P:* Conor Mahony
24 Jan	H	Dungannon	18-10	*P:* O'Mahony 5 *D:* O'Neill
31 Jan	A	Old Crescent	9-24	*P:* O'Mahony 3
14 Feb	H	Clontarf	21-46	*T:* O'Donovan, O'Connell *C:* O'Mahony *P:* O'Mahony 2 *D:* O'Mahony
21 Feb	A	Shannon	3-30	*P:* O'Mahony
28 Feb	H	Cork Constitution	29-35	*T:* Pomeroy, Mahony *C:* O'Mahony 2 *P:* O'Mahony 4 *D:* O'Mahony
28 Mar	A	St Mary's College	32-36	*T:* O'Dowd, Cian Mahony, O'Donovan, MacCoitir *C:* O'Neill, MacCoitir 2 *P:* O'Neill 2
11 Apr	H	Lansdowne	13-13	*T:* Knowles *C:* O'Mahony *P:* O'Mahony 2

Dungannon

Year of formation 1873
Ground Stevenson Park, Dungannon Tel: Dungannon 22387
Colours Blue and white hoops
Captain 1997-98 G Leslie
Insurance Corporation League Div 1 11th – *Relegated after play-off* **First Trust Bank Ulster Senior Cup** *Winners* – Beat Malone 19-16 (final)

Even the return of Willie Anderson from London Irish towards the end of the season could not save the County Tyrone side from relegation to Division Two. Their best win of the season came against high-flying Clontarf in the last match but this was not enough to prevent them from becoming the first Division One side to face a play-off for their place next season. Despite a victory in the first leg of the play-off they were well beaten at home by Buccaneers to lose 22-34 on aggregate. There were some fine individual performances at various stages of the campaign, but the side were unable to sustain a run of victories at any stage and lost to both of the other relegated sides. Robin Morrow at full-back gave some excellent displays as did Ashley Blair at outside-half, Keith Walker at the line-out, and the Hastings brothers in the back row. The only consolation was victory over Malone in an exciting Ulster Senior Cup final.

League Record 1997-98

Date	Venue	Opponents	Result	Scorers
22 Nov	A	Shannon	13-20	*T:* Hastings, Bell *P:* R Morrow
6 Dec	H	Cork Constitution	18-9	*T:* Moffett, Clarke *C:* Blair
				P: R Morrow, Blair
13 Dec	A	St Mary's College	29-70	*T:* Hastings, Carey, Bell, Simpson *C:* Clarke,
				R Morrow 2 *P:* R.Morrow
3 Jan	H	Lansdowne	28-8	*T:* Bell, Simpson, Carey, Blair *C:* Blair
				P: Blair 2
10 Jan	A	Ballymena	12-27	*P:* Blair 4
17 Jan	H	Garryowen	10-37	*T:* B Morrow *C:* Carey *P:* Carey
24 Jan	A	Dolphin	10-18	*T:* Carey, Simpson
31 Jan	H	Old Belvedere	16-12	*T:* Walker *C:* Blair *P:* Blair 3
14 Feb	A	Blackrock College	9-23	*P:* Blair 2 *D:* Blair
21 Feb	H	Terenure College	22-28	*T:* Redpath, Carey, Blair *C:* Blair 2 *P:* Blair
28 Feb	A	Young Munster	13-29	*T:* Moffett *C:* Blair *P:* Blair 2
28 Mar	A	Old Crescent	13-16	*T:* Simpson *C:* Blair *P:* Blair 2
11 Apr	H	Clontarf	47-12	*T:* Curray, Cowan, Carey, Morrow 2,
				Leslie, pen try *C:* Blair 3 *P:* Blair 2

Division 1/2 Play-Off

Date	Venue	Opponents	Result	Scorers
18 Apr	A	Buccaneers	17-11	*T:* Clarke, Morrow, Hood *C:* Blair
25 Apr	H	Buccaneers	10-27	*T:* Hood *C:* Blair *P:* Blair

Garryowen

Year of formation 1884
Ground Dooradoyle, Limerick Tel: Limerick 303099
Colours Light blue with white five-pointed star
Captain 1997-98 K Keane
Insurance Corporation League Div 1 2nd (Runners-Up in League final)   **Carling Munster Senior Cup** Withdrew from first round (Cork Constitution given walkover)

Garryowen confirmed their place as the country's, and Limerick's, second best side with a strong league campaign built upon some excellent loose play and a controlled defensive approach. David Wallace, who joined his brothers Richard and Paul on Ireland's tour of South Africa, was a key player, both going forward and in his high tackle count, and also contributed nearly a quarter of his side's league tries. His back-row colleague Andrew Bermingham, scrum-half Stephen McIvor and Dominic Crotty at full-back were also vital to the side and Crotty was unlucky not to make the tour party. Coach Phil Danaher was selected to assist with the international side part way through the season and captain Killian Keane made an excellent Ireland debut when he came on as a replacement at Twickenham. Two of their defeats were in games they should have won: against Dolphin after leading by 11 points at half-time, and against Lansdowne when they led 27-23 going into injury time. Although they gave their all in the play-off final they were unable to penetrate the Shannon defence, but they still made a major contribution to the success of the play-offs.

League Record 1997-98

Date	Venue	Opponents	Result	Scorers
23 Nov	H	Young Munster	3-3	*P:* Keane
6 Dec	A	Dolphin	24-25	*T:* Wallace, McIvor *C:* Keane *P:* Keane
				D: Everett 2, Keane

225

13 Dec	A	Old Belvedere	37-22	T: Kilroy, Wallace, Crotty, McIvor, Varley C: Kilroy 3 P: Kilroy 2
3 Jan	A	Blackrock College	29-8	T: Keane, Kilroy, Bermingham, Everett C: Kilroy 3 P: Kilroy
17 Jan	A	Dungannon	37-10	T: Crotty 2, McIvor, Wallace, Keane C: Keane 2, Kilroy P: Keane 2
24 Jan	H	Old Crescent	33-13	T: Keane, McIvor, Brooks C: Keane 3 P: Keane 4
31 Jan	A	Clontarf	16-14	T: Humphries, Kilroy P: Keane 2
14 Feb	H	Shannon	14-17	T: Clarke P: Keane 3
21 Feb	A	Cork Constitution	23-15	T: Kilroy 2 C: Keane 2 P: Keane 2 D: McIvor
28 Feb	H	St Mary's College	13-12	T: Crotty C: Keane P: Keane 2
14 Mar	H	Terenure College	38-26	T: Crotty, Clarke, Keane, Wallace 2 C: Keane 5 P: Keane
28 Mar	A	Lansdowne	27-30	T: Wallace 3 C: Keane 3 P: Keane 2
11 Apr	H	Ballymena	66-29	T: Wallace 2, Brooks 2, Tierney, Keane, Humphreys, Everitt, Hogan C: Keane 6 P: Keane 3

League Knock-out Semi-Final

| 19 Apr | H | Young Munster | 24-10 | T: O'Riordan, Crotty   C: Keane   P: Keane 4 |

League Knock-out Final

| 25 Apr | | Shannon | 9-15 | P: Keane 3 |

Lansdowne

Year of formation 1872
Ground Lansdowne Road, Dublin Tel: Dublin 6689300
Colours Red, yellow and black
Captain 1997-98 K McQuilkin
Insurance Corporation League Div 1 9th   **Heineken Leinster Senior Cup** *Winners* –
Beat Skerries 23-17 (final)

Lansdowne had high expectations this season, after finishing second last year, but were unable to match these in a year which contained many lows and one significant high. They were the only club to defeat Shannon in the league, their first ever league success over the champions. That win and the 51 points against Old Crescent should be set against some poor defensive performances when the side seemed to lack direction and a sense of attacking penetration. Initially they were coached by Paul Clinch, but he was replaced by Michael Cosgrave in January, who was assisted by Kurt McQuilkin. McQuilkin missed part of the season due to injury and his commitments as a development officer for the IRFU. The pack, which this season was spearheaded by Colin McEntee, will be bolstered next season by the arrival of internationals Reggie Corrigan from Greystones and Gabriel Fulcher from London Irish.

League Record 1997-98

Date	Venue	Opponents	Result	Scorers
19 Nov	H	Old Belvedere	35-20	T: McEntee 2, Freeman, O'Mahony C: Kearns 3 P: Kearns 3
6 Dec	A	Blackrock College	32-54	T: Dillon 2, McKean, pen try C: Kearns 3 P: Kearns 2
14 Dec	H	Terenure College	9-9	P: Kearns 3
3 Jan	A	Dungannon	8-28	T: McQuilkin P: Kearns
10 Jan	H	Old Crescent	51-6	T: Dillon 2, McNamara, O'Kelly, Horgan, Aherne, Kearns C: Kearns 5 P: Kearns 2
17 Jan	A	Clontarf	10-42	T: pen try C: Kearns P: Kearns
24 Jan	H	Shannon	18-14	P: Kearns 6

31 Jan	A	Cork Constitution	19-26	*T:* Dillon *C:* Kearns *P:* Kearns 3
				D: McQuilkin
11 Feb	H	St Mary's College	10-42	*T:* Egan, McEntee
21 Feb	H	Young Munster	9-16	*P:* Kearns 2 *D:* Dillon
14 Mar	A	Ballymena	20-31	*T:* Dillon, Glennon *C:* Kearns 2 *P:* Kearns 2
28 Mar	H	Garryowen	30-27	*T:* Egan, McKeen, Dillon *C:* Kearns 3
				P: Kearns 2 *D:* Horgan
11 Apr	A	Dolphin	13-13	*T:* McEntee *C:* Kearns *P:* Kearns 2

Old Belvedere

Year of formation 1930
Ground Anglesea Road, Ballsbridge, Dublin Tel: Dublin 6689748
Colours Black and white hoops
Captain 1997-98 F O'Beirne
Insurance Corporation League Div 1 14th – *Relegated*   **Heineken Leinster Senior Cup**
Lost 14-51 to De La Salle Palmerston (2nd round)

Old Belvedere had a dismal start to the league with six straight defeats, and were virtually condemned to relegation by early January. Although their South African outside-half Rob Rein kicked well in the early part of the season it was only at times, such as the last 20 minutes against Lansdowne, that they ran the ball enough to give their backs any opportunities. Against both Garryowen and Dolphin they missed chances to win the game, especially against Dolphin when they battled back from 11-0 down. Coach Stephen Dodds returned to play in the back row against Terenure, and ensured they got the basics right, allowing them to grind out a morale-boosting win. However, they were unable to build upon that and suffered the season's heaviest defeat at the hands of Shannon. Fergal O'Beirne, Hugh McDonnell and Bill Treacy put in solid performances throughout the season but eventually Belvedere trailed in four points adrift at the tail of the division.

League Record 1997-98

Date	Venue	Opponents	Result	Scorers
19 Nov	A	Lansdowne	20-35	*T:* Tracey, Ridge *C:* Rein 2 *P:* Rein 2
6 Dec	H	Ballymena	12-26	*P:* Rein 4
13 Dec	A	Garryowen	22-37	*T:* O'Beirne, Sexton, Henderson *C:* Rein 2
				P: Rein
3 Jan	H	Dolphin	15-23	*T:* Tracey, Browne *C:* Rein *P:* Rein
10 Jan	A	Young Munster	12-26	*T:* Walsh, pen try *C:* Rein
17 Jan	A	Blackrock College	19-44	*T:* Browne *C:* Tracey *P:* Tracey 4
24 Jan	H	Terenure College	12-10	*P:* Tracey 4
31 Jan	A	Dungannon	12-16	*P:* Tracey 4
14 Feb	H	Old Crescent	27-23	*T:* Browne 2, Sexton, O'Beirne *C:* Treacy 2
				P: Treacy
21 Feb	A	Clontarf	10-17	*T:* Browne *C:* Treacy *P:* Treacy
28 Feb	H	Shannon	20-70	*T:* Rein, Dods *C:* Treacy 2 *P:* Treacy 2
28 Mar	A	Cork Constitution	12-63	*T:* Sexton, Gleeson *C:* Treacy
11 Apr	H	St Mary's College	15-41	*T:* Ward, Cleave *C:* Treacy *P:* Treacy

Old Crescent

Year of formation 1947
Ground Rosbrien, Limerick Tel: Limerick 228083
Colours Navy, blue and white stripes
Captain 1997-98 L Dinneen
Insurance Corporation League Div 1 13th – *Relegated*   **Carling Munster Senior Cup**
Lost 24-44 to Shannon (quarter-final)

If Crescent had not missed seven kickable chances in their first game against Clontarf and had held on to the five-point lead they held with two minutes left against Constitution, their season could have been very different. As it was a late penalty try in their final game condemned them to Division Two next season. Throughout the season they lacked back-room stability with Len Dineen, Jed O'Dwyer and Tony Grant all taking the coaching reins at some stage. They had a cohesive forward unit led by the evergreen Dineen, for whom this may have been his last season. Brian Begley was as reliable as ever with his kicking, but suffered a serious ankle injury which forced him out for almost a month. Centres Anthony O'Dwyer and Leo Doyle were always solid in defence, and in flanker Paul Neville they have a real talent for the future.

League Record 1997-98

Date	Venue	Opponents	Result	Scorers
22 Nov	A	Clontarf	8-11	T: McDonagh P: Barrett
5 Dec	H	Shannon	0-50	
13 Dec	H	Cork Constitution	10-17	T: O'Malley, Hopkins
10 Jan	A	Lansdowne	6-51	P: Begley 2
17 Jan	H	Ballymena	9-6	P: Begley, Doyle D: Begley
24 Jan	A	Garryowen	13-34	T: McLoughlin C: Begley P: Begley 2
31 Jan	H	Dolphin	24-9	T: O'Malley, Barrett, Neville C: Begley 3 P: Begley
14 Feb	A	Old Belvedere	23-27	T: McLoughlin 2, McDonagh C: Begley P: Begley 2
21 Feb	H	Blackrock College	5-3	T: Walsh
28 Feb	A	Terenure College	23-41	T: Hilton-Green, Bowles, O'Malley C: Barrett P: Barrett 2
14 Mar	H	St Mary's College	16-17	T: Hilton-Greene, O'Malley P: Hallissy 2
28 Mar	A	Dungannon	16-13	T: Walsh C: Begley P: Begley 3
11 Apr	A	Young Munster	15-19	P: Begley 5

St Mary's College

Year of formation 1900
Ground Templeville Road, Templeogue, Dublin Tel: Dublin 4900440
Colours Royal Blue with five pointed white star
Captain 1997-98 S Jameson
Insurance Corporation League Div 1 3rd (Lost in League semi-final)   **Heineken Leinster Senior Cup** Lost 20-21 to Skerries (2nd round)

St Mary's looked the part from their very first match and were genuine play-off contenders throughout the season, but lost any real title hopes with defeats against Clontarf and Shannon on successive Saturdays. They revelled on firm ground and dry conditions and have the most exciting back division in Irish rugby, including internationals John McWeeney, Kevin Nowlan, Denis Hickie (the league's top try-scorer) and Conor McGuinness. These four were supported by, amongst others, the exciting Gareth Gannon, surely an international of the future, in the centre. Up front they could, as ever, rely on Steve Jameson, who made his 80th league appearance during the season, Victor Costello and Trevor Brennan. Both Costello and Brennan joined Hickie on the Ireland tour of South Africa, with Costello displacing Lion Eric Miller as Ireland's first choice No 8 during the championship. The goal-kicking of Fergus Campion, who in January returned to senior rugby for the first time in two years, was also vital. In the league play-off semi-final they matched Shannon in all departments, but the experience of the champions was just enough to see off Mary's spirited challenge.

League Record 1997-98

Date	Venue	Opponents	Result	Scorers
22 Nov	H	Blackrock College	41-23	T: Nolan, McWeeney, Hickie, Gannon
				C: Fitzpatrick 3 P: Fitzpatrick 5
6 Dec	A	Terenure College	12-18	T: McWeeney, Costello C: Ormond
13 Dec	H	Dungannon	70-29	T: McIlreavey 2, Fitzgerald, Hickie 4, Nowlan,
				Campion, McNamee C: Ormond 10
10 Jan	H	Clontarf	12-23	T: McIlreavy, Hickie C: Ormond
17 Jan	A	Shannon	11-32	T: Hickie P: Campion 2
24 Jan	H	Cork Constitution	38-23	T: McWeeney 2, Lane, Coyle, Nowlan
				C: Campion 5 P: Campion
31 Jan	H	Young Munster	13-7	T: Hickie C: Campion P: Campion 2
11 Feb	A	Lansdowne	42-10	T: McWeeney, Nowlan, Costello, Hickie 2,
				Jameson C: Campion 3 P: Campion 2
21 Feb	H	Ballymena	64-33	T: Gannon 2, McWeeney 2, Nowlan, McIlreavy,
				Hickie, Costello, Cuddihy C: Campion 5
				P: Campion 3
28 Feb	A	Garryowen	12-13	T: McWeeney, Nowlan C: Ormond
14 Mar	A	Old Crescent	17-16	T: Nowlan, Brennan, McWeeney C: Campion
28 Mar	H	Dolphin	36-32	T: McWeeney 2, Hickie 2, Fitzgerald
				C: Fitzpatrick 4 P: Fitzpatrick
11 Apr	A	Old Belvedere	41-15	T: McNamee, Hickie, Brennan, Jameson,
				Browne, Nowlan, McGuinness C: Fitzpatrick 3

League Knock-out Semi-Final

Date	Venue	Opponents	Result	Scorers
18 Apr	A	Shannon	21-28	T: McGuinness, Reilly C: Fitzpatrick
				P: Fitzpatrick 3

Shannon

Year of formation 1884
Ground Thomond Park, Limerick Tel: Limerick 452350
Colours Black and blue hoops
Captain 1997-98 A Foley
Insurance Corporation League Div 1 1st (*Winners* in League final)   **Carling Munster Senior Cup** *Winners* – Beat Young Munster 19-18 (final)

Yet again Shannon dominated Irish club rugby. They were clearly the club of the season, and have also been described as the best Irish club side of all-time. Coaches Nial O'Donovan and Pat Murray must take great credit not just for these accolades but also for the way they were achieved. The team have learnt not to panic even if the opposition build a lead, and more often than not this allows Shannon to play their own game rather than have it dictated to them. This was highlighted in the close wins over Constitution and Garryowen and in the play-off semi-final against a determined St Mary's side. During the season they recorded their record league score over Old Belvedere and amassed a staggering +225 points difference in the league.

As always Andrew Thompson's kicking was unerringly accurate and he finished the season as the league's top points-scorer with 155. The contribution from the forwards was immense, with John Hayes, Mick Galwey and Anthony Foley all touring with Ireland in South Africa. Foley's colleagues in the back row, Alan Quinlan and Eddie Halvey, were also always to the fore. Shannon are now unbeaten in league games at Thomond Park for over four years and it will be an excellent side who next season can break their domination of Irish club rugby.

League Record 1997-98

Date	Venue	Opponents	Result	Scorers
22 Nov	H	Dungannon	20-13	T: Foley, Galvin C: Thompson 2
				P: Thompson 2
5 Dec	A	Old Crescent	50-0	T: Foley, Galwey 3, Lacey, McDermott,
				McMahon C: Thompson 6 P: Ellison

13 Dec	H	Clontarf	31-6	*T:* Lacey 2, Russell, Foley, Keane
				C: Thompson 3
10 Jan	A	Cork Constitution	12-11	*P:* Thompson 3 *D:* Galvin
17 Jan	H	St Mary's College	32-11	*T:* Lacy, Ellison, Thompson *C:* Thompson
				P: Thompson 5
24 Jan	A	Lansdowne	14-18	*T:* Thompson *P:* Thompson 3
31 Jan	H	Ballymena	19-13	*T:* O'Shea *C:* Thompson *P:* Thompson 4
14 Feb	A	Garryowen	17-14	*T:* McMahon, pen try *C:* Thompson 2
				P: Thompson
21 Feb	H	Dolphin	30-3	*T:* Galwey 2 *C:* Sheehan *P:* Thompson 5
				D: Galvin
28 Feb	A	Old Belvedere	70-20	*T:* Ellison 2, McNamara, Quinlan, Galwey,
				O'Shea, Foley, Hayes, Halvey, McGrath
				C: Thompson 7 *P:* Thompson 2
14 Mar	H	Young Munster	16-10	*T:* Jason Hayes *C:* Thompson *P:* Thompson 3
28 Mar	H	Blackrock College	37-6	*T:* Lacey 2, Thompson, Halvey, Galvin
				C: Thompson 3 *P:* Thompson 2
11 Apr	A	Terenure College	19-17	*T:* Lacey *C:* Thompson *P:* Thompson 3
				D: Galvin

League Knock-out Semi-Final

18 Apr	H	St Mary's College	28-21	*T:* Foley *C:* Thompson *P:* Thompson 7

League Knock-out Final

25 Apr	A	Garryowen	15-9	*P:* Thompson 4 *D:* Thompson

Terenure College

Year of formation 1940
Ground Lakelands Park, Greenlea, Terenure, Dublin Tel: Dublin 4907572
Colours Purple, black and white
Captain 1997-98 J Kelly
Insurance Corporation League Div 1 8th   **Heineken Leinster Senior Cup** Lost 7-21 to
Skerries (semi-final)

Terenure finished the season comfortably placed in the middle of the table, and although they gained five points from their first three games, they never really changed for a play-off place. Conversely the fear of relegation never raised its head at Lakelands Park. They lost winger David Coleman with a fractured ankle in the second game and despite individual flashes from Derek Hegarty at scrum-half, Ciaran Clarke at full-back and Gareth Dempsey at outside-half, their backs collectively were unable to produce regular attacking flair. A powerful front five, which included ex-Shannon player Rory Sheriff, and in the back row Garran Sheahan, made some useful contributions. The pack's best performance came in the last game when they had the measure of Shannon for long periods, and they came within two points of beating the champions. Clarke returned to international rugby midway through the season after a long absence and he was joined on the tour to South Africa by Hegarty.

League Record 1997-98

Date	Venue	Opponents	Result	Scorers
22 Nov	A	Cork Constitution	18-15	*T:* Coleman, Smith *C:* Walsh *P:* Walsh 2
6 Dec	H	St Mary's College	18-12	*T:* Hegarty, Walsh, Hennebry *P:* Walsh
14 Dec	A	Lansdowne	9-9	*P:* Walsh 3
3 Jan	H	Ballymena	5-25	*T:* Dempsey
17 Jan	H	Dolphin	23-10	*T:* Holden, pen try *C:* Walsh 2 *P:* Walsh 3
24 Jan	A	Old Belvedere	10-12	*T:* Dempsey *C:* Walsh *P:* Walsh
31 Jan	H	Blackrock College	13-20	*T:* Pen try *C:* Hegarty *P:* Cullen, O'Connor
14 Feb	A	Young Munster	16-22	*T:* Kavanagh *C:* Walsh *P:* Dempsey 3

21 Feb	A	Dungannon	28-22	*T:* Blaney 2, Hegarty 2 *C:* Dempsey
				P: Dempsey 2
28 Feb	H	Old Crescent	41-23	*T:* Dempsey 2, Hennebery 2, Smyth, Clarke
				C: Dempsey 4 *P:* Dempsey
14 Mar	A	Garryowen	26-36	*T:* Clarke, Hyland, Hegarty 2 *C:* Dempsey 3
28 Mar	A	Clontarf	17-37	*T:* Sheriff, Hegarty *C:* Dempsey 2
				P: Dempsey
11 Apr	H	Shannon	17-19	*T:* Walsh, Kavanagh 2 *C:* Dempsey

Young Munster

Year of formation 1895
Ground Tom Clifford Park, Greenfields, Limerick Tel: Limerick 228433
Colours Black and amber hoops
Captain 1997-98 G Earls
Insurance Corporation League Div 1 4th (Lost in League semi-final)   **Carling Munster Senior Cup** Lost 18-19 to Shannon (final)

Munsters, who were coached by Brian Hickey, welcomed back Peter Clohessy this season and had also gained four players, including Stephen Tuohy at outside-half, from Old Crescent. Ger Earls led the pack to some great performances, and the side as a whole went about their task in a quiet and efficient manner, keeping sight of a play-off place throughout the season. They were fortunate in their strength in depth, especially at prop where Peter and Des Clohessy were ably supported by the talented Nial Hartigan. Throughout the season they switched between Tuohy and Aidan O'Halloran at outside-half and it was unfortunate that when Tuohy was preferred for the play-off semi-final he missed six kicks. The whole side showed immense discipline in their game all season, and it was a tribute to the whole side that both Clohessy brothers took part in the Irish tour to South Africa.

League Record 1997-98

Date	Venue	Opponents	Result	Scorers
23 Nov	A	Garryowen	3-3	*P:* A O'Halloran
6 Dec	H	Clontarf	25-19	*T:* Boland, Lynch, A O'Halloran *C:* Tuohy 2
				P: Tuohy *D:* A O'Halloran
13 Dec	A	Dolphin	31-15	*T:* Tobin, Lynch, Boland *C:* A O'Halloran 2
				P: A O'Halloran 4
10 Jan	H	Old Belvedere	26-12	*T:* Boland, P.Clohessy, D.Clohessy *C:* A O'Halloran *P:* A.O'Halloran 3
17 Jan	A	Cork Constitution	9-16	*P:* A O'Halloran 3
24 Jan	H	Blackrock College	26-16	*T:* P Clohessy, M O'Halloran *C:* Tuohy 2
				P: Tuohy 3 *D:* Tuohy
31 Jan	A	St Mary's College	7-13	*T:* D Clohessy *C:* Tuohy
14 Feb	H	Terenure College	22-16	*T:* Boland *C:* Tuohy *P:* Tuohy 5
21 Feb	A	Lansdowne	16-9	*T:* Lynch *C:* Tuohy *P:* Tuohy *D:* Tuohy, Tobin
28 Feb	H	Dungannon	29-13	*T:* Earls, Walsh, O'Herlihy *C:* A O'Halloran *P:* A O'Halloran 4
14 Mar	A	Shannon	10-16	*T:* Boland *C:* Tuohy *P:* Tuohy
28 Mar	A	Ballymena	21-13	*T:* Honan, A O'Halloran *C:* A O'Halloran *P:* Tuohy, A O'Halloran *D:* Tuohy
11 Apr	H	Old Crescent	19-15	*T:* pen try *C:* A O'Halloran *P:* A O'Halloran 4
League Knockout Semi-Final				
18 Apr	A	Garryowen	10-24	*T:* Hayes *C:* Lynch *D:* Boland

CLUBS THREATEN TO STRIKE

THE 1997-98 SEASON IN WALES

John Billot *Western Mail*

There were those who viewed Welsh rugby as a compelling case for *Doomwatch* during their most traumatic season. The virus of rebellion spread among the clubs of the two top divisions, desperate for funding while trying to get to grips with the professional era; and a bleak fatalism was evident regarding the fortunes of the national team. Coach Kevin Bowring, whose vision was for the classic open game, reflected this when, before the trip to Dublin, he exclaimed, 'I'll be happy to win in any old way!' Wales needed to reassert the ability to surprise and destabilise opponents; but the team produced little consistent quality rugby, no crystal chandelier stuff that we remember from those heroes of the Seventies. So, it was no great shock that Bowring went in May 'by mutual consent' after record defeats by England and France.

The great illusion was that Wales could keep the score close against New Zealand at Wembley Stadium (the emergency venue while the new stadium was being built in Cardiff), but it proved another rendezvous with defeat, this time by 42-7. The management brought in a sports psychologist, Peter Terry, who had helped the British bobsleigh team win bronze in the Winter Olympics, to help soothe away any hang-ups after the shuddering Twickenham disaster and a desperate victory over Scotland. Most players did not require a calming influence; they wanted a clarion call to fuel the old fire that had been virtually extinguished. From somewhere, the sound of a distant trumpet must have stirred them and three sparkling tries did for the Irish. Bowring intoned, 'Our defence won it,' as if hardly believing the outcome. From Dublin to France at Wembley was a quantum leap and this time the highly praised defence was mutilated: it was 51-0 and a Five Nations record margin.

Bowring had taken his team into hiding to grieve in private after Twickenham and sessions were held behind closed gates, which looked a bit like running away and did nothing to burnish the Bowring image. Undoubtedly, he contrived to make matters difficult for himself by perpetuating the old errors of imprudent selection. Neil Jenkins was the classic example and, after Twickenham, Jenkins vehemently reiterated his vow that he would never again be persuaded to play at full-back. Bowring imagined Arwel Thomas, the flawed genius, as the white hope for revival; but it became a choice between Mr Reliable and Mr Maybe. In times of trouble, reliability is always the more valuable asset.

The Wales squad which faced Scotland at Wembley. L-R, back row: L S Quinnell (replacement), L Mustoe (replacement), A G Bateman, A L P Lewis, D Young, A P Moore, M J Voyle, G Thomas, C L Charvis, W T Proctor, K A Morgan, L B Davies (replacement), W S Roy (replacement); front row: J M Humphreys (replacement), R C Appleyard, N R Jenkins, R Howley (capt), K P Jones, I S Gibbs, G R Jenkins, A C Thomas (replacement), P John (replacement)

In April, there arrived the threat of a match strike by Premier and First Division clubs. 'Welsh rugby is in tatters behind the scenes,' warned Newport chairman David Watkins. The cash flow to clubs was totally inadequate with attendances at games falling as never before. The WRU, in turn, threatened to stop monthly pay cheques to the clubs. The clubs could not have paid their players. The strike move collapsed.

Only Cardiff held out. They refused to sign a ten-year loyalty contract to the WRU and struggled through the season without the £400,000 hand-out that the other Premier Division clubs received. Cardiff, alleging the clause an illegal imposition, took the WRU to court; and Terry Holmes, a member of the coaching team, declared that the club's future would be among the English clubs. Welsh rugby without Cardiff was unthinkable.

It was hardly a happy time for the new secretary Dennis Gethin, 53-year-old former Cardiff and Neath full-back, to take up office in March as the 11th secretary of the WRU and the sixth secretary in fewer than ten years. Wales captain Gwyn Jones suffered a severe spinal injury during Cardiff's match with Swansea and was forced to retire from the game. Also lost to the international scene was Ieuan Evans, after a record 72 appearances for his country, 28 as captain.

The longest season in Welsh rugby – 40 weeks – opened on 16 August 1997 and ended with the SWALEC Cup final on 23 May 1998. In between, there were moments when defeats of unimaginable magnitude had to be endured by the national team. The renaissance will not be easily achieved. Indeed, it is a task to daunt a Hercules!

SUPER SWANSEA'S THIRD TITLE

WRU NATIONAL LEAGUE 1997-98

Wales no longer enjoy the bounteous arsenal of talent that was exclusively theirs during the seventies; but Swansea made the league memorable with many moments of true quality and glitter to grace a season that held so few attractions for the declining crowds. The WRU decision to prune the Premier Division from 12 to eight teams was less than popular. There were those who viewed it as a total disaster, doing more to depress interest than any other measure that could have been devised.

In winning the title for a record third time in seven seasons, Swansea suffered just one defeat (at Llanelli by 25-22 in October) and crushed Cardiff's challenge with a dazzling display by 39-20 in their penultimate game at St Helen's. It was no more than Swansea deserved for their flexibility and continuity as dedicated attackers, spearheaded, of course, by Arwel Thomas, the most difficult outside-half in Wales to pin down. There were occasions when he made it a one-man crusade; but his presence was of inestimable value behind the most ruthless scrummaging pack in Wales.

Cardiff, whose only home defeat was by Swansea by 31-22, never produced the consistency of adventure that emanated from the Swansea camp, where New Zealand coach John Plumtree proved an admirable successor to Mike Ruddock, who left to guide the fortunes of Irish provincial champions Leinster. Pontypridd, who had won the title the previous season, with only two defeats, this time lost four games (including two against Cardiff) and finished in third spot. Ebbw Vale, inspiringly led by Kingsley Jones, kept Neath and Llanelli out of the top four places despite losing three of their first four matches. Ebbw had never finished so high in the top division. For big spenders Cardiff and Llanelli the season had failed significantly to reward them in league terms.

While events were wretched for Newport, doomed to go through the campaign without a single victory, Caerphilly were never out of the headlines and became the First Division champions with just three defeats (by Aberavon and then away to Bonymaen and Merthyr). Caerphilly established a number of records, notably those by Brett Davey, a superb all-round full-back. His 393 points for the season passed the 285 by Neil Jenkins; and 42 points against Rumney was the most in a match (previous record, 39, by Colin Stephens for Llanelli at Newport). Caerphilly became the first team to aggregate 1000 points in a season with 1090 (previous best 944 by Pontypridd). This in 30 games because the division was increased from 12 to 16 teams. Caerphilly also collected most team tries for a season with 137, surpassing the record of 136 by Llanelli.

At the other end of the First Division, it was a time of tension and turmoil for Pontypool, once the most feared of Welsh clubs. They languished at the foot of the table for seven months and relegation appeared inescapable. Then, in the last-match shoot-out for the dreaded drop, they scraped a 14-8 home verdict against University of Wales Institute, Cardiff. Player/coach David Bishop, aged 37, found the vigour of youth for a final time in the hour of greatest need and lasted an exhausting mental and physical ordeal in the heat of a glorious May day. So often a hero of immense proportions in days of yore, he inspired yet again. There were emotional tears at the end. Thank you, Dai Bish, for saving a great club from the horrors of the unthinkable plunge.

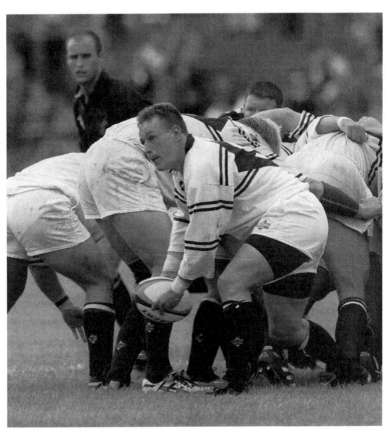

Swansea's scrum-half Andy Booth kept the All Whites moving forward throughout a successful season.

THE WRU LEAGUES
1997-98

* – Two points deducted

Premier Div.	P	W	D	L	T	Bon	F	A	Pts
Swansea	14	11	2	1	68	11	569	263	46
Cardiff	14	10	1	3	59	9	469	297	40
Pontypridd	14	8	2	4	55	9	441	299	35
Ebbw Vale	14	8	0	6	33	3	302	375	27
Neath	14	6	1	7	41	4	351	430	23
Llanelli	14	5	2	7	44	5	370	331	22
Bridgend	14	3	2	9	33	1	276	523	12
Newport *	14	0	0	14	23	2	224	484	0

Division 1	P	W	D	L	T	Bon	F	A	Pts
Caerphilly	30	27	0	3	137	18	1090	501	99
Aberavon	30	20	2	8	104	12	738	530	74
Treorchy	30	19	0	11	115	16	840	566	73
Bonymaen	30	17	0	13	86	9	656	503	60
Dunvant	30	17	1	12	87	6	723	721	58
Merthyr **	30	14	4	12	91	8	639	592	54
Llandovery	30	14	0	16	88	12	690	648	54
Rumney	30	15	1	14	94	7	710	755	53
Abertillery	30	15	1	14	66	4	559	601	50
Newbridge	30	14	0	16	61	8	554	576	50
Cross Keys **	30	14	1	15	79	6	674	700	49
S Wales Police	30	10	1	19	93	11	665	707	42
Blackwood	30	12	0	18	72	4	546	770	40
Pontypool	30	11	1	18	73	4	604	856	38
UWIC	30	8	0	22	87	11	655	858	35
Maesteg	30	7	0	23	59	2	531	990	23

** Cross Keys v Merthyr match abandoned but result understood to stand at time of going to press

Division 2	P	W	D	L	T	Bon	F	A	Pts
Tredegar	22	18	0	4	80	14	563	255	68
Tondu	22	17	1	4	74	13	524	265	65
Whitland	22	16	2	4	76	14	557	248	64
Tenby Utd	22	13	0	9	69	7	498	405	46
Pyle	22	10	1	11	43	6	390	426	37
Ystradgynlais	22	10	0	12	46	5	371	380	35
Narberth	22	9	1	12	49	5	404	392	33
Llanharan	22	7	3	12	50	3	368	468	27
Mountain Ash	22	8	0	14	32	0	314	511	24
Kenfig Hill	22	7	1	14	40	2	354	527	24
St Peter's	22	6	0	16	52	5	380	586	23
Abercynon	22	6	1	15	37	1	348	608	20

Division 3	P	W	D	L	T	Bon	F	A	Pts
Llantrisant	22	18	1	3	79	13	615	273	68
Rhymney	22	16	0	6	81	14	576	305	62
Oakdale	22	14	2	6	72	9	479	326	53
Ystrad Rhondda	22	14	0	8	65	6	446	401	48
Blaina	22	11	1	10	74	9	512	430	43
Glamorgan W.	22	11	0	11	61	9	455	389	42
Felinfoel	22	12	0	10	74	5	590	531	41
Carmarthen Q.	22	10	1	11	67	8	522	398	39
Builth Wells	22	8	1	13	54	6	371	436	31
Kidwelly	22	6	0	16	51	4	332	489	22
Glynneath	22	6	0	16	41	2	326	635	20
Penarth	22	3	0	19	38	1	324	935	10

Division 4	P	W	D	L	T	Bon	F	A	Pts
Vardre	22	18	0	4	59	7	483	282	61
Gilfach Goch	22	17	0	5	78	10	526	268	61
Carmarthen Ath	22	15	2	5	64	11	513	284	58
Pencoed	22	13	1	8	56	5	476	292	45
Seven Sisters	22	11	2	9	54	7	400	430	42
Garndiffaith	22	11	0	11	52	5	387	418	38
Abergavenny	22	10	1	11	48	5	404	352	36
Aberavon Quins	22	10	0	12	51	3	409	418	33
Tonmawr	22	8	2	12	50	5	430	393	31
Bedwas *	22	6	2	14	53	6	378	572	24
Resolven	22	7	1	14	35	0	296	520	22
Tumble	22	0	1	21	35	2	272	745	3

PROP MADDEN'S MAGIC MOMENT

SWALEC CUP 1997-98
23 May, Ashton Gate, Bristol

Llanelli 19 (1G 4PG) **Ebbw Vale 12** (3PG 1DG)

Martyn Madden's magic moment saw him score the winning try for Llanelli seven minutes from the end. Martyn who? Indeed, it may be asked. Few people in Wales recognised the name of the distinctive 18st tighthead prop, a former Cardiff Youth No 8 and Pontypool player, who was on loan to Llanelli from Penzance/ Newlyn because the Stradey club had prop problems. It was only his third appearance for the Scarlets after crossing for two tries on debut against Newport and little did anyone, least of all the 23-year-old Madden, imagine that even greater glory awaited him.

It was 12-all and Ebbw Vale must have been contemplating extra time at the unusual venue of Bristol City's Ashton Gate (because the WRU new Millennium Stadium was in process of construction). First Chris Wyatt and then Neil Boobyer (who dropped the ball in the act of diving over the line) had gone close to scoring Llanelli tries, but defences mostly ruled supreme. There were four penalty goals by Craig Warlow, as the Scarlets three times snatched the lead; and three penalty goals and a high, floated dropped goal by Byron Hayward for Ebbw. Certainly not champagne stuff for some 16,000 onlookers.

Then Rupert Moon injected the game with his typical brand of opportunism. Always a tricky customer, he decided to venture on a daring voyage of discovery through a line-out. 'I was on hand for "Big Nose" to give me the ball and I just kept going,' grinned Madden, thundering some 25 yards to become one of the few props to claim the princely prize of a cup final try. Warlow added the goal points superbly from the touchline and Llanelli, in their 13th final, had taken the cup for a 10th time in 27 years.

'We won without the ball,' reflected Llanelli captain Robin McBryde. 'We had to make sure we tackled everything.' Ebbw's Tongan full-back, Suia Taumalolo, full of adventure as usual, was voted man-of-the-match for the Lloyd Lewis Memorial Award after the most spectacular long, slashing break of the game. Chay Billen's precision in the line-out was another pleasing feature for the losers as they reduced Llanelli's possession to a trickle. But Madden's mad rush for the corner eclipsed all other emotions and Llanelli had saved their dismal season right on the bell.

Llanelli: D Williams; W T Proctor, N Boobyer, N G Davies, G Evans; C Warlow, R H StJ B Moon; A Jones, R C McBryde (*capt*), M Madden, V Cooper,

M J Voyle, C Wyatt, H Jenkins, I Jones *Substitutions:* A Gibbs for Wyatt (62 mins); M E Wintle for Boobyer (63 mins)
Scorers *Try:* Madden *Conversion:* Warlow *Penalty Goals:* Warlow (4)
Ebbw Vale: S Taumalolo; A Harries, J Hawker, J Funnell, L Woodard; B I Hayward, D Llewellyn; A Phillips, L Phillips, M Wilson, C Billen, K Faletau, R G Collins, M A Jones, K P Jones *(capt) Substitutions:* J Strange for Hawker (71 mins); S Jones for L Phillips (72 mins)
Scorers *Penalty Goals:* Hayward (3) *Dropped Goal:* Hayward
Referee C Thomas (Bryncoch)

Earlier Rounds

It was Taumalolo Day at Pontypridd in the semi-final tie that brought Ebbw Vale their record win by 44-10 against Newport. The attacker many considered tackle-proof in open spaces – or even a glimmer of space – swept away for three sparkling tries. Lennie Woodard snapped up the other two and Hayward decorated the points with a pretty drop-shot while providing 19 goal points. Seven Sisters, the first village team to reach the semi-finals, snatched the lead three times at the Gnoll before their defence crumbled during the closing 10 minutes and allowed Llanelli in for a further five tries. Eventually, it was 10 tries and victory by 61-16 for the Scarlets; but Seven can feel proud of their try by Ian Watts, conversion and two penalty goals by Andrew James and a smooth Hywel Evans dropped goal.

Ebbw Vale's path to the final was highlighted by knocking out Cardiff, the holders, by 24-9 in the sixth round, and then defeating Swansea, the previous season's losing finalists, by 27-13 in the quarter-final stage. This after losing both league fixtures to these high-flying title chasers. Swansea had crushed Ebbw Vale by 63-3 a month before their tie, though that was at St Helen's, and Ebbw were fortunate enough to enjoy home advantage in three of their four ties. Cardiff failed to score a try in their tie there and Swansea managed just one by prop John Evans.

Llanelli's most difficult tussle was at Merthyr in the fifth round, where they scraped an 8-0 verdict. Nigel Davies scored the try. Cardiff opened with a glut of tries when the Premier Division teams entered the tourney in the fourth round. There were 14 tries in victory by 82-14 against Abercarn. Then Lee Jarvis kicked 22 points at Newbridge and the score was 62-6. Then it was the end of the line at Ebbw Vale!

The end was swifter for Bridgend: in their opening match they went out by 24-21 at Garndiffaith. It was the first time that Bridgend had lost a cup-tie to a small team and giant-killers Garn, from the Fourth Division, went on to put out First Division Rumney and then Second Division Llanharan. Perhaps there was a touch of irony that it was fellow Fourth Division side Seven Sisters who stopped Garn's gallant gallop by a cruel 39-0 margin.

Pontypridd were considered one of the favourites, but that fact did not impress Newport outside-half Shaun Connor and he dropped a goal five minutes from the end at Rodney Parade to put out Ponty by a whisker at 29-27. Connor contributed 19 points to ease some of the pain of a disastrous league season.

RESULTS

Third round

Abercarn 34, Blaengarw 3; Abercwmboi 17, Newtown 15; Abercynon 56, Cowbridge 5; Bala 10, Morriston 34; Beddau w/o against Glais; Bedwas 20, Pill Harriers 17; Builth Wells 37, Abergavenny 6; Bynea 13, Penygraig 21; Carmarthen Athletic 7, Llanharan 26; Carmarthen Quins 36, Cwmgwrach 15; Cilfynydd 17, Gilfach Goch 37; Dinas Powys 14, Aberavon Quins 27; Garndiffaith 14, Oakdale 6; Glamorgan Wanderers 18, Cwmllynfell 25; Glynneath 16, Llantrisant 13; Kidwelly 30, Pencoed 21; Llanishen 28, Cwmgors 44; Maesteg Celtic 10, Pontyclun 28; Mountain Ash 35, Crumlin 10; Nantymoel 15, Croesyceiliog 28; Narberth 19, Brynmawr 16; Neath Athletic 23, Trebanos 8; Newport Saracens 5, Maesteg Quins 13; Old Illtydians 12, Blaina 51; Porthcawl 27, Birchgrove 10; Pwllheli 47, Vardre 11; Pyle 29, Rhymney 13; Rhigos 15, Kenfig Hill 25; Senghenydd 17, Felinfoel 33; Seven Sisters 38, Tycroes 8; Tenby Utd 9, Whitland 29; Tondu 33, St Peter's 25; Tonyrefail 34, Penarth 12; Tredegar 41, Ystrad Rhondda 10; Treherbert 35, Aberdare 8; Trimsaran 10, Newcastle Emlyn 8; Tylorstown 25, Chepstow 21; Wrexham 27, Tonmawr 18; Ynysybwl 60, Llandudno 12; Ystradgynlais 17, Resolven 9

Fourth round

Aberavon 26, Bedwas 10; Aberavon Quins 30, Felinfoel 17; Abercynon 7, Caerphilly 44; Beddau 14, UWIC 35; Blackwood 11, Maesteg 29; Cardiff 82, Abercarn 14; Carmarthen Quins 13, Llanharan 24; Cross Keys 67, Pontyclun 17; Cwmgors 22, Porthcawl 0; Cwmllynfell 13, Neath 32; Ebbw Vale 57, Kidwelly 14; Garndiffaith 24, Bridgend 21; Gilfach Goch 5, Seven Sisters 6; Glynneath 11, Merthyr 43; Kenfig Hill 8, Treorchy 62; Llanelli 21, Dunvant 16; Maesteg Quins 12, Llandovery 55; Morriston 16, Tredegar 17; Mountain Ash 22, Neath Athletic

12; Narberth 30, Wrexham 16; Newbridge 50, Abercwmboi 0; Newport 58, Pwllheli 16; Penygraig 29, Blaina 22; Pontypool 18, Abertillery 28; Pontypridd 43, Bonymaen 3; Swansea 25, Whitland 12; Tondu 26, Pyle 10; Tonyrefail 24, Croesyceiliog 21; Trimsaran 0, Builth Wells 18; Tylorstown 3, S Wales Police 32; Ynysybwl 15, Treherbert 13; Ystradgynlais 31, Rumney 32

Fifth round

Aberavon 35, Maesteg 15; Abertillery 15, Aberavon Quins 10; Builth Wells 23, Narberth 17; Cwmgors 0, Caerphilly 55; Garndiffaith 17, Rumney 11; Llandovery 17, Neath 36; Merthyr 0, Llanelli 8; Newbridge 6, Cardiff 62; Penygraig 3, Tredegar 8; Pontypridd 42, Treorchy 7; Seven Sisters 12, Cross Keys 9; S Wales Police 8, Newport 26; Tondu 13, Swansea 54; Tonyrefail 20, Ebbw Vale 60; UWIC 53, Mountain Ash 29; Ynysybwl 19, Llanharan 27

Sixth round

Abertillery 24, Pontypridd 33; Ebbw Vale 24, Cardiff 9; Garndiffaith 19, Llanharan 14; Llanelli 35, Caerphilly 18; Neath 41, Builth Wells 0; Swansea 66, Aberavon 12; Tredegar 11, Seven Sisters 15; UWIC 15, Newport 69

Quarter-finals

Ebbw Vale 27, Swansea 13; Llanelli 40, Neath 17; Newport 29, Pontypridd 27; Seven Sisters 39, Garndiffaith 0

Semi-finals

Ebbw Vale 44, Newport 10 (at Sardis Road, Pontypridd); Llanelli 61, Seven Sisters 16 (at The Gnoll, Neath)

Final (at Ashton Gate, Bristol)
Llanelli 19, Ebbw Vale 12

Previous finals
(all at Cardiff Arms Park)
1972 Neath 15, Llanelli 9
1973 Llanelli 30, Cardiff 7
1974 Llanelli 12, Aberavon 10

1975	Llanelli 15, Aberavon 6	1987	Cardiff 16, Swansea 15
1976	Llanelli 16, Swansea 4	1988	Llanelli 28, Neath 13
1977	Newport 16, Cardiff 15	1989	Neath 14, Llanelli 13
1978	Swansea 13, Newport 9	1990	Neath 16, Bridgend 10
1979	Bridgend 18, Pontypridd 12	1991	Llanelli 24, Pontypool 9
1980	Bridgend 15, Swansea 9	1992	Llanelli 16, Swansea 7
1981	Cardiff 14, Bridgend 6	1993	Llanelli 21, Neath 18
1982*	Cardiff 12, Bridgend 12	1994	Cardiff 15, Llanelli 8
1983	Pontypool 18, Swansea 6	1995	Swansea 17, Pontypridd 12
1984	Cardiff 24, Neath 19	1996	Pontypridd 29, Neath 22
1985	Llanelli 15, Cardiff 14	1997	Cardiff 33, Swansea 26
1986	Cardiff 28, Newport 21	* Winners on 'most tries' rule

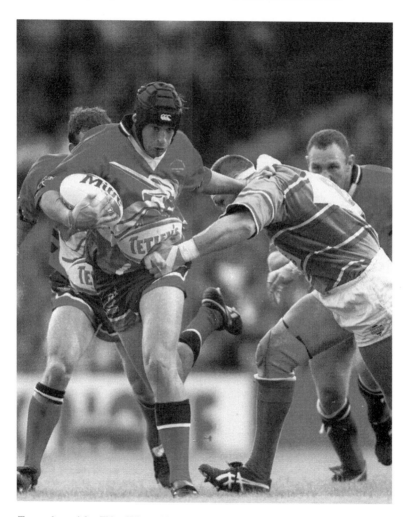

Try as they might, Ebbw Vale could not quite hang on to Llanelli in the 1998 SWALEC Cup final, Iwan Jones (Llanelli) here shrugging off a challenge.

241

CONSOLATION FOR PONTYPRIDD

WRU CHALLENGE TROPHY 1997-98
28 March, Sardis Road, Pontypridd

Pontypridd 15 (5PG) **Cardiff 10** (1G 1PG)

The reduction of the WRU Premier Division to eight teams was a disaster with so few fixtures. A Challenge Trophy was instituted by the WRU to try to compensate for lost gates. It failed lamentably to interest the public at large, though there was a goodly turn-out to see Pontypridd defeat Cardiff in an evening final arranged for the weekend between Wales's Five Nations engagements with Ireland and France.

Victory for Pontypridd provided some consolation for their disappointments in the European Cup and the Welsh league. Neil Jenkins's boot supplied all of Ponty's points. He set the champions off with two penalties before his Wales squad understudy Lee Jarvis, who had started the match on Cardiff's bench, scored a cracking try within five minutes of coming on as a substitute. Jarvis converted and kicked a penalty a couple of minutes later to put Cardiff 10-6 ahead after half-an-hour's play, but two more Jenkins penalties restored the home side's lead before the interval.

The second half was overshadowed by an injury to Welsh captain Robert Howley. He twisted his left ankle so severely that it was doubtful whether he would be fit in time to lead Wales against France at Wembley, adding strength to the argument that this competition was a pointless waste of time and money for players, spectators and clubs. A fifth Jenkins penalty in the 73rd minute was the only score of the second spell.

Pontypridd: A Barnard; G Wyatt, S Lewis, D R James, D Manley; N R Jenkins (*capt*), P John; A Griffiths, A E Lamerton, M Griffiths, W S Roy, S Bundy, G Lewis, D L M McIntosh, M E Williams *Substitutions:* G Prosser for Bundy (56 mins); M Lloyd for G Lewis (69 mins)
Scorer *Penalty Goals:* Jenkins (5)
Cardiff: C Morgan; G Thomas, M R Hall, L B Davies, S D Hill; R P Ross, R Howley; A L P Lewis, J M Humphries (*capt*), L Mustoe, T Rees, J Tait, G Kacala, E W Lewis, J Ringer *Substitutions:* L Jarvis for Ross (23 mins); W J L Thomas for Morgan (50 mins); J Hewlett for Howley (55 mins); S Williams for Ringer (temp 23-33 mins) and for Lewis (64 mins); D Jones for Tait (66 mins); S C John for Lewis (69 mins)
Scorer *Try:* Jarvis *Conversion:* Jarvis *Penalty Goal:* Jarvis
Referee W D Bevan (Clydach)

WALES TO NORTH AMERICA 1997

THE TOURING PARTY

Manager T James   **Coach** K Bowring   **Assistant Coach** D John
Captain RG Jones

Full-backs: KA Morgan (Pontypridd), MJ Back (Bridgend)

Threequarters: WT Proctor (Llanelli), LB Davies (Cardiff), G Thomas (Bridgend),
NK Walker (Cardiff), G Wyatt (Pontypridd), N Boobyer (Llanelli), J Lewis
(Pontypridd), DR James (Bridgend)

Half-backs: AC Thomas (Swansea), L Jarvis (Cardiff), P John (Pontypridd),
AP Moore (Richmond)

Forwards: CD Loader (Swansea), IM Buckett (Swansea), CT Anthony (Swansea),
RC McBryde (Llanelli), GR Jenkins (Swansea), L Mustoe (Cardiff), *A Griffiths
(Pontypridd), GO Llewellyn (Harlequins), SJ Moore (Swansea), MJ Voyle
(Llanelli), N Watkins (Neath), C Wyatt (Llanelli), A Gibbs (Newbridge),
N Thomas (Bath), RC Appleyard (Swansea), SM Williams (Cardiff), RG Jones
(Cardiff)

* *Replacement on tour*

TOUR RECORD

All matches   Played 6   Won 6   Points for 289   Against 104
International matches   Played 3   Won 3   Points for 86   Against 68

SCORING DETAILS

All matches   **International matches**
For: 43T   25C   8PG   289 Pts   For: 11T   5C   7PG   86 Pts
Against: 10T   9C   11PG   1DG   104 Pts   Against: 7T   6C   6PG   1DG   68 Pts

MATCH DETAILS

1997	OPPONENTS	VENUE	RESULT
1 July	Southern RFU	Charlotte	W 94-3
5 July	USA	Wilmington	W 30-20
8 July	USA Development XV	San Francisco	W 55-23
12 July	USA	San Francisco	W 28-23
15 July	Ontario	Hamilton	W 54-10
19 July	CANADA	Toronto	W 28-25

MATCH 1   1 July, Davidson College, Charlotte

Southern RFU 3 (1DG)   **Wales XV 94** (12G 2T)
Southern RFU: G Miller (*capt*); A Blom, D Peyroux, A Smuts, S Ryan;
S DeKoch, T Liddle; J Venus, S Nault, D Watts, G Bradley, P Dembowski,
D Walsh, C Young, G Schor *Substitution:* T Faulkner for Liddle (42 mins)
Scorer *Dropped goal:* DeKoch
Wales XV: Morgan; Wyatt, Boobyer, G Thomas, James; Jarvis, Moore; Buckett,
McBryde, Anthony, Moore, Llewellyn, Thomas, Wyatt, G Jones (*capt*)
Substitutions: Watkins for Llewellyn (41 mins); Appleyard for G Jones (43 mins); G
Jenkins for McBryde (65 mins); A Thomas for G Thomas (74 mins)
Scorers *Tries:* G Wyatt (4), James (3), Morgan (2), Jarvis (2), Moore, C Wyatt,
G Thomas *Conversions:* Jarvis (12)
Referee E Todd (California RU)

MATCH 2   5 July, University of North Carolina, Wilmington   1st Test

USA 20 (2G 2PG)   WALES 30 (2G 2PG 2T)

USA: C Morrow (Gentlemen of Aspen); V Anitoni (San Mateo), T Takau (Gentlemen of Aspen), M Scharrenberg (Reading, England), B Hightower (Gentlemen of Aspen); M Alexander (Denver Barbarians), A Bachelet (Reading, England); C Lippert (OMBAC, San Diego), TW Billups (Harlequins, England), R Lehner (Hamilton, S Africa), D Hodges (OMBAC, San Diego), L Gross Harlequins, England), J Walker (Gentlemen of Aspen), D Lyle (Bath, England) (*capt*), J Wilkerson (Pontypridd, Wales) *Substitutions:* A Saulala (San Mateo) for Scharrenberg (39 mins); S Allen (OMBAC, San Diego) for Billups (40 mins); M McLeod (OMBAC, San Diego) for Lyle (50 mins); Billups for Allen (65 mins); K Shuman (Penn State University) for Morrow (77 mins)
Scorers *Tries:* Anitoni, Takau *Conversions:* Alexander (2)
Penalty Goals: Alexander (2)
WALES: Morgan; Proctor, Davies, G Thomas, Walker; A Thomas, John; Loader, G Jenkins, Mustoe, Llewellyn, Voyle, A Gibbs, S Williams, G Jones (*capt*)
Substitutions: Anthony for Loader (63 mins); N Thomas for S Williams (75 mins)
Scorers *Tries:* A Thomas (2), Walker, G Jones *Conversions:* A Thomas (2)
Penalty Goals: A Thomas (2)
Referee KW McCartney (Scotland)

MATCH 3   8 July, Balboa Park, San Francisco

USA Development XV 23 (2G 3PG)   **Wales XV 55** (5G 4T)
USA Development XV: D Kennedy; C Curtis, M Ortiz, K Shuman, C LaBounty; E Flecton, K Dalzell; T Giuntini, K Khasigian, M Calcagno, K Quinn, G Gawronski, P Vogel, S Yungling (*capt*), J Holtzmann
Substitutions: E Reed for Gawronski (63 mins); J McBride for Calcagno (63 mins); W Whitko for Kennedy (78 mins)
Scorers *Tries:* Shuman, Holtzmann *Conversions:* Flecton (2)
Penalty Goals: Flecton (3)
Wales XV: Back; G Wyatt, Boobyer, J Lewis, James; Jarvis, Moore (*capt*); Buckett, McBryde, Anthony, Moore, Watkins, N Thomas, C Wyatt, Appleyard
Substitutions: Voyle for C Wyatt (50 mins); Walker for Boobyer (74 mins)
Scorers *Tries:* Moore (2), Back (2), J Lewis (2), James (2), Appleyard
Conversions: Jarvis (5)
Referee D Mew (Canada RFU)

MATCH 4   12 July, Balboa Park, San Francisco   2nd Test

USA 23 (2G 3PG)   WALES 28 (1G 2PG 3T)

USA: C Morrow (Gentlemen of Aspen); V Anitoni (San Mateo), T Takau (Gentlemen of Aspen), M Scharrenberg (Reading, England), B Hightower (Gentlemen of Aspen); M Alexander (Denver Barbarians), A Bachelet (Reading, England); C Lippert (OMBAC, San Diego), TW Billups (Harlequins, England), R Lehner (Hamilton, S Africa), D Hodges (OMBAC, San Diego), L Gross (Harlequins, England), D Lyle (Bath, England) (*capt*), J Walker (Gentlemen of Aspen), J Wilkerson (Pontypridd, Wales) *Substitutions:* S Yungling (University of California) for Wilkerson (49 mins); S Allen (OMBAC, San Diego) for Billups (56 mins); A Saulala (San Mateo) for Takau (77 mins); M Sika (Rhinoes) for Hightower (79 mins)

Scorers *Tries:* Walker, Anitoni *Conversions:* Alexander (2)
Penalty Goals: Alexander (3)
WALES: Morgan; Proctor, Davies, G Thomas, Walker; A Thomas, John; Buckett,
McBryde, Mustoe, Llewellyn, Voyle, A Gibbs, N Thomas, G Jones (*capt*)
Substitutions: S Williams for G Jones (41 mins); Anthony for Buckett (77 mins)
Scorers *Tries:* Proctor (3), A Thomas *Conversion:* A Thomas
Penalty Goals: A Thomas (2)
Referee CB Muir (Scotland)

MATCH 5   15 July, Mohawk Park, Hamilton

Ontario 10 (1G 1PG)   **Wales XV 54** (3G 1PG 6T)
Ontario: J Pagano; J Nichols, J Hall, A Armstrong, M Cahoon; S Pettigrew,
S Armstrong; M Jacques, S Hendry, J Ashley, B Traynor, B McCarthy,
G Musgrave, P Ross, D Swindle *Substitutions:* G Miller for S Armstrong (56
mins); A Marshall for Ashley (67 mins)
Scorers *Try:* Pagano *Conversion:* Pettigrew *Penalty Goal:* Pettigrew
Wales XV: Back; G Wyatt, Boobyer, J Lewis, James; Jarvis, Moore (*capt*); Buckett,
Jenkins, Anthony, Moore, Watkins, C Wyatt, S Williams, Appleyard *Substitutions:*
Griffiths for Buckett (60 mins); McBryde for G Jenkins (70 mins)
Scorers *Tries:* Wyatt (3), Jarvis (2), James (2), Boobyer, Appleyard *Conversions:*
Jarvis (3) *Penalty Goal:* Jarvis
Referee K Hanley (USRFU)

MATCH 6   19 July, Fletcher's Fields, Markham,
Toronto   Test Match

CANADA 25 (2G 1PG 1DG 1T)   WALES 28 (2G 3PG 1T)

CANADA: RP Ross (James Bay); W Stanley (Vancouver Kats), DC Lougheed
(Balmy Beach), S Bryan (Balmy Beach), DS Stewart (UBC Old Boys); GL Rees
(Wasps, England)(*capt*), JD Graf (UBC Old Boys); EA Evans (IBM, Japan),
K Morgan (Ajax Wanderers), RGA Snow (Newport, Wales), J Tait (Barrie &
CCSD), M James (Perpignan, France), AJ Charron (Moseley, England),
M Schmid (Abbotsford), J Hutchinson (IBM, Japan) *Substitutions:* ME Cardinal
(James Bay) for Morgan (40 mins); R Bice (Vancouver Rowing Club) for Evans
(53 mins)
Scorers *Tries:* Schmid (2), Ross *Conversions:* Rees (2) *Penalty Goal:* Rees
Dropped Goal: Ross
WALES: Morgan; Proctor, Davies, G Thomas, Walker; A Thomas, John (*capt*);
Buckett, G Jenkins, Mustoe, Moore, Voyle, A Gibbs, S Williams, Appleyard
Substitutions: N Thomas for A Gibbs (64 mins); Anthony for Buckett (75 mins)
Scorers *Tries:* Proctor, G Thomas, Davies *Conversions:* A Thomas (2)
Penalty Goals: A Thomas (3)
Referee S Borsani (Argentina)

ROMANIA TO WALES 1997

THE TOURING PARTY

Manager V Moraru   **Assistant Manager** S Fuica
Coaches M Paraschiv, A Achim   **Captain** T Brinza

Full-backs: P Mitu (Steaua Bucharest), V Maftei (Cluj University)

Threequarters: L Colceriu (Steaua Bucharest), C Haldan (Dinamo Bucharest),
I Rotaru (Dinamo Bucharest), G Solomie (Timisoara), G Brezoianu (Timisoara),
R Gontineac (Pau, France)

Half-backs: S Guranescu (Dinamo Bucharest), M Iacob (Dinamo Bucharest),
I Tofan (Coanig Giugiu)

Forwards: G Vlad (Narbonne, France), D Nicolae (Steaua Bucharest), C Stan
(Dinamo Bucharest), A Salageanu (Dinamo Bucharest), C Popescu (Timisoara),
M Radoi (Dinamo Bucharest), C Branescu (Albertville, France), V Nedelcu
(Dinamo Bucharest), M Dragomir (Dinamo Bucharest), I Doja (Dinamo
Bucharest), C Draguceanu (Steaua Bucharest), F Corodeanu (Steaua Bucharest),
E Septar (Farul Constanta), I Ruxanda (Farul Constanta), O Slusariuc (Dinamo
Bucharest), T Brinza (Narbonne, France)

TOUR RECORD

All matches   Played 2   Lost 2   Points for 42   Against 106
International matches   Played 1   Lost 1   Points for 21   Against 70

SCORING DETAILS

All matches					**International matches**				
For:	5T	4C	3PG	42 Pts	For:	2T	1C	3PG	21 Pts
Against:	16T	7C	4PG	106 Pts	Against:	11T	6C	1PG	70 Pts

MATCH DETAILS

1997	OPPONENTS	VENUE	RESULT
26 Aug	Wales A	Pontypridd	L 21-36
30 Aug	WALES	Wrexham	L 21-70

MATCH 1   26 August, Sardis Road, Pontypridd

Wales A 36 (1G 3PG 4T)   **Romanians 21** (3G)
Wales A: L Davies (Swansea); G Wyatt (Pontypridd), DR James (Pontypridd),
J Lewis (Pontypridd), NK Walker (Cardiff); M Lewis (Bridgend), Rhodri Jones
(Swansea), IM Buckett (Swansea), RC McBryde (Llanelli), CT Anthony
(Swansea), GO Llewellyn (Harlequins)(*capt*), N Watkins (Neath), A Gibbs
(Llanelli), C Wyatt (Llanelli), ME Williams (Pontypridd) *Substitutions:* D Case
(Neath) for L Davies (64 mins); M Lloyd (Pontypridd) for Watkins (73 mins)
Scorers *Tries:* M Williams (2), Wyatt (2), Llewellyn *Conversion:* L Davies
Penalty Goals: L Davies (3)
Romanians: Maftei; Colceriu, Gontineac, Solomie, Rotaru; Guranescu, Iacob;
Nicolae, Radoi, Salageanu, Branescu, Nedelcu, Corodeanu, Slusariuc (*capt*),
Septar *Substitutions:* Mitu for Maftei (8 mins); Vlad for Nicolae (37 mins); Brinza
for Branescu (53 mins); Stan for Salageanu (53 mins); Ruxanda for Slusariuc
(75 mins)
Scorers *Tries:* Solomie (2), Gontineac *Conversions:* Guranescu (3)
Referee C White (England)

MATCH 2   30 August, The Racecourse Ground, Wrexham
Test Match

WALES 70 (6G 1PG 5T)   ROMANIA 21 (1G 3PG 1T)

WALES: KA Morgan (Pontypridd); WT Proctor (Llanelli), AG Bateman (Richmond), LB Davies (Cardiff), G Thomas (Bridgend); AC Thomas (Swansea), P John (Pontypridd); CD Loader (Swansea), BH Williams (Richmond), D Young (Cardiff), SJ Moore (Moseley), MA Rowley (Pontypridd), RC Appleyard (Swansea), N Thomas (Bath), RG Jones (Cardiff)*(capt)* *Substitutions:* L Mustoe (Cardiff) for Young (40 mins); NK Walker (Cardiff) for Proctor (66 mins); SM Williams (Cardiff) for Rowley (68 mins); L Jarvis (Cardiff) for A Thomas (78 mins)
Scorers *Tries:* Bateman (2), L Davies (2), A Thomas (2), P John, Morgan, Walker, B Williams, S Williams *Conversions:* A Thomas (5), Jarvis
Penalty Goal: A Thomas
ROMANIA: Maftei; Colceriu, Gontineac, Solomie, Rotaru; Guranescu, Iacob; Vlad, Radoi, Salageanu, Brinza *(capt)*, Nedelcu, Corodeanu, Draguceanu, Septar *Substitutions:* Stan for Salageanu (48 mins); Mitu for Maftei (50 mins); Ruxanda for Septar (75 mins)
Scorers *Tries:* Draguceanu, Rotaru *Conversion:* Guranescu
Penalty Goals: Guranescu (3)
Referee DI Ramage (Scotland)

TONGA TO BRITAIN 1997

THE TOURING PARTY

Manager S Kolokihakaufisi   **Technical Director** P Kingsley-Jones
Coach L Vikalani   **Captain** D Briggs

Full-backs: K Tonga (Fasi), S Taumalolo (Ebbw Vale, Wales)

Threequarters: M Mafi (Workington RLC), S Faka'osi'folau (Toa Ko Ma'afu), S Mafile'o (Northland, New Zealand), F Tatafu (Fasi), P Tanginoa (Siutaka), S Lotima (Kolofa'ou), SJ Ngauamo (Harlequins, England), *D Tiueti (Bristol, England)

Half-backs: S Tai (Fasi), V Afeaki (Fasi), M Vunipola (Toa Ko Ma'afu), SM Tu'ipulotu (Kolomotua)

Forwards: K Tu'ipulotu (Toa Ko Ma'afu), L Katoa (Siutaka), K Ahota'e'iloa (Lavengemaile), H Pohiva (Felenite), T Matakaionga (Nelson Bays, New Zealand), S Latu (Natal, South Africa), V Vaki (Lavengemaile), S Havili (Auckland B, New Zealand), M Molitika (Toa Ko Ma'afu), K Faletau (Ebbw Vale, Wales), V Ma'asi (Fasi), S Hafoka (Siutaka), L Maka (Siutaka), H Lavaka (Fasi), N Ta'u (Police), D Briggs (Waikato, New Zealand)

* *Replacement on tour*

TOUR RECORD

All matches   Played 12   Won 5   Drawn 1   Lost 6   Points for 269   Against 337
International match   Played 1   Lost 1   Points for 12   Against 46

SCORING DETAILS

All matches					International match				
For:	35T	23C	15PG	1DG	269 Pts	For:	2T	1C		12 Pts
Against:	41T	21C	29PG	1DG	337 Pts	Against:	6T	2C	4PG	46 Pts

MATCH DETAILS

1997	OPPONENTS	VENUE	RESULT
26 Oct	Redruth President's XV	Redruth	W 64-9
29 Oct	Bristol	Bristol	L 15-35
2 Nov	Edinburgh	Edinburgh	L 14-26
5 Nov	Oxford University	Oxford	W 31-16
9 Nov	Bridgend	Bridgend	W 21-18
12 Nov	Bath	Bath	W 29-13
16 Nov	WALES	Swansea	L 12-46
18 Nov	Blackheath	Blackheath	D 20-20
20 Nov	Sale	Sale	W 26-14
23 Nov	West Hartlepool	West Hartlepool	L 14-28
26 Nov	Leeds	Leeds	L 15-29
30 Nov	Saracens	Watford	L 8-83

MATCH 1   26 October, Recreation Ground, Redruth

Redruth President's XV 9 (3PG)   **Tongans 64** (7G 3T)
Redruth President's XV: Scorer *Penalty Goals:* Thirlby (3)
Tongans: Scorers *Tries:* Mafi (2), Tai (2), Tatafu (2), Fakaosi'folau, Matakaionga, Molitika, Pohiva *Conversions:* Tonga (7)

MATCH 2   29 October, Memorial Ground, Bristol

Bristol 35 (5G)   **Tongans 15** (1G 1PG 1T)
Bristol: Scorers *Tries:* Hull, Breeze, Brownrigg, Tiueti, Bennett
Conversions: Armstrong (5)
Tongans: Scorers *Tries:* Faka'osifolau (2) *Conversion:* Tonga *Penalty Goal:* Tonga

MATCH 3   2 November, Edinburgh

Edinburgh 26 (1G 2PG 1DG 2T)   **Tongans 14** (2G)
Edinburgh: Scorers *Tries:* Burns, Clark, Reed *Conversion:* Ross
Penalty Goals: Hodge (2) *Dropped Goal:* Ross
Tongans: Scorers *Tries:* Tanginoa (2) *Conversions:* Tonga (2)

MATCH 4   5 November, Iffley Road, Oxford

Oxford University 16 (1G 3PG)   **Tongans 31** (1G 8PG)
Oxford Univ: Scorers *Try:* Kelaher *Conversion:* Kelaher
Penalty Goals: Kelaher (3)
Tongans: Scorers *Try:* K Tu'ipulotu *Conversion:* Tonga *Penalty Goals:* Tonga (8)

MATCH 5   9 November, Brewery Field, Bridgend

Bridgend 18 (1G 2PG 1T)   **Tongans 21** (1G 3PG 1T)
Bridgend: Scorers *Tries:* Boobyer, Greenaway *Conversion:* Cull
Penalty Goals: Cull (2)
Tongans: Scorers *Tries:* Faka'osi'folau, S Tu'ipolotu *Conversion:* Tonga
Penalty Goals: Tonga (3)

MATCH 6   12 November, Recreation Ground, Bath

Bath 13 (1DG 2T)   **Tongans 29** (3G 1DG 1T)
Bath: Scorers *Tries:* Tsimba (2) *Dropped Goal:* Balshaw
Tongans: Scorers *Tries:* Faka'osi'folau, Lotima, Mafile'o, Tiueti
Conversions: Tai (2), Tonga *Dropped Goal:* Lotima

MATCH 7   16 November, St Helen's, Swansea   Test Match

WALES 46 (2G 4PG 4T)   **TONGA 12** (1G 1T)

WALES: G Wyatt (Pontypridd); G Thomas (Bridgend), LB Davies (Cardiff),
IS Gibbs (Swansea), NK Walker (Cardiff); NR Jenkins (Pontypridd), P John
(Pontypridd); CD Loader (Swansea), BH Williams (Richmond), SC John
(Cardiff), SJ Moore (Moseley), MJ Voyle (Llanelli), RC Appleyard (Swansea),
N Thomas (Bath), RG Jones (Cardiff) (*capt*) *Substitutions:* CT Anthony (Swansea)
for S John (56 mins); R Howley (Cardiff) for P John (56 mins); JM Humphreys
(Cardiff) for B Williams (58 mins); B Williams for Humphreys (temp 67-74 mins);
DR James (Bridgend) for Thomas (70 mins); SM Williams (Cardiff) for Moore
(74 mins)
Scorers *Tries:* Thomas (2), Davies, Wyatt, Walker, Anthony *Conversions:* Jenkins
(2) *Penalty Goals:* Jenkins (4)
TONGA: Tonga; Tiueti, Tatafu, Tanginoa, Faka'osi'folau; Taumalolo,
S Tu'ipulotu; Briggs (*capt*), Ma'asi, Ta'u, Latu, Faletau, K Tu'ipulotu, Matakaiongo,
Pohiva *Substitutions:* Lavaka for Briggs (40 mins); Molitika for Matakaiongo
(57 mins); Hafoka for Pohiva (64 mins); Tai for Tatafu (76 mins)
Scorers *Tries:* Tatafu, Tai *Conversion:* Tonga
Referee S Borsani (Argentina)

MATCH 8   18 November, Rectory Field, Blackheath

Blackheath 20 (5PG 1T)   **Tongans 20** (1G 1PG 2T)
Blackheath: Scorers *Try:* Peters *Penalty Goals:* Braithwaite (5)
Tongans: Scorers *Tries:* Ahota'e'iloa, Katoa, Tonga *Conversion:* Tonga
Penalty Goal: Tonga

MATCH 9   20 November, Heywood Road, Sale

Sale 14 (3PG 1T)   **Tongans 26** (3G 1T)
Sale: Scorers *Try:* Mills *Penalty Goals:* Davidson (3)
Tongans: Scorers *Tries:* Faka'osi'folau, Mafile'o, Mafi. Matakaionga
Conversions: Afeaki (3)

MATCH 10   23 November, Brierton Lane, West Hartlepool

West Hartlepool 28 (2G 3PG 1T)   **Tongans 14** (2G)
West Hartlepool: Scorers *Tries:* John, Morgan, Farmer *Conversions:* Vile (2)
Penalty Goals: Vile (3)
Tongans: Scorers *Tries:* Tanginoa, Molitika *Conversions:* Tonga (2)

MATCH 11   26 November, Headingley, Leeds

Leeds 29 (3G 1PG 1T)   **Tongans 15** (1G 1PG 1T)
Leeds: Scorers *Tries:* S Tu'ipulotu, Cawthorne, Wynn, penalty try
Conversions: S Tu'ipulotu (2), Zoing *Penalty Goal:* S Tu'ipulotu
Tongans: Scorers *Tries:* Mafile'o, Tanginoa, *Conversion:* Tonga
Penalty Goal: Tonga

MATCH 12   30 November, Vicarage Road, Watford

Saracens 83 (6G 2PG 7T)   **Tongans 8** (1PG 1T)
Saracens: Scorers *Tries:* Daniel (3), Constable (3), Pienaar (2), R Wallace (2),
Ravenscroft, Watts, Bennett *Conversions:* Singer (5), Lee *Penalty Goals:* Lee (2)
Tongans: Scorers *Try:* Hafoka *Penalty Goal:* Tonga

WELSH INTERNATIONAL PLAYERS
(up to 30 April 1998)

Note: Years given for Five Nations' matches are for second half of season; eg 1972 means season 1971-72. Years for all other matches refer to the actual year of the match. When a series has taken place, figures have been used to denote the particular matches in which players have featured. Thus 1969 *NZ* 2 indicates that a player appeared in the second Test of the series.

Ackerman, R A (Newport, London Welsh) 1980 *NZ*, 1981 *E, S, A*, 1982 *I, F, E, S*, 1983 *S, I, F, R*, 1984 *S, I, F, E, A*, 1985 *S, I, F, E, Fj*
Alexander, E P (Llandovery Coll, Cambridge U) 1885 *S*, 1886 *E, S*, 1887 *E, I*
Alexander, W H (Llwynypia) 1898 *I, E*, 1899 *E, S, I*, 1901 *S, I*
Allen, A G (Newbridge) 1990 *F, E, I*
Allen, C P (Oxford U, Beaumaris) 1884 *E, S*
Andrews, F (Pontypool) 1912 *SA*, 1913 *E, S, I*
Andrews, F G (Swansea) 1884 *E, S*
Andrews, G E (Newport) 1926 *E, S*, 1927 *E, F, I*
Anthony, C T (Swansea) 1997 *US* 1 (R), 2 (R), *C* (R), *Tg* (R)
Anthony, L (Neath) 1948 *E, S, F*
Appleyard, R C (Swansea) 1997 *C, R, Tg, NZ*, 1998 *It, E* (R), *S, I, F*
Arnold, P (Swansea) 1990 *Nm* 1, 2, *Bb*, 1991 *E, S, I, F* 1, *A*, [*Arg, A*], 1993 *F* (R), *Z* 2, 1994 *Sp, Fj*, 1995 *SA*, 1996 *Bb* (R)
Arnold, W R (Swansea) 1903 *S*
Arthur, C S (Cardiff) 1888 *I, M*, 1891 *E*
Arthur, T (Neath) 1927 *S, F, I*, 1929 *E, S, F, I*, 1930 *E, S, I, F*, 1931 *E, S, F, SA*, 1933 *E, S*
Ashton, C (Aberavon) 1959 *E, S, I*, 1960 *E, S, I*, 1962 *I*
Attewell, S L (Newport) 1921 *E, S, F*

Back, M J (Bridgend) 1995 *F* (R), *E* (R), *S, I*
Badger, O (Llanelli) 1895 *E, S, I*, 1896 *E*
Baker, A (Neath) 1921 *I*, 1923 *E, S, F, I*
Baker, A M (Newport) 1909 *S, F*, 1910 *S*
Bancroft, J (Swansea) 1909 *E, S, F, I*, 1910 *F, E, S, I*, 1911 *E, F, I*, 1912 *E, S, I*, 1913 *I*, 1914 *E, S, F*
Bancroft, W J (Swansea) 1890 *S, E, I*, 1891 *E, S, I*, 1892 *E, S, I*, 1893 *E, S, I*, 1894 *E, S, I*, 1895 *E, S, I*, 1896 *E, S, I*, 1897 *E*, 1898 *I, E*, 1899 *E, S, I*, 1900 *E, S, I*, 1901 *E, S, I*
Barlow, T M (Cardiff) 1884 *I*
Barrell, R J (Cardiff) 1929 *S, F, I*, 1933 *I*
Bartlett, J D (Llanelli) 1927 *S*, 1928 *E, S*
Bassett, A (Cardiff) 1934 *I*, 1935 *E, S, I*, 1938 *E, S*
Bassett, J A (Penarth) 1929 *E, S, F, I*, 1930 *E, S, I*, 1931 *E, S, F, I, SA*, 1932 *E, S, I*
Bateman, A G (Neath, Richmond) 1990 *S, I, Nm* 1,2, 1996 *SA*, 1997 *US, S, F, E, R, NZ*, 1998 *It, E, S, I*
Bayliss, G (Pontypool) 1933 *S*
Bebb, D I E (Carmarthen TC, Swansea) 1959 *E, S, I, F*, 1960 *S, I, F, SA*, 1961 *E, S, I, F*, 1962 *E, S, F, I*, 1963 *E, F, NZ*, 1964 *E, S, F, SA*, 1965 *E, S, I, F*, 1966 *F, A*, 1967 *S, I, F, E*
Beckingham, G (Cardiff) 1953 *E, S*, 1958 *F*
Bennett, A M (Cardiff) 1995 [*NZ*] *SA, Fj*
Bennett, I (Aberavon) 1937 *I*
Bennett, P (Cardiff Harlequins) 1891 *E, S*, 1892 *S, I*
Bennett, P (Llanelli) 1969 *F* (R), 1970 *SA, S, F*, 1972 *S* (R), *NZ*, 1973 *E, S, I, F, A*, 1974 *S, I, F*, 1975 *S* (R), *I*, 1976 *E, S, I, F*, 1977 *I, F, E, S*, 1978 *E, S, I, F*
Bergiers, R T E (Cardiff Coll of Ed, Llanelli) 1972 *E, S, F, NZ*, 1973 *E, S, I, F, A*, 1974 *E, F*, 1975 *I*
Bevan, G W (Llanelli) 1947 *E*
Bevan, J A (Cambridge U) 1881 *E*
Bevan, J C (Cardiff, Cardiff Coll of Ed) 1971 *E, S, I, F*, 1972 *E, S, F, NZ*, 1973 *E, S*
Bevan, J D (Aberavon) 1975 *F, E, S, A*
Bevan, S (Swansea) 1904 *I*
Beynon, B (Swansea) 1920 *E, S*
Beynon, G E (Swansea) 1925 *F, I*
Bidgood, R A (Newport) 1992 *S*, 1993 *Z* 1,2, *Nm, J* (R)
Biggs, N W (Cardiff) 1888 *M*, 1889 *I*, 1892 *I*, 1893 *E, S, I*, 1894 *E, I*
Biggs, S H (Cardiff) 1895 *E, S*, 1896 *E*, 1897 *E*, 1898 *I, E*, 1899 *S, I*, 1900 *I*

Birch, J (Neath) 1911 *S, F*
Birt, F W (Newport) 1911 *E, S*, 1912 *E, S, I, SA*, 1913 *E*
Bishop, D J (Pontypool) 1984 *A*
Bishop, E H (Swansea) 1889 *S*
Blackmore, J H (Abertillery) 1909 *E*
Blackmore, S W (Cardiff) 1987 *I*, [*Tg* (R), *C, A*]
Blake, J (Cardiff) 1899 *E, S, I*, 1900 *E, S, I*, 1901 *E, S, I*
Blakemore, R E (Newport) 1947 *E*
Bland, A F (Cardiff) 1887 *E, S, I*, 1888 *S, I, M*, 1890 *S, E, I*
Blyth, L (Swansea) 1951 *SA*, 1952 *E, S*
Blyth, W R (Swansea) 1974 *E*, 1975 *S* (R), 1980 *F, E, S, I*
Boobyer, N (Llanelli) 1993 *Z* 1 (R), 2, *Nm*, 1994 *Fj, Tg*, 1998 *F*
Boon, R W (Cardiff) 1930 *S, F*, 1931 *E, S, F, I, SA*, 1932 *E, S, I*, 1933 *E, I*
Booth, J (Pontymister) 1898 *I*
Boots, J G (Newport) 1898 *I, E*, 1899 *I*, 1900 *E, S, I*, 1901 *E, S, I*, 1902 *E, S, I*, 1903 *E, S, I*, 1904 *E*
Boucher, A W (Newport) 1892 *E, S, I*, 1893 *E, S, I*, 1894 *E, 1895 E, S, I*, 1896 *E, I*, 1897 *E*
Bowcott, H M (Cardiff, Cambridge U) 1929 *S, F, I*, 1930 *E, 1931 E, S*, 1933 *E, I*
Bowdler, F A (Cross Keys) 1927 *A*, 1928 *E, S, I, F*, 1929 *E, S, F, I*, 1930 *E*, 1931 *SA*, 1932 *E, S, I*, 1933 *I*
Bowen, B (S Wales Police, Swansea) 1983 *R*, 1984 *S, I, F, E*, 1985 *Fj*, 1986 *E, S, I, F, Fj, Tg, WS*, 1987 [*C, E, NZ*], *US*, 1988 *E, S, I, F, WS*, 1989 *S, I*
Bowen, C A (Llanelli) 1896 *E, S, I*, 1897 *E*
Bowen, D H (Llanelli) 1883 *E*, 1886 *E, S*, 1887 *E*
Bowen, G E (Swansea) 1887 *S, I*, 1888 *S, I*
Bowen, W (Swansea) 1921 *S, F*, 1922 *E, S, I, F*
Bowen, Wm A (Swansea) 1886 *E, S*, 1887 *E, S, I*, 1888 *M*, 1889 *S, I*, 1890 *E, S, I*, 1891 *E, S*
Brace, D O (Llanelli, Oxford U) 1956 *E, S, I, F*, 1957 *E*, 1960 *S, I, F*, 1961 *I*
Braddock, K J (Newbridge) 1966 *A*, 1967 *S, I*
Bradshaw, K (Bridgend) 1964 *E, S, I, F, SA*, 1966 *E, S, I, F*
Brewer, T J (Newport) 1950 *E*, 1955 *E, S*
Brice, A B (Aberavon) 1899 *E, S, I*, 1900 *E, S, I*, 1901 *E, S, I*, 1902 *E, S, I*, 1903 *E, S, I*, 1904 *E, S, I*
Bridges, C J (Neath) 1990 *Nm* 1,2, *Bb*, 1991 *E* (R), *I, F* 1, *A*
Bridie, R H (Newport) 1882 *I*
Britton, G R (Newport) 1961 *S*
Broughton, A S (Treorchy) 1927 *A*, 1929 *S*
Brown, A (Newport) 1921 *I*
Brown, J (Cardiff) 1925 *I*
Brown, J A (Cardiff) 1907 *E, S, I*, 1908 *E, S, F*, 1909 *E*
Brown, M (Pontypool) 1983 *R*, 1986 *E, S, Fj* (R), *Tg, WS*
Bryant, D J (Bridgend) 1988 *NZ* 1,2, *WS, R*, 1989 *S, I, F, E*
Buchanan, A (Llanelli) 1987 [*Tg, E, NZ, A*], 1988 *I*
Buckett, I M (Swansea) 1994 *Tg*, 1997 *US* 2, *C*
Burcher, D H (Newport) 1977 *I, F, E, S*
Burgess, R C (Ebbw Vale) 1977 *I, F, E, S*, 1981 *I, F*, 1982 *F, E, S*
Burnett, R (Newport) 1953 *E*
Burns, J (Cardiff) 1927 *F, I*
Bush, P F (Cardiff) 1905 *NZ*, 1906 *E, SA*, 1907 *I*, 1908 *E, S*, 1910 *S, I*
Butler, E T (Pontypool) 1980 *F, E, S, I, NZ* (R), 1982 *S*, 1983 *E, S, I, F, R*, 1984 *S, I, F, E, A*

Cale, W R (Newbridge, Pontypool) 1949 *E, S, I*, 1950 *E, S, I, F*
Carter, A J (Newport) 1991 *E, S*
Cattell, A (Llanelli) 1883 *E, S*
Challinor, C (Neath) 1939 *E*
Charvis, C L (Swansea) 1996 *A* 3(R), *SA*, 1997 *US, S, I, F*, 1998 *It* (R), *E, S, I, F*

251

Dyke, J C M (Penarth) 1906 *SA*
Dyke, L M (Penarth, Cardiff) 1910 *I*, 1911 *S, F, I*

Edmunds, D A (Neath) 1990 *I* (R), *Bb*
Edwards, A B (London Welsh, Army) 1955 *E, S*
Edwards, B O (Newport) 1951 *I*
Edwards, D (Glynneath) 1921 *E*
Edwards, G O (Cardiff, Cardiff Coll of Ed) 1967 *F, E, NZ*, 1968 *E, S, I, F*, 1969 *S, I, F, E, NZ* 1,2, *A*, 1970 *SA, S, E, I, F*, 1971 *E, S, I, F*, 1972 *E, S, F, NZ*, 1973 *E, S, I, F, A*, 1974 *S, I, F, E*, 1975 *F, E, S, I, A*, 1976 *E, S, I, F*, 1977 *I, F, E, S*, 1978 *E, S, I, F*
Eidman, I H (Cardiff) 1983 *S, R*, 1984 *I, F, E, A*, 1985 *S, I, Fj*, 1986 *E, S, I, F*
Elliott, J E (Cardiff) 1894 *I*, 1898 *I, E*
Elsey, W J (Cardiff) 1895 *E*
Emyr, Arthur (Swansea) 1989 *E, NZ*, 1990 *F, E, S, I, Nm* 1,2, 1991 *F* 1,2, *[WS, Arg, A]*
Evans, A (Pontypool) 1924 *E, I, F*
Evans, B (Swansea) 1933 *S*
Evans, B (Llanelli) 1933 *E, S*, 1936 *E, S, I*, 1937 *E*
Evans, B S (Llanelli) 1920 *E*, 1922 *E, S, I, F*
Evans, C (Pontypool) 1960 *E*
Evans, D (Penygraig) 1896 *S, I*, 1897 *E*, 1898 *E*
Evans, D B (Swansea) 1926 *E*
Evans, D D (Cheshire, Cardiff U) 1934 *E*
Evans, D P (Llanelli) 1960 *SA*
Evans, D W (Cardiff) 1889 *S, I*, 1890 *E, I*, 1891 *E*
Evans, D W (Oxford U, Cardiff, Treorchy) 1989 *F, E, NZ*, 1990 *F, E, S, I, Bb*, 1991 *A* (R), *F* 2 (R), *[A* (R)], 1995 *[J* (R)]
Evans, E (Llanelli) 1937 *E*, 1939 *S, I*
Evans, F (Llanelli) 1921 *S*
Evans, G (Cardiff) 1947 *E, S, F, I, A*, 1948 *E, S, F, I*, 1949 *E, S, I*
Evans, G (Maesteg) 1981 *S* (R), *I, F, A*, 1982 *I, F, E, S*, 1983 *F, R*
Evans, G L (Newport) 1977 *F* (R), 1978 *F, A* 2 (R)
Evans, I (London Welsh) 1934 *S, I*
Evans, I (Swansea) 1922 *E, S, I, F*
Evans, I C (Llanelli, Bath) 1987 *F, E, S, I, [I, C, E, NZ, A]*, 1988 *E, S, I, F, NZ* 1,2, 1989 *I, F, E*, 1991 *E, S, I, F* 1, *A, F* 2, *[WS, Arg, A]*, 1992 *I, F, E, S, A*, 1993 *E, S, I, F, J, C*, 1994 *S, I, E, Pt, Sp, C, Fj, Tg, WS, R*, 1995 *E, S, I, [J, NZ, I]*, *SA, Fj*, 1996 *It, E, S, I, F* 1, *A* 1,2, *Bb, F* 2, *A* 3, *SA*, 1997 *US, S, I, F*, 1998 *It*
Evans, I L (Llanelli) 1991 *F* 2 (R)
Evans, J (Llanelli) 1896 *S, I*, 1897 *E*
Evans, J (Blaina) 1904 *E*
Evans, J (Pontypool) 1907 *E, S, I*
Evans, J D (Cardiff) 1958 *I, F*
Evans, J E (Llanelli) 1924 *S*
Evans, J R (Newport) 1934 *E*
Evans, O J (Cardiff) 1887 *E, S*, 1888 *S, I*
Evans, P D (Llanelli) 1951 *E, F*
Evans, R (Cardiff) 1889 *S*
Evans, R (Bridgend) 1963 *S, I, F*
Evans, R L (Llanelli) 1993 *E, S, I, F*, 1994 *S, I, F, E, Pt, Sp, C, Fj, WS, R, It, SA*, 1995 *F, [NZ, I* (R)]
Evans, R T (Newport) 1947 *F, I*, 1950 *E, S, I, F*, 1951 *E, S, I, F*
Evans, S (Swansea, Neath) 1985 *E, F*, 1986 *Fj, Tg, WS*, 1987 *F, E, [I, Tg]*
Evans, T (Swansea) 1924 *I*
Evans, T G (London Welsh) 1970 *SA, S, E, I*, 1972 *E, S, F*
Evans, T H (Llanelli) 1906 *I*, 1907 *E, S, I*, 1908 *I, A*, 1909 *E, S, F, I*, 1910 *F, E, S, I*, 1911 *E, S, F, I*
Evans, T P (Swansea) 1975 *F, E, S, I, A*, 1976 *E, S, I, F*, 1977 *I*
Evans, V (Neath) 1954 *I, F, S*
Evans, W (Llanelli) 1958 *A*
Evans, W F (Rhymney) 1882 *I*, 1883 *S*
Evans, W G (Brynmawr) 1911 *I*
Evans, W H (Llwynypia) 1914 *E, S, F, I*
Evans, W J (Pontypool) 1947 *S*
Evans, W R (Bridgend) 1958 *A, E, S, I, F*, 1960 *SA*, 1961 *E, S, I, F*, 1962 *E, S, I*
Everson, W A (Newport) 1926 *S*

Faulkner, A G (Pontypool) 1975 *F, E, S, I, A*, 1976 *E, S, I, F*, 1978 *E, S, I, F, A* 1,2, *NZ*, 1979 *S, I, F*
Faull, J (Swansea) 1957 *I, F*, 1958 *A, E, S, I, F*, 1959 *E, S, I*, 1960 *E, F*
Fauvel, T J (Aberavon) 1988 *NZ* 1 (R)

Fear, A G (Newport) 1934 *S, I*, 1935 *S, I*
Fender, N H (Cardiff) 1930 *I, F*, 1931 *E, S, F, I*
Fenwick, S P (Bridgend) 1975 *F, E, S, A*, 1976 *E, S, I, F*, 1977 *I, F, E, S*, 1978 *E, S, I, F, A* 1,2, *NZ*, 1979 *S, I, F, E*, 1980 *F, E, S, I, NZ*, 1981 *E, S*
Finch, E (Llanelli) 1924 *F, NZ*, 1925 *F, I*, 1926 *F*, 1927 *A*, 1928 *I*
Finlayson, A A J (Cardiff) 1974 *I, F, E*
Fitzgerald, D (Cardiff) 1894 *S, I*
Ford, F J V (Welch Regt, Newport) 1939 *E*
Ford, I (Newport) 1959 *E, S*
Ford, S P (Cardiff) 1990 *I, Nm* 1,2, *Bb*, 1991 *E, S, I, A*
Forward, A (Pontypool, Mon Police) 1951 *S, SA*, 1952 *E, S, I, F*
Fowler, I J (Llanelli) 1919 *NZA*
Francis, D G (Llanelli) 1919 *NZA*, 1924 *S*
Francis, P (Maesteg) 1987 *S*

Gabe, R T (Cardiff, Llanelli) 1901 *I*, 1902 *E, S, I*, 1903 *E, S, I*, 1904 *E, S, I*, 1905 *E, S, I, NZ*, 1906 *E, I, SA*, 1907 *E, S, I*, 1908 *E, S, F, I*
Gale, N R (Swansea, Llanelli) 1960 *I*, 1963 *E, S, I, NZ*, 1964 *E, S, I, F, SA*, 1965 *E, S, I, F*, 1966 *E, S, I, F, A*, 1967 *E, NZ*, 1968 *E*, 1969 *NZ* 1 (R), 2, *A*
Gallacher, I S (Llanelli) 1970 *F*
Garrett, R M (Penarth) 1888 *M*, 1889 *S*, 1890 *S, E, I*, 1891 *S, I*, 1892 *E*
Geen, W P (Oxford U, Newport) 1912 *SA*, 1913 *E, I*
George, E E (Pontypridd, Cardiff) 1895 *S, I*, 1896 *E*
George, G M (Newport) 1991 *E, S*
Gething, G I (Neath) 1913 *F*
Gibbs, A (Newbridge) 1995 *I, SA*, 1996 *A* 2, 1997 *US* 1,2, *C*
Gibbs, I S (Neath, Swansea) 1991 *E, S, I, F* 1, *A, F* 2, *[WS, Arg, A]*, 1992 *I, F, E, S, A*, 1993 *E, S, I, F, J, C*, 1996 *It, A* 3, *SA*, 1997 *US, S, I, F, Tg, NZ*, 1998 *It, E, S*
Gibbs, R A (Cardiff) 1906 *S, I*, 1907 *E, S*, 1908 *E, S, F, I*, 1910 *F, E, S, I*, 1911 *E, S, F, I*
Giles, R (Aberavon) 1983 *R*, 1985 *Fj* (R), 1987 *[C]*
Girling, B E (Cardiff) 1881 *E*
Goldsworthy, S J (Swansea) 1884 *I*, 1885 *E, S*
Gore, J H (Blaina) 1924 *I, F, NZ*, 1925 *E*
Gore, W (Newbridge) 1947 *S, F, I*
Gould, A J (Newport) 1885 *E, S*, 1886 *E, S*, 1887 *E, S, I*, 1888 *S*, 1889 *I*, 1890 *S, E, I*, 1892 *E, S, I*, 1893 *E, S, I*, 1894 *E, S*, 1895 *E, S, I*, 1896 *E, S, I*, 1897 *E*
Gould, G H (Newport) 1892 *I*, 1893 *S, I*
Gould, R (Newport) 1882 *I*, 1883 *E, S*, 1884 *E, S, I*, 1885 *E, S*, 1886 *E*, 1887 *E, S*
Graham, T C (Newport) 1890 *I*, 1891 *S, I*, 1892 *E, S*, 1893 *E, S, I*, 1894 *E, S*, 1895 *E, S*
Gravell, R W R (Llanelli) 1975 *F, E, S, I, A*, 1976 *E, S, I, F*, 1978 *E, S, I, F, A* 1,2, *NZ*, 1979 *S, I*, 1981 *I, F*, 1982 *F, E, S*
Gray, A J (London Welsh) 1968 *E, S*
Greenslade, D (Newport) 1962 *S*
Greville, H G (Llanelli) 1947 *A*
Griffin, Dr J (Edinburgh U) 1883 *S*
Griffiths, C (Llanelli) 1979 *E* (R)
Griffiths, D (Llanelli) 1888 *M*, 1889 *I*
Griffiths, G (Llanelli) 1889 *I*
Griffiths, G M (Cardiff) 1953 *E, S, I, F, NZ*, 1954 *I, F, S*, 1955 *I, F*, 1957 *E, S*
Griffiths, J L (Llanelli) 1988 *NZ* 2, 1989 *S*
Griffiths, M (Bridgend, Cardiff) 1988 *WS, R*, 1989 *S, I, F, E, NZ*, 1990 *F, E, Nm* 1,2, *Bb*, 1991 *F* 1,2, *[WS, Arg, A]*, 1992 *I, F, E, S, A*, 1993 *Z* 1,2, *Nm, J, C*, 1995 *F* (R), *E, S, I, [J, I]*
Griffiths, V M (Newport) 1924 *S, I, F*
Gronow, B (Bridgend) 1910 *F, E, S, I*
Gwilliam, J A (Cambridge U, Newport) 1947 *A*, 1948 *I*, 1949 *E, S, I, F*, 1950 *E, S, I, F*, 1951 *E, S, I, SA*, 1952 *E, S, I, F*, 1953 *E, I, F, NZ*, 1954 *E*
Gwynn, D (Swansea) 1883 *E*, 1887 *S*, 1890 *E, I*, 1891 *E, S*
Gwynn, W H (Swansea) 1884 *E, S, I*, 1885 *E, S*

Hadley, A M (Cardiff) 1983 *R*, 1984 *S, I, F, E*, 1985 *F, E, Fj*, 1986 *E, S, I, F, Fj, Tg*, 1987 *S* (R), *I, [I, Tg, C, E, NZ, A]*, *US*, 1988 *E, S, I, F*
Hall, I (Aberavon) 1967 *NZ*, 1970 *SA, S, E*, 1971 *S*, 1974 *S, I, F*

Hall, M R (Cambridge U, Bridgend, Cardiff) 1988 *NZ* 1
(R), 2, *WS, R*, 1989 *S, I, F, E, NZ*, 1990 *F, E, S*, 1991 *A, F*
2, [*WS, Arg, A*], 1992 *I, F, E, S, A*, 1993 *E, S, I*, 1994 *S, I,
F, E, Pt, Sp, C, Tg, R, It, SA*, 1995 *F, S, I, [J, NZ, I*]
Hall, W H (Bridgend) 1988 *WS*
Hancock, F E (Cardiff) 1884 *I*, 1885 *E, S*, 1886 *S*
Hannan, J (Newport) 1888 *M*, 1889 *S, I*, 1890 *S, E, I*,
1891 *E*, 1892 *E, S, I*, 1893 *E, S, I*, 1894 *E, S, I*, 1895 *E, S, I*
Harding, A F (London Welsh) 1902 *E, S, I*, 1903 *E, S, I*,
1904 *E, S, I*, 1905 *E, S, I, NZ*, 1906 *E, S, I, SA*, 1907 *I*,
1908 *E, S*
Harding, G F (Newport) 1881 *E*, 1882 *I*, 1883 *E, S*
Harding, R (Swansea, Cambridge U) 1923 *E, S, F, I*,
1924 *I, F, NZ*, 1925 *F, I*, 1926 *E, I, F*, 1927 *E, S, F, I*,
1928 *E*
Harding, T (Newport) 1888 *M*, 1889 *S, I*
Harris, D J E (Pontypridd, Cardiff) 1959 *I, F*, 1960 *S, I,
F, SA*, 1961 *E, S*
Harris, T (Aberavon) 1927 *A*
Hathway, G F (Newport) 1924 *I, F*
Havard, Rev W T (Llanelli) 1919 *NZA*
Hawkins, F (Pontypridd) 1912 *I, F*
Hayward, D (Newbridge) 1949 *E, F*, 1950 *E, S, I, F*,
1951 *E, S, I, F, SA*, 1952 *E, S, I, F*
Hayward, D J (Cardiff) 1963 *E, NZ*, 1964 *S, I, F, SA*
Hayward, G (Swansea) 1908 *S, F, I, A*, 1909 *E*
Hellings, R (Llwynypia) 1897 *E*, 1898 *I, E*, 1899 *S, I*,
1900 *E, I*, 1901 *E, S*
Herrerá, R C (Cross Keys) 1925 *S, F, I*, 1926 *E, S, I, F*,
1927 *E*
Hiams, H (Swansea) 1912 *I, F*
Hickman, A (Neath) 1930 *E*, 1933 *S*
Hiddlestone, D D (Neath) 1922 *E, S, I, F*, 1924 *NZ*
Hill, A F (Cardiff) 1885 *S*, 1886 *E, S*, 1888 *S, I, M*, 1889
S, 1890 *S, I*, 1893 *E, S, I*, 1894 *E, S, I*
Hill, S D (Cardiff) 1993 *Z* 1,2, *Nm*, 1994 *I* (R), *F, SA*,
1995 *F, SA*, 1996 *A* 2, *F* 2(R), *It*, 1997 *E*
Hinam, S (Cardiff) 1925 *I*, 1926 *E, S, I, F*
Hinton, J T (Cardiff) 1884 *I*
Hirst, G L (Newport) 1912 *S*, 1913 *S*, 1914 *E, S, F, I*
Hodder, W (Pontypool) 1921 *E, S, F*
Hodges, J J (Newport) 1899 *E, S, I*, 1900 *E, S, I*, 1901 *E,
S*, 1902 *E, S, I*, 1903 *E, S, I*, 1904 *E, S*, 1905 *E, S, I, NZ*,
1906 *E, S, I*
Hodgson, G T R (Neath) 1962 *I*, 1963 *E, S, I, F, NZ*,
1964 *E, S, I, F, SA*, 1966 *S, I, F*, 1967 *I*
Hollingdale, H (Swansea) 1912 *SA*, 1913 *E*
Hollingdale, T H (Neath) 1927 *A*, 1928 *E, S, I, F*, 1930 *E*
Holmes, T D (Cardiff) 1978 *A* 2, *NZ*, 1979 *S, I, F, E*,
1980 *F, E, S, I, NZ*, 1981 *A*, 1982 *I, F, E*, 1983 *E, S, I, F*,
1984 *E*, 1985 *S, I, F, E, Fj*
Hopkin, W H (Newport) 1937 *S*
Hopkins, K (Cardiff, Swansea) 1985 *E*, 1987 *F, E, S,
[Tg, C* (R)], *US*
Hopkins, P L (Swansea) 1908 *A*, 1909 *E, I*, 1910 *E*
Hopkins, R (Maesteg) 1970 *E* (R)
Hopkins, T (Swansea) 1926 *E, S, I, F*
Hopkins, W J (Aberavon) 1925 *E, S*
Howells, B (Llanelli) 1934 *E*
Howells, W G (Llanelli) 1957 *E, S, I, F*
Howells, W H (Swansea) 1888 *S, I*
Howley, R (Bridgend, Cardiff) 1996 *E, S, I, F* 1, *A* 1,2,
Bb, F 2, *It, A* 3, *SA*, 1997 *US, S, I, F, E, Tg* (R), *NZ*, 1998
It, E, S, I, F
Hughes, D (Newbridge) 1967 *NZ*, 1969 *NZ* 2, 1970 *SA,
S, E, I*
Hughes, G (Penarth) 1934 *E, S, I*
Hughes, H (Cardiff) 1887 *S*, 1889 *S*
Hughes, K (Cambridge U, London Welsh) 1970 *I*, 1973
A, 1974 *S*
Hullin, W (Cardiff) 1967 *S*
Humphreys, J M (Cardiff) 1995 *[NZ, I*], *SA, Fj*, 1996 *It,
E, S, I, F* 1, *A* 1,2, *Bb, It, A* 3, *SA*, 1997 *S, I, F, E, Tg* (R),
NZ (R), 1998 *It* (R), *E* (R), *S* (R), *I* (R), *F* (R)
Hurrell, J (Newport) 1959 *F*
Hutchinson, F (Neath) 1894 *I*, 1896 *S, I*
Huxtable, R (Swansea) 1920 *F, I*
Huzzey, H V P (Cardiff) 1898 *I, E*, 1899 *E, S, I*
Hybart, A J (Cardiff) 1887 *E*

Ingledew, H M (Cardiff) 1890 *I*, 1891 *E, S*
Isaacs, I (Cardiff) 1933 *E, S*

Jackson, T H (Swansea) 1895 *E*
James, B (Bridgend) 1968 *E*
James, C R (Llanelli) 1958 *A, F*
James, D (Swansea) 1891 *I*, 1892 *S, I*, 1899 *E*
James, D R (Treorchy) 1931 *F, I*
James, D R (Bridgend, Pontypridd) 1996 *A* 2(R), *It, A* 3,
SA, 1997 *I, Tg* (R), 1998 *F* (R)
James, E (Swansea) 1890 *S*, 1891 *I*, 1892 *S, I*, 1899 *E*
James, M (Cardiff) 1947 *A*, 1948 *E, S, F, I*
James, T O (Aberavon) 1935 *I*, 1937 *S*
James, W J (Aberavon) 1983 *E, S, I, F, R*, 1984 *S*, 1985
S, I, F, E, Fj, 1986 *E, S, I, F, Fj, Tg, WS*, 1987 *E, S, I*
James, W P (Aberavon) 1925 *E, S*
Jarman, H (Newport) 1910 *E, S, I*, 1911 *E*
Jarrett, K S (Newport) 1967 *E*, 1968 *E, S*, 1969 *S, I, F,
E, NZ* 1,2, *A*
Jarvis, L (Cardiff) 1997 *R* (R)
Jeffery, J J (Cardiff Coll of Ed, Newport) 1967 *NZ*
Jenkin, A M (Swansea) 1895 *I*, 1896 *E*
Jenkins, A (Llanelli) 1920 *E, S, I, F*, 1921 *S, F*, 1922 *F, I*,
1923 *E, S, F, I*, 1924 *NZ*, 1928 *S, I*
Jenkins, D M (Treorchy) 1926 *E, S, I, F*
Jenkins, D R (Swansea) 1927 *A*, 1929 *E*
Jenkins, E (Newport) 1910 *S, I*
Jenkins, E M (Aberavon) 1927 *S, F, I, A*, 1928 *E, S, I, F*,
1929 *F*, 1930 *E, S, I, F*, 1931 *E, S, F, I, SA*, 1932 *E, S, I*
Jenkins, G R (Pontypool, Swansea) 1991 *F* 2, [*WS* (R),
Arg, A], 1992 *I, F, E, S, A*, 1993 *C*, 1994 *S, I, F, E, Pt, Sp,
C, Tg, WS, R, It, SA*, 1995 *F, E, S, I, [J*], *SA* (R), *Fj* (t),
1996 *E* (R), 1997 *US, US* 1, *C*, 1998 *S, I, F*
Jenkins, J C (London Welsh) 1906 *SA*
Jenkins, J L (Aberavon) 1923 *S, F*
Jenkins, L H (Mon TC, Newport) 1954 *I*, 1956 *E, S, I, F*
Jenkins, N R (Pontypridd) 1991 *E, S, I, F* 1, 1992 *I, F, E,
S*, 1993 *E, S, I, F, Z* 1,2, *Nm, J, C*, 1994 *S, I, F, E, Pt, Sp,
C, Tg, WS, R, It, SA*, 1995 *F, E, S, I, [J, NZ, I*], *SA, Fj*,
1996 *F* 1, *A* 1,2, *Bb, F* 2, *It, A* 3(R), *SA*, 1997 *S, I, F, E,
Tg, NZ*, 1998 *It, E, S, I, F*
Jenkins, V G J (Oxford U, Bridgend, London Welsh)
1933 *E, I*, 1934 *S, I*, 1935 *E, S, NZ*, 1936 *E, S, I*, 1937 *E,
I*, 1938 *E, S*, 1939 *E*
Jenkins, W (Cardiff) 1912 *I, F*, 1913 *S, I*
John, B (Llanelli, Cardiff) 1966 *A*, 1967 *S, NZ*, 1968 *E,
S, I, F*, 1969 *S, I, F, E, NZ* 1,2, *A*, 1970 *SA, S, E, I*, 1971
E, S, I, F, 1972 *E, S, F*
John, D A (Llanelli) 1925 *I*, 1928 *E, S, I*
John, D E (Llanelli) 1923 *F, I*, 1928 *E, S, I*
John, E R (Neath) 1950 *E, S, I, F*, 1951 *E, S, I, F, SA*,
1952 *E, S, I, F*, 1953 *E, S, I, F, NZ*, 1954 *E*
John G (St Luke's Coll, Exeter) 1954 *E, F*
John, J H (Swansea) 1926 *E, S, I, F*, 1927 *E, S, F, I*
John, P (Pontypridd) 1994 *Tg*, 1996 *Bb* (t), 1997 *US* (R),
US 1,2, *C, R, Tg*
John, S C (Llanelli, Cardiff) 1995 *S, I*, 1997 *E* (R), *Tg,
NZ* (R)
Johnson, T A (Cardiff) 1921 *E, F, I*, 1923 *E, S, F*, 1924
E, S, NZ, 1925 *E, S, F*
Johnson, W D (Swansea) 1953 *E*
Jones, A H (Cardiff) 1933 *E, S*
Jones, B (Abertillery) 1914 *E, S, F, I*
Jones, Bert (Llanelli) 1934 *S, I*
Jones, Bob (Llwynypia) 1901 *I*
Jones, B J (Newport) 1960 *I, F*
Jones B Lewis (Devonport Services, Llanelli) 1950 *E, S,
I, F*, 1951 *E, S, SA*, 1952 *E, I, F*
Jones, C W (Cambridge U, Cardiff) 1934 *E, S, I*, 1935 *E,
S, I, NZ*, 1936 *E, S, I*, 1938 *E, S, I*
Jones, C W (Bridgend) 1920 *E, S, F*
Jones, D (Neath) 1927 *A*
Jones, D (Aberavon) 1897 *E*
Jones, D (Swansea) 1947 *E, F, I*, 1949 *E, S, I, F*
Jones, D (Treherbert) 1902 *E, S, I*, 1903 *E, S, I*, 1905 *E,
S, I, NZ*, 1906 *E, S, SA*
Jones, D (Newport) 1926 *E, S, I, F*, 1927 *E*
Jones, D (Llanelli) 1948 *E*
Jones, D (Cardiff) 1994 *SA*, 1995 *F, E, S*, [*J, NZ, I*], *SA,
Fj*, 1996 *It, E, S, I, F* 1, *A* 1,2, *Bb, It, A* 3
Jones, D K (Llanelli, Cardiff) 1962 *E, S, F, I*, 1963 *E, F,
NZ*, 1964 *E, S, SA*, 1966 *E, S, I, F*
Jones, D P (Pontypool) 1907 *I*
Jones, E H (Neath) 1929 *E, S*
Jones, E L (Llanelli) 1930 *F*, 1933 *E, S, I*, 1935 *E*
Jones, Elvet L (Llanelli) 1939 *S*
Jones, G (Ebbw Vale) 1963 *S, I, F*

254

Meredith, A (Devonport Services) 1949 *E, S, I*
Meredith, B V (St Luke's Coll, London Welsh, Newport) 1954 *I, F, S*, 1955 *E, S, I, F*, 1956 *E, S, I, F*, 1957 *E, S, I, F*, 1958 *A, E, S, I*, 1959 *E, S, I, F*, 1960 *E, S, F, SA*, 1961 *E, S, I*, 1962 *E, S, F, I*
Meredith, C C (Neath) 1953 *S, NZ*, 1954 *E, I, F, S*, 1955 *E, S, I, F*, 1956 *E, I*, 1957 *E, S*
Meredith, J (Swansea) 1888 *S, I*, 1890 *S, E*
Merry, A E (Pill Harriers) 1912 *I, F*
Michael, G (Swansea) 1923 *E, S, F*
Michaelson, R C B (Aberavon, Cambridge U) 1963 *E*
Miller, F (Mountain Ash) 1896 *I*, 1900 *E, S, I*, 1901 *E, S, I*
Mills, F M (Swansea, Cardiff) 1892 *E, S, I*, 1893 *E, S, I*, 1894 *E, S, I*, 1895 *E, S, I*, 1896 *E*
Moon, R H StJ B (Llanelli) 1993 *F, Z* 1,2, *Nm, J, C*, 1994 *S, I, F, E, Sp, C, Fj, WS, R, It*, 1995 *E* (R)
Moore, A P (Cardiff) 1995 *[J], SA, Fj*, 1996 *It*
Moore, A P (Swansea) 1995 *SA* (R), *Fj*, 1998 *S, I, F*
Moore, S J (Swansea, Moseley) 1997 *C, R, Tg*
Moore, W J (Bridgend) 1933 *I*
Morgan, C H (Llanelli) 1957 *I, F*
Morgan, C I (Cardiff) 1951 *I, F, SA*, 1952 *E, S, I*, 1953 *S, I, F, NZ*, 1954 *E, I, S*, 1955 *E, S, I, F*, 1956 *E, S, I, F*, 1957 *E, S, I, F*, 1958 *E, S, I, F*
Morgan, D (Swansea) 1885 *S*, 1886 *E, S*, 1887 *E, S, I*, 1889 *I*
Morgan, D (Llanelli) 1895 *I*, 1896 *E*
Morgan, D R R (Llanelli) 1962 *E, S, F, I*, 1963 *E, S, I, F, NZ*
Morgan, E (Llanelli) 1920 *I*, 1921 *E, S, F*
Morgan, Edgar (Swansea) 1914 *E, S, F, I*
Morgan, E T (London Welsh) 1902 *E, S, I*, 1903 *I*, 1904 *E, S, I*, 1905 *E, S, I, NZ*, 1906 *E, S, I, SA*, 1908 *F*
Morgan, F L (Llanelli) 1938 *E, S, I*, 1939 *E*
Morgan, H J (Abertillery) 1958 *E, S, I, F*, 1959 *I, F*, 1960 *E*, 1961 *E, S, I, F*, 1962 *E, S, F, I*, 1963 *S, I, F*, 1965 *E, S, I, F*, 1966 *E, S, I, F, A*
Morgan, H P (Newport) 1956 *E, S, I, F*
Morgan, I (Swansea) 1908 *A*, 1909 *E, S, F, I*, 1910 *F, E, S, I*, 1911 *E, F, I*, 1912 *S*
Morgan, J L (Llanelli) 1912 *SA*, 1913 *E*
Morgan, K A (Pontypridd) 1997 *US* 1,2, *C, R, NZ*, 1998 *S, I, F*
Morgan, M E (Swansea) 1938 *E, S, I*, 1939 *E*
Morgan, N (Newport) 1960 *S, I, F*
Morgan, P E J (Aberavon) 1961 *E, S, F*
Morgan, P J (Llanelli) 1980 *S* (R), *I, NZ* (R), 1981 *I*
Morgan, R (Newport) 1984 *S*
Morgan, T (Llanelli) 1889 *I*
Morgan, W G (Cambridge U) 1927 *F, I*, 1929 *E, S, F, I*, 1930 *I, F*
Morgan, W L (Cardiff) 1910 *S*
Moriarty, R D (Swansea) 1981 *A*, 1982 *I, F, E, S*, 1983 *E*, 1984 *S, I, F, E*, 1985 *S, I, F*, 1986 *Fj, Tg, WS*, 1987 *[I, Tg, C* (R), *E, NZ, A]*
Moriarty, W P (Swansea) 1986 *I, F, Fj, Tg, WS*, 1987 *F, E, S, I, [I, Tg, C, E, NZ, A], US*, 1988 *E, S, I, F, NZ* 1
Morley, J C (Newport) 1929 *E, S, F, I*, 1930 *E, I*, 1931 *E, S, F, I, SA*, 1932 *E, S, I*
Morris, G L (Swansea) 1882 *I*, 1883 *E, S*, 1884 *E, S*
Morris, H T (Cardiff) 1951 *F*, 1955 *I, F*
Morris, J I T (Swansea) 1924 *E, S*
Morris, M S (S Wales Police, Neath) 1985 *S, I, F*, 1990 *I, Nm* 1,2, *Bb*, 1991 *I, F* 1, *[WS* (R)], 1992 *E*
Morris, R R (Swansea, Bristol) 1933 *S*, 1937 *S*
Morris, S (Cross Keys) 1920 *E, S, F, I*, 1922 *E, S, I, F*, 1923 *E, S, F, I*, 1924 *E, S, F, NZ*, 1925 *E, S, F*
Morris, W (Abertillery) 1919 *NZA*, 1920 *F*, 1921 *I*
Morris, W (Llanelli) 1896 *S, I*, 1897 *E*
Morris, W D (Neath) 1967 *E, F*, 1968 *E, S, I, F*, 1969 *S, I, F, E, NZ* 1,2, *A*, 1970 *SA, S, E, I, F*, 1971 *E, S, I, F*, 1972 *E, S, F, NZ*, 1973 *E, S, I, A*, 1974 *S, I, F, E*
Morris, W J (Newport) 1965 *S*, 1966 *F*
Morris, W J (Pontypool) 1963 *S, I*
Moseley, K (Pontypool, Newport) 1988 *NZ* 2, *R*, 1989 *S, I*, 1990 *F*, 1991 *F* 2, *[WS, Arg, A]*
Murphy, C D (Cross Keys) 1935 *E, S, I*
Mustoe, L (Cardiff) 1995 *Fj*, 1996 *A* 1 (R), 2, 1997 *US* 1,2, *C, R* (R), 1998 *E* (R), *I* (R), *F* (R)

Nash, D (Ebbw Vale) 1960 *SA*, 1961 *E, S, I, F*, 1962 *F*
Newman, C H (Newport) 1881 *E*, 1882 *I*, 1883 *E, S*, 1884 *E, S*, 1885 *E, S*, 1886 *E*, 1887 *E*
Nicholas, D L (Llanelli) 1981 *E, S, I, F*

Nicholas, T J (Cardiff) 1919 *NZA*
Nicholl, C B (Cambridge U, Llanelli) 1891 *I*, 1892 *E, S, I*, 1893 *E, S, I*, 1894 *E, S*, 1895 *E, S, I*, 1896 *E, S, I*
Nicholl, D W (Llanelli) 1894 *I*
Nicholls, E G (Cardiff) 1896 *S, I*, 1897 *E*, 1898 *I, E*, 1899 *E, S, I*, 1900 *S, I*, 1901 *E, S, I*, 1902 *E, S, I*, 1903 *I*, 1904 *E*, 1905 *I, NZ*, 1906 *E, S, I, SA*
Nicholls, F E (Cardiff Harlequins) 1892 *I*
Nicholls, H (Cardiff) 1958 *I*
Nicholls, S H (Cardiff) 1888 *M*, 1889 *S, I*, 1891 *S*
Norris, C H (Cardiff) 1963 *F*, 1966 *F*
Norster, R L (Cardiff) 1982 *S*, 1983 *E, S, I, F*, 1984 *S, I, F, E, A*, 1985 *S, I, F, E, Fj*, 1986 *Fj, Tg, WS*, 1987 *F, E, S, I, [I, C, E]*, *US*, 1988 *E, S, I, F, NZ* 1, *WS*, 1989 *F, E*
Norton, W B (Cardiff) 1882 *I*, 1883 *E, S*, 1884 *E, S, I*

O'Connor, A (Aberavon) 1960 *SA*, 1961 *E, S*, 1962 *F, I*
O'Connor, R (Aberavon) 1957 *E*
O'Neill, W (Cardiff) 1904 *S, I*, 1905 *E, S, I*, 1907 *E, I*, 1908 *E, S, F, I*
O'Shea, J P (Cardiff) 1967 *S, I*, 1968 *S, I, F*
Oliver, G (Pontypool) 1920 *E, S, F, I*
Osborne, W T (Mountain Ash) 1902 *E, S, I*, 1903 *E, S, I*
Ould, W J (Cardiff) 1924 *E, S*
Owen, A (Swansea) 1924 *E*
Owen, G D (Newport) 1955 *I, F*, 1956 *E, S, I, F*
Owen, R M (Swansea) 1901 *I*, 1902 *E, S, I*, 1903 *E, S, I*, 1904 *E, S, I*, 1905 *E, S, I, NZ*, 1906 *E, S, I, SA*, 1907 *E, S*, 1908 *F, I, A*, 1909 *E, S, F, I*, 1910 *F, E, I*, 1911 *E, S, F, I*, 1912 *E, S*

Packer, H (Newport) 1891 *E*, 1895 *S, I*, 1896 *E, S, I*, 1897 *E*
Palmer, F (Swansea) 1922 *E, S, I*
Parfitt, F C (Newport) 1893 *E, S, I*, 1894 *E, S, I*, 1895 *S*, 1896 *S, I*
Parfitt, S A (Swansea) 1990 *Nm* 1 (R), *Bb*
Parker, D S (Swansea) 1924 *F, NZ*, 1925 *E, S, F, I*, 1929 *F, I*, 1930 *E*
Parker, T (Swansea) 1919 *NZA*, 1920 *E, S, I*, 1921 *E, S, F, I*, 1922 *E, S, I, F*, 1923 *E, S, F*
Parker, W (Swansea) 1899 *E, S*
Parsons, G W (Newport) 1947 *E*
Pascoe, D (Bridgend) 1923 *F, I*
Pask, A E I (Abertillery) 1961 *F*, 1962 *E, S, F, I*, 1963 *E, S, I, F, NZ*, 1964 *E, S, I, F, SA*, 1965 *E, S, I, F*, 1966 *E, S, I, F, A*, 1967 *S, I*
Payne, G W (Army, Pontypridd) 1960 *E, S, I*
Payne, H (Swansea) 1935 *NZ*
Peacock, H (Newport) 1929 *S, F, I*, 1930 *S, I, F*
Peake, E (Chepstow) 1881 *E*
Pearce, G P (Bridgend) 1981 *I, F*, 1982 *I* (R)
Pearson, T W (Cardiff, Newport) 1891 *E, I*, 1892 *E, S*, 1894 *S, I*, 1895 *E, S, I*, 1897 *E*, 1898 *I, E*, 1903 *E*
Pegge, E V (Neath) 1891 *E*
Perego, M A (Llanelli) 1990 *S*, 1993 *F, Z* 1, *Nm* (R), 1994 *S, I, F, E, Sp*
Perkins, S J (Pontypool) 1983 *S, I, F, R*, 1984 *S, I, F, E, A*, 1985 *S, I, F, E, Fj*, 1986 *E, S, I, F*
Perrett, F L (Neath) 1912 *SA*, 1913 *E, S, F, I*
Perrins, V C (Newport) 1970 *SA, S*
Perry, W (Neath) 1911 *E*
Phillips, A J (Cardiff) 1979 *E*, 1980 *F, E, S, I, NZ*, 1981 *E, S, I, F, A*, 1982 *I, F, E, S*, 1987 *[C, E, A]*
Phillips, B (Aberavon) 1925 *E, S, F, I*, 1926 *E*
Phillips, D H (Swansea) 1952 *F*
Phillips, H P (Newport) 1892 *E*, 1893 *E, S, I*, 1894 *E, S*
Phillips, H T (Newport) 1927 *E, S, F, I, A*, 1928 *E, S, I, F*
Phillips, K H (Neath) 1987 *F, [I, Tg, NZ], US*, 1988 *E, NZ* 1, 1989 *NZ*, 1990 *F, E, S, I, Nm* 1,2, *Bb*, 1991 *E, S, I, F* 1, *A*
Phillips, L A (Newport) 1900 *E, S, I*, 1901 *S*
Phillips, R (Neath) 1987 *US*, 1988 *E, S, I, F, NZ* 1,2, *WS*, 1989 *S, I*
Phillips, W D (Cardiff) 1881 *E*, 1882 *I*, 1884 *E, S, I*
Pickering, D F (Llanelli) 1983 *E, S, I, F, R*, 1984 *S, I, F, E, A*, 1985 *S, I, F, E, Fj*, 1986 *E, S, I, F, Fj*, 1987 *F, E, S, I, A*
Plummer, R C S (Newport) 1912 *S, I, F, SA*, 1913 *E*
Pook, T (Newport) 1895 *S*
Powell, G (Ebbw Vale) 1957 *I, F*
Powell, J (Cardiff) 1906 *I*
Powell, J (Cardiff) 1923 *I*
Powell, R W (Newport) 1888 *S, I*

Powell, W C (London Welsh) 1926 *S, I, F*, 1927 *E, F, I*, 1928 *S, I, F*, 1929 *E, S, F, I*, 1930 *S, I, F*, 1931 *E, S, F, I, SA*, 1932 *E, S, I*, 1935 *E, S, I*
Powell, W J (Cardiff) 1920 *E, S, F, I*
Price, B (Newport) 1961 *I, F*, 1962 *E, S*, 1963 *E, S, F, NZ*, 1964 *E, S, I, F, SA*, 1965 *E, S, I, F*, 1966 *E, S, I, F, A*, 1967 *S, I, F, E*, 1969 *S, I, F, NZ* 1,2, *A*
Price, G (Pontypool) 1975 *F, E, S, I, A*, 1976 *E, S, I, F*, 1977 *I, F, E, S*, 1978 *E, S, I, F, A* 1,2, *NZ*, 1979 *S, I, F, E*, 1980 *F, E, S, I, NZ*, 1981 *E, S, I, F, A*, 1982 *I, F, E, S*, 1983 *E, I, F*
Price, M J (Pontypool, RAF) 1959 *E, S, I, F*, 1960 *E, S, I, F*, 1962 *E*
Price, R E (Weston-s-Mare) 1939 *S, I*
Price, T G (Llanelli) 1965 *E, S, I, F*, 1966 *E, A*, 1967 *S, F*
Priday, A J (Cardiff) 1958 *I*, 1961 *I*
Pritchard, C (Pontypool) 1928 *E, S, I, F*, 1929 *E, S, F, I*
Pritchard, C C (Newport, Pontypool) 1904 *S, I*, 1905 *NZ*, 1906 *E, S*
Pritchard, C M (Newport) 1904 *I*, 1905 *E, S, NZ*, 1906 *E, S, I, SA*, 1907 *E, S, I*, 1908 *E*, 1910 *F, E, A* 1,2, *Bb, F* 2, *It, A* 3, 1997 *E* (R)
Proctor, W T (Llanelli) 1992 *A*, 1993 *E, S, Z* 1,2, *Nm, C*, 1994 *I, C, Fj, WS, R, It, SA*, 1995 *S, I, [NZ], Fj*, 1996 *It, E, S, I, A* 1,2, *Bb, F* 2, *It, A* 3, 1997 *E* (R)
Prosser, D R (Neath) 1934 *S, I*
Prosser, G (Neath) 1934 *E, S, I*, 1935 *NZ*
Prosser, G (Pontypridd) 1995 [*NZ*]
Prosser, J (Cardiff) 1921 *I*
Prosser, T R (Pontypool) 1956 *S, F*, 1957 *E, S, I, F*, 1958 *A, E, S, I, F*, 1959 *E, S, I, F*, 1960 *E, S, I, F, SA*, 1961 *I, F*
Prothero, G J (Bridgend) 1964 *S, I, F*, 1965 *E, S, I, F*, 1966 *E, S, I, F*
Pryce-Jenkins, T J (London Welsh) 1888 *S, I*
Pugh, C (Maesteg) 1924 *E, S, I, F, NZ*, 1925 *E, S*
Pugh, J D (Neath) 1987 *US*, 1988 *S* (R), 1990 *S*
Pugh, P (Neath) 1989 *NZ*
Pugsley, J (Cardiff) 1910 *E, S, I*, 1911 *E, S, F, I*
Pullman, J J (Neath) 1910 *F*
Purdon, F T (Newport) 1881 *E*, 1882 *I*, 1883 *E, S*

Quinnell, D L (Llanelli) 1972 *F* (R), *NZ*, 1973 *E, S, A*, 1974 *S, F*, 1975 *E* (R), 1977 *I* (R), *F, E, S*, 1978 *E, S, I, F, A* 1, *NZ*, 1979 *S, I, F, E*, 1980 *NZ*
Quinnell, J C (Llanelli, Richmond) 1995 *Fj*, 1996 *A* 3(R), 1997 *US* (R), *S* (R), *I, F* (R), *E* (R)
Quinnell, L S (Llanelli, Richmond) 1993 *C*, 1994 *S, I, F, E, Pt, Sp, C, WS*, 1997 *US, S, I, F, E*, 1998 *It, E, S* (R)

Radford, W J (Newport) 1923 *I*
Ralph, A R (Newport) 1931 *F, I, SA*, 1932 *E, S, I*
Ramsey, S H (Treorchy) 1896 *E*, 1904 *E*
Randell, R (Aberavon) 1924 *I, F*
Raybould, W H (London Welsh, Cambridge U, Newport) 1967 *S, I, F, E, NZ*, 1968 *I, F*, 1970 *SA, E, I, F* (R)
Rayer, M A (Cardiff) 1991 [*WS* (R), *Arg, A* (R)], 1992 *E* (R), *A*, 1993 *E, S, I, Z* 1, *Nm, J* (R), 1994 *S* (R), *I* (R), *F, E, Pt, C, Fj, WS, R, It*
Rees, Aaron (Maesteg) 1919 *NZA*
Rees, Alan (Maesteg) 1962 *E, S, F*
Rees, A M (London Welsh) 1934 *E*, 1935 *E, S, I, NZ*, 1936 *E, S, I*, 1937 *E, S, I*, 1938 *E, S*
Rees, B I (London Welsh) 1967 *S, I, F*
Rees, C F W (London Welsh) 1974 *I*, 1975 *A*, 1978 *NZ*, 1981 *F, A*, 1982 *I, F, E, S*, 1983 *S, I, F*
Rees, D (Swansea) 1968 *S, I, F*
Rees, Dan (Swansea) 1900 *E*, 1903 *E, S*, 1905 *E, S*
Rees, E B (Swansea) 1919 *NZA*
Rees, H (Cardiff) 1937 *S, I*, 1938 *E, S, I*
Rees, H E (Neath) 1979 *S, I, F, E*, 1980 *F, E, S, I, NZ*, 1983 *E, S, I, F*
Rees, J (Swansea) 1920 *E, S, F, I*, 1921 *E, S, I*, 1922 *E*, 1923 *E, F, I*, 1924 *E*
Rees, J I (Swansea) 1934 *E, S, I*, 1935 *S, NZ*, 1936 *E, S, I*, 1937 *E, S, I*, 1938 *E, S, I*
Rees, L M (Cardiff) 1933 *I*
Rees, P (Llanelli) 1947 *F, I*
Rees, P M (Newport) 1961 *E, S, I*, 1964 *I*
Rees, T (Newport) 1935 *S, I, NZ*, 1936 *E, S, I*, 1937 *E, S*
Rees, T A (Llandovery) 1881 *E*
Rees, T E (London Welsh) 1926 *I, F*, 1927 *A*, 1928 *E*

Rees-Jones, G R (Oxford U, London Welsh) 1934 *E, S*, 1935 *I, NZ*, 1936 *E*
Reeves, F (Cross Keys) 1920 *F, I*, 1921 *E*
Reynolds, A (Swansea) 1990 *Nm* 1,2 (R), 1992 *A* (R)
Rhapps, J (Penygraig) 1897 *E*
Rice-Evans, W (Swansea) 1890 *S*, 1891 *E, S*
Richards, B (Swansea) 1960 *F*
Richards, C (Pontypool) 1922 *E, S, I, F*, 1924 *I*
Richards, D S (Swansea) 1979 *F, E*, 1980 *F, E, S, I, NZ*, 1981 *E, S, I, F*, 1982 *I, F*, 1983 *E, S, I, R* (R)
Richards, E G (Cardiff) 1927 *S*
Richards, E S (Swansea) 1885 *E*, 1887 *S*
Richards, H D (Neath) 1986 *Tg* (R), 1987 [*Tg, E* (R), *NZ*]
Richards, I (Cardiff) 1925 *E, S, F*
Richards, K H L (Bridgend) 1960 *SA*, 1961 *E, S, I, F*
Richards, M C R (Cardiff) 1968 *I, F*, 1969 *S, I, F, E, NZ* 1,2, *A*
Richards, R (Aberavon) 1913 *S, F, I*
Richards, R (Cross Keys) 1956 *F*
Richards, T L (Maesteg) 1923 *I*
Richardson, S J (Aberavon) 1978 *A* 2 (R), 1979 *E*
Rickards, A R (Cardiff) 1924 *F*
Ring, J (Aberavon) 1921 *E*
Ring, M G (Cardiff, Pontypool) 1983 *E*, 1984 *A*, 1985 *S, I, F*, 1987 *I, [I, Tg, A], US*, 1988 *E, S, I, F, NZ* 1,2, 1989 *NZ*, 1990 *F, E, S, I, Nm* 1,2, *Bb*, 1991 *E, S, I, F* 1,2, [*WS, Arg, A*]
Ringer, P (Ebbw Vale, Llanelli) 1978 *NZ*, 1979 *S, I, F, E*, 1980 *F, E, NZ*
Roberts, C (Neath) 1958 *I, F*
Roberts, D E A (London Welsh) 1930 *E*
Roberts, E (Llanelli) 1886 *E*, 1887 *I*
Roberts, E J (Llanelli) 1888 *S, I*, 1889 *I*
Roberts, G J (Cardiff) 1985 *F* (R), *E*, 1987 [*I, Tg, C, E, A*]
Roberts, H M (Cardiff) 1960 *SA*, 1961 *E, S, I, F*, 1962 *S, F*, 1963 *I*
Roberts, J (Cardiff) 1927 *E, S, F, I, A*, 1928 *E, S, I, F*, 1929 *E, S, F, I*
Roberts, M G (London Welsh) 1971 *E, S, I, F*, 1973 *I, F*, 1975 *S*, 1979 *E*
Roberts, T (Newport, Risca) 1921 *S, F, I*, 1922 *E, S, I, F*, 1923 *E, S*
Roberts, W (Cardiff) 1929 *E*
Robins, J D (Birkenhead Park) 1950 *E, S, I, F*, 1951 *E, S, I, F*, 1953 *E, I, F*
Robins, R J (Pontypridd) 1953 *S*, 1954 *F, S*, 1955 *E, S, I, F*, 1956 *E, F, I*, 1957 *E, S, I, F*
Robinson, I R (Cardiff) 1974 *F, E*
Rocyn-Jones, D N (Cambridge U) 1925 *I*
Roderick, W B (Llanelli) 1884 *I*
Rosser, M A (Penarth) 1924 *S, F*
Rowland, E M (Lampeter) 1885 *E*
Rowlands, C F (Aberavon) 1926 *I*
Rowlands, D C T (Pontypool) 1963 *E, S, I, F, NZ*, 1964 *E, S, I, F, SA*, 1965 *E, S, I, F*
Rowlands, G (RAF, Cardiff) 1953 *NZ*, 1954 *E, F*, 1956 *F*
Rowlands, K A (Cardiff) 1962 *F, I*, 1963 *I*, 1965 *I, F*
Rowles, G R (Penarth) 1892 *E*
Rowley, M (Pontypridd) 1996 *SA*, 1997 *US, S, I, F, R*
Roy, W S (Cardiff) 1995 [*J* (R)]
Russell, S (London Welsh) 1987 *US*

Samuel, D (Swansea) 1891 *I*, 1893 *I*
Samuel, F (Mountain Ash) 1922 *S, I, F*
Samuel, J (Swansea) 1891 *I*
Scourfield, T (Torquay) 1930 *F*
Scrine, G F (Swansea) 1899 *E, S*, 1901 *I*
Shanklin, J L (London Welsh) 1970 *F*, 1972 *NZ*, 1973 *I, F*
Shaw, G (Neath) 1972 *NZ*, 1973 *E, S, I, F, A*, 1974 *S, I, F, E*, 1977 *I, F*
Shaw, T W (Newbridge) 1983 *R*
Shea, J (Newport) 1919 *NZA*, 1920 *E, S*, 1921 *E*
Shell, R C (Aberavon) 1973 *A* (R)
Simpson, H J (Cardiff) 1884 *E, S, I*
Skrimshire, R T (Newport) 1899 *E, S, I*
Skym, A (Llanelli) 1928 *E, S, I, F*, 1930 *E, S, I, F*, 1931 *E, S, F, I, SA*, 1932 *E, S, I*, 1933 *E, S, I*, 1935 *E*
Smith, J S (Cardiff) 1884 *E, I*, 1885 *E*
Sparks, B (Neath) 1954 *I*, 1955 *E, F*, 1956 *E, S, I*, 1957 *S*
Spiller, W J (Cardiff) 1910 *S, I*, 1911 *E, S, F, I*, 1912 *E, F, SA*, 1913 *E*

Squire, J (Newport, Pontypool) 1977 *I, F*, 1978 *E, S, I, F, A* 1, *NZ*, 1979 *S, I, F, E*, 1980 *F, E, S, I, NZ*, 1981 *E, S, I, F, A*, 1982 *I, F, E*, 1983 *E, S, I, F*
Stadden, W J W (Cardiff) 1884 *I*, 1886 *E, S*, 1887 *I*, 1888 *S, M*, 1890 *S, E*
Stephens, C (Bridgend) 1998 *E* (R)
Stephens, C J (Llanelli) 1992 *I, F, E, A*
Stephens, G (Neath) 1912 *E, S, I, F, SA*, 1913 *E, S, F, I*, 1919 *NZA*
Stephens, I (Bridgend) 1981 *E, S, I, F, A*, 1982 *I, F, E, S*, 1984 *I, F, E, A*
Stephens, Rev J G (Llanelli) 1922 *E, S, I, F*
Stephens, J R G (Neath) 1947 *E, S, F, I*, 1948 *I*, 1949 *S, I, F*, 1951 *F, SA*, 1952 *E, S, I, F*, 1953 *E, S, I, F, NZ*, 1954 *E, I*, 1955 *E, S, I, F*, 1956 *S, I, F*, 1957 *E, S, I, F*
Stock, A (Newport) 1924 *F, NZ*, 1926 *E, S*
Stone, P (Llanelli) 1949 *F*
Strand-Jones, J (Llanelli) 1902 *E, S, I*, 1903 *E, S*
Summers, R H B (Haverfordwest) 1881 *E*
Sutton, S (Pontypool, S Wales Police) 1982 *F, E*, 1987 *F, E, S, I, [C, NZ* (R), *A]*
Sweet-Escott, R B (Cardiff) 1891 *S*, 1894 *I*, 1895 *I*

Tamplin, W E (Cardiff) 1947 *S, F, I, A*, 1948 *E, S, F*
Tanner, H (Swansea, Cardiff) 1935 *NZ*, 1936 *E, S, I*, 1937 *E, S, I*, 1938 *E, S, I*, 1939 *E, S, I*, 1947 *E, S, F, I*, 1948 *E, S, F, I*, 1949 *E, S, I, F*
Tarr, D J (Swansea, Royal Navy) 1935 *NZ*
Taylor, A R (Cross Keys) 1937 *I*, 1938 *I*, 1939 *E*
Taylor, C G (Ruabon) 1884 *E, S, I*, 1885 *E, S*, 1886 *E, S*, 1887 *E, I*
Taylor, H T (Cardiff) 1994 *Pt, C, Fj, Tg, WS* (R), *R, It, SA*, 1995 *E, S, [J, NZ, I], SA, Fj*, 1996 *It, E, S, I, F* 1, *A* 1,2, *It, A* 3
Taylor, J (London Welsh) 1967 *S, I, F, E, NZ*, 1968 *I, F*, 1969 *S, I, F, E, NZ* 1, *A*, 1970 *F*, 1971 *E, S, I, F*, 1972 *E, S, F, NZ*, 1973 *E, S, I, F*
Taylor, M (Pontypool, Swansea) 1994 *SA*, 1995 *F, E, SA* (R)
Thomas, A (Newport) 1963 *NZ*, 1964 *E*
Thomas, A C (Bristol, Swansea) 1996 *It, E, S, I, F* 2(R), *SA*, 1997 *US, S, I, F, US* 1,2, *C, R, NZ* (t), 1998 *It, E, S* (R)
Thomas, A G (Swansea, Cardiff) 1952 *E, S, I, F*, 1953 *S, I, F*, 1954 *E, I, F*, 1955 *S, I, F*
Thomas, Bob (Swansea) 1900 *E, S, I*, 1901 *E*
Thomas, Brian (Neath, Cambridge U) 1963 *E, S, I, F, NZ*, 1964 *E, S, I, F, SA*, 1965 *E, S, I, F*, 1966 *E, S, I, F*, 1967 *NZ*, 1969 *S, I, F, E, NZ* 1,2
Thomas, C (Bridgend) 1925 *E, S*
Thomas, C J (Newport) 1888 *I, M*, 1889 *S, I*, 1890 *S, E, I*, 1891 *E, I*
Thomas, D (Aberavon) 1961 *I*
Thomas, D (Llanelli) 1954 *I*
Thomas, Dick (Mountain Ash) 1906 *SA*, 1908 *F, I*, 1909 *S*
Thomas, D J (Swansea) 1904 *E*, 1908 *A*, 1910 *E, S, I*, 1911 *E, S, F, I*, 1912 *E*
Thomas, D J (Swansea) 1930 *S, I*, 1932 *E, S, I*, 1933 *E, S*, 1934 *E, S, I*, 1935 *E, S, I*
Thomas, D L (Neath) 1937 *E*
Thomas, E (Newport) 1904 *S, I*, 1909 *S, F, I*, 1910 *F*
Thomas, G (Llanelli) 1923 *E, S, F, I*
Thomas, G (Newport) 1888 *M*, 1890 *I*, 1891 *S*
Thomas, G (Bridgend, Cardiff) 1995 *[J, NZ, I], SA, Fj*, 1996 *F* 1, *A* 1,2, *Bb, F* 2, *It, A* 3, 1997 *US, S, I, F, E, US* 1,2, *C, R, Tg, NZ*, 1998 *It, E, S, I, F*
Thomas, H (Llanelli) 1912 *F*
Thomas, H (Neath) 1936 *E, S, I*, 1937 *E, S, I*
Thomas, H W (Swansea) 1912 *SA*, 1913 *E*
Thomas, I (Bryncethin) 1924 *E*
Thomas, L C (Cardiff) 1885 *E, S*
Thomas, M C (Newport, Devonport Services) 1949 *F*, 1950 *E, S, I, F*, 1951 *E, S, I, F, SA*, 1952 *E, S, I, F*, 1953 *E*, 1956 *E, S, I, F*, 1957 *E, S*, 1958 *E, S, I, F*, 1959 *I, F*
Thomas, M G (St Bart's Hospital) 1919 *NZA*, 1921 *S, F, I*, 1923 *F*, 1924 *E*
Thomas, N (Bath) 1996 *SA* (R), 1997 *US* 1 (R), 2, *C* (R), *R, Tg, NZ*
Thomas, R (Pontypool) 1909 *F, I*, 1911 *S, F*, 1912 *E, S, SA*, 1913 *E*
Thomas, R C C (Swansea) 1949 *F*, 1952 *I, F*, 1953 *S, I, F, NZ*, 1954 *E, I, F, S*, 1955 *S, I*, 1956 *E, S, I*, 1957 *E, I*, 1958 *A, E, S, I, F*, 1959 *E, S, I, F*

Thomas, R L (London Welsh) 1889 *S, I*, 1890 *I*, 1891 *E, S, I*, 1892 *E*
Thomas, S (Llanelli) 1890 *S, E*, 1891 *I*
Thomas, W D (Llanelli) 1966 *A*, 1968 *S, I, F*, 1969 *E, NZ* 2, *A*, 1970 *SA, S, E, I, F*, 1971 *E, S, I, F*, 1972 *E, S, F, NZ*, 1973 *E, S, I, F*, 1974 *E*
Thomas, W G (Llanelli, Waterloo, Swansea) 1927 *E, S, F, I*, 1929 *E*, 1931 *E, S, SA*, 1932 *E, S, I*, 1933 *E, S, I*
Thomas, W H (Llandovery Coll, Cambridge U) 1885 *S*, 1886 *E, S*, 1887 *E, S*, 1888 *S, I*, 1890 *E, I*, 1891 *S, I*
Thomas, W J (Cardiff) 1961 *F*, 1963 *F*
Thomas, W J L (Llanelli, Cardiff) 1995 *SA, Fj*, 1996 *It, E, S, I, F* 1, 1996 *Bb* (R), 1997 *US*
Thomas, W L (Newport) 1894 *S*, 1895 *E, I*
Thomas, W T (Abertillery) 1930 *E*
Thompson, J F (Cross Keys) 1923 *E*
Thorburn, P H (Neath) 1985 *F, E, Fj*, 1986 *E, S, I, F*, 1987 *F, [I, Tg, C, E, NZ, A], US*, 1988 *S, I, F, WS, R* (R), 1989 *S, I, F, E, NZ*, 1990 *F, E, S, I, Nm* 1,2, *Bb*, 1991 *E, S, I, F* 1, *A*
Titley, M H (Bridgend, Swansea) 1983 *R*, 1984 *S, I, F, E, A*, 1985 *S, I, Fj*, 1986 *F, Fj, Tg, WS*, 1990 *F, E*
Towers, W H (Swansea) 1887 *I*, 1888 *M*
Travers, G (Pill Harriers) 1903 *E, S, I*, 1905 *E, S, I, NZ*, 1906 *E, S, I, SA*, 1907 *E, S, I*, 1908 *E, S, F, I, A*, 1909 *E, S, I*, 1911 *S, F, I*
Travers, W H (Newport) 1937 *S, I*, 1938 *E, S, I*, 1939 *E, S, I*, 1949 *E, S, I, F*
Treharne, E (Pontypridd) 1881 *E*, 1883 *E*
Trew, W J (Swansea) 1900 *E, S, I*, 1901 *E, S*, 1903 *S*, 1905 *S*, 1906 *S*, 1907 *E, S*, 1908 *E, S, F, I, A*, 1909 *E, S, F, I*, 1910 *F, E, S*, 1911 *E, S, F, I*, 1912 *S*, 1913 *S, F*
Trott, R F (Cardiff) 1948 *E, S, F, I*, 1949 *E, S, I, F*
Truman, W H (Llanelli) 1934 *E*, 1935 *E*
Trump, L C (Newport) 1912 *E, S, I, F*
Turnbull, B R (Cardiff) 1925 *I*, 1927 *E, S*, 1928 *E, F*, 1930 *S*
Turnbull, M J L (Cardiff) 1933 *E, I*
Turner, P (Newbridge) 1989 *I* (R), *F, E*

Uzzell, H (Newport) 1912 *E, S, I, F*, 1913 *S, F, I*, 1914 *E, S, F, I*, 1920 *E, S, F, I*
Uzzell, J R (Newport) 1963 *NZ*, 1965 *E, S, I, F*

Vickery, W E (Aberavon) 1938 *E, S, I*, 1939 *E*
Vile, T H (Newport) 1908 *E, S*, 1910 *I*, 1912 *I, F, SA*, 1913 *E*, 1921 *S*
Vincent, H C (Bangor) 1882 *I*
Voyle, M J (Newport, Llanelli) 1996 *A* 1(t), *F* 2, 1997 *E, US* 1,2, *C, Tg, NZ*, 1998 *It, E, S, I, F*

Wakeford, J D M (S Wales Police) 1988 *WS, R*
Waldron, R (Neath) 1965 *E, S, I, F*
Walker, N (Cardiff) 1993 *I, F, J*, 1994 *S, F, E, Pt, Sp*, 1995 *F, E*, 1997 *US* 1,2, *C, R* (R), *Tg, NZ*, 1998 *E*
Waller, P D (Newport) 1908 *A*, 1909 *E, S, F, I*, 1910 *F*
Walters, N (Llanelli) 1902 *E*
Wanbon, R (Aberavon) 1968 *E*
Ward, W S (Cross Keys) 1934 *S, I*
Warlow, J (Llanelli) 1962 *I*
Waters, D R (Newport) 1986 *E, S, I, F*
Waters, K (Newbridge) 1991 *[WS]*
Watkins, D (Newport) 1963 *E, S, I, F, NZ*, 1964 *E, S, I, F, SA*, 1965 *E, S, I, F*, 1966 *E, S, I, F*, 1967 *I, F, E*
Watkins, E (Neath) 1924 *E, S, I, F*
Watkins, E (Blaina) 1926 *S, I, F*
Watkins, E (Cardiff) 1935 *NZ*, 1937 *S, I*, 1938 *E, S, I*, 1939 *E, S*
Watkins, H (Llanelli) 1904 *S, I*, 1905 *E, S, I*, 1906 *E*
Watkins, I J (Ebbw Vale) 1988 *E* (R), *S, I, F, NZ* 2, *R*, 1989 *S, I, F, E*
Watkins, L (Oxford U, Llandaff) 1881 *E*
Watkins, M J (Newport) 1984 *I, F, E, A*
Watkins, S J (Newport, Cardiff) 1964 *S, I, F*, 1965 *E, S, I, F*, 1966 *E, S, I, F, A*, 1967 *S, I, F, E, NZ*, 1968 *E, S*, 1969 *S, I, F, E, NZ* 1, 1970 *E, I, F*
Watkins, W R (Newport) 1959 *F*
Watts, D (Maesteg) 1914 *E, S, F, I*
Watts, J (Llanelli) 1907 *E, S, I*, 1908 *E, S, F, I, A*, 1909 *S, F, I*
Watts, W (Llanelli) 1914 *E*
Watts, W H (Newport) 1892 *E, S, I*, 1893 *E, S, I*, 1894 *E, S, I*, 1895 *E, I*, 1896 *E*
Weaver, D (Swansea) 1964 *E*

Webb, J (Abertillery) 1907 *S*, 1908 *E, S, F, I, A,* 1909 *E, S, F, I,* 1910 *F, E, S, I,* 1911 *E, S, F, I,* 1912 *E, S*
Webb, J E (Newport) 1888 *M*, 1889 *S*
Webbe, G M C (Bridgend) 1986 *Tg* (R), *WS*, 1987 *F, E, S,* [*Tg*], *US*, 1988 *F* (R), *NZ* 1, *R*
Webster, R E (Swansea) 1987 [*A*], 1990 *Bb*, 1991 [*Arg, A*], 1992 *I, F, E, S, A,* 1993 *E, S, I, F*
Wells, G T (Cardiff) 1955 *E, S,* 1957 *I, F,* 1958 *A, E, S*
Westacott, D (Cardiff) 1906 *I*
Wetter, H (Newport) 1912 *SA*, 1913 *E*
Wetter, J J (Newport) 1914 *S, F, I,* 1920 *E, S, F, I,* 1921 *E,* 1924 *I, NZ*
Wheel, G A D (Swansea) 1974 *I, E* (R), 1975 *F, E, I, A,* 1976 *E, S, I, F,* 1977 *I, E, S,* 1978 *E, S, I, F, A* 1,2, *NZ,* 1979 *S, I,* 1980 *F, E, S, I,* 1981 *E, S, I, F, A,* 1982 *I*
Wheeler, P J (Aberavon) 1967 *NZ*, 1968 *E*
Whitefoot, J (Cardiff) 1984 *A* (R), 1985 *S, I, F, E, Fj,* 1986 *E, S, I, F, Fj, Tg, WS,* 1987 *F, E, S, I,* [*I, C*]
Whitfield, J (Newport) 1919 *NZA*, 1920 *E, S, F, I,* 1921 *E,* 1922 *E, S, I, F,* 1924 *S, I*
Whitson, G K (Newport) 1956 *F*, 1960 *S, I*
Wilkins, G (Bridgend) 1994 *Tg*
Williams, A (Bridgend, Swansea) 1990 *Nm* 2 (R), 1995 *Fj* (R)
Williams, B (Llanelli) 1920 *S, F, I*
Williams, B H (Neath, Richmond) 1996 *F* 2, 1997 *R, Tg, NZ,* 1998 *It, E*
Williams, B L (Cardiff) 1947 *E, S, F, I, A,* 1948 *E, S, F, I,* 1949 *E, S, I,* 1951 *I, SA,* 1952 *S,* 1953 *E, S, I, F, NZ,* 1954 *S,* 1955 *E*
Williams, B R (Neath) 1990 *S, I, Bb,* 1991 *E, S*
Williams, C (Llanelli) 1924 *NZ*, 1925 *E*
Williams, C (Aberavon, Swansea) 1977 *E, S,* 1980 *F, E, S, I, NZ,* 1983 *E*
Williams, C D (Cardiff, Neath) 1955 *F*, 1956 *F*
Williams, D (Ebbw Vale) 1963 *E, S, I, F,* 1964 *E, S, I, F, SA,* 1965 *E, S, I, F,* 1966 *E, S, I, A,* 1967 *F, E, NZ,* 1968 *E,* 1969 *S, I, F, E, NZ* 1,2, *A,* 1970 *SA, S, E, I,* 1971 *E, S, I, F*
Williams, D B (Newport, Swansea) 1978 *A* 1, 1981 *E, S*
Williams, E (Neath) 1924 *NZ*, 1925 *F*
Williams, E (Aberavon) 1925 *E, S*
Williams, F L (Cardiff) 1929 *S, F, I,* 1930 *E, S, I, F,* 1931 *F, I, SA,* 1932 *E, S, I,* 1933 *I*
Williams, G (Aberavon) 1936 *E, S, I*
Williams, G (London Welsh) 1950 *I, F,* 1951 *E, S, I, F, SA,* 1952 *E, S, I, F,* 1953 *NZ,* 1954 *E*
Williams, G (Bridgend) 1981 *I, F,* 1982 *E* (R), *S*
Williams, G P (Bridgend) 1980 *NZ*, 1981 *E, S, A,* 1982 *I*
Williams, J (Blaina) 1920 *E, S, F, I,* 1921 *S, F, I*
Williams, J F (London Welsh) 1905 *I, NZ,* 1906 *S, SA*
Williams, J J (Llanelli) 1973 *F* (R), *A,* 1974 *S, I, F, E,* 1975 *F, E, S, I, A,* 1976 *E, S, I, F,* 1977 *I, F, E, S,* 1978 *E, S, I, F, A* 1,2, *NZ,* 1979 *S, I, F, E*
Williams, J L (Cardiff) 1906 *SA*, 1907 *E, S, I,* 1908 *E, S, I, A,* 1909 *E, S, F, I,* 1910 *I,* 1911 *E, S, F, I*
Williams, J P R (London Welsh, Bridgend) 1969 *S, I, F, E, NZ* 1,2, *A,* 1970 *SA, S, E, I, F,* 1971 *E, S, I, F,* 1972 *E, S, F, NZ,* 1973 *E, S, I, F, A,* 1974 *S, I, F,* 1975 *F, E, S, I, A,* 1976 *E, S, I, F,* 1977 *I, F, E, S,* 1978 *E, S, I, F, A* 1,2, *NZ,* 1979 *S, I, F, E,* 1980 *NZ,* 1981 *E, S*
Williams, L (Llanelli, Cardiff) 1947 *E, S, F, I, A,* 1948 *I,* 1949 *E*

Williams, L H (Cardiff) 1957 *S, I, F,* 1958 *E, S, I, F,* 1959 *E, S, I,* 1961 *F,* 1962 *E, S*
Williams, M (Newport) 1923 *F*
Williams, M E (Pontypridd) 1996 *Bb, F* 2, *It* (t), 1998 *It, E*
Williams, O (Bridgend) 1990 *Nm* 2
Williams, O (Llanelli) 1947 *E, S, A,* 1948 *E, S, F, I*
Williams, R (Llanelli) 1954 *S,* 1957 *F,* 1958 *A*
Williams, R D G (Newport) 1881 *E*
Williams, R F (Cardiff) 1912 *SA*, 1913 *E, S,* 1914 *I*
Williams, R H (Llanelli) 1954 *I, F, S,* 1955 *S, I, F,* 1956 *E, S, I,* 1957 *E, S, I, F,* 1958 *A, E, S, I, F,* 1959 *E, S, I, F,* 1960 *E*
Williams, S (Llanelli) 1947 *E, S, F, I,* 1948 *S, F*
Williams, S A (Aberavon) 1939 *E, S, I*
Williams, S M (Neath, Cardiff) 1994 *Tg*, 1996 *E* (t), *A* 1,2, *Bb, F* 2, *It, A* 3, *SA,* 1997 *US, S, I, F, E, US* 1,2 (R), *C, R* (R), *Tg* (R), *NZ* (t + R)
Williams, T (Pontypridd) 1882 *I*
Williams, T (Swansea) 1888 *S, I*
Williams, T (Swansea) 1912 *I,* 1913 *F,* 1914 *E, S, F, I*
Williams, Tudor (Swansea) 1921 *F*
Williams, T G (Cross Keys) 1935 *S, I, NZ,* 1936 *E, S, I,* 1937 *S, I*
Williams, W A (Crumlin) 1927 *E, S, F, I*
Williams, W A (Newport) 1952 *I, F,* 1953 *E*
Williams, W E O (Cardiff) 1887 *S, I,* 1889 *S,* 1890 *S, E*
Williams, W H (Pontymister) 1900 *E, S, I,* 1901 *E*
Williams, W O G (Swansea, Devonport Services) 1951 *F, SA,* 1952 *E, S, I, F,* 1953 *E, S, I, F, NZ,* 1954 *E, I, F, S,* 1955 *E, S, I, F,* 1956 *E, S, I*
Williams, W P J (Neath) 1974 *I, F*
Williams-Jones, H (S Wales Police, Llanelli) 1989 *S* (R), 1990 *F* (R), *I,* 1991 *A,* 1992 *S, A,* 1993 *E, S, I, F, Z* 1, *Nm,* 1994 *Fj, Tg, WS* (R), *It* (t), 1995 *E* (R)
Willis, W R (Cardiff) 1950 *E, S, I, F,* 1951 *E, S, I, F, SA,* 1952 *E, S,* 1953 *S, NZ,* 1954 *E, I, F, S,* 1955 *E, S, I, F*
Wiltshire, M L (Aberavon) 1967 *NZ*, 1968 *E, S, F*
Windsor, R W (Pontypool) 1973 *A,* 1974 *S, I, F, E,* 1975 *F, E, S, I, A,* 1976 *E, S, I, F,* 1977 *I, F, E, S,* 1978 *E, S, I, F, A* 1,2, *NZ,* 1979 *S, I, F*
Winfield, H B (Cardiff) 1903 *I,* 1904 *E, S, I,* 1905 *NZ,* 1906 *E, S, I,* 1907 *S, I,* 1908 *E, S, F, I, A*
Winmill, S (Cross Keys) 1921 *E, S, F, I*
Wintle, M E (Llanelli) 1996 *It*
Wintle, R V (London Welsh) 1988 *WS* (R)
Wooller, W (Sale, Cambridge U, Cardiff) 1933 *E, S, I,* 1935 *E, S, I, NZ,* 1936 *E, S, I,* 1937 *E, S, I,* 1938 *S, I,* 1939 *E, S, I*
Wyatt, G (Pontypridd) 1997 *Tg*
Wyatt, M A (Swansea) 1983 *E, S, I, F,* 1984 *A,* 1985 *S, I,* 1987 *E, S, I*

Young, D (Swansea, Cardiff) 1987 [*E, NZ*], *US,* 1988 *E, S, I, F, NZ* 1,2, *WS, R,* 1989 *S, NZ,* 1990 *F,* 1996 *A* 3, *SA,* 1997 *US, S, I, F, E, R, NZ,* 1998 *It, E, S, I, F*
Young, G A (Cardiff) 1886 *E, S*
Young, J (Harrogate, RAF, London Welsh) 1968 *S, I, F,* 1969 *S, I, F, E, NZ* 1, 1970 *E, I, F,* 1971 *E, S, I, F,* 1972 *E, S, F, NZ,* 1973 *E, S, I, F*

WELSH INTERNATIONAL RECORDS
(*up to 30 April 1998*)

MATCH RECORDS

MOST CONSECUTIVE TEST WINS
11 1907 *I*, 1908 *E*, *S*, *F*, *I*, *A*, 1909 *E*, *S*, *F*, *I*, 1910 *F*
8 1970 *F*, 1971 *E*, *S*, *I*, *F*, 1972 *E*, *S*, *F*

MOST CONSECUTIVE TESTS WITHOUT DEFEAT

P	W	D	Period
11	11	0	1907–10
8	8	0	1970–72

MOST POINTS IN A MATCH
by the team

Pts	Opp	Venue	Year
102	Pt	Lisbon	1994
70	R	Wrexham	1997
57	J	Bloemfontein	1995
55	J	Cardiff	1993
54	Sp	Madrid	1994

by a player

24 by N R Jenkins v Canada at Cardiff — 1993
24 by N R Jenkins v Italy at Cardiff — 1994
23 by A C Thomas v Romania at Wrexham — 1997
22 by N R Jenkins v Portugal at Lisbon — 1994
22 by N R Jenkins v Japan at Bloemfontein — 1995
21 by P H Thorburn v Barbarians at Cardiff — 1990

MOST TRIES IN A MATCH
by the team

T	Opp	Venue	Year
16	Pt	Lisbon	1994
11	F	Paris	1909
11	R	Wrexham	1997
10	F	Swansea	1910
9	F	Cardiff	1908
9	J	Cardiff	1993

by a player

4 by W Llewellyn v England at Swansea — 1899
4 by R A Gibbs v France at Cardiff — 1908
4 by M C R Richards v England at Cardiff — 1969
4 by I C Evans v Canada at Invercargill — 1987
4 by N Walker v Portugal at Lisbon — 1994

MOST CONVERSIONS IN A MATCH
by the team

C	Opp	Venue	Year
11	Pt	Lisbon	1994
8	F	Swansea	1910
7	F	Paris	1909

by a player

11 by N R Jenkins v Portugal at Lisbon — 1994
8 by J Bancroft v France at Swansea — 1910
6 by J Bancroft v France at Paris — 1909

MOST PENALTY GOALS IN A MATCH
by the team

P	Opp	Venue	Year
8	C	Cardiff	1993
7	It	Cardiff	1994
6	F	Cardiff	1982
6	Tg	Nuku'alofa	1994

by a player

8 by N R Jenkins v Canada at Cardiff — 1993
7 by N R Jenkins v Italy at Cardiff — 1994
6 by G Evans v France at Cardiff — 1982
6 by N R Jenkins v Tonga at Nuku'alofa — 1994

MOST DROPPED GOALS IN A MATCH
by the team

D	Opp	Venue	Year
2	S	Swansea	1912
2	S	Cardiff	1914
2	E	Swansea	1920
2	S	Swansea	1921
2	F	Paris	1930
2	E	Cardiff	1971
2	F	Cardiff	1978
2	E	Twickenham	1984

| 2 | I | Wellington | 1987 |
| 2 | S | Cardiff | 1988 |

by a player

2 by J Shea v England at Swansea 1920
2 by A Jenkins v Scotland at Swansea 1921
2 by B John v England at Cardiff 1971
2 by M Dacey v England at Twickenham 1984
2 by J Davies v Ireland at Wellington 1987
2 by J Davies v Scotland at Cardiff 1988

CAREER RECORDS

MOST CAPPED PLAYERS

Caps	Player	Career
72	I C Evans	1987–98
62	G O Llewellyn	1989–98
57	N R Jenkins	1991–98
55	J P R Williams	1969–81
54	R N Jones	1986–95
53	G O Edwards	1967–78
46	T G R Davies	1966–78
46	P T Davies	1985–95
44	K J Jones	1947–57
42	M R Hall	1988–95

MOST CONSECUTIVE TESTS

Tests	Player	Span
53	G O Edwards	1967–78
43	K J Jones	1947–56
39	G Price	1975–83
38	T M Davies	1969–76
33	W J Bancroft	1890–1901

MOST TESTS AS CAPTAIN

Tests	Captain	Span
28	I C Evans	1991–95
18	A J Gould	1889–97
17	J M Humphreys	1995–97
14	D C T Rowlands	1963–65
14	W J Trew	1907–13

MOST TESTS IN INDIVIDUAL POSITIONS

Full-back J P R Williams	54	1969–81
Wing I C Evans	72	1987–98
Centre ⎰M R Hall	32	1988–95
⎱I S Gibbs	32	1991–98

Fly-half N R Jenkins	40	1991–98
Scrum-half ⎰G O Edwards	53	1967–78
⎱R N Jones	53	1986–95
Prop G Price	41	1975–83
Hooker G R Jenkins	35	1991–98
Lock G O Llewellyn	61	1989–98
Flanker W D Morris	32	1967–74
No 8 T M Davies	38	1969–76

MOST POINTS IN TESTS

Pts	Player	Tests	Career
594	N R Jenkins	57	1991–98
304	P H Thorburn	37	1985–91
166	P Bennett	29	1969–78
157	I C Evans	72	1987–98
152	S P Fenwick	30	1975–81

MOST TRIES IN TESTS

Tries	Player	Tests	Career
33	I C Evans	72	1987–98
20	G O Edwards	53	1967–78
20	T G R Davies	46	1966–78
17	R A Gibbs	16	1906–11
17	J L Williams	17	1906–11
17	K J Jones	44	1947–57

MOST CONVERSIONS IN TESTS

Cons	Player	Tests	Career
76	N R Jenkins	57	1991–98
43	P H Thorburn	37	1985–91
38	J Bancroft	18	1909–14
20	W J Bancroft	33	1890–1901
20	A C Thomas	18	1996–98

MOST PENALTY GOALS IN TESTS

Pens	Player	Tests	Career
133	N R Jenkins	57	1991–98
70	P H Thorburn	37	1985–91
36	P Bennett	29	1969–78
35	S P Fenwick	30	1975–81
22	G Evans	10	1981–83
22	A C Thomas	18	1996–98

MOST DROPPED GOALS IN TESTS

Drops	Player	Tests	Career
13	J Davies	32	1985–97
8	B John	25	1966–72
7	W G Davies	21	1978–85

INTERNATIONAL CHAMPIONSHIP RECORDS

Record	Detail		Set
Most points in season	102	in four matches	1976
Most tries in season	21	in four matches	1910
Highest score	49	49–14 v France	1910
Biggest win	35	49–14 v France	1910
Highest score conceded	60	26–60 v England	1998
Biggest defeat	51	0–51 v France	1998
Most appearances	45	G O Edwards	1967–78
Most points in matches	220	N R Jenkins	1991–98
Most points in season	52	P H Thorburn	1986
Most points in match	20	N R Jenkins	v Ireland, 1998
Most tries in matches	18	G O Edwards	1967–78
Most tries in season	6	M C R Richards	1969
Most tries in match	4	W Llewellyn	v England, 1899
	4	M C R Richards	v England, 1969
Most cons in matches	32	J Bancroft	1909–1914
Most cons in season	9	J Bancroft	1910
	9	J A Bassett	1931
Most cons in match	8	J Bancroft	v France, 1910
Most pens in matches	52	N R Jenkins	1991–98
Most pens in season	16	P H Thorburn	1986
Most pens in match	6	G Evans	v France, 1982
Most drops in matches	8	J Davies	1985–97
Most drops in season	4	J Davies	1988
Most drops in match	2	J Shea	v England, 1920
	2	A Jenkins	v Scotland, 1921
	2	B John	v England, 1971
	2	M Dacey	v England, 1984
	2	J Davies	v Scotland, 1988

MAJOR TOUR RECORDS

Record	Detail	Year	Place
Most individual points	89 by N R Jenkins	1993	Africa
Most points in match	34 by L Jarvis	1997 v Southern RFU USA	Namibia
Most tries in match	5 by G Thomas	1996 v W Australia	Perth

MISCELLANEOUS RECORDS

Record	Holder	Detail
Longest Test career	W J Trew	14 seasons, 1899–1900 to 1912–13
	T H Vile	14 seasons, 1907–08 to 1920–21
	H Tanner	14 seasons, 1935–36 to 1948–49
Youngest Test cap	N Biggs	18 yrs 49 days in 1888
Oldest Test cap	T H Vile	38 yrs 152 days in 1921

WELSH INTERNATIONAL CAREER RECORDS (*up to 30 April 1998*)

Player	Debut	Caps since last season	Caps	T	C	PG	DG	Pts
K A Morgan	1997 v US	1997 *US* 1,2, *C, R, NZ,* 1998 *S, I, F*	8	2	0	0	0	10
G Wyatt	1997 v Tg	1997 *Tg*	1	1	0	0	0	5
I C Evans	1987 v F	1998 *It*	72	33	0	0	0	157
N K Walker	1993 v I	1997 *US* 1,2, *C, R* (R), *Tg,* *NZ,* 1998 *E*	17	12	0	0	0	60
W T Proctor	1992 v A	1997 *US* 1,2, *C, R,* 1998 *E* (R), *S, I, F*	37	10	0	0	0	50
D R James	1996 v A	1997 *Tg* (R), 1998 *F* (R)	7	1	0	0	0	5
G Thomas	1995 v J	1997 *US* 1,2, *C, R, Tg,* *NZ,* 1998 *It, E, S, I, F*	28	13	0	0	0	65
N Boobyer	1993 v Z	1998 *F*	6	0	0	0	0	0
A G Bateman	1990 v S	1997 *R, NZ,* 1998 *It, E, S,* *I*	15	6	0	0	0	30
L B Davies	1996 v It	1997 *US* 1,2, *C, R, Tg, NZ* (R), 1998 *E* (R), *I, F*	18	4	0	0	0	20
I S Gibbs	1991 v E	1997 *Tg, NZ,* 1998 *It, E, S*	32	4	0	0	0	20
N R Jenkins	1991 v E	1997 *Tg, NZ,* 1998 *It, E,* *S, I, F*	57	7	76	133	3	594
A C Thomas	1996 v It	1997 *US* 1,2, *C, R, NZ* (t), 1998 *It, E, S* (R)	18	7	20	22	0	141
L Jarvis	1997 v R	1997 *R* (R)	1	0	1	0	0	2
Paul John	1994 v Tg	1997 *US* 1,2, *C, R, Tg*	8	1	0	0	0	5
R Howley	1996 v E	1997 *Tg* (R), *NZ,* 1998 *It,* *E, S, I, F*	23	5	0	0	0	25
G R Jenkins	1991 v F	1997 *US* 1, *C,* 1998 *S, I, F*	36	1	0	0	0	5
J M Humphreys	1995 v NZ	1997 *Tg* (R), *NZ* (R), 1998 *It* (R), *E* (R), *S* (R), *I* (R), *F* (R)	26	2	0	0	0	10
B H Williams	1996 v F	1997 *R, Tg, NZ,* 1998 *It, E*	6	2	0	0	0	10
R C McBryde	1994 v Fj	1997 *US* 2	3	0	0	0	0	0
C D Loader	1995 v SA	1997 *US* 1, *R, Tg, NZ*	19	0	0	0	0	0
S C John	1995 v S	1997 *Tg, NZ* (R)	5	0	0	0	0	0
A L P Lewis	1996 v It	1998 *It, E, S, I, F*	10	0	0	0	0	0
I M Buckett	1994 v Tg	1997 *US* 2, *C*	3	0	0	0	0	0
D Young	1987 v E	1997 *R, NZ,* 1998 *It, E, S,* *I, F*	28	1	0	0	0	4
L Mustoe	1995 v Fj	1997 *US* 1,2, *C, R* (R), 1998 *E* (R), *I* (R), *F* (R)	10	0	0	0	0	0
C T Anthony	1997 v US	1997 *US* 1 (R),2 (R), *C* (R), *Tg* (R)	4	1	0	0	0	5
G O Llewellyn	1989 v NZ	1997 *US* 1,2, *NZ,* 1998 *It,* *E*	62	5	0	0	0	24
M A Rowley	1996 v SA	1997 *R*	6	0	0	0	0	0
C Stephens	1998 v E	1998 *E* (R)	1	0	0	0	0	0
A P Moore	1995 v SA	1998 *S, I, F*	5	0	0	0	0	0
S J Moore	1997 v C	1997 *C, R, Tg*	3	0	0	0	0	0
M J Voyle	1996 v A	1997 *US* 1,2, *C, Tg,* *NZ,* 1998 *It, E, S, I, F*	13	0	0	0	0	0

N Thomas	1996 v SA	1997 *US* 1 (R),2, *C* (R), *R*, *Tg*, *NZ*	7	0	0	0	0	0
K P Jones	1996 v Bb	1998 *S*, *I*, *F* (R)	9	0	0	0	0	0
M E Williams	1996 v Bb	1998 *It*, *E*	5	0	0	0	0	0
R G Jones	1996 v It	1997 *US* 1,2, *R*, *Tg*, *NZ*	13	1	0	0	0	5
A Gibbs	1995 v I	1997 *US* 1,2, *C*	6	0	0	0	0	0
C L Charvis	1996 v A	1998 *It* (R), *E*, *S*, *I*, *F*	11	0	0	0	0	0
R C Appleyard	1997 v C	1997 *C*, *R*, *Tg*, *NZ*, 1998 *It*, *E* (R), *S*, *I*, *F*	9	0	0	0	0	0
S M Williams	1994 v Tg	1997 *US* 1,2 (R), *C*, *R* (R), *Tg* (R), *NZ* (t&R)	20	1	0	0	0	5
S Davies	1992 v I	1998 *I* (R), *F*	17	2	0	0	0	9
L S Quinnell	1993 v C	1998 *It*, *E*, *S* (R)	17	5	0	0	0	25

Arwel Thomas rode the roller coaster for all it was worth last season; in and out of favour with Wales, the Swansea fly-half finished on top with his club.

WELSH CLUBS 1997-98

Bridgend

Year of formation 1878
Ground Brewery Field, Tondu Road, Bridgend, Mid Glamorgan Tel: Bridgend (01656) 652707 and 659032
Colours Blue and white hoops
Captain 1997-98 G Thomas/M Lewis/J Burnell
WRU Leagues 1997-98 Div 1 7th   **SWALEC Cup 1997-98** Lost 21-24 Garndiffaith (4th round)

There were few happy faces at the Brewery Field. New captain Gareth Thomas requested a transfer in October, but this was refused initially. Then he was released to Cardiff in a deal worth around £110,000 (a record for a transfer between Welsh clubs) and Matthew Lewis took over the captaincy. Dafydd James was a big loss when he went to Pontypridd, and John Graf, Chris Bradshaw, Kevin Ellis, Ian Greenslade, Cliff Vogl and Chris Michaluk were others released. New Zealander John Phillips, former Canterbury flanker, was appointed director of rugby, but quit on Christmas Eve, four days after Bridgend had lost to a small club for the first time in the cup. They went out 24-21 at Garndiffaith and Phillips launched a vitriolic attack on his players' lack of professionalism. J P R Williams took over the running of the team with coaches Steve Brown and Alun Donovan. Justin Burnell then assumed duties as captain and he encouraged some outstanding youngsters in Gareth Cull (102 league points), Stephen Winn, Gareth Bowen, Andrew Jenkins and Gareth Downes. Only Newport finished below them in the division and just three victories illustrated their doleful season.

League Record 1997-98

Date	Venue	Opponents	Result	Scorers
17 Aug	A	Newport	27-19	*T:* J Dodds, M Lewis, S Winn *C:* G Cull 3 *P:* G Cull 2
23 Aug	H	Llanelli	22-21	*T:* G Thomas, S Winn *P:* G Cull 4
18 Oct	H	Cardiff	27-27	*T:* L Davies, G Cull, D Francis *C:* G Cull 3 *P:* G Cull 2
25 Oct	A	Neath	10-52	*T:* S Greenaway *C:* M Lewis *P:* G Cull
6 Dec	H	Swansea	15-63	*T:* S Greenaway, G A Thomas *C:* M Lewis *P:* G Cull
13 Dec	A	Pontypridd	10-46	*T:* A Williams *C:* G Cull *P:* G Cull
27 Dec	H	Ebbw Vale	26-33	*T:* S Greenaway, A Durston *C:* G Cull 2 *P:* G Cull 4
31 Jan	A	Llanelli	14-14	*T:* L Manning, S Winn *C:* G Bowen 2
14 Feb	H	Neath	26-32	*T:* J Burnell, G Cull, O Thomas, C Kinsey *C:* G Cull 2, G Bowen
14 Mar	H	Newport	24-13	*T:* G Wilkins 2, O Thomas *P:* G Bowen 3
18 Apr	A	Cardiff	17-52	*T:* R Boobyer, A Durston *C:* G Cull, G Bowen *P:* G Bowen
2 May	A	Swansea	19-71	*T:* G Cull, S Ford, O Lloyd *C:* G Cull 2
9 May	H	Pontypridd	27-46	*T:* O Thomas, G Wilkins, A Williams *C:* G Cull 3 *P:* G Cull 2
15 May	A	Ebbw Vale	12-34	*T:* G A Thomas, S Winn *C:* G Cull

Cardiff

Year of formation 1876
Ground Cardiff Arms Park, Westgate Street, Cardiff CF1 1JA Tel: Cardiff (01222) 383546
Colours Cambridge blue and black
Captain 1997-98 J M Humphreys
WRU Leagues 1997-98 Div 1 2nd **SWALEC Cup 1997-98** Lost 9-24 to Ebbw Vale (6th round)

'We are spending too much on players' wages,' said chief executive Gareth Davies after Cardiff lost £1.1m in the first six months of their financial year. Davies admitted that the high expenditure in building a team had not brought the anticipated success on the field. With attendances dropping through lack of meaningful fixtures and the WRU withholding funding because Cardiff refused to sign a 10-year loyalty contract, there were mounting problems. They were strongly criticised for an obsession with forward domination and a lack of adventure. Ebbw Vale knocked them out of the cup by 24-9 and then Swansea completed a double victory to end any hopes of challenging for the league title. Pontypridd defeated Cardiff in the final of the unpopular WRU Challenge Trophy at Sardis Road by 15-10 and Bath put them out of the European Cup by 32-21 in the quarter-final at Bath.

Recruiting brought in Gregori Kacala and Tony Rees from Brive, Steve Williams (Neath), Spencer John (Llanelli), Gareth Thomas (Bridgend), Liam Botham (West Hartlepool), Steve Wake (Dunvant) and Canada stars Bob Ross and John Tait. Record try-scorer Steve Ford left to join Rumney after 13 years with the club. Lee Jarvis broke his own scoring record with 492 points, including 16 tries, in all matches. The season was darkened by the serious spinal injury Gwyn Jones suffered during the home match with Swansea in December. His condition was such that he was forced to retire from the game.

League Record 1997-98

Date	Venue	Opponents	Result	Scorers
16 Aug	A	Pontypridd	19-16	*T:* L Jarvis *C:* L Jarvis *P:* L Jarvis 4
23 Aug	A	Neath	46-12	*T:* Gareth Jones, Gwyn Jones, L Jarvis, J Humphreys, pen try *C:* L Jarvis 3 *P:* L Jarvis 5
18 Oct	A	Bridgend	27-27	*T:* R Howley, J Humphreys, G Kacala, pen try *C:* L Jarvis 2 *P:* L Jarvis
25 Oct	H	Ebbw Vale	30-24	*T:* L Davies, Gwyn Jones, S Hill *C:* L Jarvis 3 *P:* L Jarvis 3
6 Dec	A	Newport	26-25	*T:* G Thomas 2 *C:* L Jarvis 2 *P:* L Jarvis 4
13 Dec	H	Swansea	22-31	*T:* G Thomas 2 *P:* L Jarvis 4
27 Dec	A	Llanelli	24-26	*T:* J Thomas, L Davies, L Jarvis, pen try *C:* J Thomas, L Jarvis
31 Jan	H	Neath	50-11	*T:* N Walker 2, G Thomas, L Davies, G Kacala, A Lewis, C Morgan *C:* L Jarvis 3 *P:* L Jarvis 3
14 Feb	A	Ebbw Vale	33-18	*T:* L Davies, R Howley, L Jarvis, C Morgan *C:* L Jarvis 2 *P:* L Jarvis 3
18 Apr	H	Bridgend	52-17	*T:* R Howley 2, S Hill, L Davies, E Lewis, J Tait, J Thomas, D Young *C:* L Jarvis 6
25 Apr	H	Pontypridd	28-0	*T:* G Thomas 3, L Jarvis *C:* L Jarvis *P:* L Jarvis 2
9 May	A	Swansea	20-39	*T:* L Jarvis, J Ringer *C:* L Jarvis 2 *P:* L Jarvis 2
13 May	H	Newport	61-24	*T:* L Davies 2, J Thomas 2, L Botham, L Jarvis, J Tait, S Williams, S Hill *C:* L Jarvis 8
16 May	H	Llanelli	31-27	*T:* L Botham 2, S Hill, H Taylor *C:* L Jarvis 4 *P:* L Jarvis

Ebbw Vale

Year of formation 1880
Ground Eugene Cross Park, Ebbw Vale, Gwent Tel: Ebbw Vale (01495) 302995
Colours Red, white and green
Captain 1997-98 K P Jones
WRU Leagues 1997-98 Div 1 4th   **SWALEC Cup 1997-98** Lost 12-19 to Llanelli (final)

After twice defeating Llanelli in the league, Kingsley Jones's team failed against the Scarlets in their first cup final. It was a double disappointment for the Ebbw captain: during the same week he had been left out of the Wales team to tour South Africa. As an outstanding motivator and openside breakaway, he always set an inspiring example and his side put holders Cardiff and league champions Swansea out of the cup. The influence of the Tongans proved highly beneficial: the 21-year-old Suia Taumalolo was a fast, elusive attacking full-back, while 31-year-old lock Kuli Faletau proved of inestimable value in a rugged pack. Richie Collins, recruited from Bristol, was another key performer. The half-back unit of David Llewellyn and Byron Hayward triggered numerous successes and Hayward finished with 154 league points. Fourth was their highest finishing position in the league. This after losing their opening two matches against Swansea and Pontypridd while conceding 103 points. An explanation was that Hayward missed the early matches of the season. Still, they achieved far more than was anticipated.

League Record 1997-98

Date	Venue	Opponents	Result	Scorers
16 Aug	H	Swansea	11-47	T: A Harries P: A Harries D: G Bisp
23 Aug	A	Pontypridd	12-56	T: N Thomas, D Llewellyn C: A Harries
18 Oct	H	Newport	24-19	T: D Llewellyn, G Mason C: B Hayward P: B Hayward 4
25 Oct	A	Cardiff	24-30	T: B Hayward, G Williams C: B Hayward P: B Hayward 4
6 Dec	A	Llanelli	15-12	T: M Jones, K Jones C: B Hayward P: B Hayward
13 Dec	H	Neath	31-11	T: K Faletau, A Harries, G Mason, D Llewellyn C: B Hayward 4 P: B Hayward
27 Dec	A	Bridgend	33-26	T: A Harries, J Hawker, D Llewellyn, B Hayward, L Woodard C: B Hayward 4
31 Jan	H	Pontypridd	29-13	T: K Faletau, A Harries C: B Hayward 2 P: B Hayward 5
14 Feb	H	Cardiff	18-33	T: A Harries, pen try C: B Hayward P: B Hayward 2
14 Mar	A	Swansea	3-63	D: B Hayward
18 Apr	A	Newport	18-10	T: J Hawker, A Harries C: B Hayward P: B Hayward 2
2 May	H	Llanelli	26-15	T: C Billen, B Hayward C: B Hayward 2 P: B Hayward 4
9 May	A	Neath	24-28	T: A Harries, G Mason, pen try C: B Hayward 3 P: B Hayward
15 May	H	Bridgend	34-12	T: B Hayward 2, D Llewellyn, S Taumalolo C: B Hayward 4 P: B Hayward 2

Llanelli

Year of formation 1872
Ground Stradey Park, Llanelli, Dyfed SA15 4BT Tel: Llanelli (01554) 774060 and 0891 660221
Colours Scarlet and white
Captain 1997-98 R C McBryde

WRU Leagues 1997-98 Div 1 6th **SWALEC Cup 1997-98** *Winners* – beat Ebbw Vale 19-12 (Final)

A 10th cup triumph in their 13th final saw Llanelli finish with a flourish, though it was a disappointing season in the league with seven defeats. They lost Ieuan Evans, a legendary figure at Stradey, to Bath and injuries plagued the team. They had to call 34-year-old Hugh Williams-Jones out of retirement to prop and then negotiated with Penzance/Newlyn to play another prop, Martyn Madden, on loan. He made a dramatic impact with two tries on debut against Newport and then the winning try in the cup final. There was criticism of the high cost of Frano Botica's two seasons with the club: he played 42 games and reputedly received approximately £13,000 per game. Llanelli paid him two £50,000 signing-on fees, one for each of two seasons, and he was paid a basic £75,000 per season. Chairman Ron Jones attacked the previous committee for lack of financial control. He said, 'The keeping of records and financial documentation was shambolic.' Llanelli were the only side to inflict a league defeat on Swansea, but they won only one of their last seven league fixtures. Darril Williams, signed from Bonymaen, quickly became a great success at full-back and Craig Warlow continued to mature as fly-half successor to Botica. The ever-reliable Wayne Proctor completed his 100th try for the club.

League Record 1997-98

Date	Venue	Opponents	Result	Scorers
16 Aug	H	Neath	52-23	*T:* N Boobyer 2, D Williams, P Morris, W Proctor, S Ford, R Moon, I Jones *C:* F Botica 6
23 Aug	A	Bridgend	21-22	*T:* A Gibbs 2, C Davies *C:* C Warlow 3
18 Oct	A	Pontypridd	23-27	*T:* G Evans, C Warlow *C:* C Warlow 2 *P:* C Warlow 3
25 Oct	H	Swansea	25-22	*T:* I Jones *C:* C Warlow *P:* C Warlow 6
6 Dec	H	Ebbw Vale	12-15	*T:* N Boobyer, D Williams *C:* C Warlow
13 Dec	A	Newport	32-24	*T:* W Proctor 2, R McBryde, R Moon *C:* F Botica 3 *P:* F Botica 2
27 Dec	H	Cardiff	26-24	*T:* pen try, D Williams *C:* Botica 2 *P:* F Botica 4
3 Jan	A	Neath	6-31	*P:* F Botica, C Warlow
31 Jan	H	Bridgend	14-14	*T:* N Boobyer *P:* C Warlow 3
14 Feb	A	Swansea	26-26	*T:* C Warlow, N Boobyer *C:* C Warlow 2 *P:* C Warlow 4
18 Apr	H	Pontypridd	25-36	*T:* I Jones, S Jones, M Wintle *C:* C Warlow, N Boobyer *P:* C Warlow 2
2 May	A	Ebbw Vale	15-26	*T:* G Evans, A Gibbs *C:* S Jones *P:* S Jones
9 May	H	Newport	66-10	*T:* M Madden 2, W Proctor 2, G Evans, S Jones, I Jones, A Thomas, M Wintle, D Williams *C:* C Warlow 5, S Jones 3
16 May	A	Cardiff	27-31	*T:* W Proctor 3, A Gibbs *C:* C Warlow 2 *D:* N Boobyer

Neath

Year of formation 1871
Ground The Gnoll, Gnoll Park Road, Neath, West Glamorgan Tel: Neath (01639) 636547
Colours All black with white Maltese cross
Captain 1997-98 G Evans
WRU Leagues 1997-98 Div 1 5th **SWALEC Cup 1997-98** Lost 17-40 to Llanelli (quarter-final)

Chairman John Davies stood down at the end of the season, saying, 'The quality of rugby had degenerated. That is because clubs and players have not come to terms with professionalism. We have to go down a road of semi-professionalism or go back to amateur days because there is not enough cash around to sustain professional rugby. Players don't behave the same and the relationship that has evolved between players and committees is alien to me. Gates are dwindling and it is crippling the top clubs. We are all in a hell of a mess!' It was not an encouraging summing up and Neath struggled with only six league victories and exit from the cup by 40-17 at Llanelli in the quarter-final stage. Lyn Jones returned as coach and Ron Waldron also came back as team manager when Darryl Jones resigned as director of rugby in August, only for Waldron to quit again in May. Paul Thorburn joined the coaching team and turned out to make his 300th appearance. They lost international prop John Davies to Richmond (his three-year contract brought around £180,000) while Steve Williams went to Cardiff. Glyn Llewellyn returned when released by Harlequins.

League Record 1997-98

Date	Venue	Opponents	Result	Scorers
16 Aug	A	Llanelli	23-52	*T:* S Rees, A Palfrey, P Horgan *C:* I Calder *P:* I Calder 2
23 Aug	H	Cardiff	12-46	*T:* G Newman, G Evans *C:* D Case
18 Oct	A	Swansea	18-27	*T:* G Evans, P Horgan *C:* J Price *P:* J Price 2
25 Oct	H	Bridgend	52-10	*T:* G Bernard 3, I Boobyer, M Evans, S Martin *C:* J Price 5 *P:* J Price 4
6 Dec	H	Pontypridd	22-22	*T:* G Davies, L Jones, A Palfrey *C:* J Price 2 *P:* J Price
13 Dec	A	Ebbw Vale	11-31	*T:* Richard Jones *P:* J Price 2
27 Dec	H	Newport	23-22	*T:* G Evans, pen try *C:* C John 2 *P:* C John 3
3 Jan	H	Llanelli	31-6	*T:* M Davies, T Davies, G Evans, D Williams *C:* C John *P:* C John 3
31 Jan	A	Cardiff	11-50	*T:* P Horgan *P:* C John 2
14 Feb	A	Bridgend	32-26	*T:* G Evans, C John, D Williams, L Jones *C:* C John 3 *P:* C John 2
18 Apr	H	Swansea	28-36	*T:* pen tries 2, D Case *C:* C John 2 *P:* C John 3
2 May	A	Pontypridd	19-61	*T:* M Davies, P Horgan, I Jones *C:* C John 2
9 May	H	Ebbw Vale	28-24	*T:* M Bennett, G Newman *P:* C Bridges 4, C John 2
16 May	A	Newport	41-17	*T:* D Case, G Evans, D Williams, P Horgan, L Gerrard *C:* D Case 2 *P:* D Case 4

Newport

Year of formation 1874
Ground Rodney Parade, Newport, Gwent NP9 0UU Tel: Newport (01633) 258193 or 267410
Colours Black and amber
Captain 1997-98 I Jones
WRU Leagues 1997-98 Div 1 8th   **SWALEC Cup 1997-98** Lost 10-44 to Ebbw Vale (semi-final)

'Disaster' summed up a dismal record on the field and an undercurrent of unrest behind the scenes. New captain Ian Jones never faltered in trying to maintain enthusiasm, but the bleak fact was that his team lost all 14 league fixtures. Coach Steve Jones must have suffered numerous sleepless nights and there were frustrations, too, for Steve Fenwick when he joined as backs coach. Secretary Campbell Black resigned after nine years in the post because of a 'personality clash' with a member of the executive committee; and then Tom David gave up his post as director of rugby in December 1997 for work and family reasons. Centre John

Colderley went to Moseley, Adam Palfrey and Chris John to Neath, and David Waters, legendary second row, moved to help Merthyr. The opportunism of Shaun Connor was the redeeming factor behind the scrum; this maturing fly-half supplied 120 league points. Jan Machacek worked like five men at No 8, always impressive on the drive, while Rod Snow was a human dynamo at prop in scrum and open. Ian Gough was an athletic jumper and Matthew Watkins a runner to watch, but Newport have the proverbial mountain to climb.

League Record 1997-98

Date	Venue	Opponents	Result	Scorers
17 Aug	H	Bridgend	19-27	*T:* M Llewellyn *C:* S Connor *P:* S Connor 4
23 Aug	A	Swansea	14-38	*T:* M Llewellyn, A Lewis *C:* C John 2
18 Oct	A	Ebbw Vale	19-24	*T:* S Connor, M Llewellyn *P:* S Connor 3
25 Oct	A	Pontypridd	11-26	*T:* A Lawson *P:* S Connor, A Lawson
6 Dec	H	Cardiff	25-26	*T:* J Machacek *C:* S Connor *P:* S Connor 6
13 Dec	H	Llanelli	24-32	*T:* pen try, J Machacek, D Price
				C: S Connor 3 *P:* S Connor
27 Dec	A	Neath	22-23	*T:* S Connor, M Llewellyn, M Robinson
				C: S Connor 2 *P:* S Connor
31 Jan	H	Swansea	11-37	*T:* D Gray *P:* S Connor *D:* S Connor
14 Feb	A	Pontypridd	5-41	*T:* N Lloyd
14 Mar	A	Bridgend	13-24	*T:* M Llewellyn *C:* S Connor *P:* S Connor 2
18 Apr	H	Ebbw Vale	10-18	*T:* M Workman *C:* A Lawson *P:* S Connor
9 May	A	Llanelli	10-66	*T:* D Burn *C:* S Connor *P:* S Connor
13 May	A	Cardiff	24-61	*T:* S Connor, M Watkins, M Workman
				C: S Connor 3 *P:* S Connor
16 May	H	Neath	17-41	*T:* S Connor, B Davies *C:* S Connor 2
				P: S Connor

Pontypridd

Year of formation 1876
Ground Sardis Road Ground, Pwllgwaun, Pontypridd Tel: Pontypridd (01443) 405006 and 407170
Colours Black and white hoops
Captain 1997-98 N R Jenkins
WRU Leagues 1997-98 Div 1 3rd **SWALEC Cup 1997-98** Lost 27-29 to Newport (quarter-final)

'The Battle of Brive' is the match most remembered in a campaign that proved a keen disappointment for Pontypridd. They lost their league title to Swansea, were knocked out of the cup at Newport by the team who could not win a league match, and failed to reach the quarter-finals of the European Cup in a play-off at Brive. It was the previous visit that caused the rumpus. Dale McIntosh was sent off after being set upon by a few home players, who took exception to his late tackle on Philippe Carbonneau. Ponty players swarmed to the aid of the beleaguered No 8 and quickly a full scale action was in progress. Lionel Mallier was also ordered off, but a charge against McIntosh of bringing the game into disrepute was dropped. After the match there was an incident in the Bar Toulzac and the police delayed the team's return to Wales for a day while McIntosh, Phil John and André Barnard were questioned. Brive won 32-31 and did not want to play the return match. However, they were ordered to do so and drew 29-all at Sardis Road. The third meeting, in Brive, was a play-off for the quarter-final spot and Brive won by 25-20. 'They thought they could push us around, but we would not let them,' explained Neil Jenkins, the Ponty captain. Brive coach Laurent Seigne called the Pontypridd players 'semi-civilised animals'. All round, it was an ugly episode.

At the end of the season, rugby administrator Eddie Jones, a former captain and coach of the club, resigned after internal disagreement over the club signing a 10-year loyalty contract with the WRU. Ponty signed Dafydd James and Stuart Roy from Cardiff and also recruited Andrew Lamerton, Matthew McCarthy and Mike Griffiths.

League Record 1997-98

Date	Venue	Opponents	Result	Scorers
16 Aug	H	Cardiff	16-19	T: G Wyatt C: N Jenkins P: N Jenkins 2, G Wyatt
23 Aug	H	Ebbw Vale	56-12	T: K Morgan 2, M Rowley, D Manley, G Wyatt, Paul John, M Williams, D James, G Prosser C: A Barnard 4 P: A Barnard
18 Oct	H	Llanelli	27-23	T: D Manley, Paul John C: N Jenkins P: N Jenkins 5
25 Oct	A	Newport	26-11	T: Paul John 3, M Williams C: N Jenkins 3
6 Dec	A	Neath	22-22	T: M Williams, K Morgan P: N Jenkins 4
13 Dec	H	Bridgend	46-10	T: D McIntosh, A Griffiths, G Wyatt, A Barnard, G Prosser, S Lewis, G Lewis C: N Jenkins 4 P: N Jenkins
27 Dec	A	Swansea	24-24	T: K Morgan, G Wyatt C: N Jenkins P: N Jenkins 3 D: N Jenkins
31 Jan	A	Ebbw Vale	13-29	T: J Evans, G Prosser P: A Barnard
14 Feb	H	Newport	41-5	T: D James 2, G Lewis 2, N Jenkins, M Williams C: N Jenkins 4 P: N Jenkins
18 Apr	A	Llanelli	36-25	T: G Lewis, S Enoch, N Jenkins C: N Jenkins 3 P: N Jenkins 4 D: N Jenkins
25 Apr	A	Cardiff	0-28	
2 May	H	Neath	61-19	T: Paul John 2, G Lewis 2, S Enoch, S Bundy, D McIntosh, G Wyatt, S Lewis C: N Jenkins 8
9 May	A	Bridgend	46-27	T: G Lewis 2, G Wyatt 2, S Enoch, Paul John C: N Jenkins 4, M McCarthy P: N Jenkins 2
16 May	H	Swansea	27-45	T: S Enoch 2 C: N Jenkins P: N Jenkins 5

Swansea

Year of formation 1873
Ground St Helen's Ground, Bryn Road, Swansea, West Glamorgan SA2 0AR Tel: Swansea (01792) 466593
Colours All white
Captain 1997-98 G R Jenkins
WRU Leagues 1997-98 Div 1 – *Winners*   **SWALEC Cup 1997-98** Lost 13-27 to Ebbw Vale (quarter-final)

Success in the league for a third time in seven years was a well-deserved record and the prime ambition of Garin Jenkins's team. They fancied their chances in the cup against Ebbw Vale in the quarter-final after destroying Ebbw 63-3 at St Helen's in the match before their cup meeting. Alas, Kingsley Jones put the Indian sign on Arwel Thomas and Swansea went out on the valley club's ground by 27-13. New Zealander John Plumtree proved the ideal successor as coaching supremo to Mike Ruddock (who left to coach Leinster) and Swansea lost only one league match (to Llanelli). They defeated their closest challengers Cardiff twice and, ironically, Ebbw Vale twice. However, their European Cup experience was disappointing and they did not reach the quarter-finals. Wasps defeated them twice, the second time by a whisker at 29-28. Arwel Thomas was top-scorer in the Premier Division with 246 points (five tries). No 8 Stuart Davies proved a key figure in a dominating pack and was recalled by Wales. A testimonial match was held for Anthony Clement on 29 April 1998 and Clement's Invitation XV defeated Swansea 57-51. Swansea's running game made them the most entertaining team in the division.

League Record 1997-98

Date	Venue	Opponents	Result	Scorers
16 Aug	A	Ebbw Vale	47-11	*T:* A Thomas, R Appleyard, M Back, D Thomas, Simon Davies, M Taylor, D Weatherley *C:* A Thomas 6
23 Aug	H	Newport	38-14	*T:* A Harris 2, P Arnold, A Thomas, R Rees, R Appleyard *C:* A Thomas 4
18 Oct	H	Neath	27-18	*T:* A Booth, M Back, A Grabham, T Maulin *C:* A Williams, A Thomas *P:* A Thomas
25 Oct	A	Llanelli	22-25	*T:* M Back, A Harris *P:* A Thomas 2, L Davies 2
6 Dec	A	Bridgend	63-15	*T:* Stuart Davies 3, M Taylor, pen try, R Rees, G Jenkins, A Booth, D Thomas *C:* A Thomas 6 *P:* A Thomas 2
13 Dec	A	Cardiff	31-22	*T:* R Appleyard, Stuart Davies, S Gibbs *C:* A Thomas 2 *P:* A Thomas 3 *D:* A Thomas
27 Dec	H	Pontypridd	24-24	*P:* A Thomas 8
31 Jan	A	Newport	37-11	*T:* A Thomas 2, R Rees, A Moore *C:* A Thomas 4 *P:* A Thomas 3
14 Feb	H	Llanelli	26-26	*T:* R Rees *P:* A Thomas 7
14 Mar	H	Ebbw Vale	63-3	*T:* S Gibbs 2, G Jenkins 2, P Moriarty 2, R Rees, Stuart Davies, T Maullin *C:* A Thomas 6 *P:* A Thomas *D:* A Thomas
18 Apr	A	Neath	36-28	*T:* Rhodri Jones, M Taylor, T Maullin, P Moriarty *C:* A Thomas 2 *P:* A Thomas 4
2 May	H	Bridgend	71-19	*T:* R Rees 4, M Taylor 2, P Arnold, A Booth, Simon Davies, P Moriarty, D Weatherley *C:* A Thomas 8
9 May	H	Cardiff	39-20	*T:* Simon Davies, S Gibbs, A Thomas *C:* A Thomas 3 *P:* A Thomas 6
16 May	A	Pontypridd	45-27	*T:* P Moriarty 2, S Gibbs, A Booth, C Charvis *C:* A Thomas 4 *P:* A Thomas 4

EN ROUTE TO THE WORLD CUP

THE 1997-98 SEASON IN FRANCE

Bob Donahue *International Herald Tribune*

Here was a dramatic season. French emotions ranged from despair in November to jubilation in April. Coaches Jean-Claude Skrela and Pierre Villepreux tried 40 players in 11 Tests. Call it a learning experience for all involved, supporters included.

The coaches stuck to their plan to raise the national squad to southern hemisphere level. The leaders of the French Rugby Federation supported the coaches. Distinguished players who failed to convert to the new faith were dropped. At the end of the season, Skrela said he reckoned he had 13 starters for the 1999 World Cup.

The World Cup was an obsession. Sometimes it seemed that tours and the Five Nations matches, win or lose, were really little more than training outings. Poor Celtic showings heightened fears that the northern hemisphere was sinking. Said Skrela in April: 'If we want to compete one day with the south, we need strong teams in Wales, Scotland and Ireland. We'll succeed together or not at all.'

In France, as in England, the major clubs and their money worries confronted the game as a whole. So tangled was the struggle that the season ended without an agreed structure for the 1998-99 club championship. 'Fifteen Months of Muddle,' complained *L'Equipe*. Adaptation to the professional era was proving very difficult. All these obdurate gentlemen needed a referee. The interminable fracas did nothing for rugby's good name.

The story of the international season starts in Australia in June 1997. France had achieved a Grand Slam in the Five Nations and seemed on its way to fine things. Instead, both Tests were lost ingloriously.

Next came a home series against Italy, Romania and Argentina, amid much grumbling. People asked what the point was. Aren't we told constantly that the players turn out much too often? Why inflict these meaningless Tests on them? In the event, all three French victories were lacklustre. The team were whistled off the pitch.

And then South Africa arrived. A late French surge in Lyon brought a flattering losing scoreline. A week later, on November 22, the sky fell in on France's farewell to the Parc des Princes – 10-52! The big black headline in *Midi Olympique* used just one word: 'Nightmare'.

Manager Jo Maso and the coaches did an unusual thing, publishing an open letter to the stunned rugby community. The Springboks, they argued, had given a magnificent illustration of the sort of

The France squad which faced England in Paris. L-R, back row: T Cléda (replacement), M Dal Maso (replacement), C Califano, F Tournaire, C Soulette (replacement), M Lièvremont (replacement), O Magne, T Lièvremont, P Benetton, F Pelous, O Brouzet; front row: D Aucagne (replacement), P Bernat-Salles, C Dominici, X Garbajosa (replacement), J-L Sadourny, R Ibañez (capt), C Lamaison, P Carbonneau, T Castaignède, S Glas, F Galthié (replacement)

rugby that France must learn to play. So, let's get on with it.

Villepreux later commented that the Springbok lesson had been a blessing because it helped get rid of some foot-dragging veterans. By the time Five Nations play began, Olivier Merle, Laurent Cabannes, Abdel Benazzi, Thierry Lacroix, Philippe Saint-André and Laurent Leflamand were international has-beens.

Tension was high before the England match in February. Defeat was unthinkable, but were France any good at all? Hooker Raphael Ibañez of Dax was the new captain. Thomas Castaignède of Castres had been shifted to stand-off. The new No 8 was Thomas Lièvremont of Perpignan, soon to be joined in the back row by his elder brother Marc of Stade Français in Paris. A crowd of close to 80,000 saw England well beaten in rugby's debut at the State de France in Saint-Denis.

It was felt that France, on the day, should have won by a larger margin. Mostly, though, there was worry that after a one-off exploit at home, Ibañez and company would flop at Murrayfield. But they certainly did not flop. Now Frenchmen let themselves be happy – until Ireland came to Saint-Denis and were unlucky to lose.

The finale at Wembley, where dashing Castaignède led a rout of Wales, brought another Grand Slam – two in a row for France for the first time. The French had totalled 18 Five Nations tries. Skrela confessed that the months between the Springboks and England had been 'awful' for him. Now he would set out soon for Argentina and Fiji in good heart.

Tighthead Franck Tournaire and full-back Jean-Luc Sadourny started all 11 Tests. Loosehead Christian Califano, locks Fabien Pelous and Olivier Brouzet and centre Christophe Lamaison started 10 of them. There were five half-back pairings, with Philippe Carbonneau and Castaignède finally settling in.

The bad news, meanwhile, was that the English clubs were pulling out of the Heineken European Championship, which had proved a big success in France. This season, three French clubs made it to the semi-finals, where Brive bettered Toulouse while Bath knocked out Agen. Bath proceeded to beat Brive in the final in Bordeaux.

Toulouse salvaged a disappointing season by winning the French Cup final against the Stade Français.

FRENCH CLUB CHAMPIONSHIP FINAL
16 May, Stade de France (Saint-Denis)
STADE FRANÇAIS 34 (3G 1PG 2T)   PERPIGNAN 7 (1G)

The meteoric rise of an old Paris club from the Second Division to the lower half of the First Division to the upper half in consecutive years was already impressive. To then promptly reach the final, and make it a one-sided romp, was even more so. A tycoon's money helped, of course, but the squad, coached by Bernard Laporte, played some fine rugby.

Perpignan were game but helpless against the aggressive defence and technical precision of the Parisians, who seemed to be forever going forward. The score was 24-0 within an hour. The first final at the new Stade de France, featuring a Lièvremont brother on each side, was spectacular and clean.

Stade Français: A Gomès; C Dominici, F Comba, C Mytton, E Bolo-Bolo; D Dominguez, C Laussucq; S Simon, V Moscato (*capt*), P Gimbert, D Auradou, H Chaffardon, M Lièvremont, C Juillet, R Pool-Jones *Substitutions:* G Abadie for Bolo-Bolo; C Moni for Pool-Jones; G Ross for Chaffardon; O Roumat for Auradou; S Marconnet for Gimbert; L Pedrosa for Moscato
Scorers *Tries:* Simon, Mytton, Bolo-Bolo, Gomès, Dominici
Conversions: Dominguez (3)   *Penalty Goal:* Dominguez
Perpignan: G Bastide; A Joubert, D Plana, M Barrau, G Tutard; L Saliès, J Basset; R Peillard, J Lançon, S De Besombes, J Pradal, M James, S Deroeux, T Lièvremont (*capt*), G Majoral *Substitutions:* H Laporte for Barrau; M Arandiga for Saliès; C Pérarnau for Basset; O Oilbeau for Deroeux; A Fourny for Pradal; M Koniekiewicz for Lançon; P Meya for Peillard
Scorers *Try:* Pérarnau   *Conversion:* Arandiga
Referee J Dumé (Côte d'Argent)

FRANCE TO AUSTRALIA 1997

THE TOURING PARTY

Manager J Maso   **Tour Director** J Dunyach   **Coach** J-C Skrela
Assistant Coaches P Villepreux, M Godemet   **Captain** A Benazzi

Full-backs: J-L Sadourny (Colomiers), S Viars (Brive), N Brusque (Pau)

Threequarters: P Bernat-Salles (Pau), D Venditti (Brive), P Bondouy (Narbonne), R Dourthe (Dax), D Dantiacq (Pau), T Castaignède (Stade Toulousain), C Lamaison (Brive), S Viars (Brive)

Half-backs: D Aucagne (Pau), A Penaud (Brive), F Torossian (Pau), G Accoceberry (Bègles-Bordeaux), P Carbonneau (Brive)

Forwards: M Dal Maso (Agen), R Ibañez (Dax), D Casadei (Brive), F Tournaire (Narbonne), P Triep-Capdeville (Pau), C Califano (Stade Toulousain), D Laperne (Dax), T Cléda (Pau), H Miorin (Stade Toulousain), O Merle (Montferrand), O Brouzet (Bègles-Bordeaux), O Magne (Dax), R Castel (Béziers), A Benazzi (Agen), P Raschi (Bourgoin-Jallieu), F Pelous (Dax), M Lièvremont (Perpignan), *T Lièvremont (Perpignan)

* *Replacement on tour*

TOUR RECORD

All matches   Played 6   Won 3   Lost 3   Points for 189   Against 140
International matches   Played 2   Lost 2   Points for 34   Against 55

SCORING DETAILS

All matches					International matches				
For:	27T	15C	8PG	189 Pts	For:	3T	2C	5PG	34 Pts
Against:	13T	6C	21PG	140 Pts	Against:	5T	3C	8PG	55 Pts

MATCH DETAILS

1997	OPPONENTS	VENUE	RESULT
10 June	Victoria	Melbourne	W 65-13
13 June	ACT President's XV	Canberra	W 31-22
17 June	Queensland	Brisbane	W 34-24
21 June	AUSTRALIA	Sydney	L 15-29
24 June	Australian Barbarians	Newcastle	L 25-26
28 June	AUSTRALIA	Sydney	L 19-26

MATCH 1   10 June, Olympic Park, Melbourne

Victoria 13 (1PG 2T)   **France XV 65** (5G 6T)
Victoria: A Pilli; P Ioane, M Nasalio, L Strauss, G Low; A Hendry, L Daley; A Charles, D Thompson *(capt)*, S Iakodvidis, B Parsons, T Booth, C Fraser, N Urika, J Deans *Substitutions:* Holsted for Fraser (54 mins); Chirila for Low (61 mins); Naituku for Iakovidis (66 mins); Hardley for Parsons (77 mins)
Scorers *Tries:* Nasalio (2) *Penalty Goal:* Hendry
France XV: Brusque; Viars, Dourthe, Castaignède, Bondouy; Aucagne, Accoceberry *(capt)*; Triep-Capdeville, Dal Maso, Califano, Cléda, Merle, Magne, Raschi, Castel *Substitutions:* Miorin for Merle (47 mins); Tournaire for Califano (57 mins); Lamaison for Castaignède (61 mins); Ibañez for Dal Maso (67 mins)

Scorers *Tries:* Dourthe (3), Viars (2), Castaignède, Bondouy, Aucagne, Lamaison, Magne, Raschi *Conversions:* Dourthe (5)
Referee M Keogh (ACT)

MATCH 2   13 June, Bruce Stadium, Canberra

ACT President's XV 22 (2G 1PG 1T)   **France XV 31** (3G 2T)
ACT President's XV: R Kafer (*capt*); MD Hardy, J Holbeck, G Logan, L O'Connor; DJ Knox, A Cairns; D Zammit, T Tavalea, P Noreiga, JF Langford, J Harrison, T Jaques, ODA Finegan, I Fenukitau *Substitutions:* J Ross for Jaques (10 mins); A Obad for Hardy (46 mins); J McGrath for Logan (69 mins)
Scorers *Tries:* Knox, Fenukitau, penalty try *Conversions:* Knox (2)
Penalty Goal: Knox
France XV: Sadourny; Bernat-Salles, Lamaison, Castaignède, Venditti; Penaud, Carbonneau; Califano, Dal Maso, Tournaire, Merle, Brouzet, Benazzi (*capt*), Pelous, T Lièvremont *Substitutions:* Miorin for Brouzet (50 mins); Magne for Lièvremont (50 mins); Dourthe for Lamaison (75 mins)
Scorers *Tries:* Sadourny (2), Bernet-Salles, Venditti, Benazzi
Conversions: Lamaison (3)
Referee S Dickinson (NSW)

MATCH 3   17 June, Ballymore, Brisbane

Queensland 24 (1G 4PG 1T)   **France XV 34** (3G 1PG 2T)
Queensland: N Williams; DPP Smith, DJ Herbert, N Grey, D McInally; EJ Flatley, B Johnstone (*capt*); M Ryan, C Knapp, J Watkins, M Gabey, R Johnston, T Kefu, M Connors, A Coombe *Substitutions:* T Mandrusiak for Flatley (18 mins); L Grant for Herbert (27 mins); GJ Morgan for Johnston (53 mins); D Barrett for Knapp (70 mins)
Scorers *Tries:* McInally, Gabey *Conversion:* Mandrusiak *Penalty Goals:* Flatley (2), Mandrusiak (2)
France XV: Brusque; Viars, Dourthe, Dantiacq, Bondouy; Aucagne, Torossian; Casedei, Ibañez (*capt*), Triep-Capdeville, Brouzet, Cléda, M Lièvremont, Raschi, Castel *Substitution:* Magne for Lièvremont (75 mins)
Scorers *Tries:* Viars (2), Brusque, Ibañez, Dourthe *Conversions:* Dourthe (3)
Penalty Goal: Dourthe
Referee A Cole (Queensland)

MATCH 4   21 June, Sydney Football Stadium   1st Test
AUSTRALIA 29 (2G 5PG)   FRANCE 15 (1G 1PG 1T)

AUSTRALIA: SJ Larkham (ACT); BN Tune (Queensland), JS Little (Queensland), PW Howard (ACT), JW Roff (ACT); TJ Horan (Queensland), GM Gregan (ACT); RLL Harry (NSW), M Caputo (ACT), EJA McKenzie (NSW), D Giffin (ACT), JA Eales (Queensland)(*capt*), BJ Robinson (ACT), DT Manu (NSW), DJ Wilson (Queensland) *Substitutions:* T Coker (Queensland) for Wilson (51 mins); MD Hardy (ACT) for Larkham (temp 59-72 mins); SJ Payne (NSW) for Little (temp 68-71 mins)
Scorers *Tries:* Hardy (2) *Conversions:* Eales (2) *Penalty Goals:* Eales (5)
FRANCE: Sadourny; Bernat-Salles, Dourthe, Castaignède, Venditti; Aucagne, Carbonneau; Califano, Dal Maso, Tournaire, Merle, Brouzet, Benazzi (*capt*), Pelous, Magne *Substitutions:* Viars for Venditti (39 mins); Castel for Magne (57 mins)

Scorers *Tries:* Bernat-Salles, Castaignède *Conversion:* Dourthe
Penalty Goal: Dourthe
Referee C Thomas (Wales)

MATCH 5   24 June, Breakers Stadium, Newcastle

Australian Barbarians 26 (7PG 1T)   **France XV 25** (2G 2PG 1T)
Australian Barbarians: C Latham (ACT); MD Hardy (ACT), S Taupeaafe
(NSW), J Holbeck (ACT), DPP Smith (Queensland); C Warner (NSW),
C Whitaker (NSW); CD Blades (NSW), PN Kearns (NSW)(*capt*), A Heath
(NSW), S Domoni (NSW), JF Langford (ACT), S Pinkerton (NSW), ODA
Finegan (ACT), SF Finau (NSW) *Substitutions:* A Murdoch (NSW) for Hardy
(64 mins); D Zammit (ACT) for C Blades (67 mins); BT Gavin (NSW) for
Domoni (69 mins); M Edmunds (NSW) for Warner (74 mins)
Scorers *Try:* Hardy *Penalty Goals:* Warner (6), Edmunds
France XV: Brusque; Viars, Lamaison, Dantiacq, Bondouy; Penaud, Accoceberry
(*capt*); Casedei, Ibañez, Triep-Capdeville, Merle, Miorin, Cléda, Raschi, M
Lièvremont *Substitutions:* Dourthe for Dantiacq (47 mins); Magne for Merle
(64 mins)
Scorers *Tries:* Dantiacq, Casedei, Lamaison *Conversions:* Viars, Dourthe
Penalty Goals: Viars, Dourthe
Referee S Dickinson

MATCH 6   28 June, Ballymore, Brisbane   2nd Test
AUSTRALIA 26 (1G 3PG 2T)   FRANCE 19 (1G 4PG)

AUSTRALIA: SJ Larkham (ACT); BN Tune (Queensland), JS Little
(Queensland), PW Howard (ACT), JW Roff (ACT); TJ Horan (Quennsland),
GM Gregan (ACT); RLL Harry (NSW), M Caputo (ACT), EJA McKenzie
(NSW), D Giffin (ACT), JA Eales (Queensland)(*capt*), BJ Robinson (ACT),
T Coker (Queensland), DJ Wilson (Queensland) *Substitutions:* MD Hardy (ACT)
for Little (60 mins); M Cockbain (Queensland) for Wilson (70 mins)
Scorers *Tries:* Harry, Tune, Little *Conversion:* Eales *Penalty Goals:* Eales (3)
FRANCE: Sadourny; Bernat Salles, Lamaison, Castaignède, Viars; Penaud,
Carbonneau; Califano, Dal Maso, Tournaire, Merle, Brouzet, Benazzi (*capt*),
Pelous, Magne *Substitutions:* M Lièvremont for Pelous (70 mins); Bondouy for
Viars (77 mins)
Scorers *Try:* Castaignède *Conversion:* Lamaison *Penalty Goals:* Lamaison (4)
Referee C Thomas (Wales)

FRENCH INTERNATIONAL PLAYERS
(*up to 30 April 1998*)

Note: Years given for Five Nations matches are for second half of season, eg 1972 refers to season 1971-72. Years for all other matches refer to the actual year of the match. When a series has taken place, or more than one match has been played against a country in the same year, figures have been used to denote the particular matches in which players have featured. Thus 1967 *SA* 2,4 indicates that a player appeared in the second and fourth Tests of the 1967 series against South Africa. This list includes only those players who have appeared in FFR International Matches '*donnant droit au titre d'international*'.

Abadie, A (Pau) 1964 *I*
Abadie, A (Graulhet) 1965 *R*, 1967 *SA* 1, 3, 4, *NZ*, 1968 *S, I*
Abadie, L (Tarbes) 1963 *R*
Accoceberry, G (Bègles) 1994 *NZ* 1,2, *C* 2, 1995 *W, E, S, I, R* 1, [*Iv, S*], *It*, 1996 *I, W* 1, *R, Arg* 1, *W* 2(R), *SA* 2, 1997 *S, It* 1
Aguerre, R (Biarritz O) 1979 *S*
Aguilar, D (Pau) 1937 *G*
Aguirre, J-M (Bagnères) 1971 *A* 2, 1972 *S*, 1973 *W, I, J, R*, 1974 *I, W, Arg* 2, *R, SA* 1, 1976 *W* (R), *E, US, A* 2, *R*, 1977 *W, E, S, I, Arg* 1,2, *NZ* 1,2, *R*, 1978 *E, S, I, W, R*, 1979 *I, W, E, S, NZ* 1,2, *R*, 1980 *W, I*
Ainciart, E (Bayonne) 1933 *G*, 1934 *G*, 1935 *G*, 1937 *G, It*, 1938 *G* 1
Albaladejo, P (Dax) 1954 *E, It*, 1960 *W, I, It, R*, 1961 *S, SA, E, W, I, NZ* 1,2, *A*, 1962 *S, E, W, I*, 1963 *S, I, E, W, It*, 1964 *S, NZ, W, It, I, SA, Fj*
Alvarez, A-J (Tyrosse) 1945 *B*2, 1946 *B, I, K, W*, 1947 *S, I, W, E*, 1948 *I, A, S, W, E*, 1949 *I, E, W*, 1951 *S, E, W*
Amand, H (SF) 1906 *NZ*
Ambert, A (Toulouse) 1930 *S, I, E, G, W*
Amestoy, J-B (Mont-de-Marsan) 1964 *NZ, E*
André, G (RCF) 1913 *SA, E, W, I*, 1914 *I, W, E*
Andrieu, M (Nîmes) 1986 *Arg* 2, *NZ* 1, *R* 2, *NZ* 2, 1987 [*R, Z*], *R*, 1988 *E, S, I, W, Arg* 1,2,3,4, *R*, 1989 *I, W, E, S, NZ* 2, *B, A* 2, 1990 *W, E, I* (R)
Anduran, J (SCUF) 1910 *W*
Araou, R (Narbonne) 1924 *R*
Arcalis, R (Brive) 1950 *S, I*, 1951 *I, E, W*
Arino, M (Agen) 1962 *R*
Aristouy, P (Pau) 1948 *S*, 1949 *Arg* 2, 1950 *S, I, E, W*
Arlettaz, P (Perpignan) 1995 *R* 2
Armary, L (Lourdes) 1987 [*R*], *R*, 1988 *S, I, W, Arg* 3,4, *R*, 1989 *W, S, A* 1,2, 1990 *W, E, S, I, A* 1,2,3, *NZ* 1, 1991 *W* 2, 1992 *S, I, R, Arg* 1,2, *SA* 1, 2, *Arg*, 1993 *E, S, I, W, SA* 1,2, *R* 2, *A* 1,2, 1994 *I, W, NZ* 1 (t), 2 (t), 1995 *I, R* 1 [*Tg, I, SA*]
Arnal, J-M (RCF) 1914 *I, W*
Arnaudet, M (Lourdes) 1964 *I*, 1967 *It, W*
Arotca, R (Bayonne) 1938 *R*
Arrieta, J (SF) 1953 *E, W*
Arthapignet, P (see Harislur-Arthapignet)
Astre, R (Béziers) 1971 *R*, 1972 *I* 1, 1973 *E* (R), 1975 *E, S, I, SA* 1,2, *Arg* 2, 1976 *A* 2, *R*
Aucagne, D (Pau) 1997 *W* (R), *S, It* 1, *R* 1 (R), *A* 1, *R* 2 (R), *SA* 2 (R), 1998 *S* (R), *W* (R)
Aué, J-M (Castres) 1998 *W* (R)
Augé, J (Dax) 1929 *S, W*
Augras-Fabre, L (Agen) 1931 *I, S, W*
Averous, J-L (La Voulte) 1975 *S, I, SA* 1,2, 1976 *I, W, E, US, A* 1,2, *R*, 1977 *W, E, S, I, Arg* 1, *R*, 1978 *E, S, I*, 1979 *NZ* 1,2, 1980 *E, S*, 1981 *A* 2
Azam, O (Montferrand) 1995 *R* 2, *Arg* (R)
Azarete, J-L (Dax, St Jean-de-Luz) 1969 *W, R*, 1970 *S, I, W, R*, 1971 *S, I, E, SA* 1,2, *A* 1, 1972 *E, W, I* 2, *A* 1, *R*, 1973 *NZ, W, I, R*, 1974 *I, R, SA* 1,2, 1975 *W*

Bacqué, N (Pau) 1997 *R* 2
Bader, E (Primevères) 1926 *M*, 1927 *I, S*
Badin, C (Chalon) 1973 *W, I*, 1975 *Arg* 1
Baillette, M (Perpignan) 1925 *I, NZ, S*, 1926 *W, M*, 1927 *I, W, G* 2, 1929 *G*, 1930 *S, I, E, G*, 1931 *I, E*, 1932 *G*
Baladie, G (Agen) 1945 *B* 1,2, *W*, 1946 *B, I, K*
Ballarin, J (Tarbes) 1924 *E*, 1925 *NZ, W*
Baquey, J (Toulouse) 1921 *I*
Barbazanges, A (Roanne) 1932 *G*, 1933 *G*
Barrau, M (Beaumont, Toulouse) 1971 *S, E, W*, 1972 *E, W, A* 1,2, 1973 *S, NZ, E, I, J, R*, 1974 *I, S*

Barrère, P (Toulon) 1929 *G*, 1931 *W*
Barrière, R (Béziers) 1960 *R*
Barthe, E (SBUC) 1925 *W, E*
Barthe, J (Lourdes) 1954 *Arg* 1,2, 1955 *S*, 1956 *I, W, It, E, Cz*, 1957 *S, I, E, W, R* 1,2, 1958 *S, E, A, W, It, I, SA* 1,2, 1959 *S, E, It, W*
Basauri, R (Albi) 1954 *Arg* 1
Bascou, P (Bayonne) 1914 *E*
Basquet, G (Agen) 1945 *W*, 1946 *B, I, K, W*, 1947 *S, I, W, E*, 1948 *I, A, S, W, E*, 1949 *S, I, E, W, Arg* 1, 1950 *S, I, E, W*, 1951 *S, I, E, W*, 1952 *S, I, SA, W, E, It*
Bastiat, J-P (Dax) 1969 *R*, 1970 *S, I, W*, 1971 *S, I, SA* 2, 1972 *A* 1, 1973 *E*, 1974 *Arg* 1,2, *SA* 2, 1975 *W, Arg* 1,2, *R*, 1976 *S, I, W, E, A* 1,2, *R*, 1977 *W, E, S, I*, 1978 *E, S, I, W*
Baudry, N (Montferrand) 1949 *S, I, W, Arg* 1,2
Baulon, R (Vienne, Bayonne) 1954 *S, NZ, W, E, It*, 1955 *I, E, W, It*, 1956 *S, I, W, It, E, Cz*, 1957 *S, I, It*
Baux, J-P (Lannemezan) 1968 *NZ* 1,2, *SA* 1,2
Bavozet, J (Lyon) 1911 *S, E, W*
Bayard, J (Toulouse) 1923 *S, W, E*, 1924 *W, R, US*
Bayardon, J (Chalon) 1964 *S, NZ, E*
Beaurin-Gressier, C (SF) 1907 *E*, 1908 *E*
Bégu, J (Dax) 1982 *Arg* 2 (R), 1984 *E, S*
Béguerie, C (Agen) 1979 *NZ* 1
Beguet, L (RCF) 1922 *I*, 1923 *S, W, E, I*, 1924 *S, I, E, R, US*
Behoteguy, A (Bayonne, Cognac) 1923 *E*, 1924 *S, I, E, W, R, US*, 1926 *E*, 1927 *E, G* 1,2, 1928 *A, I, E, G, W*, 1929 *S, W, E*
Behoteguy, H (RCF, Cognac) 1923 *W*, 1928 *A, I, E, G, W*
Belascain, C (Bayonne) 1977 *R*, 1978 *E, S, I, W, R*, 1979 *I, W, E, S*, 1982 *W, E, S, I*, 1983 *E, S, I, W*
Belletante, G (Nantes) 1951 *I, E, W*
Benazzi, A (Agen) 1990 *A* 1,2,3, *NZ* 1,2, 1991 *E, US* 1 (R), 2, [*R, Fj, C*], 1992 *SA* 1 (R), 2, *Arg*, 1993 *E, S, I, W, A* 1,2, 1994 *I, W, E, S, C* 1, *NZ* 1,2, *C* 2, 1995 *W, E, S, I*, [*Tg, Iv, S, SA, E*], *NZ* 1,2, 1996 *E, S, I, W* 1, *Arg* 1,2, *W* 2, *SA* 1,2, 1997 *I, W, E, S, R* 1, *A* 1,2, *It* 2, *R* 2 (R), *Arg, SA* 1,2
Bénésis, R (Narbonne) 1969 *W, R*, 1970 *S, I, W, E, R*, 1971 *S, I, E, W, A* 2, 1972 *S, I* 1, *E, W, I* 2, *A* 1, *R*, 1973 *NZ, E, W, I, J, R*, 1974 *W, E, S*
Benetiere, J (Roanne) 1954 *It, Arg* 1
Benetton, P (Agen) 1989 *B*, 1990 *NZ* 2, 1991 *US* 2, 1992 *Arg* 1,2 (R), *SA* 1 (R), 2, *Arg*, 1993 *E, S, I, W, SA* 1,2, *R* 2, *A* 1,2, 1994 *I, W, E, S, C* 1, *NZ* 1,2, *C* 2, 1995 *W, E, S, I*, [*Tg, Iv* (R), *S*], *It, R* 2 (R), *Arg, NZ* 1, 2, 1996 *Arg* 1,2, *W* 2, *SA* 1,2, 1997 *I, It* 1,2 (R), *R* 2, *Arg, SA* 1,2 1998 *E, S* (R), *I* (R), *W* (R)
Benezech, L (RCF) 1994 *E, S, C* 1, *NZ* 1,2, *C* 2, 1995 *W, E*, [*Iv, S, E*], *R* 2, *Arg, NZ* 1, 2
Berbizier, P (Lourdes, Agen) 1981 *S, I, W, E, NZ* 1,2, 1982 *I, R*, 1983 *S, I*, 1984 *S, I, W, E, NZ* 1,2, 1985 *Arg* 1,2, 1986 *S, I, W, E, R* 1, *Arg* 1, *A, NZ* 1, *R* 2, *NZ* 2,3, 1987 *W, E, S, I*, [*S, R, Fj, A, NZ*], *R*, 1988 *E, S, I, W, Arg* 1,2,3, 1989 *I, W, E, S, NZ* 1,2, *B, A* 1, 1990 *W, E*, 1991 *S, I, W* 1, *E*
Berejnoi, J-C (Tulle) 1963 *R*, 1964 *S, W, It, I, SA, Fj, R*, 1965 *S, I, E, W, It, R*, 1966 *S, I, E, W, It, R*, 1967 *S, A, E, It, W, I, R*
Berges, B (Toulouse) 1926 *I*
Berges-Cau, R (Lourdes) 1976 *E* (R)
Bergese, F (Bayonne) 1936 *G* 2, 1937 *G, It*, 1938 *G* 1, *R, G* 2
Bergougnan, Y (Toulouse) 1945 *B* 1, *W*, 1946 *B, I, K, W*, 1947 *S, I, W, E*, 1948 *S, W, E*, 1949 *S, E, Arg* 1,2
Bernard, R (Bergerac) 1951 *S, I, E, W*

Bernat-Salles, P (Pau, Bègles-Bordeaux) 1992 *Arg*, 1993 *R* 1, *SA* 1,2, *R* 2, *A* 1,2, 1994 *I*, 1995 *E, S*, 1996 *E* (R), 1997 *R* 1, *A* 1,2, 1998 *E, S, I, W*

Bernon, J (Lourdes) 1922 *I*, 1923 *S*

Bérot, J-L (Toulouse) 1968 *NZ* 3, *A*, 1969 *S, I*, 1970 *E, R*, 1971 *S, I, E, W, SA* 1,2, *A* 1,2, *R*, 1972 *S, I* 1, *E, W, A* 1, 1974 *I*

Bérot, P (Agen) 1986 *R* 2, *NZ* 2, 3, 1987 *W, E, S, I, R*, 1988 *S, I, Arg* 1, 2, 3, 4, *R*, 1989 *S, NZ* 1, 2

Bertrand, P (Bourg) 1951 *I, E, W*, 1953 *S, I, E, W, It*

Bertranne, R (Bagnères) 1971 *E, W, SA* 2, *A* 1,2, 1972 *S, I* 1, 1973 *NZ, E, J, R*, 1974 *I, W, E, S, Arg* 1,2, *R, SA* 1,2, 1975 *W, E, S, I, SA* 1,2, *Arg* 1,2, *R*, 1976 *S, I, W, E, US, A* 1,2, *R*, 1977 *W, E, S, I, Arg* 1,2, *NZ* 1,2, *R*, 1978 *E, S, I, W, R*, 1979 *I, W, E, S, R*, 1980 *W, E, S, I, SA, R*, 1981 *S, I, W, E, R, NZ* 1,2

Berty, D (Toulouse) 1990 *NZ* 2, 1992 *R* (R), 1993 *R* 2, 1995 *NZ* 1 (R), 1996 *W* 2(R), *SA* 1

Besset, E (Grenoble) 1924 *S*

Besset, L (SCUF) 1914 *W, E*

Besson, M (CASG) 1924 *I*, 1925 *I, E*, 1926 *S, W*, 1927 *I*

Besson, P (Brive) 1963 *S, I, E*, 1965 *R*, 1968 *SA* 1

Betsen, S (Biarritz) 1997 *It* 1 (R)

Bianchi, J (Toulon) 1986 *Arg* 1

Bichindaritz, J (Biarritz O) 1954 *It, Arg* 1,2

Bidart, L (La Rochelle) 1953 *W*

Biemouret, P (Agen) 1969 *E, W*, 1970 *I, W, E*, 1971 *W, SA* 1,2, *A* 1, 1972 *E, W, I* 2, *A* 2, *R*, 1973 *S, NZ, E, W, I*

Biénès, R (Cognac) 1950 *S, I, E, W*, 1951 *S, I, E, W*, 1952 *S, I, SA, W, E, It*, 1953 *S, I, E*, 1954 *S, I, NZ, W, E, Arg* 1,2, 1956 *S, I, W, It, E*

Bigot, C (Quillan) 1930 *S, E*, 1931 *I, S*

Bilbao, L (St Jean-de-Luz) 1978 *I*, 1979 *I*

Billac, E (Bayonne) 1920 *S, E, W, I, US*, 1921 *S, W*, 1922 *W*, 1923 *E*

Billière, M (Toulouse) 1968 *NZ* 3

Bioussa, A (Toulouse) 1924 *W, US*, 1925 *I, NZ, S, E*, 1926 *S, I, E*, 1928 *E, G, W*, 1929 *I, S, W, E*, 1930 *S, I, E, G, W*

Bioussa, C (Toulouse) 1913 *W, I*, 1914 *I*

Biraben, M (Dax) 1920 *W, I, US*, 1921 *S, W, E, I*, 1922 *S, E, I*

Blain, A (Carcassonne) 1934 *G*

Blanco, S (Biarritz O) 1980 *SA, R*, 1981 *S, W, E, A* 1,2, *R, NZ* 1,2, 1982 *W, E, S, I, R, Arg* 1,2, 1983 *E, S, I, W*, 1984 *I, W, E, S, NZ* 1,2, *R*, 1985 *E, S, I, W, Arg* 1,2, 1986 *S, I, W, E, R* 1, *Arg* 2, *A, NZ* 1, *R* 2, *NZ* 2,3, 1987 *W, E, S, I*, [*S, R, Fj, A, NZ*], *R*, 1988 *E, S, I, W, Arg* 1,2,3,4, *R*, 1989 *I, W, E, S, NZ* 1,2, *B, A* 1, 1990 *E, S, I, R, A* 1,2,3, *NZ* 1,2, 1991 *S, I, W* 1, *E, R, US* 1,2, *W* 2, [*R, Fj, C, E*]

Blond, J (SF) 1935 *G*, 1936 *G* 2, 1937 *G*, 1938 *G* 1, *R, G* 2

Blond, X (RCF) 1990 *A* 3, 1991 *S, I, W* 1, *E*, 1994 *NZ* 2 (R)

Boffelli, V (Aurillac) 1971 *A* 2, *R*, 1972 *S, I* 1, 1973 *J, R*, 1974 *I, W, E, S, Arg* 1,2, *R, SA* 1,2, 1975 *W, S, I*

Bonal, J-M (Toulouse) 1968 *E, W, Cz, NZ* 2,3, *SA* 1,2, 1969 *S, I, E, R*, 1970 *W, E*

Bonamy, R (SB) 1928 *A, I*

Bondouy, P (Narbonne) 1997 *S* (R), *It* 1, *A* 2 (R), *R* 2

Boniface, A (Mont-de-Marsan) 1954 *I, NZ, W, E, It, Arg* 1,2, 1955 *S, I*, 1956 *S, I, W, It, Cz*, 1957 *S, I, W, R* 2, 1958 *S, E*, 1959 *E*, 1961 *NZ* 1,3, *A, R*, 1962 *E, W, I, It, R*, 1963 *S, I, E, W, It, R*, 1964 *S, NZ, E, W, It, R*, 1965 *W, It, E, W*

Boniface, G (Mont-de-Marsan) 1960 *W, I, It, R, Arg* 1,2,3, 1961 *S, A, SA, E, W, It, I, NZ* 1,2,3, *R*, 1962 *R, 1963 *S, I, E, W, It, R*, 1964 *S, I, E, W, It, R*, 1966 *S, I, E, W*

Bonnes, E (Narbonne) 1924 *W, R, US*

Bonneval, E (Toulouse) 1984 *NZ* 2 (R), 1985 *W, Arg* 1, 1986 *W, E, R* 1, *Arg* 1,2, *A, R* 2, *NZ* 2,3, 1987 *W, E, S, I*, [*Z*], 1988 *E*

Bonnus, F (Toulon) 1950 *S, I, E, W*

Bonnus, M (Toulon) 1937 *It*, 1938 *G* 1, *R, G* 2, 1940 *B*

Bontemps, D (La Rochelle) 1968 *SA* 2

Borchard, G (RCF) 1908 *E*, 1909 *E, W, I*, 1911 *I*

Borde, F (RCF) 1920 *I, US*, 1921 *S, W, E, I*, 1922 *S, W*, 1923 *S, I*, 1924 *E*, 1925 *I*, 1926 *E*

Bordenave, L (Toulon) 1948 *A, S, W, E*, 1949 *S*

Boubée, J (Tarbes) 1921 *S, E, I*, 1922 *E, W*, 1923 *E, I*, 1925 *NZ, S*

Boudreaux, R (SCUF) 1910 *W, S*

Bouet, D (Dax) 1989 *NZ* 1,2, *B, A* 2, 1990 *A* 3

Bouguyon, G (Grenoble) 1961 *SA, E, W, It, I, NZ* 1,2,3, *A*

Bouic, G (Agen) 1996 *SA* 1

Boujet, C (Grenoble) 1968 *NZ* 2, *A* (R), *SA* 1

Bouquet, J (Bourgoin, Vienne) 1954 *S*, 1955 *E*, 1956 *S, I, W, It, E, Cz*, 1957 *S, E, W, R* 2, 1958 *S, E*, 1959 *S, It, W, I*, 1960 *S, E, W, I, R*, 1961 *S, SA, E, W, It, I, R*, 1962 *S, E, W, I*

Bourdeu, J R (Lourdes) 1952 *S, I, SA, W, E, It*, 1953 *S, I, E*

Bourgarel, R (Toulouse) 1969 *R*, 1970 *S, I, E, R*, 1971 *W, SA* 1,2, 1973 *S*

Bourguignon, G (Narbonne) 1988 *Arg* 3, 1989 *I, E, B, A* 1, 1990 *R*

Bousquet, A (Béziers) 1921 *E, I*, 1924 *R*

Bousquet, R (Albi) 1926 *M*, 1927 *I, S, W, E, G* 1, 1929 *W, E*, 1930 *W*

Boyau, M (SBUC) 1912 *I, S, W, E*, 1913 *W, I*

Boyer, P (Toulon) 1935 *G*

Branca, G (SF) 1928 *S*, 1929 *I, S*

Branlat, A (RCF) 1906 *NZ, E*, 1908 *W*

Brejassou, R (Tarbes) 1952 *S, I, SA, W, E*, 1953 *W, E*, 1954 *S, I, NZ*, 1955 *S, I, E, W, It*

Brethes, R (St Sever) 1960 *Arg* 2

Bringeon, A (Biarritz O) 1925 *W*

Brouzet, O (Grenoble, Bègles) 1994 *S, NZ* 2 (R), 1995 *E, S, I, R* 1, [*Tg, Iv, E* (t)], *It, Arg* (R), 1996 *W* 1 (R), 1997 *R* 1, *A* 1,2, *It* 2, *Arg, SA* 1,2, 1998 *E, S, I, W*

Brun, G (Vienne) 1950 *E, W*, 1951 *S, E, W*, 1952 *S, I, SA, W, E, It, W, It*

Bruneau, M (SBUC) 1910 *W, E*, 1913 *SA, E*

Brunet, Y (Perpignan) 1975 *SA* 1, 1977 *Arg* 1

Brusque, N (Pau) 1997 *R* 2 (R)

Buchet, E (Nice) 1980 *R*, 1982 *E, R* (R), *Arg* 1,2

Buisson, H (see Empereur-Buisson)

Buonomo, Y (Béziers) 1971 *A* 2, *R*, 1972 *I* 1

Burgun, M (RCF) 1909 *I*, 1910 *W, S, I*, 1911 *S, E*, 1912 *I, S*, 1913 *S, E*, 1914 *E*

Bustaffa, D (Carcassonne) 1977 *Arg* 1,2, *NZ* 1,2, 1978 *W, R*, 1980 *W, E, S, SA, R*

Buzy, C-E (Lourdes) 1946 *K, W*, 1947 *S, I, W, E*, 1948 *I, A, S, W, E*, 1949 *S, I, E, W, Arg* 1,2

Cabanier, J-M (Montauban) 1963 *R*, 1964 *S, Fj*, 1965 *S, I, W, It, R*, 1966 *S, I, E, W, It, R*, 1967 *S, A, E, It, W, I, SA* 1,3, *NZ, R*, 1968 *S, I*

Cabannes, L (RCF, Harlequins) 1990 *NZ* 2 (R), 1991 *S, I, W* 1, *E, US* 2, *W* 2, [*R, Fj, C, E*], 1992 *W, E, S, I, R, Arg* 2, *SA* 1,2, 1993 *E, S, I, W, R* 1, *SA* 1,2, 1994 *C, S* 1, *NZ* 1,2, 1995 *W, E, S, R* 1, [*Tg* (R), *Iv, S, I, SA, E*], 1996 *E, S, I, W* 1, 1997 *It* 2, *Arg, SA* 1,2

Cabrol, H (Béziers) 1972 *A* 1 (R), 2, 1973 *J*, 1974 *SA* 2

Cadenat, J (SCUF) 1910 *S, E*, 1911 *W, I*, 1912 *W, E*, 1913 *I*

Cadieu, J-M (Toulouse) 1991 *R, US* 1, [*R, Fj, C, E*], 1992 *W, I, R, Arg* 1,2, 1994 *S, C*

Cahuc, F (St Girons) 1922 *S*

Califano, C (Toulouse) 1994 *NZ* 1,2, *C* 2, 1995 *W, E, S, I*, [*Iv, S, I, SA, E*], *It, Arg, NZ* 1, 2, 1996 *E, S, I, W* 1, *R, Arg* 1,2, *SA* 1,2, 1997 *I, W, E, A* 1,2, *It* 2, *R* 2 (R), *Arg, SA* 1,2, 1998 *E, S, I, W*

Cals, R (RCF) 1938 *G* 1

Calvo, G (Lourdes) 1961 *NZ* 1,3

Camberabero, D (La Voulte, Béziers) 1982 *R, Arg* 1,2, 1983 *E, W*, 1987 [*R* (R), *Z, Fj* (R), *A, NZ*], 1988 *I*, 1989 *B, A* 1, 1990 *W, S, I, R, A* 1,2,3, *NZ* 1,2, 1991 *S, I, W* 1, *E, R, US* 1,2, *W* 2, [*R, Fj, C*], 1993 *E, S, I*

Camberabero, G (La Voulte) 1961 *NZ* 3, 1962 *R*, 1964 *R*, 1967 *A, E, It, W, I, SA* 1,3,4, 1968 *S, E, W*

Camberabero, L (La Voulte) 1964 *R*, 1965 *S, I*, 1966 *E, W*, 1967 *A, E, It, W, I*, 1968 *S, E, W*

Cambré, T (Oloron) 1920 *E, W, I, US*

Camel, A (Toulouse) 1928 *S, A, I, E, G, W*, 1929 *W, E, G*, 1930 *S, I, E, G, W*, 1935 *G*

Camel, M (Toulouse) 1929 *S, W, E*

Camicas, F (Tarbes) 1927 *G* 2, 1928 *S, I, E, G, W*, 1929 *I, S, W, E*

Camo, E (Villeneuve) 1931 *I, S, W, E, G*, 1932 *G*

Campaes, A (Lourdes) 1965 *W*, 1967 *NZ*, 1968 *S, I, E, W, Cz, NZ* 1,2, *A*, 1969 *S, W*, 1972 *R*, 1973 *NZ*

Campan, O (Agen) 1993 *SA* 1 (R), 2 (R), *R* 2 (R), 1996 *I, W, R*

Cantoni, J (Béziers) 1970 *W, R*, 1971 *S, I, E, W, SA* 1,2, *A* 1, *R*, 1972 *S, I*, 1973 *S, NZ, E, W, I*, 1975 *W* (R)

Capdouze, J (Pau) 1964 *SA, Fj, R*, 1965 *S, I, E*

Capendeguy, J-M (Bègles) 1967 *NZ, R*

Capitani, P (Toulon) 1954 *Arg* 1,2

Capmau, J-L (Toulouse) 1914 *E*
Carabignac, G (Agen) 1951 *S, I,* 1952 *SA, W, E,* 1953 *S, I*
Carbonne, J (Perpignan) 1927 *W*
Carbonneau, P (Toulouse, Brive) 1995 *R* 2, *Arg, NZ* 1, 2, 1996 *E, S, R* (R), *Arg* 2, *W* 2, *SA* 1, 1997 *I* (R), *W, E, S* (R), *R* 1 (R), *A* 1,2, 1998 *E, S, I, W*
Carminati, A (Béziers, Brive) 1986 *R* 2, *NZ* 2, 1987 [*R, Z*], 1988 *I, W, Arg* 1,2, 1989 *I, W, S, NZ* 1 (R), 2, *A* 2, 1990 *S,* 1995 *It, R* 2, *Arg, NZ* 1, 2
Caron, L (Lyon O, Castres) 1947 *E,* 1948 *I, A, W, E,* 1949 *S, I, E, W, Arg* 1
Carpentier, M (Lourdes) 1980 *E, SA, R,* 1981 *S, I, A* 1, 1982 *E, S*
Carrère, C (Toulon) 1966 *R,* 1967 *S, A, E, W, I, SA* 1,3,4, *NZ, R,* 1968 *S, I, E, W, Cz, NZ* 3, *A, R,* 1969 *S, I,* 1970 *S, I, W, E,* 1971 *E, W*
Carrère, J (Vichy, Toulon) 1956 *S,* 1957 *E, W, R* 2, 1958 *S, SA* 1,2, 1959 *I*
Carrère, R (Mont-de-Marsan) 1953 *E, It*
Casadei, D (Brive) 1997 *S, R* 1, *SA* 2 (R)
Casaux, L (Tarbes) 1959 *I, It,* 1962 *S*
Cassagne, P (Pau) 1957 *It*
Cassayet-Armagnac, A (Tarbes, Narbonne) 1920 *S, E, W, US,* 1921 *W, E, I,* 1922 *S, E, W,* 1923 *S, W, E, I,* 1924 *S, E, W, R, US,* 1925 *I, NZ, S, W,* 1926 *S, I, E, W, M,* 1927 *I, S, W*
Cassiède, M (Dax) 1961 *NZ* 3, *A, R*
Castaignède, T (Toulouse, Castres) 1995 *R* 2, *Arg, NZ* 1, 2, 1996 *E, S, I, W* 1, *Arg* 1,2, 1997 *I, A* 1,2, *It* 2, 1998 *E, S, I, W*
Castel, R (Toulouse, Béziers) 1996 *I, W* 1, *W* 2, *SA* 1(R),2, 1997 *I* (R), *W, E* (R), *S* (R), *A* 1 (R)
Castets, J (Toulon) 1923 *W, E, I*
Caujolle, J (Tarbes) 1909 *E,* 1913 *SA, E,* 1914 *W, E*
Caunègre, R (SB) 1938 *R, G* 2
Caussade, A (Lourdes) 1978 *R,* 1979 *I, W, E, NZ* 1,2, *R,* 1980 *W, E, S,* 1981 *S* (R), *I*
Caussarieu, G (Pau) 1929 *I*
Cayrefourcq, E (Tarbes) 1921 *E*
Cazalbou, J (Toulouse) 1997 *It* 2 (R), *R* 2, *Arg, SA* 2 (R)
Cazals, P (Mont-de-Marsan) 1961 *NZ* 1, *A, R*
Cazenave, A (Pau) 1927 *E, G* 1, 1928 *S, A, G*
Cazenave, F (RCF) 1950 *E,* 1952 *S,* 1954 *I, NZ, W, E*
Cecillon, M (Bourgoin) 1988 *I, W, Arg* 2,3,4, *R,* 1989 *I, E, NZ* 1,2, *A* 1, 1991 *S, I, E* (R), *R, US* 1, *W* 2, [*E*], 1992 *W, E, S, I, R, Arg* 1,2, *SA* 1,2, 1993 *E, S, I, W, R* 1, *SA* 1,2, *R* 2, *A* 1,2, 1994 *I, W, NZ* 1 (R), 1995 *I, R* 1, [*Tg, S* (R), *I, SA*]
Celaya, M (Biarritz O, SBUC) 1953 *E, W, It,* 1954 *I, E, It, Arg* 1,2, 1955 *S, I, E, W, It,* 1956 *S, I, W, It, E, Cz* 1957 *S, I, E, W, R* 2, 1958 *S, E, A, W, It,* 1959 *S, E,* 1960 *S, E, W, I, R, Arg* 1,2,3, 1961 *S, SA, E, W, It, I, NZ* 1,2,3, *A, R*
Celhay, M (Bayonne) 1935 *G,* 1936 *G* 1, 1937 *G, It,* 1938 *G* 1, 1940 *B*
Cessieux, N (Lyon) 1906 *NZ*
Cester, E (TOEC, Valence) 1966 *S, I, E,* 1967 *W,* 1968 *S, I, E, W, Cz, NZ* 1,3, *A, SA* 1,2, *R,* 1969 *S, I, E,* 1970 *S, I, W, E,* 1971 *A* 1, 1972 *R,* 1973 *S, NZ, W, I, J, R,* 1974 *I, W, E, S*
Chaban-Delmas, J (CASG) 1945 *B* 2
Chabowski, H (Nice, Bourgoin) 1985 *Arg* 2, 1986 *R* 2, *NZ* 2, 1989 *B* (R)
Chadebech, P (Brive) 1982 *R, Arg* 1,2, 1986 *S, I*
Champ, E (Toulon) 1985 *Arg* 1,2, 1986 *I, W, E, R* 1, *Arg* 1,2, *A, NZ* 1, *R* 2, *NZ* 2,3, 1987 *W, E, S, I,* [*S, R, Fj, A, NZ*], *R,* 1988 *E, S, Arg* 1,3,4, *R,* 1989 *W, S, A* 1,2, 1990 *W, E, NZ* 1, 1991 *R, US* 1, [*R, Fj, C, E*]
Chapuy, L (SF) 1926 *S*
Charpentier, G (SF) 1911 *E,* 1912 *W, E*
Charton, P (Montferrand) 1940 *B*
Charvet, D (Toulouse) 1986 *W, E, R* 1, *Arg* 1, *A, NZ* 1,3, 1987 *W, E, S, I,* [*S, R, Z, Fj, A, NZ*], *R,* 1989 *E* (R), 1990 *W, E,* 1991 *S, I*
Chassagne, J (Montferrand) 1938 *G* 1
Chatau, A (Bayonne) 1913 *SA*
Chaud, E (Toulon) 1932 *G,* 1934 *G,* 1935 *G*
Chenevay, C (Grenoble) 1968 *SA* 1
Chevallier, B (Montferrand) 1952 *S, I, SA, W, E, It,* 1953 *E, W, It,* 1954 *S, I, NZ, W, E, It, Arg* 1, 1955 *S, I, E, W, It,* 1956 *S, I, W, It, E, Cz,* 1957 *S*
Chiberry, J (Chambéry) 1955 *It*
Chilo, A (RCF) 1920 *S, W,* 1925 *I, NZ*

Cholley, G (Castres) 1975 *E, S, I, SA* 1,2, *Arg* 1,2, *R,* 1976 *S, I, W, E, A* 1,2, *R,* 1977 *W, E, S, I, Arg* 1,2, *NZ* 1,2, *R,* 1978 *E, S, I, W, R,* 1979 *I, S*
Choy, J (Narbonne) 1930 *S, I, E, G, W,* 1931 *I,* 1933 *G,* 1934 *G,* 1935 *G,* 1936 *G* 2
Cigagna, A (Toulouse) 1995 [*E*]
Cimarosti, J (Castres) 1976 *US* (R)
Clady, A (Lezignan) 1929 *G,* 1931 *I, S, E, G*
Clarac, H (St Girons) 1938 *G* 1
Claudel, R (Lyon) 1932 *G,* 1934 *G*
Clauzel, F (Béziers) 1924 *E, W,* 1925 *W*
Clavé, J (Agen) 1936 *G* 2, 1938 *R, G* 2
Claverie, H (Lourdes) 1954 *NZ, W*
Cléda, T (Pau) 1998 *E* (R), *S* (R), *I* (R), *W* (R)
Clément, G (RCF) 1931 *W*
Clément, J (RCF) 1921 *S, W, E,* 1922 *S, E, W, I,* 1923 *S, W, I*
Clemente, M (Oloron) 1978 *R,* 1980 *S, I*
Cluchague, L (Biarritz O) 1924 *S,* 1925 *E*
Coderc, J (Chalon) 1932 *G,* 1933 *G,* 1934 *G,* 1935 *G,* 1936 *G* 1
Codorniou, D (Narbonne) 1979 *NZ* 1,2, *R,* 1980 *W, E, S, I,* 1981 *S, W, E, A* 2, 1983 *E, S, I, W, A* 1,2, *R,* 1984 *I, W, E, S, NZ* 1,2, *R,* 1985 *E, S, I, W, Arg* 1,2
Coeurveille, C (Agen) 1992 *Arg* 1 (R), 2
Cognet, L (Montferrand) 1932 *G,* 1936 *G* 1,2, 1937 *G, It*
Colombier, J (St Junien) 1952 *SA, W, E*
Colomine, G (Narbonne) 1979 *NZ* 1
Combe, J (SF) 1910 *S, E, I,* 1911 *S*
Combes, G (Fumel) 1945 *B* 2
Communeau, M (SF) 1906 *NZ, E,* 1907 *E,* 1908 *E, W,* 1909 *E, W, I,* 1910 *S, E, I,* 1911 *S, E, I,* 1912 *I, S, W, E,* 1913 *SA, E, W*
Condom, J (Boucau, Biarritz O) 1982 *R,* 1983 *E, S, I, W, A* 1,2, *R,* 1984 *I, W, E, S, NZ* 1,2, *R,* 1985 *E, S, I, W, Arg* 1,2, 1986 *S, I, W, E, R* 1, *Arg* 1,2, *NZ* 1, *R* 2, *NZ* 2,3, 1987 *W, E, S, I,* [*S, R, Z, A, NZ*], *R,* 1988 *S, I, W, E, A* 1,2,3,4, *R,* 1989 *I, W, E, S, NZ* 1,2, *A* 1, 1990 *I, R, A* 2,3 (R)
Conilh de Beyssac, J-J (SBUC) 1912 *I, S,* 1914 *I, W, E*
Constant, G (Perpignan) 1920 *W*
Coscolla, G (Béziers) 1921 *S, W*
Costantino, J (Montferrand) 1973 *R*
Costes, A (Montferrand) 1994 *C* 2, 1995 *R* 1, [*Iv*], 1997 *It* 1
Costes, F (Montferrand) 1979 *E, S, NZ* 1,2, *R,* 1980 *W, I*
Couffignal, H (Colomiers) 1993 *R* 1
Coulon, E (Grenoble) 1928 *S*
Courtiols, M (Bègles) 1991 *R, US* 1, *W* 2
Crabos, R (RCF) 1920 *S, E, W, I, US,* 1921 *S, W, E, I,* 1922 *S, E, W, I,* 1923 *S, I,* 1924 *S, I*
Crampagne, J (Bègles) 1967 *SA* 4
Crancee, R (Lourdes) 1960 *Arg* 3, 1961 *S*
Crauste, M (RCF, Lourdes) 1957 *R* 1,2, 1958 *S, E, A, W, It, I,* 1959 *E, It, W, I,* 1960 *S, E, W, I, It, R, Arg* 1,3, 1961 *S, SA, E, W, It, I, NZ* 1,2,3, *A, R,* 1962 *S, E, W, I, It,* 1963 *S, I, E, W, It, R,* 1964 *S, NZ, E, W, It, I, SA, Fj, R,* 1965 *S, I, E, W, It, R,* 1966 *S, I, E, W, It, R*
Cremaschi, M (Lourdes) 1980 *R,* 1981 *R, NZ* 1,2, 1982 *W, S,* 1983 *A* 1,2, *R,* 1984 *I, W*
Crenca, J-J (Agen) 1996 *SA* 2(R)
Crichton, W H (Le Havre) 1906 *NZ, E*
Cristina, J (Montferrand) 1979 *R*
Cussac, P (Biarritz O) 1934 *G*
Cutzach, A (Quillan) 1929 *G*

Daguerre, F (Biarritz O) 1936 *G* 1
Daguerre, J (CASG) 1933 *G*
Dal Maso, M (Mont-de-Marsan, Agen) 1988 *R* (R), 1990 *NZ* 2, 1996 *SA* 1(R),2, 1997 *I, W, E, S, It* 1, *R* 1 (R), *A* 1,2, *It* 2, *Arg, SA* 1,2, 1998 *W* (R)
Danion, J (Toulon) 1924 *I*
Danos, P (Toulon, Béziers) 1954 *Arg* 1,2, 1957 *R* 2, 1958 *S, E, W, It, I, SA* 1,2, 1959 *S, E, It, W, I,* 1960 *S, E*
Dantiacq, D (Pau) 1997 *R* 1
Darbos, P (Dax) 1969 *R*
Darracq, R (Dax) 1957 *It*
Darrieussecq, A (Biarritz O) 1973 *E*
Darrieussecq, J (Mont-de-Marsan) 1953 *It*
Darrouy, C (Mont-de-Marsan) 1957 *I, E, W, It, R* 1, 1959 *E,* 1961 *NZ* 1, 1963 *S, I, E, W, It, I, SA, Fj, R,* 1964 *NZ, E, W, It, I, SA, Fj, R,* 1965 *S, I, E, It, R,* 1966 *S, I, E, W, It, R,* 1967 *S, A, E, It, W, I, SA* 1, 2, 4
Daudignon, G (SF) 1928 *S*

Dauga, B (Mont-de-Marsan) 1964 *S, NZ, E, W, It, I, SA, Fj, R*, 1965 *S, I, E, W, It, R*, 1966 *S, I, E, W, It, R*, 1967 *S, A, E, It, W, I, SA* 1,2,3,4, *NZ, R*, 1968 *S, I, NZ* 1,2,3, *A, SA* 1,2, *R*, 1969 *S, I, E, R*, 1970 *S, I, W, E, R*, 1971 *S, I, E, W, SA* 1,2, *A* 1,2, *R*, 1972 *S, I* 1, *W*
Dauger, J (Bayonne) 1945 *B* 1,2, 1953 *S*
Daulouede, P (Tyrosse) 1937 *G, It*, 1938 *G* 1, 1940 *B*
Decamps, P (RCF) 1911 *S*
Dedet, J (SF) 1910 *S, E, I*, 1911 *W, I*, 1912 *S*, 1913 *E, I*
Dedeyn, P (RCF) 1906 *NZ*
Dedieu, P (Béziers) 1963 *E, It*, 1964 *W, It, I, SA, Fj, R*, 1965 *S, I, E, W*
De Gregorio, J (Grenoble) 1960 *S, E, W, I, It, R, Arg* 1,2, 1961 *S, SA, E, W, It, I*, 1962 *S, E, W*, 1963 *S, W, It*, 1964 *NZ, E*
Dehez, J-L (Agen) 1967 *SA* 2, 1969 *R*
De Jouvencel, E (SF) 1909 *W, I*
De Laborderie, M (RCF) 1921 *I*, 1922 *I*, 1925 *W, E*
Delage, C (Agen) 1983 *S, I*
De Malherbe, H (CASG) 1932 *G*, 1933 *G*
De Malmann, R (RCF) 1908 *E, W*, 1909 *E, W, I*, 1910 *E, I*
De Muizon, J J (SF) 1910 *I*
Delaigue, G (Toulon) 1973 *J, R*
Delaigue, Y (Toulon) 1994 *S, NZ* 2 (R), *C* 2, 1995 *I, R* 1, [*Tg, Iv*], *It, R* 2 (R), 1997 *It* 1
Delque, A (Toulouse) 1937 *It*, 1938 *G* 1, *R, G* 2
De Rougemont, M (Toulon) 1995 *E* (t), *R* 1 (t), [*Iv*], *NZ* 1, 2, 1996 *I* (R), *Arg* 1,2, *W* 2, *SA* 1, 1997 *E* (R), *S* (R), *It* 1
Descamps, P (SB) 1927 *G* 2
Desclaux, F (RCF) 1949 *Arg* 1,2, 1953 *It*
Desclaux, J (Perpignan) 1934 *G*, 1935 *G*, 1936 *G* 1,2, 1937 *G, It*, 1938 *G* 1, *R, G* 2, 1945 *B* 1
Deslandes, C (RCF) 1990 *A* 1, *NZ* 2, 1991 *W* 1, 1992 *R, Arg* 1,2
Desnoyer, L (Brive) 1974 *R*
Destarac, L (Tarbes) 1926 *S, I, E, W, M*, 1927 *W, E, G* 1,2
Desvouges, R (SF) 1914 *W*
Detrez, P-E (Nîmes) 1983 *A* 2 (R), 1986 *Arg* 1 (R), 2, *A* (R), *NZ1*
Devergie, T (Nîmes) 1988 *R*, 1989 *NZ* 1,2, *B, A* 2, 1990 *W, E, S, I, R, A* 1,2,3, 1991 *US* 2, *W* 2, 1992 *R* (R), *Arg* 2 (R)
Deygas, M (Vienne) 1937 *It*
Deylaud, C (Toulouse) 1992 *R, Arg* 1,2, *SA* 1, 1994 *C* 1, *NZ* 1,2, 1995 *W, E, S*, [*Iv* (R), *S, I, SA*], *It, Arg*
Dintrans, P (Tarbes) 1979 *NZ* 1,2, *R*, 1980 *E, S, I, SA, R*, 1981 *S, I, W, E, A* 1,2, *R, NZ* 1,2, 1982 *W, E, S, I, R, Arg* 1,2, 1983 *E, W, A* 1,2, *R*, 1984 *I, W, E, S, NZ* 1,2, *R*, 1985 *E, S, I, W, Arg* 1,2, 1987 [*R*], 1988 *Arg* 1,2,3, 1989 *W, E, S*, 1990 *R*
Dispagne, S (Toulouse) 1996 *I* (R), *W* 1
Dizabo, P (Tyrosse) 1948 *A, S, E*, 1949 *S, I, E, W, Arg* 2, 1950 *S, I*, 1960 *Arg* 1,2,3
Domec, A (Carcassonne) 1929 *W*
Domec, H (Lourdes) 1953 *W, It*, 1954 *S, I, NZ, W, E, It*, 1955 *S, I, E, W*, 1956 *I, W, It*, 1958 *E, A, W, It, I*
Domenech, A (Vichy, Brive) 1954 *W, E, It*, 1955 *S, I, E, W*, 1956 *S, I, W, It, E, Cz*, 1957 *S, I, E, W, It, R* 1,2, 1958 *S, E, It*, 1959 *It*, 1960 *S, E, W, I, It, R, Arg* 1,2,3, 1961 *S, SA, E, W, It, I, NZ* 1,2,3, *A, R*, 1962 *S, E, W, I, It, R*, 1963 *W, It*
Domercq, J (Bayonne) 1912 *I, S*
Dominici, C (SF) 1998 *E, S*
Dorot, J (RCF) 1935 *G*
Dospital, P (Bayonne) 1977 *R*, 1980 *I*, 1981 *S, I, W, E*, 1982 *I, R, Arg* 1,2, 1983 *E, S, I, W*, 1984 *E, S, NZ* 1,2, *R*, 1985 *E, S, I, W, Arg* 1
Dourthe, C (Dax) 1966 *R*, 1967 *S, A, E, W, I, SA* 1,2,3, *NZ*, 1968 *W, NZ* 3, *SA* 1,2, 1969 *W*, 1971 *SA* 2 (R), *R*, 1972 *I* 1,2, *A* 1,2, *R*, 1973 *S, NZ, E*, 1974 *I, Arg* 1,2, *SA* 1,2, 1975 *W, E, S*
Dourthe, R (Dax) 1995 *R* 2, *Arg, NZ* 1, 2, 1996 *E, R*, 1996 *Arg* 1,2, *W* 2, *SA* 1,2, 1997 *W, A* 1
Doussau, E (Angoulême) 1938 *R*
Droitecourt, M (Montferrand) 1972 *R*, 1973 *NZ* (R), *E*, 1974 *E, S, Arg* 1, *SA* 2, 1975 *SA* 1,2, *Arg* 1,2, *R*, 1976 *S, I, W, A* 1, 1977 *Arg* 2
Dubertrand, A (Montferrand) 1971 *A* 2, *R*, 1972 *I* 2, 1974 *I, W, E, SA* 2, 1975 *Arg* 1,2, *R*, 1976 *S, US*
Dubois, D (Bègles) 1971 *S*

Dubroca, D (Agen) 1979 *NZ* 2, 1981 *NZ* 2 (R), 1982 *E, S*, 1984 *W, E, S*, 1985 *Arg* 2, 1986 *S, I, W, E, R* 1, *Arg* 2, *A, NZ* 1, *R* 2, *NZ* 2,3, 1987 *W, E, S, I*, [*S, Z, Fj, A, NZ*], *R*, 1988 *E, S, I, W*
Duché, A (Limoges) 1929 *G*
Duclos, A (Lourdes) 1931 *S*
Ducousso, J (Tarbes) 1925 *S, W, E*
Dufau, G (RCF) 1948 *I, A*, 1949 *I, W*, 1950 *S, E, W*, 1951 *S, I, E, W*, 1952 *SA, W*, 1953 *S, I, E, W*, 1954 *S, I, NZ, W, E, It*, 1955 *S, I, E, W, It*, 1956 *S, I, W, It*, 1957 *S, I, E, W, It, R* 1
Dufau, J (Biarritz) 1912 *I, S, W, E*
Duffaut, Y (Agen) 1954 *Arg* 1,2
Duffour, R (Tarbes) 1911 *W*
Dufourcq, J (SBUC) 1906 *NZ, E*, 1907 *E*, 1908 *W*
Duhard, Y (Bagnères) 1980 *E*
Duhau, J (SF) 1928 *I,1930 I, G*, 1931 *I, S, W*, 1933 *G*
Dulaurens, C (Toulouse) 1926 *I*, 1928 *S*, 1929 *W*
Duluc, A (Béziers) 1934 *G*
Du Manoir, Y le P (RCF) 1925 *I, NZ, S, W, E*, 1926 *S, 1927 I, E*
Dupont, C (Lourdes) 1923 *S, W, I*, 1924 *S, I, W, R, US*, 1925 *S, 1927 E, G* 1,2, 1928 *A, G, W*, 1929 *I*
Dupont, J-L (Agen) 1983 *S*
Dupont, L (RCF) 1934 *G*, 1935 *G*, 1936 *G* 1,2, 1938 *R, G* 2
Dupouy, A (SB) 1924 *W, R*
Duprat, B (Bayonne) 1966 *E, W, It, R*, 1967 *S, A, E, SA* 2,3, 1968 *S, I*, 1972 *E, W, I* 2, *A* 1
Dupré, P (RCF) 1909 *W*
Dupuy, J (Tarbes) 1956 *S, I, W, It, E, Cz*, 1957 *S, I, E, W, It, R* 2, 1958 *S, E, SA* 1,2, 1959 *S, E, It, W, I*, 1960 *W, I, It, Arg* 1,3, 1961 *S, SA, E, NZ* 2, *R*, 1962 *S, E, W, I, It*, 1963 *W, It, R*, 1964 *S*
Du Souich, C J (see Judas du Souich)
Dutin, B (Mont-de-Marsan) 1968 *NZ* 2, *A, SA* 2, *R*
Dutour, F X (Toulouse) 1911 *E, I*, 1912 *S, W, E*, 1913 *S*
Dutrain, H (Toulouse) 1945 *W*, 1946 *B, I*, 1947 *E*, 1949 *I, E, W, Arg* 1
Dutrey, J (Lourdes) 1940 *B*
Duval, R (SF) 1908 *E, W*, 1909 *E*, 1911 *E, W, I*

Echavé, L (Agen) 1961 *S*
Elissalde, E (Bayonne) 1936 *G* 2, 1940 *B*
Elissalde, J-P (La Rochelle) 1980 *SA, R*, 1981 *A* 1,2, *R*
Empereur-Buisson, H (Béziers) 1931 *E, G*
Erbani, D (Agen) 1981 *A* 1,2, *NZ* 1,2, 1982 *Arg* 1,2, 1983 *S* (R), *I, W, A* 1,2, *R*, 1984 *W, E, R*, 1985 *E, W* (R), *Arg* 2, 1986 *S, I, W, E, R* 1, *Arg* 2, *NZ* 1,2 (R), 3, 1987 *W, E, S, I*, [*S, R, Fj, A, NZ*], 1988 *E, S*, 1989 *I* (R), *W, E, S, NZ* 1, *A* 2, 1990 *W, E*
Escaffre, P (Narbonne) 1933 *G*, 1934 *G*
Escommier, M (Montelimar) 1955 *It*
Esponda, J-M (RCF) 1967 *SA* 1,2, *R*, 1968 *NZ* 1,2, *SA* 2, *R*, 1969 *S, I* (R), *E*
Estève, A (Béziers) 1971 *SA* 1, 1972 *I* 1, *E, W, I* 2, *A* 2, *R*, 1973 *S, NZ, E, I*, 1974 *I, W, E, S, R, SA* 1,2, 1975 *W, E*
Estève, P (Narbonne, Lavelanet) 1982 *R, Arg* 1,2, 1983 *E, S, I, W, A* 1,2, *R*, 1984 *I, W, E, S, NZ* 1,2, *R*, 1985 *E, S, I, W*, 1986 *S, I*, 1987 [*S, Z*]
Etcheberry, J (Rochefort, Cognac) 1923 *W, I*, 1924 *S, I, E, W, R, US*, 1926 *S, I, E, M*, 1927 *I, S, W, G* 2
Etchenique, J-M (Biarritz O) 1974 *R, SA* 1, 1975 *E, Arg* 2
Etchepare, A (Bayonne) 1922 *I*
Etcheverry, M (Pau) 1971 *S, I*
Eutrope, A (SCUF) 1913 *I*

Fabre, E (Toulouse) 1937 *It*, 1938 *G* 1,2
Fabre, J (Toulouse) 1963 *S, I, E, W, It*, 1964 *S, NZ, E*
Fabre, L (Lezignan) 1930 *G*
Fabre, M (Béziers) 1981 *A* 1, *R, NZ* 1,2, 1982 *I, R*
Failliot, P (RCF) 1911 *S, W, I*, 1912 *I, S, E*, 1913 *E, W*
Fargues, G (Dax) 1923 *I*
Fauré, F (Tarbes) 1914 *I, W, E*
Fauvel, J-P (Tulle) 1980 *R*
Favre, M (Lyon) 1913 *E, W*
Ferrand, L (Chalon) 1940 *B*
Ferrien, R (Tarbes) 1950 *S, I, E, W*
Finat, R (CASG) 1932 *G*, 1933 *G*
Fite, R (Brive) 1963 *W, It*
Forestier, J (SCUF) 1912 *W*
Forgues, F (Bayonne) 1911 *S, E, W*, 1912 *I, W, E*, 1913 *S, SA, W*, 1914 *I, E*
Fort, J (Agen) 1967 *It, W, I, SA* 1,2,3,4

Fourcade, G (BEC) 1909 *E, W*
Foures, H (Toulouse) 1951 *S, I, E, W*
Fournet, F (Montferrand) 1950 *W*
Fouroux, J (La Voulte) 1972 *I* 2, *R,* 1974 *W, E, Arg* 1,2, *R, SA* 1,2, 1975 *W, Arg* 1, *R,* 1976 *S, I, W, E, US, A* 1, 1977 *W, E, S, I, Arg* 1,2, *NZ* 1,2, *R*
Francquenelle, A (Vaugirard) 1911 *S,* 1913 *W, I*
Furcade, R (Perpignan) 1952 *S*

Gabernet, S (Toulouse) 1980 *E, S,* 1981 *S, I, W, E, A* 1,2, *R, NZ* 1,2, 1982 *I,* 1983 *A* 2, *R*
Gachassin, J (Lourdes) 1961 *S, I,* 1963 *R,* 1964 *S, NZ, E, W, It, I, SA, Fj, R,* 1965 *S, I, E, W, It, R,* 1966 *S, I, E, W,* 1967 *S, A, It, W, I, NZ,* 1968 *I, E,* 1969 *S, I*
Galau, H (Toulouse) 1924 *S, I, E, W, US.*
Galia, J (Quillan) 1927 *E, G* 1,2, 1928 *S, A, I, E, W,* 1929 *I, E, G,* 1930 *S, I, E, G, W,* 1931 *S, W, E, G*
Gallart, P (Béziers) 1990 *R, A* 1,2 (R), 3, 1992 *S, I, R, Arg* 1,2, *SA* 1,2, *Arg,* 1994 *I, W, E,* 1995 *I* (t), *R* 1, [*Tg*]
Gallion, J (Toulon) 1978 *E, S, I, W,* 1979 *I, W, E, S, NZ* 2, *R,* 1980 *W, E, S, I,* 1983 *A* 1,2, *R,* 1984 *I, W, E, S, R,* 1985 *E, S, I, W,* 1986 *Arg* 2
Galthié, F (Colomiers) 1991 *R, US* 1, [*R, Fj, C, E*], 1992 *W, E, S, R, Arg,* 1994 *I, W, E,* 1995 [*SA, E*], 1996 *W* 1(R), 1997 *I, It* 2, *SA* 1,2, 1998 *W* (R)
Galy, J (Perpignan) 1953 *W*
Garbajosa, X (Toulouse) 1998 *I, W*
Garuet-Lempirou, J-P (Lourdes) 1983 *A* 1,2, *R,* 1984 *I, NZ* 1,2, *R,* 1985 *E, S, I, W, Arg* 1, 1986 *S, I, W, E, R* 1, *Arg* 1, *NZ* 1, *R* 2, *NZ* 2,3, 1987 *W, E, S, I,* [*S, R, Fj, A, NZ*], 1988 *E, S, Arg* 1,2, *R,* 1989 *E* (R), *S, NZ* 1,2, 1990 *W, E*
Gasc, J (Graulhet) 1977 *NZ* 2
Gasparotto, G (Montferrand) 1976 *A* 2, *R*
Gauby, G (Perpignan) 1956 *Cz*
Gaudermen, P (RCF) 1906 *E*
Gayraud, W (Toulouse) 1920 *I*
Geneste, R (BEC) 1945 *B* 1, 1949 *Arg* 2
Genet, J-P (RCF) 1992 *S, I, R*
Gensane, R (Béziers) 1962 *S, E, W, I, It, R,* 1963 *S*
Gerald, G (RCF) 1927 *E, G* 2, 1928 *S,* 1929 *I, S, W, E, G,* 1930 *S, I, E, G, W,* 1931 *I, S, E, G*
Gerintes, G (CASG) 1924 *R,* 1925 *I,* 1926 *W*
Geschwind, P (RCF) 1936 *G* 1,2
Giacardy, M (SBUC) 1907 *E*
Gimbert, P (Bègles) 1991 *R, US* 1, 1992 *W, E*
Glas, S (Bourgoin) 1996 *S* (t), *I* (R), *W* 1, *R, Arg* 2(R), *W* 2, *SA* 1,2, 1997 *I, W, E, S, It* 2 (R), *R* 2, *Arg, SA* 1,2, 1998 *E, S, I, W*
Gommes, J (RCF) 1909 *I*
Gonnet, C-A (Albi) 1921 *E, I,* 1922 *E, W,* 1924 *S, E,* 1926 *S, I, E, W, M,* 1927 *I, S, W, E, G* 1
Gonzalez, J-M (Bayonne) 1992 *Arg* 1,2, *SA* 1,2, *Arg,* 1993 *R* 1, *SA* 1,2, *R* 2, *A* 1,2, 1994 *I, W, E, S, C* 1, *NZ* 1,2, *C* 2, 1995 *W, E, S, I, R* 1, [*Tg, S, I, SA, E*], *It, Arg,* 1996 *E, S, I, W* 1
Got, R (Perpignan) 1920 *I, US,* 1921 *S, W,* 1922 *S, E, W, I,* 1924 *I, E, W, R, US*
Gourdon, J-F (RCF, Bagnères) 1974 *S, Arg* 1, 2, *R, SA* 1, 2, 1975 *W, E, S, I, R,* 1976 *S, I, W, E,* 1978 *E, S,* 1979 *W, E, S, R,* 1980 *I*
Gourragne, J-F (Béziers) 1990 *NZ* 2, 1991 *W* 1
Goyard, A (Lyon U) 1936 *G* 1,2, 1937 *G, It,* 1938 *G* 1, *R, G* 2
Graciet, R (SBUC) 1926 *I, W,* 1927 *S, G* 1, 1929 *E,* 1930 *W*
Graou, S (Auch, Colomiers) 1992 *Arg* (R), 1993 *SA* 1,2, *R* 2, *A* 2 (R), 1995 *R* 2, *Arg* (t), *NZ* 2 (R)
Gratton, J (Agen) 1984 *NZ* 2, *R,* 1985 *E, S, I, W, Arg* 1,2, 1986 *S, NZ* 1
Graule, V (Perpignan) 1926 *I, E, W,* 1927 *S, W,* 1931 *G*
Greffe, M (Grenoble) 1968 *W, Cz, NZ* 1,2, *SA* 1
Griffard, J (Lyon U) 1932 *G,* 1933 *G,* 1934 *G*
Gruarin, A (Toulon) 1964 *W, It, I, SA, Fj, R,* 1965 *S, I, E, W, It,* 1966 *S, I, E, W, It, R,* 1967 *S, A, E, It, W, I, NZ,* 1968 *S, I*
Guelorget, P (RCF) 1931 *E, G*
Guichemerre, A (Dax) 1920 *E,* 1921 *E, I,* 1923 *S*
Guilbert, A (Toulon) 1975 *E, S, I, SA* 1,2, 1976 *A* 1, 1977 *Arg* 1,2, *NZ* 1,2, *R,* 1979 *I, W, E*
Guillemin, P (RCF) 1908 *E, W,* 1909 *E, I,* 1910 *W, S, E, I,* 1911 *S, E, W*
Guilleux, P (Agen) 1952 *SA, It*
Guiral, M (Agen) 1931 *G,* 1932 *G,* 1933 *G*
Guiraud, H (Nîmes) 1996 *R*

Haget, A (PUC) 1953 *E,* 1954 *I, NZ, E, Arg* 2, 1955 *E, W, It,* 1957 *I, E, It, R* 1, 1958 *It, SA* 2
Haget, F (Agen, Biarritz O) 1974 *Arg* 1,2, 1975 *SA* 2, *Arg* 1,2, *R,* 1976 *S,* 1978 *S, I, W, R,* 1979 *I, W, E, S, NZ* 1,2, *R,* 1980 *W, S, I,* 1984 *S, NZ* 1,2, *R,* 1985 *E, S, I,* 1986 *S, I, W, E, R* 1, *Arg* 1, *A, NZ* 1, 1987 *S, I,* [*R, Fj*]
Haget, H (CASG) 1928 *S,* 1930 *G*
Halet, R (Strasbourg) 1925 *NZ, S, W*
Harislur-Arthapignet, P (Tarbes) 1988 *Arg* 4 (R)
Harize, D (Cahors, Toulouse) 1975 *SA* 1,2, 1976 *A* 1,2, *R,* 1977 *W, E, S, I*
Hauc, J (Toulon) 1928 *E, G,* 1929 *I, S, G*
Hauser, M (Lourdes) 1969 *E*
Hedembaigt, M (Bayonne) 1913 *S, SA,* 1914 *W*
Hericé, D (Bègles) 1950 *I*
Herrero, A (Toulon) 1963 *R,* 1964 *NZ, E, W, It, I, SA, Fj, R,* 1965 *S, I, E, W,* 1966 *W, It, R,* 1967 *S, A, E, It, I, R*
Herrero, B (Nice) 1983 *I,* 1986 *Arg* 1
Heyer, F (Montferrand) 1990 *A* 2
Hiquet, J-C (Agen) 1964 *E*
Hoche, M (PUC) 1957 *I, E, W, It, R* 1
Hondagné-Monge, M (Tarbes) 1988 *Arg* 2 (R)
Hontas, P (Biarritz) 1990 *S, I, R,* 1991 *R,* 1992 *Arg,* 1993 *E, S, I, W*
Hortoland, J-P (Béziers) 1971 *A* 2
Houblain, H (SCUF) 1909 *E,* 1910 *W*
Houdet, R (SF) 1927 *S, W, G* 1, 1928 *G, W,* 1929 *I, S, E,* 1930 *S, E*
Hourdebaigt, A (SBUC) 1909 *I,* 1910 *W, S, E, I*
Hubert, A (ASF) 1906 *E,* 1907 *E,* 1908 *E, W,* 1909 *E, W, I*
Hueber, A (Lourdes, Toulon) 1990 *A* 3, *NZ* 1, 1991 *US* 2, 1992 *I, Arg* 1,2, *SA* 1,2, 1993 *E, S, I, W, R* 1, *SA* 1,2, *R* 2, *A* 1,2, 1995 [*Tg, S* (R), *I*]
Hutin, R (CASG) 1927 *I, S, W*
Hyardet, A (Castres) 1995 *It, Arg* (R)

Ibanez, R (Dax) 1996 *W* 1(R), 1997 *It* 1 (R), *R* 1, *It* 2 (R), *R* 2, *SA* 2 (R), 1998 *E, S, I, W*
Icard, J (SF) 1909 *E, W*
Iguiniz, E (Bayonne) 1914 *E*
Ihingoué, D (BEC) 1912 *I, S*
Imbernon, J-F (Perpignan) 1976 *I, W, E, US, A* 1, 1977 *W, E, S, I, Arg* 1,2, *NZ* 1,2, 1978 *E, R,* 1979 *I,* 1981 *S, I, W, E,* 1982 *I,* 1983 *I, W*
Iraçabal, J (Bayonne) 1968 *NZ* 1,2, *SA* 1, 1969 *S, I, W, R,* 1970 *S, I, W, E, R,* 1971 *W, SA* 1,2, *A* 1, 1972 *E, W, I* 2, *A* 2, *R,* 1973 *S, NZ, E, W, I* 2, 1974 *I, W, E, S, Arg* 1,2, *SA* 2 (R)
Isaac, H (RCF) 1907 *E,* 1908 *E*
Ithurra, E (Biarritz O) 1936 *G* 1,2, 1937 *G*

Janeczek, T (Tarbes) 1982 *Arg* 1,2, 1990 *R*
Janik, K (Toulouse) 1987 *R*
Jarasse, A (Brive) 1945 *B* 1
Jardel, J (SB) 1928 *I, E*
Jauréguy, A (RCF, Toulouse, SF) 1920 *S, E, W, I, US,* 1922 *S, W,* 1923 *S, W, E, I,* 1924 *S, W, R, US,* 1925 *I, NZ,* 1926 *S, E, W, M,* 1927 *I, E,* 1928 *S, A, E, G, W,* 1929 *I, S, E*
Jauréguy, P (Toulouse) 1913 *S, SA, W, I*
Jeangrand, M-H (Tarbes) 1921 *I*
Jeanjean, P (Toulon) 1948 *I*
Jérôme, G (SF) 1906 *NZ, E*
Joinel, J-L (Brive) 1977 *NZ* 1, 1978 *R,* 1979 *I, W, E, S, NZ* 1,2, *R,* 1980 *W, E, S, I, SA,* 1981 *S, I, W, E, R, NZ* 1,2, 1982 *E, S, I, W,* 1983 *E, S, I, W, A* 1,2, *R,* 1984 *I, W, E, S, NZ* 1,2, 1985 *S, I, W, Arg* 1, 1986 *S, I, W, E, R* 1, *Arg* 1,2, *A,* 1987 [*Z*]
Jol, M (Biarritz O) 1947 *S, I, W, E,* 1949 *S, I, E, W, Arg* 1,2
Jordana, J-L (Pau, Toulouse) 1996 *R* (R), *Arg* 1(t),2, *W* 2, 1997 *I* (t), *W, S* (R)
Judas du Souich, C (SCUF) 1911 *W, I*
Juillet, C (Montferrand) 1995 *R* 2, *Arg*
Junquas, L (Tyrosse) 1945 *B* 1,2, *W,* 1946 *B, I, K, W,* 1947 *S, I, W, E,* 1948 *S, W*

Kaczorowski, D (Le Creusot) 1974 *I* (R)
Kaempf, A (St Jean-de-Luz) 1946 *B*

Labadie, P (Bayonne) 1952 *S, I, SA, W, E, It,* 1953 *S, I, It,* 1954 *S, I, NZ, W, E, Arg* 2, 1955 *I, E, W,* 1956 *I,* 1957 *I*
Labarthete, R (Pau) 1952 *S*
Labazuy, A (Lourdes) 1952 *I,* 1954 *S, W,* 1956 *E,* 1958 *A, W, I,* 1959 *S, E, It, W*

A delighted Raphael Ibañez lifts the Five Nations trophy for France after the victory over Wales at Wembley, 5 April 1998.

Laborde, C (RCF) 1962 *It, R*, 1963 *R*, 1964 *SA*, 1965 *E*
Labrousse, T (Brive) 1996 *R, SA* 1
Lacans, P (Béziers) 1980 *SA*, 1981 *W, E, A* 2, *R*, 1982 *W*
Lacassagne, H (SBUC) 1906 *NZ*, 1907 *E*
Lacaussade, R (Bègles) 1948 *A, S*
Lacaze, C (Lourdes, Angoulême) 1961 *NZ* 2,3, *A, R*, 1962 *E, W, I, It*, 1963 *W, R*, 1964 *S, NZ, E*, 1965 *It, R*, 1966 *S, I, E, W, It, R*, 1967 *S, E, SA* 1,3,4, *R*, 1968 *S, E, W, Cz, NZ* 1, 1969 *E*
Lacaze, H (Périgueux) 1928 *I, G, W*, 1929 *I, W*
Lacaze, P (Lourdes) 1958 *SA* 1,2, 1959 *S, E, It, W, I*
Lacazedieu, C (Dax) 1923 *W, I*, 1928 *A, I*, 1929 *S*
Lacombe, B (Agen) 1989 *B*, 1990 *A* 2
Lacome, M (Pau) 1960 *Arg* 2
Lacoste, R (Tarbes) 1914 *I, W, E*
Lacrampe, F (Béziers) 1949 *Arg* 2
Lacroix, P (Mont-de-Marsan, Agen) 1958 *A*, 1960 *W, I, It, R, Arg* 1,2,3, 1961 *S, SA, E, W, I, NZ* 1,2,3, *A, R*, 1962 *S, E, W, I, R*, 1963 *S, I, E, W*
Lacroix, T (Dax, Harlequins) 1989 *A* 1 (R), 2, 1991 *W* 1 (R), 2 (R), *[R, C* (R), *E]*, 1992 *SA* 2, 1993 *E, S, I, W, SA* 1,2, *R* 2, *A* 1,2, 1994 *I, W, E, S, C* 1, *NZ* 1,2, *C* 2, 1995 *W, E, S, R* 1, *[Tg, Iv, S, I, SA, E]*, 1996 *E, S, I*, 1997 *It* 2, *R* 2, *Arg, SA* 1,2
Lafarge, Y (Montferrand) 1978 *R*, 1979 *NZ* 1, 1981 *I* (R)
Laffitte, R (SCUF) 1910 *W, S*
Laffont, H (Narbonne) 1926 *W*
Lafond, A (Bayonne) 1922 *E*
Lafond, J-B (RCF) 1983 *A* 1, 1985 *Arg* 1,2 1986 *S, I, W, E, R* 1, 1987 *I* (R), 1988 *W*, 1989 *I, W, E*, 1990 *W, A* 3 (R), *NZ* 2, 1991 *S, I, W* 1, *E, R, US* 1, *W* 2, *[R* (R), *Fj, C, E]*, 1992 *W, E, S, I* (R), *SA* 2, 1993 *E, S, I, W*
Lagisquet, P (Bayonne) 1983 *A* 1,2, *R*, 1984 *I, W, NZ* 1,2, 1986 *R* 1 (R), *Arg* 1,2, *A, NZ* 1, 1987 *[S, R, Fj, A, NZ]*, *R*, 1988 *S, I, W, Arg* 1,2,3,4, *R*, 1989 *I, W, E, S, NZ* 1,2, *B, A* 1,2, 1990 *W, E, S, I, A* 1,2,3, 1991 *S, I, US* 2, *[R]*
Lagrange, J-C (RCF) 1966 *It*
Lalande, M (RCF) 1923 *S, W, I*
Lamaison, C (Brive) 1996 *SA* 1(R),2, 1997 *W, E, S, R* 1, *A* 2, *It* 2, *R* 2, *Arg, SA* 1,2, 1998 *E, S, I, W*
Lane, G (RCF) 1906 *NZ, E*, 1907 *E*, 1908 *E, W*, 1909 *E, W, I*, 1910 *W, E*, 1911 *S, W*, 1912 *I, W, E*, 1913 *S*
Langlade, J-C (Hyères) 1990 *R, A* 1, *NZ* 1
Laperne, D (Dax) 1997 *R* 1 (R)
Laporte, G (Graulhet) 1981 *I, W, E, R, NZ* 1,2, 1986 *S, I, W, E, R* 1, *Arg* 1, *A* (R), 1987 *[R, Z* (R), *Fj]*

Larreguy, P (Bayonne) 1954 *It*
Larribau, J (Périgueux) 1912 *I, S, W, E*, 1913 *S*, 1914 *I, E*
Larrieu, J (Tarbes) 1920 *I, US*, 1921 *W*, 1923 *S, W, E, I*
Larrieux, M (SBUC) 1927 *G* 2
Larrue, H (Carmaux) 1960 *W, I, It, R, Arg* 1,2,3
Lasaosa, P (Dax) 1950 *I*, 1952 *S, I, E, It*, 1955 *It*
Lascubé, G (Agen) 1991 *S, I, W* 1, *E, US* 2, *W* 2, *[R, Fj, C, E]*, 1992 *W, E*
Lassegue, J-B (Toulouse) 1946 *W*, 1947 *S, I, W*, 1948 *W*, 1949 *I, E, W, Arg* 1
Lasserre, F (René) (Bayonne, Cognac, Grenoble) 1914 *I*, 1920 *S*, 1921 *S, W, I*, 1922 *S, E, W, I*, 1923 *W, E*, 1924 *S, I, E*
Lasserre, J-C (Dax) 1963 *It*, 1964 *S, NZ, E, W, It, I, Fj*, 1965 *W, It, R*, 1966 *R*, 1967 *S*
Lasserre, M (Agen) 1967 *SA* 2,3, 1968 *E, W, Cz, NZ* 3, *A, SA* 1,2, 1969 *S, I, E*, 1970 *E*, 1971 *E, W, R, US*
Laterrade, G (Tarbes) 1910 *E, I*, 1911 *S, E, I*
Laudouar, J (Soustons, SBUC) 1961 *NZ* 1,2, *R*, 1962 *I, R*
Lauga, P (Vichy) 1950 *S, I, E, W*
Laurent, A (Biarritz O) 1925 *NZ, S, W, E*, 1926 *W*
Laurent, J (Bayonne) 1920 *S, E, W*
Laurent, M (Auch) 1932 *G*, 1933 *G*, 1934 *G*, 1935 *G*, 1936 *G* 1
Lavail, G (Perpignan) 1937 *G*, 1940 *B*
Lavaud, R (Carcassonne) 1914 *I, W*
Lavergne, P (Limoges) 1950 *S*
Lavigne, B (Agen) 1984 *R*, 1985 *E*
Lavigne, J (Dax) 1920 *E, W*
Lazies, H (Auch) 1954 *Arg* 2, 1955 *It*, 1956 *E*, 1957 *S*
Le Bourhis, R (La Rochelle) 1961 *R*
Lecointre, M (Nantes) 1952 *It*
Le Droff, J (Auch) 1963 *It, R*, 1964 *S, NZ, E*, 1970 *E, R*, 1971 *S, I*
Lefevre, R (Brive) 1961 *NZ* 2
Leflamand, L (Bourgoin) 1996 *SA* 2, 1997 *W, E, S, It* 2, *Arg, SA* 1,2 (R)
Lefort, J-B (Biarritz O) 1938 *G* 1
Le Goff, R (Métro) 1938 *R, G* 2
Legrain, M (SF) 1909 *I*, 1910 *I*, 1911 *S, E, W, I*, 1913 *S, SA, E, I*, 1914 *I, W*
Lemeur, Y (RCF) 1993 *R* 1
Lenient, J-J (Vichy) 1967 *R*
Lepatey, J (Mazamet) 1954 *It*, 1955 *S, I, E, W*
Lepatey, L (Mazamet) 1924 *S, I, E*

285

Lescarboura, J-P (Dax) 1982 *W, E, S, I,* 1983 *A* 1,2, *R,* 1984 *I, W, E, S, NZ* 1,2, *R,* 1985 *E, S, I, W, Arg* 1,2, 1986 *Arg* 2, *A, NZ* 1, *R* 2, *NZ* 2, 1988 *S, W,* 1990 *R*
Lesieur, E (SF) 1906 *E,* 1908 *E, W,* 1909 *E, W, I,* 1910 *S, E, I,* 1911 *E, I,* 1912 *W*
Leuvielle, M (SBUC) 1908 *W,* 1913 *S, SA, E, W,* 1914 *W, E*
Levasseur, R (SF) 1925 *W, E*
Levée, H (RCF) 1906 *NZ*
Lewis, E W (Le Havre) 1906 *E*
Lhermet, J-M (Montferrand) 1990 *S, I,* 1993 *R* 1
Libaros, G (Tarbes) 1936 *G* 1, 1940 *B*
Lievremont, M (Perpignan) 1995 *It, R* 2, *Arg* (R), *NZ* 2 (R), 1996 *R, Arg* 1(R), *SA* 2 (R), 1997 *R* 1, *A* 2 (R), 1998 *E* (R), *S, I, W*
Lievremont, T (Perpignan, SF) 1996 *W* 2 (R), 1998 *E, S, I, W*
Lira, M (La Voulte) 1962 *R,* 1963 *I, E, W, It, R,* 1964 *W, It, I, SA,* 1965 *S, I, R*
Llari, R (Carcassonne) 1926 *S*
Lobies, J (RCF) 1921 *S, W, E*
Lombard, F (Narbonne) 1934 *G,* 1937 *It*
Lombarteix, R (Montferrand) 1938 *R, G* 2
Londios, J (Montauban) 1967 *SA* 3
Loppy, L (Toulon) 1993 *R* 2
Lorieux, A (Grenoble, Aix) 1981 *A* 1, *R, NZ* 1,2, 1982 *W,* 1983 *A* 2, *R,* 1984 *I, W, E,* 1985 *Arg* 1,2 (R), 1986 *R* 2, *NZ* 2,3, 1987 *W, E,* [*S, Z, Fj, A, NZ*], 1988 *S, I, W, Arg* 1,2,4, 1989 *W, A* 2
Loury, A (RCF) 1927 *E, G* 1,2, 1928 *S, A, I*
Loustau, M (Dax) 1923 *E*
Lubin-Lebrère, M-F (Toulouse) 1914 *I, W, E,* 1920 *S, E, W, I, US,* 1921 *S,* 1922 *S, E, W,* 1924 *W, US,* 1925 *I*
Lubrano, A (Béziers) 1972 *A* 2, 1973 *S*
Lux, J-P (Tyrosse, Dax) 1967 *E, It, W, I, SA* 1,2,4, *R,* 1968 *I, E, Cz, NZ* 3, *A, SA* 1,2, 1969 *S, I, E,* 1970 *S, I, W, E, R,* 1971 *S, I, E, W, A* 1,2, 1972 *S, I* 1, *E, W, I* 2, *A* 1,2, *R,* 1973 *S, NZ, E,* 1974 *I, W, E, S, Arg* 1,2, 1975 *W*

Macabiau, A (Perpignan) 1994 *S, C* 1
Maclos, P (SF) 1906 *E,* 1907 *E*
Magne, O (Dax, Brive) 1997 *W* (R), *E, S, R* 1 (R), *A* 1,2, *It* 2 (R), *R* 2, *Arg* (R), 1998 *E, S, I, W*
Magnanou, C (RCF) 1923 *E,* 1925 *W, E,* 1926 *S,* 1929 *S, W,* 1930 *S, I, E, W*
Magnol, L (Toulouse) 1928 *S,* 1929 *S, W, E*
Magois, H (La Rochelle) 1968 *SA* 1,2, *R*
Majerus, R (SF) 1928 *W,* 1929 *I, S,* 1930 *S, I, E, G, W*
Malbet, J-C (Agen) 1967 *SA* 2,4
Maleig, A (Oloron) 1979 *W, E, NZ* 2, 1980 *W, E, SA, R*
Malquier, Y (Narbonne) 1979 *S*
Manterola, T (Lourdes) 1955 *It,* 1957 *R* 1
Mantoulan, C (Pau) 1959 *I*
Marcet, J (Albi) 1925 *I, NZ, S, W, E,* 1926 *I, E*
Marchal, J-F (Lourdes) 1979 *S, R,* 1980 *W, S, I*
Marchand, R (Poitiers) 1920 *S, W*
Marfaing, M (Toulouse) 1992 *R, Arg* 1
Marocco, P (Montferrand) 1968 *S, I, W, E, R* 1, *Arg* 1,2, *A,* 1988 *Arg* 4, 1989 *I,* 1990 *E* (R), *NZ* 1 (R), 1991 *S, I, W* 1, *E, US* 2, [*R, Fj, C, E*]
Marot, A (Brive) 1969 *R,* 1970 *S, I, W,* 1971 *SA* 1, 1972 *I* 2, 1976 *A* 1
Marquesuzaa, A (RCF) 1958 *It, SA* 1,2, 1959 *S, E, It, W,* 1960 *S, E, Arg* 1
Marracq, H (Pau) 1961 *R*
Martin, C (Lyon) 1909 *I,* 1910 *W, S*
Martin, H (SBUC) 1907 *E,* 1908 *W*
Martin, J-L (Béziers) 1971 *A* 2, 1972 *S, I* 1
Martin, L (Pau) 1948 *I, A, S, W, E,* 1950 *S*
Martine, R (Lourdes) 1952 *S, I, It,* 1953 *It,* 1954 *S, I, NZ, W, E, It, Arg* 2, 1955 *S, I, W,* 1958 *A, W, It, I, SA* 1,2, 1960 *S, E, Arg* 3, 1961 *S, It*
Martinez, G (Toulouse) 1982 *W, E, S, Arg* 1,2, 1983 *E, W*
Mas, F (Béziers) 1962 *R,* 1963 *S, I, E, W*
Maso, J (Perpignan, Narbonne) 1966 *It, R,* 1967 *S, R,* 1968 *S, W, Cz, NZ* 1,2,3, *A, R,* 1969 *S, I, W,* 1971 *SA* 1,2, *R,* 1972 *E, W, A* 2, 1973 *W, I, J, R*
Massare, J (PUC) 1945 *B* 1,2, *W,* 1946 *B, I, W*
Massé, A (SBUC) 1908 *W,* 1909 *E, W,* 1910 *W, S, E, I*
Masse, H (Grenoble) 1937 *G*
Matheu-Cambas, J (Agen) 1945 *W,* 1946 *B, I, K, W,* 1947 *S, I, W, E,* 1948 *I, A, S, W, E,* 1949 *S, I, E, W, Arg* 1,2, 1950 *E, W,* 1951 *S, I*

Mauduy, G (Périgueux) 1957 *It, R* 1,2, 1958 *S, E,* 1961 *W, It*
Mauran, J (Castres) 1952 *SA, W, E, It,* 1953 *I, E*
Mauriat, P (Lyon) 1907 *E,* 1908 *E, W,* 1909 *W, I,* 1910 *W, S, E, I,* 1911 *E, S, W, I,* 1912 *I, S,* 1913 *S, SA, W, I*
Maurin, G (ASF) 1906 *E*
Maury, A (Toulouse) 1925 *I, NZ, S, W, E,* 1926 *S, I, E*
Mayssonnié, A (Toulouse) 1908 *E, W,* 1910 *W*
Mazas, L (Colomiers, Biarritz) 1992 *Arg,* 1996 *SA* 1
Melville, E (Toulon) 1990 *I* (R), *A* 1,2,3, *NZ* 1, 1991 *US* 2
Menrath, R (SCUF) 1910 *W*
Menthiller, Y (Romans) 1964 *W, It, SA, R,* 1965 *E*
Meret, F (Tarbes) 1940 *B*
Mericq, S (Agen) 1959 *I,* 1960 *S, E, W,* 1961 *I*
Merle, O (Grenoble, Montferrand) 1993 *SA* 1,2, *R* 2, *A* 1,2, 1994 *I, W, E, S, C* 1, *NZ* 1,2, *C* 2, 1995 *W, I, R* 1, [*Tg, S, I, SA, E*], *It, R* 2, *Arg, NZ* 1, 2, 1996 *E, S, R, Arg* 1,2, *W* 2, *SA* 2, 1997 *I, W, E, S, It* 1, *R* 1, *A* 1,2, *It* 2, *R* 2, *SA* 1 (R), 2
Merquey, J (Toulon)1950 *S, I, E, W*
Mesnel, F (RCF) 1986 *NZ* 2 (R), 3, 1987 *W, E, S, I,* [*S, Z, Fj, A, NZ*], *R,* 1988 *E, Arg* 1,2,3,4, *R,* 1989 *I, W, E, S, NZ* 1, 4, 1,2, 1990 *E, S, I, A* 2,3, *NZ* 1,2, 1991 *S, I, W* 1, *E, R, US* 1,2, *W* 2, [*R, Fj, C, E*], 1992 *W, E, S, I, SA* 1,2, 1993 *E* (R), *W,* 1995 *I, R* 1, [*Iv, E*]
Mesny, P (RCF, Grenoble) 1979 *NZ* 1,2, 1980 *SA, R,* 1981 *I, W, E, A* 1,2, *R, NZ* 1,2, 1982 *I, Arg* 1,2
Meyer, G-S (Périgueux) 1960 *S, E, It, R, Arg* 2
Meynard, J (Cognac) 1954 *Arg* 1, 1956 *Cz*
Mias, L (Mazamet) 1951 *S, I, E, W,* 1952 *I, SA, W, E, It,* 1953 *S, I, W, It,* 1954 *S, I, NZ, W,* 1957 *R* 2, 1958 *S, E, A, W, I, SA* 1,2, 1959 *S, It, W, I*
Mignoni, P (Béziers) 1997 *R* 2 (R), *Arg* (t)
Milliand, P (Grenoble) 1936 *G* 2, 1937 *G, It*
Minjat, R (Lyon) 1945 *B* 1
Miorin, H (Toulouse) 1996 *R, SA* 1, 1997 *I, W, E, S, It* 1
Mir, J-H (Lourdes) 1967 *R,* 1968 *I*
Mir, J-P (Lourdes) 1967 *A*
Modin, R (Brive) 1987 [*Z*]
Moga, A-M-A (Bègles) 1945 *B* 1,2, *W,* 1946 *B, I, K, W,* 1947 *S, I, W, E,* 1948 *I, A, S, W, E,* 1949 *S, I, E, W, Arg* 1,2
Mola, U (Dax) 1997 *S* (R)
Mommejat, B (Cahors, Albi) 1958 *It, I, SA* 1,2, 1959 *S, E, It, W, I,* 1960 *S, E, I, R,* 1962 *S, E, W, I, It, R,* 1963 *S, I, W*
Moncla, F (RCF, Pau) 1956 *Cz,* 1957 *I, E, W, It, R* 1, 1958 *SA* 1,2, 1959 *S, E, It, W, I,* 1960 *S, E, W, I, It, R, Arg* 1,2,3, 1961 *S, SA, E, W, It, I, NZ* 1,2,3
Moni, C (Nice) 1996 *R*
Monié, R (Perpignan) 1956 *Cz,* 1957 *E*
Monier, R (SBUC) 1911 *I,* 1912 *S*
Monniot, M (RCF) 1912 *W, E*
Montade, A (Perpignan) 1925 *I, NZ, S, W,* 1926 *W*
Montlaur, P (Agen) 1992 *E* (R), 1994 *S* (R)
Moraitis, B (Toulon) 1969 *E, W*
Morel, A (Grenoble) 1954 *Arg* 2
Morere, J (Toulouse) 1927 *E, G* 1, 1928 *S, A*
Moscato, V (Bègles) 1991 *R, US* 1, 1992 *W, E*
Mougeot, C (Bègles) 1992 *W, E, Arg*
Mouniq, P (Toulouse) 1911 *S, E, W, I,*1912 *I, E,* 1913 *S, SA, E*
Moure, H (SCUF) 1908 *E*
Moureu, P (Béziers) 1920 *I, US,* 1921 *W, E, I,* 1922 *S, W, I,* 1923 *S, W, E, I,* 1924 *S, I, E, W,* 1925 *E*
Mournet, A (Bagnères) 1981 *A* 1 (R)
Mouronval, F (SF) 1909 *I*
Muhr, A H (RCF) 1906 *NZ, E,* 1907 *E*
Murillo, G (Dijon) 1954 *It, Arg* 1

Namur, R (Toulon) 1931 *E, G*
Noble, J-C (La Voulte) 1968 *E, W, Cz, NZ* 3, *A, R*
Normand, A (Toulouse) 1957 *R* 1
Novès, G (Toulouse) 1977 *NZ* 1,2, *R,* 1978 *W, R,* 1979 *I, W*
Ntamack, E (Toulouse) 1994 *W, C* 1, *NZ* 1,2, *C* 2, 1995 *W, I, R* 1, [*Tg, S, I, SA, E*], *It, R* 2, *Arg, NZ* 1, 2, 1996 *E, S, I, W* 1, *R* (R), *Arg* 1,2, *W* 2, 1997 *I*

Olive, D (Montferrand) 1951 *I,* 1952 *I*
Ondarts, P (Biarritz O) 1986 *NZ* 3, 1987 *W, E, S, I,* [*S, Z, Fj, A, NZ*], *R,* 1988 *E, I, W, Arg* 1,2,3,4, *R,* 1989 *I, W, E, NZ* 1,2, *A* 2, 1990 *W, E, S, I, R* (R), *NZ* 1,2, 1991 *S, I, W* 1, *E, US* 2, *W* 2, [*R, Fj, C, E*]

Orso, J-C (Nice, Toulon) 1982 *Arg* 1,2, 1983 *E, S, A* 1, 1984 *E* (R), *S, NZ* 1, 1985 *I* (R), *W*, 1988 *I*
Othats, J (Dax) 1960 *Arg* 2,3
Ougier, S (Toulouse) 1992 *R, Arg* 1, 1993 *E* (R), 1997 *It* 1

Paco, A (Béziers) 1974 *Arg* 1,2, *R, SA* 1,2, 1975 *W, E, Arg* 1,2, *R*, 1976 *S, I, W, E, US, A* 1,2, *R*, 1977 *W, E, S, I, NZ* 1,2, *R*, 1978 *E, S, I, W, R*, 1979 *I, W, E, S*, 1980 *W*
Palat, J (Perpignan) 1938 *G* 2
Palmié, M (Béziers) 1975 *SA* 1,2, *Arg* 1,2, *R*, 1976 *S, I, W, E, US*, 1977 *W, E, S, I, Arg* 1,2, *NZ* 1,2, *R*, 1978 *E, S, I, W*
Paoli, R (see Simonpaoli)
Paparemborde, R (Pau) 1975 *SA* 1,2, *Arg* 1,2, *R*, 1976 *S, I, W, E, US, A* 1,2, *R*, 1977 *W, E, S, I, Arg* 1, *NZ* 1,2, 1978 *E, S, I, W, R*, 1979 *I, W, E, S, NZ* 1,2, *R*, 1980 *W, E, S, SA, R*, 1981 *S, I, W, E, A* 1,2, *R, NZ* 1,2, 1982 *W, I, R, Arg* 1,2 1983 *E, S, I, W*
Pardo, L (Hendaye) 1924 *I, E*
Pardo, L (Bayonne) 1980 *SA, R*, 1981 *S, I, W, E, A* 1, 1982 *W, E, S*, 1983 *A* 1 (R), 1985 *S, I, Arg* 2
Pardgade, J-H (Lyon U) 1953 *It*
Paries, L (Biarritz O) 1968 *SA* 2, *R*, 1970 *S, I, W*, 1975 *E, S, I*
Pascalin, P (Mont-de-Marsan) 1950 *I, E, W*, 1951 *S, I, E, W*
Pascarel, J-R (TOEC) 1912 *W, E*, 1913 *S, SA, E, I*
Pascot, J (Perpignan) 1922 *S, E, I*, 1923 *S*, 1926 *I*, 1927 *G* 2
Paul, R (Montferrand) 1940 *B*
Pauthe, G (Graulhet) 1956 *E*
Pebeyre, E-J (Fumel, Brive) 1945 *W*, 1946 *I, K, W*, 1947 *S, I, W, E*
Pebeyre, M (Vichy, Montferrand) 1970 *E, R*, 1971 *I, SA* 1,2, *A* 1, 1973 *W*
Pecune, J (Tarbes) 1974 *W, E, S*, 1975 *Arg* 1,2, *R*, 1976 *I, W, E, US*
Pedeutour, P (Begles) 1980 *I*
Pellissier, L (RCF) 1928 *A, I, E, G, W*
Pelous, F (Dax) 1995 *R* 2, *Arg, NZ* 1, 2, 1996 *E, S, I, R* (R), *Arg* 1,2, *W* 2, *SA* 1,2, 1997 *I, W, E, S, It* 1, *R* 1, *A* 1,2, *It* 2, *R* 2, *Arg, SA* 1,2 (R), 1998 *E, S, I, W*
Penaud, A (Brive) 1992 *W, E, S, I, R, Arg* 1,2, *SA* 1,2, *Arg*, 1993 *R* 1, *SA* 1,2, *R* 2, *A* 1,2, 1994 *I, W, E*, 1995 *NZ* 1, 2, 1996 *S, R, Arg* 1,2, *W* 2, 1997 *I, E, R* 1, *A* 2
Périé, M (Toulon) 1996 *E, S, I* (R)
Peron, P (RCF) 1975 *SA* 1,2
Perrier, P (Bayonne) 1982 *W, E, S, I* (R)
Pesteil, J-P (Béziers) 1975 *SA* 1, 1976 *A* 2, *R*
Petit, C (Lorrain) 1931 *W*
Peyrelade, H (Tarbes) 1940 *B*
Peyroutou, G (Périgueux) 1911 *S, E*
Phliponeau, J-F (Montferrand) 1973 *W, I*
Piazza, A (Montauban) 1968 *NZ* 1, *A*
Picard, T (Montferrand) 1985 *Arg* 2, 1986 *R* 1 (R), *Arg* 2
Pierrot, G (Pau) 1914 *I, W, E*
Pilon, J (Périgueux) 1949 *E*, 1950 *E*
Piqué, J (Pau) 1961 *NZ* 2,3, *A*, 1962 *S, It*, 1964 *NZ, E, W, It, I, SA, Fj, R*, 1965 *S, I, E, W*
Piquemal, M (Tarbes) 1927 *I, S*, 1929 *I, G*, 1930 *S, I, E, G, W*
Piquiral, E (RCF) 1924 *S, I, E, W, R, US*, 1925 *E*, 1926 *S, I, E, W, M*, 1927 *I, S, W, E, G* 1,2, 1928 *E*
Piteu, P (Pau) 1921 *S, W, E, I*, 1922 *S, E, W, I*, 1923 *E*, 1924 *E*, 1925 *I, NZ, W, E*, 1926 *E*
Plantefol, A (RCF) 1967 *SA* 2,3,4, *NZ, R*, 1968 *E, W, Cz, NZ* 2, 1969 *E, W*
Plantey, S (RCF) 1961 *A*, 1962 *It*
Podevin, G (SF) 1913 *W, I*
Poeydebasque, F (Bayonne) 1914 *I, W*
Poirier, A (SCUF) 1907 *E*
Pomathios, M (Agen, Lyon U, Bourg) 1948 *I, A, S, W, E*, 1949 *S, I, E, W, Arg* 1,2, 1950 *S, I, W*, 1951 *S, I, E, W*, 1952 *W, E*, 1953 *S, I, W*, 1954 *S*
Pons, P (Toulouse) 1920 *S, E, W*, 1921 *S, W*, 1922 *S*
Porra, M (Lyon) 1931 *I*
Porthault, A (RCF) 1951 *S, E, W*, 1952 *I*, 1953 *S, I, E*
Portolan, C (Toulouse) 1986 *A*, 1989 *I, E*
Potel, A (Begles) 1932 *G*
Prat, J (Lourdes) 1945 *B* 1,2, *W*, 1946 *B, I, K, W*, 1947 *S, I, W, E*, 1948 *I, A, S, W, E*, 1949 *S, I, E, W, Arg* 1,2, 1950 *S, I, E, W*, 1951 *S, E, W*, 1952 *S, I, SA, W, E, It*, 1953 *S, I, E, W, It*, 1954 *S, I, NZ, W, E, It*, 1955 *S, I, E, W, It*

Prat, M (Lourdes) 1951 *I*, 1952 *S, I, SA, W, E*, 1953 *S, I, E*, 1954 *I, NZ, W, E, It*, 1955 *S, I, E, W, It*, 1956 *I, W, It, Cz*, 1957 *S, I, W, It, R* 1, 1958 *A, W, I*
Prevost, A (Albi) 1926 *M*, 1927 *I, S, W*
Prin-Clary, J (Cavaillon, Brive) 1945 *B* 1,2, *W*, 1946 *B, I, K, W*, 1947 *S, I, W*
Puech, L (Toulouse) 1920 *S, E, I*, 1921 *E, I*
Puget, M (Toulouse) 1961 *It*, 1966 *S, I, It*, 1967 *SA* 1,3,4, *NZ*, 1968 *Cz, NZ* 1,2, *SA* 1,2, *R*, 1969 *E, R*, 1970 *W*
Puig, A (Perpignan) 1926 *S, E*
Pujol, A (SOE Toulouse) 1906 *NZ*
Pujolle, M (Nice) 1989 *B, A* 1, 1990 *S, I, R, A* 1,2, *NZ* 2

Quaglio, A (Mazamet) 1957 *R* 2, 1958 *S, E, A, W, I, SA* 1,2, 1959 *S, E, It, W, I*
Quilis, A (Narbonne) 1967 *SA* 1,4, *NZ*, 1970 *R*, 1971 *I*

Ramis, R (Perpignan) 1922 *E, I*, 1923 *W*
Rancoule, H (Lourdes, Toulon, Tarbes) 1955 *E, W, It*, 1958 *A, W, It, I, SA* 1, 1959 *S, It, W*, 1960 *I, It, R, Arg* 1,2, 1961 *SA, E, W, It, NZ* 1,2, 1962 *S, E, W, I, It*
Rapin, A (SBUC) 1938 *R*
Raymond, F (Toulouse) 1925 *S*, 1927 *W*, 1928 *I*
Raynal, F (Perpignan) 1935 *G*, 1936 *G* 1,2, 1937 *G, It*
Raynaud, F (Carcassonne) 1933 *G*
Razat, J-P (Agen) 1962 *R*, 1963 *S, I, R*
Rebujent, R (RCF) 1963 *E*
Revailler, D (Graulhet) 1981 *S, I, W, E, A* 1,2, *R, NZ* 1,2, 1982 *W, S, I, R, Arg* 1
Revillon, J (RCF) 1926 *I, E*, 1927 *S*
Ribère, E (Perpignan, Quillan) 1924 *I*, 1925, *I, NZ, S*, 1926 *S, I, W, M*, 1927 *I, S, W, E, G* 1,2, 1928 *S, A, I, E, G, W*, 1929 *I, E, G*, 1930 *S, I, E, W*, 1931 *I, S, W, E, G*, 1932 *G*, 1933 *G*
Rives, J-P (Toulouse, RCF) 1975 *E, S, I, Arg* 1,2, *R*, 1976 *S, I, W, E, US, A* 1,2, *R*, 1977 *W, E, S, I, Arg* 1,2, *R*, 1978 *E, S, I, W, R*, 1979 *I, W, E, S, NZ* 1,2, *R*, 1980 *W, E, S, I, SA*, 1981 *S, I, W, E, A* 2, 1982 *W, E, S, I, R*, 1983 *E, S, I, W, A* 1,2, 1984 *S, I, W*
Rochon, A (Montferrand) 1936 *G* 1
Rodrigo, M (Mauléon) 1931 *I, W*
Rodriguez, L (Mont-de-Marsan, Montferrand, Dax) 1981 *A* 1,2, *R, NZ* 1,2, 1982 *W, E, S, I, R, Arg*, 1984 *I, NZ* 1,2, *R*, 1985 *E, S, I, W*, 1986 *Arg* 1, *A, R* 2, *NZ* 2,3, 1987 *W, E, S, I*, [*S, Z, Fj, A, NZ*], *R*, 1988 *E, S, I, W, Arg* 1,2,3,4, 1989 *I, E, S, NZ* 1,2, *B, A* 1, 1990 *W, E, S, I, NZ* 1
Rogé, L (Béziers) 1952 *It*, 1953 *E, W, It*, 1954 *S, Arg* 1,2, 1955 *S, I*, 1956 *W, It, E*, 1957 *S*, 1960 *S, E*
Rollet, J (Bayonne) 1960 *Arg* 3, 1961 *NZ* 3, *A*, 1962 *It*, 1963 *I*
Romero, H (Montauban) 1962 *S, E, W, I, It, R*, 1963 *E*
Romeu, J-P (Montferrand) 1972 *R*, 1973 *S, NZ, E, W, I, R*, 1974 *W, S, Arg* 1,2, *R, SA* 1,2 (R), 1975 *W, SA* 2, *Arg* 1,2, *R*, 1976 *S, I, W, E, US*, 1977 *W, E, S, I, Arg* 1,2, *NZ* 1,2, *R*
Roques, A (Cahors) 1958 *A, W, It, I, SA* 1,2, 1959 *S, E, W, I*, 1960 *S, E, W, I, It, Arg* 1,2,3, 1961 *S, SA, E, W, It, I*, 1962 *S, E, W, I, It*, 1963 *S*
Roques, J-C (Brive) 1966 *S, I, It, R*
Rossignol, J-C (Brive) 1972 *A* 2
Rouan, J (Narbonne) 1953 *S, I*
Roucaries, G (Perpignan) 1956 *S*
Rouffia, L (Narbonne) 1945 *B* 2, *W*, 1946 *W*, 1948 *I*
Rougerie, J (Montferrand) 1973 *J*
Rougé-Thomas, P (Toulouse) 1989 *NZ* 1,2
Roujas, F (Tarbes) 1910 *I*
Roumat, O (Dax) 1989 *NZ* 2 (R), *B*, 1990 *W, E, S, I, R, A* 1,2,3, *NZ* 1,2, 1991 *S, I, W* 1, *E, R, US* 1, *W* 2, [*R, Fj, C, E*], 1992 *W* (R), *E* (R), *S, I, SA* 1,2, *Arg*, 1993 *E, S, I, W, R* 1, *SA* 1,2, *R* 2, *A* 1,2, 1994 *I, W, E, C* 1, *NZ* 1,2, *C* 2, 1995 *W, E, S*, [*Iv, S, I, SA, E*], 1996 *E, S, I, W* 1, *Arg* 1
Rousie, M (Villeneuve) 1931 *S, G*, 1932 *G*, 1933 *G*
Rousset, G (Béziers) 1975 *SA* 1, 1976 *US*
Ruiz, A (Tarbes) 1968 *SA* 2, *R*
Rupert, J-J (Tyrosse) 1963 *R*, 1964 *S, Fj*, 1965 *E, W, It*, 1966 *S, I, E, W, It*, 1967 *It, R*, 1968 *S*

Sadourny, J-L (Colomiers) 1991 *W* 2 (R), [*C* (R)], 1992 *E* (R), *S, I, Arg* 1 (R), 2, *SA* 1,2, 1993 *R* 1, *SA* 1,2, *R* 2, *A* 1,2, 1994 *I, W, E, C* 1, *NZ* 1,2, *C* 2, 1995 *W, E, S, I, R* 1, [*Tg, S, I, SA, E*], *It, R* 2, *Arg, NZ* 1, 2, 1996 *E, S, I, W* 1, *Arg* 1,2, *W* 2, *SA* 1,2, 1997 *I, W, E, S, It* 1, *R* 1, *A* 1,2, *It* 2, *R* 2, *Arg, SA* 1,2, 1998 *E, S, I, W*

Sagot, P (SF) 1906 *NZ*, 1908 *E*, 1909 *W*
Sahuc, A (Métro) 1945 *B* 1,2
Sahuc, F (Toulouse) 1936 *G* 2
Saint-André, P (Montferrand, Gloucester) 1990 *R, A* 3, *NZ* 1,2, 1991 *I* (R), *W* 1, *E, US* 1,2, *W* 2, [*R, Fj, C, E*], 1992 *W, E, S, I, R, Arg* 1,2, *SA* 1,2, 1993 *E, S, I, W, SA* 1,2, *A* 1,2, 1994 *I, W, E, S, C* 1, *NZ* 1,2, *C* 2, 1995 *W, E, S, I, R* 1, [*Tg, Iv, S, I, SA, E*], *It, R* 2, *Arg, NZ* 1, 2, 1996 *E, S, I, W* 1, *R, Arg* 1,2, *W* 2, 1997 *It* 1,2, *R* 2, *Arg, SA* 1,2
Saisset, O (Béziers) 1971 *R*, 1972 *S, I* 1, *A* 1,2, 1973 *S, NZ, E, W, I, J, R*, 1974 *I, Arg* 2, *SA* 1,2, 1975 *W*
Salas, P (Narbonne) 1979 *NZ* 1,2, *R*, 1980 *W, E*, 1981 *A* 1, 1982 *Arg* 2
Salinié, R (Perpignan) 1923 *E*
Sallefranque, M (Dax) 1981 *A* 2, 1982 *W, E, S*
Salut, J (TOEC) 1966 *R*, 1967 *S*, 1968 *I, E, Cz, NZ* 1, 1969 *I*
Samatan, R (Agen) 1930 *S, I, E, G, W*, 1931 *I, S, W, E, G*
Sanac, A (Perpignan) 1952 *It*, 1953 *S, I*, 1954 *E*, 1956 *Cz*, 1957 *S, I, E, W, It*
Sangalli, F (Narbonne) 1975 *I, SA* 1,2, 1976 *S, A* 1,2, *R*, 1977 *W, E, S, I, Arg* 1,2, *NZ* 1,2
Sanz, H (Narbonne) 1988 *Arg* 3,4, *R*, 1989 *A* 2, 1990 *S, I, R, A* 1,2, *NZ* 2, 1991 *W* 2
Sappa, M (Nice) 1973 *J, R*, 1977 *R*
Sarrade, R (Pau) 1929 *I*
Saux, J-P (Pau) 1960 *W, It, Arg* 1,2, 1961 *SA, E, W, It, I, NZ* 1,2,3, *A*, 1962 *S, E, W, I, It*, 1963 *S, I, E, It*
Savitsky, M (La Voulte) 1969 *R*
Savy, M (Montferrand) 1931 *I, S, W, E*, 1936 *G* 1
Sayrou, J (Perpignan) 1926 *W, M*, 1928 *E, G, W*, 1929 *S, W, E, G*
Scohy, R (BEC) 1931 *S, W, E, G*
Sébedio, J (Tarbes) 1913 *S, E*, 1914 *I*, 1920 *S, I, US*, 1922 *S, E*, 1923 *S*
Seguier, N (Béziers) 1973 *J, R*
Seigne, L (Agen, Merignac) 1989 *B, A* 1, 1990 *NZ* 1, 1993 *E, S, I, W, R* 1, *A* 1,2, 1994 *S, C* 1, 1995 *E* (R), *S*
Sella, P (Agen) 1982 *R, Arg* 1,2, 1983 *E, S, I, W, A* 1,2, *R*, 1984 *I, W, E, S, NZ* 1,2, *R*, 1985 *E, S, I, W, Arg* 1,2, 1986 *S, I, W, E, R* 1, *Arg* 1,2, *A, NZ* 1, *R* 2, *NZ* 2,3, 1987 *W, E, S, I, [S, R, Z* (R)*, Fj, A, NZ*], 1988 *E, S, I, W, Arg* 1,2,3,4, *R*, 1989 *I, W, E, S, NZ* 1,2, *B, A* 1,2, 1990 *W, E, S, I, A* 1,2,3, 1991 *W* 1, *E, R, US* 1,2, *W* 2, [*Fj, C, E*], 1992 *W, E, S, I, Arg*, 1993 *E, S, I, W, R* 1, *SA* 1,2, *R* 2, *A* 1,2, 1994 *I, W, E, S, C* 1, *NZ* 1,2, *C* 2, 1995 *W, E, S, I*, [*Tg, S, I, SA, E*]
Semmartin, J (SCUF) 1913 *W, I*
Senal, G (Béziers) 1974 *Arg* 1,2, *R, SA* 1,2, 1975 *W*
Sentilles, J (Tarbes) 1912 *W, E*, 1913 *S, SA*
Serin, L (Béziers) 1928 *E*, 1929 *W, E, G*, 1930 *S, I, E, G, W*, 1931 *I, W, E*
Serre, P (Perpignan) 1920 *S, E*
Serrière, P (RCF) 1986 *A*, 1987 *R*, 1988 *E*
Servole, L (Toulon) 1931 *I, S, W, E, G*, 1934 *G*, 1935 *G*
Sicart, N (Perpignan) 1922 *I*
Sillières, J (Tarbes) 1968 *R*, 1970 *S, I*, 1971 *S, I, E*, 1972 *E, W*
Siman, M (Montferrand) 1948 *E*, 1949 *S*, 1950 *S, I, E, W*
Simon, S (Bègles) 1991 *R, US* 1
Simonpaoli, R (SF) 1911 *I*, 1912 *I, S*
Sitjar, M (Agen) 1964 *W, It, I, R*, 1965 *It, R*, 1967 *A, E, It, W, I, SA* 1,2
Skrela, J-C (Toulouse) 1971 *SA* 2, *A* 1,2, 1972 *I* 1 (R), *E, W, I* 2, *A* 1, 1973 *W, J, R*, 1974 *W, E, S, Arg* 1, *R*, 1975 *W* (R), *E, S, I, SA* 1,2, *Arg* 1,2, *R*, 1976 *S, I, W, E, US, A* 1,2, *R*, 1977 *W, E, S, I, Arg* 1,2, *NZ* 1,2, *R*, 1978 *E, S, I, W*
Soler, M (Quillan) 1929 *G*
Soro, R (Lourdes, Romans) 1945 *B* 1,2, *W*, 1946 *B, I, K*, 1947 *S, I, W, E*, 1948 *I, A, S, W, E*, 1949 *S, I, E, W, Arg* 1,2
Sorondo, L-M (Montauban) 1946 *K*, 1947 *S, I, W, E*, 1948 *I*
Soulette, C (Béziers) 1997 *R* 2, 1998 *S* (R), *I* (R), *W* (R)
Soulié, E (CASG) 1920 *E, I, US*, 1921 *S, E, I*, 1922 *E, W, I*
Sourgens, J (Bègles) 1926 *M*
Spanghero, C (Narbonne) 1971 *E, W, SA* 1,2, *A* 1,2, *R*, 1972 *S, E, W, I* 2, *A* 1,2, 1974 *I, W, E, S, R, SA* 1, 1975 *E, S, I*
Spanghero, W (Narbonne) 1964 *SA, Fj, R*, 1965 *S, I, E, W, It, R*, 1966 *S, I, E, W, It, R*, 1967 *S, A, E, SA* 1,2,3,4, *NZ*, 1968 *S, I, E, W, NZ* 1,2,3, *A, SA* 1,2, *R*, 1969 *S, I, W*, 1970 *R*, 1971 *E, W, SA* 1, 1972 *E, I* 2, *A* 1,2, 1973 *S, NZ, E, W, I*
Stener, G (PUC) 1956 *S, I, E*, 1958 *SA* 1,2

Struxiano, P (Toulouse) 1913 *W, I*, 1920 *S, E, W, I, US*
Sutra, G (Narbonne) 1967 *SA* 2, 1969 *W*, 1970 *S, I*
Swierczinski, C (Bègles) 1969 *E*, 1977 *Arg* 2

Tachdjian, M (RCF) 1991 *S, I, E*
Taffary, M (RCF) 1975 *W, E, S, I*
Taillantou, J (Pau) 1930 *I, G, W*
Tarricq, P (Lourdes) 1958 *A, W, It, I*
Tavernier, H (Toulouse) 1913 *I*
Techoueyres, W (SBUC) 1994 *E, S*, 1995 [*Iv*]
Terreau, M-M (Bourg) 1945 *W*, 1946 *B, I, K, W*, 1947 *S, I, W, E*, 1948 *I, A, W, E*, 1949 *S, Arg* 1,2, 1951 *S*
Theuriet, A (SCUF) 1909 *E, W*, 1910 *S*, 1911 *W*, 1913 *E*
Thevenot, M (SCUF) 1910 *W, E, I*
Thierry, R (RCF) 1920 *S, E, W, US*
Thiers, P (Montferrand) 1936 *G* 1,2, 1937 *G, It*, 1938 *G* 1,2, 1940 *B*, 1945 *B*, 1,2
Tignol, P (Toulouse) 1953 *S*
Tilh, H (Nantes) 1912 *W, E*, 1913 *S, SA, E, W*
Tolot, J-L (Agen) 1987 [*Z*]
Tordo, J-F (Nice) 1991 *US* 1 (R), 1992 *W, E, S, I, R, Arg* 1,2, *SA* 1, *Arg*, 1993 *E, S, I, W, R* 1
Torossian, F (Pau) 1997 *R* 1
Torreilles, S (Perpignan) 1956 *S*
Tournaire, F (Narbonne) 1995 *It*, 1996 *I, W* 1, *R, Arg* 1,2(R), *W* 2, *SA* 1,2, 1997 *I, E, S, It* 1, *R* 1, *A* 1,2, *It* 2, *R* 2, *Arg, SA* 1,2, 1998 *E, S, I, W*
Tourte, R (St Girons) 1940 *B*
Trillo, J (Bègles) 1967 *SA* 3,4, *NZ, R*, 1968 *S, I, NZ* 1,2,3, *A*, 1969 *I, E, W, R*, 1970 *E, R*, 1971 *S, I, SA* 1,2, *A* 1,2, 1972 *S, A* 1,2, *R*, 1973 *S, E*
Triviaux, R (Cognac) 1931 *E, G*
Tucco-Chala, M (PUC) 1940 *B*

Ugartemendia, J-L (St Jean-de-Luz) 1975 *S, I*

Vaills, G (Perpignan) 1928 *A*, 1929 *G*
Vallot, C (SCUF) 1912 *S*
Van Heerden, A (Tarbes) 1992 *E, S*
Vannier, M (RCF, Chalon) 1953 *W*, 1954 *S, I, Arg* 1,2, 1955 *S, I, E, W, It*, 1956 *S, I, W, It, E*, 1957 *S, I, E, W, It, R* 1,2, 1958 *S, E, A, W, It, I*, 1960 *S, E, W, I, It, R, Arg* 1,3, 1961 *SA, E, W, It, I, NZ* 1, *A*
Vaquer, F (Perpignan) 1921 *S, W*, 1922 *W*
Vaquerin, A (Béziers) 1971 *R*, 1972 *S, I* 1, *A* 1, 1973 *S*, 1974 *W, E, S, Arg* 1,2, *R, SA* 1,2, 1975 *W, E, S, I*, 1976 *US, A* 1 (R), 2, *R*, 1977 *Arg* 2, 1979 *W, E*, 1980 *S, I*
Vareilles, C (SF) 1907 *E*, 1908 *E, W*, 1910 *S, E*
Varenne, F (RCF) 1952 *S*
Varvier, T (RCF) 1906 *E*, 1909 *E, W*, 1911 *E, W*, 1912 *I*
Vassal, G (Carcassonne) 1938 *R, G* 2
Vaysse, J (Albi) 1924 *US*, 1926 *M*
Vellat, E (Grenoble) 1927 *I, E, G* 1,2, 1928 *A*
Venditti, D (Bourgoin, Brive) 1996 *R, SA* 1(R),2, 1997 *I, W, E, S, R* 1, *A* 1, *SA* 2
Vergé, L (Bègles) 1993 *R* 1 (R)
Verger, A (SF) 1927 *W, E, G* 1, 1928 *I, E, G, W*
Verges, S-A (SF) 1906 *NZ, E*, 1907 *E*
Viard, G (Narbonne) 1969 *W*, 1970 *S, R*, 1971 *S, I*
Viars, S (Brive) 1992 *W, E, S, I, R, SA* 1,2 (R), *Arg*, 1993 *R* 1, 1994 *C* 1 (R), *NZ* 1 (t), 1995 *E* (R), [*Iv*], 1997 *R* 1 (R), *A* 1 (R), 2
Vigerie, M (Agen) 1931 *W*
Vigier, R (Montferrand) 1956 *S, W, It, E, Cz*, 1957 *S, E, W, It, R* 1,2, 1958 *S, E, A, W, It, I, SA* 1,2, 1959 *S, E, It, W, I*
Vigneau, A (Bayonne) 1935 *G*
Vignes, C (RCF) 1957 *R* 1,2, 1958 *S, E*
Vila, E (Tarbes) 1926 *M*
Vilagra, J (Vienne) 1945 *B* 2
Villepreux, P (Toulouse) 1967 *It, I, SA* 2, *NZ*, 1968 *I, Cz, NZ* 1,2,3, *A*, 1969 *S, I, E, W, R*, 1970 *S, I, W, E, R*, 1971 *S, I, E, W, A* 1,2, *R*, 1972 *S, I* 1, *E, W, I* 2
Viviès, B (Agen) 1978 *E, S, I, W*, 1980 *SA, R*, 1981 *S, A* 1, 1983 *A* 1 (R)
Volot, M (SF) 1945 *W*, 1946 *B, I, K, W*

Weller, S (Grenoble) 1989 *A* 1,2, 1990 *A* 1, *NZ* 1
Wolf, J-P (Béziers) 1980 *SA, R*, 1981 *A* 2, 1982 *E*

Yachvili, M (Tulle, Brive) 1968 *E, W, Cz, NZ* 3, *A, R*, 1969 *S, I, R*, 1971 *E, SA* 1,2 *A* 1, 1972 *R*, 1975 *SA* 2

Zago, F (Montauban) 1963 *I, E*

FRENCH INTERNATIONAL RECORDS
(up to 30 April 1998)

MATCH RECORDS

MOST CONSECUTIVE TEST WINS

10 1931 *E, G*, 1932 *G*, 1933 *G*, 1934 *G*,
1935 *G*, 1936 *G* 1,2, 1937 *G, It*
7 1954 *E, It, Arg* 1,2, 1955 *S, I, E*
7 1991 *R, US* 1,2, *W* 2, *R, Fj, C*

MOST CONSECUTIVE TESTS WITHOUT DEFEAT

P	W	D	Period
10	10	0	1931–38
10	8	2	1958–59
10	9	1	1986–87

MOST POINTS IN A MATCH
by the team

Pts	Opp	Venue	Year
70	Z	Auckland	1987
64	R	Aurillac	1996
60	It	Toulon	1967
59	R	Paris	1924
55	R	Wellington	1987

by a player
30 by D Camberabero v Zimbabwe
  at Auckland 1987
27 by G Camberabero v Italy at
  Toulon 1967
26 by T Lacroix v Ireland at
  Durban 1995
25 by J-P Romeu v United States
  at Chicago 1976
25 by P Berot v Romania at Agen 1987
25 by T Lacroix v Tonga at
  Pretoria 1995

MOST TRIES IN A MATCH
by the team

T	Opp	Venue	Year
13	R	Paris	1924
13	Z	Auckland	1987
11	It	Toulon	1967
10	R	Aurillac	1996

by a player
4 by A Jauréguy v Romania at
  Paris 1924
4 by M Celhay v Italy at Paris 1937

MOST CONVERSIONS IN A MATCH
by the team

C	Opp	Venue	Year
9	It	Toulon	1967
9	Z	Auckland	1987
8	R	Wellington	1987

by a player
9 by G Camberabero v Italy at
  Toulon 1967
9 by D Camberabero v Zimbabwe
  at Auckland 1987
8 by G Laporte v Romania at
  Wellington 1987

MOST PENALTY GOALS IN A MATCH
by the team

P	Opp	Venue	Year
8	I	Durban	1995
6	Arg	Buenos Aires	1977
6	S	Paris	1997
6	It	Auch	1997

by a player
8 by T Lacroix v Ireland at Durban 1995
6 by J-M Aguirre v Argentina at
  Buenos Aires 1977
6 by C Lamaison v Scotland at
  Paris 1997
6 by C Lamaison v Italy at Auch 1997

MOST DROPPED GOALS IN A MATCH
by the team

D	Opp	Venue	Year
3	I	Paris	1960
3	E	Twickenham	1985
3	NZ	Christchurch	1986
3	A	Sydney	1990
3	S	Paris	1991
3	NZ	Christchurch	1994

by a player
3 by P Albaladejo v Ireland at Paris 1960
3 by J-P Lescarboura v England at
  Twickenham 1985
3 by J-P Lescarboura v New
  Zealand at Christchurch 1986
3 by D Camerabero v Australia at
  Sydney 1990

CAREER RECORDS

MOST CAPPED PLAYERS

Caps	Player	Career
111	P Sella	1982–95
93	S Blanco	1980–91
69	R Bertranne	1971–81
69	P Saint-André	1990–97
64	J-L Sadourny	1991–98
63	M Crauste	1957–66
63	B Dauga	1964–72
61	J Condom	1982–90
61	O Roumat	1989–96
61	A Benazzi	1990–97

MOST CONSECUTIVE TESTS

Tests	Player	Span
46	R Bertranne	1973–79
45	P Sella	1982–87
44	M Crauste	1960–66
35	B Dauga	1964–68

MOST TESTS AS CAPTAIN

Tests	Captain	Span
34	J-P Rives	1978–84
34	P Saint-André	1994–97
25	D Dubroca	1986–88
24	G Basquet	1948–52
22	M Crauste	1961–66

MOST TESTS IN INDIVIDUAL POSITIONS

Full-back	S Blanco	81	1980–91
Wing	P Saint-André	67	1990–97
Centre	P Sella	104	1982–95
Fly-half	J-P Romeu	33	1972–77
Scrum-half	P Berbizier	56	1981–91
Prop	R Paparemborde	55	1975–83
Hooker	P Dintrans	50	1979–90
Lock	J Condom	61	1982–90
Flanker	J-P Rives	59	1975–84
No 8	G Basquet	33	1945–52

MOST POINTS IN TESTS

Pts	Player	Tests	Career
367	T Lacroix	43	1989–97
354	D Camberabero	36	1982–93
265	J-P Romeu	34	1972–77
233	S Blanco	93	1980–91
200	J-P Lescarboura	28	1982–90

MOST TRIES IN TESTS

Tries	Player	Tests	Career
38	S Blanco	93	1980–91
33	P Saint-André	69	1990–97
30	P Sella	111	1982–95
23	C Darrouy	40	1957–67
20	P Lagisquet	46	1983–91

MOST CONVERSIONS IN TESTS

Cons	Player	Tests	Career
48	D Camberabero	36	1982–93
45	M Vannier	43	1953–61
32	T Lacroix	43	1989–97
29	P Villepreux	34	1967–72
27	J-P Romeu	34	1972–77

MOST PENALTY GOALS IN TESTS

Pens	Player	Tests	Career
89	T Lacroix	43	1989–97
59	D Camberabero	36	1982–93
56	J-P Romeu	34	1972–77
33	P Villepreux	34	1967–72
33	P Bérot	19	1986–89
33	C Lamaison	16	1996–98

MOST DROPPED GOALS IN TESTS

Drops	Player	Tests	Career
15	J-P Lescarboura	28	1982–90
12	P Albaladejo	30	1954–64
11	G Camberabero	14	1961–68
11	D Camberabero	36	1982–93
9	J-P Romeu	34	1972–77

INTERNATIONAL CHAMPIONSHIP RECORDS

Record	Detail		Set
Most points in season	144	in four matches	1998
Most tries in season	18	in four matches	1998
Highest score	51	51–16 v Scotland	1998
	51	51–0 v Wales	1998
Biggest win	51	51–0 v Wales	1998
Highest score conceded	49	14–49 v Wales	1910
Biggest defeat	37	0–37 v England	1911
Most appearances	50	P Sella	1983–95
Most points in matches	113	D Camberabero	1983–93
Most points in season	54	J-P Lescarboura	1984
Most points in match	24	S Viars	v Ireland, 1992
	24	C Lamaison	v Scotland, 1997
Most tries in matches	14	S Blanco	1981–91
	14	P Sella	1983–95
Most tries in season	5	P Estève	1983
	5	E Bonneval	1987
Most tries in match	3	M Crauste	v England, 1962
	3	C Darrouy	v Ireland, 1963
	3	E Bonneval	v Scotland, 1987
	3	D Venditti	v Ireland, 1997
Most cons in matches	18	P Villepreux	1967–72
Most cons in season	9	C Lamaison	1998
Most cons in match	5	P Villepreux	v England, 1972
	5	S Viars	v Ireland, 1992
	5	T Castaignède	v Ireland, 1996
	5	C Lamaison	v Wales, 1998
Most pens in matches	22	T Lacroix	1991–96
Most pens in season	10	J-P Lescarboura	1984
Most pens in match	6	C Lamaison	v Scotland, 1997
Most drops in matches	9	J-P Lescarboura	1982–88
Most drops in season	5	G Camberabero	1967
Most drops in match	3	P Albaladejo	v Ireland, 1960
	3	J-P Lescarboura	v England, 1985

MAJOR TOUR RECORDS

Record	Detail	Year	Place
Most individual points	112 by S Viars	1992	Argentina
Most points in match	28 by P Lagisquet	1988 v Paraguayan XV	Ascunción (Paraguay)
Most tries in match	7 by P Lagisquet	1988 v Paraguayan XV	Ascunción (Paraguay)

MISCELLANEOUS RECORDS

Record	Holder	Detail
Longest Test career	F Haget	14 seasons, 1974 to 1987
Youngest Test cap	C Dourthe	18 yrs 7 days in 1966
Oldest Test cap	A Roques	37 yrs 329 days in 1963

FRENCH INTERNATIONAL CAREER RECORDS (*up to 30 April 1998*)

Player	Debut	Caps since last season	Caps	T	C	PG	DG	Pts
J-L Sadourny	1991 v W	1997 *R* 1, *A* 1, 2, *It* 2, *R* 2, *Arg, SA* 1,2, 1998 *E, S, I, W*	64	14	0	0	4	81
N Brusque	1997 v R	1997 *R* 2 (R)	1	0	0	0	0	0
P Bernat-Salles	1992 v Arg	1997 *R* 1, *A* 1,2, 1998 *E, S, I, W*	18	13	0	0	0	65
P Saint-André	1990 v R	1997 *It* 2, *R* 2, *Arg, SA* 1,2	69	33	0	0	0	156
C Dominici	1998 v E	1998 *E, S*	2	1	0	0	0	5
X Garbajosa	1998 v I	1998 *I, W*	2	2	0	0	0	10
E Ntamack	1994 v W		27	17	1	1	0	90
D Venditti	1996 v R	1997 *R* 1, *A* 1, *SA* 2	10	6	0	0	0	30
S Glas	1996 v S	1997 *It* 2 (R), *R* 2, *Arg, SA* 1,2, 1998 *E, S, I, W*	21	6	0	0	0	30
R Dourthe	1995 v R	1997 *A* 1	13	2	16	15	0	87
D Dantiacq	1997 v R	1997 *R* 1	1	0	0	0	0	0
P Bondouy	1997 v S	1997 *A* 2 (R), *R* 2	4	2	0	0	0	10
J-M Aué	1998 v W	1998 *W* (R)	1	0	0	0	0	0
S Viars	1992 v W	1997 *R* 1 (R), *A* 1 (R),2	17	9	17	17	0	127
L Leflamand	1996 v SA	1997 *It* 2, *Arg, SA* 1,2 (R)	8	5	0	0	0	25
C Lamaison	1996 v SA	1997 *R* 1, *A* 2, *It* 2, *R* 2, *Arg, SA* 1,2, 1998 *E, S, I, W*	16	1	25	33	1	157
T Castaignède	1995 v R	1997 *A* 1,2, *It* 2, 1998 *E, S, I, W*	18	7	20	11	3	117
T Lacroix	1989 v A	1997 *It* 2, *R* 2, *Arg, SA* 1,2	43	6	32	89	2	367
A Penaud	1992 v W	1997 *R* 1, *A* 2	30	8	0	0	5	52
D Aucagne	1997 v W	1997 *R* 1 (R), *A* 1, *R* 2 (R), *SA* 2 (R), 1998 *S* (R), *W* (R)	9	0	4	3	0	17
P Carbonneau	1995 v R	1997 *R* 1 (R), *A* 1,2, 1998 *E, S, I, W*	21	3	0	0	0	15
F Torossian	1997 v R	1997 *R* 1	1	0	0	0	0	0
J Cazalbou	1997 v It	1997 *It* 2 (R), *R* 2, *Arg, SA* 2 (R)	4	0	0	0	0	0
F Galthié	1991 v R	1997 *It* 2, *SA* 1,2, 1998 *W* (R)	22	4	0	0	0	19
P Mignoni	1997 v R	1997 *R* 2 (R), *Arg* (t)	2	0	0	0	0	0
M Dal Maso	1988 v R	1997 *R* 1 (R), *A* 1,2, *It* 2, *Arg, SA* 1,2, 1998 *W* (R)	17	1	0	0	0	5
R Ibañez	1996 v W	1997 *R* 1, *It* 2 (R), *R* 2, *SA* 2 (R), 1998 *E, S, I, W*	10	2	0	0	0	10
F Tournaire	1995 v It	1997 *R* 1, *A* 1,2, *It* 2, *R* 2, *Arg, SA* 1,2, 1998 *E, S, I, W*	25	2	0	0	0	10
D Casadei	1997 v S	1997 *R* 1, *SA* 2 (R)	3	0	0	0	0	0
D Laperne	1997 v R	1997 *R* 1 (R)	1	0	0	0	0	0
C Califano	1994 v NZ	1997 *A* 1,2, *It* 2, *R* 2 (R), *Arg, SA* 1,2, 1998 *E, S, I, W*	39	6	0	0	0	30

C Soulette	1997 v R	1997 *R* 2, 1998 *S* (R), *I* (R), *W* (R)	4	0	0	0	0	0
F Pelous	1995 v R	1997 *R* 1, *A* 1,2, *It* 2, *R* 2, *Arg*, *SA* 1,2 (R), 1998 *E*, *S*, *I*, *W*	30	2	0	0	0	10
T Cléda	1998 v E	1998 *E* (R), *S* (R), *I* (R), *W* (R)	4	0	0	0	0	0
O Merle	1993 v SA	1997 *R* 1, *A* 1,2, *It* 2, *R* 2, *SA* 1 (R),2	45	6	0	0	0	30
O Brouzet	1994 v S	1997 *R* 1, *A* 1,2, *It* 2, *Arg*, *SA* 1,2, 1998 *E*, *S*, *I*, *W*	23	1	0	0	0	5
T Lièvremont	1996 v W	1998 *E*, *S*, *I*, *W*	5	1	0	0	0	5
L Cabannes	1990 v NZ	1997 *It* 2, *Arg*, *SA* 1,2	49	2	0	0	0	8
R Castel	1996 v I	1997 *A* 1 (R)	10	2	0	0	0	10
P Benetton	1989 v BL	1997 *It* 2 (R), *R* 2, *Arg*, *SA* 1,2, 1998 *E*, *S* (R), *I* (R), *W* (R)	53	7	0	0	0	34
O Magne	1997 v W	1997 *R* 1 (R), *A* 1,2, *It* 2 (R), *R* 2, *Arg* (R), 1998 *E*, *S*, *I*, *W*	13	1	0	0	0	5
M Lièvremont	1995 v It	1997 *R* 1, *A* 2 (R), 1998 *E* (R), *S*, *I*, *W*	13	3	0	0	0	15
N Bacqué	1997 v R	1997 *R* 2	1	0	0	0	0	0
A Benazzi	1990 v A	1997 *R* 1, *A* 1,2, *It* 2, *R* 2 (R), *Arg*, *SA* 1,2	61	7	0	0	0	35

ITALY ADMITTED TO SIX NATIONS

THE 1997-98 SEASON IN ITALY
Giampaolo Tassinari

It was the most important rugby season in Italy's history. Victories against Ireland and Scotland, together with good displays in the Latin Cup and in the Tests against South Africa and Wales, confirmed the increasing strength and skill of the Italian team. Above all, though, it was the season in which the decision was made to include Italy from 2000 in an enlarged Six Nations Championship.

In their eight cap matches of the season the *azzurri* played as the international scene nowadays demands. With the forwards performing particularly well, Italy did not cave in towards the ends of games as frequently as they had done in the past. The intelligent work directed by coach Georges Coste in training sessions paid dividends.

The contributions made by those playing abroad were huge. Massimo Cuttitta (Harlequins) along with Alessandro Stoica, Massimo Giovanelli and Diego Dominguez (all with French sides) played a big role in Italy's fortunes. Abroad they faced more competitive seasons, thus improving their own styles. The efforts of those who remained faithful to Italy's domestic rugby, however, were significant. In particular, wings Paolo Vaccari and Marcello Cuttitta plus the creative genius of Alessandro Troncon at scrum-half were, once again, mainstays of the national side.

The Italian Federation is strengthening its development policy so as to provide a steady supply of quality international players for the future. With the year 2000 already in sight, everything possible must be done to ensure that Italy stays amongst Europe's elite.

ITALIAN CLUB CHAMPIONSHIP FINAL

6 June, Stadio Dall'Ara, Bologna
Benetton Treviso 9 (3PG) **Petrarca Padova 3** (1PG)

Team experience and Lance Sherrell's boot carried Benetton to victory in an all-Venetian clash devoid of tries. It was Treviso's seventh overall title, their second in successive seasons and their fourth since the inception of play-offs in 1988. Petrarca were appearing in their first final.

The sides played a tight match seldom opening the play for their talented backs. As a spectacle there was little for the 5000 spectators to savour, big-match tension and a hot day sapping the players' energy. Despite the absence of seasoned international players Julian Gardner and Andrea Sgorlon, Benetton led for most of the match. Lance Sherrell kicked penalties into the wind in the 18th and 26th minutes to give them a 6-0 lead at the break. Midway through the second half the former All Black Marty Berry pulled back three points for Petrarca with his only successful penalty from six attempts, but Sherrell completed the scoring with his final goal six minutes later. In the closing minutes Petrarca went close to scoring four times, only poor finishing robbing them of a try at a time when the Treviso defence seemed too tired to offer effective resistance.

Benetton Treviso: C Pilat; M Perziano, I Francescato, M Dallan, D Dallan; L Sherrell, A Troncon (*capt*); M Dal Sie, A Moscardi, G Grespan, W Cristofoletto, D Scaglia, C Glendinning, C Checchinato, S Rigo
Substitutions: F Mazzariol for Francescato (40 mins); L Bot for Rigo (57 mins); S Saviozzi for Moscardi (65 mins)
Scorer *Penalty Goals:* Sherrell (3)
Petrarca Padova: K Rolleston; V D'Anna, M Piovene, L Martin, F Rampazzo; M J Berry, F Dalla Nora; P-G Menapace, A Moretti, A Muraro, A Giacon, S Stocco, R Saetti, R Rampazzo, C Covi (*capt*) *Substitutions:* P Vigolo for Muraro (65 mins); A Zulian for Giacon (77 mins); D Piovan for Rolleston (83 mins)
Scorer *Penalty Goal:* Berry
Referee R Faccioli (Rovigo)

The Italian XV which faced Scotland at Treviso. L-R, back row: A Castellani, C Orlandi, G de Carli, W Cristofoletto, G Croci, J M Gardner, A Sgorlon; front row: M Cuttitta, P Vaccari, C Pilat, D Dominguez, M Giovanelli (capt), A Troncon, L Martin, C Stoica

ITALIAN INTERNATIONAL RECORDS
(up to 30 April 1998)

MATCH RECORDS

MOST CONSECUTIVE TEST WINS
6 1968 *Pt, G,Y,* 1969 *Bu, Sp, Be*

MOST CONSECUTIVE TESTS WITHOUT DEFEAT

P	W	D	Period
6	6	0	1968-69
5	4	1	1982-83

MOST POINTS IN A MATCH
by the team

Pts	Opp	Venue	Year
104	Cz	Viadana	1994
78	Cr	Perpignan	1993
70	Mo	Carcassonne	1993
64	Pt	Lisbon	1996

by a player

29 by S Bettarello v Canada at Toronto	1983
28 by D Dominguez v Holland at Calvisano	1994
27 by D Dominguez v Ireland at Bologna	1997
25 by D Dominguez v Romania at Tarbes	1997
24 by L Troiani v Spain at Parma	1994

MOST TRIES IN A MATCH
by the team

T	Opp	Venue	Year
16	Cz	Viadana	1994
11	Cr	Perpignan	1993
10	Be	Paris	1937
10	Mo	Carcassonne	1993
10	Pt	Lisbon	1996

by a player

4 by R Cova v Belgium at Paris	1937
4 by I Francescato v Morocco at Carcassonne	1993

MOST CONVERSIONS IN A MATCH
by the team

C	Opp	Venue	Year
12	Cz	Viadana	1994
10	Cr	Perpignan	1993

10	Mo	Carcassonne	1993
8	Sp	Parma	1994

by a player

12 by L Troiani v Czech Republic at Viadana	1994
10 by L Troiani v Croatia at Perpignan	1993
10 by G Filizzola v Morocco at Carcassonne	1993
8 by L Troiani v Spain at Parma	1994

MOST PENALTIES IN A MATCH
by the team

P	Opp	Venue	Year
8	R	Catania	1994
6	S	Rovigo	1993
6	Arg	Lourdes	1997
6	I	Bologna	1997
6	S	Treviso	1998

by a player

8 by D Dominguez v Romania at Catania	1994
6 by D Dominguez v Scotland at Rovigo	1993
6 by D Dominguez v Argentina at Lourdes	1997
6 by D Dominguez v Ireland at Bologna	1997
6 by D Dominguez v Scotland at Treviso	1998

CAREER RECORDS

MOST CAPPED PLAYERS

Caps	Player	Career
60	S Ghizzoni	1977-87
59	Massimo Cuttitta	1990-98
55	S Bettarello	1979-88
54	M Mascioletti	1977-90
53	G Pivetta	1979-93
52	Marcello Cuttitta	1987-98

MOST CONSECUTIVE TESTS

Tests	Player	Span
29	M Bollesan	1968-72
27	Massimo Cuttitta	1991-94
25	C Orlandi	1995-98
23	A Sgorlon	1995-98
20	A Colella	1984-87
20	A Troncon	1994-96

MOST TESTS AS CAPTAIN

Tests	Captain	Span
34	M Bollesan	1969-75
24	M Giovanelli	1992-98
21	Massimo Cuttitta	1993-97
20	M Innocenti	1985-88

MOST TESTS IN INDIVIDUAL POSITIONS

Full-back	L Troiani	41	1985-95
Wing	S Ghizzoni	53	1977-87
Centre	N Francescato	39	1972-82
Fly-half	S Bettarello	55	1979-88
Scrum-half	F Lorigiola	34	1979-88
Prop	M Cuttitta	59	1990-98
Hooker	C Orlandi	40	1992-98
Lock	R Favaro	42	1988-96
Flanker	M Giovanelli	44	1989-98
No 8	M Bollesan	28	1967-73
	C Checchinato	28	1991-97

MOST POINTS IN TESTS

Pts	Player	Tests	Career
609	D Dominguez	43	1991-98
483	S Bettarello	55	1979-88
296	L Troiani	47	1985-95
133	E Ponzi	20	1973-77
110	Marc Cuttitta	52	1987-98

MOST TRIES IN TESTS

Tries	Player	Tests	Career
25	Marc Cuttitta	52	1987-98
21	M Marchetto	43	1972-81
19	P Vaccari	48	1991-98
17	S Ghizzoni	60	1977-87
17	M Mascioletti	54	1977-90

MOST CONVERSIONS IN TESTS

Cons	Player	Tests	Career
81	D Dominguez	43	1991-98
58	L Troiani	47	1985-95
46	S Bettarello	55	1979-88
17	E Ponzi	20	1973-77
16	G Filizzola	12	1993-95

MOST PENALTY GOALS IN TESTS

Pens	Player	Tests	Career
132	D Dominguez	43	1991-98
104	S Bettarello	55	1979-88
57	L Troiani	47	1985-95
31	E Ponzi	20	1973-77

MOST DROPPED GOALS IN TESTS

Drops	Player	Tests	Career
17	S Bettarello	55	1979-88
7	D Dominguez	43	1991-98
5	M Bonomi	34	1988-96
5	O Collodo	15	1977-87

ITALIAN INTERNATIONAL CAREER RECORDS (*up to 30 April 1998*)

Player	Debut	Caps since last season	Caps	T	C	PG	DG	Pts
J A Pertile	1994 v R	1997 *SA*, 1998 *Ru*	10	1	0	0	0	5
C Pilat	1997 v I	1997 *I*, 1998 *S, W*	3	1	0	0	0	5
F Mazzariol	1995 v F	1997 *R* (R), *SA* (R)	8	1	0	0	0	5
M Ravazzolo	1993 v Cr	1997 *F 2, Arg, R, SA* (R)	23	3	0	0	0	15
F Roselli	1995 v F	1998 *Ru*	4	2	0	0	0	10
P Vaccari	1991 v Nm	1997 *F 2, Arg, R, SA, I,* 1998 *S, W*	48	19	0	0	0	92
Marc Cuttitta	1987 v Pt	1997 *F 2, Arg, R, SA, I,* 1998 *S, W, Ru*	52	25	0	0	0	110
I Francescato	1990 v R	1997 *F 2, Arg, R, SA*	38	16	0	0	0	77
M Dallan	1997 v Arg	1997 *Arg, R, I*	3	1	0	0	0	5
L Martin	1997 v F	1997 *F 2* (R), *R* (R), 1998 *S, W, Ru*	5	1	0	0	0	5
C-A Stoica	1997 v I	1997 *F 2, SA, I,* 1998 *S, W, Ru*	7	3	0	0	0	15
D Dominguez	1991 v F	1997 *F 2, Arg, R, SA, I,* 1998 *S, W, Ru*	43	6	81	132	7	609
G L Guidi	1996 v Pt	1997 *Arg* (R), *R*	5	0	0	0	0	0
A Troncon	1994 v Sp	1997 *F 2, Arg, SA, I,* 1998 *S, W, Ru*	33	5	0	0	0	25
G P De Carli	1996 v W	1997 *R,* 1998 *S, Ru* (R)	4	1	0	0	0	5
S Saviozzi	1998 v Ru	1998 *Ru*	1	0	0	0	0	0
A Moretti	1997 v R	1997 *R* (R), 1998 *Ru* (R)	2	0	0	0	0	0
C Orlandi	1992 v S	1997 *F 2, Arg, R, SA, I,* 1998 *S, W*	40	4	0	0	0	20
A Castellani	1994 v Cz	1997 *Arg* (t), *R, I,* 1998 *S, W, Ru*	11	1	0	0	0	5
Mass Cuttitta	1990 v Po	1997 *F 2, Arg, SA, I,* 1998 *W, Ru*	59	6	0	0	0	29
F Properzi-Curti	1990 v Po	1997 *F 2, Arg, SA*	41	3	0	0	0	15
C Caione	1995 v R	1997 *F 2* (R), *R* (R), 1998 *Ru*	5	0	0	0	0	0
W Cristofoletto	1992 v R	1997 *F 2, Arg, SA* (R), *I* (R), 1998 *S, W, Ru*	17	0	0	0	0	0
G Croci	1990 v Sp	1997 *F 2, Arg, R, SA, I,* 1998 *S, W*	24	3	0	0	0	13
J M Gardner	1992 v R	1997 *SA, I,* 1998 *S, W*	20	4	0	0	0	20
R Piovan	1996 v Pt	1997 *R*	2	0	0	0	0	0
A Sgorlon	1993 v Pt	1997 *F 2, Arg, R, SA, I,* 1998 *S, W, Ru*	34	2	0	0	0	10
M Giovanelli	1989 v Z	1997 *F 2, Arg, R, SA, I,* 1998 *S, W, Ru*	45	3	0	0	0	14
O Arancio	1993 v Ru	1997 *I* (t), 1998 *S* (R)	26	2	0	0	0	10
C Checchinato	1990 v Sp	1997 *F 2, Arg, R, SA, I, Ru*	39	8	0	0	0	40

YOUNG GUNS COME OUT BLAZING

THE 1997 SEASON IN SOUTH AFRICA
Dan Retief

For South African rugby the mood at the end of 1997 could not have been more buoyant with the Springboks having turned in one record performance after another in sacking France, England and Scotland.

Young players such as Percy Montgomery, Pieter Rossouw, Andre Snyman, Werner Swanepoel, Johan 'Rassie' Erasmus and Krynauw Otto had matured into respected internationals while the rest, James Small, Dick Muir, Henry Honiball, Joost van der Westhuizen, Gary Teichmann, Andre Venter, Mark Andrews, Adrian Garvey, James Dalton and Os du Randt, had re-discovered a unity of purpose and a determination to be the best which had been lacking in a winter of discontent when the Boks had lost the series to the British Lions and been humiliated by the All Blacks.

Nothing which had gone before in the eventful years of 1995 and 1996 could have prepared South Africa's rugby followers for the roller coaster ride of 1997. The season had not even begun when the game was rocked by revelations of a tape recording in which incumbent coach, Andre Markgraaff, was heard to make crass and racist remarks about certain key figures in the game's administration. The 'Andregate' tape had been made clandestinely by the disaffected former captain of Markgraaff's Griqualand West province, Andre Bester, and the upshot was that the man who, after axing Francois Pienaar at the end of 1996, had guided the Boks to a record of six successive Test victories, was forced to resign.

His place was taken by Carel du Plessis, considered by many to be the greatest of Springbok wings but a man with precious little experience of coaching at any level. Du Plessis spoke romantically of adventurous rugby, but his vision turned out to be blurred as the lack of a goal-kicker, primarily, cost the Springboks the series against the Lions before they suffered back-to-back Tri-Nations humiliations against the Wallabies and the All Blacks in Brisbane and Auckland respectively – with the concession of 55 points at Eden Park proving particularly galling to officials and fans alike.

Not even a record 61-22 thrashing of the Wallabies at Loftus Versfeld could rescue the young coach who had lost the confidence of his senior players and the SARFU were forced to appoint in Nick Mallett a man they had not too long before deemed to be too controversial for the post.

Former Springbok No 8 Mallett set about correcting the managerial mistakes he had resented as a player and then took the

Springboks on a tour of Italy, France, England and Scotland which produced astounding results – France were trounced 52-10 in what was billed as rugby's farewell to the Parc des Princes, a record 29-11 result against England at Twickenham, and the obliteration of the famous 44-0 score at Murrayfield in 1951 as the Scots were smashed 68-10.

Although Mallett managed to restore South Africa's winning habit with sound selection, focused preparation and participative tactics, he also demonstrated the strength in depth of Springbok rugby. The best performances were achieved without players once considered to be essential – Andre Joubert, Japie Mulder, Joost van der Westhuizen and Ruben Kruger – while the team played a brand of rugby which others will want to emulate. In the normal course of events Western Province's long overdue return to prominence by winning the Currie Cup and James Small becoming South Africa's most-capped player (up to 47) and leading try-scorer (20) would have enjoyed a good few column centimetres. In 1997 they received just a passing mention.

This was South African rugby's year for living litigiously. The year in which Natal took the SARFU to court over the proposed new Super-12 system and won; in which President Nelson Mandela instituted a commission of enquiry into the running of the game; during which the deposed Carel du Plessis sued SARFU for breach of contract; and during which Uli Schmidt and Kitch Christie forced Northern Transvaal to concede unfair dismissal when the World Cup coach was relieved of his duties while lying sick in hospital. There was also an outcry regarding the dropping of Hennie le Roux and Kobus Wiese, two players who just six months previously had been linchpins in a team which won six Tests, while the World Cup Springboks, as a species, continued to be whittled down to near extinction.

But most of all 1997 was an All Black year. A year in which the New Zealanders finally acquired a credit balance in Tests played against the Springboks. The year had started with the historical record tied at 22 victories apiece, with three drawn, from 47 internationals but with victories at Ellis Park and *that* record 55-point score at Eden Park, New Zealand moved ahead to 24-22. Since the Springboks forced the All Blacks in the first Test back from isolation at Ellis Park in 1992, the teams have met 12 times with New Zealand registering nine victories, two losses and one draw.

BANKFIN CURRIE CUP 1997

	P	W	D	L	F	A	Bonus	Pts
Western Province	13	12	0	1	567	286	10	58
Natal Sharks	13	12	0	1	566	241	9	57
FS Cheetahs	13	11	0	2	651	234	10	54
Gauteng Lions	13	9	0	4	562	399	9	45
Blue Bulls	13	8	0	5	382	341	8	40
Griqualand West	13	7	1	5	410	313	9	39
Boland	13	6	1	6	464	386	12	38
SWD Eagles	13	7	0	6	362	365	8	36
Mpumalanga	13	4	0	9	321	438	6	22
Gauteng Falcons	13	3	0	10	349	600	6	18
Border	13	3	0	10	277	569	5	17
Northern FS	13	3	0	10	344	744	5	17
North West	13	3	0	10	346	507	4	16
Eastern Province	13	2	0	11	284	462	4	12

*The competition was played on the Super-12 format of four points for a win, two points for a draw, one point for a defeat by seven points or less, a bonus point for four tries or more.

Semi-finals
Western Province 88, Gauteng Lions 18; Free State Cheetahs 38, Natal 22

Final
Western Province 14 (3PG 1T)   **Free State Cheetahs 12** (4PG)
Western Province *Try:* J Swart   *Penalty Goals:* L Koen (3)
Free State *Penalty Goals:* J de Beer (4)

Bankfin President's Shield: Western Province 51, Gauteng Lions 21
Bankfin Under-21 (A Section): Natal Sharks 21, Gauteng Lions 17
Supersport Club Championship: Stellenbosch University 30, Rand Afrikaans University 15

TONGA TO AFRICA 1997

THE TOURING PARTY

Manager D Havea   **Technical Director** P Kingsley-Jones   **Coach** T Felilani
Captain L Katoa

Full-backs: K Tonga (Fasi), *C Schumkel (Fasi)

Threequarters: S Faka'osi'folau (Toa Ko Ma'afu), F Tatafu (Fasi), V Uhi (Toa Ko Ma'afu), SM Latu (Toa Ko Ma'afu), T Manako (Siutaka & Northland, NZ)

Half-backs: M Vunipola (Toa Ko Ma'afu), S Tau'ma'lolo (Toa Ko Ma'afu & Otahuhu, NZ), T Alatini (Siutaka & Otahuhu, NZ), A Alatini (Siutaka & Otahuhu, NZ), S Mafile'o (Siutaka)

Forwards: D Penisini (Wellington, NZ), D Benisa (Horowhenua, NZ), L Maka (Siutaka), N Ta'u (Police), H Lavaka (Fasi), F Vunipola (Toa Ko Ma'afu), T Siale (Siutaka & Northland, NZ), F Finefiuaki (Kolofo'ou), K Faletau (Toa Ko Ma'afu), P Moala (Siutaka), S Valu (Mt Roskill, Auckland, NZ), K Tu'ipolutu (Toa Ko Ma'afu), A Ta'ufo'ou (Kolomotu'a), M Molitika (Toa Ko Ma'afu), L Katoa (Siutaka), T Tohi (Siutaka)

* *Replacement on tour*

TOUR RECORD

All matches   Played 8   Won 6   Lost 2   Points for 232   Against 226
International matches   Played 3   Won 2   Lost 1   Points for 72   Against 101

MATCH DETAILS

1997	OPPONENTS	VENUE	RESULT
13 May	Zimbabwe Goshawks	Harare	W 62-22
17 May	ZIMBABWE	Harare	W 42-13
21 May	Namibian President's XV	Windhoek	W 31-28
24 May	NAMIBIA	Windhoek	W 20-14
28 May	North West (W Transvaal)	Potchefstroom	L 6-46
1 June	Eastern Province XV	Port Elizabeth	W 34-19
4 June	Border	East London	W 27-10
10 June	SOUTH AFRICA	Cape Town	L 10-74

10 June, Newlands, Cape Town   Test Match

SOUTH AFRICA 74 (7G 5T)   TONGA 10 (1G 1PG)

SOUTH AFRICA: AJ Joubert (Natal); JT Small (Western Province), JC Mulder (Gauteng Lions), E Lubbe (Griqualand West), AH Snyman (Blue Bulls); HW Honiball (Natal), JH van der Westhuizen (Blue Bulls); JP du Randt (Free State), AE Drotské (Free State), AC Garvey (Natal), FJ van Heerden (Western Province), JJ Strydom (Gauteng Lions), RJ Kruger (Blue Bulls), GH Teichmann (*capt*), AG Venter (Free State) *Substitutions:* MG Andrews (Natal) for Teichmann (23 mins); J Dalton (Gauteng Lions) for van Heerden (50 mins); RG Bennett (Border) for Small (54 mins)
Scorers *Tries:* Snyman (3), Small (2), Garvey (2), Kruger (2), van Heerden, van der Westhuizen, Drotské *Conversions:* Lubbe (7)
TONGA: Tonga; Fakaosi'folau, Schumkel, Uhi, Mafileo; Tau'ma'lolo, M Vunipola; Ta'u, F Vunipola (*capt*), Lavaka, Ta'ufo'ou, Faletau, Molitika, K Tu'ipolutu, Tohi *Substitution:* Tulikifanga for M Vunipola (47 mins)
Scorers *Try:* Ta'u *Conversion:* Tau'ma'lolo *Penalty Goal:* Tonga
Referee M Wildes (Zimbabwe)

SOUTH AFRICA TO EUROPE 1997

THE TOURING PARTY

Manager A Petersen   **Chief Coach** NVH Mallett
Assistant Coaches A Solomons, P de Villiers   **Captain** GH Teichmann

Full-backs: PC Montgomery (Western Province), **GM Delport (Gauteng Lions)

Threequarters: DJ Muir (Western Province), AH Snyman (Western Province),
JT Small (Western Province), PWG Rossouw (Western Province), M Hendricks
(Boland), **JW Gillingham (Gauteng Lions), **B Paulse (Western Province),
PF Smith (Griqualand West), J Swart (Western Province)

Half-backs: HW Honiball (Natal), JH de Beer (Free State), **JC Wessels
(Griqualand West), JH van der Westhuizen (Blue Bulls), W Swanepoel
(Free State), D van Zyl (Mpumalanga)

Forwards: J Dalton (Gauteng Lions), AE Drotské (Free State), **D Santon
(Boland), JP du Randt (Free State), AC Garvey (Natal), W Meyer (Free State),
DF Theron (Griqualand West), A van der Linde (Western Province),
*A-H le Roux (Natal), MG Andrews (Natal), K Otto (Blue Bulls), WW Els
(Free State), **WW Basson (Blue Bulls), JC Erasmus (Free State), AD Aitken
(Western Province), +CPJ Krige (Western Province), PL Smit (Griqualand West),
RB Skinstad (Western Province), AG Venter (Free State), GH Teichmann (Natal),
**W Brosnihan (Gauteng Lions)

+ *selected for tour, injured and replaced by Brosnihan*
* *replacement on tour but returned home before England & Scotland Tests*
** *returned home before England & Scotland Tests*

TOUR RECORD

All matches   Played 7   Won 5   Lost 2   Points for 276   Against 155
International matches   Played 5   Won 5   Points for 247   Against 94

SCORING DETAILS

All matches					International matches				
For:	40T	32C	4PG		276 Pts	For:	35T	30C	4PG	247 Pts
Against:	16T	9C	18PG	1DG	155 Pts	Against:	9T	5C	13PG	94 Pts

MATCH DETAILS

1997	OPPONENTS	VENUE	RESULT
8 Nov	ITALY	Bologna	W 62-31
11 Nov	French Barbarians	Biarritz	L 22-40
15 Nov	FRANCE	Lyon	W 36-32
18 Nov	France A	Toulon	L 7-21
22 Nov	FRANCE	Paris	W 52-10
29 Nov	ENGLAND	Twickenham	W 29-11
6 Dec	SCOTLAND	Murrayfield	W 68-10

MATCH 1   8 November, Stadio Dall'Ara, Bologna   Test Match
ITALY 31 (2G 4PG 1T)   SOUTH AFRICA 62 (7G 1PG 2T)

ITALY: J-A Pertile (Roma); P Vaccari (Calvisano), C Stoica (Narbonne, France), I Francescato (Treviso), Marcello Cuttitta (Milan); D Dominguez (SF-CASG, France), A Troncon (Treviso); Massimo Cuttitta (Harlequins, England), C Orlandi (Milan), F Properzi Curti (Milan), C Checchinato (Treviso), G Croci (Milan), M Giovanelli (Narbonne, France)(*capt*), JM Gardner (Treviso), A Sgorlon (Treviso) *Substitutions:* M Ravazzolo (Calvisano) for Pertile (51 mins); W Cristofoletto (Treviso) for Checchinato (57 mins); F Mazzariol (Treviso) for Ravazzolo (79 mins)
Scorers *Tries:* Gardner, Francescato, Vaccari *Conversions:* Dominguez (2) *Penalty Goals:* Dominguez (4)
SOUTH AFRICA: Swart; Small, Snyman, Muir, Rossouw; Honiball, van der Westhuizen; du Randt, Dalton, Garvey, Otto, Andrews, Erasmus, Teichmann (*capt*), Venter
Scorers *Tries:* Rossouw (2), Small (2), Erasmus (2), du Randt, Swart, Muir *Conversions:* Honiball (7) *Penalty Goal:* Honiball
Referee P Deluca (Argentina)

MATCH 2   11 November, Stade Aguilera, Biarritz

French Barbarians 40 (3G 2PG 1DG 2T)   South Africans 22 (1G 3T)
French Barbarians: N Brusque (Pau); P Bernat-Salles (Pau), D Dantiacq (Pau), E Artiguste (Castres), C Dominici (SF-CASG); W Serevi (Leicester, England), F Corrihons (SF-CASG); J-J Crenca (Agen), V Moscato (SF-CASG)(*capt*), P de Villiers (SF-CASG), J Matiu (Biarritz), O Roumat (SF-CASG), S Betsen (Biarritz), T Lièvremont (Perpignan), M Lièvremont (SF-CASG) *Substitutions:* S Puleoto (Biarritz) for Matiu (40 mins); S Dispagne (Toulouse) for M Lièvremont (52 mins); M Vunibaka (Leicester, England) for Bernat-Salles (52 mins); C Laussucq (SF) for Corrihons (73 mins); B Bellot (Perpignan) for Dantiacq (80 mins)
Scorers *Tries:* T Lièvremont (2), Matiu, de Villiers, Vunibaka *Conversions:* Serevi (3) *Penalty Goals:* Serevi (2) *Dropped Goal:* Serevi
South Africans: Montgomery; Hendricks, Gillingham, Smith, Paulse; de Beer, Swanepoel; van der Linde, Drotské, Theron, Basson, Els, Smit, Aitken (*capt*), Skinstad *Substitutions:* Brosnihan for Smit (15 mins); Meyer for Brosnihan (40 mins); Delport for Paulse (74 mins)
Scorers *Tries:* Drotské, Skinstad, Montgomery, de Beer *Conversion:* de Beer
Referee J Dumé (Côte d'Argent)

MATCH 3   15 November, Stade Gerland, Lyon   1st Test
FRANCE 32 (1G 5PG 2T)   SOUTH AFRICA 36 (4G 1PG 1T)

FRANCE: J-L Sadourny (Colomiers); L Leflamand (Bourgoin-Jallieu), C Lamaison (Brive), S Glas (Bourgoin-Jallieu), P Saint-André (Gloucester, England)(*capt*); T Lacroix (Harlequins, England), F Galthié (Colomiers); C Califano (Toulouse), M Dal Maso (Agen), F Tournaire (Toulouse), O Brouzet (Bègles-Bordeaux), F Pelous (Toulouse), P Benetton (Agen), A Benazzi (Agen), L Cabannes (Harlequins, England) *Substitution:* O Merle (Montferrand) for Pelous (50 mins)
Scorers *Tries:* Merle, Califano, Glas *Conversion:* Lamaison
Penalty Goals: Lamaison (5)

SOUTH AFRICA: Montgomery; Small, Snyman, Muir, Rossouw; Honiball, van der Westhuizen; du Randt, Dalton, Garvey, Otto, Andrews, Erasmus, Teichmann (*capt*), Venter *Substitution:* Swanepoel for van der Westhuizen (79 mins)
Scorers *Tries:* Muir, Montgomery, Rossouw, Dalton, Small
Conversions: Honiball (4) *Penalty Goal:* Honiball
Referee WD Bevan (Wales)

MATCH 4   18 November, Stade Mayol, Toulon

France A 21 (1G 3PG 1T)   **South Africans 7** (1G)
France A: N Brusque (Pau); P Bondouy (Toulouse), F Leloir (Pau), J-M Aué (Castres), D Bory (Montferrand); B Bellot (Perpignan), P Mignoni (Béziers); C Soulette (Béziers), Y Bru (Colomiers), R Crespy (Brive), H Miorin (Toulouse), T Cléda (Pau), N Bacqué (Pau), T Lièvremont (Perpignan)(*capt*), P Tabacco (Colomiers) *Substitution:* P Escale (Castres) for Brusque (40 mins)
Scorers *Tries:* Cléda, Bondouy *Conversion:* Bellot *Penalty Goals:* Bellot (3)
South Africans: Delport; Hendricks, Gillingham, Smith, Paulse; Wessels, van Zyl; Theron, Santon, le Roux, Basson, Els, Skinstad, Aitken (*capt*), Brosnihan
Substitutions: Venter for Basson (temp 10-20 mins); Drotské for Santon (26 mins)
Scorers *Try:* Smith *Conversion:* Gillingham
Referee P Thomas (Drome-Ardeche)

MATCH 5   22 November, Parc des Princes, Paris   2nd Test
FRANCE 10 (1G 1PG)   SOUTH AFRICA 52 (7G 1PG)

FRANCE: J-L Sadourny (Colomiers); D Venditti (Brive), C Lamaison (Brive), S Glas (Bourgoin-Jallieu), P Saint-André (Gloucester, England)(*capt*); T Lacroix (Harlequins, England), F Galthié (Colomiers); C Califano (Toulouse), M Dal Maso (Agen), F Tournaire (Toulouse), O Brouzet (Bègles-Bordeaux), O Merle (Montferrand), P Benetton (Agen), A Benazzi (Agen), L Cabannes (Harlequins, England) *Substitutions:* R Ibañez (Pau) for Dal Maso (temp 15-21 mins and 58 mins); F Pelous (Toulouse) for Cabannes (40 mins); L Leflamand (Bourgoin-Jallieu) for Venditti (47 mins); J Cazalbou (Toulouse) for Galthié (54 mins); D Aucagne (Pau) for Cazalbou (68 mins); D Casedeï (Brive) for Saint-André (75 mins)
Scorers *Try:* Ibañez *Conversion:* Lamaison *Penalty Goal:* Lamaison
SOUTH AFRICA: Montgomery; Small, Snyman, Muir, Rossouw; Honiball, Swanepoel; du Randt, Dalton, Garvey, Otto, Andrews, Erasmus, Teichmann (*capt*), Venter *Substitutions:* Aitken for Erasmus (48 mins); de Beer for Rossouw (79 mins)
Scorers *Tries:* Rossouw (4), Snyman, Teichmann, Honiball
Conversions: Honiball (7) *Penalty Goal:* Honiball
Referee PD O'Brien (New Zealand)

MATCH 6   29 November, Twickenham   Test Match
ENGLAND 11 (2PG 1T)   SOUTH AFRICA 29 (3G 1PG 1T)

ENGLAND: MB Perry (Bath); J Bentley (Newcastle), WJH Greenwood (Leicester), NJJ Greenstock (Wasps), DL Rees (Sale); MJ Catt (Bath), MJS Dawson (Northampton); J Leonard (Harlequins), R Cockerill (Leicester), DJ Garforth (Leicester), DJ Grewcock (Saracens), GS Archer (Newcastle), LBN Dallaglio (Wasps)(*capt*), RA Hill (Saracens), NA Back (Leicester) *Substitutions:* PJ Grayson (Northampton) for Catt (40 mins); CMA Sheasby (Wasps) for Hill (57 mins); AS Healey (Leicester) for Bentley (64 mins); SD Shaw (Wasps) for Grewcock (68 mins)
Scorers *Try:* Greenstock *Penalty Goals:* Catt (2)

SOUTH AFRICA: Montgomery; Small, Snyman, Muir, Rossouw; Honiball, Swanepoel; du Randt, Dalton, Garvey, Otto, Andrews, Aitken, Teichmann (*capt*), Venter *Substitution:* Skinstad for Venter (temp 31-38 mins)
Scorers *Tries:* Garvey, Snyman, Andrews, Swanepoel *Conversions:* Honiball (2), Montgomery *Penalty Goal:* Honiball
Referee CJ Hawke (New Zealand)

Pieter Roussow (South Africa) beats Laurent Leflamand (France) to score one of his four tries in the final Test at the Parc des Princes on 22 November 1997.

MATCH 7	**6 December, Murrayfield**	**Test Match**

SCOTLAND 10 (1G 1PG) SOUTH AFRICA 68 (9G 1T)

SCOTLAND: RJS Shepherd (Melrose); CA Joiner (Leicester), AG Stanger (Hawick), CM Chalmers (Melrose), DA Stark (Glasgow Hawks); GPJ Townsend (Northampton), AD Nicol (Bath); DIW Hilton (Bath), GC Bulloch (West of Scotland), MJ Stewart (Northampton), SJ Campbell (Dundee HSFP), S Murray (Bedford), RI Wainwright (Dundee HSFP)(*capt*), EW Peters (Bath), IR Smith (Moseley) *Substitutions:* DW Hodge (Watsonians) for Stanger (temp 21-29 mins) and for Chalmers (51 mins); G Armstrong (Newcastle) for Nicol (63 mins); P Walton (Newcastle) for Peters (72 mins); G Graham (Newcastle) for Hilton (73 mins)
Scorers *Try:* Stark *Conversion:* Shepherd *Penalty Goal:* Shepherd
SOUTH AFRICA: Montgomery; Small, Snyman, Muir, Rossouw; de Beer, Swanepoel; du Randt, Dalton, Garvey, Otto, Andrews, Erasmus, Teichmann (*capt*), Venter *Substitutions:* Smith for de Beer (35 mins); Swart for Small (71 mins); Meyer for du Randt (71 mins)
Scorers *Tries:* Montgomery (2), Small (2), Erasmus, Rossouw, Teichmann, Venter, Snyman, Smith *Conversions:* Montgomery (8), de Beer
Referee P Thomas (France)

SOUTH AFRICAN INTERNATIONAL PLAYERS (*up to 30 April 1998*)

Ackermann, D S P (WP) 1955 *BI* 2,3,4, 1956 *A* 1,2, *NZ* 1,3, 1958 *F* 2
Ackermann, J N (NT) 1996 *Fj*, *A* 1, *NZ* 1, *A* 2
Aitken, A D (WP) 1997 *F* 2 (R), *E*
Albertyn, P K (SWD) 1924 *BI* 1,2,3,4
Alexander, F A (GW) 1891 *BI* 1,2
Allan, J (N) 1993 *A* 1 (R), *Arg* 1,2 (R), 1994 *E* 1,2, *NZ* 1,2,3, 1996 *Fj*, *A* 1, *NZ* 1, *A* 2, *NZ* 2
Allen, P B (EP) 1960 *S*
Allport, P H (WP) 1910 *BI* 2,3
Anderson, J W (WP) 1903 *BI* 3
Anderson, J H (WP) 1896 *BI* 1,3,4
Andrew, J B (Tvl) 1896 *BI* 2
Andrews, K S (WP) 1992 *E*, 1993 *F* 1,2, *A* 1 (R), 2,3, *Arg* 1 (R), 2, 1994 *NZ* 3
Andrews, M G (N) 1994 *E* 2, *NZ* 1,2,3, *Arg* 1,2, *S*, *W*, 1995 *WS*, [*A*, *WS*, *F*, *NZ*], *W*, *It*, *E*, 1996 *Fj*, *A* 1, *NZ* 1, *A* 2, *NZ* 2,3,4,5, *Arg* 1,2, *F* 1,2, *W*, 1997 *Tg* (R), *BI* 1,2, *NZ* 1, *A* 1, *NZ* 2, *A* 2, *It*, *F* 1,2, *E*, *S*
Antelme, M J G (Tvl) 1960 *NZ* 1,2,3,4, 1961 *F*
Apsey, J T (WP) 1933 *A* 4,5, 1938 *BI* 2
Ashley, S (WP) 1903 *BI* 2
Aston, F T D (Tvl) 1896 *BI* 1,2,3,4
Atherton, S (N) 1993 *Arg* 1,2, 1994 *E* 1,2, *NZ* 1,2,3, 1996 *NZ* 2
Aucamp, J (WT) 1924 *BI* 1,2

Baard, A P (WP) 1960 *I*
Babrow, L (WP) 1937 *A* 1,2, *NZ* 1,2,3
Badenhorst, C (OFS) 1994 *Arg* 2, 1995 *WS* (R)
Barnard, A S (EP) 1984 *S Am* 1,2, 1986 *Cv* 1,2
Barnard, J H (Tvl) 1965 *S*, *A* 1,2, *NZ* 3,4
Barnard, R W (Tvl) 1970 *NZ* 2 (R)
Barnard, W H M (NT) 1949 *NZ* 4, 1951 *W*
Barry, J (WP) 1903 *BI* 1,2,3
Bartmann, W J (Tvl, N) 1986 *Cv* 1,2,3,4, 1992 *NZ*, *A*, *F*, 1,2
Bastard, W E (N) 1937 *A* 1, *NZ* 1,2,3, 1938 *BI* 1,3
Bates, A J (WT) 1969 *E*, 1970 *NZ* 1,2, 1972 *E*
Bayvel, P C R (Tvl) 1974 *BI* 2,4, *F* 1,2, 1975 *F* 1,2, 1976 *NZ* 1,2,3,4
Beck, J J (WP) 1981 *NZ* 2 (R), 3 (R), *US*
Bedford, T P (N) 1963 *A* 1,2,3,4, 1964 *W*, *F*, 1965 *I*, *A* 1,2, 1968 *BI* 1,2,3,4, *F* 1,2, 1969 *A* 1,2,3,4, *S*, *E*, 1970 *I*, *W*, 1971 *F* 1,2
Bekker, H J (WP) 1981 *NZ* 1,3
Bekker, H P J (NT) 1952 *E*, *F*, 1953 *A* 1,2,3,4, 1955 *BI* 2,3,4, 1956 *A* 1,2, *NZ* 1,2,3,4
Bekker, M J (NT) 1960 *S*
Bekker, R P (NT) 1953 *A* 3,4
Bekker, S (NT) 1997 *A* 2 (t)
Bennett, R G (Border) 1997 *Tg* (R), *BI* 1 (R), 3, *NZ* 1, *A* 1, *NZ* 2
Bergh, W F (SWD) 1931 *W*, *I*, 1932 *E*, *S*, 1933 *A* 1,2,3,4,5, 1937 *A* 1,2, *NZ* 1,2,3, 1938 *BI* 1,2,3
Bestbier, A (OFS) 1974 *F* 2 (R)
Bester, J J N (WP) 1924 *BI* 2,4
Bester, J L A (WP) 1938 *BI* 2,3
Beswick, A M (Bor) 1896 *BI* 2,3,4
Bezuidenhoudt, C E (NT) 1962 *BI* 2,3,4
Bezuidenhoudt, N S E (NT) 1972 *E*, 1974 *BI* 2,3,4, *F* 1,2, 1975 *F* 1,2, 1977 *Wld*
Bierman, J N (Tvl) 1931 *I*
Bisset, W M (WP) 1891 *BI* 1,3
Blair, R (WP) 1977 *Wld*
Bosch, G R (Tvl) 1974 *BI* 2, *F* 1,2, 1975 *F* 1,2, 1976 *NZ* 1,2,3,4
Bosman, N J S (Tvl) 1924 *BI* 2,3,4
Botha, D S (NT) 1981 *NZ* 1
Botha, H E (NT) 1980 *S Am* 1,2, *BI* 1,2,3,4, *S Am* 3,4, *F*, 1981 *I* 1,2, *NZ* 1,2,3, *US*, 1982 *S Am* 1,2, 1986 *Cv* 1,2,3,4, 1989 *Wld* 1,2, 1992 *NZ*, *A*, *F* 1,2, *E*
Botha, J A (Tvl) 1903 *BI* 3
Botha, J P F (NT) 1962 *BI* 2,3,4
Botha, P H (Tvl) 1965 *A* 1,2
Boyes, H C (GW) 1891 *BI* 1,2
Brand, G H (WP) 1928 *NZ* 2,3, 1931 *W*, *I*, 1932 *E*, *S*, 1933 *A* 1,2,3,4,5, 1937 *A* 1,2, *NZ* 2,3, 1938 *BI* 1

Bredenkamp, M J (GW) 1896 *BI* 1,3
Breedt, J C (Tvl) 1986 *Cv* 1,2,3,4, 1989 *Wld* 1,2, 1992 *NZ*, *A*
Brewis, J D (NT) 1949 *NZ* 1,2,3,4, 1951 *S*, *I*, *W*, 1952 *E*, *F*, 1953 *A* 1
Briers, T P D (WP) 1955 *BI* 1,2,3,4, 1956 *NZ* 2,3,4
Brink, D J (WP) 1906 *S*, *W*, *E*
Brink, R (WP) 1995 [*R*, *C*]
Brooks, D (Bor) 1906 *S*
Brosnihan, W (GL) 1997 *A* 2
Brown, C B (WP) 1903 *BI* 1,2,3
Brynard, G S (WP) 1965 *A* 1, *NZ* 1,2,3,4, 1968 *BI* 3,4
Buchler, J U (Tvl) 1951 *S*, *I*, *W*, 1952 *E*, *F*, 1953 *A* 1,2,3,4, 1956 *A* 2
Burdett, A F (WP) 1906 *S*, *I*
Burger, J M (WP) 1989 *Wld* 1,2
Burger, M B (NT) 1980 *BI* 2 (R), *S Am* 3, 1981 *US* (R)
Burger, S W P (WP) 1984 *E* 1,2, 1986 *Cv* 1,2,3,4
Burger, W A G (Bor) 1906 *S*, *I*, *W*, 1910 *BI* 2

Carelse, G (EP) 1964 *W*, *F*, 1965 *I*, *S*, 1967 *F* 1,2,3, 1968 *F* 1,2, 1969 *A* 1,2,3,4, *S*
Carlson, R A (WP) 1972 *E*
Carolin, H W (WP) 1903 *BI* 3, 1906 *S*, *I*
Castens, H H (WP) 1891 *BI* 1
Chignell, T W (WP) 1891 *BI* 3
Cilliers, G D (OFS) 1963 *A* 1,3,4
Cilliers, N V (WP) 1996 *NZ* 3 (t)
Claassen, J T (WT) 1955 *BI* 1,2,3,4,6, 1956 *A* 1,2, *NZ* 1,2,3,4, 1958 *F* 1,2, 1960 *S*, *NZ* 1,2,3, *W*, *I*, 1961 *E*, *S*, *F*, *I*, *A* 1,2, 1962 *BI* 1,2,3,4
Claassen, W (N) 1981 *I* 1,2, *NZ* 2,3, *US*, 1982 *S Am* 1,2
Clark, W H G (Tvl) 1933 *A* 3
Clarkson, W A (N) 1921 *NZ* 1,2, 1924 *BI* 1
Cloete, H A (WP) 1896 *BI* 4
Cockrell, C H (WP) 1969 *S*, 1970 *I*, *W*
Cockrell, R J (WP) 1974 *F* 1,2, 1975 *F* 1,2, 1976 *NZ* 1,2, 1977 *Wld*, 1981 *NZ* 1,2 (R), 3, *US*
Coetzee, J H H (WP) 1974 *BI* 1, 1975 *F* 2 (R), 1976 *NZ* 1,2,3,4
Cope, D K (Tvl) 1896 *BI* 2
Cotty, W (GW) 1896 *BI* 3
Crampton, G (GW) 1903 *BI* 2
Craven, D H (WP) 1931 *W*, *I*, 1932 *S*, 1933 *A* 1,2,3,4,5, 1937 *A* 1,2, *NZ* 1,2,3, 1938 *BI* 1,2,3, 1946 *NZ* 1,2,3, 1937 *A* 1,2, *NZ* 1,2,3
Cronje, P A (Tvl) 1971 *F* 1,2, *A* 1,2,3, 1974 *BI* 3,4
Crosby, J H (Tvl) 1896 *BI* 2
Crosby, N J (Tvl) 1910 *BI* 1,3
Currie, C (GW) 1903 *BI* 2

D'Alton, G (WP) 1933 *A* 1
Dalton, J (Tvl, GL) 1994 *Arg* 1 (R), 1995 [*A*, *C*], *W*, *It*, *E*, 1996 *NZ* 4 (R), 5, *Arg* 1,2, *F* 1,2, *W*, 1997 *Tg* (R), *BI* 3, *NZ* 2, *A* 2, *It*, *F* 1,2, *E*, *S*
Daneel, G M (WP) 1928 *NZ* 1,2,3,4, 1931 *W*, *I*, 1932 *E*, *S*
Daneel, H J (WP) 1906 *S*, *I*, *W*, *E*
Davison, P M (EP) 1910 *BI* 1
De Beer, J H (OFS) 1997 *BI* 3, *NZ* 1, *A* 1, *NZ* 2, *A* 2, *F* 2 (R), *S*
De Bruyn, J (OFS) 1974 *BI* 3
De Jongh, H P K (WP) 1928 *NZ* 3
De Klerk, I J (Tvl) 1969 *E*, 1970 *I*, *W*
De Klerk, K B H (Tvl) 1974 *BI* 1,2,3 (R), 1975 *F* 1,2, 1976 *NZ* 2 (R), 3,4, 1980 *S Am* 1,2, *BI* 2, 1981 *I* 1,2
De Kock, A N (GW) 1891 *BI* 2
De Kock, J S (WP) 1921 *NZ* 3, 1924 *BI* 3
Delport, W H (EP) 1951 *S*, *I*, *W*, 1952 *E*, *F*, 1953 *A* 1,2,3,4
De Melker, S C (GW) 1903 *BI* 2, 1906 *E*
Devenish, C E (GW) 1896 *BI* 2
Devenish, G St L (Tvl) 1896 *BI* 2
Devenish, G E (Tvl) 1891 *BI* 1
De Villiers, D I (Tvl) 1910 *BI* 1,2,3
De Villiers, D J (WP, Bol) 1962 *BI* 2,3, 1965 *I*, *NZ* 1,3,4, 1967 *F* 1,2,3,4, 1968 *BI* 1,2,3,4, *F* 1,2, 1969 *A* 1,4, *E*, 1970 *I*, *W*, *NZ* 1,2,3,4
De Villiers, H A (WP) 1906 *S*, *W*, *E*

307

Johnson, G K (Tvl) 1993 *Arg* 2, 1994 *NZ* 3, *Arg* 1, 1995 *WS*, [*R, C, WS*]
Johnstone, P G A (WP) 1951 *S, I, W*, 1952 *E, F*, 1956 *A* 1, *NZ* 1,2,4
Jones, C H (Tvl) 1903 *BI* 1,2
Jones, P S T (WP) 1896 *BI* 1,3,4
Jordaan, R P (NT) 1949 *NZ* 1,2,3,4
Joubert, A J (OFS, N) 1989 *Wld* 1 (R), 1993 *A* 3, *Arg* 1, 1994 *E* 1,2, *NZ* 1,2 (R), 3, *Arg* 2, *S, W*, 1995 [*A, C, WS, F, NZ*], *W, It, E*, 1996 *Fj, A* 1, *NZ* 1,3,4,5, *Arg* 1,2, *F* 1,2, *W*, 1997 *Tg, BI* 1,2, *A* 2
Joubert, S J (WP) 1906 *I, W, E*

Kahts, W J H (NT) 1980 *BI* 1,2,3, *S Am* 3,4, *F*, 1981 *I* 1,2, *NZ* 1, 1982 *S Am* 1,2
Kaminer, J (Tvl) 1958 *F* 2
Kebble, G R (N) 1993 *Arg* 1,2, 1994 *NZ* 1 (R), 2
Kelly, E W (GW) 1896 *BI* 3
Kenyon, B J (Bor) 1949 *NZ* 4
Kipling, H G (GW) 1931 *W, I*, 1932 *E, S*, 1933 *A* 1,2,3,4,5
Kirkpatrick, A I (GW) 1953 *A* 2, 1956 *NZ* 2, 1958 *F* 1, 1960 *S, NZ* 1,2,3,4, *W, I*, 1961 *E, S, F*
Knight, A S (Tvl) 1912 *S, I, W*, 1913 *E, F*
Knoetze, F (WP) 1989 *Wld* 1,2
Koch, A C (Bol) 1949 *NZ* 2,3,4, 1951 *S, I, W*, 1952 *E, F*, 1953 *A* 1,2,4, 1955 *BI* 1,2,3,4, 1956 *A* 1, *NZ* 2,3, 1958 *F* 1,2, 1960 *NZ* 1,2
Koch, H V (WP) 1949 *NZ* 1,2,3,4
Kotze, G J M (WP) 1967 *F* 1,2,3,4
Krantz, E F W (OFS) 1976 *NZ* 1, 1981 *I* 1,
Krige, J D (WP) 1903 *BI* 1,3, 1906 *S, I, W*
Kritzinger, J L (Tvl) 1974 *BI* 3,4, *F* 1,2, 1975 *F* 1,2, 1976 *NZ* 4
Kroon, C M (EP) 1955 *BI* 1
Kruger, P E (Tvl) 1986 *Cv* 3,4
Kruger, R J (NT) 1993 *Arg* 1,2, 1994 *S, W*, 1995 *WS*, [*A, R, WS, F, NZ*], *W, It, E*, 1996 *Fj, A* 1, *NZ* 1, *A* 2, *NZ* 2,3,4,5, *Arg* 1,2, *F* 1,2, *W*, 1997 *Tg, BI* 1,2, *NZ* 1, *A* 1, *NZ* 2
Kruger, T L (Tvl) 1921 *NZ* 1,2, 1924 *BI* 1,2,3,4, 1928 *NZ* 1,2
Kuhn, S P (Tvl) 1960 *NZ* 3,4, *W, I*, 1961 *E, S, F, I, A* 1,2, 1962 *BI* 1,2,3,4, 1963 *A* 1,2,3, 1965 *I, S*

La Grange, J B (WP) 1924 *BI* 3,4
Larard, A (Tvl) 1896 *BI* 2,4
Lategan, M T (WP) 1949 *NZ* 1,2,3,4, 1951 *S, I, W*, 1952 *E, F*, 1953 *A* 1,2
Laubscher, T G (WP) 1994 *Arg* 1,2, *S, W*, 1995 *It, E*
Lawless, M J (WP) 1964 *F*, 1969 *E* (R), 1970 *I, W*
Ledger, S H (GW) 1912 *S, I*, 1913 *E, F*
Le Roux, A H (OFS) 1994 *E* 1
Le Roux, H P (Tvl) 1993 *F* 1,2, 1994 *E* 1,2, *NZ* 1,2,3, *Arg* 2, *S, W*, 1995 *WS* [*A, R, C* (R), *WS, F, NZ*], *W, It, E*, 1996 *Fj, NZ* 2, *Arg* 1,2, *F* 1,2
Le Roux, J H S (Tvl) 1994 *E* 2, *NZ* 1,2
Le Roux, M (OFS) 1980 *BI* 1,2,3,4, *S Am* 3,4, *F*, 1981 *I* 1
Le Roux, P A (WP) 1906 *I, W, E*
Little, E M (GW) 1891 *BI* 1,3
Lochner, G P (WP) 1955 *BI* 3, 1956 *A* 1,2, *NZ* 1,2,3,4, 1958 *F* 1,2
Lochner, G P (EP) 1937 *NZ* 3, 1938 *BI* 1,2
Lockyear, R J (GW) 1960 *NZ* 1,2,3,4, 1960 *I*, 1961 *F*
Lombard, A C (EP) 1910 *BI* 2
Lötter, D (Tvl) 1993 *F* 2, *A* 1,2
Lotz, J W (Tvl) 1937 *A* 1,2, *NZ* 1,2,3, 1938 *BI* 1,2,3
Loubser, J A (WP) 1903 *BI* 3, 1906 *S, I, W, E*, 1910 *BI* 1,3
Lourens, M J (NT) 1968 *BI* 2,3,4
Louw, J S (Tvl) 1891 *BI* 1,2,3
Louw, M J (Tvl) 1971 *A* 2,3
Louw, M M (WP) 1928 *NZ* 3,4, 1931 *W, I*, 1932 *E, S*, 1933 *A* 1,2,3,4,5, 1937 *A* 1,2, *NZ* 2,3, 1938 *BI* 1,2,3
Louw, R J (WP) 1980 *S Am* 1,2, *BI* 1,2,3,4 *S Am* 3,4, *F*, 1981 *I* 1,2, *NZ* 1,3, 1982 *S Am* 1,2, 1984 *E* 1,2, *S Am* 1,2
Louw, S C (WP) 1933 *A* 1,2,3,4,5, 1937 *A* 1, *NZ* 1,2,3, 1938 *BI* 1,2,3
Lubbe, E (GW) 1997 *Tg, BI* 1
Luyt, F P (WP) 1910 *BI* 1,2,3, 1912 *S, I, W*, 1913 *E*
Luyt, J D (EP) 1912 *S, W*, 1913 *E, F*
Luyt, R R (W P) 1910 *BI* 2,3, 1912 *S, I, W*, 1913 *E, F*
Lyons, D J (EP) 1896 *BI* 1
Lyster, P J (N) 1933 *A* 2,5, 1937 *NZ* 1

McCallum, I D (WP) 1970 *NZ* 1,2,3,4, 1971 *F* 1,2, *A* 1,2,3, 1974 *BI* 1,2
McCallum, R J (WP) 1974 *BI* 1
McCulloch, J D (GW) 1913 *E, F*
MacDonald, A W (R) 1965 *A* 1, *NZ* 1,2,3,4
Macdonald, A W (R) 1974 *BI* 2
Macdonald, I (Tvl) 1992 *NZ, A*, 1993 *F* 1, *A* 3, 1994 *E* 2, 1995 *WS* (R)
McDonald, J A J (WP) 1931 *W, I*, 1932 *E, S*
McEwan, W M C (Tvl) 1903 *BI* 1,3
McHardy, E E (OFS) 1912 *S, I, W*, 1913 *E, F*
McKendrick, J A (WP) 1891 *BI* 3
Malan, A S (Tvl) 1960 *NZ* 1,2,3,4, *W, I*, 1961 *E, S, F*, 1962 *BI* 1, 1963 *A* 1,2,3, 1964 *W*, 1965 *I, S*
Malan, A W (NT) 1989 *Wld* 1,2, 1992 *NZ, A, F* 1,2, *E*
Malan, E (NT) 1980 *BI* 3 (R), 4
Malan, G F (WP) 1958 *F* 2, 1960 *NZ* 1,3,4, 1961 *E, S, F*, 1962 *BI* 1,2,3, 1963 *A* 1,2,4, 1964 *W*, 1965 *A* 1,2, *NZ* 1,2
Malan, P (Tvl) 1949 *NZ* 4
Mallett, N V H (WP) 1984 *S Am* 1,2
Mans, W J (WP) 1965 *I, S*
Marais, F P (Bol) 1949 *NZ* 1,2, 1951 *S*, 1953 *A* 1,2
Marais, J F K (WP) 1963 *A* 3, 1964 *W, F*, 1965 *I, S, A* 2, 1968 *BI*, 1,2,3,4, *F* 1,2, 1969 *A* 1,2,3,4, *S, E*, 1970 *I, W, NZ* 1,2,3,4, 1971 *F* 1,2, *A* 1,2,3, 1974 *BI* 1,2,3,4, *F* 1,2
Maré, D S (Tvl) 1906 *S*
Marsberg, A F W (GW) 1906 *S, W, E*
Marsberg, P A (GW) 1910 *BI* 1
Martheze, W C (GW) 1903 *BI* 2, 1906 *I, W*
Martin, H J (Tvl) 1937 *A* 2
Mellet, T B (GW) 1896 *BI* 2
Mellish, F W (WP) 1921 *NZ* 1,3, 1924 *BI* 1,2,3,4
Merry, J (EP) 1891 *BI* 1
Metcalf, H D (Bor) 1903 *BI* 2
Meyer, C du P (WP) 1921 *NZ* 1,2,3
Meyer, P J (GW) 1896 *BI* 1
Meyer, W (OFS) 1997 *S* (R)
Michau, J M (Tvl) 1921 *NZ* 1
Michau, J P (WP) 1921 *NZ* 1,2,3
Millar, W A (WP) 1906 *E*, 1910 *BI* 2,3, 1912 *I, W*, 1913 *F*
Mills, W J (WP) 1910 *BI* 2
Moll, T (Tvl) 1910 *BI* 2
Montini, P E (WP) 1956 *A* 1,2
Montgomery, P C (WP) 1997 *BI* 2,3, *NZ* 1, *A* 1, *NZ* 2, *A* 2, *F* 1,2, *E, S*
Moolman, L C (NT) 1977 *Wld*, 1980 *S Am* 1,2, *BI* 1,2,3,4, *S Am* 3,4, *F*, 1981 *I* 1,2, *NZ* 1,2,3, *US*, 1982 *S Am* 1,2, 1984 *S Am* 1,2, 1986 *Cv* 1,2,3,4
Mordt, R H (Z-R, NT) 1980 *S Am* 1,2, *BI* 1,2,3,4, *S Am* 3,4, *F*, 1981 *I* 2, *NZ* 1,2,3, *US*, 1982 *S Am* 1,2, 1984 *S Am* 1,2
Morkel, D A (Tvl) 1903 *BI* 1
Morkel, D F T (Tvl) 1906 *I, E*, 1910 *BI* 1,3, 1912 *S, I, W*, 1913 *E, F*
Morkel, H J (WP) 1921 *NZ* 1
Morkel, H W (WP) 1921 *NZ* 1,2
Morkel, J A (WP) 1921 *NZ* 2,3
Morkel, J W H (WP) 1912 *S, I, W*, 1913 *E, F*
Morkel, P G (WP) 1912 *S, I, W*, 1913 *E, F*, 1921 *NZ* 1,2,3
Morkel, P K (WP) 1928 *NZ* 4
Morkel, W H (WP) 1910 *BI* 3, 1912 *S, I, W*, 1913 *E, F*, 1921 *NZ* 1,2,3
Morkel, W S (Tvl) 1906 *S, I, W, E*
Moss, C (N) 1949 *NZ* 1,2,3,4
Mostert, P J (WP) 1921 *NZ* 1,2,3, 1924 *BI* 1,2,4, 1928 *NZ* 1,2,3,4, 1931 *W, I*, 1932 *E, S*
Mulder, J C (Tvl, GL) 1994 *NZ* 2,3, *S, W*, 1995 *WS*, [*A, WS, F, NZ*], *W, It, E*, 1996 *Fj, A* 1, *NZ* 1, *A* 2, *NZ* 2,5, *Arg* 1,2, *F* 1,2, *W*, 1997 *Tg, BI* 1
Muller, G H (WP) 1969 *A* 3,4, *S*, 1970 *W, NZ* 1,2,3,4, 1971 *F* 1,2, 1972 *E*, 1974 *BI* 1,3,4
Muller, H L (OFS) 1986 *Cv* 4 (R), 1989 *Wld* 1 (R)
Muller, H S V (Tvl) 1949 *NZ* 1,2,3,4, 1951 *S, I, W*, 1952 *E, F*, 1953 *A* 1,2,3,4
Muller, L J J (N) 1992 *NZ, A*
Muller, P G (N) 1992 *NZ, A, F* 1,2, *E*, 1993 *F* 1,2, *A* 1,2,3, *Arg* 1,2, 1994 *E* 1,2, *NZ* 1, *S, W*
Muir, D J (WP) 1997 *It, F* 1,2, *E, S*
Myburgh, F R (EP) 1896 *BI* 1
Myburgh, J L (NT) 1962 *BI* 1, 1963 *A* 4, 1964 *W, F*, 1968 *BI* 1,2,3, *F* 1,2, 1969 *A* 1,2,3,4, *E*, 1970 *I, W, NZ* 3,4
Myburgh, W H (WT) 1924 *BI* 1

Naude, J P (WP) 1963 *A* 4, 1965 *A* 1,2, *NZ* 1,3,4, 1967 *F* 1,2,3,4, 1968 *BI* 1,2,3,4
Neethling, J B (WP) 1967 *F* 1,2,3,4, 1968 *BI* 4, 1969 *S*, 1970 *NZ* 1,2
Nel, J A (Tvl) 1960 *NZ* 1,2, 1963 *A* 1,2, 1965 *A* 2, *NZ* 1,2,3,4, 1970 *NZ* 3,4
Nel, J J (WP) 1956 *A* 1,2, *NZ* 1,2,3,4, 1958 *F* 1,2
Nel, P A R O (Tvl) 1903 *BI* 1,2,3
Nel, P J (N) 1928 *NZ* 1,2,3,4, 1931 *W, I,* 1932 *E, S,* 1933 *A* 1,3,4,5, 1937 *A* 1,2, *NZ* 2,3
Nimb, C F (WP) 1961 *I*
Nomis, S H (Tvl) 1967 *F* 4, 1968 *BI* 1,2,3,4, *F* 1,2, 1969 *A* 1,2,3,4, *S, E,* 1970 *I, W, NZ* 1,2,3,4, 1971 *F* 1,2, *A* 1,2,3, 1972 *E*
Nykamp, J L (Tvl) 1933 *A* 2

Ochse, J K (WP) 1951 *I, W,* 1952 *E, F,* 1953 *A* 1,2,4
Oelofse, J S A (Tvl) 1953 *A* 1,2,3,4
Oliver, J F (Tvl) 1928 *NZ* 3,4
Olivier, E (WP) 1967 *F* 1,2,3,4, 1968 *BI* 1,2,3,4, *F* 1,2, 1969 *A* 1,2,3,4, *S, E*
Olivier, J (NT) 1992 *F* 1,2, *E,* 1993 *F* 1,2 *A* 1,2,3, *Arg* 1, 1995 *W, It* (R), *E,* 1996 *Arg* 1,2, *F* 1,2, *W*
Olver, E (EP) 1896 *BI* 1
Oosthuizen, J J (WP) 1974 *BI* 1, *F* 1,2, 1975 *F* 1,2, 1976 *NZ* 1,2,3,4
Oosthuizen, O W (NT, Tvl) 1981 *I* 1 (R), 2, *NZ* 2,3, *US,* 1982 *S Am* 1,2, 1984 *E* 1,2
Osler, B L (WP) 1924 *BI* 1,2,3,4, 1928 *NZ* 1,2,3,4, 1931 *W, I,* 1932 *E, S,* 1933 *A* 1,2,3,4,5
Osler, S G (WP) 1928 *NZ* 1
Otto, K (NT, BB) 1995 [*R, C* (R), *WS* (R)], 1997 *BI* 3, *A* 1, *NZ* 2, *A* 2, *It, F* 1,2, *E, S*
Oxlee, K (N) 1960 *NZ* 1,2,3,4, *W, I,* 1961 *S, A* 1,2, 1962 *BI* 1,2,3,4, 1963 *A* 1,2,4, 1964 *W,* 1965 *NZ* 1,2

Pagel, G L (WP) 1995 [*A* (R), *R, C, NZ* (R)], 1996 *NZ* 5 (R)
Parker, W H (EP) 1965 *A* 1,2
Partridge, J E C (Tvl) 1903 *BI* 1
Payn, C (N) 1924 *BI* 1,2
Pelser, H J M (Tvl) 1958 *F* 1, 1960 *NZ* 1,2,3,4, *W, I,* 1961 *F, I, A* 1,2
Pfaff, B D (WP) 1956 *A* 1
Pickard, J A J (WP) 1953 *A* 3,4, 1956 *NZ* 2, 1958 *F* 2
Pienaar, J F (Tvl) 1993 *F* 1,2, *A* 1,2,3, *Arg* 1,2, 1994 *E* 1,2, *NZ* 2,3, *Arg* 1,2, *S, W,* 1995 *WS,* [*A, C, WS, F, NZ*], *W, It, E,* 1996 *Fj, A* 1, *NZ* 1, *A* 2, *NZ* 2
Pienaar, Z M J (OFS) 1980 *S Am* 2 (R), *BI* 1,2,3,4, *S Am* 3,4, *F,* 1981 *I* 1,2, *NZ* 1,2,3
Pitzer, G (NT) 1967 *F* 1,2,3,4, 1968 *BI* 1,2,3,4, *F* 1,2, 1969 *A* 3,4
Pope, C F (WP) 1974 *BI* 1,2,3,4, 1975 *F* 1,2, 1976 *NZ* 2,3,4
Potgieter, H J (OFS) 1928 *NZ* 1,2
Potgieter, H L (OFS) 1977 *Wld*
Powell, A W (GW) 1896 *BI* 3
Powell, J M (GW) 1891 *BI* 2, 1896 *BI* 3, 1903 *BI* 1,2
Prentis, R B (Tvl) 1980 *S Am* 1,2, *BI* 1,2,3,4, *S Am* 3,4, *F,* 1981 *I* 1,2
Pretorius, N F (Tvl) 1928 *NZ* 1,2,3,4
Prinsloo, J (Tvl) 1958 *F* 1,2
Prinsloo, J (NT) 1963 *A* 3
Prinsloo, J P (Tvl) 1928 *NZ* 1
Putter, D J (WT) 1963 *A* 1,2,4

Raaff, J W E (GW) 1903 *BI* 1,2, 1906 *S, W, E,* 1910 *BI* 1
Ras, W J de Wet (OFS) 1976 *NZ* 1 (R), 1980 *S Am* 2 (R)
Reece-Edwards, H (N) 1992 *F* 1,2, 1993 *A* 2
Reid, A (WP) 1903 *BI* 3
Reid, B C (Bor) 1933 *A* 4
Reinach, J (OFS) 1986 *Cv* 1,2,3,4
Rens, I J (Tvl) 1953 *A* 3,4
Retief, D F (NT) 1955 *BI* 1,2,4, 1956 *A* 1,2, *NZ* 1,2,3,4
Reyneke, H J (WP) 1910 *BI* 3
Richards, A R (WP) 1891 *BI* 1,2,3
Richter, A (NT) 1992 *F* 1,2, *E,* 1994 *E* 2, *NZ* 1,2,3, 1995 [*R, C, WS* (R)]
Riley, N M (ET) 1963 *A* 3
Riordan, C A (Tvl) 1910 *BI* 1,2
Robertson, I W (R) 1974 *F* 1,2, 1976 *NZ* 1,2,4
Rodgers, P H (NT, Tvl) 1989 *Wld* 1,2, 1992 *NZ, F* 1,2
Rogers, C D (Tvl) 1984 *E* 1,2, *S Am* 1,2
Roos, G D (WP) 1910 *BI* 2,3

Roos, P J (WP) 1903 *BI* 3, 1906 *I, W, E*
Rosenberg, W (Tvl) 1955 *BI* 2,3,4, 1956 *NZ* 3, 1958 *F* 1
Rossouw, C L C (Tvl) 1995 *WS,* [*R, WS, F, NZ*]
Rossouw, D H (WP) 1953 *A* 3, 4
Rossouw, P W G (WP) 1997 *BI* 2,3, *NZ* 1, *A* 1, *NZ* 2 (R), *A* 2 (R), *It, F* 1,2, *E, S*
Rousseau, W P (WP) 1928 *NZ* 3,4
Roux, F du T (WP) 1960 *W,* 1961 *A* 1,2, 1962 *BI* 1,2,3,4, 1963 *A* 2, 1965 *A* 1,2, *NZ* 1,2,3,4, 1968 *BI* 3,4, *F* 1,2 1969 *A* 1,2,3,4, 1970 *I, NZ* 1,2,3,4
Roux, J P (Tvl) 1994 *E* 2, *NZ* 1,2,3, *Arg* 1, 1995 [*R, C, F* (R)], 1996 *A* 1 (R), *NZ* 1, *A* 2, *NZ* 3
Roux, O A (NT) 1969 *S, E,* 1970 *I, W,* 1972 *E,* 1974 *BI* 3,4

Samuels, T A (GW) 1896 *BI* 2,3,4
Sauermann, J T (Tvl) 1971 *F* 1,2, *A* 1, 1972 *E,* 1974 *BI* 1
Schlebusch, J J J (OFS) 1974 *BI* 3,4, 1975 *F* 2
Schmidt, L U (NT) 1958 *F* 2, 1962 *BI* 2
Schmidt, U L (NT, Tvl) 1986 *Cv* 1,2,3,4, 1989 *Wld* 1,2, 1992 *NZ, A,* 1993 *F* 1,2, *A* 1,2,3, 1994 *Arg* 1,2, *S, W*
Schoeman, J (WP) 1963 *A* 3,4, 1965 *I, S, A* 1, *NZ* 1,2
Scholtz, C P (WP, Tvl) 1994 *Arg* 1, 1995 [*R, C, WS*]
Scholtz, H H (WP) 1921 *NZ* 1,2
Schutte, P J W (Tvl) 1994 *S, W*
Scott, P A (Tvl) 1896 *BI* 1,2,3,4
Sendin, W D (GW) 1921 *NZ* 2
Serfontein, D J (WP) 1980 *BI* 1,2,3,4, *S Am* 3,4, *F,* 1981 *I* 1,2, *NZ* 1,2,3, *US,* 1982 *S Am* 1,2, 1984 *E* 1,2, *S Am* 1,2
Shand, R (GW) 1891 *BI* 2,3
Sheriff, A R (Tvl) 1938 *BI* 1,2,3
Shum, E H (Tvl) 1913 *E*
Sinclair, D J (Tvl) 1955 *BI* 1,2,3,4
Sinclair, J H (Tvl) 1903 *BI* 1
Skene, A L (WP) 1958 *F* 2
Skinstad, R B (WP) 1997 *E* (t)
Slater, J T (EP) 1924 *BI* 3,4, 1928 *NZ* 1
Smal, G P (WP) 1986 *Cv* 1,2,3,4, 1989 *Wld* 1,2
Small, J T (Tvl, N, WP) 1992 *NZ, A, F* 1,2, *E,* 1993 *F* 1,2, *A* 1,2,3, *Arg* 1,2, 1994 *E* 1,2, *NZ* 1,2,3 (t), *Arg* 1, 1995 *WS,* [*A, R, F, NZ*], *W, It, E* (R), 1996 *Fj, A* 1, *NZ* 1, *A* 2, *NZ* 2, *Arg* 1,2, *F* 1,2, *W,* 1997 *Tg, BI* 1, *NZ* 1 (R), *A* 1 (R), *NZ* 2, *A* 2, *It, F* 1,2, *E, S*
Smit, F C (WP) 1992 *E*
Smith, C M (OFS) 1963 *A* 3,4, 1964 *W, F,* 1965 *A* 1,2, *NZ* 2
Smith, C W (GW) 1891 *BI* 2, 1896 *BI* 2,3
Smith, D (GW) 1891 *BI* 2
Smith D J (Z-R) 1980 *BI* 1,2,3,4
Smith, G A C (EP) 1938 *BI* 3
Smith, P F (GW) 1997 *S* (R)
Smollan, F C (Tvl) 1933 *A* 3,4,5
Snedden, R C D (GW) 1891 *BI* 2
Snyman, A H (NT, BB) 1996 *NZ* 3,4, *Arg* 2 (R), *W* (R), 1997 *Tg, BI* 1,2,3, *NZ* 1, *A* 1, *NZ* 2, *It, F* 1,2, *E, S*
Snyman, D S L (WP) 1972 *E,* 1974 *BI* 1,2, *F* 1,2, 1975 *F* 1,2, 1976 *NZ* 2,3, 1977 *Wld*
Snyman, J C P (OFS) 1974 *BI* 2,3,4
Sonnekus, G H H (OFS) 1974 *BI* 3, 1984 *E* 1,2
Spies, J J (NT) 1970 *NZ* 1,2,3,4
Stander, J C J (OFS) 1974 *BI* 4 (R), 1976 *NZ* 1,2,3,4
Stapelberg, W P (NT) 1974 *F* 1,2
Starke, J J (WP) 1956 *NZ* 4
Starke, K T (WP) 1924 *BI* 1,2,3,4
Steenekamp, J G A (Tvl) 1958 *F* 1
Stegmann, A C (WP) 1906 *S, I*
Stegmann, J A (Tvl) 1912 *S, I, W,* 1913 *E, F*
Stewart, D A (WP) 1960 *S,* 1961 *E, S, F, I,* 1963 *A* 1,3,4, 1964 *W, F,* 1965 *I*
Stofberg, M T S (OFS, NT, WP) 1976 *NZ* 2,3, 1977 *Wld,* 1980 *S Am* 1,2, *BI* 1,2,3,4, *S Am* 3,4, *F,* 1981 *I* 1,2, *NZ* 1,2, *US,* 1982 *S Am* 1,2, 1984 *E* 1,2
Strachan, L C (Tvl) 1932 *E, S,* 1937 *A* 1,2, *NZ* 1,2,3, 1938 *BI* 1,2,3
Stransky, J (N, WP) 1993 *A* 1,2,3, *Arg* 1, 1994 *Arg* 1,2, 1995 *WS,* [*A, R* (t), *C, F, NZ*], *W, It, E,* 1996 *Fj* (R), *NZ* 1, *A* 2, *NZ* 2,3,4,5 (R)
Straeuli, R A W (Tvl) 1994 *NZ* 1, *Arg* 1,2, *S, W,* 1995 *WS,* [*A, WS, NZ* (R)], *E* (R)
Strauss, C P (WP) 1992 *F* 1,2, *E,* 1993 *F* 1,2, *A* 1,2,3, *Arg* 1,2, 1994 *E* 1, *NZ* 1,2, *Arg* 1,2
Strauss, J A (WP) 1984 *S Am* 1,2
Strauss, J H P (Tvl) 1976 *NZ* 3,4, 1980 *S Am* 1

Record-breakers come face to face as South Africa's most capped player, winger James Small, attempts to evade the clutches of Wales' Ieuan Evans.

SOUTH AFRICAN INTERNATIONAL RECORDS (*up to 30 April 1998*)

MATCH RECORDS

MOST CONSECUTIVE TEST WINS

15 1994 *Arg* 1,2, *S, W* 1995 *WS, A, R, C, WS, F, NZ, W, It,* E 1996 *Fj*
10 1949 *NZ* 1,2,3,4, 1951 *S, I, W,* 1952 *E, F,* 1953 *A* 1

MOST CONSECUTIVE TESTS WITHOUT DEFEAT

P	W	D	Period
16	15	1	1994–96
15	12	3	1960–63
11	9	2	1967–69

MOST POINTS IN A MATCH
by the team

Pts	Opp	Venue	Year
74	Tg	Cape Town	1997
68	S	Murrayfield	1997
62	It	Bologna	1997
61	A	Pretoria	1997
60	WS	Johannesburg	1995

by a player

28 by G K Johnson v Western Samoa at Johannesburg — 1995
26 by J H de Beer v Australia at Pretoria — 1997
26 by P C Montgomery v Scotland at Murrayfield — 1997
25 by J T Stransky v Australia at Bloemfontein — 1996

MOST TRIES IN A MATCH
by the team

T	Opp	Venue	Year
12	Tg	Cape Town	1997
10	I	Dublin	1912
10	S	Murrayfield	1997

by a player

4 by C M Williams v Western Samoa at Johannesburg — 1995
4 by P W G Rossouw v France at Parc des Princes — 1997
3 by E E McHardy v Ireland at Dublin — 1912
3 by J A Stegmann v Ireland at Dublin — 1912
3 by K T van Vollenhoven v British Isles at Cape Town — 1955

3 by H J van Zyl v Australia at Johannesburg — 1961
3 by R H Mordt v New Zealand at Auckland — 1981
3 by R H Mordt v United States at New York — 1981
3 by D M Gerber v South America at Pretoria — 1982
3 by D M Gerber v England at Johannesburg — 1984
3 by G K Johnson v Western Samoa at Johannesburg — 1995
3 by J H van der Westhuizen v Wales at Cardiff — 1996
3 by A H Snyman v Tonga at Cape Town — 1997

MOST CONVERSIONS IN A MATCH
by the team

C	Opp	Venue	Year
9	S	Murrayfield	1997
7	S	Murrayfield	1951
7	Tg	Cape Town	1997
7	It	Bologna	1997
7	F	Parc des Princes	1997

by a player

8 by P C Montgomery v Scotland at Murrayfield — 1997
7 by A Geffin v Scotland at Murrayfield — 1951
7 by E Lubbe v Tonga at Cape Town — 1997
7 by H W Honiball v Italy at Bologna — 1997
7 by H W Honiball v France at Parc des Princes — 1997

MOST PENALTY GOALS IN A MATCH
by the team

P	Opp	Venue	Year
7	F	Pretoria	1975
6	A	Bloemfontein	1996
5	several instances		

by a player

6 by G R Bosch v France at Pretoria — 1975
6 by J T Stransky v Australia at Bloemfontein — 1996
5 by A Geffin v New Zealand at Cape Town — 1949

5 by R Blair v World XV at
Pretoria — 1977
5 by H E Botha v New Zealand at
Wellington — 1981
5 by J W Heunis v England at Port
Elizabeth — 1984
5 by H E Botha v New Zealand
Cavaliers at Johannesburg — 1986
5 by J T J van Rensburg v France
at Durban — 1993
5 by A J Joubert v England at
Pretoria — 1994

MOST DROPPED GOALS IN A MATCH
by the team

D	Opp	Venue	Year
3	SAm	Durban	1980
3	I	Durban	1981

by a player

3 by H E Botha v South America at
Durban — 1980
3 by H E Botha v Ireland at
Durban — 1981
2 by B L Osler v New Zealand at
Durban — 1928
2 by H E Botha v New Zealand
Cavaliers at Cape Town — 1986
2 by J T Stransky v New Zealand
at Johannesburg — 1995

CAREER RECORDS

MOST CAPPED PLAYERS

Caps	Player	Career
47	J T Small	1992–97
41	M G Andrews	1994–97
38	F C H du Preez	1961–71
38	J H Ellis	1965–76
38	J H van der Westhuizen	1993–97
35	J F K Marais	1963–74
34	A J Joubert	1989–97
33	J P Engelbrecht	1960–69
33	J L Gainsford	1960–67
32	R J Kruger	1993–97

MOST CONSECUTIVE TESTS

Tests	Player	Span
26	G H Teichmann	1996–97
25	S H Nomis	1967–72
23	J L Gainsford	1961–67
23	J F K Marais	1968–71
22	L G Wilson	1961–65
22	R J Kruger	1995–97

MOST TESTS AS CAPTAIN

Tests	Captain	Span
29	J F Pienaar	1993–96
22	D J de Villiers	1965–70
21	G H Teichmann	1996–97
15	M du Plessis	1975–80
11	J F K Marais	1971–74

MOST TESTS IN INDIVIDUAL POSITIONS

Full-back A J Joubert		34	1989–97
Wing J T Small		43★	1992–97
Centre J L Gainsford		33	1960–67
Fly-half H E Botha		28	1980–92
Scrum-half J H van der Westhuizen		36	1993–97
Prop J F K Marais		35	1963–74
Hooker J Dalton		22	1994–97
Lock M G Andrews		38	1994–97
Flanker J H Ellis		38	1965–76
No 8 G H Teichmann		27	1995–97

★ *excludes an appearance as a temporary replacement*

MOST POINTS IN TESTS

Pts	Player	Tests	Career
312	H E Botha	28	1980–92
240	J T Stransky	22	1993–96
143	H W Honiball	23	1993–97
130	P J Visagie	25	1967–71
117	A J Joubert	34	1989–97

MOST TRIES IN TESTS

Tries	Player	Tests	Career
20	J T Small	47	1992–97
19	D M Gerber	24	1980–92
17	J H van der Westhuizen	38	1993–97
13	C M Williams	16	1993–95
12	J S Germishuys	20	1974–81
12	R H Mordt	18	1980–84

MOST CONVERSIONS IN TESTS

Cons	Player	Tests	Career
50	H E Botha	28	1980–92
36	H W Honiball	23	1993–97
30	J T Stransky	22	1993–96
20	P J Visagie	25	1967–71
15	J H de Beer	7	1997
14	K Oxlee	19	1960–65
14	G K Johnson	7	1993–95

MOST PENALTY GOALS IN TESTS

Pens	Player	Tests	Career
50	H E Botha	28	1980–92
47	J T Stransky	22	1993–96
23	G R Bosch	9	1974–76
22	H W Honiball	23	1993–97
19	P J Visagie	25	1967–71
17	A J Joubert	34	1989–97

MOST DROPPED GOALS IN TESTS

Drops	Player	Tests	Career
18	H E Botha	28	1980–92
5	J D Brewis	10	1949–53
5	P J Visagie	25	1967–71
4	B L Osler	17	1924–33

TRI-NATIONS RECORDS

Record	Detail	Holder	Set
Most points in matches	64	J H de Beer	1997
Most points in season	64	J H de Beer	1997
Most points in match	26	J H de Beer	v Australia (h) 1997
Most tries in matches	3	P C Montgomery	1997
Most tries in season	3	P C Montgomery	1997
Most tries in match	2	P C Montgomery	v Australia (h) 1997
Most cons in matches	12	J H de Beer	1997
Most cons in season	12	J H de Beer	1997
Most cons in match	6	J H de Beer	v Australia (h)1997
Most pens in matches	10	J T Stransky	1996
Most pens in season	10	J T Stransky	1996
Most pens in match	6	J T Stransky	v Australia (h) 1996

SERIES RECORDS

Record	Holder	Detail
Most tries	P W G Rossouw	8 in Europe 1997
Most points	H E Botha	69 v Cavaliers, 1986

MAJOR TOUR RECORDS

Record	Detail	Year	Place
Most team points	753	1937	A & NZ
Most team tries	161	1937	A & NZ
Most individual points	190 by G H Brand	1937	A & NZ
Most individual tries	22 by J A Loubser	1906–07	Europe
Most points in match	38 by A J Joubert	1994 v Swansea	Swansea
Most tries in match	6 by R G Dryburgh	1956 v Queensland	Brisbane

MISCELLANEOUS RECORDS

Record	Holder	Detail
Longest Test career	J M Powell/B H Heatlie/ D M Gerber/ H E Botha	13 seasons, 1891–1903/ 1891–1903/1980–1992/ 1980–1992
Youngest Test cap	A J Hartley	17 yrs 18 days in 1891
Oldest Test cap	W H Morkel	36 yrs 258 days in 1921

SOUTH AFRICAN INTERNATIONAL CAREER RECORDS *(up to 30 April 1998)*

Player	Debut	Caps since last season	Caps	T	C	PG	DG	Pts
A J Joubert	1989 v Wld	1997 *Tg, BI* 1,2, *A* 2	34	10	8	17	0	117
G K Johnson	1993 v Arg		7	5	14	11	0	86
R G Bennett	1997 v Tg	1997 *Tg*(R), *BI* 1(R),3, *NZ* 1, *A* 1, *NZ* 2	6	2	0	0	0	10
J Olivier	1992 v F		17	3	0	0	0	15
J T Small	1992 v NZ	1997 *Tg, BI* 1, *NZ* 1(R), *A* 1(R), *NZ* 2, *A* 2, *It, F* 1,2, *E, S*	47	20	0	0	0	100
C M Williams	1993 v Arg		16	13	0	0	0	65
P Hendriks	1992 v NZ		14	2	0	0	0	10
P W G Rossouw	1997 v BI	1997 *BI* 2,3, *NZ* 1, *A* 1, *NZ* 2(R), *A* 2(R), *It, F* 1,2, *E, S*	11	11	0	0	0	55
J Swart	1996 v Fj	1997 *BI* 3(R), *It, S*(R)	10	1	0	0	0	5
D van Schalkwyk	1996 v Fj	1997 *BI* 2,3, *NZ* 1, *A* 1	8	2	0	0	0	10
A H Snyman	1996 v NZ	1997 *Tg, BI* 1,2,3, *NZ* 1, *A* 1, *NZ* 2, *A* 2, *It, F* 1,2, *E, S*	17	7	0	0	0	35
D J Muir	1997 v It	1997 *It, F* 1,2, *E, S*	5	2	0	0	0	10
H P le Roux	1993 v F		27	4	1	4	0	34
E Lubbe	1997 v Tg	1997 *Tg, BI* 1	2	0	7	1	0	17
P C Montgomery	1997 v BI	1997 *BI* 2,3, *NZ* 1, *A* 1, *NZ* 2, *A* 2, *F* 1,2, *E, S*	10	8	9	0	0	58
B Venter	1994 v E		14	1	0	0	0	5
J C Mulder	1994 v NZ	1997 *Tg, BI* 1	25	6	0	0	0	30
H W Honiball	1993 v A	1997 *Tg, BI* 1,2,3(R), *NZ* 1(R), *A* 1(R), *NZ* 2, *A* 2, *It, F* 1,2, *E*	23	1	36	22	0	143
N V Cilliers	1996 v NZ		1	0	0	0	0	0
P F Smith	1997 v S	1997 *S*(R)	1	1	0	0	0	5
J T Stransky	1993 v A		22	6	30	47	3	240
J H de Beer	1997 v BI	1997 *BI* 3, *NZ* 1, *A* 1, *NZ* 2, *A* 2, *F* 2(R), *S*	7	2	15	11	2	79
J P Roux	1994 v E		12	2	0	0	0	10
J H van der Westhuizen	1993 v Arg	1997 *Tg, BI* 1,2,3, *NZ* 1, *A* 1, *NZ* 2, *A* 2, *It, F* 1	38	17	0	0	0	85
W Swanepoel	1997 v BI	1997 *BI* 3(R), *A* 2(R), *F* 1(R),2, *E, S*	6	1	0	0	0	5
A E Drotské	1993 v Arg	1997 *Tg, BI* 1,2,3(R), *NZ* 1, *A* 1, *NZ* 2(R)	10	2	0	0	0	10
J Dalton	1994 v Arg	1997 *Tg*(R), *BI* 3, *NZ* 2, *A* 2, *It, F* 1,2, *E, S*	22	3	0	0	0	15

Name	Debut	1997						
H Tromp	1996 v NZ		4	0	0	0	0	0
G L Pagel	1995 v A		5	0	0	0	0	0
J P du Randt	1994 v Arg	1997 *Tg, BI* 1,2,3, *NZ* 1, *A* 1, *NZ* 2, *A* 2, *It, F* 1,2, *E, S*	29	4	0	0	0	20
W Meyer	1997 v S	1997 *S*(R)	1	0	0	0	0	0
A van der Linde	1995 v It		6	0	0	0	0	0
A C Garvey	1996 v Arg	1997 *Tg, BI* 1,2,3(R), *A* 1(t), *It, F* 1,2, *E, S*	15	3	0	0	0	15
M H Hurter	1995 v R	1997 *NZ* 1,2, *A* 2	13	0	0	0	0	0
I S Swart	1993 v A		16	0	0	0	0	0
D F Theron	1996 v A	1997 *BI* 2(R),3, *NZ* 1(R), *A* 1, *NZ* 2(R)	13	0	0	0	0	0
J Ackermann	1996 v Fj		4	0	0	0	0	0
K Otto	1995 v R	1997 *BI* 3, *A* 1, *NZ* 2, *A* 2, *It, F* 1,2, *E, S*	12	0	0	0	0	0
M G Andrews	1994 v E	1997 *Tg*(R), *BI* 1,2, *NZ* 1, *A* 1, *NZ* 2, *A* 2, *It, F* 1,2, *E, S*	41	8	0	0	0	40
J J Wiese	1993 v F		18	1	0	0	0	5
F J van Heerden	1994 v E	1997 *Tg, BI* 2(t&R),3(R) *NZ* 1(R),2(R)	13	1	0	0	0	5
J J Strydom	1993 v F	1997 *Tg, BI* 1,2,3, *A* 2	21	1	0	0	0	5
W W Els	1997 v A	1997 *A* 2(R)	1	0	0	0	0	0
S Atherton	1993 v Arg		8	0	0	0	0	0
J F Pienaar	1993 v F		29	3	0	0	0	15
R J Kruger	1993 v Arg	1997 *Tg, BI* 1,2, *NZ* 1, *A* 1, *NZ* 2	32	7	0	0	0	35
W Brosnihan	1997 v A	1997 *A* 2	1	1	0	0	0	5
J C Erasmus	1997 v BI	1997 *BI* 3, *A* 2, *It, F* 1,2, *S*	6	4	0	0	0	20
R B Skinstad	1997 v E	1997 *E* (t)	1	0	0	0	0	0
W Fyvie	1996 v NZ		3	0	0	0	0	0
S Bekker	1997 v A	1997 *A* 2(t)	1	0	0	0	0	0
A G Venter	1996 v NZ	1997 *Tg, BI* 1,2,3, *NZ* 1, *A* 1, *NZ* 2, *It, F* 1,2, *E, S*	20	3	0	0	0	15
A D Aitken	1997 v F	1997 *F* 2(R), *E*	2	0	0	0	0	0
G H Teichmann	1995 v W	1997 *Tg, BI* 1,2,3, *NZ* 1, *A* 1, *NZ* 2, *A* 2, *It, F* 1,2, *E, S*	27	4	0	0	0	20

A TEASING END TO A THRILLING YEAR

THE 1997 SEASON IN NEW ZEALAND

Donald Cameron *New Zealand Herald*

The beginning of the end, or the end of the beginning. As they approached their Christmas holidays New Zealand rugby folk would have dearly liked to know the answer.

Had they seen an All Black team reaching yet another peak in going through the 12 Tests of 1997 unbeaten, or had the tingling draw with England in the last international of the long hard year been the signal that the All Blacks' unchallenged time at the top was running out?

Were several of the All Blacks, especially among the tight forwards, past their use-by date? Was the published comment of a leading All Black back that playing for the All Blacks was not fun any more the sign that the fabric of the great side of recent years was wearing thin?

Was John Hart leaning on his players too heavily? Players talked after the November-December tour of being 'meeting-ed out', suggesting that Hart was becoming too autocratic.

And how, after Hart had claimed that no-one, not even Jonah Lomu, would tour if they were not fit, was Sean Fitzpatrick retained in the side when he was plainly below peak condition? Were Zinzan Brooke and Fitzpatrick Hart's security blankets?

None of these niggling worries was being offered as an excuse for not completing their season with a win at Twickenham over England. In fact, the signs that England was moving into the high-speed game polished up by South Africa, New Zealand and Australia (and sometimes resurrected by France) were warmly greeted by those New Zealanders who saw the danger of such imbalance between northern and southern hemispheres. But that nerve-wracking finish at Twickenham did confirm some doubts that were being raised about the life span of some of the All Blacks.

Zinzan Brooke had resigned, and it was a measure of Hart's determination that he chose to retain him rather than mould a new player as close as possible to the Brooke style. Fitzpatrick's various injuries suggest that his body is sending out retirement messages. Olo Brown, Robin Brooke, Craig Dowd, Ian Jones and Michael Jones are not far from the last round-up. Frank Bunce may have another season, as may Walter Little. The supply and/or encouragement of quick-witted backs is not deep, although there are any number of bang-and-bash people who can, as they say, 'take the ball up'.

These may be the signs of the beginning of the end of the new All Black era.

The other viewpoint is that the New Zealand Rugby Football Union, after some expensive tinkering, has arrived at a suitable system of contracts for the international, Super-12 and national championship players. The first contracts were thrown together to stifle the appeal, however flimsy, of World Championship Rugby. In a new field the NZRFU overspent, and lost $6 million in 1996. Now the contracts are more sensibly arranged. The flow of unsecured and quality New Zealand players to Japan and the Continent has been slowed down. With a new contract system, and with money pouring in from international, Super-12 and provincial championship matches that are creating extraordinarily high interest, the NZRFU last year gathered in that deficit, and returned a $1 million profit.

But there is still the worry that the top-heavy financial success will further erode the wealth and strength of the clubs. The Auckland Rugby Union made a $1m profit last year for the first time. At least $600,000 will be diverted to support of the ARU clubs. Not all the other unions are so lucky – even Canterbury which has taken over Auckland's championship-winning mantle, and Waikato which removed the Ranfurly Shield from Auckland in what became the last challenge of the year.

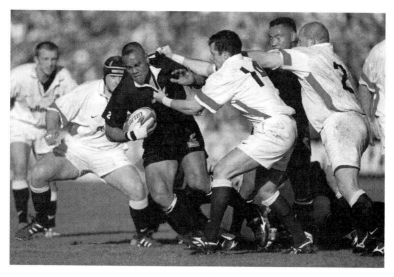

New Zealand wing Jonah Lomu is tackled by Tom Beim (England) during New Zealand's 40-10 2nd Test victory over England at Eden Park, 27 June 1998.

The Auckland Blues – mostly Auckland players with a smattering of help from Counties-Manukau – retained their Super-12 title. In their own right Auckland, who had won the national First Division title for the three preceding years, made unusually erratic progress. They lost their first game, to the newly promoted Taranaki side. They lost two other round-robin matches: the second of these and the Ranfurly Shield to Waikato.

Auckland were twice beaten by Canterbury, the new and vibrant power in the land, who have taken over Auckland's old expansive mantle. Auckland self-destructed against Canterbury in the championship semi-final, and sadly Canterbury's last points came from penalties awarded against curmudgeonly play by Zinzan Brooke and Fitzpatrick.

Canterbury have now closed the gap to Auckland, and perhaps England and South Africa and the rest are about to do the same to the All Blacks.

NATIONAL CHAMPIONSHIP

Division 1	P	W	D	L	F	A	Pts
Waikato	8	7	0	1	233	132	32
Canterbury	8	6	0	2	259	137	29
Auckland	8	5	0	3	217	198	27
Counties-Manukau	8	6	0	2	225	161	26
Otago	8	4	0	4	211	193	21
Wellington	8	3	0	5	207	287	18
Taranaki	8	2	0	6	216	260	12
North Harbour	8	2	0	6	116	179	10
Southland	8	1	0	7	171	308	9

Semi-finals: Counties-Manukau 43, Waikato 40; Canterbury 21, Auckland 15
Final: Canterbury 44, Counties-Manukau 13

Division 2	P	W	D	L	F	A	Pts
Northland	8	8	0	0	567	101	40
Bay of Plenty	8	6	0	2	311	122	30
Central Vikings	8	6	0	2	450	154	30
King Country	8	5	0	3	216	224	26
Nelson Bays	8	5	0	3	191	321	22
Wairarapa Bush	8	3	0	5	172	343	14
Wanganui	8	1	1	6	134	279	8
Thames Valley	8	1	0	7	102	371	5
South Canterbury	8	0	1	7	96	324	3

Semi-finals: Central Vikings 29, Bay of Plenty 6; Northland 51, King Country 12
Final: Northland 63, Central Vikings 10

Division 3	P	W	D	L	F	A	Pts
North Otago	7	6	0	1	236	152	28
Poverty Bay	7	5	0	2	224	146	27
Marlborough	7	5	0	2	271	188	26
Horowhenua	7	3	1	3	199	164	19
Mid-Canterbury	7	4	0	3	160	144	17
East Coast	7	2	1	4	157	189	12
Buller	7	1	0	6	118	238	6
West Coast	7	1	0	6	114	258	4

Semi-finals: North Otago 37, Horowhenua-Kapiti 7; Marlborough 17, Poverty Bay 14
Final: Marlborough 32, North Otago 17

RANFURLY SHIELD:
Auckland 115, East Coast 6; Auckland 47, Northland 14; Auckland 34, Southland 32; Auckland 27, Counties-Manukau 12; Auckland 93, West Coast 20; Waikato 31, Auckland 29

FIJI TO NEW ZEALAND 1997

THE TOURING PARTY

Manager S Vuetaki   **Assistant Manager** M Kurisaru   **Coach** BR Johnstone
Captain G Smith

Full-backs: F Rayasi (Kintetsu, Japan)

Threequarters: FT Lasagavibau (Nadroga), M Bari (Otago, NZ), A Uluinayau (Suntory, Japan), S Sorovaki (Kentetsu, Japan), N Little (Waikato, NZ), L Little (North Harbour & Rugby, England), S Nasilasila (Nadroga), A Tuilevu (Waikato, NZ), *L Duvuduvukula (Suva)

Half-backs: J Waqa (Queensland, Australia), W Serevi (Nasinu, Japan), M Rauluni (Queensland, Australia), J Rauluni (Queensland, Australia)

Forwards: D Rouse (Canterbury, NZ), J Veitayaki (King Country, NZ), G Smith (Waikato, NZ), E Natuivau (Queensland, Australia), E Katalau (Dunvant, Wales), S Raiwalui (Queensland, Australia), A Naevo (Counties, NZ), E Tuvunivono (NSW, Aus), A Natuiyaga (Nadroga), I Tawake (Nadroga), *VB Cavubati (Wellington, NZ), M Taga (Suva), E Batimala (Nadroga), M Korovou (Nadi), A Mocelutu (Japan), *S Niqara (Nadroga)

* *Replacement on tour*

TOUR RECORD

All matches   Played 6   Won 3   Lost 3   Points for 151   Against 178
International match   Played 1   Lost 1   Points for 5   Against 71

SCORING DETAILS

All matches					International match			
For:	22T	13C	5PG	151 Pts	For:	1T		5 Pts
Against:	25T	13C	9PG	178 Pts	Against:	11T	8C	71 Pts

MATCH DETAILS

1997	OPPONENTS	VENUE	RESULT
27 May	South Island Invitation XV	Westport	L 24-31
30 May	Mid & South Canterbury	Timaru	W 55-24
2 June	Central Vikings	Palmerston North	W 19-10
6 June	Wanganui	Wanganui	W 28-19
10 June	Counties	Pukekohe	L 20-23
14 June	NEW ZEALAND	Albany	L 5-71

MATCH 1   **27 May, Victoria Square, Westport**

South Island Invitation XV 31 (2G 4PG 1T)   **Fijians 24** (2G 2T)
South Island Invitation XV: Scorers *Tries:* Mayerhofler, Flynn, Barrell
Conversions: Lilley (2) *Penalty Goals:* Lilley (4)
Fijians: Scorers *Tries:* Lasagavibau (4) *Conversions:* N Little (2)

MATCH 2   30 May, Alpine Energy Stadium, Timaru

Mid & South Canterbury 24 (2G 2T)   **Fijians 55** (5G 4T)
Mid & South Canterbury: Scorers *Tries:* Mawhinney, McCrea, Doig, penalty try *Conversions:* Butterick (2)
Fijians: Scorers *Tries:* Waqa (3), Duvuduvukula (2), Tuilevu, Nasilasila, Tawake, Naevo *Conversions:* Waqa (4), Tawake

MATCH 3   2 June, Showgrounds Oval, Palmerton North

Central Vikings 10 (2T)   **Fijians 19** (2G 1T)
Central Vikings: Scorers *Tries:* Waldegrave, Watts
Fijians: Scorers *Tries:* Bari, L Little, Waqa *Conversions:* Waqa (2)

MATCH 4   6 June, Cook's Gardens, Wanganui

Wanganui 19 (1G 4PG)   **Fijians 28** (2G 3PG 1T)
Wanganui: Scorers *Try:* Hamlin *Conversion:* Nahona *Penalty Goals:* Nahona (4)
Fijians: Scorers *Tries:* Natuiyaga, Lasagavibau, Mocelutu
Conversions: N Little (2) *Penalty Goals:* N Little (3)

MATCH 5   10 June, Pukekohe Stadium

Counties 23 (1PG 4T)   **Fijians 20** (2G 2PG)
Counties: Scorers *Tries:* D Mika (2), Qio, Filipo *Penalty Goal:* Jack
Fijians: Scorers *Tries:* J Rauluni, Bari *Conversions:* N Little (2)
Penalty Goals: N Little (2)

MATCH 6   14 June, North Harbour Stadium, Albany   Test Match

NEW ZEALAND 71 (8G 3T)   FIJI 5 (1T)

NEW ZEALAND: CM Cullen (Manawatu); JW Wilson (Otago), FE Bunce (North Harbour), L Stensness (Auckland), TJF Umaga (Wellington); AP Mehrtens (Canterbury), JW Marshall (Canterbury); CW Dowd (Auckland), SBT Fitzpatrick (Auckland)(*capt*), OM Brown (Auckland), ID Jones (North Harbour), RM Brooke (Auckland), MN Jones (Auckland), TC Randell (Otago), JA Kronfeld (Otago) *Substitutions:* AD Oliver (Otago) for Fitzpatrick (temp 26-37 mins); CC Riechelmann (Auckland) for M Jones (39 mins); SJ McLeod (Waikato) for Mehrtens (58 mins); OFJ Tonu'u (Auckland) for Marshall (60 mins); MP Carter (Auckland) for Kronfeld (68 mins)
Scorers *Tries:* Wilson (5), Cullen (2), M Jones, Marshall, Umaga, Riechelmann *Conversions:* Mehrtens (6), Cullen (2)
FIJI: Rayasi; Lasagavibau, Uluinayau, Sorovaki, Bari; Waqa, J Rauluni; Rouse, Smith (capt), Natuivau, Katalau, Raiwalui, Naevo, Tuvunivono, Natuiyaga *Substitutions:* N Little for Rayasi (40 mins); Tawake for Tuvunivono (40 mins); J Veitayaki for Natuivau (40 mins); Cavubati for Rouse (40 mins); Taga for Naevo (60 mins)
Scorer *Try:* Lasagavibau
Referee WJ Erickson (Australia)

ARGENTINA TO NEW ZEALAND 1997

THE TOURING PARTY

Manager JL Rolandi   **Assistant Manager** A Cafoncelli   **Coach** JL Imhoff
Assistant Coach JJ Fernandez   **Technical Advisor** AJ Wyllie
Captain L Arbizu

Full-backs: E Jurado (Jockey Club, Rosario), F Soler (Tala)

Threequarters: DL Albanese (San Isidro Club), L Arbizu (Belgrano Athletic),
GE Aristide (Gimnasia y Esgrima), O Bartolucci (Atletico Rosario), F Garcia
(Alumni), J Legora (La Tablada), E Simone (Liceo Naval), T Solari (Hindu)

Half-backs: G Quesada (Hindu), JL Cilley (San Isidro Club), N Fernandez
Miranda (Hindu), C Barrea (Cordoba Athletic)

Forwards: M Ledesma (Curupayti), C Promanzio (Duendes), M Reggiardo
(Castres, France), RD Grau (Gauteng Lions, S Africa), O Hasan-Jalil
(Natacion y Gymnasia), GA Llanes (Bath, England), PL Sporleder (Curupayti),
J Simes (Tala), G Ugartemendia (Los Matreros), RA Martin (San Isidro Club),
P Bouza (Duendes), PJ Camerlinckx (Regatas Bella Vista), I Fernandez Lobbe
(Liceo Naval), M Ruiz (Teque, Cuyo), R Travaglini (CA San Isidro),
C Viel (Newman), F Werner (CA San Isidro)

TOUR RECORD

All matches Played 5 Won 1 Lost 4 Points for 87 Against 230
International matches Played 2 Lost 2 Points for 18 Against 230

SCORING DETAILS

All matches					International matches				
For:	13T	5C	4PG	87 Pts	For:	2T	1C	2PG	18 Pts
Against:	34T	24C	4PG	230 Pts	Against:	23T	17C	2PG	155 Pts

MATCH DETAILS

1997	OPPONENTS	VENUE	RESULT	
14 June	NZ Maori	Napier	L	17-39
17 June	Nelson Bays/Marlborough	Nelson	W	42-10
21 June	NEW ZEALAND	Wellington	L	8-93
24 June	Taranaki	New Plymouth	L	10-26
28 June	NEW ZEALAND	Hamilton	L	10-62

MATCH 1   14 June, McLean Park, Napier

NZ Maori 39 (4G 2PG 1T)   **Argentinians 17** (2G 1PG)
NZ Maori Scorers *Tries:* Duggan, Cashmore, Hewitt, M Going, Martin
Conversions: Cashmore (4) *Penalty Goals:* Cashmore (2)
Argentinians Scorers *Tries:* Jurado, Simone *Conversions:* Quesada (2)
Penalty Goal: Quesada

MATCH 2   17 June, Rugby Park, Nelson

Nelson Bays/Marlborough 10 (2T)   **Argentinians 42** (1G 7T)
Nelson Bays/Marlborough Scorers *Tries:* Henderson, Holder
Argentinians Scorers *Tries:* Bouza (2), Viel, Garcia, Solari, Aristide, Ledesma,
Bartolucci *Conversion:* Cilley

MATCH 3   21 June, Athletic Park, Wellington   1st Test
NEW ZEALAND 93 (10G 1PG 4T)   ARGENTINA 8 (1PG 1T)

NEW ZEALAND: CM Cullen (Manawatu); JW Wilson (Otago), FE Bunce
(North Harbour), L Stensness (Auckland), TJF Umaga (Wellington); CJ Spencer
(Auckland), JW Marshall (Canterbury); CW Dowd (Auckland), SBT Fitzpatrick
(Auckland)*(capt)*, OM Brown (Auckland), ID Jones (North Harbour), RM Brooke
(Auckland), TC Randell (Otago), ZV Brooke (Auckland), JA Kronfeld (Otago)
Substitutions: MR Allen (Manawatu) for Brown (57 mins); CC Riechelmann
(Auckland) for Jones (58 mins); GM Osborne (North Harbour) for Cullen
(65 mins)
Scorers *Tries:* Umaga (2), Cullen (2), Spencer (2), Jones, Marshall, Kronfeld,
Fitzpatrick, Brown, R Brooke, Stensness, penalty try *Conversions:* Spencer (10)
Penalty Goal: Spencer
ARGENTINA: Jurado; Solari, Simone, Arbizu *(capt)*, Soler; Quesada,
Fernandez-Mirnada; Grau, Promanzio, Reggiardo, Sporleder, Llanes, Martin,
Camerlinckx, Viel *Substitutions:* Garcia for Jurado (temp 3-9 mins); Ruiz for Viel
(61 mins); Bouza for Llanes (62 mins); Ledesma for Promanzio (62 mins)
Scorers *Try:* Solari *Penalty Goal:* Quesada
Referee B Campsall (England)

MATCH 4   24 June, Rugby Park, New Plymouth

Taranaki 26 (3G 1T)   **Argentinians 10** (1G 1PG)
Taranaki: Scorers *Tries:* Robinson, Barrett, Potauta, Toala
Conversions: Holland (3)
Argentinians: Scorers *Try:* Albanese *Conversion:* Cilley *Penalty Goal:* Cilley

MATCH 5   28 June, Rugby Park, Hamilton   2nd Test
NEW ZEALAND 62 (7G 1PG 2T)   ARGENTINA 10 (1G 1PG)

NEW ZEALAND: CM Cullen (Manawatu); JW Wilson (Otago), FE Bunce
(North Harbour), L Stensness (Auckland), TJF Umaga (Wellington); CJ Spencer
(Auckland), JW Marshall (Canterbury); CW Dowd (Auckland), SBT Fitzpatrick
(Auckland)*(capt)*, OM Brown (Auckland), ID Jones (North Harbour), RM Brooke
(Auckland), TC Randell (Otago), ZV Brooke (Auckland), JA Kronfeld (Otago)
Substitutions: MR Allen (Manawatu) for Dowd (52 mins); SJ McLeod (Waikato)
for Spencer (temp 39-40 mins) and for Bunce (67 mins)
Scorers *Tries:* Randell, Brown, Stensness, Cullen, Kronfeld, R Brooke, Allen,
Umaga, Spencer *Conversions:* Spencer (6), Cullen *Penalty Goal:* Spencer
ARGENTINA: Jurado; Albanese, Simone, Arbizu *(capt)* Soler; Quesada,
Fernandez-Miranda; Grau, Ledesma, Reggiardo, Sporleder, Llanes, Martin,
Camerlinckx, Travaglini *Substitutions:* Bouza for Travaglini (39 mins); Solari for
Jurado (41 mins); Hasan-Jalil for Reggiardo (57 mins)
Scorers *Try:* Grau *Conversion:* Quesada *Penalty Goal:* Quesada
Referee B Campsall (England)

NEW ZEALAND TO BRITAIN & IRELAND 1997

THE TOURING PARTY

Manager M Banks   **Coach** JB Hart   **Assistant Coaches** R Cooper, G Hunter
Captain SBT Fitzpatrick

Full-backs: CM Cullen (Central Vikings), TJ Miller (Waikato)

Threequarters: JW Wilson (Otago), TJF Umaga (Wellington), GM Osborne (North Harbour), JT Lomu (Counties), JC Stanley (Auckland), FE Bunce (North Harbour), A Ieremia (Wellington), SJ McLeod (Waikato), WK Little (North Harbour)

Half-backs: CJ Spencer (Auckland), AP Mehrtens (Canterbury), MD Robinson (North Harbour), JP Preston (Wellington), JW Marshall (Canterbury)

Forwards: MR Allen (Manawatu), CW Dowd (Auckland), OM Brown (Auckland), CK Barrell (Canterbury), G Slater (Taranaki), SBT Fitzpatrick (Auckland), NJ Hewitt (Southland), AD Oliver (Otago), RM Brooke (Auckland), ID Jones (North Harbour), MSB Cooksley (Waikato), CC Riechelmann (Auckland), AR Hopa (Waikato), TJ Blackaddder (Canterbury), JA Kronfeld (Otago), AF Blowers (Auckland), TC Randell (Otago), ZV Brooke (Auckland), MP Carter (Auckland), SD Surridge (Canterbury)

TOUR RECORD

All matches   Played 9   Won 8   Drawn 1   Points for 395   Against 119
International matches   Played 4   Won 3   Drew 1   Points for 156   Against 56

SCORING DETAILS

All matches | **International matches**

For:	51T	31C	25PG	1DG	395 Pts	For:	17T 13C 14PG 1DG	156 Pts	
Against:	11T	5C	18PG		119 Pts	Against:	7T 3C 5PG	56 Pts	

MATCH DETAILS

1997	OPPONENTS	VENUE	RESULT
8 Nov	Llanelli	Llanelli	W 81-3
11 Nov	Wales A	Pontypridd	W 51-8
15 Nov	IRELAND	Dublin	W 63-15
18 Nov	Emerging England XV	Huddersfield	W 59-22
22 Nov	ENGLAND	Manchester	W 25-8
25 Nov	ERP XV	Bristol	W 18-11
29 Nov	WALES	Wembley	W 42-7
2 Dec	England A	Leicester	W 30-19
6 Dec	ENGLAND	Twickenham	D 26-26

MATCH 1   8 November, Stradey Park, Llanelli

Llanelli 3 (1PG)   **New Zealanders 81** (5G 2PG 8T)
Llanelli: D Williams; WT Proctor, N Boobyer, S Jones, W Leech; C Warlow, RHStJB Moon; R Jones, RC McBryde (*capt*), S Gale, S Ford, MJ Voyle, C Wyatt, H Jenkins, I Jones *Substitutions:* P Morris for Jenkins (40 mins); H Williams-Jones for R Jones (60 mins); A Thomas for Moon (75 mins); A Gibbs for I Jones (58 mins)
Scorer *Penalty Goal:* Warlow

New Zealanders: Cullen; Wilson, Bunce, Ieremia, Osborne; Mehrtens, Marshall (*capt*); Dowd, Hewitt, Brown, Jones, R Brooke, Blowers, Randell, Kronfeld *Substitutions:* Z Brooke for Kronfeld (51 mins); Stanley for Wilson (56 mins); Preston for Mehrtens (72 mins)
Scorers Cullen (4), Wilson (2), Hewitt (2), Jones, Kronfeld, Marshall, Z Brooke, Ieremia *Conversions:* Mehrtens (2), Wilson (2), Preston *Penalty Goals:* Mehrtens (2)
Referee B Campsall (England)

MATCH 2   11 November, Sardis Road, Pontypridd

Wales A 8 (1PG 1T)   **New Zealanders 51** (5G 2PG 2T)
Wales A: MJ Back (Swansea); G Thomas (Bridgend), N Boobyer (Llanelli), J Lewis (Pontypridd), DR James (Pontypridd); BI Hayward (Ebbw Vale), AP Moore (Richmond); IM Buckett (Swansea), GR Jenkins (Swansea), CT Anthony (Swansea), GO Llewellyn (Harlequins)(*capt*), C Stephens (Bridgend), M Spiller (Pontypridd), C Wyatt (Llanelli), ME Williams (Pontypridd)
Substitutions: L Jarvis (Cardiff) for Thomas (45 mins); N Eynon (Pontypridd) for Buckett (47 mins); D Thomas (Swansea) for Wyatt (67 mins); WS Roy (Pontypridd) for Stephens (78 mins); H Harries (Harlequins) for Hayward (78 mins)
Scorers *Try:* James *Penalty Goal:* Hayward
New Zealanders: Miller; Umaga, McLeod, Little, Lomu; Spencer, Robinson; Allen, Oliver, Barrell, Riechelmann, Cooksley, Blackadder (*capt*), Surridge, Carter
Substitutions: Hopa for Riechelmann (63 mins); Slater for Barrell (69 mins)
Scorers *Tries:* McLeod (2), Carter, Lomu, Miller, Oliver, Robinson *Conversions:* Spencer (5) *Penalty Goals:* Spencer (2)
Referee J Pearson (England)

MATCH 3   15 November, Lansdowne Road, Dublin Test Match

IRELAND 15 (1G 1PG 1T)   **NEW ZEALAND 63** (5G 6PG 2T)

IRELAND: KW Nowlan (St Mary's College); DA Hickie (St Mary's College), RAJ Henderson (Wasps), MC McCall (London Irish), JPJ McWeeney (St Mary's College); EP Elwood (Galwegians), CD McGuinness (St Mary's College); NJ Popplewell (Newcastle), KGM Wood (Harlequins)(*capt*), PS Wallace (Saracens), PS Johns (Saracens), ME O'Kelly (London Irish), EO Halvey (Shannon), ERP Miller (Leicester), K Dawson (London Irish)
Substitutions: RP Nesdale (Newcastle) for Wood (40 mins); KM Maggs (Bristol) for McWeeney (60 mins); DJ Erskine (Sale) for Halvey (60 mins); BT O'Meara (Cork Constitution) for McGuiness (73 mins)
Scorers *Tries:* Wood (2) *Conversion:* Elwood *Penalty Goal:* Elwood
NEW ZEALAND: Cullen; Wilson, Bunce, Ieremia, Osborne; Mehrtens, Marshall (*capt*); Dowd, Hewitt, Brown, Jones, R Brooke, Randell, Z Brooke, Blowers
Substitutions: Riechelmann for R Brooke (51 mins); Kronfeld for Blowers (60 mins); McLeod for Bunce (65 mins), Preston for Mehrtens (75 mins)
Scorers *Tries:* Wilson (2), Osborne (2), Mehrtens, Marshall, Ieremia *Conversions:* Mehrtens (5) *Penalty Goals:* Mehrtens (6)
Referee AJ Spreadbury (England)

MATCH 4   18 November, McAlpine Stadium, Huddersfield

Emerging England 22 (1G 5PG)   **New Zealanders 59** (5G 3PG 3T)
Emerging England: J Mallinder (Sale); J Bentley (Newcastle), NJJ Greenstock (Wasps), MC Allen (Northampton), TD Beim (Sale); PJ Grayson (Northampton), AS Healey (Leicester); GC Rowntree (Leicester), MP Regan (Bath), DJ Garforth (Leicester), SD Shaw (Wasps), DJ Grewcock (Saracens), RHJ Jenkins

(Harlequins), CMA Sheasby (Wasps), NA Back (Leicester)*(capt)*
Substitutions: MJ Corry (Leicester) for Jenkins (56 mins); KP Yates (Bath) for Garforth (60 mins); N McCarthy (Gloucester) for Regan (78 mins); D Sims (Gloucester) for Shaw (78 mins)
Scorers *Try:* Greenstock *Conversion:* Grayson *Penalty Goals:* Grayson (5)
New Zealanders: Miller; Umaga, McLeod, Little, Lomu; Spencer, Robinson; Allen, Oliver, Slater, Riechelmann, Cooksley, Blackadder *(capt)*, Surridge, Kronfeld *Substitutions:* Hopa for Surridge (60 mins); Stanley for Umaga (71 mins)
Scorers *Tries:* Miller (3), Lomu (2), Kronfeld, Surridge, Riechelmann *Conversions:* Spencer (5) *Penalty Goals:* Spencer (3)
Referee P Deluca (Argentina)

MATCH 5   22 November, Old Trafford, Manchester   1st Test
ENGLAND 8 (1PG 1T)   NEW ZEALAND 25 (2G 2PG 1T)

ENGLAND: MB Perry (Bath); DL Rees (Sale), WJH Greenwood (Leicester), PR de Glanville (Bath), AA Adebayo (Bath); MJ Catt (Bath), KPP Bracken (Saracens); J Leonard (Harlequins), R Cockerill (Leicester), DJ Garforth (Leicester), MO Johnson (Leicester), GS Archer (Newcastle), LBN Dallaglio (Wasps)*(capt)*, AJ Diprose (Saracens), RA Hill (Saracens) *Substitutions:* NA Back (Leicester) for Diprose (40 mins); AS Healey (Leicester) for Adebayo (55 mins)
Scorers *Try:* de Glanville *Penalty Goal:* Catt
NEW ZEALAND: Cullen; Wilson, Bunce, Ieremia, Lomu; Mehrtens, Marshall *(capt)*; Dowd, Hewitt, Brown, Jones, R Brooke, Randell, Z Brooke, Kronfeld *Substitutions:* Blowers for Z Brooke (52 mins); McLeod for Ieremia (59 mins); Preston for Wilson (79 mins)
Scorers *Tries:* Jones, Wilson, Randell *Conversions:* Mehrtens (2)
Penalty Goals: Mehrtens (2)
Referee PL Marshall (Australia)

MATCH 6   25 November, Ashton Gate, Bristol

England Rugby Partnership XV 11 (2PG 1T)   New Zealanders 18 (1G 2PG 1T)
ERP XV: TRG Stimpson (Newcastle); J Bentley (Newcastle), NJJ Greenstock (Wasps), MC Allen (Northampton), S Brown (Richmond); R de V Butland (Bath), M Wood (Wasps); KP Yates (Bath), MP Regan (Bath), PJ Vickery (Gloucester), D Sims (Gloucester), R Fidler (Gloucester), TAK Rodber (Northampton)*(capt)*, CMA Sheasby (Wasps), PH Sanderson (Sale)
Substitutions: AE Long (Bath) for Regan (40 mins); PJ Grayson (Northampton) for Butland (46 mins); R Winters (Bedford) for Sims (65 mins); S Benton (Gloucester) for Wood (73 mins); J Worsley (Wasps) for Sanderson (78 mins)
Scorers *Try:* Wood *Penalty Goals:* Stimpson (2)
New Zealanders: Miller; Umaga, Stanley, McLeod, Osborne; Spencer, Preston; Allen, Oliver, Barrell, Riechelmann, Cooksley, Blackadder *(capt)*, Hopa, Carter
Substitutions: Fitzpatrick for Oliver (59 mins); Little for Stanley (64 mins)
Scorers *Tries:* Spencer, Hopa *Conversion:* Spencer *Penalty Goals:* Spencer (2)
Referee R Davies (Wales)

MATCH 7   29 November, Wembley Stadium   Test Match
WALES 7 (1G)   NEW ZEALAND 42 (4G 2PG 1DG 1T)

WALES: KA Morgan (Pontypridd); G Thomas (Bridgend), AG Bateman (Richmond), IS Gibbs (Swansea), NK Walker (Cardiff); NR Jenkins (Pontypridd), R Howley (Cardiff); CD Loader (Swansea), BH Williams (Richmond), D Young (Cardiff), GO Llewellyn (Harlequins), MJ Voyle (Llanelli), RC Appleyard

The New Zealand team perform the ritual 'haka' before the drawn 2nd Test match against England on 6 December 1997.

(Swansea), N Thomas (Bath), RG Jones (Cardiff)*(capt) Substitutions:* LB Davies (Cardiff) for Gibbs (26 mins); SM Williams (Cardiff) for G Jones (temp 38-39 mins) & for N Thomas (63 mins); AC Thomas (Swansea) for Bateman (temp 38-40 mins); JM Humphreys (Cardiff) for B Williams (56 mins); SC John (Cardiff) for Loader (73 mins)
Scorers *Try:* Walker *Conversion:* Jenkins
NEW ZEALAND: Cullen; Wilson, Bunce, Little, Lomu; Mehrtens, Marshall (*capt*); Dowd, Hewitt, Brown, Jones, R Brooke, Randell, Z Brooke, Kronfeld
Substitutions: Fitzpatrick for Brown (55 mins); Allen for Brown (58 mins); Blowers for Randell (67 mins); McLeod for Little (temp 26-30 mins)
Scorers *Tries:* Cullen (3), Randell, Marshall *Conversions:* Mehrtens (4)
Penalty Goals: Mehrtens (2) *Dropped Goal:* Z Brooke
Referee WJ Erickson (Australia)

MATCH 8   2 December, Welford Road, Leicester

England A 19 (1G 4PG)   **New Zealanders 30** (2G 2PG 2T)
England A: TRG Stimpson (Newcastle); S Brown (Richmond), S Potter (Leicester), MC Allen (Northampton), AA Adebayo (Bath); R deV Butland (Bath), S Benton (Gloucester); GC Rowntree (Leicester), MP Regan (Bath), PJ Vickery (Gloucester), D Sims (Gloucester), R Fidler (Gloucester), RHJ Jenkins (Harlequins), BB Clarke (Richmond)(*capt*), PH Sanderson (Sale)
Substitutions: VE Ubogu (Bath) for Vickery (57 mins); R Winters (Bedford) for Jenkins (68 mins); MS Mapletoft (Gloucester) for Butland (71 mins); N McCarthy (Gloucester) for Regan (78 mins)
Scorers *Try:* Benton *Conversion:* Stimpson *Penalty Goals:* Stimpson (4)
New Zealanders: Miller; Umaga, McLeod, Ieremia, Osborne; Spencer, Robinson; Allen, Oliver, Slater, Riechelmann, Cooksley, Blackadder (*capt*), Surridge, Carter
Substitutions: Preston for Robinson (30 mins); Blowers for Carter (40 mins); Hopa for Cooksley (72 mins)
Scorers *Tries:* McLeod, Oliver, Riechelmann, Umaga *Conversions:* Spencer (2)
Penalty Goals: Spencer, Preston
Referee A Lewis (Ireland)

MATCH 9   6 December, Twickenham   2nd Test

ENGLAND 26 (1G 3PG 2T)   **NEW ZEALAND 26** (2G 4PG)

ENGLAND: MB Perry (Bath); DL Rees (Sale), WJH Greenwood (Leicester), PR de Glanville (Bath), AS Healey (Leicester); PJ Grayson (Northampton), KPP Bracken (Saracens); J Leonard (Harlequins), R Cockerill (Leicester), DJ Garforth (Leicester), MO Johnson (Leicester), GS Archer (Newcastle), LBN Dallaglio (Wasps)(*capt*), RA Hill (Saracens), NA Back (Leicester)
Substitutions: TRG Stimpson (Newcastle) for Rees (temp 6-17 mins) & for de Glanville (59 mins); CMA Sheasby (Wasps) for Back (19-28 mins); MJS Dawson (Northampton) for Bracken (59 mins); MP Regan (Bath) for Cockerill (63 mins)
Scorers *Tries:* Rees, Hill, Dallaglio *Conversion:* Grayson *Penalty Goals:* Grayson (3)
NEW ZEALAND: Cullen; Wilson, Bunce, Little, Lomu; Mehrtens, Marshall (*capt*); Allen, Hewitt, Brown, Jones, R Brooke, Randell, Z Brooke, Kronfeld
Substitutions: Riechelmann for Kronfeld (temp 31-34 mins); Spencer for Little (65 mins); McLeod for Bunce (75 mins)
Scorers *Tries:* Mehrtens, Little *Conversions:* Mehrtens (2)
Penalty Goals: Mehrtens (4)
Referee JM Fleming (Scotland)

NEW ZEALAND INTERNATIONAL PLAYERS (*up to 30 April 1998*)

Abbott, H L (Taranaki) 1906 *F*
Aitken, G G (Wellington) 1921 *SA* 1,2
Allen, F R (Auckland) 1946 *A* 1,2, 1947 *A* 1,2, 1949 *SA* 1,2
Allen, M R (Taranaki, Manawatu) 1993 *WS* (t), 1996 *S* 2 (t), 1997 *Arg* 1 (R), 2 (R), *SA* 2 (R), *A* 3 (R), *E* 2, *W* (R)
Allen, N H (Counties) 1980 *A* 3, *W*
Alley, G T (Canterbury) 1928 *SA* 1,2,3
Anderson, A (Canterbury) 1983 *S, E,* 1984 *A* 1,2,3, 1987 [*Fj*]
Anderson, B L (Wairarapa-Bush) 1986 *A* 1
Archer, W R (Otago, Southland) 1955 *A* 1,2, 1956 *SA* 1,3
Argus, W G (Canterbury) 1946 *A* 1,2, 1947 *A* 1,2
Arnold, D A (Canterbury) 1963 *I, W,* 1964 *E, F*
Arnold, K D (Waikato) 1947 *A* 1,2
Ashby, D L (Southland) 1958 *A* 2
Asher, A A (Auckland) 1903 *A*
Ashworth, B G (Auckland) 1978 *A* 1,2
Ashworth, J C (Canterbury, Hawke's Bay) 1978 *A* 1,2,3, 1980 *A* 1,2,3, 1981 *SA* 1,2,3, 1982 *A* 1,2, 1983 *BI* 1,2,3,4, *A,* 1984 *F* 1,2, *A* 1,2,3, 1985 *E* 1,2, *A*
Atkinson, H (West Coast) 1913 *A* 1
Avery, H E (Wellington) 1910 *A* 1,2,3

Bachop, G T M (Canterbury) 1989 *W, I,* 1990 *S* 1,2, *A* 1,2,3, *F* 1,2, 1991 *Arg* 1,2, *A* 1,2, [*E, US, C, A, S*], 1992 *Wld* 1, 1994 *SA* 1,2,3, *A,* 1995 *C,* [*I, W, S, E, SA*], *A* 1,2
Bachop, S J (Otago) 1994 *F* 2, *SA* 1,2,3, *A*
Badeley, C E O (Auckland) 1921 *SA* 1,2
Baird, J A S (Otago) 1913 *A* 2
Ball, N (Wellington) 1931 *A,* 1932 *A* 2,3, 1935 *W,* 1936 *E*
Barrett, J (Auckland) 1913 *A* 2,3
Barry, E F (Wellington) 1934 *A* 2
Barry, L J (North Harbour) 1995 *F* 2
Batty, G B (Wellington, Bay of Plenty) 1972 *W, S,* 1973 *E* 1, *I, F, E* 2, 1974 *A* 1,3, *I,* 1975 *S,* 1976 *SA* 1,2,3,4, 1977 *BI* 1
Batty, W (Auckland) 1930 *BI* 1,3,4, 1931 *A*
Beatty, G E (Taranaki) 1950 *BI* 1
Bell, R H (Otago) 1951 *A* 3, 1952 *A* 1,2
Bellis, E A (Wanganui) 1921 *SA* 1,2,3
Bennet, R (Otago) 1905 *A*
Berghan, T (Otago) 1938 *A* 1,2,3
Berry, M J (Wairarapa-Bush) 1986 *A* 3 (R)
Bevan, V D (Wellington) 1949 *A* 1,2, 1950 *BI* 1,2,3,4
Birtwistle, W M (Canterbury) 1965 *SA* 1,2,3,4, 1967 *E, W, S*
Black, J E (Canterbury) 1977 *F* 1, 1979 *A,* 1980 *A* 3
Black, N W (Auckland) 1949 *SA* 3
Black, R S (Otago) 1914 *A* 1
Blake, A W (Wairarapa) 1949 *A* 1
Blowers, A F (Auckland) 1996 *SA* 2 (R), 4 (R), 1997 *I, E* 1 (R), *W* (R)
Boggs, E G (Auckland) 1946 *A* 2, 1949 *SA* 1
Bond, J G (Canterbury) 1949 *A* 2
Booth, E E (Otago) 1906 *F,* 1907 *A* 1,3
Boroevich, K G (Wellington) 1986 *F* 1, *A* 1, *F* 3 (R)
Botica, F M (North Harbour) 1986 *F* 1, *A* 1,2,3, *F* 2,3, 1989 *Arg* 1 (R)
Bowden, N J G (Taranaki) 1952 *A* 2
Bowers, R G (Wellington) 1954 *I, F*
Bowman, A W (Hawke's Bay) 1938 *A* 1,2,3
Braid, G J (Bay of Plenty) 1983 *S, E*
Bremner, S G (Auckland, Canterbury) 1952 *A* 2, 1956 *SA* 2
Brewer, M R (Otago, Canterbury) 1986 *F* 1, *A* 1,2,3, *F* 2,3, 1988 *A* 1, 1989 *A, W, I,* 1990 *S* 1,2, *A* 1,2,3, *F* 1,2, 1992 *I* 2, *A* 1, 1994 *F* 1,2, *SA* 1,2,3, *A,* 1995 *C,* [*I, W, E, SA*], *A* 1,2
Briscoe, K C (Taranaki) 1959 *BI* 2, 1960 *SA* 1,2,3,4, 1963 *I, W,* 1964 *E, S*
Brooke, R M (Auckland) 1992 *I* 2, *A* 1,2,3, *SA,* 1993 *BI* 1,2,3, *A, WS,* 1994 *SA* 2,3, 1995 *C,* [*J, S, E, SA*], *A* 1,2, *It, F* 1,2, 1996 *WS, S* 1, 2, *A* 1, *SA* 1, *A* 2, *SA* 2,3,4,5, 1997 *Fj, Arg* 1,2, *A* 1, *SA* 1, *A* 2, *SA* 2, *A* 3, *I, E* 1, *W, E* 2

Brooke, Z V (Auckland) 1987 [*Arg*], 1989 *Arg* 2 (R), 1990 *A* 1,2,3, *F* 1 (R), 1991 *Arg* 2, *A* 1,2, [*E, It, C, A, S*], 1992 *A* 2,3, *SA,* 1993 *BI* 1,2,3 (R), *WS* (R), *S, E,* 1994 *F* 2, *SA* 1,2,3, *A,* 1995 [*J, S, E, SA*], *A* 1,2, *It, F* 1,2, 1996 *WS, S* 1,2, *A* 1, *SA* 1, *A* 2, *SA* 2,3,4,5, 1997 *Arg* 1,2, *A* 1, *SA* 1, *A* 2, *SA* 2, *A* 3, *I, E* 1, *W, E* 2
Brooke-Cowden, M (Auckland) 1986 *F* 1, *A* 1, 1987 [*W*]
Brown, C (Taranaki) 1913 *A* 2,3
Brown, O M (Auckland) 1992 *I* 2, *A* 1,2,3, *SA,* 1993 *BI* 1,2,3, *A, S, E,* 1994 *F* 1,2, *SA* 1,2,3, *A,* 1995 *C,* [*I, W, S, E, SA*], *A* 1,2, *It, F* 1,2, 1996 *WS, S* 1,2, *A* 1, *SA* 1, *A* 2, *SA* 2,3,4,5, 1997 *Fj, Arg* 1,2, *A* 1, *SA* 1, *A* 2, *SA* 2, *A* 3, *I, E* 1, *W, E* 2
Brown, R H (Taranaki) 1955 *A* 3, 1956 *SA* 1,2,3,4, 1957 *A* 1,2, 1958 *A* 1,2,3, 1959 *BI* 1,3, 1961 *F* 1,2,3, 1962 *A* 1
Brownlie, C J (Hawke's Bay) 1924 *W,* 1925 *E, F*
Brownlie, M J (Hawke's Bay) 1924 *I, W,* 1925 *E, F,* 1928 *SA* 1,2,3,4
Bruce, J A (Auckland) 1914 *A* 1,2
Bruce, O D (Canterbury) 1976 *SA* 1,2,4, 1977 *BI* 2,3,4, *F* 1,2, 1978 *A* 1,2, *I, W, E, S*
Bryers, R F (King Country) 1949 *A* 1
Budd, T A (Southland) 1946 *A* 2, 1949 *A* 2
Bullock-Douglas, G A H (Wanganui) 1932 *A* 1,2,3, 1934 *A* 1,2
Bunce, F E (North Harbour) 1992 *Wld* 1,2,3, *I* 1,2, *A* 1,2,3, *SA,* 1993 *BI* 1,2,3, *A, WS, S, E,* 1994 *F* 1,2, *SA* 1,2,3, *A,* 1995 *C,* [*I, W, S, E, SA*], *A* 1,2, *It, F* 1,2, 1996 *WS, S* 1,2, *A1, SA* 1, *A* 2, *SA* 2,3,4,5, 1997 *Fj, Arg* 1,2, *A* 1, *SA* 1, *A* 2, *SA* 2, *A* 3, *I, E* 1, *W, E* 2
Burgess, G A J (Auckland) 1981 *SA* 2
Burgess, G F (Southland) 1905 *A*
Burgess, R E (Manawatu) 1971 *BI* 1,2,3, 1972 *A* 3, *W,* 1973 *I, F*
Burke, P S (Taranaki) 1955 *A* 1, 1957 *A* 1,2
Burns, P J (Canterbury) 1908 *AW* 2, 1910 *A* 1,2,3, 1913 *A* 3
Bush, R G (Otago) 1931 *A*
Bush, W K (Canterbury) 1974 *A* 1,2, 1975 *S,* 1976 *I, SA,* 2,4, 1977 *BI* 2,3,4 (R), 1978 *I, W,* 1979 *A*
Buxton, J B (Canterbury) 1955 *A* 3, 1956 *SA* 1

Cain, M J (Taranaki) 1913 *US,* 1914 *A* 1,2,3
Callesen, J A (Manawatu) 1974 *A* 1,2,3, 1975 *S*
Cameron, D (Taranaki) 1908 *AW* 1,2,3
Cameron, L M (Manawatu) 1980 *A* 3, 1981 *SA* 1 (R), 2,3, *R*
Carleton, S R (Canterbury) 1928 *SA* 1,2,3, 1929 *A* 1,2,3
Carrington, K R (Auckland) 1971 *BI* 1,3,4
Carter, M P (Auckland) 1991 *A* 2, [*It, A*], 1997 *Fj* (R), *A* 1 (R)
Casey, S T (Otago) 1905 *S, I, E, W,* 1907 *A* 1,2,3, 1908 *AW* 1
Cashmore, A R (Auckland) 1996 *S2* (R), 1997 *A* 2 (R)
Catley, E H (Waikato) 1946 *A* 1, 1947 *A* 1,2, 1949 *SA* 1,2,3,4
Caughey, T H C (Auckland) 1932 *A* 1,3, 1934 *A* 1,2, 1935 *S, I,* 1936 *E, A* 1, 1937 *SA* 3
Caulton, R W (Wellington) 1959 *BI* 2,3,4, 1960 *SA* 1,4, 1961 *F* 2, 1963 *E* 1,2, *I, W,* 1964 *E, S, F, A* 1,2,3
Cherrington, N P (North Auckland) 1950 *BI* 1
Christian, D L (Auckland) 1949 *SA* 4
Clamp, M (Wellington) 1984 *A* 2,3
Clark, D W (Otago) 1964 *A* 1,2
Clark, W H (Wellington) 1953 *W,* 1954 *I, E, S,* 1955 *A* 1,2, 1956 *SA* 2,3,4
Clarke, A H (Auckland) 1958 *A* 3, 1959 *BI* 4, 1960 *SA* 1
Clarke, D B (Waikato) 1956 *SA* 3,4, 1957 *A* 1,2, 1958 *A* 1,3, 1959 *BI* 1,2,3,4, 1960 *SA* 1,4, 1961 *F* 1,2,3, 1962 *A* 1,2,3,4,5, 1963 *E* 1,2, *I, W,* 1964 *E, S, F, A* 2,3
Clarke, E (Auckland) 1992 *Wld* 2,3, *I* 1,2, 1993 *BI* 1,2, *S* (R), *E*
Clarke, I J (Waikato) 1953 *W,* 1955 *A* 1,2,3, 1956 *SA* 1,2,3,4, 1957 *A* 1,2, 1958 *A* 1,3, 1959 *BI* 1,2, 1960 *SA* 2,4, 1961 *F* 2,3, 1962 *A* 1,2,3, 1963 *E* 1,2
Clarke, R L (Taranaki) 1932 *A* 2,3
Cobden, D G (Canterbury) 1937 *SA* 1

330

Cockerill, M S (Taranaki) 1951 *A* 1,2,3
Cockroft, E A P (South Canterbury) 1913 *A* 3, 1914 *A* 2,3
Codlin, B W (Counties) 1980 *A* 1,2,3
Collins, A H (Taranaki) 1932 *A* 2,3, 1934 *A* 1
Collins, J L (Poverty Bay) 1964 *A* 1, 1965 *SA* 1,4
Colman, J T H (Taranaki) 1907 *A* 1,2, 1908 *AW* 1,3
Connor, D M (Auckland) 1961 *F* 1,2,3, 1962 *A* 1,2,3,4,5, 1963 *E* 1,2, 1964 *A* 2,3
Conway, R J (Otago, Bay of Plenty) 1959 *BI* 2,3,4, 1960 *SA* 1,3,4, 1965 *SA* 1,2,3,4
Cooke, A E (Auckland, Wellington) 1924 *I, W*, 1925 *E, F*, 1930 *BI* 1,2,3,4
Cooke, R J (Canterbury) 1903 *A*
Cooksley, M S B (Counties, Waikato) 1992 *Wld* 1, 1993 *BI* 2,3 (R), *A*, 1994 *F* 1,2, *SA* 1,2, *A*
Cooper, G J L (Auckland, Otago) 1986 *F* 1, *A* 1,2, 1992 *Wld* 1,2,3, *I* 1
Cooper, M J A (Waikato) 1992 *I* 2, *SA* (R), 1993 *BI* 1 (R), 3 (t), *WS* (t), *S*, 1994 *F* 1,2
Corner, M M N (Auckland) 1930 *BI* 2,3,4, 1931 *A*, 1934 *A* 1, 1936 *E*
Cossey, R R (Counties) 1958 *A* 1
Cottrell, A I (Canterbury) 1929 *A* 1,2,3, 1930 *BI* 1,2,3,4, 1931 *A*, 1932 *A* 1,2,3
Cottrell, W D (Canterbury) 1968 *A* 1,2, *F* 2,3, 1970 *SA* 1, 1971 *BI* 1,2,3,4
Couch, M B R (Wairarapa) 1947 *A* 1, 1949 *A* 1,2
Coughlan, T D (South Canterbury) 1958 *A* 1
Creighton, J N (Canterbury) 1962 *A* 4
Crichton, S (Wellington) 1983 *S, E*
Cross, T (Canterbury) 1904 *BI*, 1905 *A*
Crowley, K J (Taranaki) 1985 *E* 1,2, *A, Arg* 1,2, 1986 *A* 3, *F* 2,3, 1987 *[Arg]*, 1990 *S* 1,2, *A* 1,2,3, *F* 1,2, 1991 *Arg* 1,2, *[A]*
Crowley, P J B (Auckland) 1949 *SA* 3,4, 1950 *BI* 1,2,3,4
Culhane, S D (Southland) 1995 *[J], It, F* 1,2, 1996 *SA* 3,4
Cullen C M (Manawatu, Central Vikings) 1996 *WS, S* 1,2, *A* 1, *SA* 1, *A* 2, *SA* 2,3,4,5, 1997 *Fj, Arg* 1,2, *A* 1, *SA* 1, *A* 2, *SA* 2, *A* 3, *I, E* 1, *W, E* 2
Cummings, W (Canterbury) 1913 *A* 2,3
Cundy, R T (Wairarapa) 1929 *A* 2 (R)
Cunningham, G R (Auckland) 1979 *A, S, E*, 1980 *A* 1,2
Cunningham, W (Auckland) 1905 *S, I*, 1906 *F*, 1907 *A* 1,2,3, 1908 *AW* 1,2,3
Cupples, L F (Bay of Plenty) 1924 *I, W*
Currie, C J (Canterbury) 1978 *I, W*
Cuthill, J E (Otago) 1913 *A* 1, *US*

Dalley, W C (Canterbury) 1924 *I*, 1928 *SA* 1,2,3,4
Dalton, A G (Counties) 1977 *F* 2, 1978 *A* 1,2,3, *I, W, E, S*, 1979 *F* 1,2, *S*, 1981 *S* 1,2, *SA* 1,2,3, *R, F* 1,2, 1982 *A* 1,2,3, 1983 *BI* 1,2,3,4, *A*, 1984 *F* 1,2, *A* 1,2,3, 1985 *E* 1,2, *A*
Dalton, D (Hawke's Bay) 1935 *I, W*, 1936 *A* 1,2, 1937 *SA* 1,2,3, 1938 *A* 1,2
Dalton, R A (Wellington) 1947 *A* 1,2
Dalzell, G N (Canterbury) 1953 *W*, 1954 *I, E, S, F*
Davie, M G (Canterbury) 1983 *E* (R)
Davies, W A (Auckland, Otago) 1960 *SA* 4, 1962 *A* 4,5
Davis, K (Auckland) 1952 *A* 2, 1953 *W*, 1954 *I, E, S, F*, 1955 *A* 2, 1958 *A* 1,2,3
Davis, L J (Canterbury) 1976 *I*, 1977 *BI* 3,4
Davis, W L (Hawke's Bay) 1967 *A, E, W, F, S*, 1968 *A* 1,2, *F* 1, 1969 *W* 1,2, 1970 *SA* 2
Deans, I B (Canterbury) 1988 *W* 1,2, *A* 1,2,3, 1989 *F* 1,2, *Arg* 1,2, *A*
Deans, R G (Canterbury) 1905 *S, I, E, W*, 1908 *AW* 3
Deans, R M (Canterbury) 1983 *S, E*, 1984 *A* 1 (R), 2,3
Delamore, G W (Wellington) 1949 *SA* 4
Dewar, H (Taranaki) 1913 *A* 1, *US*
Diack, E S (Otago) 1959 *BI* 2
Dick, J (Auckland) 1937 *SA* 1,2, 1938 *A* 3
Dick, M J (Auckland) 1963 *I, W*, 1964 *E, S, F*, 1965 *SA* 3, 1966 *BI* 4, 1967 *A, E, W, F*, 1969 *W* 1,2, 1970 *SA* 1,4
Dixon, M J (Canterbury) 1954 *I, E, S, F*, 1956 *SA* 1,2,3,4, 1957 *A* 1,2
Dobson, R L (Auckland) 1949 *A* 1
Dodd, E H (Wellington) 1905 *A*
Donald, A J (Wanganui) 1983 *S, E*, 1984 *F* 1,2, *A* 1,2,3
Donald, J G (Wairarapa) 1921 *SA* 1,2
Donald, Q (Wairarapa) 1924 *I, W*, 1925 *E, F*

Donaldson, M W (Manawatu) 1977 *F* 1,2, 1978 *A* 1,2,3, *I, E, S*, 1979 *F* 1,2, *A, S* (R), 1981 *SA* 3 (R)
Dougan, J P (Wellington) 1972 *A* 1, 1973 *E* 2
Dowd, C W (Auckland) 1993 *BI* 1,2,3, *A, WS, S, E*, 1994 *SA* 1 (R), 1995 *C*, *[I, W, J, E, SA]*, *A* 1,2, *It, F* 1,2, 1996 *WS, S* 1,2, *A* 1, *SA* 1, *A* 2, *SA* 2,3,4,5, 1997 *Fj, Arg* 1,2, *A* 1, *SA* 1, *A* 2, *SA* 2, *A* 3, *I, E* 1, *W*
Dowd, G W (North Harbour) 1992 *I* 1 (R)
Downing, A J (Auckland) 1913 *A* 1, *US*, 1914 *A* 1,2,3
Drake, J A (Auckland) 1986 *F* 2,3, 1987 *[Fj, Arg, S, W, F], A*
Duff, R H (Canterbury) 1951 *A* 1,2,3, 1952 *A* 1,2, 1955 *A* 2,3, 1956 *SA* 1,2,3,4
Duncan, J (Otago) 1903 *A*
Duncan, M G (Hawke's Bay) 1971 *BI* 3 (R), 4
Duncan, W D (Otago) 1921 *SA* 1,2,3
Dunn, E J (North Auckland) 1979 *S*, 1981 *S* 1
Dunn, I T W (North Auckland) 1983 *BI* 1,4, *A*
Dunn, J M (Auckland) 1946 *A* 1

Earl, A T (Canterbury) 1986 *F* 1, *A* 1, *F* 3 (R), 1987 *[Arg]*, 1989 *W, I*, 1991 *Arg* 1 (R), 2, *A* 1, *[E* (R), *US, S]*, 1992 *A* 2,3 (R)
Eastgate, B P (Canterbury) 1952 *A* 1,2, 1954 *S*
Elliott, K G (Wellington) 1946 *A* 1,2
Ellis, M C G (Otago) 1993 *S, E*, 1995 *C*, *[I* (R), *W, J, S, SA* (R)]
Elsom, A E G (Canterbury) 1952 *A* 1,2, 1953 *W*, 1955 *A* 1,2,3
Elvidge, R R (Otago) 1946 *A* 1,2, 1949 *SA* 1,2,3,4, 1950 *BI* 1,2,3
Erceg, C P (Auckland) 1951 *A* 1,2,3, 1952 *A* 1
Evans, D A (Hawke's Bay) 1910 *A* 2
Eveleigh, K A (Manawatu) 1976 *SA* 2,4, 1977 *BI* 1,2

Fanning, A H N (Canterbury) 1913 *A* 3
Fanning, B J (Canterbury) 1903 *A*, 1904 *BI*
Farrell, C P (Auckland) 1977 *BI* 1,2
Fawcett, C L (Auckland) 1976 *SA* 2,3
Fea, W R (Otago) 1921 *SA* 3
Finlay, B E L (Manawatu) 1959 *BI* 1
Finlay, J (Manawatu) 1946 *A* 1
Finlayson, I (North Auckland) 1928 *SA* 1,2,3,4, 1930 *BI* 1,2
Fitzgerald, J T (Wellington) 1952 *A* 1
Fitzpatrick, B B J (Wellington) 1953 *W*, 1954 *I, F*
Fitzpatrick, S B T (Auckland) 1986 *F* 1, *A* 1, *F* 2,3, 1987 *[It, Fj, Arg, S, W, F], A*, 1988 *W* 1,2, *A* 1,2,3, 1989 *F* 1,2, *Arg* 1,2, *A, W, I*, 1990 *S* 1,2, *A* 1,2,3, *F* 1,2, 1991 *Arg* 1,2, *A* 1,2, *[E, US, It, C, A, S]*, 1992 *Wld* 1,2,3, *I* 1,2, *A* 1,2,3, *SA*, 1993 *BI* 1,2,3, *A, WS, S, E*, 1994 *SA* 1,2,3, *A*, 1995 *C*, *[I, W, S, E, SA]*, *A* 1,2, *It, F* 1,2, 1996 *WS, S* 1,2, *A* 1, *SA* 1, *A* 2, *SA* 2,3,4,5, 1997 *Fj, Arg* 1,2, *A* 1, *SA* 1, *A* 2, *SA* 2, *A* 3, *W* (R)
Fleming, J K (Wellington) 1979 *S, E*, 1980 *A* 1,2,3
Fletcher, C J C (North Auckland) 1921 *SA* 3
Fogarty, R (Taranaki) 1921 *SA* 1,3
Ford, B R (Marlborough) 1977 *BI* 3,4, 1978 *I*, 1979 *E*
Forster, S T (Otago) 1993 *S, E*, 1994 *F* 1,2, 1995 *It, F* 1
Fox, G J (Auckland) 1985 *Arg* 1, 1987 *[It, Fj, Arg, S, W, F], A*, 1988 *W* 1,2, *A* 1,2,3, 1989 *F* 1,2, *Arg* 1,2, *A, W, I*, 1990 *S* 1,2, *A* 1,2,3, *F* 1,2, 1991 *Arg* 1,2, *A* 1,2, *[E, It, C, A]*, 1992 *Wld* 1,2 (R), *A* 1,2,3, *SA*, 1993 *BI* 1,2,3, *A, WS*
Francis, A R H (Auckland) 1905 *A*, 1907 *A* 1,2,3, 1908 *AW* 1,2,3, 1910 *A* 1,2,3
Francis, W C (Wellington) 1913 *A* 2,3, 1914 *A* 1,2,3
Fraser, B G (Wellington) 1979 *S, E*, 1980 *A* 3, *W*, 1981 *S* 1,2, *SA* 1,2,3, *R, F* 1,2, 1982 *A* 1,2,3, 1983 *BI* 1,2,3,4, *A, S, E*, 1984 *A* 1
Frazer, H F (Hawke's Bay) 1946 *A* 1,2, 1947 *A* 1, 1949 *SA* 2
Fryer, F C (Canterbury) 1907 *A* 1,2,3, 1908 *AW* 2
Fuller, W B (Canterbury) 1910 *A* 1,2
Furlong, B D M (Hawke's Bay) 1970 *SA* 4

Gallagher, J A (Wellington) 1987 *[It, Fj, S, W, F], A*, 1988 *W* 1,2, *A* 1,2,3, 1989 *F* 1,2, *Arg* 1,2, *A, W, I*
Gallaher, D (Auckland) 1903 *A*, 1904 *BI*, 1905 *S, E, W*, 1906 *F*
Gard, P C (North Otago) 1971 *BI* 4
Gardiner, A J (Taranaki) 1974 *A* 3
Geddes, J H (Southland) 1929 *A* 1
Geddes, W McK (Auckland) 1913 *A* 2
Gemmell, B McL (Auckland) 1974 *A* 1,2

George, V L (Southland) 1938 *A* 1,2,3
Gilbert, G D M (West Coast) 1935 *S, I, W,* 1936 *E*
Gillespie, C T (Wellington) 1913 *A* 2
Gillespie, W D (Otago) 1958 *A* 3
Gillett, G A (Canterbury, Auckland) 1905 *S, I, E, W,* 1907 *A* 2,3, 1908 *AW* 1,3
Gillies, C C (Otago) 1936 *A* 2
Gilray, C M (Otago) 1905 *A*
Glasgow, F T (Taranaki, Southland) 1905 *S, I, E, W,* 1906 *F,* 1908 *AW* 3
Glenn, W S (Taranaki) 1904 *BI,* 1906 *F*
Goddard, M P (South Canterbury) 1946 *A* 2, 1947 *A* 1,2, 1949 *SA* 3,4
Going, S M (North Auckland) 1967 *A, F,* 1968 *F* 3, 1969 *W* 1,2, 1970 *SA* 1 (R), 4, 1971 *BI* 1,2,3,4, 1972 *A* 1,2,3, *W, S,* 1973 *E* 1, *I, F, E* 2, 1974 *I,* 1975 *S,* 1976 *I* (R), *SA* 1,2,3,4, 1977 *BI* 1,2
Gordon, S B (Waikato) 1993 *S, E*
Graham, D J (Canterbury) 1958 *A* 1,2, 1960 *SA* 2,3, 1961 *F* 1,2,3, 1962 *A* 1,2,3,4,5, 1963 *E* 1,2, *I, W,* 1964 *E, S, F, A* 1,2,3
Graham, J B (Otago) 1913 *US,* 1914 *A* 1,3
Graham, W G (Otago) 1979 *F* 1 (R)
Grant, L A (South Canterbury) 1947 *A* 1,2, 1949 *SA* 1,2
Gray, G D (Canterbury) 1908 *AW* 2, 1913 *A* 1, *US*
Gray, K F (Wellington) 1963 *I, W,* 1964 *E, S, F, A* 1,2,3, 1965 *SA* 1,2,3,4, 1966 *BI* 1,2,3,4, 1967 *W, F, S,* 1968 *A* 1, *F* 2,3, 1969 *W* 1,2
Gray, W N (Bay of Plenty) 1955 *A* 2,3, 1956 *SA* 1,2,3,4
Green, C I (Canterbury) 1983 *S* (R), *E,* 1984 *A* 1,2,3, 1985 *E* 1,2, *A, Arg* 1,2, 1986 *A* 2,3, *F* 2,3, 1987 [*It, Fj, S, W, F*], *A*
Grenside, B A (Hawke's Bay) 1928 *SA* 1,2,3,4, 1929 *A* 2,3
Griffiths, J L (Wellington) 1934 *A* 2, 1935 *S, I, W,* 1936 *A* 1,2, 1938 *A* 3
Guy, R A (North Auckland) 1971 *BI* 1,2,3,4

Haden, A M (Auckland) 1977 *BI* 1,2,3,4, *F* 1,2, 1978 *A* 1,2,3, *I, W, E, S,* 1979 *F* 1,2, *A, S, E,* 1980 *A* 1,2,3, *W,* 1981 *S* 2, *SA* 1,2,3, *R, F* 1,2, 1982 *A* 1,2,3, 1983 *BI* 1,2,3,4, *A,* 1984 *F* 1,2, 1985 *Arg* 1,2
Hadley, S (Auckland) 1928 *SA* 1,2,3,4
Hadley, W E (Auckland) 1934 *A* 1,2, 1935 *S, I, W,* 1936 *E, A* 1,2
Haig, J S (Otago) 1946 *A* 1,2
Haig, L S (Otago) 1950 *BI* 2,3,4, 1951 *A* 1,2,3, 1953 *W,* 1954 *E, S*
Hales, D A (Canterbury) 1972 *A* 1,2,3, *W*
Hamilton, D C (Southland) 1908 *AW* 2
Hammond, I A (Marlborough) 1952 *A* 2
Harper, E T (Canterbury) 1904 *BI,* 1906 *F*
Harris, P C (Manawatu) 1976 *SA* 3
Hart, A H (Taranaki) 1924 *I*
Hart, G F (Canterbury) 1930 *BI* 1,2,3,4, 1931 *A,* 1934 *A* 1, 1935 *S, I, W,* 1936 *A* 1,2
Harvey, B A (Wairarapa-Bush) 1986 *F* 1
Harvey, I H (Wairarapa) 1928 *SA* 4
Harvey, L R (Otago) 1949 *SA* 1,2,3,4, 1950 *BI* 1,2,3,4
Harvey, P (Canterbury) 1904 *BI*
Hasell, E W (Canterbury) 1913 *A* 2,3
Hayward, H O (Auckland) 1908 *AW* 3
Hazlett, E J (Southland) 1966 *BI* 1,2,3,4, 1967 *A, E*
Hazlett, W E (Southland) 1928 *SA* 1,2,3,4, 1930 *BI* 1,2,3,4
Heeps, T R (Wellington) 1962 *A* 1,2,3,4,5
Heke, W R (North Auckland) 1929 *A* 1,2,3
Hemi, R C (Waikato) 1953 *W,* 1954 *I, E, S, F,* 1955 *A* 1,2,3, 1956 *SA* 1,3,4, 1957 *A* 1,2, 1959 *BI* 1,3,4
Henderson, P (Wanganui) 1949 *SA* 1,2,3,4, 1950 *BI* 2,3,4
Henderson, P W (Otago) 1991 *Arg* 1, [*C*], 1992 *Wld* 1,2,3, *I* 1, 1995 [*J*]
Herewini, M A (Auckland) 1962 *A* 5, 1963 *I,* 1964 *S, F,* 1965 *SA* 4, 1966 *BI* 1,2,3,4, 1967 *A*
Hewett, J A (Auckland) 1991 [*It*]
Hewitt, N J (Auckland) 1995 [*I* (t), *J*], 1996 *A* 1 (R), 1997 *SA* 1 (R), *I, E* 1, *W, E* 2
Hewson, A R (Wellington) 1981 *S* 1,2, *SA* 1,2,3, *R, F* 1,2, 1982 *A* 1,2,3, 1983 *BI* 1,2,3,4, *A,* 1984 *F* 1,2, *A* 1
Higginson, G (Canterbury, Hawke's Bay) 1980 *W,* 1981 *S* 1, *SA* 1, 1982 *A* 1,2, 1983 *A* 1
Hill, S F (Canterbury) 1955 *A* 3, 1956 *SA* 1,3,4, 1957 *A* 1,2, 1958 *A* 3, 1959 *BI* 1,2,3,4

Hines, G R (Waikato) 1980 *A* 3
Hobbs, M J B (Canterbury) 1983 *BI* 1,2,3,4, *A, S, E,* 1984 *F* 1,2, *A* 1,2,3, 1985 *E* 1,2, *A, Arg* 1,2, 1986 *A* 2,3, *F* 2,3
Holder, E C (Buller) 1934 *A* 2
Hook, L S (Auckland) 1929 *A* 1,2,3
Hooper, J A (Canterbury) 1937 *SA* 1,2,3
Hopkinson, A E (Canterbury) 1967 *S,* 1968 *A* 2, *F* 1,2,3, 1969 *W* 2, 1970 *SA* 1,2,3
Hore, J (Otago) 1930 *BI* 2,3,4, 1932 *A* 1,2,3, 1934 *A* 1,2, 1935 *S,* 1936 *E*
Horsley, R H (Wellington) 1960 *SA* 2,3,4
Hotop, J (Canterbury) 1952 *A* 1,2, 1955 *A* 3
Howarth, S P (Auckland) 1994 *SA* 1,2,3, *A*
Hughes, A M (Auckland) 1949 *A* 1,2, 1950 *BI* 1,2,3,4
Hughes, E (Southland, Wellington) 1907 *A* 1,2,3, 1908 *AW* 1, 1921 *SA* 1,2
Hunter, B A (Otago) 1971 *BI* 1,2,3
Hunter, J (Taranaki) 1905 *S, I, E, W,* 1906 *F,* 1907 *A* 1,2,3, 1908 *AW* 1,2,3
Hurst, I A (Canterbury) 1973 *I, F, E* 2, 1974 *A* 1,2

Ieremia, A I (Wellington) 1994 *SA* 1,2,3, 1995 [*J*], 1996 *SA* 2 (R), 5 (R), 1997 *A* 1 (R), *SA* 1 (R), *A* 2, *SA* 2, *A* 3, *I, E* 1
Ifwersen, K D (Auckland) 1921 *SA* 3
Innes, C R (Auckland) 1989 *W, I,* 1990 *A* 1,2,3, *F* 1,2, 1991 *Arg* 1,2, *A* 1,2, [*E, US, It, C, A, S*]
Innes, G D (Canterbury) 1932 *A* 2
Irvine, I B (North Auckland) 1952 *A* 1
Irvine, J G (Otago) 1914 *A* 1,2,3
Irvine, W R (Hawke's Bay, Wairarapa) 1924 *I, W,* 1925 *E, F,* 1930 *BI* 1
Irwin, M W (Otago) 1955 *A* 1,2, 1956 *SA* 1, 1958 *A* 2, 1959 *BI* 3,4, 1960 *SA* 1

Jackson, E S (Hawke's Bay) 1936 *A* 1,2, 1937 *SA* 1,2,3, 1938 *A* 3
Jaffray, J L (Otago, South Canterbury) 1972 *A* 2, 1975 *S,* 1976 *I, SA* 1, 1977 *BI* 2, 1979 *F* 1,2
Jarden, R A (Wellington) 1951 *A* 1,2, 1952 *A* 1,2, 1953 *W,* 1954 *I, E, S, F,* 1955 *A* 1,2,3, 1956 *SA* 1,2,3,4
Jefferd, A C R (East Coast) 1981 *S* 1,2, *SA* 1
Jessep, E M (Wellington) 1931 *A,* 1932 *A* 1
Johnson, L M (Wellington) 1928 *SA* 1,2,3,4
Johnston, W (Otago) 1907 *A* 1,2,3
Johnstone, B R (Auckland) 1976 *SA* 2, 1977 *BI* 1,2, *F* 1,2, 1978 *I, W, E, S,* 1979 *F* 1,2, *S, E*
Johnstone, P (Otago) 1949 *SA* 2,4, 1950 *BI* 1,2,3,4, 1951 *A* 1,2,3
Jones, I D (North Auckland, North Harbour) 1990 *S* 1,2, *A* 1,2,3, *F* 1,2, 1991 *Arg* 1,2, *A* 1,2, [*E, US, It, C, A, S*], 1992 *Wld* 1,2,3, *I* 1,2, *A* 1,2,3, *SA,* 1993 *BI* 1,2 (R), 3, *WS, S, E,* 1994 *F* 1,2, *SA* 1,3, *A,* 1995 *C,* [*I, W, S, E, SA*], *A* 1,2, *It, F* 1,2, 1996 *WS, S* 1,2, *A* 1, *SA* 1, *A* 2, *SA* 2,3,4,5, 1997 *Fj, Arg* 1,2, *A* 1, *SA* 1, *A* 2, *SA* 2, *A* 3, *I, E* 1, *W, E* 2
Jones, M G (North Auckland) 1973 *E* 2
Jones, M N (Auckland) 1987 [*It, Fj, S, F*], *A,* 1988 *W* 1,2, *A* 2,3, 1989 *F* 1,2, *Arg* 1,2, 1990 *F* 1,2, 1991 *Arg* 1,2, *A* 1,2, [*E, US, S*], 1992 *Wld* 1,3, *I* 2, *A* 1,3, *SA,* 1993 *BI* 1,2,3, *A, WS,* 1994 *SA* 3 (R), *A,* 1995 *A* 1 (R), 2, *It, F* 1,2, 1996 *WS, S* 1,2, *A* 1, *SA* 1, *A* 2, *SA* 2,3,4,5, 1997 *Fj*
Jones, P F H (North Auckland) 1954 *E, S,* 1955 *A* 1,2, 1956 *SA* 3,4, 1958 *A* 1,2,3, 1959 *BI* 1, 1960 *SA* 1
Joseph, H T (Canterbury) 1971 *BI* 2,3
Joseph, J W (Otago) 1992 *Wld* 2,3 (R), *I* 1, *A* 1 (R), 3, *SA,* 1993 *BI* 1,2,3, *A, WS, S, E,* 1994 *SA* 2 (t), 1995 *C,* [*I, W, J* (R), *S, SA* (R)]

Karam, J F (Wellington, Horowhenua) 1972 *W, S,* 1973 *E* 1, *I, F,* 1974 *A* 1,2,3, *I,* 1975 *S*
Katene, T (Wellington) 1955 *A* 2
Kearney, J C (Otago) 1947 *A* 2, 1949 *SA* 1,2,3
Kelly, J W (Auckland) 1949 *A* 1,2
Kember, G F (Wellington) 1970 *SA* 4
Ketels, R C (Counties) 1980 *W,* 1981 *S* 1,2, *R, F* 1
Kiernan, H A D (Auckland) 1903 *A*
Kilby, F D (Wellington) 1932 *A* 1,2,3, 1934 *A* 2
Killeen, B A (Auckland) 1936 *A* 1
King, R R (West Coast) 1934 *A* 2, 1935 *S, I, W,* 1936 *E, A* 1,2, 1937 *SA* 1,2,3, 1938 *A* 1,2,3
Kingstone, C N (Taranaki) 1921 *SA* 1,2,3

Meads, S T (King Country) 1961 *F* 1, 1962 *A* 4,5, 1963 *I*, 1964 *A* 1,2,3, 1965 *SA* 1,2,3,4, 1966 *BI* 1,2,3,4
Meates, K F (Canterbury) 1952 *A* 1,2
Meates, W A (Otago) 1949 *SA* 2,3,4, 1950 *BI* 1,2,3,4
Mehrtens, A P (Canterbury) 1995 *C*, [*I, W, S, E, SA*], *A* 1,2, 1996 *WS, S* 1,2, *A* 1, *SA* 1, *A* 2, *SA* 2,5, 1997 *Fj, SA* 2 (R), *I, E* 1, *W, E* 2
Metcalfe, T C (Southland) 1931 *A*, 1932 *A* 1
Mexted, G G (Wellington) 1950 *BI* 4
Mexted, M G (Wellington) 1979 *S, E*, 1980 *A* 1,2,3, *W*, 1981 *S* 1,2, *SA* 1,2,3, *R, F* 1,2, 1982 *A* 1,2,3, 1983 *BI* 1,2,3,4, *A, S, E*, 1984 *F* 1,2, *A* 1,2,3, 1985 *E* 1,2, *A, Arg* 1,2
Mill, J J (Hawke's Bay, Wairarapa) 1924 *W*, 1925 *E, F*, 1930 *BI* 1
Milliken, H M (Canterbury) 1938 *A* 1,2,3
Milner, H P (Wanganui) 1970 *SA* 3
Mitchell, N A (Southland, Otago) 1935 *S, I, W*, 1936 *E, A* 2, 1937 *SA* 3, 1938 *A* 1,2
Mitchell, T W (Canterbury) 1976 *SA* 4 (R)
Mitchell, W J (Canterbury) 1910 *A* 2,3
Mitchinson, F E (Wellington) 1907 *A* 1,2,3, 1908 *AW* 1,2,3, 1910 *A* 1,2,3, 1913 *A* 1 (R), *US*
Moffitt, J E (Wellington) 1921 *SA* 1,2,3
Moore, G J T (Otago) 1949 *A* 1
Moreton, R C (Canterbury) 1962 *A* 3,4, 1964 *A* 1,2,3, 1965 *SA* 2,3
Morgan, J E (North Auckland) 1974 *A* 3, *I*, 1976 *SA* 2,3,4
Morris, T J (Nelson Bays) 1972 *A* 1,2,3
Morrison, T C (South Canterbury) 1938 *A* 1,2,3
Morrison, T G (Otago) 1973 *E* 2 (R)

Morrissey, P J (Canterbury) 1962 *A* 3,4,5
Mourie, G N K (Taranaki) 1977 *BI* 3,4, *F* 1,2, 1978 *I, W, E, S*, 1979 *F* 1,2, *A, S, E*, 1980 *W*, 1981 *S* 1,2, *F* 1,2, 1982 *A* 1,2,3
Muller, B L (Taranaki) 1967 *A, E, W, F*, 1968 *A* 1, *F* 1, 1969 *W* 1, 1970 *SA* 1,2,4, 1971 *BI* 1,2,3,4
Mumm, W J (Buller) 1949 *A* 1
Murdoch, K (Otago) 1970 *SA* 4, 1972 *A* 3, *W*
Murdoch, P H (Auckland) 1964 *A* 2,3, 1965 *SA* 1,2,3
Murray, H V (Canterbury) 1913 *A* 1, *US*, 1914 *A* 2,3
Murray, P C (Wanganui) 1908 *AW* 2
Myers, R G (Waikato) 1978 *A* 3
Mynott, H J (Taranaki) 1905 *I, W*, 1906 *F*, 1907 *A* 1,2,3, 1910 *A* 1,3

Nathan, W J (Auckland) 1962 *A* 1,2,3,4,5, 1963 *E* 1,2, *W*, 1964 *F*, 1966 *BI* 1,2,3,4, 1967 *A*
Nelson, K A (Otago) 1962 *A* 4,5
Nepia, G (Hawke's Bay, East Coast) 1924 *I, W*, 1925 *E, F*, 1929 *A* 1, 1930 *BI* 1,2,3,4
Nesbit, S R (Auckland) 1960 *SA* 2,3
Newton, F (Canterbury) 1905 *E, W*, 1906 *F*
Nicholls, H E (Wellington) 1921 *SA* 1
Nicholls, M F (Wellington) 1921 *SA* 1,2,3, 1924 *I, W*, 1925 *E, F*, 1928 *SA* 4, 1930 *BI* 2,3
Nicholson, G W (Auckland) 1903 *A*, 1904 *BI*, 1907 *A* 2,3
Norton, R W (Canterbury) 1971 *BI* 1,2,3,4, 1972 *A* 1,2,3, *W, S*, 1973 *E* 1, *I, F, E* 2, 1974 *A* 1,2,3, *I*, 1975 *S*, 1976 *I, SA* 1,2,3,4, 1977 *BI* 1,2,3,4

The New Zealand place-kicker Andrew Mehrtens lines up a kick in the World Cup match against Wales on 31 May 1995.

O'Brien, J G (Auckland) 1914 *A* 1
O'Callaghan, M W (Manawatu) 1968 *F* 1,2,3
O'Callaghan, T R (Wellington) 1949 *A* 2
O'Donnell, D H (Wellington) 1949 *A* 2
Old, G H (Manawatu) 1981 *SA* 3, *R* (R), 1982 *A* 1 (R)
O'Leary, M J (Auckland) 1910 *A* 1,3, 1913 *A* 2,3
Oliver, A D (Otago) 1997 *Fj* (t)
Oliver, C J (Canterbury) 1929 *A* 1,2, 1934 *A* 1, 1935 *S, I, W,* 1936 *E*
Oliver, D J (Wellington) 1930 *BI* 1,2
Oliver, D O (Otago) 1954 *I, F*
Oliver, F J (Southland, Otago, Manawatu) 1976 *SA* 4, 1977 *BI* 1,2,3,4, *F* 1,2, 1978 *A* 1,2,3, *I, W, E, S,* 1979 *F* 1,2, 1981 *SA* 2
Orr, R W (Otago) 1949 *A* 1
Osborne, G M (North Harbour) 1995 *C,* [*I, W, J, E, SA*], *A* 1,2, *F* 1 (R), 2, 1996 *SA* 2,3,4,5, 1997 *Arg* 1 (R), *A* 2,3, *I*
Osborne, W M (Wanganui) 1975 *S,* 1976 *SA* 2 (R), 4 (R), 1977 *BI* 1,2,3,4, *F* 1,2, 1978 *I, W, E, S,* 1980 *W,* 1982 *A* 1,3
O'Sullivan, J M (Taranaki) 1905 *S, I, E, W,* 1907 *A* 3
O'Sullivan, T P A (Taranaki) 1960 *SA* 1, 1961 *F* 1, 1962 *A* 1,2

Page, J R (Wellington) 1931 *A,* 1932 *A* 1,2,3, 1934 *A* 1,2
Palmer, B P (Auckland) 1929 *A* 2, 1932 *A* 2,3
Parker, J H (Canterbury) 1924 *I, W,* 1925 *E*
Parkhill, A A (Otago) 1937 *SA* 1,2,3, 1938 *A* 1,2,3
Parkinson, R M (Poverty Bay) 1972 *A* 1,2,3, *W, S,* 1973 *E* 1,2
Paterson, A M (Otago) 1908 *AW* 2,3, 1910 *A* 1,2,3
Paton, H (Otago) 1910 *A* 1,3
Pene, A R B (Otago) 1992 *Wld* 1 (R), 2,3, *I* 1,2, *A* 1,2 (R), 1993 *BI* 3, *A, WS, S, E,* 1994 *F* 1,2 (R), *SA* 1 (R)
Phillips, W J (King Country) 1937 *SA* 2, 1938 *A* 1,2
Philpott, S (Canterbury) 1991 [*It* (R), *S* (R)]
Pickering, E A R (Waikato) 1958 *A* 2, 1959 *BI* 1,4
Pierce, M J (Wellington) 1985 *F* 1,2, *A, Arg* 1, 1986 *A* 2,3, *F* 2,3, 1987 [*It, Arg, S, W, F*], *A,* 1988 *W* 1,2, *A* 1,2,3, 1989 *F* 1,2, *Arg* 1,2, *A, W, I*
Pokere, S T (Southland, Auckland) 1981 *SA* 3, 1982 *A* 1,2,3, 1983 *BI* 1,2,3,4, *A, S, E,* 1984 *F* 1,2, *A* 2,3, 1985 *E* 1,2, *A*
Pollock, H R (Wellington) 1932 *A* 1,2,3, 1936 *A* 1,2
Porter, C G (Wellington) 1925 *F,* 1929 *A* 2,3, 1930 *BI* 1,2,3,4
Preston, J P (Canterbury, Wellington) 1991 [*US, S*], 1992 *SA* (R), 1993 *BI* 2,3, *A, WS,* 1996 *SA* 4 (R), 1997 *I* (R), *E* 1 (R)
Procter, A C (Otago) 1932 *A* 1
Purdue, C A (Southland) 1905 *A*
Purdue, E (Southland) 1905 *A*
Purdue, G B (Southland) 1931 *A,* 1932 *A* 1,2,3
Purvis, G R (Waikato) 1991 [*US*], 1993 *WS*
Purvis, N A (Otago) 1976 *I*

Quaid, C E (Otago) 1938 *A* 1,2

Randell, T C (Otago) 1997 *Fj, Arg* 1,2, *A* 1, *SA* 1, *A* 2, *SA* 2, *A* 3, *I, E* 1, *W, E* 2
Rangi, R E (Auckland) 1964 *A* 2,3, 1965 *SA* 1,2,3,4, 1966 *BI* 1,2,3,4
Rankin, J G (Canterbury) 1936 *A* 1,2, 1937 *SA* 2
Reedy, W J (Wellington) 1908 *AW* 2,3
Reid, A R (Waikato) 1952 *A* 1, 1956 *SA* 3,4, 1957 *A* 1,2
Reid, H R (Bay of Plenty) 1980 *A* 1,2, *W,* 1983 *S, E,* 1985 *Arg* 1,2, 1986 *A* 2,3
Reid, K H (Wairarapa) 1929 *A* 1,3
Reid, S T (Hawke's Bay) 1935 *I, W,* 1936 *E, A* 1,2, 1937 *SA* 1,2,3
Reside, W B (Wairarapa) 1929 *A* 1
Rhind, P K (Canterbury) 1946 *A* 1,2
Richardson, J (Otago, Southland) 1921 *SA* 1,2,3, 1924 *I, W,* 1925 *E, F*
Rickit, H (Waikato) 1981 *S* 1,2
Riechelmann, C C (Auckland) 1997 *Fj* (R), *Arg* 1 (R), *A* 1 (R), *SA* 2 (t), *I* (R), *E* 2 (t)
Ridland, A J (Southland) 1910 *A* 1,2,3
Roberts, E J (Wellington) 1914 *A* 1,2,3, 1921 *SA* 2,3
Roberts, F (Wellington) 1905 *S, I, E, W,* 1907 *A* 1,2,3, 1908 *AW* 1,3, 1910 *A* 1,2,3
Roberts, R W (Taranaki) 1913 *A* 1, *US,* 1914 *A* 1,2,3

Robertson, B J (Counties) 1972 *A* 1,3, *S,* 1973 *E* 1, *I, F,* 1974 *A* 1,2,3, *I,* 1976 *I, SA* 1,2,3,4, 1977 *BI* 1,3,4, *F* 1,2, 1978 *A* 1,2,3, *W, E, S,* 1979 *F* 1,2, *A,* 1980 *A* 2,3, *W,* 1981 *S* 1,2
Robertson, D J (Otago) 1974 *A* 1,2,3, *I,* 1975 *S,* 1976 *I, SA* 1,3,4, 1977 *BI* 1
Robilliard, A C C (Canterbury) 1928 *SA* 1,2,3,4
Robinson, C E (Southland) 1951 *A* 1,2,3, 1952 *A* 1,2
Rollerson, D L (Manawatu) 1980 *W,* 1981 *S* 2, *SA* 1,2,3, *R, F* 1 (R), 2
Roper, R A (Taranaki) 1949 *A* 2, 1950 *BI* 1,2,3,4
Rowley, H C B (Wanganui) 1949 *A* 2
Rush, E J (North Harbour) 1995 [*W* (R), *J*], *It, F* 1,2, 1996 *S* 1 (R), 2, *A* 1 (t), *SA* 1 (R)
Rutledge, L M (Southland) 1978 *A* 1,2,3, *I, W, E, S,* 1979 *F* 1,2, *A,* 1980 *A* 1,2,3
Ryan, J (Wellington) 1910 *A* 2, 1914 *A* 1,2,3

Sadler, B S (Wellington) 1935 *S, I, W,* 1936 *A* 1,2
Salmon, J L B (Wellington) 1981 *R, F* 1,2 (R)
Savage, L T (Canterbury) 1949 *SA* 1,2,4
Saxton, C K (South Canterbury) 1938 *A* 1,2,3
Schuler, K J (Manawatu, North Harbour) 1990 *A* 2 (R), 1992 *A* 2, 1995 [*I* (R), *J*]
Schuster, N J (Wellington) 1988 *A* 1,2,3, 1989 *F* 1,2, *Arg* 1,2, *A, W, I*
Scott, R W H (Auckland) 1946 *A* 1,2, 1947 *A* 1,2, 1949 *SA* 1,2,3,4, 1950 *BI* 1,2,3,4, 1953 *W,* 1954 *I, E, S, F*
Scown, A I (Taranaki) 1972 *A* 1,2,3, *W* (R), *S*
Scrimshaw, G (Canterbury) 1928 *SA* 1
Seear, G A (Otago) 1977 *F* 1,2, 1978 *A* 1,2,3, *I, W, E, S,* 1979 *F* 1,2, *A*
Seeling, C E (Auckland) 1904 *BI,* 1905 *S, I, E, W,* 1906 *F,* 1907 *A* 1,2, 1908 *AW* 1,2,3
Sellars, G M V (Auckland) 1913 *A* 1, *US*
Shaw, M W (Manawatu, Hawke's Bay) 1980 *A* 1,2,3 (R), *W,* 1981 *S* 1,2, *SA* 1,2, *R, F* 1,2, 1982 *A* 1,2,3, 1983 *BI* 1,2,3,4, *A, S, E,* 1984 *F* 1,2, *A* 1, 1985 *E* 1,2, *A, Arg* 1,2, 1986 *A* 3
Shelford, F N K (Bay of Plenty) 1981 *SA* 3, *R,* 1984 *A* 2,3
Shelford, W T (North Harbour) 1986 *F* 2,3, 1987 [*It, Fj, S, W, F*], *A,* 1988 *W* 1,2, *A* 1,2,3, 1989 *F* 1,2, *Arg* 1,2, *A, W, I,* 1990 *S* 1,2
Siddells, S K (Wellington) 1921 *SA* 3
Simon, H J (Otago) 1937 *SA* 1,2,3
Simpson, J G (Auckland) 1947 *A* 1,2, 1949 *SA* 1,2,3,4, 1950 *BI* 1,2,3,4
Simpson, V L J (Canterbury) 1985 *Arg* 1,2
Sims, G S (Otago) 1972 *A* 2
Skeen, J R (Auckland) 1952 *A* 2
Skinner, K L (Otago, Counties) 1949 *SA* 1,2,3,4, 1950 *BI* 1,2,3,4, 1951 *A* 1,2,3, 1952 *A* 1,2, 1953 *W,* 1954 *I, E, S, F,* 1956 *SA* 3,4
Skudder, G R (Waikato) 1969 *W* 2
Sloane, P H (North Auckland) 1979 *E*
Smith, A E (Taranaki) 1969 *W* 1,2, 1970 *SA* 1
Smith, B W (Waikato) 1984 *F* 1,2, *A* 1
Smith, G W (Auckland) 1905 *S, I*
Smith, I S T (Otago, North Otago) 1964 *A* 1,2,3, 1965 *SA* 1,2,4, 1966 *BI* 1,2,3
Smith, J B (North Auckland) 1946 *A* 1, 1947 *A* 2, 1949 *A* 1,2
Smith, R M (Canterbury) 1955 *A* 1
Smith, W E (Nelson) 1905 *A*
Smith, W R (Canterbury) 1980 *A* 1, 1982 *A* 1,2,3, 1983 *BI* 2,3, *S, E,* 1984 *F* 1,2, *A* 1,2,3, 1985 *E* 1,2, *A, Arg* 2
Snow, E M (Nelson) 1929 *A* 1,2,3
Solomon, F (Auckland) 1931 *A,* 1932 *A* 2,3
Sonntag, W T C (Otago) 1929 *A* 1,2,3
Speight, M W (Waikato) 1986 *A* 1
Spencer, C J (Auckland) 1997 *Arg* 1,2, *A* 1, *SA* 1, *A* 2, *SA* 2, *A* 3, *E* 2 (R)
Spencer, J C (Wellington) 1905 *A,* 1907 *A* 1 (R)
Spiers, J E (Counties) 1979 *S, E,* 1981 *R, F* 1,2
Spillane, A P (South Canterbury) 1913 *A* 2,3
Stanley, J T (Auckland) 1986 *F* 1, *A* 1,2,3, *F* 2,3, 1987 [*It, Fj, Arg, S, W, F*], *A,* 1988 *W* 1,2, *A* 1,2,3, 1989 *F* 1,2, *Arg* 1,2, *A, W, I,* 1990 *S* 1,2
Stead, J W (Southland) 1904 *BI,* 1905 *S, I, E,* 1906 *F,* 1908 *AW* 1,3
Steel, A G (Canterbury) 1966 *BI* 1,2,3,4, 1967 *A, F, S,* 1968 *A* 1,2
Steel, J (West Coast) 1921 *SA* 1,2,3, 1924 *W,* 1925 *E, F*

Steele, L B (Wellington) 1951 *A* 1,2,3
Steere, E R G (Hawke's Bay) 1930 *BI* 1,2,3,4, 1931 *A*, 1932 *A* 1
Stensness, L (Auckland) 1993 *BI* 3, *A*, *WS*, 1997 *Fj*, *Arg* 1,2, *A* 1, *SA* 1
Stephens, O G (Wellington) 1968 *F* 3
Stevens, I N (Wellington) 1972 *S*, 1973 *E* 1, 1974 *A* 3
Stewart, A J (Canterbury, South Canterbury) 1963 *E* 1,2, *I*, *W*, 1964 *E*, *S*, *F*, *A* 3
Stewart, J D (Auckland) 1913 *A* 2,3
Stewart, K W (Southland) 1973 *E* 2, 1974 *A* 1,2,3, *I*, 1975 *S*, 1976 *I*, *SA* 1,3, 1979 *S*, *E*, 1981 *SA* 1,2
Stewart, R T (South Canterbury, Canterbury) 1928 *SA* 1,2,3,4, 1930 *BI* 2
Stohr, L B (Taranaki) 1910 *A* 1,2,3
Stone, A M (Waikato, Bay of Plenty) 1981 *F* 1,2, 1983 *BI* 3 (R), 1984 *A* 3, 1986 *F* 1, *A* 1,3, *F* 2,3
Storey, P W (South Canterbury) 1921 *SA* 1,2
Strachan, A D (Auckland, North Harbour) 1992 *Wld* 2,3, *I* 1,2, *A* 1,2,3, *SA*, 1993 *BI* 1, 1995 [*J*, *SA* (t)]
Strahan, S C (Manawatu) 1967 *A*, *E*, *W*, *F*, *S*, 1968 *A* 1,2, *F* 1,2,3, 1970 *SA* 1,2,3, 1972 *A* 1,2,3, 1973 *E* 2
Strang, W A (South Canterbury) 1928 *SA* 1,2, 1930 *BI* 3,4, 1931 *A*
Stringfellow, J C (Wairarapa) 1929 *A* 1 (R), 3
Stuart, K C (Canterbury) 1955 *A* 1
Stuart, R C (Canterbury) 1949 *A* 1,2, 1953 *W*, 1954 *I*, *E*, *S*, *F*
Stuart, R L (Hawke's Bay) 1977 *F* 1 (R)
Sullivan, J L (Taranaki) 1937 *SA* 1,2,3, 1938 *A* 1,2,3
Sutherland, A R (Marlborough) 1970 *SA* 2,4, 1971 *BI* 1, 1972 *A* 1,2,3, *W*, 1973 *E* 1, *I*, *F*
Svenson, K S (Wellington) 1924 *I*, *W*, 1925 *E*, *F*
Swain, J P (Hawke's Bay) 1928 *SA* 1,2,3,4

Tanner, J M (Auckland) 1950 *BI* 4, 1951 *A* 1,2,3, 1953 *W*
Tanner, K J (Canterbury) 1974 *A* 1,2,3, *I*, 1975 *S*, 1976 *I*, *SA* 1
Taylor, G L (Northland) 1996 *SA* 5 (R)
Taylor, H M (Canterbury) 1913 *A* 1, *US*, 1914 *A* 1,2,3
Taylor, J M (Otago) 1937 *SA* 1,2,3, 1938 *A* 1,2,3
Taylor, M B (Waikato) 1979 *F* 1,2, *A*, *S*, *E*, 1980 *A* 1,2
Taylor, N M (Bay of Plenty, Hawke's Bay) 1977 *BI* 2, 4 (R), *F* 1,2, 1978 *A* 1,2,3, *I*, 1982 *A* 2
Taylor, R (Taranaki) 1913 *A* 2,3
Taylor, W T (Canterbury) 1983 *BI* 1,2,3,4, *A*, *S*, 1984 *F* 1,2, *A* 1,2, 1985 *E* 1,2, *A*, *Arg* 1,2, 1986 *A* 2, 1987 [*It*, *Fj*, *S*, *W*, *F*], *A*, 1988 *W* 1,2
Tetzlaff, P L (Auckland) 1947 *A* 1,2
Thimbleby, N W (Hawke's Bay) 1970 *SA* 3
Thomas, B T (Auckland, Wellington) 1962 *A* 5, 1964 *A* 1,2,3
Thomson, H D (Wellington) 1908 *AW* 1
Thorne, G S (Auckland) 1968 *A* 1,2, *F* 1,2,3, 1969 *W* 1, 1970 *SA* 1,2,3,4
Thornton, N H (Auckland) 1947 *A* 1,2, 1949 *SA* 1
Tilyard, J T (Wellington) 1913 *A* 3
Timu, J K R (Otago) 1991 *Arg* 1, *A* 1,2, [*E*, *US*, *C*, *A*], 1992 *Wld* 2, *I* 2, *A* 1,2,3, *SA*, 1993 *BI* 1,2,3, *A*, *WS*, *S*, *E*, 1994 *F* 1,2, *SA* 1,2,3, *A*
Tindill, E W T (Wellington) 1936 *E*
Tonu'u, O F J (Auckland) 1997 *Fj* (R), *A* 3 (R)
Townsend, L J (Otago) 1955 *A* 1,3
Tremain, K R (Canterbury, Hawke's Bay) 1959 *BI* 2,3,4, 1960 *SA* 1,2,3,4, 1961 *F* 2,3 1962 *A* 1,2,3, 1963 *E* 1,2, *I*, *W*, 1964 *E*, *S*, *F*, *A* 1,2,3, 1965 *SA* 1,2,3,4, 1966 *BI* 1,2,3,4, 1967 *A*, *E*, *W*, *S*, 1968 *A* 1, *F* 1,2,3
Trevathan, D (Otago) 1937 *SA* 1,2,3
Tuck, J M (Waikato) 1929 *A* 1,2,3
Tuigamala, V L (Auckland) 1991 [*US*, *It*, *C*, *S*], 1992 *Wld* 1,2,3, *I* 1, *A* 1,2,3, *SA*, 1993 *BI* 1,2,3, *A*, *WS*, *S*, *E*
Turner, R S (North Harbour) 1992 *Wld* 1,2 (R)
Turtill, H S (Canterbury) 1905 *A*
Twigden, T M (Auckland) 1980 *A* 2,3
Tyler, G A (Auckland) 1903 *A*, 1904 *BI*, 1905 *S*, *I*, *E*, *W*, 1906 *F*

Udy, D K (Wairarapa) 1903 *A*
Umaga, T J F (Wellington) 1997 *Fj*, *Arg* 1,2, *A* 1, *SA* 1,2
Urbahn, R J (Taranaki) 1959 *BI* 1,3,4
Urlich, R A (Auckland) 1970 *SA* 3,4
Uttley, I N (Wellington) 1963 *E* 1,2

Vincent, P B (Canterbury) 1956 *SA* 1,2
Vodanovich, I M H (Wellington) 1955 *A* 1,2,3

Wallace, W J (Wellington) 1903 *A*, 1904 *BI*, 1905 *S*, *I*, *E*, *W*, 1906 *F*, 1907 *A* 1,2,3, 1908 *AW* 2
Walsh, P T (Counties) 1955 *A* 1,2,3, 1956 *SA* 1,2,4, 1957 *A* 1,2, 1958 *A* 1,2,3, 1959 *BI* 1, 1963 *E* 2
Ward, R H (Southland) 1936 *A* 2, 1937 *SA* 1,3
Waterman, A C (North Auckland) 1929 *A* 1,2
Watkins, E L (Wellington) 1905 *A*
Watt, B A (Canterbury) 1962 *A* 1,4, 1963 *E* 1,2, *W*, 1964 *E*, *S*, *A* 1
Watt, J M (Otago) 1936 *A* 1,2
Watt, J R (Wellington) 1958 *A* 2, 1960 *SA* 1,2,3,4, 1961 *F* 1,3, 1962 *A* 1,2
Watts, M G (Taranaki) 1979 *F* 1,2, 1980 *A* 1,2,3 (R)
Webb, D S (North Auckland) 1959 *BI* 2
Wells, J (Wellington) 1936 *A* 1,2
West, A H (Taranaki) 1921 *SA* 2,3
Whetton, A J (Auckland) 1984 *A* 1 (R), 3 (R), 1985 *A* (R), *Arg* 1 (R), 1986 *A* 2, 1987 [*It*, *Fj*, *Arg*, *S*, *W*, *F*], *A*, 1988 *W* 1,2, *A*, 1989 *F* 1,2, *Arg* 1,2, *A*, 1990 *S* 1,2, *A* 1,2,3, *F* 1,2, 1991 *Arg* 1, [*E*, *US*, *It*, *C*, *A*]
Whetton, G W (Auckland) 1981 *SA* 3, *R*, *F* 1,2, 1982 *A* 3, 1983 *BI* 1,2,3,4, 1984 *F* 1,2, *A* 1,2,3, 1985 *E* 1,2, *A*, *Arg* 2, 1986 *A* 2,3, *F* 2,3, 1987 [*It*, *Fj*, *Arg*, *S*, *W*, *F*], *A*, 1988 *W* 1,2, *A*, 1989 *F* 1,2, *Arg* 1,2, *A*, *W*, *I*, 1990 *S* 1,2, *A* 1,2,3, *F* 1,2, 1991 *Arg* 1,2, *A* 1,2, [*E*, *US*, *It*, *C*, *A*, *S*]
Whineray, W J (Canterbury, Waikato, Auckland) 1957 *A* 1,2, 1958 *A* 1,2,3, 1959 *BI* 1,2,3,4, 1960 *SA* 1,2,3,4, 1961 *F* 1,2,3, 1962 *A* 1,2,3,4,5, 1963 *E* 1,2, *I*, *W*, 1964 *E*, *S*, *F*, 1965 *SA* 1,2,3,4
White, A (Southland) 1921 *SA* 1, 1924 *I*, 1925 *E*, *F*
White, H L (Auckland) 1954 *I*, *E*, *F*, 1955 *A* 3
White, R A (Poverty Bay) 1949 *A* 1,2, 1950 *BI* 1,2,3,4, 1951 *A* 1,2,3, 1952 *A* 1,2, 1953 *W*, 1954 *I*, *E*, *S*, *F*, 1955 *A* 1,2,3, 1956 *SA* 1,2,3,4
White, R M (Wellington) 1946 *A* 1,2, 1947 *A* 1,2
Whiting, G J (King Country) 1972 *A* 1,2, *S*, 1973 *E* 1, *I*, *F*
Whiting, P J (Auckland) 1971 *BI* 1,2,4, 1972 *A* 1,2,3, *W*, *S*, 1973 *E* 1, *I*, *F*, 1974 *A* 1,2,3, *I*, 1976 *I*, *SA* 1,2,3,4
Williams, B G (Auckland) 1970 *SA* 1,2,3,4, 1971 *BI* 1,2,4, 1972 *A* 1,2,3, *W*, *S*, 1973 *E* 1, *I*, *F*, *E* 2, 1974 *A* 1,2,3, *I*, 1975 *S*, 1976 *I*, *SA* 1,2,3,4, 1977 *BI* 1,2,3,4, *F* 1, 1978 *A* 1,2,3, *I*, *W*, *E*, *S*
Williams, G C (Wellington) 1967 *E*, *W*, *F*, *S*, 1968 *A* 2
Williams, P (Otago) 1913 *A* 1
Williment, M (Wellington) 1964 *A* 1, 1965 *SA* 1,2,3, 1966 *BI* 1,2,3,4, 1967 *A*
Willocks, C (Otago) 1946 *A* 1,2, 1949 *SA* 1,3,4
Wilson, B W (Otago) 1977 *BI* 3,4, 1978 *A* 1,2,3, 1979 *F* 1,2, *A*
Wilson, D D (Canterbury) 1954 *E*, *S*
Wilson, H W (Otago) 1949 *A* 1, 1950 *BI* 4, 1951 *A* 1,2,3
Wilson, J W (Otago) 1993 *S*, *E*, 1994 *A*, 1995 *C*, [*I*, *J*, *S*, *E*, *SA*], *A* 1,2, *It*, *F* 1, 1996 *WS*, *S* 1,2, *A* 1, *SA* 1, *A* 2, *SA* 2,3,4,5, 1997 *Fj*, *Arg* 1,2, *A* 1, *SA* 1, *A* 2, *SA* 2, *A* 3, *I*, *E* 1, *W*, *E* 2
Wilson, N A (Wellington) 1908 *AW* 1,2, 1910 *A* 1,2,3, 1913 *A* 2,3, 1914 *A* 1,2,3
Wilson, N L (Otago) 1951 *A* 1,2,3
Wilson, R G (Canterbury) 1979 *S*, *E*
Wilson, S S (Wellington) 1977 *F* 1,2, 1978 *A* 1,2,3, *I*, *W*, *E*, *S*, 1979 *F* 1,2, *A*, *S*, *E*, 1980 *A* 1, *W*, 1981 *S* 1,2, *A* 1,2,3, *R*, *F* 1,2, 1982 *A* 1,2,3, 1983 *BI* 1,2,3,4, *A*, *S*
Wolfe, T N (Wellington, Taranaki) 1961 *F* 1,2,3, 1962 *A* 2,3, 1963 *E* 1
Wood, M E (Canterbury, Auckland) 1903 *A*, 1904 *BI*
Woodman, F A (North Auckland) 1981 *SA* 1,2, *F* 2
Wrigley, E (Wairarapa) 1905 *A*
Wright, T J (Auckland) 1986 *F* 1, *A* 1, 1987 [*Arg*], 1988 *W* 1,2, *A* 1,2, 1989 *F* 1,2, *Arg* 1,2, *A*, *W*, *I*, 1990 *S* 1,2, *A* 1,2,3, *F* 1,2, 1991 *Arg* 1,2, *A* 1,2, [*E*, *US*, *It*, *S*]
Wylie, J T (Auckland) 1913 *A* 1, *US*
Wyllie, A J (Canterbury) 1970 *SA* 2,3, 1971 *BI* 2,3,4, 1972 *W*, *S*, 1973 *E* 1, *I*, *F*, *E* 2

Yates, V M (North Auckland) 1961 *F* 1,2,3
Young, D (Canterbury) 1956 *SA* 2, 1958 *A* 1,2,3, 1960 *SA* 1,2,3,4, 1961 *F* 1,2,3, 1962 *A* 1,2,3,5, 1963 *E* 1,2, *I*, *W*, 1964 *E*, *S*, *F*

NEW ZEALAND INTERNATIONAL RECORDS (*up to 30 April 1998*)

MATCH RECORDS

MOST CONSECUTIVE TEST WINS

17 1965 *SA* 4, 1966 *BI* 1,2,3,4, 1967 *A,E,W,F,S,* 1968 *A* 1,2, *F* 1,2,3, 1969 *W* 1,2

12 1988 *A* 3, 1989 *F* 1,2, *Arg* 1,2, *A,W,I,* 1990 *S* 1,2, *A* 1,2

MOST CONSECUTIVE TESTS WITHOUT DEFEAT

P	W	D	Period
23	22	1	1987–90
17	15	2	1961–64
17	17	0	1965–69

MOST POINTS IN A MATCH
by the team

Pts	Opp	Venue	Year
145	J	Bloemfontein	1995
93	Arg	Wellington	1997
74	Fj	Christchurch	1987
73	C	Auckland	1995
71	Fj	Albany	1997

by a player

45 by S D Culhane v Japan at Bloemfontein — 1995
33 by C J Spencer v Argentina at Wellington — 1997
33 by A P Mehrtens v Ireland at Dublin — 1997
30 by M C G Ellis v Japan at Bloemfontein — 1995
28 by A P Mehrtens v Canada at Auckland — 1995

MOST TRIES IN A MATCH
by the team

T	Opp	Venue	Year
21	J	Bloemfontein	1995
14	Arg	Wellington	1997
13	US	Berkeley	1913
12	It	Auckland	1987
12	Fj	Christchurch	1987

by a player

6 by M C G Ellis v Japan at Bloemfontein — 1995
5 by J W Wilson v Fiji at Albany — 1997
4 by D McGregor v England at Crystal Palace — 1905

4 by C I Green v Fiji at Christchurch — 1987
4 by J A Gallagher v Fiji at Christchurch — 1987
4 by J J Kirwan v Wales at Christchurch — 1988
4 by J T Lomu v England at Cape Town — 1995
4 by C M Cullen v Scotland at Dunedin — 1996

MOST CONVERSIONS IN A MATCH
by the team

C	Opp	Venue	Year
20	J	Bloemfontein	1995
10	Fj	Christchurch	1987
10	Arg	Wellington	1997
8	It	Auckland	1987
8	W	Auckland	1988
8	Fj	Albany	1997

by a player

20 by S D Culhane v Japan at Bloemfontein — 1995
10 by C J Spencer v Argentina at Wellington — 1997
10 by G J Fox v Fiji at Christchurch — 1987
8 by G J Fox v Italy at Auckland — 1987
8 by G J Fox v Wales at Auckland — 1988

MOST PENALTY GOALS IN A MATCH
by the team

P	Opp	Venue	Year
7	WS	Auckland	1993
6	BI	Dunedin	1959
6	E	Christchurch	1985
6	Arg	Wellington	1987
6	S	Christchurch	1987
6	F	Paris	1990
6	SA	Auckland	1994
6	A	Brisbane	1996
6	I	Dublin	1997

by a player

7 by G J Fox v Western Samoa at Auckland — 1993
6 by D B Clarke v British Isles at Dunedin — 1959
6 by K J Crowley v England at Christchurch — 1985

6 by G J Fox v Argentina at
Wellington | 1987
6 by G J Fox v Scotland at
Christchurch | 1987
6 by G J Fox v France at Paris | 1990
6 by S P Howarth v South Africa
at Auckland | 1994
6 by A P Mehrtens v Australia at
Brisbane | 1996
6 by A P Mehrtens v Ireland at
Dublin | 1997

MOST DROPPED GOALS IN A MATCH
by the team

D	Opp	Venue	Year
3	F	Christchurch	1986

by a player

2 by O D Bruce v Ireland at Dublin 1978
2 by F M Botica v France at
Christchurch | 1986
2 by A P Mehrtens v Australia at
Auckland | 1995

CAREER RECORDS

MOST CAPPED PLAYERS

Caps	Player	Career
92	S B T Fitzpatrick	1986–97
70	I D Jones	1990–97
63	J J Kirwan	1984–94
58	G W Whetton	1981–91
58	Z V Brooke	1987–97
55	C E Meads	1957–71
55	F E Bunce	1992–97
51	M N Jones	1987–97
50	O M Brown	1992–97
49	R W Loe	1987–95

MOST CONSECUTIVE TESTS

Tests	Player	Span
63	S B T Fitzpatrick	1986–95
40	G W Whetton	1986–91
38	I A Kirkpatrick	1968–77
38	S C McDowell	1987–92
34	M G Mexted	1979–85

MOST TESTS AS CAPTAIN

Tests	Captain	Span
51	S B T Fitzpatrick	1992–97
30	W J Whineray	1958–65
19	G N K Mourie	1977–82
18	B J Lochore	1966–70
17	A G Dalton	1981–85

MOST TESTS IN INDIVIDUAL POSITIONS

Full-back D B Clarke	31	1956–64
Wing J J Kirwan	63	1984–94
Centre F E Bunce	55	1992–97
Fly-half G J Fox	46	1985–93
Scrum-half G T M Bachop	31	1989–95
Prop O M Brown	50	1992–97
Hooker S B T Fitzpatrick	92	1986–97
Lock I D Jones	70	1990–97
Flanker M N Jones	49	1987–97
No 8 Z V Brooke	52	1987–97

MOST POINTS IN TESTS

Pts	Player	Tests	Career
645	G J Fox	46	1985–93
364	A P Mehrtens	22	1995–97
207	D B Clarke	31	1956–64
201	A R Hewson	19	1981–84
147	C J Spencer	8	1997

MOST TRIES IN TESTS

Tries	Player	Tests	Career
35	J J Kirwan	63	1984–94
24	J W Wilson	35	1993–97
21	C M Cullen	22	1996–97
20	F E Bunce	55	1992–97
19	S S Wilson	34	1977–83
19	T J Wright	30	1986–91

MOST CONVERSIONS IN TESTS

Cons	Player	Tests	Career
118	G J Fox	46	1985–93
68	A P Mehrtens	22	1995–97
33	D B Clarke	31	1956–64
32	S D Culhane	6	1995–96
31	C J Spencer	8	1997

MOST PENALTY GOALS IN TESTS

Pens	Player	Tests	Career
128	G J Fox	46	1985–93
60	A P Mehrtens	22	1995–97
43	A R Hewson	19	1981–84
38	D B Clarke	31	1956–64
24	W F McCormick	16	1965–71

MOST DROPPED GOALS IN TESTS

Drops	Player	Tests	Career
7	G J Fox	46	1985–93
6	A P Mehrtens	22	1995–97
5	D B Clarke	31	1956–64
5	M A Herewini	10	1962–67
5	O D Bruce	14	1976–78

TRI-NATIONS RECORDS

Record	Detail	Holder	Set
Most points in matches	84	C J Spencer	1997
Most points in season	84	C J Spencer	1997
Most points in match	25	C J Spencer	v S Africa (h) 1997
Most tries in matches	5	C M Cullen	1996–97
Most tries in season	4	C M Cullen	1997
Most tries in match	2	F E Bunce	v S Africa (a) 1997
	2	C M Cullen	v S Africa (h) 1997
Most cons in matches	13	C J Spencer	1997
Most cons in season	13	C J Spencer	1997
Most cons in match	4	C J Spencer	v S Africa (h) 1997
Most pens in matches	19	A P Mehrtens	1996
Most pens in season	19	A P Mehrtens	1996
Most pens in match	6	A P Mehrtens	v Australia (a) 1996

SERIES RECORDS

Record	Holder	Detail
Most tries	J J Kirwan	6 v Wales 1988
Most points	A P Mehrtens	78 v Home Unions 1997

MAJOR TOUR RECORDS

Record	Detail	Year	Place
Most team points	976	1905–06	Europe & N Am
Most team tries	243	1905–06	Europe & N Am
Most individual points	246 by W J Wallace	1905–06	Europe & N Am
Most individual tries	44 by J Hunter	1905–06	Europe & N Am
Most points in match	43 by R M Deans	1984 v S Australia	Adelaide
Most tries in match	8 by T R Heeps	1962 v N NSW	Quirindi

MISCELLANEOUS RECORDS

Record	Holder	Detail
Longest Test career	E Hughes/C E Meads	15 seasons, 1907–21/1957–71
Youngest Test cap	J T Lomu	19 yrs 45 days in 1994
Oldest Test cap	E Hughes	40 yrs 123 days in 1921

NEW ZEALAND INTERNATIONAL CAREER RECORDS *(up to 30 April 1998)*

Player	Debut	Caps since last season	Caps	T	C	PG	DG	Pts
T Miller	None		0	0	0	0	0	0
C M Cullen	1996 v WS	1997 *Fj, Arg* 1,2, *A* 1, *SA* 1, *A* 2, *SA* 2, *A* 3, *I, E* 1, *W, E* 2	22	21	3	0	0	111
A R Cashmore	1996 v S	1997 *A* 2(R)	2	0	0	0	0	0
G M Osborne	1995 v C	1997 *Arg* 1(R), *A* 2,3, *I*	18	9	0	0	0	45
J Vidiri	None		0	0	0	0	0	0
J W Wilson	1993 v S	1997 *Fj, Arg* 1,2, *A* 1, *SA* 1, *A* 2, *SA* 2, *A* 3, *I, E* 1, *W, E* 2	35	24	1	3	0	131
J T Lomu	1994 v F	1997 *E* 1, *W, E* 2	20	14	0	0	0	70
E J Rush	1995 v W		9	5	0	0	0	25
T J F Umaga	1997 v Fj	1997 *Fj, Arg* 1,2, *A* 1, *SA* 1,2	6	5	0	0	0	25
F E Bunce	1992 v Wd	1997 *Fj, Arg* 1,2, *A* 1, *SA* 1, *A* 2, *SA* 2, *A* 3, *I, E* 1, *W, E* 2	55	20	0	0	0	96
A Ieremia	1994 v SA	1997 *A* 1(R), *SA* 1(R), *A* 2, *SA* 2, *A* 3, *I, E* 1	13	3	0	0	0	15
S J McLeod	1996 v WS	1997 *Fj* (R), *Arg* 2(t&R), *I*(R), *E* 1(R), *W* (t), *E* 2(R)	8	1	0	0	0	5
J Stanley	None		0	0	0	0	0	0
W K Little	1990 v S	1997 *W, E* 2	46	9	0	0	0	44
M Ranby	None		0	0	0	0	0	0
L Stensness	1993 v BI	1997 *Fj, Arg* 1,2, *A* 1, *SA* 1	8	3	0	0	0	15
C J Spencer	1997 v Arg	1997 *Arg* 1,2, *A* 1, *SA* 1, *A* 2, *SA* 2, *A* 3, *E* 2(R)	8	5	31	20	0	147
A P Mehrtens	1995 v C	1997 *Fj, SA* 2(R), *I, E* 1, *W, E* 2	22	6	68	60	6	364
S D Culhane	1995 v J		6	1	32	15	0	114
J P Preston	1991 v US	1997 *I* (R), *E* 1(R)	10	1	4	7	0	34
J W Marshall	1995 v F	1997 *Fj, Arg* 1,2, *A* 1, *SA* 1, *A* 2, *SA* 2, *A* 3, *I, E* 1, *W, E* 2	23	11	0	0	0	55
S T Forster	1993 v S		6	0	0	0	0	0
O F J Tonu'u	1997 v Fj	1997 *Fj* (R), *A* 3(R)	2	0	0	0	0	0
M D Robinson	None		0	0	0	0	0	0
S B T Fitzpatrick	1986 v F	1997 *Fj, Arg* 1,2, *A* 1, *SA* 1, *A* 2, *SA* 2, *A* 3, *W* (R)	92	12	0	0	0	55
N J Hewitt	1995 v I	1997 *SA* 1(R), *I, E* 1, *W, E* 2	8	0	0	0	0	0
A D Oliver	1997 v Fj	1997 *Fj* (t)	1	0	0	0	0	0
M R Allen	1993 v WS	1997 *Arg* 1(R),2(R), *SA* 2(R), *A* 3(R), *E* 2, *W* (R)	8	1	0	0	0	5
C K Barrell	None		0	0	0	0	0	0
G Slater	None		0	0	0	0	0	0

C W Dowd	1993 v BL	1997 *Fj, Arg* 1,2, *A* 1, *SA* 1, *A* 2, *SA* 2, *A* 3, *I*, *E* 1, *W*	40	2	0	0	0	10
O M Brown	1992 v I	1997 *Fj, Arg* 1,2, *A* 1, *SA* 1, *A* 2, *SA* 2, *A* 3, *I*, *E* 1, *W*, *E* 2	50	4	0	0	0	20
I D Jones	1990 v S	1997 *Fj, Arg* 1,2, *A* 1, *SA* 1, *A* 2, *SA* 2, *A* 3, *I*, *E* 1, *W*, *E* 2	70	8	0	0	0	37
C C Riechelmann	1997 v Fj	1997 *Fj* (R), *Arg* 1(R), *A* 1(R), *SA* 2(t), *I*(R), *E* 2(t)	6	1	0	0	0	5
R M Brooke	1992 v I	1997 *Fj, Arg* 1,2, *A* 1, *SA* 1, *A* 2, *SA* 2, *A* 3, *I*, *E* 1, *W*, *E* 2	44	4	0	0	0	20
M S B Cooksley	1992 v Wd		9	0	0	0	0	0
B P Larsen	1992 v Wd		17	1	0	0	0	4
A R Hopa	None		0	0	0	0	0	0
A F Blowers	1996 v SA	1997 *I*, *E* 1(R), *W* (R)	5	0	0	0	0	0
M N Jones	1987 v It	1997 *Fj*	51	13	0	0	0	56
J A Kronfeld	1995 v C	1997 *Fj, Arg* 1,2, *A* 1, *SA* 1, *A* 2, *SA* 2, *A* 3, *I* (R), *E* 1, *W*, *E* 2	30	9	0	0	0	45
M P Carter	1991 v A	1997 *Fj* (R), *A* 1(R)	5	0	0	0	0	0
G L Taylor	1996 v SA		1	0	0	0	0	0
T C Randell	1997 v Fj	1997 *Fj, Arg* 1,2, *A* 1, *SA* 1, *A* 2, *SA* 2, *A* 3, *I*, *E* 1, *W*, *E* 2	12	5	0	0	0	25
S D Surridge	None		0	0	0	0	0	0
Z V Brooke	1987 v Arg	1997 *Arg* 1,2, *A* 1, *SA* 1, *A* 2, *SA* 2, *A* 3, *I*, *E* 1, *W*, *E* 2	58	17	0	0	3	89
T J Blackadder	None		0	0	0	0	0	0

CHANGE OF COACH DOES NOT MAKE FOR SMOOTHER RIDE

THE 1997 SEASON IN AUSTRALIA
Peter Jenkins

It was a year when the coach was sacked; his replacement, touted as a guru, failed to right the listing ship and Australian administrators finally realised that perhaps the problem really lay at the feet of their highly-paid players. The 1997 season was pockmarked by poor performances. None worse than the record loss to South Africa in Pretoria, a 61-22 pounding. It came at the tail-end of the Tri-Nations Championship, and three days later coach Greg Smith would jump, knowing that if he did not, he would be pushed soon enough.

Rod Macqueen took over the helm for the end-of-season tour to South America and Britain. Four Tests were on the programme and Macqueen, the man who would work miracles if a number of officials behind-the-scenes were to be believed, was expected to bring his side back with an unblemished record. Instead, he returned with a team beaten by Argentina in one of two Tests and held to a draw by an experimental England line-up fielding five new caps. It was not the introduction Macqueen or his supporters had been counting on. The style of play he had fostered at the ACT Brumbies during two impressive Super-12 campaigns had not been carried successfully into the international environment. The Australians rarely sought physical confrontation among the forwards, and where their backs attempted intricate, angle-changing ploys behind the advantage line they were frequently picked off by waiting defences.

Adding to Macqueen's problems was his reliance on Brumbies players. The hinge of his side, the back row and three backs closest to the scrum, were all ACT during the Argentina Test: Robinson, Coker and Finegan in the back row, with Gregan, Knox and Howard behind. But by tour's end, Macqueen had been forced to change his thinking. Robinson was reduced to half a game in the England and Scotland Tests, sharing the openside role with the more constructive David Wilson. Willie Ofahengaue had come into the pack at No 8 to give more drive and Elton Flatley debuted at fly-half, in the absence of an injured Knox.

But the Australians, having continued to experiment with their line-ups, a common gripe during the Smith coaching regime, ended their visit to Britain in a state of further confusion, with a plethora of questions still unanswered. For instance, what shape is the Wallaby pack likely to take at the World Cup in 1999? Who knows?

The Australian team celebrate winning the Cook Cup after their record 76-0 victory over England at the Suncorp Stadium on 6 June 1998.

The only selection certainty is the skipper, John Eales. And the backline? There is unquestionably world-class talent there in wingers Roff and Tune, full-backs Burke and Larkham, half-back Gregan and centres Horan and Little. But a fly-half needs to be discovered and persevered with. At the close of 1997, it was a position causing anxiety attacks in the Wallaby ranks, so crucial is it to the functioning of any successful side. Clearly the Australians were without a Lynagh-like figure.

In 1997, the Wallabies used Tim Horan, David Knox and Flatley in the role. The previous year they had also tried Scott Bowen, Pat Howard, even Tim Wallace and Larkham on tour. But the youngster considered the most likely to succeed, NSW's Manuel Edmonds, was overlooked for the Argentina-Britain trip.

Back though to the beginning: the dramas that would unfold as the season progressed could not have been imagined after the first two Tests for the year. The Wallabies took on France and won the series with 29-15 and 26-19 victories. The first Test highlight was a two-try performance from blood bin replacement, winger Mitch Hardy. He was on the field for 13 minutes, and his two tries swung the game. Larkham filled the full-back spot in both games in the absence of the injured Burke and would do so, with great aplomb, for all but two matches in Australia's 12-Test programme. The coaching record of Smith was also extended, after the French series, to 10 wins from 13 games; but he would last only another six Tests.

After France came the All Blacks, a Bledisloe Cup encounter but not part of the Tri-Nations series. New Zealand hammered the Wallabies 30-13 in Christchurch, after leading 23-3 at half-time. Four tries to one was the harsh reality. Australia had not even been close.

An England side, its ranks filled by leg-weary players from the British Lions tour to South Africa, made an ill-timed visit to Australia in July and were soundly beaten 25-6 as Australia scored four tries to nil. A crowd of more than 40,000 at the Sydney Football Stadium saw Horan score one try and become only the sixth Australian player to reach 100 points in Tests.

The Tri-Nations series opened for the Wallabies with another flogging, this time in front of an Australian record crowd of 90,119 at the Melbourne Cricket Ground. Two mistakes by back-rower Michael Brial led to New Zealand tries. The All Blacks led 23-6 at half-time and, at the end, it was 33-18. The Wallabies had made no impression against their trans-Tasman rivals in two outings, their pattern of play was slated as boring and predictable, and the powerbrokers were starting to whisper among themselves. For them, the answer, eventually, would be a change of coach.

Following the Melbourne disappointment, the Wallabies recovered to strike form against South Africa in Brisbane. Winger Ben Tune, with two tries, and the playmaking skills of fly-half Knox, recalled to the side after Horan was injured, led a first-half onslaught in which the Australians raced to 26-10. The final scoreline of 32-20 was deceptive. For once, the Wallabies had won and won well.

Former Wallaby coach Alan Jones used to warn his players that they could be roosters one week and feather dusters the next. Greg Smith might have been wise to counsel his players with the same analogy. A fortnight after their cock-of-the-walk performance against the Springboks, the Wallabies were reduced to cleaning implements. The All Blacks wiped the floor with them 36-24. A 12-point margin might not appear too traumatic, but the half-time score was 36-nil.

On to Pretoria went the Wallabies and on to a 61-22 thrashing. Even the Titanic had not sunk this quickly. At half-time it was 18-15 to the Springboks, but the Wallabies showed little taste for the fight after the break. Apart from full-back Larkham, not a single Wallaby left Loftus Versfeld with reputation intact. Days later, Smith resigned. And few players were weeping over his exit. Privately, many blamed the coach's techniques and his inconsistent selections for the side's poor performances. But as Argentina would show in beating the Wallabies in the second of two Tests a couple of months later, there was plenty wrong with the on-field personnel as well.

The South American tour was a failure, a drawn series saw to that, while the two Tests in Britain were far from vintage displays. The 15-all draw with England was a case of missed opportunities, with the Wallabies scoring two tries to nil and failing to kick their goals. The 37-8 scoreline against Scotland, while impressive at first glance, did camouflage several deficiencies. At half-time, with the score 8-all, both sides were making elementary errors. International standard this match was not. But two wonderful solo tries from Larkham helped put the Wallabies into gear. At least in a season where there were few highs to enjoy, they managed to end the year with a solid 40 minutes.

Ironically, while the Test results were disappointing, the 1997 Super-12 proved a triumph for Australia as the ACT Brumbies, in their second season, advanced to the tournament final before going down to Auckland. The Brumbies had proved unbeatable at home, their support in Canberra continued to grow and the fledglings of the previous year avoided second-year syndrome. Teams might have known their pattern, they no longer underestimated them; but the Brumbies kept on winning.

The same could not be said for the traditional heavyweights of Australian rugby, NSW and Queensland. The Waratahs, with by far the biggest nursery of players in the country, failed to give the semi-finals a shake for the second year running. As for Queensland, injuries to key players, a lack of depth in certain positions, particularly in the pack, and a reluctance to adopt the bullet-fast playing style of rival provinces, brought them back to the field. The Reds had topped the Super-12 table in 1996 before losing their semi-final to Natal. But in 1997, they finished towards the back of the pack in 10th position. As for head-to-head battles between NSW and the Reds, Queensland won the Super-12 encounter between the two sides, 26-16 in Sydney. In the separate State of the Union series, Queensland won the opening game 30-14 before losing the second 33-9.

On the club scene, Easts won their first Brisbane premiership, in their 50th anniversary year, downing title favourites Souths 18-16. In NSW, Manly won their first grand final since 1983, beating Eastwood 34-19.

George Gregan sets up an attack for Australia with Kyran Bracken (England) in pursuit during the drawn Test at Twickenham on 15 November 1997.

AUSTRALIA TO ARGENTINA & BRITAIN 1997

THE TOURING PARTY

Manager J McKay **Coach** R Macqueen **Assistant Coaches** TA Lane, JS Miller
Trainer D Williams **Captain** JA Eales

Full-backs: SJ Larkham (Canberra Kookaburras & ACT), S Mortlock (Gordon & NSW)

Threequarters: BN Tune (GPS & Queensland), DP Smith (Easts & Queensland), JW Roff (Canberra Kookaburras & ACT), A Magro (Randwick & ACT), MD Hardy (Gordon & ACT), J Holbeck (Randwick & ACT), TJ Horan (Souths & Queensland), DJ Herbert (GPS & Queensland), PW Howard (Queensland University & ACT), J Jones-Hughes (Randwick & NSW)

Half-backs: GM Gregan (Randwick & ACT), SJ Payne (Eastern Suburbs & NSW), DJ Knox (Randwick & ACT), EJ Flatley (Brothers & Queensland)

Forwards: AT Blades (Gordon & NSW), CD Blades (Randwick & NSW), RLL Harry (Sydney University & NSW), A Heath (Eastern Suburbs & NSW), MA Foley (Souths & Queensland), M Caputo (Canberra Kookaburras & ACT), B Cannon (Souths & Queensland), JA Eales (Brothers & Queensland), JF Langford (Gordon & ACT), TM Bowman (Eastern Suburbs & NSW), BJ Robinson (Souths & ACT), DJ Wilson (Easts & Queensland), ODA Finegan (Randwick & ACT), WW Waugh (Souths & ACT), T Kefu (Souths & Queensland), V Ofahengaue (Manly & NSW), M Cockbain (GPS & Queensland), T Coker (Canberra Kookaburras & ACT)

TOUR RECORD

All matches Played 7 Won 5 Drawn 1 Lost 1 Points for 213 Against 101
International matches Played 4 Won 2 Drawn 1 Lost 1 Points for 91 Against 56

SCORING DETAILS

All matches					**International matches**				
For:	29T	16C	12PG		213 Pts	For:	10T	4C	11PG	91 Pts
Against:	5T	2C	21PG	3DG	101 Pts	Against:	3T	1C	13PG	56 Pts

MATCH DETAILS

1997	OPPONENTS	VENUE	RESULT
25 Oct	Tucuman	Tucuman	W 76-15
28 Oct	Rosario	Rosario	W 29-18
1 Nov	ARGENTINA	Buenos Aires	W 23-15
4 Nov	Buenos Aires	Buenos Aires	W 17-12
8 Nov	ARGENTINA	Buenos Aires	L 16-18
15 Nov	ENGLAND	Twickenham	D 15-15
22 Nov	SCOTLAND	Murrayfield	W 37-8

MATCH 1   25 October, Tucuman

Tucuman 15 (1G 1PG 1T)   **Australians 76** (8G 4T)
Tucuman: *Tries:* Garcia, Santamarina *Conversion:* Albornoz *Penalty Goal:* Sauze
Australians: *Tries:* Larkham (3), Tune (3), Howard, Horan, Foley, Harry, Roff,
Finegan *Conversions:* Knox (6), Roff, Larkham

MATCH 2   28 October, Rosario

Rosario 18 (3PG 3DG)   **Australians 29** (3G 1T 1PG)
Rosario: *Penalty Goals:* G del Castillo (3) *Dropped Goals:* G del Castillo (2),
L Bouza
Australians: *Tries:* Ofahengaue (2), Howard, Hardy *Conversions:* Payne (3)
Penalty Goal: Payne

MATCH 3   1 November, Ferrocarril Oeste Stadium, Buenos Aires   1st Test

ARGENTINA 15 (5PG)   AUSTRALIA 23 (6PG 1T)

ARGENTINA: E Jurado (Jockey Club, Rosario); D Albanese (San Isidro Club),
E Simone (Liceo Naval), F Turnes (Banco Nacion), D Giannantonio (Piacenza,
Italy); L Arbizu (Brive, France), A Pichot (Richmond, England); R Grau (Gauteng
Lions, S Africa), M Ledesma (Curupayti), M Reggiardo (Castres, France),
P Sporleder (Curupayti)*(capt)*, A Allub (Jockey Club, Cordoba), R Martin
(Richmond, England), P Camerlinckx (Regatas Bella Vista), M Ruiz (Teque,
Cuyo) *Substitution:* M Scelzo (Hindu) for Ledesma (65 mins)
Scorer *Penalty Goals:* Giannantonio (5)
AUSTRALIA: Larkham; Tune, Horan, Howard, Roff; Knox, Gregan; Harry,
Foley, A Blades, Waugh, Eales *(capt)*, Finegan, Coker, Robinson
Substitutions: Ofahengaue for Coker (temp 40-59 mins and 77 mins); Hardy for
Larkham (75 mins)
Scorers *Try:* Finegan *Penalty Goals:* Knox (6)
Referee HA Smith (Ireland)

MATCH 4   4 November, Buenos Aires

Buenos Aires 12 (4PG)   **Australians 17** (1G 2T)
Buenos Aires: *Penalty Goals:* Cilley (4)
Australians: *Tries:* Kefu, Wilson, Payne *Conversion:* Flatley

MATCH 5   8 November, Ferrocarril Oeste Stadium, Buenos Aires   2nd Test

ARGENTINA 18 (1G 2PG 1T)   AUSTRALIA 16 (2PG 2T)

ARGENTINA: E Jurado (Jockey Club, Rosario); D Albanese (San Isidro Club),
E Simone (Liceo Naval), F Turnes (Banco Nacion), D Giannantonio (Piacenza,
Italy); L Arbizu (Brive, France), A Pichot (Richmond, England); R Grau (Gauteng
Lions, S Africa), M Ledesma (Curupayti), M Reggiardo (Castres, France),
P Sporleder (Curupayti)*(capt)*, A Allub (Jockey Club, Cordoda), R Martin
(Richmond, England), P Camerlinckx (Regatas Bella Vista), M Ruiz (Teque,
Cuyo) *Substitution:* O Hasan-Jalil (Natacion y Gimnasia) for Reggiardo (54 mins)
Scorers *Tries:* Pichot, Martin *Conversion:* Giannantonio
Penalty Goals: Giannantonio (2)

AUSTRALIA: Larkham; Tune, Horan, Howard, Roff; Knox, Gregan; Harry, Foley, A Blades, Waugh, Eales *(capt)*, Finegan, Coker, Robinson
Substitutions: Ofahengaue for Coker (55 mins); Hardy for Knox (77 mins); Payne for Gregan (temp 57-62 mins)
Scorers *Tries:* Tune, Finegan *Penalty Goals:* Knox (2)
Referee DTM McHugh (Ireland)

MATCH 6   15 November, Twickenham   Test Match
ENGLAND 15 (5PG)   AUSTRALIA 15 (1G 1PG 1T)

ENGLAND: MB Perry (Bath); DL Rees (Sale), WJH Greenwood (Leicester), PR de Glanville (Bath), AA Adebayo (Bath); MJ Catt (Bath), KPP Bracken (Saracens); J Leonard (Harlequins), AE Long (Bath), WR Green (Wasps), MO Johnson (Leicester), GS Archer (Newcastle), LBN Dallaglio (Wasps) *(capt)*, AJ Diprose (Saracens), RA Hill (Saracens) *Substitutions:* PJ Grayson (Northampton) for de Glanville (temp 7-23 mins); R Cockerill (Leicester) for Long (temp 15-16 mins; 40 mins); AS Healey (Leicester) for Adebayo (65 mins)
Scorer *Penalty Goals:* Catt (5)
AUSTRALIA: Larkham; Tune, Horan, Howard, Roff; Flatley, Gregan; Harry, Foley, A Blades, Langford, Eales *(capt)*, Finegan, Ofahengaue, Robinson
Substitutions: Wilson for Robinson (40 mins); Heath for A Blades (65 mins)
Scorers *Tries:* Gregan, Tune *Conversion:* Roff *Penalty Goal:* Roff
Referee A Watson (South Africa)

MATCH 7   22 November, Murrayfield   Test Match
SCOTLAND 8 (1PG 1T)   AUSTRALIA 37 (3G 2PG 2T)

SCOTLAND: DW Hodge (Watsonians); JM Craig (West of Scotland), AG Stanger (Hawick), AV Tait (Newcastle), KM Logan (Wasps); GPJ Townsend (Northampton), AD Nicol (Bath)*(capt)*; DIW Hilton (Bath), G McKelvey (Watsonians), MJ Stewart (Northampton), SJ Campbell (Dundee HSFP), S Murray (Bedford), AJ Roxburgh (Kelso), EW Peters (Bath), IR Smith (Moseley)
Substitutions: SB Grimes (Watsonians) for Smith (temp 20-28 mins) and for Roxburgh (40 mins); G Graham (Newcastle) for Stewart (65 mins); CM Chalmers (Melrose) for Stanger (75 mins); Stewart for Hilton (83 mins)
Scorers *Try:* Murray *Penalty Goal:* Hodge
AUSTRALIA: Larkham; Tune, Horan, Howard, Roff; Flatley, Gregan; Harry, Foley, A Blades, Langford, Eales *(capt)*, Finegan, Ofahengaue, Robinson
Substitution: Wilson for Robinson (40 mins)
Scorers *Tries:* Larkham (2), Ofahengaue, Roff, Gregan *Conversions:* Eales (3)
Penalty Goals: Eales (2)
Referee WTS Henning (South Africa)

AUSTRALIAN INTERNATIONAL PLAYERS (*up to 30 April 1998*)

N.B. In the summer of 1986, the ARU retrospectively granted full Australian Test status to the five international matches played by the 1927-28 touring team to Europe. In 1988 Test status was extended to all those who played overseas in the 1920s.

Abrahams, A M F (NSW) 1967 *NZ*, 1968 *NZ* 1, 1969 *W*
Adams, N J (NSW) 1955 *NZ* 1
Adamson, R W (NSW) 1912 *US*
Allan, T (NSW) 1946 *NZ* 1, *M*, *NZ* 2, 1947 *NZ* 2, *S*, *I*, *W*, 1948 *E*, *F*, 1949 *M* 1,2,3, *NZ* 1,2
Anlezark, E A (NSW) 1905 *NZ*
Armstrong, A R (NSW) 1923 *NZ* 1,2
Austin, L R (NSW) 1963 *E*

Baker, R L (NSW) 1904 *BI* 1,2
Baker, W H (NSW) 1914 *NZ* 1,2,3
Ballesty, J P (NSW) 1968 *NZ* 1,2, *F*, *I*, *S*, 1969 *W*, *SA* 2,3,4,
Bannon, D P (NSW) 1946 *M*
Bardsley, E J (NSW) 1928 *NZ* 1,3, *M* (R)
Barker, H S (NSW) 1952 *Fj* 1,2, *NZ* 1,2, 1953 *SA* 4, 1954 *Fj* 1,2
Barnett, J T (NSW) 1907 *NZ* 1,2,3, 1908 *W*, 1909 *E*
Barry, M J (Q) 1971 *SA* 3
Barton, R F D (NSW) 1899 *BI* 3
Batch, P G (Q) 1975 *S*, *W*, 1976 *E*, *Fj* 1,2,3, *F* 1,2, 1978 *W* 1,2, *NZ* 1,2,3, 1979 *Arg* 2
Batterham, R P (NSW) 1967 *NZ*, 1970 *S*
Battishall, B R (NSW) 1973 *E*
Baxter, A J (NSW) 1949 *M* 1,2,3, *NZ* 1,2, 1951 *NZ* 1,2, 1952 *NZ* 1,2
Baxter, T J (Q) 1958 *NZ* 3
Beith, B McN (NSW) 1914 *NZ* 3
Bell, K R (Q) 1968 *S*
Bell, M D NSW) 1996 *C*
Bennett, W G (Q) 1931 *M*, 1933 *SA* 1,2,3,
Bermingham, J V (Q) 1934 *NZ* 1,2, 1937 *SA* 1
Berne, J E (NSW) 1975 *S*
Besomo, K S (NSW) 1979 *I* 2
Betts, T N (Q) 1951 *NZ* 2,3, 1954 *Fj* 2
Biilmann, R R (NSW) 1933 *SA* 1,2,3,4
Birt, R (Q) 1914 *NZ* 2
Black, J W (NSW) 1985 *C* 1,2, *NZ*, *Fj* 1
Blackwood, J G (NSW) 1923 *NZ* 1,2,3, 1925 *NZ*, 1927 *I*, *W*, *S*, 1928 *E*, *F*
Blades, A T (NSW) 1996 *S*, *I*, *W* 3, 1997 *NZ* 1 (R), *E* 1 (R), *SA* 1 (R), *NZ* 3, *SA* 2, *Arg* 1,2, *E* 2, *S*
Blades, C D (NSW) 1997 *E* 1
Blair, M R (NSW) 1928 *F*, 1931 *M*, *NZ*
Bland, G V (NSW) 1928 *NZ* 3, *M*, 1932 *NZ* 1,2,3, 1933 *SA* 1,2,4,5
Blomley, J (NSW) 1949 *M* 1,2,3, *NZ* 1,2, 1950 *BI* 1,2
Boland, S B (Q) 1899 *BI* 3,4, 1903 *NZ*
Bond, J H (NSW) 1921 *NZ*
Bonis, E T (Q) 1929 *NZ* 1,2,3, 1930 *BI*, 1931 *M*, *NZ*, 1932 *NZ* 1,2,3, 1933 *SA* 1,2,3,4,5, 1934 *NZ* 1,2, 1936 *NZ* 1,2, *M*, 1937 *SA* 1, 1938 *NZ* 1
Bosler, J M (NSW) 1953 *SA* 1
Bouffler, R G (NSW) 1899 *BI* 3
Bourke, T K (Q) 1947 *NZ* 2
Bowen, S (NSW) 1993 *SA* 1,2,3, 1995 [*R*], *NZ* 1,2, 1996 *C*, *NZ* 1, *SA* 2
Bowers, A J A (NSW) 1923 *NZ* 3, 1925 *NZ*, 1927 *I*
Boyce, E S (NSW) 1962 *NZ* 1,2, 1964 *NZ* 1,2,3, 1965 *SA* 1,2, 1966 *W*, *S*, 1967 *E*, *I* 1, *F* 1 2
Boyce, J S (NSW) 1962 *NZ* 3,4,5, 1963 *E*, *SA* 1,2,3,4, 1964 *NZ* 1,3, 1965 *SA* 1,2
Boyd, A (NSW) 1899 *BI* 3
Boyd, A F McC (Q) 1958 *M* 1
Brass, J E (NSW) 1966 *BI* 2, *W*, *S*, 1967 *E*, *I* 1, *F*, *I* 2, *NZ*, 1968 *NZ* 1, *F*, *I*, *S*
Breckenridge, J W (NSW) 1927 *I*, *W*, *S*, 1928 *E*, *F*, 1929 *NZ* 1,2,3, 1930 *BI*
Brial, M C (NSW) 1993 *F* 1 (R), 2, 1996 *W* 1 (R), 2, *C*, *NZ* 1, *SA* 1, *NZ* 2, *SA* 2, *It*, *I*, *W* 3, 1997 *NZ* 2
Bridle, O L (V) 1931 *M*, 1932 *NZ* 1,2,3, 1933 *SA* 3,4,5, 1934 *NZ* 1,2, 1936 *NZ* 1,2, *M*
Broad, E G (Q) 1949 *M* 1

Brockhoff, J D (NSW) 1949 *M* 2,3, *NZ* 1,2, 1950 *BI* 1,2, 1951 *NZ* 2,3
Brown, B R (Q) 1972 *NZ* 1,3
Brown, J V (NSW) 1956 *SA* 1,2, 1957 *NZ* 1,2, 1958 *W*, *I*, *E*, *S*, *F*
Brown, R C (NSW) 1975 *E* 1,2
Brown, S W (NSW) 1953 *SA* 2,3,4
Bryant, H (NSW) 1925 *NZ*
Buchan, A J (NSW) 1946 *NZ* 1,2, 1947 *NZ* 1,2, *S*, *I*, *W*, 1948 *E*, *F*, 1949 *M* 3
Bull, D (NSW) 1928 *M*
Buntine, H (NSW) 1923 *NZ* 1 (R)
Burdon, A (NSW) 1903 *NZ*, 1904 *BI* 1,2, 1905 *NZ*
Burge, A B (NSW) 1907 *NZ* 3, 1908 *W*
Burge, P H (NSW) 1907 *NZ* 1,2,3
Burge, R (NSW) 1928 *NZ* 1,2,3 (R), *M* (R)
Burke, B T (NSW) 1988 *S* (R)
Burke, C T (NSW) 1946 *NZ* 2, 1947 *NZ* 1,2, *S*, *I*, *W*, 1948 *E*, *F*, 1949 *M* 2,3, *NZ* 1,2, 1950 *BI* 1,2, 1951 *NZ* 1,2,3, 1953 *SA* 2,3,4, 1954 *Fj* 1, 1955 *NZ* 1,2,3, 1956 *SA* 1,2,
Burke, M (NSW) 1993 *SA* 3 (R), *F* 1, 1994 *I* 1,2, *It* 1,2, 1995 [*C*, *R*, *E*], *NZ* 1,2, 1996 *W* 1,2, *C*, *NZ* 1, *SA* 1, *NZ* 2, *SA* 2, *It*, *S*, *I*, *W* 3, 1997 *E* 1, *NZ* 2
Burke, M P (NSW) 1984 *E* (R), *I*, 1985 *C* 1,2, *NZ*, *Fj* 1,2, 1986 *It* (R), *F*, *Arg* 1,2, *NZ* 1,2,3, 1987 *SK*, [*US*, *J*, *I*, *F*, *W*], *NZ*, *Arg* 1,2
Burnet, D R (NSW) 1972 *F* 1,2, *NZ* 1,2,3, *Fj*
Butler, O F (NSW) 1969 *SA* 1,2, 1970 *S*, 1971 *SA* 2,3, *F* 1,2

Calcraft, W J (NSW) 1985 *C* 1, 1986 *It*, *Arg* 2
Caldwell, B C (NSW) 1928 *NZ* 3
Cameron, A S (NSW) 1951 *NZ* 1,2,3, 1952 *Fj* 1,2, *NZ* 1,2, 1953 *SA* 1,2,3,4, 1954 *Fj* 1,2, 1955 *NZ* 1,2,3, 1956 *SA* 1,2, 1957 *NZ* 1, 1958 *I*
Campbell, J D (NSW) 1910 *NZ* 1,2,3
Campbell, W A (Q) 1984 *Fj*, 1986 *It*, *F*, *Arg* 1,2, *NZ* 1,2,3, 1987 *SK*, [*E*, *US*, *J* (R), *I*, *F*], *NZ*, 1988 *E*, 1989 *BI* 1,2,3, *NZ*, 1990 *NZ* 2,3
Campese, D I (ACT, NSW) 1982 *NZ* 1,2,3, 1983 *US*, *Arg* 1,2, *NZ*, *It*, *F* 1,2, 1984 *Fj*, *NZ* 1,2,3, *E*, *I*, *W*, *S*, 1985 *Fj* 1,2, 1986 *It*, *F*, *Arg* 1,2, *NZ* 1,2,3, 1987 [*E*, *US*, *J*, *I*, *F*, *W*], *NZ*, 1988 *E* 1,2, *NZ* 1,2,3, *E*, *S*, *It*, 1989 *BI* 1,2,3, *NZ*, *F* 1,2, 1990 *F* 2,3, *US*, *NZ* 1,2,3, 1991 *W*, *E*, *NZ* 1,2, [*Arg*, *WS*, *W*, *I*, *NZ*, *E*], 1992 *S* 1,2, *NZ* 1,2,3, *SA*, *I*, *W*, 1993 *Tg*, *NZ*, *SA* 1,2,3, *C*, *F* 1,2, 1994 *I* 1,2, *It* 1,2, *WS*, *NZ*, 1995 *Arg* 1,2, [*SA*, *C*, *E*], *NZ* 2 (R), 1996 *W* 1,2, *C*, *NZ* 1, *SA* 1, *NZ* 2, *SA* 2, *It*, *W* 3
Canniffe, W D (Q) 1907 *NZ* 2
Caputo, M E (ACT) 1996 *W* 1,2, 1997 *F* 1,2, *NZ* 1
Carberry, C M (NSW, Q) 1973 *Tg* 2, *E*, 1976 *I*, *US*, *Fj* 1,2,3, 1981 *F* 1,2, *I*, *W*, *S*, 1982 *E*
Cardy, A M (NSW) 1966 *BI* 1,2, *W*, *S*, 1967 *E*, *I* 1, *F*, 1968 *NZ* 1,2
Carew, P J (Q) 1899 *BI* 1,2,3,4
Carmichael, P (Q) 1904 *BI* 2, 1907 *NZ* 1, 1908 *W*, 1909 *E*
Carozza, P V (Q) 1990 *F* 1,2,3, *NZ* 2,3, 1992 *S* 1,2, *NZ* 1,2,3, *SA*, *I*, *W*, 1993 *Tg*, *NZ*
Carpenter, M G (V) 1938 *NZ* 1,2
Carr, E T A (NSW) 1913 *NZ* 1,2,3, 1914 *NZ* 1,2,3
Carr, E W (NSW) 1921 *NZ* 1 (R)
Carroll, D B (NSW) 1908 *W*, 1912 *US*
Carroll, J C (NSW) 1953 *SA* 1
Carroll, J H (NSW) 1958 *M* 2,3, *NZ* 1,2,3, 1959 *BI* 1,2
Carson, J (NSW) 1899 *BI* 1
Carson, P J (NSW) 1979 *NZ*, 1980 *NZ* 3
Carter, D G (NSW) 1988 *E* 1,2, *NZ* 1, 1989 *F* 1,2
Casey, T V (NSW) 1963 *SA* 2,3,4, 1964 *NZ* 1,2,3
Catchpole, K W (NSW) 1961 *Fj* 1,2,3, *SA* 1,2, *F*, 1962 *NZ* 1,2,4, 1963 *SA* 2,3,4, 1964 *NZ* 1,2,3, 1965 *SA* 1,2, 1966 *BI* 1,2, *W*, *S*, 1967 *E*, *I* 1, *F*, *I* 2, *NZ*, 1968 *NZ* 1

Cawsey, R M (NSW) 1949 *M* 1, *NZ* 1,2
Cerutti, W H (NSW) 1928 *NZ* 1,2,3, *M*, 1929 *NZ* 1,2,3, 1930 *BI*, 1931 *M, NZ*, 1932 *NZ* 1,2,3, 1933 *SA* 1,2,3,4,5, 1936 *M*, 1937 *SA* 1,2
Challoner, R L (NSW) 1899 *BI* 2
Chapman, G A (NSW) 1962 *NZ* 3,4,5
Clark, J G (Q) 1931 *M, NZ*, 1932 *NZ* 1,2, 1933 *SA* 1
Clarken, J C (NSW) 1905 *NZ*, 1910 *NZ* 1,2,3
Cleary, M A (NSW) 1961 *Fj* 1,2,3, *SA* 1,2, *F*
Clements, P (NSW) 1982 *NZ* 3
Clifford, M (NSW) 1938 *NZ* 3
Cobb, W G (NSW) 1899 *BI* 3,4
Cockbain, M (Q) 1997 *F* 2 (R), *NZ* 1, *SA* 1,2
Cocks, M R (NSW, Q) 1972 *F* 1,2, *NZ* 2,3, *Fj*, 1973 *Tg* 1,2, *W, E*, 1975 *J* 1
Codey, D (NSW Country, Q) 1983 *Arg* 1, 1984 *E, W, S*, 1985 *C* 2, *NZ*, 1986 *F, Arg* 1, 1987 [*US, J, F* (R), *W*], *NZ*
Cody, E W (NSW) 1913 *NZ* 1,2,3
Coker, T (Q, ACT) 1987 [*E, US, F, W*], 1991 *NZ* 2, [*Arg, WS, NZ, E*], 1992 *NZ* 1,2,3, *W* (R), 1993 *Tg, NZ*, 1995 *Arg* 2, *NZ* 1 (R), 1997 *F* 1 (R), 2, *NZ* 1, *E* 1, *NZ* 2 (R), *SA* 1 (R), *NZ* 3, *SA* 2, *Arg* 1,2
Colbert, R (NSW) 1952 *Fj* 2, *NZ* 1,2, 1953 *SA* 2,3,4
Cole, J W (NSW) 1968 *NZ* 1,2, *F, I, S*, 1969 *W, SA* 1,2,3,4, 1970 *S*, 1971 *SA* 1,2,3, *F* 1,2, 1972 *NZ* 1,2,3, 1973 *Tg* 1,2, 1974 *NZ* 1,2,3
Collins, P K (NSW) 1937 *SA* 2, 1938 *NZ* 2,3
Colton, A J (Q) 1899 *BI* 1,3
Colton, T (Q) 1904 *BI* 1,2
Comrie-Thomson, I R (NSW) 1928 *NZ* 1,2,3 *M*
Connor, D M (Q) 1958 *W, I, E, S, F, M* 2,3, *NZ* 1,2,3, 1959 *BI* 1,2
Constable, R (Q) 1994 *I* 2 (t & R)
Cook, M T (Q) 1986 *F*, 1987 *SK*, [*J*], 1988 *E* 1,2, *NZ* 1,2,3, *E, S, It*
Cooke, B P (Q) 1979 *I* 1
Cooke, G M (Q) 1932 *NZ* 1,2,3, 1933 *SA* 1,2,3, 1946 *NZ* 2, 1947 *NZ* 2, *S, I, W*, 1948 *E, F*
Coolican, J E (NSW) 1982 *NZ* 1, 1983 *It, F* 1,2
Corfe, A C (Q) 1899 *BI* 2
Cornelsen, G (NSW) 1974 *NZ* 2,3, 1975 *J* 2, *S, W*, 1976 *E, F* 1,2, 1978 *W* 1,2, *NZ* 1,2,3, 1979 *I* 1,2, *NZ, Arg* 1,2, 1980 *NZ* 1,2,3, 1981 *I, W, S*, 1982 *E*
Cornes, J R (Q) 1972 *Fj*
Cornforth, R G W (NSW) 1947 *NZ* 1, 1950 *BI* 2
Cornish, P (ACT) 1990 *F* 2,3, *NZ* 1
Costello, P P S (Q) 1950 *BI* 2
Cottrell, N V (Q) 1949 *M* 1,2,3, *NZ* 1,2, 1950 *BI* 1,2, 1951 *NZ* 1,2,3, 1952 *Fj* 1,2, *NZ* 1,2
Cowper, D L (V) 1931 *NZ*, 1932 *NZ* 1,2,3, 1933 *SA* 1,2,3,4,5
Cox, B P (NSW) 1952 *Fj* 1,2, *NZ* 1,2, 1954 *Fj* 2, 1955 *NZ* 1, 1956 *SA* 2, 1957 *NZ* 1,2
Cox, M H (NSW) 1981 *W, S*
Cox, P A (NSW) 1979 *Arg* 1,2, 1980 *Fj, NZ* 1,2, 1981 *W* (R), *S*, 1982 *S* 1,2, *NZ* 1,2,3, 1984 *Fj, NZ* 1,2,3
Craig, R R (NSW) 1908 *W*
Crakanthorp, J S (NSW) 1923 *NZ* 3
Cremin, J F (NSW) 1946 *NZ* 1,2, 1947 *NZ* 1
Crittle, C P (NSW) 1962 *NZ* 4, 5, 1963 *SA* 2,3,4, 1964 *NZ* 1,2,3, 1965 *SA* 1,2, 1966 *BI* 1,2, *S*, 1967 *E, I*
Croft, B H D (NSW) 1928 *M*
Cross, J R (NSW) 1955 *NZ* 1,2,3
Cross, K A (NSW) 1949 *M* 1, *NZ* 1,2, 1950 *BI* 1,2, 1951 *NZ* 2,3, 1952 *NZ* 1, 1953 *SA* 1,2,3,4, 1954 *Fj* 1,2, 1955 *NZ* 3, 1956 *SA* 1,2, 1957 *NZ* 1,2
Crossman, O C (NSW) 1925 *NZ*, 1929 *NZ* 2, 1930 *BI*
Crowe, P J (NSW) 1976 *F* 2, 1978 *W* 1,2, 1979 *I* 2, *NZ, Arg* 1
Crowley, D J (Q) 1989 *BI* 1,2,3, 1991 [*WS*], 1992 *I, W*, 1993 *C* (R), 1995 *Arg* 1,2, [*SA, E*], *NZ* 1, 1996 *W* 2 (R), *C, NZ* 1, *SA* 1,2, *I, W* 3
Curley, T G P (NSW) 1957 *NZ* 1,2, 1958 *W, I, E, S, F, M* 1, *NZ* 1,2,3
Curran, D J (NSW) 1980 *NZ* 3, 1981 *F* 1,2, *W*, 1983 *Arg* 1
Currie, E W (Q) 1899 *BI* 2
Cutler, S A G (NSW) 1982 *NZ* 2 (R), 1984 *NZ* 1,2,3, *E, I, W, S*, 1985 *C* 1,2, *NZ, Fj* 1,2, 1986 *It, F, NZ* 1,2,3, 1987 *SK*, [*E, J, I, F, W*], *NZ, Arg* 1,2, 1988 *E* 1,2, *NZ* 1,2,3, *E, S, It*, 1989 *BI* 1,2,3, *NZ*, 1991 [*WS*]

Daly, A J (NSW) 1989 *NZ, F* 1,2, 1990 *F* 1,2,3, *US, NZ* 1,2,3, 1991 *W, E, NZ* 1,2, [*Arg, W, I, NZ, E*], 1992 *S* 1,2, *NZ* 1,2,3, *SA*, 1993 *Tg, NZ, SA* 1,2,3, *C, F* 1,2, 1994 *I* 1,2, *It* 1,2, *WS, NZ*, 1995 [*C, R*]
D'Arcy, A M (Q) 1980 *Fj, NZ* 3, 1981 *F* 1,2, *I, W, S*, 1982 *E, S* 1,2
Darveniza, P (NSW) 1969 *W, SA* 2,3,4
Davidson, R A L (NSW) 1952 *Fj* 1,2, *NZ* 1,2, 1953 *SA* 1, 1957 *NZ* 1,2, 1958 *W, I, E, S, F, M* 1
Davis, C C (NSW) 1949 *NZ* 1, 1951 *NZ* 1,2,3
Davis, E H (V) 1947 *S, W*, 1949 *M* 1,2
Davis, G V (NSW) 1963 *E, SA* 1,2,3,4, 1964 *NZ* 1,2,3, 1965 *SA* 1, 1966 *BI* 1,2, *W, S*, 1967 *E, I* 1, *F, I* 2, *NZ*, 1968 *NZ* 1,2, *F, I, S*, 1969 *W, SA* 1,2,3,4, 1970 *S*, 1971 *SA* 1,2,3, *F* 1,2, 1972 *F* 1,2, *NZ* 1,2,3
Davis, G W G (NSW) 1955 *NZ* 2,3
Davis, R A (NSW) 1974 *NZ* 1,2,3
Davis, T S R (NSW) 1921 *NZ*, 1923 *NZ* 1,2,3
Davis, W (NSW) 1899 *BI* 1,3,4
Dawson, W L (NSW) 1946 *NZ* 1,2
Diett, L J (NSW) 1959 *BI* 1,2
Dix, W (NSW) 1907 *NZ* 1,2,3, 1909 *E*
Dixon, E J (Q) 1904 *BI* 3
Donald, K J (Q) 1957 *NZ* 1, 1958 *W, I, E, S, M* 2,3, 1959 *BI* 1,2
Dore, E (Q) 1904 *BI* 1
Dore, M J (Q) 1905 *NZ*
Dorr, R W (V) 1936 *M*, 1937 *SA* 1
Douglas, J A (V) 1962 *NZ* 3,4,5
Dowse, J H (NSW) 1961 *Fj* 1,2, *SA* 1,2
Dunbar, A R (NSW) 1910 *NZ* 1,2,3, 1912 *US*
Dunlop, E E (V) 1932 *NZ* 3, 1934 *NZ* 1
Dunn, P K (NSW) 1958 *NZ* 1,2,3, 1959 *BI* 1,2
Dunn, V A (NSW) 1921 *NZ*
Dunworth, D A (Q) 1971 *F* 1,2, 1972 *F* 1,2, 1976 *Fj* 2
Dwyer, L J (NSW) 1910 *NZ* 1,2,3, 1912 *US*, 1913 *NZ* 3, 1914 *NZ* 1,2,3

Eales, J A (Q) 1991 *W, E, NZ* 1,2, [*Arg, WS, W, I, NZ, E*], 1992 *S* 1,2, *NZ* 1,2,3, *SA, I*, 1994 *I* 1,2, *It* 1,2, *WS, NZ*, 1995 *Arg* 1,2, [*SA, C, R, E*], *NZ* 1, 1996 *W* 1,2, *C, NZ* 1, *SA* 1, *NZ* 2, *SA* 2, *It, S, I*, 1997 *F* 1,2, *NZ* 1, *E* 1, *NZ* 2, *SA* 1, *Arg* 1,2, *E* 2, *S*
Eastes, C C (NSW) 1946 *NZ* 1,2, 1947 *NZ* 1,2, 1949 *M* 1,2
Egerton, R H (NSW) 1991 *W, E, NZ* 1,2, [*Arg, W, I, NZ, E*]
Ella, G A (NSW) 1982 *NZ* 1,2, 1983 *F* 1,2, 1988 *E* 2, *NZ* 1
Ella, G J (NSW) 1982 *S* 1, 1983 *It*, 1985 *C* 2 (R), *Fj* 2
Ella, M G (NSW) 1980 *NZ* 1,2,3, 1981 *F* 2, *S*, 1982 *E, S* 1, *NZ* 1,2,3, 1983 *US, Arg* 1,2, *NZ, It, F* 1,2, 1984 *Fj, NZ* 1,2,3, *E, I, W, S*
Ellem, M A (NSW) 1976 *Fj* 3 (R)
Elliott, F M (NSW) 1957 *NZ* 1
Elliott, R E (NSW) 1921 *NZ*, 1923 *NZ* 1,2,3
Ellis, C S (NSW) 1899 *BI* 1,2,3,4
Ellis, K J (NSW) 1958 *NZ* 1,2,3, 1959 *BI* 1,2
Ellwood, B J (NSW) 1958 *NZ* 1,2,3, 1961 *Fj* 2,3, *SA* 1, *F*, 1962 *NZ* 1,2,3,4,5, 1963 *SA* 1,2,3,4, 1964 *NZ* 3, 1965 *SA* 1,2, 1966 *BI* 1
Emanuel, D M (NSW) 1957 *NZ* 2, 1958 *W, I, E, S, F, M* 1,2,3
Emery, N A (NSW) 1947 *NZ* 2, *S, I, W*, 1948 *E, F*, 1949 *M* 2,3, *NZ* 1,2
Erasmus, D J (NSW) 1923 *NZ* 1,2
Erby, A B (NSW) 1923 *NZ* 2,3
Evans, L J (Q) 1903 *NZ*, 1904 *BI* 1,3
Evans, W T (Q) 1899 *BI* 1,2

Fahey, E J (NSW) 1912 *US*, 1913 *NZ* 1,2, 1914 *NZ* 3
Fairfax, R L (NSW) 1971 *F* 1,2, 1972 *F* 1,2, *NZ* 1, *Fj*, 1973 *W, E*
Farmer, E H (Q) 1910 *NZ* 1
Farr-Jones, N C (NSW) 1984 *E, I, W, S*, 1985 *C* 1,2, *NZ, Fj* 1,2, 1986 *It, F, Arg* 1,2, *NZ* 1,2,3, 1987 *SK*, [*E, I, F, W* (R)], *NZ, Arg* 2, 1988 *E* 2, *NZ* 1,2,3, *E, S, It*, 1989 *BI* 1,2,3, *NZ, F* 1,2, 1990 *F* 1,2,3, *US, NZ* 1,2,3, 1991 *W, E, NZ* 1,2, [*Arg, WS, I, NZ, E*], 1992 *S* 1,2, *NZ* 1,2,3, *SA*, 1993 *NZ, SA* 1,2,3
Fay, G (NSW) 1971 *SA* 2, 1972 *NZ* 1,2,3, 1973 *Tg* 1,2, *W, E*, 1974 *NZ* 1,2,3, 1975 *E* 1,2, *J* 1, *S, W*, 1976 *I, US*, 1978 *W* 1,2, *NZ* 1,2,3, 1979 *I* 1

How, R A (NSW) 1967 *I* 2

Howard, J (Q) 1938 *NZ* 1,2

Howard, J L (NSW) 1970 *S*, 1971 *SA* 1, 1972 *F* 1 (R), *NZ* 2, 1973 *Tg* 1,2, *W*

Howard, P W (Q, ACT) 1993 *NZ*, 1994 *WS, NZ*, 1995 *NZ* 1 (R), 2 (t), 1996 *W* 1,2, *SA* 1, *NZ* 2, *SA* 2, *It, S, W* 3, 1997 *F* 1,2, *NZ* 1, *Arg* 1,2, *E* 2, *S*

Howell, M L (NSW) 1946 *NZ* 1 (R), 1947 *NZ* 1, *S, I, W*

Hughes, B D (NSW) 1913 *NZ* 2,3

Hughes, J C (NSW) 1907 *NZ* 1,3

Hughes, N McL (NSW) 1953 *SA* 1,2,3,4, 1955 *NZ* 1,2,3, 1956 *SA* 1,2, 1958 *W, I, E, S, F*

Humphreys, O W (NSW) 1921 *NZ*

Hutchinson, E E (NSW) 1937 *SA* 1,2

Hutchinson, F E (NSW) 1936 *NZ* 1,2, 1938 *NZ* 1,3

Ide, W P J (Q) 1938 *NZ* 2,3

Ives, W N (NSW) 1929 *NZ* 3

James, P M (Q) 1958 *M* 2,3

James, S L (NSW) 1987 *SK* (R), [*E* (R)], *NZ*, *Arg* 1,2, 1988 *NZ* 2 (R)

Jessep, E M (V) 1934 *NZ* 1,2

Johnson, A P (NSW) 1946 *NZ* 1, *M*

Johnson, B B (NSW) 1952 *Fj* 1,2, *NZ* 1,2, 1953 *SA* 2,3,4, 1955 *NZ* 1,2

Johnson, P G (NSW) 1959 *BI* 1,2, 1961 *Fj* 1,2,3, *SA* 1,2, *F*, 1962 *NZ* 1,2,3,4,5, 1963 *E, SA* 1,2,3,4, 1964 *NZ* 1,2,3, 1965 *SA* 1,2, 1966 *BI* 1,2, *W, S*, 1967 *E, I* 1, *F, I* 2, *NZ*, 1968 *NZ* 1,2, *F, I, S*, 1970 *S*, 1971 *SA* 1,2, *F* 1,2

Johnstone, B (Q) 1993 *Tg* (R)

Jones, G G (Q) 1952 *Fj* 1,2, 1953 *SA* 1,2,3,4, 1954 *Fj* 1,2, 1955 *NZ* 1,2,3, 1956 *SA* 1

Jones, H (NSW) 1913 *NZ* 1,2,3

Jones, P A (NSW) 1963 *E, SA* 1

Jorgensen, P (NSW) 1992 *S* 1 (R), 2 (R)

Joyce, J E (NSW) 1903 *NZ*

Judd, H A (NSW) 1903 *NZ*, 1904 *BI* 1,2,3, 1905 *NZ*

Judd, P B (NSW) 1925 *NZ*, 1927 *I, W, S*, 1928 *E*, 1931 *M, NZ*

Junee, D K (NSW) 1989 *F* 1 (R), 2 (R), 1994 *WS* (R), *NZ* (R)

Kahl, P R (Q) 1992 *W*

Kassulke, N (Q) 1985 *C* 1,2

Kay, A R (V) 1958 *NZ* 2, 1959 *BI* 2

Kay, P (NSW) 1988 *E* 2

Kearney, K H (NSW) 1947 *NZ* 1,2, *S, I, W*, 1948 *E, F*

Kearns, P N (NSW) 1989 *NZ, F* 1,2, 1990 *F* 1,2,3, *US*, *NZ* 1,2,3, 1991 *W, E, NZ* 1,2, [*Arg, WS, W, I, NZ, E*], 1992 *S* 1,2, *NZ* 1,2,3, *SA, I, W*, 1993 *Tg, NZ, SA* 1,2,3, *C, F* 1,2, 1994 *I* 1,2, *It* 1,2, *WS, NZ*, 1995 *Arg* 1,2, [*SA, C, E*], *NZ* 1,2

Kefu, T (Q) 1997 *SA* 2 (R)

Kelaher, J D (NSW) 1933 *SA* 1,2,3,4,5, 1934 *NZ* 1,2, 1936 *NZ* 1,2, *M*, 1937 *SA* 1,2, 1938 *NZ* 3

Kelaher, T P (NSW) 1992 *NZ* 1, *I* (R), 1993 *NZ*

Kelleher, R J (Q) 1969 *SA* 2,3

Keller, D H (NSW) 1947 *NZ* 1, *S, I, W*, 1948 *E, F*

Kelly, A J (NSW) 1899 *BI* 1

Kelly, R L F (NSW) 1936 *NZ* 1,2, *M*, 1937 *SA* 1,2, 1938 *NZ* 1,2

Kent, A (Q) 1912 *US*

Kerr, F R (V) 1938 *NZ* 1

King, S C (NSW) 1927 *W, S*, 1928 *E, F*, 1929 *NZ* 1,2,3, 1930 *BI*, 1932 *NZ* 1,2

Knight, M (NSW) 1978 *W* 1,2, *NZ* 1

Knight, S O (NSW) 1969 *SA* 2,4, 1970 *S*, 1971 *SA* 1,2,3

Knox, D J (NSW, ACT) 1994 *WS*, 1996 *It, S, I*, 1997 *SA* 1, *NZ* 3, *SA* 2, *Arg* 1,2

Kraefft, D F (NSW) 1947 *NZ* 2, *S, I, W*, 1948 *E, F*

Kreutzer, S D (Q) 1914 *NZ* 2

Lamb, J S (NSW) 1928 *NZ* 1,2, *M*

Lambie, J K (NSW) 1974 *NZ* 1,2,3, 1975 *W*

Lane, T A (Q) 1985 *C* 1,2, *NZ*

Lang, C W P (V) 1938 *NZ* 2,3

Langford, J F (ACT) 1997 *NZ* 3, *SA* 2, *E* 2, *S*

Larkham, S J (ACT) 1996 *W* 2 (R), 1997 *F* 1,2, *NZ* 1,2 (R), *SA* 1, *NZ* 3, *SA* 2, *Arg* 1,2, *E* 2, *S*

Larkin, E R (NSW) 1903 *NZ*

Larkin, K K (NSW) 1958 *M* 2,3

Latimer, N B (NSW) 1957 *NZ* 2

Lawton, R (Q) 1988 *E* 1, *NZ* 2 (R), 3, *S*

Lawton, T (NSW, Q) 1925 *NZ*, 1927 *I, W, S*, 1928 *E, F*, 1929 *NZ* 1,2,3, 1930 *BI*, 1932 *NZ* 1,2

Lawton, T A (Q) 1983 *F* 1 (R), 2, 1984 *Fj, NZ* 1,2,3, *E, I, W, S*, 1985 *C* 1,2, *NZ*, *Fj* 1, 1986 *It, F, Arg* 1,2, *NZ* 1,2,3, 1987 *SK*, [*E, US, I, F, W*], *NZ*, *Arg* 1,2, 1988 *E* 1,2, *NZ* 1,2,3, *E, S, It*, 1989 *BI* 1,2,3

Laycock, W M B (NSW) 1925 *NZ*

Leeds, A J (NSW) 1986 *NZ* 3, 1987 [*US, W*], *NZ*, *Arg* 1,2, 1988 *E* 1,2, *NZ* 1,2,3, *E, S, It*

Lenehan, J K (NSW) 1958 *W, E, S, F, M* 1,2,3, 1959 *BI* 1,2, 1961 *SA* 1,2, *F*, 1962 *NZ* 2,3,4,5, 1965 *SA* 1,2, 1966 *W, S*, 1967 *E, I* 1, *F, I* 2

L'Estrange, D (Q) 1971 *F* 1,2, 1972 *NZ* 1,2,3, 1973 *Tg* 1,2, *W, E*, 1974 *NZ* 1,2,3, 1975 *S, W*, 1976 *I, US*

Lewis, L S (Q) 1934 *NZ* 1,2, 1936 *NZ* 2, 1938 *NZ* 1

Lidbury, S (NSW) 1987 *Arg* 1, 1988 *E* 2

Lillicrap, C P (Q) 1985 *Fj* 2, 1987 [*US, I, F, W*], 1989 *BI* 1, 1991 [*WS*]

Lindsay, R T G (Q) 1932 *NZ* 3

Lisle, R J (NSW) 1961 *Fj* 1,2,3, *SA* 1

Little, J S (Q) 1989 *F* 1,2, 1990 *F* 1,2,3, *US*, 1991 *W, E, NZ* 1,2, [*Arg, W, I, NZ, E*], 1992 *NZ* 1,2,3, *SA, I, W*, 1993 *Tg, NZ, SA* 1,2,3, *C, F* 1,2, 1994 *WS, NZ*, 1995 *Arg* 1,2, [*SA, C, E*], *NZ* 1,2, 1996 *It* (R), *I, W* 3, 1997 *F* 1,2, *E* 1, *NZ* 2, *SA* 1, *NZ* 3, *SA* 2

Livermore, A E (Q) 1946 *NZ* 1, *M*

Loane, M E (Q) 1973 *Tg* 1,2, 1974 *NZ* 1, 1975 *E* 1,2, *J* 1, 1976 *E, I, Fj* 1,2,3, *F* 1,2, 1978 *W* 1,2, 1979 *I* 1,2, *NZ*, *Arg* 1,2, 1981 *F* 1,2, *I, W, S*, 1982 *E, S* 1,2

Logan, D L (NSW) 1958 *M* 1

Loudon, D B (NSW) 1921 *NZ*

Loudon, R B (NSW) 1923 *NZ* 1 (R), 2,3, 1928 *NZ* 1,2,3, *M*, 1929 *NZ* 2, 1933 *SA* 2,3,4,5, 1934 *NZ* 2

Love, E W (NSW) 1932 *NZ* 1,2,3

Lowth, D R (NSW) 1958 *NZ* 1

Lucas, B C (Q) 1905 *NZ*

Lucas, P W (NSW) 1982 *NZ* 1,2,3

Lutge, D (NSW) 1903 *NZ*, 1904 *BI* 1,2,3

Lynagh, M P (Q) 1984 *Fj, E, I, W, S*, 1985 *C* 1,2, *NZ*, 1986 *It, F, Arg* 1,2, *NZ* 1,2,3, 1987 [*E, US, J, I, F, W*], *Arg* 1,2, 1988 *E* 1,2, *NZ* 1,3 (R), *E, S, It*, 1989 *BI* 1,2,3, *NZ, F* 1,2, 1990 *F* 1,2,3, *US, NZ* 1,2,3, 1991 *W, E, NZ* 1,2, [*Arg, WS, W, I, NZ, E*], 1992 *S* 1,2, *NZ* 1,2,3, *SA, I*, 1993 *Tg, C, F* 1,2, 1994 *I* 1,2, *It* 1, 1995 *Arg* 1,2, [*SA, C, E*]

McArthur, M (NSW) 1909 *E*

McBain, M I (Q) 1983 *It, F* 1, 1985 *Fj* 2, 1986 *It* (R), 1987 [*J*], 1988 *E* 2 (R), 1989 *BI* 1 (R)

MacBride, J W T (NSW) 1946 *NZ* 1, *M, NZ* 2, 1947 *NZ* 1,2, *S, I, W*, 1948 *E, F*

McCabe, A J M (NSW) 1909 *E*

McCall, R J (Q) 1989 *F* 1,2, 1990 *F* 1,2,3, *US, NZ* 1,2,3, 1991 *W, E, NZ* 1,2, [*Arg, W, I, NZ, E*], 1992 *S* 1,2, *NZ* 1,2,3, *SA, I, W*, 1993 *Tg, NZ, SA* 1,2,3, *C, F* 1,2, 1994 *It* 2, 1995 *Arg* 1,2, [*SA, R, E*]

McCarthy, F J C (Q) 1950 *BI* 1

McCowan, R H (Q) 1899 *BI* 1,2,4

McCue, P A (NSW) 1907 *NZ* 1,3, 1908 *W*, 1909 *E*

McDermott, L C (Q) 1962 *NZ* 1,2

McDonald, B S (NSW) 1969 *SA* 4, 1970 *S*

McDonald, J C (Q) 1938 *NZ* 2,3

Macdougall, D G (NSW) 1961 *Fj* 1, *SA* 1

Macdougall, S G (NSW, ACT) 1971 *SA* 3, 1973 *E*, 1974 *NZ* 1,2,3, 1975 *E* 1,2, 1976 *E*

McGhie, G J (Q) 1929 *NZ* 2,3, 1930 *BI*

McGill, A N (NSW) 1968 *NZ* 1,2, *F*, 1969 *W, SA* 1,2,3,4, 1970 *S*, 1971 *SA* 1,2,3, *F* 1,2, 1972 *F* 1,2, *NZ* 1,2,3, 1973 *Tg* 1,2

McIntyre, A J (Q) 1982 *NZ* 1,2,3, 1983 *F* 1,2, 1984 *Fj, NZ* 1,2,3, *E, I, W, S*, 1985 *C* 1,2, *NZ, Fj* 1,2, 1986 *It, F, Arg* 1,2, 1987 [*E, US, I, F, W*], *NZ, Arg* 2, 1988 *E* 1,2, *NZ* 1,2,3, *E, S, It*, 1989 *NZ*

McKenzie, E J A (NSW, ACT) 1990 *F* 1,2,3, *US, NZ* 1,2,3, 1991 *W, E, NZ* 1,2, [*Arg, W, I, NZ, E*], 1992 *S* 1,2, *NZ* 1,2,3, *SA, I, W*, 1993 *Tg, NZ, SA* 1,2,3, *C, F* 1,2, 1994 *I* 1,2, *It* 1,2, *WS, NZ*, 1995 *Arg* 1,2, [*SA, C* (R), *R, E*], *NZ* 2, 1996 *W* 1,2, 1997 *F* 1,2, *NZ* 1, *E* 1

McKid, W A (NSW) 1976 *E, Fj* 1, 1978 *NZ* 2,3, 1979 *I* 1,2

McKinnon, A (Q) 1904 *BI* 2

McKivat, C H (NSW) 1907 *NZ* 1,3, 1908 *W*, 1909 *E*

McLaughlin, R E M (NSW) 1936 *NZ* 1,2

McLean, A D (Q) 1933 *SA* 1,2,3,4,5, 1934 *NZ* 1,2, 1936 *NZ* 1,2, *M*

McLean, J D (Q) 1904 *BI* 2,3, 1905 *NZ*
McLean, J J (Q) 1971 *SA* 2,3, *F* 1,2, 1972 *F* 1,2, *NZ* 1,2,3, *Fj*, 1973 *W, E*, 1974 *NZ* 1
McLean, P E (Q) 1974 *NZ* 1,2,3, 1975 *J* 1,2, *S, W*, 1976 *E, I, Fj* 1,2,3, *F* 1,2, 1978 *W* 1,2, *NZ* 2, 1979 *I* 1,2, *NZ, Arg* 1,2, 1980 *Fj*, 1981 *F* 1,2, *I, W, S*, 1982 *E, S* 2
McLean, P W (Q) 1978 *NZ* 1,2,3, 1979 *I* 1,2, *NZ, Arg* 1,2, 1980 *Fj* (R), *NZ* 3, 1981 *I, W, S*, 1982 *E, S* 1,2
McLean, R A (NSW) 1971 *SA* 1,2,3, *F* 1,2
McLean, W M (Q) 1946 *NZ* 1, *M, NZ* 2, 1947 *NZ* 1,2
McMahon, M J (Q) 1913 *NZ* 1
McMaster, R E (Q) 1946 *NZ* 1, *M, NZ* 2, 1947 *NZ* 1,2, *I, W*
MacMillan, D I (Q) 1950 *BI* 1,2
McMullen, K V (NSW) 1962 *NZ* 3,5, 1963 *E, SA* 1
McShane, J M S (NSW) 1937 *SA* 1,2
Mackney, W A R (NSW) 1933 *SA* 1,5, 1934 *NZ* 1,2
Magrath, E (NSW) 1961 *Fj* 1, *SA* 2, *F*
Maguire, D J (Q) 1989 *BI* 1,2,3
Malcolm, S J (NSW) 1927 *S*, 1928 *E, F, NZ* 1,2, *M*, 1929 *NZ* 1,2,3, 1930 *BI*, 1931 *NZ*, 1932 *NZ* 1,2,3, 1933 *SA* 4,5, 1934 *NZ* 1,2
Malone, J H (NSW) 1936 *NZ* 1,2, *M*, 1937 *SA* 2
Malouf, B P (NSW) 1982 *NZ* 1
Mandible, E F (NSW) 1907 *NZ* 2,3, 1908 *W*
Manning, J (NSW) 1904 *BI* 2
Manning, R C S (Q) 1967 *NZ*
Mansfield, B W (NSW) 1975 *J* 2
Manu, D T (NSW) 1995 [*R* (t)], *NZ* 1,2, 1996 *W* 1,2 (R), *SA* 1, *NZ* 2, *It, S, I*, 1997 *F* 1, *NZ* 1 (t), *E* 1, *NZ* 2, *SA* 1
Marks, H (NSW) 1899 *NZ* 1,2
Marks, R J P (Q) 1962 *NZ* 4,5, 1963 *E, SA* 2,3,4, 1964 *NZ* 1,2,3, 1965 *SA* 1,2, 1966 *W, S*, 1967 *E, I* 1, *F, I* 2
Marrott, W J (NSW) 1923 *NZ* 1,2
Marshall, J S (NSW) 1949 *M* 1
Martin, G J (Q) 1989 *BI* 1,2,3, *NZ, F* 1,2, 1990 *F* 1,3 (R), *NZ* 1
Martin, M C (NSW) 1980 *Fj, NZ* 1,2, 1981 *F* 1,2, *W* (R)
Massey-Westropp, M (NSW) 1914 *NZ* 3
Mathers, M J (NSW) 1980 *Fj, NZ* 2 (R)
Maund, J W (NSW) 1903 *NZ*
Meadows, J E C (V, Q) 1974 *NZ* 1, 1975 *S, W*, 1976 *I, US, Fj* 1,3, *F* 1,2, 1978 *NZ* 1,2,3, 1979 *I* 1,2, 1981 *I, S*, 1982 *E, NZ* 2,3, 1983 *US, Arg* 2, *NZ*
Meadows, R W (NSW) 1958 *M* 1,2,3, *NZ* 1,2,3
Meagher, F W (NSW) 1923 *NZ* 3, 1925 *NZ*, 1927 *I, W*
Meibusch, J H (Q) 1904 *BI* 3
Meibusch, L S (Q) 1912 *US*
Melrose, T C (NSW) 1978 *NZ* 3, 1979 *I* 1,2, *NZ, Arg* 1,2
Merrick, S (NSW) 1995 *NZ* 1,2
Messenger, H H (NSW) 1907 *NZ* 2,3
Middleton, S A (NSW) 1909 *E*, 1910 *NZ* 1,2,3
Miller, A R (NSW) 1952 *Fj* 1,2, *NZ* 1,2, 1953 *SA* 1,2,3,4, 1954 *Fj* 1,2, 1955 *NZ* 1,2,3, 1956 *SA* 1,2, 1957 *NZ* 1,2, 1958 *W, E, S, F, M* 1,2,3, 1959 *BI* 1,2, 1961 *Fj* 1,2,3, *SA* 2, *F*, 1962 *NZ* 1,2, 1966 *BI* 1,2, *W, S*, 1967 *I* 1, *F, I* 2
Miller, J M (NSW) 1962 *NZ* 1, 1963 *E, SA* 1, 1966 *W, S*, 1967 *E*
Miller, J S (Q) 1986 *NZ* 2,3, 1987 *SK*, [*US, I, F*], *NZ, Arg* 1,2, 1988 *E* 1,2, *NZ* 2,3, *E, S, It*, 1989 *BI* 1,2,3, *NZ*, 1990 *F* 1,3, 1991 *W*, [*WS, W, I*]
Miller, S W J (NSW) 1899 *BI* 3
Mingey, N (NSW) 1923 *NZ* 1,2
Monaghan, L E (NSW) 1973 *E*, 1974 *NZ* 1,2,3, 1975 *E* 1,2, *S, W*, 1976 *E, I, US, F* 1, 1978 *W* 1,2, *NZ* 1, 1979 *I* 1,2
Monti, C I A (Q) 1938 *NZ* 2
Moon, B J (Q) 1978 *NZ* 2,3, 1979 *I* 1,2, *NZ, Arg* 1,2, 1980 *Fj, NZ* 1,2,3, 1981 *F* 1,2, *I, W, S*, 1982 *E, S* 1,2, 1983 *US, Arg* 1,2, *NZ, It, F* 1,2, 1984 *Fj, NZ* 1,2,3, *E*, 1986 *It, F, Arg* 1,2
Mooney, T P (Q) 1954 *Fj* 1,2
Moran, H M (NSW) 1908 *W*
Morgan, G (Q) 1992 *NZ* 1 (R), 3 (R), *W*, 1993 *Tg, NZ, SA* 1,2,3, *C, F* 1,2, 1994 *I* 1,2, *It* 1, *WS, NZ*, 1996 *W* 1,2, *C, NZ* 1, *SA* 1, *NZ* 2, 1997 *E* 1, *NZ* 2
Morrissey, C V (NSW) 1925 *NZ*
Morrissey, W (NSW) 1914 *NZ* 2
Morton, A R (NSW) 1957 *NZ* 1,2, 1958 *F, M* 1,2,3, *NZ* 1,2,3, 1959 *BI* 1,2
Mossop, R P (NSW) 1949 *NZ* 1, 1950 *BI* 1,2, 1951 *NZ* 1
Moutray, I E (NSW) 1963 *SA* 2
Munsie, A (NSW) 1928 *NZ* 2

Murdoch, A R (NSW) 1993 *F* 1, 1996 *W* 1
Murphy, P J (Q) 1910 *NZ* 1,2,3, 1913 *NZ* 1,2,3, 1914 *NZ* 1,2,3
Murphy, W (Q) 1912 *US*

Nasser, B P (Q) 1989 *F* 1,2, 1990 *F* 1,2,3, *US, NZ* 2, 1991 [*WS*]
Nicholson, F C (Q) 1904 *BI* 3
Nicholson, F V (Q) 1903 *NZ*, 1904 *BI* 1
Niuqila, A S (NSW) 1988 *S, It*, 1989 *BI* 1
Nothling, O E (NSW) 1921 *NZ*, 1923 *NZ* 1,2,3
Nucifora, D V (Q) 1991 [*Arg* (R)], 1993 *C* (R)

O'Brien, F W H (NSW) 1937 *SA* 2, 1938 *NZ* 3
O'Connor, J A (NSW) 1928 *NZ* 1,2,3, *M*
O'Connor, M (ACT) 1994 *I* 1
O'Connor, M D (ACT, Q) 1979 *Arg* 1,2, 1980 *Fj, NZ* 1,2,3, 1981 *F* 1,2, *I*, 1982 *E, S* 1,2
O'Donnell, C (NSW) 1913 *NZ* 1,2
O'Donnell, I C (NSW) 1899 *BI* 3,4
O'Donnell, J B (NSW) 1928 *NZ* 1,3, *M*
O'Donnell, J M (NSW) 1899 *BI* 4
O'Gorman, J F (NSW) 1961 *Fj* 1, *SA* 1,2, *F*, 1962 *NZ* 2, 1963 *E, SA* 1,2,3,4, 1965 *SA* 1,2, 1966 *W, S*, 1967 *E, I* 1, *F, I* 2
O'Neill, D J (Q) 1964 *NZ* 1,2
O'Neill, J M (Q) 1952 *NZ* 1,2, 1956 *SA* 1,2
Ofahengaue, V (NSW) 1990 *NZ* 1,2,3, 1991 *W, E, NZ* 1,2, [*Arg, W, I, NZ, E*], 1992 *S* 1,2, *SA, I, W*, 1994 *WS, NZ*, 1995 *Arg* 1,2 (R), [*SA, C, E*], *NZ* 1,2, 1997 *Arg* 1 (t + R), 2 (R), *E* 2, *S*
Osborne, D H (V) 1975 *E* 1,2, *J* 1
Outterside, R (NSW) 1959 *BI* 1,2
Oxenham, A McE (Q) 1904 *BI* 2, 1907 *NZ* 2
Oxlade, A M (Q) 1904 *BI* 2,3, 1905 *NZ*, 1907 *NZ* 2
Oxlade, B D (Q) 1938 *NZ* 1,2,3

Palfreyman, J R L (NSW) 1929 *NZ* 1, 1930 *BI*, 1931 *NZ*, 1932 *NZ* 3
Papworth, B (NSW) 1985 *Fj* 1,2, 1986 *It, Arg* 1,2, *NZ* 1,2,3, 1987 [*E, US, J* (R), *I, F*], *NZ, Arg* 1,2
Parker, A J (Q) 1983 *Arg* 1 (R), 2, *NZ*
Parkinson, C E (Q) 1907 *NZ* 2
Pashley, J J (NSW) 1954 *Fj* 1,2, 1958 *M* 1,2,3
Pauling, T P (NSW) 1936 *NZ* 1, 1937 *SA* 1
Payne, S J (NSW) 1996 *W* 2, *C, NZ* 1, *S*, 1997 *F* 1 (t), *NZ* 2 (R), *Arg* 2 (t)
Pearse, G K (NSW) 1975 *W* (R), 1976 *I, US, Fj* 1,2,3, 1978 *NZ* 1,2,3
Penman, A P (NSW) 1905 *NZ*
Perrin, P D (Q) 1962 *NZ* 1
Perrin, T D (NSW) 1931 *M, NZ*
Phelps, R (NSW) 1955 *NZ* 2,3, 1956 *SA* 1,2, 1957 *NZ* 1,2, 1958 *W, I, E, S, F, M* 1, *NZ* 1,2,3, 1961 *Fj* 1,2,3, *SA* 1,2, *F*, 1962 *NZ* 1,2
Phipps, J A (NSW) 1953 *SA* 1,2,3,4, 1954 *Fj* 1,2, 1955 *NZ* 1,2,3, 1956 *SA* 1,2
Phipps, W J (NSW) 1928 *NZ* 2
Pilecki, S J (Q) 1978 *W* 1,2, *NZ* 1,2, 1979 *I* 1,2, *NZ, Arg* 1,2, 1980 *Fj, NZ* 1,2,3, 1982 *S* 1,2, 1983 *US, Arg* 1,2, *NZ*
Pini, M (Q) 1994 *I* 1, *It* 2, *WS, NZ*, 1995 *Arg* 1,2, [*SA, R* (t)]
Piper, B J C (NSW) 1946 *NZ* 1, *M, NZ* 2, 1947 *NZ* 1, *S, I, W*, 1948 *E, F*, 1949 *M*, 1,2,3
Poidevin, S P (NSW) 1980 *Fj, NZ* 1,2,3, 1981 *F* 1,2, *I, W, S*, 1982 *NZ* 1,2,3, 1983 *US, Arg* 1,2, *NZ, It, F* 1,2, 1984 *Fj, NZ* 1,2,3, *E, I, W, S*, 1985 *C* 1,2, *NZ, Fj* 1,2, 1986 *It, F, Arg* 1,2, *NZ* 1,2,3, 1987 *SK*, [*E, J, I, F, W*], *Arg* 1, 1988 *NZ* 1,2,3, 1989 *NZ*, 1991 *E, NZ* 1,2, [*Arg, W, I, NZ, E*]
Pope, A M (Q) 1968 *NZ* 2 (R)
Potter, R T (Q) 1961 *Fj* 2
Potts, J M (NSW) 1957 *NZ* 1,2, 1958 *W, I*, 1959 *BI* 1
Prentice, C W (NSW) 1914 *NZ* 3
Prentice, W S (NSW) 1908 *W*, 1909 *E*, 1910 *NZ* 1,2,3, 1912 *US*
Price, R A (NSW) 1974 *NZ* 1,2,3, 1975 *E* 1,2, *J* 1,2, 1976 *US*
Primmer, C J (Q) 1951 *NZ* 1,3
Proctor, I J (NSW)) 1967 *NZ*
Prosser, R B (NSW) 1967 *E, I* 1,2, *NZ*, 1968 *NZ* 1,2, *F, I, S*, 1969 *W, SA* 1,2,3,4, 1971 *SA* 1,2,3, *F* 1,2, 1972 *F* 1,2, *NZ* 1,2,3, *Fj*
Pugh, G H (NSW) 1912 *US*

354

Purcell, M P (Q) 1966 *W, S*, 1967 *I* 2
Purkis, E M (NSW) 1958 *S, M* 1

Ramalli, C (NSW) 1938 *NZ* 2,3
Ramsay, K M (NSW) 1936 *M*, 1937 *SA* 1, 1938 *NZ* 1,3
Rankin, R (NSW) 1936 *NZ* 1,2, *M*, 1937 *SA* 1,2, 1938 *NZ* 1,2
Rathie, D S (Q) 1972 *F* 1,2
Raymond, R L (NSW) 1921 *NZ*
Redwood, C (Q) 1903 *NZ*, 1904 *BI* 1,2,3
Reid, E J (NSW) 1925 *NZ*
Reid, T W (NSW) 1961 *Fj* 1,2,3, *SA* 1, 1962 *NZ* 1
Reilly, N P (Q) 1968 *NZ* 1,2, *F, I, S*, 1969 *W, SA* 1,2,3,4
Reynolds, L J (NSW) 1910 *NZ* 2 (R), 3
Reynolds, R J (NSW) 1984 *Fj, NZ* 1,2,3, 1985 *Fj* 1,2, 1986 *Arg* 1,2, *NZ* 1, 1987 *[J]*
Richards, E W (Q) 1904 *BI* 1,3, 1905 *NZ*, 1907 *NZ* 1 (R), 2
Richards, G (NSW) 1978 *NZ* 2 (R), 3, 1981 *F* 1
Richards, T J (Q) 1908 *W*, 1909 *E*, 1912 *US*
Richards, V S (NSW) 1936 *NZ* 1,2 (R), *M*, 1937 *SA* 1, 1938 *NZ* 1
Richardson, G C (Q) 1971 *SA* 1,2,3, 1972 *NZ* 2,3, *Fj*, 1973 *Tg* 1,2, *W*
Rigney, W A (NSW) 1925 *NZ*
Riley, S A (NSW) 1903 *NZ*
Roberts, B T (NSW) 1956 *SA* 2
Roberts, H F (Q) 1961 *Fj* 1,3, *SA* 2, *F*
Robertson, I J (NSW) 1975 *J* 1,2
Robinson, B J (ACT) 1996 *It* (R), *S* (R), *I* (R), 1997 *F* 1,2, *NZ* 1, *E* 1, *NZ* 2, *SA* 1 (R), *NZ* 3 (R), *SA* 2 (R), *Arg* 1,2, *E* 2, *S*
Roche, C (Q) 1982 *S* 1,2, *NZ* 1,2,3, 1983 *US, Arg* 1,2, *NZ, It, F* 1,2, 1984 *Fj, NZ* 1,2,3, *I*
Rodriguez, E E (NSW) 1984 *Fj, NZ* 1,2,3, *E, I, W, S*, 1985 *C* 1,2, *NZ, Fj* 1, 1986 *It, F, Arg* 1,2, *NZ* 1,2,3, 1987 *SK, [E, J, W* (R)]*, *NZ, Arg* 1,2
Roebuck, M C (NSW) 1991 *W, E, NZ* 1,2, *[Arg, WS, W, I, NZ, E]*, 1992 *S* 1,2, *NZ* 2,3, *SA, I, W*, 1993 *Tg, SA* 1,2,3, *C, F* 2
Roff, J W (ACT) 1995 *[C, R]*, *NZ* 1,2, 1996 *W* 1,2, *NZ* 1, *SA* 1, *NZ* 2, *SA* 2 (R), *S, I, W* 3, 1997 *F* 1,2, *NZ* 1, *E* 1, *NZ* 2, *SA* 1, *NZ* 3, *SA* 2, *Arg* 1,2, *E* 2, *S*
Rose, H A (NSW), 1967 *I* 2, 1968 *NZ* 1,2, *F, I, S*, 1969 *W, SA* 1,2,3,4, 1970 *S*
Rosenblum, M E (NSW) 1928 *NZ* 1,2,3, *M*
Rosenblum, R G (NSW) 1969 *SA* 1,3, 1970 *S*
Rosewell, J S H (NSW) 1907 *NZ* 1,3
Ross, A W (NSW) 1927 *I, W, S*, 1928 *E, F*, 1929 *NZ* 1, 1930 *BI*, 1931 *M, NZ*, 1932 *NZ* 2,3, 1933 *SA* 5, 1934 *NZ* 1,2
Ross, W S (Q) 1979 *I* 1,2, *Arg* 2, 1980 *Fj, NZ* 1,2,3, 1982 *S* 1,2, 1983 *US, Arg* 1,2, *NZ*
Rothwell, P R (NSW) 1951 *NZ* 1,2,3, 1952 *Fj* 1
Row, F L (NSW) 1899 *BI* 1,3,4
Row, N E (NSW) 1907 *NZ* 1,3, 1909 *E*, 1910 *NZ* 1,2,3
Rowles, P G (NSW) 1972 *Fj*, 1973 *E*
Roxburgh, J R (NSW) 1968 *NZ* 1,2, *F*, 1969 *W, SA* 1,2,3,4, 1970 *S*
Ruebner, G (NSW) 1966 *BI* 1,2
Russell, C J (NSW) 1907 *NZ* 1,2,3, 1908 *W*, 1909 *E*
Ryan, J R (NSW) 1975 *J* 2, 1976 *I, US, Fj* 1,2,3
Ryan, K J (NSW) 1958 *E, M* 1, *NZ* 1,2,3
Ryan, P F (NSW) 1963 *E, SA* 1, 1966 *BI* 1,2

Sampson, J H (NSW) 1899 *BI* 4
Sayle, J L (NSW) 1967 *NZ*
Schulte, B G (Q) 1946 *NZ* 1, *M*
Scott, P R I (NSW) 1962 *NZ* 1,2
Scott-Young, S J (Q) 1990 *F* 2,3 (R), *US, NZ* 3, 1992 *NZ* 1,2,3
Shambrook, G G (Q) 1976 *Fj* 2,3
Shaw, A A (Q) 1973 *W, E*, 1975 *E* 1,2, *J* 2, *S, W*, 1976 *E, I, US, Fj* 1,2,3, *F* 1,2, 1978 *W* 1,2, *NZ* 1,2,3, 1979 *I* 1,2, *NZ, Arg* 1,2, 1980 *Fj, NZ* 1,2,3, 1981 *F* 1,2, *I, W, S*, 1982 *S* 1,2
Shaw, C (NSW) 1925 *NZ* (R)
Shaw, G A (NSW) 1969 *W, SA* 1 (R), 1970 *S*, 1971 *SA* 1,2,3, *F* 1,2, 1973 *W, E*, 1974 *NZ* 1,2,3, 1975 *E* 1,2, *J* 1,2, *W*, 1976 *E, I, US, Fj* 1,2,3, *F* 1,2, 1979 *NZ*
Sheehan, W B J (NSW) 1923 *NZ* 1,2,3, 1927 *W, S*

Shehadie, N M (NSW) 1947 *NZ* 2, 1948 *E, F*, 1949 *M* 1,2,3, *NZ* 1,2, 1950 *BI* 1,2, 1951 *NZ* 1,2,3, 1952 *Fj* 1,2, *NZ* 2, 1953 *SA* 1,2,3,4, 1954 *Fj* 1,2, 1955 *NZ* 1,2,3, 1956 *SA* 1,2, 1957 *NZ* 2, 1958 *W, I*
Sheil, A G R (Q) 1956 *SA* 1
Shepherd, D J (V) 1964 *NZ* 3, 1965 *SA* 1,2, 1966 *BI* 1,2
Simpson, R J (NSW) 1913 *NZ* 2
Skinner, A J (NSW) 1969 *W, SA* 4, 1970 *S*
Slack, A G (Q) 1978 *W* 1,2, *NZ* 1,2, 1979 *NZ, Arg* 1,2, 1980 *Fj*, 1981 *I, W, S*, 1982 *E, S* 1, *NZ* 3, 1983 *US, Arg* 1,2 *NZ, It*, 1984 *Fj, NZ* 1,2,3, *E, I, W, S*, 1986 *It, F, NZ* 1,2,3, 1987 *SK, [E, US, J, I, F, W]*
Slater, S H (NSW) 1910 *NZ* 3
Slattery, P J (Q) 1990 *US* (R), 1991 *W* (R), *E* (R), *[WS* (R), *W, I* (R)]*, 1992 *I, W*, 1993 *Tg, C, F* 1,2, 1994 *I* 1 1,2, *It* 1 (R), 1995 *[C, R* (R)]*
Smairl, A M (NSW) 1928 *NZ* 1,2,3
Smith, B A (Q) 1987 *SK, [US, J, I* (R), *W]*, *Arg* 1
Smith, D P (Q) 1993 *SA* 1,2,3, *C, F* 2, 1994 *I* 1,2, *It* 1,2, *WS, NZ*, 1995 *Arg* 1,2, *[SA, R, E]*, *NZ* 1,2
Smith, F B (NSW) 1905 *NZ*, 1907 *NZ* 1,2,3
Smith, L M (NSW) 1905 *NZ*
Smith, N C (NSW) 1923 *NZ* 1
Smith, P V (NSW) 1967 *NZ*, 1968 *NZ* 1,2, *F, I, S*, 1969 *W, SA* 1
Smith, R A (NSW) 1971 *SA* 1,2, 1972 *F* 1,2, *NZ* 1,2 (R), 3, *Fj*, 1975 *E* 1,2, *J* 1,2, *S, W*, 1976 *E, I, US, Fj* 1,2,3, *F* 1,2
Smith, T S (NSW) 1921 *NZ*, 1925 *NZ*
Snell, H W (NSW) 1928 *NZ* 3
Solomon, H J (NSW) 1949 *M* 3, *NZ* 2, 1950 *BI* 1,2, 1951 *NZ* 1,2, 1952 *Fj* 1,2, *NZ* 1,2, 1953 *SA* 1,2,3, 1955 *NZ* 1
Spragg, S A (NSW) 1899 *BI* 1,2,3,4
Stanley, R G (NSW) 1921 *NZ*, 1923 *NZ* 1,2,3
Stapleton, E T (NSW) 1951 *NZ* 1,2,3, 1952 *Fj* 1,2, *NZ* 1,2, 1953 *NZ* 1,2,3,4, 1954 *Fj* 1, 1955 *NZ* 1,2,3, 1958 *NZ* 1
Steggall, J C (Q) 1931 *M, NZ*, 1932 *NZ* 1,2,3, 1933 *SA* 1,2,3,4,5
Stegman, T R (NSW) 1973 *Tg* 1,2
Stephens, O G (NSW) 1973 *Tg* 1,2, *W*, 1974 *NZ* 2,3
Stewart, A A (NSW) 1979 *NZ, Arg* 1,2
Stone, A H (NSW) 1937 *SA* 2, 1938 *NZ* 2,3
Stone, C G (NSW) 1938 *NZ* 1
Stone, J M (NSW) 1946 *M, NZ* 2
Storey, G P (NSW) 1927 *I, W, S*, 1928 *E, F*, 1929 *NZ* 3 (R), 1930 *BI*
Storey, K P (NSW) 1936 *NZ* 2
Storey, N J D (NSW) 1962 *NZ* 1
Strachan, D J (NSW) 1955 *NZ* 2,3
Street, N O (NSW) 1899 *BI* 2
Streeter, S F (NSW) 1978 *NZ* 1
Stuart, R (NSW) 1910 *NZ* 2,3
Stumbles, B D (NSW) 1972 *NZ* 1 (R), 2,3, *Fj*
Sturtridge, G S (V) 1929 *NZ* 2, 1932 *NZ* 1,2,3, 1933 *SA* 1,2,3,4,5
Sullivan, P D (NSW) 1971 *SA* 1,2,3, *F* 1,2, 1972 *F* 1,2, *NZ* 1,2, *Fj*, 1973 *Tg* 1,2, *W*
Summons, A J (NSW) 1958 *W, I, E, S, M* 2, *NZ* 1,2,3, 1959 *BI* 1,2
Suttor, D C (NSW) 1913 *NZ* 1,2,3
Swannell, B I (NSW) 1905 *NZ*
Sweeney, T L (Q) 1953 *SA* 1

Taafe, B S (NSW) 1969 *NZ* 1, 1972 *F* 1,2
Tabua, I (Q) 1993 *SA* 2,3, *C, F* 1, 1994 *I* 1,2, *It* 1,2, 1995 *[C, R]*
Tancred, A J (NSW) 1927 *I, W, S*
Tancred, J L (NSW) 1928 *F*
Tanner, W H (Q) 1899 *BI* 1,2
Tasker, W G (NSW) 1913 *NZ* 1,2,3, 1914 *NZ* 1,2,3
Tate, M J (NSW) 1951 *NZ* 3, 1952 *Fj* 1,2, *NZ* 1,2, 1953 *SA* 1, 1954 *Fj* 1,2
Taylor, D A (Q) 1968 *NZ* 1,2, *F, I, S*
Taylor, H C (NSW) 1923 *NZ* 1,2,3
Taylor, J I (NSW) 1971 *SA* 1, 1972 *F* 1,2, *Fj*
Teitzel, R G (Q) 1966 *W, S*, 1967 *E, I* 1, *F, I* 2, *NZ*
Thompson, C E (NSW) 1923 *NZ* 1
Thompson, E G (Q) 1929 *NZ* 1,2,3, 1930 *BI*
Thompson, F (NSW) 1913 *NZ* 1,2,3, 1914 *NZ* 1,2,3
Thompson, J (Q) 1914 *NZ* 1
Thompson, P D (Q) 1950 *BI* 1
Thompson, R J (WA) 1971 *SA* 3, *F* 2 (R), 1972 *Fj*
Thorn, A M (NSW) 1921 *NZ*

Thorn, E J (NSW) 1923 *NZ* 1,2,3
Thornett, J E (NSW) 1955 *NZ* 1,2,3, 1956 *SA* 1,2, 1958 *W, I, S, F, M* 2,3, *NZ* 2,3, 1959 *BI* 1,2, 1961 *Fj* 2,3, *SA* 1,2, *F*, 1962 *NZ* 2,3,4,5, 1963 *E, SA* 1,2,3,4, 1964 *NZ* 1,2,3, 1965 *SA* 1,2, 1966 *BI* 1,2, 1967 *F*
Thornett, R N (NSW) 1961 *Fj* 1,2,3, *SA* 1,2, *F*, 1962 *NZ* 1,2,3,4,5
Thorpe, A C (NSW) 1929 *NZ* 1 (R)
Timbury, F R V (Q) 1910 *NZ* 1,2,
Tindall, E N (NSW) 1973 *Tg* 2
Toby, A E (NSW) 1925 *NZ*
Tolhurst, H A (NSW) 1931 *M, NZ*
Tombs, R C (NSW) 1992 *S* 1,2, 1994 *I* 2, *It* 1, 1996 *NZ* 2
Tonkin, A E J (NSW) 1947 *S, I, W*, 1948 *E, F*, 1950 *BI* 2
Tooth, R M (NSW) 1951 *NZ* 1,2,3, 1954 *Fj* 1,2, 1955 *NZ* 1,2,3, 1957 *NZ* 1,2
Towers, C H T (NSW) 1927 *I*, 1928 *E, F, NZ* 1,2,3, *M*, 1929 *NZ* 1,3, 1930 *BI*, 1931 *M, NZ*, 1934 *NZ* 1,2, 1937 *SA* 1,2
Trivett, R K (Q) 1966 *BI* 1,2
Tune, B N (Q) 1996 *W* 2, *C, NZ* 1, *SA* 1, *NZ* 2, *SA* 2, 1997 *F* 1,2, *NZ* 1, *E* 1, *NZ* 2, *SA* 1, *NZ* 3, *SA* 2, *Arg,* 1,2, *E* 2, *S*
Turnbull, A (V) 1961 *Fj* 3
Turnbull, R V (NSW) 1968 *I*
Tuynman, S N (NSW) 1983 *F* 1,2, 1984 *E, I, W, S*, 1985 *C* 1,2, *NZ, Fj* 1,2, 1986 *It, F, Arg* 1,2, *NZ* 1,2,3, 1987 *SK, [E, US, J, I, W], NZ, Arg* 1 (R), 2, 1988 *E, It*, 1989 *BI* 1,2,3, *NZ*, 1990 *NZ* 1
Tweedale, E (NSW) 1946 *NZ* 1,2, 1947 *NZ* 2, *S, I*, 1948 *E, F*, 1949 *M* 1,2,3

Vaughan, D (NSW) 1983 *US, Arg* 1, *It, F* 1,2
Vaughan, G N (V) 1958 *E, S, F, M* 1,2,3
Verge, A (NSW) 1904 *BI* 1,2

Walden, R J (NSW) 1934 *NZ* 2, 1936 *NZ* 1,2, *M*
Walker, A K (NSW) 1947 *NZ* 1, 1948 *E, F*, 1950 *BI* 1,2
Walker, A S B (NSW) 1912 *US*, 1921 *NZ*
Walker, L F (NSW) 1988 *NZ* 2,3, *S, It*, 1989 *BI* 1,2,3, *NZ*
Walker, L R (NSW) 1982 *NZ* 2,3
Wallace, A C (NSW) 1921 *NZ*, 1927 *I, W, S*, 1928 *E, F*
Wallace, T M (NSW) 1994 *It* 1 (R), 2
Wallach, C (NSW) 1913 *NZ* 1,3, 1914 *NZ* 1,2,3
Walsh, J J (NSW) 1953 *SA* 1,2,3,4
Walsh, P B (NSW) 1904 *BI* 1,2,3
Walsham, K P (NSW) 1962 *NZ* 3, 1963 *E*
Ward, P G (NSW) 1899 *BI* 1,2,3,4
Ward, T (Q) 1899 *BI* 2
Watson, G W (Q) 1907 *NZ* 1
Watson, W T (NSW) 1912 *US*, 1913 *NZ* 1,2,3, 1914 *NZ* 1

Waugh, W W (NSW, ACT) 1993 *SA* 1, 1995 [*C*], *NZ* 1,2, 1996 *S, I*, 1997 *Arg* 1,2
Weatherstone, L J (ACT) 1975 *E* 1,2, *J* 1,2, *S* (R), 1976 *E, I*
Webb, W (NSW) 1899 *BI* 3,4
Welborn, J (NSW) 1996 *SA* 2, *It*
Wells, B G (NSW) 1958 *M* 1
Westfield, R E (NSW) 1928 *NZ* 1,2,3, *M*, 1929 *NZ* 2,3
White, C J B (NSW) 1899 *BI* 1, 1903 *NZ*, 1904 *BI* 1
White, J M (NSW) 1904 *BI* 3
White, J P L (NSW) 1958 *NZ* 1,2,3, 1961 *Fj* 1,2,3, *SA* 1,2, *F*, 1962 *NZ* 1,2,3,4,5, 1963 *E, SA* 1,2,3,4, 1964 *NZ* 1,2,3, 1965 *SA* 1,2
White, M C (Q) 1931 *M, NZ* 1932 *NZ* 1,2, 1933 *SA* 1,2,3,4,5
White, S W (NSW) 1956 *SA* 1,2, 1958 *I, E, S, M* 2,3
White, W G S (Q) 1933 *SA* 1,2,3,4,5, 1934 *NZ* 1,2, 1936 *NZ* 1,2, *M*
White, W J (NSW) 1928 *NZ* 1, *M*, 1932 *NZ* 1
Wickham, S M (NSW) 1903 *NZ*, 1904 *BI* 1,2,3, 1905 *NZ*
Williams, D (NSW) 1913 *NZ* 3, 1914 *NZ* 1,2,3
Williams, I M (NSW) 1987 *Arg* 1,2, 1988 *E* 1,2, *NZ* 1,2,3, 1989 *BI* 2,3, *NZ, F* 1,2, 1990 *F* 1,2,3, *US, NZ* 1
Williams, J L (NSW) 1963 *SA* 1,3,4
Williams, S A (NSW) 1980 *Fj, NZ* 1,2, 1981 *F* 1,2, 1982 *E, NZ* 1,2,3, 1983 *US, Arg* 1 (R), 2, *NZ, It, F* 1,2, 1984 *NZ* 1,2,3, *E, I, W, S*, 1985 *C* 1,2, *NZ, Fj* 1,2
Wilson, B J (NSW) 1949 *NZ* 1,2
Wilson, C R (Q) 1957 *NZ* 1, 1958 *NZ* 1,2,3
Wilson, D J (Q) 1992 *S* 1,2, *NZ* 1,2,3, *SA, I, W*, 1993 *Tg, NZ, SA* 1,2,3, *C, F* 1,2, 1994 *I* 1,2, *It* 1,2, *WS, NZ*, 1995 *Arg* 1,2, [*SA, R, E*], 1996 *W* 1,2, *C, NZ* 1, *SA* 1, *NZ* 2, *SA* 2, *It, S, I, W* 3, 1997 *F* 1,2, *NZ* 1, *E* 1 (t + R), *NZ* 2 (R), *SA* 1, *NZ* 3, *SA* 2, *E* 2 (R), *S* (R)
Wilson, V W (Q) 1937 *SA* 1,2, 1938 *NZ* 1,2,3
Windon, C J (NSW) 1946 *NZ* 1,2, 1947 *NZ* 1, *S, I, W*, 1948 *E, F*, 1949 *M* 1,2,3, *NZ* 1,2, 1951 *NZ* 1,2,3, 1952 *Fj* 1,2, *NZ* 1,2
Windon, K S (NSW) 1937 *SA* 1,2, 1946 *M*
Windsor, J C (Q) 1947 *NZ* 2
Winning, K C (Q) 1951 *NZ* 1
Wogan, L W (NSW) 1913 *NZ* 1,2,3, 1914 *NZ* 1,2,3, 1921 *NZ*
Wood, F (NSW) 1907 *NZ* 1,2,3, 1910 *NZ* 1,2,3, 1913 *NZ* 1,2,3, 1914 *NZ* 1,2,3
Wood, R N (Q) 1972 *Fj*
Woods, H F (NSW) 1925 *NZ*, 1927 *I, W, S*, 1928 *E*
Wright, K J (NSW) 1975 *E* 1,2, *J* 1, 1976 *US, F* 1,2, 1978 *NZ* 1,2,3

Yanz, K (NSW) 1958 *F*

AUSTRALIAN INTERNATIONAL RECORDS (*up to 30 April 1998*)

MATCH RECORDS

MOST CONSECUTIVE TEST WINS

10 1991 *Arg, WS, W, I, NZ, E,* 1992 *S* 1,2, *NZ* 1,2
 9 1993 *F* 2, 1994 *I* 1,2, *It* 1,2, *WS, NZ,* 1995 *Arg* 1,2

MOST CONSECUTIVE TESTS WITHOUT DEFEAT

P	W	D	Period
10	10	0	1991–92
9	9	0	1993–95
7	7	0	1985–86

MOST POINTS IN A MATCH
by the team

Pts	Opp	Venue	Year
74	C	Brisbane	1996
73	WS	Sydney	1994
67	US	Brisbane	1990
65	SK	Brisbane	1987
63	W	Brisbane	1991

by a player

39 by M Burke v Canada at Brisbane — 1996
28 by M P Lynagh v Argentina at Brisbane — 1995
24 by M P Lynagh v United States at Brisbane — 1990
24 by M P Lynagh v France at Brisbane — 1990
23 several instances

MOST TRIES IN A MATCH
by the team

T	Opp	Venue	Year
13	SK	Brisbane	1987
12	US	Brisbane	1990
12	W	Brisbane	1991
11	WS	Sydney	1994
10	C	Brisbane	1996

by a player

4 by G Cornelsen v New Zealand at Auckland — 1978
4 by D I Campese v United States at Sydney — 1983
3 by A D McLean v New Zealand Maoris at Palmerston N — 1936
3 by J R Ryan v Japan at Brisbane — 1975
3 by M P Burke v Canada at Brisbane — 1985
3 by M P Burke v South Korea at Brisbane — 1987
3 by D I Campese v It{{}}alty at Rome — 1988
3 by A S Nuiqila v Italy at Rome — 1988
3 by D I Campese v Canada at Calgary — 1993
3 by M Burke v Canada at Brisbane — 1996

MOST CONVERSIONS IN A MATCH
by the team

C	Opp	Venue	Year
9	C	Brisbane	1996
8	It	Rome	1988
8	US	Brisbane	1990
7	C	Sydney	1985

by a player

9 by M Burke v Canada at Brisbane — 1996
8 by M P Lynagh v Italy at Rome — 1988
8 by M P Lynagh v United States at Brisbane — 1990
7 by M P Lynagh v Canada at Sydney — 1985

MOST PENALTY GOALS IN A MATCH
by the team

P	Opp	Venue	Year
6	NZ	Sydney	1984
6	F	Sydney	1986
6	E	Brisbane	1988
6	Arg	Buenos Aires	1997
5	several instances		

by a player

6 by M P Lynagh v France at Sydney — 1986
6 by M P Lynagh v England at Brisbane — 1988
6 by D J Knox v Argentina at Buenos Aires — 1997
5 several instances

MOST DROPPED GOALS IN A MATCH

by the team

D	Opp	Venue	Year
3	E	Twickenham	1967
3	I	Dublin	1984
3	Fj	Brisbane	1985

by a player

3 by P F Hawthorne v England at Twickenham		1967
2 by M G Ella v Ireland at Dublin		1984
2 by D J Knox v Fiji at Brisbane		1985

CAREER RECORDS

MOST CAPPED PLAYERS

Caps	Player	Career
101	D I Campese	1982–96
72	M P Lynagh	1984–95
63	N C Farr Jones	1984–93
59	S P Poidevin	1980–91
56	T J Horan	1989–97
51	E J A McKenzie	1990–97
51	J A Eales	1991–97
49	P N Kearns	1989–95
48	J S Little	1989–97
48	D J Wilson	1992–97

MOST CONSECUTIVE TESTS

Tests	Player	Span
46	P N Kearns	1989–95
42	D I Campese	1990–95
37	P G Johnson	1959–68
34	M P Lynagh	1988–92

MOST TESTS AS CAPTAIN

Tests	Captain	Span
36	N C Farr Jones	1988–92
20	J A Eales	1996–97
19	A G Slack	1984–87
16	J E Thornett	1962–67
16	G V Davis	1969–72

MOST TESTS IN INDIVIDUAL POSITIONS

Full-back R G Gould		25	1980–87
Wing D I Campese		85	1982–96
Centre T J Horan		49	1989–97
Fly-half M P Lynagh		64	1984–95
Scrum-half N C Farr Jones		62	1984–93
Prop E J A McKenzie		51	1990–97
Hooker P N Kearns		49	1989–95
Lock J A Eales		49	1991–97
Flanker S P Poidevin		59	1980–91
No 8 T B Gavin		43	1988–96

MOST POINTS IN TESTS

Pts	Player	Tests	Career
911	M P Lynagh	72	1984–95
315	D I Campese	101	1982–96
260	P E McLean	30	1974–82
239	M Burke	24	1993–97
117	D J Knox	13	1985–97

MOST TRIES IN TESTS

Tries	Player	Tests	Career
64	D I Campese	101	1982–96
22	T J Horan	56	1989–97
17	M P Lynagh	72	1984–95
15	M P Burke	23	1984–87
14	B J Moon	35	1978–86

MOST CONVERSIONS IN TESTS

Cons	Player	Tests	Career
140	M P Lynagh	72	1984–95
33	M Burke	24	1993–97
27	P E McLean	30	1974–82
19	D J Knox	13	1985–97
14	R G Gould	25	1980–87

MOST PENALTY GOALS IN TESTS

Pens	Player	Tests	Career
177	M P Lynagh	72	1984–95
62	P E McLean	30	1974–82
41	M Burke	24	1993–97
23	M C Roebuck	23	1991–93
21	D J Knox	13	1985–97

MOST DROPPED GOALS IN TESTS

Drops	Player	Tests	Career
9	P F Hawthorne	21	1962–67
9	M P Lynagh	72	1984–95
8	M G Ella	25	1980–84
4	P E McLean	30	1974–82

TRI-NATIONS RECORDS

Record	Detail	Holder	Set
Most points in matches	48	M Burke	1996 to 1997
Most points in season	40	M Burke	1996
Most points in match	20	M Burke	v N Zealand (h) 1996
Most tries in matches	4	B N Tune	1996 to 1997
Most tries in season	3	B N Tune	1997
Most tries in match	2	B N Tune	v S Africa (h) 1997
Most cons in matches	7	D J Knox	1997
Most cons in season	7	D J Knox	1997
Most cons in match	3	D J Knox	v S Africa (h) 1997
Most pens in matches	13	M Burke	1996 to 1997
Most pens in season	11	M Burke	1996
Most pens in match	5	M Burke	v N Zealand (h) 1996

SERIES RECORDS

Record	Holder	Detail
Most tries	D I Campese	6 in Europe 1988
Most points	M Burke	74 in Europe 1996

MAJOR TOUR RECORDS

Record	Detail	Year	Place
Most team points	500	1947–48	Europe
Most team tries	115	1947–48	Europe
Most individual points	154 by P E McLean	1975–76	Britain & Ireland
Most individual tries	23 by C J Russell	1908–09	Britain
Most points in match	26 by A J Leeds	1986 v Buller (NZ)	Westport
	26 by M C Roebuck	1993 v Fr Barbarians	Clermont Ferrand
Most tries in match	6 by J S Boyce	1962 v Wairarapa (NZ)	Masterton

MISCELLANEOUS RECORDS

Record	Holder	Detail
Longest Test career	G M Cooke/A R Miller	16 seasons, 1932–1947–48/1952–67
Youngest Test cap	B W Ford	18 yrs 90 days in 1957
Oldest Test cap	A R Miller	38 yrs 113 days in 1967

AUSTRALIAN INTERNATIONAL CAREER RECORDS (*up to 30 April 1998*)

Player	Debut	Caps since last season	Caps	T	C	PG	DG	Pts
S Mortlock	None		0	0	0	0	0	0
M Burke	1993 v SA	1997 *E* 1, *NZ* 2	24	10	33	41	0	239
S J Larkham	1996 v W	1997 *F* 1,2, *NZ* 1,2(R), *SA* 1, *NZ* 3, *SA* 2, *Arg* 1,2, *E* 2, *S*	12	5	0	0	0	25
D I Campese	1982 v NZ		101	64	8	7	2	315
M D Hardy	1997 v F	1997 *F* 1(t), 2(R), *NZ* 1(R),3(R), *Arg* 1(R),2(R)	6	2	0	0	0	10
A R Murdoch	1993 v F		2	1	0	0	0	5
J W Roff	1995 v C	1997 *F* 1,2, *NZ* 1, *E* 1, *NZ* 2, *SA* 1, *NZ* 3, *SA* 2, *Arg* 1,2, *E* 2, *S*	25	9	2	3	0	58
B N Tune	1996 v W	1997 *F* 1,2, *NZ* 1, *E* 1, *NZ* 2, *SA* 1, *NZ* 3, *SA* 2, *Arg* 1,2, *E* 2, *S*	18	9	0	0	0	45
D P Smith	1993 v SA		18	8	0	0	0	40
A Magro	None		0	0	0	0	0	0
J Jones-Hughes	None		0	0	0	0	0	0
J S Little	1989 v F	1997 *F* 1,2, *E* 1, *NZ* 2, *SA* 1, *NZ* 3, *SA* 2	48	13	0	0	0	62
J Holbeck	1997 v NZ	1997 *NZ* 1(R), *E* 1, *NZ* 2, *SA* 1, *NZ* 3, *SA* 2	6	0	0	0	0	0
D J Herbert	1994 v I	1997 *NZ* 1	14	4	0	0	0	20
T J Horan	1989 v NZ	1997 *F* 1,2, *NZ* 1, *E* 1, *NZ* 2, *Arg* 1,2, *E* 2, *S*	56	22	0	0	0	100
R C Tombs	1992 v S		5	0	0	0	0	0
S Bowen	1993 v SA		9	0	0	0	0	0
E J Flatley	1997 v E	1997 *E* 2, *S*	2	0	0	0	0	0
P W Howard	1993 v NZ	1997 *F* 1,2, *NZ* 1, *Arg* 1,2, *E* 2, *S*	20	2	0	0	0	10
D J Knox	1985 v Fj	1997 *SA* 1, *NZ* 3, *SA* 2, *Arg* 1,2	13	2	19	21	2	117
T M Wallace	1994 v It		2	0	1	6	0	20
G M Gregan	1994 v It	1997 *F* 1,2, *NZ* 1, *E* 1, *NZ* 2, *SA* 1, *NZ* 3, *SA* 2, *Arg* 1,2, *E* 2, *S*	30	6	0	0	0	30
S J Payne	1996 v W	1997 *F* 1(t), *NZ* 2(R), *Arg* 2(t)	7	1	0	0	0	5
B Cannon	None		0	0	0	0	0	0
M A Foley	1995 v C	1997 *NZ* 1(R), *E* 1, *NZ* 2, *SA* 1, *NZ* 3, *SA* 2, *Arg* 1,2, *E* 2, *S*	21	3	0	0	0	15
M E Caputo	1996 v W	1997 *F* 1,2, *NZ* 1	5	1	0	0	0	5
M D Bell	1996 v C		1	0	0	0	0	0
E J A McKenzie	1990 v F	1997 *F* 1,2, *NZ* 1, *E* 1	51	2	0	0	0	9
A Heath	1996 v C	1997 *NZ* 2, *SA* 1, *E* 2(R)	8	0	0	0	0	0
R L L Harry	1996 v W	1997 *F* 1,2, *NZ* 1,2, *SA* 1, *NZ* 3, *SA* 2, *Arg* 1,2, *E* 2, *S*	18	1	0	0	0	5

D J Crowley	1989 v BL		19	0	0	0	0	0
A T Blades	1996 v S	1997 *NZ* 1(R), *E* 1(R), *SA* 1(R), *NZ* 3, *SA* 2, *Arg* 1,2, *E* 2, *S*	12	0	0	0	0	0
C D Blades	1997 v E	1997 *E* 1	1	0	0	0	0	0
J Welborn	1996 v SA		2	0	0	0	0	0
G J Morgan	1992 v NZ	1997 *E* 1, *NZ* 2	24	3	0	0	0	15
D Giffin	1996 v W	1997 *F* 1,2	3	0	0	0	0	0
T M Bowman	None		0	0	0	0	0	0
J F Langford	1997 v NZ	1997 *NZ* 3, *SA* 2, *E* 2, *S*	4	0	0	0	0	0
M J Cockbain	1997 v F	1997 *F* 2(R), *NZ* 1, *SA* 1,2	4	0	0	0	0	0
J A Eales	1991 v W	1997 *F* 1,2, *NZ* 1, *E* 1, *NZ* 2, *SA* 1, *Arg* 1,2, *E* 2, *S*	51	2	13	16	0	83
W W Waugh	1993 v SA	1997 *Arg* 1,2	8	1	0	0	0	5
D J Wilson	1992 v S	1997 *F* 1,2, *NZ* 1, *E* 1(t&R), *NZ* 2(R), *SA* 1, *NZ* 3, *SA* 2, *E* 2(R), *S*(R)	48	9	0	0	0	45
B J Robinson	1996 v It	1997 *F* 1,2, *NZ* 1, *E* 1, *NZ* 2, *SA* 1(R), *NZ* 3(R), *SA* 2(R), *Arg* 1,2, *E* 2, *S*	15	0	0	0	0	0
D T Manu	1995 v R	1997 *F* 1, *NZ* 1(t), *E* 1, *NZ* 2, *SA* 1	15	2	0	0	0	10
O D A Finegan	1996 v W	1997 *SA* 1, *NZ* 3, *SA* 2, *Arg* 1,2, *E* 2, *S*	14	3	0	0	0	15
V Ofahengaue	1990 v NZ	1997 *Arg* 1(t&R),2(R), *E* 2, *S*	30	9	0	0	0	41
S F Finau	1997 v NZ	1997 *NZ* 3	1	0	0	0	0	0
T S Kefu	1997 v SA	1997 *SA* 2(R)	1	0	0	0	0	0
T Coker	1987 v E	1997 *F* 1(R),2, *NZ* 1, *E* 1, *NZ* 2(R), *SA* 1(R), *NZ* 3, *SA* 2, *Arg* 1,2	27	0	0	0	0	0
M C Brial	1993 v F	1997 *NZ* 2	13	1	0	0	0	5
T B Gavin	1988 v NZ		47	9	0	0	0	40

INTERNATIONAL MATCH APPEARANCES FOR BRITISH ISLES TEAMS (*up to 30 April 1998*)

From 1910 onwards, when British Isles teams first became officially representative of the four Home Unions. (*Uncapped when first selected to play in a Test match for the British Isles.)

Aarvold, C D (Cambridge U, Blackheath and England) 1930 *NZ* 1,2,3,4, *A*
Ackerman, R A (London Welsh and Wales) 1983 *NZ* 1,4 (R)
Ackford, P J (Harlequins and England) 1989 *A* 1,2,3
Alexander, R (NIFC and Ireland) 1938 *SA* 1,2,3
Andrew, C R (Wasps and England) 1989 *A* 2,3, 1993 *NZ* 1,2,3
Arneil, R J (Edinburgh Acads and Scotland) 1968 *SA* 1,2,3,4
Ashcroft, A (Waterloo and England) 1959 *A* 1, *NZ* 2

Back, N A (Leicester and England) 1997 *SA* 2 (R), 3
Bainbridge, S J (Gosforth and England) 1983 *NZ* 3,4
Baird, G R T (Kelso and Scotland) 1983 *NZ* 1,2,3,4
Baker, A M (Newport and Wales) 1910 *SA* 3
Baker, D G S (Old Merchant Taylors' and England) 1955 *SA* 3,4
Bassett, J (Penarth and Wales) 1930 *NZ* 1,2,3,4, *A*
Bateman, A G (Richmond and Wales) 1997 *SA* 3 (R)
Bayfield, M C (Northampton and England) 1993 *NZ* 1,2,3
Beamish, G R (Leicester, RAF and Ireland) 1930 *NZ* 1,2,3,4, *A*
Beattie, J R (Glasgow Acads and Scotland) 1983 *NZ* 2 (R)
Beaumont, W B (Fylde and England) 1977 *NZ* 2,3,4, 1980 *SA* 1,2,3,4
Bebb, D I E (Swansea and Wales) 1962 *SA* 2,3, 1966 *A* 1,2, *NZ* 1,2,3,4
Bennett, P (Llanelli and Wales) 1974 *SA* 1,2,3,4, 1977 *NZ* 1,2,3,4
Bentley, J (Newcastle and England) 1997 *SA* 2,3
Bevan, J C (Cardiff Coll of Ed, Cardiff and Wales) 1971 *NZ* 1
Black, A W (Edinburgh U and Scotland) 1950 *NZ* 1,2
Black, B H (Oxford U, Blackheath and England) 1930 *NZ* 1,2,3,4, *A*
Blakiston, A F (Northampton and England) 1924 *SA* 1,2,3,4
Bowcott, H M (Cambridge U, Cardiff and Wales) 1930 *NZ* 1,2,3,4, *A*
Boyle, C V (Dublin U and Ireland) 1938 *SA* 2,3
Brand, T N (NIFC and *Ireland) 1924 *SA* 1,2
Bresnihan, F P K (UC Dublin and Ireland) 1968 *SA* 1,2,4
Brophy, N H (UC Dublin and Ireland) 1962 *SA* 1,4
Brown, G L (W of Scotland and Scotland) 1971 *NZ* 3,4, 1974 *SA* 1,2,3, 1977 *NZ* 2,3,4
Budge, G M (Edinburgh Wands and Scotland) 1950 *NZ* 4
Burcher, D H (Newport and Wales) 1977 *NZ* 3
Burnell, A P (London Scottish and Scotland) 1993 *NZ* 1
Butterfield, J (Northampton and England) 1955 *SA* 1, 2,3,4

Calder, F (Stewart's-Melville FP and Scotland) 1989 *A* 1,2,3
Calder, J H (Stewart's-Melville FP and Scotland) 1983 *NZ* 3
Cameron, A (Glasgow HSFP and Scotland) 1955 *SA* 1,2
Campbell, S O (Old Belvedere and Ireland) 1980 *SA* 2 (R), 3,4, 1983 *NZ* 1,2,3,4
Campbell-Lamerton, M J (Halifax, Army and Scotland) 1962 *SA* 1,2,3,4, 1966 *A* 1,2, *NZ* 1,3
Carleton, J (Orrell and England) 1980 *SA* 1,2,4, 1983 *NZ* 2,3,4
Carling, W D C (Harlequins and England) 1993 *NZ* 1
Catt, M J (Bath and England) 1997 *SA* 3
Chalmers, C M (Melrose and Scotland) 1989 *A* 1

Clarke, B B (Bath and England) 1993 *NZ* 1,2,3
Cleaver, W B (Cardiff and Wales) 1950 *NZ* 1,2,3
Clifford, T (Young Munster and Ireland) 1950 *NZ* 1,2,3, *A* 1,2
Cobner, T J (Pontypool and Wales) 1977 *NZ* 1,2,3
Colclough, M J (Angoulême and England) 1980 *SA* 1,2,3,4, 1983 *NZ* 1,2,3,4
Connell, G C (Trinity Acads and Scotland) 1968 *SA* 4
Cotton, F E (Loughborough Colls, Coventry and England) 1974 *SA* 1,2,3,4, 1977 *NZ* 2,3,4
Coulman, M J (Moseley and England) 1968 *SA* 3
Cove-Smith, R (Old Merchant Taylors' and England) 1924 *SA* 1,2,3,4
Cowan, R C (Selkirk and Scotland) 1962 *SA* 4
Cromey, G E (Queen's U, Belfast and Ireland) 1938 *SA* 3
Cunningham, W A (Lansdowne and Ireland) 1924 *SA* 3

Dallaglio, L B N (Wasps and England) 1997 *SA* 1,2,3
Dancer, G T (Bedford) 1938 *SA* 1,2,3
Davidson, J W (London Irish and Ireland) 1997 *SA* 1,2,3
Davies, C (Cardiff and Wales) 1950 *NZ* 4
Davies, D M (Somerset Police and Wales) 1950 *NZ* 3,4, *A* 1
Davies, D S (Hawick and Scotland) 1924 *SA* 1,2,3,4
Davies, H J (Newport and Wales) 1924 *SA* 2
Davies, T G R (Cardiff, London Welsh and Wales) 1968 *SA* 3, 1971 *NZ* 1,2,3,4
Davies, T J (Llanelli and Wales) 1959 *NZ* 2,4
Davies, T M (London Welsh, Swansea and Wales) 1971 *NZ* 1,2,3,4, 1974 *SA* 1,2,3,4
Davies, W G (Cardiff and Wales) 1980 *SA* 2
Davies, W P C (Harlequins and England) 1955 *SA* 1,2,3
Dawes, S J (London Welsh and Wales) 1971 *NZ* 1,2,3,4
Dawson, A R (Wanderers and Ireland) 1959 *A* 1,2, *NZ* 1,2,3,4
Dawson, M J S (Northampton and England) 1997 *SA* 1,2,3
Dixon, P J (Harlequins and England) 1971 *NZ* 1,2,4
Dodge, P W (Leicester and England) 1980 *SA* 3,4
Dooley, W A (Preston Grasshoppers and England) 1989 *A* 2,3
Doyle, M G (Blackrock Coll and Ireland) 1968 *SA* 1
Drysdale, D (Heriot's FP and Scotland) 1924 *SA* 1,2,3,4
Duckham, D J (Coventry and England) 1971 *NZ* 2,3,4
Duggan, W P (Blackrock Coll and Ireland) 1977 *NZ* 1,2,3,4
Duff, P L (Glasgow Acads and Scotland) 1938 *SA* 2,3

Edwards, G O (Cardiff and Wales) 1968 *SA* 1,2, 1971 *NZ* 1,2,3,4, 1974 *SA* 1,2,3,4
Evans, G (Maesteg and Wales) 1983 *NZ* 3,4
Evans, G L (Newport and Wales) 1977 *NZ* 2,3,4
Evans, I C (Llanelli and Wales) 1989 *A* 1,2,3, 1993 *NZ* 1,2,3, 1997 *SA* 1
Evans, R T (Newport and Wales) 1950 *NZ* 1,2,3,4, *A* 1,2
Evans, T P (Swansea and Wales) 1977 *NZ* 1
Evans, W R (Cardiff and Wales) 1959 *A* 2, *NZ* 1,2,3

Farrell, J L (Bective Rangers and Ireland) 1930 *NZ* 1,2,3,4, *A*
Faull, J (Swansea and Wales) 1959 *A* 1, *NZ* 1,3,4
Fenwick, S P (Bridgend and Wales) 1977 *NZ* 1,2,3,4
Fitzgerald, C F (St Mary's Coll and Ireland) 1983 *NZ* 1,2,3,4
Foster, A R (Queen's U, Belfast and Ireland) 1910 *SA* 1,2

Gibbs, I S (Swansea and Wales) 1993 *NZ* 2,3, 1997 *SA* 1,2,3

Gibson, C M H (Cambridge U, NIFC and Ireland) 1966 *NZ* 1,2,3,4, 1968 *SA* 1 (R), 2,3,4, 1971 *NZ* 1,2,3,4
Giles, J L (Coventry and England) 1938 *SA* 1,3
Gravell, R W R (Llanelli and Wales) 1980 *SA* 1 (R), 2,3,4
Graves, C R A (Wanderers and Ireland) 1938 *SA* 1,3
Greenwood, J T (Dunfermline and Scotland) 1955 *SA* 1,2,3,4
Grieve, C F (Oxford U and Scotland) 1938 *SA* 2,3
Griffiths, G M (Cardiff and Wales) 1955 *SA* 2,3,4
Griffiths, V M (Newport and Wales) 1924 *SA* 3,4
Guscott, J C (Bath and England) 1989 *A* 2,3, 1993 *NZ* 1,2,3, 1997 *SA* 1,2,3

Hall, M R (Bridgend and Wales) 1989 *A* 1
Handford, F G (Manchester and England) 1910 *SA* 1,2,3
Harding, W R (Cambridge U, Swansea and Wales) 1924 *SA* 2,3,4
Harris, S W (Blackheath and England) 1924 *SA* 3,4

Hastings, A G (London Scottish, Watsonians and Scotland) 1989 *A* 1,2,3, 1993 *NZ* 1,2,3
Hastings, S (Watsonians and Scotland) 1989 *A* 2,3
Hay, B H (Boroughmuir and Scotland) 1980 *SA* 2,3,4
Hayward, D J (Newbridge and Wales) 1950 *NZ* 1,2,3
Healey, A S (Leicester and England) 1997 *SA* 2 (R), 3 (R)
Henderson, N J (Queen's U, Belfast, NIFC and Ireland) 1950 *NZ* 3
Henderson, R G (Northern and Scotland) 1924 *SA* 3,4
Hendrie, K G P (Heriot's FP and Scotland) 1924 *SA* 2
Hewitt, D (Queen's U, Belfast, Instonians and Ireland) 1959 *A* 1,2, *NZ* 1,3,4, 1962 *SA* 4
Higgins, R (Liverpool and England) 1955 *SA* 1
Hill, R A (Saracens and England) 1997 *SA* 1,2
Hinshelwood, A J W (London Scottish and Scotland) 1966 *NZ* 2,4, 1968 *SA* 2
Hodgson, J McD (Northern and *England) 1930 *NZ* 1,3
Holmes, T D (Cardiff and Wales) 1983 *NZ* 1

Jeremy Guscott celebrates his famous winning drop goal with Scott Gibbs, South Africa-British Lions, 2nd Test, King's Park, Durban, 28 June 1997.

Hopkins, R (Maesteg and Wales) 1971 *NZ* 1 (R)
Horrocks-Taylor, J P (Leicester and England) 1959 *NZ* 3
Horton, A L (Blackheath and England) 1968 *SA* 2,3,4
Howard, W G (Old Birkonians) 1938 *SA* 1
Howie, R A (Kirkcaldy and Scotland) 1924 *SA* 1,2,3,4

Irvine, A R (Heriot's FP and Scotland) 1974 *SA* 3,4, 1977 *NZ* 1,2,3,4, 1980 *SA* 2,3,4
Irwin, D G (Instonians and Ireland) 1983 *NZ* 1,2,4
Isherwood, G A M (Old Alleynians, Sale) 1910 *SA* 1,2,3

Jackson, P B (Coventry and England) 1959 *A* 1,2, *NZ* 1,3,4
Jarman, H (Newport and Wales) 1910 *SA* 1,2,3
Jeeps, R E G (Northampton and *England) 1955 *SA* 1,2,3,4, 1959 *A* 1,2, *NZ* 1,2,3, 1962 *SA* 1,2,3,4
Jenkins, N R (Pontypridd and Wales) 1997 *SA* 1,2,3
Jenkins, V G J (Oxford U, London Welsh and Wales) 1938 *SA* 1
John, B (Cardiff and Wales) 1968 *SA* 1, 1971 *NZ* 1,2,3,4
John, E R (Neath and Wales) 1950 *NZ* 1,2,3,4, *A* 1,2
Johnson, M O (Leicester and England) 1993 *NZ* 2,3, 1997 *SA* 1,2,3
Jones, B L (Devonport Services, Llanelli and Wales) 1950 *NZ* 4, *A* 1,2
Jones, D K (Llanelli, Cardiff and Wales) 1962 *SA* 1,2,3, 1966 *A* 1,2, *NZ* 1
Jones, E L (Llanelli and *Wales) 1938 *SA* 1,3
Jones, Ivor (Llanelli and Wales) 1930 *NZ* 1,2,3,4, *A*
Jones, J P (Newport and Wales) 1910 *SA* 1,2,3
Jones, K D (Cardiff and Wales) 1962 *SA* 1,2,3,4
Jones, K J (Newport and Wales) 1950 *NZ* 1,2,4
Jones, R N (Swansea and Wales) 1989 *A* 1,2,3
Jones, S T (Pontypool and Wales) 1983 *NZ* 2,3,4

Keane, M I (Lansdowne and Ireland) 1977 *NZ* 1
Kennedy, K W (CIYMS, London Irish and Ireland) 1966 *A* 1,2, *NZ* 1,4
Kiernan, M J (Dolphin and Ireland) 1983 *NZ* 2,3,4
Kiernan, T J (Cork Const and Ireland) 1962 *SA* 3, 1968 *SA*, 1,2,3,4
Kininmonth, P W (Oxford U, Richmond and Scotland) 1950 *NZ* 1,2,4
Kinnear, R M (Heriot's FP and *Scotland) 1924 *SA* 1,2,3,4
Kyle, J W (Queen's U, Belfast, NIFC and Ireland) 1950 *NZ* 1,2,3,4, *A* 1,2

Laidlaw, F A L (Melrose and Scotland) 1966 *NZ* 2,3
Laidlaw, R J (Jedforest and Scotland) 1983 *NZ* 1 (R), 2,3,4
Lamont, R A (Instonians and Ireland) 1966 *NZ* 1,2,3,4
Lane, M F (UC Cork and Ireland) 1950 *NZ* 4, *A* 2
Larter, P J (Northampton, RAF and England) 1968 *SA* 2
Leonard, J (Harlequins and England) 1993 *NZ* 2,3, 1997 *SA* 1 (R)
Lewis, A R (Abertillery and Wales) 1966 *NZ* 1,2,3,4
Lynch, J F (St Mary's Coll and Ireland) 1971 *NZ* 1,2,3,4

McBride, W J (Ballymena and Ireland) 1962 *SA* 3,4, 1966 *NZ* 2,3,4, 1968 *SA* 1,2,3,4, 1971 *NZ* 1,2,3,4, 1974 *SA* 1,2,3,4
Macdonald, R (Edinburgh U and Scotland) 1950 *NZ* 1, *A* 2
McFadyean, C W (Moseley and England) 1966 *NZ* 1,2,3,4
McGeechan, I R (Headingley and Scotland) 1974 *SA* 1,2,3,4, 1977 *NZ* 1,2,3 (R), 4
McKay, J W (Queen's U, Belfast and Ireland) 1950 *NZ* 1,2,3,4, *A* 1,2
McKibbin, H R (Queen's U, Belfast and Ireland) 1938 *SA* 1,2,3
McLauchlan, J (Jordanhill and Scotland) 1971 *NZ* 1,2,3,4, 1974 *SA* 1,2,3,4
McLeod, H F (Hawick and Scotland) 1959 *A* 1,2, *NZ* 1,2,3,4
McLoughlin, R J (Gosforth, Blackrock Coll and Ireland) 1966 *A* 1,2, *NZ* 4
MacNeill, H P (Oxford U and Ireland) 1983 *NZ* 1,2,4 (R)
Macpherson, N C (Newport and Scotland) 1924 *SA* 1,2,3,4
Macrae, D J (St Andrew's U and Scotland) 1938 *SA* 1

McVicker, J (Collegians and Ireland) 1924 *SA* 1,3,4
Marques, R W D (Harlequins and England) 1959 *A* 2, *NZ* 2
Marsden-Jones, D (London Welsh and Wales) 1924 *SA* 1,2
Martin, A J (Aberavon and Wales) 1977 *NZ* 1
Martindale, S A (Kendal and England) 1930 *A*
Matthews, J (Cardiff and Wales) 1950 *NZ* 1,2,3,4, *A* 1,2
Maxwell, R B (Birkenhead Park) 1924 *SA* 1
Mayne, R B (Queen's U, Belfast and Ireland) 1938 *SA* 1,2,3
Meredith, B V (Newport and Wales) 1955 *SA* 1,2,3,4, 1962 *SA* 1,2,3,4
Meredith, C C (Neath and Wales) 1955 *SA* 1,2,3,4
Millar, S (Ballymena and Ireland) 1959 *A* 1,2, *NZ* 2, 1962 *SA* 1,2,3,4, 1968 *SA* 1,2
Miller, E R P (Leicester and England) 1997 *SA* 2 (R)
Milliken, R A (Bangor and Ireland) 1974 *SA* 1,2,3,4
Milne, K S (Heriot's FP and Scotland) 1993 *NZ* 1
Moore, B C (Nottingham, Harlequins and England) 1989 *A* 1,2,3, 1993 *NZ* 2,3
Morgan, C I (Cardiff and Wales) 1955 *SA* 1,2,3,4
Morgan, D W (Stewart's-Melville FP and Scotland) 1977 *NZ* 3 (R), 4
Morgan, G J (Clontarf and Ireland) 1938 *SA* 3
Morgan, H J (Abertillery and Wales) 1959 *NZ* 3,4, 1962 *SA* 2,3
Morgan, M E (Swansea and Wales) 1938 *SA* 1,2
Morley, J C (Newport and Wales) 1930 *NZ* 1,2,3
Morris, C D (Orrell and England) 1993 *NZ* 1,2,3
Mulcahy, W A (UC Dublin and Ireland) 1959 *A* 1, *NZ* 4, 1962 *SA* 1,2,3,4
Mullen, K D (Old Belvedere and Ireland) 1950 *NZ* 1,2, *A* 2
Mulligan, A A (Wanderers, London Irish and Ireland) 1959 *NZ* 4
Mullin, B J (London Irish and Ireland) 1989 *A* 1
Murphy, N A A (Cork Const and Ireland) 1959 *A* 2, *NZ* 1,2,4, 1966 *A* 1,2, *NZ* 3,4
Murray, P F (Wanderers and Ireland) 1930 *NZ* 1,2,4, *A*

Neale, M E (Bristol, Blackheath and *England) 1910 *SA* 1,2,3
Neary, A (Broughton Park and England) 1977 *NZ* 4
Nelson, J E (Malone and Ireland) 1950 *NZ* 3,4, *A* 1,2
Nicholson, B E (Harlequins and England) 1938 *SA* 2
Norris, C H (Cardiff and Wales) 1966 *NZ* 1,2,3
Norster, R L (Cardiff and Wales) 1983 *NZ* 1,2, 1989 *A* 1
Novis, A L (Blackheath and England) 1930 *NZ* 2, 4, *A*

O'Donnell, R C (St Mary's Coll and Ireland) 1980 *SA* 1
O'Driscoll, J B (London Irish and Ireland) 1980 *SA* 1,2,3,4, 1983 *NZ* 2,4
O'Neill, H O'H (Queen's U, Belfast and Ireland) 1930 *NZ* 1,2,3,4, *A*
O'Reilly, A J F (Old Belvedere and Ireland) 1955 *A* 1,2,3,4, 1959 *A* 1,2, *NZ* 1,2,3,4
Orr, P A (Old Wesley and Ireland) 1977 *NZ* 1
O'Shea, J P (Cardiff and Wales) 1968 *SA* 1

Parker, D (Swansea and Wales) 1930 *NZ* 1,2,3,4, *A*
Pask, A E I (Abertillery and Wales) 1962 *SA* 1,2,3, 1966 *A* 1,2, *NZ* 1,3,4
Patterson, C S (Instonians and Ireland) 1980 *SA* 1,2,3
Patterson, W M (Sale and *England) 1959 *NZ* 2
Paxton, I A M (Selkirk and Scotland) 1983 *NZ* 1,2,3,4
Pedlow, A C (CIYMS and Ireland) 1955 *SA* 1,4
Pillman, C H (Blackheath and England) 1910 *SA* 2,3
Piper, O J S (Cork Const and Ireland) 1910 *SA* 1
Poole, H (Cardiff) 1930 *NZ* 3
Popplewell, N J (Greystones and Ireland) 1993 *NZ* 1,2,3
Preece, I (Coventry and England) 1950 *NZ* 1
Prentice, F D (Leicester and England) 1930 *NZ* 2, *A*
Price, B (Newport and Wales) 1966 *A* 1,2, *NZ* 1,4
Price, G (Pontypool and Wales) 1977 *NZ* 1,2,3,4, 1980 *SA* 1,2,3,4, 1983 *NZ* 1,2,3,4
Price, M J (Pontypool and Wales) 1959 *A* 1,2, *NZ* 1,2,3
Prosser, T R (Pontypool and Wales) 1959 *NZ* 4
Pullin, J V (Bristol and England) 1968 *SA* 2,3,4, 1971 *NZ* 1,2,3,4

Quinnell, D L (Llanelli and *Wales) 1971 *NZ* 3, 1977 *NZ* 2,3, 1980 *SA* 1,2

Ralston, C W (Richmond and England) 1974 *SA* 4
Reed, A I (Bath and Scotland) 1993 *NZ* 1
Rees, H E (Neath and *Wales) 1977 *NZ* 4
Reeve, J S R (Harlequins and England) 1930 *NZ* 1,3,4, *A*
Regan, M P (Bristol and England) 1997 *SA* 3
Reid, T E (Garryowen and Ireland) 1955 *SA* 2,3
Renwick, J M (Hawick and Scotland) 1980 *SA* 1
Rew, H (Blackheath, Army and England) 1930 *NZ* 1,2,3,4
Reynolds, F J (Old Cranleighans and England) 1938 *SA* 1,2
Richards, D (Leicester and England) 1989 *A* 1,2,3, 1993 *NZ* 1,2,3
Richards, D S (Swansea and Wales) 1980 *SA* 1
Richards, M C R (Cardiff and Wales) 1968 *SA* 1,3,4
Richards, T J (Bristol and Australia) 1910 *SA* 1,2
Rimmer, G (Waterloo and England) 1950 *NZ* 3
Ringland, T M (Ballymena and Ireland) 1983 *NZ* 1
Risman, A B W (Loughborough Colls and England) 1959 *A* 1,2, *NZ* 1,4
Robbie, J C (Greystones and Ireland) 1980 *SA* 4
Robins, J D (Birkenhead Park and Wales) 1950 *NZ* 1,2,3, *A* 1,2,3,4
Robins, R J (Pontypridd and Wales) 1955 *SA* 1,2,3,4
Rodber, T A K (Northampton and England) 1997 *SA* 1,2
Rogers, D P (Bedford and England) 1962 *SA* 1,4
Rowlands, K A (Cardiff and Wales) 1962 *SA* 1,2,4
Rutherford, D (Gloucester and England) 1966 *A* 1
Rutherford, J Y (Selkirk and Scotland) 1983 *NZ* 3

Savage, K F (Northampton and England) 1968 *SA* 1,2,3,4
Scotland, K J F (Cambridge U, Heriot's FP and Scotland) 1959 *A* 1,2, *NZ* 1,3,4
Sharp, R A W (Oxford U, Redruth and England) 1962 *SA* 3,4
Slattery, J F (Blackrock Coll and Ireland) 1974 *SA* 1,2,3,4
Slemen, M A C (Liverpool and England) 1980 *SA* 1
Smith, A R (Edinburgh Wands, London Scottish and Scotland) 1962 *SA* 1,2,3
Smith, D F (Richmond and England) 1910 *SA* 1,2,3
Smith, D W C (London Scottish and Scotland) 1950 *A* 1
Smith, G K (Kelso and Scotland) 1959 *A* 1,2, *NZ* 1,3
Smith, I S (Oxford U, London Scottish and Scotland) 1924 *SA* 1,2
Smith, T J (Watsonians and Scotland) 1997 *SA* 1,2,3
Smyth, T (Malone, Newport and Ireland) 1910 *SA* 2,3
Sole, D M B (Edinburgh Acads and Scotland) 1989 *A* 1,2,3
Spong, R S (Old Millhillians and England) 1930 *NZ* 1,2,3,4, *A*
Spoors, J A (Bristol) 1910 *SA* 1,2,3
Squire, J (Newport, Pontypool and Wales) 1977 *NZ* 4, 1980 *SA* 1,2,3,4, 1983 *NZ* 1
Squires, P J (Harrogate and England) 1977 *NZ* 1
Stagg, P K (Oxford U, Sale and Scotland) 1968 *SA* 1,3,4
Steele, W C C (Bedford, RAF and Scotland) 1974 *SA* 1,2
Stephens, I (Bridgend and Wales) 1983 *NZ* 1
Stephens, J R G (Neath and Wales) 1950 *A* 1,2
Stevenson, R C (St Andrew's U and Scotland) 1910 *SA* 1,2,3
Stimpson, T R G (Newcastle and England) 1997 *SA* 3 (R)

Tait, A V (Newcastle and Scotland) 1997 *SA* 1,2
Tanner, H (Swansea and Wales) 1938 *SA* 2
Taylor, A R (Cross Keys and Wales) 1938 *SA* 1,2
Taylor, J (London Welsh and Wales) 1971 *NZ* 1,2,3,4
Taylor, R B (Northampton and England) 1968 *SA* 1,2,3,4
Teague, M C (Gloucester, Moseley and England) 1989 *A* 2,3, 1993 *NZ* 2 (t)
Telfer, J W (Melrose and Scotland) 1966 *A* 1,2, *NZ* 1,2,4, 1968 *SA* 2,3,4
Thomas, M C (Devonport Services, Newport and Wales) 1950 *NZ* 2,3, *A* 1, 1959 *NZ* 2

Thomas, R C C (Swansea and Wales) 1955 *SA* 3,4
Thomas, W D (Llanelli and *Wales) 1966 *NZ* 2,3, 1968 *SA* 3 (R), 4, 1971 *NZ* 1,2,4 (R)
Thompson, R H (Instonians, London Irish and Ireland) 1955 *SA* 1,2,4
Townsend, G P J (Northampton and Scotland) 1997 *SA* 1,2
Travers, W H (Newport and Wales) 1938 *SA* 2,3
Tucker, C C (Shannon and Ireland) 1980 *SA* 3,4
Turner, J W C (Gala and Scotland) 1968 *SA* 1,2,3,4

Underwood, R (RAF, Leicester and England) 1989 *A* 1,2,3, 1993 *NZ* 1,2,3
Underwood, T (Newcastle and England) 1997 *SA* 3
Unwin, E J (Rosslyn Park, Army and England) 1938 *SA* 1,2
Uttley, R M (Gosforth and England) 1974 *SA* 1,2,3,4

Voyce, A T (Gloucester and England) 1924 *SA* 3,4

Waddell, G H (Cambridge U, London Scottish and Scotland) 1962 *SA* 1,2
Waddell, H (Glasgow Acads and Scotland) 1924 *SA* 1,2,4
Wainwright, R I (Watsonians and Scotland) 1997 *SA* 3
Walker, S (Instonians and Ireland) 1938 *SA* 1,2,3
Wallace, P S (Saracens and Ireland) 1997 *SA* 1,2,3
Wallace, W (Percy Park) 1924 *SA* 1
Waller, P D (Newport and Wales) 1910 *SA* 1,2,3
Ward, A J P (Garryowen and Ireland) 1980 *SA* 1
Waters, J A (Selkirk and Scotland) 1938 *SA* 3
Watkins, D (Newport and Wales) 1966 *A* 1,2, *NZ* 1,2,3,4
Watkins, S J (Newport and Wales) 1966 *A* 1,2, *NZ* 3
Webb, J (Abertillery and Wales) 1910 *SA* 1,2,3
Welsh, W B (Hawick and Scotland) 1930 *NZ* 4
Weston, M P (Richmond, Durham City and England) 1962 *SA* 1,2,3,4, 1966 *A* 1,2
Wheeler, P J (Leicester and England) 1977 *NZ* 2,3,4, 1980 *SA* 1,2,3,4
White, D B (London Scottish and Scotland) 1989 *A* 1
Whitley, H (Northern and *England) 1924 *SA* 1,3,4
Willcox, J G (Oxford U, Harlequins and England) 1962 *SA* 1,2,4
Williams, B L (Cardiff and Wales) 1950 *NZ* 2,3,4, *A* 1,2
Williams, C (Swansea and Wales) 1980 *SA* 1,2,3,4
Williams, D (Ebbw Vale and Wales) 1966 *A* 1,2, *NZ* 1,2,4
Williams, D B (Cardiff and *Wales) 1977 *NZ* 1,2,3
Williams, J J (Llanelli and Wales) 1974 *SA* 1,2,3,4, 1977 *NZ* 1,2,3
Williams, J P R (London Welsh and Wales) 1971 *NZ* 1,2,3,4, 1974 *SA* 1,2,3,4
Williams, R H (Llanelli and Wales) 1955 *SA* 1,2,3,4, 1959 *A* 1,2, *NZ* 1,2,3,4
Williams, S H (Newport and *England) 1910 *SA* 1,2,3
Williams, W O G (Swansea and Wales) 1955 *SA* 1,2,3,4
Willis, W R (Cardiff and Wales) 1950 *NZ* 4, *A* 1,2
Wilson, S (London Scottish and Scotland) 1966 *A* 2, *NZ* 1,2,3,4
Windsor, R W (Pontypool and Wales) 1974 *SA* 1,2,3,4, 1977 *NZ* 1
Winterbottom, P J (Headingley, Harlequins and England) 1983 *NZ* 1,2,3,4, 1993 *NZ*, 1,2,3
Wood, B G M (Garryowen and Ireland) 1959 *NZ* 1,3
Wood, K B (Leicester) 1910 *SA* 3
Wood, K G M (Harlequins and Ireland) 1997 *SA* 1,2
Woodward, C R (Leicester and England) 1980 *SA* 2,3

Young, A T (Cambridge U, Blackheath and England) 1924 *SA* 2
Young, D (Cardiff and Wales) 1989 *A* 1,2,3
Young, J (Harrogate, RAF and Wales) 1968 *SA* 1
Young, J R C (Oxford U, Harlequins and England) 1959 *NZ* 2
Young, R M (Queen's U, Belfast, Collegians and Ireland) 1966 *A* 1,2, *NZ* 1, 1968 *SA* 3

RESULTS OF BRITISH ISLES MATCHES (*up to 30 April 1998*)

From 1910 onwards – the tour to South Africa in that year was the first fully representative one in which the four Home Unions co-operated.

BRITISH ISLES v SOUTH AFRICA
Played 33   British Isles won 10, South Africa won 19, Drawn 4
Highest scores: British Isles 28–9 in 1974, South Africa 35–16 in 1997
Biggest wins: British Isles 28–9 in 1974, South Africa 34–14 in 1962

1910 *1* Johannesburg **South Africa** 14–10
 2 Port Elizabeth **British Isles** 8–3
 3 Cape Town **South Africa** 21–5
 South Africa won series 2-1
1924 *1* Durban **South Africa** 7–3
 2 Johannesburg **South Africa** 17–0
 3 Port Elizabeth **Drawn** 3–3
 4 Cape Town **South Africa** 16–9
 South Africa won series 3-0, with 1 draw
1938 *1* Johannesburg **South Africa** 26–12
 2 Port Elizabeth **South Africa** 19–3
 3 Cape Town **British Isles** 21–16
 South Africa won series 2-1
1955 *1* Johannesburg **British Isles** 23–22
 2 Cape Town **South Africa** 25–9
 3 Pretoria **British Isles** 9–6
 4 Port Elizabeth **South Africa** 22–8
 Series drawn 2-2
1962 *1* Johannesburg **Drawn** 3–3
 2 Durban **South Africa** 3–0
 3 Cape Town **South Africa** 8–3

 4 Bloemfontein **South Africa** 34–14
 South Africa won series 3-0, with 1 draw
1968 *1* Pretoria **South Africa** 25–20
 2 Port Elizabeth **Drawn** 6–6
 3 Cape Town **South Africa** 11–6
 4 Johannesburg **South Africa** 19–6
 South Africa won series 3-0, with 1 draw
1974 *1* Cape Town **British Isles** 12–3
 2 Pretoria **British Isles** 28–9
 3 Port Elizabeth **British Isles** 26–9
 4 Johannesburg **Drawn** 13–13
 British Isles won series 3-0, with 1 draw
1980 *1* Cape Town **South Africa** 26–22
 2 Bloemfontein **South Africa** 26–19
 3 Port Elizabeth **South Africa** 12–10
 4 Pretoria **British Isles** 17–13
 South Africa won series 3-1
1997 *1* Cape Town **British Isles** 25-16
 2 Durban **British Isles** 18-15
 3 Johannesburg **South Africa** 35-16
 British isles won series 2-1

BRITISH ISLES v NEW ZEALAND
Played 31   British Isles won 6, New Zealand won 23, Drawn 2
Highest scores: British Isles 20–7 in 1993, New Zealand 38–6 in 1983
Biggest wins: British Isles 20–7 in 1993, New Zealand 38–6 in 1983

1930 *1* Dunedin **British Isles** 6–3
 2 Christchurch **New Zealand** 13–10
 3 Auckland **New Zealand** 15–10
 4 Wellington **New Zealand** 22–8
 New Zealand won series 3-1
1950 *1* Dunedin **Drawn** 9–9
 2 Christchurch **New Zealand** 8–0
 3 Wellington **New Zealand** 6–3
 4 Auckland **New Zealand** 11–8
 New Zealand won series 3-0, with 1 draw
1959 *1* Dunedin **New Zealand** 18–17
 2 Wellington **New Zealand** 11–8
 3 Christchurch **New Zealand** 22–8
 4 Auckland **British Isles** 9–6
 New Zealand won series 3-1
1966 *1* Dunedin **New Zealand** 20–3
 2 Wellington **New Zealand** 16–12
 3 Christchurch **New Zealand** 19–6
 4 Auckland **New Zealand** 24–11
 New Zealand won series 4-0

1971 *1* Dunedin **British Isles** 9–3
 2 Christchurch **New Zealand** 22–12
 3 Wellington **British Isles** 13–3
 4 Auckland **Drawn** 14–14
 British Isles won series 2-1, with 1 draw
1977 *1* Wellington **New Zealand** 16–12
 2 Christchurch **British Isles** 13–9
 3 Dunedin **New Zealand** 19–7
 4 Auckland **New Zealand** 10–9
 New Zealand won series 3-1
1983 *1* Christchurch **New Zealand** 16–12
 2 Wellington **New Zealand** 9–0
 3 Dunedin **New Zealand** 15–8
 4 Auckland **New Zealand** 38–6
 New Zealand won series 4-0
1993 *1* Christchurch **New Zealand** 20–18
 2 Wellington **British Isles** 20–7
 3 Auckland **New Zealand** 30–13
 New Zealand won series 2-1

BRITISH ISLES v AUSTRALIA
Played 10   British Isles won 8, Australia won 2, Drawn 0
Highest scores: British Isles 31–0 in 1966, Australia 30–12 in 1989
Biggest wins: British Isles 31–0 in 1966, Australia 30–12 in 1989

1930 Sydney **Australia** 6–5
1950 *1* Brisbane **British Isles** 19–6
    2 Sydney **British Isles** 24–3
    British Isles won series 2-0
1959 *1* Brisbane **British Isles** 17–6
    2 Sydney **British Isles** 24–3
    British Isles won series 2-0

1966 *1* Sydney **British Isles** 11–8
    2 Brisbane **British Isles** 31–0
    British Isles won series 2-0
1989 *1* Sydney **Australia** 30–12
    2 Brisbane **British Isles** 19–12
    3 Sydney **British Isles** 19–18
    British Isles won series 2-1

BRITISH ISLES INTERNATIONAL RECORDS (*up to 30 April 1998*)

From 1910 onwards – the tour to South Africa in that year was the first fully representative one in which the four Home Unions co-operated.

MATCH RECORDS

MOST CONSECUTIVE TEST WINS
3 1950 *A* 1,2, 1955 *SA* 1
3 1974 *SA* 1,2,3

MOST CONSECUTIVE TESTS WITHOUT DEFEAT

P	W	D	Period
6	4	2	1971–74

MOST POINTS IN A MATCH
by the team

Pts	Opp	Venue	Year
31	A	Brisbane	1966
28	SA	Pretoria	1974
26	SA	Port Elizabeth	1974
25	SA	Cape Town	1997

by a player
18 by A J P Ward v South Africa at
  Cape Town   1980
18 by A G Hastings v New Zealand
  at Christchurch   1993
17 by T J Kiernan v South Africa at
  Pretoria   1968
16 by B L Jones v Australia at
  Brisbane   1950

15 by A G Hastings v Australia at
  Sydney   1989
15 by N R Jenkins v South Africa at
  Cape Town   1997
15 by N R Jenkins v South Africa at
  Durban   1997

MOST TRIES IN A MATCH
by the team

T	Opp	Venue	Year
5	A	Sydney	1950
5	SA	Johannesburg	1955
5	A	Sydney	1959
5	A	Brisbane	1966
5	SA	Pretoria	1974

by a player
2 by C D Aarvold v New Zealand at
  Christchurch   1930
2 by J E Nelson v Australia at
  Sydney   1950
2 by M J Price v Australia at
  Sydney   1959
2 by M J Price v New Zealand at
  Dunedin   1959
2 by D K Jones v Australia at
  Brisbane   1966
2 by T G R Davies v New Zealand
  at Christchurch   1971
2 by J J Williams v South Africa at
  Pretoria   1974
2 by J J Williams v South Africa at
  Port Elizabeth   1974

MOST CONVERSIONS IN A MATCH
by the team

C	Opp	Venue	Year
5	A	Brisbane	1966
4	SA	Johannesburg	1955
3	A	Sydney	1950
3	A	Sydney	1959

by a player
5 by S Wilson v Australia at Brisbane 1966
4 by A Cameron v South Africa at Johannesburg 1955
2 several instances

MOST PENALTY GOALS IN A MATCH
by the team

P	Opp	Venue	Year
6	NZ	Christchurch	1993
5	SA	Pretoria	1968
5	SA	Cape Town	1980
5	A	Sydney	1989
5	SA	Cape Town	1997
5	SA	Durban	1997

by a player
6 by A G Hastings v New Zealand at Christchurch 1993
5 by T J Kiernan v South Africa at Pretoria 1968
5 by A J P Ward v South Africa at Cape Town 1980
5 by A G Hastings v Australia at Sydney 1989
5 by N R Jenkins v South Africa at Cape Town 1997
5 by N R Jenkins v South Africa at Durban 1997

MOST DROPPED GOALS IN A MATCH
by the team

D	Opp	Venue	Year
2	SA	Port Elizabeth	1974

by a player
2 by P Bennett v South Africa at Port Elizabeth 1974

CAREER RECORDS

MOST CAPPED PLAYERS

Caps	Player	Career
17	W J McBride	1962–74
13	R E G Jeeps	1955–62
12	C M H Gibson	1966–71
12	G Price	1977–83
10	A J F O'Reilly	1955–59
10	R H Williams	1955–59
10	G O Edwards	1968–74

MOST CONSECUTIVE TESTS

Tests	Player	Span
15	W J McBride	1966–74
12	C M H Gibson	1966–71
12	G Price	1977–83

MOST TESTS AS CAPTAIN

Tests	Captain	Span
6	A R Dawson	1959
4	R Cove-Smith	1924
4	M J Campbell-Lamerton	1966
4	T J Kiernan	1968
4	S J Dawes	1971
4	W J McBride	1974
4	P Bennett	1977
4	W B Beaumont	1980
4	C F Fitzgerald	1983

MOST TESTS IN INDIVIDUAL POSITIONS

Full-back	J P R Williams	8	1971–74
Wing	A J F O'Reilly	9	1955–59
Centre {	C M H Gibson	8	1966–71
{	J C Guscott	8	1989–97
Fly-half	P Bennett	8	1974–77
Scrum-half	R E G Jeeps	13	1955–62
Prop	G Price	12	1977–83
Hooker	B V Meredith	8	1955–62
Lock	W J McBride	17	1962–74
Flanker	N A A Murphy	8	1959–66
No 8	T M Davies	8	1971–74

MOST POINTS IN TESTS

Pts	Player	Tests	Career
66	A G Hastings	6	1989–93
44	P Bennett	8	1974–77
41	N R Jenkins	3	1997
35	T J Kiernan	5	1962–68
30	S Wilson	5	1966
30	B John	5	1968–71

MOST TRIES IN TESTS

Tries	Player	Tests	Career
6	A J F O'Reilly	10	1955–59
5	J J Williams	7	1974–77
4	M J Price	5	1959

MOST CONVERSIONS IN TESTS

Cons	Player	Tests	Career
6	S Wilson	5	1966
4	B L Jones	3	1950
4	A Cameron	2	1955

MOST PENALTY GOALS IN TESTS

Pens	Player	Tests	Career
20	A G Hastings	6	1989–93
13	N R Jenkins	3	1997
11	T J Kiernan	5	1962–68
10	P Bennett	8	1974–77
7	S O Campbell	7	1980–83

MOST DROPPED GOALS IN TESTS

Drops	Player	Tests	Career
2	D Watkins	6	1966
2	B John	5	1968–71
2	P Bennett	8	1974–77
2	C R Andrew	5	1989–93

SERIES RECORDS

Record	Holder	Detail
Most team points		79 in S Africa 1974
Most team tries		10 in S Africa 1955 & 1974
Most points by player	N R Jenkins	41 in S Africa 1997
Most tries by player	J J Williams	4 in S Africa 1974

MAJOR TOUR RECORDS

Record	Detail	Year	Place
Most team points	842	1959	A, NZ & C
Most team tries	165	1959	A, NZ & C
Most individual points	188 by B John	1971	A & NZ
Most individual tries	22 by A J F O'Reilly	1959	A, NZ & C
Most points in match	37 by A G B Old	1974 v SW Districts	Mossel Bay, SA
Most tries in match	6 by D J Duckham	1971 v W Coast/ Buller	Greymouth, NZ
	6 by J J Williams	1974 v SW Districts	Mossel Bay, SA

MISCELLANEOUS RECORDS

Record	Holder	Detail
Longest Test career	W J McBride	13 seasons, 1962–74
Youngest Test cap	A J F O'Reilly	19 yrs 91 days in 1955
Oldest Test cap	W J McBride	34 yrs 51 days in 1974

RESULTS OF INTERNATIONAL MATCHES (*up to 30 April 1998*)

Cap matches only.

Years for Five Nations matches are for the second half of the season: eg 1972 means season 1971-72. Years for matches against touring teams from the Southern Hemisphere refer to the actual year of the match.

Points-scoring was first introduced in 1886, when an International Board was formed by Scotland, Ireland and Wales. Points values varied between countries until 1890, when England agreed to join the Board, and uniform values were adopted.

Northern Hemisphere seasons	Try	Conversion	Penalty goal	Dropped goal	Goal from mark
1890-91	1	2	2	3	3
1891-92 to 1892-93	2	3	3	4	4
1893-94 to 1904-05	3	2	3	4	4
1905-06 to 1947-48	3	2	3	4	3
1948-49 to 1970-71	3	2	3	3	3
1971-72 to 1991-92	4	2	3	3	3*
1992-93 onwards	5	2	3	3	–

*The goal from mark ceased to exist when the free-kick clause was introduced, 1977-78.

WC indicates a fixture played during the Rugby World Cup finals. LC indicates a fixture played in the Latin Cup. TN indicates a fixture played in the Tri-Nations.

ENGLAND v SCOTLAND

Played 115   England won 59, Scotland won 39, Drawn 17

Highest scores England 41-13 in 1997, Scotland 33-6 in 1986

Biggest wins England 41-13 in 1997, Scotland 33-6 in 1986

1871 Raeburn Place (Edinburgh) **Scotland** 1G 1T to 1T
1872 The Oval (London) **England** 1G 1DG 2T to 1DG
1873 Glasgow **Drawn** no score
1874 The Oval **England** 1DG to 1T
1875 Raeburn Place **Drawn** no score
1876 The Oval **England** 1G 1T to 0
1877 Raeburn Place **Scotland** 1 DG to 0
1878 The Oval **Drawn** no score
1879 Raeburn Place **Drawn** Scotland 1DG England 1G
1880 Manchester **England** 2G 3T to 1G
1881 Raeburn Place **Drawn** Scotland 1G 1T England 1DG 1T
1882 Manchester **Scotland** 2T to 0
1883 Raeburn Place **England** 2T to 1T
1884 Blackheath (London) **England** 1G to 1T
1885 No Match
1886 Raeburn Place **Drawn** no score
1887 Manchester **Drawn** 1T each
1888 No Match
1889 No Match
1890 Raeburn Place **England** 1G 1T to 0
1891 Richmond (London) **Scotland** 9-3
1892 Raeburn Place **England** 5-0
1893 Leeds **Scotland** 8-0
1894 Raeburn Place **Scotland** 6-0
1895 Richmond **Scotland** 6-3

1896 Glasgow **Scotland** 11-0
1897 Manchester **England** 12-3
1898 Powderhall (Edinburgh) **Drawn** 3-3
1899 Blackheath **Scotland** 5-0
1900 Inverleith (Edinburgh) **Drawn** 0-0
1901 Blackheath **Scotland** 18-3
1902 Inverleith **England** 6-3
1903 Richmond **Scotland** 10-6
1904 Inverleith **Scotland** 6-3
1905 Richmond **Scotland** 8-0
1906 Inverleith **England** 9-3
1907 Blackheath **Scotland** 8-3
1908 Inverleith **Scotland** 16-10
1909 Richmond **Scotland** 18-8
1910 Inverleith **England** 14-5
1911 Twickenham **England** 13-8
1912 Inverleith **Scotland** 8-3
1913 Twickenham **England** 3-0
1914 Inverleith **England** 16-15
1920 Twickenham **England** 13-4
1921 Inverleith **England** 18-0
1922 Twickenham **England** 11-5
1923 Inverleith **England** 8-6
1924 Twickenham **England** 19-0
1925 Murrayfield **Scotland** 14-11
1926 Twickenham **Scotland** 17-9
1927 Murrayfield **Scotland** 21-13
1928 Twickenham **England** 6-0
1929 Murrayfield **Scotland** 12-6

1930 Twickenham **Drawn** 0-0
1931 Murrayfield **Scotland** 28-19
1932 Twickenham **England** 16-3
1933 Murrayfield **Scotland** 3-0
1934 Twickenham **England** 6-3
1935 Murrayfield **Scotland** 10-7
1936 Twickenham **England** 9-8
1937 Murrayfield **England** 6-3
1938 Twickenham **Scotland** 21-16
1939 Murrayfield **England** 9-6
1947 Twickenham **England** 24-5
1948 Murrayfield **Scotland** 6-3
1949 Twickenham **England** 19-3
1950 Murrayfield **Scotland** 13-11
1951 Twickenham **England** 5-3
1952 Murrayfield **England** 19-3
1953 Twickenham **England** 26-8
1954 Murrayfield **England** 13-3
1955 Twickenham **England** 9-6
1956 Murrayfield **England** 11-6
1957 Twickenham **England** 16-3
1958 Murrayfield **Drawn** 3-3
1959 Twickenham **Drawn** 3-3
1960 Murrayfield **England** 21-12
1961 Twickenham **England** 6-0
1962 Murrayfield **Drawn** 3-3
1963 Twickenham **England** 10-8
1964 Murrayfield **Scotland** 15-6
1965 Twickenham **Drawn** 3-3
1966 Murrayfield **Scotland** 6-3
1967 Twickenham **England** 27-14
1968 Murrayfield **England** 8-6
1969 Twickenham **England** 8-3

1970 Murrayfield **Scotland** 14-5
1971 Twickenham **Scotland** 16-15
1971 Murrayfield **Scotland** 26-6
Special centenary match – non-championship
1972 Murrayfield **Scotland** 23-9
1973 Twickenham **England** 20-13
1974 Murrayfield **Scotland** 16-14
1975 Twickenham **England** 7-6
1976 Murrayfield **Scotland** 22-12
1977 Twickenham **England** 26-6
1978 Murrayfield **England** 15-0
1979 Twickenham **Drawn** 7-7
1980 Murrayfield **England** 30-18
1981 Twickenham **England** 23-17
1982 Murrayfield **Drawn** 9-9
1983 Twickenham **Scotland** 22-12
1984 Murrayfield **Scotland** 18-6
1985 Twickenham **England** 10-7
1986 Murrayfield **Scotland** 33-6
1987 Twickenham **England** 21-12
1988 Murrayfield **England** 9-6
1989 Twickenham **Drawn** 12-12
1990 Murrayfield **Scotland** 13-7
1991 Twickenham **England** 21-12
1991 Murrayfield *WC* **England** 9-6
1992 Murrayfield **England** 25-7
1993 Twickenham **England** 26-12
1994 Murrayfield **England** 15-14
1995 Twickenham **England** 24-12
1996 Murrayfield **England** 18-9
1997 Twickenham **England** 41-13
1998 Murrayfield **England** 34-20

ENGLAND v IRELAND

Played 111   England won 65, Ireland won 38, Drawn 8
Highest scores England 46-6 in 1997, Ireland 26-21 in 1974
Biggest wins England 46-6 in 1997, Ireland 22-0 in 1947

1875 The Oval (London) **England** 1G 1DG
      1T to 0
1876 Dublin **England** 1G 1T to 0
1877 The Oval **England** 2G 2T to 0
1878 Dublin **England** 2G 1T to 0
1879 The Oval **England** 2G 1DG 2T to 0
1880 Dublin **England** 1G 1T to 1T
1881 Manchester **England** 2G 2T to 0
1882 Dublin **Drawn** 2T each
1883 Manchester **England** 1G 3T to 1T
1884 Dublin **England** 1G to 0
1885 Manchester **England** 2T to 1T
1886 Dublin **England** 1T to 0
1887 Dublin **Ireland** 2G to 0
1888 No Match
1889 No Match
1890 Blackheath (London) **England** 3T to 0
1891 Dublin **England** 9-0
1892 Manchester **England** 7-0
1893 Dublin **England** 4-0
1894 Blackheath **Ireland** 7-5
1895 Dublin **England** 6-3
1896 Leeds **Ireland** 10-4

1897 Dublin **Ireland** 13-9
1898 Richmond (London) **Ireland** 9-6
1899 Dublin **Ireland** 6-0
1900 Richmond **England** 15-4
1901 Dublin **Ireland** 10-6
1902 Leicester **England** 6-3
1903 Dublin **Ireland** 6-0
1904 Blackheath **England** 19-0
1905 Cork **Ireland** 17-3
1906 Leicester **Ireland** 16-6
1907 Dublin **Ireland** 17-9
1908 Richmond **England** 13-3
1909 Dublin **England** 11-5
1910 Twickenham **Drawn** 0-0
1911 Dublin **Ireland** 3-0
1912 Twickenham **England** 15-0
1913 Dublin **England** 15-4
1914 Twickenham **England** 17-12
1920 Dublin **England** 14-11
1921 Twickenham **England** 15-0
1922 Dublin **England** 12-3
1923 Leicester **England** 23-5
1924 Belfast **England** 14-3

1925 Twickenham **Drawn** 6-6
1926 Dublin **Ireland** 19-15
1927 Twickenham **England** 8-6
1928 Dublin **England** 7-6
1929 Twickenham **Ireland** 6-5
1930 Dublin **Ireland** 4-3
1931 Twickenham **Ireland** 6-5
1932 Dublin **England** 11-8
1933 Twickenham **England** 17-6
1934 Dublin **England** 13-3
1935 Twickenham **England** 14-3
1936 Dublin **Ireland** 6-3
1937 Twickenham **England** 9-8
1938 Dublin **England** 36-14
1939 Twickenham **Ireland** 5-0
1947 Dublin **Ireland** 22-0
1948 Twickenham **Ireland** 11-10
1949 Dublin **Ireland** 14-5
1950 Twickenham **England** 3-0
1951 Dublin **Ireland** 3-0
1952 Twickenham **England** 3-0
1953 Dublin **Drawn** 9-9
1954 Twickenham **England** 14-3
1955 Dublin **Drawn** 6-6
1956 Twickenham **England** 20-0
1957 Dublin **England** 6-0
1958 Twickenham **England** 6-0
1959 Dublin **England** 3-0
1960 Twickenham **England** 8-5
1961 Dublin **Ireland** 11-8
1962 Twickenham **England** 16-0
1963 Dublin **Drawn** 0-0
1964 Twickenham **Ireland** 18-5
1965 Dublin **Ireland** 5-0
1966 Twickenham **Drawn** 6-6

1967 Dublin **England** 8-3
1968 Twickenham **Drawn** 9-9
1969 Dublin **Ireland** 17-15
1970 Twickenham **England** 9-3
1971 Dublin **England** 9-6
1972 Twickenham **Ireland** 16-12
1973 Dublin **Ireland** 18-9
1974 Twickenham **Ireland** 26-21
1975 Dublin **Ireland** 12-9
1976 Twickenham **Ireland** 13-12
1977 Dublin **England** 4-0
1978 Twickenham **England** 15-9
1979 Dublin **Ireland** 12-7
1980 Twickenham **England** 24-9
1981 Dublin **England** 10-6
1982 Twickenham **Ireland** 16-15
1983 Dublin **Ireland** 25-15
1984 Twickenham **England** 12-9
1985 Dublin **Ireland** 13-10
1986 Twickenham **England** 25-20
1987 Dublin **Ireland** 17-0
1988 Twickenham **England** 35-3
1988 Dublin **England** 21-10
Non-championship match
1989 Dublin **England** 16-3
1990 Twickenham **England** 23-0
1991 Dublin **England** 16-7
1992 Twickenham **England** 38-9
1993 Dublin **Ireland** 17-3
1994 Twickenham **Ireland** 13-12
1995 Dublin **England** 20-8
1996 Twickenham **England** 28-15
1997 Dublin **England** 46-6
1998 Twickenham **England** 35-17

ENGLAND v WALES
Played 104   England won 44, Wales won 48, Drawn 12
Highest scores England 60-26 in 1998, Wales 34-21 in 1967
Biggest wins England 60-26 in 1998, Wales 25-0 in 1905

1881 Blackheath (London) **England** 7G
   1DG 6T to 0
1882 No Match
1883 Swansea **England** 2G 4T to 0
1884 Leeds **England** 1G 2T to 1G
1885 Swansea **England** 1G 4T to 1G 1T
1886 Blackheath **England** 1GM 2T to 1G
1887 Llanelli **Drawn** no score
1888 No Match
1889 No Match
1890 Dewsbury **Wales** 1T to 0
1891 Newport **England** 7-3
1892 Blackheath **England** 17-0
1893 Cardiff **Wales** 12-11
1894 Birkenhead **England** 24-3
1895 Swansea **England** 14-6
1896 Blackheath **England** 25-0
1897 Newport **Wales** 11-0
1898 Blackheath **England** 14-7
1899 Swansea **Wales** 26-3
1900 Gloucester **Wales** 13-3

1901 Cardiff **Wales** 13-0
1902 Blackheath **Wales** 9-8
1903 Swansea **Wales** 21-5
1904 Leicester **Drawn** 14-14
1905 Cardiff **Wales** 25-0
1906 Richmond (London) **Wales** 16-3
1907 Swansea **Wales** 22-0
1908 Bristol **Wales** 28-18
1909 Cardiff **Wales** 8-0
1910 Twickenham **England** 11-6
1911 Swansea **Wales** 15-11
1912 Twickenham **England** 8-0
1913 Cardiff **England** 12-0
1914 Twickenham **England** 10-9
1920 Swansea **Wales** 19-5
1921 Twickenham **England** 18-3
1922 Cardiff **Wales** 28-6
1923 Twickenham **England** 7-3
1924 Swansea **England** 17-9
1925 Twickenham **England** 12-6
1926 Cardiff **Drawn** 3-3

1927 Twickenham **England** 11-9
1928 Swansea **England** 10-8
1929 Twickenham **England** 8-3
1930 Cardiff **England** 11-3
1931 Twickenham **Drawn** 11-11
1932 Swansea **Wales** 12-5
1933 Twickenham **Wales** 7-3
1934 Cardiff **England** 9-0
1935 Twickenham **Drawn** 3-3
1936 Swansea **Drawn** 0-0
1937 Twickenham **England** 4-3
1938 Cardiff **Wales** 14-8
1939 Twickenham **England** 3-0
1947 Cardiff **England** 9-6
1948 Twickenham **Drawn** 3-3
1949 Cardiff **Wales** 9-3
1950 Twickenham **Wales** 11-5
1951 Swansea **Wales** 23-5
1952 Twickenham **Wales** 8-6
1953 Cardiff **England** 8-3
1954 Twickenham **England** 9-6
1955 Cardiff **Wales** 3-0
1956 Twickenham **Wales** 8-3
1957 Cardiff **England** 3-0
1958 Twickenham **Drawn** 3-3
1959 Cardiff **Wales** 5-0
1960 Twickenham **England** 14-6
1961 Cardiff **Wales** 6-3
1962 Twickenham **Drawn** 0-0
1963 Cardiff **England** 13-6
1964 Twickenham **Drawn** 6-6
1965 Cardiff **Wales** 14-3
1966 Twickenham **Wales** 11-6

1967 Cardiff **Wales** 34-21
1968 Twickenham **Drawn** 11-11
1969 Cardiff **Wales** 30-9
1970 Twickenham **Wales** 17-13
1971 Cardiff **Wales** 22-6
1972 Twickenham **Wales** 12-3
1973 Cardiff **Wales** 25-9
1974 Twickenham **England** 16-12
1975 Cardiff **Wales** 20-4
1976 Twickenham **Wales** 21-9
1977 Cardiff **Wales** 14-9
1978 Twickenham **Wales** 9-6
1979 Cardiff **Wales** 27-3
1980 Twickenham **England** 9-8
1981 Cardiff **Wales** 21-19
1982 Twickenham **England** 17-7
1983 Cardiff **Drawn** 13-13
1984 Twickenham **Wales** 24-15
1985 Cardiff **Wales** 24-15
1986 Twickenham **England** 21-18
1987 Cardiff **Wales** 19-12
1987 Brisbane *WC* **Wales** 16-3
1988 Twickenham **Wales** 11-3
1989 Cardiff **Wales** 12-9
1990 Twickenham **England** 34-6
1991 Cardiff **England** 25-6
1992 Twickenham **England** 24-0
1993 Cardiff **Wales** 10-9
1994 Twickenham **England** 15-8
1995 Cardiff **England** 23-9
1996 Twickenham **England** 21-15
1997 Cardiff **England** 34-13
1998 Twickenham **England** 60-26

ENGLAND v FRANCE
Played 75   England won 40, France won 28, Drawn 7
Highest scores England 41-13 in 1907, France 37-12 in 1972
Biggest wins England 37-0 in 1911, France 37-12 in 1972

1906 Paris **England** 35-8
1907 Richmond (London) **England** 41-13
1908 Paris **England** 19-0
1909 Leicester **England** 22-0
1910 Paris **England** 11-3
1911 Twickenham **England** 37-0
1912 Paris **England** 18-8
1913 Twickenham **England** 20-0
1914 Paris **England** 39-13
1920 Twickenham **England** 8-3
1921 Paris **England** 10-6
1922 Twickenham **Drawn** 11-11
1923 Paris **England** 12-3
1924 Twickenham **England** 19-7
1925 Paris **England** 13-11
1926 Twickenham **England** 11-0
1927 Paris **France** 3-0
1928 Twickenham **England** 18-8
1929 Paris **England** 16-6
1930 Twickenham **England** 11-5
1931 Paris **France** 14-13
1947 Twickenham **England** 6-3
1948 Paris **France** 15-0

1949 Twickenham **England** 8-3
1950 Paris **France** 6-3
1951 Twickenham **France** 11-3
1952 Paris **England** 6-3
1953 Twickenham **England** 11-0
1954 Paris **France** 11-3
1955 Twickenham **France** 16-9
1956 Paris **France** 14-9
1957 Twickenham **England** 9-5
1958 Paris **England** 14-0
1959 Twickenham **Drawn** 3-3
1960 Paris **Drawn** 3-3
1961 Twickenham **Drawn** 5-5
1962 Paris **France** 13-0
1963 Twickenham **England** 6-5
1964 Paris **England** 6-3
1965 Twickenham **England** 9-6
1966 Paris **France** 13-0
1967 Twickenham **France** 16-12
1968 Paris **France** 14-9
1969 Twickenham **England** 22-8
1970 Paris **France** 35-13
1971 Twickenham **Drawn** 14-14

1972 Paris **France** 37-12
1973 Twickenham **England** 14-6
1974 Paris **Drawn** 12-12
1975 Twickenham **France** 27-20
1976 Paris **France** 30-9
1977 Twickenham **France** 4-3
1978 Paris **France** 15-6
1979 Twickenham **England** 7-6
1980 Paris **England** 17-13
1981 Twickenham **France** 16-12
1982 Paris **England** 27-15
1983 Twickenham **France** 19-15
1984 Paris **France** 32-18
1985 Twickenham **Drawn** 9-9
1986 Paris **France** 29-10

1987 Twickenham **France** 19-15
1988 Paris **France** 10-9
1989 Twickenham **England** 11-0
1990 Paris **England** 26-7
1991 Twickenham **England** 21-19
1991 Paris *WC* **England** 19-10
1992 Paris **England** 31-13
1993 Twickenham **England** 16-15
1994 Paris **England** 18-14
1995 Twickenham **England** 31-10
1995 Pretoria *WC* **France** 19-9
1996 Paris **France** 15-12
1997 Twickenham **France** 23-20
1998 Paris **France** 24-17

ENGLAND v NEW ZEALAND
Played 20   England won 4, New Zealand won 15, Drawn 1
Highest scores England 29-45 in 1995, New Zealand 45-29 in 1995
Biggest wins England 13-0 in 1936, New Zealand 42-15 in 1985

1905 Crystal Palace (London) **New Zealand** 15-0
1925 Twickenham **New Zealand** 17-11
1936 Twickenham **England** 13-0
1954 Twickenham **New Zealand** 5-0
1963 *1* Auckland **New Zealand** 21-11
    2 Christchurch **New Zealand** 9-6
    New Zealand won series 2-0
1964 Twickenham **New Zealand** 14-0
1967 Twickenham **New Zealand** 23-11
1973 Twickenham **New Zealand** 9-0
1973 Auckland **England** 16-10

1978 Twickenham **New Zealand** 16-6
1979 Twickenham **New Zealand** 10-9
1983 Twickenham **England** 15-9
1985 *1* Christchurch **New Zealand** 18-13
    2 Wellington **New Zealand** 42-15
    New Zealand won series 2-0
1991 Twickenham *WC* **New Zealand** 18-12
1993 Twickenham **England** 15-9
1995 Cape Town *WC* **New Zealand** 45-29
1997 *1* Manchester **New Zealand** 25-8
    2 Twickenham **Drawn** 26-26
    New Zealand won series 1-0, with 1 draw

ENGLAND v SOUTH AFRICA
Played 14   England won 4, South Africa won 9, Drawn 1
Highest scores England 33-16 in 1992, South Africa 35-9 in 1984
Biggest wins England 33-16 in 1992 & 32-15 in 1994, South Africa 35-9 in 1984

1906 Crystal Palace (London) **Drawn** 3-3
1913 Twickenham **South Africa** 9-3
1932 Twickenham **South Africa** 7-0
1952 Twickenham **South Africa** 8-3
1961 Twickenham **South Africa** 5-0
1969 Twickenham **England** 11-8
1972 Johannesburg **England** 18-9
1984 *1* Port Elizabeth **South Africa** 33-15

    2 Johannesburg **South Africa** 35-9
    South Africa won series 2-0
1992 Twickenham **England** 33-16
1994 *1* Pretoria **England** 32-15
    2 Cape Town **South Africa** 27-9
    Series drawn 1-1
1995 Twickenham **South Africa** 24-14
1997 Twickenham **South Africa** 29-11

ENGLAND v AUSTRALIA
Played 21   England won 7, Australia won 13, Drawn 1
Highest scores England 28-19 in 1988, Australia 40-15 in 1991
Biggest wins England 20-3 in 1973 & 23-6 in 1976, Australia 40-15 in 1991

1909 Blackheath (London) **Australia** 9-3
1928 Twickenham **England** 18-11
1948 Twickenham **Australia** 11-0
1958 Twickenham **England** 9-6
1963 Sydney **Australia** 18-9
1967 Twickenham **Australia** 23-11

1973 Twickenham **England** 20-3
1975 *1* Sydney **Australia** 16-9
    2 Brisbane **Australia** 30-21
    Australia won series 2-0
1976 Twickenham **England** 23-6
1982 Twickenham **England** 15-11

1984 Twickenham **Australia** 19-3
1987 Sydney *WC* **Australia** 19-6
1988 *1* Brisbane **Australia** 22-16
    2 Sydney **Australia** 28-8
    Australia won series 2-0
1988 Twickenham **England** 28-19

1991 Sydney **Australia** 40-15
1991 Twickenham *WC* **Australia** 12-6
1995 Cape Town *WC* **England** 25-22
1997 *1* Sydney **Australia** 25-6
    2 Twickenham **Drawn** 15-15
    Australia won series 1-0, with 1 draw

ENGLAND v NEW ZEALAND NATIVES
Played 1   England won 1
Highest score England 7-0 in 1889, NZ Natives 0-7 in 1889
Biggest win England 7-0 in 1889, NZ Natives no win

1889 Blackheath **England** 1G 4T to 0

ENGLAND v RFU PRESIDENT'S XV
Played 1   President's XV won 1
Highest score England 11-28 in 1971, RFU President's XV 28-11 in 1971
Biggest win RFU President's XV 28-11 in 1971

1971 Twickenham **President's XV** 28-11

ENGLAND v ARGENTINA
Played 9   England won 6, Argentina won 2, Drawn 1
Highest scores England 51-0 in 1990, Argentina 33-13 in 1997
Biggest wins England 51-0 in 1990, Argentina 33-13 in 1997

1981 *1* Buenos Aires **Drawn** 19-19
    2 Buenos Aires **England** 12-6
    England won series 1-0 with 1 draw
1990 *1* Buenos Aires **England** 25-12
    2 Buenos Aires **Argentina** 15-13
    Series drawn 1-1

1990 Twickenham **England** 51-0
1995 Durban *WC* **England** 24-18
1996 Twickenham **England** 20-18
1997 *1* Buenos Aires **England** 46-20
    2 Buenos Aires **Argentina** 33-13
    Series drawn 1-1

ENGLAND v ROMANIA
Played 3   England won 3
Highest scores England 58-3 in 1989, Romania 15-22 in 1985
Biggest win England 58-3 in 1989, Romania no win

1985 Twickenham **England** 22-15
1989 Bucharest **England** 58-3

1994 Twickenham **England** 54-3

ENGLAND v JAPAN
Played 1   England won 1
Highest score England 60-7 in 1987, Japan 7-60 in 1987
Biggest win England 60-7 in 1987, Japan no win

1987 Sydney *WC* **England** 60-7

ENGLAND v UNITED STATES
Played 2   England won 2
Highest scores England 37-9 in 1991, United States 9-37 in 1991
Biggest win England 37-9 in 1991, United States no win

1987 Sydney *WC* **England** 34-6

1991 Twickenham *WC* **England** 37-9

ENGLAND v FIJI
Played 3   England won 3
Highest scores England 58-23 in 1989, Fiji 23-58 in 1989
Biggest win England 58-23 in 1989, Fiji no win

1988 Suva **England** 25-12
1989 Twickenham **England** 58-23

1991 Suva **England** 28-12

ENGLAND v ITALY
Played 3   England won 3
Highest scores England 54-21 in 1996, Italy 21-54 in 1996
Biggest win England 54-21 in 1996, Italy no win

1991 Twickenham *WC* **England** 36-6
1995 Durban *WC* **England** 27-20

1996 Twickenham **England** 54-21

ENGLAND v CANADA
Played 2   England won 2
Highest scores England 60-19 in 1994, Canada 19-60 in 1994
Biggest win England 60-19 in 1994, Canada no win

1992 Wembley **England** 26-13

1994 Twickenham **England** 60-19

ENGLAND v WESTERN SAMOA
Played 2   England won 2
Highest scores England 44-22 in 1995, Western Samoa 22-44 in 1995
Biggest win England 44-22 in 1995, Western Samoa no win

1995 Durban *WC* **England** 44-22

1995 Twickenham **England** 27-9

SCOTLAND v IRELAND
Played 110   Scotland won 59, Ireland won 45, Drawn 5, Abandoned 1
Highest scores Scotland 38-10 in 1997, Ireland 26-8 in 1953
Biggest wins Scotland 38-10 in 1997, Ireland 21-0 in 1950

1877 Belfast **Scotland** 4G 2DG 2T to 0
1878 No Match
1879 Belfast **Scotland** 1G 1DG 1T to 0
1880 Glasgow **Scotland** 1G 2DG 2T to 0
1881 Belfast **Ireland** 1DG to 1T
1882 Glasgow **Scotland** 2T to 0
1883 Belfast **Scotland** 1G 1T to 0
1884 Raeburn Place (Edinburgh) **Scotland** 2G 2T to 1T
1885 Belfast **Abandoned** Ireland 0 Scotland 1T
1885 Raeburn Place **Scotland** 1G 2T to 0
1886 Raeburn Place **Scotland** 3G 1DG 2T to 0
1887 Belfast **Scotland** 1G 1GM 2T to 0
1888 Raeburn Place **Scotland** 1G to 0
1889 Belfast **Scotland** 1DG to 0
1890 Raeburn Place **Scotland** 1DG 1T to 0
1891 Belfast **Scotland** 14-0
1892 Raeburn Place **Scotland** 2-0
1893 Belfast **Drawn** 0-0

1894 Dublin **Ireland** 5-0
1895 Raeburn Place **Scotland** 6-0
1896 Dublin **Drawn** 0-0
1897 Powderhall (Edinburgh) **Scotland** 8-3
1898 Belfast **Scotland** 8-0
1899 Inverleith (Edinburgh) **Ireland** 9-3
1900 Dublin **Drawn** 0-0
1901 Inverleith **Scotland** 9-5
1902 Belfast **Ireland** 5-0
1903 Inverleith **Scotland** 3-0
1904 Dublin **Scotland** 19-3
1905 Inverleith **Ireland** 11-5
1906 Dublin **Scotland** 13-6
1907 Inverleith **Scotland** 15-3
1908 Dublin **Ireland** 16-11
1909 Inverleith **Scotland** 9-3
1910 Belfast **Scotland** 14-0
1911 Inverleith **Ireland** 16-10
1912 Dublin **Ireland** 10-8
1913 Inverleith **Scotland** 29-14
1914 Dublin **Ireland** 6-0

1920 Inverleith **Scotland** 19-0
1921 Dublin **Ireland** 9-8
1922 Inverleith **Scotland** 6-3
1923 Dublin **Scotland** 13-3
1924 Inverleith **Scotland** 13-8
1925 Dublin **Scotland** 14-8
1926 Murrayfield **Ireland** 3-0
1927 Dublin **Ireland** 6-0
1928 Murrayfield **Ireland** 13-5
1929 Dublin **Scotland** 16-7
1930 Murrayfield **Ireland** 14-11
1931 Dublin **Ireland** 8-5
1932 Murrayfield **Ireland** 20-8
1933 Dublin **Scotland** 8-6
1934 Murrayfield **Scotland** 16-9
1935 Dublin **Ireland** 12-5
1936 Murrayfield **Ireland** 10-4
1937 Dublin **Ireland** 11-4
1938 Murrayfield **Scotland** 23-14
1939 Dublin **Ireland** 12-3
1947 Murrayfield **Ireland** 3-0
1948 Dublin **Ireland** 6-0
1949 Murrayfield **Ireland** 13-3
1950 Dublin **Ireland** 21-0
1951 Murrayfield **Ireland** 6-5
1952 Dublin **Ireland** 12-8
1953 Murrayfield **Ireland** 26-8
1954 Belfast **Ireland** 6-0
1955 Murrayfield **Scotland** 12-3
1956 Dublin **Ireland** 14-10
1957 Murrayfield **Ireland** 5-3
1958 Dublin **Ireland** 12-6
1959 Murrayfield **Ireland** 8-3
1960 Dublin **Scotland** 6-5
1961 Murrayfield **Scotland** 16-8
1962 Dublin **Scotland** 20-6
1963 Murrayfield **Scotland** 3-0

1964 Dublin **Scotland** 6-3
1965 Murrayfield **Ireland** 16-6
1966 Dublin **Scotland** 11-3
1967 Murrayfield **Ireland** 5-3
1968 Dublin **Ireland** 14-6
1969 Murrayfield **Ireland** 16-0
1970 Dublin **Ireland** 16-11
1971 Murrayfield **Ireland** 17-5
1972 No Match
1973 Murrayfield **Scotland** 19-14
1974 Dublin **Ireland** 9-6
1975 Murrayfield **Scotland** 20-13
1976 Dublin **Scotland** 15-6
1977 Murrayfield **Scotland** 21-18
1978 Dublin **Ireland** 12-9
1979 Murrayfield **Drawn** 11-11
1980 Dublin **Ireland** 22-15
1981 Murrayfield **Scotland** 10-9
1982 Dublin **Ireland** 21-12
1983 Murrayfield **Ireland** 15-13
1984 Dublin **Scotland** 32-9
1985 Murrayfield **Ireland** 18-15
1986 Dublin **Scotland** 10-9
1987 Murrayfield **Scotland** 16-12
1988 Dublin **Ireland** 22-18
1989 Murrayfield **Scotland** 37-21
1990 Dublin **Scotland** 13-10
1991 Murrayfield **Scotland** 28-25
1991 Murrayfield *WC* **Scotland** 24-15
1992 Dublin **Scotland** 18-10
1993 Murrayfield **Scotland** 15-3
1994 Dublin **Drawn** 6-6
1995 Murrayfield **Scotland** 26-13
1996 Dublin **Scotland** 16-10
1997 Murrayfield **Scotland** 38-10
1998 Dublin **Scotland** 17-16

SCOTLAND v WALES

Played 102 Scotland won 44, Wales won 56, Drawn 2
Highest scores Scotland 35-10 in 1924, Wales 35-12 in 1972
Biggest wins Scotland 35-10 in 1924, Wales 35-12 in 1972 & 29-6 in 1994

1883 Raeburn Place (Edinburgh) **Scotland**
    3G to 1G
1884 Newport **Scotland** 1DG 1T to 0
1885 Glasgow **Drawn** no score
1886 Cardiff **Scotland** 2G 8T to 0
1887 Raeburn Place **Scotland** 4G 8T to 0
1888 Newport **Wales** 1T to 0
1889 Raeburn Place **Scotland** 2T to 0
1890 Cardiff **Scotland** 1G 2T to 1T
1891 Raeburn Place **Scotland** 15-0
1892 Swansea **Scotland** 7-2
1893 Raeburn Place **Wales** 9-0
1894 Newport **Wales** 7-0
1895 Raeburn Place **Scotland** 5-4
1896 Cardiff **Wales** 6-0
1897 No Match
1898 No Match
1899 Inverleith (Edinburgh) **Scotland** 21-10
1900 Swansea **Wales** 12-3

1901 Inverleith **Scotland** 18-8
1902 Cardiff **Wales** 14-5
1903 Inverleith **Scotland** 6-0
1904 Swansea **Wales** 21-3
1905 Inverleith **Wales** 6-3
1906 Cardiff **Wales** 9-3
1907 Inverleith **Scotland** 6-3
1908 Swansea **Wales** 6-5
1909 Inverleith **Wales** 5-3
1910 Cardiff **Wales** 14-0
1911 Inverleith **Wales** 32-10
1912 Swansea **Wales** 21-6
1913 Inverleith **Wales** 8-0
1914 Cardiff **Wales** 24-5
1920 Inverleith **Scotland** 9-5
1921 Swansea **Scotland** 14-8
1922 Inverleith **Drawn** 9-9
1923 Cardiff **Scotland** 11-8
1924 Inverleith **Scotland** 35-10

1925 Swansea **Scotland** 24-14
1926 Murrayfield **Scotland** 8-5
1927 Cardiff **Scotland** 5-0
1928 Murrayfield **Wales** 13-0
1929 Swansea **Wales** 14-7
1930 Murrayfield **Scotland** 12-9
1931 Cardiff **Wales** 13-8
1932 Murrayfield **Wales** 6-0
1933 Swansea **Scotland** 11-3
1934 Murrayfield **Wales** 13-6
1935 Cardiff **Wales** 10-6
1936 Murrayfield **Wales** 13-3
1937 Swansea **Scotland** 13-6
1938 Murrayfield **Scotland** 8-6
1939 Cardiff **Wales** 11-3
1947 Murrayfield **Wales** 22-8
1948 Cardiff **Wales** 14-0
1949 Murrayfield **Scotland** 6-5
1950 Swansea **Wales** 12-0
1951 Murrayfield **Scotland** 19-0
1952 Cardiff **Wales** 11-0
1953 Murrayfield **Wales** 12-0
1954 Swansea **Wales** 15-3
1955 Murrayfield **Scotland** 14-8
1956 Cardiff **Wales** 9-3
1957 Murrayfield **Scotland** 9-6
1958 Cardiff **Wales** 8-3
1959 Murrayfield **Scotland** 6-5
1960 Cardiff **Wales** 8-0
1961 Murrayfield **Scotland** 3-0
1962 Cardiff **Scotland** 8-3
1963 Murrayfield **Wales** 6-0
1964 Cardiff **Wales** 11-3
1965 Murrayfield **Wales** 14-12

1966 Cardiff **Wales** 8-3
1967 Murrayfield **Scotland** 11-5
1968 Cardiff **Wales** 5-0
1969 Murrayfield **Wales** 17-3
1970 Cardiff **Wales** 18-9
1971 Murrayfield **Wales** 19-18
1972 Cardiff **Wales** 35-12
1973 Murrayfield **Scotland** 10-9
1974 Cardiff **Wales** 6-0
1975 Murrayfield **Scotland** 12-10
1976 Cardiff **Wales** 28-6
1977 Murrayfield **Wales** 18-9
1978 Cardiff **Wales** 22-14
1979 Murrayfield **Wales** 19-13
1980 Cardiff **Wales** 17-6
1981 Murrayfield **Scotland** 15-6
1982 Cardiff **Scotland** 34-18
1983 Murrayfield **Wales** 19-15
1984 Cardiff **Scotland** 15-9
1985 Murrayfield **Wales** 25-21
1986 Cardiff **Wales** 22-15
1987 Murrayfield **Scotland** 21-15
1988 Cardiff **Wales** 25-20
1989 Murrayfield **Scotland** 23-7
1990 Cardiff **Scotland** 13-9
1991 Murrayfield **Scotland** 32-12
1992 Cardiff **Wales** 15-12
1993 Murrayfield **Scotland** 20-0
1994 Cardiff **Wales** 29-6
1995 Murrayfield **Scotland** 26-13
1996 Cardiff **Scotland** 16-14
1997 Murrayfield **Wales** 34-19
1998 Wembley **Wales** 19-13

SCOTLAND v FRANCE
Played 70   Scotland won 32, France won 35, Drawn 3
Highest scores Scotland 31-3 in 1912, France 51-16 in 1998
Biggest wins Scotland 31-3 in 1912, France 51-16 in 1998

1910 Inverleith (Edinburgh) **Scotland** 27-0
1911 Paris **France** 16-15
1912 Inverleith **Scotland** 31-3
1913 Paris **Scotland** 21-3
1914 No Match
1920 Paris **Scotland** 5-0
1921 Inverleith **France** 3-0
1922 Paris **Drawn** 3-3
1923 Inverleith **Scotland** 16-3
1924 Paris **France** 12-10
1925 Inverleith **Scotland** 25-4
1926 Paris **Scotland** 20-6
1927 Murrayfield **Scotland** 23-6
1928 Paris **Scotland** 15-6
1929 Murrayfield **Scotland** 6-3
1930 Paris **France** 7-3
1931 Murrayfield **Scotland** 6-4
1947 Paris **France** 8-3
1948 Murrayfield **Scotland** 9-8
1949 Paris **Scotland** 8-0
1950 Murrayfield **Scotland** 8-5
1951 Paris **France** 14-12

1952 Murrayfield **France** 13-11
1953 Paris **France** 11-5
1954 Murrayfield **France** 3-0
1955 Paris **France** 15-0
1956 Murrayfield **Scotland** 12-0
1957 Paris **Scotland** 6-0
1958 Murrayfield **Scotland** 11-9
1959 Paris **France** 9-0
1960 Murrayfield **France** 13-11
1961 Paris **France** 11-0
1962 Murrayfield **France** 11-3
1963 Paris **Scotland** 11-6
1964 Murrayfield **Scotland** 10-0
1965 Paris **France** 16-8
1966 Murrayfield **Drawn** 3-3
1967 Paris **Scotland** 9-8
1968 Murrayfield **France** 8-6
1969 Paris **Scotland** 6-3
1970 Murrayfield **France** 11-9
1971 Paris **France** 13-8
1972 Murrayfield **Scotland** 20-9
1973 Paris **France** 16-13

1974 Murrayfield **Scotland** 19-6
1975 Paris **France** 10-9
1976 Murrayfield **France** 13-6
1977 Paris **France** 23-3
1978 Murrayfield **France** 19-16
1979 Paris **France** 21-17
1980 Murrayfield **Scotland** 22-14
1981 Paris **France** 16-9
1982 Murrayfield **Scotland** 16-7
1983 Paris **France** 19-15
1984 Murrayfield **Scotland** 21-12
1985 Paris **France** 11-3
1986 Murrayfield **Scotland** 18-17
1987 Paris **France** 28-22

1987 Christchurch *WC* **Drawn** 20-20
1988 Murrayfield **Scotland** 23-12
1989 Paris **France** 19-3
1990 Murrayfield **Scotland** 21-0
1991 Paris **France** 15-9
1992 Murrayfield **Scotland** 10-6
1993 Paris **France** 11-3
1994 Murrayfield **France** 20-12
1995 Paris **Scotland** 23-21
1995 Pretoria *WC* **France** 22-19
1996 Murrayfield **Scotland** 19-14
1997 Paris **France** 47-20
1998 Murrayfield **France** 51-16

SCOTLAND v NEW ZEALAND

Played 20   Scotland won 0, New Zealand won 18, Drawn 2
Highest scores Scotland 31-62 in 1996, New Zealand 62-31 in 1996
Biggest wins Scotland no win, New Zealand 51-15 in 1993

1905 Inverleith (Edinburgh) **New Zealand** 12-7
1935 Murrayfield **New Zealand** 18-8
1954 Murrayfield **New Zealand** 3-0
1964 Murrayfield **Drawn** 0-0
1967 Murrayfield **New Zealand** 14-3
1972 Murrayfield **New Zealand** 14-9
1975 Auckland **New Zealand** 24-0
1978 Murrayfield **New Zealand** 18-9
1979 Murrayfield **New Zealand** 20-6
1981 *1* Dunedin **New Zealand** 11-4
     2 Auckland **New Zealand** 40-15
New Zealand won series 2-0

1983 Murrayfield **Drawn** 25-25
1987 Christchurch *WC* **New Zealand** 30-3
1990 *1* Dunedin **New Zealand** 31-16
     2 Auckland **New Zealand** 21-18
New Zealand won series 2-0
1991 Cardiff *WC* **New Zealand** 13-6
1993 Murrayfield **New Zealand** 51-15
1995 Pretoria *WC* **New Zealand** 48-30
1996 *1* Dunedin **New Zealand** 62-31
     2 Auckland **New Zealand** 36-12
New Zealand won series 2-0

SCOTLAND v SOUTH AFRICA

Played 10   Scotland won 3, South Africa won 7, Drawn 0
Highest scores Scotland 10-18 in 1960 & 10-34 in 1994 & 10-68 in 1997, South Africa 68-10 in 1997
Biggest wins Scotland 6-0 in 1906, South Africa 68-10 in 1997

1906 Glasgow **Scotland** 6-0
1912 Inverleith **South Africa** 16-0
1932 Murrayfield **South Africa** 6-3
1951 Murrayfield **South Africa** 44-0
1960 Port Elizabeth **South Africa** 18-10

1961 Murrayfield **South Africa** 12-5
1965 Murrayfield **Scotland** 8-5
1969 Murrayfield **Scotland** 6-3
1994 Murrayfield **South Africa** 34-10
1997 Murrayfield **South Africa** 68-10

SCOTLAND v AUSTRALIA

Played 16   Scotland won 7, Australia won 9, Drawn 0
Highest scores Scotland 24-15 in 1981, Australia 37-12 in 1984 & 37-13 in 1992 & 37-8 in 1997
Biggest wins Scotland 24-15 in 1981, Australia 37-8 in 1997

1927 Murrayfield **Scotland** 10-8
1947 Murrayfield **Australia** 16-7
1958 Murrayfield **Scotland** 12-8
1966 Murrayfield **Scotland** 11-5
1968 Murrayfield **Scotland** 9-3
1970 Sydney **Australia** 23-3

1975 Murrayfield **Scotland** 10-3
1981 Murrayfield **Scotland** 24-15
1982 *1* Brisbane **Scotland** 12-7
     2 Sydney **Australia** 33-9
Series drawn 1-1
1984 Murrayfield **Australia** 37-12

Percival Montgomery (South Africa) takes on Gregor Townsend (Scotland) in the Scotland–South Africa Test at Murrayfield, 6 December 1997.

1988 Murrayfield **Australia** 32-13	1996 Murrayfield **Australia** 29-19
1992 *1* Sydney **Australia** 27-12	1997 Murrayfield **Australia** 37-8
2 Brisbane **Australia** 37-13	
Australia won series 2-0	

SCOTLAND v SRU PRESIDENT'S XV
Played 1   Scotland won 1
Highest scores Scotland 27-16 in 1972, SRU President's XV 16-27 in 1973
Biggest win Scotland 27-16 in 1973, SRU President's XV no win

1973 Murrayfield **Scotland** 27-16

SCOTLAND v ROMANIA
Played 7   Scotland won 5, Romania won 2, Drawn 0
Highest scores Scotland 55-28 in 1987, Romania 28-55 in 1987 & 28-22 in 1984
Biggest wins Scotland 49-16 in 1995, Romania 28-22 in 1984 & 18-12 in 1991

1981 Murrayfield **Scotland** 12-6	1989 Murrayfield **Scotland** 32-0
1984 Bucharest **Romania** 28-22	1991 Bucharest **Romania** 18-12
1986 Bucharest **Scotland** 33-18	1995 Murrayfield **Scotland** 49-16
1987 Dunedin *WC* **Scotland** 55-28	

SCOTLAND v ZIMBABWE
Played 2   Scotland won 2
Highest scores Scotland 60-21 in 1987, Zimbabwe 21-60 in 1987
Biggest win Scotland 60-21 in 1987 & 51-12 in 1991, Zimbabwe no win

1987 Wellington *WC* **Scotland** 60-21	1991 Murrayfield *WC* **Scotland** 51-12

SCOTLAND v FIJI
Played 1   Scotland won 1
Highest scores Scotland 38-17 in 1989, Fiji 17-38 in 1989
Biggest win Scotland 38-17 in 1989, Fiji no win

1989 Murrayfield **Scotland** 38-17

SCOTLAND v ARGENTINA
Played 3   Scotland won 1, Argentina won 2, Drawn 0
Highest scores Scotland 49-3 in 1990, Argentina 19-17 in 1994
Biggest wins Scotland 49-3 in 1990, Argentina 19-17 in 1994

1990 Murrayfield **Scotland** 49-3	*2* Buenos Aires **Argentina** 19-17
1994 *1* Buenos Aires **Argentina** 16-15	*Argentina won series 2-0*

SCOTLAND v JAPAN
Played 1   Scotland won 1
Highest scores Scotland 47-9 in 1991, Japan 9-47 in 1991
Biggest win Scotland 47-9 in 1991, Japan no win

1991 Murrayfield *WC* **Scotland** 47-9

SCOTLAND v WESTERN SAMOA
Played 2   Scotland won 1, Drawn 1
Highest scores Scotland 28-6 in 1991, Western Samoa 15-15 in 1995
Biggest win Scotland 28-6 in 1991, Western Samoa no win

1991 Murrayfield *WC* **Scotland** 28-6   1995 Murrayfield **Drawn** 15-15

SCOTLAND v CANADA
Played 1   Scotland won 1
Highest scores Scotland 22-6 in 1995, Canada 6-22 in 1995
Biggest win Scotland 22-6 in 1995, Canada no win

1995 Murrayfield **Scotland** 22-6

SCOTLAND v IVORY COAST
Played 1   Scotland won 1
Highest scores Scotland 89-0 in 1995, Ivory Coast 0-89 in 1995
Biggest win Scotland 89-0 in 1995, Ivory Coast no win

1995 Rustenburg *WC* **Scotland** 89-0

SCOTLAND v TONGA
Played 1   Scotland won 1
Highest scores Scotland 41-5 in 1995, Tonga 5-41 in 1995
Biggest win Scotland 41-5 in 1995, Tonga no win

1995 Pretoria *WC* **Scotland** 41-5

SCOTLAND v ITALY
Played 2   Scotland won 1, Italy won 1
Highest scores Scotland 29-22 in 1996, Italy 25-21 in 1998
Biggest wins Scotland 29-22 in 1996, Italy 25-21 in 1998

1996 Murrayfield **Scotland** 29-22   1998 Treviso **Italy** 25-21

IRELAND v WALES
Played 102   Ireland won 37, Wales won 59, Drawn 6
Highest scores Ireland 30-17 in 1996, Wales 34-9 in 1976
Biggest wins Ireland 19-3 in 1925, Wales 29-0 in 1907

1882 Dublin **Wales** 2G 2T to 0	1897 No Match
1883 No Match	1898 Limerick **Wales** 11-3
1884 Cardiff **Wales** 1DG 2T to 0	1899 Cardiff **Ireland** 3-0
1885 No Match	1900 Belfast **Wales** 3-0
1886 No Match	1901 Swansea **Wales** 10-9
1887 Birkenhead **Wales** 1DG 1T to 3T	1902 Dublin **Wales** 15-0
1888 Dublin **Ireland** 1G 1DG 1T to 0	1903 Cardiff **Wales** 18-0
1889 Swansea **Ireland** 2T to 0	1904 Belfast **Ireland** 14-12
1890 Dublin **Drawn** 1G each	1905 Swansea **Wales** 10-3
1891 Llanelli **Wales** 6-4	1906 Belfast **Ireland** 11-6
1892 Dublin **Ireland** 9-0	1907 Cardiff **Wales** 29-0
1893 Llanelli **Wales** 2-0	1908 Belfast **Wales** 11-5
1894 Belfast **Ireland** 3-0	1909 Swansea **Wales** 18-5
1895 Cardiff **Wales** 5-3	1910 Dublin **Wales** 19-3
1896 Dublin **Ireland** 8-4	1911 Cardiff **Wales** 16-0

1912 Belfast **Ireland** 12-5	1963 Cardiff **Ireland** 14-6
1913 Swansea **Wales** 16-13	1964 Dublin **Wales** 15-6
1914 Belfast **Wales** 11-3	1965 Cardiff **Wales** 14-8
1920 Cardiff **Wales** 28-4	1966 Dublin **Ireland** 9-6
1921 Belfast **Wales** 6-0	1967 Cardiff **Ireland** 3-0
1922 Swansea **Wales** 11-5	1968 Dublin **Ireland** 9-6
1923 Dublin **Ireland** 5-4	1969 Cardiff **Wales** 24-11
1924 Cardiff **Ireland** 13-10	1970 Dublin **Ireland** 14-0
1925 Belfast **Ireland** 19-3	1971 Cardiff **Wales** 23-9
1926 Swansea **Wales** 11-8	1972 No Match
1927 Dublin **Ireland** 19-9	1973 Cardiff **Wales** 16-12
1928 Cardiff **Ireland** 13-10	1974 Dublin **Drawn** 9-9
1929 Belfast **Drawn** 5-5	1975 Cardiff **Wales** 32-4
1930 Swansea **Wales** 12-7	1976 Dublin **Wales** 34-9
1931 Belfast **Wales** 15-3	1977 Cardiff **Wales** 25-9
1932 Cardiff **Ireland** 12-10	1978 Dublin **Wales** 20-16
1933 Belfast **Ireland** 10-5	1979 Cardiff **Wales** 24-21
1934 Swansea **Wales** 13-0	1980 Dublin **Ireland** 21-7
1935 Belfast **Ireland** 9-3	1981 Cardiff **Wales** 9-8
1936 Cardiff **Wales** 3-0	1982 Dublin **Ireland** 20-12
1937 Belfast **Ireland** 5-3	1983 Cardiff **Wales** 23-9
1938 Swansea **Wales** 11-5	1984 Dublin **Wales** 18-9
1939 Belfast **Wales** 7-0	1985 Cardiff **Ireland** 21-9
1947 Swansea **Wales** 6-0	1986 Dublin **Wales** 19-12
1948 Belfast **Ireland** 6-3	1987 Cardiff **Ireland** 15-11
1949 Swansea **Ireland** 5-0	1987 Wellington *WC* **Wales** 13-6
1950 Belfast **Wales** 6-3	1988 Dublin **Wales** 12-9
1951 Cardiff **Drawn** 3-3	1989 Cardiff **Ireland** 19-13
1952 Dublin **Wales** 14-3	1990 Dublin **Ireland** 14-8
1953 Swansea **Wales** 5-3	1991 Cardiff **Drawn** 21-21
1954 Dublin **Wales** 12-9	1992 Dublin **Wales** 16-15
1955 Cardiff **Wales** 21-3	1993 Cardiff **Ireland** 19-14
1956 Dublin **Ireland** 11-3	1994 Dublin **Wales** 17-15
1957 Cardiff **Wales** 6-5	1995 Cardiff **Ireland** 16-12
1958 Dublin **Wales** 9-6	1995 Johannesburg *WC* **Ireland** 24-23
1959 Cardiff **Wales** 8-6	1996 Dublin **Ireland** 30-17
1960 Dublin **Wales** 10-9	1997 Cardiff **Ireland** 26-25
1961 Cardiff **Wales** 9-0	1998 Dublin **Wales** 30-21
1962 Dublin **Drawn** 3-3	

IRELAND v FRANCE

Played 72   Ireland won 25, France won 42, Drawn 5
Highest scores Ireland 25-5 in 1911 & 25-6 in 1975, France 45-10 in 1996
Biggest wins Ireland 24-0 in 1913, France 45-10 in 1996

1909 Dublin **Ireland** 19-8	1931 Paris **France** 3-0
1910 Paris **Ireland** 8-3	1947 Dublin **France** 12-8
1911 Cork **Ireland** 25-5	1948 Paris **Ireland** 13-6
1912 Paris **Ireland** 11-6	1949 Dublin **France** 16-9
1913 Cork **Ireland** 24-0	1950 Paris **Drawn** 3-3
1914 Paris **Ireland** 8-6	1951 Dublin **Ireland** 9-8
1920 Dublin **France** 15-7	1952 Paris **Ireland** 11-8
1921 Paris **France** 20-10	1953 Belfast **Ireland** 16-3
1922 Dublin **Ireland** 8-3	1954 Paris **France** 8-0
1923 Paris **France** 14-8	1955 Dublin **France** 5-3
1924 Dublin **Ireland** 6-0	1956 Paris **France** 14-8
1925 Paris **Ireland** 9-3	1957 Dublin **Ireland** 11-6
1926 Belfast **Ireland** 11-0	1958 Paris **France** 11-6
1927 Paris **Ireland** 8-3	1959 Dublin **Ireland** 9-5
1928 Belfast **Ireland** 12-8	1960 Paris **France** 23-6
1929 Paris **Ireland** 6-0	1961 Dublin **France** 15-3
1930 Belfast **France** 5-0	1962 Paris **France** 11-0

1963 Dublin **France** 24-5	1981 Dublin **France** 19-13
1964 Paris **France** 27-6	1982 Paris **France** 22-9
1965 Dublin **Drawn** 3-3	1983 Dublin **Ireland** 22-16
1966 Paris **France** 11-6	1984 Paris **France** 25-12
1967 Dublin **France** 11-6	1985 Dublin **Drawn** 15-15
1968 Paris **France** 16-6	1986 Paris **France** 29-9
1969 Dublin **Ireland** 17-9	1987 Dublin **France** 19-13
1970 Paris **France** 8-0	1988 Paris **France** 25-6
1971 Dublin **Drawn** 9-9	1989 Dublin **France** 26-21
1972 Paris **Ireland** 14-9	1990 Paris **France** 31-12
1972 Dublin **Ireland** 24-14	1991 Dublin **France** 21-13
Non-championship match	1992 Paris **France** 44-12
1973 Dublin **Ireland** 6-4	1993 Dublin **France** 21-6
1974 Paris **France** 9-6	1994 Paris **France** 35-15
1975 Dublin **Ireland** 25-6	1995 Dublin **France** 25-7
1976 Paris **France** 26-3	1995 Durban *WC* **France** 36-12
1977 Dublin **France** 15-6	1996 Paris **France** 45-10
1978 Paris **France** 10-9	1997 Dublin **France** 32-15
1979 Dublin **Drawn** 9-9	1998 Paris **France** 18-16
1980 Paris **France** 19-18	

IRELAND v NEW ZEALAND

Played 14   Ireland won 0, New Zealand won 13, Drawn 1
Highest scores Ireland 21-24 in 1992, New Zealand 63-15 in 1997
Biggest win Ireland no win, New Zealand 59-6 in 1992

1905 Dublin **New Zealand** 15-0	1978 Dublin **New Zealand** 10-6
1924 Dublin **New Zealand** 6-0	1989 Dublin **New Zealand** 23-6
1935 Dublin **New Zealand** 17-9	1992 *1* Dunedin **New Zealand** 24-21
1954 Dublin **New Zealand** 14-3	*2* Wellington **New Zealand** 59-6
1963 Dublin **New Zealand** 6-5	*New Zealand won series 2-0*
1973 Dublin **Drawn** 10-10	1995 Johannesburg *WC* **New Zealand** 43-19
1974 Dublin **New Zealand** 15-6	1997 Dublin **New Zealand** 63-15
1976 Wellington **New Zealand** 11-3	

IRELAND v SOUTH AFRICA

Played 10   Ireland won 1, South Africa won 8, Drawn 1
Highest scores Ireland 15-23 in 1981, South Africa 38-0 in 1912
Biggest wins Ireland 9-6 in 1965, South Africa 38-0 in 1912

1906 Belfast **South Africa** 15-12	1965 Dublin **Ireland** 9-6
1912 Dublin **South Africa** 38-0	1970 Dublin **Drawn** 8-8
1931 Dublin **South Africa** 8-3	1981 *1* Cape Town **South Africa** 23-15
1951 Dublin **South Africa** 17-5	*2* Durban **South Africa** 12-10
1960 Dublin **South Africa** 8-3	*South Africa won series 2-0*
1961 Cape Town **South Africa** 24-8	

IRELAND v AUSTRALIA

Played 17   Ireland won 6, Australia won 11, Drawn 0
Highest scores Ireland 27-12 in 1979, Australia 42-17 in 1992
Biggest wins Ireland 27-12 in 1979, Australia 42-17 in 1992

1927 Dublin **Australia** 5-3	1976 Dublin **Australia** 20-10
1947 Dublin **Australia** 16-3	1979 *1* Brisbane **Ireland** 27-12
1958 Dublin **Ireland** 9-6	*2* Sydney **Ireland** 9-3
1967 Dublin **Ireland** 15-8	*Ireland won series 2-0*
1967 Sydney **Ireland** 11-5	1981 Dublin **Australia** 16-12
1968 Dublin **Ireland** 10-3	1984 Dublin **Australia** 16-9

1987 Sydney *WC* **Australia** 33-15
1991 Dublin *WC* **Australia** 19-18
1992 Dublin **Australia** 42-17
1994 *1* Brisbane **Australia** 33-13

2 Sydney **Australia** 32-18
Australia won series 2-0
1996 Dublin **Australia** 22-12

IRELAND v NEW ZEALAND NATIVES
Played 1   New Zealand Natives won 1
Highest scores Ireland 4-13 in 1888, Zew Zealand Natives 13-4 in 1888
Biggest win Ireland no win, New Zealand Natives 13-4 in 1888

1888 Dublin **New Zealand Natives**
    4G 1T to 1G 1T

IRELAND v IRU PRESIDENT'S XV
Played 1   Drawn 1
Highest scores Ireland 18-18 in 1974, IRFU President's XV 18-18 in 1974

1974 Dublin **Drawn** 18-18

IRELAND v ROMANIA
Played 2   Ireland won 2
Highest scores Ireland 60-0 in 1986, Romania 3-25 in 1993
Biggest win Ireland 60-0 in 1986, Romania no win

1986 Dublin **Ireland** 60-0   1993 Dublin **Ireland** 25-3

IRELAND v CANADA
Played 2   Ireland won 2
Highest scores Ireland 46-19 in 1987, Canada 19-46 in 1987
Biggest win Ireland 46-19 in 1987, Canada no win

1987 Dunedin *WC* **Ireland** 46-19   1997 Dublin **Ireland** 33-11

IRELAND v TONGA
Played 1   Ireland won 1
Highest scores Ireland 32-9 in 1987, Tonga 9-32 in 1987
Biggest win Ireland 32-9 in 1987, Tonga no win

1987 Brisbane *WC* **Ireland** 32-9

IRELAND v WESTERN SAMOA
Played 2   Ireland won 1, Western Samoa won 1, Drawn 0
Highest scores Ireland 49-22 in 1988, Western Samoa 40-25 in 1996
Biggest wins Ireland 49-22 in 1988, Western Samoa 40-25 in 1996

1988 Dublin **Ireland** 49-22   1996 Dublin **Western Samoa** 40-25

IRELAND v ITALY
Played 4   Ireland won 1, Italy won 3, Drawn 0
Highest scores Ireland 31-15 in 1988, Italy 37-29 in 1997 & 37-22 in 1997
Biggest wins Ireland 31-15 in 1988, Italy 37-22 in 1997

1988 Dublin **Ireland** 31-15   1997 Dublin **Italy** 37-29
1995 Treviso **Italy** 22-12   1997 Bologna **Italy** 37-22

IRELAND v ARGENTINA
Played 1   Ireland won 1
Highest scores Ireland 20-18 in 1990, Argentina 18-20 in 1990
Biggest win Ireland 20-18 in 1990, Argentina no win

1990 Dublin **Ireland** 20-18

IRELAND v NAMIBIA
Played 2   Namibia won 2
Highest scores Ireland 15-26 in 1991, Namibia 26-15 in 1991
Biggest win Ireland no win, Namibia 26-15 in 1991

1991 *1* Windhoek **Namibia** 15-6   *2* Windhoek **Namibia** 26-15
Namibia won series 2-0

IRELAND v ZIMBABWE
Played 1   Ireland won 1
Highest scores Ireland 55-11 in 1991, Zimbabwe 11-55 in 1991
Biggest win Ireland 55-11 in 1991, Zimbabwe no win

1991 Dublin *WC* **Ireland** 55-11

IRELAND v JAPAN
Played 2   Ireland won 2
Highest scores Ireland 50-28 in 1995, Japan 28-50 in 1995
Biggest win Ireland 50-28 in 1995, Japan no win

1991 Dublin *WC* **Ireland** 32-16   1995 Bloemfontein *WC* **Ireland** 50-28

IRELAND v UNITED STATES
Played 2   Ireland won 2
Highest scores Ireland 26-15 in 1994, United States 18-25 in 1996
Biggest win Ireland 26-15 in 1994, United States no win

1994 Dublin **Ireland** 26-15   1996 Atlanta **Ireland** 25-18

IRELAND v FIJI
Played 1   Ireland won 1
Highest scores Ireland 44-8 in 1995, Fiji 8-44 in 1995
Biggest win Ireland 44-8 in 1995, Fiji no win

1995 Dublin **Ireland** 44-8

WALES v FRANCE
Played 73   Wales won 38, France won 32, Drawn 3
Highest scores Wales 49-14 in 1910, France 51-0 in 1998
Biggest wins Wales 47-5 in 1909, France 51-0 in 1998

1908 Cardiff **Wales** 36-4	1914 Swansea **Wales** 31-0
1909 Paris **Wales** 47-5	1920 Paris **Wales** 6-5
1910 Swansea **Wales** 49-14	1921 Cardiff **Wales** 12-4
1911 Paris **Wales** 15-0	1922 Paris **Wales** 11-3
1912 Newport **Wales** 14-8	1923 Swansea **Wales** 16-8
1913 Paris **Wales** 11-8	1924 Paris **Wales** 10-6

1925 Cardiff **Wales** 11-5		1972 Cardiff **Wales** 20-6
1926 Paris **Wales** 7-5		1973 Paris **France** 12-3
1927 Swansea **Wales** 25-7		1974 Cardiff **Drawn** 16-16
1928 Paris **France** 8-3		1975 Paris **Wales** 25-10
1929 Cardiff **Wales** 8-3		1976 Cardiff **Wales** 19-13
1930 Paris **Wales** 11-0		1977 Paris **France** 16-9
1931 Swansea **Wales** 35-3		1978 Cardiff **Wales** 16-7
1947 Paris **Wales** 3-0		1979 Paris **France** 14-13
1948 Swansea **France** 11-3		1980 Cardiff **Wales** 18-9
1949 Paris **France** 5-3		1981 Paris **France** 19-15
1950 Cardiff **Wales** 21-0		1982 Cardiff **Wales** 22-12
1951 Paris **France** 8-3		1983 Paris **France** 16-9
1952 Swansea **Wales** 9-5		1984 Cardiff **France** 21-16
1953 Paris **Wales** 6-3		1985 Paris **France** 14-3
1954 Cardiff **Wales** 19-13		1986 Cardiff **France** 23-15
1955 Paris **Wales** 16-11		1987 Paris **France** 16-9
1956 Cardiff **Wales** 5-3		1988 Cardiff **France** 10-9
1957 Paris **Wales** 19-13		1989 Paris **France** 31-12
1958 Cardiff **France** 16-6		1990 Cardiff **France** 29-19
1959 Paris **France** 11-3		1991 Paris **France** 36-3
1960 Cardiff **France** 16-8		1991 Cardiff **France** 22-9
1961 Paris **France** 8-6		*Non-championship match*
1962 Cardiff **Wales** 3-0		1992 Cardiff **France** 12-9
1963 Paris **France** 5-3		1993 Paris **France** 26-10
1964 Cardiff **Drawn** 11-11		1994 Cardiff **Wales** 24-15
1965 Paris **France** 22-13		1995 Paris **France** 21-9
1966 Cardiff **Wales** 9-8		1996 Cardiff **Wales** 16-15
1967 Paris **France** 20-14		1996 Cardiff **France** 40-33
1968 Cardiff **France** 14-9		*Non-championship match*
1969 Paris **Drawn** 8-8		1997 Paris **France** 27-22
1970 Cardiff **Wales** 11-6		1998 Wembley **France** 51-0
1971 Paris **Wales** 9-5		

WALES v NEW ZEALAND
Played 17 Wales won 3, New Zealand won 14, Drawn 0
Highest scores Wales 16-19 in 1972, New Zealand 54-9 in 1988
Biggest wins Wales 13-8 in 1953, New Zealand 52-3 in 1988

1905 Cardiff **Wales** 3-0	1978 Cardiff **New Zealand** 13-12
1924 Swansea **New Zealand** 19-0	1980 Cardiff **New Zealand** 23-3
1935 Cardiff **Wales** 13-12	1987 Brisbane *WC* **New Zealand** 49-6
1953 Cardiff **Wales** 13-8	1988 *1* Christchurch **New Zealand** 52-3
1963 Cardiff **New Zealand** 6-0	*2* Auckland **New Zealand** 54-9
1967 Cardiff **New Zealand** 13-6	*New Zealand won series 2-0*
1969 *1* Christchurch **New Zealand** 19-0	1989 Cardiff **New Zealand** 34-9
2 Auckland **New Zealand** 33-12	1995 Johannesburg *WC* **New Zealand** 34-9
New Zealand won series 2-0	1997 Wembley **New Zealand** 42-7
1972 Cardiff **New Zealand** 19-16	

WALES v SOUTH AFRICA
Played 10 Wales won 0, South Africa won 9, Drawn 1
Highest scores Wales 20-37 in 1996, South Africa 37-20 in 1996
Biggest win Wales no win, South Africa 40-11 in 1995

1906 Swansea **South Africa** 11-0	1964 Durban **South Africa** 24-3
1912 Cardiff **South Africa** 3-0	1970 Cardiff **Drawn** 6-6
1931 Swansea **South Africa** 8-3	1994 Cardiff **South Africa** 20-12
1951 Cardiff **South Africa** 6-3	1995 Johannesburg **South Africa** 40-11
1960 Cardiff **South Africa** 3-0	1996 Cardiff **South Africa** 37-20

WALES v AUSTRALIA

Played 19   Wales won 8, Australia won 11, Drawn 0
Highest scores Wales 28-3 in 1975, Australia 63-6 in 1991
Biggest wins Wales 28-3 in 1975, Australia 63-6 in 1991

1908 Cardiff **Wales** 9-6
1927 Cardiff **Australia** 18-8
1947 Cardiff **Wales** 6-0
1958 Cardiff **Wales** 9-3
1966 Cardiff **Australia** 14-11
1969 Sydney **Wales** 19-16
1973 Cardiff **Wales** 24-0
1975 Cardiff **Wales** 28-3
1978 *1* Brisbane **Australia** 18-8
   2 Sydney **Australia** 19-17
   Australia won series 2-0

1981 Cardiff **Wales** 18-13
1984 Cardiff **Australia** 28-9
1987 Rotorua *WC* **Wales** 22-21
1991 Brisbane **Australia** 63-6
1991 Cardiff *WC* **Australia** 38-3
1992 Cardiff **Australia** 23-6
1996 *1* Brisbane **Australia** 56-25
   2 Sydney **Australia** 42-3
   Australia won series 2-0
1996 Cardiff **Australia** 28-19

WALES v NEW ZEALAND NATIVES

Played 1   Wales won 1
Highest scores Wales 5-0 in 1888, New Zealand Natives 0-5 in 1888
Biggest win Wales 5-0 in 1888, New Zealand Natives no win

1888 Swansea **Wales** 1G 2T to 0

WALES v NEW ZEALAND ARMY

Played 1   New Zealand Army won 1
Highest scores Wales 3-6 in 1919, New Zealand Army 6-3 in 1919
Biggest win Wales no win, New Zealand Army 6-3 in 1919

1919 Swansea **New Zealand Army** 6-3

WALES v ROMANIA

Played 4   Wales won 2, Romania won 2
Highest scores Wales 70-21 in 1997, Romania 24-6 in 1983
Biggest wins Wales 70-21 in 1997, Romania 24-6 in 1983

1983 Bucharest **Romania** 24-6
1988 Cardiff **Romania** 15-9

1994 Bucharest **Wales** 16-9
1997 Wrexham **Wales** 70-21

WALES v FIJI

Played 4   Wales won 4
Highest scores Wales 40-3 in 1985, Fiji 15-22 in 1986 & 15-19 in 1995
Biggest win Wales 40-3 in 1985, Fiji no win

1985 Cardiff **Wales** 40-3
1986 Suva **Wales** 22-15

1994 Suva **Wales** 23-8
1995 Cardiff **Wales** 19-15

WALES v TONGA

Played 4   Wales won 4
Highest scores Wales 46-12 in 1997, Tonga 16-29 in 1987
Biggest win Wales 46-12 in 1997, Tonga no win

1986 Nuku'Alofa **Wales** 15-7
1987 Palmerston North *WC* **Wales** 29-16

1994 Nuku'Alofa **Wales** 18-9
1997 Swansea **Wales** 46-12

WALES v WESTERN SAMOA
Played 4   Wales won 2, Western Samoa won 2, Drawn 0
Highest scores Wales 32-14 in 1986, Western Samoa 34-9 in 1994
Biggest wins Wales 28-6 in 1988, Western Samoa 34-9 in 1994

1986 Apia **Wales** 32-14	1991 Cardiff *WC* **Western Samoa** 16-13
1988 Cardiff **Wales** 28-6	1994 Moamoa **Western Samoa** 34-9

WALES v CANADA
Played 4   Wales won 3, Canada won 1, Drawn 0
Highest scores Wales 40-9 in 1987, Canada 26-24 in 1993
Biggest wins Wales 40-9 in 1987, Canada 26-24 in 1993

1987 Invercargill *WC* **Wales** 40-9	1994 Toronto **Wales** 33-15
1993 Cardiff **Canada** 26-24	1997 Toronto **Wales** 28-25

WALES v UNITED STATES
Played 4   Wales won 4
Highest scores Wales 46-0 in 1987, United States 23-28 in 1997
Biggest win Wales 46-0 in 1987, United States no win

1987 Cardiff **Wales** 46-0	*2* San Francisco **Wales** 28-23
1997 Cardiff **Wales** 34-14	*Wales won series 2-0*
1997 *1* Wilmington **Wales** 30-20	

WALES v NAMIBIA
Played 3   Wales won 3
Highest scores Wales 38-23 in 1993, Namibia 30-34 in 1990
Biggest win Wales 38-23 in 1993, Namibia no win

1990 *1* Windhoek **Wales** 18-9	1993 Windhoek **Wales** 38-23
2 Windhoek **Wales** 34-30	
Wales won series 2-0	

WALES v BARBARIANS
Played 2   Wales won 1, Barbarians won 1
Highest scores Wales 31-10 in 1996, Barbarians 31-24 in 1990
Biggest wins Wales 31-10 in 1996, Barbarians 31-24 in 1990

1990 Cardiff **Barbarians** 31-24	1996 Cardiff **Wales** 31-10

WALES v ARGENTINA
Played 1   Wales won 1
Highest scores Wales 16-7 in 1991, Argentina 7-16 in 1991
Biggest win Wales 16-7 in 1991, Argentina no win

1991 Cardiff *WC* **Wales** 16-7

WALES v ZIMBABWE
Played 2 Wales won 2
Highest scores Wales 42-13 in 1993, Zimbabwe 14-35 in 1993
Biggest win Wales 42-13 in 1993, Zimbabwe no win

1993 *1* Bulawayo **Wales** 35-14
2 Harare **Wales** 42-13
Wales won series 2-0

WALES v JAPAN
Played 2 Wales won 2
Highest scores Wales 57-10 in 1995, Japan 10-57 in 1995
Biggest win Wales 55-5 in 1993, Japan no win

1993 Cardiff **Wales** 55-5
1995 Bloemfontein *WC* **Wales** 57-10

WALES v PORTUGAL
Played 1 Wales won 1
Highest scores Wales 102-11 in 1994, Portugal 11-102 in 1994
Biggest win Wales 102-11 in 1994, Portugal no win

1994 Lisbon **Wales** 102-11

WALES v SPAIN
Played 1 Wales won 1
Highest scores Wales 54-0 in 1994, Spain 0-54 in 1994
Bigegst win Wales 54-0 in 1994, Spain no win

1994 Madrid **Wales** 54-0

WALES v ITALY
Played 4 Wales won 4
Highest scores Wales 31-26 in 1996 & 31-22 in 1996, Italy 26-31 in 1996
Biggest win Wales 29-19 in 1994, Italy no win

1994 Cardiff **Wales** 29-19
1996 Cardiff **Wales** 31-26
1996 Rome **Wales** 31-22
1998 Llanelli **Wales** 23-20

FRANCE v NEW ZEALAND
Played 32 France won 8, New Zealand won 24, Drawn 0
Highest scores France 24-19 in 1979, New Zealand 38-8 in 1906
Biggest wins France 22-8 in 1994, New Zealand 38-8 in 1906

1906 Paris **New Zealand** 38-8
1925 Toulouse **New Zealand** 30-6
1954 Paris **France** 3-0
1961 *1* Auckland **New Zealand** 13-6
   2 Wellington **New Zealand** 5-3
   3 Christchurch **New Zealand** 32-3
   New Zealand won series 3-0
1964 Paris **New Zealand** 12-3
1967 Paris **New Zealand** 21-15
1968 *1* Christchurch **New Zealand** 12-9
   2 Wellington **New Zealand** 9-3
   3 Auckland **New Zealand** 19-12
   New Zealand won series 3-0

1973 Paris **France** 13-6
1977 *1* Toulouse **France** 18-13
   2 Paris **New Zealand** 15-3
   Series drawn 1-1
1979 *1* Christchurch **New Zealand** 23-9
   2 Auckland **France** 24-19
   Series drawn 1-1
1981 *1* Toulouse **New Zealand** 13-9
   2 Paris **New Zealand** 18-6
   New Zealand won series 2-0
1984 *1* Christchurch **New Zealand** 10-9
   2 Auckland **New Zealand** 31-18
   New Zealand won series 2-0

1986 Christchurch **New Zealand** 18-9
1986 *1* Toulouse **New Zealand** 19-7
    2 Nantes **France** 16-3
    Series drawn 1-1
1987 Auckland *WC* **New Zealand** 29-9
1989 *1* Christchurch **New Zealand** 25-17
    2 Auckland **New Zealand** 34-20
    New Zealand won series 2-0
1990 *1* Nantes **New Zealand** 24-3

    2 Paris **New Zealand** 30-12
    New Zealand won series 2-0
1994 *1* Christchurch **France** 22-8
    2 Auckland **France** 23-20
    France won series 2-0
1995 *1* Toulouse **France** 22-15
    2 Paris **New Zealand** 37-12
    Series drawn 1-1

FRANCE v SOUTH AFRICA
Played 28 France won 5, South Africa won 18, Drawn 5
Highest scores France 32-36 in 1997, South Africa 52-10 in 1997
Biggest wins France 29-16 in 1992, South Africa 52-10 in 1997

1913 Bordeaux **South Africa** 38-5
1952 Paris **South Africa** 25-3
1958 *1* Cape Town **Drawn** 3-3
    2 Johannesburg **France** 9-5
    France won series 1-0, with 1 draw
1961 Paris **Drawn** 0-0
1964 Springs (SA) **France** 8-6
1967 *1* Durban **South Africa** 26-3
    2 Bloemfontein **South Africa** 16-3
    3 Johannesburg **France** 19-14
    4 Cape Town **Drawn** 6-6
    South Africa won series 2-1, with 1 draw
1968 *1* Bordeaux **South Africa** 12-9
    2 Paris **South Africa** 16-11
    South Africa won series 2-0
1971 *1* Bloemfontein **South Africa** 22-9
    2 Durban **Drawn** 8-8
    South Africa won series 1-0, with 1 draw
1974 *1* Toulouse **South Africa** 13-4

    2 Paris **South Africa** 10-8
    South Africa won series 2-0
1975 *1* Bloemfontein **South Africa** 38-25
    2 Pretoria **South Africa** 33-18
    South Africa won series 2-0
1980 Pretoria **South Africa** 37-15
1992 *1* Lyons **South Africa** 20-15
    2 Paris **France** 29-16
    Series drawn 1-1
1993 *1* Durban **Drawn** 20-20
    2 Johannesburg **France** 18-17
    France won series 1-0, with 1 draw
1995 Durban *WC* **South Africa** 19-15
1996 *1* Bordeaux **South Africa** 22-12
    2 Paris **South Africa** 13-12
    South Africa won series 2-0
1997 *1* Lyons **South Africa** 36-32
    2 Paris **South Africa** 52-10
    South Africa won series 2-0

FRANCE v AUSTRALIA
Played 27 France won 13, Australia won 12, Drawn 2
Highest scores France 34-6 in 1976, Australia 48-31 in 1990
Biggest wins France 34-6 in 1976, Australia 24-3 in 1993

1928 Paris **Australia** 11-8
1948 Paris **France** 13-6
1958 Paris **France** 19-0
1961 Sydney **France** 15-8
1967 Paris **France** 20-14
1968 Sydney **Australia** 11-10
1971 *1* Toulouse **Australia** 13-11
    2 Paris **France** 18-9
    Series drawn 1-1
1972 *1* Sydney **Drawn** 14-14
    2 Brisbane **France** 16-15
    France won series 1-0, with 1 draw
1976 *1* Bordeaux **France** 18-15
    2 Paris **France** 34-6
    France won series 2-0
1981 *1* Brisbane **Australia** 17-15
    2 Sydney **Australia** 24-14
    Australia won series 2-0

1983 *1* Clermont-Ferrand **Drawn** 15-15
    2 Paris **France** 15-6
    France won series 1-0, with 1 draw
1986 Sydney **Australia** 27-14
1987 Sydney *WC* **France** 30-24
1989 *1* Strasbourg **Australia** 32-15
    2 Lille **France** 25-19
    Series drawn 1-1
1990 *1* Sydney **Australia** 21-9
    2 Brisbane **Australia** 48-31
    3 Sydney **France** 28-19
    Australia won series 2-1
1993 *1* Bordeaux **France** 16-13
    2 Paris **Australia** 24-3
    Series drawn 1-1
1997 *1* Sydney **Australia** 29-15
    2 Brisbane **Australia** 26-19
    Australia won series 2-0

FRANCE v UNITED STATES
Played 5   France won 4, United States won 1, Drawn 0
Highest scores France 41-9 in 1991, United States 17-3 in 1924
Biggest wins France 41-9 in 1991, United States 17-3 in 1924

1920 Paris **France** 14-5
1924 Paris **United States** 17-3
1976 Chicago **France** 33-14
1991 *1* Denver **France** 41-9

2 Colorado Springs **France** 10-3*
Abandoned after 43 mins
France won series 2-0

FRANCE v ROMANIA
Played 45   France won 35, Romania won 8, Drawn 2
Highest scores France 64-12 in 1996, Romania 21-33 in 1991
Biggest wins France 59-3 in 1924, Romania 15-0 in 1980

1924 Paris **France** 59-3
1938 Bucharest **France** 11-8
1957 Bucharest **France** 18-15
1957 Bordeaux **France** 39-0
1960 Bucharest **Romania** 11-5
1961 Bayonne **Drawn** 5-5
1962 Bucharest **Romania** 3-0
1963 Toulouse **Drawn** 6-6
1964 Bucharest **France** 9-6
1965 Lyons **France** 8-3
1966 Bucharest **France** 9-3
1967 Nantes **France** 11-3
1968 Bucharest **Romania** 15-14
1969 Tarbes **France** 14-9
1970 Bucharest **France** 14-3
1971 Béziers **France** 31-12
1972 Constanza **France** 15-6
1973 Valence **France** 7-6
1974 Bucharest **Romania** 15-10
1975 Bordeaux **France** 36-12
1976 Bucharest **Romania** 15-12
1977 Clermont-Ferrand **France** 9-6
1978 Bucharest **France** 9-6

1979 Montauban **France** 30-12
1980 Bucharest **Romania** 15-0
1981 Narbonne **France** 17-9
1982 Bucharest **Romania** 13-9
1983 Toulouse **France** 26-15
1984 Bucharest **France** 18-3
1986 Lille **France** 25-13
1986 Bucharest **France** 20-3
1987 Wellington *WC* **France** 55-12
1987 Agen **France** 49-3
1988 Bucharest **France** 16-12
1990 Auch **Romania** 12-6
1991 Bucharest **France** 33-21
1991 Béziers *WC* **France** 30-3
1992 Le Havre **France** 25-6
1993 Bucharest **France** 37-20
1993 Brive **France** 51-0
1995 Bucharest **France** 24-15
1995 Tucumán *LC* **France** 52-8
1996 Aurillac **France** 64-12
1997 Bucharest **France** 51-20
1997 Lourdes *LC* **France** 39-3

FRANCE v NEW ZEALAND MAORIS
Played 1   New Zealand Maoris won 1
Highest scores France 3-12 in 1926, New Zealand Maoris 12-3 in 1926
Biggest win France no win, New Zealand Maoris 12-3 in 1926

1926 Paris **New Zealand Maoris** 12-3

FRANCE v GERMANY
Played 15   France won 13, Germany won 2, Drawn 0
Highest scores France 38-17 in 1933, Germany 17-16 in 1927 & 17-38 in 1933
Biggest wins France 34-0 in 1931, Germany 3-0 in 1938

1927 Paris **France** 30-5
1927 Frankfurt **Germany** 17-16
1928 Hanover **France** 14-3
1929 Paris **France** 24-0
1930 Berlin **France** 31-0
1931 Paris **France** 34-0
1932 Frankfurt **France** 20-4

1933 Paris **France** 38-17
1934 Hanover **France** 13-9
1935 Paris **France** 18-3
1936 *1* Berlin **France** 19-14
2 Hanover **France** 6-3
France won series 2-0
1937 Paris **France** 27-6

1938 Frankfurt **Germany** 3-0   1938 Bucharest **France** 8-5

FRANCE v ITALY
Played 20   France won 19, Italy won 1, Drawn 0
Highest scores France 60-13 in 1967, Italy 40-32 in 1997
Biggest wins France 60-13 in 1967, Italy 40-32 in 1997

1937 Paris **France** 43-5	1961 Chambéry **France** 17-0
1952 Milan **France** 17-8	1962 Brescia **France** 6-3
1953 Lyons **France** 22-8	1963 Grenoble **France** 14-12
1954 Rome **France** 39-12	1964 Parma **France** 12-3
1955 Grenoble **France** 24-0	1965 Pau **France** 21-0
1956 Padua **France** 16-3	1966 Naples **France** 21-0
1957 Agen **France** 38-6	1967 Toulon **France** 60-13
1958 Naples **France** 11-3	1995 Buenos Aires *LC* **France** 34-22
1959 Nantes **France** 22-0	1997 Grenoble **Italy** 40-32
1960 Treviso **France** 26-0	1997 Auch *LC* **France** 30-19

FRANCE v BRITISH XVs
Played 5   France won 2, British XVs won 3, Drawn 0
Highest scores France 27-29 in 1989, British XV 36-3 in 1940
Biggest wins France 21-9 in 1945, British XV 36-3 in 1940

1940 Paris **British XV** 36-3	1946 Paris **France** 10-0
1945 Paris **France** 21-9	1989 Paris **British XV** 29-27
1945 Richmond **British XV** 27-6	

FRANCE v NEW ZEALAND ARMY
Played 1   New Zealand Army won 1
Highest scores France 9-14 in 1946, New Zealand Army 14-9 in 1946
Biggest win France no win, New Zealand Army 14-9 in 1946

1946 Paris **New Zealand Army** 14-9

FRANCE v ARGENTINA
Played 30   France won 25, Argentina won 4, Drawn 1
Highest scores France 47-12 in 1995, Argentina 27-31 in 1974 & 27-34 in 1996
& 27-32 in 1997
Biggest wins France 47-12 in 1995, Argentina 18-6 in 1988

1949 *1* Buenos Aires **France** 5-0	*2* Buenos Aires **Drawn** 18-18
2 Buenos Aires **France** 12-3	*France won series 1-0, with 1 draw*
France won series 2-0	1982 *1* Toulouse **France** 25-12
1954 *1* Buenos Aires **France** 22-8	*2* Paris **France** 13-6
2 Buenos Aires **France** 30-3	*France won series 2-0*
France won series 2-0	1985 *1* Buenos Aires **Argentina** 24-16
1960 *1* Buenos Aires **France** 37-3	*2* Buenos Aires **France** 23-15
2 Buenos Aires **France** 12-3	*Series drawn 1-1*
3 Buenos Aires **France** 29-6	1986 *1* Buenos Aires **Argentina** 15-13
France won series 3-0	*2* Buenos Aires **France** 22-9
1974 *1* Buenos Aires **France** 20-15	*Series drawn 1-1*
2 Buenos Aires **France** 31-27	1988 *1* Buenos Aires **France** 18-15
France won series 2-0	*2* Buenos Aires **Argentina** 18-6
1975 *1* Lyons **France** 29-6	*Series drawn 1-1*
2 Paris **France** 36-21	1988 *1* Nantes **France** 29-9
France won series 2-0	*2* Lille **France** 28-18
1977 *1* Buenos Aires **France** 26-3	*France won series 2-0*

1992 *1* Buenos Aires **France** 27-12
    2 Buenos Aires **France** 33-9
    France won series 2-0
1992 Nantes **Argentina** 24-20
1995 Buenos Aires *LC* **France** 47-12

1996 *1* Buenos Aires **France** 34-27
    2 Buenos Aires **France** 34-15
    France won series 2-0
1997 Tarbes *LC* **France** 32-27

FRANCE v CZECHOSLOVAKIA
Played 2   France won 2
Highest scores France 28-3 in 1956, Czechoslovakia 6-19 in 1968
Biggest win France 28-3 in 1956, Czechoslovakia no win

1956 Toulouse **France** 28-3

1968 Prague **France** 19-6

FRANCE v FIJI
Played 3   France won 3
Highest scores France 33-9 in 1991, Fiji 16-31 in 1987
Biggest win France 33-9 in 1991, Fiji no win

1964 Paris **France** 21-3
1987 Auckland *WC* **France** 31-16

1991 Grenoble *WC* **France** 33-9

FRANCE v JAPAN
Played 1   France won 1
Highest scores France 30-18 in 1973, Japan 18-30 in 1973
Biggest win France 30-18 in 1973, Japan no win

1973 Bordeaux **France** 30-18

FRANCE v ZIMBABWE
Played 1   France won 1
Highest scores France 70-12 in 1987, Zimbabwe 12-70 in 1987
Biggest win France 70-12 in 1987, Zimbabwe no win

1987 Auckland *WC* **France** 70-12

FRANCE v CANADA
Played 3   France won 2, Canada won 1, Drawn 0
Highest scores France 28-9 in 1994, Canada 18-16 in 1994
Biggest wins France 28-9 in 1994, Canada 18-16 in 1994

1991 Agen *WC* **France** 19-13
1994 Nepean **Canada** 18-16

1994 Besançon **France** 28-9

FRANCE v TONGA
Played 1   France won 1
Highest scores France 38-10 in 1995, Tonga 10-38 in 1995
Biggest win France 38-10 in 1995, Tonga no win

1995 Pretoria *WC* **France** 38-10

394

FRANCE v IVORY COAST

Played 1   France won 1
Highest scores France 54-18 in 1995, Ivory Coast 18-54 in 1995
Biggest win France 54-18 in 1995, Ivory Coast no win

1995 Rustenburg *WC* **France** 54-18

NEW ZEALAND v SOUTH AFRICA

Played 49   New Zealand won 24, South Africa won 22, Drawn 3
Highest scores New Zealand 55-35 in 1997, South Africa 35-55 in 1997
Biggest wins New Zealand 55-35 in 1997, South Africa 17-0 in 1928

1921 *1* Dunedin **New Zealand** 13-5
    2 Auckland **South Africa** 9-5
    3 Wellington **Drawn** 0-0
    Series drawn 1-1, with 1 draw
1928 *1* Durban **South Africa** 17-0
    2 Johannesburg **New Zealand** 7-6
    3 Port Elizabeth **South Africa** 11-6
    4 Cape Town **New Zealand** 13-5
    Series drawn 2-2
1937 *1* Wellington **New Zealand** 13-7
    2 Christchurch **South Africa** 13-6
    3 Auckland **South Africa** 17-6
    South Africa won series 2-1
1949 *1* Cape Town **South Africa** 15-11
    2 Johannesburg **South Africa** 12-6
    3 Durban **South Africa** 9-3
    4 Port Elizabeth **South Africa** 11-8
    South Africa won series 4-0
1956 *1* Dunedin **New Zealand** 10-6
    2 Wellington **South Africa** 8-3
    3 Christchurch **New Zealand** 17-10
    4 Auckland **New Zealand** 11-5
    New Zealand won series 3-1
1960 *1* Johannesburg **South Africa** 13-0
    2 Cape Town **New Zealand** 11-3
    3 Bloemfontein **Drawn** 11-11
    4 Port Elizabeth **South Africa** 8-3
    South Africa won series 2-1, with 1 draw
1965 *1* Wellington **New Zealand** 6-3
    2 Dunedin **New Zealand** 13-0
    3 Christchurch **South Africa** 19-16

    4 Auckland **New Zealand** 20-3
    New Zealand won series 3-1
1970 *1* Pretoria **South Africa** 17-6
    2 Cape Town **New Zealand** 9-8
    3 Port Elizabeth **South Africa** 14-3
    4 Johannesburg **South Africa** 20-17
    South Africa won series 3-1
1976 *1* Durban **South Africa** 16-7
    2 Bloemfontein **New Zealand** 15-9
    3 Cape Town **South Africa** 15-10
    4 Johannesburg **South Africa** 15-14
    South Africa won series 3-1
1981 *1* Christchurch **New Zealand** 14-9
    2 Wellington **South Africa** 24-12
    3 Auckland **New Zealand** 25-22
    New Zealand won series 2-1
1992 Johannesburg **New Zealand** 27-24
1994 *1* Dunedin **New Zealand** 22-14
    2 Wellington **New Zealand** 13-9
    3 Auckland **Drawn** 18-18
    New Zealand won series 2-0, with 1 draw
1995 Johannesburg *WC* **South Africa** 15-12
    (*aet*)
1996 Christchurch *TN* **New Zealand** 15-11
1996 Cape Town *TN* **New Zealand** 29-18
1996 *1* Durban **New Zealand** 23-19
    2 Pretoria **New Zealand** 33-26
    3 Johannesburg **South Africa** 32-22
    New Zealand won series 2-1
1997 Johannesbury *TN* **New Zealand** 35-32
1997 Auckland *TN* **New Zealand** 55-35

NEW ZEALAND v AUSTRALIA

Played 105   New Zealand won 73, Australia won 27, Drawn 5
Highest scores New Zealand 43-6 in 1996, Australia 30-16 in 1978
Biggest wins New Zealand 43-6 in 1996, Australia 26-10 in 1980

1903 Sydney **New Zealand** 22-3
1905 Dunedin **New Zealand** 14-3
1907 *1* Sydney **New Zealand** 26-6
    2 Brisbane **New Zealand** 14-5
    3 Sydney **Drawn** 5-5
    New Zealand won series 2-0, with 1 draw
1910 *1* Sydney **New Zealand** 6-0

    2 Sydney **Australia** 11-0
    3 Sydney **New Zealand** 28-13
    New Zealand won series 2-1
1913 *1* Wellington **New Zealand** 30-5
    2 Dunedin **New Zealand** 25-13
    3 Christchurch **Australia** 16-5
    New Zealand won series 2-1

1914 *1* Sydney **New Zealand** 5-0
   2 Brisbane **New Zealand** 17-0
   3 Sydney **New Zealand** 22-7
   New Zealand won series 3-0
1929 *1* Sydney **Australia** 9-8
   2 Brisbane **Australia** 17-9
   3 Sydney **Australia** 15-13
   Australia won series 3-0
1931 Auckland **New Zealand** 20-13
1932 *1* Sydney **Australia** 22-17
   2 Brisbane **New Zealand** 21-3
   3 Sydney **New Zealand** 21-13
   New Zealand won series 2-1
1934 *1* Sydney **Australia** 25-11
   2 Sydney **Drawn** 3-3
   Australia won series 1-0, with 1 draw
1936 *1* Wellington **New Zealand** 11-6
   2 Dunedin **New Zealand** 38-13
   New Zealand won series 2-0
1938 *1* Sydney **New Zealand** 24-9
   2 Brisbane **New Zealand** 20-14
   3 Sydney **New Zealand** 14-6
   New Zealand won series 3-0
1946 *1* Dunedin **New Zealand** 31-8
   2 Auckland **New Zealand** 14-10
   New Zealand won series 2-0
1947 *1* Brisbane **New Zealand** 13-5
   2 Sydney **New Zealand** 27-14
   New Zealand won series 2-0
1949 *1* Wellington **Australia** 11-6
   2 Auckland **Australia** 16-9
   Australia won series 2-0
1951 *1* Sydney **New Zealand** 8-0
   2 Sydney **New Zealand** 17-11
   3 Brisbane **New Zealand** 16-6
   New Zealand won series 3-0
1952 *1* Christchurch **Australia** 14-9
   2 Wellington **New Zealand** 15-8
   Series drawn 1-1
1955 *1* Wellington **New Zealand** 16-8
   2 Dunedin **New Zealand** 8-0
   3 Auckland **Australia** 8-3
   New Zealand won series 2-1
1957 *1* Sydney **New Zealand** 25-11
   2 Brisbane **New Zealand** 22-9
   New Zealand won series 2-0
1958 *1* Wellington **New Zealand** 25-3
   2 Christchurch **Australia** 6-3
   3 Auckland **New Zealand** 17-8
   New Zealand won series 2-1
1962 *1* Brisbane **New Zealand** 20-6
   2 Sydney **New Zealand** 14-5
   New Zealand won series 2-0
1962 *1* Wellington **Drawn** 9-9
   2 Dunedin **New Zealand** 3-0
   3 Auckland **New Zealand** 16-8
   New Zealand won series 2-0, with1 draw
1964 *1* Dunedin **New Zealand** 14-9
   2 Christchurch **New Zealand** 18-3
   3 Wellington **Australia** 20-5
   New Zealand won series 2-1
1967 Wellington **New Zealand** 29-9

1968 *1* Sydney **New Zealand** 27-11
   2 Brisbane **New Zealand** 19-18
   New Zealand won series 2-0
1972 *1* Wellington **New Zealand** 29-6
   2 Christchurch **New Zealand** 30-17
   3 Auckland **New Zealand** 38-3
   New Zealand won series 3-0
1974 *1* Sydney **New Zealand** 11-6
   2 Brisbane **Drawn** 16-16
   3 Sydney **New Zealand** 16-6
   New Zealand won series 2-0, with 1 draw
1978 *1* Wellington **New Zealand** 13-12
   2 Christchurch **New Zealand** 22-6
   3 Auckland **Australia** 30-16
   New Zealand won series 2-1
1979 Sydney **Australia** 12-6
1980 *1* Sydney **Australia** 13-9
   2 Brisbane **New Zealand** 12-9
   3 Sydney **Australia** 26-10
   Australia won series 2-1
1982 *1* Christchurch **New Zealand** 23-16
   2 Wellington **Australia** 19-16
   3 Auckland **New Zealand** 33-18
   New Zealand won series 2-1
1983 Sydney **New Zealand** 18-8
1984 *1* Sydney **Australia** 16-9
   2 Brisbane **New Zealand** 19-15
   3 Sydney **New Zealand** 25-24
   New Zealand won series 2-1
1985 Auckland **New Zealand** 10-9
1986 *1* Wellington **Australia** 13-12
   2 Dunedin **New Zealand** 13-12
   3 Auckland **Australia** 22-9
   Australia won series 2-1
1987 Sydney **New Zealand** 30-16
1988 *1* Sydney **New Zealand** 32-7
   2 Brisbane **Drawn** 19-19
   3 Sydney **New Zealand** 30-9
   New Zealand won series 2-0, with 1 draw
1989 Auckland **New Zealand** 24-12
1990 *1* Christchurch **New Zealand** 21-6
   2 Auckland **New Zealand** 27-17
   3 Wellington **Australia** 21-9
   New Zealand won series 2-1
1991 *1* Sydney **Australia** 21-12
   2 Auckland **New Zealand** 6-3
1991 Dublin *WC* **Australia** 16-6
1992 *1* Sydney **Australia** 16-15
   2 Brisbane **Australia** 19-17
   3 Sydney **New Zealand** 26-23
   Australia won series 2-1
1993 Dunedin **New Zealand** 25-10
1994 Sydney **Australia** 20-16
1995 Auckland **New Zealand** 28-16
1995 Sydney **New Zealand** 34-23
1996 Wellington *TN* **New Zealand** 43-6
1996 Brisbane *TN* **New Zealand** 32-25
   New Zealand won series 2-0
1997 Christchurch **New Zealand** 30-13
1997 Melbourne *TN* **New Zealand** 33-18
1997 Dunedin *TN* **New Zealand** 36-24
   New Zealand won series 3-0

NEW ZEALAND v UNITED STATES

Played 2   New Zealand won 2
Highest scores New Zealand 51-3 in 1913, United States 6-46 in 1991
Biggest win New Zealand 51-3 in 1913, United States no win

1913 Berkeley **New Zealand** 51-3   1991 Gloucester *WC* **New Zealand** 46-6

NEW ZEALAND v ROMANIA

Played 1   New Zealand won 1
Highest score New Zealand 14-6 in 1981, Romania 6-14 in 1981
Biggest win New Zealand 14-6 in 1981, Romania no win

1981 Bucharest **New Zealand** 14-6

NEW ZEALAND v ARGENTINA

Played 9   New Zealand won 8, Drawn 1
Highest scores New Zealand 93-8 in 1997, Argentina 21-21 in 1985
Biggest win New Zealand 93-8 in 1997, Argentina no win

1985 *1* Buenos Aires **New Zealand** 33-20
 2 Buenos Aires **Drawn** 21-21
 New Zealand won series 1-0, with 1 draw
1987 Wellington *WC* **New Zealand** 46-15
1989 *1* Dunedin **New Zealand** 60-9
 2 Wellington **New Zealand** 49-12
 New Zealand won series 2-0

1991 *1* Buenos Aires **New Zealand** 28-14
 2 Buenos Aires **New Zealand** 36-6
 New Zealand won series 2-0
1997 *1* Wellington **New Zealand** 93-8
 2 Hamilton **New Zealand** 62-10
 New Zealand won series 2-0

NEW ZEALAND v ITALY

Played 3   New Zealand won 3
Highest scores New Zealand 70-6 in 1987 & 70-6 in 1995, Italy 21-31 in 1991
Biggest win New Zealand 70-6 in 1987 & 70-6 in 1995, Italy no win

1987 Auckland *WC* **New Zealand** 70-6   1995 Bologna **New Zealand** 70-6
1991 Leicester *WC* **New Zealand** 31-21

NEW ZEALAND v FIJI

Played 2   New Zealand won 2
Highest scores New Zealand 74-13 in 1987, Fiji 13-74 in 1987
Biggest win New Zealand 71-5 in 1997, Fiji no win

1987 Christchurch *WC* **New Zealand** 74-13   1997 Albany **New Zealand** 71-5

NEW ZEALAND v CANADA

Played 2   New Zealand won 2
Highest scores New Zealand 73-7 in 1995, Canada 13-29 in 1991
Biggest win New Zealand 73-7 in 1995, Canada no win

1991 Lille *WC* **New Zealand** 29-13   1995 Auckland **New Zealand** 73-7

NEW ZEALAND v WORLD XVs
Played 3 New Zealand won 2, World XV won 1, Drawn 0
Highest scores New Zealand 54-26 in 1992, World XV 28-14 in 1992
Biggest wins New Zealand 54-26 in 1992, World XV 28-14 in 1992

1992 *1* Christchurch **World XV** 28-14   *3* Auckland **New Zealand** 26-15
       2 Wellington **New Zealand** 54-26   *New Zealand won series 2-1*

NEW ZEALAND v WESTERN SAMOA
Played 2 New Zealand won 2
Highest scores New Zealand 51-10 in 1996, Western Samoa 13-35 in 1993
Biggest win New Zealand 51-10 in 1996, Western Samoa no win

1993 Auckland **New Zealand** 35-13   1996 Napier **New Zealand** 51-10

NEW ZEALAND v JAPAN
Played 1 New Zealand won 1
Highest scores New Zealand 145-17 in 1995, Japan 17-145 in 1995
Biggest win New Zealand 145-17 in 1995, Japan no win

1995 Bloemfontein *WC* **New Zealand** 145-17

SOUTH AFRICA v AUSTRALIA
Played 37 South Africa won 25, Australia won 12, Drawn 0
Highest scores South Africa 61-22 in 1997, Australia 32-20 in 1997
Biggest wins South Africa 61-22 in 1997, Australia 26-3 in 1992

1933 *1* Cape Town **South Africa** 17-3
     2 Durban **Australia** 21-6
     3 Johannesburg **South Africa** 12-3
     4 Port Elizabeth **South Africa** 11-0
     5 Bloemfontein **Australia** 15-4
     South Africa won series 3-2
1937 *1* Sydney **South Africa** 9-5
     2 Sydney **South Africa** 26-17
     South Africa won series 2-0
1953 *1* Johannesburg **South Africa** 25-3
     2 Cape Town **Australia** 18-14
     3 Durban **South Africa** 18-8
     4 Port Elizabeth **South Africa** 22-9
     South Africa won series 3-1
1956 *1* Sydney **South Africa** 9-0
     2 Brisbane **South Africa** 9-0
     South Africa won series 2-0
1961 *1* Johannesburg **South Africa** 28-3
     2 Port Elizabeth **South Africa** 23-11
     South Africa won series 2-0
1963 *1* Pretoria **South Africa** 14-3
     2 Cape Town **Australia** 9-5
     3 Johannesburg **Australia** 11-9

     4 Port Elizabeth **South Africa** 22-6
     Series drawn 2-2
1965 *1* Sydney **Australia** 18-11
     2 Brisbane **Australia** 12-8
     Australia won series 2-0
1969 *1* Johannesburg **South Africa** 30-11
     2 Durban **South Africa** 16-9
     3 Cape Town **South Africa** 11-3
     4 Bloemfontein **South Africa** 19-8
     South Africa won series 4-0
1971 *1* Sydney **South Africa** 19-11
     2 Brisbane **South Africa** 14-6
     3 Sydney **South Africa** 18-6
     South Africa won series 3-0
1992 Cape Town **Australia** 26-3
1993 *1* Sydney **South Africa** 19-12
     2 Brisbane **Australia** 28-20
     3 Sydney **Australia** 19-12
     Australia won series 2-1
1995 Cape Town *WC* **South Africa** 27-18
1996 Sydney *TN* **Australia** 21-16
1996 Bloemfontein *TN* **South Africa** 25-19
1997 Brisbane *TN* **Australia** 32-20
1997 Pretoria *TN* **South Africa** 61-22

SOUTH AFRICA v WORLD XVs
Played 3   South Africa won 3
Highest scores South Africa 45-24 in 1977, World XV 24-45 in 1977
Biggest win South Africa 45-24 in 1977, World XV no win

1977 Pretoria **South Africa** 45-24	*2* Johannesburg **South Africa** 22-16
1989 *1* Cape Town **South Africa** 20-19	*South Africa won series 2-0*

SOUTH AFRICA v SOUTH AMERICA
Played 8   South Africa won 7, South America won 1, Drawn 0
Highest scores South Africa 50-18 in 1982, South America 21-12 in 1982
Biggest wins South Africa 50-18 in 1982, South America 21-12 in 1982

1980 *1* Johannesburg **South Africa** 24-9	1982 *1* Pretoria **South Africa** 50-18
2 Durban **South Africa** 18-9	*2* Bloemfontein **South America** 21-12
South Africa won series 2-0	*Series drawn 1-1*
1980 *1* Montevideo **South Africa** 22-13	1984 *1* Pretoria **South Africa** 32-15
2 Santiago **South Africa** 30-16	*2* Cape Town **South Africa** 22-13
South Africa won series 2-0	*South Africa won series 2-0*

SOUTH AFRICA v UNITED STATES
Played 1   South Africa won 1
Highest scores South Africa 38-7 in 1981, United States 7-38 in 1981
Biggest win South Africa 38-7 in 1981, United States no win

1981 Glenville **South Africa** 38-7

SOUTH AFRICA v NEW ZEALAND CAVALIERS
Played 4   South Africa won 3, New Zealand Cavaliers won 1, Drawn 0
Highest scores South Africa 33-18 in 1986, New Zealand Cavaliers 19-18 in 1986
Biggest wins South Africa 33-18 in 1986, New Zealand Cavaliers 19-18 in 1986

1986 *1* Cape Town **South Africa** 21-15	*4* Johannesburg **South Africa** 24-10
2 Durban **New Zealand Cavaliers** 19-18	*South Africa won series 3-1*
3 Pretoria **South Africa** 33-18	

SOUTH AFRICA v ARGENTINA
Played 6   South Africa won 6
Highest scores South Africa 52-23 in 1993, Argentina 26-29 in 1993 & 26-46 in 1994
Biggest wins South Africa 46-15 in 1996, Argentina no win

1993 *1* Buenos Aires **South Africa** 29-26	*2* Johannesburg **South Africa** 46-26
2 Buenos Aires **South Africa** 52-23	*South Africa won series 2-0*
South Africa won series 2-0	1996 *1* Buenos Aires **South Africa** 46-15
1994 *1* Port Elizabeth **South Africa** 42-22	*2* Buenos Aires **South Africa** 44-21
	South Africa win series 2-0

SOUTH AFRICA v WESTERN SAMOA
Played 2   South Africa won 2
Highest scores South Africa 60-8 in 1995, Western Samoa 14-42 in 1995
Biggest win South Africa 60-8 in 1995, Western Samoa no win

1995 Johannesburg **South Africa** 60-8	1995 Johannesburg *WC* **South Africa** 42-14

SOUTH AFRICA v ROMANIA
Played 1   South Africa won 1
Highest score South Africa 21-8 in 1995, Romania 8-21 in 1995
Biggest win South Africa 21-8 in 1995, Romania no win

1995 Cape Town *WC* **South Africa** 21-8

SOUTH AFRICA v CANADA
Played 1   South Africa won 1
Highest scores South Africa 20-0 in 1995, Canada 0-20 in 1995
Biggest win South Africa 20-0 in 1995, Canada no win

1995 Port Elizabeth *WC* **South Africa** 20-0

SOUTH AFRICA v ITALY
Played 2   South Africa won 2
Highest scores South Africa 62-31 in 1997, Italy 31-62 in 1997
Biggest win South Africa 62-31 in 1997, Italy no win

1995 Rome **South Africa** 40-21   1997 Bologna **South Africa** 62-31

SOUTH AFRICA v FIJI
Played 1   South Africa won 1
Highest scores South Africa 43-18 in 1996, Fiji 18-43 in 1996
Biggest win South Africa 43-18 in 1996, Fiji no win

1996 Pretoria **South Africa** 43-18

SOUTH AFRICA v TONGA
Played 1   South Africa won 1
Higest scores South Africa 74-10 in 1997, Tonga 10-74 in 1997
Biggest win South Africa 74-10 in 1997, Tonga no win

1997 Cape Town **South Africa** 74-10

AUSTRALIA v UNITED STATES
Played 5   Australia won 5
Highest scores Australia 67-9 in 1990, United States 12-24 in 1976 & 12-47 in 1987
Biggest win Australia 67-9 in 1990, United States no win

1912 Berkeley **Australia** 12-8   1987 Brisbane *WC* **Australia** 47-12
1976 Los Angeles **Australia** 24-12   1990 Brisbane **Australia** 67-9
1983 Sydney **Australia** 49-3

AUSTRALIA v NEW ZEALAND MAORIS
Played 10   Australia won 4, New Zealand Maoris won 4, Drawn 2
Highest scores Australia 31-6 in 1936, New Zealand Maoris 20-0 in 1946
Biggest wins Australia 31-6 in 1936, New Zealand Maoris 20-0 in 1946

1928 Wellington **New Zealand Maoris** 9-8   1949 *1* Sydney **New Zealand Maoris** 12-3
1931 Palmerston North **Australia** 14-3   *2* Brisbane **Drawn** 8-8
1936 Palmerston North **Australia** 31-6   *3* Sydney **Australia** 18-3
1946 Hamilton **New Zealand Maoris** 20-0   *Series drawn 1-1, with 1 draw*

1958 *1* Brisbane **Australia** 15-14
    2 Sydney **Drawn** 3-3

3 Melbourne **New Zealand Maoris** 13-6
Series drawn 1-1, with 1 draw

AUSTRALIA v FIJI
Played 15   Australia won 12, Fiji won 2, Drawn 1
Highest scores Australia 52-28 in 1985, Fiji 28-52 in 1985
Biggest wins Australia 52-28 in 1985, Fiji 17-15 in 1952 & 18-16 in 1954

1952 *1* Sydney **Australia** 15-9
    2 Sydney **Fiji** 17-15
    Series drawn 1-1
1954 *1* Brisbane **Australia** 22-19
    2 Sydney **Fiji** 18-16
    Series drawn 1-1
1961 *1* Brisbane **Australia** 24-6
    2 Sydney **Australia** 20-14
    3 Melbourne **Drawn** 3-3
    Australia won series 2-0, with 1 draw

1972 Suva **Australia** 21-19
1976 *1* Sydney **Australia** 22-6
    2 Brisbane **Australia** 21-9
    3 Sydney **Australia** 27-17
    Australia won series 3-0
1980 Suva **Australia** 22-9
1984 Suva **Australia** 16-3
1985 *1* Brisbane **Australia** 52-28
    2 Sydney **Australia** 31-9
    Australia won series 2-0

AUSTRALIA v TONGA
Played 3   Australia won 2, Tonga won 1, Drawn 0
Highest scores Australia 52-14 in 1993, Tonga 16-11 in 1973
Biggest wins Australia 52-14 in 1993, Tonga 16-11 in 1973

1973 *1* Sydney **Australia** 30-12
    2 Brisbane **Tonga** 16-11
    Series drawn 1-1

1993 Brisbane **Australia** 52-14

AUSTRALIA v JAPAN
Played 3   Australia won 3
Highest scores Australia 50-25 in 1975, Japan 25-50 in 1973
Biggest win Australia 50-25 in 1975, Japan no win

1975 *1* Sydney **Australia** 37-7
    2 Brisbane **Australia** 50-25
    Australia won series 2-0

1987 Sydney *WC* **Australia** 42-23

AUSTRALIA v ARGENTINA
Played 13   Australia won 8, Argentina won 4, Drawn 1
Highest scores Australia 53-7 in 1995, Argentina 27-19 in 1987
Biggest wins Australia 53-7 in 1995, Argentina 18-3 in 1983

1979 *1* Buenos Aires **Argentina** 24-13
    2 Buenos Aires **Australia** 17-12
    Series drawn 1-1
1983 *1* Brisbane **Argentina** 18-3
    2 Sydney **Australia** 29-13
    Series drawn 1-1
1986 *1* Brisbane **Australia** 39-19
    2 Sydney **Australia** 26-0
    Australia won series 2-0
1987 *1* Buenos Aires **Drawn** 19-19

    2 Buenos Aires **Argentina** 27-19
    Argentina won series 1-0, with 1 draw
1991 Llanelli *WC* **Australia** 32-19
1995 *1* Brisbane **Australia** 53-7
    2 Sydney **Australia** 30-13
    Australia won series 2-0
1997 *1* Buenos Aires **Australia** 23-15
    2 Buenos Aires **Argentina** 18-16
    Series drawn 1-1

AUSTRALIA v WESTERN SAMOA
Played 2   Australia won 2
Highest scores Australia 73-3 in 1994, Western Samoa 3-9 in 1991 & 3-73 in 1994
Biggest win Australia 73-3 in 1994, Western Samoa no win

1991 Pontypool *WC* **Australia** 9-3   1994 Sydney **Australia** 73-3

AUSTRALIA v ITALY
Played 6   Australia won 6
Highest scores Australia 55-6 in 1988, Italy 20-23 in 1994
Biggest win Australia 55-6 in 1988, Italy no win

1983 Rovigo **Australia** 29-7
1986 Brisbane **Australia** 39-18
1988 Rome **Australia** 55-6
1994 *1* Brisbane **Australia** 23-20

2 Melbourne **Australia** 20-7
Australia won series 2-0
1996 Padua **Australia** 40-18

AUSTRALIA v CANADA
Played 5   Australia won 5
Highest scores Australia 74-9 in 1996, Canada 16-43 in 1993
Biggest win Australia 74-9 in 1996, Canada no win

1985 *1* Sydney **Australia** 59-3
    2 Brisbane **Australia** 43-15
    Australia won series 2-0

1993 Calgary **Australia** 43-16
1995 Port Elizabeth *WC* **Australia** 27-11
1996 Brisbane **Australia** 74-9

AUSTRALIA v KOREA
Played 1   Australia won 1
Highest scores Australia 65-18 in 1987, Korea 18-65 in 1987
Biggest win Australia 65-18 in 1987, Korea no win

1987 Brisbane **Australia** 65-18

AUSTRALIA v ROMANIA
Played 1   Australia won 1
highest scores Australia 42-3 in 1995, Romania 3-42 in 1995
Biggest win Australia 42-3 in 1995, Romania no win

1995 Stellenbosch *WC* **Australia** 42-3

INTERNATIONAL HONOURS

WORLD CUP WINNERS
New Zealand once: 1987
Australia once: 1991
South Africa once: 1995

GRAND SLAM WINNERS
England 11 times: 1913, 1914, 1921, 1923, 1924, 1928, 1957, 1980, 1991, 1992, 1995.
Wales 8 times: 1908, 1909, 1911, 1950, 1952, 1971, 1976, 1978. **France** 6 times: 1968, 1977, 1981, 1987, 1997, 1998. **Scotland** 3 times; 1925, 1984, 1990. **Ireland** once: 1948.

TRIPLE CROWN WINNERS
England 21 times: 1883, 1884, 1892, 1913, 1914, 1921, 1923, 1924, 1928, 1934, 1937, 1954, 1957, 1960, 1980, 1991, 1992, 1995, 1996, 1997, 1998. **Wales** 17 times: 1893, 1900, 1902, 1905, 1908, 1909, 1911, 1950, 1952, 1965, 1969, 1971, 1976, 1977, 1978, 1979, 1988.
Scotland 10 times: 1891, 1895, 1901, 1903, 1907, 1925, 1933, 1938, 1984, 1990.
Ireland 6 times: 1894, 1899, 1948, 1949, 1982, 1985.

INTERNATIONAL CHAMPIONSHIP WINNERS

Year	Winner	Year	Winner	Year	Winner	Year	Winner
1883	England	1912	England / Ireland	1947	Wales / England	1972*	—
1884	England	1913	England	1948	Ireland	1973	Quintuple tie
1885*	—	1914	England	1949	Ireland	1974	Ireland
1886	England / Scotland	1920	England / Scotland / Wales	1950	Wales	1975	Wales
1887	Scotland	1921	England	1951	Ireland	1976	Wales
1888*	—	1922	Wales	1952	Wales	1977	France
1889*	—	1923	England	1953	England	1978	Wales
1890	England / Scotland	1924	England	1954	England / France / Wales	1979	Wales
1891	Scotland	1925	Scotland	1955	France / Wales	1980	England
1892	England	1926	Scotland / Ireland	1956	Wales	1981	France
1893	Wales	1927	Scotland / Ireland	1957	England	1982	Ireland
1894	Ireland	1928	England	1958	England	1983	France / Ireland
1895	Scotland	1929	Scotland	1959	France	1984	Scotland
1896	Ireland	1930	England	1960	France / England	1985	Ireland
1897*	—	1931	Wales	1961	France	1986	France / Scotland
1898*	—	1932	England / Wales / Ireland	1962	France	1987	France
1899	Ireland	1933	Scotland	1963	England	1988	Wales / France
1900	Wales	1934	England	1964	Scotland / Wales	1989	France
1901	Scotland	1935	Ireland	1965	Wales	1990	Scotland
1902	Wales	1936	Wales	1966	Wales	1991	England
1903	Scotland	1937	England	1967	France	1992	England
1904	Scotland	1938	Scotland	1968	France	1993	France
1905	Wales	1939	England / Wales / Ireland	1969	Wales	1994**	Wales
1906	Ireland / Wales			1970	France / Wales	1995	England
1907	Scotland			1971	Wales	1996**	England
1908	Wales					1997	France
1909	Wales					1998	France
1910	England						
1911	Wales						

*Matches not completed, for various reasons
** Indicates winners of the Five Nations Trophy (introduced 1993) on points difference

Wales and England have won the title outright 22 times each; Scotland 13 times; France 12 and Ireland 10.

LATIN CUP WINNERS
France twice: 1995, 1997

TRI-NATIONS WINNERS
New Zealand twice: 1996, 1997

INTERNATIONAL REFEREES 1997-98

Leading Referees

Up to 30 April 1998, in major international matches. These include all matches for which senior members of the International Board have awarded caps, and also all matches played in the World Cup final stages.

15 or more internationals

W D Bevan	Wales	35	A E Freethy	Wales	18
J M Fleming	Scotland	29	R C Quittenton	England	18
C Norling	Wales	25	J R West	Ireland	18
D J Bishop	New Zealand	24	J B Anderson	Scotland	18
K D Kelleher	Ireland	23	R Hourquet	France	18
D G Walters	Wales	23	D P D'Arcy	Ireland	17
M Joseph	Wales	22	F Palmade	France	17
R C Williams	Ireland	21	S R Hilditch	Ireland	17
K V J Fitzgerald	Australia	21	B S Cumberlege	England	16
E F Morrison	England	21	O E Doyle	Ireland	16
F A Howard	England	20	D I H Burnett	Ireland	15
A M Hosie	Scotland	19	C H Gadney	England	15
Capt M J Dowling	Ireland	18			

Major International Match Appearances 1997-98

Matches controlled between 1 May 1997 and 30 April 1998

1997

Arg v E	I Rogers (South Africa)	Arg v A	D T M McHugh (Ireland)
R v F	* C Giacomel (Italy)	E v A	A Watson (South Africa)
Arg v E	* J Kaplan (South Africa)	F v SA	W D Bevan (Wales)
SA v Tg	* M Wildes (Zimbabwe)	I v NZ	A J Spreadbury (England)
NZ v Fj	W J Erickson (Australia)	W v Tg	S Borsani (Argentina)
NZ v Arg (2)	B Campsall (England)	E v NZ	P L Marshall (Australia)
A v F (2)	C Thomas (Wales)	F v SA	P D O'Brien (New Zealand)
SA v BI	C J Hawke (New Zealand)	S v A	W T S Henning (South Africa)
SA v BI	D Mené (France)	E v SA	C J Hawke (New Zealand)
NZ v A	E F Morrison (England)	W v NZ	W J Erickson (Australia)
SA v BI	W J Erickson (Australia)	I v C	C Giacomel (Italy)
US v W	K W McCartney (Scotland)	E v NZ	J M Fleming (Scotland)
A v E	P D O'Brien (New Zealand)	S v SA	P Thomas (France)
US v W	* C B Muir (Scotland)	It v I	D Mené (France)
SA v NZ	P L Marshall (Australia)	**1998**	
C v W	S Borsani (Argentina)	It v S	*D Davies (Wales)
A v NZ	E F Morrison (England)	F v E	D T M McHugh (Ireland)
A v SA	C J Hawke (New Zealand)	I v S	A Watson (South Africa)
NZ v SA	W D Bevan (Wales)	W v It	S Lander (England)
NZ v A	J Dumé (France)	E v W	C J Hawke (New Zealand)
SA v A	P D O'Brien (New Zealand)	S v F	P D O'Brien (New Zealand)
W v R	D I Ramage (Scotland)	F v I	J M Fleming (Scotland)
F v It	S Borsani (Argentina)	W v S	J Dumé (France)
F v R	S Borsani (Argentina)	I v W	E F Morrison (England)
F v Arg	C Giacomel (Italy)	S v E	C Thomas (Wales)
Arg v A	H A Smith (Ireland)	E v I	W D Bevan (Wales)
It v SA	P Deluca (Argentina)	W v F	P L Marshall (Australia)

* Denotes debut in a major international

Dismissals in Major International Matches (*up to 30 April 1998*)

A E Freethy	sent off	C J Brownlie (NZ)	E v NZ	1925
K D Kelleher	sent off	C E Meads (NZ)	S v NZ	1967
R T Burnett	sent off	M A Burton (E)	A v E	1975
W M Cooney	sent off	J Sovau (Fj)	A v Fj	1976
N R Sanson	sent off	G A D Wheel (W)	W v I	1977
N R Sanson	sent off	W P Duggan (I)	W v I	1977
D I H Burnett	sent off	P Ringer (W)	E v W	1980
C Norling	sent off	J-P Garuet (F)	F v I	1984
K V J Fitzgerald	sent off	H D Richards (W)	NZ v W	*1987
F A Howard	sent off	D Codey (A)	A v W	*1987
K V J Fitzgerald	sent off	M Taga (Fj)	Fj v E	1988
O E Doyle	sent off	A Lorieux (F)	Arg v F	1988
B W Stirling	sent off	T Vonolagi (Fj)	E v Fj	1989
B W Stirling	sent off	N Nadruku (Fj)	E v Fj	1989
F A Howard	sent off	K Moseley (W)	W v F	1990
F A Howard	sent off	A Carminati (F)	S v F	1990
F A Howard	sent off	A Stoop (Nm)	Nm v W	1990
A J Spreadbury	sent off	A Benazzi (F)	A v F	1990
C Norling	sent off	P Gallart (F)	A v F	1990
C J Hawke	sent off	F E Mendez (Arg)	E v Arg	1990
E F Morrison	sent off	C Cojocariu (R)	R v F	1991
J M Fleming	sent off	P L Sporleder (Arg)	WS v Arg	*1991
J M Fleming	sent off	M G Keenan (WS)	WS v Arg	*1991
S R Hilditch	sent off	G Lascubé (F)	F v E	1992
S R Hilditch	sent off	V Moscato (F)	F v E	1992
D J Bishop	sent off	O Roumat (Wld)	NZ v Wld	1992
E F Morrison	sent off	J T Small (SA)	A v SA	1993
I Rogers	sent off	M E Cardinal (C)	C v F	1994
I Rogers	sent off	P Sella (F)	C v F	1994
D Mené	sent off	J D Davies (W)	W v E	1995
S Lander	sent off	F Mahoni (Tg)	F v Tg	*1995
D T M McHugh	sent off	J Dalton (SA)	SA v C	*1995
D T M McHugh	sent off	R G A Snow (C)	SA v C	*1995
D T M McHugh	sent off	G L Rees (C)	SA v C	*1995
J Dumé	sent off	G R Jenkins (W)	SA v W	1995
W J Erickson	sent off	V B Cavubati (Fj)	NZ v Fj	1997
W D Bevan	sent off	A G Venter (SA)	NZ v SA	1997
C Giacomel	sent off	R Travaglini (Arg)	F v Arg	1997

* Matches in World Cup final stages

WORLD INTERNATIONAL RECORDS

Both match and career records are for official cap matches played by senior members of the International Board, up to 30 April 1998. Figures include Test performances for the Lions (shown in brackets).

MATCH RECORDS

MOST CONSECUTIVE TEST WINS

17 by N Zealand 1965 *SA* 4, 1966 *BI* 1,2,3,4, 1967 *A, E, W, F, S*, 1968 *A* 1,2, *F* 1,2,3, 1969 *W* 1,2

15 by S Africa 1994 *Arg* 1,2,*S,W* 1995 *WS, A, R, C, WS, F, NZ, W, It, E*, 1996 *Fj*

MOST CONSECUTIVE TESTS WITHOUT DEFEAT

P	W	D	Period
23 by NZ	22	1	1987–90
17 by NZ	15	2	1961–64
17 by NZ	17	0	1965–69

MOST POINTS IN A MATCH
by the team

Pts	Opps	Venue	Year
145 by NZ	J	Bloemfontein	1995
102 by W	Pt	Lisbon	1994
93 by NZ	Arg	Wellington	1997
89 by S	Iv	Rustenburg	1995
74 by NZ	Fj	Christchurch	1987
74 by A	C	Brisbane	1996
74 by SA	Tg	Cape Town	1997

by a player

45 by S D Culhane, New Zealand v Japan at Bloemfontein	1995
44 by A G Hastings, Scotland v Ivory Coast at Rustenburg	1995
39 by M Burke, Australia v Canada at Brisbane	1996
33 by C J Spencer, New Zealand v Argentina at Wellington	1997
33 by A P Mehrtens, New Zealand v Ireland at Dublin	1997
31 by A G Hastings, Scotland v Tonga at Pretoria	1995
30 by D Camberabero, France v Zimbabwe at Auckland	1987
30 by C R Andrew, England v Canada at Twickenham	1994
30 by M C G Ellis, New Zealand v Japan at Bloemfontein	1995

MOST TRIES IN A MATCH
by the team

Tries	Opps	Venue	Year
21 by NZ	J	Bloemfontein	1995
16 by W	Pt	Lisbon	1994
14 by NZ	Arg	Wellington	1997
13 by E	W	Blackheath	1881
13 by NZ	US	Berkeley	1913
13 by F	R	Paris	1924
13 by A	SK	Brisbane	1987
13 by F	Z	Auckland	1987
13 by S	Iv	Rustenburg	1995

by a player

6 by M C G Ellis, New Zealand v Japan at Bloemfontein	1995
5 by G C Lindsay, Scotland v Wales at Raeburn Place	1887
5 by D Lambert, England v France at Richmond	1907
5 by R Underwood, England v Fiji at Twickenham	1989
5 by J W Wilson, New Zealand v Fiji at Albany	1997

MOST CONVERSIONS IN A MATCH
by the team

Cons	Opps	Venue	Year
20 by NZ	J	Bloemfontein	1995
11 by W	Pt	Lisbon	1994
10 by NZ	Fj	Christchurch	1987
10 by NZ	Arg	Wellington	1997
9 by F	It	Toulon	1967
9 by F	Z	Auckland	1987
9 by S	Iv	Rustenburg	1995
9 by A	C	Brisbane	1996
9 by SA	S	Murrayfield	1997

by a player

20 by S D Culhane, New Zealand v Japan at Bloemfontein	1995
11 by N R Jenkins, Wales v Portugal at Lisbon	1994
10 by G J Fox, New Zealand v Fiji at Christchurch	1987

10 by C J Spencer, New Zealand v
Argentina at Wellington 1997
9 by G Camberabero, France v
Italy at Toulon 1967
9 by D Camberabero, France v
Zimbabwe at Auckland 1987
9 by A G Hastings, Scotland v
Ivory Coast at Rustenburg 1995
9 by M Burke, Australia v Canada
at Brisbane 1996

MOST PENALTY GOALS IN A MATCH
by the team

Penalties	Opps	Venue	Year
8 by W	C	Cardiff	1993
8 by S	Tg	Pretoria	1995
8 by F	I	Durban	1995
8 by I	It	Dublin	1997

by a player

8 by N R Jenkins, Wales v Canada
at Cardiff 1993
8 by A G Hastings, Scotland v
Tonga at Pretoria 1995
8 by T Lacroix, France v Ireland at
Durban 1995
8 by P A Burke, Ireland v Italy at
Dublin 1997

MOST DROPPED GOALS IN A MATCH
by the team

Drops	Opps	Venue	Year
3 by F	I	Paris	1960
3 by A	E	Twickenham	1967
3 by S	I	Murrayfield	1973
3 by SA	SAm	Durban	1980
3 by SA	I	Durban	1981
3 by A	I	Dublin	1984
3 by F	E	Twickenham	1985
3 by A	Fj	Brisbane	1985
3 by F	NZ	Christchurch	1986
3 by NZ	F	Christchurch	1986
3 by F	A	Sydney	1990
3 by F	S	Paris	1991
3 by F	NZ	Christchurch	1994

by a player

3 by P Albaladejo, France v
Ireland at Paris 1960
3 by P F Hawthorne, Australia v
England at Twickenham 1967
3 by H E Botha, South Africa v
S America at Durban 1980
3 by H E Botha, South Africa v
Ireland at Durban 1981
3 by J-P Lescarboura, France v
England at Twickenham 1985
3 by J-P Lescarboura, France v
New Zealand at Christchurch 1986
3 by D Camberabero, France v
Australia at Sydney 1990

CAREER RECORDS

MOST CAPPED PLAYERS

Caps	Player	Career
111	P Sella (France)	1982–95
101	D I Campese (Australia)	1982–96
93	S Blanco (France)	1980–91
92	S B T Fitzpatrick (New Zealand)	1986–97
91 (6)	R Underwood (England/Lions)	1984–96
81(12)	C M H Gibson (Ireland/Lions)	1964–79
80(17)	W J McBride (Ireland/Lions)	1962–75
79 (7)	I C Evans (Wales/Lions)	1987–98
76 (5)	C R Andrew (England/Lions)	1985–97
73 (1)	W D C Carling (England/Lions)	1988–97
72	M P Lynagh (Australia)	1984–95

MOST CONSECUTIVE TESTS

Tests	Player	Span
63	S B T Fitzpatrick (New Zealand)	1986–95
53	G O Edwards (Wales)	1967–78
52	W J McBride (Ireland)	1964–75

The world's most capped player, Philippe Sella (France), bowed out at the end of this season.

49	A B Carmichael (Scotland)	1967–78
49	P A Orr (Ireland)	1976–86

MOST TESTS AS CAPTAIN

Tests	Captain	Span
59	W D C Carling (England)	1988–96
51	S B T Fitzpatrick (New Zealand)	1992–97
36	N C Farr-Jones (Australia)	1988–92
34	J-P Rives (France)	1978–84
34	P Saint-André (France)	1994–97
30	W J Whineray (New Zealand)	1958–65
29	J F Pienaar (South Africa)	1993–96

MOST TESTS IN INDIVIDUAL POSITIONS

Position	Player		Span
Full-back	S Blanco (France)	81	1980–91
Wing	R Underwood (England/Lions)	91 (6)	1984–96
Centre	P Sella (France)	104	1982–95
Fly-half	C R Andrew (England/Lions)	75 (5)	1985–97
Scrum-half	G O Edwards (Wales/Lions)	63(10)	1967–78
Prop	J Leonard (England/Lions)	66 (3)	1990–98
Hooker	S B T Fitzpatrick (New Zealand)	92	1986–97
Lock	W J McBride (Ireland/Lions)	80(17)	1962–75
Flanker	J F Slattery (Ireland/Lions)	65 (4)	1970–84
	P J Winterbottom (England/Lions)	65 (7)	1982–93
No 8	D Richards (England/Lions)	53*(6)	1986–96

* excludes an appearance as a temporary replacement

MOST POINTS IN TESTS

Points	Player	Tests	Career
911	M P Lynagh (Australia)	72	1984–95
733(66)	A G Hastings (Scotland/Lions)	67(6)	1986–95
645	G J Fox (New Zealand)	46	1985–93
635(41)	N R Jenkins (Wales/Lions)	60(3)	1991–98
407(11)	C R Andrew (England/Lions)	76(5)	1985–97

MOST TRIES IN TESTS

Tries	Player	Tests	Career
64	D I Campese (Australia)	101	1982–96
50(1)	R Underwood (England/Lions)	91(6)	1984–96
38	S Blanco (France)	93	1980–91
35	J J Kirwan (N Zealand)	63	1984–94
34(1)	I C Evans (Wales/Lions)	79(7)	1987–98

MOST CONVERSIONS IN TESTS

Cons	Player	Tests	Career
140	M P Lynagh (Australia)	72	1984–95
118	G J Fox (N Zealand)	46	1985–93
87(1)	A G Hastings (Scotland/Lions)	67(6)	1986–95
77(1)	N R Jenkins (Wales/Lions)	60(3)	1991–98
68	A P Mehrtens (N Zealand)	22	1995-97
50	H E Botha (S Africa)	28	1980–92

MOST PENALTY GOALS IN TESTS

Penalties	Player	Tests	Career
177	M P Lynagh (Australia)	72	1984–95
160(20)	A G Hastings (Scotland/Lions)	67(6)	1986–95
146(13)	N R Jenkins (Wales/Lions)	60(3)	1991–98
128	G J Fox (N Zealand)	46	1985–93
89	T Lacroix (France)	38	1989–97
87 (1)	C R Andrew (England/Lions)	76(5)	1985–97

MOST DROPPED GOALS IN TESTS

Drops	Player	Tests	Career
23(2)	C R Andrew (England/Lions)	76(5)	1985–97
18	H E Botha (S Africa)	28	1980–92
15	J-P Lescarboura (France)	28	1982–90
13	J Davies (Wales)	32	1985–97
12	P Albaladejo (France)	30	1954–64
12(0)	J Y Rutherford (Scotland/Lions)	43(1)	1979–87

INTERNATIONAL CHAMPIONSHIP RECORDS

Record	Detail		Set
Most points in season	146 by England	in four matches	1998
Most tries in season	21 by Wales	in four matches	1910
Highest Score	60 by England	60-26 v Wales	1998
Biggest win	51 by France	51-0 v Wales	1998
Most appearances	56 for Ireland	C M H Gibson	1964–79
Most points in matches	288 for Scotland	A G Hastings	1986–95
Most points in season	67 for England	J M Webb	1992
Most points in match	24 for France	S Viars	v Ireland, 1992
	24 for England	C R Andrew	v Scotland, 1995
	24 for France	C Lamaison	v Scotland, 1997
Most tries in matches	24 for Scotland	I S Smith	1924–1933
Most tries in season	8 for England	C N Lowe	1914
	8 for Scotland	I S Smith	1925
Tries in all four games	For England	H C Catcheside	1924
	For Scotland	A C Wallace	1925
	For France	P Estève	1983
	For France	P Sella	1986
Most tries in match	5 for Scotland	G C Lindsay	v Wales, 1887
Most cons in matches	32 for Wales	J Bancroft	1909–14
Most cons in season	14 for England	P J Grayson	1998
Most cons in match	8 for Wales	J Bancroft	v France, 1910
Most pens in matches	77 for Scotland	A G Hastings	1986–95
Most pens in season	18 for England	S D Hodgkinson	1991
Most pens in match	7 for England	S D Hodgkinson	v Wales, 1991
	7 for England	C R Andrew	v Scotland, 1995
Most drops in matches	9 for France	J-P Lescarboura	1982–88
	9 for England	C R Andrew	1985–97
Most drops in season	5 for France	G Camberabero	1967
Drops in all four games	For France	J-P Lescarboura	1984
Most drops in match	3 for France	P Albaladejo	v Ireland, 1960
	3 for France	J-P Lescarboura	v England, 1985

PARTNERSHIP RECORDS

Position	Holders	Detail	Span
Centre threequarters	W D C Carling & J C Guscott	45(1) for England/ Lions	1989–96
Half-backs	M P Lynagh & N C Farr-Jones	47 for Australia	1985–92
Front row	A J Daly, P N Kearns & E J A McKenzie	37 for Australia	1990–95
Second row	I D Jones & R M Brooke	41 for N Zealand	1992–97
Back row	J Matheu, G Basquet & J Prat	22 for France	1945–51

OTHER MAJOR TEST RECORDS

Record	Holder	Detail
Fastest to 100 points	A P Mehrtens	in his 5th Test for N Zealand
	S D Culhane	in his 5th Test for N Zealand
	C J Spencer	in his 5th Test for N Zealand
Fastest to ten tries	M C G Ellis	in his 6th Test for N Zealand

MAJOR TOUR RECORDS

Record	Detail	Year	Place
Most team points	976 by NZ	1905–06	Europe & NAm
Most team tries	243 by NZ	1905–06	Europe & NAm
Biggest win	117-6 by NZ	1974 v S Australia	Adelaide
Most individual points	246 by W J Wallace	1905–06 for NZ	Europe & NAm
Most individual tries	44 by J Hunter	1905–06 for NZ	Europe & NAm
Most points in match	43 by R M Deans	1984 v S Australia for NZ	Adelaide
Most tries in match	8 by T R Heeps	1962 v Northern NSW for NZ	Quirindi

OTHER INTERNATIONAL MATCH RECORDS

Up to 30 April 1998. These are included for comparison and cover performances since 1971 by teams and players in Test matches for nations which are not senior members of the International Board.

Most points in a match
By a team
164 Hong Kong v Singapore 1994 Kuala Lumpar
By a player
50 A Billington Hong Kong v Singapore 1994

Most tries in a match
By a team
26 Hong Kong v Singapore 1994 Kuala Lumpar
By a player
10 A Billington Hong Kong v Singapore 1994

Most conversions in a match
By a team
17 Hong Kong v Singapore 1994 Kuala Lumpar

By a player
17 J McKee Hong Kong v Singapore 1994

Most penalty goals in a match
By a team
8 Canada v Scotland 1991 St John
8 Italy v Romania 1994 Catania
8 Argentina v Canada 1995 Buenos Aires
By a player
8 M A Wyatt Canada v Scotland 1991 St John
8 D Dominguez Italy v Romania 1994 Catania
8 S E Meson Argentina v Canada 1995 Buenos Aires

Most dropped goals in a match
By a team
3 Argentina v SA Gazelles 1971 Pretoria

3 Argentina v Australia 1979 Buenos
  Aires
3 Argentina v New Zealand 1985 Buenos
  Aires
3 Romania v France 1995 Bucharest

By a player
3 T A Harris-Smith Argentina v SA
  Gazelles 1971
3 H Porta Argentina v Australia 1979
3 H Porta Argentina v New Zealand
  1985
3 N Nichitean Romania v France 1995

Most points in matches
609 D Dominguez (Italy)
530 H Porta (Argentina/S America)
483 S Bettarello (Italy)

Most tries in matches
25 Marcello Cuttitta (Italy)

Most conversions in matches
81 D Dominguez (Italy)
54 H Porta (Argentina/S America)
46 S Bettarello (Italy)

Most penalty goals in matches
132 D Dominguez (Italy)
109 H Porta (Argentina/S America)
104 S Bettarello (Italy)

Most dropped goals in matches
25 H Porta (Argentina/S America)
17 S Bettarello (Italy)

Most matches as captain
43 H Porta (Argentina/S America)

Biggest win on a major tour
128-0 W Samoa v Marlborough
  (New Zealand) 1993 Blenheim

BAABAAS VISIT SOUTH AMERICA

THE BARBARIANS 1997-98
Geoff Windsor-Lewis

A new fixture against Combined Services, regular fixtures against Leicester and East Midlands in their centenary year, another Middlesex Sevens triumph and a visit to South America, kept the club active and innovative in another unsettled professional season.

The fixture against the Combined Services at Portsmouth named The Remembrance Match, which took place on 11 November, provided an entertaining game and a particularly spirited performance from the Combined Services. The Barbarians, who had eight internationals in their ranks, began slowly and took until half-time to produce team work and confidence. The Services led 28-7 at half-time, but the second half was a different story and the BaaBaas produced some glorious moves and showed a large crowd some fine attacking rugby.

In March the club enjoyed a record victory over Leicester at Welford Road. The outstanding effort came from Tongan Siua Taumalolo who scored 33 points from three tries and nine conversions. In appalling weather a crowd of nearly 10,000 loyal Leicester supporters turned up to watch some brilliant rugby from the BaaBaas.

The annual visit to Franklins Gardens for the Mobbs Match against the East Midlands in their centenary year produced a game which was contested in the usual free-playing entertaining spirit from start to finish. Unusually the visitors began in great form and led by Sporleder, the Argentinian No 8, thoroughly tested a valiant defence and after 45 minutes the game looked over with the BaaBaas leading 45-14.

However, late in the second half East Midlands managed to claw themselves back to 40-45 points amid high excitement. Deep into injury-time East Midlands were desperate to make that final score and after some continuous passages of play eventually produced a two-man overlap within sight of the BaaBaa line. Unfortunately the final pass did not go to hand and the Cambridge winger Mark Robinson pounced on the loose ball and ran the length of the field to score in the corner. The game ended with the visitors running out winners by 50 points to 40.

The BaaBaas won the Middlesex Charity Sevens at Twickenham for the second successive year and wound up their season with an enjoyable tour of South America. There, the BaaBaas were ably led by Mike Brewer and Steve Cottrell, who produced a New Zealand influence both in training and playing the game. Younger players such as Adam Jones, James Ponton and Jon Ufton will have benefited from the tour, whilst the presence of older players such as Greg Prosser, Harvey Thorneycroft and John Phillips ably supported by Alan Buzza kept the Barbarian spirit very much alive.

The club remains very grateful to Scottish Amicable, their sponsors since 1990, who have now donated £98,400 to youth rugby in the four Home Unions, a magnificent and generous gesture of support both to the Barbarians and to British rugby.

RESULTS 1997-98 (up to 8 June 1998)

Played 6 Won 4 Lost 2 Drawn 0 Points for 252 (26G 14T) **Points against 227** (24G 3PG 10T)

11 Nov 1997	**Beat Combined Services** at Portsmouth (The Remembrance Match) 40 (5G 1T) to 33 (2G 3PG 2T)
11 Mar 1998	**Beat East Midlands** at Franklins Gardens (The Mobbs Memorial Match) 50 (5G 3T) to 40 (5G 1T)
17 Mar	**Beat Leicester** at Welford Road 73 (9G 2T) to 19 (2G 1T)
31 May	**Beat South American Barbarians** at The British School, Montevideo 25 (5T) to 14 (2G)
4 Jun	**Lost to South American Barbarians** at Tucuman 44 (2G 6T) to 33 (4G 1T)
8 Jun	**Lost to South American Barbarians** at Buenos Aires 77 (11G) to 31 (3G 2T)

PLAYERS 1997-98 (up to 8 June 1998)

Abbreviations: *CS* – Combined Services; *EM* – East Midlands; *L* – Leicester; *MS* – Middlesex Sevens; *SA1* – South American Barbarians at Montevideo; *SA2* – South American Barbarians at Tucuman; *SA3* – South American Barbarians at Buenos Aires; (R) – Replacement; * – New Barbarian

Full-backs: J Gallagher (Blackheath & New Zealand) *CS*; *R Byrom (Nottingham) *EM*; *J Mallinder (Sale & England) *L*; *J Ufton (Wasps) *SA1*, *SA2*(R), *SA3*; *A Buzza (Rotherham) *SA2*.

Wings: *A Bernard (Pontypridd) *CS*; *P Sampson (Wasps) *CS*; *S Lewis (Pontypridd) *EM*; N Hill (Cambridge University) *EM*; *M Hoskin (Manchester) *L*; *Marcello Cuttitta (Amatori Milan & Italy) *L*; *A Jones (London Welsh) *SA1*, *SA2*, *SA3*(R); H Thorneycroft (Northampton & England) *SA1*, *SA2*, *SA3*; *D Quaqua (Baravi Exiles & Fiji) *MS*, *SA3*; *N Warne (Cambridge University) *EM*(R); *R Elliott (Cambridge University) *EM*(R); *M Denney (Wasps) *L*(R); *P Moran (Cambridge University) *L*(R); *P Belgian (West Hartlepool) *SA1*(R).

Centres: M Allen (Northampton) *CS*; M Field (Malone & Ireland) *CS*; *E Simone (Liceo Noval & Argentina) *EM*, *L*; *M Robinson (Cambridge University) *EM*, *L*; *P Burns (Furness) *SA1*, *SA3*; S Cottrell (Richmond) *SA1*, *SA2*, *SA3*; *M Shaw (Newcastle) *SA1*(R), *SA2*.

Fly-halves: N Malone (Leicester & Ireland) *CS*; *S Binns (Rotherham) *EM*; *S Tuamalolo (Ebbw Vale & Tonga) *L*; *I Kiliraki (Naitasivi) *MS*, *SA1*, *SA3*; P Belgian (West Hartlepool) *SA2*, *SA3*(R).

Scrum-halves: *D Patterson (Heriots FP & Scotland) *CS*; *S Benton (Gloucester) *CS*(R); P John (Pontypridd & Wales) *EM*; D Scully (Wakefield) *L*, *MS*; A Gommarsall (Wasps & England) *SA1*, *SA2*(R), *SA3*; G Downes (Bridgend) *SA1*(R), *SA2*; *N McCarthy (Pontypridd) *EM*(R).

Forwards: R Hardwick (Coventry) *CS*; P John (Pontypridd) *CS*; *D Barnes (Newcastle) *CS*, *SA2*, *SA3*(R); G Prosser (Pontypridd & Wales) *CS*, *SA1*, *SA2*(R), *SA3*; N Redman (Bath & England) *CS*; J Worsley (Wasps) *CS*; D Lyle (Bath & USA) *CS*; M White (Wasps) *CS*; *D Rees (Rugby) *EM*; *W Bullock (Coventry) *EM*(R), *L*; *J Brammer (Newbury & Army) *EM*, *L*(R); *S Cronk (Newport) *EM*, *SA2*, *SA3*; *R Malone (Tabard) *EM*; *R Bramley (Cambridge University) *EM*(R); P Sporleder (Curapaity & Argentina) *EM*, *L*; K O'Connell (London Irish & Ireland) *EM*; *J Wilde (Manchester) *EM*; *M Williams (Pontypridd & Wales) *EM*; C Hillman (South Wales Police) *EM*(R); *S Diamond (Sale) *L*; *Massimo Cuttitta (Harlequins & Italy) *L*; *A Craig (Cambridge University) *L*; *S Tatupu (Northampton & Western Samoa) *L*; *J Machacek (Newport & Czech Republic) *L*; *S Foale (Northampton) *L*; *L Mooney (London Irish) *SA1*; D West (Leicester & England) *SA1*, *SA2*(R), *SA3*; *A Deacon (Gloucester) *SA1*, *SA3*; *J Phillips (Northampton) *SA1*, *SA2*; *S Nawavi (Baravi Exiles & Fiji) *MS*, *SA1*, *SA2*(R), *SA3*(R); *M Corry (Leicester) *SA1*, *SA2*, *SA3*; *N Carter (Gloucester) *SA1*, *SA2*(R), *SA3*; *C Fortey (Gloucester) *SA1*(R), *SA2*, *SA3*(R); *J Ponton (West Hartlepool) *SA2*, *SA3*; M Brewer (West Hartlepool & New Zealand) *SA2*, *SA3*; *C Bird (London Irish) *SA2*, *SA3*(R).

LOSS OF A TRADITION

THE VARSITY MATCH 1997 (*for the Bowring Bowl*)

9 December 1997, Twickenham
Cambridge University 29 (3G 1PG 1T)
Oxford University 17 (2G 1PG)

The RFU referees' committee decreed before the game that only qualified officials should in future run the touchlines at the Varsity Match. So, 125 years after the series had been launched, one of Rugby Union's last great amateur events lost one of its longest traditions: that of the previous year's captains operating as touch judges. Another cherished convention – that of the universities choosing the match official – was also ceded to the referees' committee.

It didn't make any difference to the occasion of course. More than 70,000 made their way to Twickenham to see Cambridge win the 116th match of the series by the handsome margin of four tries to two. It was the Light Blues' fourth win on the trot, leaving them one short of the record for successive victories set by the Cambridge sides of 1972-76 and 1980-84. It was, moreover, one of the brightest matches of the 22 played for the Bowring Bowl.

Cambridge possessed an effective pack that, as a unit, had enjoyed a successful match against the ACT Brumbies a month earlier, setting up the platform for a 36-27 win over the team that had reached the final of the Super-12s in May. Cambridge had no hesitation in selecting the same pack to face Oxford and entered the match as favourites. Their pre-match record was impressive. Besides beating the Brumbies, they had scored an average of nearly 35 points a match, winning nine of the 16 played. Oxford, on the other hand, had averaged 21 and had lost more than they had won.

The Dark Blues were effectively beaten in the first quarter as Cambridge's fired-up forwards drove into rucks and mauls to win quality second-phase possession for their gifted backs. Richard Bramley, in his fifth Varsity Match, opened the scoring in the sixth minute when the rest of his pack forced him over from a line-out. Bramley was then the active agent in the next try, setting up Nick Walne's 19th-minute corner score from a tap penalty. Surridge converted both tries to put Cambridge 14-0 ahead.

Yet Oxford played their part in a thoroughly entertaining match, running the ball back at Cambridge at every opportunity. They had the better of the play leading up to the break, but the tight defence of Mark Denney and Mark Robinson in midfield restricted Oxford's efforts to a solitary penalty kicked by David Kelaher.

Thomas Murphy (Cambridge) lifts the Bowring Bowl after the Light Blues' fourth Varsity Match victory in succession, Twickenham, 9 December 1997.

Denney turned defence to offence early in the second half to score on the blind side and stretch the lead to 19-3, before Kevin Spicer responded with an Oxford try from a scrum. Then, in the 21st minute of the second half, Cambridge scored the try that really demonstrated their forward superiority. From a line-out on the Oxford 22, a forward drive carried play to the goal line where Paul Surridge, the Cambridge full-back no less, popped out of the rolling maul to score. Surridge then converted and added a late penalty after Nick Booth had put in a powerful run to score Oxford's second try.

Cambridge University: P A Surridge (St Kentigern College, Auckland & Hughes Hall); N J Walne (Caerleon Comprehensive & St Catherine's), M P Robinson (Opunake HS, NZ & Hughes Hall), M C A Denney (Bedford Modern & St Edmund's), N J Hill (St Ignatius College, Sydney & St Edmund's); R W Ashforth (Bradford GS & Peterhouse), R J Elliott (Durham School & St Edmund's); G M Reynolds (Cheshunt School & Hughes Hall), T D Murphy (St Joseph's College, Brisbane & St Edmund's) *(capt)*, M T Foulds (Christ's College, Canterbury & Sidney Sussex), R A Bramley (Queen Elizabeth GS, Wakefield & St Edmund's), A M Craig (Tauranga Boys College, NZ & Hughes Hall), M J Hyde (St Ignatius College, Sydney & St Edmund's), J F T Cocks (Newington College, Sydney & St Edmund's), H M D Whitford (The Leys School & Homerton) *Substitutions:* A M Goldsmith (Oundle & Homerton) for Surridge (81 mins); G Williams (Hinchingbrooke School & Homerton) for Hill (84 mins)
Scorers *Tries:* Bramley, Walne, Denney, Surridge *Conversions:* Surridge (3) *Penalty Goal:* Surridge
Oxford University: R A P Maher (St Ignatius College, Sydney & University) *(capt)*; N J Booth (Lytham St Anne's HS & Worcester), N A Larsen (Hilton College, Durban & Lincoln), B Rudge (St Edward's College, Liverpool & Keble), R J Pollock (Diocesan College, Cape Town & Keble); T P P Jensen (St Edward's College, Canberra & St Anne's), N A Hogan (Terenure College, Dublin & Merton); R P Lehner (Jesuit HS, Sacramento & St Anne's), M J Collard (The King's School, Sydney & St Anne's), A E Reuben (Solihull School & University), T S Eisenhauer (St Ignatius College, Sydney & St Anne's), A J Roberts (Ampleforth College & New), M G P S Orsler (King's School, Canterbury & Christ Church), K M J Spicer (Clongowes Wood College, Dublin & St Anne's), D J Kelaher (St Joseph's College, Sydney & St Cross) *Substitutions:* G C Lewis (Cheadle Hulme School & St Anne's) for Pollock (32 mins); S W van Reenan (Paul Roos Gymnasium, Stellenbosch & St Anne's) for Roberts (40 mins); J R J Sharples (Sydney C of E GS & St Edmund Hall) for Lehner (79 mins); C A Lavin (King Edward's School, Lytham & St Edmund Hall) for Kelaher (83 mins)
Scorers *Tries:* Spicer, Booth *Conversions:* Kelaher (2) *Penalty Goal:* Kelaher
Referee B Campsall (Yorkshire Society)

VARSITY MATCH RESULTS

116 Matches played   Oxford 48 wins   Cambridge 55 wins   13 Draws

*Match played at Oxford 1871-72; Cambridge 1872-73; The Oval 1873-74 to 1879-80; Blackheath 1880-81 to 1886-87; Queen's Club 1887-88 to 1920-21; then Twickenham. *At this date no match could be won unless a goal was scored.* † Penalty try.*

1871-72	**Oxford**	1G 1T to 0
1872-73	**Cambridge**	1G 2T to 0
1873-74	Drawn	1T each
1874-75*	Drawn	Oxford 2T to 0
1875-76	**Oxford**	1T to 0
1876-77	**Cambridge**	1G 2T to 0
1877-78	**Oxford**	2T to 0
1878-79	Drawn	No score
1879-80	**Cambridge**	1G 1DG to 1DG
1880-81	Drawn	1T each
1881-82	**Oxford**	2G 1T to 1G
1882-83	**Oxford**	1T to 0
1883-84	**Oxford**	3G 4T to 1G
1884-85	**Oxford**	3G 1T to 1T
1885-86	**Cambridge**	2T to 0
1886-87	**Cambridge**	3T to 0
1887-88	**Cambridge**	1DG 2T to 0
1888-89	**Cambridge**	1G 2T to 0
1889-90	**Oxford**	1G 1T to 0
1890-91	Drawn	1G each
1891-92	**Cambridge**	2T to 0
1892-93	Drawn	No score
1893-94	**Oxford**	1T to 0
1894-95	Drawn	1G each
1895-96	**Cambridge**	1G to 0
1896-97	**Oxford**	1G 1DG to 1G 1T
1897-98	**Oxford**	2T to 0
1898-99	**Cambridge**	1G 2T to 0
1899-1900	**Cambridge**	2G 4T to 0
1900-01	**Oxford**	2G to 1G 1T
1901-02	**Oxford**	1G 1T to 0
1902-03	Drawn	1G 1T each
1903-04	**Oxford**	3G 1T to 2G 1T
1904-05	**Cambridge**	3G to 2G
1905-06	**Cambridge**	3G (15) to 2G 1T (13)
1906-07	**Oxford**	4T (12) to 1G 1T (8)
1907-08	**Oxford**	1G 4T (17) to 0
1908-09	Drawn	1G (5) each
1909-10	**Oxford**	4G 5T (35) to 1T (3)
1910-11	**Oxford**	4G 1T (23) to 3G 1T (18)
1911-12	**Oxford**	2G 3T (19) to 0
1912-13	**Cambridge**	2G (10) to 1T (3)
1913-14	**Cambridge**	1DG 3T (13) to 1T (3)
1914-18	No matches	
1919-20	**Cambridge**	1PG 1DG (7) to 1G (5)
1920-21	**Oxford**	1G 4T (17) to 1G 3T (14)
1921-22	**Oxford**	1G 2T (11) to 1G (5)
1922-23	**Cambridge**	3G 2T (21) to 1G 1T (8)
1923-24	**Oxford**	3G 2T (21) to 1G 1PG 2T (14)
1924-25	**Oxford**	1G 2T (11) to 2T (6)
1925-26	**Cambridge**	3G 6T (33) to 1T (3)
1926-27	**Cambridge**	3G 5T (30) to 1G (5)
1927-28	**Cambridge**	2G 2PG 2T (22) to 1G 3T (14)
1928-29	**Cambridge**	1G 3T (14) to 1PG 1DG 1T (10)
1929-30	**Oxford**	1G 1DG (9) to 0
1930-31	Drawn	Oxford 1PG (3) Cambridge 1T (3)
1931-32	**Oxford**	1DG 2T (10) to 1T (3)
1932-33	**Oxford**	1G 1T (8) to 1T (3)
1933-34	**Oxford**	1G (5) to 1T (3)
1934-35	**Cambridge**	2G 1PG 1DG 4T (29) to 1DG (4)
1935-36	Drawn	No score
1936-37	**Cambridge**	2T (6) to 1G (5)
1937-38	**Oxford**	1G 4T (17) to 1DG (4)
1938-39	**Cambridge**	1G 1PG (8) to 2PG (6)
1939-45	War-time series	
1945-46	**Cambridge**	1G 2T (11) to 1G 1PG (8)
1946-47	**Oxford**	1G 1DG 2T (15) to 1G (5)
1947-48	**Cambridge**	2PG (6) to 0
1948-49	**Oxford**	1G 1DG 2T (14) to 1G 1PG (8)
1949-50	**Oxford**	1T (3) to 0
1950-51	**Oxford**	1G 1PG (8) to 0
1951-52	**Oxford**	2G 1T (13) to 0
1952-53	**Cambridge**	1PG 1T (6) to 1G (5)
1953-54	Drawn	Oxford 1PG 1T (6) Cambridge 2PG (6)
1954-55	**Cambridge**	1PG (3) to 0
1955-56	**Oxford**	1PG 2T (9) to 1G (5)
1956-57	**Cambridge**	1G 1PG 1DG 1T (14) to 2PG 1T (9)
1957-58	**Oxford**	1T (3) to 0
1958-59	**Cambridge**	1G 1PG 3T (17) to 1PG 1T (6)
1959-60	**Oxford**	3PG (9) to 1PG (3)
1960-61	**Cambridge**	2G 1T (13) to 0
1961-62	**Cambridge**	1DG 2T (9) to 1DG (3)
1962-63	**Cambridge**	1G 1PG 1DG 1T (14) to 0
1963-64	**Cambridge**	2G 1PG 2T (19) to 1G 1PG 1DG (11)
1964-65	**Oxford**	2G 1PG 2T (19) to 1PG 1GM (6)
1965-66	Drawn	1G (5) each
1966-67	**Oxford**	1G 1T (8) to 1DG 1T (6)
1967-68	**Cambridge**	1T 1PG (6) to 0
1968-69	**Cambridge**	1T 1PG 1DG (9) to 2T (6)
1969-70	**Oxford**	3PG (9) to 2PG (6)
1970-71	**Oxford**	1G 1DG 2T (14) to 1PG (3)
1971-72	**Oxford**	3PG 3T (21) to 1PG (3)
1972-73	**Cambridge**	1G 1PG 1DG 1T (16) to 2PG (6)
1973-74	**Cambridge**	1PG 1DG 2T (14) to 1G 2PG (12)
1974-75	**Cambridge**	1G 2PG 1T (16) to 5PG (15)
1975-76	**Cambridge**	2G 5PG 1DG 1T (34) to 3PG 1DG (12)
1976-77	**Cambridge**	1G 3PG (15) to 0
1977-78	**Oxford**	4PG 1T (16) to 2PG 1T (10)
1978-79	**Cambridge**	2G 3PG 1T (25) to 1PG 1T (7)
1979-80	**Oxford**	2PG 1DG (9) to 1PG (3)
1980-81	**Cambridge**	3PG 1T (13) to 3PG (9)
1981-82	**Cambridge**	3PG (9) to 2PG (6)
1982-83	**Cambridge**	3PG 1DG 2T (20) to 1G 1PG 1T (13)
1983-84	**Cambridge**	4PG 2T (20) to 3PG (9)
1984-85	**Cambridge**	4G (32) to 2PG (6)
1985-86	**Oxford**	1PG 1T (7) to 2PG (6)
1986-87	**Oxford**	3PG 2DG (15) to 1PG 1DG 1T (10)
1987-88	**Cambridge**	1DG 3T (15) to 2PG 1T (10)
1988-89	**Oxford**	2G 1DG 3T (27) to 1DG 1T (7)
1989-90	**Cambridge**	2G 2PG 1T (22) to 1G 1PG 1T (13)
1990-91	**Oxford**	2G 2PG 1DG (21) to 1G 2PG (12)
1991-92	**Cambridge**	2PG 1DG 2T (17) to 1DG 2T (11)
1992-93	**Cambridge**	1G 2PG 2DG (19) to 1PG 1DG 1T (11)
1993-94	**Oxford**	3PG 2DG 1T (20) to 1DG 1T (8)
1994-95	**Cambridge**	1G 1PG 2DG 2T (26) to 1G 2PG 1DG 1T (21)
1995-96	**Cambridge**	1G† 3PG 1T (21) to 1G 3PG 1DG (19)
1996-97	**Cambridge**	2G 2PG 2DG (23) to 1G (7)
1997-98	**Cambridge**	3G 1PG 1T (29) to 2G 1PG (17)

EVERYONE A WINNER

TETLEY'S BITTER COUNTY CHAMPIONSHIP 1998

18 April 1998, Twickenham
Cheshire 21 (1G 2PG 1DG 1T)   Cornwall 14 (3PG 1T)

There were smiles all round after the 98th official County title went to Cheshire: from their 500 supporters who saw the county's first appearance in a Twickenham final; and from the 30,000 Cornish faithful who enjoyed another weekend in London. The RFU, too, could laugh all the way to their bank. The appearance of Cornwall in the County Championship final added roughly £½million to the gate.

Steve Swindells put Cheshire ahead with a sixth-minute penalty and added another 15 minutes later, before Alex Guest dropped a goal for Cheshire to lead 9-0 on the half-hour. Danny Sloman pulled back three points for Cornwall with a penalty on the stroke of half-time and then kicked his second early in the second half to set up an exciting final 30 minutes.

The match turned dramatically when Cheshire grabbed two tries in two minutes midway through the half. First Nick Briers (from a line-out drive) and then Mike Blood (finishing a spectacular 65-metre attack) scored to put the northerners 21-6 clear. Eddie Nancekivell stole five points back from a tapped penalty before four minutes from time Sloman kicked his final penalty.

Cheshire: S Swindells (Manchester); M Blood (Manchester), C Ball (Widnes), R Hughes (New Brighton), M Hoskin (Manchester); A Guest (New Brighton), N Briers (London Irish); M Dorrington (New Brighton), L Hewson (Manchester), M Hill (Widnes), D Craddock (Manchester), M Kirke (Macclesfield), G Jones (New Brighton), S Beeley (Widnes), K Brookman (New Brighton) (*capt*)
Substitutions: S Dorrington (New Brighton) for Hill (54 mins); T Wasdell (Chester) for Jones (60 mins); A Yates (Lymm) for Hewson (66 mins); M King (Widnes) for Swindells (73 mins); S Wright (New Brighton) for Briers (75 mins); I Kennedy (New Brighton) for Hughes (temp 27-32 mins) and for Blood (79 mins)
Scorers *Tries:* Briers, Blood *Conversion:* Swindells *Penalty Goals:* Swindells (2) *Dropped Goal:* Guest

Cornwall: D Sloman (Launceston); R Thirlby (Redruth), J Tucker (Launceston), K Thomas (Truro), R Newton (Redruth); S Whitworth (Redruth), C Whitworth (Redruth); P Risdon (Launceston), B Lucas (Launceston), S Rush (Launceston), G Hutchings (Launceston), T Cook (Hayle), J Willcocks (Launceston), D Shipton (Launceston) (*capt*), M Addinall (Penryn) *Substitutions:* L Mruk (Penzance-Newlyn) for Cook (45 mins); E Nancekivell (Launceston) for Newton (52 mins); J Atkinson (St Ives) for Willcocks (62 mins); R Nancekivell (Launceston) for C Whitworth (71 mins)
Scorers *Try:* E Nancekivell *Penalty Goals:* Sloman (3)
Referee A Rowden (Berkshire)

Lancashire and Gloucestershire have won the title 16 times each, Yorkshire 12, Warwickshire 10, Middlesex 8, Durham 8 (twice jointly), Devon 7 (once jointly), Kent and Cheshire 3 times each, Hampshire, East Midlands, Cheshire, Northumberland, Cumbria (formerly Cumberland) twice each, Surrey twice (once jointly), and Midlands, Somerset, Leicestershire, Staffordshire and North Midlands once each.

NEWCASTLE RULE THE WORLD

SANYO CUP CHALLENGE 1998
23 May 1998, Twickenham
Newcastle 47 (6G 1T) **Sanyo World XV 41** (3G 4T)

Previous Sanyo challenges to the English champions had been exhibition matches pitting strong World XVs against makeshift club sides. Newcastle made sure that particular mould was broken in 1998. They fielded their strongest possible squad and staged a determined second-half recovery to win an absorbing match.

Nearly 20,000 turned up at Twickenham to see Philippe Sella, in the last competitive senior match of a brilliant career, lead the World XV. But it was another Philippe, Bernat-Salles on the right wing, who captivated the crowd with his sumptuous running in the first half-hour. Three times he ripped apart the Newcastle defence to help the invitation side to a 31-7 lead, before tries by Alan Tait (Newcastle's captain on the day of his last game for the club) and Ross Nesdale made it 31-19 at the break.

Young Jonny Wilkinson, who had played with assurance in his first senior start at No 10, slipped off at half-time with a minor injury for Rob Andrew to come on in the second half. Agustin Pichot snatched two cheeky tries soon after the interval, but as the World XV relaxed and began to lose its way, so Andrew and Gary Armstrong's experience began to tell. Newcastle's 28 points without reply in the final 25 minutes were enough to see them to victory.

Newcastle: S Legg; J Naylor, V Tuigamala, M Shaw, A Tait (*capt*); J Wilkinson, C Simpson-Daniel; G Graham, R Nesdale, P Van-Zandvliet, R Beattie, G Weir, P Lam, P Walton, R Arnold *Substitutions:* R Andrew for Wilkinson (40 mins); G Armstrong for Simpson-Daniel (40 mins); D Barnes for Van-Zandvliet (40 mins); S O'Neill for Arnold (47 mins); R Horton for Nesdale (60 mins); G Childs for Shaw (63 mins); N Frankland for Walton (68 mins); Van-Zandvliet for Graham (71 mins)
Scorers *Tries:* Tait (2), Nesdale, Graham, Armstrong, Lam, Tuigamala *Conversions:* Wilkinson (2), Andrew (4)
Sanyo World XV: P Vaccari (Italy); P Bernat-Salles (France), P Sella (France) (*capt*), S Glas (France), C M Williams (South Africa); D J Knox (Australia), A Pichot (Argentina); C D Blades (Australia), R Ibañez (France), M H Hurter (South Africa), J J Strydom (South Africa), W W Waugh (Australia), M Giovanelli (Italy), C P Strauss (South Africa), J F Pienaar (South Africa) *Substitutions:* G E Leaupepe (Western Samoa) for Sella (40 mins); T Coker (Australia) for Strydom (40 mins); S T Latu (Japan) for Pienaar (40 mins); R Cockerill (England) for Ibañez (49 mins); E J Rush (New Zealand) for Vaccari (50 mins); D J Garforth (England) for Hurter (55 mins); Strydom for Waugh (58 mins); Sella for Glas (58 mins); Pienaar for Giovanelli (58 mins); A C Thomas (Wales) for Knox (66 mins)
Scorers *Tries:* Bernat-Salles (3), Pichot (2), Williams, Sella *Conversions:* Knox (3)
Referee S W Piercy (England)
Previous Results: **1996** Leicester 31, Sanyo World XV 40 **1997** Wasps 31, Sanyo World XV 52

ANOTHER FIJIAN TRIUMPH

HONG KONG SEVENS 1998
27-29 March 1998, Hong Kong
Final: Fiji 28 (4G) **Western Samoa 19** (2G 1T)

Fiji returned to Hong Kong, the scene of their World Cup Sevens triumph in 1997, to pick up their eighth title in this event and with it the £75,000 winner's purse. It was the first time that the competition, sponsored by Credit Suisse First Boston, had offered prize money. Controversially, none of the Home Unions sent a side to the first tournament held in Hong Kong since the former colony was handed back to the Chinese.

Fiji were made to work hard for their title. After big wins against South Africa and Canada they struggled to hold the Argentinians to a draw in the qualifying pool, while on the final day of the event they opened with demanding quarter-final and semi-final matches against Australia and New Zealand respectively. Inspired by Waisale Serevi, the undisputed king of the shortened game, and with Marika Vunibaka to score their tries, the Fijians nevertheless overcame all the obstacles placed in front of them to win through to a final with Western Samoa. The Samoans, on the other hand, had enjoyed a relatively easy path to the showdown with their South Seas rivals and went into the final fancying their chances against a side that was well below full strength owing to injuries.

Yet the Fijians set about the business of retaining their Sevens supremacy with typical flair. Vunibaka opened the scoring before Toa Samania equalised for the Samoans. By half-time, the Fijians had established a 21-7 lead thanks to tries by Jope Tuikabe and Inoki Maraiwai, but the game was far from over. Ailaoa Samania grabbed two tries after the pause for the Samoans to threaten an upset, but with the match delicately balanced at 21-19 Bruce Rauque scampered over beneath the goal for Fiji's final score.

CUP RESULTS
Quarter-finals: Western Samoa 52, Canada 0; South Africa 24, France 19 (aet); Fiji 21, Australia 7; New Zealand 19, Argentina 7
Semi-finals: Western Samoa 45, South Africa 7; Fiji 24, New Zealand 7
FINAL: Fiji 28, Western Samoa 19

PLATE RESULTS
Quarter-finals: South Korea 24, United States 19; Spain 14, Holland 12; Papua New Guinea 19, Tonga 12; Japan 27, Hong Kong 21
Semi-finals: South Korea 40, Spain 0; Papua New Guinea 26, Japan 12
FINAL: South Korea 40, Papua New Guinea 14

BOWL RESULTS
Quarter-finals: Morocco 29, China 5; Malaysia 26, Singapore 17; Taiwan 19, Thailand 17; Zimbabwe 36, Sri Lanka 14
Semi-finals: Morocco 17, Malaysia 10; Taiwan 19, Zimbabwe 7
FINAL: Morocco 31, Taiwan 14

BARBARIANS RETAIN TITLE

MIDDLESEX SEVENS 1998
16 May 1998, Twickenham
Barbarians 38 (4G 2T) **Leicester 28** (4G)

The Barbarians, with pretty much the same recipe as in 1997, retained their Middlesex Sevens title. A team made up once again around four Fijians and captained by Wakefield's Dave Scully gave notice of its winning potential with an athletic performance to beat a London Welsh VII that pushed them hard in the opening round of the finals. The Welsh went on to underline their strength by winning the Plate competition.

Taniela Qauqau was the outstanding player of the afternoon, scoring eight tries in the Barbarians' four matches, including a scorching run for the opening score against a spirited Leicester Seven in the final. The Barbarians led 31-28 in the final when the Fijian, who had run in a hat-trick of tries in the first seven minutes, rounded off the scoring with a try from the last attack of the game.

After handing the greater share of the £50,000 prize money over to charity, Barbarians spokesman Geoff Windsor-Lewis revealed that his side were unlikely to defend their title for a third year in 1999. Instead, the club is likely to take part in the increasingly prestigious Paris Air Sevens. That will give the organisers of the Middlesex event even more to ponder as they consider plans to rejuvenate a competition that has run, uninterrupted even by war, for 73 seasons.

RESULTS
Sixth round: Saracens 31, Rosslyn Park 12; Sale 0, Wasps 33; Leicester 35, Nottingham 7; Reading 12, Emerging London Broncos 38; Kenya 24, Chichester Inst of HE 5; Gloucester 26, London Nigerian 10; Harlequins 26, Northampton 14; London Welsh 19, Barbarians 24
Seventh round: Saracens 26, Wasps 21; Leicester 31, Emerging London Broncos 0; Kenya 33, Gloucester 7; Harlequins 17, Barbarians 38
Semi-finals: Leicester 26, Saracens 14; Barbarians 33, Kenya 14
Final: Barbarians 38, Leicester 28

Teams in the final
Barbarians: T Quaqua, D A Stark, K Kiliraki, D Scully (*capt*); G Flockhart, D Eves, S Nawaui *Substitutions:* A Bose for Stark; P Buxton for Flockhart
Scorers *Tries:* Quaqua (4), Flockhart, Scully *Conversions:* Kiliraki (4)
Leicester: M Briggs, G Murphy, D Roke, T Barlow; O Wingham, L Moody, D Addison *Substitutions:* S Read for Briggs; R Edwards for Barlow
Scorers *Tries:* Barlow, Moody, penalty try, Murphy *Conversions:* Roke (2), Murphy (2)
Referee T J Miller (London Society)

Harlequins have won the title 13 times, Richmond nine (including one win by their second VII), London Welsh eight, London Scottish seven, St Mary's Hospital and Loughborough Colleges five each, Rosslyn Park and Wasps four each, Barbarians three, Blackheath and St Luke's College (now Exeter University) twice each, Sale, Met Police, Cardiff, Cambridge University, Notts (now Nottingham), Heriot's FP, Stewart's-Melville, Western Samoa, Bath, Leicester and Wigan (RL) once each.

SERVICES TAKE TO THE ROAD

WILLIS CORROON INTER-SERVICES TOURNAMENT 1998

Services rugby broke new ground in 1998 when, for the first time, matches in the Inter-Services tournament were staged away from Twickenham. The tournament opened in the familiar enough surrounds of the famous stadium where the Army, strengthened by Scotland captain Rob Wainwright, were too powerful up front for the Royal Navy. A crowd of 12,000 saw the soldiers, captained once again by hooker Julian Brammer, put on a splendid display of free-flowing rugby to win a high-scoring match that yielded 58 points, included ten tries and was unsullied by penalty points. A disappointing feature of the match, however, was the number of interruptions to play caused by injuries and riotous behaviour among the crowd. All told, there were seven substitutions and nine streakers (which must be a record for Twickenham). On top of that, five male spectators deemed it necessary to bare their posteriors at the end of the game.

Eleven days later the tournament took to the road for the first time. The Royal Navy deserved their win at Portsmouth against the RAF, if only for the heroic defence of their backs in a scrappy and at times ill-tempered match. As a spectacle the occasion came nowhere near to matching the Twickenham game. A week later at Kingsholm the Army duly retained the Willis Corroon title with a convincing victory against the RAF, for whom Rory Underwood, playing in the centre, created a new record by appearing in his 30th Inter-Service match.

The experiment of taking games away from Twickenham was deemed a success. Army supporters from their Salisbury Plain camps and RAF recruits from a number of nearby bases found Gloucester the ideal venue for a midweek evening match.

RESULTS
25 April, Twickenham Army 36, Royal Navy 22
6 May, Portsmouth Royal Navy 11, Royal Air Force 8
13 May, Gloucester Royal Air Force 7, Army 23

FINAL TABLE

	P	W	D	L	F	A	Pts
Army	2	2	0	0	59	29	4
Navy	2	1	0	1	33	44	2
RAF	2	0	0	2	15	34	0

The Army have won the Inter-Services tournament 30 times, the Royal Navy 17 times and the Royal Air Force 14 times. The Army and the Royal Air Force have shared it on two occasions and there have been ten triple ties.

JUNIOR CLUBS TAKE IT ALL THE WAY

NPI CUP & TETLEY'S BITTER VASE 1997-98

Bedford Athletic, winners of the NPI Cup for Junior clubs, provided Twickenham with its tensest finish of the season. A last-minute penalty kicked by Ashley Tapper in front of a crowd of 9000 rescued Bedford when all seemed lost at 21-24 down and with 80 minutes up on the clock. So, for the second year running, the final went into extra time (Harpenden having beaten Crewe Nantwich in 1997). Bedford emerged the stronger side and their winning score came when Alf Bartlett dashed over on the wing.

In the curtain-raiser, Huddersfield YMCA won an all-Yorkshire final against West Leeds to lift the Tetley's Bitter Vase.

2 May 1998, Twickenham
Bedford Athletic 29 (1G 4PG 2T)   **Stroud 24** (1G 4PG 1T) –
after extra time

Bedford Athletic: C Glanville; A Bartlett, G Witheat, J Chandler, T Cassidy; A Tapper (*capt*), C Eldridge; R Porter, D Stapleton, L Mansell, M Curry, C Wright, I Skingsley, T Gray, J Egan *Substitutions:* M Swift for Skingsley (29 mins); D Goodwin for Gray (40 mins); S Turner for Glanville (40 mins); M Norman for Cassidy (99 mins); N Paterson for Stapleton (99 mins)
Scorers *Tries:* Bartlett (2), Cassidy *Conversion:* Tapper *Penalty Goals:* Tapper (4)
Stroud: S Reed; M Nicholson, J Perrins, C Bayliss, A Sharp; S Thompson, L Moore; P Morris, G Trott, P Phillips, A Bean, R Davey, S Miles, S Bewick, S Cale *Substitutions:* C Ward for Cale (temp 18-29 mins and from 66 mins); A Cambridge for Bayliss (67 mins); G Fenwick for Reed (77 mins); M Bulley for Davey (77 mins); S Viggers for Moore (80 mins); I Gibbons for Trott (80 mins)
Scorers *Tries:* Sharp, Nicholson *Conversion:* Thompson *Penalty Goals:* Thompson (3), Fenwick
Referee N Yates (Manchester)

2 May 1998, Twickenham
Huddersfield YMCA 40 (2G 1PG 1DG 4T) **West Leeds 8** (1PG 1T)

Huddersfield YMCA: T Horner; M Kersey-Brown, J Campbell, J Marsden, M Ellis; K Gillespie, D O'Hehir; K Fleming, D Mellor, P Thompson, P Harrison, G Toomes (*capt*), R Davis, M Throssell, P Ounsley *Substitutions:* M Hunt for Thompson (17 mins); A Crossley for Gillespie (17 mins); P Harris for Harrison (40 mins); N Walker for Ounsley (40 mins); P Hopkins for O'Hehir (72 mins); K McCallion for Mellor (75 mins)
Scorers *Tries:* Ellis (2), Toomes, Davis, Campbell, Gillespie *Conversions:* Campbell, Marsden *Penalty Goal:* Marsden *Dropped Goal:* Campbell
West Leeds: S Evans; T Chard, B Salkeld, P Christopher, T Wrigglesworth; D Breakwell (*capt*), J Chard; R Dawson, D Broadbent, G Gatenby, C Taylor, J Cundale, P Davis, G Hudson, P Shaw *Substitutions:* D Tate for T Chard (76 mins); P Howitt for Christopher (76 mins); D Field for Breakwell (76 mins); C Jewell for Broadbent (76 mins); R Bedford for Hudson (76 mins); G Forbes for Dawson (76 mins)
Scorers *Try:* J Chard *Penalty Goal:* Breakwell
Referee T Ashworth (London)

WILKINSON BREAKS RECORD

UNDER-21 RUGBY 1997-98
Tony Simpson

The pace at which emerging talent can be catapulted into senior representative rugby was emphasised by the fact that three players at the junior end of the under-21 scale at the start of the season found themselves on tour with the England senior squad in Australia and New Zealand by the end of it.

Jonny Wilkinson had the advantage of having made his England debut against Ireland in the Five Nations Championship when he appeared as a replacement to become the youngest player for 71 years to wear an England senior shirt. That experience, however, did not prevent the teenager from experiencing the harsh realities of the senior game in the southern hemisphere during the summer, a daunting experience that he was to share with his England under-21 team-mates Josh Lewsey and Patrick Sanderson.

5 December 1997	England U21 42	New Zealand U21 13
23 January 1998	Italy U21 15	Scotland U21 41
6 February	France U21 15	England U21 16
6 February	Ireland U21 23	Scotland U21 7
20 February	England U21 46	Wales U21 7
20 February	Scotland U21 9	France U21 22
6 March	France U21 36	Ireland U21 28
6 March	Wales U21 3	Scotland U21 10
20 March	Scotland U21 16	England U21 32
20 March	Ireland U21 27	Wales U21 25
3 April	England U21 7	Ireland U21 9
3 April	Wales U21 14	France U21 3
23 May	England U21 42	France U21 27

NEW HORIZONS BECKON

STUDENT RUGBY 1997-98
Harry Townsend

Two years ago, Toulouse beat Cardiff at Wales's National Stadium in the final of the first Heineken European Cup; now, by strange coincidence, on 17 March 1998 at the Paul Sabatier University, Toulouse met the University of Wales Institute Cardiff (UWIC) in the final of the first European Students Cup, sponsored by *The Times* and supported by a grant from the Foundation for Sport and the Arts, on the Cardiff club ground. An enthralling final saw Toulouse triumph 52-37, although a 12-minute hat-trick of tries by centre Gwion Bowen had tied the half-time score at 27-27.

The BUSA Championship had long produced embarrassing mismatches in the early regional rounds; the introduction of Northern and Southern Premier Leagues meant meaningful fixtures through the first term. Undefeated Newcastle, beating Loughborough 25-0, won the northern title; Brunel (West London) were similarly unbeaten in the south and swamped Newcastle 48-8 at Welford Road to win the first English Universities Championship. UWIC, 33-30 victors over Swansea, won the Welsh title; Dundee took the Scottish title ahead of Glasgow.

Ireland, their university teams hardened in the senior club leagues, again won the Universities Triple Crown, trouncing England 80-30 on the way.

Representative matches: France Students 34, England Students 20 (Bordeaux); France Students 64, England Students 16 (PUC); England Students 24, Wales Students 15 (Blackheath); Wales Students 6, France Students 15 (London Welsh); Irish Universities 25, Scottish Universities 11 (Old Belvedere); English Universities 15, Welsh Universities 24 (Iffley Road); Welsh Universities 7, Scottish Universities 0 (UWIC) (abandoned through injury); Irish Universities 44, Welsh Universities 24 (Trinity College, Dublin); Scottish Universities 46, English Universities 10 (Peffermill); English Universities 30, Irish Universities 80 (Rosslyn Park); Scottish Universities 35, Glasgow Under-21 28 (Old Anniesland); Scottish Universities 45, Nice University 11 (Peffermill); England Students Under-21 16, Anglo Irish Under-21 14 (Brunel West London); England Students Under-21 31, Combined Services Under-21 19 (Twickenham)

BRITISH UNIVERSITIES SPORTS ASSOCIATION (BUSA) CHAMPIONSHIP 1997-98

Sponsored by Halifax

25 March, Twickenham
University of Wales, Swansea 17 (2G 1PG) **Northumbria University 3** (1PG)

Swansea, eight times the bridesmaid since their last championship success in 1939, at last rewarded long time coach Stan Addicott with an emphatic victory over 1994 champions Northumbria. Prop James Meredith crashed over for the opening try after 24 minutes, converted by Lee Davies. Although Northumbria reduced the arrears with a second-half penalty by Gareth McCullough, the result was in the balance until the last seven minutes when Davies kicked a penalty goal and converted his own interception try.

University of Wales, Swansea: G John; B Davies, B Williams (*capt*), O Jones, R Jones; L Davies, E Lewsey; N Hennessey, G Thomas, J Meredith, P Langley, A Wright, B Martin, R Griffiths, A Grabham *Substitutions:* A Cox for R Jones (50 mins); A Winter for Thomas (75 mins); R Lewis for Martin (75 mins); S Lodder for Hennessey (77 mins); G Roberts for Griffiths (77 mins); N Bennett (for Lewsey (77 mins)
Scorers *Tries:* Meredith, L Davies *Conversions:* L Davies (2)
Penalty Goal: L Davies
University of Northumbria: G Thompson, M Thomson (*capt*), G Foreman, G McCullough; A Herper; A Chilton; J Brannigan, J McNeish, D Corwood, C Yeoman, H Quigley, E Thorpe, C Yeoman, S Hobson, R Beattie
Substitutions: T Richardson for Gandy (30 mins); P Davies for Chilton (65 mins)
Scorer *Penalty Goal:* McCullough
Referee A Rowden (RFU)
Second XV final: UWIC 28   Brunel (West London) 19
Third XV final: Loughborough 49   Durham 0

BUSA CHAMPIONSHIPS
Sponsored by Halifax
Knock-out rounds
1st play-off round: Durham 14, Leeds 16; Glasgow 3, Hull 10; Durham 65, Teeside 5; Loughborough 78, Heriot Watt/St Andrews 5; Harper Adams 5, Nene 12; Manchester 31, Worcester 7; UWIC 34, St Mary's Hospital 5; UW Swansea 26, Wolverhampton 12; Bristol 15, Bath 10; Chichester Institute 48, South Bank 21; St Mary's UC 26, Plymouth 17; Birmingham 26, UW Aberystwyth 7; Brunel (West London), Exeter, Northumbria and Newcastle received byes
2nd play-off round: Northumbria 31, Chichester Institute 3; Leeds 6, Bristol 25; Hull 5, Durham 32; St Mary's UC 19, Harper Adams 22; Exeter 10, UWIC 23; Loughborough 23, Brunel (West London) 9; Manchester 11, Newcastle 31; UW Swansea 31, Birmingham 7
Quarter-finals: UW Swansea 28, Newcastle 3; UWIC 43, Loughborough 0; Bristol 20, Durham 5; Harper Adams 10, Northumbria 15
Semi-finals: UW Swansea, UWIC 20; Northumbria 18, Bristol 15
Final: UW Swansea, Northumbria 3
Loughborough have won the title 25 times, Durham and Swansea eight, Liverpool seven, Bristol five, Cardiff and Manchester four, Bangor, Brunel (West London) (formerly Brunel University College and West London Institute) and UWIST two, Aberystwyth, Birmingham, Leeds, Newcastle, Nortumbria and UWIC once each.

BUSA SHIELD
Final: Trinity College, Carmarthen 25, Cheltenham and Gloucester 19

BUSA PLATE
Final: Newport 35, Royal Agricultural College 5

BUSA SEVEN-A-SIDE TOURNAMENT
15 April 1998, Bristol University
Final: Bristol 12, Exeter 10

EUROPEAN STUDENTS CUP
Sponsored by The Times and supported by The Foundation for Sport and The Arts
Semi-finals: University Paul Sabatier, Toulouse 48, University College Cork, 29; UWIC 14, UW Swansea 10
Final: 17 March 1998, National Stadium, Cardiff
Paul Sabatier University, Toulouse 52, UWIC 37

THE CUPS THAT CHEER

COLTS AND YOUTH RUGBY 1997-98
Harry Townsend

It was a marvellous year for Irish junior rugby. University and under-21 Triple Crown champions, they were also unbeaten at under-18 and under-19 youth levels, culminating in winning the FIRA Junior title (effectively the junior World Cup) in France, where they beat their stunned hosts 18-0 in the final in Toulouse.

The Irish had earlier come back from 17-0 down against South Africa to draw 17-17 and survived a 'penalty-shoot-out' on appeal after their opponents had used an illegal kicker, but their 18-3 semi-final win over reigning champions Argentina and their defeat of France proved them worthy champions. Wales (9th) host the 1999 championships; Scotland (13th) will be there also. England, absent once more from FIRA, were again robbed of an unbeaten season by France. Jon Wilkinson (Newcastle) was capped at senior level.

Representative matches: Scotland U19 39, Canada U19 6; Scotland U18 Youth 6, Scotland Schools 3; Ireland U18 Youth 14, Italy U18 Juniors 11; Portugal Juniors 6, Wales U18 Youth 19; Wales FIRA Group Youth 33, Welsh Schools 12; Wales FIRA Group Youth 29, Romania Juniors 13; Ireland FIRA Group Youth 26, Italy Juniors 19; Wales U18 Youth 0, Ireland U18 Youth 15; France Juniors 15, Wales U19 Youth 6; Scotland U18 Youth 27, Scotland Schools 12; Ireland FIRA Group Youth 63, Spain Juniors 0; Scotland U18 Youth 33, Spain Juniors 7; Wales FIRA Group Youth 23, Italy Juniors 14; England Colts 41, Scotland U19 Youth 0; England Colts 10, Argentine Pumitas 3; Ireland U18 Youth 25, Scotland U18 Youth 14; Wales U19 Youth 20, England Colts 29; Scotland U18 Youth 11, Wales U18 Youth 13; England Colts 17, France Juniors 18.

FIRA YOUTH TOURNAMENT, FRANCE 1998

4 April	Ireland 47	USA 13
4 April	Scotland 3	Chile 7
4 April	Wales 19	Canada 23
6 April	Ireland 17	South Africa 17
6 April	Wales 20	Scotland 7
9 April	Scotland 56	Spain 10
9 April	Wales 39	Japan 10
9 April – Semi-Final	Ireland 18	Argentina 3
12 April	Scotland 45	Russia 5
12 April	Wales 34	Romania 19
12 April – Final	Ireland 18	France 0

The following players took part in Youth/Junior International matches. Countries played against are shown after the name.
Abbreviations: *Arg* – Argentina; *C* – Canada; *Ch* – Chile; *E* – England; *F* – France; *I* – Ireland; *It* – Italy; *J* – Japan; *P* – Portugal; *R* – Romania; *Ru* – Russia; *S* – Scotland; *SS* – Scottish Schools; *SA* – South Africa; *Sp* – Spain; *US* – USA; *W* – Wales; *WS* – Welsh Schools; (R) – Replacement.

ENGLAND
Colts
Full-backs: L Best (Richmond) *S, Arg, W, F*; I Balshaw (Bath) *Arg, W*
Threequarters: B Johnston (Waterloo) *S, Arg, W, F*; M Tindall (Bath) *S, W, F*; T May (Richmond) *S, Arg, W, F*; R Jewell (Gloucester) *S, Arg, F*; P Greenaway (Moseley) *W* (R), *F* (R)
Half-backs: J Lofthouse (Bath) *S, Arg, W, F*; M Taylor (Pontypridd) *S, Arg, W, F*; S Amor (London Irish) *W* (R), *F* (R); D Taberner (Richmond) *Arg* (R)
Forwards: R Siveter (Bath) *S, Arg, W, F*; L Mears (Bath) *S, Arg, W, F*; M Ward (Newcastle Falcons) *S, Arg, W, F*; A Brown (Pontypool) *S, Arg, W, F*; K Roche (Loughborough U/Old MidWhitgiftians) *S, Arg, W, F*; M Jarvis (London Irish) *S, Arg, W, F*; A Roques (Saracens) *S, Arg, W, F*; A Beattie (Richmond) *S, Arg, W, F*; S Williams (Saracens) *S* (R); S Williams (Moseley) *Arg* (R)

SCOTLAND
Under-18s
Full-backs: B Ruthven (Melrose) *SS*; M Mallinson (Watsonians) *SS* (R), *SS, Sp, I, W*

Threequarters: E Adie (Aberdeen GS) *SS (2), Sp, I*; R Couper (Ardrossan) *SS, Sp, I, W*; G Hill (Jed-Thistle) *I, W*; A McNair (Millfield) *SS* (R), *Sp* (R), *I* (R), *W* (R); J Pattison (Newcastle Falsons) *SS, I* (R); J Steel (Northampton) *SS (2), Sp*; R Kerr (Strathendrick) *SS, I* (R), *W* (R)

Half-backs: I Black (Angus Colts) *SS, Sp, I, W*; B Irving (Sevenoaks) *SS, Sp, W*; J Burnett (Watsonians) *SS (2), Sp, I, W*; M Dinwoodie (Watsonians) *SS, I* (R), *W* (R)

Forwards: A Meikle (Ary) *SS*; E Stewart (East Kilbride) *SS, SS* (2) (R); B Douglas (Heriot's FP) *SS (2), Sp, I, W*; I Whiteley (Hutchinsons/Aloy.) *SS*; A Davidson (Ormskirk) *SS (2), Sp, I, W*; C Hamilton (Wigtownshire) *SS (2), Sp, I, W*; G Lind (Stewart's Melville) *SS, Sp, I, W* (R); A Walters (Harrogate) *SS*; D Clark (Newcastle Falcons) *SS, Sp, I, W*; A Brown (Morgan) *SS, Sp, I* (R), *W*; S Swankie (Dunfermline/Rosyth) *SS, Sp, I, W*; O Hughes (Angus Colts) *SS, Sp* (R); S Caulfield (Dalziel) *SS* (R), *Sp* (R), *I* (R), *W*; K Dickinson (Dunfermline/Rosyth) *SS* (R), *Sp* (R), *W* (R); A Spalding (Gala Wanderers) *SS* (R), *Sp* (R), *I* (R); E Murray (Glasgow South) *SS, Sp, I, W* (R); C Sutherland (Hawuck PSA) *SS, I, W*; L Hamilton (Morley) *SS* (R)

Lind was captain in the first match against Scottish Schools; Mallinson in the second match against Scottish Schools, Spain, Ireland and Wales.

Under-19s
Full-back: B Ruthven (Melrose) *C, E*

Threequarters: R Kerr (Strathendrick) *C, E*; I McInroy (Garnock) *C, E*; R Stewart (Guildford and Godalming) *C, E*; R Haddow (Leicester Tigers) *C, E* (R); P Cumming (Liverpool St Helens) *E*; K Davidson *C* (R)

Half-backs: D Adamson (Boroughmuir) *C*; P Drought (Bath University) *E*; C Nichol (London Scottish) *C, E* (R); S Grant (Heriot's FP) *E*

Forwards: J Henderson (Jed-Forest) *C, E*; B McMahon (London Scottish) *C*; R Mathieson (Harlequins) *C, E*; W Mitchell (Melrose) *C* (R), *E*; T Palmer (Leeds) *C, E*; R Maxton (Stewart's Melville FP) *C, E*; S Taylor (Heriot's FP) *C, E*; R McKay (Gordonians) *C, E*; S Alborough (Watsonians) *C*; L Hamilton (Morley) *E*; B Douglas (Heriot's FP) *C* (R), M Welch (Dunfermline) *E* (R)

Taylor was captain in both matches.

FIRA Tournament
Full-backs: D Millard (Merchiston Castle School) *Ch*; B Ruthven (Melrose) *Ch* (R), *W, Sp, Ru*

Threequarters: P Cumming (Liverpool St Helens), *Ch, Sp, Ru* (R); C Milne (Dundee HSFP) *Ch, Sp, Ru*; I McInroy (Garnock) *W, Sp, Ru*; R Stewart (Guildford and Godalming) *W, Sp, Ru*; K Davidson (Hawick) *Ch, W, Sp* (R), *Ru*; R Haddow (Leicester Tigers) *Ch, W, Sp* (R), Ru

Half-backs: D Adamson (Dunfermline) *Ch, W*; P Drought (Bath University) *Ch* (R), *W* (R), *Sp* (R); S Grant (Heriot's FP) *Ch* (R), *W* (R), *Sp, Ru*; C Nichol (London Scottish) *Ch* (R), *W, Sp*, (R)

Forwards: M Welch (Dunfermline) *Ch, W* (R), *Sp* (R), *Ru* (R); J Henderson (Jed-Forest) *W, Sp, Ru*; S Linden (Dunfermline) *Ch, Sp* 9R), *Ru* (R); W Mitchell (Melrose) *W, Sp, Ru*; A McLean (Currie) *Ch, Sp* (R), *R* (R); R Mathieson (Harlequins) *Ch, W, Sp, Ru*; A Kennedy (Dundee HSFP) *Ch, Sp* (R); T Palmer (Leeds) *W, Sp, Ru*; R Maxton (Stewart's Melville FP) *Ch, W, Sp, Ru*; T Parratt (Dundee HSFP) *Ch* (R), *W, Sp*; A Hall (Moseley) *Ch, W* (R), *Sp, Ru* (R); S Taylor (Heriot's FP) *W, Sp, Ru*; R McKay (Glasgow Hawks) *Ch, W, Ru*; L Hamilton (Morley) *Ch, Ru*

Haddow was captain against Chile, Taylor against Wales, Spain and Russia.

IRELAND
Under-18s
Full-backs: G Brady (Ballina) *It, W, S*

Threequarters: G Duggan (Richmond) *It*; B Davis (Boyne) *It, W, S*; D Dunne (Athy) *It, W*; C Blanchfield (Athy) *It, W, S*; J Murray-Tait (Ballymena) *W, S*, C Richardson (Thurles) *W* (R), *S*; B Walsh (Portarlington) *S* (R); D Hunt (Athlone) *S* (R)

Half-backs: J Staunton (Garryowen) *It, W, S*; M Walls (Mullingar) *It, W*; P Jennings (Westport) *S*; F Farrell (Monivea) *S*

Forwards: N Foxe (Kilkenny) *It, W, S*; P Whateley (Dundalk) *It, W, S*; G Horan (Portarlington) *It, W, S*; T Hogan (Nenagh) *It, W, S*; G Logan (Guinness) *It*; D Quinn (Boyne) *It, W, S*; J Walsh (Westport) *It, W, S*; P Fitzgerald (Shannon) *It*; K Dowling (Skerries) *W, S*; D O'Kane (Portsdown) *W, S*; A Hanley (Athlone) *It* (R); P Flanagan (Athlone) *S* (R); D Vennard (Portadown) *S* (R); G Collings (Boyne) *S* (R)

Foxe was captain against Italy; Staunton against Wales and Scotland.

Under-19s and FIRA Tournament

Full-back: D Rossi (Clontarf) *It, Sp, US, SA, Arg, F*

Threequarters: J Reynolds (Watsonians) *It, Sp, Arg* (R), *F* (R); S Moore (UCD) *It, US, SA, Arg, F*; A Considine (Bective Rangers) *It, Arg* (R), *F* (R); D Holt (UCC) *It, SA, Arg, F*; M Cupitt (Instonians) *Sp, US, SA, Arg, F*; B McCracken (CIYMS) *It* (R), *Sp, US*; E Binham (Coventry) *It* (R)

Half-backs: B O'Driscoll (UCD) *It, Sp, US* (R), *SA, Arg, F*; K Campbell (London Irish) *It, Sp* (R) *SA, Arg, F*; P Wallace (Campbell College) *Sp, US, SA, Arg, F*; D Mescall (Ballina/UCG) *It* (R), *Sp, UA, F* (R); B Ronan (CBC) *US*

Forwards: A O'Brien (UCD) *It, SA, Arg, F*; A Flavin (London Irish) *It, SA, Arg, F*; F Roche (Bohemians) *It, US, SA, Arg, F*; D O'Callaghan (Cork Constitution) *It, Sp, US* (R), *SA, Arg, F*; C Fitzgerald (Garryowen) *It, Arg* (R), *F* (R); C McCarey (Ballymena) *It, Sp* (R), *US, SA, Arg, F*; N Coughlan (UCD) *It, Sp, SA, Arg, F*; C McMahon (Castleknock College) *Sp,* B Urquhart (MCB) *Sp, US, SA* (R), *Arg* (R), *F* (R); C Schofield (Bangor) *It* (R), *Sp, US, SA* (R), *Arg* (R), *F* (R); D Broughall (UCD) *Sp, US, SA, Arg, F*; B Cahill (UCC) *Sp, US*; A Kearney (St Michael's College) *It, Sp, US, SA, Arg, F*; J Sheahan (PBC) *US*; S Walsh (Old Belvedere) *It* (R); B Powell (Lansdowne) *It* (R); C Good (RBAI) *US* (R), *F* (R) A Bohane (Highfield) *Sp* (R)

Mescall was captain against Spain; Moore against Italy, USA, South Africa, Argentina and France.

WALES

Under-18s

Full-backs: R Potter (Abercarn) *P, I*; N Jones (Dunvant) *S*

Threequarters: N McKim (Newport) *P, I, S*; J Bowd (Abertillery) *P, I, S*; S Thomas (Bradford Bulls) *P*; M Jones (Builth Wells) *P, I, S*; B Tyler (Llanelli Wanderers) *P* (R), *I* (R); T Duval (Dunvant) *I*

Half-backs: M Lovell (Newport), *P, I, S*; A Williams (Dunvant) *P, I, S*; P Burridge (Pontypridd) *P* (R), *I* (R), *S*; R Goodfellow (Llandeilo) *S* (R)

Forwards: R Mills (Builth Wells) *P, I, S*; J Jones (Swansea) *P, I*; J Fallon (Northampton) *P*; D Adams (Pontypridd) *P, I, S*; G Phillips (Newport) *P, I*; W Morris (Builth Wells) *P*; T Morris (Abercarn) *P, I, S*; M Sweeney (Neath Colts) *P*; M Jenkins (Builth Wells) *P* (R); W Lloyd (Llandovery College) *P* (R), *I* (R), *S*; A Edwards (Neath Colts) *P* (R), *I* (R); M Dixon (Pencoed) *P* (R), *I* (R), *S*; D Evans (Carmarthen Athletic) *I*; T Snelgrove (Risca) *I, S*; R Jones (Risca) *I, S*; K Lawrence (Builth Wells) *I* (R), *S* (R); A Popham (Newport) *S*; A Luff (Pencoed) *S*

Bowd was captain in all three matches.

Under-19s

Full-backs: G King (Newport) *F*; H Rees (Pencoed) *F*

Threequarters: J Taylor (Neath Colts) *F, E*; M J Watkins (Newport) *F, E*; B Jeffries (Pontypool) *F, E*; C Batsford (Glais) *F, E*; C Landry (Pontypool) *F* (R); G Bowen (Bridgend) *F* (R); T Green (Neath Colts) (R)

Half-backs: R Davies (Neath) *F, E*; A Jenkins (Bridgend) *F*; G Cooper (Pencoed/UWIC) *F* (R), *E*

Forwards: D Jones (Neath Colts) *F, E*; G Williams (UWIC) *F, E*; G Mason (Ebbw Vale) *F, E*; J Pemberton (Neath Colts) *F, E*; S Morgan (Neath Colts) *F, E*; C Hughes (Llanelli) *F, E*; D Bowles (Llanelli Wanderers) *F, E*; M Prosser (Pontypridd) *F*; R Bowen (Abertillery) *F* (R), *E* (R); B Scrivens (Bridgend) *F* (R); A Popham (Newport) *E*; J Stenner (Cornelly/Kenfig Hill) *E* (R)

Williams was captain in both matches.

FIRA Group and Tournament

Full-backs: G King (Newport) *WS, R, It, C, J, R*; C Rees (Llandovery) *S, J, R*

Threequarters: D Rogers (Llanelli) *WS, R*; J Evans (Llanelli) *WS, R, It* (R), *C, S, J, R*; P Davies (Pontyberem) *WS, S, R* (R); C Landry (Pontypool) *WS, R, It, C, S, R*; M Jones (Builth Wells) *R, It*; I Higgins (Cardiff) *R, It*; L Davies (Llanelli) *It, C, J*; E Davies (Carmarthen Quins) *It* (R), *C, J* (R), *R*; N McKim (Newport) *S, J*; G John (Neath) *J, R* (R)

Half-backs: G Bowen (Bridgend) *WS, R, It, C, S, J, R*; G Cooper (Pencoed/UWIC) *WS, R, It, C, S* (R), *J, R*; C Rees (Llandovery) *WS* (R); E Lewsey (Swansea University) *WS* (R), *R* (R), *S*

Forwards: R Mills (Builth Wells) *WS, R* (R), *S* (R), *J* (R); C Hawkins (Dunvant) *WS, R, It, C, S, J, R*; A Low (Rumney) *WS*; G Evans (Morriston/UWIC) *WS, R, S, J, R* (R); M Morgan (Llanelli) *WS, R, It, C, S, J* (R), *R*; A Bowen (Abertillery) *WS, R, It, C, S, R*; M Wood (Bridgend) *WS, R, S* (R), *J, R* (R); R Jones (Bridgend) *WS, R, It, C, J* (R), *R* (R); R Robinson (Newport) *WS* (R); R Sidoli (Merthyr) *WS* (R), *R* (R), *It, C, S* (R), *J, R*; M Dixon (Pencoed) *WS* (R), *J* (R), *R* (R); J Stenner (Cornelly/Kenfig Hill) *WS* (R), *R* (R), *It, C* (R), *S, J, R*; E Ross (Newport) *It* (R), *C, S, J, R*; L Howell *It* (R), *I, R* (R)

Bowen was captain in all seven matches.

BIG DAY FOR HIGH WYCOMBE

SCHOOLS RUGBY 1997-98
Tony Simpson

England 18 Group suffered only their second defeat in 16 matches under coach Geoff Wappett when they were beaten by France in their only defeat of the season, but they still managed a Triple Crown success to mark the end of the Sedbergh man's period at the helm. The rapid advance of Jonny Wilkinson from 18 Group player to senior international in 12 months was one of the major talking points of the season, while elsewhere, the focus was on the Daily Mail Schools Cup competitions, which once again provided a jamboree atmosphere for Schools Day at Twickenham.

True to form, Colston's Collegiate from Bristol carried off the under-18 Cup for the fourth year in succession when they defeated RGS High Wycombe 21-9 in the final, while at under-15 level, a 5-5 draw between QEGS Wakefield and High Wycombe provided arguably the most entertaining encounter of the three-match programme.

The day also marked a milestone in the history of the Daily Mail competitions, High Wycombe being the first school to have a team in both finals on the same day.

22 December 1997	Scotland 3	France 20
14 February 1998	Wales 18	France 25
31 March	Scotland 5	England 56
3 April	England 11	Wales 10
7 April	Ireland 49	Scotland 0
11 April	France 22	England 8
11 April	Ireland 13	Wales 6
18 April	England 26	Ireland 22

ENGLAND

J Shaw (Old Swinford Hospital) *S, W, F, I*; S Danielli (Cheltenham College) *S, W, F, I*; S Marsden (Bristol Grammar) *S, W, F, I*; M Tucker (Oundle) *S, W, F*; C Brain (Eltham College) *S* (R), *F* (R), *I*; S Obanjo (Christ's Hospital) *S*; M Stephenson (Durham School) *W, F, I*; A Goode (Bromsgrove) *S, W, F, I*; H Charlton (Durham School) *S, W, F, I* (R); R Blake (Bristol Grammar) *S* (R), *F* (R), *I*; D Flatman (Dulwich College) *S, W, F, I*; M Williams (Bromsgrove) *S, W, F*; O Julyan (Harrow) *I*; C Balshen (Durham School) *S* (R), *I* (R); J Dawson (Dulwich College) *S, W, F, I*; G Davis (Colston's Collegiate) *S* (R), *F* (R), *I* (R); D Giles (Kirkham) *S* (R); R Tyrrell (Sir John Dean's College) *I* (R); A Sheridan (Dulwich College) *S, W, F*; S Borthwick (Hutton Grammar) *S, W, F, I*; R Birkett (Millfield) *S* (R), *I*; J Dunbar (Abingdon College) *S, W, F, I*; M Soden (Uppingham) *S* (R), *W* (R), *F* (R), *I* (R); A Sanderson (Kirkham) *S, W, F, I*; A Balding (Caludon Castle School) *S, W, F, I*.
Alex Sanderson captained England in every game.

IRELAND

G D'Arcy (Clongowes Wood College) *S, W, E*; J Norton (St Mary's College) *S, W, E*; K Lewis (St Mary's College) *S, W, E*; R Miliken (Bangor Grammar) *S, W, E*; D McCombe (Royal Belfast Academical Institute) *S, W, E*; A Dunne (Belvedere College) *S, W, E*; D Spence (Wallace High School) *S, W, E*; N Brady (Royal School, Dungannon) *S, W*; N O'Connor (Clongowes Wood School) *E*; G Ryan (Clongowes Wood College) *S, W*; R Henson (St Mary's College) *E*; N Treston (Blackrock College) *S, W, E*; D Dillon (Clongowes Wood School) *S, W, E*; P O'Connell (Ard Scoil Ris) *S, W, E*; A Hickey (CBC Cork) *S, W, E*; A Hughes (Royal School, Dungannon) *S, W, E*; D O'Loughlin (Cistercean College, Roscrea) *S, W, E. Replacements:* N Beggs (Campbell College), G Duffy (Cistercian College, Roscrea), S Keogh (St Michael's College), A Cullen (Belvedere College), R McGrath (CBC Cork), A Emerson (Portora Royal School), G Hickey (St Mary's College), G Cleary (St Michael's College).
Andrew Hughes captain Ireland in every game.

SCOTLAND

K Swan (Dundee HS) *F* (R), *I* (R); G Ross (Dunfermline HS) *W, E, I*; R Brown (Earlston HS) *F* (R), *W* (R), *E, I*; P Liston (Edinburgh Acad) *W* (R); J Thomson (Edinburgh Acad) *F, W, E, I*; M Blair (Edinburgh Acad) *I*; J Bertinussen (Galashiels Acad); P Cockburn (Galashiels Acad) *F, W*; D Hall (Glenalmond College) *F, W, E, I*; T McBride (Glenalmond College) *F*; H Smuts-Muller (Glenalmond College) *I*; C Cusiter (Robert Gordon's College) *W, E, I* (R); A Frost (Robert Gordon's College); J Stewart (Robert Gordon's College) *F*; S Cranston (Hawick HS) *W, E, I*; N Stenhouse (Hawick HS) *F*; J Gibbon (Hutchestons' GS) *F*; D Hutton (Inverkeithing HS) *F, W, E, I*; C Pothan (Kelvinside Acad) *W*; E Goodman (Merchiston Castle) *E* (R), *I* (R); D Millard (Merchiston Castle) *F, W*; J Russell (Merchiston Castle) *W, E, I*; E Smith (Merchiston Castle) *F, W, E, I*; M Reay (Merchiston Castle) *E, I*; E Milligan (Stewarton Acad) *F, W, E, I*; A Moffat (George Watson's) *F, W, E, I*; J Nicholson (George Watson's) *F, W*; C Duck (George Watson's) *E, I*; R Armour (Williamwood HS) *F, W, E* (R), *I* (R); C Shaw (Peebles HS) *F*; M Teague (George Heriot's) *E, I*; D Lyall (Hutchesons' GS) *E, I* (R); T Beaver (Gordonstoun) *E, I*; M Hart (Dollar Acad) *I* (R).
E Smith captained Scotland against France and Wales; J Russell was captain against England and Ireland.

FRANCE

S Azouli (Rene Cassin, Bayonne) *W, E*; F Berneau (Jolimont, Toulouse) *S, W*; W Bonet (Lycee Agricole, Rodilhan) *W, E*; C Charrier (Francisque Sarcey, Dourdan) *S, W, E*; J-F Coux (Louis Armand, Gleize) *W, E*; L Dauchy (Jean-Moulin, Beziers) *S, W*; O Gargallo (Jolimont, Toulouse) *S, W*; M Girard (Prof Argouge, Grenoble) *S*; J Guiard (Jolimont, Toulouse) *E*; V Jaffres (Alain Fournier, Mirande) *W, E*; R Jahouer (Loiselet, Bourgoin) *S, W, E*; R Ladauge (Lacanal, Sceaux) *S, E*; N Laharrague (Prof Lautreamont, Tarbes) *S, W, E*; P Lannes (Saint Criq, Pau) *S, W*; Y Larguet (Les Eaux Claires, Grenoble) *S, W, E*; M Larrouy (Cantau, Anglet) *S, W, E*; A Mela (Prof de L'arrouza, Lourdes) *S, E*; Y Misse (Borde Basse, Castres) *S, W, E*; C Moulet (Raymond Naves, Toulouse) *S, W, E*; W Nolihan (Rene Cassin, Bayonne) *S*; T Pascal (Jolimont, Toulouse) *S, W, E*; J Pauthe (Jolimont, Toulouse) *E*; C Payet-Morice (Louis Armand, Gleize) *S, W*; P Rabadan (Sacre Coeur, Aix-en-Provence) *S, W, E*; A Rougerie (Bernard de Ventadour, Ussel) *S, W, E*; C Savignat (Parc de Vilgenis, Massy) *E*; E Serna (Lycee Agricole, Montardon) *E*; F Sestaret (Jolimont, Toulouse) *S, E*; J Stylite (Andre Malraux) *S*; J Tastet (Rene Cassin, Bayonne) *W*; H Vermis (Rene Cassin, Bayonne) *W, E*; R Wild (J M Boivin, Chevigny St Sauveur) *S*.

ENGLISH GAME COMES INTO ITS OWN

WOMEN'S RUGBY
Christine Kenrick

A burgeoning game at junior level; a 64-strong Student Cup competition; a successful National Car Parks (NCP) Regional and Divisional Championship. Put these encouraging developments to one side – the 1997-98 season will be remembered for a performance which established beyond doubt that the game of women's rugby had come into its own in England. For, despite losing their world crown, England gave a display that Stephen Jones of the *Sunday Times* described as 'probably the greatest performance in the history of the England side.' The game? England against New Zealand on a blisteringly hot afternoon in the semi-final of the third Women's World Cup, hosted this year by the Dutch.

England's preparations for the World Cup had begun almost as soon as they had won the title four years before, but gathered pace with a pre-season tour to New Zealand in August. Despite the dubious timing of the Test – off the plane and almost immediately onto the pitch for a resounding 67-0 defeat – England were forced to acknowledge that there was a significant difference between the two sides. The task was then to bridge that gap by May 1998.

The 1997-98 season began with a victory over Spain in the finals of the European Championships, with successes over the Nomads and Spain to follow. The Home Nations Championship in early 1998 was a crucial period of experimentation for the World Cup. France, Wales and Ireland all fell to England, but in a timely reminder of their lack of invincibility England then lost to Scotland, who thereby annexed the Championship title for the first time.

If that was a slap in the face, it was followed by a shot in the arm with the announcement of sufficient funding from the Sports Council to enable the 29-player squad to enjoy a pre-World Cup training camp at Lilleshall, which included specialist help from a team of sports experts and professional tactical advice.

And so to Holland. After victories over Sweden (75-0), Canada (70-6) and Australia (30-13), England faced the All Blacks in the semi-final. In a tremendously hard-fought and skilful game the New Zealand side confirmed their superiority with a 44-11 victory and then went on to a 46-12 defeat of the USA in the final. England secured their position as third best in the world by beating Canada 81-15.

The other home nations also competed: Scotland were unlucky to face the All Blacks in their second game and eventually lost

25-15 to Australia in the plate final; Ireland were runners-up in the Bowl competition and Wales third in the 'best of the rest'.

Of the 29-strong England squad, 12 play their rugby with Saracens, so it is perhaps not surprising that the London side completed a clean sweep of the domestic competitions. They came out on top in the newly created Premier Division One; overturned an early Wasps lead to retain the National Sevens title by 24-17; and Sky TV televised their victory over Wasps in the Bread for Life Cup final.

Saracens may reign supreme at the moment, but the talent base is widening all the time and they are sure to face stiffer competition in the future, which can only be to the benefit of the national team. All eyes are now on World Cup 2002 and the RFUW's attempts to consolidate and maintain its position as the best organised and most progressive union world-wide.

WORLD CUP RESULTS

Quarter-finals: England 30, Australia 13; United States 25, Scotland 10; Canada 9, France 7; New Zealand 46, Spain 3

Semi-finals: New Zealand 44, England 11; United States 46, Canada 6

Third/Fourth Play-Off: England 81, Canada 15

FINAL: New Zealand 44, United States 12

Student Cup: Loughborough 17, Staffordshire 12

OBITUARY 1997-98 (*up to 30 April 1998*)

Geoffrey Coker Arding ADAMS MBE (Cambridge University), the newspaper proprietor who died in Geelong, Australia on 10 February at the age of 88, was an accomplished sportsman in his youth. He played cricket and rugby for Hampshire and won his rugby Blue as a centre for Cambridge in 1929.

William Francis BLACKADDER DFC (West of Scotland, Northern), who died at the age of 84 on 27 November, won his only cap for Scotland at Twickenham in 1938 as an eleventh-hour replacement prop. The match went down in history as one of the most thrilling of the inter-war years, Scotland winning 21-16 in perfect conditions to take the Triple Crown and Championship. Played county rugby for Northumberland.

Cecil Albert BLAZEY OBE, chairman of the New Zealand Rugby Football Union from 1977 to 1986, died in Wellington on 20 February at the age of 88. He was also a long-serving chairman of New Zealand's Athletics Association, bringing integrity and wisdom to administrative duties at a time when his nation's sports organisations faced difficult political challenges.

Brian John BRENNAN MC (Old Alleynians), the former deputy chairman of Lloyd's who died aged 79 on April 14, was a well-known forward on the London Old Boys scene in the seasons after the last War and toured South Wales with the Barbarians in 1950.

George Moir CHRISTIE was the coach of the South African side that won the 1995 World Cup. He played a major role in the senior management team that masterminded that victory, for apart from his charismatic leadership he was a knowledgeable coach who drew up his match strategies after making meticulous studies of opposing sides. After running the Transvaal side, he was invited to take over as national coach only nine months before the World Cup, yet working productively with François Pienaar he built up a side that enjoyed a run of 14 consecutive Test victories before his contract was terminated. Kitch Christie died aged 58 in Pretoria on April 22. On hearing the news Pienaar said, 'He was like a father to me.'

Ian James CLARKE (Waikato) played more than 250 first-class matches including 24 Tests for New Zealand in the 1950s and 1960s. He captained the All Blacks in 1955 and was a versatile enough forward to win caps as prop and No 8. In 1963-64, when he became the first New Zealander to make a second tour of Britain, he was invited by the Barbarians to appear against his compatriots. He made his mark on that game by contributing the Baa-Baas' only points with a soaring drop-kick from 40 yards out near the South Stand touchline. From 1956 onwards he was regularly joined in the national side by his younger brother Don, a goal-kicking full-back. Died on his Morrinsville farm on 29 June, the day after watching New Zealand play its first Test match in Hamilton. He was 66.

Patrick John COSTELLO (Palmerston, Bective Rangers) was a dual international for Ireland, representing his nation at athletics (as a shot putter) and rugby. He was the mainstay of the Bective pack that ruled the Leinster roost in 1955 and 1956 and won his only international cap in the second row against France in Paris in 1960. The father of Victor, the current Ireland No 8, Paddy Costello died on 6 October aged 66.

Brigadier Bernard Turing Vionnée COWEY DSO, OBE, DL (Army, Newport, London Welsh) who died in Nottingham on 20 August aged 85, scored three tries as Wales's right wing in four international matches in 1934 and 1935. Bun Cowey made his debut as one of 13 new caps in the Welsh side beaten 9-0 by England at Cardiff in 1934, but was never again on a losing Welsh side. He was awarded the DSO for outstanding leadership of his battalion during the Burma Campaign in 1945.

Donald CRICHTON-MILLER (Cambridge University, Gloucester, Bath), who died at Compton on 5 August aged 90, chose a teaching career in preference to Colonial Service when he realised that the former offered him the opportunity to advance his rugby career. He won a Cambridge Blue in 1928 and made his Scotland debut three years later, scoring two tries against Wales in Cardiff. Altogether he gained three caps as a back-row player of genuine pace.

Commander Trevor George Payne CRICK OBE, DSC (Royal Navy, United Services), the celebrated war-time naval commander who died aged 95 on 20 June, served Royal Navy rugby sides of the 1920s as a burly prop. Captained both the Navy and United Services.

Raymond Alfred DALTON (Wellington, Otago), who toured with the All Blacks to Australia (1947 winning two caps) and South Africa (1949 as vice-captain, though injury kept him out of the Test series), was a rugged prop whose early rugby was played in the second and back rows. He was an early master of the intricacies of the rucking techniques developed by the Otago provincial side in the post-war years. The father of the 1977 All Black Andy Dalton, he died 2 February in Auckland, aged 77.

Raffaele DOLFATO (Treviso) died in a traffic accident on 7 July, aged 34. A robust flanker, he helped bring Italian rugby to the fore as a member of the side that went to New Zealand in 1987 for the inaugural World Cup. He won nine caps for the *azzurri* and scored 65 tries in 257 matches for his club between 1981 and 1994.

Carel FOURIE (Eastern Province, NE Cape, Transvaal), who died of malaria aged 46 on 5 May in Johannesburg, was a determined wing capped four times by South Africa in 1974 and 1975. Scored a try and kicked two penalties in Tests and with his elder brother toured France in 1974 with the Springboks.

Joseph GALY (Perpignan, Toulon), whose death aged 67 was reported in June, appeared in the 1952 French Championship final for Perpignan, scoring a try in a 20-11 defeat by Lourdes, and played centre for France against Wales in 1953. From 1979 to 1984 he was the Perpignan club's much-respected president.

Robert GENESTE (Bègles-Bordeaux, Angoulême) was a French wing who would have won many more than two caps had War not interrupted his career. He made his Test debut on New Year's Day 1945 against a British Army XV of Union and League talents that was spearheaded from fly-half by Gus Risman. France won that match 21-9 and Geneste was again on the winning side in his only other international, against Argentina four years later. A distinguished orthopaedic surgeon, he died in August aged 76.

John Clifford GIBBS (Harlequins) won seven caps for England between 1925 and 1927 when he was considered the fastest wing in the country. Attack was the stronger part of his game and he was a natural sevens player, appearing for Harlequins in the side that won the first Middlesex tournament in 1926. Played for Kent when they won the County Championship in 1927 and later captained both his county and club. At the time of his death on 11 January he was, at 95, the senior England international.

Noel Joseph HENDERSON (Queen's University, Belfast, NIFC) enjoyed a successful international rugby career that brought him 40 Irish caps between 1949 and 1959 and a Lions tour to New Zealand/Australia in 1950. As a bone-jarring tackler and strong-running centre he helped Ireland remain unbeaten to win the Five Nations title in 1951, lining up alongside his brother-in-law Jackie Kyle, and later captained his country 11 times, including the match against Australia in 1958 when his lung-bursting 50-yard run for a try brought Ireland her first ever victory over a touring side. His last five Tests in 1958 and 1959 were as a full-back yet within three years of hanging up his international rugby boots he further demonstrated his all-round sporting talents by representing his country at badminton. Later, his wise counsel as a selector and ultimately as president of the IRFU was greatly valued in Irish rugby's administrative circles. He died on 27 August, aged 69.

John Cairns HUBBARD (Blackheath, Harlequins), whose father George was capped in 1892, won his only England cap at full-back in the scoreless Calcutta Cup match of 1930. His death at the age of 95 was reported in September.

Peter JOHNSTONE (Otago) was a fixture in New Zealand's back row from 1949 to 1951, winning nine caps. He took over from Ron Elvidge as captain of the national side for the fourth Test of the 1950 series against the Lions and went on to lead the side through an unbeaten tour of Australia the next year. He died at Wanaka on 18 October aged 75.

James Mitchell KERR (Edinburgh University, Heriot's FP), one of the eight Heriot's full-backs capped by Scotland, died on 3 January aged 87. He won his five Scotland caps between 1935 and 1937, proving a good reader of the game and a safe last line of defence. Gave up serious rugby to concentrate on his medical career.

James William McKAY (Queen's University, Belfast), a member with Des O'Brien and Jim McCarthy of the renowned back row that carried Ireland to its only Grand Slam in 1948, died in Gisborne, New Zealand on 15 October after a long illness. He was 76. He had spent such a happy period at Gisborne recuperating from injury when he toured New Zealand with the 1950 Lions that he chose to emigrate there as a GP a few years later. All told, he won 23 successive caps for Ireland between 1947 and 1952 (14 of them alongside McCarthy and O'Brien), scored three tries (including one on his debut) and helped Ireland win the Five Nations title three times.

Neville Athol Channon McMILLAN, who died suddenly at the age of 75 on 12 December in Auckland, was New Zealand's leading rugby historian. From 1978 until his death he used his expertise as a trained historian to produce a clutch of rugby classics, often working with the late Rod Chester as his reliable statistician.

Sir John MEGAW PC, CBE (Cambridge University, Richmond), the distinguished judge who was a Lord Justice of Appeal from 1969 to 1980, played twice for Ireland as a strapping forward in 1934 and 1938. At Cambridge he narrowly failed to win his Blue, though his devotion to the game was never in doubt. Indeed his call to the Bar was delayed a term in 1933 because he opted to appear in an important match in Ireland instead of attending Call Day. Died on 27 December at the age of 88.

Air Commodore Herbert Waldemar MERMAGEN CB, CBE, AFC (Richmond, RAF) was a noted wartime fighter pilot who, despite his stocky appearance, was a useful wing in the RAF and Richmond sides of the early 1930s. Tubby Mermagen died on 10 January aged 85.

Philip Edward John MORGAN (Aberavon) was a sturdy prop who graduated via the Welsh Schools and Youth sides to a place in the Welsh front row in three internationals in 1961 when he displaced Ray Prosser. His 11-season playing connection with Aberavon began in 1958 and he was a key member of the side that were unofficial Welsh champions in 1960-61. Captained the club in 1963-64 and became chairman and president before being made a life member in 1997. A former steelworker, he died in Porthcawl on 9 April aged 60.

Lieutenant-Colonel Anthony Leslie NOVIS MC (Oxford University, Army, Blackheath, Headingley), who died on 2 November at the age of 91, was one of the shortest players to appear for England, yet his incisive breaks as a centre or wing made him a popular player with crowds. Tony Novis played three Tests for the 1930 Lions, won seven England caps (1929-33) and was an Oxford Blue. He later became an inspirational captain of England and of the Army at a time when they dominated the Services Tournament. In the North Africa Campaign of 1940 he was awarded an immediate MC for his bravery at the Battle of Sidi Barrani.

Dr Desmond Oswald OLIVER (Otago, Wellington), the 1953-54 All Black, died at his Horton-cum-Studley home in Oxfordshire on 25 October, the day before his 67th birthday. Born in Palmerston North, he toured Europe and North America as a flanker with the Fourth All Blacks, making 20 appearances on that visit, including the Tests against Ireland and France. He retired from first-class rugby at 24 to concentrate on his medical studies. In 1960, he emigrated to England and from 1967 until his retirement in 1995 was Director of the Oxford Renal Unit.

Lucien PARIÈS (Biarritz, Narbonne, Mazamet), enjoyed his finest hour of Test rugby at Twickenham in 1975 when he orchestrated a wonderful 27-20 win over England in a match that marked the international debut of Jean-Pierre Rives. Lulu Pariès was heavily-built for a fly-half and unlucky to find himself competing for French Test honours with the likes of Jean-Louis Bérot and Jean-Pierre Romeu, otherwise he would have won many more than eight caps between 1968 and 1975. Even so, he maintained good club form for a decade and in 1979 was a member of the Narbonne side that won the French Championship. Died at Aix-les-Bains on 28 January aged 50.

Air Commodore Robert Henry PRATT (Dublin University, Lansdowne, RAF), Ireland's full-back in five successive internationals in 1933 and 1934 before he qualified as a doctor, died on 4 August at the age of 85. He was best remembered in Dublin rugby circles as the first player to use a round-the-corner approach to place kicking.

David SOLOMON (Waikato, Auckland), who died in Auckland on 15 August, was the utility back of the 1935-36 All Blacks in Britain. He appeared as a full-back, inside-centre and outside-half on that tour but was unable to force his way into the Test side. Transferred to League in 1939 and was immediately selected for a New Zealand tour of Britain that had to be abandoned owing to the outbreak of War. He was 84 at the time of his death.

John Rees Glyn STEPHENS (Neath) played in 32 official Welsh internationals between 1947 and 1957 before retiring as his country's most-capped forward. He was an integral member of the 1951-52 Welsh Grand Slam side and played a part in the last Welsh victory over the All Blacks, at Cardiff in 1953. In many ways he was a forward ahead of his time for, apart from being blessed with traditional scrummaging skills and toughness, he was an athletic player who showed a surprising turn of speed in the loose and could also place goals. He captained Wales six times and led them to five victories, including two in 1957 when his father (who had also captained Wales) was president of the WRU. Rees Stephens died on 4 February aged 75.

Pietro STIEVANO (Rovigo), who died in Padua on 18 September, aged 78, was a forceful wing in the Rovigo sides that ruled the Italian Championship between 1951 and 1954. He won eight caps for Italy between 1948 and 1955, later coached Petrarca and was instrumental in bringing mini-rugby to the north-eastern region of Italy.

Commander Sir Geoffrey William VAVASOUR Bt (Royal Navy), whose wartime exploits included a leading part in the chase of the German battle cruiser *Scharnhorst*, died aged 82 in August. He was one of the Navy's best all-round sportsmen in his youth, representing them at four different sports. As a useful fly-half he spearheaded the XV that won the Services Triangular tournament in 1938 and was captain of the side that retained the title in 1939.

Alfred Clarence WATERMAN (North Auckland) was, at 93 when he died in Whangarei on 22 October, the oldest living New Zealand Test player. After scoring four tries against Newcastle in the second match of the 1929 tour of Australia, he gained his international spurs as a wing in the first two Tests of a series that Australia took by three wins to nil.

James WHITE (Border) toured Britain and Ireland as a teenager with Bennie Osler's Third Springboks in 1931-32, playing nine times including the Test with Wales at Swansea. He was a centre on that visit but later became a valued utility back and made ten Test appearances in all, appearing also at wing and full-back. His death at the age of 85 was reported in June.

Graham George WILLARS (Leicester), who died on 19 September at the age of 57, was a Tigers stalwart from his late teens. He played nearly 350 games for the club as a loose forward between 1959 and 1987, coached the side in the 1980s and was Leicester's president from 1991 to 1993.

FIXTURES 1998-99

As of 14 August, when the book went to press, the fixtures for the Allied Dunbar Premiership were not confirmed, and no fixtures had been released for Allied Dunbar One beyond 4 October because of the discussions regarding whether there should be a British league.

Venues and fixtures are subject to alteration. We should like to thank all those who have assisted in the compilation of this list, particularly those at the various headquarters of the Home Unions and Chris Burns of Twickenham Services.

Saturday, 15 August 1998
SOUTH AFRICA v NEW ZEALAND
(Durban)
ARGENTINA v USA (Buenos Aires)
CANADA v URUGUAY
(Buenos Aires)

Wednesday, 19 August
ARGENTINA v URUGUAY (Buenos Aires)
CANADA v USA (Buenos Aires)

Saturday, 22 August
SOUTH AFRICA v AUSTRALIA
(Johannesburg)
URUGUAY v USA (Buenos Aires)
ARGENTINA v CANADA
(Buenos Aires)

Saturday, 29 August
AUSTRALIA v NEW ZEALAND
(Sydney)
WRU League
Division 1
Bridgend v Swansea
Caerphilly v Pontypridd
Llanelli v Ebbw Vale
Neath v Cardiff

Saturday, 5 September
RFU Allied Dunbar Premiership
Allied Premiership 1
Bath v Wasps
Gloucester v London Irish
Leicester v NEC Harlequins
London Scottish v Manchester Sale
Richmond v Newcastle
Allied Premiership 2
Exeter v Bristol
Fylde v Orrell
Leeds v London Welsh
Moseley v Wakefield
Rugby v Blackheath
Waterloo v Rotherham
Worcester v Coventry
RFU Jewson National League
Division 1
Camberley v Wharfedale
Henley v Harrogate
Lydney v Birmingham Solihull

Morley v Liverpool St Helens
Newbury v Reading
Nottingham v Manchester
Otley v Rosslyn Park
RFU Tetley's Bitter Cup:
Preliminary round
SRU Premiership
Division 1
Currie v Boroughmuir
Glasgow Hawks v Heriot's FP
Jed-Forest v West of Scotland
Stirling County v Hawick
Watsonians v Melrose
WRU League
Division 1
Ebbw Vale v Bridgend
Neath v Caerphilly
Pontypridd v Llanelli
Swansea v Cardiff

Sunday, 6 September
RFU Allied Dunbar Premiership
Allied Premiership 1
Saracens v Northampton

Tuesday/Wednesday, 8/9 September
WRU League
Division 1
Bridgend v Pontypridd
Caerphilly v Cardiff
Llanelli v Neath
Swansea v Ebbw Vale

Saturday, 12 September
MOROCCO v ZIMBABWE
(Casablanca)
IVORY COAST v NAMIBIA
(Casablanca)
RFU Allied Dunbar Premiership
Allied Premiership 1
London Scottish v Leicester
Manchester Sale v Bedford
Newcastle v Bath
Northampton v NEC Harlequins
Richmond v Gloucester
West Hartlepool v London Irish
Allied Premiership 2
Blackheath v London Welsh
Bristol v Fylde
Coventry v Waterloo
Moseley v Leeds

Orrell v Rugby
Rotherham v Exeter
Wakefield v Worcester
RFU Jewson National League
Division 1
Birmingham Solihull v Otley
Harrogate v Morley
Liverpool St Helens v Lydney
Manchester v Camberley
Nottingham v Newbury
Rosslyn Park v Reading
Wharfedale v Henley
SRU Premiership
Division 1
Boroughmuir v Stirling County
Hawick v Glasgow Hawks
Heriot's FP v Jed-Forest
Melrose v Currie
West of Scotland v Watsonians
WRU League
Division 1
Caerphilly v Llanelli
Ebbw Vale v Cardiff
Neath v Bridgend
Pontypridd v Swansea

Wednesday, 16 September

IVORY COAST v ZIMBABWE
  (Casablanca)
MOROCCO v NAMIBIA (Casablanca)

Friday, 18 September

AUSTRALIA v FIJI (Sydney)
WESTERN SAMOA v TONGA
  (Sydney)

Saturday, 19 September

IVORY COAST v MOROCCO
  (Casablanca)
ZIMBABWE v NAMIBIA
  (Casablanca)
RFU Allied Dunbar Premiership
Allied Premiership 1
Bath v Richmond
Bedford v London Scottish
Gloucester v West Hartlepool
Leicester v Northampton
London Irish v Wasps
Allied Premiership 2
Exeter v Coventry
Fylde v Rotherham
Leeds v Blackheath
London Welsh v Orrell
Rugby v Bristol
Waterloo v Wakefield
Worcester v Moseley
RFU Jewson National League
Division 1
Camberley v Nottingham
Henley v Manchester
Lydney v Harrogate
Morley v Wharfedale

Newbury v Rosslyn Park
Otley v Liverpool St Helens
Reading v Birmingham Solihull
RFU Tetley's Bitter Cup: *1st round*
SRU Premiership
Division 1
Currie v Stirling County
Glasgow Hawks v Boroughmuir
Jed-Forest v Hawick
Melrose v West of Scotland
Watsonians v Heriot's FP

Sunday, 20 September

RFU Allied Dunbar Premiership
Allied Premiership 1
Saracens v Manchester Sale

Tuesday, 22 September

AUSTRALIA v TONGA (Canberra)
WESTERN SAMOA v FIJI (Canberra)

Saturday, 26 September

AUSTRALIA v WESTERN SAMOA
  (Brisbane)
FIJI v TONGA (Brisbane)
RFU Allied Dunbar Premiership
Allied Premiership 1
Bath v Gloucester
Bedford v Leicester
London Scottish v Saracens
Manchester Sale v NEC Harlequins
Newcastle v London Irish
Wasps v Wast Hartlepool
Allied Premiership 2
Bristol v London Welsh
Coventry v Fylde
Moseley v Waterloo
Orrell v Blackheath
Rotherham v Rugby
Wakefield v Exeter
Worcester v Leeds
RFU Jewson National League
Division 1
Birmingham Solihull v Rosslyn Park
Camberley v Newbury
Harrogate v Otley
Liverpool St Helens v Reading
Manchester v Morley
Nottingham v Henley
Wharfedale v Lydney
SRU Premiership
Division 1
Boroughmuir v Jed-Forest
Hawick v Watsonians
Heriot's FP v Melrose
Stirling County v Glasgow Hawks
West of Scotland v Currie
WRU SWALEC Cup: *1st round*

Saturday, 3 October

RFU Allied Dunbar Premiership
Allied Premiership 1
Gloucester v Wasps
London Irish v Richmond
NEC Harlequins v London Scottish
Northampton v Manchester Sale
West Hartlepool v Newcastle
Allied Premiership 2
Blackheath v Bristol
Exeter v Moseley
Fylde v Wakefield
Leeds v Orrell
London Welsh v Rotherham
Rugby v Coventry
Waterloo v Worcester
RFU Jewson National League
Division 1
Henley v Camberley
Lydney v Manchester
Morley v Nottingham
Newbury v Birmingham Solihull
Otley v Wharfedale
Reading v Harrogate
Rosslyn Park v Liverpool St Helens
SRU Premiership
Division 1
Currie v Glasgow Hawks
Jed-Forest v Stirling County
Melrose v Hawick
Watsonians v Boroughmuir
West of Scotland v Heriot's FP
WRU League
Division 1
Bridgend v Caerphilly
Ebbw Vale v Pontypridd
Llanelli v Cardiff
Swansea v Neath

Sunday, 4 October

RFU Allied Dunbar Premiership
Allied Premiership 1
Saracens v Bedford

Saturday, 10 October

RFU Allied Dunbar Premiership
Allied Premiership 2
Bristol v Orrell
Coventry v London Welsh
Moseley v Fylde
Rotherham v Blackheath
Wakefield v Rugby
Waterloo v Leeds
Worcester v Exeter
RFU Jewson National League
Division 1
Camberley v Morley
Harrogate v Rosslyn Park
Henley v Newbury
Liverpool St Helens v Birmingham Solihull
Nottingham v Lydney

Manchester v Otley
Wharfedale v Reading
SRU Premiership
Division 1
Boroughmuir v Melrose
Glasgow Hawks v Jed-Forest
Hawick v West of Scotland
Heriot's FP v Currie
Stirling County v Watsonians

Saturday, 17 October

RFU Allied Dunbar Premiership
Allied Premiership 2
Blackheath v Coventry
Exeter v Waterloo
Fylde v Worcester
Leeds v Bristol
London Welsh v Wakefield
Orrell v Rotherham
Rugby v Moseley
RFU Tetley's Bitter Cup: *2nd round*
SRU Premiership
Division 1
Currie v Jed-Forest
Heriot's FP v Hawick
Melrose v Stirling County
Watsonians v Glasgow Hawks
West of Scotland v Boroughmuir

Saturday, 24 October

HONG KONG v CHINESE TAIPEI
(Singapore)
JAPAN v KOREA (Singapore)
RFU Allied Dunbar Premiership
Allied Premiership 2
Coventry v Orrell
Exeter v Leeds
Moseley v London Welsh
Rotherham v Bristol
Wakefield v Blackheath
Waterloo v Fylde
Worcester v Rugby
RFU Jewson National League
Division 1
Birmingham Solihull v Harrogate
Lydney v Camberley
Morley v Henley
Newbury v Liverpool St Helens
Otley v Nottingham
Reading v Manchester
Rosslyn Park v Wharfedale
SRU Premiership
Division 1
Boroughmuir v Heriot's FP
Currie v Hawick
Glasgow Hawks v Melrose
Jed-Forest v Watsonians
Stirling County v West of Scotland
WRU League
Division 1
Caerphilly v Swansea
Cardiff v Pontypridd

Llanelli v Bridgend
Neath v Ebbw Vale
WRU SWALEC Cup: *2nd round*

Tuesday, 27 October
HONG KONG v KOREA (Singapore)
JAPAN v CHINESE TAIPEI
(Singapore)

Saturday, 31 October
JAPAN v HONG KONG (Singapore)
KOREA v CHINESE TAIPEI
(Singapore)
RFU Allied Dunbar Premiership
Allied Premiership 2
Blackheath v Moseley
Bristol v Coventry
Fylde v Exeter
Leeds v Rotherham
London Welsh v Worcester
Orrell v Wakefield
Rugby v Waterloo
RFU Jewson National League
Division 1
Camberley v Otley
Harrogate v Liverpool St Helens
Henley v Lydney
Manchester v Rosslyn Park
Morley v Newbury
Nottingham v Reading
Wharfedale v Birmingham Solihull
SRU Premiership
Division 1
Hawick v Boroughmuir
Heriot's FP v Stirling County
Melrose v Jed-Forest
Watsonians v Currie
West of Scotland v Glasgow Hawks

Saturday, 7 November
RFU Allied Dunbar Premiership
Allied Premiership 2
Coventry v Rotherham
Exeter v Rugby
Fylde v Leeds
Moseley v Orrell
Wakefield v Bristol
Waterloo v London Welsh
Worcester v Blackheath
RFU Jewson National League
Division 1
Birmingham Solihull v Manchester
Liverpool St Helens v Wharfedale
Lydney v Morley
Newbury v Harrogate
Otley v Henley
Reading v Camberley
Rosslyn Park v Nottingham
SRU Premiership
Division 1
Boroughmuir v Currie
Hawick v Stirling County

Heriot's FP v Glasgow Hawks
Melrose v Watsonians
West of Scotland v Jed-Forest

Tuesday, 10 November
France A v Argentinians (Toulouse)

Saturday, 14 November
WALES v SOUTH AFRICA
(Wembley)
ENGLAND v HOLLAND
(Huddersfield)
IRELAND v GEORGIA (Dublin)
Scotland XV v NZ Maori (Murrayfield)
RFU Allied Dunbar Premiership
RFU Tetley's Bitter Cup: *3rd round*

Sunday, 15 November
FRANCE v ARGENTINA (Nantes)

Tuesday, 17 November
France A v Australians (Lille)

Wednesday, 18 November
ITALY v HOLLAND (Huddersfield)
ROMANIA v GEORGIA (Dublin)
Wales A v Argentinians (Pontypridd)

Saturday, 21 November
SCOTLAND v SOUTH AFRICA
(Murrayfield)
FRANCE v AUSTRALIA (Stade de
France)
WALES v ARGENTINA (Llanelli)
IRELAND v ROMANIA (Dublin)
RFU Allied Dunbar Premiership
Allied Premiership 2
Blackheath v Waterloo
Bristol v Moseley
Leeds v Coventry
London Welsh v Exeter
Orrell v Worcester
Rotherham v Wakefield
Rugby v Fylde
RFU Jewson National League
Division 1
Camberley v Rosslyn Park
Henley v Reading
Lydney v Newbury
Manchester v Liverpool St Helens
Morley v Otley
Nottingham v Birmingham Solihull
Wharfedale v Harrogate

Sunday, 22 November
ENGLAND v ITALY (Huddersfield)

Saturday, 28 November

ENGLAND v AUSTRALIA
(Twickenham)
IRELAND v SOUTH AFRICA
(Dublin)
SCOTLAND v PORTUGAL
(Murrayfield)
RFU Jewson National League
Division 1
Birmingham Solihull v Camberley
Harrogate v Manchester
Liverpool St Helens v Nottingham
Newbury v Wharfedale
Otley v Lydney
Reading v Morley
Rosslyn Park v Henley
WRU League
Division 1
Bridgend v Cardiff
Ebbw Vale v Caerphilly
Pontypridd v Neath
Swansea v Llanelli
WRU SWALEC Cup: *3rd round*

Tuesday/Wednesday, 1/2 December

WRU League
Division 1
Cardiff v Neath
Ebbw Vale v Llanelli
Pontypridd v Caerphilly
Swansea v Bridgend

Wednesday, 2 December

SPAIN v PORTUGAL (Murrayfield)

Saturday, 5 December

ENGLAND v SOUTH AFRICA
(Twickenham)
SCOTLAND v SPAIN (Murrayfield)
RFU Jewson National League
Division 1
Camberley v Liverpool St Helens
Henley v Birmingham Solihull
Lydney v Reading
Manchester v Wharfedale
Morley v Rosslyn Park
Nottingham v Harrogate
Otley v Newbury
IRFU AIB League
Division 1
Ballymena v Shannon
Blackrock Coll v Terenure Coll
Buccaneers v Galwegians
Garryowen v Clontarf
Lansdowne v Cork Constitution
Young Munster v St Mary's Coll
WRU League
Division 1
Bridgend v Ebbw Vale
Cardiff v Swansea

Caerphilly v Neath
Llanelli v Pontypridd

Tuesday, 8 December

**Oxford University v Cambridge
University** (Twickenham)

Saturday, 12 December

RFU Allied Dunbar Premiership
Allied Premiership 2
Exeter v Blackheath
Fylde v London Welsh
Moseley v Rotherham
Rugby v Leeds
Wakefield v Coventry
Waterloo v Orrell
Worcester v Bristol
RFU Jewson National League
Division 1
Birmingham Solihull v Morley
Harrogate v Camberley
Liverpool St Helens v Henley
Newbury v Manchester
Reading v Otley
Rosslyn Park v Lydney
Wharfedale v Nottingham
SRU Premiership
Division 1
Currie v Melrose
Glasgow Hawks v Hawick
Jed-Forest v Heriot's FP
Stirling County v Boroughmuir
Watsonians v West of Scotland
IRFU AIB League
Division 1
Clontarf v Buccaneers
Cork Constitution v Ballymena
Galwegians v Blackrock Coll
Shannon v Garryowen
St Mary's Coll v Lansdowne
Terenure Coll v Young Munster

Saturday, 19 December

RFU Allied Dunbar Premiership
Allied Premiership 2
Blackheath v Fylde
Bristol v Waterloo
Coventry v Moseley
Leeds v Wakefield
London Welsh v Rugby
Orrell v Exeter
Rotherham v Worcester
RFU Jewson National League
Division 1
Camberley v Birmingham Solihull
Henley v Rosslyn Park
Lydney v Otley
Manchester v Harrogate
Morley v Reading
Nottingham v Liverpool St Helens
Wharfedale v Newbury

SRU Premiership
Division 1
Boroughmuir v Glasgow Hawks
Hawick v Jed-Forest
Heriot's FP v Watsonians
Stirling County v Currie
West of Scotland v Melrose
IRFU AIB League
Division 1
Ballymena v St Mary's Coll
Blackrock Coll v Shannon
Buccaneers v Terenure Coll
Garryowen v Galwegians
Lansdowne v Clontarf
Young Munster v Cork Constitution
WRU SWALEC Cup: *4th round*

Saturday, 26 December
RFU Allied Dunbar Premiership
RFU Jewson National League
Division 1
Birmingham Solihull v Nottingham
Harrogate v Wharfedale
Newbury v Lydney
Otley v Morley
Rosslyn Park v Camberley
WRU League
Division 1
Cardiff v Caerphilly
Ebbw Vale v Swansea
Neath v Llanelli
Pontypridd v Bridgend

Monday, 28 December
RFU Jewson National League
Division 1
Liverpool St Helens v Manchester
Reading v Henley

Saturday, 2 January 1999
RFU Allied Dunbar Premiership
Allied Premiership 2
Coventry v Leeds
Exeter v London Welsh
Fylde v Rugby
Moseley v Bristol
Wakefield v Rotherham
Waterloo v Blackheath
Worcester v Orrell
RFU Jewson National League
Division 1
Camberley v Reading
Harrogate v Newbury
Henley v Otley
Manchester v Birmingham Solihull
Morley v Lydney
Nottingham v Rosslyn Park
Wharfedale v Liverpool St Helens
IRFU AIB League
Division 1
Clontarf v Ballymena
Cork Constitution v Blackrock Coll

Galwegians v Young Munster
Shannon v Buccaneers
St Mary's Coll v Garryowen
Terenure Coll v Lansdowne
WRU League
Division 1
Bridgend v Neath
Cardiff v Ebbw Vale
Llanelli v Caerphilly
Swansea v Pontypridd

Saturday, 9 January
WALES v WESTERN SAMOA –
provisional
RFU Tetley's Bitter Cup: *4th round*
IRFU AIB League
Division 1
Ballymena v Terenure Coll
Blackrock Coll v Clontarf
Buccaneers v St Mary's Coll
Garryowen v Cork Constitution
Lansdowne v Galwegians

Sunday, 10 January
IRFU AIB League
Division 1
Young Munster v Shannon

Saturday, 16 January
RFU Allied Dunbar Premiership
Allied Premiership 2
Blackheath v Worcester
Bristol v Wakefield
Leeds v Fylde
London Welsh v Waterloo
Orrell v Moseley
Rotherham v Coventry
Rugby v Exeter
RFU Jewson National League
Division 1
Birmingham Solihull v Wharfedale
Liverpool St Helens v Harrogate
Lydney v Henley
Newbury v Morley
Otley v Camberley
Reading v Nottingham
Rosslyn Park v Manchester
SRU Premiership
Division 1
Currie v West of Scotland
Glasgow Hawks v Stirling County
Jed-Forest v Boroughmuir
Melrose v Heriot's FP
Watsonians v Hawick
IRFU AIB League
Division 1
Clontarf v Young Munster
Cork Constitution v Buccaneers
Galwegians v Ballymena
Shannon v Lansdowne
St Mary's Coll v Blackrock Coll
Terenure Coll v Garryowen

Saturday, 23 January
RFU Allied Dunbar Premiership
Allied Premiership 2
Coventry v Bristol
Exeter v Fylde
Moseley v Blackheath
Rotherham v Leeds
Wakefield v Orrell
Waterloo v Rugby
Worcester v London Welsh
RFU Jewson National League
Division 1
Camberley v Lydney
Harrogate v Birmingham Solihull
Henley v Morley
Liverpool St Helens v Newbury
Manchester v Reading
Nottingham v Otley
Wharfedale v Rosslyn Park
SRU Premiership
Division 1
Boroughmuir v Watsonians
Glasgow Hawks v Currie
Hawick v Melrose
Heriot's FP v West of Scotland
Stirling County v Jed-Forest
IRFU AIB League
Division 1
Buccaneers v Garryowen
Clontarf v St Mary's Coll
Cork Constitution v Galwegians
Lansdowne v Blackrock Coll
Shannon v Terenure Coll
Young Munster v Ballymena

Saturday, 30 January
RFU Tetley's Bitter Cup: *5th round*
RFU Jewson National League
Division 1
Birmingham Solihull v Liverpool St
  Helens
Lydney v Nottingham
Morley v Camberley
Newbury v Henley
Otley v Manchester
Reading v Wharfedale
Rosslyn Park v Harrogate
SRU Premiership
Division 1
Currie v Heriot's FP
Jed-Forest v Glasgow Hawks
Melrose v Boroughmuir
Watsonians v Stirling County
West of Scotland v Hawick
WRU SWALEC Cup: *5th round*

Friday, 5 February
Scotland A v Wales A
Ireland A v France A

Saturday, 6 February
SCOTLAND v WALES (Murrayfield)
IRELAND v FRANCE (Dublin)
RFU Allied Dunbar Premiership
Allied Premiership 2
Blackheath v Wakefield
Bristol v Rotherham
Fylde v Waterloo
Leeds v Exeter
London Welsh v Moseley
Orrell v Coventry
Rugby v Worcester
RFU Jewson National League
Division 1
Birmingham Solihull v Newbury
Camberley v Henley
Harrogate v Reading
Liverpool St Helens v Rosslyn Park
Manchester v Lydney
Nottingham v Morley
Wharfedale v Otley

Saturday, 13 February
RFU Allied Dunbar Premiership
Allied Premiership 2
Bristol v Leeds
Coventry v Blackheath
Moseley v Rugby
Rotherham v Orrell
Wakefield v London Welsh
Waterloo v Exeter
Worcester v Fylde
RFU Jewson National League
Division 1
Henley v Nottingham
Lydney v Wharfedale
Morley v Manchester
Otley v Harrogate
Newbury v Camberley
Reading v Liverpool St Helens
Rosslyn Park v Birmingham Solihull
IRFU AIB League
Division 1
Ballymena v Buccaneers
Blackrock Coll v Young Munster
Galwegians v Clontarf
Garryowen v Lansdowne
St Mary's Coll v Shannon
Terenure Coll v Cork Constitution
WRU League
Division 1
Caerphilly v Bridgend
Cardiff v Llanelli
Neath v Swansea
Pontypridd v Ebbw Vale

Friday, 19 February
England A v Scotland A
Wales A v Ireland A (Ebbw Vale)

Saturday, 20 February

ENGLAND v SCOTLAND
(Twickenham)
WALES v IRELAND (Wembley)

Saturday, 27 February

RFU Tetley's Bitter Cup: *Quarter-finals*
RFU Allied Dunbar Premiership
Allied Premiership 2
Blackheath v Rotherham
Exeter v Worcester
Fylde v Moseley
Leeds v Waterloo
London Welsh v Coventry
Orrell v Bristol
Rugby v Wakefield
RFU Jewson National League
Division 1
Birmingham Solihull v Reading
Harrogate v Lydney
Liverpool St Helens v Otley
Manchester v Henley
Nottingham v Camberley
Rosslyn Park v Newbury
Wharfedale v Morley
SRU Premiership
Division 1
Boroughmuir v West of Scotland
Glasgow Hawks v Watsonians
Hawick v Heriot's FP
Jed-Forest v Currie
Stirling County v Melrose
IRFU AIB League
Division 1
Ballymena v Garryowen
Blackrock Coll v Buccaneers
Clontarf v Shannon
Cork Constitution v St Mary's Coll
Terenure Coll v Galwegians
Young Munster v Lansdowne
WRU SWALEC Cup: *6th round*

Friday, 5 March

Ireland A v England A
France A v Wales A
Scotland A v Italy A

Saturday, 6 March

IRELAND v ENGLAND (Dublin)
FRANCE v WALES (Paris)
SCOTLAND v ITALY (Murrayfield)

Saturday, 13 March

RFU Allied Dunbar Premiership
Allied Premiership 2
Bristol v Blackheath
Coventry v Rugby
Moseley v Exeter
Orrell v Leeds
Rotherham v London Welsh
Wakefield v Fylde

Worcester v Waterloo
RFU Jewson National League
Division 1
Camberley v Manchester
Henley v Wharfedale
Lydney v Liverpool St Helens
Morley v Harrogate
Newbury v Nottingham
Otley v Birmingham Solihull
Reading v Rosslyn Park
SRU Premiership
Division 1
Hawick v Currie
Heriot's FP v Boroughmuir
Melrose v Glasgow Hawks
Watsonians v Jed-Forest
West of Scotland v Stirling County
IRFU AIB League
Division 1
Buccaneers v Young Munster
Clontarf v Cork Constitution
Garryowen v Blackrock Coll
Lansdowne v Ballymena
Shannon v Galwegians
St Mary's Coll v Terenure Coll
WRU League
Division 1
Bridgend v Llanelli
Ebbw Vale v Neath
Pontypridd v Cardiff
Swansea v Caerphilly

Friday, 19 March

Scotland A v Ireland A
England A v France A

Saturday, 20 March

SCOTLAND v IRELAND
(Murrayfield)
ENGLAND v FRANCE (Twickenham)
ITALY v WALES

Wednesday, 24 March

BUSA FINAL (Twickenham)

Saturday, 27 March

HONG KONG SEVENS
RFU Allied Dunbar Premiership
Allied Premiership 2
Blackheath v Orrell
Exeter v Wakefield
Fylde v Coventry
Leeds v Worcester
London Welsh v Bristol
Rugby v Rotherham
Waterloo v Moseley
RFU Jewson National League
Division 1
Birmingham Solihull v Lydney
Harrogate v Henley
Liverpool St Helens v Morley

Manchester v Nottingham
Reading v Newbury
Rosslyn Park v Otley
Wharfedale v Camberley
SRU Premiership
Division 1
Boroughmuir v Hawick
Currie v Watsonians
Glasgow Hawks v West of Scotland
Jed-Forest v Melrose
Stirling County v Heriot's FP
IRFU AIB League
Division 1
Blackrock Coll v Ballymena
Buccaneers v Lansdowne
Cork Constitution v Shannon
Galwegians v St Mary's Coll
Terenure Coll v Clontarf
Young Munster v Garryowen
WRU SWALEC Cup: *Quarter-finals*

Sunday, 28 March

HONG KONG SEVENS

Saturday, 3 April

RFU Tetley's Bitter Cup: *Semi-finals*
RFU Allied Dunbar Premiership
Allied Premiership 2
Blackheath v Leeds
Bristol v Rugby
Coventry v Exeter
Moseley v Worcester
Orrell v London Welsh
Rotherham v Fylde
Wakefield v Waterloo
RFU Jewson National League
Division 1
Camberley v Harrogate
Henley v Liverpool St Helens
Lydney v Rosslyn Park
Manchester v Newbury
Morley v Birmingham Solihull
Nottingham v Wharfedale
Otley v Reading
RFU Tetley's Bitter County
   Championship
Berkshire v Sussex
Buckinghamshire v Somerset
Cornwall v Oxfordshire
Cheshire v Lancashire
Cumbria v Notts, Lincs & Derbys
Eastern Counties v Hertfordshire
Gloucestershire v Surrey
Kent v Hampshire
Leicestershire v Staffordshire
Middlesex v Dorset & Wilts
North Midlands v Yorkshire
Northumberland v Durham
WRU League
Division 1
Caerphilly v Ebbw Vale

Cardiff v Bridgend
Llanelli v Swansea
Neath v Pontypridd

Friday, 9 April

Wales A v England A (Swansea)
France A v Scotland A

Saturday, 10 April

FRANCE v SCOTLAND (Paris)
IRELAND v ITALY (Dublin)
RFU Tetley's Bitter County
   Championship
Cheshire v Northumberland
Cornwall v Berkshire
Dorset & Wilts v Hampshire
Eastern Counties v Buckinghamshire
Hertfordshire v Somerset
Lancashire v Durham
Notts, Lincs & Derbys v
   Warwickshire
Middlesex v Kent
North Midlands v Leicestershire
Oxfordshire v Sussex
Surrey v Devon
Yorkshire v Staffordshire

Sunday, 11 April

WALES v ENGLAND (Wembley)

Saturday, 17 April

RFU Allied Dunbar Premiership
Allied Premiership 2
Exeter v Rotherham
Fylde v Bristol
Leeds v Moseley
London Welsh v Blackheath
Rugby v Orrell
Waterloo v Coventry
Worcester v Wakefield
RFU Jewson National League
Division 1
Birmingham Solihull v Henley
Harrogate v Nottingham
Liverpool St Helens v Camberley
Newbury v Otley
Reading v Lydney
Rosslyn Park v Morley
Wharfedale v Manchester
WRU SWALEC Cup: *Semi-finals*

Saturday, 24 April

Army v Royal Navy (Twickenham)
RFU Allied Dunbar Premiership
Allied Premiership 2
Blackheath v Rugby
Bristol v Exeter
Coventry v Worcester
London Welsh v Leeds

Orrell v Fylde
Rotherham v Waterloo
Wakefield v Moseley
**RFU Tetley's Bitter County
Championship**
Berkshire v Oxfordshire
Buckinghamshire v Hertfordshire
Devon v Gloucestershire
Durham v Cheshire
Hampshire v Middlesex
Kent v Dorset & Wilts
Leicestershire v Yorkshire
Northumberland v Lancashire
Somerset v Eastern Counties
Staffordshire v North Midlands
Sussex v Cornwall
Warwickshire v Cumbria

Saturday, 1 May

RFU Allied Dunbar Premiership
Allied Premiership 2
Exeter v Orrell
Fylde v Blackheath
Moseley v Coventry
Rugby v London Welsh
Wakefield v Leeds
Waterloo v Bristol
Worcester v Rotherham
**RFU Tetley's Bitter County
Championship** *Quarter-finals*

Saturday, 8 May

RFU Allied Dunbar Premiership
Allied Premiership 2
Blackheath v Exeter
Bristol v Worcester
Coventry v Wakefield
Leeds v Rugby
London Welsh v Fylde
Orrell v Waterloo
Rotherham v Moseley
**RFU Tetley's Bitter County
Championship** *Semi-finals*

Saturday, 15 May

RFU Tetley's Bitter Cup: FINAL
(Twickenham)
WRU SWALEC Cup: FINAL

Saturday, 22 May

**RFU Tetley's Bitter County
Championship: FINAL**
(Twickenham)

Sunday, 23 May

Sanyo World Challenge (Twickenham)

Saturday, 29 May

Middlesex Sevens Finals
(Twickenham)